PELICAN BOOKS

THE MAKING OF
THE ENGLISH WORKING CLASS

E. P. Thompson was born in 1924, and his time at Cambridge, where he read history, was interrupted by war service in Italy. From 1948 until 1965 he was extra-mural Lecturer at Leeds University in the West Riding, and he was also Reader at the Centre for the Study of Social History at the University of Warwick. He is a freelance writer and historian, founder of END and a Vice-President of CND. E. P. Thompson is a Foreign Honorary Member of the American Academy of Arts and Sciences.

E. P. Thompson is the author of *William Morris, Romantic to Revolutionary* (1955), *Whigs and Hunters* (Penguin) and *The Poverty of Theory and Other Essays*; editor of *Out of Apathy* (1960); joint-editor of *The New Reasoner* (1957–60) and of *The Unknown Mayhew* (Penguin); and a contributor to the *May Day Manifesto* (1968: a Penguin Special) and *Albion's Fatal Tree* (Penguin). His more recent publications are *Writing by Candlelight* (1980), *Beyond the Cold War* (1982), *Protest and Survive* (1980) and its sequel *From Protest to Survival* (to be published in 1986), both of which he co-edited with Dan Smith. Among recent publications on peace questions are *The Heavy Dancers* and *Double Exposure*. In 1985 he edited *Star Wars*, a Penguin Special.

THE MAKING OF
THE ENGLISH WORKING CLASS

E. P. THOMPSON

PENGUIN BOOKS

PENGUIN BOOKS

Published by the Penguin Group
27 Wrights Lane, London W8 5TZ, England
Viking Penguin Inc., 40 West 23rd Street, New York, New York 10010, USA
Penguin Books Australia Ltd, Ringwood, Victoria, Australia
Penguin Books Canada Ltd, 2801 John Street, Markham, Ontario, Canada L3R 1B4
Penguin Books (NZ) Ltd, 182–190 Wairau Road, Auckland 10, New Zealand

Penguin Books Ltd, Registered Offices: Harmondsworth, Middlesex, England

First published by Victor Gollancz 1963
Published with revisions in Pelican Books 1968
Reprinted with new preface 1980
7 9 10 8

Made and printed in Great Britain by
Hazell Watson & Viney Limited
Member of BPCC Limited
Aylesbury, Bucks, England
Set in Linotype Times

TO DOROTHY AND
JOSEPH GREENALD

Contents

A

3102413 £8.99

PART THREE: THE WORKING-CLASS PRESENCE

Preface

THIS book has a clumsy title, but it is one which meets its purpose. *Making*, because it is a study in an active process, which owes as much to agency as to conditioning. The working class did not rise like the sun at an appointed time. It was present at its own making.

Class, rather than classes, for reasons which it is one purpose of this book to examine. There is, of course, a difference. 'Working classes' is a descriptive term, which evades as much as it defines. It ties loosely together a bundle of discrete phenomena. There were tailors here and weavers there, and together they make up the working classes.

By class I understand a historical phenomenon, unifying a number of disparate and seemingly unconnected events, both in the raw material of experience and in consciousness. I emphasize that it is a *historical* phenomenon. I do not see class as a 'structure', nor even as a 'category', but as something which in fact happens (and can be shown to have happened) in human relationships.

More than this, the notion of class entails the notion of historical relationship. Like any other relationship, it is a fluency which evades analysis if we attempt to stop it dead at any given moment and anatomize its structure. The finest-meshed sociological net cannot give us a pure specimen of class, any more than it can give us one of deference or of love. The relationship must always be embodied in real people and in a real context. Moreover, we cannot have two distinct classes, each with an independent being, and then bring them *into* relationship with each other. We cannot have love without lovers, nor deference without squires and labourers. And class happens when some men, as a result of common experiences (inherited or shared), feel and articulate the identity of their interests as between themselves, and as against other men whose interests are different from (and usually opposed to) theirs. The class experience is largely determined by the productive relations into which men are born – or enter involuntarily. Class-consciousness is the way in which these experiences are handled in cultural terms: embodied in traditions, value-systems, ideas, and institutional forms. If the experience appears as determined, class-consciousness does not. We can see a *logic* in the responses of similar occupational groups undergoing similar experiences, but we cannot predicate any *law*. Consciousness of class arises in the same way in different times and places, but never in just the same way.

There is today an ever-present temptation to suppose that class is a thing. This was not Marx's meaning, in his own historical writing, yet the error vitiates much latter-day 'Marxist' writing. 'It', the working class, is assumed to have a real existence, which can be defined almost mathematically – so many men who stand in a certain relation to the means of production. Once this is assumed it becomes possible to deduce the class-consciousness which 'it' ought to have (but seldom does have) if 'it' was properly aware of its own position and real interests. There is a cultural superstructure, through which this recognition dawns in inefficient ways. These cultural 'lags' and distortions are a nuisance, so that it is easy to pass from this to some theory of substitution: the party, sect, or theorist, who disclose class-consciousness, not as it is, but as it ought to be.

But a similar error is committed daily on the other side of the ideological divide. In one form, this is a plain negative. Since the crude notion of class attributed to Marx can be faulted without difficulty, it is assumed that any notion of class is a pejorative theoretical construct, imposed upon the evidence. It is denied that class has happened at all. In another form, and by a curious inversion, it is possible to pass from a dynamic to a static view of class. 'It' – the working class – exists, and can be defined with some accuracy as a component of the social structure. Class-consciousness, however, is a bad thing, invented by displaced intellectuals, since everything which disturbs the harmonious coexistence of groups performing different 'social rôles' (and which thereby retards economic growth) is to be deplored as an 'unjustified dis-turbance-symptom'.[1] The problem is to determine how best 'it' can be conditioned to accept its social rôle, and how its grievances may best be 'handled and channelled'.

If we remember that class is a relationship, and not a thing, we cannot think in this way. 'It' does not exist, either to have an ideal interest or consciousness, or to lie as a patient on the Adjustor's table. Nor can we turn matters upon their heads, as has been done by one authority who (in a study of class obsessively concerned with methodology, to the exclusion of the examination of a single real class situation in a real his-torical context) has informed us:

Classes are based on the differences in legitimate power associated with certain positions, i.e. on the structure of social rôles with re-spect to their authority expectations. . . . An individual becomes a member of a class by playing a social rôle relevant from the point of view of authority. . . . He belongs to a class because he occupies a position in a social organization; i.e. class membership is derived from the incumbency of a social rôle.[2]

The question, of course, is how the individual got to be in this 'social rôle', and how the particular social organization (with its property-rights and structure of authority) got to be there. And these are historical questions. If we stop history at a given point, then there are no classes but simply a multitude of individuals with a multitude of experiences. But if we watch these men over an adequate period of social change, we observe patterns in their relationships, their ideas, and their institutions. Class is defined by men as they live their own history, and, in the end, this is its only definition.

If I have shown insufficient understanding of the methodo-logical preoccupations of certain sociologists, nevertheless I hope this book will be seen as a contribution to the under-standing of class. For I am convinced that we cannot under-

1. An examp e of this approach, covering the period of this book, is to be found in the work of a co..eague of Professor Ta.cott Parsons: N. J. Smelser, *Social Change in the Industrial Revolution* (1959).

2. R. Dahrendorf, *Class and Class Conflict in Industrial Society* (1959), pp. 148–9,

stand class unless we see it as a social and cultural formation, arising from processes which can only be studied as they work themselves out over a considerable historical period. In the years between 1780 and 1832 most English working people came to feel an identity of interests as between themselves, and as against their rulers and employers. This ruling class was itself much divided, and in fact only gained in cohesion over the same years because certain antagonisms were resolved (or faded into relative insignificance) in the face of an insurgent working class. Thus the working-class presence was, in 1832, the most significant factor in British political life.

The book is written in this way. In Part One I consider the continuing popular traditions in the eighteenth century which influenced the crucial Jacobin agitation of the 1790s. In Part Two I move from subjective to objective influences – the experiences of groups of workers during the Industrial Revolution which seem to me to be of especial significance. I also attempt an estimate of the character of the new industrial work-discipline, and the bearing upon this of the Methodist Church. In Part Three I pick up the story of plebeian Radicalism, and carry it through Luddism to the heroic age at the close of the Napoleonic Wars. Finally, I discuss some aspects of political theory and of the consciousness of class in the 1820s and 1830s.

This is a group of studies, on related themes, rather than a consecutive narrative. In selecting these themes I have been conscious, at times, of writing against the weight of prevailing orthodoxies. There is the Fabian orthodoxy, in which the great majority of working people are seen as passive victims of *laissez faire*, with the exception of a handful of far-sighted organizers (notably, Francis Place). There is the orthodoxy of the empirical economic historians, in which working people are seen as a labour force, as migrants, or as the data for statistical series. There is the 'Pilgrim's Progress' orthodoxy, in which the period is ransacked for forerunners–pioneers of the Welfare State, progenitors of a Socialist Commonwealth, or (more recently) early exemplars of rational industrial relations. Each of these orthodoxies has a certain validity. All have added to our knowledge. My quarrel with the first and second is that they tend to obscure the agency of working people, the degree to which they contributed by conscious efforts, to the making of history. My quarrel with the third is that it reads history in the light of subsequent preoccupations, and not as in fact it occurred. Only the successful (in the sense of those whose aspirations anticipated subsequent evolution) are remembered. The blind alleys, the lost causes, and the losers themselves are forgotten.

I am seeking to rescue the poor stockinger, the Luddite cropper, the 'obsolete' hand-loom weaver, the 'utopian' artisan, and even the deluded follower of Joanna Southcott, from the enormous condescension of posterity. Their crafts and traditions may have been dying. Their hostility to the new industrialism may have been backward-looking. Their communitarian ideals may have been fantasies. Their insurectionary conspiracies may have been foolhardy. But they lived through these times of acute social disturbance, and we did not. Their aspirations were valid in terms of their own experience; and, if they were casualties of history, they remain, condemned in their own lives, as casualties.

Our only criterion of judgement should not be whether or not a man's actions are justified in the light of subsequent evolution. After all, we are not at the end of social evolution ourselves. In some of the lost causes of the people of the Industrial Revolution we may discover insights into social evils which we have yet to cure. Moreover, the greater part of the world today is still undergoing problems of industrialization, and of the formation of democratic institutions, analogous in many ways to our own experience during the Industrial Revolution. Causes which were lost in England might, in Asia or Africa, yet be won.

Finally, a note of apology to Scottish and Welsh readers. I have neglected these histories, not out of chauvinism, but out of respect. It is because class is a cultural as much as an economic formation that I have been cautious as to generalizing beyond English experience. (I have considered the Irish, not in Ireland, but as immigrants to England.) The Scottish record, in particular, is quite as dramatic, and as tormented, as our own. The Scottish Jacobin agitation was more intense and more heroic. But the Scottish story is significantly different. Calvinism was not the same thing as Methodism, although it is difficult to say which, in the early nineteenth century, was worse. We had no peasantry in England comparable to the Highland migrants. And the popular culture was very different. It is possible, at least until the 1820s, to regard the English and Scottish experiences as distinct, since trade union and political links were impermanent and immature.

This book was written in Yorkshire, and is coloured at times by West Riding sources. My grateful acknowledgements are due to the University of Leeds and to Professor S. G. Raybould for enabling me, some years ago, to commence the research which led to this book; and to the Leverhulme Trustees for the award of a Research Fellowship, which has enabled me to complete the work. I have also learned a great deal from members of my tutorial classes, with whom I have discussed many of the themes treated here. Acknowledgements are due also to the authorities who have allowed me to quote from manuscript and copyright sources: particular acknowledgements will be found at the end of the first edition.

I have also to thank many others. Mr Christopher Hill, Professor Asa Briggs, and Mr John Saville criticized parts of the book in draft, although they are in no sense responsible for my judgements. Mr R. W. Harris showed great editorial patience, when the book burst the bounds of a series for which it was first commissioned. Mr Perry Anderson, Mr Denis Butt, Mr Richard Cobb, Mr Henry Collins, Mr Derrick Crossley, Mr Tim Enright, Dr E. P. Hennock, Mr Rex Russell, Dr John Rex, Dr E. Sigsworth, and Mr H. O. E. Swift, have helped me at different points. I have also to thank Mrs Dorothy Thompson, an historian to whom I am related by the accident of marriage. Each chapter has been discussed with her, and I have been well placed to borrow not only her ideas but material from her notebooks. Her collaboration is to be found, not in this or that particular, but in the way the whole problem is seen.

Halifax, August 1963

Preface to 1980 edition

When a contract was signed between myself and Victor Gollancz Ltd, in August 1959, it was for a book on 'Working-Class Politics, 1790–1921', to be 'approximately 60,000 words in length'. This is, I suppose, the first chapter of such a book, and I am grateful to the publishers for the good-humoured and encouraging way in which they received my large and untidy manuscript. Looking back, I am puzzled to know when and how the book got itself written, since in 1959–62 I was also heavily engaged in the work of the first New Left, the Campaign for Nuclear Disarmament, and so on. The writing was only possible because some part of the research had already been laid down during the previous ten years in the course of my work as a tutor in extra-mural classes in the West Riding. Discussion in these classes, as well as practical political activity of several kinds, undoubtedly prompted me to see the problems of political consciousness and organization in certain ways.

Many readers have noted that the book is structured by a double-sided critique: on the one hand, of the positivist orthodoxies then dominant in the more conservative academic schools of economic history – orthodoxies more recently marketed under the name of 'modernization theory'; on the other hand, of a certain 'Marxist' orthodoxy (then waning in influence in this country), which supposed that the working class was the more-or-less spontaneous generation of new productive forces and relations. Some critics of the first persuasion found the book to be a matter of scandal, and I replied to certain of their criticisms in a postscript to the Pelican edition of 1968 (reprinted here), not because I suppose that my work should be beyond criticism but because important matters of principle are involved. As regards critics of the second persuasion, I have been engaged in a running argument of a more theoretical kind for some years, culminating in *The Poverty of Theory* (Merlin Press, 1978).

I do not intend to write a further postscript, reviewing the new work of the past decade. This book has been generously received and has passed into historical discourse, and it would be self-important to try and adjudicate between other scholars in the light of my own findings. However, my own research was continuing while this book went through the press – as the galley-proofs testified – and in work on the crowd and customary consciousness in the eighteenth century I have myself extended and revised some of the material in the first four chapters. Meanwhile much new and important work has been published, and more lies in theses or is forthcoming. Work on the 1790s has been reopened, as can be seen from the bibliography to Professor Albert Goodwin's weighty study, *The Friends of Liberty* (Hutchinson, 1979). The prophetic roles of Richard Brothers and Joanna Southcott have now been fully examined in J. F. C. Harrison, *The Second Coming* (Routledge & Kegan Paul, 1979). Most important revisions and additions to my account of London artisans, London radical politics, and the Queen Caroline affair, are made in Dr Iorwerth Prothero's study of John Gast, *Artisans and Politics in Early Nineteenth-Century London* (Dawsons, 1979). I am happy to say that my note that the struggle of the unstamped press 'has not yet found its historian' has now been overtaken by two admirable studies: Patricia Hollis, *The Pauper Press* (Oxford University Press, 1970) and Joel H. Wiener, *The War of the Unstamped* (Cornell University Press, 1969).

Other areas remain more controversial. I should, perhaps, briefly indicate that I remain unrepentant as to my treatment of Methodism; that, despite criticisms, I maintain my view as to a small 'underground' Jacobin presence in the war years; that several works by Dr Malcolm Thomis on the Luddite movement have not led me to alter my own interpretation; and that Dr Duncan Bythell's study of *The Handloom Weavers* (Cambridge University Press, 1969), some part of which is structured around a critique of my Chapter 9, seems to me to be at fault in general arguments and in matters of detail. But to follow up any one of these questions would require close and prolonged attention to evidence.

The work of research and of critique will continue, and if I

have passed by important work without mention, this is only for
fear of being drawn into a bibliography. I wish only to indicate
that, for its author, the major theses of this book still stand as
hypotheses which, in their turn, must never be petrified into
orthodoxies.

Worcester, October 1979

Part One

THE LIBERTY TREE

'You are wrestling with the Enemies of the human Race, not for yourself merely, for you may not see the full Day of Liberty, but for the Child hanging at the Breast.'

*Instructions of the London Corresponding
Society to its travelling delegates, 1796*

'The Beast & the Whore rule without control.'

WILLIAM BLAKE, 1798

Part One

THE LIBERTY TREE

'You are wrestling with the Enemies of the human Race, not for yourself merely, for you may not see the full Day of Liberty, but for the Child hanging at the Breast.'

Instructions of the London Corresponding Society to its travelling delegates, 1796

'The Beast & the Whore rule without control.'

WILLIAM BLAKE, 1793

[1]

Members Unlimited

'THAT the number of our Members be unlimited.' This is the first of the 'leading rules' of the London Corresponding Society, as cited by its Secretary when he began to correspond with a similar society in Sheffield in March 1792.[1] The first meeting of the London society had been held two months before in a tavern off the Strand ('The Bell' in Exeter Street) and nine 'well-meaning, sober and industrious men' were present. The founder and first Secretary, Thomas Hardy, later recalled this meeting:

After having had their bread and cheese and porter for supper, as usual, and their pipes afterwards, with some conversation on the hardness of the times and the dearness of all the necessaries of life ... the business for which they had met was brought forward – *Parliamentary Reform* – an important subject to be deliberated upon and dealt with by such a class of men.

Eight of the nine present became founder-members that night (the ninth thought it over and joined the next week) and paid their first weekly subscription of one penny. Hardy (who was also Treasurer) went back to his home at No. 9 Piccadilly with the entire funds of the organization in his pocket: 8*d*. towards paper for the purpose of corresponding with like-minded groups in the country.

Within a fortnight twenty-five members were enrolled and the sum in the Treasurer's hands was 4*s*. 1*d*. (Six months later more than 2,000 members were claimed.) Admission to membership was simple, the test being an affirmative reply to three questions, of which the most important was:

Are you thoroughly persuaded that the welfare of these kingdoms require that every adult person, in possession of his reason, and not incapacitated by crimes, should have a vote for a Member of Parliament?

1. *Memoir of Thomas Hardy ... Written by Himself* (1832), p. 16.

In the first month of its existence the society debated for five nights in succession the question – 'Have we, who are Tradesmen, Shopkeepers, and Mechanics, any right to obtain a Parliamentary Reform?' – turning it over 'in every point of view in which we were capable of presenting the subject to our minds'. They decided that they had.

Two years later, on 12 May 1794, the King's Messenger, two Bow Street Runners, the private secretary to Home Secretary Dundas, and other dignitaries arrived at No. 9 Piccadilly to arrest Thomas Hardy, shoemaker, on a charge of high treason. The Hardys watched while the officers ransacked the room, broke open a bureau, rummaged among Mrs Hardy's clothes (she was pregnant and remained in bed), filled four large silk handkerchiefs with letters and a corn-sack with pamphlets, books and manuscripts. On the same day a special message from the King was brought to the House of Commons, concerning the seditious practices of the Corresponding Societies; and two days later a Committee of Secrecy of the House was appointed to examine the shoemaker's papers.

The shoemaker was examined several times by the Privy Council itself. Hardy left little record of these encounters; but one of his fellow prisoners entertained his readers with a dramatic reconstruction of his own interrogation by the highest council in the land. 'I was called in,' related John Thelwall, 'and beheld the whole Dramatis Personae intrenched chin deep in Lectures and manuscripts ... all scattered about in the utmost confusion.' The Lord Chancellor, the Home Secretary, and the Prime Minister (Pitt) were all present:

ATTORNEY-GENERAL [*piano*]. Mr Thelwall, what is your Christian name?

T. [*somewhat sullenly*]. John.

ATT. GEN. [*piano still*] ... With two l's at the end or with one?

T. With two – but it does not signify. [*Carelessly, but rather sullen, or so.*] You need not give yourself any trouble. I do not intend to answer any questions.

PITT. What does he say? [*Darting round, very fiercely, from the other side of the room, and seating himself by the side of the* CHANCELLOR.]

LORD CHANCELLOR [*with silver softness, almost melting to a whisper*]. He does not mean to answer any questions.
PITT. What is it? – What is it? – What? [*fiercely*] . . .[1]

John Thelwall then turned his back on the august company and 'began to contemplate a drawing in water-colours'. The Prime Minister dismissed him and summoned for interrogation a fourteen-year-old lad, Henry Eaton, who had been living with the Thelwalls. But the boy stood his ground and 'entered into a political harangue, in which he used very harsh language against Mr Pitt; upbraiding him with having taxed the people to an enormous extent . . .'[2]

By the standards of the next 100 years the antagonists appear to be strangely amateurish and uncertain of their rôles, rehearsing in curiously personal encounters the massive impersonal encounters of the future.[3] Civility and venom are mixed together; there is still room for acts of personal kindness alongside the malice of class hatred. Thelwall, Hardy, and ten other prisoners were committed to the Tower and later to Newgate. While there, Thelwall was for a time confined in the charnel-house; and Mrs Hardy died in childbirth as a result of shock sustained when her home was beseiged by a 'Church and King' mob. The Privy Council determined to press through with the charge of high treason: and the full penalty for a traitor was that he should be hanged by the neck, cut down while still alive, disembowelled (and his entrails burned before his face) and then beheaded and quartered. A Grand Jury of respectable citizens had no stomach for this. After a nine-day trial, Hardy was acquitted (on Guy Fawkes Day, 1794). The Foreman of the Jury fainted after delivering his 'Not Guilty', while the London crowd went wild with enthusiasm and dragged Hardy in triumph through the streets. Acquittals for Horne Tooke and

1. *Tribune*, 4 April 1795. Compare the Privy Council's own record of Thelwall's examination: 'Being asked by the Clerk of the Council how he spelt his Name – Answered: He might spell it according to his own discretion for that he should answer no Questions of any kind. . . .' T.S. 11.3509 f. 83.
2. *Morning Post*, 16 May 1794.
3. Later, when John Binns, the Jacobin, was imprisoned without trial in Gloucester Castle, the Home Secretary, his wife, and two daughters, paid him a social visit.

Thelwall (and the dismissal of the other cases) followed. But the celebrations of the crowd were premature. For in the next year the steady repression of reformers – or 'Jacobins' – was renewed. And by the end of the decade it seemed as if the entire agitation had been dispersed. The London Corresponding Society had been outlawed. Tom Paine's *Rights of Man* was banned. Meetings were prohibited. Hardy was running a shoe-shop near Covent Garden, appealing to old reformers to patronize him in tribute to his past services. John Thelwall had retired to an isolated farm in South Wales. It seemed, after all, that 'tradesmen, shopkeepers, and mechanics' had no right to obtain a Parliamentary Reform.

The London Corresponding Society has often been claimed as the first definitely working-class political organization formed in Britain. Pedantry apart (the Sheffield, Derby and Manchester societies were formed before the Society in London) this judgement requires definition. On the one hand, debating societies in which working men took part existed sporadically in London from the time of the American War. On the other hand, it may be more accurate to think of the L.C.S. as a 'popular Radical' society than as 'working-class'.

Hardy was certainly an artisan. Born in 1752, he had been apprenticed as a shoemaker in Stirlingshire: had seen something of the new industrialism as a bricklayer at the Carron Iron Works (he was nearly killed when the scaffolding collapsed when he was at work on ironmaster Roebuck's house); and had come to London as a young man, shortly before the American War. Here he worked in one of those numerous trades where a journeyman looked forward to becoming independent, with luck to becoming a master himself – as Hardy eventually became. He married the daughter of a carpenter and builder. One of his colleagues, a Chairman of the L.C.S., was Francis Place, on his way to becoming a master-tailor. The line between the journeymen and the small masters was often crossed – the Journeymen Boot and Shoemakers struck against Hardy in his new rôle as a small employer in 1795, while Francis Place, before becoming a master-tailor, helped to organize a strike of Journeymen Breeches-makers in 1793. And the line between the artisan of independent status (whose workroom was also his 'shop') and the small shopkeeper or tradesmen was even fainter. From here it was another step to the world of self-employed engravers, like William Sharp and William Blake, of printers and apothecaries, teachers and journalists, surgeons and Dissenting clergy.

At one end, then, the London Corresponding Society reached out to the coffee-houses, taverns and dissenting churches off Piccadilly, Fleet Street and the Strand, where the self-educated journeyman might rub shoulders with the printer, the shopkeeper, the engraver or the young attorney. At the other end, to the east, and south of the river, it touched those older working-class communities – the waterside workers of Wapping, the silk-weavers of Spitalfields, the old dissenting stronghold of Southwark. For 200 years 'Radical London' has always been more heterogeneous and fluid in its social and occupational definition than the Midlands or Northern centres grouped around two or three staple industries. Popular movements in London have often lacked the coherence and stamina which results from the involvement of an entire community in common occupational and social tensions. On the other hand, they have generally been more subject to intellectual and 'ideal' motivations. A propaganda of ideas has had a larger audience than in the North. London Radicalism early acquired a greater sophistication from the need to knit diverse agitations into a common movement. New theories, new arguments, have generally first effected a junction with the popular movement in London, and travelled outwards from London to the provincial centres.

The L.C.S. was a junction-point of this sort. And we must remember that its first organizer lived in Piccadilly, not in Wapping or in Southwark. But there are features, in even the brief description of its first meetings, which indicate that a new kind of organization had come into being – features which help us to define (in the context of 1790–1850) the nature of a 'working-class organization'. There is the working man as Secretary. There is the low weekly subscription. There is the intermingling of economic and political themes – 'the hardness of the times' and Parliamentary Reform. There is the function of the meeting, both as a social occasion and as a centre for political activity. There is the realistic attention to procedural formalities. Above all, there is the determination to propagate opinions and to organize the converted, embodied in the leading rule: 'That the number of our Members be unlimited.'

Today we might pass over such a rule as a commonplace: and yet it is one of the hinges upon which history turns. It signified the end to any notion of exclusiveness, of politics as the preserve of any hereditary élite or property group. Assent to this rule meant that the L.C.S. was turning its back upon the century-old identification of political with property-rights – turning its back also upon the Radicalism of the days of 'Wilkes and Liberty', when 'the Mob' did not organize *itself* in pursuance of its own ends but was called into spasmodic action by a faction – even a Radical faction – to strengthen its hand and frighten the authorities. To throw open the doors to propaganda and agitation in this 'unlimited' way implied a new notion of democracy, which cast aside ancient inhibitions and trusted to self-activating and self-organizing processes among the common people. Such a revolutionary challenge was bound to lead on to the charge of high treason.

The challenge had, of course, been voiced before – by the seventeenth-century Levellers. And the matter had been argued out between Cromwell's officers and the Army agitators in terms which look forward to the conflicts of the 1790s. In the crucial debate, at Putney,[1] the representatives of the soldiers argued that since they had won the victory they should benefit by being admitted to a greatly extended popular franchise. The claim of the Leveller Colonel Rainborough is well known:

For really I think that the poorest he that is in England hath a life to live, as the greatest he; and therefore truly, sir, I think it's clear, that every man that is to live under a government ought first by his own consent to put himself under that government. ... I should doubt whether he was an Englishman or no, that should doubt of these things.

The reply of Cromwell's son-in-law, General Ireton – the spokesman of the 'Grandees' – was that 'no person hath a right

1. A. S. P. Woodhouse, *Puritanism and Liberty* (1938), pp. 53 et seq.

to an interest or share in the disposing of the affairs of the kingdom ... that hath not a permanent fixed interest in this kingdom'. When Rainborough pressed him, Ireton grew warm in return:

All the main thing that I speak for, is because I would have an eye to property. I hope we do not come to contend for victory – but let every man consider with himself that he do not go that way to take away all property. For here is the case of the most fundamental part of the constitution of the kingdom, which if you take away, you take all by that.

'If you admit any man that hath a breath and being,' he continued, a majority of the Commons might be elected who had no 'local and permanent interest'. 'Why may not those men vote against all property? ... Show me what you will stop at; wherein you will fence any man in a property by this rule.'

This unqualified identification of political and property rights brought angry expostulations. From Sexby –

There are many thousands of us soldiers that have ventured our lives; we have had little propriety in the kingdom as to our estates, yet we have had a birthright. But it seems now, except a man hath a fixed estate in this kingdom, he hath no right. ... I wonder we were so much deceived.

And Rainborough broke in ironically:

Sir, I see that it is impossible to have liberty but all property must be taken away. If it be laid down for a rule ... it must be so. But I would fain know what the soldier hath fought for all this while? He hath fought to enslave himself, to give power to men of riches, men of estates, to make him a perpetual slave.

To which Ireton and Cromwell replied with arguments which seem like prescient apologetics for the compromise of 1688. The common soldier had fought for three things: the limitation of the prerogative of the Crown to infringe his personal rights and liberty of conscience: the right to be governed by representatives, even though he had no part in choosing them: and the 'freedom of trading to get money, to get estates by' – and of entering upon political rights in this way. On such terms, 'Liberty may be had and property not be destroyed.'

For 100 years after 1688 this compromise – the oligarchy of landed and commercial property – remained unchallenged, although with a thickening texture of corruption, purchase, and interest whose complexities have been lovingly chronicled by Sir Lewis Namier and his school. The Leveller challenge was altogether dispersed – although the spectre of a Leveller revival was often conjured up, as the Scylla to the Charybdis of Papists and Jacobites between which the good ship Constitution must steer her course. But until the last quarter of the eighteenth century the temperate republican and libertarian impulses of the 'Eighteenth-Century Commonwealthsman' seem to be transfixed within the limits of Ireton's definition.[1] To read the controversies between reformers and authority, and between different reforming groups, in the 1790s is to see the Putney Debates come to life once again. The 'poorest he' in England, the man with a 'birthright', becomes the *Rights of Man*: while the agitation of 'unlimited' members was seen by Burke as the threat of the 'swinish multitude'. The great semi-official agency for the intimidation of reformers was called the Association for 'Protecting Liberty and Property against Republicans and Levellers'. The moderate Yorkshire reformer, the Reverend Christopher Wyvill, as to whose devotion there can be no question, nevertheless believed that a reform on the principle of universal suffrage 'could not be effected without a Civil War':

In times of warm political debate, the Right of Suffrage communicated to an ignorant and ferocious Populace would lead to tumult and confusion. ... After a series of Elections disgraced by the most shameful corruption, or disturbed by the most furious commotion, we expect that the turbulence or venality of the English Populace would at last disgust the Nation so greatly, that to get rid of the intolerable evils of a profligate Democracy, they would take refuge ... under the protection of Despotic Power.[2]

'If Mr Paine should be able to rouze up the lower classes,' he wrote in 1792, 'their interference will probably be marked by wild work, and all we now possess, whether in private property

1. See Caroline Robbins, *The Eighteenth-Century Commonwealthsman* (Harvard, 1959).
2. C. Wyvill to John Cartwright, 16 December 1797, in Wyvill's *Political Papers* (York, 1804), V. pp. 381–2.

or public liberty, will be at the mercy of a lawless and furious rabble.'[1]

It is the old debate continued. The same aspirations, fears, and tensions are there: but they arise in a new context, with new language and arguments, and a changed balance of forces. We have to try to understand both things – the continuing traditions and the context that has changed. Too often, since every account must start somewhere, we see only the things which are new. We start at 1789, and English Jacobinism appears as a by-product of the French Revolution. Or we start in 1819 and with Peterloo, and English Radicalism appears to be a spontaneous generation of the Industrial Revolution. Certainly the French Revolution precipitated a new agitation, and certainly this agitation took root among working people, shaped by new experiences, in the growing manufacturing districts. But the question remains – what were the elements precipitated so swiftly by these events? And we find at once the long traditions of the urban artisans and tradesmen, so similar to the *menu peuple* whom George Rudé has shown to be the most volatile revolutionary element in the Parisian crowd.[2] We may see something of the complexities of these continuing traditions if we isolate three problems: the tradition of Dissent, and its modification by the Methodist revival: the tradition made up of all those loose popular notions which combine in the idea of the Englishman's 'birthright'; and the ambiguous tradition of the eighteenth-century 'mob', of which Wyvill was afraid and which Hardy was trying to organize into committees, divisions, and responsible demonstrations.

1. Ibid., V, p. 23.
2. See G. Rudé, *The Crowd in the French Revolution* (1959).

[2]

Christian and Apollyon

DISSENT is a misleading term. It covers so many sects, so many conflicting intellectual and theological tendencies, finds so many different forms in differing social milieux. The old dissenting groups, Quakers, and Baptists – show certain similarities of development after the Glorious Revolution. As persecution gave way to greater toleration, the congregations became less zealous and more prosperous. Where the clothiers and farmers of the Spen Valley had met, in 1670, in secret and at night, in a farmhouse called 'Ye Closes' or 'in the barn near Chapel Fold', 100 years later we find a sturdy church with a prosperous deacon, Joseph Priestley, who confided in his devotional diary such entries as this:

The world smiles. I had some agreeable engagements by this post. What shall I render my Lord, was my language when I went to Leeds. I determined to give four or five loads of wheat to Christ's poor. Had much reason to complain this day that I did not set God before me in all my thoughts. Find it difficult in the hurry of business. . .

And the next week:

This morning I . . . dined with a company of officers who all appeared to be ignorant of the way of salvation. I had some pleasure in reading 45th Isiah. . . . Ordered brother Obadiah to give a load of wheat among Christ's poor.[1]

This Priestley was still a Calvinist, albeit a somewhat guilt-stricken one. (No doubt 'brother Obadiah' was a Calvinist too.) But his younger cousin, also a Joseph Priestley, was at this time studying at the Daventry Academy, where he sadly disappointed his kinsmen and church by being touched by the

1. Frank Peel, *Nonconformity in Spen Valley* (Heckmondwike, 1891), p. 136.

spirit of the rational enlightenment, becoming a Unitarian, a scientist, and a political reformer. It was this Dr Priestley whose books and laboratory were destroyed by a 'Church and King' mob in Birmingham in 1791.

That is a thumb-nail sketch of one part of the Dissenting tradition. Their liberty of conscience tolerated, but still disabled in public life by the Test and Corporations Acts, the Dissenters continued throughout the century to work for civil and religious liberties. By the mid-century many of the younger educated ministers prided themselves on their broad-minded rational theology. The Calvinist self-righteousness of the persecuted sect was left behind, and they gravitated through Arian and Socinian 'heresy' towards Unitarianism. From Unitarianism it was only a further step to Deism, although few took this step until the 1790s; and even fewer in the second half of the eighteenth century wished or dared to make a public avowal of scepticism – in 1763 the seventy-year-old schoolmaster, Peter Annet, was imprisoned and stocked for translating Voltaire and for publishing 'free-thinking' tracts in popular form, while shortly afterwards the sceptical Robin Hood debating society was closed down. It was from Socinian or Unitarian positions that liberal principles were argued : the famous figures are Dr Price, whose *Observations on Civil Liberty* (1776) at the time of the American War achieved the remarkable sale of 60,000 within a few months, and who lived to enrage Burke by his sermon in welcome to the French Revolution; Dr Priestley himself; and a score of lesser figures, several of whom – Thomas Cooper of Bolton and William Frend of Cambridge – took an active part in the reform agitation of the 1790s.[1]

So far the story seems clear. But this is deceptive. These liberal notions prevailed widely among dissenting clergy, teachers, and educated city communities. But many of the ministers had left their congregations behind. It was the Presby-

1. See Anthony Lincoln, *Social and Political Ideas of English Dissent, 1763–1830* (Cambridge, 1938), and R. V. Holt, *The Unitarian Contribution to Social Progress in England* (1938). For briefer surveys, see Robbins, op. cit., ch. 7 and H. W. Carless Davis, *The Age of Grey and Peel* (Oxford, 1929), pp. 49–58.

terian Church, in which the impulse to Unitarianism was most strongly felt, which was declining in strength most markedly in relation to other dissenting groups. In the mid-eighteenth century the Presbyterians and the Independents (taken together) were strongest in the south-west (Devonshire, Dorset, Gloucestershire, Hampshire, Somerset, Wiltshire), in the industrial north (notably Lancashire, Northumberland and Yorkshire), in London, and in East Anglia (notably Essex and Suffolk). The Baptists contested some of these strongholds, and were also well-rooted in Bedfordshire, Buckinghamshire, Kent, Leicestershire, and Northamptonshire. Thus the Presbyterians and Independents would appear to have been strongest in the commercial and wool manufacturing centres, while the Baptists held ground in areas where petty tradesmen, small farmers and rural labourers must have made up a part of their congregations.[1] It was in the greatest of the older woollen centres, the West Country, that the broad-minded, 'rational' religion which tended towards the denial of Christ's divinity and to Unitarianism both made its most rapid advances and lost it the allegiance of its congregations. In Devonshire, by the end of the eighteenth century, more than twenty Presbyterian meeting-houses had been closed, and the historians of Dissent, writing in 1809, declared:

Devonshire, the cradle of arianism, has been the grave of the arian dissenters; and there is not left in that populous county a twentieth part of the presbyterians who were to be found at the time of her birth.[2]

But elsewhere the story was different. In matters of church organization the dissenting sects often carried the principles of self-government and of local autonomy to the borders of anarchy. Any centralized authority – even consultation and association between churches – was seen as 'productive of the great anti-christian apostasy',

1. D. Bogue and J. Bennett, *History of Dissenters* (1809), III, p. 333 estimate that in 1760 the 'principal strength' of Dissent of all varieties was among tradesmen and in some counties farmers, while 'mechanics of all descriptions composed a large portion of their congregations in towns, and labourers in husbandry in country villages'.

2. Ibid., IV, p. 319.

An apostasy so fatal to the civil and religious liberties of mankind, and particularly to those of the brave old puritans and nonconformists, that the very words synod and session, council and canon, yet make both the ears of a sound Protestant Dissenter to tingle.[1]

Where the Calvinist tradition was strong, as in parts of Lancashire and Yorkshire, the congregations fought back against the drift towards Unitarianism; and stubborn deacons, trustees and Obadiahs tormented the lives of their ministers, investigating their heresies, expelling them or breaking away to form more righteous sects. (Thomas Hardy gained some of his first experiences of organization in the factional struggles of the Presbyterian congregation in Crown Court, off Russell Street.) But what of 'Christ's poor', to whom Dr Price offered enlightenment and Deacon Priestley loads of wheat? The Spen Valley lay at the centre of a thickly populated and expanding manufacturing district – here one might have expected the dissenting churches to have reaped at last the reward for their endurance in the years of persecution. And yet 'Christ's poor' seemed little touched by either the Established Church or old Dissent. 'A wilder people I never saw in England.' John Wesley noted in his *Journal*, when he rode through near-by Huddersfield in 1757; 'the men, women, and children filled the street as we rode along, and appeared just ready to devour us.'

The rational Christianity of the Unitarians, with its preference for 'candour' and its distrust of 'enthusiasm', appealed to some of the tradesmen and shopkeepers of London, and to similar groups in the large cities. But it seemed too cold, too distant, too polite, and too much associated with the comfortable values of a prospering class to appeal to the city or village poor. Its very language and tone served as a barrier: 'No other preaching will do for Yorkshire,' John Nelson told Wesley, 'but the old sort that comes like a thunderclap upon the conscience. Fine preaching does more harm than good here.' And yet old Calvinism had erected its own barriers which inhibited any evangelistic zeal. The persecuted sect only too easily made a virtue of its own exclusiveness, and this in turn reinforced the hardest tenets of Calvinist dogma. 'Election,' ran

1. J. Ivimey, *History of the English Baptists* (1830), IV, p. 40.

one article of the Savoy Confession (1658), 'was not out of the corrupt lump or mass of mankind foreseen.' 'Christ's poor' and the 'corrupt lump' were of course the same people: from another aspect the 'wildness' of the poor was a sign that they lived outwith the bounds of grace. The Calvinist elect tended to narrow into a kinship group.

And there were other reasons for this process. Some go right back to the defeat of the Levellers in the Commonwealth. When the millennial hopes for a rule of the Saints were dashed to the ground, there followed a sharp dissociation between the temporal and spiritual aspirations of the poor man's Puritanism. Already in 1654, before the Restoration, the General Association of the General Baptists issued a manifesto (aimed at the Fifth Monarchy men in their midst) declaring that they did not 'know any ground for the saints, as such, to expect that the Rule and Government of the World should be put into their hands' until the Last Judgement. Until such time it was their portion 'patiently to suffer from the world ... than anywhere to attain the Rule of Government thereof'.[1] At the end of the Commonwealth, the rebellious tradition of Antinomianism 'curved back from all its claims'. Where the ardent sectaries had been zealous – indeed, ruthless – social gardeners, they were now content to say: 'let the tares (if tares) alone with the wheat ...'[2] Gerrard Winstanley, the Digger, helps us to understand the movement of feeling, turning away from the 'kingdom without' to the 'kingdom within':

The living soul and the creating spirit are not one, but divided, the one looking after a kingdom without him, the other drawing him to look and wait for a kingdom within him, which moth and rust doth not corrupt and thieves cannot break through and steal. This is a kingdom that will abide, the outward kingdom must be taken from you.[3]

An understanding of this withdrawal – and of what was preserved despite the withdrawal – is crucial to an understanding

1. A. C. Underwood, *History of the English Baptists* (1947), pp. 84–5.
2. G. Huehns, *Antinomianism in English History* (1951), p. 146.
3. *Fire in the Bush* in *Selections ... from Gerrard Winstanley*, ed. L. Hamilton (1944), pp. 30–1.

of the eighteenth century and of a continuing element in later working-class politics. In one sense, the change can be seen in the different associations called up by two words: the positive energy of *Puritanism*, the self-preserving retreat of *Dissent*. But we must also see the way in which the resolution of the sects to 'patiently suffer from the world' while abstaining from the hope of attaining to its 'Rule and Government' enabled them to combine political quietism with a kind of slumbering Radicalism – preserved in the imagery of sermons and tracts and in democratic form of organization –which might, in any more hopeful context, break into fire once more. We might expect to find this most marked among the Quakers and the Baptists. By the 1790s, however, the Quakers – who numbered fewer than 20,000 in the United Kingdom – seem little like a sect which once contained such men as Lilbourne, Fox and Penn. They had prospered too much: had lost some of their most energetic spirits in successive emigrations to America: their hostility to State, and authority had diminished to formal symbols – the refusal to swear oath or to bare the head: the continuing tradition, at its best, gave more to the social conscience of the middle class than to the popular movement. In the mid-century there were still humble congregations like that which met in the meeting-house in Cage Lane, Thetford – adjoining the gaol, with its pillory and stocks – where young Tom Paine received (by his own avowal) 'an exceeding good moral education'. But few Quakers seem to have come forward when Paine, in 1791, combined some of their own notions of service to humanity with the intransigent tone of *Rights of Man*. In 1792 the Yorkshire Quarterly Meeting of Friends urged on its members 'true quietude of mind' in the 'state of unsettlement which at present exists in our nation'. They should not unite in political associations, nor should they promote 'a spirit of disaffection to the King and to the Government under which we live and enjoy many privileges and favours which merit our grateful subjection thereto'.[1]

Their forebears had not accepted *subjection*, nor would they have admitted the word *grateful*. The tension between the

1. Rufus M. Jones, *The Later Periods of Quakerism* (1921), I, p. 315.

kingdoms 'without' and 'within' implied a *rejection* of the ruling powers except at points where coexistence was inevitable: and much nice argument had once turned on what was 'lawful' to the conscience and what was not. The Baptists, perhaps, showed the greatest consistency: and they remained most Calvinist in their theology and most plebeian in their following. And it is above all in Bunyan that we find the slumbering Radicalism which was preserved through the eighteenth century and which breaks out again and again in the nineteenth. *Pilgrim's Progress* is, with *Rights of Man*, one of the two foundation texts of the English working-class movement: Bunyan and Paine, with Cobbett and Owen, contributed most to the stock of ideas and attitudes which make up the raw material of the movement from 1790-1850. Many thousands of youths found in *Pilgrim's Progress* their first adventure story, and would have agreed with Thomas Cooper, the Chartist, that it was their 'book of books'.[1]

'I seek an inheritance incorruptible, undefiled, and that fadeth not away ... laid up in heaven, and safe there ... to be bestowed, at the time appointed, on them that diligently seek it. Read it so, if you will, in my book.' Here is Winstanley's kingdom which 'moth and rust doth not corrupt', here is the other-worldly millennium of the Saints, who must 'patiently suffer from' this world. Here is the 'lamentable cry' – 'What shall I do?' – of those who lost at Putney, and who had no share in the settlement of 1688. Here is Old Man P O P E, whom Christian feels that *his* forebears have tamed, and who has now 'grown so crazy and stiff in his joints', that he can do little but sit in his cave's mouth, saying to the pilgrims – 'You will never mend till more of you be burned' – 'grinning ... as they go by, and biting his nails because he cannot come at them.' Here is the inner spiritual landscape of the poor man's Dissent – of the 'tailors, leather-sellers, soap-boilers, brewers, weavers and tinkers' who were among Baptist preachers [2] – a landscape seeming all the more lurid, suffused with passionate energy and conflict, from the frustration of these passions in

1. See Q. D. Leavis, *Fiction and the Reading Public* (1932), ch. 2.
2. R. M. Jones, *Studies in Mystical Religion* (1923), p. 418. See also J. Lindsay, *John Bunyan* (1937).

the outer world: Beelzebub's Castle, the giants Bloody-man, Maul, and Slay-good, the Hill Difficulty, Doubting Castle, Vanity Fair, the Enchanted Ground; a way 'full of snares, pits, traps, and gins'. Here are Christian's aristocratic enemies – 'the Lord Carnal Delight, the Lord Luxurious, the Lord Desire of Vain Glory, my old Lord Lechery, Sir Having Greedy, with all the rest of our nobility'. And here is the Valley of Humiliation in which Bunyan's readers were to be found: 'a Valley that nobody walks in, but those that love a pilgrim's life'. It is MERCY who says:

I love to be in such places where there is no rattling with coaches, nor rumbling with wheels; methinks, here one may, without much molestation, be thinking what he is, whence he came, what he has done ... here one may think, and break at heart, and melt in one's spirit, until one's eyes become like 'the fishpools of Heshbon'.

And it is GREAT-HEART who replies, with the spiritual pride of the persecuted and unsuccessful: 'It is true ... I have gone through this Valley many a time, and never was better than when here.'

But the world of the spirit – of righteousness and spiritual liberty – is constantly under threat from the other world. First, it is threatened by the powers of the State: when we encounter APOLLYON we seem to be in a world of fantasy:

He was clothed with scales, like a fish (and they are 'his pride), he had wings like a dragon, feet like a bear, and out of his belly came fire and smoke...

But when this monster turns upon CHRISTIAN ('with a disdainful countenance') he turns out to be very like the perplexed country magistrates who tried, with alternating arguments and threats, to make Bunyan promise to desist from field-preaching. APOLLYON, opens his mouth – which was 'as the mouth of a lion' – for a very muted roar: 'I am willing to pass by all, if now thou wilt yet turn again and go back.' Only when persuasion has failed does he straddle 'over the whole breadth of the way' and declare: 'I swear by my infernal den, that thou shalt go no further.' And it is APOLLYON'S subtlety which enables him to find allies among CHRISTIAN'S own company and fellow pilgrims. These – and they are by far the most numerous and deceptive – are the second source of threat to CHRISTIAN's incorruptible inheritance; one by one, Bunyan brings forward all the slippery arguments of comfort and compromise preparing the way for an accommodation between APOLLYON and Dissent. There is Mr By-ends of Fair-Speech: and Mr Hold-the-world, Mr Money-love, and Mr Save-all, all pupils of 'a schoolmaster in Love-gain, which is a market town in the county of Coveting, in the north'. It is Mr By-ends who condemns those 'that are righteous over-much':

BY-ENDS: Why, they ... rush on their journey all weathers; and I am for waiting for wind and tide. They are for hazarding all for God at a clap; and I am for taking all advantages to secure my life and estate. They are for holding their notions, though all other men are against them; but I am for religion in what, and so far as the times, and my safety will bear it. They are for religion when in rags and contempt; but I am for him when he walks in his golden slippers, in the sunshine, with applause.

MR HOLD-THE-WORLD: Aye, and hold you there still, good Mr By-Ends. ... Let us be wise as serpents; it is best to make hay when the sun shines. ..

MR SAVE-ALL: I think that we are all agreed in this matter, and therefore there needs no more words about it.

MR MONEY-LOVE: No, there needs no more words about this matter, indeed; for he that believes neither Scripture nor reason (and you see we have both on our side), neither knows his own liberty, nor seeks his own safety.

It is a splendid passage, foreshadowing so much in the development of eighteenth-century Dissent. Bunyan knew that in a sense Mr By-end's friends *did* have both Scripture and reason on their side: he worked into his apologia the arguments of security, comfort, enlightenment and liberty. What they have lost is their moral integrity and their compassion; the incorruptible inheritance of the spirit, it seems, could not be preserved if the inheritance of struggle was forgotten.

This is not all that *Pilgrim's Progress* is about. As Weber noted, the 'basic atmosphere' of the book is one in which 'the after-life was not only more important, but in many ways also more certain, than all the interests of life in this world'.[1] And this reminds us that faith in a life to come served not only as a consolation to the poor but also as some emotional compensation for present sufferings and grievances: it was possible not only to imagine the 'reward' of the humble but also to enjoy some revenge upon their oppressors, by imagining their torments to come. Moreover, in stressing the positives in Bunyan's imagery we have said little of the obvious negatives – the unction, the temporal submissiveness, the egocentric pursuit of personal salvation – with which they are inseparably intermingled; and this ambivalence continues in the language of humble Nonconformity far into the eighteenth century. The story seemed to Bamford to be 'mournfully soothing, like that of a light coming from an eclipsed sun'. When the context is hopeful and mass agitations arise, the active energies of the tradition are most apparent: Christian does battle with Apollyon in the real world. In times of defeat and mass apathy, quietism is in the ascendant, reinforcing the fatalism of the poor: Christian suffers in the Valley of Humiliation, far from the rattling of coaches, turning his back on the City of Destruction and seeking the way to a spiritual City of Zion.

Moreover, Bunyan, in his fear of the erosion of the inheritance by compromise, added to the forbidding Puritan joylessness his own figurative portrayal of the 'straight and narrow' path, which emphasized the jealous sectarianism of the Calvinist elect. By 1750 those very sects which had sought to be most loyal to 'Christ's poor' were least welcoming to new converts, least evangelistic in temper. Dissent was caught in the tension between opposing tendencies, both of which led away from any popular appeal: on the other hand, the tendency towards rational humanitarianism and fine preaching – too intellectual and genteel for the poor; on the other hand, the rigid Elect, who might not marry outside the church, who expelled all back-sliders and heretics, and who stood apart from the 'corrupt mass' predestined to be damned. 'The Calvinism

1. M. Weber, *The Protestant Ethic and the Spirit of Capitalism* (1930), pp. 109–10, 227. See also A. Kettle, *Introduction to the English Novel* (1951), pp. 44–5.

of the former,' Halévy noted, 'was undergoing decomposition, the Calvinism of the latter petrification.'[1]

Even Bunyan's Baptists were deeply divided in this way, the 'Arminian' General Baptists losing ground to the zealously Calvinist Particular Baptists (with their strongholds in Northamptonshire, Bedfordshire, Lincolnshire) whose very Calvinism, however, prevented the progagation of the sect.[2] It was not until 1770 that the Particular Baptists began to break out of the trap of their own dogma, issuing a circular letter (from Northamptonshire) which offered a formula by which evangelism and the notion of election might be reconciled: 'Every soul that comes to Christ to be saved ... is to be encouraged ... The coming soul need not fear that he is not elected, for none but such would be willing to come.' But the revival was slow; and it was competition with the Methodists, rather than an inner dynamic, which drove the Baptists back to the poor. When, in the 1760s, Dan Taylor, a Yorkshire collier who had worked in the pit from the age of five and who had been converted by the Methodists, looked around for a Baptist sect with an evangelistic temper, he could find nothing that suited. He built his own meeting-house, digging the stone out of the moors above Hebden Bridge and carrying it on his own back;[3] then he walked down from the weaving township of Heptonstall (a Puritan stronghold during the Civil War) to Lincolnshire and Northamptonshire, making contact with restive Baptist groups, and finally forming (in 1770) the Baptist New Connexion. Travelling in the next years 25,000 miles and preaching 20,000 sermons he is a man to be remembered by the side of Wesley and Whitefield; but he came from neither the Particular nor the General Baptist societies: spiritually, perhaps, he came from Bunyan's inheritance, but literally he just came out of the ground.

We should remember both Dr Price and Dan Taylor; and

1. See Halévy's excellent summary, *A History of the English People in 1815* (Penguin edn), III, pp. 28–32, 40–8.

2. Bogue and Bennett, op. cit., III, pp. 332–3; Ivimey, op. cit., III, pp. 160 ff.

3. John Wesley notes in his *Journal* (31 July 1766) that 'renegade Methodists, first turning Calvinist, then Anabaptist have made confusion at Heptonstall'.

we should recall that they *did* enjoy liberty of conscience, they
were not threatened by the Inquisition or the dungeon of the
'Scarlet Whore of Babylon'.[1] The very anarchy of Old Dissent,
with its self-governing churches and its schisms, meant that
the most unexpected and unorthodox ideas might suddenly
appear – in a Lincolnshire village, a Midlands market-town, a
Yorkshire pit. In the Somerset woollen town of Frome (Wesley
noted in his *Journal* in 1768) there was 'a mixture of men of all
opinions, Anabaptists, Quakers, Presbyterians, Arians, Antinomians, Moravians and what not'. Scottish tradesmen and
artisans brought other sects into England; in the last decades
of the eighteenth century the Glasites or Sandemanians made
a little headway with their zealous church discipline, their belief that the 'distinctions of civil life [were] annihilated in the
church' and that membership implied some community of
goods, and – in the view of critics – their inordinate spiritual
pride and 'neglect of the poor, ignorant, perishing multitude'.[2]
By the end of the century, there were Sandemanian societies in
London, Nottingham, Liverpool, Whitehaven and Newcastle.

The intellectual history of Dissent is made up of collisions,
schisms, mutations; and one feels often that the dormant seeds
of political Radicalism lie within it, ready to germinate whenever planted in a beneficent and hopeful social context.
Thomas Spence, who was brought up in a Sandemanian family,
delivered a lecture to the Newcastle Philosophical Society in
1775 which contained in outline his whole doctrine of agrarian
Socialism; and yet it was not until the 1790s that he commenced
his serious public propaganda. Tom Paine, with his Quaker
background, had shown little sign of his outrageously hetero-
dox political views during his humdrum life as an exciseman

1. Dissent's term for Erastianism – in the first place the Papacy and the
Roman Church, but often attached to the Church of England or *any*
church accused of prostituting its spiritual virtue to reasons of State and
worldly power. Cobbett recalled: 'I most firmly believed when I was a
boy, that the Pope was a prodigious woman, dressed in a dreadful robe,
which had been made red by being dipped in the blood of Protestants.'
Political Register, 13 January 1821.
2. Bogue and Bennett, op. cit., IV, pp. 107–24. Despite their severity,
the Sandemanians were less bigoted than other Dissenters about some
social observances, and approved of the theatre.

at Lewes; the context was hopeless, politics seemed a mere species of 'jockeyship'. Within one year of his arrival in America (November 1774) he had published *Common Sense* and the *Crisis* articles which contain all the assumptions of *Rights of Man*. 'I have an aversion to monarchy, as being too debasing to the dignity of man,' he wrote. 'But I never troubled others with my notions till very lately, nor ever published a syllable in England in my life.' What had changed was not Paine, but the context in which he wrote. The seed of *Rights of Man* was English: but only the hope brought by the American and French Revolutions enabled it to strike.

If some sect of Old Dissent had set the pace of the evangelical revival – instead of John Wesley – then nineteenth-century Nonconformity might have assumed a more intellectual and democratic form. But it was Wesley – High Tory in politics, sacerdotal in his approach to organization – who first reached 'Christ's poor', breaking the Calvinist taboo with the simple message: 'You have nothing to do but save souls.'

> Outcasts of men, to you I call,
>   Harlots, and publicans, and thieves!
> He spreads his arms to embrace you all;
>   Sinners alone His grace receives:
> No need for him the righteous have;
> He came the lost to seek and save.
>
> Come, O my guilty brethren, come,
>   Groaning beneath your load of sin!
> His bleeding heart shall make you room,
>   His open side shall take you in;
> He calls you now, invites you home:
> Come, O my guilty brethren, come.

There is, of course, a certain logic in the fact that the evangelical revival should have come from within the Established Church. The Puritan emphasis upon a 'calling' was, as Weber and Tawney have shown, particularly well adapted to the experience of prospering and industrious middle class or petty bourgeois groups. The more Lutheran traditions of Anglican Protestantism were less adapted to exclusive doctrines of 'election'; while as the *established* Church it had a peculiar charge over the souls of the poor – indeed, the duty to incul-

cate in them the virtues of obedience and industry. The lethargy
and materialism of the eighteenth-century Church were such
that, in the end and against Wesley's wishes, the evangelical
revival resulted in the distinct Methodist Church. And yet
Methodism was profoundly marked by its origin; the poor
man's Dissent of Bunyan, of Dan Taylor, and – later – of the
Primitive Methodists was a religion *of* the poor; orthodox
Wesleyanism remained as it had commenced, a religion *for* the
poor.

As preachers and evangelists, Whitefield and other early
field-preachers were more impressive than Wesley. But it was
Wesley who was the superlatively energetic and skilful organizer, administrator, and law-giver. He succeeded in combining
in exactly the right proportions democracy and discipline,
doctrine and emotionalism; his achievement lay not so much
in the hysterical revivalist meetings (which were not uncommon in the century of Tyburn) but in the organization of self-
sustaining Methodist societies in trading and market centres,
and in mining, weaving, and labouring communities, the democratic participation of whose members in the life of the Church
was both enlisted and strictly superintended and disciplined.
He facilitated entry to these societies by sweeping away all barriers of sectarian doctrines. In order to gain admission, he
wrote, Methodists

do not impose ... any opinions whatever. Let them hold particular
or general redemption, absolute or conditional decrees; let them be
Churchmen or Dissenters, Presbyterians or Independents, it is no
obstacle. ... The Independent or Anabaptist [may] use his own
mode of worship; so may the Quaker, and none will contend with
him about it. ... One condition, and one only, is required, – a real
desire to save their souls.[1]

But once within the Methodist societies, the converted were
subjected to a discipline which challenges comparison with the
more zealous Calvinist sects. Wesley wished the Methodists to
be a 'peculiar people'; to abstain from marriage outside the
societies; to be distinguished by their dress and by the gravity
of their speech and manners; to avoid the company even of

1. R. Southey, *Life of Wesley and the Rise of Methodism*, (1890 edn),
p. 545.

relatives who were still in 'Satan's kingdom'. Members were expelled for levity, for profanity and swearing, for lax attendance at class meetings. The societies, with their confessional band-meetings, classes, watch-nights and visiting, made up a lay order within which, as Southey noted, there was a 'spiritual police' constantly alert for any sign of relapse.[1] The 'grass roots' democracy, by which the societies were officered by tradesmen and working people, extended not at all to matters of doctrine or Church government. In nothing did Wesley break more sharply with the traditions of Dissent than in his opposition to local autonomy, and in the authoritarian rule of himself and of his nominated ministers.

And yet it was often in areas with a long Dissenting tradition – Bristol, the West Riding, Manchester, Newcastle – that Methodism made most rapid headway among the poor. In the 1760s, two miles from Heckmondwike, where Deacon Priestley and Obadiah were still supporting a church of Calvinist Independents, John Nelson, a Birstall stone-mason, was already drawing great congregations of clothing workers and miners to hear the new message of personal salvation. On his way to work at the quarry Nelson would pass the old Dissenting minister's house, exchange texts, and argue the doctrines of sin, redemption by grace and predestination. (Such disputations became more rare in later years as orthodox Methodist theology became more opportunist, anti-intellectual, and otiose.) Nelson had been converted while in London, when hearing John Wesley preach in Moorfields. His *Journal* is very different from that of Deacon Priestley:

One night ... I dreamed that I was in Yorkshire, in my working clothes going home; and as I went by Paul Champion's, I heard a mighty cry, as of a multitude of people in distress. ... All on a sudden they began to scream and tumble over one another; I asked, what was the matter; and they told me, Satan was let loose among them. ... Then I thought I saw him in the shape of a red bull, running through the people, as a beast runs through the standing corn, yet did not offer to gore any of them, but made directly at me, as if he would run his horns into my heart. Then I cried out, 'Lord, help me!' and immediately caught him by the horns, and twisted

1. Ibid., pp. 382, 545.

him on his back, setting my right foot on his neck, in the presence of a thousand people. . .

From this dream he awoke perspiring and exhausted. On another night 'my soul was filled with such a sense of God's love, as made me weep before him':

I dreamed I was in Yorkshire, going from Gomersal-Hill-Top to Cleckheaton; and about the middle of the lane, I thought I saw Satan coming to meet me in the shape of a tall, black man, and the hair of his head like snakes; . . . But I went on, ript open my clothes, and shewed him my naked breast, saying, 'See, here is the blood of Christ.' Then I thought he fled from me as fast as a hare could run.

John Nelson was very much in earnest. He was pressed into the Army, refused to serve, he and his wife were mobbed and stoned in their work. But it occurs to one, nevertheless, that Nelson's Satan belongs more to a world of fantasy than Bunyan's Apollyon, for all the latter's fire and scales. And the fantasy has undertones of hysteria and of impaired or frustrated sexuality which – along with the paroxysms which often accompanied conversion [1] – are among the hallmarks of the Methodist revival. Where Bunyan disclosed the challenge of Apollyon in a world of magistrates, backsliders and worldly excuses for compromise, this Methodist Satan is a disembodied force located somewhere in the psyche, discovered through introspection or springing forward as a phallic image opposed to the feminine imagery of Christ's love in the gusts of mass hysteria which climaxed revivalist campaigns.

From one aspect this Satan may be seen as an emanation of the misery and despair of the eighteenth-century poor; from another we may see the energies thwarted of effective outlet in social life and constricted by the life-denying tenets of Puritanism taking a monstrous revenge on the human spirit. We can see Methodism as a mutation of that tradition which reaches back to the seventeenth-century 'Ranters', whose cousins the Moravians so deeply influenced Wesley. But the cult of 'Love'

1. See W. E. H. Lecky, *History of the English People in the 18th Century* (1891), III, pp. 582–8. Despite all that has been written in this century, on the subject of Methodism the accounts in Lecky and in Southey remain essential reading.

was brought to a point of poise between the affirmations of 'social religion' and the pathological aberrations of frustrated social and sexual impulses. On the one hand, genuine compassion for 'harlots, and publicans, and thieves': on the other hand, morbid preoccupation with sin and with the sinner's confessional. On one hand, real remorse for real wrong-doing: on the other, luxuriating refinements of introspective guilt. On one hand, the genuine fellowship of some early Methodist societies: on the other, social energies denied outlet in public life which were released in sanctified emotional onanism. On one hand, a religion which found a place for humble men, as local preachers and class leaders, which taught them to read and gave them self-respect and experience in speaking and in organization: on the other hand, a religion hostile to intellectual enquiry and to artistic values, which sadly abused their intellectual trust. Here was a cult of 'Love' which feared love's effective expression, either as sexual love or in any social form which might irritate relations with Authority. Its authentic language of devotion was that of sexual sublimation streaked through with masochism: the 'bleeding love', the wounded side, the blood of the Lamb:

> Teach me from every pleasing snare
> To keep the issues of my heart.
> Be Thou my Love, my Joy, my Fear!
> Thou my Eternal Portion art.
> Be Thou my never-failing Friend,
> And love, O love me to the end.

In London a Jacobin engraver went to the 'Garden of Love' and found 'a Chapel ... built in the midst,/Where I used to play on the green':

> And the gates of this Chapel were shut,
> And 'Thou shalt not' writ over the door ...

In the Garden were 'tomb-stones where flowers should be':

> And Priests in black gowns were walking their rounds,
> And binding with briars my joys & desires.

So much has been said, in recent years, of Methodism's positive contribution to the working-class movement that it is necessary to remind ourselves that Blake and Cobbett, Leigh Hunt and Hazlitt, saw the matter differently. We might suppose, from some popular accounts, that Methodism was no more than a nursing-ground for Radical and trade union organizers, all formed in the image of the Tolpuddle martyr, George Loveless, with his 'small theological library' and his forthright independence. The matter is a great deal more complex. At one level the reactionary – indeed, odiously subservient – character of official Wesleyanism can be established without the least difficulty. Wesley's few active interventions into politics included pamphleteering against Dr Price and the American colonists. He rarely let pass any opportunity to impress upon his followers the doctrines of submission, expressed less at the level of ideas than of superstition.[1] His death (1791) coincided with the early enthusiasm for the French Revolution; but successive Methodist Conferences continued the tradition of their founder, reaffirming their 'unfeigned loyalty to the King and sincere attachment to the Constitution' (Leeds Conference, 1793). The statutes drawn up in the year after Wesley's death were explicit: 'None of us shall either in writing or in conversation speak lightly or irreverently of the Government.'[2]

Thus, at this level Methodism appears as a politically regressive, or 'stabilizing', influence, and we find some confirmation of Halévy's famous thesis that Methodism prevented revolution in England in the 1790s. But, at another level, we are familiar with the argument that Methodism was indirectly responsible for a growth in the self-confidence and capacity for organization of working people. This argument was stated, as early as 1820, by Southey:

1. For a succinct account of Wesley's political prejudices, see Maldwyn Edwards, *John Wesley and the Eighteenth Century* (1933).

2. Cited in Halévy, op. cit., III, p. 49. Halévy adds the comment: 'Such conduct ensured that . . . the unpopularity of Jacobin principles did not prejudice the Methodist propaganda.' However, since Jacobin principles were gaining in popularity in 1792 (see pp. 111–23 below), it is more true that the Methodist propaganda was designed to *make* these principles unpopular, and that this was prejudicial to the liberties of the English people. See also Hobsbawm's critique of Halévy, 'Methodism and the Threat of Revolution', *History Today*, February 1957.

Perhaps the manner in which Methodism has familiarized the lower classes to the work of combining in associations, making rules for their own governance, raising funds, and communicating from one part of the kingdom to another, may be reckoned among the incidental evils which have resulted from it . . .

And, more recently, it has been documented in Dr Wearmouth's interesting books; although readers of them will do well to remember Southey's important qualification – 'but in this respect it has only facilitated a process to which other causes had given birth'.[1] Most of the 'contributions' of Methodism to the working-class movement came in spite of and not because of the Wesleyan Conference.

Indeed, throughout the early history of Methodism we can see a shaping democratic spirit which struggled against the doctrines and the organizational forms which Wesley imposed. Lay preachers, the break with the Established Church, self-governing forms within the societies – on all these questions Wesley resisted or temporized or followed after the event. Wesley could not escape the consequences of his own spiritual egalitarianism. If Christ's poor came to believe that their souls were as good as aristocratic or bougeois souls then it might lead them on to the arguments of the *Rights of Man*. The Duchess of Buckingham was quick to spot this, and observed to the Methodist Countess of Huntingdon:

I Thank Your Ladyship for the information concerning the Methodist preachers; their doctrines are most repulsive and strongly tinctured with impertinence and disrespect towards their Superiors, in perpetually endeavouring to level all ranks and to do away with all distinctions. It is monstrous to be told you have a heart as sinful as the common wretches that crawl on the earth.[2]

Smollett had pointed out much the same thing, in the high comedy of a coachman, Humphrey Clinker, preaching to the London rabble. And – for their part – hundreds of lay preachers who followed in John Nelson's footsteps were learning this in a very different way. Again and again Establishment writers voice this fear. An anti-Jacobin pamphleteer, in 1800, laid blame upon the 'beardless boys, and mechanics or

1. Southey, op. cit., p. 571.
2. Cited in J. H. Whiteley, *Wesley's England* (1938), p. 328.

labourers' who preached in Spa Fields, Hackney, and Islington Green. Among the preachers of the sects he found a Dealer in Old Clothes, a Grinder, a Sheep's-Head Seller, a Coach-painter, a Mangle-maker, a Footman, a Tooth-drawer, a Peruke-maker and Phlebotomist, a Breeches-maker, and a Coal-heaver. The Bishop of Lincoln saw in this a darker threat: 'the same means might, with equal efficacy, be employed to sap and overturn the state, as well as the church'.[1]

And from preaching to organization. There are two questions here: the temporary permeation of Methodism by some of the self-governing traditions of Dissent, and the transmission to working-class societies of forms of organization peculiar to the Methodist Connexion. For the first, Wesley did not only (as is sometimes supposed) take his message to 'heathen' outside the existing churches; he also offered an outlet for the land-locked emotions of Old Dissent. There were Dissenting minis-ters, and whole congregations, who joined the Methodists. Some passed through the revival, only to rejoin their own sects in disgust at Wesley's authoritarian government; while by the 1790s Dissent was enjoying its own evangelistic revival. But others maintained a somewhat restive membership, in which their older traditions struggled within the sacerdotal Wesleyan forms. For the second, Methodism provided not only the forms of the class meeting, the methodical collection of penny sub-scriptions and the 'ticket', so frequently borrowed by radical and trade union organizations, but also an experience of effi-cient centralized organization – at district as well as national level – which Dissent had lacked. (Those Wesleyan Annual Conferences, with their 'platform', their caucuses at work on the agendas, and their careful management, seem uncomfort-ably like another 'contribution' to the Labour movement of more recent times.)

Thus late eighteenth-century Methodism was troubled by alien democratic tendencies within itself, while at the same time it was serving despite itself as a model of other organizational forms. During the last decade of Wesley's life internal demo-cratic pressures were restrained only by reverence for the

1. W. H. Reid, *The Rise and Dissolution of the Infidel Societies of the Metropolis* (1800), pp. 45–8.

founder's great age – and by the belief that the old autocrat could not be far from entering upon his 'great reward'. There were a score of demands being voiced in dissident societies: for an elected Conference, for greater local autonomy, for the final break with the Church, for lay participation in district and quarterly meetings. Wesley's death, when the general radical tide was rising, was like a 'signal gun'. Rival schemes of organization were canvassed with a heat which is as significant as were the matters under dispute. 'We detest the conduct of persecuting Neros, and all the bloody actions of the great Whore of Babylon, and yet in our measure, we tread in their steps,' declared Alexander Kilham in a pamphlet entitled *The Progress of Liberty*.[1] And he set forward far-reaching proposals for self-government, which were canvassed throughout the Connexion, by means of pamphlets, and in class meetings and local preachers' meetings, and whose discussion must itself have been an important part of the process of democratic education.[2]

In 1797 Kilham led the first important Wesleyan secession, the Methodist New Connexion, which adopted many of his proposals for a more democratic structure. The greatest strength of the Connexion was in manufacturing centres, and (it is probable) among the artisans and weavers tinged with Jacobinism.[3] Kilham himself sympathized with the reformers, and although his political convictions were kept in the background, his opponents in the orthodox Connexion were at pains to bring them forward. 'We shall lose all the turbulent disturbers of our Zion,' the Conference addressed the members of the Church in Ireland, when accounting for the secession:

1. *The Progress of Liberty Amongst the People Called Methodists* (Alnwick, 1795).

2. See *An Appeal to the Members of the Methodist Connexion* (Manchester, 1796); E. R. Taylor, *Methodism and Politics, 1791–1851* (Cambridge, 1935), ch. 2; W. J. Warner, *The Wesleyan Movement in the Industrial Revolution* (1930), pp. 128–31.

3. Kilham's support was strong in Sheffield, Nottingham, Manchester, Leeds, Huddersfield, Plymouth Dock, Liverpool, Bristol, Birmingham, Burslem, Macclesfield, Bolton, Wigan, Blackburn, Oldham, Darlington, Newcastle, Alnwick, Sunderland, Ripon, Otley, Epworth, Chester, Banbury. See E. R. Taylor, op. cit., p. 81; J. Blackwell, *Life of Alexander Kilham* (1838), pp. 290, 343.

'all who have embraced the sentiments of Paine ...' In Huddersfield the members of the New Connexion were known as the 'Tom Paine Methodists'. We may guess at the complexion of his following from an account of the principal Kilhamite chapel in Leeds, with a congregation of 500 'in the midst of a dense, poor, and unruly population, at the top of Ebeneezer Street where strangers of the middle class could not reasonably be expected to go'. And in several places the link between the New Connexion and actual Jacobin organization is more than a matter of inference. In Halifax, at the Bradshaw chapel, a reading club and debating society was formed. The people of this weaving village discussed in their class meetings not only Kilham's *Progress of Liberty* but also Paine's *Rights of Man*. Writing forty years later, the historian of Halifax Methodism still could not restrain his abomination of 'that detestable knot of scorpions' who, in the end, captured the chapel, excluded the orthodox circuit minister, bought the site, and continued it as a 'Jacobin' chapel of their own.[1]

The progress of the New Connexion was unspectacular. Kilham himself died in 1798, and his following was weakened by the general political reaction of the later 1790s. By 1811 the New Connexion could claim only 8,000 members. But its existence leads one to doubt Halévy's thesis. On Wesley's death it was estimated that about 80,000 people made up the Methodist societies. Even if we suppose that every one of them shared the Tory principles of their founder, this was scarcely sufficient to have stemmed a revolutionary tide. In fact, whatever Annual Conferences resolved, there is evidence that the Radical groundswell of 1792 and 1793 extended through Dissent generally and into most Methodist societies. The Mayor of Liverpool may have shown sound observation when he wrote to the Home Office in 1792:

In all these places are nothing but Methodist and other Meeting houses and ... thus the Youth of the Countery are training up under the Instruction of a Set of Men not only Ignorant, but whom I

1. J. Blackwell, op. cit., p. 339; E. R. Taylor, op. cit., p. 85; J. Wray, 'Facts Illustrative of Methodism in Leeds' [c. 1835], MS. in Leeds Reference Library; J. U. Walker, *Wesleyan Methodism in Halifax* (Halifax, 1836), pp. 216–23.

believe we have of late too Much Reason to imagine, are inimical to Our Happy Constitution.[1]

It was in the counter-revolutionary years *after* 1795 that Methodism made the most headway amongst working people and acted most evidently as a stabilizing or regressive social force. Drained of its more democratic and intellectual elements by the Kilhamite secession, and subjected to severer forms of discipline, it appears during these years almost as a new phenomenon – and as one which may be seen as the consequence of political reaction as much as it was a cause.[2]

Throughout the whole period of the Industrial Revolution, Methodism never overcame this tension between authoritarian and democratic tendencies. It is in the seceding sects – the New Connexion and (after 1806) the Primitive Methodists – that the second impulse was felt most strongly. Moreover, as Dr Hobsbawm has pointed out, wherever Methodism was found it performed, in its rupture with the Established Church, certain of the functions of anti-clericalism in nineteenth-century France.[3] In the agricultural or mining village, the polarization of chapel and Church might facilitate a polarization which took political or industrial forms. For years the tension might seem to be contained; but when it did break out it was sometimes charged with a moral passion – where the old Puritan God of Battles raised his banners once again – which secular leaders could rarely touch. So long as Satan remained undefined and of no fixed class abode, Methodism condemned working people to a kind of moral civil war – between the chapel and the pub, the wicked and the redeemed, the lost and the saved. Samuel Bamford related in his *Early Days* the missionary zeal with which he and his companions would tramp to prayer-meetings in neighbouring villages 'where Satan had as yet many strongholds'. 'These prayers were looked upon as so many assaults on "the powers of the Prince of the Air".' (A similar zeal inspired, on the other side of the Pennines, the notable hymn: 'On Bradford likewise look Thou down, Where Satan keeps

1. Cited in J. L. Hammond, *The Town Labourer* (2nd edn, 1925), p. 270.
2. See below, ch. 11.
3. E. J. Hobsbawm, *Primitive Rebels* (1959), p. 146.

his seat.') Only a few years later Cobbett had taught the weavers of upland Lancashire to look for Satan, not in the ale-houses of a rival village, but in 'the Thing' and Old Corruption. It was such a swift identification of Apollyon with Lord Liverpool and Oliver the Spy which led the weavers to Peterloo.

Two other features of the Dissenting tradition should be noted. While neither was of great influence in the eighteenth century, both assumed new significance after 1790. In the first place, there is a continuous thread of communitarian ideas and experiments, associated with the Quakers, Camisards, and in particular the Moravians. It was in Bolton and Manchester that a ferment in a small group of dissident Quakers culminated in the departure, in 1774, of 'Mother Ann' and a small party to found the first Shaker communities in the United States; forty years later Robert Owen was to find encouragement in the success of the Shakers, whose ideas he popularized in secular form.[1] The Moravians, to whom Wesley owed his conversion, never became fully naturalized in England in the eighteenth century. Although many English people entered their communities at Fulneck (Pudsey), and Dukinfield and Fairfield (near Manchester), as well as the Moravian congregation in London, the societies remained dependent upon German preachers and administrators. While the first Methodist societies arose in association with the Moravian Brotherhood, the latter were distinguished from the former by their 'stillness', their avoidance of enthusiasm', and their practical communitarian values; 'the calm, soft, steady, sweet and impressive character of the service [at Fulneck] was such as appeared as a kind of rebuke to the earnestness, noise, and uproar of a [Methodist] revival meeting'. The influence of the Moravians was three-fold: first, through their educational activities – Richard Oastler and James Montgomery (the Radical poet and editor of the Sheffield *Iris*) were educated at Fulneck; second, through the evident success of their communities, which – along with those of the Shakers – were often cited by early nineteenth-century Owenites; and third, through the perpetuation within the Methodist societies – long after Wesley had

1. W. H. G. Armytage, *Heavens Below* (1961), I, chs. 3 and 5.

disowned the Moravian connection – of the yearning for communitarian ideals expressed in the language of 'brotherhood' and 'sisterhood'.[1]

The communitarian tradition was sometimes found in association with another underground tradition, that of millennarianism. The wilder sectaries of the English Revolution – Ranters and Fifth Monarchy Men – were never totally extinguished, with their literal interpretations of the Book of Revelation and their anticipations of a New Jerusalem descending from above. The Muggletonians (or followers of Ludovic Muggleton) were still preaching in the fields and parks of London at the end of the eighteenth century. The Bolton society from which the Shakers originated was presided over by Mother Jane Wardley who paced the meeting-room 'with a mighty trembling', declaiming:

Repent. For the Kingdom of God is at Hand. The new heaven and new earth prophesied of old is about to come. . . . And when Christ appears again, and the true church rises in full and transcendant glory, then all anti-Christian denominations – the priests, the church, the pope – will be swept away.[2]

Any dramatic event, such as the Lisbon earthquake of 1755, aroused apocalyptic expectations. There was, indeed, a millennarial instability within the heart of Methodism itself. Wesley, who was credulous to a degree about witches, Satanic possession, and bibliomancy (or the search for guidance from texts opened at random in the Bible), sometimes voiced premonitions as to the imminence of the Day of Judgement. An early hymn of the Wesleys employs the customary millennarial imagery:

> Erect Thy tabernacle here,
> The *New Jerusalem* send down,
> Thyself amidst Thy saints appear,
> And seat us on Thy dazzling throne.

1. See C. W. Towlson, *Moravian and Methodist* (1957); Armytage, op. cit., I, ch. 6; J. Lawson, *Letters to the Young on Progress in Pudsey* (Stanningley, 1887), ch. 15; C. Driver, *Tory Radical* (Oxford, 1946), pp. 15–17.

2. E. D. Andrews, *The People Called Shakers* (New York, 1953), p. 6.

Begin the great millennial day;
Now, Saviour, with a shout descend,
Thy standard in the heavens display,
And bring the joy which ne'er shall end.

Even if literal belief in the millennium was discouraged, the apocalyptic manner of Methodist revival meetings inflamed the imagination and prepared the way for the acceptance of chiliastic prophets after 1790. In London, Bristol and Birmingham small congregations of the Swedenborgian Church of the New Jerusalem were preparing some artisans for more intellectual and mystical millennarial beliefs.[1]

Although historians and sociologists have recently given more attention to millennarial movements and fantasies, their significance has been partly obscured by the tendency to discuss them in terms of maladjustment and 'paranoia'. Thus Professor Cohn, in his interesting study of *The Pursuit of the Millennium*, is able – by a somewhat sensational selection of the evidence – to proceed to generalizations as to the paranoiac and megalomaniac notion of 'the Elect', and the 'chronically impaired sense of reality' of 'chiliastically minded movements'. When messianic movements gain mass support –

It is as though units of paranoia hitherto diffused through the population suddenly coalesce to form a new entity: a collective paranoiac fanaticism.[2]

One doubts such a process of 'coalescence'. Given such a phenomenon, however, the historical problem remains – why should grievances, aspirations, or even psychotic disorders, 'coalesce' into influential movements only at certain times and in particular forms?

1. For Wesleyanism, see Southey, op. cit., p. 367; Joseph Nightingale, *Portraiture of Methodism* (1807), pp. 443 ff.; J. E. Rattenbury, *The Eucharistic Hymns of John and Charles Wesley* (1948), p. 249. For Swedenborgianism, Bogue and Bennett, op. cit., IV, pp. 126–34; R. Southey, *Letters from England* (1808), III, pp. 113 ff. For the end of the seventeenth-century millennarialism, see Christopher Hill, 'John Mason and the End of the World', in *Puritanism and Revolution* (1958). For some indications of the eighteenth-century tradition, see W. H. G. Armytage, op. cit., I, ch. 4.

2. N. Cohn, *The Pursuit of the Millennium* (1957), p. 312.

What we must not do is confuse pure 'freaks' and fanatical aberrations with the *imagery* – of Babylon and the Egyptian exile and the Celestial City and the contest with Satan – in which minority groups have articulated their experience and projected their aspirations for hundreds of years. Moreover, the extravagant imagery used by certain groups does not always reveal their objective motivations and effective assumptions. This is a difficult question; when we speak of 'imagery' we mean much more than figures of speech in which ulterior motives were 'clothed'. The imagery is itself evidence of powerful subjective motivations, fully as 'real' as the objective, fully as effective, as we see repeatedly in the history of Puritanism, in their historical agency. It is the sign of how men felt and hoped, loved and hated, and of how they preserved certain values in the very texture of their language. But because the luxuriating imagery points sometimes to goals that are clearly illusory, this does not mean that we can lightly conclude that it indicates a 'chronically impaired sense of reality'. Moreover, abject 'adjustment' to suffering and want at times may indicate a sense of reality as impaired as that of the chiliast. Whenever we encounter such phenomena, we must try to distinguish between the psychic energy stored – and released – in language, however apocalyptic, and actual psychotic disorder.

Throughout the Industrial Revolution we can see this tension between the 'kingdom without' and the 'kingdom within' in the Dissent of the poor, with chiliasm at one pole, and quietism at the other. For generations the most commonly available education came by way of pulpit and Sunday School, the Old Testament and *Pilgrim's Progress*. Between this imagery and that social experience there was a continual interchange – a dialogue between attitudes and reality which was sometimes fruitful, sometimes arid, sometimes masochistic in its submissiveness, but rarely 'paranoiac'. The history of Methodism suggests that the morbid deformities of 'sublimation' are the most common aberrations of the poor in periods of social reaction; while paranoiac fantasies belong more to periods when revolutionary enthusiasms are released. It was in the immediate aftermath of the French Revolution that the millennarial current, so long underground, burst into the open with unexpected force:

For the real Chiliast, the present becomes the breach through which what was previously inward bursts out suddenly, takes hold of the outer world and transforms it.[1]

Image and reality again became confused. Chiliasm touched Blake with its breath: it walked abroad, not only among the Jacobins and Dissenters of artisan London, but in the mining and weaving villages of the Midlands and the north and the villages of the south-west.

But in most minds a balance was held between outer experience and the kingdom within, which the Powers of the World could not touch and which was stored with the evocative language of the Old Testament. Thomas Hardy was a sober, even prosaic, man, with a meticulous attention to the practical detail of organization. But when recalling his own trial for high treason, it seemed the most natural thing in the world that he should draw upon the Book of Kings for the language which most common Englishmen understood:

The people said 'what portion have we in David? Neither have we inheritance in the son of Jesse. To your tents, O Israel. . . . So Israel rebelled against the House of David unto this day.'

No easy summary can be offered as to the Dissenting tradition which was one of the elements precipitated in the English Jacobin agitation. It is its diversity which defies generalization and yet which is, in itself, its most important characteristic. In the complexity of competing sects and seceding chapels we have a forcing-bed for the variants of nineteenth-century working-class culture. Here are Unitarians or Independents, with a small but influential artisan following, nurtured in a strenuous intellectual tradition. There are the Sandemanians, among whom William Godwin's father was a minister; the Moravians with their communitarian heritage; the Inghamites, the Muggletonians, the Swedenborgian sect which originated in a hairdresser's off Cold Bath Fields and which published a *Magazine of Heaven and Hell.* Here are the two old Dissenting

1. Karl Mannheim, *Ideology and Utopia* (1960 edn), p 193. See below pp. 127–30 and 421–6.

ministers whom Hazlitt observed stuffing raspberry leaves in their pipes, in the hope of bringing down Old Corruption by boycotting all taxed articles. There are the Calvinist Methodist immigrants from Wales, and immigrants brought up in the Covenanting sects of Scotland – Alexander Somerville, who became a famous anti-Corn Law publicist, was educated as a strict Anti-Burgher in a family of Berwickshire field-labourers. There is the printing-worker, Zachariah Coleman, the beautifully re-created hero of *The Revolution in Tanner's Lane*, with his portraits of Burdett, Cartwright, and Sadler's Bunyan on the wall: 'he was not a ranter or revivalist, but what was called a moderate Calvinist; that is to say, he held to Calvinism as his undoubted creed, but when it came to the push in actual practice he modified it'. And there are curious societies, like the Ancient Deists of Hoxton, who spoke of dreams and (like Blake) of conversations with departed souls and Angels, and who (like Blake) 'almost immediately yielded to the stronger impulse of the French Revolution' and became '*politicians*'.[1]

Liberty of conscience was the one great value which the common people had preserved from the Commonwealth. The countryside was ruled by the gentry, the towns by corrupt corporations, the nation by the corruptest corporation of all: but the chapel, the tavern and the home were their own. In the 'unsteepled' places of worship there was room for a free intellectual life and for democratic experiments with 'members unlimited'. Against the background of London Dissent, with its fringe of deists and earnest mystics, William Blake seems no longer the cranky untutored genius that he must seem to those who know only the genteel culture of the time.[2] On the contrary, he is the original yet authentic voice of a long popular tradition. If some of the London Jacobins were strangely unperturbed by the execution of Louis and Marie Antoinette it was because they remembered that their own forebears had

---

1. W. H. Reid, op. cit., p. 90.

2. David V. Erdman, in his Blake, *Prophet against Empire* (Princeton, 1954), has helped us to see Blake in this context and – in doing so – has thrown much light upon the intellectual life of Jacobin London. See also (for Blake's 'Ranting' and Muggletonian forebears) A. L. Morton, *The Everlasting Gospel* (1958).

once executed a king. No one with Bunyan in their bones could have found many of Blake's aphorisms strange:

> The strongest poison ever known
> Came from Caesar's laurel crown.

And many, like Blake, felt themselves torn between a rational Deism and the spiritual values nurtured for a century in the 'kingdom within'. When Paine's *Age of Reason* was published in the years of repression, many must have felt with Blake when he annotated the final page of the Bishop of Llandaff's *Apology for the Bible* (written in reply to Paine):

It appears to me Now that Tom Paine is a better Christian than the Bishop.

When we see Dissent in this way we are seeing it as an intellectual tradition: out of this tradition came many original ideas and original men. But we should not assume that the 'Old Dissenters' as a body were willing to take the popular side. Thomas Walker, the Manchester reformer, who – a Churchman himself – had laboured hard for the repeal of the Test and Corporation Acts – was contemptuous of their timidity:

Dissenters ... have as a body constantly fallen short of their own principles; ... through fear or some other motive they have been so strongly the advocates of an Overstrained Moderation that they have rather been the enemies than the friends of those who have ventured the most and effected the most for the rights of the people.[1]

We see here, perhaps, a tension between London and the industrial centres. The Dissenters at Manchester, the members of the Old Meeting at Birmingham or the Great Meeting at Leicester, included some of the largest employers in the district. Their attachment to civil and religious liberty went hand in hand with their attachment to the dogmas of free trade. They contributed a good deal – and especially in the 1770s and 1780s – to forms of extra-parliamentary agitation and pressure-group politics which anticipate the pattern of middle-class politics of the nineteenth century. But their enthusiasm for

1. T. Walker, *Review of some Political Events in Manchester* (1794), p. 125.

civil liberty melted away with the publication of *Rights of Man*
and in very few of them did it survive the trials and persecution of the early 1790s. In London, and in pockets in the great
cities, many of the Dissenting artisans graduated in the same
period from Dissent through Deism to a secular ideology.
'Secularism,' Dr Hobsbawm has written,

is the ideological thread which binds London labour history together, from the London Jacobins and Place, through the anti-
religious Owenites and cooperators, the anti-religious journalists
and booksellers, through the free-thinking Radicals who followed
Holyoake and flocked to Bradlaugh's Hall of Science, to the Social
Democratic Federation and the London Fabians with their uncon-
cealed distaste for chapel rhetoric.[1]

Nearly all the theorists of the working-class movement are in
that London tradition – or else, like Bray the Leeds printer,
they are analogues of the skilled London working men.

But the list itself reveals a dimension that is missing – the
moral force of the Luddites, of Brandreth and young Bamford, of the Ten Hour men, of Northern Chartists and I.L.P.
And some of this difference in traditions can be traced to the
religious formations of the eighteenth century. When the
democratic revival came in the last years of the century, Old
Dissent had lost much of its popular following, and those artisans who still adhered to it were permeated by the values of
enlightened self-interest which led on, in such a man as
Francis Place, to the acceptance of a limited Utilitarian
philosophy. But in those great areas in the provinces where
Methodism triumphed in the default of Dissent, it nearly
destroyed the democratic and anti-authoritarian elements in
the older tradition, interposing between the people and their
revolutionary heritage a callow emotionalism which served
as auxiliary to the Established Church. And yet the Methodist
rebel was marked by a special earnestness and vigour of moral
concern. South and North, intellect and enthusiasm, the arguments of secularism and the rhetoric of love – the tension is
perpetuated in the nineteenth century. And each tradition
seems enfeebled without the complement of the other.

1. Hobsbawm, op. cit., p. 128.

[3]

'Satan's Strongholds'

BUT what of the denizens of 'Satan's strongholds', the 'harlots and publicans and thieves' whose souls the evangelists wrestled for? If we are concerned with historical change we must attend to the articulate minorities. But these minorities arise from a less articulate majority whose consciousness may be described as being, at this time, 'sub-political' – made up of superstition or passive irreligion, prejudice and patriotism.

The inarticulate, by definition, leave few records of their thoughts. We catch glimpses in moments of crisis, like the Gordon Riots, and yet crisis is not a typical condition. It is tempting to follow them into the archives of crime. But before we do this we must warn against the assumption that in the late eighteenth century 'Christ's poor' can be divided between penitent sinners on the one hand, and murderers, thieves and drunkards on the other.

It is easy to make a false division of the people into the organized or chapel-going good and the dissolute bad in the Industrial Revolution, since the sources push us towards this conclusion from at least four directions. Such facts as are available were often presented in sensational form, and marshalled for pejorative purposes. If we are to credit one of the most industrious investigators, Patrick Colquhoun, there were, at the turn of the century, 50,000 harlots, more than 5,000 publicans, and 10,000 thieves in the metropolis alone; his more extended estimates of criminal classes, taking in receivers of stolen property, coiners, gamblers, lottery agents, cheating shopkeepers, riverside scroungers, and colourful characters like Mudlarks, Scufflehunters, Bludgeon Men, Morocco Men, Flash Coachmen, Grubbers, Bear Baiters and Strolling Minstrels totals (with the former groups) 115,000 out of a metropolitan population of less than one million. His estimate of the same classes, for the whole country, – and including one million in receipt of parish relief – totals 1,320,716. But these estimates lump together indiscriminately gipsies, vagrants, unemployed, and pedlars and the grandparents of Mayhew's street-sellers; while his prostitutes turn out, on closer inspection to be 'lewd and immoral women', including 'the prodigious number among the lower classes who cohabit together without marriage' (and this at a time when divorce for the poor was an absolute impossibility).[1]

The figures then are impressionistic estimates. They reveal as much about the mentality of the propertied classes (who assumed – not without reason – that any person out of steady employment and without property must maintain himself by illicit means) as they do about the actual criminal behaviour of the unpropertied. And the date of Colquhoun's investigations is as relevant as his conclusions; for they were conducted in the atmosphere of panic in the aftermath of the French Revolution. In the two decades before this there was an important access of humanitarian concern amongst the upper classes; we can see this in the work of Howard, Hanway, Clarkson, Sir Frederick Eden, and in the growing concern for civil and religious liberties among the small gentry and the Dissenting tradesmen. But the awakening of the labouring classes, after the first shocks of the French Revolution, made the upper classes tremble', Frances, Lady Shelley, noted in her *Diary*: 'Every man felt the necessity for putting his house in order ...'[2]

To be more accurate, most men and women of property felt the necessity for putting the houses of the poor in order. The remedies proposed might differ; but the impulse behind Colquhoun, with his advocacy of more effective police. Hannah More, with her halfpenny tracts and Sunday Schools, the Methodists with their renewed emphasis upon order and submissiveness, Bishop Barrington's more humane Society for Bettering the Conditions of the Poor, and William Wilberforce and Dr John Bowdler, with their Society for the Suppression

1. Patrick Colquhoun, *Treatise on the Police of the Metropolis* (1797), pp. vii-xi; *Observations and Facts Relative to Public Houses* (1796), Appendix; *Treatise on Indigence* (1806), pp. 38–43.

2. *The Diary of Frances Lady Shelley, 1787–1817*, ed. R. Edgcumbe (1912), pp. 8–9.

of Vice and Encouragement of Religion, was much the same. The message to be given to the labouring poor was simple, and was summarized by Burke in the famine year of 1795: 'Patience, labour, sobriety, frugality and religion, should be recommended to them; all the rest is downright fraud.' 'I know nothing better calculated to fill a country with barbarians ready for any mischief,' wrote Arthur Young, the agricultural propagandist, 'than extensive commons and divine service only once a month. ... Do French principles make so slow a progress, that you should lend them such helping hands?'[1] The sensibility of the Victorian middle class was nurtured in the 1790s by frightened gentry who had seen miners, potters and cutlers reading *Rights of Man*, and its foster-parents were William Wilberforce and Hannah More. It was in these counter-revolutionary decades that the humanitarian tradition became warped beyond recognition. The abuses which Howard had exposed in the prisons in the 1770s and 1780s crept back in the 1790s and 1800s; and Sir Samuel Romilly, in the first decade of the nineteenth century, found that his efforts to reform the criminal law were met with hostility and timidity; the French Revolution had produced (he recalled) 'among the higher orders ... a horror of every kind of innovation'. 'Everything rung and was connected with the Revolution in France,' recalled Lord Cockburn (of his Scottish youth): 'Everything, not this thing or that thing, but literally everything, was soaked in this one event.' It was the pall of moral equivocation which settled upon Britain in these years which stung Blake to fury:

Because of the Oppressors of Albion in every City and Village ...
They compell the Poor to live upon a crust of bread by soft mild
   arts:
They reduce the Man to want, then give with pomp and ceremony:
The praise of Jehovah is chaunted from lips of hunger and thirst.[2]

Such a disposition on the part of the propertied classes was not (as we have seen in the case of Colquhoun) conducive to

1. *General View of the Agriculture of the County of Lincoln* (1799), p. 439.
2. See also the challenging analysis of V. Kiernan, 'Evangelicalism and the French Revolution', *Past and Present*, I, February 1952.

accurate social observation. And it reinforced the natural tendency of authority to regard taverns, fairs, any large congregations of people, as a nuisance – sources of idleness, brawls, sedition or contagion. And this general disposition, at the end of the eighteenth century, to 'fudge' the evidence was abetted from three other directions. First, we have the utilitarian attitudes of the new manufacturing class, whose need to impose a work discipline in the factory towns made it hostile to many traditional amusements and levities. Second, there is the Methodist pressure itself, with its unending procession of breast-beating sinners, pouring confessional biographies from the press. 'Almighty Father, why didst thou bear with such a rebel?' asks one such penitent, a redeemed sailor. In his dissolute youth he –

went to horse-races, wakes, dances, fairs, attended the play-house, nay, so far had he forsaken the fear of his Maker and the counsel of his mother, that he several times got intoxicated with liquor. He was an adept in singing profane songs, cracking jokes, and making risible and ludicrous remarks . . .

As for the common sailor –

His song, his bumper and his sweetheart (perhaps a street-pacing harlot) form his trio of pleasure. He rarely thinks, seldom reads, and never prays. . . . Speak to him about the call of God, he tells you he hears enough of the boatswain's call. . . . If you talk of Heaven, he hopes he shall get a good berth aloft: is hell mentioned? he jokes about being put under the hatchway.

'O my children, what a miracle that such a victim of sin should become a preacher of salvation!'[1]

Such literature as this must be held up to a Satanic light and read backwards if we are to perceive what the 'Jolly Tar' or the apprentice or the Sandgate lass thought about Authority or Methodist preachers. If this is not done, the historian may be led to judge the eighteenth century most harshly for some of the things which made life endurable for the common people.

1. Joshua Marsden, *Sketches of the Early Life of a Sailor* . . . (Hull, n.d. 1812?): for a different view of the eighteenth-century sailor, see R. B. Rose, 'A Liverpool Sailor's Strike in the 18th Century'. *Trans. Lancs. and Chesh. Antiq. Soc., LXVIII*, 1958.

And, when we come to assess the early working-class movement, this kind of evidence is supplemented from a third direction. Some of the first leaders and chroniclers of the movement were self-educated working men, who raised themselves by efforts of self-discipline which required them to turn their backs upon the happy-go-lucky tavern world. 'I cannot, like many other men, go to a tavern,' wrote Francis Place: 'I hate taverns and tavern company. I cannot drink, I cannot for any considerable time consent to converse with fools.'[1] The self-respecting virtues often carried with them corresponding narrowing attitudes – in Place's case leading him on to the acceptance of Utilitarian and Malthusian doctrines. And since Place was the greatest archivist of the early movement, his own abhorrence of the improvidence, ignorance, and licentiousness of the poor is bound to colour the record. Moreover, the struggle of the reformers was one for enlightenment, order, sobriety, in their own ranks; so much so that Windham, in 1802, was able to declare with some colour that the Methodists and the Jacobins were leagued together to destroy the amusements of the people:

By the former ... everything joyous was to be prohibited, to prepare the people for the reception of their fanatical doctrines. By the Jacobins, on the other hand, it was an object of important consideration to give to the disposition of the lower orders a character of greater seriousness and gravity, as the means of facilitating the reception of their tenets.[2]

Those who have wished to emphasise the sober constitutional ancestry of the working-class movement have sometimes minimized its more robust and rowdy features. All that we can do is bear the warning in mind. We need more studies of the social attitudes of criminals, of soldiers and sailors, of tavern life; and we should look at the evidence, not with a moralizing eye ('Christ's poor' were not always pretty), but with an eye for Brechtian values – the fatalism, the irony in the face of Establishment homilies, the tenacity of self-preservation. And we must also remember the 'underground' of the ballad-singer and

1. Graham Wallas, *Life of Francis Place* (1918), p. 195.
2. Windham was speaking in a debate on bull-baiting, and on this issue no doubt most Methodists and Jacobins were united. See L. Radzinowicz, *History of the English Criminal Law* (1948–56), III, 205–6.

the fair-ground which handed on traditions to the nineteenth century (to the music-hall, or Dickens' circus folk, or Hardy's pedlars and showmen); for in these ways the 'inarticulate' conserved certain values – a spontaneity and capacity for enjoyment and mutual loyalties – despite the inhibiting pressures of magistrates, mill-owners, and Methodists.

We may isolate two ways in which these 'sub-political' traditions affect the early working-class movement; the phenomena of riot and of the mob, and the popular notions of an Englishman's 'birthright'. For the first, we must realize that there have always persisted popular attitudes towards crime, amounting at times to an unwritten code, quite distinct from the laws of the land. Certain crimes were outlawed by both codes: a wife or child murderer would be pelted and execrated on the way to Tyburn. Highwaymen and pirates belonged to popular ballads, part heroic myth, part admonition to the young. But other crimes were actively condoned by whole communities – coining, poaching, the evasion of taxes (the window tax and tithes) or excise or the press-gang. Smuggling communities lived in a state of constant war with authority, whose unwritten rules were understood by both sides; the authorities might seize a ship or raid the village, and the smugglers might resist arrest – 'but it was no part of the smuggling tactics to carry war farther than defence, or at times a rescue, because of the retaliatory measures that were sure to come . . .'[1] On the other hand, other crimes, which were easily committed and yet which struck at the livelihood of particular communities – sheep-stealing or stealing cloth off the tenters in the open field – excited popular condemnation.[2]

This distinction between the legal code and the unwritten popular code is a commonplace at any time. But rarely have the two codes been more sharply distinguished from each other than in the second half of the eighteenth century. One may even see these years as ones in which the class war is fought out in terms of Tyburn, the hulks and the Bridewells on the one hand; and crime, riot, and mob action on the other. Professor

1. Serjeant Paul Swanston, *Memoirs of . . . a Soldier's Life* (n.d.).
2. For insight into the unwritten traditions of the transported, see Russel Ward, *The Australian Legend* (Melbourne, 1958), ch. 2.

Radzinowicz's researches into the *History of English Criminal Law* have added a depressing weight of evidence to the picture long made familiar by Goldsmith:

> Each wanton judge new penal statutes draw,
> Laws grind the poor, and rich men rule the law. ...

It was not (an important reservation) the judge but the legislature which was responsible for enacting ever more capital punishments for crimes against property: in the years between the Restoration and the death of George III the number of capital offences was increased by about 190 – or more than one for every year: no less than sixty-three of these were added in the years 1760–1810. Not only petty theft, but primitive forms of industrial rebellion – destroying a silk loom, throwing down fences when commons were enclosed, and firing corn ricks – were to be punished by death. It is true that the police force was totally inadequate and the administration of 'justice' haphazard. It is true also that in the latter years of the eighteenth century, while capital offences multiplied, some juries became reluctant to convict, and the proportion of convicted offenders who were actually brought to execution fell.[1] But the death sentence, if respited, was generally exchanged to the terrible living death of the hulks or to transportation. The procession to Tyburn (later, the scaffold outside Newgate) was a central ceremonial of eighteenth-century London. The condemned in the carts – the men in gaudy attire, the women in white, with baskets of flowers and oranges which they threw to the crowds – the ballad-singers and hawkers, with their 'last speeches' (which were sold even before the victims had given the sign of the dropped handkerchief to the hangman to do his

1. See Radzinowicz, op. cit., I, Parts 1 and 2. Dr Radzinowicz shows that of 527 sentenced to death in London and Middlesex between 1749 and 1758 365 were executed; whereas in 1790–99 745 were sentenced and only 220 executed. Thus the ratio of executed to sentenced falls from roughly two in three to one in three: and continues to fall in the 1800s. On the other hand, the majority of executions were for offences against property; e.g. of ninety-seven executions in London and Middlesex in 1785, only one was for murder, forty-three for burglary, and the remainder for offences against property (forgery, horse-stealing, etc.). He concludes that these figures indicate national tendencies, and that 'in 1785 the death penalty was inflicted almost exclusively for economic offences'.

work): all the symbolism of 'Tyburn Fair' was a ritual at the heart of London's popular culture.

The commercial expansion, the enclosure movement, the early years of the Industrial Revolution – all took place within the shadow of the gallows. The white slaves left our shores for the American plantations and later for Van Diemen's Land, while Bristol and Liverpool were enriched with the profits of black slavery; and slave-owners from West Indian plantations grafted their wealth to ancient pedigrees at the marriage-market in Bath. It is not a pleasant picture. In the lower depths, police officers and gaolers grazed on the pastures of crime – blood-money, garnish money, and sales of alcohol to their victims. The system of graduated rewards for thief-takers incited them to magnify the offence of the accused. The poor lost their rights in the land and were tempted to crime by their poverty and by the inadequate measures of prevention; the small tradesman or master was tempted to forgery or illicit transactions by fear of the debtor's prison. Where no crime could be proved, the J.P.s had wide powers to consign the vagabond or sturdy rogue or unmarried mother to the Bridewell (or 'House of Correction') – those evil, disease-ridden places, managed by corrupt officers, whose conditions shocked John Howard more than the worst prisons. The greatest offence against property was to have none.

The law was hated, but it was also despised. Only the most hardened criminal was held in as much popular odium as the informer who brought men to the gallows. And the resistance movement to the laws of the propertied took not only the form of individualistic criminal acts, but also that of piecemeal and sporadic insurrectionary actions where numbers gave some immunity. When Wyvill warned Major Cartwright of the 'wild work' of the 'lawless and furious rabble' he was not raising imaginary objections. The British people were noted throughout Europe for their turbulence, and the people of London astonished foreign visitors by their lack of deference. The eighteenth and early nineteenth century are punctuated by riot, occasioned by bread prices, turnpikes and tolls, excise, 'rescue', strikes, new machinery, enclosures, press-gangs and a score of other grievances. Direct action on particular grievances merges on one hand into the great political risings of the 'mob' – the Wilkes agitation of the 1760s and 1770s, the Gordon Riots (1780), the mobbing of the King in the London streets (1795 and 1820), the Bristol Riots (1831) and the Birmingham Bull Ring riots (1839). On the other hand it merges with organized forms of sustained illegal action or quasi-insurrection – Luddism (1811–13), the East Anglian Riots (1816), the 'Last Labourer's Revolt' (1830), the Rebecca Riots (1839 and 1842) and the Plug Riots (1842).

This second, quasi-insurrectionary, form we shall look at more closely when we come to consider Luddism. It was a form of direct action which arose in specific conditions, which was often highly organized and under the protection of the local community, and as to which we should be chary of generalization. The first form is only now beginning to receive the attention of historians. Dr Rudé, in his study of *The Crowd in the French Revolution*, suggests that 'the term "mobs", in the sense of hired bands operating on behalf of external interests ... should be invoked with discretion and only when justified by the particular occasion'. Too often historians have used the term lazily, to evade further analysis, or (with the suggestion of criminal elements motivated by the desire for loot) as a gesture of prejudice. And Dr Rudé suggests that the term 'revolutionary crowd' may be more useful when discussing riot in late eighteenth-century England as well as in revolutionary France.

The distinction is useful. In eighteenth-century Britain riotous actions assumed two different forms: that of more or less spontaneous popular direct action; and that of the deliberate use of the crowd as an instrument of pressure, by persons 'above' or apart from the crowd. The first form has not received the attention which it merits. It rested upon more articulate popular sanctions and was validated by more sophisticated traditions than the word 'riot' suggests. The most common example is the bread or food riot, repeated cases of which can be found in almost every town and county until the 1840s.[1] This was rarely a mere uproar which culminated in the breaking open of barns or the looting of shops. It was legitimized

1. For the incidence of riots, see R. F. W. Wearmouth, *Methodism and the Common People of the Eighteenth Century* (1946).

by the assumptions of an older moral economy, which taught the immorality of any unfair method of forcing up the price of provisions by profiteering upon the necessities of the people.

In urban and rural communities alike, a consumer-consciousness preceded other forms of political or industrial antagonism. Not wages, but the cost of bread, was the most sensitive indicator of popular discontent. Artisans, self-employed craftsmen, or such groups as the Cornish tin miners (where the traditions of the 'free' miner coloured responses until the nineteenth century),[1] saw their wages as regulated by custom or by their own bargaining. They expected to buy their provisions in the open market, and even in times of shortage they expected prices to be regulated by custom also. (The God-provided 'laws' of supply and demand, whereby scarcity inevitably led to soaring prices, had by no means won acceptance in the popular mind, where older notions of face-to-face bargaining still persisted.) Any sharp rise in prices precipitated riot. An intricate tissue of legislation and of custom regulated the 'Assize of Bread', the size and quality of the loaf.[2] Even the attempt to impose the standard Winchester measure for the sale of wheat, in the face of some customary measure, could ensue in riots. When the North Devon Agricultural Society imposed the standard Winchester bushel in Bideford market in 1812, one of its leading members was the recipient of a blood-chilling letter:

... Winter Nights is not past therefore your person shall not go home alive – or if you chance to escape the hand that guides this pen, a lighted Match will do eaqual execution. Your family I know not But the whole shall be inveloped in flames, your Carkase if any such should be found will be given to the Dogs if it Contains any Moisture for the Annimals to devour it . . . [3]

1. The Cornish 'tributers' or 'tut-workers' were direct contract workers, a minority of whom still in the late eighteenth century varied their work with pilchard fishing, small-holding (as did some Yorkshire lead miners), etc.: see J. Rowe, *Cornwall in the Age of the Industrial Revolution* (Liverpool, 1953), pp. 26–7.

2. For this complex position, see C. R. Fay, *The Corn Laws and Social England* (Cambridge, 1932), ch. 4.

3. Enclosure from 'Thomas Certain', in Skurray to H.O., 25 March 1812, H.O. 42.121.

Food riots were sometimes uproarious, like the 'Great Cheese Riot' at Nottingham's Goose Fair in 1764, when whole cheeses were rolled down the streets; or the riot in the same city, in 1788, caused by the high price of meat, when the doors and shutters of the shambles were torn down and burned, together with the butcher's books, in the market-place.[1] But even this violence shows a motive more complex than hunger: retailers were being punished, on account of their prices and the poor quality of the meat. More often the 'mobs' showed self-discipline, within a customary pattern of behaviour. Perhaps the only occasion in his life when John Wesley commended a disorderly action was when he noted in his journal the actions of a mob in James' Town, Ireland; the mob –

had been in motion all the day; but their business was only with the forestallers of the market, who had bought up all the corn far and near, to starve the poor, and load a Dutch ship, which lay at the quay; but the mob brought it all out into the market, and sold it for the owners at the common price. And this they did with all the calmness and composure imaginable, and without striking or hurting anyone.

In Honiton in 1766 lace-workers seized corn on the premises of the farmers, took it to market themselves, sold it, and returned the money and even the sacks back to the farmers.[2] In the Thames Valley in the same year the villages and towns (Abingdon, Newbury, Maidstone) were visited by large parties of labourers, who styled themselves 'the Regulators', enforcing a popular price on all provisions. (The action commenced with gangs of men working on the turnpike road, who said 'with one Voice, Come one & all to Newbury in a Body to Make the Bread cheaper'.)[3] A Halifax example of 1783 repeats the same pattern of mass intimidation and self-discipline. The crowd was gathered from weaving villages outside the town, and descended upon the market-place in some sort of order (formed into 'twos') with an ex-soldier and coiner, Thomas Spencer, at

1. J. Blackner, *History of Nottingham* (Nottingham, 1815), pp. 383–4.
2. See R. B. Rose, '18th Century Price-Riots, the French Revolution, and the Jacobin Maximum', *International Review of Social History*, IV, 1959, p. 435.
3. T.S. 11 3707.

their head. The corn merchants were besieged, and forced to
sell oats at 30s. and wheat at 21s. a load. When Spencer and a
fellow rioter were subsequently executed, a strong force of
military was brought out in expectation of a rescue attempt;
and the funeral cart went up the Calder Valley to Spencer's
home village on a road thronged for several miles with
mourners.[1]

Such 'riots' were popularly regarded as acts of justice, and
their leaders held as heroes. In most cases they culminated in
the enforced sale of provisions at the customary or popular
price, analogous to the French 'taxation populaire',[2] the proceeds being given to the owners. Moreover, they required more
preparation and organization than is at first apparent; sometimes the 'mob' controlled the market-place for several days,
waiting for prices to come down; sometimes actions were preceded by hand-written (and, in the 1790s, printed) handbills;
sometimes the women controlled the market-place, while parties of men intercepted grain on the roads, at the docks, on the
rivers; very often the signal for the action was given by a man
or woman carrying a loaf aloft, decorated with black ribbon,
and inscribed with some slogan. A Nottingham action in September 1812 commenced with several women,

sticking a half penny loaf on the top of a fishing rod, after having
streaked it with red ochre, and tied around it a shred of black crape,
emblematic ... of 'bleeding famine decked in Sackecloth'.[3]

The climactic year for such 'riots' was 1795, a year of European famine or extreme scarcity, when the older popular
tradition was stiffened by the Jacobin consciousness of a minority. As prices soared, direct action spread throughout the
country. In Nottingham women 'went from one baker's shop
to another, set their own price on the stock therein, and putting
down the money, took it away'. The Mayor of Gloucester
wrote anxiously:

I have great reason to be apprehensive of a visit from the Colliers
in the Forest of Dean, who have for some days been going round to

1. H. Ling Roth, The Yorkshire Coiners (Halifax, 1906), p. 108.
2. See R. B. Rose, op. cit.
3. J. F. Sutton, The Date-Book of Nottingham (Nottingham, 1880 edn),
p. 286.

the Townes in their Neighbourhood, & selling the Flour, Wheat, & Bread belonging to the Millers & Bakers, at a reduced price.

In Newcastle the crowd enforced the sale of butter at 8*d.* a lb., wheat at 12*s.* per boll, and potatoes at 5*s.* a load, in the presence of the town's officers: no violence was committed. At Wisbech the 'Bankers' ('a most Outrageous Set of Men, whose numbers make them formidable') – gangs of rural workers engaged in ditching, enclosure work, etc. – led a riot in the market headed by a man with a sixpenny loaf on a pitch-fork. At Carlisle grain hidden in a warehouse was located, and its contents, as well as the cargo of a ship, were brought to the Town Hall and sold at 18*s.* a load. In Cornwall the 'tinners' swarmed into the farmlands, enforcing their 'Laws of the Maximum'.[1]

Actions on such a scale (and there were many others) indicate an extraordinarily deep-rooted pattern of behaviour and belief. Moreover, they were so extensive that the Privy Council (which was largely concerned with the problem of grain supplies from May to December 1795) could scarcely ensure the transport of supplies from one county to the next. Something in the nature of a war between the countryside and the towns grew up. The people of the rural districts believed that their corn would be sent to the cities, while they would be left to starve. The farmers refused to send grain to market, for fear it would be sold at the popular price. In the ports grain-ships were stopped, since the people believed that factors were sending it abroad. Magistrates connived at the retaining of corn in their own districts. At Witney 'the Inhabitants ... seized some Grain as it was going to be sent out of the Country, brought it back, and sold it at a low price'. Loads of wheat were stopped in Cambridge, and sold off in the market-place. In the West Riding, barges on the Calder and Aire were stopped and impounded by mobs. At Burford the people prevented a load of corn from being sent out of the town, and sold it at 8*s.*

1. Nottingham: J. F. Sutton, op. cit., p. 207; Gloucester, Wisbech and Carlisle: H.O. 42.35; Newcastle: E. Mackenzie, *Descriptive and Historical Account of Newcastle-upon-Tyne* (Newcastle, 1827), p. 72; Cornwall: Rowe, op. cit. pp. 104–5, and, for later actions, pp. 142, 158–62, 181–4. See also W. P. Hall, *British Radicalism,* 1791–97 (New York, 1912), pp. 202–15.

a bushel; a magistrate feared that the people of Birmingham
might sally out and attack Burford. At Wells 'a great many
Women' prevented grain ships from sailing to London.[1]

These popular actions were legitimized by the old paternalist
moral economy. Although the old legislation against forestallers and regraters had been largely repealed or abrogated by the
end of the eighteenth century, it endured with undiminished
vigour, both in popular tradition and in the minds of some
Tory paternalists, including no less a person than the Lord
Chief Justice (Kenyon), who made known his view, in 1795,
that forestalling and engrossing remained offences at common
law.[2] In the popular mind, these offences encompassed any
exploitive action calculated to raise the price of provisions, and
in particular the activities of factors, millers, bakers, and all
middlemen. 'Those Cruall Villions the Millers Bakers etc
Flower Sellers rases Flowe under a Comebination to what price
they please on purpose to make an Artificall Famine in a Land
of plenty' – so runs a handbill of 1795, from Retford. 'The
corn factors and the sort of peopul which we call huckstors
and mealmen which have got the corn in to there hands and
thay hold it up and Sell it to the poor at thare owne price' – so
runs a petition from some labourers in Leeds.[3] The great millers
were believed to corner the grain in order to enhance its price;
in Birmingham a large flour mill, powered by steam, at Snow
Hill was attacked in 1795; while London's great Albion Flour
Mills burned down on two occasions. On the first occasion,
arson was rumoured, since the Mills were believed to practise
forms of adulteration; the people were 'willing spectators', and
'ballads of rejoicing were printed and sung on the spot'. On the
second occasion (1811), 'the populace rejoiced at the conflagra-
tion'.[4]

1. P.C. A.56/8; H.O. 42.35/7.
2. The ancient statutes were repealed in 1772 and 1791, but for the
complicated situation existing in the 1790s, see Fay, op. cit., ch. 4, and
D. G. Barnes, *History of the English Corn Laws* (1930), ch. 5.
3. Fay, op. cit., p. 44; Leeds petition to Duke of Portland, 20 July
1795, H.O. 42.35.
4. C. Gill, *History of Birmingham* (O.U.P., 1952), I, p. 128; R. Southey,
Letters from England (2nd edn 1808), III, 179–81; *Alfred*, 25 October
1811.

Hence the final years of the eighteenth century saw a last desperate effort by the people to reimpose the older moral economy as against the economy of the free market. In this they received some support from old-fashioned J.P.s, who threatened to prosecute forestallers, tightened controls over markets, or issued proclamations against engrossers who brought up growing corn in the fields.[1] The Speenhamland decision of 1795, to subsidize wages in relation to the price of bread, must be seen as arising out of this background; where the custom of the market-place was in dissolution, paternalists attempted to evoke it in the scale of relief. But the old customary notions died hard. There was a scatter of prosecutions for forestalling between 1795 and 1800; in 1800 a number of private prosecuting societies were formed, which offered rewards for convictions; and an important conviction for forestalling was upheld in the High Courts, to the evident satisfaction of Lord Kenyon.[2] But this was the last attempt to enforce the old paternalist consumer-protection. Thereafter the total breakdown of customary controls contributed much to popular bitterness against a Parliament of protectionist landlords and *laissez faire* commercial magnates.

In considering only this one form of 'mob' action we have come upon unsuspected complexities, for behind every such form of popular direct action some legitimizing notion of right is to be found. On the other hand, the employment of the

1. See, e.g H.O. 42.35 for resolutions of a committee of the leading inhabitants of Gloucester (26 June 1795), threatening prosecutions for forestalling and regrating; and extracts from the *Blackburn Mail*, July–September 1795, in G. C. Miller, *Blackburn: The Evolution of a Cotton Town* (Blackburn, 1951), pp. 23, 60–3.

2. See Fay, op. cit., p. 55; Barnes, op. cit., pp. 81–3; J. Ashton, *The Dawn of the 19th Century in England* (1906), pp. 240-41; W. Smart, *Economic Annals of the 19th Century* (1910), I, pp. 5–6; Miller, op. cit., pp. 94, 103; J. A. Langford, *A Century of Birmingham Life* (Birmingham, 1868), II, pp. 101-2; and especially J. S. Girdler, *Observations on the Pernicious Consequences of Forestalling, Regrating, and Ingrossing* (1800), pp. 209–15. The Earl of Warwick, who moved unsuccessfully a resolution in the House of Lords authorizing J.P.s to fix the price of corn, declared that 'there had been no less than 400 convictions for forestalling, regrating, and monopolizing' within the previous months: *Parliamentary History*, XXXV (1800), 839.

'mob' in a sense much closer to Dr Rudé's definition ('hired bands operating on behalf of external interests') was an established technique in the eighteenth century; and – what is less often noted – it had long been employed by authority itself. The 1688 settlement was, after all, a compromise; and it was convenient for the beneficiaries to seek to confirm their position by encouraging popular antipathy towards Papists (potential Jacobites) on the one hand, and Dissenters (potential Levellers) on the other. A mob was a very useful supplement to the magistrates in a nation that was scarcely policed. John Wesley, in his early years, and his first field-preachers, often encountered these mobs who acted under a magistrate's licence. One of the most violent encounters was at Wednesbury and Walsall in 1743. By Wesley's account the mob was highly volatile and confused as to its own intentions. The 'captains of the rabble' were the 'heroes of the town': but the only ones identified are an 'honest butcher' and a 'prize-fighter at the bear-garden' who both suddenly changed sides and took Wesley's part. The matter becomes more clear when we learn that the mob was backed by the local magistrates, and by a local vicar, who was outraged by Wesley's local preachers ('a Bricklayer, and then a Plumber-Glazier') who had 'alienated the Affections' of Colliers from the Church, and called the clergy 'dumb Dogs'. Indeed, by Wesley's account, 'some of the gentlemen ... threatened to turn away collier or miner out of their service that did not come and do his part'.[1] John Nelson's *Journal* gives us an example from Grimsby where it was the minister of the Church of England who –

got a man to beat the town drum through the town, and went before the drum, and gathered all the rabble he could, giving them liquor to go with him to fight for the Church.

At the door of the house where Nelson was preaching it was the parson who cried out to the mob, 'Pull down the house! Pull down the house!'

But of greater importance than these provincial manifestations of popular feeling upon particular issues was the London

---

1. Wesley's *Journal* (Everyman), I, pp. 438–44, 455; *Some Papers giving an Account of the Rise and Progress of Methodism at Wednesbury* (1744), p. 8.

mob, whose presence is continually felt in the political history
of the eighteenth century and which Wilkes removed altogether
from the control of the agents of authority in the 1760s. In a
sense, this was a transitional mob, on its way to becoming a
self-conscious Radical crowd; the leaven of Dissent and of
political education was at work, giving to the people a predis-
position to turn out in defence of popular liberties, in defiance
of authority, and in 'movements of social protest, in which the
underlying conflict of poor against rich ... is clearly visible ...'[1] The Spitalfields silk-weavers and their apprentices
had long been noted for their anti-authoritarian turbulence;
Dr Rudé, in his study of *Wilkes and Liberty*, notes occasions
where industrial conflict slips over into Wilkite demonstration,
and where the slogans of the crowd took a republican or revolutionary turn: 'Damn the King, damn the Government, damn
the Justices!', 'This is the most glorious opportunity for a Revolution that ever offered!' For nearly a decade London and the
south seemed (in the words of one critic) to be 'a great Bedlam
under the dominion of a beggarly, idle and intoxicated mob
without keepers, actuated solely by the word *Wilkes* ...'[2]
These were the supporters who:

demonstrated in St George's Fields, at Hyde Park Corner, at the
Mansion House, in Parliament Square and St James's Palace; who
shouted, or chalked up, 'Wilkes and Liberty' in the streets of the
City, Westminster and Southwark; who pelted Sheriff Harley and
the common hangman at the Royal Exchange when they attempted
to burn No. 45 of *The North Briton*; who smashed the windows of
Lords Bute and Egremont and daubed the boots of the Austrian
Ambassador; who paraded the Boot and Petticoat in the City
streets, and burned Colonel Luttrell and Lords Sandwich and Barrington in effigy outside the Tower of London. These are the elements whom contemporaries and later historians have – either from
indolence, prejudice or lack of more certain knowledge – called
'the mob' ...[3]

They were also the people – tradesmen, servants, coal-heavers, sailors, artisans and wage-earners of all descriptions – who

1. G. Rudé, op. cit., p. 237.
2. G. Rudé, *Wilkes and Liberty* (Oxford, 1962), pp. 50, 173.
3. Ibid., p. 181.

demonstrated for Wilkes on the hustings and who dragged him in triumph through the streets whenever he was victorious.

Dr Rudé is right to rescue the London crowd from the imputation of being mere hooligans and 'criminal elements'; and the distinction which he draws between the hired ruffians brought in to support the anti-Wilkite candidate, Proctor, and the spontaneous ebullience of the Wilkite majority is significant. However, in protesting against the 'prejudice' of historians, he protests too much. For the London crowd of the 1760s and 1770s had scarcely begun to develop its own organization or leaders; had little theory distinct from that of its 'managers'; and there is a sense in which it was manipulated and called out by Wilkes to 'operate on behalf of external interests' – the interests of the wealthy tradesmen, merchants, and manufacturers of the City who were Wilkes's most influential supporters. Wilkes himself affected a cynical contempt for the huzzas of his own plebeian following: 'Do you suppose,' it is said that he asked his opponent, Colonel Luttrell, while watching the cheering throngs on the hustings, 'that there are more fools or rogues in that assembly?' And the anomaly between the libertarian aspirations of the crowd and the mob-technique of its management, is further emphasized when we recall that the Wilkite merchants and tradesmen captured key posts in the government of the City, so that the Londoners who mobbed the carriages and broke the windows of the Great knew – no less than the Walsall miners – that they were acting under licence. The Wilkite crowd was in fact at a half-way house in the emergence of popular political consciousness; while its most popular slogan was 'Liberty!' many of its members were highly volatile and might equally well swing round to attack 'alien' elements or smash the windows of citizens who failed to illuminate them on 'patriotic' occasions.[1]

1. For Proctor, see Rudé, *Wilkes and Liberty*, pp. 59–60. Since Dr Rudé is the foremost pioneer in this important field, it is perhaps ungrateful to suggest the deficiencies in his analysis. But it should be noted that he shows no interest in the dissenting tradition of London artisans; and little interest in the debating clubs and tavern societies which would be intellectual and organizing foci for the crowd; nor in the underground politics of the ballad-vendors and 'patterers'. For further insight into plebeian politics in London, see G. Rudé. 'The London "Mob" of the

This is most clearly revealed in the Gordon Riots of 1780. Here we see a popular agitation which passed swiftly through three phases. In the first phase the 'revolutionary crowd', well organized by the popular Protestant Association, marched in fair order behind great banners to present a petition against Catholic toleration to the Houses of Parliament. Those foremost in the demonstration were 'the better sort of tradesmen ... well-dressed, decent sort of people ... exceeding quiet and orderly and very civil'. This was Dissenting London, and among them Gibbon described some fanatical 'Puritans', 'such as they might be in the time of Cromwell ... started out from their graves'. The refusal of the House of Commons to debate the petition – and Lord George Gordon's harangues – led on to angry scenes which introduced the second phase. This phase may be described as one of licensed spontaneity, leading on to mob violence informed by 'a groping desire to settle accounts with the rich, if only for a day'; some of the 'better sort of tradesmen' faded away, while journeymen, apprentices, and servants – and some criminals – thronged the streets.[1] The cry 'No Popery' had reverberated in the popular consciousness since the Commonwealth and 1688; and no doubt swept in many whose sub-political responses were described by Defoe many years before – 'stout fellows that would spend the last drop of their blood against Popery that do not know whether it be a man or a horse'. The riots were directed in the first place against Catholic chapels and the houses of wealthy Catholics, then against prominent personalities in authority – including Lord Chief Justice Mansfield and the Archbishop of York –

Eighteenth Century', *Historical Journal*, ii (1959); Lucy S. Sutherland, *The City and the Opposition to Government, 1768–1774* (1959) and 'The City in Eighteenth-Century Politics', in *Essays presented to Sir Lewis Namier*, ed. R. Pares and A. J. P. Taylor (1956); and, for tavern life, M. D. George, *London Life in the Eighteenth Century* (1928), ch. 6

1. See G. Rudé, 'The Gordon Riots', *Trans. Royal Hist. Soc.* (1956), Fifth Series, Vol. 6 and Christopher Hibbert, *King Mob* (1958). Dr Rudé places less emphasis than Mr Hibbert upon the degree to which criminals and prostitutes were involved in the final stages of the riots – Dr Rudé analysing a sample of prisoners (the majority wage-earners) brought before the Courts, Mr Hibbert relying more upon eyewitness accounts of the riots. See also J. P. de Castro, *The Gordon Riots* (Oxford, 1926).

who were believed to sympathize with Catholic emancipation, then against the prisons – whose inmates were released – and finally culminated in an attack on the Bank itself. Throughout this second phase, the sense of a 'licensed' mob continued: the Wilkite city authorities were conspicuous by their inactivity or absence, in part through fear of incurring popular odium, in part through actual connivance at disorders which strengthened their hands against the King and his Government. It was only when the third phase commenced – the attack on the Bank on one hand, and indiscriminate orgies of drunkenness, arson, and pickpocketing on the other – that the 'licence' was withdrawn: the inactive Lord Mayor at last sent a desperate message to the Commander-in-Chief calling for 'Horse and Foot to assist the civil power' and Alderman Wilkes himself went out to repel the mob on the steps of the Bank. The rapidity with which the riots were quelled emphasizes the previous inactivity of the City authorities.

We have here, then, something of a mixture of manipulated mob and revolutionary crowd. Lord George Gordon had tried to emulate Wilkes, but he had nothing of Wilkes's well-judged audacity and splendid sense of the popular mood. He released a spontaneous process of riot, which yet was under the immunity of the Wilkite City fathers. Groups of rioters threw up their own temporary leaders, reminiscent of Thomas Spencer the Halifax coiner – James Jackson, a watch-wheelcutter, who rode a carthorse and waved a red and black flag, and Enoch Foster, a circus strong man, who amused the mob by hurling floorboards through the windows of a Whitechapel house. But this kind of mixture is never seen in the metropolis again. In 1780 the London people, despite their excesses, were under the protection of the libertarian Whigs, who saw them as a counter-weight to the pretensions of the Throne: Burke deplored the use of the military in subduing the riots, while Fox declared that he would 'much rather be governed by a mob than a standing army'. But after the French Revolution no Whig politician would have risked, no City father condoned, the tampering with such dangerous energies; while the reformers, for their part, worked to create an organized public opinion, and despised the technique of unleashing the mob. 'Mobility' was a

term proudly adopted by nineteenth-century Radicals and
Chartists for their peaceable and well-conducted demonstrations.

The last great action of an eighteenth-century mob was at
Birmingham in 1791, in a form which should make us especially
chary as to generalizations about the 'revolutionary crowd'.[1]
Birmingham was perhaps the greatest centre of middle-class
Dissent; its Old and New Unitarian Meetings included some of
the largest employers in the district; Dissenters played so large
a part in the economic, intellectual, and corporate life of the
city that the 'Church and King' party had long felt the bitterness which came, not from strength, but from waning power
and prestige. The ostensible occasion for the riots was a dinner
held by middle-class reformers (many of them Dissenters) on
14 July 1791, to celebrate the fall of the Bastille. That night
and for the next three days the 'bunting, beggarly, brass-mak-
ing, brazen-faced, brazen-hearted, blackguard, bustling, booby
Birmingham mob' ran amuck in the city and its environs,
sacking two Unitarian and one Baptist meeting-house, burning
or looting a score of houses and many shops of wealthy Dissenters (or supposed sympathizers), and releasing prisoners
from the Town Prison. While Dissenters were the chief victims
(especially those associated with the cause of reform) 'it was
not always clear' (Mr Rose comments), 'whether rich dissenters
were attacked because they were dissenters or because they
were rich'. The cries of their assailants ranged from 'Church
and King!' to 'No Popery!'

As to the authenticity of popular resentment against some
of the wealthy Dissenters there can be no doubt. (For example,
one of the victims, William Hutton, had earned particular unpopularity in his office as a commissioner for the Birmingham
Court of Requests, a court for the enforcement of the payment
of small debts.) But there are a number of peculiarly suspicious
circumstances in the Birmingham riots which recall John Wesley's treatment nearly fifty years previously at the hands of the
Walsall mobs. First, there is the undoubted complicity of

1. In the account which follows I have drawn largely upon the definitive
study by R. B. Rose, 'The Priestley Riots of 1791', *Past and Present*,
November 1960, pp. 68–88.

several prominent Tory magistrates and clergy, who encouraged the rioters at their commencement, directed them to the
meeting-houses, intervened only half-heartedly, refused to
prosecute offenders, and may even have indicated 'legitimate'
targets for mob violence. Second, there is the small number of
effective rioters in the important actions. Apart from miners
and others from surrounding villages who joined in the week-
end looting, the marauding mob was rarely estimated at above
250, while repeated accounts speak of a hard core of about
thirty incendiaries who did most of the serious damage. Third,
there is the evidence that this hard core (which may not even
have been composed of local men) worked to a definite plan of
campaign and was exceptionally well-briefed as to the religious
and political affiliations of prominent Birmingham citizens.
The riots may have been motivated – as Priestley charged –
by 'religious bigotry', and the Bastille Day celebrations certainly served as their pretext. But it was a discriminatory outburst, under the licence of a part of the local Establishment,
and it should be regarded 'as an episode in which the "country
gentlemen" called out the urban mob to draw the dissenting
teeth of the aggressive and successful Birmingham bourgeoisie'. At the same time, it was 'an explosion of latent class
hatred and personal lawlessness triggered-off by the fortuitous
coming together of old religious animosities and new social and
political grievances',[1] in which the actions of the mob went beyond the limits anticipated at their permissive origin.

But it is a serious error to generalize from the Birmingham
riots as to the general hostility of the urban poor to French
Revolutionary or 'Jacobin' ideas. As we shall see, the welcome
to the first stages of the French Revolution came largely from
middle-class and Dissenting groups. It was not until 1792 that
these ideas gained a wide popular following, mainly through
the agency of Paine's *Rights of Man*. Thus the Priestley riots
can be seen as a late backward eddy of the transitional mob,
before the Painite propaganda had started in earnest the formation of a new democratic consciousness. Riots, of course, continued for many years after 1792: either upon specific issues
– Bamford's *Passages in the Life of a Radical* commences with

1. R. B. Rose, op. cit., p. 84.

a roll-call of the riots, at Bridport, Bideford, Bury, Newcastle, Glasgow, Ely, Preston, Nottingham, Merthyr, Birmingham, Walsall, at the close of the Napoleonic Wars – or (notably at Bristol, Merthyr, Nottingham and Derby in 1831 and at Birmingham in 1839) as insurrectionary climaxes to Radical agitation. In the Bristol riots we meet again some of the features of the Gordon and Priestley Riots: the sack of the Bishop's Palace and the Mansion House, the release of prisoners from the gaols, the looting and burning of unpopular citizens' houses and shops. But the authorities could find no conspiracy behind the rioters – at the most an excited free-thinking tradesman, Charles Davis, who went about waving his hat on the end of his umbrella, shouting 'Down with the churches and mend the roads with them!', and who was hanged for his pains.[1] The riots took place, not under the slogan of 'Church and King!' but of 'King and Reform!' and the King was only coupled with the latter cry because it was believed that he favoured a Reform Ministry. It was not the Dissenters but leading Churchmen (many of whom were West India slave-holders) who were the main target. At the same time, the democratic sentiments informing the rioters should not mislead us into mistaking the Bristol Riots for a politically conscious revolutionary action. Bristol in 1831 exemplifies the persistence of older, backward-looking patterns of behaviour, just as much as Manchester in 1819 exemplifies the emergence of the self-disciplined patterns of the new working-class movement. Ignorance and superstition had been jerked from loyalist into Radical courses; but we get a whiff of the Gordon and Priestley Riots in the words of the Bristol rioter who threw an armful of manuscripts and books from the Cathedral Chapter Library into the fire-declaring *'there could be no reform without books were burnt'.*[2]

The true *mobs*, in the sense of 'hired bands operating on

1. Another similar feature is the sense of *licence* given to the crowd by magistrates who were 'stupefied with terror' and who refused to accompany the troops; and by the humane Commanding Officer, Lt-Col. Brereton, who rode among the crowd huzzaing for 'The King and Reform'. See 'A Citizen' [John Eagles], *The Bristol Riots* (Bristol, 1832).

2. Eyewitness account in *Bristol Times*, 30 October 1931.

behalf of external interests', are the 'Church and King' mobs employed from 1792 onwards to terrorize the English Jacobins.[1] While these mobs were sometimes directed against wealthy and prominent reformers – as in the case of Thomas Walker of Manchester – they belong to the tradition of the Walsall mine-owners and the Grimsby Parson, and were so highly organized by – and sometimes paid by – 'external interests' that it is difficult to take them as indicative of any authentic independent popular sentiment. Moreover, despite the complete licence offered in many places by clergy and J.Ps to anti-Jacobin mobs they rarely involved more than a small group of picked hooligans, and they never sparked off popular violence on the scale of Birmingham in 1791. There were important urban centres – notably Sheffield and Norwich – where the 'Church and King' mob acted with very limited success. Nor was it possible to employ these mobs on any scale in London. The acquittal of the Jacobin prisoners in 1794 was the signal for popular triumph on the scale of the Wilkite celebrations. In 1795 the London crowd was revolutionary in mood and (through the London Corresponding Society) was discovering new forms of organization and leadership. Perhaps the crucial encounter was in October 1797, at the height of anti-Jacobin repression, when there was an inspired attempt to destroy Thomas Hardy's premises when he refused to illuminate on the occasion of a naval victory. The attack was beaten off by a guard of 100 members of the L.C.S., 'many of them Irish, armed with good shillelahs'. It was an historic victory: as one of the 'guard' recalled, 'I never was in so long-continued and well-conducted a fight as was that night made by those who defended Hardy's house.' When Hardy looked back on the incident his own feelings were decided: 'I do not relish the government of a mob.'[2] And we may see in the events of four years later an ironic sequel. In 1801 London was once again illuminated, but this time it was in honour of the preliminaries of peace which had been signed between Britain and France. This time the mob vented its feelings by breaking every window in

1. See pp. 122 ff. below.
2. John Binns, *Recollections* (Philadelphia, 1854); Hardy, op. cit., pp. 85–6.

the house of a bellicose anti-Jacobin journalist, who refused to illuminate for the peace. There was no popular guard and even the City authorities were tardy in sending protection. The journalist was William Cobbett.[1]

1. G. D. H. Cole, *Life of William Cobbett* (1924), p. 76. War recommenced, with Cobbett's full support, in May 1803.

[4]

The Free-born Englishman

IN 1797 the defenders of Hardy's house were fighting a rear-guard action. In the next few years, when a French invasion was possible, there is no doubt that the patriotic sentiments of the populace threatened the surviving Jacobins with mob terrorism. In Westminster, with its wide franchise, it was still possible to defeat the Radicals in 1806 by deploying the resources of bribery and deference. Francis Place saw servants of the Duke of Northumberland 'in their showy dress liveries, throwing lumps of bread and cheese among the dense crowd of vagabonds':

To see these vagabonds catching the lumps, shouting, swearing, fighting, and blackguarding in every possible way, women as well as men, all the vile wretches from the courts and alleys in St Giles and Westminster, the Porridge Islands, and other miserable places; to see these people representing, as it was said, the electors of Westminster, was certainly the lowest possible step of degradation ...

Beer was given to the crowd, the heads of the butts were knocked in and 'coal-heavers ladled the beer out with their long-tailed, broad-brimmed hats ... but the mob pressing on, the butts were upset, and the beer flowed along the gutters, from whence some made efforts to obtain it'. Place looked on, appalled at this 'disgraceful scene'. But in the next year (1807) Place and his friends organized a Radical election committee which worked among the people with such effect that Westminster returned two Radical Members, Sir Francis Burdett and Lord Cochrane.[1] And from that time forward, the tradition of 'Radical London' is almost unbroken. Burdett was able in 1810 to model his tactics upon those of Wilkes, and assume the support of the populace in his contest with the

1. Add. MSS. 27850 ff., 19–20: 27838 ff., 19–20; G. D. H. Cole and A. W. Filson, *British Working Class Movements* (1951), pp. 79–80. See below, ch. 13.

Government. In the main provincial centres much the same is true by 1812: 'the mob' (a Sheffield diarist noted), 'dislike all but a thorough Reformer'.[1] By the time that the Wars ended (1815), it was not possible, either in London or in the industrial North or Midlands, to employ a 'Church and King' mob to terrorize the Radicals.

From time to time, between 1815 and 1850, Radicals, Owenites, or Chartists complained of the apathy of the people. But – if we leave out of account the usual election tumults – it is generally true that reformers were shielded by the support of working-class communities. At election times in the large towns, the open vote by show of hands on the 'hustings' which preceded the poll usually went overwhelmingly for the most radical candidate. The reformers ceased to fear 'the mob', while the authorities were forced to build barracks and take precautions against the 'revolutionary crowd'. This is one of those facts of history so big that it is easily overlooked, or assumed without question; and yet it indicates a major shift in emphasis in the inarticulate, 'sub-political' attitudes of the masses.

The shift in emphasis is related to popular notions of 'independence', patriotism, and the Englishman's 'birthright'. The Gordon Rioters of 1780 and the 'Church and King' rioters in Birmingham in 1791 had this in common: they felt themselves, in some obscure way, to be defending the 'Constitution' against alien elements who threatened their 'birthright'. They had been taught for so long that the Revolution settlement of 1688, embodied in the Constitution of King, Lords and Commons, was the guarantee of British independence and liberties, that the reflex had been set up – Constitution equals Liberty – upon which the unscrupulous might play. And yet it is likely that the very rioters who destroyed Dr Priestley's precious library and laboratory were proud to regard themselves as 'free-born Englishmen'. Patriotism, nationalism, even bigotry and repression, were all clothed in the rhetoric of liberty. Even Old Corruption extolled British liberties; not national honour, or power, but freedom was the coinage of patrician, demagogue and radical alike. In the name of freedom Burke denounced, and Paine championed, the French Revolution: with the open-

1. T. A. Ward, *Peeps into the Past*, ed. A. B. Bell (1909), p. 192.

ing of the French Wars (1793), patriotism and liberty occupied every poetaster:

> Thus Britons guard their ancient fame,
>   Assert their empire o'er the sea,
> And to the envying world proclaim,
>   One nation still is brave and free –
>
> Resolv'd to conquer or to die,
> True to their KING, their LAWS, their LIBERTY.[1]

The invasion scare resulted in a torrent of broadsheets and ballads on such themes, which form a fitting background for Wordsworth's smug and sonorous patriotic sonnets:

> It is not to be thought of that the Flood
> Of British freedom, which, to the open sea
> Of the world's praise, from dark antiquity
> Hath flowed, 'with pomp of waters, unwithstood,' ...

'Not to be thought of': and yet, at this very time, freedom of the press, of public meeting, of trade union organization, of political organization and of election, were either severely limited or in abeyance. What, then, did the common Englishman's 'birthright' consist in? 'Security of property!' answered Mary Wollstonecraft: 'Behold ... the definition of English liberty'.[2] And yet the rhetoric of liberty means much more – first of all, of course, freedom from foreign domination. And, within this enveloping haze of patriotic self-congratulation, there were other less distinct notions which Old Corruption felt bound to flatter and yet which were to prove dangerous to it in the long run. Freedom from absolutism (the constitutional monarchy), freedom from arbitrary arrest, trial by jury, equality before the law, the freedom of the home from arbitrary entrance and search, some limited liberty of thought, of speech, and of conscience, the vicarious participation in liberty (or in its semblance) afforded by the right of parliamentary opposition and by elections and election tumults (although the people had no vote they had the right to parade, huzza and jeer on the hustings), as well as freedom to travel, trade, and sell one's own labour. Nor were any of these freedoms insignificant; taken

1. *Anti-Jacobin*, 1 January 1798.
2. *A Vindication of the Rights of Men* (1790), p. 23.

together, they both embody and reflect a moral consensus in which authority at times shared, and of which at all times it was bound to take account.[1]

Indefinite as such a notion as 'moral consensus' may be, this question of the *limits* beyond which the Englishman was not prepared to be 'pushed around', and the limits beyond which authority did not dare to go, is crucial to an understanding of this period. The stance of the common Englishman was not so much democratic, in any positive sense, as anti-absolutist. He felt himself to be an individualist, with few affirmative rights, but protected by the laws against the intrusion of arbitrary power. More obscurely, he felt that the Glorious Revolution afforded a consitutional precedent for the right to riot in resistance to oppression. And this indeed was the central paradox of the eighteenth century, in both intellectual and practical terms: constitutionalism was the 'illusion of the epoch'. Political theory, of traditionalists and reformers alike, was transfixed within the Whiggish limits established by the 1688 settlement, by Locke or by Blackstone. For Locke, the chief ends of government were the maintenance of civil peace, and the security of the person and of property. Such a theory, diluted by self-interest and prejudice, might provide the propertied classes with a sanction for the most bloody code penalizing offenders against property; but it provided no sanction for *arbitrary* authority, intruding upon personal or property rights, and uncontrolled by the rule of law. Hence the paradox, which surprised many foreign observers, of a bloody penal code alongside a *liberal* and, at times, meticulous administration and interpretation of the laws. The eighteenth century was indeed a great century for constitutional theorists, judges and lawyers. The poor man might often feel little protection when caught up in the law's toils. But the jury system *did* afford a measure of protection, as Hardy, Horne Tooke, Thelwall and Binns discovered. Wilkes *was* able to defy King, Parliament and administration – and to establish important new precedents – by using alternately the law courts and the mob. There was no *droit administratif*, no right of arbitrary arrest or search. Even in the 1790s, each attempt to introduce a 'continental' spy

1. See E. Halévy, op. cit., I, pp. 193–212.

system, each suspension of Habeas Corpus, each attempt to pack juries, aroused an outcry beyond the reformers' own ranks. If any – faced by the records of Tyburn and of repression – are inclined to question the value of these limits, they should contrast the trial of Hardy and his colleagues with the treatment of Muir, Gerrald, Skirving and Palmer in 1793–4 in the Scottish courts.[1]

This constitutionalism coloured the less articulate responses of the 'free-born Englishman'. He claimed few rights except that of being left alone. No institution was as much hated, in the eighteenth century, as the press-gang. A standing Army was deeply distrusted, and few of Pitt's repressive measures aroused as much discontent as the erection of barracks near the industrial towns. The right of individuals to bear arms in their own defence was claimed by reformers. The profession of a soldier was held to be dishonourable. 'In arbitrary Monarchies,' wrote one pamphleteer,

where the Despot who reigns can say to his wretched subjects, 'Eat straw', and they eat straw, no wonder that they can raise Armies of human Butchers, to destroy their fellow creatures; but, in a country like Great Britain, which at least is *pretended to be free*, it becomes a matter of no small surprize that so many thousands of men should deliberately renounce the privileges and blessings attendant on Freemen, and voluntarily sell themselves to the most humiliating and degrading *Slavery*, for the miserable pittance of sixpence a day . . .[2]

The 'crimping-houses' used for military recruiting in Holborn, the City, Clerkenwell and Shoreditch were mobbed and destroyed in three days of rioting in August 1794.[3] At the height

1. See pp. 135 ff. below. The evidence is fully discussed in Lord Cockburn's learned and lively *Examination of the Trials of Sedition . . . in Scotland* (Edinburgh, 1888).

2. Anon., *Letters on the Impolicy of a Standing Army in Time of Peace, and on the unconstitutional and illegal Measure of Barracks* (1793). John Trenchard's *History of Standing Armies in England* (1698) was republished in 1731, 1739, 1780 and in the Jacobin *Philanthropist* (1795).

3. See Rudé, *Wilkes and Liberty*, p. 14; S. Maccoby, *English Radicalism 1786–1832* (1955), p. 91. It was said that prostitutes, known as 'gallows bitches', enticed men into the house where they were forcibly 'recruited': see H. M. Saunders, *The Crimps* (1794).

of the agitation by the framework knitters for protective legislation in 1812, the secretary of the Mansfield branch wrote in
alarm when he learned that the workers' representatives were
proposing a clause authorizing powers of inspection and search
into the houses of manufacturers suspected of evading the proposed regulations: 'if iver that bullwark is broke down of every
english mans hous being his Castil then that strong barrer is for
iver broke that so many of our ancestors have bled for and in
vain'.[1] Resistance to an effective police force continued well
into the nineteenth century. While reformers were prepared to
agree that a more effective *preventive* police was necessary, with
more watchmen and a stronger nightly guard over property,
any centralized force with larger powers was seen as:

a system of tyranny; an organized army of spies and informers,
for the destruction of all public liberty, and the disturbance of all
private happiness. Every other system of police is the curse of
despotism . . .[2]

The Parliamentary Committee of 1818 saw in Bentham's proposals for a Ministry of Police 'a plan which would make every
servant of every house a spy on the actions of his master, and
all classes of society spies on each other'. Tories feared the
over-ruling of parochial and chartered rights, and of the powers
of local J.P.s; Whigs feared an increase in the powers of Crown
or of Government; Radicals like Burdett and Cartwright preferred the notion of voluntary associations of citizens or rotas
of householders; the radical populace until Chartist times saw
in any police an engine of oppression. A quite surprising consensus of opinion resisted the establishment of 'one supreme
and resistless tribunal, such as is denominated in other
countries the "High Police" – an engine . . . invented by despotism . . .'[3]

In hostility to the increase in the powers of any centralized
authority, we have a curious blend of parochial defensiveness,
Whig theory, and popular resistance. Local rights and customs

1. *Records of the Borough of Nottingham*, VIII (1952), p. 152.
2. J. P. Smith, *An Account of a Successful Experiment* (1812).
3. *The Times*, 31 January 1823: see Radzinowicz, op. cit., III, pp.
354–64.

were cherished against the encroachment of the State by gentry and common people alike; hostility to 'the Thing' and to 'Bashaws' contributed much to the Tory-Radical strain which runs through from Cobbett to Oastler, and which reached its meridian in the resistance to the Poor Law of 1834. (It is ironic that the main protagonists of the State, in its political and administrative authority, were the middle-class Utilitarians, on the other side of whose Statist banner were inscribed the doctrines of economic *laissez faire*.) Even at the peak of the repression of the Jacobins, in the middle 1790s, the fiction was maintained that the intimidation was the work of 'voluntary' associations of 'private' citizens (Reeves' Anti-Jacobin Society or Wilberforce's Society for the Suppression of Vice); while the same fiction was employed in the persecution of Richard Carlile after the Wars. State subsidies to the 'official' press during the Wars were administered guiltily, and with much hedging and diplomatic denial. The employment of spies and of *agents provocateurs* after the Wars was the signal for a genuine outburst of indignation in which very many who were bitterly opposed to manhood suffrage took part.

Moreover, not only freedom from the intrusions of the State but also belief in the equality of rich and poor before the law was a source of authentic popular congratulation. Sensational reading-matter, such as the *New Newgate Calendar: or Malefactor's Bloody Register*, recorded with satisfaction instances of the noble and influential brought to Tyburn. Local annalists noted smugly such cases as that of Leeds' 'domineering villanous lord of the manor' who was executed in 1748 for killing one of his own tenants in a fit of temper. Radicals might affect a well-based cynicism. If the law is open alike to rich and poor, said Horne Tooke, so is the London Tavern: 'but they will give you a very sorry welcome, unless you come with money sufficient to pay for your entertainment'.[1] But the conviction that the rule of law was the distinguishing inheritance of the 'free-born Englishman', and was his defence against arbitrary power, was upheld even by the Jacobins. The London Corresponding Society, in an *Address* of 1793, sought to define the difference

1. T. Walker, *Review of some Political Events in Manchester* (1794), p. 87.

in status between the English commoner and the commoner in pre-revolutionary France: 'our persons were protected by the laws, while their lives were at the mercy of every titled individual. ... We were MEN while they were SLAVES.'

This defensive ideology nourished, of course, far larger claims to positive rights. Wilkes had known well how to strike this chord – the champion defending his individual rights passed imperceptibly into the free-born citizen challenging King and Ministers and claiming rights for which there was no precedent. In 1776 Wilkes went so far as to plead in the House of Commons for the political rights of 'the meanest mechanic, the poorest peasant and day labourer', who –

has important rights respecting his personal liberty, that of his wife and children, his property however inconsiderable, his wages ... which are in many trades and manufactures regulated by the power of Parliament. ... Some share therefore in the power of making those laws which deeply interest them ... should be reserved even to this inferior but most useful set of men ...

The argument is still that of Ireton (or Burke) but property-rights are interpreted in a far more liberal sense; and Wilkes rounded it off with the customary appeal to tradition and precedent:

Without a true representation of the Commons our constitution is essentially defective ... and all other remedies to recover the pristine purity of the form of government established by our ancestors would be ineffectual.

'Pristine purity', 'our ancestors' – these are key-phrases, and for twenty years arguments among reformers turned upon nice interpretations of these terms. *Which* model was pure and pristine, to *which* ancestors should reformers refer? To the founding fathers of the United States, breaking free from the trammels of precedent, it seemed sufficient to find certain truths 'self-evident'. But to Major John Cartwright (1740–1824), publishing his pamphlet *Take Your Choice* in the same year as the Declaration of Independence (1776), it seemed necessary to shore up his case for annual parliaments, equal electoral districts, payment of Members, and adult manhood suffrage, with reference to Saxon precedent. The 'good, grey

Major' (as he became known nearly half a century later) defined as early as this the main claims of advanced political reformers, from 1776 to the Chartists and beyond.[1] And from these claims he never swerved. Incapable of compromise, eccentric and courageous, the Major pursued his single-minded course, issuing letters, appeals, and pamphlets, from his seat in Boston, Lincs, surviving trials, tumults, dissension and repression. It was he who set out, before the Napoleonic Wars had ended, to found the first reform societies of a new era, the Hampden Clubs, in those northern industrial regions where his clerical brother had accelerated other processes of change with his invention of the power-loom. But although the Major's principles and proposals outlived his own long lifetime, his arguments did not.

In a moment, we shall see why. (The answer, in two words, is Tom Paine.) But we should first note that in twenty years before the French Revolution a new dimension was *in practice* being added to the accepted procedures of the Constitution. The press had already established indefinite rights independent of King, Lords and Commons; and the agitation surrounding Wilkes's *North Briton* revealed both the precariousness of these rights and the sensitivity of a large public in their defence. But the second half of the eighteenth century sees also the rise of the Platform,[2] – the 'extra-parliamentary' pressure-group, campaigning for more or less limited aims, mobilizing opinion 'without doors' by means of publications, great meetings, and petitions. Different uses of platform and petition were adopted by bodies as various as Wilkes's supporters, Wyvill's county associations, the Protestant Association (which figured at the start of the Gordon Riots), the 'economical' reformers, the anti-slavery agitation, agitation for the repeal of disabilities upon Nonconformists. While Wilberforce or Wyvill might wish to limit their agitation to gentlemen, or to freeholders, precedents were established, and the example was contagious. A new cog was added to the complicated machinery of constitu-

1. Major Cartwright also came to advocate the secret ballot, but not the sixth Chartist point, the abolition of property qualifications for M.P.s.

2. I use here the term of Henry Jephson, whose two-volume history of *The Platform* (1892) is still the only consecutive study of this institution.

tion; Erksine and Wyvill, using the familiar mechanical imagery of checks and balances,[1] called for 'Clock-Work Regularity in the movements of the People'. Major John Cartwright went further – the more fuss stirred up, for the most far-reaching demands, among all classes of people, the better:

On the old maxim of teaching a young archer to shoot at the moon [he wrote to Wyvill] in order that he may acquire the power of throwing his arrow far enough for practical purposes, I have always thought that a free discussion of the principle of Universal Suffrage the most likely means of obtaining any Reform at all worth contending for.

For the Major – although he couched his arguments in terms of precedent and tradition – believed in methods of agitation among 'members unlimited'. In the years of repression, 1797–9, the squire of Boston issued a reproof to the caution of the north Yorkshire reformer. 'I am but little afraid of your Yeomanry,' he wrote to Wyvill, 'but your *Gentlemen* I dread. ... It is fortunate for me that hitherto all the *Gentlemen*, except one, have been on the *other side*. My efforts, therefore, have not been maimed by their councils, and I have on all occasions spoken out':

I feel as if nothing but strong cordials, and the most powerful stimulants, can awaken the People to any thing energetic. ... Unless our appeals convince all under-standings, and the truths we utter irresistibly seize on the heart, we shall do nothing. ... If you should, in order to get on at all, be compelled to propose mere expedients short of such energetic appeals, I hope in God you will be rescued from the situation by some strong-minded men at your Meeting ...[2]

Similar constitutional arguments might, then, conceal deep differences in tone and in means of propaganda. But all reformers before Paine commenced with 'the corruptions of the Constitution'. And their degree of Radicalism can generally be inferred from the historical precedents cited in their writings. The Wilkite, but largely aristocratic, Supporters of the Bill of Rights (and its successors, the 'Revolution Societies' (1788) and

1. See Asa Briggs, *The Age of Improvement* (1959), pp. 88 ff.
2. C. Wyvill, *Political Papers*, V, pp. 389–90, 399–400.

The Friends of the People (1792)) were content to enforce the precedent of the settlement of 1688. The advanced Society for Constitutional Information, founded in 1780, whose pamphlets by Dr Jebb, Cartwright, and Capel Lofft provided Thomas Hardy with his first introduction to the theory of reform, ranged widely – to the Magna Carta and beyond – for precedents, and drew upon both Anglo-Saxon and American example.[1] And, after the French Revolution, theorists of the popular societies dealt largely in Anglo-Saxon 'tythings', the Witenagemot, and legends of Alfred's reign. 'Pristine purity', and 'our ancestors', became – for many Jacobins – almost any constitutional innovation for which a Saxon precedent could be vamped up. John Baxter, a Shoreditch silversmith, a leader of the L.C.S. and a fellow prisoner with Hardy during the treason trials, found time to publish in 1796 an 830-page *New and Impartial History of England*, in which Saxon precedent is almost indistinguishable from the state of nature, the noble savage, or the original social compact. 'Originally,' Baxter supposed, 'the constitution must have been free.' History was the history of its corruption, 'the Britons having been subdued first by the Romans, next by the Saxons, these again by the Danes, and, finally, all by the Normans ...' As for the Revolution of 1688 it 'did no more than expel a tyrant, and confirm the Saxon laws'. But there were plenty of these laws still to be restored; and, next to manhood suffrage, the ones which John Baxter liked best were the absence of a standing Army, and the right of each citizen to go armed. He had arrived, by industrious constitutional arguments, at the right of the people to defy the Constitution.

Nevertheless, as Mr Christopher Hill has shown in his study of the theory of the 'Norman Yoke', these elaborate and often specious constitutional controversies were of real significance.[2] Even the forms of antiquarian argument conceal important differences in political emphasis. From the anonymous *Historical Essay on the English Constitution* (1771) to the early 1790s,

1. The Constitutional Society became quiescent in the later 1780s, but – with Horne Tooke as a prominent member – was most active after 1790.

2. In *Democracy and the Labour Movement*, ed. P. Saville, (1954), esp. pp. 42–54.

the more advanced reformers were marked out by their fondness for citing Saxon example. Long before this Tom Paine had published his *Common Sense* (1776) whose arguments were scarcely conducive to the appeal to precedent:

A French bastard landing with an armed banditti and establishing himself King of England, against the consent of the natives, is, in plain terms, a very paltry, rascally original. It certainly hath no divinity in it. ... The plain truth is that the antiquity of English monarchy will not bear looking into.

But this was published on American soil; and, as we shall see, it was only after the French Revolution and the publication of *Rights of Man* that such iconoclasm was heard in England: 'If the succession runs in the line of the Conqueror, the nation runs in the line of being conquered, and ought to rescue itself from this approach.' Meanwhile, the thory of the 'Norman Yoke' showed astonishing vitality; and even had a revival, in Jacobin circles, after 1793, when Paine was driven into exile and his *Rights of Man* was banned as seditious libel.

This was, in part, a matter of expediency. Paine's prosecution revealed the limits of freedom permitted within the conventions of constitutionalism. To deny altogether the appeal to 'our ancestors' was actively dangerous. When Henry Yorke, the Sheffield reformer, was on trial in 1795, his defence turned upon this point: 'In almost every speech I took essential pains in controverting the doctrines of Thomas Paine, who denied the existence of our constitution. ... I constantly asserted on the contrary, that we had a good constitution', 'that magnanimous government which we derived from our Saxon fathers, and from the prodigious mind of the immortal Alfred'. Even John Baxter, whose 'Saxons' were Jacobin and *sans-culottes* to a man, felt it expedient to dissociate himself from Paine's total lack of reverence:

Much as we respect the opinions of Mr Thomas Paine ... we cannot agree with him, that we have no constitution; his mistake seems to arise from having carried his views no further than the Norman Conquest.

But it was more than expediency. According to legend, Saxon precedent provided legitimation for a constitutional monarchy, a free Parliament based on manhood suffrage, and the rule of law. In coming forward as 'Patriots' and constitutionalists, men like Major Cartwright and Baxter were attempting to take over the rhetoric of the age.[1] It seemed that if matters were to be posed as bluntly as Paine posed them in *Common Sense*, then reformers would be forced to disengage from the constitutional debate altogether, and rest their claims upon reason, conscience, self-interest, 'self-evident' truths. For many eighteenth-century Englishmen whose minds were nurtured in a constitutionalist culture the idea was shocking, unnerving, and, in its implications, dangerous.

And yet it was necessary that this rhetoric should be broken through, because – even when tricked out in Baxter's improbable Saxon terms – it implied the absolute sanctity of certain conventions: respect for the institution of monarchy, for the hereditary principle, for the traditional rights of the great landowners and the Established Church, and for the representation, not of human rights, but of property rights. Once enmeshed in constitutionalist arguments – even when these were used to advance the claims of manhood suffrage – reformers became caught up in the trivia of piecemeal constitutional renovation. For a plebeian movement to arise it was essential to escape from these categories altogether and set forward far wider democratic claims. In the years between 1770 and 1790 we can observe a dialectical paradox by means of which the rhetoric of constitutionalism contributed to its own destruction or transcendence. Those in the eighteenth century who read Locke or Blackstone's commentaries found in them a searching criticism of the workings of faction and interest in the unreformed House of Commons.[2] The first reaction was to criticize the practice of

1. This rhetoric turns up in unlikely places. A late eighteenth-century bill advertises 'that Most antient, Loyal, National, Constitutional and Lawful Diversion: BEAR-BAITING'. Provincial Jacobin societies, between 1792 and 1796, usually described themselves as Constitutional or Patriotic. John Thelwall's widow, when compiling his life, was at pains to note that her husband was 'descended from a Saxon family', while Joseph Gerrald, when proposing the dangerous expedient of a National Convention, cited as precedents the 'folk-motes' of 'our Saxon ancestors'.

2. Erskine rested his defence of Paine, at his trial *in absentia*, upon passages from Blackstone, while the Sheffield reformer, Yorke, read extracts from Locke at public demonstrations. Student in the Temple, *Trial of Thomas Hardy* (1794), p. 108.

the eighteenth century in the light of its own theory; the second, more delayed, reaction was to bring the theory itself into discredit. And it was at this point that Paine entered, with *Rights of Man*.

The French Revolution had set a precedent of a larger kind: a new constitution drawn up, in the light of reason and from first principles, which threw 'the meagre, stale, forbidding ways/Of custom, law, and statute' into the shadows. And it was not Paine, but Burke, who effected the first major evacuation of the grounds of constitutional argument. The French example, on one hand, and the industrious reformers quarrying for pre-1688 or pre-Norman precedent, on the other, had made the old ground untenable. In his *Reflections on the French Revolution* (1790) Burke supplemented the authority of precedent by that of wisdom and experience, and reverence for the Constitution by reverence for tradition – that 'partnership ... between those who are living, those who are dead, and those who are to be born'. The theory of checks and balances upon the exercise of specific powers was translated into the moody notion of checks and balances upon the imperfections of man's nature:

The science of constructing a commonwealth ... is not to be taught *a priori*. ... The nature of man is intricate; the objects of society are of the greatest possible complexity: and therefore no simple disposition or direction of power can be suitable either to man's nature, or to the quality of his affairs. ... The rights of men in governments are ... often in balances between differences of good; in compromises sometimes between good and evil, and sometimes between evil and evil ...

Radical reformers 'are so taken up with their theories about the rights of man, that they have totally forgotten his nature'. 'By their violent haste and their defiance of the process of nature, they are delivered over blindly to every projector and adventurer, to every alchymist and empiric.'[1]

The argument is deduced from man's moral nature in general; but we repeatedly glimpse sight of the fact that it was not the moral nature of a corrupt aristocracy which alarmed

1. *Reflections on the French Revolution* (Everyman edn) pp. 58–9, 62, 166.

Burke so much as the nature of the populace, 'the swinish multitude'. Burke's great historical sense was brought to imply a 'process of nature' so complex and procrastinating that any innovation was full of unseen dangers – a process in which the common people might have no part. If Paine was wrong to dismiss Burke's cautions (for his *Rights of Man* was written in reply to Burke), he was right to expose the inertia of class interests which underlay his special pleading. Academic judgement has dealt strangely with the two men. Burke's reputation as a political philosopher has been inflated, very much so in recent years. Paine has been dismissed as a mere popularizer. In truth, neither writer was systematic enough to rank as a major political theorist. Both were publicists of genius, both are less remarkable for what they say than for the *tone* in which it is said. Paine lacks any depth of reading, any sense of cultural security, and is betrayed by his arrogant and impetuous temper into writing passages of a mediocrity which the academic mind still winces at and lays aside with a sigh. But the popular mind remembers Burke less for his insight than for his epochal indiscretion – 'the swinish multitude' – the give-away phrase which revealed another kind of insensitivity of which Paine was incapable. Burke's blemish vitiates the composure of eighteenth-century polite culture. In all the angry popular pamphleteering which followed it might almost seem that issues could be defined in five words: Burke's two-word epithet on the one hand, Paine's three-word banner on the other. With dreary invention the popular pamphleteers performed satirical variations upon Burke's theme: *Hog's Wash, Pig's Meat, Mast and Acorns: Collected by Old Hubert, Politics for the People: A Salmagundy for Swine* (with contributions from 'Brother Grunter', 'Porculus' and *ad nauseam*) were the titles of the pamphlets and periodicals. The stye, the swineherds, the bacon – so it goes on. 'Whilst ye are ... gorging yourselves at troughs filled with the daintiest wash; we, with our numerous train of *porkers*, are employed, from the rising to the setting sun, to obtain the means of subsistence, by ... picking up a few acorns,' runs an *Address to the Hon. Edmund Burke from the Swinish Multitude* (1793). No other words have ever made the 'free-born Englishman' so angry – nor so ponderous in reply.

Since the *Rights of Man* is a foundation-text of the English working-class movement, we must look at its arguments and tone more closely.[1] Paine wrote on English soil, but as an American with an international reputation who had lived for close on fifteen years in the bracing climate of experiment and constitutional iconoclasm. 'I wished to know,' he wrote in the Preface to the Second Part, 'the manner in which a work, written in a style of thinking and expression different to what had been customary in England, would be received.' From the outset he rejected the framework of constitutional argument: 'I am contending for the rights of the *living*, and against their being willed away, and controuled, and contracted for, by the manuscript-assumed authority of the dead.' Burke wished to 'consign over the rights of posterity for ever, on the authority of a mouldy parchment', while Paine asserted that each successive generation was competent to define its rights and form of government anew.

As for the English Constitution, no such thing existed. At the most, it was a 'sepulchre of precedents', a kind of 'Political Popery'; and 'government by precedent, without any regard to the principle of the precedent, is one of the vilest systems that can be set up'. All governments, except those in France and America, derived their authority from conquest and superstition: their foundations lay upon 'arbitrary power'. And Paine reserved his particular invective for the superstitious regard attached to the means by which the continuation of this power was secured – the hereditary principle. 'A banditti of ruffians overrun a country, and lay it under contributions. Their power being thus established, the chief of the band contrived to lose the name of Robber in that of Monarch; and hence the origin of Monarchy and Kings.' As for the right of inheritance, 'to inherit a Government, is to inherit the People, as if they were

1. Paine returned to England in 1787, and was much preoccupied with his experiments in bridge-building. The First Part of *Rights of Man* was published in 1791: the Second Part in 1792. The most recent biography of Paine – A. O. Aldridge, *Man of Reason* (1960) – is thorough but pedestrian, and adds little to our knowledge of Paine's English influence and connexions. It should be read beside the lively but partisan *Life* (1892) by Moncure D. Conway; or the brief sketch by H. N. Brailsford in *Shelley, Godwin and their Circle*.

flocks and herds'. 'Kings succeed each other, not as rationals, but as animals. ... It requires some talents to be a common mechanic; but to be a King, requires only the animal figure of a man – a sort of breathing automaton':

The time is not very far distant when England will laugh at itself for sending to Holland, Hanover, Zell, or Brunswick for men, at the expense of a million a year, who understood neither her laws, her language, nor her interest, and whose capacities would scarcely have fitted them for the office of a parish constable.

'What are those men kept for?,' he demanded.

Placemen, Pensioners, Lords of the Bed-chamber, Lords of the Kitchen, Lords of the Necessary-house, and the Lord knows what besides, can find as many reasons for monarchy as their salaries, paid at the expence of the country, amount to: but if I ask the farmer, the manufacturer, the merchant, the tradesman ... the common labourer, what service monarchy is to him, he can give me no answer. If I ask him what monarchy is, he believes it is something like a sinecure.

The hereditary system in general was consigned to the same oblivion: 'an hereditary governor is as inconsistent as an hereditary author'.

All this was (and has some of the dare-devil air of) blasphemy. Even the sacred Bill of Rights Paine found to be 'a bill of wrongs and of insult'. It is not that Paine was the first man to think in this way: many eighteenth-century Englishmen must have held these thoughts privately. He was the first to dare to express himself with such irreverence; and he destroyed with one book century-old taboos. But Paine did very much more than this. In the first place he pointed towards a theory of the State and of class power, although in a confused, ambiguous manner. In *Common-Sense* he had followed Locke in seeing government as a 'necessary evil'. In the 1790s the ambiguities of Locke seem to fall into two halves, one Burke, the other Paine. Where Burke assumes government and examines its operation in the light of experience and tradition, Paine speaks for the governed, and assumes that the authority of government derives from conquest and inherited power in a class-divided society. The classes are roughly defined – 'there are two distinct

classes of men in the nation, those who pay taxes, and those
who receive and live upon taxes' – and as for the Constitution,
it is a good one for –

courtiers, placemen, pensioners, borough-holders, and the leaders
of the Parties . . . ; but it is a bad Constitution for at least ninety-
nine parts of the nation out of a hundred.

From this also, the war of the propertied and the unpropertied:
'when the rich plunder the poor of his rights, it becomes an
example to the poor to plunder the rich of his property'.[1] By
this argument, government appears as court parasitism: taxes
are a form of robbery, for pensioners and for wars of conquest:
while 'the whole of the Civil Government is executed by the
People of every town and country, by means of parish
officers, magistrates, quarterly sessions, juries, and assize, without any trouble to what is called the Government'. So that – at
this point – we are close to a theory of anarchism. What is required is less the reform than the abolition of government: 'the
instant formal Government is abolished, society begins to act'.

On the other hand, 'society', acting through a representative
system as a government opened up new possibilities which suddenly caught fire in Paine's mind while writing the crucial fifth
chapter of the Second Part of *Rights of Man*. Here, after extolling commerce and industrial enterprise, clouting colonial
domination (and – later – proposing international arbitration in
place of war), hitting out at the penal code ('legal barbarity'),
denouncing closed charters, corporations, and monopolies, and
exclaiming against the burden of taxation, he came to rest for
a moment on the sins of the landed aristocracy:

Why . . . does Mr Burke talk of this House of Peers, as the pillar of
the landed interest? Were that pillar to sink into the earth, the
same landed property would continue, and the same ploughing, sow-
ing, and reaping would go on. The Aristocracy are not the farmers
who work the land . . . but are the mere consumers of the rent . . .

And this led him on to far-reaching impressionistic proposals
for cutting the costs of government, Army and Navy; remitting
taxes and poor rates; raising additional taxation by means of

1. These last three passages are taken from Paine's *Letter Addressed to
the Addressers* (1792), pp. 19, 26, 69. All others from *Rights of Man*.

a graduated income-tax (rising to twenty shillings in the £ at £23,000 p.a.); and paying out the moneys raised or saved in sums to alleviate the position of the poor. He proposed family allowances: public funds to enable general education of all children: old age pensions – 'not as a matter of grace and favour, but of right' (for the recipients would receive back only a portion of what they had contributed in taxation): a maternity benefit, a benefit for newly-wedded couples, a benefit for funerals for the necessitous: and the building in London of combined lodging-houses and workshops to assist immigrants and unemployed:

By the operation of this plan, the poor laws, those instruments of civil torture, will be superceded. ... The dying poor will not be dragged from place to place to breathe their last, as a reprisal of parish upon parish. Widows will have a maintenance for their children ... and children will no longer be considered as encreasing the distresses of their parents. ... The number of petty crimes, the offspring of distress and poverty, will be lessened. The poor, as well as the rich, will then be interested in the support of Government, and the cause and apprehension of riots and tumults will cease. Ye who sit in ease, and solace yourselves in plenty ... have ye thought of these things?

This is Paine at his strongest. The success of the First Part of *Rights of Man* was great, but the success of the Second Part was phenomenal. It was this part – and especially such sections as these – which effected a bridge between the older traditions of the Whig 'commonwealthsman' and the radicalism of Sheffield cutlers, Norwich weavers and London artisans. Reform was related by these proposals, to their daily experience of economic hardship. However specious some of Paine's financial calculations may have been, the proposals gave a new constructive cast to the whole reform agitation. If Major Cartwright formulated the specific demands for manhood suffrage which were to be the basis of a hundred years of agitation (and Mary Wollstonecraft, with her *Rights of Women*, initiated for the second sex an even longer era of struggle), Paine, in this chapter, set a sourse towards the social legislation of the twentieth century.

Few of Paine's ideas were original, except perhaps in this

'social' chapter. 'Men who give themselves to their Energetic Genius in the manner that Paine does are no Examiners' – the comment is William Blake's. What he gave to English people was a new rhetoric of radical egalitarianism, which touched the deepest responses of the 'free-born Englishman' and which penetrated the sub-political attitudes of the urban working people. Cobbett was not a true Painite, and Owen and the early Socialists contributed a new strand altogether; but the Paine tradition runs strongly through the popular journalism of the nineteenth century – Wooler, Carlile, Hetherington, Watson, Lovett, Holyoake, Reynolds, Bradlaugh. It is strongly challenged in the 1880s, but the tradition and the rhetoric are still alive in Blatchford and in the popular appeal of Lloyd George. We can almost say that Paine established a new framework within which Radicalism was confined for nearly 100 years, as clear and as well defined as the constitutionalism which it replaced.

What was this framework? Contempt for monarchical and hereditary principles, we have seen:

I disapprove of monarchical and aristocratical governments, however modified. Hereditary distinctions, and privileged order of every species . . . must necessarily counteract the progress of human improvement. Hence it follows that I am not among the admirers of the British Constitution.

The words happen to be Wordsworth's – in 1793. And Wordsworth's also the retrospective lines which recapture more than any other the optimism of those revolutionary years when – walking with Beaupuy – he encountered a 'hunger-bitten' peasant girl—

　　　　. . . and at the sight my friend
　　In agitation said, ' 'Tis against *that*
　　That we are fighting,' I with him believed
　　That a benignant spirit was abroad
　　Which might not be withstood, that poverty
　　Abject as this would in a little time
　　Be found no more, that we should see the earth
　　Unthwarted in her wish to recompense
　　The meek, the lowly, patient child of toil,
　　All institutes for ever blotted out

> That legalised exclusion, empty pomp
> Abolished, sensual state and cruel power,
> Whether by edict of the one or few;
> And finally, as sum and crown of all,
> Should see the people having a strong hand
> In framing their own laws; whence better days
> To all mankind.

An optimism (which Wordsworth was soon to lose) but to which Radicalism clung tenaciously, founding it upon premisses which Paine did not stop to examine: unbounded faith in representative institutions: in the power of reason: in (Paine's words) 'a mass of sense lying in a dormant state' among the common people, and in the belief that 'Man, were he not corrupted by Governments, is naturally the friend of Man, and that human nature is not of itself vicious.' And all this expressed in an intransigent, brash, even cocksure tone, with the self-educated man's distrust of tradition and institutes of learning ('He knew by heart all his own writings and knew nothing else', was the comment of one of Paine's acquaintances), and a tendency to avoid complex theoretical problems with a dash of empiricism and an appeal to 'Common Sense'.

Both the strengths and the weaknesses of this optimism were reproduced again and again in nineteenth-century working-class Radicalism. But Paine's writings were in no special sense aimed at the working people, as distinct from farmers, tradesmen and professional men. His was a doctrine suited to agitation among 'members unlimited'; but he did not challenge the property-rights of the rich nor the doctrines of *laissez faire*. His own affiliations were most obviously with men of the unrepresented manufacturing and trading classes; with men like Thomas Walker and Holcroft; with the Constitutional Society rather than the L.C.S. His proposals for a graduated income tax anticipate more far-reaching notions of property redistribution; but they were aimed at the great landed aristocracy, where the hereditary principle involved in the custom of primogeniture gave him offence. In terms of political democracy he wished to level all inherited distinctions and privileges; but he gave no countenance to economic levelling. In political society every man must have equal rights as a citizen: in economic society he must naturally remain employer or employed, and the State should not interfere with the capital of the one or the wages of the other. The *Rights of Man* and the *Wealth of Nations* should supplement and nourish each other. And in this also the main tradition of nineteenth-century working-class Radicalism took its cast from Paine. There were times, at the Owenite and Chartist climaxes, when other traditions became dominant. But after each relapse, the substratum of Painite assumptions remained intact. The aristocracy were the main target; their property might be threatened – even as far as Land Nationalization or Henry George's Single Tax – and their rents regarded as a feudal exaction dating from 'a French bastard' and his 'armed banditti'; but – however hard trade unionists might fight against their employers – industrial capital was assumed to be the fruit of enterprise and beyond reach of political intrusion. Until the 1880s, it was, by and large, within this framework that working-class Radicalism remained transfixed.

One other element Paine contributed to the nineteenth-century tradition: the true Painite – Carlile or James Watson or Holyoake – was also a free-thinker. 'My religion is to do good,' Paine wrote in *Rights of Man*, and left the matter there. But he saw himself as the champion of these rights against 'the age of fiction and political superstition, and of craft and mystery': and it was natural that he should complete his work with *The Age of Reason*, a sustained invective against State religion and every form of priestcraft. Paine wrote, not as an atheist, but as a Deist; the First Part, written in France in 1793 under the shadow of the guillotine, saw proofs of a God in the act of Creation and in the universe itself, and appealed to Reason as opposed to Mystery, Miracle or Prophecy. It was published in England in 1795, by Daniel Isaac Eaton who sustained no fewer than seven prosecutions and – by 1812 fifteen months of imprisonment and three years of outlawry – for his activities as a printer. Despite the brash provocations of its tone, *The Age of Reason* contained little that would have surprised the eighteenth-century Deist or advanced Unitarian. What was new was the popular audience to which Paine appealed, and the great authority of his name. The Second Part –

published in 1796 (also by the courageous Eaton)[1] – was an assault on the ethics of the Old Testament, and the veracity of the New, a pell-mell essay in biblical criticism:

> I have ... gone through the Bible, as a man would go through a wood with an axe on his shoulders, and fell trees. Here they lie; and the priests, if they can, may replant them. They may, perhaps, stick them in the ground, but they will never make them grow.

It has to be said that there are other uses for woods. Blake acknowledged the force and attack of Paine's arguments, rephrasing them in his own inimitable shorthand:

> That the Bible is all a State Trick, thro' which tho' the People at all times could see, they never had the power to throw off. Another Argument is that all the Commentators on the Bible are Dishonest Designing Knaves, who in hopes of a good living adopt the State religion ... I could name an hundred such.

But Paine was incapable of reading any part of the Bible as (in Blake's words) 'a Poem of probable impossibilities'. For many of Paine's English followers during the years of repression, *The Age of Reason* was as 'a sword sent to divide'. Some Jacobins who maintained their membership of Dissenting or Methodist churches resented both Paine's book and the opportunity which it afforded to their enemies to mount a renewed attack upon 'atheists' and 'republicans'. The authorities, for their part, saw Paine's latest offence as surpassing all his previous outrages; he had taken the polite periods of the comfortable Unitarian ministers and the scepticism of Gibbon, translated them into literal-minded polemical English, and thrown them to the groundlings. He ridiculed the authority of the Bible with arguments which the collier or country girl could understand:

> ... the person they call Jesus Christ, begotten, they say, by a ghost, whom they call holy, on the body of a woman engaged in marriage and afterwards married, and whom they call a virgin seven hundred years after this foolish story was told. ... Were any girl that is now with child to say ... that she was gotten with child by a ghost, and that an angel told her so, would she be believed?

1. Eaton published a 'Third Part' in 1811, and was sentenced in 1812 – at the age of sixty – to a further eighteen months imprisonment and to the pillory. T. S. Howell, *State Trials* (1823), XXXI, pp. 927 ff.

When we consider the barbaric and evil superstitions which the churches and Sunday schools were inculcating at this time,[1] we can see the profoundly liberating effect which Paine's writing had on many minds. It helped men to struggle free from a pall of religious deference which reinforced the deference due to magistrate and employer, and it launched many nineteenth-century artisans upon a course of sturdy intellectual self-reliance and enquiry. But the limitations of Paine's 'reason' must also be remembered; there was a glibness and lack of imaginative resource about it which remind one of Blake's strictures on the 'single vision'. In the Book of Ecclesiastes Paine could see only 'the solitary reflection of a worn-out debauchee ... who, looking back on scenes he can no longer enjoy, cries out, *All is Vanity*! A great deal of the metaphor and of the sentiment is obscure ...'

The Age of Reason was not the only source-book for nineteenth-century free thought. Many other tracts and translations (abridgements of Voltaire, D'Holbach, Rousseau) were circulated in Jacobin circles in the 1790s, the most influential of which was Volney's *Ruins of Empire*. This was a profounder and more imaginative book than Paine's, an original study in comparative religion. Moreover, Volney's allegory of the evolution of priestcraft was correlated with an allegory of the growth of political despotism; in its conclusions it offered a more general message of toleration and of internationalism than did Paine. Unlike William Godwin's *Political Justice* (1793), whose influence was confined to a small and highly literate circle,[2] Volney's *Ruins* was published in cheap pocket-book form and remained in the libraries of many artisans in the nineteenth century. Its fifteenth chapter, the vision of a 'New Age', was frequently circulated as a tract. In this the narrator sees a civilized nation determined to divide itself into two groups: those who 'by useful labours contribute to the support and maintenance of society', on the one hand, and their

1. See below, ch. 11.
2. Godwin's philosophical anarchism reached a working-class public only after the Wars; and then mainly through the Notes to Shelley's *Queen Mab*, in Richard Carlile's pirated editions.

enemies, on the other. The overwhelming majority are found in the first group: 'labourers, artisans, tradesmen, and every profession useful to society'. The second was 'a petty group, a valueless fraction' – 'none but priests, courtiers, public accountants, commanders of troops, in short, the civil, military, or religious agents of government'. A dialogue takes place between the two groups:

People. .... What labour do you perform in the society?

Privileged Class. None: we are not made to labour.

People. How then have you acquired your wealth?

Privileged Class. By taking the pains to govern you.

People. To govern us! ... We toil, and you enjoy; we produce and you dissipate; wealth flows from us, and you absorb it. Privileged men, class distinct from the people, form a nation apart and govern yourselves.

A few of the privileged class join the people (the vision continues) but the remainder attempt to cow the people with troops. The soldiers, however, ground their arms, and say: 'We are a part of the people.' The privileged class next attempt to delude the people with priests, but these are rebuffed: 'Courtiers and priests, your services are too expensive; henceforth we take our affairs into our own hands.' By a curious effect of translation, Volney's views appeared more radical in English than in French. The notion of the parasitic aristocratic estate or order comes through as the more generalized 'class' of the wealthy and idle. From this the sociology of post-war Radicalism was to be derived, which divided society between the 'Useful' or 'Productive Classes' on the one hand, and courtiers, sinecurists, fund-holders, speculators and parasitic middlemen on the other.[1]

Volney's, however, was a somewhat later influence. Paine dominated the popular radicalism of the early 1790s. It is true that his polemical literalness of mind gave a narrowness to the movement which (with the more sophisticated euphoria of Godwin) was bitterly caricatured by disenchanted reformers when French revolutionary Convention passed, by way of

1. See especially the discussion of Wade and the *Gorgon*, below, pp. 848 ff.

Terror, into Bonapartism. The critique and the caricature, expressed with the combined genius of Burke, Wordsworth, Coleridge, have dominated the judgements of many contemporary scholars, themselves exposed to similar experiences of revolutionary disenchantment in the past twenty-five years.

There was certainly a star-struck, messianic mood among some of the disciples of Godwin and of Paine, which prepared them for the acceptance of facile (and ultimately disenchanting) notions of human perfectibility:

O, PAINE! next to *God*, how infinitely are millions beholden to you for the small remnant of their liberties ... Alexanders, Caesars, Ferdinands, Capets, Frederics, Josephs, and Czarinas have ... fought ferociously to enslave mankind; but it was reserved to you ... to wave the celestial banners of the rights of man, over the tottering bastiles of Europe; to break the shackles of despotism from the ankles of millions, and destroy those yokes of oppression ... for the necks of millions more as yet unborn.[1]

Such moods are always to be found in periods of revolutionary excitement. But if the myth of Jacobin 'totalitarianism' is applied to the English context, then it is necessary to rebut it with the simplest truths. Paine and his English followers did not preach the extermination of their opponents, but they did preach against Tyburn and the sanguinary penal code. The English Jacobins argued for internationalism, for arbitration in place of war, for the toleration of Dissenters, Catholics and free-thinkers, for the discernment of human virtue in 'heathen, Turk or Jew'. They sought, by education and agitation, to transform 'the mob' (in Paine's words) from 'followers of the *camp*' to followers of 'the *standard* of liberty'.

This is not to dismiss the charges against some English Jacobins, of doctrinaire notions and shallow moral experimentalism, whose most notable expression is in Book III of Wordsworth's *Excursion*. These have often been the vices of the 'Left.' Paine had little historical sense, his view of human nature was facile, and his optimism ('I do not believe that Monarchy and Aristocracy will continue seven years longer in any of the

1. Citizen Randol, of Ostend, *A Political Catechism of Man* (1795), p. 8.

enlightened countries in Europe') is of a kind which the twentieth-century mind finds tedious. But so great has been the reaction in our own time against Whig or Marxist interpretations of history, that some scholars have propagated a ridiculous reversal of historical rôles: the persecuted are seen as forerunners of oppression, and the oppressors as victims of persecution. And so we have been forced to go over these elementary truths. It was Paine who put his faith in the free operation of opinion in the 'open society': 'mankind are not now to be told they shall not think, or they shall not read'; Paine also who saw that in the constitutional debates of the eighteenth century 'the Nation was always left out of the question'. By bringing the nation *into* the question, he was bound to set in motion forces which he could neither control nor foresee. That is what democracy is about.

[5]

Planting the Liberty Tree

WE must now return to Thomas Hardy and his companions who met in 'The Bell' in Exeter Street in January 1792. We have gone round this long way in order to break down the Chinese walls which divide the 18th from the 19th century, and the history of working-class agitation from the cultural and intellectual history of the rest of the nation. Too often events in England in the 1790s are seen only as a reflected glow from the storming of the Bastille.[1] But the elements precipitated by the French example – the Dissenting and libertarian traditions – reach far back into English history. And the agitation of the 1790s, although it lasted only five years (1792-6) was extraordinarily intensive and far-reaching. It altered the sub-political attitudes of the people, affected class alignments, and initiated traditions which stretch forward into the present century. It was not an agitation about France, although French events both inspired and bedevilled it. It was an English agitation, of impressive dimensions, for an English democracy.[2]

Constitutionalism was the flood-gate which the French example broke down. But the year was 1792, not 1789, and the waters which flowed through were those of Tom Paine. One way of approaching this is by way of some impressions of the north of England in the second half of 1792. In the summer

1. For the popular societies, see G. S. Veitch, *The Genesis of Parliamentary Reform* (1913); W. P. Hall, *British Radicalism, 1791-97* (New York, 1912), and P. A. Brown, *The French Revolution in English History* (1918). See also J. Dechamps, *Les Iles Britanniques et La Revolution Française* (Brussels, 1949); H. Collins, 'The London Corresponding Society', in *Democracy and the Labour Movement*, ed. J. Saville (1954); W. A. L. Seaman, 'British Democratic Societies in the French Revolution', (unpublished Ph.D. thesis, London, 1954).

2. It was, of course, in an even more intense form an agitation for Irish independence and for Scottish democracy. See H. W. Meikle, *Scotland and the French Revolution* (Glasgow, 1912); R. B. Madden, *The United Irishmen* (1842-6).

the Secretary at War considered the situation serious enough to send the Deputy Adjutant-General on tour to ascertain the disposition of the troops and their dependability in time of emergency. At Sheffield he 'found that the seditious doctrines of Paine and the factious people who are endeavouring to disturb the peace of the country had extended to a degree very much beyond my conception'. He saw in Sheffield a 'centre of all their seditious machinations': 2,500 'of the lowest mechanics' were enrolled in the principal reform association (the Constitutional Society):

Here they read the most violent publications, and comment on them, as well as on their correspondence not only with the dependent Societies in the towns and villages in the vicinity, but with those . . . in other parts of the kingdom. . .[1]

In the autumn and winter of 1792, Wilberforce (the Member for Yorkshire) received alarming reports from various correspondents. Wyvill wrote to him of 'the disposition of the lower people in the county of Durham':

Considerable numbers in Bernard Castle have manifested disaffection to the constitution, and the words, 'No King,' 'Liberty,' and 'Equality,' have been written there upon the Market Cross. During the late disturbances amongst the keelmen at Shields and Sunderland, General Lambton was thus addressed: 'Have you read this little work of Tom Paine's?' 'No.' 'Then read it – we like it much. You have a great estate, General; we shall soon divide it amongst us.'[2]

In November a correspondent was writing from North Shields direct to Pitt, describing the seamen's strikes and riots ('P.S. Shocking to relate, the mob at this moment are driving some seamen or officers that have discovered a reluctance to comply with their mode of proceedings naked through the town before them') in terms bordering on panic:

When I look round and see this Country covered with thousands of Pittmen, Keelmen, Waggonmen and other labouring men, hardy fellows strongly impressed with the new doctrine of equality, and at present composed of such combustible matter that the least spark will set them in a blaze, I cannot help thinking the supineness of the Magistrates very reprehensible.[3]

1. Cited in A. Aspinall, *The Early English Trade Unions* (1949), pp. 4–5.
2. R. I. and S. Wilberforce, *Life of William Wilberforce* (1838), II, p. 2.
3. Powditch to Pitt, 3 November 1792, H.O. 42.22.

From Leeds a prominent man wrote to Wilberforce of 'Paine's mischievous work ... compressed into a sixpenny pamphlet, and sold and given away in profusion. ... You may see them in the houses of our journeymen cloth-dressers. The soldiers are every where tampered with.' 'The state of the country ... seems very critical,' Wilberforce noted in his diary. And he informed his Leeds correspondent, 'I think of proposing to the Archbishop of Canterbury ... the appointment of a day of fasting and humiliation.' But from Leeds there came better news: a loyal mob had paraded the streets,

carrying an image of Tom Paine upon a pole, with a rope round his neck which was held by a man behind, who continually lashed the effigy with a carter's whip. The effigy was at last burned in the market-place, the market-bell tolling slowly. ... A smile sat on every face ... 'God Save the King' resounded in the streets. . .[1]

The streets of Sheffield, however, witnessed scenes of a very different nature. Demonstrations were held at the end of November to celebrate the successes of the French armies at Valmy, and they were reported in the *Sheffield Register* (30 November 1792), a weekly newspaper which supported the reformers. A procession of five or six thousand drew a quartered roasted ox through the streets amid the firing of cannon. In the procession were –

a caricature painting representing Britannia – Burke riding on a swine – and a figure, the upper part of which was the likeness of a Scotch Secretary,[2] and the lower part that of an Ass ... the pole of Liberty lying broken on the ground, inscribed 'Truth is Libel' – the Sun breaking from behind a Cloud, and the Angel of Peace, with one hand dropping the 'Rights of Man', and extending the other to raise up Britannia.

— 'As resolute and determined a set of villains as I ever saw', remarked a hostile observer.

Here is something unusual – pitmen, keelmen, cloth-dressers, cutlers: not only the weavers and labourers of Wapping and Spitalfields, whose colourful and rowdy demonstrations had

1. Wilberforce, op. cit., I I, pp. 1–5.
2. Henry Dundas, Home Secretary.

often come out in support of Wilkes, but working men in villages and towns over the whole country claiming *general* rights for themselves. It was this – and not the French Terror – which threw the propertied classes into panic.

We may see this if we look more closely at the events surrounding the publication of *Rights of Man*. The first popular societies were not formed until more than two years after the storming of the Bastille. There was a general disposition among the middle and upper classes to welcome the first events of the Revolution – even traditionalists argued that France was coming belatedly into line with British notions of the 'mixed constitution'. Dissenters – and notably Dr Price – were some of the first to turn the French example to account by drawing British parallels and by deriving from the Glorious Revolution the right to bring our own 'chief magistrate' to account. The agitation for the repeal of disabilities on Dissenters (the Test and Corporation Acts) reached its climax in the winter of 1789-90; and in the high feelings aroused by this campaign (and the rejection of Repeal) the first provincial Constitutional Societies of the reformers, as well as the first 'Church and King' Clubs of their aristocratic opponents were formed. Burke's *Reflections* (in which Dr Price was taken to task) was the first major sign of a general reaction and preceded the proclamation of the French Republic and the first terror against counter-revolutionaries. Indeed, Burke surprised many tentative reformers (among whom Pitt as well as Burke himself had once been numbered) and even traditionalists by the heat of his arguments. As we have seen, the 'Church and King' riots in Birmingham in the summer of 1791 scarcely belong to the 'French revolutionary' era. Although the pretext for the riots was a dinner to celebrate the anniversary of the fall of the Bastille, the propaganda of Jacobins and of anti-Jacobins had scarcely penetrated the populace. From May 1792 onwards anti-Jacobin demonstrations of the kind described by Wilberforce in Leeds were more highly organized, more often composed of the demoralized and the dependent, and more openly directed towards the intimidation of plebeian reformers.

Nevertheless, the Birmingham riots signify a moment of

transition.[1] The evident complicity and satisfaction of the authorities angered and stiffened the reformers who, in many other parts of the country, had celebrated the fall of the Bastille without molestation. They served also, in a perverse way, as an advertisement of their activities, at a time when the First Part of *Rights of Man* was gaining in popularity. Lancashire magistrates detected a 'general ill-humour', to which the Birmingham events had contributed, and they related this to 'a very general spirit of combination amongst all sorts of labourers and artisans, who are in a state of disaffection to all legal control'.[2] In London in August, perhaps in reply to the events in Birmingham, Horne Tooke, the former lieutenant of Wilkes, presided over a 'Select Meeting of the FRIENDS OF UNIVERSAL PEACE and LIBERTY' at the Thatched House Tavern, issuing an *Address and Declaration*, in the form of a broadsheet, which pointed out in blunt terms the relevance to Britain of the French example.

The pace quickens in the winter of 1791–2, when several of the reform societies – in the provinces and in London – were founded. In February 1792 the Second Part of *Rights of Man*, with its crucial 'social' chapter, was published. In March the Constitutional Society[3] was reorganized, with Horne Tooke, who was to act as the energetic go-between of different sections of reformers, as a leading spirit. In April a number of Whig peers and parliamentarians founded an exclusive 'Society of Friends of the People', one of the aims of which was to *offset* the unconstitutional extremism of Paine, and whose most important positive contribution was the publication of the report of a committee which investigated, with Fabian thoroughness, the state of parliamentary representation, corrup-

1. They have a further significance in inhibiting the later development of the Birmingham Radical movement. If it had not been for the riots, Birmingham – with its numerous small masters and artisans – might have become a leading Jacobin centre alongside Norwich and Sheffield.

2. Aspinall, op. cit., p. 1.

3. That is, the London or national Society for Constitutional Information, which did not have provincial branches. Constitutional Societies (like those at Sheffield, Manchester and Derby) corresponded with London – and often with the L.C.S. as much as with the S.C.I. – but were founded and conducted independently.

tion, and influence. In May 1792 a Royal Proclamation against seditious publications was issued, aimed in particular at Paine. That summer Austro-Prussian armies entered France: the King and Queen were arrested: and the first terror against supporters of the *ancien régime* commenced. The National Convention met in September, and the first year of the Republic was proclaimed. In November John Reeves founded his anti-Jacobin association: in December Paine was outlawed (in his absence) and *Rights of Man* was condemned as seditious libel. In January 1793 Louis was executed, and in February war between England and France commenced.

Events strung together baldly in this way can be misleading. What is remarkable is the very dramatic change which took place in the twelve months between February 1792 and February 1793. At the beginning of this year Pitt confidently expected 'fifteen years' of peace. More than six months later he still hoped to profit from France's turmoil while preserving British neutrality. The Proclamation of May 1792 signified the first serious alarm on the part of the Government as to the extent of the Painite propaganda; but this was still regarded as a purely domestic issue. Three factors altered the situation. First, the rapid radicalization of the French Revolution after the September massacres. Second, the direct threat to British interests and to the diplomatic balance in Europe presented by the expansionist fervour of the new Republic. Third, dangerous signs of confluence between the revolutionary exhilaration in France and the growing Jacobin movement at home. In November 1792 the Convention had issued its famous decree of 'fraternity and assistance' to all peoples; later in the same month, fraternal delegations attended upon the Convention from London and Scotland, and a deputy (Grégoire) saluted the new republic soon to arise on the banks of the Thames. Paine, in his French exile, was elected deputy for the Pas-de-Calais. By December the expansionist policy of the vacillating Girondins was confirmed in Savoy, the Rhineland, Nice and Belgium, and the slogan was sounded, 'War upon *châteaux*; peace to cottages'. The actual occasions for war (the execution of Louis and the control of the Scheldt) came at the conclusion of twelve months which had transformed Pitt from the Prime

Minister of economic retrenchment, peace, and piecemeal reform into the diplomatic architect of European counter-revolution.[1] And this transformation was not of one man but of a class; of the patricians as well as of the commercial and manufacturing *bourgeoisie* who had seen in Pitt their hope for economic rationalization and cautious political reform.

It is the third of these factors – the depth and intensity of the democratic agitation in England – which is commonly underestimated. The panic, and the counter-revolutionary offensive, of the propertied in Britain commenced some months before the arrest of the King and the September massacres in France; and when the latter did take place, every organ of authority here used every means to publicize the sufferings of the victims of the guillotine, and of French *émigrés*, not only from a sense of shock and compassion but also – and, perhaps, mainly – as a means of counteracting English Jacobin propaganda.

For the success of the Second Part of *Rights of Man* was, in a true sense, phenomenal. The estimate (in a pamphlet of 1793) that sales totalled 200,000 by that year has been widely accepted: this in a population of ten millions.[2] The Second Part went immediately into a 6*d*. edition, sponsored by the Constitutional Society and by local societies. Hannah More complained that 'the friends of insurrection, infidelity and vice, carried their exertions so far as to load asses with their pernicious pamphlets and to get them dropped, not only in cottages, and in highways, but into mines and coal-pits'.[3] In Sheffield it was said that 'every cutler' had a copy. At Newcastle (Staffs.) Paine's publications were said to be 'in almost every

1. See G. Lefebvre, *The French Revolution* (1962), pp. 274–83.

2. Burke's *Reflections* was sold at 3*s*. and 30,000 copies went in the first two years. Part One of *Rights of Man* was also priced at 3*s*., and sold 50,000 copies in 1791. By 1802 Paine claimed a circulation for both parts of four or five hundred thousand – and 1,500,000 was claimed by 1809 – but this included the enormous Irish sales as well as European translations. I am inclined to accept the claim of 200,000 sales in England, Wales and Scotland (taking account of both parts, and of abridged editions issued by local clubs) in 1791 to 1793, even though R. D. Altick warns us that 'no single piece of nonce literature . . . had ever approached such a circulation'. See *The English Common Reader* (1957), pp. 69–73.

3. W. Roberts, *Memoirs of . . . Mrs Hannah More* (1834), II, pp. 424–5.

hand', and in particular in those of the journeymen potters: 'more than Two Thirds of this populous Neighbourhood are ripe for a Revolt, especially the lower class of Inhabitants'.[1] Paine's book was found in Cornish tin-mines, in Mendip villages, in the Scottish Highlands, and, a little later, in most parts of Ireland. 'The Northern parts of Wales', a correspondent complained,

are infested by itinerant Methodist preachers who descant on the Rights of Man and attack Kingly Government.[2]

'The book', wrote an English correspondent, 'is now made as much a Standard book in this Country as Robinson Crusoe & the Pilgrim's Progress.'[3]

At Paine's trial *in absentia* the Attorney-General complained that *Rights of Man* was 'thrust into the hands of subjects of every description, even children's sweetmeats being wrapped in it'. Dundas explained that the Royal Proclamation of May 1792 was justified 'when great bodies of men in large manufacturing towns adopted and circulated doctrines so pernicious in their tendency'. It was clearly stated that the cheapness of the abridged editions was an aggravation of the offence. The Proclamation was endorsed by carefully sponsored meetings throughout the country. Local magistrates and clergy promoted loyal addresses condemning Paine, and societies of gentry were formed 'to preserve inviolable the GLORIOUS CONSTITU-TION of OLD ENGLAND'. Twenty-two thousand copies of a scurrilous pamphlet attacking Paine were printed and subsidized through the Secret Service fund.[4] Paine replied to the mounting attack with a stinging *Letter Addressed to the Addressers*, in which he also took issue with the aristocratic Friends of the People, and poured ridicule upon the use of petitions as a means of reform:

1. J. Massey, 22 November 1792, H.O. 42.22; F. Knight, *The Strange Case of Thomas Walker* (1957), p. 117.

2. 'Memorandum on Clubs', October 1792, in H.O. 42.22. For Jacobinism in Wales, see D. Davies, *The Influence of the French Revolution on Welsh Life and Literature* (Carmarthen, 1926) and M. P. Jones, 'John Jones of Glan-y-Gors', *Trans. Cymmrodorian Society* (1909–10).

3. Benjamin Vaughan, 30 November 1792, H.O. 42.22.

4. In the winter of 1792–3: see A. Aspinall, *Politics and the Press* (1949), pp. 152–3.

I consider the reform of Parliament, by an application to Parliament ... to be a worn-out, hackneyed subject, about which the nation is tired. ... The right, and the exercise of that right, appertains to the nation only, and the proper means is by a national convention, elected for the purpose by all the people.[1]

This, with a king across the Channel under arrest as the consequence of a National Convention, was revolutionary talk. But before the *Letter* was published, Paine had crossed the Channel himself, to avoid arrest. His parting shot was a letter, addressed to the Attorney-General, from 'Paris, 11th of November, 1st year of the Republic', to be read at his trial. A verdict against him (he said) would mean as much as a verdict against 'the Man in the Moon': it would signify in reality a verdict against the rights of the people of England:

The time, Sir, is becoming too serious to play with Court prosecutions. ... The terrible examples that have taken place here, upon men who less than a year ago thought themselves as secure as any prosecuting Judge, Jury, or Attorney General can now do in England, ought to have some weight with men in your situation. That the government of England is as great, if not the greatest, perfection of fraud and corruption that ever took place since governments began, is what you cannot be a stranger to. ... Is it possible that you, or I can believe ... that the capacity of such a man as Mr Guelph, or any of his profligate sons, is necessary to the government of a nation ... ? [2]

But even before Paine had adopted so truculent a tone, his writings had served as a touchstone to distinguish different emphases among reformers. The aristocratic Friends of the People was at pains to affirm its allegiance to the settlement of 1688, to dissociate itself from any notion of National Convention, and from Paine's 'indefinite language of delusion, which ... tends to excite a spirit of innovation, of which no wisdom can forsee the effect, and no skill direct the course' (May 1792).[3] Christopher Wyvill, the Yorkshire gentleman

1. Paine, loc. cit., p. 56. Eaton, who published the *Letter*, was prosecuted but acquitted (on this occasion) by a friendly jury.

2. All duly published in Joseph Gurney's *Proceedings on the Trial ... against Thomas Paine* (1793).

3. Wyvill, *Political Papers*, III, Appendix, pp. 154–5.

reformer, published *A Defence of Dr Price* (1791) against Burke, in which he took occasion to deplore the 'mischievous effects' of Paine's work, in tending to 'excite the lowest classes of the People to acts of violence and injustice'.[1] After the publication of Part Two of *Rights of Man* Wyvill's tone hardened. In his nation-wide correspondence with moderate reformers he exerted his considerable influence to urge them to mount a counter-agitation to minimize the effect of 'Mr Paine's illtimed, and ... pernicious counsels'. In April 1792 he was urging the London Constitutional Society to dissociate itself from the 'popular party':

As Mr Paine ... backs his proposal by holding out to the Poor annuities to be had out of the superfluous wealth of the Rich, I thought the extremely dangerous tendency of his licentious doctrines required opposition ...

There can be no doubt that it was the sharper spirit of class antagonism precipitated by Paine's linking of political with economic demands which gave Wyvill greatest alarm: 'it is unfortunate for the public cause,' he wrote to a Sheffield gentleman in May 1792, 'that Mr Paine took such unconstitutional ground, and has formed a party for the Republic among the lower classes of the people, by holding out to them the prospect of plundering the rich'.[2]

Wyvill's supporters in the Constitutional Society in London (of which Paine was himself a member) were outnumbered by Painites. The Society had officially welcomed Part One of *Rights of Man*, while at the same time passing a general resolution affirming support for the mixed constitution (March and May 1791). Throughout the rest of the year the moderates lost ground to the inflexible Major Cartwright, to the opportunist but adventurous Horne Tooke, to the Jacobin attorney John Frost, and to Paine's immediate circle. 'Hey for the New Jerusalem! The millennium! And peace and eternal beatitude be unto the soul of Thomas Paine,' Thomas Holcroft, the dramatist, wrote ecstatically to Godwin. In the reorganization of the Society in the early spring of 1792 the adherents of Paine

1. Ibid., III, Appendix, pp. 67–8. It is to Wyvill's credit that he opposed any prosecution of Paine.
2. Ibid., V, pp. 1, 23–4, 51.

gained unquestioned control. Part Two of *Rights of Man* was officially welcomed – and in particular the 'social' proposals – and the Society initiated a very much more vigorous agitational policy. Tooke and Frost assisted Hardy in promoting the Corresponding Society; correspondence was opened with provincial societies and (in May 1792) with the Jacobin Club in Paris; handbills, pamphlets and a cheap edition of Paine were published; the Society opened a public subscription for Paine's defence, while in November and December 1792 John Frost went as a delegate of the Society to Paris, where he attended the trial of the King. The Painite sympathies of the L.C.S. and of provincial societies in Manchester, Norwich, Sheffield, were equally pronounced. Thomas Cooper, a young Bolton merchant and Unitarian, and a very able propagandist, was overcome with enthusiasm on the appearance of Part Two: 'it has made me more politically mad than I ever was. It is choque full, crowded with good sense ... heightened also with a profusion of libellous matter. I regard it as the very jewel of a book ... Burke is done up for ever and ever by it.' [1]

1792, then, was the *annus mirabilis* of Tom Paine. In twelve months his name became a household word. There were few places in the British Isles where his book had not penetrated. It served as a touchstone, dividing the gentlemen reformers and patrician Whigs from a minority of radical manufacturers and professional men who sought an alliance with the labourers and artisans, welcomed Paine's social and economic proposals, and looked in the direction of a Republic. Pitt's long-delayed decision to prosecute Paine signalled the opening of the era of repression. The outlawry of Paine (and the banning of *Rights of Man*) was preceded and accompanied by a sustained effort by authority to meet the reformers in the field. 'As we have now got the stone to roll,' Paine wrote to Walker in the summer of 1792, 'it must be kept going by cheap publications. This will embarrass the Court gentry more than anything else, because it is a ground they are not used to.' [2] But the 'Court gentry' mounted their own publications offensive; and stimulated their own 'Clockwork Regularity' in the movements of their sup-

1. Cited in Knight, op. cit., pp. 63–4.
2. Blanchard Jerrold, *The Original* (1874), p. 41.

porters. Reeves' Association for the Protection of Property against Republicans and Levellers only consolidated and strengthened numerous societies of magistrates and gentry already formed in reply to the popular societies. In the winter of 1792–3 these sought to revive and inflame the technique of mob violence, so effective in Birmingham the previous year. In December 1792, a drunken mob was deliberately directed against the premises of Thomas Walker in Manchester: he and his supporters defended themselves successfully by firing into the air. 'The same contrivances were used as at a contested election,' wrote Walker: 'Parties were collected in different public houses, and from thence paraded the streets with a fiddler before them, and carrying a board, on which was painted CHURCH and KING.'[1]

'Guy Fawkes'-type demonstrations against Tom Paine, on the same lines as that reported to Wilberforce from Leeds, were promoted throughout the country. In the small Pennine weaving township of Ripponden a prosperous lawyer noted in his diary for 7 January 1793 that he paid certain people 'who carried about Tom Payne's Effigy and shot at it, 10s. 6d.'[2] A Heckmondwike mill-owner himself impersonated Paine and had himself 'discovered' reading *Rights of Man* among the coal-pits; his mask was transferred to a straw effigy which was dragged around the village and 'executed'. At near-by Littletown a wooden image of Paine was pounded to bits with a sledge-hammer with such vigour that the executioner's hands ran with blood.[3] In December 1792:

The effigy of Thomas Paine was, with great solemnity, drawn on a sledge from Lincoln Castle to the gallows, and then hanged, amidst a vast multitude of spectators. After being suspended the usual time it was taken to the Castle-hill and there hung on a gibbet post erected for the purpose. In the evening a large fire was made under the effigy, which ... was consumed to ashes, amidst the acclama-

1. Walker, op. cit., p. 55. See also the excellent account in Knight, op. cit., and A. Prentice, *Historical Sketches of Manchester* (1851), pp. 419 ff.

2. J. H. Priestley, 'John Howarth, Lawyer', *Trans. Halifax Antiq. Soc.*, 1949.

3. Frank Peel, *Spen Valley: Past and Present* (Heckmondwike, 1893), pp. 307–8.

tions of many hundreds of people, accompanied with a grand band of music playing 'God Save the King ' . . .

Even at small market-towns like Brigg and Caistor branches of Reeves' Association were formed, among whose purposes (to quote the Caistor Society) was the exertion of 'Vigilance and Activity in discovering and bringing to Justice all Persons who shall, either by publishing or distributing seditious Papers or Writings, or by engaging in any illegal Associations or Conspiracies, endeavour to disturb the public Peace . . .'[1]

If the distribution of *Rights of Man* was nation wide, so also was the promotion of anti-Jacobin societies. Hence in England the revolutionary impulse had scarcely begun to gather force before it was exposed to a counter-revolutionary assault backed by the resources of established authority. 'Thenceforth,' Georges Lefebvre has noted,

whenever the people happened to stir, their leaders throughout Europe agreed that they must be brought to their senses, as tradition dictated. The very success of the French Revolution provoked outside its borders a development exactly contrary to the series of events which had secured its victory in France.[2]

But these carefully fostered demonstrations of loyalty, however popular the momentary bribery and license may have made them, have an increasingly artificial air. Each bonfire of the effigy of Paine served to light up, in an unintended way, the difference between the Constitution of the gentry and the rights of the people. 'Church and King' actions signify less the blind *pogrom* of prejudice against an out-group and more a skirmish in a political civil war. Thomas Walker dismissed the mob which attacked him as 'wretched tools of a most unprincipled faction'. 'All . . . will continue quiet if the people are left to themselves; or rather the Mob, as the people, in my opinion, are with us.'[3]

How far was Walker right? Of all questions, it is the most difficult to answer. And we must address ourselves once again to a brief narrative of the events of the next two years.

1. *Stamford Mercury*, 8 December 1792, 11 January 1793. I am indebted to Mr Rex Russell for this reference.

2. Lefebvre, op. cit., p. 187.   3. Knight, op. cit., pp. 101, 105.

After each great shift in popular mood, a hardening and contraction commonly takes place. And this was reinforced in the first months of 1793 by three causes: the execution of the French King, the opening of war, and the commencement of legal persecution of the reformers. Among the latter were a Dissenting minister, the Rev. William Winterbotham, imprisoned for four years for a sermon which scarcely went further than the views as to the Sovereign's accountability already popularized by Dr Price: and John Frost, the attorney, sentenced to the pillory and to eighteen months imprisonment, in reality for serving as an English delegate to the French Convention, but on the pretext of his saying in a Marylebone coffee-house: 'I am for equality.... Why, no kings!' A printer named Holt, at Newark, was jailed for four years for reprinting an early address of the Constitutional Society. At Leicester, the bookseller, Richard Phillips, who published the pro-reform *Leicester Herald*, was imprisoned for eighteen months, ostensibly for selling *Rights of Man*. And many humble men were harassed in a score of ways. The authorities exerted themselves, with great success, to post spies in the popular societies. Already, in the autumn of 1792, 186 Manchester publicans had signed a declaration refusing the use of their rooms to 'any CLUB or societies ... that have a tendency to put in force what those INFERNALS so *ardently* and *devoutly wish for*, namely, the DESTRUCTION OF THIS COUNTRY'. Those who failed to sign were visited and warned that their licences would not be renewed. Gilt signs were placed over the bars. 'NO JACOBINS ADMITTED HERE'. 'The Enymies to Reform in this Town,' wrote the Secretary of the Manchester Reformation Society to the L.C.S., 'are exerting all their powers to depress the noble spirit of Liberty...'[1]

The same quasi-legal forms of intimidation were employed

1. T.S. 11.3510 A (3); A. Prentice, *Historical Sketches of Manchester* (1851), pp. 7–8. For similar action against Leicester inn-keepers, see A. Temple Patterson, *Radical Leicester* (Leicester, 1954), p. 71. For provincial prosecutions, see R. Phillips, *Original Papers Published in the Leicester Herald &c.* (Leicester Gaol, 1793); *Account of the Trial of Alexander Whyte, Baker* (Newcastle, 1793); Daniel Holt, *Vindication of the Conduct and Principles of the Printer of the Newark Herald* (Newark, 1794).

in London, where divisions of the L.C.S. were harried from tavern to tavern. 'An official heresy hunt was soon on foot in almost every town from Portsmouth to Newcastle and from Swansea to Chelmsford.'[1] In Ipswich the magistrates dispersed a 'Disputing Club' in an ale-house, 'consisting of very Inferior People': in Wiltshire a schoolmaster was sacked for 'traitorous expressions': in Northamptonshire villages a house-to-house loyalty canvass took place. Agents were appointed in various districts to visit bookshops and prosecute any found selling *Rights of Man*: at least one illiterate bill-sticker was imprisoned for posting bills in favour of reform.

Nor did external events make the work of the English Jacobins more easy. There can be little doubt that the French war, unpopular at its outset, reactivated the long tradition of anti-Gallican sentiment among the people. Each fresh execution, reported with copious detail – the September massacres – the King – Marie Antoinette – added to these feelings. In September 1793, also, Paine's friends the Girondins were expelled from the Convention, and their leaders sent to the guillotine, while in the last week of 1793 Paine himself was imprisoned in the Luxembourg. These experiences provoked the first phase of that profound disenchantment, in an intellectual generation which had identified its beliefs in too ardent and utopian a way with the cause of France. The unity between intellectual and plebeian reformers of 1792 was never to be regained.

In 1794 the war fever became more intense. Volunteer corps were formed: public subscriptions raised: traditional fairs were made the occasion for military demonstrations. The Government increased its subsidies to, and influence over, the newspaper press: popular anti-Jacobin sheets multiplied. In Exeter a handbill was circulated:

... as for them that do not like ... the present CONSTITUTION, let them have their deserts, that is a HALTER and a GIBBET, and be burnt afterwards, not as PAINE hath been, in effigy, but in body and person. To which every loyal heart will say Amen.

In Birmingham a scurrilous anti-Jacobin pamphleteer, 'Job Nott', addressed reformers:

1. P. A. Brown, op. cit., p. 85.

Do be off – only think of the New Drop – you may be recorded in the Newgate Calendar – transportation may reform you – you deserve to be highly exalted – Did you ever see the New Drop?

In London parishes, where the influence of Reeves' Association was strongest, house-to-house inquiries were made: in St Anne's a register was kept with the 'complexion, age, employment, &c. of lodgers and strangers': in St James' inhabitants were called upon to denounce for 'incivism' all housekeepers who would not oblige their servants, workmen and apprentices to sign a declaration of loyalty to the Constitution, no tradesman was to be employed who had not been cleared by Reeves' agents, and publicans were refused licences who failed to report 'suspected persons'. Collections of flannel waistcoats for the troops were pressed forward by members of Reeves' Committee, as an auxiliary means of testing loyalty; and from waistcoats collections went on to 'mitts, drawers, caps, shirts, Welch-wigs, stockings, shoes, trowsers, boots, sheets, greatcoats, gowns, petticoats, blankets ...'[1]

The existence of a heresy-hunt of these proportions, in time of war, does not *prove* the widespread existence of heresy. 'Loyalism' at such times always supposes the existence of 'treason', if only as a foil to itself. And yet something more than 'war fever', or the guilt and uneasiness of the propertied classes, is indicated by the outpourings of tracts and sermons, and the attacks on specific Jacobins in outlying parts. It was in April 1794 that a gang of roughs, armed with cudgels, terrified young Samuel Bamford, as they passed through Middleton – with curses and broken windows for the 'Painites' – on their way to Royton. Here they smashed up the 'Light Horseman' public house, where reformers were meeting, and beat up those in attendance. Meanwhile the magistrates refused to stir from his home, a few score yards from the scene of the riot, and the parson stood on a hillock pointing out fugitives to the ruffians: 'There goes one. ... That's a Jacobin; that's

1. Several of the examples in this paragraph are taken from an anonymous pamphlet, *Peace and Reform; against War and Corruption* (1794). For anti-Jacobin publications (including Job Nott) see also R. K. Webb, *The British Working Class Reader* (1955), pp 41–51; M. J. Jones, *Hannah More* (Cambridge, 1952), ch. 6.

another!'[1] It is as if the authorities sensed some sea-change in the opinion of the masses, some subterranean alteration in mood – not such as to make the English nation Painite and Jacobin, but yet such as disposed it to harbour and tolerate the seditious. Some slight event might be enough to set all that 'combustible matter' aflame. Reformers must be watched and intimidated, the societies isolated and ringed round with suspicion, the prejudices of the ignorant whipped up and given licence. In particular, professional men with access to printing-press, bookshop, pulpit or rostrum, who associated with plebeian reformers, were the subject of intimidation.

A confirmation of this sea-change in the attitudes of the inarticulate – or in the structure of feeling of the poor – may be found in an unexpected place. 1793 and 1794 saw a sudden emergence of millennarial fantasies, on a scale unknown since the seventeenth century. Where Holcroft's 'New Jerusalem' was a rational conceit, and Blake's 'Jerusalem' was a visionary image (although owing more to the millennarial background than critics have noted), the poor and the credulous found a more literal prophet in Richard Brothers, a retired naval captain on half pay. His *Revealed Knowledge of the Prophecies and Times* was published early in 1794. His prophecies combined a great knowingness as to the intentions of the Almighty, with the usual paraphernalia from the Book of Revelation, in a language which combined the 'combustible matter' of poor men's dissent with that of a revolutionary era:

All nations have drunk of the wine of the wrath of Babylon's fornication, and the kings of the earth have committed fornication with her, and the merchants of the earth are waxed rich through the abundance of her delicacies ...

Among his visions was that of 'a large River run(ning) through London coloured with human blood'. A prediction that London was to be destroyed on a certain date coincided fortuitously with a thunderstorm of exceptional severity; John Binns, on his way to a meeting of the L.C.S., took shelter in an ale-house where he found the people (to his amusement and surprise)

1. Bamford, *Early Days* (1893 edn), pp. 55–6.

awaiting the consummation of all things.[1] Shortly afterwards Brothers announced that London had been spared only as the result of his personal last minute intervention; and since he obviously wielded such influence with the Almighty his following was doubled at a stroke.

There was published -- whether with or without his authority is unclear -- an 8-page leaflet of *Brother's Prophecy of all the Remarkable and Wonderful Events which will come to pass ... foretelling the Downfall of the Pope; a Revolution in Spain, Portugal, and Germany; the Death of Certain Great Persons in this and other Countries. Also a dreadful Famine, Pestilence, and Earthquake. ...* In England there was to be 'sorrow and great woe, mingled with joy unspeakable'; 'the proud and lofty shall be humbled, even to the dust; but the righteous and poor shall flourish on the ruins of the wicked; the Palaces shall be — — and Cottages shall be —.' As for the Famine, Pestilence, and Earthquake, these were to be seen as metaphorical:

The Famine shall destroy none but the Caterpillars of *Spain* and —. The Pestilence shall sweep away the Locusts that eat up the harvest of Industry; and the Earthquake shall swallow up the monstrous *Leviathan*, with all his train. In all these things the poor, the honest, the virtuous, and the patriotic, shall rejoice.

'*France* must bleed afresh, but none but contaminated blood shall flow.' '*Italy* shall hurl the Antechrist from his throne...' Turkey and Russia will be plunged in war, ending in the destruction of the Ottoman Porte, the Mahometan Faith, the Russian Empire and the Greek Church. At the end of these signs of mercy, there will be an era of universal brotherhood. 'All shall be as one people, and of one mind. ... The *Christian*, the *Turk*, and the *Pagan* shall no longer be distinguished the one from the other':

The time is come, and now is the whore of Babylon falling, and will fall to rise no more. Go forth, then, ye Sons of Eternal Light, and instruct the Sons of Ignorance and Darkness. ...

Then shall there be no more war, no more want, no more wickedness; but all shall be peace, plenty, and virtue.

1. Binns, op. cit., pp. 47–8.

The influence of Brothers may have been much greater than has been supposed.[1] Some of his vague predictions could not fail to appear to be fulfilled, and they were recalled to mind when the French armies were victorious. Members of the L.C.S. used to visit him: they perhaps even prompted him. An M.P. was found (as there usually is) ready to testify as to the authenticity of Brothers's prophetic powers; William Sharp, the famous engraver and political reformer, became a disciple. The Privy Council regarded him seriously enough to arrest him in March 1795, and to ensure his confinement for the next few years in a lunatic asylum. His followers, like George Turner of Leeds, continued until the turn of the century to agitate for his release (threatening destruction upon the English Babylon if the Prophet remained confined), and they thereby prepared the way for the even greater cult of Joanna Southcott.[2] Rival prophetic schools grew up, and there was much thumbing through the Book of Revelation; while Methodist and Baptist Ministers tried to drive out this new heresy. In 1798 a 'True Baptist' preacher was wrestling with his flock among the poor of Norwich, Wisbech and Liverpool, dealing out blow for blow from Revelation, and recalling them from too literal an encounter with Apollyon and back to the pilgrimage of the spirit:

The gospel of Christ has no tendency to fraternize mankind in a state of worldly or political intercourse. It calls individuals out of the world, and considers them only as strangers and pilgrims on the earth. As well ... might a traveller, who is hastening to his wife and family at a distance, and where all his felicity centres, interfere with the internal regulations of every town and village through which he passeth; as that a christian should intermeddle with the constitution ...

As for the Millennium, that was put firmly forward into the next world, when –

The high and the low, the oppressor and the oppressed, shall be reduced to one perfect level. The pampered tyrant, and his

1. See Cecil Roth, *The Nephew of the Almighty* (1933); G. R. Balleine, *Past Finding Out* (1956), ch. 4; R. Southey, *Letters from England by Don Manual Alvarez* (1808, 2nd edn) I I I, pp. 223 f.

2. G. Turner, *A Call to All the World* (Leeds, 1800). For Joanna Southcott, see below pp. 420–26.

indigent vassal; the wealthy peer, and the neglected pauper, shall receive an equitable and impartial sentence . . .[1]

The millennarial spirit which visited Wisbech and Liverpool indicated a restiveness, which authority decried as 'the spirit of innovation', an indefinite social optimism of the credulous which was kin to the revolutionary aspirations of the more sophisticated. 'It's comin' yet, for a' that,' Burns had written, 'when man to man, the warld o'er,/Shall brithers be for a' that.' 'Nor Can Man Exist But By Brotherhood,' echoed Blake; and the same spirit underlies his own 'prophetic books' and his own beautiful vision of Jerusalem:

> In my Exchanges every Land
> Shall walk, & mine in every Land,
> Mutual shall build Jerusalem,
> Both heart in heart & hand in hand.

The spirit, whether in its visionary or in its superstitious form, is a curious paradox of the advent of 'The Age of Reason'. But, in its modification of attitudes and nourishment of new aspirations, it was perhaps as long-lasting in its influence as the arguments of Tom Paine.

Perhaps it is a testimony to the quality of elation aroused in 1792 that the popular societies survived the shocks and the witch-hunting of the first months of 1793. Where the societies were well established in 1792, they held most of their ground and even improved their organization: this was true of London, Sheffield and Norwich, and perhaps of Derby and Nottingham. Most societies suffered some loss in membership, and the withdrawal of many of their influential middle-class supporters. Manchester (with Thomas Walker awaiting trial for high treason for defending his premises against the mob) was much weakened, while the Leicester Constitutional Society was disbanded when Phillips was imprisoned. But in both centres more plebeian societies continued after the respectable parent-bodies had failed. (In Manchester the field was shared

1. S. Fisher, *Unity and Equality in the Kingdom of God* (Norwich, 1798); *The Christian's Monitor* (Wisbech, 1798).

by Walker's Constitutional Society, and the Reformation and Patriotic Societies which were alleged to be made up of 'mechanicks of the lowest class'.)[1]

Sheffield, the strongest society, which had recorded close on 2,000 members in 1792, seems to have been little affected. In April it passed a series of outspoken resolutions condemning the war. In May it reported nearly 10,000 signatures collected for a national petition for manhood suffrage. Norwich, an ancient stronghold of Dissent, with an abundance of small masters and of artisans with strong traditions of independence, may even have surpassed Sheffield as the leading provincial centre of Jacobinism, although the records of the movement are imperfect. In August 1792, when the Norwich Revolution Society sponsored a cheap edition of *Rights of Man*, it claimed to have forty-eight associated clubs. By October it claimed that the 'associated brethren' were not fewer than 2,000.[2] In March 1793 it remained at the centre of a constellation of small clubs, with 'between 30 and 40 separate Societies' in the city, 'besides many in the country villages'.[3] But the tone of a letter sent to the L.C.S. in June suggests that they had encountered difficulties:

... when we consider how many sweat and toil and starve to support it, how can we be persuaded but that there is a contrivance between the land owners and the merchant to hold the people in vassalage; for they eat up the people as they eat bread; – the influence of the aristocracy and hierarchy is becoming very alarming, for they have absorbed and swallowed up the people; but a rumour is spread from the south, and it is terrible to tyrants ...[4]

The position in London is more difficult to establish. The Constitutional Society appears to have fallen away seriously after the commencement of war; until the autumn of 1793 its activities went little further than the passing of formal motions.

1. Memorandum in T.S. 11.3035. Walker's co-defendants included artisans from these societies – William Paul, a paper-stainer, James Cheetham, a hatter, Oliver Pearsall, a weaver; see J. Gurney, *The Whole Proceedings on the Trial ... of T. Walker and Others* (1794), Appendix, pp. 122–6.   2. T.S. 11.3510 A (3).

3. *Report of the Committee of Secrecy* (1794), p. 140.

4. Ibid., p. 150. For 'the South' read 'France'.

The L.C.S. also encountered great difficulties. In the last months of 1792 it had claimed a membership of some thousands. In January 1793 (according to a spy at Hardy's trial) measures were taken to subsidize the rent for the meeting-rooms of the divisions in Spitalfields and Moorfields, which, although poor, were 'as many in number as the other divisions put together'. But it proved necessary to re-form the Moorfields division in September, together with another which 'appeared very violent ... at the Grove in Bandy-legged-walk'. The L.C.S. succeeded in collecting only 6,000 signatures to the national petition, despite the energy of the committee – Joseph Gerrald collecting 200 signatures and marks from inmates of the King's Bench (debtor's) prison.[1] On 30 May 1793 (according to the spy) 'Mr Hardy proposed to the society to break up for three months. The proposition negatived.' 'We have made a stand against the place and pension clubs,' Hardy wrote, more confidently, to a new Constitutional Society in Leeds in July:

We have been abused in the senate, calumniated in public, persecuted in private, and worried out of public houses, yet we continue meeting numerously entire ... and our doctrine makes numerous proselytes ...[2]

The confidence was not misplaced, for the summer saw a definite revival of provincial correspondence – old societies re-awakening or new societies formed – for which the L.C.S., rather than the Constitutional Society, served as a centre. A Birmingham society, formed in the last months of 1792, cautiously extended its activities in the early summer, and received an especial welcome: 'the increase of your numbers will soon do away the stigma thrown on your town by the unjustifiable behaviour of a Church and King mob'. From Leeds a new society of 'a company of poor Mechanics' asked to be admitted to 'fraternization' with the London Constitutional Society:

1. An informer's report (in T.S. 11.3510 A (3)) lists twenty-nine divisions in April 1793, of which at least sixteen were actively engaged in collecting signatures.

2. *Report from the Committee of Secrecy* (1794), pp. 152, 154; A Student in the Temple, *Trial of Thomas Hardy* (1794), pp. 142, 144; F. Knight, op. cit., p. 134.

Aristocratic Tirany and Democratic Ignorance, seem to pervade and overawe the Town of Leeds to that Amazing Degree that in the General we are beheld more like Monsters than the friends of the People, and I believe that this six months past the Ignorant part of the People (through the Insinuations of the Aristocracy and the priests) have expected us to fall upon them and destroy them. ... Our numbers amount to near two hundred and we constantly keep increasing ...

In July new societies were writing to the L.C.S. from Hertfordshire and Tewksbury. 'Your fellow citizen, and Co-operator in the glorious cause of liberty', as the Tewksbury secretary signed himself, described how –

The burning of Thomas Paine's Effigy, together with the *blessed effects* of the present war, has done more good to the cause than the most substantial arguments; 'tis amazing the increase of friends to liberty, and the spirit of enquiry that is gone abroad; scarcely an old woman but is talking politics.

In August the L.C.S. was renewing correspondence with societies in Derby, Stockport, Manchester, Nottingham and Coventry – asking them to 'point out a safer mode of conveyance for our letters than the post' – and had some plans (shelved for the time being) of asking them to adopt its title and to form a 'Universal Society'. The Society's minute-books show well-attended and well-conducted meetings, the formation of new divisions, and an influx of new members into the old.[1]

The popular societies had weathered their first storm. But they emerged from it with significant changes in emphasis and tone. Paine's name dropped into the background, and his outspoken republican tone gave way to renewed emphasis upon restoring the 'purity' of the Constitution. (In June 1793, the L.C.S. went so far as to define this in terms of the 1688 settlement.) But while this modification was made necessary by the evident intention of the authorities to prosecute any rhetoric which went beyond these limits, in other respects persecution led to a radicalization of the societies. In the first place, the pace was now being set, not in London, but in Scotland,

---

1. *Report from the Committee of Secrecy* (1794), pp. 148–57; Minutes of L.C.S., Add. MSS. 27812.

Sheffield, Norwich. In the second place, while a few ardent members of the professions were taking a leading part alongside artisans like Hardy and Baxter in London – Joseph Gerrald, Maurice Margarot, John Thelwall – the great majority of the reformers organized in the societies of 1793 were artisans, wage-earners, small masters and small tradesmen. And two new themes are emphasized with great insistence – economic grievances and social remedies, and the imitation of French example, forms of organization and of address.

Thomas Hardy, if we may judge from his minute books, was an able and conscientious organizer, an honourable prototype for those scores of voluntary secretaries who were to follow him. According to Binns he 'dressed plainly, talked frankly, never at any time assuming airs or making pretentions'. Maurice Margarot, a Chairman of the L.C.S., was the son of a wine merchant. He had spent much of his childhood in Portugal and Switzerland (where he had been educated at the University of Geneva) and was sometimes referred to as a 'Frenchman'. He was energetic and audacious, but badly bitten by the characteristic vice of the English Jacobins – self-dramatization.[1] Joseph Gerrald and John Thelwall were closer than any others to having the metal of national leaders and theorists. It was Gerrald, a brilliant pupil of Dr Samuel Parr, the 'Whig Johnson' and doyen of West Country learning, who advocated most forcefully the dangerous proposal of Paine – the calling of a National Convention of British reformers.[2] It was this threat, of a general combination of reformers, and – an even more serious, and growing, threat – of an alliance between English and Scottish reformers and the United Irishmen, that determined the Government to act.

The dilemma of the authorities arose out of the paradox of constitutionalism. While there was law enough for summary convictions by local magistrates, the Law Officers of the Crown

1. Entries in *D.N.B.*; Binns, op. cit., p. 42; M Roe, 'Maurice Margarot: A Radical in Two Hemispheres', *Bulletin of the Institute of Historical Research*, XXXI (1958), p. 68.

2. See Joseph Gerrald, *A Convention the only Means of Saving Us from Ruin* (1793), pp. 111ff., and Henry Collins, 'The London Corresponding Society', in *Democracy and the Labour Movement*, ed. Saville (1954), pp. 117–18. For Thelwall, see below pp. 172–6.

were reluctant to advise major prosecutions. The law of sedition was indefinite, and the Attorney-General was faced with the choice of the appalling indictment of high treason or the lesser charge of seditious libel. But Fox's Libel Act had reached the statute book in the temperate early months of 1792, making the jury the judge of the matter as well as of the fact. It was, perhaps, Fox's greatest service to the common people, passed at the eleventh hour before the tide turned towards repression.[1] Thus, in England, the Government was faced with a series of obstacles: an indefinite law, the jury system (which humiliated authority by twice acquitting Daniel Eaton and by acquitting Thomas Walker in 1794), a small but brilliant Foxite opposition among whose number was the great advocate Thomas Erskine (who led the defence in several trials), a public opinion saturated with constitutionalist rhetoric and willing to spring to the defence of any invasion of individual liberties.

But Scottish law was different. Here the judges were docile or partisan, the juries could be picked with impunity. Here also the Scottish 'Friends of the People' had held a National Convention in December 1792. The Scottish trials of 1793–4 were aimed not only at the very vigorous Scottish Jacobin societies, but also at the societies in England. The first blow was struck in August 1793, when Thomas Muir, the most gifted Scottish leader, was sentenced to fourteen years transportation after a scandalous mock trial. Braxfield, the Lord Justice-Clerk, was more virulent in his conduct than the prosecution: 'Come awa', Maaster Horner, come awa', and help us to hang ane o' thae damned scoondrels,' he whispered to a juror who passed behind the bench. In his charge to the jury he treated Muir's ability and his propaganda among 'ignorant country people, and among the lower classes, making them leave off their work', as an aggravation:

Mr Muir might have known that no attention could be paid to such a rabble. What right had they to representation? ... A Gov-

1. It passed its third reading in the Lords on 21 May 1792, the same day as the proclamation was issued against seditious writings. The Lord Chancellor, Lord Thurlow, predicted 'the confusion and destruction of the law of England'.

ernment ... should be just like a corporation; and, in this country, it is made up of the landed interest, which alone has a right to be represented.

One thing, he informed the jury, required 'no proof': 'the British constitution is the best that ever was since the creation of the world, and it is not possible to make it better'. His learned fellow judges concurred in all this, one of them – Lord Swinton – opining that the crime of sedition included 'every sort of crime, murder, robbery, rapine, fire-raising. ... If punishment adequate to the crime ... were to be sought for, it could not be found in our law, now that torture is happily abolished.'[1] In September a second blow followed: the Rev. T. F. Palmer, an English Unitarian minister and Fellow of Queen's College, Cambridge, then ministering in Dundee, was tried at Perth. His 'crime' was that of encouraging the reading of Paine, and membership of the Dundee Friends of Liberty – described as a society of 'low weavers and mechanics'. A bench of crocodiles wept copiously as they sentenced him to their 'mildest punishment' of seven years transportation to Botany Bay.

The example was made upon two gifted professional men, who had been unreserved in their willingness to cooperate with plebeian reformers. Both men endured their trials with great firmness and dignity. And the Scottish reformers, over whose heads these sentences now hung, refused to be intimidated. It semed to them possible that greater unity with the English societies might afford them some protection, and they urged an early National Convention. Hardy, Margarot and Gerrald assented, and a Convention was summoned to meet in Edinburgh on less than three weeks' notice. The L.C.S. appointed Margarot and Gerrald as delegates, confirming them at their first open-air demonstration, in Hackney, on 24 October 1793. Some thousands of supporters attended, together with the curious who were attracted by rumours that the French Jacobins had landed or that 'Tom Paine was come to plant the tree of liberty'. The Minutes faithfully record the expenses voted for the delegates (£10 for the fare there and

1. Lord Cockburn, op. cit., I, pp. 175 ff. See also Meikle, op. cit., ch. 6; *The Life and Trial of Thomas Muir* (Rutherglen, 1919).

back and £4 expenses on the journey, with 9s. per day expenses in Edinburgh), and the Society was hard pressed in the next few weeks to raise these 'supplies'. And yet it was fare enough to take their delegates as far as the antipodes.

The invitation was at too short notice for the provincial societies to raise the money to send delegates. Sheffield was the exception. On 1 November it sent a biting letter to the London Constitutional Society, criticizing it for its inactivity:

The measures lately adopted in the sister kingdom, measures as opposite to ... a free Constitution, as fire and water ... have hitherto been viewed only with a degree of apathy by the great bodies of the kingdom, which we little folks in the country look up to for examples, styling themselves patriotic, such as 'The Society for Constitutional Information in London,' 'The Friends of the People,' ... that we begin almost to think here, it is time to nip those buds of freedom ... lest they should be exposed to the danger of being blighted by those torpid frosts ...

It appointed as its delegate to Edinburgh M. C. Brown, a 'player' turned attorney, who was also deputed to represent the society at Leeds. The Norwich societies authorized Margarot to represent them, and assisted with 'supplies'. There is a new note of desperation in the air, to which the Scottish verdicts, the French victory at Valenciennes, rising prices and unemployment, and the actual bravado of calling a Convention contributed. The Birmingham society regretted its inability to send a delegate,

in consequence of Mr Pitt's war of humanity having almost utterly annihilated our trade in this town, and driven a great number of our best members and mechanics across the Atlantic. ... However, upon the whole ... it has tended greatly to abate the pride, assuage the malice, and confound many of the devices of the enemies to reform ... and has made many proselytes to the cause of liberty.

Sheffield also was feeling the effects of the war:

We have many thousands members, but a vast majority of them being working men, the war, which has deprived many of them of *all* employment, and almost every one of *half* his earnings, we have been crippled more than any other in the kingdom.[1]

1. *Report of the Committee of Secrecy* (1794), pp. 160–65.

Margarot and Gerrald knew perfectly well the danger they were running. They were rushing 'supplies' of moral solidarity to their Scottish comrades which – if withheld at that moment – would have resulted in the demoralization of the Scottish and English movements. And they were challenging Braxfield's bench to treat Englishmen as they had treated Muir and Palmer. The supplies arrived only just in time. The Convention in Edinburgh had met briefly, at the end of October, and broken up in the absence of the English delegates. Upon their arrival it was hastily re-convened, in greater strength than before, and Margarot, Gerrald, and the Scottish secretary, Skirving, dominated the proceedings. It met through the last two weeks of November and into the first week of December 1793, when it was broken up and its leaders arrested. (Before this, Margarot and Gerrald had applied urgently to Hardy for more supplies to enable them to tour the main Scottish societies: 'no excuse for recal can be valid, unless founded on *fear*; and that we must remind you is our concern, not yours'.) The proceedings of the Convention were moderate, if somewhat histrionic; but a more revolutionary colour was given by certain circumstances – the fact of the Convention meeting at all – the presence of observers from the United Irishmen – and the French forms of procedure and address (although the term 'Citizen' had long been used in Sheffield) which burgeoned in the pro-Gallican climate of Edinburgh. Minutes were dated, 'First Year of the British Convention', and a resolution was passed (whose terms were disputed at the ensuing trials) authorizing the calling of an immediate emergency Convention at a secret place in the event of the suspension of Habeas Corpus, or the introduction of legislation against the reformers.[1]

Trials followed, on the pattern of those of Muir and Palmer. Skirving and Margarot acquitted themselves well; they were sentenced to fourteen years transportation. 'My Lords, I know that what has been done these two days will be rejudged; – that

1. According to the prosecution, in the event of other circumstances, including the landing of French troops in Britain. See also 'A Member', *Account . . . of the British Convention* (1794), pp. 24, 34, 45; Meikle, op. cit., ch. 7.

is my comfort and all my hope', said Skirving, as he left the bar. Margarot, who was accompanied to his trial by a procession holding a 'tree of liberty' in the shape of a letter M above his head, overplayed his hand and was too eager for the crown of martyrdom. But he challenged Braxfield with great audacity of having boasted at a dinner-party before the trial that he would have the reformers whipped before transportation, and that 'the mob would be the better for losing a little blood'. He was, Lord Cockburn (who saw him when he was a boy) recalled, 'a little, dark creature, dressed in black, with silk stockings and white metal buttons, something like one's idea of a puny Frenchman, a most impudent and provoking body'.[1]

Joseph Gerrald secured bail, returned to London to report to the L.C.S. and to wind up his affairs, and went back to face trial in March 1794. He had no need to do so – his colleagues and friends implored him to jump his bail. His constitution had been weakened by illness when in the West Indies in the 1780s, and transportation was a probable sentence of death, as it proved to be. But he argued that his 'honour was pledged', not to the Scottish Courts, but to humbler men who 'have been brought into similar peril by the influence of my own arguments'. He offered only one provocation, refusing to powder his hair in the 'loyalist' fashion, and appearing at the bar 'with unpowdered hair hanging loosely down behind – his neck nearly bare, and his shirt with a large collar, doubled over. This was the French costume of the day.' For the rest, in the view of Lord Cockburn, 'the manner and tone of no prisoner ever contrasted more strikingly with that of his judges'.[2] When Gerrald urged that Jesus Christ had himself been a reformer,

1. Cockburn, op. cit., II, p. 25. The excess of the histrionic in Margarot's character appears to be borne out by his subsequent history. He wrote a most injudicious letter to Norwich, while awaiting transportation in the hulks at Spithead: 'Rumour ... says there are 70 sail of French at sea; if so ... a descent may probably be the consequence. – For God's Sake, my worthy friends, do not relax. ..' (10 March 1794, *Committee of Secrecy*, p. 81.) He quarrelled with his fellow prisoners on the way out, and suspicions hung round his name. He was the only victim to return – in 1810 – and he then resumed some part in Radical politics, until his death in 1815. See M. Roe, 'Maurice Margarot', op. cit.

2. Cockburn, op. cit., II, pp. 41–3.

Braxfield chuckled to his fellow judges: 'Muckle he made o'
that; *he* was hanget.' Gerrald, who had legal training, followed
the example of the other reformers in conducting his own
defence. Without withdrawing a syllable of the reformers'
demands, he drew extensively upon Hooker, Locke and
Blackstone in arguing the right to agitate for reform. It was
a constitutionalist case which exposed the rhetoric of constitutionalism:

The word *constitution, constitution*! is rung in our ears with un-
ceasing perseverance. This is the *talisman* which the enemies of
reform wield over the heads of the credulous and the simple; and,
like old and wicked enchanters, having first bound them in the spell,
take advantage of the drowsiness which their arts have created. But
to hear placemen and pensioners talking of a constitution, when
their whole lives are one uniform violation of its principles is like
a monk preaching population . . .[1]

'When you see Mr Gerrald . . . making speeches such as you
have heard today,' observed Braxfield, in his 'charge' to the
jury, 'I look upon him as a very dangerous member of society,
for I dare say, he has eloquence enough to persuade the
people to rise in arms.' 'Oh my lord! My lord!' interjected
the prisoner, 'this is a very improper way of addressing a
jury. . . .'

Gerrald received fourteen years. He and Skirving died less
than a year after their arrival in New South Wales.[2] Braxfield
and the mysteries of 'Scottish law' have received too much
credit for these verdicts at the hands of English historians.
It was as much a verdict of the English Government as of the
Scottish Judiciary. Pitt, Dundas, Loughborough, Thurlow,
were at pains to defend every jot and iota of the proceedings
in ensuing Parliamentary debates. Dundas thought the judges,
in awarding sentence, had exercised a 'sound discretion': Pitt,
attempting to parry a most damaging assault from Fox, thought

1. *Trial of Joseph Gerrald* (Edinburgh, 1794), pp. 197–8, 241. Gerrald
may have practised in the Courts in Pennsylvania in the 1780s; see *Trial
of Gerrald* (Glasgow, 1835), p. 4.

2. Gerrald was held for over a year in Newgate and other London
prisons, and there is some reason to suppose that he was offered a pardon
if he would renounce his principles.

the judges would have been 'highly culpable' if they had *not* employed their discretionary powers to punish 'such daring delinquents' and to suppress 'doctrines so dangerous to the country'. (These doctrines, reformers were at pains to point out, were ostensibly little different from ones which Pitt himself had advocated in the 1780s.) And Wilberforce 'ridiculed the idea of humanity as applying to Mr Palmer although he had not read his trial'; 'he declared upon his conscience that he did not conceive the sentence ought to be suspended'.[1]

Persecution, we know, is a two-edged weapon. Men in the next decade looked back, not to the times of Braxfield, but – like De Quincey – to the 'times of Gerrald'. The image of Tom Paine across the water, conspiring with the King's enemies, might inspire fear or hatred. But the image of a sick man, returning voluntarily to face this kind of 'judgement', could not. Moreover, in a curious way, national prejudice helped the cause of the reformers. The guilt felt by the moderate 'free-born Englishman' was allayed by the thought that such things might happen in Scotland but could not happen 'here'. The revulsion of feeling among 'decent, respectable' Englishmen is indicated by Eaton's third acquittal (February 1794) and Thomas Walker's acquittal in April. It was strong enough to stem the opposite sentiments of horror aroused by Robespierre's Terror. Gerrald and his companions, by their example, contributed materially to the saving of the lives of Hardy, Tooke and Thelwall. By sacrificing themselves, they helped to save England from a White Terror.

The example of the Scottish victims stiffened, rather than intimidated, the English societies. When John Frost (imprisoned in the previous year) was released from Newgate in a state of collapse on 19 December 1793, he was drawn through the London streets in triumph, the crowd stopping outside the house of the Prince of Wales to jeer. John Thelwall, who now replaced Gerrald as the most able theorist of the L.C.S., opened a series of lectures to provide funds for the prisoners' defence. On 17 January 1794, Gerrald (who was a member of both societies, and who was now on bail) attended a meeting

1. Once again, a brilliant summary of the debates is in Cockburn, II, pp. 133–49.

of the Constitutional Society, which was jolted back into activity, voted him with acclamation into the Chair, and passed a resolution 'to oppose tyranny by the same means by which it is exercised'. 'Rebellion to Tyrants,' Gerrald had already reminded English reformers, 'is Obedience to God.' Three days later the Globe Tavern was so packed at a General Meeting of the L.C.S. that the floor gave way. A new British Convention, to be held this time on English soil, was proposed. Citizen John Martin presented a defiant Address from the chair:

We are at issue. We must now choose at once either liberty or slavery for ourselves and our posterity. Will you wait till BAR-RACKS are created in every village, and till *subsidized* Hessians and Hanoverians are upon us?

Four days later the Constitutional Society resolved that 'the London Corresponding Society have deserved well of their country', and ordered that 40,000 copies of its Address be printed and distributed. The effect of the Address was to rally provincial societies. On its receipt, wrote the Bristol secretary, 'I collected as many friends as I conveniently could that evening – we read – we blushed – we took courage ... your second epistle has quickened our courage, and vivified our patriotism ... and more, our number is now considerably increased.'[1]

Letters came in from other inactive societies. From New-castle (for long silent) it turned out that a number of 'societies' were in existence, which 'meet weekly, admitting none but known friends; and have assumed no name but that of news-paper companies'. It is clear that very many other societies existed – or revived – which had no formal correspondence with London, such as the Royston society or the society at Halifax which came forward for the first time, in April 1794,

1. *Report of Committee of Secrecy* (1794), pp. 185 ff.; Joseph Gerrald, *A Convention the Only Means of Saving Us from Ruin*, p. 59; *The Address published by the L.C.S. ... 20 January 1794*. John Martin wrote to Margarot in Edinburgh's Tolbooth (22 January 1794): 'The Society is increasing rapidly both in spirit & in numbers, and the *rich* now begin to come among us and to sit down with pleasure among the honest men with the leathern aprons.' T.S. 11.3510 (B).

with an apology for the fact that they had 'hitherto adopted the greatest prudence and circumspection' in their proceedings:

We wish the public in general to know that in this town and parish there are number of men, who violently oppose ... all free discussion. ... To see one of the advocates for Liberty in this town, fined, piloried, or imprisoned, would unspeakably gratify their rage ...

In the same month an open-air demonstration was held at Halifax 'at which were many friends from Leeds, Wakefield, Huddersfield, Bradford, and the adjacent neighbourhood' attended; plans for a general delegate meeting (at Bristol) and a National Convention were approved. In Leicester several clubs and 'Democratical lectures' were being held in public houses. In London the L.C.S. and the Constitutional Society had formed a joint committee to call a Convention – although the latter wanted some other name. A successful open-air demonstration at Chalk Farm in April, addressed by Thelwall and others, resolved that any further attempts 'to violate those yet remaining laws ... ought to be considered as dissolving entirely the social compact between the English Nation and their Governors'.[1]

This was the harvest, not only of persecution, but also of rising prices and of economic hardship. There is some evidence that the agitation was penetrating the poorer parts of the East End. Where the Hackney meeting in October had been a novelty, Francis Place recalled that the Chalk Farm meeting was attended by an 'immense multitude ... of all descriptions of persons – men and women ... in the greatest order I ever witnessed ... although they received many insults and provocaations from the Bow Street runners and different police officers and Government spies and reporters ... they were *thinking* and *reasoning* men'.[2] At Sheffield, also in April, a meeting of six or seven thousand was held (the reformers claimed 12,000),

1. *Report of the Committee of Secrecy* (1794), pp. 185–9: *An Account of a Meeting of the Constitutional Society of Halifax* (Halifax, 1794); P. A. Brown, op. cit., pp. 111–17: A. Temple Patterson, op. cit., p. 74.

2. Add. MSS. 27814. These meetings helped to establish important precedents, since the calling of public meetings by commoners without authority – and without the specific intention of petitioning Parliament – was of doubtful legality: see Jephson, op. cit., I, p. 277.

to protest against the Scottish sentences; a very young, elo-quent, and unstable gentleman from Derby, Henry Yorke, took the Chair and looked forward to the time when 'the command-ing voice of the whole people shall recommend the 558 Gentle-men in St Stephen's Chapel to go about their business'. 'Drunken fellows in the night' were attacking the houses of Sheffield reformers, and the Secretary of the society, Davison, encouraged a plan to furnish 'a quantity of pikes to the patriots, great enough to make them formidable'. Enormous weight was placed upon this in the subsequent trials of Hardy and of Yorke. The Prosecution offered it as proof of insurrec-tionary intent: the Defence witnesses denied the fact or pleaded that the furthest intent was self-defence from 'Church and King' thugs. In fact, both intentions were probably to be found within the societies. In Edinburgh a fragmentary com-mittee left over from the British Convention was still meeting secretly, and had passed under the control of a former govern-ment spy, Robert Watt. A few pikeheads and battle-axes were made, and Watt, in a dying confession, claimed that he had become converted to the cause of reform, and was planning simultaneous insurrections in Edinburgh, Dublin and London. Whatever Watt's own motives, a score of Scottish weavers and artisans were deeply implicated in his intrigues.[1]

These were the circumstances which preceded Pitt's sudden assault, in May 1794, upon the societies. The leaders of the London Constitutional Society and L.C.S. were arrested, their papers impounded, and a Committee of Secrecy ap-pointed by Parliament to examine them.[2] Habeas Corpus was suspended. In Norwich Isaac Saint and other committee members were arrested. In Sheffield (whose delegate to the Edinburgh Convention, M. C. Browne, was already awaiting trial) Henry Yorke and members of the committee were seized. The Secretary of the society, Richard Davison, evaded arrest, and the Editor of the *Sheffield Register*, Joseph Gales, was also

---

1. *Trial of Hardy, passim; Trial of Henry Yorke* (1795), pp. 26, 80–81; *Trial of Robert Watt* (Edinburgh, 1795), p. 353; Meikle, op. cit., pp. 150–53, *The Life and Character of Robert Watt* (Edinburgh, 1795), p. 76.
2. For the circumstances of the arrest of the London reformers, see pp. 19–21 above.

indicted for conspiracy (in June) but escaped to America. In the immediate aftermath of these arrests, with sensational 'disclosures' of conspiracy in the House, and rumours of insurrectionary plots and of liaison between the societies and the French, public opinion was stampeded against the societies. Ballad and broadsheet-vendors ran through the streets with sheets headed 'TREASON! TREASON! TREASON!' Bills were posted throughout the city. It was in celebration of the naval victory of the 'Glorious First of June' that a mob attacked Mrs Hardy's house; and one London newspaper jeered that 'the woman died in consequence of being haunted by visions of her dear Tommy's being hanged, drawn, and quartered'. Some clubs broke up in alarm, while those who stood their corner were occupied in raising funds for the prisoners' dependants. (Members of the L.C.S. were prosecuted when they sought to raise a fund for the prisoners' defence.) *The Times* published a mock account of an English Revolution, in which the prisoners were portrayed in enjoyment of sanguinary power.[1] In Lincolnshire 'ballad-singers were paid, and stationed at the end of streets, to chant the downfall of the Jacobins . . .' In genteel company, even silence on the subject of the trials provoked suspicion.[2] In Nottingham there was 'Church and King' Jacobin-baiting of exceptional violence. As in the previous year, the houses of reformers were 'broken open and persons dragged out, halters were put round their necks, and they were plunged into the muddy brook by the side of the town'. A loyalist committee paid the 'navigators' employed in cutting a new canal to attack the Jacobins, to whom the Mayor refused to afford protection.[3] At Failsworth at about this time a leading Jacobin was 'tied in the saddle of a dragoon's horse, whilst the mad and bigoted populace stuck pins into his legs'.[4]

The London Corresponding Society, however, was far from

1. [James Parkinson], *A Vindication of the L.C.S.* (1795), pp. 1–6: *The Times*, 5 September 1794.

2. W. Gardiner, *Music and Friends* (1838), I, p. 222.

3. F. D. Cartwright, *Life and Correspondence of Major Cartwright* (1826), I, p. 312; Blackner, op. cit., pp. 396–401; Sutton, op. cit., pp. 193–9.

4. B. Brierley, *Failsworth, My Native Village* (Oldham, 1895), p. 14.

breaking up. A secret executive committee of nine was set up, whose most active members were Richard Hodgson, a hatter, John Bone, a bookseller, and 'Citizen Groves'. According to an official memorandum, which had perhaps influenced Pitt in his determination to act, the L.C.S. had been recruiting vigorously throughout the spring. Not only did it number forty-eight divisions in May 1794, but in addition to tradesmen and artisans 'a new description of Persons has lately appeared among them: viz. several Persons from the Waterside Porters and Shopmen from Warehouses in the City and some Gentlemen's Servants'. Fifty Irishmen had joined one section in a body, while divisions had been set up in Woolwich and Deptford.[1] After the arrests of Hardy, Thelwall, and the other leaders, Hodgson, Bone and 'Citizen Groves' were able to rally most of their new recruits. In July it was reported that '18 Divisions panicstruck do not meet', and that delegates had been sent to revive them; but the remaining thirty divisions continued to function. The consequence of persecution was in fact to press further the process of radicalization within the Society. If in August some divisions had 'gone to sleep', and if members had withdrawn from others, in the result (an informer noted) 'the Society, at present, consists chiefly of the daring & the desperate'. The language of meetings had formerly been confined to Parliamentary Reform: '*Now* the intention to overturn the Government of the Country is openly avowed.' In the autumn, as the shock of the arrests wore off, there was another change of popular mood. The treatment of the prisoners improved, and Hardy noted that the common felons at Newgate began to treat the reformers with respect. 'The violent proceedings of the Government frightened away many,' Place recalled:

Many persons, however, of whom I was one, considered it meritorious and the performance of a duty to become members now. . . . This improved the character of the Society, as most of those who

1. Memorandum *re* Corresponding Societies, especially in the 'Eastern end of the Town and in the City', 6 May 1794, in T.S. 11.3510 A (3). According to this, Sheffield, Bristol and Norwich reported a similar increase in the same period.

joined it were men of decided character, sober thinking men, not likely to be easily put from their purpose.[1]

Meanwhile, the secret executive of the Society went through its own troubles. It had difficulty in finding *'proper ways and means for safe conveyance'* for its letters to provincial clubs. In August its most able member, Citizen Hodgson, would have been seized on a warrant for high treason if the Bow Street Runners had not 'laid hold of a wrong person', which (when reported to the surviving members of the executive) 'occasioned great mirth'. Thereafter he could only communicate with his executive by letters headed 'On the *Tramp*'. On 3 September the Bow Street Runners rudely intruded upon the executive and arrested the acting secretary. 'Citizen Groves' challenged their authority, and then led the others to a tavern to make a collection for the family of the arrested man. But on the next day there was a more remarkable occurrence. Groves was accused by Hardy's foreman of being a Government spy, and defended himself in a formal trial before the full General Committee of the Society. His speech was moving, if a trifle histrionic, in its sincerity. He brought forward many proofs of his devotion, as well as witnesses to his Jacobin character. He was triumphantly acquitted.

But 'Citizen Groves' *was*, in fact, a spy – one of the most able in the long line which runs through Oliver to the Chartist years and beyond. After each meeting of the secret executive, his full reports came in, for the perusal of Pitt or Dundas or the Treasury Solicitor. It is only thanks to his peculiar skill that we are able to describe the events of these months at all.[2]

1. G. Wallas, *Life of Place*, p. 21. Place's MS. 'History' must be treated with some reserve. Written many years after the event, when he was a lukewarm Benthamite reformer, it is in part a personal *apologia*, in which the 'sober thinking men' (i.e, Francis Place) are elevated, and the less temperate denigrated. Thelwall's lectures are described as 'loose declamation' which 'entertained all the vulgar prejudices of the day': a brief examination of *The Tribune* will reveal the bias of this judgement.

2. Both the minutes of the 'secret executive' and Groves's reports are preserved in T.S. 11.3510 A (3). Groves's reports run from May until mid-October 1794: I have been unable to find out why they end – perhaps, despite his formal acquittal, he was no longer trusted after his 'trial'. For an example of his observant reporting, see below, p. 171. On the question of spies more generally, see below, pp. 533 ff.

Hardy's trial came up at the Old Bailey on 25 October 1794. The charge was high treason. And as if to emphasize the horror of the charge, Robert Watt – the genuine conspirator and perhaps 'double agent' – had been beheaded in Edinburgh only ten days before. The public, and the jury, knew that the prisoners were on trial for their lives. (The only man in the courtroom who refused to recognize the gravity of the proceedings was John Horne Tooke, who combined the affectation of boredom with irreverent wit, in the true Wilkes manner. When asked if he would be tried 'By God and his Country' he 'eyed the court for some seconds with an air of significancy few men are so well able to assume, and shaking his head, emphatically answered 'I *would* be tried by God and my country, *but* —!') As the trial dragged on, for eight days, the evidence of dangerous 'conspiracy' seemed more and more pitiful, and Erskine's high-handed, even brutal, cross-questioning of the Prosecution's witnesses, made it appear even more flimsy than it was. The public found in Hardy once again one of those images of independence in which the free-born Englishman delighted: a firm and dignified commoner, defying the power of the State. The circumstances of Mrs Hardy's death attracted further sympathy. Excitement rose: in the provinces travellers and posts were stopped in the roads and asked for news: on the eve of the day when the verdict came, it was rumoured that Hardy had been acquitted, and Erskine's horses were taken from his carriage and he was dragged in triumph through the streets. On the final day – as the jury retired for three hours – the streets around the Old Bailey were packed with excited crowds: a verdict of 'Guilty' would undoubtedly have provoked a riot. A delegate from the Norwich Patriotic Society, named Davey, was in London to watch the trials. On the news of the acquittal, he posted back to Norwich, travelling all night, and arriving on the Sunday morning during the hours of divine service. He went directly to the Baptist meeting-house in St Paul's, whose minister was an ardent reformer, Mark Wilks – one of the old-style Baptist ministers who combined an occupation (as a farmer) with his unpaid ministry. Wilks was in the pulpit when Davey entered, and he broke off to enquire: 'What news, brother?' 'Not guilty!'

'Then let us sing, "Praise God from whom all blessings flow".'

The Government persisted with its case against Horne Tooke. But the proceedings were a source of even greater humiliation. The Prime Minister, Pitt, was subpoenaed for the defence, and was forced to admit that he had attended Wyvill's county meetings for reform. Tooke's acquittal was followed by a last effort, in December, to secure a verdict against Thelwall. But the result was a foregone conclusion. Not perhaps quite so. Thelwall, who had a dash of the histrionic in his character, had occupied himself in Newgate by writing poems on the theme of Hampden, Sidney and Tyranny:

> Within the Dungeon's noxious gloom
> The Patriot still, with dauntless breast,
> The cheerful aspect can assume –
> And smile – in conscious Virtue blest![1]

At the close of his trial he was seized with the desire to deliver a harangue to the jury himself. 'I'll be hanged if I don't,' he told Erskine. 'You'll be hanged if you do,' was Erskine's reply. On Thelwall's acquittal the charges against the remaining prisoners were dropped.

One might expect to find an immediate access of membership to the societies. But it is difficult to untangle the events of the next year. In the first place, most of the provincial societies had dissolved themselves during the summer of 1794, or else they continued in 'underground' forms which have left little trace. (The Committee of Secrecy had advertised clearly enough the danger of correspondence, and the trials advertised the widespread employment of Government spies.) At Sheffield the society remained quiescent, since Yorke was still in prison: his trial did not take place until July 1795, and he was sentenced to two years imprisonment for conspiracy. Moreover, these trials were only the show-pieces. In the provinces the magistrates had considerable powers of summary jurisdic-

---

1. J. Thelwall, *Poems Written in Close Confinement in the Tower and Newgate* ... (1795), p. 9.

tion, and humble reformers could expect no Erskines to come to the defence.[1]

Moreover the costs of that defence still had to be met. (At Norwich, where influential citizens still supported the Patriotic Society, two thundering Jacobin Collection Sermons were preached in St Paul's Chapel by Mark Wilks in April 1795 to defray the expenses of the Trials.) If the acquittals had prevented a general Terror – Hardy was informed, on good authority, that no fewer than 800 warrants against reformers had been drawn up (and 300 actually signed) which were to be served immediately upon a verdict being obtained against him – the trials nevertheless revealed the length to which the Government was prepared to go. And the acquittals drove the publicists of the Establishment to the point of incoherence. Burke, who had taken a hand in the preparation of the Report of the Committee of Secrecy, and who was now in possession of a pension of £4,000 a year, became, after 1794, the intellectual analogue of James Reeves. He regarded one-fifth of the electorate and most of the unenfranchised as 'pure Jacobins; utterly incapable of amendment; objects of eternal vigilance'. He implied that the acquitted men were 'assassins', and urged that the diseases of the body politic demanded the 'critical terrors of the cautery and the knife'.[2]

In the second place, some among the reformers' leaders had had enough. The Constitutional Society never revived, and Horne Tooke withdrew from public affairs, until the 1796 election. Hardy was much preoccupied with his own affairs after the death of his wife, and did not resume an active part in the L.C.S. And the London society was now torn by dissension.

1. For example, James Hindley of Leeds was sentenced in 1794 to two years imprisonment for selling seditious writings. At Leicester George Bown was arrested in 1794, but released after several months without facing trial. At Sheffield James Montgomery, who tried to continue Joseph Gales' work by publishing the more cautious *Iris*, was twice imprisoned (for three months and six months) in 1795. There has been no systematic research into the extent of such provincial prosecutions.

2. Hardy, *Memoir*, pp. 42–3; Mark Wilks, *Athaliah: or the Tocsin Sounded* (Norwich, 1795); Thelwall, *The Rights of Nature* (1796), Letter I, pp. 40, 56–7; Sarah Wilks, *Memoirs of the Reverend Mark Wilks* (1821), pp. 78–9; E. Burke, *Two Letters addressed to a Member of the Present Parliament, &c.* (1796).

Weeks were spent in wrangling over whether the society ought to have a new constitution, one section arguing that *all* constitutions were an impediment to direct democracy, the other section arguing that persecution should be met by a stricter internal discipline. (Even the chance use, in a letter, of the words our 'leaders', led to a democratical hue-and-cry within the society.) In a welter of personalities, two divisions seceded to form new societies. John Bone became Secretary of a London Reforming Society, which maintained friendly relations with the parent body. John Baxter appears to have initiated the other breakaway, a Society of the Friends of Liberty which specialized in grandiloquent libertarian histrionics. Described by a spy as a 'mean-looking man ... thin-faced, black hair queued, dark brown coat, black snuff waistcoat, about forty', Baxter appears to have been an advocate of more forceful measures, and he was delivering lectures on *Resistance to Oppression*: 'While the whole Power of the State is confided to Men of Landed Property, it may be truly said, they have the *means* of LIFE and DEATH in their hands.' A former Newcastle schoolmaster, Thomas Spence, was now gaining a following with 'another *Rights of Man* ... that goes farther than Paine's'. The aristocracy must be expropriated of their land, and Spence's new cooperatives take their place – 'Do you think Mankind will ever enjoy any tolerable degree of Liberty and Felicity, by having a Reform in Parliament, if Landlords were still suffered to remain? ... A Convention or Parliament of the People would be at eternal War with the Aristocracy.'[1]

These tensions were only to be expected. As early as October 1793 the Minutes of the L.C.S. record a motion from one division calling for the expulsion of persons propagating levelling principles. As the cost of living rose – and as the society made headway in East and South London – the 'social' question came more and more into the foreground. A characteristic pamphlet of 1794 held up as the consequences of Reform a

1. *The Correspondence of the L.C.S.* (1795), pp. 4, 20–21, 26, 42–3; Hardy, *Memoir, passim*; P.A. Brown, op. cit., pp. 142, 151; J Baxter, *Resistance to Oppression*, (1795); Anon. [T. Spence], *The End of Oppression* (1795). For Spence, see below, pp. 176–8.

reduction of taxes and excise, reform of the Poor Laws and
Game Laws, an end to restrictions upon trade unions, work for
the unemployed, and an end to the press-gang and to the
quartering of the military upon publicans.[1] Such demands
might win universal acceptance in the society, where the more
extreme views of Spence and of Baxter might not. But it is clear
that the society was also divided upon tactics. Two newcomers
to the London leadership may be taken to exemplify the different trends. Place himself, with his sober manner, his great
capacity for organization, his intellectual application, and his
experience of trade union organization was in the tradition of
Hardy. In the summer of 1795 he was frequently Chairman of
the weekly General Committee, and according to his own
account he saw the main function of the society as that of
political education among working men:

I believed that Ministers would go on until they brought the Government to a standstill – that was until they could carry it on no
longer. It appeared to me that the only chance the people either
had or could have for good and cheap government was in their
being taught the advantages of representation ... so that whenever
the conduct of Ministers should produce a crisis they should be
qualified to support those who were most likely to establish a cheap
and simple form of government. I therefore advised that the Society
should proceed as quietly and privately as possible.

This has too much of hindsight about it: 'cheap and
simple government' is a phrase from Place's later Benthamite
jargon, whereas the society in 1795 wanted an end to repression, and manhood suffrage, on grounds of liberty and equity.
But Place is probably accurate in saying that, as early as 1795,
he saw the rôle of the working-class reformers as *accessories* to
middle-class or aristocratic reformers in Parliament. Working
men could not hope to bring about reform by and for themselves, but should give support to others 'most likely' to win
concessions. This was in one sense a far-seeing tactical compromise; but it entailed attending on a crisis – awaiting, per-

1. Anon. [James Parkinson], *Revolutions without Bloodshed* (1794).
This admirable example of moderate Jacobin demands, forcefully stated,
is printed in Cole and Filson, *British Working Class Movements*, pp.
48–52.

haps, financial dislocation, food riots and tumults among the populace – rather than a policy of *hastening* the crisis by popular agitation. It is the policy of those self-respecting tradesmen or artisans who preferred to build bridges towards the middle class than to try and bridge the gulf between themselves and the tumultuous poor. As such, it represents a withdrawal from the agitation among 'members unlimited', while at the same time embodying the strengths of self-education and painstaking organization.[1]

The other trend is represented by John Binns, a young man from a tradesman's family in Dublin, who was now working as a plumber in London. He also joined the L.C.S. in 1794, rose rapidly to the Chairmanship of committees and of demonstrations. He belonged to the majority of members who argued that, in the aftermath of the acquittals, the society should propagate its message more widely, and should organize large public demonstrations so that the Government might be 'compelled to grant a reform'. And the reform for which he was working was, in effect, reform by revolution; although reform was their avowed object (he noted in his *Recollections*) 'the wishes and the hopes of many of [the society's] influential members carried them to the overthrow of the monarchy and the establishment of a republic.'[2]

By March 1795 the society had been reduced, as a result of the secessions, to only seventeen divisions.[3] Even more serious, the provincial correspondence had fallen off, so that the movement lacked any national centre. John Thelwall also resigned, ostensibly because (he argued) it was better for him to serve as an independent lecturer and publicist, but more probably because he was wearied of the dissensions. But after the secessions, the society appeared more united and its activity revived. Against the arguments of Place – that public meetings would

1. G. Wallas, op. cit., pp. 24–5.
2. Binns, op. cit., p. 45.
3. In the winter of 1794–5 there was another 'Treason' scare, three members of the Society – Smith, Higgins, and Lemaitre – being held on the accusation of plotting to assassinate the King with a poisoned dart from an air-gun. The accusation arose from a malicious informer, and the accused were released without trial: see J. Smith, *The Conspirators Exposed* (1795); P. T. Lemaitre, *Narrative of Arrest* (1795); P.C. A.35/6.

call down renewed persecution and suspension of Habeas Corpus – the policy of Gale Jones and Binns, for agitation on the widest scale, won the day after a referendum of all London divisions. As a consequence, a great meeting was held in St George's Fields at the end of June in support of manhood suffrage and annual parliaments. It was certainly the largest reform demonstration ever held in London, even if we scale down the figure of 100,000 claimed by the L.C.S. Citizen John Gale Jones took the Chair, and presented an Address whose flamboyant language is far from the Benthamite recollections of Place:

Are we Britons, and is not liberty our birthright? ... Bring forth your whips and racks, ye ministers of vengeance. Produce your scaffolds. ... Erect barracks in every street and bastiles in every corner! Persecute and banish every innocent individual; but you will not succeed. ... The holy blood of Patriotism, streaming from the severing axe, shall carry with it the infant seeds of Liberty ...

The demonstrators, reeling under these sanguinary mixed metaphors, were nevertheless peaceable and orderly, and quietly dispersed.[1]

From this time until the end of the year, the society grew apace. It broke out from its fairly restricted circle of artisans and tradesmen, and commanded increasing support among the wage-earning population. Four hundred new members were claimed in June, 700–800 in July: the seventeen divisions of March had grown to forty-one at the end of July and seventy or eighty by October. Meanwhile the two seceding societies also prospered. Auxiliary discussion groups and reading clubs sprang up. Deism and free-thought gained ground, so that Gale Jones was writing in the next year, as a matter of course, 'Although I do not profess to be a Christian ...' The Society struck token coinage and medallions, in celebration of the acquittals of 1794 and on other occasions. Thelwall was regularly drawing audiences of some hundreds to his twice-weekly lectures, and could not forbear to posture in his letters to his wife:

1. *Correspondence of L.C.S.* (1795), pp. 4–5 *et passim*; *Tribune*, 20 June 1795; Add. MSS. 27808; Anon., *History of Two Acts*, pp. 91 ff.

Two nights I have had nearly six hundred persons. . . . Two lectures in particular . . . have shaken the pillars of corruption till every stone of the rotten edifice trembled. Every sentence darted from breast to breast with electric contagion, and the very aristocrats themselves – numbers of whom throng to hear me – were frequently compelled . . . to join in the acclamations.

Moreover, around the societies there grew up other groups and tavern clubs with a new stridency of republican rhetoric. A 'Citizen Lee' (sometimes described as a Methodist) issued from the 'British Tree of Liberty, No. 98 Berwick-Street, Soho' a series of inflammatory and provocative tracts whose titles included *King Killing, The Reign of the English Robespierre,* and *The Happy Reign of George the Last.* His emphasis (like that of Spence) was upon '*parochial* and *village associations*', and he was also one of the few English Jacobins who referred to the guillotine in terms of warm approval. It was probably his output of chapbooks, Jacobinical stories, and broadsheets, which inspired Hannah More to counter-attack with her Cheap Repository Tracts, although D. I. Eaton and several of the provincial societies also engaged in the cheap tract trade.[1]

After June 1795 the provincial correspondence also revived. An open-air meeting was held at Sheffield in August, with a Chairman sent down for the purpose from London. An attendance of 10,000 was claimed.[2] But Norwich was, in other respects, by far the most impressive provincial centre. Nineteen divisions of the Patriotic Society were active in September, and, in addition to the weavers, cordwainers, artisans, and shopkeepers who made up the society. it still carried the cautious support of the patrician merchant families, the Gurneys and the Taylors. Moreover, Norwich owned a gifted group of professional people, who published throughout 1795 a periodical – *The Cabinet* – which was perhaps the most impressive of the quasi-Jacobin intellectual publications of the period. Its articles ranged from close analysis of European affairs and the conduct

1. *Correspondence of the L.C.S.* (1795), pp. 4–5, 29, 35; J. G. Jones, *Sketch of a Political Tour* . . . (1796), p. 33; Mrs Thelwall, *Life of John Thelwall* (1837), p. 367.

2. *Proceedings of the Public Meeting on Crooke's Moor at Sheffield* (Sheffield, 1795).

of the war, through poetic effusions, to disquisitions upon Machiavelli, Rousseau, the Rights of Women and Godwinian Socialism. Despite the many different degrees of emphasis, Norwich displayed a most remarkable consensus of anti-Ministerial feeling, from the Baptist chapels to the aspiring *philosophes* of *The Cabinet*, from the 'Weavers Arms' (the headquarters of the Patriotic Society) to the House of Gurney, from the Foxite Coke of Holkham to the labourers in the villages near the city.[1] The organization extended from Norwich to Yarmouth, Lynn, Wisbech and Lowestoft. Some similar movement was arising in the Medway towns, Chatham, Rochester, Maidstone, extending from the surgeons and professional men to the artificers in the docks. Nottingham witnessed a revival, with (once again) some alliance between the manufacturers and the stocking-weavers. And the published *Correspondence* of the L.C.S. shows activity in Leeds, Bradford, Birmingham, Leominster, Whitchurch (Salop), Melbourne (near Derby), Sunbury (Middlesex), High Wycombe, Truro, and Portsmouth.

'A new instructor was busy amongst the masses – WANT': the words are those of the Manchester historian, Prentice. 1795 was the year of crisis, in France and in England alike. The exceptionally severe winter of 1794–5, war dislocation, crop failures, – all sent the price of provisions soaring. May 1795 is the date of the famous Speenhamland decision, regulating the relief of wages in relation to the price of bread. The price of wheat reached impossible heights: 108s. a quarter in London, 160s. in Leicester, while in many places it was unobtainable. During the unprecedented rash of food rioting which swept the country in the summer and autumn, there were several occasions when the Militia took the part of the rioters.[2] There were signs of disaffection in the armed forces; Ireland was moving towards rebellion; manufacturers in Norwich,

1. *Correspondence*, op. cit., pp. 27–8, 63–4; *Cabinet* (Norwich, 1795), 3 volumes; Sarah Wilks, *Memoirs of the Reverend Mark Wilks* (1821).

2. For the riots of 1795, see above, pp. 70–72. See also *Morning Post*, 20 May 1795, reporting 'riot' in Oakhampton (Devon) when the Staffordshire Militia 'all . . . to a man joined the People'; T.S. 11.3431; Hammonds, *Town Labourer* (1920 edn.), pp. 85–6; Maccoby, op. cit., p. 90; J. H. Rose, *William Pitt and the Great War* (1911), pp. 282–8.

Manchester, the West Riding, petitioned for peace. John Thelwall addressed several of his most cogent lectures to the theme of want. In Jacobin Norwich (he declared) no fewer than 25,000 workers were claiming relief: the poor rates had reached 12s. or 13s. in the pound. The great Spitalfields silk industry, he claimed, was derelict:

Even in my short remembrance, bare-foot ragged children ... in that part of the town were very rare. ... I remember the time ... when a man who was a tolerable workman in the fields, had generally, beside the apartment in which he carried on his vocation, a small summer house and a narrow slip of a garden, at the outskirts of the town, where he spent his *Monday*, either in flying his pidgeons, or raising his tulips. But those gardens are now fallen into decay. The little summer-house and the Monday's recreation are no more; and you will find the poor weavers and their families crowded together in vile, filthy and unwholesome chambers, destitute of the most common comforts, and even of the common necessaries of life.

Here is a picture of the passing of old England which – even more than the theme of the 'Deserted Village' (which Thelwall also drew upon) – touched deep sources of feeling in the memories of Jacobin journeymen and artisans.[1]

On 26 October 1795 the L.C.S. called a further great demonstration, in Copenhagen Fields, Islington, with Citizen John Binns (aged twenty-two) in the Chair. 'An injudicious proceeding,' in the view of Place, who refused to take any official part in the meeting. Thelwall was one of the main speakers, using his considerable powers of oratory to keep the crowd in peaceable mood. He was now entertaining a vision of 'the whole nation ... combined in one grand political Association, or Corresponding Society, from the Orkneys to the Thames, from the Cliffs of Dover to the Land's End'; and the meeting passed a resolution to send deputies to the principal towns throughout the kingdom. (Thelwall himself rejoined the society in November.) The claim that 100,000 to 150,000 attended cannot be dismissed.[2] Despite the use of three platforms, or 'tribunes',

1. *Tribune*, XXIX, 23 September 1795.
2. Place, who was generally willing to deflate rhetorical claims, and who was writing (in 1824) out of a wide experience of political agitation, would only say that 150,000 'may be an exaggeration'.

'not half of the spectators could get near enough to hear a single word'. This time a 'Remonstrance' was addressed to the King – 'Whencefore, in the midst of apparent plenty, are we thus compelled to starve? Why, when we incessantly toil and labour, must we pine in misery and want? ... *Parliamentary Corruption* ... like a foaming whirlpool, swallows the fruit of all our labours.' 'The utmost harmony, regularity, and good order prevailed,' declares the anonymous historian of the Two Acts: 'it was a day *sacred to liberty*.' [1]

Three days later there was a day which – if not sacred to liberty – most certainly scared authority. The King, going in state to open Parliament, was hissed, hooted, and his carriage pelted: 'Down with Pitt!', 'No war!', 'No King!', 'No Pitt!', 'Peace!'. Perhaps 200,000 Londoners thronged the streets. Some brandished small loaves on sticks, decorated with black crepe. A hawker in the crowd who was selling 'The Rights of Man for a penny' was taken in custody, rescued, and chaired in triumph. The King's carriage window was fractured, probably by a pebble, but he is alleged to have gasped out as he reached the House of Lords: 'My Lord, I, I, I've been shot at!' [2] On the next day, when the King insisted on attending the theatre, the streets were cleared and he was attended by 100 foot, 200 horse, and 500 constables.

The London Corresponding Society disclaimed all responsibility. But it may well have intended some such demonstration, and in any case could not hope to control the anger of its followers. (In a tavern, on the evening after the riots, a member of the society boasted to John Binns that he had climbed on the carriage and attempted to assault the King.) In any case, the response of the authorities was immediate. A proclamation was issued against seditious assemblies, and Pitt at once introduced the Two Acts. By the first of these it became a treasonable offence to incite the people by speech or writing to hatred

1. L.C.S., *Account of the Proceedings of a Meeting ... 26 October 1795*; Add. MSS. 27808; J. Thelwall, *An Appeal to Popular Opinion against Kidnapping and Murder* (1796), p. 8; Thelwall, *Life*, pp. 379 ff.; *The History of Two Acts*, pp. 97 ff.

2. Anon., *Truth and Treason! or a Narrative of the Royal Procession* (1795).

or contempt of King, Constitution or Government. By the second no meetings of over fifty persons could be held without notifying a magistrate, who had wide powers to stop speeches, arrest speakers, and disperse the meetings. Yet one more capital offence was added to the statute book – defiance of the magistrate's orders was punishable by death. A special clause, aimed in particular at Thelwall, enabled reformers' lecture-rooms to be closed as 'disorderly houses'.

The interval between the introduction of this Act (10 November 1795) and its receipt of the Royal Assent (18 December) was the last, and greatest, period of popular agitation. The small Foxite oppposition fought every stage of its passage, and for the first and last time campaigned in the country alongside the popular societies. The L.C.S. called an emergency demonstration on 12 November (200,000 claimed this time)[1] in Copenhagen Fields: 'the meeting, as is usual on such occasions,' recalled Place, 'was attended by men, women, and children'. But neither the occasion of the meeting, nor the practice of bringing children, were 'usual'; and the latter is an indication of peaceable intent which became traditional in the later working-class movement. In December, in Marylebone Fields, the society held a final great demonstration, of which there is an account in Joseph Farington's diary. The speakers at the several 'tribunes' included William Frend, Thelwall, and John Gale Jones. Jones, the 'shabby, genteel' surgeon, who had some 'paralytic affection' with an 'almost constant convulsive twitching of his head, shoulders & arms', nevertheless had 'an excellent voice; sharp, clear, and distinct ...' His speech included a threat that Pitt would be brought to 'publick execution':

No tumult took place: nor was any offence given to such as did not hold up hands, or join in the plaudit.[2]

In the rest of the country great demonstrations were held, nearly all in opposition to the Acts. 'My head would be off in six months, were I to resign,' said Pitt. The major setback was

1. In fact, one *Account* published by the L.C.S. claimed 'upwards of 300,000' Britons!
2. *The Farington Diary* (ed. J. Greig, 1922), I, pp. 118–19.

in Yorkshire. Wilberforce, one of the county Members, had worked privately with Pitt on 'the Sedition Bill – altered it much for the better by enlarging'. (He was careful to uphold his reputation for 'independence' by opposing one clause in the House.) Meanwhile in Yorkshire Christopher Wyvill, true to his moderate principles, requisitioned a county meeting to protest, and issued a call, on four days notice – a Friday – to all freeholders of the West Riding to attend at York the next Tuesday: 'Come forth from your looms, ye honest and industrious clothiers; quit the labours of your fields for one day, ye stout and independent yeomen: come forth in the spirit of your ancestors. . .' Wilberforce, on his way to church in London ('Let me remember the peculiar character of a Christian; gravity in the House, cheerfulness, kindness, and placability, with a secret guard and hidden seriousness,' he had noted in his diary a few days before), was intercepted by an express message from Yorkshire. Overcoming, without difficulty, his scruples against travelling on the Sabbath, he drove to see Pitt. Pitt said he must attend the county meeting. But Wilberforce's carriage was not ready. 'Mine,' said Pitt, 'is ready, set off in that.' ('If they find out whose carriage you have got,' said someone in the group, 'you will run the risk of being murdered.') In Pitt's borrowed carriage, he made the 'forced march' up to the north. The whole county seemed to be pouring into York, the clothiers, or 'Billy-men', riding on their pack-horses. The meeting, once started, was going strongly against the Government when Wilberforce drove into York. He addressed 'the largest assemblage of gentlemen and freeholders ever met in Yorkshire' with an eloquence 'never exceeded', breathing 'energy and vigour into the desponding souls of timid loyalists'. Wilberforce's great reputation for independence and Christian philanthropy won over the West Riding yeomen and clothiers. The assembly broke apart, the vast majority of the 4,000 freeholders supporting Wilberforce's address in favour of King and Constitution, while 'that mad fellow Colonel Thornton stood up in his regimentals', and addressed the 'York rabble . . . in favour of the Jacobins. . . . He told them that many of the soldiers were ready to join them whenever they should rise.' Thornton concluded by 'throwing off his regimentals to the rabble', who chaired him in triumph to the Guildhall.[1]

It is one of those moments in history which seems to reveal a crisis between epochs. Elections apart, the next massive West Riding meeting to be held in York was to be Oastler's 'Pilgrimage' of the factory slaves (1832). As the York meeting split into loyalist freeholders and seditious non-electors, so nineteenth-century society was to be split, until 1850, between the electors and the workers on the hustings. And it symbolizes another division. 'Yorkshire and Middlesex between them make all England,' Fox said. The nonconformist conscience of Yorkshire had proved itself to be vulnerable: where Church and King might fail, Wilberforce and the Methodists could reach. But in Middlesex the traditional dissent of tradesmen and artisans now swung more markedly towards free-thought. And this also was a consequence of the Two Acts, and of the declarations of 'loyalty' by leaders of the Church and chapel alike.

It has been argued that the bark of the Two Acts was worse than their bite. The death penalty was never exacted under their provisions. Although Habeas Corpus remained suspended for eight years, it seems that only a few score were detained for any period without trial.[2] It was, of course, the bark which Pitt wanted: fear, spies, watchful magistrates with undefined powers, the occasional example. Between the bark and the bite of the Two Acts there remained, in any case, the barrier of an English jury; and Place's judgement (in 1842) that 'the mass of the shopkeepers and working people may be said to have approved them [the Acts] without understanding them,'[3] is questionable.

The Acts, in any case, succeeded. The L.C.S. at first risked a policy of defiance: delegates were sent into the provinces in

1. Wilberforce, op. cit. II, pp. 112–33; Wyvill, *Political Papers*, V, *passim*.

2. Among the Place MSS. is a 'Narrative of John Oxlade', a member of the L.C.S., seized in May 1798, in which it was estimated that during the peak years (1798–1800) about forty members of the L.C.S. were confined without trial, and about thirty-five United Englishmen. See also 'Lists of Suspects' in P.C. A.158.

3. Wallas, op. cit., p. 25.

the hope of rebuilding a national organization. John Binns was sent to Portsmouth, the principal naval station, but was recalled when the London committee learned that he was being shadowed and was liable to arrest. John Gale Jones toured the Kent towns – Rochester, Chatham, Maidstone, Gillingham, Gravesend; at Rochester he found a society nine or ten divisions strong, at Chatham when someone in the audience enquired whether the meeting did not exceed the fifty permitted in the Act 'he was angrily desired by another to leave the room and contribute by *his* absence to the diminution'. He learned that the Chatham dockers had refused to sign an address to the King in support of the Acts, and had signed a petition in protest instead. The attention of the society to these naval stations throws doubt upon Place's vehement denial (many years later) that any members looked with favour upon 'the formation of a Republic by the assistance of France'. These visits to the dockyards may be one among the threads which link the Jacobins to the naval mutineers at Spithead and the Nore in 1797.[1]

Jones and Binns then went as delegates to Birmingham, where they were arrested, while addressing a meeting on 11 March 1796. They were tried separately, Jones being imprisoned in 1797, but Binns securing an acquittal. (Dr Samuel Parr, Gerrald's old master, contributed materially to the verdict, by sitting directly in front of the jury throughout the trial, scowling ferociously and unbelievingly during the evidence for the prosecution, and nodding benignly at every point made by the defence.) Meanwhile, Thelwall, after continuing his lectures under the disguise of 'Roman history', lost his lecture-rooms and was forced to end publication of *The Tribune*. He toured East Anglia, delivering a series of twenty-two lectures in Norwich; but at Yarmouth he and his audience were brutally assaulted by ninety sailors, armed with cutlasses and bludgeons, who had been sent for this purpose from a naval frigate lying in harbour. The London society, with its leaders absent or under arrest, and with only a sketchy corre-

1. John Binns, op. cit., pp. 63–4; J. G. Jones, *Sketch of a Political Tour through Rochester, Chatham, Maidstone, Gravesend* ... (1796), pp. 27, 81; Wallas, op. cit., pp. 27–8.

spondence with the provinces, turned in upon itself and entered into a phase of internal dissension and disintegration.[1]

The dissension was not uncreative. It arose in part from religious—or anti-religious—issues. These men had pitted themselves against the State: now many of them were eager to pit their minds against the State religion. Place took a hand in the publication of a cheap edition of *The Age of Reason*. The support given to this by a majority of the society's committee resulted in secessions by the religious.[2] A Jacobin 'renegade', William Hamilton Reid, published an account of the society in these years which bears the mark of authenticity. In choosing delegates from the divisions to the general committee, it became common to recommend men as 'A good Democrat and a Deist', or 'He is no Christian'. Clubs and reading-groups had a fugitive existence, hounded from tavern to tavern. One debating society originated in the 'Green Dragon' in Cripplegate in 1795 and moved successively to Finsbury Square, Fetter Lane, the 'Scouts Arms' in Little Britain, thence to two public houses in Moorfields, and finally, in 1798, to Hoxton 'beyond the limits of the city-officers': until its last days the meetings were crowded. A more ambitious venture was the opening of a Temple of Reason in the spring of 1796, at Nichol's Sale Room in Whitecross Street. Its members furnished it and built up a library. It did not prosper, but it was preparing the soil in which Owenism, a generation later, was to strike.[3]

Before we conclude the narrative, we may pause to take stock of the societies and examine what kind of bodies they were. We may take the Sheffield and London societies as examples

1. Binns, op. cit., *passim*; Thelwall, *Narrative of the late Atrocious Proceedings at Yarmouth* (1796); C. Cestre, *John Thelwall* (1906), pp. 127–9.

2. James Powell, another spy who secured election to the General Committee (and on occasion to the executive) in 1795–6, reported that on 24 September 1795 'a letter was read from a numerous meeting of Methodists, belonging to the Society, requesting the expulsion of Atheists & Deists from the Society'. When their resolution was rejected, they seceded to form 'The Friends of Religious & Civil Liberty'. Powell thought that six entire divisions and several hundred individual members would follow them. P.C. A.38.

3. W. H. Reid, *The Rise and Dissolution of the Infidel Societies of this Metropolis* (1800), pp. 5, 9–12, 22–3.

since they were the strongest, and about them most is known.

The Sheffield Society originated, like the L.C.S., from a gathering of 'five or six mechanics ... conversing about the enormous high price of provisions'. It grew so rapidly that by January 1792 it comprised eight societies 'which meet each at their different houses, all on the same evening'. 'None are admitted without a ticket ... and perfect regular good order kept up.' The societies met fortnightly, the General Meeting, 'at which some hundreds attend', monthly. There were 1,400 subscribers for a pamphlet edition (at 6d.) of the First Part of *Rights of Man*, which was 'read with avidity in many of the workshops of Sheffield'. In March 1792, after four months in existence, the society claimed nearly 2,000 members. In May a new method of organization was adopted:

viz. dividing them into small bodies or meetings of ten persons each, and these ten to appoint a delegate: Ten of these delegates form another meeting, and so on ... till at last are reduced to a proper number for constituting the Committee or Grand Council.

These divisions were described, in the Saxon manner, as *tythyngs*. From the outset local gentry were alarmed at a society composed of 'persons of the lowest order', but the reports of outsiders well-disposed to moderate reform, in these early months, laid emphasis on the members' sober and orderly behaviour. A correspondent tried to reassure Wyvill, in May 1792, that it was composed of 'persons of good characters ... men of sound understanding, with their minds open to information'. A few Quakers were members (although not acknowledged by the body) and 'a number of Methodists':

One of the Meetings, at which a person was accidentally present, was conducted with order and regularity, it began with the Chairman's reading the minutes ... and afterwards several Members in succession read selected passages ... for the instruction of the Meeting, all in favour of Liberty and peaceable Reforms ...[1]

1. Fitzwilliam Papers (Sheffield Reference Library), F.44 (a); Wyvill, *Political Papers*, V, pp. 43–50; H. McLachlan, *Letters of Theophilus Lindsay* (1920), p. 132; *A Complete Refutation of the Malevolent Charges Exhibited against the Friends of Reform in and about Sheffield* (Sheffield, 1793); *Report of the Committee of Secrecy* (1794), pp. 85, 116, 119; W. A. L. Seaman, 'Reform Politics at Sheffield', *Trans. Hunter Arch. Soc.* VII, pp. 215 ff.

Of all societies, in the years 1792–4, Sheffield was most pain-staking and prompt in its correspondence. (Since it was technically illegal to form a national society, correspondence – together with the formal admission of members to honorary membership in each other's societies – was the means by which national association was maintained.) Although, as we have seen, the members had a preference for histrionic talent on the platform – M.C. Brown and Henry Yorke – their own officers were all journeymen or craftsmen in the Sheffield industries. Sheffield was a town of small masters and of highly skilled – and relatively well-paid – craftsmen; and (the Deputy Adjutant-General complained) 'no civil power'. In 1792 the two magis-trates lived out of town, one at a distance of fourteen miles the other 'having made some efforts during the riots last year relative to some enclosures, the populace burned part of his property, and since that time he has been very little in the country'.[1] It was thus an ideal centre for the Jacobin agitation, with little aristocratic influence, many skilled and literate workers, and a tradition of democratic independence. Among the few professional men, there were several who were well-disposed; a 'Quaker physician', was among the first members, and two Dissenting ministers gave evidence for the defence at Yorke's trial; while some substantial master cutlers were re-formers. Outstanding in organization, the Sheffield cutlers do not appear to have found a notable orator among their own ranks. But the witnesses, drawn from their committee, at the trials of Hardy and of Yorke are impressive in their solidarity and their refusal to be brow-beaten or tricked in cross-questioning. A witness at Hardy's trial defined the object of the society:

To enlighten the people, to show the people the reason, the ground of all their sufferings; when a man works hard for thirteen or four-teen hours of the day, the week through, and is not able to maintain his family; that is what I understood of it; to show the people the ground of this; why they were not able.

'I did not come here to learn my lesson, but to tell the truth,' another expostulated when cross-examined at the trial of Yorke.

1. Aspinall, op. cit., pp. 4–5.

It is possible that some of them meditated armed rebellion in the depression (and repression) of 1793-4. Certainly they were intransigent in their opposition to the war, and they were the first to come to the support of Palmer and Muir.

Sheffield had one outstanding advantage; a capable publisher and editor, Joseph Gales, with a weekly newspaper, the *Sheffield Register* which supported the society. (A more intellectual journal, *The Patriot*, was also published in Sheffield for a time.) Founded in 1787, it achieved the high circulation for that time of 2,000 weekly in 1794. The 'democratic' spirit of the time affected manners as much as politics: 'democrats' were dress reformers, rambled instead of hacked in the countryside, abrogated all formal titles, including 'Mr' or 'Esquire', and – if they were Jacobins – wore their hair short-cropped. In the same way, the democratic journals in the provinces – the *Sheffield Register, Manchester Herald, Cambridge Intelligencer* (edited by Benjamin Flower, a Unitarian reformer) and *Leicester Herald* – set new standards in provincial journalism, abandoning the paste-and-scissors copying of the London press, and presenting original editorial articles. The policy which Gales pioneered was also expressed in the opening number of the *Manchester Herald* (31 March 1792):

We shall spare little room for articles of *fashionable* intent – for accounts of Court Dresses or Court Intrigues – of Hunting Parties, Drinking Parties or Visiting Parties – interesting only to the Butterflies of Society ...

Gales' journal, his bookshop, and his pamphlet press were an integral part of the Sheffield movement.[1]

The Sheffield society was from its inception based on 'the inferior sort of Manufacturers & Workmen' in the cutlery industry.[2] (Although there is mention of propaganda in the surrounding villages, no collier or rural labourer appears to figure in any committee rôle.) The membership of the London society was, of course, very much more diverse. It drew its members from scores of societies, in the tradition of Coachmaker's Hall

1. See Donald Read, *Press and People* (1861), pp. 69–73; also F. Knight, op. cit., p. 72 and J. Taylor, 'The Sheffield Constitutional Society', *Trans. Hunter Arch. Soc.*, V., 1939.

2. Fitzwilliam papers, F.44 (a).

and the 'Society for Free Debate' (in which Thelwall served an apprenticeship) or the later societies of 'infidels' described by Reid. The L.C.S. was by far the strongest of these, but many groups always continued on its periphery.

The society was organized into 'divisions', each to be thirty strong, and to form new divisions at either forty-five or sixty. A delegate from each division attended the weekly General Committee (as well as a sub-delegate without voting powers); and divisions could recall their delegate and had the right to be consulted on questions of principle. The well-kept minute books reveal a lively interchange between the committee and the divisions, resolutions continually coming up from the membership, who jealously watched the committee's powers. On the other hand, fear of spies after 1794 led to the delegation of considerable powers to an executive, or committee of correspondence of the General Committte, composed of about five members.[1]

It is exceedingly difficult to offer an accurate estimate of the society's membership. Its peaks were achieved in the autumn of 1792, the spring of 1794, and (probably the highest of all) the last six months of 1795. The society itself made large claims, at times in scores of thousands, while historians have made claims which appear a great deal too modest. (It is often suggested that the membership never exceeded the figure of 2,000, which, there is good reason to suppose, was exceeded both in Sheffield and in Norwich.) The position is not made easier by the fact that two leading members of its committee of 1795-6 flatly contradict each other in their reminiscences. Francis Place, who was occasional Chairman of the General Committee, said that in the summer of 1795 there were seventy divisions and 2,000 actually *meeting* weekly. John Binns goes into more detail. The income of the society (in his account) was for some time over £50 per week: and at 1d. per week this would have required 'the regular attendance of 12,000 members'.

1. For a fuller account see H. Collins, op. cit., p. 110, and for a thorough investigation of procedures, see Dr Seaman's unpublished thesis. The rules were changed on several occasions, and the account above is based largely upon impressions gained from the minute books of the first two or three years.

Since many members seldom contributed, or attended only occasionally, he suggests an overall *average* attending membership of 18,000 to 20,000, 'the great mass ... shopkeepers, artisans, mechanics, and labourers'. When he was occasional Chairman of the General Committee (in 1795–6) the average attendance of divisional delegates and sub-delegates, at Thelwall's lecture-room in Beaufort's Buildings, was 160 to 180.

Both accounts were written some decades after the event. Place's account is more reliable, but it is biased by his desire to underplay the rôle of the 'agitators' in the society. The bias of Binns was in the direction of throwing a romantic colour over his Jacobin youth. One of the problems is in estimating the numbers in each division. The rule that divisions should divide at forty-five was not kept in the first years. Surviving records of divisions from the years 1792-4 show extremes of 17 and 170 members, while Hardy, in his sober and reserved replies before the Privy Council (1794), claimed that his own division numbered 600 members. But only 50 or 60 of these actually *met* each week – a not unusual proportion of non-attending members in a popular movement. Margarot claimed at the British Convention (December 1793) that the society had 12,000 to 13,000 members – almost certainly an exaggeration. In May 1794 a well-informed spy (probably 'Citizen Groves') reported: 'They themselves say that they amount to above 18,000 ... but this appears perfectly incredible.' At this time (he reported) the society's income of £280 per quarter would indicate (at 13*d*. per quarter per member) a paying membership of around 5,500. In the autumn of 1795 another spy (Powell) reported regularly the weekly divisional statements of new members and of members meeting in divisions. These show that while Place's estimate of rather fewer than 2,000 regular weekly attenders is accurate, several times that number must have been on the society's books. At the end of 1795 (Powell reported) 'a General State of the Society has been made out from the Division Books, it appears there are actually upwards of 10,000 set down'. But he regarded this as a 'false account' as it included many who had lapsed since 1794 as well as 'numbers who enter their names, pay the 13*d*. & never come to the Society again'. Thus Place and Binns are brought a little closer to each other. Pitt was many things, but not a fool; he would scarcely have sanctioned unpopular treason trials and the Two Acts for fear of a body never more than 2,000 strong. An active membership of at least that number, a paying membership of 5,000, and a paper membership of above 10,000 appear credible for early 1794 and late 1795.[1]

The business and finances of the society were conducted with great punctiliousness, and severe attention to democratic principle. At the fateful October meeting which nominated Margarot and Gerrald to attend the British Convention (1793), objection was made to a delegate who volunteered to attend *without reward* (i.e. at his own expense) as 'contrary to the principles of our Society'. This – at a time when the society was short of funds – was in emphasis of the principle of payment for services, to prevent the taking over of its affairs by men of means or leisure. On the other hand, Binns recalled, 'while I was their deputy, travelling on their business, they paid my expenses liberally'.[2]

Accounts of the work of the divisions are various. Place, who was most interested in tracing a sober constitutional pedigree, put most emphasis on educational activities: his L.C.S. was not Pitt's at all, it was a premature Worker's Educational Association. His division met in a private house: 'I met with many inquisitive, clever, upright men. . . . We had book subscriptions. . . . We had Sunday evening parties . . . readings, conversations, and discussions.'

The usual mode of proceeding at these weekly meetings was this. The chairman (each man was chairman in rotation) read from some book . . . and the persons present were invited to make remarks thereon, as many as chose did so, but without rising. Then another portion was read and a second invitation given. Then the remainder was read and a third invitation was given when they who had not

1. Divisional records and Powell's reports in P.C. A.38; 'Examinations before the Privy Council', T.S. 11.3509; Grove in T.S. 11.3510(A); Place's account, Add. MSS 27808; Binns, *Recollections*, pp. 45-6; A Member, Account of the British Convention, p. 40; *Correspondence of the L.C.S.* (1795), p. 29, 35. 2,600 new members were made between June and November 1795.

2. Minutes of L.C.S., Add. MSS. 27812; Binns, op. cit., p. 36.

before spoken were expected to say something. Then there was a general discussion.

'The moral effects of the Society were very great indeed. It induced men to read books instead of spending their time at public houses. It taught them to think, to respect themselves, and to desire to educate their children. It elevated them in their own opinions.' [1]

All this is very well: it is a splendid account of the first stages in the political self-education of a class: and, containing an important part of the truth, it is partly true. But we cannot fail to be aware that Place was also sitting to James Mill for his own portrait, as the White Man's Uncle Tom. The contemporary reports of spies have a touch of animation which Place has missed. 'Almost everybody speaks,' said a London porter, 'and there is always a very great noise, till the delegate gets up. People grow very outrageous and won't wait, then the delegate gets up and tries to soften them.' Moreover, we know that the divisions did not *always* meet on Sundays in private houses: many divisions, in the poorer districts, were harried from tavern to tavern. And W. H. Reid's account of club meetings in the later 1790s – with 'songs, in which the clergy were a standing subject of abuse', 'pipes and tobacco', 'the tables strewed with penny, two-penny, and three-penny publications' – seems as credible as (and not incompatible with) the account of Place.[2]

Of the social composition of the society there need be no doubt. It was, above all, a society of artisans. Surviving divisional registers show silk-weavers, watchmakers, cordwainers, cabinet-makers, carpenters, tailors. The register of one division, with ninety-eight members, shows 9 watchmakers, 8 weavers, 8 tailors, 6 cabinet-makers, 5 shoemakers, 4 cordwainers, 3 carpenters, dyers, hairdressers, 2 merchants, ribbon-dressers, butchers, hosiers, carvers, bricklayers, frame-work cutters, breeches-makers, bedstead-makers, and china burners, and one

1. Add. MSS 27808; G. Wallas, op. cit., p. 22; R. Birley, *The English Jacobins* (1924), Appendix II, p. 5.

2. P. A. Brown, op. cit., p. 73; Reid, op. cit., p. 8. Place's account may describe artisans and tradesmen in Central London, the other accounts divisions in the East and South.

stationer, hatter, baker, upholsterer, locksmith, wire-worker, musician, surgeon, founder, glazier, tinplate-worker, japanner, bookseller, engraver, mercer, warehouseman, and labourer, with the remainder unclassified.[1] If several of the society's most active propagandists, like Gale Jones and Thelwall, were medical men and journalists, most of the committeemen were artisans or tradesmen: Ashley, a shoemaker, Baxter, a journeyman silversmith, Binns, a plumber, John Bone, a Holborn bookseller, Alexander Galloway, a mathematical machine-maker (later to become the leading engineering employer in London), Thomas Evans, a colourer of prints and (later) patent brace-maker, Richard Hodgson, a master hatter, John Lovett, a hairdresser, Luffman, a goldsmith, Oxlade, a master book-binder, while others can be identified as shoemakers, bakers, turners, booksellers and tailors. In June 1794 'Citizen Groves' gave to his employers a revealing account of the society's social composition:

There are some of decent tradesmanlike appearance, who possess strong, but unimproved faculties, and tho' bold, yet cautious. The delegates of this description are but few. There are others of an apparent lower order – no doubt journeymen, who though they seem to possess no abilities and say nothing, yet they appear resolute ... and regularly vote for every motion which carries with it a degree of boldness. The last description ... and which is the most numerous, consist of the very lowest order of society – few are ever decent in appearance, some of them are filthy and ragged, and others such wretched looking blackguards that it requires some mastery over that innate pride, which every well-educated man must necessarily possess, even to sit down in their company; and I have seen at one Oyer & Terminer at the Old Bailey much more decent figures discharged by proclamation at the end of the Session, for want of prosecution. These appear very violent & seem ready to adopt every thing tending [to] Confusion & Anarchy.[2]

These English Jacobins were more numerous, and more closely resembled the *menu peuple* who made the French Revolution, than has been recognized. Indeed, they resemble less the Jacobins than the *sans-culottes* of the Paris 'sections', whose zealous egalitarianism underpinned Robespierre's revolutionary war

1. P.C. A.38.   2. T.S. 11.3510 A (3).

dictatorship of 1793–4.[1] Their strongholds were not yet in the new mill towns, but among urban craftsmen with longer intellectual traditions: in the old industrial city of Norwich, which had not yet lost its pre-eminence in the worsted industry to the West Riding: in Spitalfields, where the silk industry, with its notoriously turbulent apprentices, was suffering from competition with Lancashire cottons: and in Sheffield, where many journeymen cutlers were half-way to being little masters. Just as in Paris in the Year II, the shoemakers were always prominent. These artisans took the doctrines of Paine to their extreme – absolute democracy: root-and-branch opposition to monarchy and the aristocracy, to the State and to taxation. In times of enthusiasm, they were the hard centre of a movement which drew the support of thousands of small shopkeepers, of printers and booksellers, medical men, schoolmasters, engravers, small masters, and Dissenting clergy at one end; and of porters, coal-heavers, labourers, soldiers and sailors at the other.

The movement produced only two considerable theorists; and they reveal the tensions at its heart. John Thelwall, the son of a silk mercer, was the most important – he straddled the world of Wordsworth and of Coleridge, and the world of the Spitalfields weavers. After the decline of the movement it became customary to disparage 'poor Thelwall': in the early nineteenth century he was a figure of pathos – vain, haunted by a not unjustifiable sense of persecution, earning his living as a teacher of elocution. He also had the misfortune to be a mediocre poet – a crime which, although it is committed around us every day, historians and critics cannot forgive. De Quincey, who was brought up 'in a frenzied horror of jacobinism ... and to worship the name of Pitt' was only expressing the opinion current amongst the next generation of intellectual radicals when he referred to 'poor empty tympanies of men, such as Thelwall'. The opinion has followed him to this day.

But it required more than an empty tympany to stand forward, in the aftermath of the trials of Gerrald and of Margarot,

1. Cf. A. Soboul, *Les sans-culottes parisiens en l'an II* (Paris, 1958), Book II, and the valuable discussion of the social basis of the *sectionaires* in R. Cobb, 'The People in the French Revolution', *Past and Present*, XV, April 1959.

as the outstanding leader of the Jacobins: to face trial for high treason: and to continue (as Tooke and Hardy did not do) until – and beyond – the time of the Two Acts. To do this required, perhaps, a dash of the actor in his temperament; the vice of the English Jacobins (except for Hardy) was self-dramatization, and in their histrionic postures they sometimes seem ridiculous. But it was an age of rhetoric, and the rhetoric of a *parvenu* is bound to be less composed than the rhetoric of a Burke. The flourishes of the Tribunes of Liberty (who really were tribunes of real liberty) can surely be forgiven if they served to give them courage. Moreover, in the press of political engagement, between 1793 and 1795, Thelwall was both courageous and judicious. Throughout 1793 he fought a public battle with the London authorities to secure the right to lecture and debate: after being driven from hall to hall, he eventually secured (with the help of a committee of patrons) the premises at Beaufort Buildings which served both as a centre for his lectures and for the general activities of the society in 1794 and 1795.[1] On Hardy's arrest, he immediately rallied the society. When spies attended his lectures, he turned the tables by lecturing on the spy system; when an attempt was made to provoke riot, he led the audience quietly out of the hall. He modified intemperate resolutions and was watchful for provocations. His command over crowds was great, and when at the final demonstration against the Two Acts the cry went up of 'Soldiers, soldiers!' he is said to have turned a wave of panic into a wave of solidarity, by preaching the society's doctrine of fraternization with the troops.

In 1795 and 1796 his lectures and writings have a depth and consistency much in advance of that in any other active Jacobin. He defined clearly an English estimate of events in France:

That which I glory in, in the French Revolution, is this: That it has been upheld and propagated as a principle of that Revolution, that ancient abuses are not by their antiquity converted into virtues ... that man has rights which no statutes or usages can take away ... that thought ought to be free ... that intellectual beings are entitled to the use of their intellects ... that one order of society has no right, how many years soever they have been guilty of the pillage,

1. See C. Cestre, op. cit., pp. 74 ff.

to plunder and oppress the other parts of the community. . . . These are the principles that I admire, and that cause me, notwithstanding all its excesses, to exult in the French Revolution.

He stood up during Robespierre's Terror to declare that 'the excesses and violences in France have not been the consequence of the new doctrines of the Revolution; but of the old leaven of revenge, corruption and suspicion which was generated by the systematic cruelties of the old despotism'. He identified his support neither with the ineffective Girondins nor with the Mountain, criticizing 'the imbecility of the philosophic and the ferocity of the energetic party'. But on the death of Robespierre he immediately lectured 'on a parallel between the characters of Pitt and of Robespierre':

Robespierre unjustly oppressed the rich, that he might support his popularity among the poor. *Pitt* has neglected, and by his wars and consequent taxes, oppressed the poor, to secure his popularity among the rich. . . . *Robespierre* set up a free constitution, and tyrannized in direct opposition to it. *Pitt* praises another *free* constitution, and tramples all its provisions under foot.[1]

This also required courage.

His twice-weekly lectures, published in *The Tribune*, combine political education with commentary upon events in a way which looks forward to Cobbett. He expressed a generous spirit of internationalism, arousing his audience with descriptions of the suppression of Poland's struggle for national independence under Kosciuszco. His radicalism was generally confined within the area defined by Paine; but his emphasis, far more than Paine's, was upon economic and social questions. He voiced the claim of the artisan for an independent livelihood by moderate labour; denounced legislation which penalized 'the poor journeymen who associate together . . . while the rich manufacturers, the contractors, the monopolists . . . may associate as they please'.[2] He disclaimed 'levelling' notions and criticized as 'speculative' and remote schemes of land nationalization or Pantisocracy. He upheld the independent

1. *Tribune*, 25 April, 23 May 1795; C. Cestre, op. cit., p. 173.

2. Although the Combination Act was not passed until 1799, this only strengthened *existing* legislation against trade unions.

manufacturer, who might raise himself by 'the sweat of his own brow'. But 'production was a mockery, if it was not accompanied with just distribution. ... A small quantity of labour would be sufficient to supply necessaries and comforts, if property was well distributed.' Enemies to wise distribution were 'land monopoly' and enclosures, and the 'accumulation of capital.' The *Rights of Man* he extended to *The Rights of Nature*:

I affirm that *every* man, and *every* woman, and *every* child, ought to obtain something more, in the general distribution of the fruits of labour, than food, and rags, and a wretched hammock with a poor rug to cover it; and that, without working twelve or fourteen hours a day ... from six to sixty. – They have a claim, a sacred and inviolable claim ... to some comfort and enjoyment ... to some tolerable leisure for such discussions, and some means of or such information as may lead to an understanding of their *rights* ...

These 'rights' included 'a right to the share of the produce ... proportionate to the profits of the employer', and the right to education through which the labourer's child might rise to the 'highest station of society'. And, among a score of other ideas and proposals which entered into the stream of nineteenth-century working-class politics (for *The Tribune* and *The Rights of Nature* were still found in the library of nineteenth-century Radicals), Thelwall tried to trace the ancestry of the eight-hour day as the traditional 'norm' for the labouring man.

We can say that Thelwall offered a consistent ideology to the artisan. His further examination of *The Rights of Nature* consisted in the analysis of the 'Origin and Distribution of Property' and the 'Feudal System'. While, like Paine, he stopped short at the criticism of private capital accumulation *per se*, he sought to limit the operation of 'monopoly' and 'commercial' exploitation, seeking to depict an ideal society of smallholders, small traders and artisans, and of labourers whose conditions and hours of labour, and health and old age, were protected.[1]

Thelwall took Jacobinism to the borders of Socialism; he

1. *Tribune*, 3 Volumes, *passim*; Cestre, op. cit., pp. 175 f.; J. Thelwall, *The Rights of Nature* (1796), Letters I and II.

also took it to the borders of revolutionism. The dilemma here was not in his mind but in his situation: it was the dilemma of all Radical reformers to the time of Chartism and beyond. How were the unrepresented, their organizations faced with persecution and repression, to effect their objects? As the Chartists termed it, 'moral' or 'physical' force? Thelwall rejected Place's policy of educational gradualism, as the auxiliary of the middle class. He accepted an unlimited agitation; but rejected the extreme course of underground revolutionary organization. It was this predicament which was to face him (and subsequent reformers) with the choice between defiant rhetoric and capitulation. Again and again, between 1792 and 1848, this dilemma was to recur. The Jacobin or Chartist, who implied the threat of overwhelming numbers but who held back from actual revolutionary preparation, was always exposed, at some critical moment, both to the loss of the confidence of his own supporters and the ridicule of his opponents.

It is clear that some members of the L.C.S. were prepared to go further. It goes without saying that much will always remain obscure about groups engaged in illegal actions, who took care to commit little to paper. But the revolutionists in the L.C.S. are persistently connected in some way with the name of Thomas Spence. Spence, a poor schoolmaster from Newcastle (where he had developed his theories of land nationalization as early as 1775), came to London in December 1792. He was arrested almost at once for selling *Rights of Man*, but acquitted. He published and sold tracts, at first from a shop in Chancery Lane, then from 8 Little Turnstile, later still from 9 Oxford Street and finally from a barrow which also sold saloop (hot sassifras). He was, Place recalled, 'not more than five feet high, very honest, simple, single-minded, who loved mankind, and firmly believed that a time would come when men would be virtuous, wise and happy. He was unpractical in the ways of the world to an extent hardly imaginable.' Throughout the 1790s he was a source of handbills, chalked notices, broadsheets, and a periodical, *Pig's Meat* (1793-6). Between May and December 1794, he was imprisoned under the suspension of Habeas Corpus. Between 1795 and 1797 he supplemented his sale of tracts by dealing in Jacobin token coinage. He was imprisoned again in 1801. On his release, the small Spencean society continued to be a centre for agitation until, and beyond, his death in 1814.

It is easy to see Spence, with his peripheral panaceas and his phonetic alphabet (in which he published an account of his own trial of 1801) as little more than a crank. But there is some sketchy evidence of arming and drilling connected with his shop, adduced at the treason trials of 1794; while in the later stages of the L.C.S. several of its leading members, including Thomas Evans and Alexander Galloway, were undoubted Spenceans. Spence took up Paine's arguments against hereditary aristocracy and carried them to their conclusion: 'we must destroy not only personal and hereditary Lordship, but the cause of them, which is Private Property in Land':

The public mind being suitably prepared by reading my little Tracts ... a few Contingent Parishes have only to declare the land to be theirs and form a convention of Parochial Delegates. Other adjacent Parishes would ... follow the example, and send also their Delegates and thus would a beautiful and powerful New Republic instantaneously arise in full vigour. The power and re-sources of War passing in this manner in a moment into the hands of the People ... their Tyrants would become weak and harmless .
And being ... scalped of their Revenues and the Lands that pro-duced them their Power would never more grow to enable them to overturn our Temple of Liberty.

Whether Spence was himself directly implicated in insurrectionary conspiracy (as distinct from general incitement) is not clear. But he certainly believed in the methods of the underground – the secret press, the anonymous handbill, the charcoaled pavement, the tavern club, perhaps the food riot. At his trial he described himself as 'the unfee'd Advocate of the disinherited seed of Adam'. His propaganda was scarcely likely to win any massive following in urban centres, and never appears to have reached any rural districts. But it was one of his followers, Thomas Evans, who was the first to give to Spence's agrarian socialism a more general application. In his *Christian Polity the Salvation of the Empire*, published at the close of the Wars, he demanded:

All the land, the waters, the mines, the houses, and all permanent feudal property, must return to the people ... and be administered in partnership, like that of the church.

The emphasis is still upon 'feudal', as opposed to commercial or industrial wealth. But the definition of class is clearer than any offered by Paine:

First, settle the property, the national domains, of the people, on a fair and just foundation, and that one settlement will do for all ... and produce a real radical reform in everything; all attempts to reform without this *are but so many approaches to actual ruin* ... that will not disturb the relative classes of society.

Evans's writing really belongs to the post-War years. But he was one of the last Secretaries of the L.C.S. and this reminds us of the importance of the Spenceans as the only English Jacobin grouping to succeed in maintaining an unbroken continuity throughout the Wars. And one other tradition is particularly linked with this grouping. The *Rights of Women*, and the cause of sexual liberation, were, in the main, championed within a small intellectual coterie – Mary Wollstonecraft, Godwin, Blake (and, later, Shelley). Spence was one of the only Jacobin propagandists to address his writing to working women themselves. *The Rights of Infants*; *or, the Imprescriptable* RIGHT *of* MOTHERS *to such share of the Elements as is sufficient to enable them to suckle and bring up their Young* is the title of a critique of Paine's *Agrarian Justice*, published in the form of a dialogue between a woman and an aristocrat. Since women have found their husbands 'woefully negligent and deficient about their own rights', the woman is made to say, 'we women mean to take up the business ourselves'. And in a later pamphlet, Spence championed the right of the common people to easy divorce:

This subject is so feelingly understood in this country, that it is supposed the Chains of Hymen would be among the first that would be broken ... in case of a Revolution, and the family business of life turned over to Cupid, who though he may be a little whimsical, is not so stern an jailor-like Deity.

'What signifies Reforms of Government or Redress of Public Grievances, if people cannot have their domestic grievances redressed?'[1]

After the Two Acts, 'some thought it dangerous, others thought it useless, to meet again,' wrote Place. 'The whole matter fell rapidly to decay. ... The business of the Society increased after its members fell off.' Deputations from the General Committee had to visit inactive or sluggish divisions: 'I remember having to attend in this way as many as three divisions on one evening, and having to harangue each of them on their neglect. ... The correspondence with the country was also very considerable.'[2]

The society felt itself to be surrounded by spies: if Thelwall went into an oyster-house, or an *à la mode* beef shop (said Binns), 'he would conceit that one-half of the boxes in the room had Government spies in them'. 'No news,' wrote Blake's friend and fellow engraver, George Cumberland, 'save that *Great Britain* is hanging the Irish, hunting the Maroons, feeding the Vendée, and establishing the human flesh trade.' He had only to enter a coffee-room and order breakfast when 'some strange but well-dressed man would seat himself on the opposite side of my box'.[3] Thelwall, after being attacked by the sailors in Yarmouth, continued his lecture tour. He was again attacked by 'sailors, armed associators, and the

1. Materials for the life of Spence in Place Collection, Add. MSS. 27808; O. D. Rudkin, *Thomas Spence and his Connections* (1927); A. W. Waters, *Trial of Spence in 1801, &c.* (Leamington Spa, 1917); A. Davenport, *The Life, Writings and Principles of Thomas Spence* (1836); T. Spence, *Pig's Meat: The Rights of Infants* (1797): *The Restorer of Society to its Natural State* (1801): Cole and Filson, op. cit., pp. 124–8; T. Evans, *Christian Polity the Salvation of the Empire* (1816), pp. 14, 33, and *Life of Spence* (Manchester, 1821).

2. Add. MSS. 27808. In the summer of 1796 Place resigned from the Executive, in March 1797 from the General Committee, and in June 1797 from the society. Powell's reports (P.C. A.38) show that the intake of new members almost stopped after the passing of the Two Acts: 16 divisions failed to meet in January 1796: 1094 were still meeting regularly in divisions in February: 826 in March: 626 in May: 459 in June: and only 209 in November. Place was still named as Assistant Secretary in December 1796.

3. Binns, op. cit., p. 44; D. V. Erdman, op. cit., p. 272.

Inniskilling dragoons' (and was refused protection by the magistrates) at meetings in Lynn, Wisbech, Derby, Stockport, and Ashby-de-la-Zouch. For a fortnight he was made Editor of the *Derby Courier*, but he was forced out of the post.

He had at last reached his breaking-point. The 'artisans, shopkeepers, dissenting ministers, schoolmasters' who entertained him during his tour of East Anglia and the north were intimidated from every side. In 1797 the invasion scare was growing, armed loyal associations and volunteer corps were formed, as much against internal conspiracy as against the French.[1] Thelwall had started to correspond, in 1796, with young Coleridge, who had been editing the *Watchman* in Bristol, and who liked his *Rights of Nature*. 'He is intrepid, eloquent, and honest', Coleridge was writing to a friend in 1797, and 'If the day of darkness and tempest should come, it is most probable that the influence of Thelwall would be great on the lower classes.' But in the summer of 1797 Thelwall's spirits were subdued; he visited Coleridge at Stowey in July, tramped with him and Wordsworth in the countryside, and envied their peace:

> ... it would be sweet
> With kindly interchange of mutual aid
> To delve our little garden plots, the while
> Sweet converse flow'd, suspending oft the arm
> And half-driven spade, while, eager, one propounds
> And listens one, weighing each pregnant word,
> And pondering fit reply ...

It was the year of the germination of *Lyrical Ballads*, and the poets were themselves the subject of the attentions of a Government spy, who reported their excited converse with the Jacobin – 'a little stout man with dark crop of hair and wore a white hat'. Thelwall determined to renounce public life:

> Ah! let me then, far from the strifeful scenes
> Of public life (where Reason's warning voice
> Is heard no longer, and the trump of Truth
> Who blows but wakes The Ruffian Crew of Power

1. In February 1797 the French actually made a small landing near Fishguard, on the Pembrokeshire coast: see E. H. S. Jones, *The Last Invasion of Britain* (Cardiff, 1950).

> To deeds of maddest anarchy and blood).
> Ah! let me, far in some sequester'd dell,
> Build my low cot; most happy might it prove,
> My Samuel! near to thine, that I might oft
> Share thy sweet converse, best-belov'd of friends!

But Coleridge was tiring of the 'trump of Truth', and was preparing to break his own 'squeaking trumpet of sedition'. His reply to Thelwall was friendly but firm: 'at present I see that much evil and little good would result from your settling here'.[1]

Meanwhile the L.C.S., with Binns and Jones awaiting trial, refused to give up. In the General Election of 1796, there was an informal Whig-Radical alliance in Westminster, where Fox declared on the hustings: 'A more detestable [Government] never existed in British History.... This Government has destroyed more human beings in its foreign wars, than Louis the Fourteenth; and attempted the lives of more innocent men at home, than Henry the Eighth.' And throughout the next ten years the Foxite opposition (so incomprehensible to historians of the Namier School) was, together with the jury system, the last defence of English liberties. Fox himself carried Westminster without difficulty; and one of Burke's 'assassins', Horne Tooke, polled nearly 3,000 votes.[2] In Norwich, the patrician Quaker, Bartlett Gurney, stood with the support of the Patriotic Society against the War Minister, Windham. As in Westminster there was a wide franchise, and he secured a majority of the resident freemen, but was swamped by out-voters imported from London. In Thelwall's view the 'labouring freemen' would have carried the day if Gurney had not been an ineffectual absentee candidate, who even failed to appear on the hustings. In Nottingham, Dr Crompton, with Jacobin support, achieved a respectable poll.[3]

1. J. Thelwall, *Poems Chiefly written in Retirement* (Hereford, 1801), pp. xxx, 129; Cestre, op. cit., p. 142 ff.; H.O. 42.41; E. Blunden (ed.), *Coleridge Studies* (1934).

2. C. J. Fox, 5160, Sir A. Gardner, 4814 (elected). John Horne Tooke, 2819 (not elected).

3. Thelwall, *The Rights of Nature*, Letter I, pp. 25–9. Norwich: Hon. H. Hobart, 1622, W. Windham, 1159 (elected). Bartlett Gurney, 1076 (not elected). Nottingham: Lord Carrington, 1211, D. P. Coke, 1070 (elected). Dr Crompton, 560 (not elected).

The collapse came at the end of 1796. In the autumn of that year the society was still strong enough to publish a weighty *Moral and Political Magazine*, although Place wisely warned that this would overstrain its finances, and it appears to have drawn largely upon Thelwall for its intellectual resources. Eighteen divisions of the society still paid contributions in January 1797, although in the same month the new Secretary, John Bone (reconciled from the Reforming Society), issued a printed circular to all members, reproving them for their non-attendance. In the summer the society inaugurated the long tradition of open-air political propaganda, taking their example from the Dissenting and Methodist field-preachers: every Sunday they spoke near the City Road, and at Islington, Hoxton, Hackney, Hornsey, Bethnal Green, mixing Jacobin propaganda with the advocacy of Deism and Atheism. They also (says Reid) began the systematic penetration of benefit societies – a development of great importance for the history of trade unionism during the years of illegality. In July 1797 they attempted to defy the Two Acts, by calling a public demonstration in St Pancras: a considerable crowd attended, was dispersed by the magistrates, and six members of the platform (including Binns) arrested. A provincial correspondence still continued, the Norwich Patriotic Society writing in July: 'We continue firm at our Post ... prepared rather to make a Public exit than to abandon ...' But it was more difficult to pass letters: five new addresses were given, of shopkeepers whose mail was unlikely to be suspected, and 'we think it would be as well to change the address sometimes as above'. After the July arrests, Thomas Evans the Spencean, became Secretary: a meeting of the General Committee, in November, issued a declaration denouncing 'weak minded persons' who propagate the view that popular associations are fruitless: it pledged the continuance of the L.C.S. to the uttermost end, but it was signed by only seven persons.[1]

But there is some evidence that there were now at least two sections of the L.C.S., one attempting a quasi-legal existence

1. *Moral and Political Magazine of the L.C.S.*, November 1796; P.C. A.38; H.O. 65.1; L.C.S. Letter-book, Add. MSS. 27815; Reid, op. cit., pp. 17–20.

(and still publishing openly its proceedings), the other committed to illegal organization. Some persons – John Binns, his brother, Benjamin, and John Bone – were probably members of both. Historians have scoffed at the evidence of underground activity, and yet, in the circumstances of 1796-1801, it would have been more surprising if this development had not taken place. Working men were not, after all, strangers to these forms of activity; couriers passed regularly, on illicit trade union business, between all parts of Britain. And while the authorities tampered with papers and presented them in selective and sensational manner, there is no evidence to suggest that such documents as those presented in the *Report of the Committee of Secrecy* of 1799 were forgeries.

The Jacobin 'underground' would lead us to the colony of English émigrés in Paris, to the insurrection of Scottish weavers (Tranent 1797), and most of all to relations between the English Jacobins and the United Irishmen, whose smouldering rebellion broke into open war in 1798. But the greatest revolutionary portents for England were the naval mutinies at Spithead and the Nore in April and May 1797. There is no doubt that appaling conditions of food, pay and discipline precipitated the mutinies, but there is also some evidence of direct Jacobin instigation. There were Corresponding Society members among the mutineers; Richard Parker himself, the unwilling 'Admiral' of the 'Floating Republic' of the Nore, exemplifies the rôle of educated 'quota-men' who brought into the fleet the language of *Rights of Man* and some experience in committee organization. The presence of 11,500 Irish sailors, and 4,000 Irish Marines added another revolutionary ingredient. 'Damn my eyes if I understand your lingo or long Proclamations,' wrote one mutineer to the 'Lord Commissioners of the Board of Admiralty',

but in short give us our Due at Once and no more at it, till we go in search of the Rascals the Eneymes of our Country.

This may have been the language of the majority. But for a critical week, when the Thames was blockaded, there was talk among the mutineers of removing the fleet to France (where indeed several ships, in desperation, finally sailed). What is remarkable about the conduct of the sailors is neither their 'fundamental loyalty' nor their Jacobinism but the 'wild and extravagent nature' of their changes in mood. It was this vola-tility against which Richard Parker, in a dying testament, warned his friends:

Remember, never to make yourself the busy body of the lower classes, for they are cowardly, selfish, and ungrateful; the least trifle will intimidate them, and him whom they have exalted one moment as their Demagogue, the next they will not scruple to exalt upon the gallows. I own it is with pain that I make such a re-mark to you, but . . . I have experimentally proved it, and very soon am to be made the example of it.

But in the same breath he declared that he died 'a Martyr in the cause of Humanity'.[1]

These great mutinies, and the Irish rebellion of the following year, were indeed events of world-wide significance, and they show how precarious was the hold of the English *ancien régime*. For the British fleet – the most important instrument of European expansion, and the only shield between revolution-ary France and her greatest rival – to proclaim that 'the Age of Reason has at length revolved', was to threaten to subvert the whole edifice of world power. It is foolish to argue that, because the majority of the sailors had few clear political notions, this was a parochial affair of ship's biscuits and arrears of pay, and not a revolutionary movement. This is to mistake the nature of popular revolutionary crises, which arise from exactly this kind of conjunction between the grievances of the majority and the aspirations articulated by the politically con-scious minority. But at the same time the attitude adopted by the L.C.S. towards the mutinies remains problematical. There is evidence that sailors attended Jacobin meetings at Chatham and Portsmouth, and that individual L.C.S. members made contact with the ships' delegates and even harangued groups of mutineers. A shadowy 'gentleman in black' is supposed to have been in contact with Parker and his fellows; and this may

1. G. E. Manwaring and B. Dobrée, *The Floating Republic* (Penguin edn), esp. pp. 200, 246, 265–8.This account underplays the evidence as to Jacobin influence in the fleet, which is very much more fully examined in C. Gill, *The Naval Mutinies of 1797* (1913).

have been Dr Watson who was certainly at this time working for a French invasion, but who (according to a later deposition) was disowned by the L.C.S.[1]

The mutinies posed in the most acute form possible the conflict between the republican sympathies and the national loyalties of the members of the L.C.S. It is at about this time that a pro-Gallican and revolutionary party (which included many Irish emigrants) can be distinguished from the more constitutionally minded reformers, many of whom (like Place) were now falling away. In June 1797, shortly after the mutiny, a certain Henry Fellowes was apprehended at Maidstone distributing handbills to the troops. He was an emissary of the London society, and a letter addressed to John Bone in London reported two divisions of the Maidstone society active (with sixty in attendance), and ordered more handbills (particularly for the Irish soldiers), as well as copies of 'Bonaparte's Address' and Paine's *Agrarian Justice*. Following these events, two further Acts were passed, imposing the death penalty for illegal oaths and for attempts to seduce the armed forces from their allegiance.[2] Immediately afterwards a Richard Fuller was apprehended and condemned to death for giving an inflammatory address to a member of the Coldstream Guards.

The London society itself had adopted a new constitution, better adapted to underground organization and to the prevention of penetration by spies. Side by side with this, a secret committee was meeting in Furnival's Inn Cellar, in Holborn. This was quite possibly a centre of the United Englishmen, an organization which was in the main an auxiliary to the United Irishmen – indeed, in England the two appear to be almost indistinguishable. Its communications were by word of mouth or by cypher: its emissaries had pass-words and signs:

1. C. Gill, op. cit., pp. 301, 319, 327, 339 et seq., and Appendix A; and, for Watson, deposition of Henry Hastings in P.C. A.152, and entry in *D.N.B.* Sensational stories as to a European-wide secret conspiracy of illuminism and Jacobinical freemasonry appear to be baseless in their relation to England, although they may have some bearing on Irish events: see Abbé Barruel, *Memoirs Illustrating the History of Jacobinism*, translated and annotated by Hon. R. Clifford (1798), IV., pp. 529 f.

2. This Act against illegal oaths was that used against the Luddites and the 'Tolpuddle Martyrs'.

... you reached out your left hand to shake hands with his left hand, then pressing with your Thumb the first joint of the fore finger and he pressing the same with you was a sure token – one saying Unity, the other answering, Truth – one saying, Liberty, the other saying Death ...

In London, John Binns, Benjamin Binns, and Colonel Despard were among the initiates. Of one of the divisions, which met at the 'Cock and Neptune' in Well Close Square, an informer reported it was 'chiefly attended by Coal Heavers'. If its strength here was among the Irish labourers on the Thames, it was also alleged to have no fewer than fifty divisions in Liverpool and Manchester, with further divisions in the south-east Lancashire weaving villages.[1] In Manchester some success was gained in penetrating the Army, where oaths were administered to members of the Light Dragoons:

In a ful Presence of God. I a.b. doo swear not to abey the Cornall but the ... Peapell. Not the officers but the Committey of United Inglashmen ... and to assist with arms as fare as lise in my power to astablish a Republican Government in this Country and others and to asist the french on ther Landing to free this Contray.

(The Irish lilt is betrayed even in the orthography.) But while secret organization undoubtedly extended beyond the ranks of the Irish, it seems that in the spring of 1798 there were differences of outlook among the conspirators. On the one hand, the native Jacobins appear to have been continuing their work under various disguises. The 'Friends of Freedom' in Rochdale and in Royton (summer 1797) appear to have been linked with a centre in Manchester calling itself the 'Institute for the Promulgation of Knowledge amongst the Working People of Manchester and its Vicinity'. In Bolton (February 1798) a spy succeeded in gaining admission (by means of an oath) to the United Englishmen; the local leader 'recommended a Book

1. A prisoner examined in May 1798 deposed that the Manchester Society 'had much fallen off' in 1796 'owing to a quarrel between the Gentlemen who belonged to it & the Mechanics of the Society'. It would seem that the mechanics proceeded to form branches of the United Englishmen, 29 divisions of which are listed in another deposition in H.O. 42.45.

Club as useful to make Proselytes'. At Thornley in February 1798 an Irish priest was approached by a fellow countryman and freemason (a 'Knight Templar') who boasted of 20,000 United Englishmen in Manchester: 'as I was a *Holy Father*' (he wrote to the authorities) the man felt that he could safely be entrusted with his secrets. 'It appears,' a Bolton clergyman wrote to the Duke of Portland in the same month, 'that they are not wholly agreed in their wishes of French interference – Some say they can manage their own business themselves . . .'[1]

In the winter of 1797–8 an Irish priest, Father O'Coigly, passed between Lancashire, Ireland and France, under the name of 'Captain Jones'. Early in 1798 he came to London, and John Binns was attempting to find a smuggler in one of the Kent ports who would carry O'Coigly and Arthur O'Connor to France when all three men were arrested. A paper was found on O'Coigly, discussing the possible reception of the French in England in the event of an invasion. Although Englishmen had many grievances, they were also anxious lest the French should reduce Britain to a province. Therefore the French were advised that, upon landing, they should issue a proclamation: 1. That the British islands should form 'distinct republicks'; 2. That each should choose its own form of government; 3. That all who joined the invaders would be given arms; 4. That no contributions would be levied, beyond those necessary for meeting the cost of the invasion; 5. That France would limit her acquisitions to ships and to overseas possessions taken from her by the allies. O'Coigly, who refused, with great heroism, to reveal his associates, was executed. Binns, who bore a charmed life, was acquitted of high treason and – before a lesser charge could be preferred – took refuge under an assumed name in the 'counties of Derby and Nottingham, where I had many friends'.[2]

Sympathy with the Irish rebellion was certainly not confined to Irishmen like Binns. The L.C.S. published, on 30 January 1798, an Address to the Irish Nation, signed by R. T. Crossfield, President, and Thomas Evans, Secretary:

1. *Report of Committee of Secrecy* (1799), *passim*; various sources in T.S. 11.333 and 4406; P.C. A.152, A.158, A.161; H.O. 42.43/6.
2. *Committee of Secrecy* (1799), *passim*; T.S. 11.333; P.C. A.152; Binns, op. cit., chs. 4 to 6.

GENEROUS, GALLANT NATION

May the present Address convince you how truly we sympathize in all your sufferings. . . . May Nations . . . learn that 'existing circumstances' have been the Watchword of Despotism in all Ages and in all Countries; and that when a People once permits Government to violate the genuine Principles of Liberty, Encroachment will be grafted upon Encroachment; Evil will grow upon Evil; Violation will follow Violation, and Power will engender Power, till the Liberties of ALL will be held at despotic command . . .

It is a moving address, which redeems the English from the charge of total complicity in the Irish repression, and which included an appeal to English soldiers in Ireland to refuse to act as 'Agents of enslaving Ireland'. And it dignified the 'public exit' of the society. Evans and the surviving committee members of the L.C.S. were rounded up in April 1798, in the course of a heated discussion as to what action they should take in the event of a French invasion. Thomas Evans took the view that the French Government had betrayed the revolutionary cause, and seemed to be 'more desirous of establishing an extensive military despotism, than of propagating republican principles'. He therefore proposed that members of the society should join the Volunteers. Dr Crossfield agreed with his strictures, but declared that the L.C.S. could not defend the bad against the worse. The Bow Street Runners ended the argument.[1]

On the previous day, Colonel Despard and three members of the United Englishmen had been rounded up. The alarmist reports as to the strength of this organization given by the Committee of Secrecy of 1799 can certainly be discounted:

Most of the societies through England, which had used to correspond with the London Corresponding Society had . . . adopted the same plan of forming societies of United Englishmen . . . and the influence of the destructive principles from which they proceeded, was still further extended by the establishment of clubs, among the lowest classes of the community . . . in which songs were sung, toasts given, and language held, of the most seditious nature.

1. See H. Collins, op. cit., p. 132; R. Hodgson, *Proceedings of General Committee of L.C.S.* (Newgate, 1798); *Committee of Secrecy* (1799), Appendix, pp. 70–3; H. C. Davis, op. cit., pp. 92–3.

But, at the same time, there is no reason why historians should have accepted without hesitation Place's account, according to which the United Englishmen was stillborn, and never had more than a dozen members.[1] Place had long been opposed, not only to illegal organization, but to any form of open agitation, and had favoured a policy of educational quietism. He had withdrawn from the society in 1797, and would certainly not have been in the confidence of conspirators. The evidence as to its existence in Lancashire is strong; and there are informers' reports in the Treasury Solicitor's and Privy Council papers on the activities of several London divisions. *Two* spies claimed to be on a General Committee, with delegates from a scatter of branches in Shoreditch, Hoxton, Bethnal Green; delegates were instructed in military drill (September 1798) in Epping Forest; there was a competing body known as the 'Sons of Liberty'.[2] 'Fortunately we have no Leader,' proclaimed the 'Address from the Secret Committee of England to the Executive Directory in France', which was found upon O'Coigly:

Some few of the opulent have indeed, by Speeches, professed themselves the Friends of Democracy, but they have not acted they have considered themselves as distinct from the People, and the People will, in its turn, consider their Claims to its Favour as unjust and frivolous. . . .

We now only wait with Impatience to see the Hero of Italy, and the brave Veterans of the great Nation. Myriads will hail their Arrival with Shouts of Joy . . .[3]

The truth would appear to be complex. On the one hand, the 'myriads', so far from adopting the stance claimed by the 'Secret Committee of England', were caught up by 1798 in the wave of patriotic feeling aroused by the expectation of a French invasion. Indeed, the Volunteer Movement in these years may not have alarmed the French, but it was a very powerful auxi-

---

1. Add. MSS. 35142 ff. 62–6. Possibly Place's account has gained acceptance because an underground organization by its nature, leaves almost no papers behind it, and therefore has, for the historian, no existential reality.

2. Reports of John Tunbridge and Gent, P.C. A.144.

3. *Report of Committee of Secrecy* (1799), p. 74.

liary force to the other resources of Church and State in repressing native Jacobins.[1] Place is probably right that in extremist London circles there were now some congenital conspirators, who lived in a tavern world of paranoiac fantasies, who had few real contacts, and whose Addresses (if they had been believed in France) would have been wholly misleading. One such man was (it seems) Dr Richard Watson, a former member of the L.C.S. whom we have already noted as having been associated in some manner with the naval mutinies. In 1797 he was arrested for smuggling information to France by way of Hamburg. Released in 1799, 'le Citoyen Watson' addressed a memorial to the French Directory, describing himself as 'President of the Executive Committee of the London Corresponding Society, Member of the British Union, and Representative of the Associations of Bath, Bristol, &c.' Escaping to France, he began to address the British nation in the same grandiloquent tone.[2]

But other conspirators were more serious, as Colonel Despard was to testify on the scaffold in 1803.[3] By 1797 it is clear that some of the extreme Jacobins had come to despair of constitutional agitation. From this time forward, for more than twenty years, there was a small group of London democrats (Spencean or republican) who saw no hope but in a *coup d'état*, perhaps aided by French arms, in which some violent action would encourage the London 'mob' to rise, in their support. It was this tradition which was inherited by Arthur Thistlewood and by another Dr Watson in 1816. Several of the group, including Richard Hodgson and John Ashley (shoemaker and former Secretary of the L.C.S.) took refuge in France in the late 1790s, where they still remained in 1817. Indeed, the return of two members of this group to London in this year was sufficient to provoke an alarmist report to Lord Sidmouth himself.[4]

1. See J. R. Western, 'The Volunteer Movement as an Anti-Revolutionary Force, 1793–1801', *English Hist. Rev.*, 1956, p. 603; and, for the deficiencies of the Volunteers, *The Town Labourer*, pp. 87–9.

2. Various papers in P.C. A.152; Meikle, op. cit., pp. 171, 191–2; *Clef du Cabinet des Souverains*, 2 Frimaire, an VII; *D.N.B.*

3. For Despard, see below, pp. 521–8.

4. G. Sangster to Sidmouth, 13 April 1817, H.O. 42. 163.

Thus the Jacobin conspirators did exist. And they were in earnest enough to risk their lives and to endure imprisonment and exile. But their kind of conspiracy had a certain stridency and abstract republican zeal which did not run with the grain of the times. Moreover, with the execution of O'Coigly, the defeat of the Irish rebellion, and the arrest of the leading men at London and at Manchester, the conspiracy ceased to have a *national* existence. In the provinces, where underground organization existed, it either withered in isolation or struck a new kind of root in its own industrial context. In 1799 special legislation was introduced 'utterly suppressing and prohibiting' by name the L.C.S. and the United Englishmen. Even the indefatigable conspirator, John Binns, felt that further national organization was hopeless, and attempted to enter into a non-aggression pact with the Privy Council, although this only resulted in his serving a sentence as its guest in Gloucester gaol. When arrested he was found in possession of a ticket which was perhaps one of the last 'covers' for the old L.C.S.: 'Admit for the Season to the School of Eloquence'.[1]

By 1799 nearly all the old leaders were in gaol or in exile: among the prisoners were Evans, Hodgson, Bone, Binns, Galloway, Despard, John Baxter. Their entertainment in prison, when contrasted with that of Wilkes thirty years before, left a great deal to be desired. Thomas Evans, by his own account,

was conveyed to the Bastile, and there confined many months in a cell, with the accomodation of a bog of straw, a blanket, and rug; denied books, pen, ink, paper, candle, and much of the time access to fire.

His house was seized by the Bow Street magistrates and his wife and baby confined. He was held for two years and eleven months. The treatment of the prisoners by Governor Aris in Coldbath Fields provoked a scandal, in the exposure of which Sir Francis Burdett took a leading part. The libertarian disposition of the London crowd is shown by the fact that his campaign on behalf of the prisoners won him a popularity only comparable to that formerly enjoyed by Wilkes. For years

1. P.C. A.152; Binns, op. cit., pp. 140–1.

London's most popular slogan was 'Burdett and No Bastille!' One of the prisoners whose release he helped to secure was Colonel Edmund Despard. The story of nineteenth-century Radicalism commences with these two men.[1]

What is the price of Experience? do men buy it for a song?
Or wisdom for a dance in the street? No, it is bought with the price
Of all that a man hath, his house, his wife, his children.
Wisdom is sold in the desolate market where none come to buy,
And in the wither'd field, where the farmer plows for bread in vain.

Thus William Blake, writing *Vala, or the Four Zoas* in 1796–7. As the Jacobin current went into more hidden underground channels, so his own prophecies became more mysterious and private. Through the years the imprisonment went on: Kyd Wake, a Gosport bookbinder, sentenced at the end of 1796 to five years hard labour, and to the pillory, for saying 'No George, no war' (in 1803 Blake was himself to escape narrowly from such a charge): Johnson, the bookseller and friend of Godwin, imprisoned; prosecutions for sedition in Lancashire and Lincolnshire; a Somerset basket-maker imprisoned for saying 'I wish success to the French'.[2] The Duke of Portland, at the Home Office, himself sent out instructions to shut down tavern societies, and to commit to the House of Correction little children selling Spence's $\frac{1}{2}d$. sheets.[3] At Hackney the eccentric classical scholar, Gilbert Wakefield, looked out from his books and offered the opinion that the labouring classes had little to lose by a French invasion: 'Within three miles of the house, where I am writing these pages, there is a much greater number of starving, miserable human beings ... than on any equal portion of ground through the habitable globe.'[4] Fox's friendship and his own scholarship did not save him from prison. 'The Beast and the Whore rule without control,' Blake noted on the title-page of Bishop Watson's *Apology for the Bible*: 'To defend the Bible in this year 1798 would cost a man

1. T. Evans, *Christian Polity*, p. iv; *Reasoner*, 26 March 1808; 'Narrative of John Oxlade', Add. MSS. 27809; P.C. A.161.
2. T.S. 11.5390.
3. H.O. 119.1; H.O. 65.1.
4. G. Wakefield, *Reply to the Bishop of Llandaff* (1798), p. 36.

his life.' Kyd Wake indeed died in prison, while Wakefield was
released only in time to die.

The persecution tore the last Jacobin intellectuals apart from
the artisans and labourers. In France, as it seemed to Wordsworth,

> ... all was quieted by iron bonds
> Of military sway. The shifting aims,
> The varied functions and high attributes
> Of civil action, yielded to a power
> Formal, and odious, and contemptible.
> – In Britain ruled a panic dread of change;
> The weak were praised, rewarded, and advanced;
> And, from the impulse of a just disdain,
> Once more did I retire into myself.

There commenced, for an intellectual generation, that pattern
of revolutionary disenchantment which foreshadows the shod-
dier patterns of our own century. Balked of their pantisocratic
fantasies, the penitents accused the Jacobins of their own intellectual follies. Walking with Thelwall in the Quantocks in the
summer of 1797, the poets came to a beautiful secluded dell.
'Citizen John,' said Coleridge, 'this is a fine place to talk
treason in.' 'Nay, Citizen Samuel,' replied Thelwall, 'it is
rather a place to make a man forget that there is any necessity
for treason.' The anecdote foreshadows the decline of the first
Romantics into political 'apostasy' – most abject in Southey,
most complex in Coleridge, most agonizing and self-question-
ing in Wordsworth. 'I wish you would write a poem in blank
verse,' Coleridge wrote to Wordsworth, in 1799, 'addressed to
those who, in consequence of the complete failure of the French
Revolution, have thrown up all hopes for the amelioration of
mankind, and are sinking into an almost epicurean selfishness,
disguising the same under the soft titles of domestic attachment
and contempt for visionary *philosophes* ...' By this time Thelwall had retired to an isolated farm in South Wales. (Arriving
there he was astonished to find himself trailed by a spy. Or was
this persecution mania?) It was here that Wordsworth paid
him a last visit; and it was in such isolated surroundings as
these that he was to depict the Solitary in *The Excursion*,

meditating upon the delusions of those millennarial years.[1]

At the other pole, we have the disorganized and persecuted working men, without national leadership, struggling to maintain some kind of illegal organization. Their predicament is well expressed in a letter to the L.C.S. from a Leeds society, written on behalf of about a hundred members in October 1797:

> We are chiefly Working Mecanicks as those tradesmen hear who are friends to our cause have few of them Virtue enough to come Publickley forward as the Aristocratic influence is so great that they have got all the trade under their own hand so that they have got Power to distress any tradesman who exposes the Villany of a Corrupt System. There was a very good Society hear about 3 years since but the arbitrary proceedings of our Justices operated in so terrifying a manner on our Friends in general that their spirits have been sunk under the Standard of Moderation & the Sacred flame which had been kindled in their Breasts was almost extinguished ...

No publican dare take them in, and they are 'quite fast' for membership tickets 'as there is not a printer in the town who dare do anything for us'.[2]

It is wrong to see this as the end, for it was also a beginning. In the 1790s something like an 'English Revolution' took place, of profound importance in shaping the consciousness of the post-war working class. It is true that the revolutionary impulse was strangled in its infancy; and the first consequence was that of bitterness and despair. The counter-revolutionary panic of the ruling classes expressed itself in every part of social life; in attitudes to trade unionism, to the education of the people to their sports and manners, to their publications and societies, and their political rights. And the reflex of despair among the

1. Thelwall, unlike the Solitary, remained in radical politics. Subsisting during the Wars as a teacher of elocution, he reappeared on a radical platform at Westminster in November 1818, 'to the no small astonishment of the Company,' noted the *Gorgon*, 'like a man risen from the dead' (21 November 1818). Thereafter he edited the *Champion*, was harassed by the prosecuting societies, and took part in the Réform Bill agitation of 1831–2. But he was not in tune with the new movement, and his work lacked his early originality and challenge.

2. L.C.S. Letter-book, Add. MSS. 27815.

common people can be seen, during the war years, in the inverted chiliasm of the Southcottians and the new Methodist revival. In the decades after 1795 there was a profound alienation between classes in Britain, and working people were thrust into a state of *apartheid* whose effects – in the niceties of social and educational discrimination – can be felt to this day. England differed from other European nations in this, that the flood-tide of counter-revolutionary feeling and discipline coincided with the flood-tide of the Industrial Revolution; as new techniques and forms of industrial organization advanced, so political and social rights receded. The 'natural' alliance between an impatient radically-minded industrial bourgeoisie and a formative proletariat was broken as soon as it was formed. The ferment among the industrialists and the wealthy dissenting tradesmen of Birmingham and the northern industrial towns belongs in the main to 1791 and 1792; the peak of 'disaffection' among artisans and wage-earners in London, Norwich and Sheffield – whether caused by Jacobin agitation or by hunger – belongs to 1795. Only for a few months in 1792 do the two coincide; and after the September massacres all but a small minority of the manufacturers had been frightened from the cause of reform. If there was no revolution in England in the 1790s it was not because of Methodism but because the only alliance strong enough to effect it fell apart; after 1792 there were no Girondins to open the doors through which the Jacobins might come. If men like Wedgwood, Boulton and Wilkinson had acted together with men like Hardy, Place and Binns – and if Wyvill's small gentry had acted with them – then Pitt (or Fox) would have been forced to grant a large instalment of reform. But the French Revolution *consolidated* Old Corruption by uniting landowners and manufacturers in a common panic; and the popular societies were too weak and too inexperienced to effect either revolution or reform on their own.[1]

1. For studies of the connexions between reformers and the manufacturing interest in the early 1790s, see E. Robinson, 'An English Jacobin: James Watt', *Camb. Hist. Journal*, XI (1953–5), p. 351; W. H. Chaloner, 'Dr Joseph Priestley, John Wilkinson, and the French Revolution', *Trans. Royal Hist. Soc.* 5th Series, VIII (1958), p. 25.

Something of this was felt even by Thelwall, when he visited Sheffield in 1796. He rejoiced at the intelligence and political awareness of the Sheffield '*Sanscullotterie*'. 'But it is a body without a head. They have unfortunately no leader.' While several people 'of considerable property and influence ... *think* with them', none had the courage to take their part:

If any three or four persons of weight and pecuniary consequence in that place, would but take these honest, intelligent manufacturers and their cause fairly and publicly by the hand (as persons of that description ... have done in Norwich), in Sheffield, as in Norwich, the petty tyranny of provincial persecution would presently be at an end ...[1]

Nor was this a symptom of Jacobin apostasy on Thelwall's part. He was faced, in 1796, with a real dilemma: on the one hand, the reformist paternalism which when he met it in practice – as in the case of Gurney at Norwich – he disliked; on the other hand, the exposure of plebeian reformers to victimization on a scale which was destroying the movement or driving it underground.

Moreover, the movement badly needed the intellectual resources of those men of the educated middle class, some of whom had been most afflicted by revolutionary disenchantment. It had early lost, through forcible and voluntary emigration, two of its most able propagandists and organizers, Gerrald and Cooper.[2] It could not survive for ever on *Rights of Man*, and the imitation of French forms, or in Roman togas and Saxon smocks. But at its peak, in 1795, the movement was scarcely of four years' growth; its thinking had to be done in the press of organization, amongst alarms and accusations of treason, with supporters defaulting and with Robespierre punctuating the florid periods of their Addresses with the more taciturn guillotine. Thelwall's lectures were thought out

1. Thelwall, *The Rights of Nature*, Letter I, p. 20.

2. Two of the most cogent pamphlets on their side were Gerrald's, *A Convention the Only Means of Saving Us from Ruin* (1793) and T. Cooper, *Reply to Mr Burke's Invective against Mr Cooper and Mr Watt* (Manchester, 1792). For Cooper's emigration to America, see D. Malone, *The Public Life of Thomas Cooper* (New Haven, 1926).

on his feet, to an audience which always included one of His Majesty's informers. His best work (significantly) was not done until the comparative calm of 1796 when the movement began to fall apart. It is scarcely surprising that the English Jacobins were guilty of immaturities and suffered through their inexperience, and that many of their speakers made themselves look foolish by their exaggerated postures.

So far, it would seem, it is a record of frustration and of failure. But the experience had another, and an altogether more positive side. Not one, but many, traditions find their origin in these years. There is the intellectual tradition of Godwin and of Mary Wollstonecraft, which Shelley was to reaffirm. There is the tradition of Deism and of free-thought; the Wars had scarcely ended before Richard Carlile commenced the re-publication of all of Paine's works. There is the tradition of the advanced Unitarians and 'free-thinking Christians', carried forward by such men as Benjamin Flower and William Frend, to the *Monthly Depository* of W. J. Fox.[1] There is the tradition of Place, and of the sober, constitutionally minded tradesmen and artisans (some of whom, like Hardy, Galloway and Place himself later prospered as small or large employers) who re-emerged in the Westminster Election of 1807, in support of Tooke's disciple Sir Francis Burdett, and who from that time remained in active association.

These traditions are embodied not only in ideas but in persons. While some Jacobins retired and others – John Gales, Thomas Cooper, 'Citizen Lee', John Binns, Daniel Isaac Eaton and many others – emigrated to America,[2] others watched for every opportunity to re-open the propaganda. John Gale Jones and John Frost were members of London debating clubs during the Wars, where they influenced a younger Radical generation; and Jones remained prominent in London Radical

1. See F. E. Mineka, *The Dissidence of Dissent* (1944).
2. Eaton was the only one of these who returned. See below, p. 662. There was also a small colony of English Jacobin *émigrés* in Paris, including Sampson Perry, Ashley, Goldsmith, Dr Maxwell, and John Stones, who published the anti-Pitt *Argus*, and most of whom became profoundly disillusioned with Bonapartism. See S. Perry, *Argus* (1796), p. 257; J. G. Alger, *Englishmen in the French Revolution* (1889).

circles until the 1820s.[1] And in many provincial centres the
same continuity can be witnessed. Few centres can boast a
record as long as that of George Bown of Leicester, who was
Secretary of its Constitutional Society in 1792, was arrested in
1794, and who was still writing as an advocate of 'physical
force' Chartism in 1848.[2] But in many towns like-minded
tradesmen and artisans, opponents of the Wars, continued to
meet together. The great engraver, Thomas Bewick, recalls the
'set of staunch advocates for the liberties of mankind', who
met in Newcastle at the 'Blue Bell', the 'Unicorn', and the News
Room. These were 'men of sense and consequence', 'tradesmen
of the genteel sort', 'bankers' clerks, artisans, and agents'.
Bewick's particular associates included a shoemaker, a builder,
a founder, a white-smith, an editor, a fencing-master, a radical
gentleman, and several actors. All were united in condemnation of the war and of its social consequences:

The shipping interest wallowed in riches; the gentry whirled about
in aristocratic pomposity, they forgot what their demeanour and
good, kind, behaviour used to be to those in inferior stations of life;
and seemed now far too often to look upon them like dirt. The
character of the farmers was also changed. They acted the gentleman very awkwardly, and could not, in these times, drink anything
but wine. ... When these upstart gentlemen left the market, they
were ready to ride over all they met ... on the way; but this was as
nothing compared to the pride and folly which took possession of
their empty or fume-charged heads, when they got dressed in
scarlet ... and were called 'yeomanry cavalry'. .... Not so with the
industrious labourer. His privations were great ...[3]

If many among the small masters, clerks, and tradesmen felt
hostility to the gentry, capitalists, and large farmers, and
sympathy with the 'industrious labourer' (and this is an extremely important feature of Radical consciousness for fifty

1. Among those influenced by Gale Jones and John Frost was Frost's
namesake, the former Mayor of Newport, who led the Chartist insurrection of 1839 in Wales: see D. Williams, *John Frost* (Cardiff, 1939), pp.
13–14.

2. A. T. Patterson, op. cit., pp. 70, 74; J. F. C. Harrison, 'Chartism in
Leicester', *Chartist Studies*, ed. A. Briggs (1959), p. 132; G. Bown,
Physical Force (Leicester, 1848).

3. T. Bewick. *A. Memoir*, ed. M. Weekley (Cresset, 1961), pp. 146–8,
153.

years after 1795), nevertheless they were, like the Leeds tradesmen, intimidated by 'Aristocratic influence'. Even Bewick, with
his puritanical zeal, was careful during the Wars to associate
only with those who might 'set the example of propriety of
conduct to those of a more violent turn of mind', and whose
indignation with 'the political enormities of the times' was
kept 'within bounds'. Hence, the plebeian Jacobins were isolated and driven back upon themselves, and forced to discover
means of independent quasi-legal or underground organization.
(In Bewick's Newcastle, scores of tavern friendly societies were
formed during the Wars, many of which were undoubtedly
covers for trade union activity, in which former Jacobins
contributed to the 'warm debate and violent language' of club
meetings.)[1] Isolated from other classes, radical mechanics,
artisans and labourers had perforce to nourish traditions and
forms of organization of their own. So that, while the years
1791–5 provided the democratic impulse, it was in the repression years that we can speak of a distinct 'working-class consciousness' maturing.

Even in the darkest war years the democratic impulse can
still be felt at work beneath the surface. It contributed an
affirmation of rights, a glimpse of a plebeian millennium,
which was never extinguished. The Combination Acts
(1799–1800) served only to bring illegal Jacobin and trade
union strands closer together.[2] Even beneath the fever of the
'invasion' years, new ideas and new forms of organization
continue to ferment. There is a radical alteration in the sub-
political attitudes of the people to which the experiences of
tens of thousands of unwilling soldiers contributed. By 1811
we can witness the simultaneous emergence of a new popular
Radicalism and of a newly-militant trade unionism. In part,
this was the product of new experiences, in part it was the
inevitable response to the years of reaction: '*I have not forgot
the English Reign of Terror*; there you have the source of my
political tendencies,' wrote Ebenezer Elliott, the 'Corn-Law
Rhymer', whose father was a Jacobin clerk at an ironworks
near Sheffield, with whom 'the yeomanry used to amuse them-'

1. See below, pp. 458–61.   2. See below, pp. 546–8.

selves periodically by backing their horses through his windows'.[1]

The history of reform agitation between 1792 and 1796 was (in general terms) the story of the simultaneous default of the middle-class reformers and the rapid 'leftwards' movement of the plebeian Radicals. The experience marked the popular consciousness for fifty years, and throughout this time the dynamic of Radicalism came not from the middle class but from the artisans and labourers. The men of the popular societies are rightly designated Jacobins. Several of their leaders, including Thelwall, were willing to accept the term:

> I adopt the term *Jacobinism* without hesitation − 1. Because it is fixed upon us, as a stigma, by our enemies. . . . 2. Because, though I abhor the sanguinary ferocity of the late Jacobins in France, yet their principles . . . are the most consonant with my ideas of reason, and the nature of man, of any that I have met with . . . I use the term Jacobinism simply to indicate *a large and comprehensive system of reform, not professing to be built upon the authorities and principles of the Gothic customary*.[2]

The particular quality of their Jacobinism is to be felt in their emphasis on *égalité*. 'Equality' is too negative a term (in its usual English connotations) for the sharp, positive doctrines as to the erasure of all distinctions of status which informed their proceedings. The working-class movement of later years was to continue and enrich the traditions of fraternity and liberty. But the very existence of its organizations, and the protection of its funds, required the fostering of a cadre of experienced officials, as well as a certain deference or exaggerated loyalty towards its leadership, which proved to be a source of bureaucratic forms and controls. The English Jacobins of the 1790s initiated quite different traditions. There was a piquancy in *égalité*, in the outrage to eighteenth-century forms, as when the Jacobin Lord Daer sat with artisans and weavers as plain 'Citizen Daer'. But the belief that 'a man's a man, for a' that' found expression in other ways which may

1. Cited in *Poor Man's Guardian*, 17 November 1832, which adds (of the memory of the Terror) 'this holds in thousands of instances besides that of Mr Elliott'.

2. J. Thelwall, *Rights of Nature* (1796), II, p. 32.

still be recalled in criticism of the practices of our own day. *Every* citizen on a committee was expected to perform some part, the chairmanship of committees was often taken in rotation, the pretensions of leaders were watched, proceedings were based on the deliberate belief that every man was capable of reason and of a growth in his abilities, and that deference and distinctions of status were an offence to human dignity. These Jacobin strengths, which contributed much to Chartism, declined in the movement of the late nineteenth century, when the new Socialism shifted emphasis from political to economic rights. The strength of distinctions of class and status in twentieth-century England is in part a consequence of the lack, in the twentieth-century labour movement, of Jacobin virtues.

It is unnecessary to stress the evident importance of other aspects of the Jacobin tradition; the tradition of self-education and of the rational criticism of political and religious institutions; the tradition of conscious republicanism; above all, the tradition of internationalism. It is extraordinary that so brief an agitation should have diffused its ideas into so many corners of Britain.[1] Perhaps the consequence of English Jacobinism which was most profound, although least easy to define, was the breaking-down of taboos upon agitation among 'members unlimited'. Wherever Jacobin ideas persisted, and wherever hidden copies of *Rights of Man* were cherished, men were no longer disposed to wait upon the example of a Wilkes or a Wyvill before they commenced a democratic agitation. Throughout the war years there were Thomas Hardys in every town and in many villages throughout England, with a kist or shelf full of Radical books, biding their time, putting in a word at the tavern, the chapel, the smithy, the shoemaker's shop, waiting for the movement to revive. And the movement for which they waited did not belong to gentlemen, manufacturers, or rate-payers; it was their own.

As late as 1849 a shrewd Yorkshire satirist published a sketch of such a 'Village Politician' which has the feel of authenticity. He is, typically, a cobbler, an old man and the sage of his industrial village:

1. W. A. L. Seaman, op. cit., p. 20 notes evidence of societies in over 100 places in England and Scotland.

He has a library that he rather prides himself upon. It is a strange collection. ... There is the 'Pearl of Great Price' and 'Cobbett's Twopenny Trash'. The 'Pilgrim's Progress' ... and 'The Go-a-head Journal', 'The Wrongs of Labour' and 'The Rights of Man'. 'The History of the French Revolution' and Bunyan's 'Holy War' ... 'The Age of Reason' and a superannuated Bible.

He is 'of course a great admirer of Bonaparte'. 'It warms his old heart like a quart of mulled ale, when he hears of a success-ful revolution, – a throne tumbled, kings flying, and princes scattered abroad. He thinks the dreams of his youth are about their fulfilment.' He indulges in grandiloquent metaphors about the 'sun of freedom' rising above 'the horizontal atmosphere', and professes knowledge of Russian affairs.

He recollects the day when he durst scarcely walk the streets. He can tell how he was hooted, pelted and spurned ... and people told him he might be thankful if he was not burned alive some night, along with an effigy of Tom Paine. ... He makes younkers stare when he tells them about a time when there was no Habeas Corpus ... and the Attorney General went up and down the country like a raging lion. ... He tells of a man who said ... that the king was born without shirt, and was in consequence transported for sedition ...[1]

The Revolution of which he had dreamed never took place, but there was a revolution of a sort, none the less. It was the loyalists, James Watt the younger complained in 1793, who – by stirring up the mob against reformers – had 'tampered' with the 'lower order of people':

They little think how dangerous it is to let the people know their power and that the day will come when they shall curse the senseless cry of Church & King, & feel their own weapons turned upon themselves.[2]

After the near-famine year of 1795, the change can be sensed in a score of places. In Nottingham, where Jacobins had been ducked in 1794, they were strong enough to meet and defeat their opponents in open combat in the election of 1796.[3] 'At

1. E. Sloane, *Essays, Tales and Sketches* (1849), pp. 61 ff.
2. See E. Robinson, op. cit., p. 355.
3. J. F. Sutton, *Date-book of Nottingham* (1880), p. 212.

most of the entrances into this town,' wrote a scandalized loyalist in 1798, 'a post is set up with a board fixed upon it, on which is written "All Vagrants will be apprehended and punished as the Law directs." ' Now, over the word 'Vagrants' the word 'Tyrants' had been pasted, and no one stirred to take it down.[1] 'Long have we been endeavouring to find ourselves men,' declared the mutineers of the fleet in 1797: 'We now find ourselves so. We will be treated as such.'[2]

In 1812, looking round him in dismay at the power of Scottish trade unionism and of Luddism in England, Scott wrote to Southey: 'The country is mined below our feet.' It was Pitt who had driven the 'miners' underground. Men like our 'Village Politician' were scarcely to be found in the villages of 1789. Jacobin ideas driven into weaving villages, the shops of the Nottingham framework knitters and the Yorkshire croppers, the Lancashire cotton-mills, were propagated in every phase of rising prices and of hardship. It was not Pitt but John Thelwall who had the last word. 'A sort of Socratic spirit will necessarily grow up, wherever large bodies of men assemble':

... Monopoly, and the hideous accumulation of capital in a few hands ... carry in their own enormity, the seeds of cure ... Whatever presses men together ... though it may generate some vices, is favourable to the diffusion of knowledge, and ultimately promotive of human liberty. Hence every large workshop and manufactory is a sort of political society, which no act of parliament can silence, and no magistrate disperse.[3]

1. J. W. Cartwright to Duke of Portland, 19 June 1798, H.O. 42.43.
2. C. Gill, *The Naval Mutinies of 1797*, p. 300.
3. Thelwall, *Rights of Nature*, I. pp. 21, 24.

Part Two

THE CURSE OF ADAM

'In the sweat of thy face shalt thou eat bread, till thou
return unto the ground; for out of it wast thou taken:
for dust thou art, and unto dust shalt thou return.'

GENESIS, III, 19

[6]

Exploitation

JOHN THELWALL was not alone in seeing in every 'manufactory' a potential centre of political rebellion. An aristocratic
traveller who visited the Yorkshire Dales in 1792 was alarmed
to find a new cotton-mill in the 'pastoral vale' of Aysgarth –
'why, here now is a great flaring mill, whose back stream has
drawn off half the water of the falls above the bridge':

> With the bell ringing, and the clamour of the mill, all the vale is
> disturb'd; treason and levelling systems are the discourse; and
> rebellion may be near at hand.

The mill appeared as symbol of social energies which were
destroying the very 'course of Nature'. It embodied a double
threat to the settled order. First, from the owners of industrial
wealth, those upstarts who enjoyed an unfair advantage over
the landowners whose income was tied to their rent-roll:

> If men thus start into riches; or if riches from trade are too easily
> procured, woe to us men of middling income, and settled revenue;
> and woe it has been to all the Nappa Halls, and the Yeomanry of
> the land.

Second, from the industrial working population, which our
traveller regarded with an alliterative hostility which betrays
a response not far removed from that of the white racialist
towards the coloured population today:

> The people, indeed, are employ'd; but they are all abandon'd to
> vice from the throng. ... At the times when people work not in the
> mill, they issue out to poaching, profligacy and plunder ...[1]

The equation between the cotton-mill and the new industrial
society, and the correspondence between new forms of productive and of social relationship, was a commonplace among

1. *The Torrington Diaries*, ed. C. B. Andrews (1936), III, pp. 81–2.

observers in the years between 1790 and 1850. Karl Marx was only expressing this with unusual vigour when he declared: 'The hand-mill gives you society with the feudal lord: the steam-mill, society with the industrial capitalist.' And it was not only the mill-owner but also the working population brought into being within and around the mills which seemed to contemporaries to be 'new'. 'The instant we get near the borders of the manufacturing parts of Lancashire', a rural magistrate wrote in 1808, 'we meet a fresh race of beings, both in point of manners, employments and subordination ...'; while Robert Owen, in 1815, declared that 'the general diffusion of manufactures throughout a country generates a new character in its inhabitants ... an essential change in the general character of the mass of the people'.

Observers in the 1830s and 1840s were still exclaiming at the novelty of the 'factory system'. Peter Gaskell, in 1833, spoke of the manufacturing population as 'but a Hercules in the cradle'; it was 'only since the introduction of steam as a power that they have acquired their paramount importance'. The steam-engine had 'drawn together the population into dense masses' and already Gaskell saw in working-class organizations an ' "imperium in imperio" of the most obnoxious description'.[1] Ten years later Cooke Taylor was writing in similar terms:

The steam-engine had no precedent, the spinning-jenny is without ancestry, the mule and the power-loom entered on no prepared heritage: they sprang into sudden existence like Minerva from the brain of Jupiter.

But it was the human consequence of these 'novelties' which caused this observer most disquiet:

As a stranger passes through the masses of human beings which have accumulated round the mills and print works ... he cannot contemplate these 'crowded hives' without feelings of anxiety and apprehension almost amounting to dismay. The population, like the system to which it belongs, is NEW; but it is hourly increasing

1. P. Gaskell, *The Manufacturing Population of England* (1833), p. 6; Asa Briggs, 'The Language of "Class" in Early Nineteenth-century England', in *Essays in Labour History*, ed. Briggs and Saville (1960), p. 63.

in breadth and strength. It is an aggregate of masses, our conceptions of which clothe themselves in terms that express something portentous and fearful ... as of the slow rising and gradual swelling of an ocean which must, at some future and no distant time, bear all the elements of society aloft upon its bosom, and float them Heaven knows whither. There are mighty energies slumbering in these masses. ... The manufacturing population is not new in its formation alone: it is new in its habits of thought and action, which have been formed by the circumstances of its condition, with little instruction, and less guidance, from external sources ...[1]

For Engels, describing the *Condition of the Working Class in England in 1844* it seemed that 'the first proletarians were connected with manufacture, were engendered by it ... the factory hands, eldest children of the industrial revolution, have from the beginning to the present day formed the nucleus of the Labour Movement'.

However different their judgements of value, conservative, radical, and socialist observers suggested the same equation: steam power and the cotton-mill=new working class. The physical instruments of production were seen as giving rise in a direct and more-or-less compulsive way to new social relationships, institutions, and cultural modes. At the same time the history of popular agitation during the period 1811–50 appears to confirm this picture. It is as if the English nation entered a crucible in the 1790s and emerged after the Wars in a different form. Between 1811 and 1813, the Luddite crisis; in 1817 the Pentridge Rising; in 1819, Peterloo; throughout the next decade the proliferation of trade union activity, Owenite propaganda, Radical journalism, the Ten Hours Movement, the revolutionary crisis of 1831–2; and, beyond that, the multitude of movements which made up Chartism. It is, perhaps, the scale and intensity of this multiform popular agitation which has, more than anything else, given rise (among contemporary observers and historians alike) to the sense of some catastrophic change.

Almost every radical phenomenon of the 1790s can be found reproduced tenfold after 1815. The handful of Jacobin sheets

1. W. Cooke Taylor, *Notes of a Tour in the Manufacturing Districts of Lancashire* (1842), pp. 4–6.

gave rise to a score of ultra-Radical and Owenite periodicals. Where Daniel Eaton served imprisonment for publishing Paine, Richard Carlile and his shopmen served a total of more than 200 years imprisonment for similar crimes. Where Corresponding Societies maintained a precarious existence in a score of towns, the post-war Hampden Clubs or political unions struck root in small industrial villages. And when this popular agitation is recalled alongside the dramatic pace of change in the cotton industry, it is natural to assume a direct causal relationship. The cotton-mill is seen as the agent not only of industrial but also of social revolution, producing not only more goods but also the 'Labour Movement' itself. The Industrial Revolution, which commenced as a description, is now invoked as an explanation.

From the time of Arkwright through to the Plug Riots and beyond, it is the image of the 'dark, Satanic mill' which dominates our visual reconstruction of the Industrial Revolution. In part, perhaps, because it is a dramatic visual image – the barrack-like buildings, the great mill chimneys, the factory children, the clogs and shawls, the dwellings clustering around the mills as if spawned by them. (It is an image which forces one to think first of the industry, and only secondly of the people connected to it or serving it.) In part, because the cotton-mill and the new mill-town – from the swiftness of its growth, ingenuity of its techniques, and the novelty or harshness of its discipline – seemed to contemporaries to be dramatic and portentous: a more satisfactory symbol for debate on the 'condition-of-England' question than those anonymous or sprawling manufacturing *districts* which figure even more often in the Home Office 'disturbance books'. And from this both a literary and an historical tradition is derived. Nearly all the classic accounts by contemporaries of conditions in the Industrial Revolution are based on the cotton industry – and, in the main, on Lancashire: Owen, Gaskell, Ure, Fielden, Cooke Taylor, Engels, to mention a few. Novels such as *Michael Armstrong* or *Mary Barton* or *Hard Times* perpetuate the tradition. And the emphasis is markedly found in the subsequent writing of economic and social history.

But many difficulties remain. Cotton was certainly the pacemaking industry of the Industrial Revolution,[1] and the cotton-mill was the pre-eminent model for the factory-system. Yet we should not assume any automatic, or over-direct, correspondence between the dynamic of economic growth and the dynamic of social or cultural life. For half a century after the 'breakthrough' of the cotton-mill (around 1780) the mill workers remained as a minority of the adult labour force in the cotton industry itself. In the early 1830s the cotton hand-loom weavers alone still outnumbered all the men and women in spinning and weaving mills of cotton, wool, and silk combined.[2] Still, in 1830, the adult male cotton-spinner was no more typical of that elusive figure, the 'average working man', than is the Coventry motor-worker of the 1960s.

The point is of importance, because too much emphasis upon the newness of the cotton-mills can lead to an underestimation of the continuity of political and cultural traditions in the making of working-class communities. The factory hands, so far from being the 'eldest children of the industrial revolution', were late arrivals. Many of their ideas and forms of organization were anticipated by domestic workers, such as the woollen workers of Norwich and the West Country, or the small-ware weavers of Manchester. And it is questionable whether factory hands – except in the cotton districts – 'formed the nucleus of the Labour Movement' at any time before the late 1840s (and, in some northern and Midland towns, the years 1832–4, leading up to the great lock-outs). Jacobinism, as we have seen, struck root most deeply among artisans. Luddism was the work of skilled men in small workshops. From 1817 onwards to Chartism, the outworkers in the north and the Midlands were as prominent in every radical agitation as the factory hands. And in many towns the actual nucleus from which the labour movement derived ideas, organization, and leadership, was made up of such men as shoemakers, weavers, saddlers and

1. For an admirable restatement of the reasons for the primacy of the cotton industry in the Industrial Revolution, see E. J. Hobsbawm, *The Age of Revolution* (1962), ch. 2.

2. Estimates for U.K., 1833. Total adult labour force in all textile mills, 191,671. Number of cotton hand-loom weavers, 213,000. See below, p. 327.

harnessmakers, booksellers, printers, building workers, small tradesmen, and the like. The vast area of Radical London between 1815 and 1850 drew its strength from no major heavy industries (shipbuilding was tending to decline, and the engineers only made their impact later in the century) but from the host of smaller trades and occupations.[1]

Such diversity of experiences has led some writers to question both the notions of an 'industrial revolution' and of a 'working class'. The first discussion need not detain us here.[2] The term is serviceable enough in its usual connotations. For the second, many writers prefer the term working *classes*, which emphasizes the great disparity in status, acquisitions, skills, conditions, within the portmanteau phrase. And in this they echo the complaints of Francis Place:

> If the character and conduct of the working-people are to be taken from reviews, magazines, pamphlets, newspapers, reports of the two Houses of Parliament and the Factory Commissioners, we shall find them all jumbled together as the 'lower orders', the most skilled and the most prudent workman, with the most ignorant and imprudent labourers and paupers, though the difference is great indeed, and indeed in many cases will scarce admit of comparison.[3]

Place is, of course, right: the Sunderland sailor, the Irish navvy, the Jewish costermonger, the inmate of an East Anglian village workhouse, the compositor on *The Times* – all might be seen by their 'betters' as belonging to the 'lower classes' while they themselves might scarcely understand each others' dialect.

Nevertheless, when every caution has been made, the outstanding fact of the period between 1790 and 1830 is the formation of 'the working class'. This is revealed, first, in the growth of class-consciousness: the consciousness of an identity of interests as between all these diverse groups of working people and as against the interests of other classes. And, second, in the growth of corresponding forms of political and indus-

1. Cf. Hobsbawm, op. cit., ch. 2.

2. There is a summary of this controversy in E. E. Lampard, *Industrial Revolution* (American Historical Association, 1957). See also Hobsbawm, op. cit., ch. 2.

3. Cit. M. D. George, *London Life in the Eighteenth Century* (1930), p 210.

trial organization. By 1832 there were strongly based and self-conscious working-class institutions – trade unions, friendly societies, educational and religious movements, political organizations, periodicals – working-class intellectual traditions, working-class community-patterns, and a working-class structure of feeling.

The making of the working class is a fact of political and cultural, as much as of economic, history. It was not the spontaneous generation of the factory system. Nor should we think of an external force – the 'industrial revolution' – working upon some nondescript undifferentiated raw material of humanity, and turning it out at the other end as a 'fresh race of beings'. The changing productive relations and working conditions of the Industrial Revolution were imposed, not upon raw material, but upon the free-born Englishman – and the free-born Englishman as Paine had left him or as the Methodists had moulded him. The factory hand or stockinger was also the inheritor of Bunyan, of remembered village rights, of notions of equality before the law, of craft traditions. He was the object of massive religious indoctrination and the creator of political traditions. The working class made itself as much as it was made.

To see the working class in this way is to defend a 'classical' view of the period against the prevalent mood of contemporary schools of economic history and sociology. For the territory of the Industrial Revolution, which was first staked out and surveyed by Marx, Arnold Toynbee, the Webbs and the Hammonds, now resembles an academic battlefield. At point after point, the familiar 'catastrophic' view of the period has been disputed. Where it was customary to see the period as one of economic disequilibrium, intense misery and exploitation, political repression and heroic popular agitation, attention is now directed to the rate of economic growth (and the difficulties of 'take-off' into self-sustaining technological reproduction). The enclosure movement is now noted, less for its harshness in displacing the village poor, than for its success in feeding a rapidly growing population. The hardships of the period are seen as being due to the dislocations consequent upon the Wars, faulty communications, immature banking and exchange,

uncertain markets, and the trade-cycle, rather than to exploitation or cut-throat competition. Popular unrest is seen as
consequent upon the unavoidable coincidence of high wheat
prices and trade depressions, and explicable in terms of an
elementary 'social tension' chart derived from these data.[1] In
general, it is suggested that the position of the industrial worker
in 1840 was better in most ways than that of the domestic
worker of 1790. The Industrial Revolution was an age, not of
catastrophe or acute class-conflict and class oppression, but
of improvement.[2]

The classical catastrophic orthodoxy has been replaced by a
new anti-catastrophic orthodoxy, which is most clearly distinguished by its empirical caution and, among its most notable
exponents (Sir John Clapham, Dr Dorothy George, Professor
Ashton) by an astringent criticism of the looseness of certain
writers of the older school. The studies of the new orthodoxy
have enriched historical scholarship, and have qualified and
revised in important respects the work of the classical school.
But as the new orthodoxy is now, in its turn, growing old and
entrenched in most of the academic centres, so it becomes
open to challenge in its turn. And the successors of the great
empiricists too often exhibit a moral complacency, a narrowness of reference, and an insufficient familiarity with the actual
movements of the working people of the time. They are more
aware of the orthodox empiricist postures than of the changes
in social relationship and in cultural modes which the Industrial Revolution entailed. What has been lost is a sense of the
whole process – the whole political and social context of the
period. What arose as valuable qualifications have passed by
imperceptible stages to new generalizations (which the evidence
can rarely sustain) and from generalizations to a ruling
attitude.

1. See W. W. Rostow, *British Economy in the Nineteenth Century*
(1948), esp. pp. 122–5.
2. Some of the views outlined here are to be found, implicitly or explicitly, in T. S. Ashton, *Industrial Revolution* (1948) and A. Radford,
The Economic History of England (2nd edn 1960). A sociological variant
is developed by N. J. Smelser, *Social Change in the Industrial Revolution* (1959), and a knockabout popularization is in John Vaizey, *Success
Story* (W.E.A., n.d.).

The empiricist orthodoxy is often defined in terms of a running critique of the work of J. L. and Barbara Hammond. It is true that the Hammonds showed themselves too willing to moralize history, and to arrange their materials too much in terms of 'outraged emotion'.[1] There are many points at which their work has been faulted or qualified in the light of subsequent research, and we intend to propose others. But a defence of the Hammonds need not only be rested upon the fact that their volumes on the labourers with their copious quotation and wide reference, will long remain among the most important source-books for this period. We can also say that they displayed throughout their narrative an understanding of the political context within which the Industrial Revolution took place. To the student examining the ledgers of one cotton-mill, the Napoleonic Wars appear only as an abnormal influence affecting foreign markets and fluctuating demand. The Hammonds could never have forgotten for one moment that it was also a war against Jacobinism. 'The history of England at the time discussed in these pages reads like a history of civil war.' This is the opening of the introductory chapter of *The Skilled Labourer*. And in the conclusion to *The Town Labourer*, among other comments of indifferent value, there is an insight which throws the whole period into sudden relief:

At the time when half Europe was intoxicated and the other half terrified by the new magic of the word citizen, the English nation was in the hands of men who regarded the idea of citizenship as a challenge to their religion and their civilization; who deliberately sought to make the inequalities of life the basis of the state, and to emphasize and perpetuate the position of the workpeople as a subject class. Hence it happened that the French Revolution has divided the people of France less than the Industrial Revolution has divided the people of England ...

'Hence it happened ...' The judgement may be questioned, And yet it is in this insight — that the revolution which did *not* happen in England was fully as devastating, and in some features more divisive, than that which did happen in France — that we find a clue to the truly catastrophic nature of the

1. See E. E. Lampard, op. cit., p. 7.

period. Throughout this time there are three, and not two, great influences simultaneously at work. There is the tremendous increase in population (in Great Britain, from 10·5 millions in 1801 to 18·1 millions in 1841, with the greatest rate of increase between 1811–21). There is the Industrial Revolution, in its technological aspects. And there is the political *counter*-revolution, from 1792–1832.

In the end, it is the political context as much as the steam-engine, which had most influence upon the shaping consciousness and institutions of the working class. The forces making for political reform in the late eighteenth century – Wilkes, the city merchants, the Middlesex small gentry, the 'mob' – or Wyvill, and the small gentry and yeomen, clothiers, cutlers, and tradesmen – were on the eve of gaining at least some piecemeal victories in the 1790s: Pitt had been cast for the rôle of reforming Prime Minister. Had events taken their 'natural' course we might expect there to have been some show-down long before 1832, between the oligarchy of land and commerce and the manufacturers and petty gentry, with working people in the tail of the middle-class agitation. And even in 1792, when manufacturers and professional men were prominent in the reform movement, this was still the balance of forces. But, after the success of *Rights of Man*, the radicalization and terror of the French Revolution, and the onset of Pitt's repression, it was the plebeian Corresponding Society which alone stood up against the counter-revolutionary wars. And these plebeian groups, small as they were in 1796, did nevertheless make up an 'underground' tradition which ran through to the end of the Wars. Alarmed at the French example, and in the patriotic fervour of war, the aristocracy and the manufacturers made common cause. The English *ancien régime* received a new lease of life, not only in national affairs, but also in the perpetuation of the antique corporations which misgoverned the swelling industrial towns. In return, the manufacturers received important concessions: and notably the abrogation or repeal of 'paternalist' legislation covering apprenticeship, wage-regulation, or conditions in industry. The aristocracy were interested in repressing the Jacobin 'conspiracies' of the people, the manufacturers were interested in defeating their 'conspiracies' to increase wages: the Combination Acts served both purposes.

Thus working people were forced into political and social *apartheid* during the Wars (which, incidentally, they also had to fight). It is true that this was not altogether new. What was new was that it was coincident with a French Revolution: with growing self-consciousness and wider aspirations (for the 'liberty tree' had been planted from the Thames to the Tyne): with a rise in population, in which the sheer sense of numbers, in London and in the industrial districts, became more impressive from year to year (and as numbers grew, so deference to master, magistrate, or parson was likely to lessen): and with more intensive or more transparent forms of economic exploitation. More intensive in agriculture and in the old domestic industries: more transparent in the new factories and perhaps in mining. In agriculture the years between 1760 and 1820 are the years of wholesale enclosure, in which, in village after village, common rights are lost, and the landless and – in the south – pauperized labourer is left to support the tenant-farmer, the landowner, and the tithes of the Church. In the domestic industries, from 1800 onwards, the tendency is widespread for small masters to give way to larger employers (whether manufacturers or middlemen) and for the majority of weavers, stockingers, or nail-makers to become wage-earning outworkers with more or less precarious employment. In the mills and in many mining areas these are the years of the employment of children (and of women underground); and the large-scale enterprise, the factory-system with its new discipline, the mill communities – where the manufacturer not only made riches out of the labour of the 'hands' but could be *seen* to make riches in one generation – all contributed to the transparency of the process of exploitation and to the social and cultural cohesion of the exploited.

We can now see something of the truly catastrophic nature of the Industrial Revolution; as well as some of the reasons why the English working class took form in these years. The people were subjected simultaneously to an intensification of two intolerable forms of relationship: those of economic exploitation and of political oppression. Relations between employer and labourer were becoming both harsher and less personal; and while it is true that this increased the potential freedom of the worker, since the hired farm servant or the journeyman in domestic industry was (in Toynbee's words) 'halted half-way between the position of the serf and the position of the citizen', this 'freedom' meant that he felt his *un*freedom more. But at each point where he sought to resist exploitation, he was met by the forces of employer or State, and commonly of both.

For most working people the crucial experience of the Industrial Revolution was felt in terms of changes in the nature and intensity of exploitation. Nor is this some anachronistic notion, imposed upon the evidence. We may describe some parts of the exploitive process as they appeared to one remarkable cotton operative in 1818 – the year in which Marx was born. The account – an Address to the public of strike-bound Manchester by 'A Journeyman Cotton Spinner' – commences by describing the employers and the workers as 'two distinct classes of persons':

First, then, as to the employers: with very few exceptions, they are a set of men who have sprung from the cotton-shop without education or address, except so much as they have acquired by their intercourse with the little world of merchants on the exchange at Manchester; but to counterbalance that deficiency, they give you enough of appearances by an ostentatious display of elegant mansions, equipages, liveries, parks, hunters, hounds, &c. which they take care to shew off to the merchant stranger in the most pompous manner. Indeed their houses are gorgeous palaces, far surpassing in bulk and extent the neat charming retreats you see round London ... but the chaste observer of the beauties of nature and art combined will observe a woeful deficiency of taste. They bring up their families at the most costly schools, determined to give their offspring a double portion of what they were so deficient in themselves. Thus with scarcely a second idea in their heads, they are literally petty monarchs, absolute and despotic, in their own particular districts; and to support all this, their whole time is occupied in contriving how to get the greatest quantity of work turned off with the least expence. ... In short, I will venture to say, without fear of contradiction, that there is a greater distance observed between the master there and the spinner, than there is between the first merchant in London and his lowest servant or the lowest artisan. Indeed there is no comparison. I know it to be a fact, that the greater part of the master spinners are anxious to keep wages low for the purpose of keeping the spinners indigent and spiritless ... as for the purpose of taking the surplus to their own pockets.

The master spinners are a class of men unlike all other master tradesmen in the kingdom. They are ignorant, proud, and tyrannical. What then must be the men or rather beings who are the instruments of such masters? Why, they have been for a series of years, with their wives and their families, patience itself – bondmen and bondwomen to their cruel taskmasters. It is in vain to insult our common understandings with the observation that such men are free; that the law protects the rich and poor alike, and that a spinner can leave his master if he does not like the wages. True; so he can: but where must he go? why to another, to be sure. Well: he goes; he is asked where did you work last: 'did he discharge you?' No; we could not agree about wages. Well I shall not employ you nor anyone who leaves his master in that manner. Why is this? Because there is an abominable *combination existing amongst the masters*, first established at Stockport in 1802, and it has since become so general, as to embrace all the great masters for a circuit of many miles round Manchester, though not the little masters: they are excluded. They are the most obnoxious beings to the great ones that can be imagined. ... When the combination first took place, one of their first articles was, that no master should take on a man until he had first ascertained whether his last master had discharged him. What then is the man to do? If he goes to the parish, that grave of all independence, he is there told – We shall not relieve you; if you dispute with your master, and don't support your family, we will send you to prison; so that the man is bound, by a combination of circumstances, to submit to his master. He cannot travel and get work in any town like a shoe-maker, joiner, or taylor; he is confined to the district.

The workmen in general are an inoffensive, unassuming, set of well-informed men, though how they acquire their information is almost a mystery to me. They are docile and tractable, if not goaded too much; but this is not to be wondered at, when we consider that they are trained to work from six years old, from five in a morning to eight and nine at night. Let one of the advocates for obedience to his master take his stand in an avenue leading to a factory a little before five o'clock in the morning, and observe the squalid appearance of the little infants and their parents taken from their beds at so early an hour in all kinds of weather; let him examine the miserable pittance of food, chiefly composed of water gruel and oatcake broken into it, a little salt, and sometimes coloured with a little milk, together with a few potatoes, and a bit of bacon or fat for dinner; would a London mechanic eat this? There they are (and if late a few minutes, a quarter of a day is stopped in wages) locked up until night in rooms heated above the hottest days we have had this summer, and allowed no time, except three-quarters of an hour at dinner in the whole day: whatever they eat at any other time must be as they are at work. The negro slave in the West Indies, if he works under a scorching sun, has probably a little breeze of air sometimes to fan him: he has a space of ground, and time allowed to cultivate it. The English spinner slave has no enjoyment of the open atmosphere and breezes of heaven. Locked up in factories eight stories high, he has no relaxation till the ponderous engine stops, and then he goes home to get refreshed for the next day; no time for sweet association wtih his family; they are all alike fatigued and exhausted. This is no over-drawn picture: it is literally true. I ask again, would the mechanics in the South of England submit to this?

When the spinning of cotton was in its infancy, and before those terrible machines for superseding the necessity of human labour, called steam engines, came into use, there were a great number of what were then called *little masters*; men who with a small capital, could procure a few machines, and employ a few hands, men and boys (say to twenty or thirty), the produce of whose labour was all taken to Manchester central mart, and put into the hands of brokers. . . . The brokers sold it to the merchants, by which means the master spinner was enabled to stay at home and work and attend to his workmen. The cotton was then always given out in its raw state from the bale to the wives of the spinners at home, when they heat and cleansed it ready for the spinners in the factory. By this they could earn eight, ten, or twelve shillings a week, and cook and attend to their families. But none are thus employed now; for all the cotton is broke up by a machine, turned by the steam engine, called a devil: so that the spinners' wives have no employment, except they go to work in the factory all day at what can be done by children for a few shillings, four or five per week. If a man then could not agree with his master, he left him, and could get employed elsewhere. A few years, however, changed the face of things. Steam engines came into use, to purchase which, and to erect buildings sufficient to contain them and six or seven hundred hands, required a great capital. The engine power produced a more marketable (though not a better) article than the little master could at the same price. The consequence was their ruin in a short time; and the overgrown capitalists triumphed in their fall; for they were the only obstacle that stood between them and the complete controul of the workmen.

Various disputes then originated between the workmen and masters as to the fineness of the work, the workmen being paid according to the number of hanks or yards of thread he produced from a given quantity of cotton, which was always to be proved by the overlooker, whose interest made it imperative on him to lean to his master, and call the material coarser than it was. If the workman would not submit *he must summon his employer before a magistrate*; the whole of the acting magistrates in that district, with the exception of two worthy clergymen, being gentlemen who have sprung from the same source with the master cotton spinners. The employer generally contented himself with sending his overlooker to answer any such summons, thinking it beneath him to meet his servant. The magistrate's decision was generally in favour of the master, though on the statement of the overlooker only. The workman dared not appeal to the sessions on account of the expense. . . .

These evils to the men have arisen from that dreadful monopoly which exists in those districts where wealth and power are got into the hands of the few, who, in the pride of their hearts, think themselves the lords of the universe.[1]

This reading of the facts, in its remarkable cogency, is as much an *ex parte* statement as is the 'political economy' of Lord Brougham. But the 'Journeyman Cotton Spinner' was describing facts of a different order. We need not concern ourselves with the soundness of all his judgements. What his address does is to itemize one after another the grievances felt by working people as to changes in the character of capitalist exploitation: the rise of a master-class without traditional authority or obligations; the growing distance between master and man; the transparency of the exploitation at the source of their new wealth and power; the loss of status and above all of independence for the worker, his reduction to total dependence on the master's instruments of production; the partiality of the law; the disruption of the traditional family economy; the discipline, monotony, hours and conditions of work; loss of

1. *Black Dwarf*, 30 September 1818.

leisure and amenities; the reduction of the man to the status of an 'instrument'.

That working people felt these grievances at all – and felt them passionately – is itself a sufficient fact to merit our attention. And it reminds us forcibly that some of the most bitter conflicts of these years turned on issues which are not encompassed by cost-of-living series. The issues which provoked the most intensity of feeling were very often ones in which such values as traditional customs, 'justice', 'independence', security, or family-economy were at stake, rather than straightforward 'bread-and-butter' issues. The early years of the 1830s are aflame with agitations which turned on issues in which wages were of secondary importance; by the potters, against the Truck System; by the textile workers, for the 10-Hour Bill; by the building workers, for cooperative direct action; by all groups of workers, for the right to join trade unions. The great strike in the north-east coalfield in 1831 turned on security of employment, 'tommy shops', child labour.

The exploitive relationship is more than the sum of grievances and mutual antagonisms. It is a relationship which can be seen to take distinct forms in different historical contexts, forms which are related to corresponding forms of ownership and State power. The classic exploitive relationship of the Industrial Revolution is depersonalized, in the sense that no lingering obligations of mutuality – of paternalism or deference, or of the interests of 'the Trade' – are admitted. There is no whisper of the 'just' price, or of a wage justified in relation to social or moral sanctions, as opposed to the operation of free market forces. Antagonism is accepted as intrinsic to the relations of production. Managerial or supervisory functions demand the repression of all attributes except those which further the expropriation of the maximum surplus value from labour. This is the political economy which Marx anatomized in *Das Kapital*. The worker has become an 'instrument', or an entry among other items of cost.

In fact, no complex industrial enterprise could be conducted according to such a philosophy. The need for industrial peace, for a stable labour-force, and for a body of skilled and experienced workers, necessitated the modification of managerial techniques – and, indeed, the growth of new forms of paternalism – in the cotton-mills by the 1830s. But in the overstocked outwork industries, where there was always a sufficiency of unorganized 'hands' competing for employment, these considerations did not operate. Here, as old customs were eroded, and the old paternalism was set aside, the exploitive relationship emerged supreme.

This does not mean that we can lay all the 'blame' for each hardship of the Industrial Revolution upon 'the masters' or upon *laissez faire*. The process of industrialization must, in any conceivable social context, entail suffering and the destruction of older and valued ways of life. Much recent research has thrown light upon the particular difficulties of the British experience; the hazards of markets; the manifold commercial and financial consequences of the Wars; the post-war deflation; movements in the terms of trade; and the exceptional stresses resulting from the population 'explosion'. Moreover, twentieth-century preoccupations have made us aware of the overarching problems of economic growth. It can be argued that Britain in the Industrial Revolution was encountering the problems of 'take-off'; heavy long-term investment – canals, mills, railways, foundries, mines, utilities – was at the expense of current consumption; the generations of workers between 1790 and 1840 sacrificed some, or all, of their prospects of increased consumption to the future.[1]

These arguments all deserve close attention. For example, studies of the fluctuations in the demand of the South American market, or of the crisis in country banking, may tell us much about the reasons for the growth or retardation of particular industries. The objection to the reigning academic orthodoxy is not to empirical studies *per se*, but to the fragmentation of our comprehension of the full historical process. First, the empiricist segregates certain events from this process and examines them in isolation. Since the conditions which gave rise to these events are assumed, they appear not only as explicable in their own terms but as inevitable. The Wars had to be paid for out of heavy taxation; they accelerated growth in

1. See S. Pollard, 'Investment, Consumption, and the Industrial Revolution', *Econ. Hist. Review*, 2nd Series, XI (1958), pp. 215–26.

this way and retarded it in that. Since this can be shown, it is also implied that this was *necessarily* so. But thousands of Englishmen at the time agreed with Thomas Bewick's condemnation of 'this superlatively wicked war'.[1] The unequal burden of taxation, fund-holders who profited from the National Debt, paper-money – these were not accepted as given data by many contemporaries, but were the staple of intensive Radical agitation.

But there is a second stage, where the empiricist may put these fragmentary studies back together again, constructing a model of the historical process made up from a multiplicity of interlocking inevitabilities, a piecemeal processional. In the scrutiny of credit facilities or of the terms of trade, where each event is explicable and appears also as a self-sufficient cause of other events, we arrive at a *post facto* determinism. The dimension of human agency is lost, and the context of class relations is forgotten.

It is perfectly true that what the empiricist points to was there. The Orders in Council had in 1811 brought certain trades almost to a standstill; rising timber prices after the Wars inflated the costs of building; a passing change of fashion (lace for ribbon) might silence the looms of Coventry; the power-loom competed with the hand-loom. But even these open-faced facts, with their frank credentials, deserve to be questioned. Whose Council, why the Orders? Who profited most from corners in scarce timber? Why should looms remain idle when tens of thousands of country girls fancied ribbons but could not afford to buy. By what social alchemy did inventions for saving labour become engines of immiseration? The raw fact – a bad harvest – may seem to be beyond human election. But the way that fact worked its way out was in terms of a particular complex of human relationship: law, ownership, power. When we encounter some sonorous phrase such as 'the strong ebb and flow of the trade cycle' we must be put on our guard. For behind this trade cycle there is a structure of social relations, fostering some sorts of expropriation (rent, interest, and profit) and outlawing others (theft, feudal dues), legitimizing some types of conflict (competition, armed warfare) and inhibit-

1. T. Bewick, *Memoir* (1961 edn), p. 151.

ing others (trade unionism, bread riots, popular political organization) – a structure which may appear, in the eyes of the future, to be both barbarous and ephemeral.

It might be unnecessary to raise these large questions, since the historian cannot always be questioning the credentials of the society which he studies. But all these questions were, in fact, raised by contemporaries: not only by men of the upper classes (Shelley, Cobbett, Owen, Peacock, Thompson, Hodgskin, Carlyle) but by thousands of articulate working men. Not the political institutions alone, but the social and economic structure of industrial capitalism, were brought into question by their spokesmen. To the facts of orthodox political economy they opposed their own facts and their own arithmetic. Thus as early as 1817 the Leicester framework knitters put forward, in a series of resolutions, an under-consumption theory of capitalist crisis:

That in proportion as the Reduction of Wages makes the great Body of the People poor and wretched, in the same proportion must the consumption of our manufacturers be lessened.

That if liberal Wages were given to the Mechanics in general throughout the Country, the Home Consumption of our Manufactures would be immediately more than doubled, and consequently every hand would soon find full employment.

That to Reduce the Wage of the Mechanic in this Country so low that he cannot live by his labour, in order to undersell Foreign Manufacturers in a Foreign Market, is to gain one customer abroad, and lose two at home . . .[1]

If those in employment worked shorter hours, and if child labour were to be restricted, there would be more work for hand-workers and the unemployed could employ themselves and exchange the products of their labour directly – short-circuiting the vagaries of the capitalist market – goods would be cheaper and labour better-rewarded. To the rhetoric of the free market they opposed the language of the 'new moral order'. It is because alternative and irreconcilable views of human order – one based on mutuality, the other on competi-

1. H.O. 42.160. See also Hammonds, *The Town Labourer*, p. 303, and Oastler's evidence on the hand-loom weavers, below, p. 329.

tion – confronted each other between 1815 and 1850 that the historian today still feels the need to take sides.

It is scarcely possible to write the history of popular agitations in these years unless we make at least the imaginative effort to understand how such a man as the 'Journeyman Cotton Spinner' read the evidence. He spoke of the 'masters', not as an aggregate of individuals, but as a class. As such, 'they' denied him political rights. If there was a trade recession, 'they' cut his wages. If trade improved, he had to fight 'them' and their state to obtain any share in the improvement. If food was plentiful, 'they' profited from it. If it was scarce, some of 'them' profited more. 'They' conspired, not in this or that fact alone, but in the essential exploitive relationship within which all the facts were validated. Certainly there were market fluctuations, bad harvests, and the rest; but the experience of intensified exploitation was constant, whereas these other causes of hardship were variable. The latter bore upon working people, not directly, but through the refraction of a particular system of ownership and power which distributed the gains and losses with gross partiality.

These larger considerations have been, for some years, overlaid by the academic exercise (through which all students must march and counter-march) known as the 'standard-of-living controversy'. Did the living standards of the bulk of the people rise or fall between 1780 and 1830 – or 1800 and 1850?[1] To understand the significance of the argument, we must look briefly at its development.

The debate on values is as old as the Industrial Revolution. The controversy on the standard-of-living is more recent. The ideological *muddle* is more recent still. We may start at one of the more lucid points of the controversy. Sir John Clapham, in his Preface to the first edition of his *Economic History of Modern Britain* (1926) wrote:

The legend that everything was getting worse for the working man, down to some unspecified date between the drafting of the People's Charter and the Great Exhibition [1837 and 1851: E.P.T.], dies

1. The futility of one part of this discussion is shown by the fact that if different datum-lines are taken, different answers may come up. 1780–1830 favours the 'pessimists'; 1800–1850 favours the 'optimists'.

hard. The fact that, after the price fall of 1820–21, the purchasing power of wages in general – not, of course, of everyone's wages – was definitely greater than it had been just before the revolutionary and Napoleonic wars, fits so ill with the tradition that it is very seldom mentioned, the work of statisticians on wages and prices being constantly ignored by social historians.

To this, J. L. Hammond offered a reply in the *Economic History Review* (1930) of two kinds: first, he criticized Clapham's statistics of agricultural earnings. These had been based on totting up the country averages, and then dividing them by the number of counties in order to reach a national average; whereas the population in the low wage-earning counties of the south was more numerous than that of the high wage-earning counties (where agricultural earnings were inflated by the proximity of industry) so that Hammond was able to show that the 'national average' concealed the fact that 60% of the labouring population was in counties where wages were below the 'average' figure. The second part of his reply consisted in a switch to discussions of value (happiness) in his most cloudy and unsatisfactory manner. The first part of this reply Clapham, in his Preface to his second edition (1930), accepted; the second part he met with dry caution ('a curve in words', 'higher matters') but nevertheless acknowledged: 'I agree most profoundly ... that statistics of material well-being can never measure a people's happiness.' Moreover, he asserted that when he had criticized the view that 'everything was getting worse' – 'I did not mean that everything was getting better. I only meant that recent historians have too often ... stressed the worsenings and slurred over or ignored the betterings.' The Hammonds, for their part, in a late revision of *The Bleak Age* (1947 edition), made their own peace: 'statisticians tell us that ... they are satisfied that earnings increased and that most men and women were less poor when this discontent was loud and active than they were when the eighteenth century was beginning to grow old in a silence like that of autumn. The evidence, of course, is scanty, and its interpretation not too simple, but this general view is probably more or less correct.' The explanation for discontent 'must be sought outside the sphere of strictly economic conditions'.

So far, so good. The most fertile – but loose – social historians of the period had encountered the astringent criticism of a notable empiricist; and in the result both sides had given ground. And. despite the heat which has subsequently been generated, the actual divergence between the hard economic conclusions of the protagonists is slight. If no serious scholar is now willing to argue that everything was getting worse, no serious scholar will argue that everything was getting better. Both Dr Hobsbawm (a 'pessimist') and Professor Ashton (an 'optimist') agree that real wages declined during the Napoleonic Wars and in their immediate aftermath. Dr Hobsbawm will not vouch for any marked general rise in the standard-of-living until the mid-1840s: whereas Professor Ashton notes a more genial economic climate after 1821 – a 'marked upward movement broken only by the slumps of 1825–6 and 1831'; and in view of increasing imports of tea. coffee, sugar, etc, 'it is difficult to believe that workers had no share in the gain'. On the other hand his own table of prices in the Oldham and Manchester districts show that 'in 1831 the standard diet of the poor can hardly have cost much less than in 1791', while he offers no corresponding wage-tables. His conclusion is to suggest two main groups within the working-class – 'a large class raised well above the level of mere subsistence' and 'masses of unskilled or poorly skilled workers – seasonally employed agricultural workers and hand-loom weavers in particular – whose incomes were almost wholly absorbed in paying for the bare necessaries of life'. 'My *guess* would be that the number of those who were able to share in the benefits of economic progress was larger than the number of those who were shut out from these benefits and that it was steadily growing.'[1]

In fact, so far as the period 1790–1830 goes, there is very little in it. The condition of the majority was bad in 1790; it remained bad in 1830 (and forty years is a long time) but there is some disagreement as to the size of the relative groups within

1. My italics. T. S. Ashton, 'The Standard of Life of the Workers in England, 1790–1830', in *Capitalism and the Historians* (ed. F. A. Hayek), pp. 127 ff.; E. J. Hobsbawm, 'The British Standard of Living, 1790–1850', *Economic History Review*, X, August 1957.

the working class. And matters are little clearer in the next decade. There were undoubted increases in real wages among organized workers during the burst of trade union activity between 1832–4: but the period of good trade between 1833 and 1837 was accompanied by the smashing of the trade unions by the concerted efforts of Government, magistrates, and employers; while 1837–42 are depression years. So that it is indeed at 'some unspecified date between the drafting of the People's Charter and the Great Exhibtion' that the tide begins to turn; let us say, with the railway boom in 1843. Moreover, even in the mid-40s the plight of very large groups of workers remains desperate, while the railway crash led to the depression years of 1847–8. This does not look very much like a 'success story'; in half a century of the fullest development of industrialism, the standard-of-living still remained – for very large but indeterminate groups – at the point of subsistencey.

This is not, however, the impression given in much contemporary writing. For, just as an earlier generation of historians who were also social reformers (Thorold Rogers, Arnold Toynbee, the Hammonds) allowed their sympathy with the poor to lead on occasions to a confusion of history with ideology, so we find that the sympathies of some economic historians today for the capitalist entrepreneur have led to a confusion of history and apologetics.[1] The point of transition was marked by the publication, in 1954, of a symposium on *Capitalism and the Historians*, edited by Professor F. A. Hayek, itself the work of a group of specialists 'who for some years have been meeting regularly to discuss the problems of the preservation of a free society against the totalitarian threat'. Since

1. Lest the reader should judge the historian too harshly, we may record Sir John Clapham's explanation as to the way in which this selective principle may order the evidence. 'It is very easy to do this unawares. Thirty years ago I read and marked Arthur Young's *Travels in France*, and taught from the marked passages. Five years ago I went through it again, to find that whenever Young spoke of a wretched Frenchman I had marked him, but that many of his references to happy or prosperous Frenchmen remained unmarked.' One suspects that for ten or fifteen years most economic historians have been busy marking up the happy and prosperous evidence in the text.

this group of international specialists regarded 'a free society' as by definition a capitalist society, the effects of such an admixture of economic theory and special pleading were deplorable; and not least in the work of one of the contributors, Professor Ashton, whose cautious findings of 1949 are now transmuted – without further evidence – into the flat statement that 'generally it is now agreed that for the majority the gain in real wages was substantial'.[1] It is at this stage that the controversy degenerated into a muddle And despite more recent attempts to rescue it for scholarship,[2] in many respects it is as a muddle of assertion and special pleading that the controversy remains.

The controversy falls into two parts. There is, first, the very real difficulty of constructing wage-series, price-series, and statistical indices from the abundant but patchy evidence. We shall examine some of the difficulties in interpreting such evidence when we come to the artisans. But at this point a further series of difficulties begins, since the term 'standard' leads us from data amenable to statistical measurement (wages or articles of consumption) to those satisfactions which are sometimes described by statisticans as 'imponderables'. From food we are led to homes, from homes to health, from health to family life, and thence to leisure, work-discipline, education and play, intensity of labour, and so on. From standard-of-life we pass to way-of-life. But the two are not the same. The first is a measurement of quantities: the second a description (and sometimes an evaluation) of qualities. Where statistical evidence is appropriate to the first, we must rely largely upon 'literary evidence' as to the second. A major source of confusion arises from the drawing of conclusions as to one from evidence appropriate only to the other. It is at times as if statisticians have been arguing: 'the indices reveal an increased *per capita* consumption of tea, sugar, meat and soap, *therefore* the working

1. T. S. Ashton, 'The Treatment of Capitalism by Historians', in *Capitalism and the Historians*, p. 41. Professor Ashton's essay on 'The Standard of Life of the Workers in England', reprinted in this volume, originally appeared in the *Journal of Economic History*, 1949.

2. The most constructive appraisal of the controversy is in A. J. Taylor's 'Progress and Poverty in Britain, 1780–1850', *History*, February 1960.

class was happier', while social historians have replied: 'literary sources show that people were unhappy, *therefore* their standard-of-living must have deteriorated'.

This is to simplify. But simple points must be made. It is quite possible for statistical averages and human experiences to run in opposite directions. A *per capita* increase in quantitative factors may take place at the same time as a great qualitative disturbance in people's way of life, traditional relationships, and sanctions. People may consume more goods and become less happy or less free at the same time. Next to the agricultural workers the largest single group of working people during the whole period of the Industrial Revolution were the domestic servants. Very many of them were household servants, living-in with the employing family, sharing cramped quarters, working excessive hours, for a few shillings' reward. Nevertheless, we may confidently list them among the more favoured groups whose standards (or consumption of food and dress) improved on average slightly during the Industrial Revolution. But the hand-loom weaver and his wife, on the edge of starvation, still regarded their status as being superior to that of a 'flunkey'. Or again, we might cite those trades, such as coal-mining, in which real wages advanced between 1790 and 1840, but at the cost of longer hours and greater intensity of labour, so that the breadwinner was 'worn out' before the age of forty. In statistical terms, this reveals an upward curve. To the families concerned it might feel like immiseration.

Thus it is perfectly possible to maintain two propositions which, on a casual view, appear to be contradictory. Over the period 1790–1840 there was a slight improvement in average material standards. Over the same period there was intensified exploitation, greater insecurity, and increasing human misery. By 1840 most people were 'better off' than their forerunners had been fifty years before, but they had suffered and continued to suffer this slight improvement as a catastrophic experience. In order to explore this experience, out of which the political and cultural expression of working-class consciousness arose, we shall do these things. First, we shall examine the changing life-experience of three groups of workers: the field labourers, the urban artisans, and the hand-loom weavers.[1] Second, we shall discuss some of the less 'ponderable' elements in the people's standard-of-life. Third, we shall discuss the inner compulsions of the industrial way of life, and the bearing upon them of Methodism. Finally, we shall examine some of the elements in the new working-class communities.

1. These groups have been selected because their experience seems most to colour the social consciousness of the working class in the first half of the century. The miners and metal-workers do not make their influence fully felt until later in the century. The other key group – the cotton-spinners – are the subject of an admirable study in the Hammonds, *The Skilled Labourer*.

[7]

The Field Labourers

THE difficulties of assessing 'standards' may be seen if we examine the history, between 1790 and 1830, of the largest group of workers in any industry – the agricultural labourers.[1] It is not altogether true (as the Hammonds implied) that the evidence is 'scanty'. The difficulty lies more often in its interpretation. There are abundant records as to early nineteenth-century wages and prices, but continuous runs of reliable figures for the same job or the same region are more scarce. Anyone who has examined the dense undergrowth of evidence in Sir John Clapham's *Economic History of Modern Britain*, with its diversity in regional and occupational practices, may well feel overwhelmed by its luxuriance. And, indeed, Clapham's chapters on 'Agrarian Organization' and 'Industrial Organization' are in themselves an education – but an education, not in the interpretation of evidence so much as in its qualifications.

Throughout this painstaking investigation, the great empiricist eschews all generalizations except for one – the pursuit of the mythical 'average'. In his discussion of agriculture we encounter the 'average farm', the 'average small-holding', the 'average' ratio of labourers to employers, – notions which often obscure more than they reveal, since they are arrived at by lumping together evidence from Welsh mountains and Norfolk corn-lands which Clapham himself has been at pains to distinguish. We go on to encounter 'the average cottager in an area affected by enclosure', the 'average' loss to rural earnings from industrial by-employments, the gross earnings of 'that rather vague figure, the average English (with Welsh) labourer', and so on. We have already seen that this 'averaging' can give us very odd results: the 60% of the labourers who, in 1830,

1. The 1831 Census showed 961,000 families employed in agriculture – 28% of all families in Great Britain.

were in low-wage counties which fell *below* the 'average' line.[1]
'In any average,' Clapham admitted, 'some 50% of the figures
averaged may be expected to fall below the line.' But if the
average itself is based on the conventional wage of a worker in
regular employment – that is, if the squire looks through his
books and informs the Board of Agriculture that the conventional wage of a ploughman or carter is 12s. – then we may
expect all or most of the casual labourers to fall below the line.

But it is in his discussion of supplementary earnings and of
the effect of enclosures – as Clapham shuttles us between empirical minutiae ('love reapings' in Glamorgan and half-acre
gardens in Ludlow) and 'average' estimates – that we feel we
have parted company with social reality:

If the pig and the cottage garden brought in less to the average
British labourer in 1824 than in 1794 ... very possibly the potato
patch would, again on the average, balance the loss. Certainly,
lost access to commons in those thirty years had worsened the lot of
many men in many places, though it is doubtful whether, averaged
over Britain, the loss in well-being due to the enclosures of the
commons would amount to very much. It has been exaggerated in
popular retrospect; for it had little significance in many parts of
England; still less in Wales; and in Scotland, for the pure labourer,
none at all.[2]

Now what is being averaged? The first part of this statement
might be of some value if it could be shown that in the same
villages where cottage gardens were lost potato patches came
in (although we should also examine relative rents). But the
second part, which has already passed into comfortable tradition, is not an example of averaging but of statistical *dilution*.
We are being invited to dilute the figures for those parts of
Britain where enclosure *did* take place with those where it did
not, divide the sum of this weak solution by the number of
counties, and come up with an 'average' loss in well-being
'due to enclosures'. But this is nonsense. One may not take an

1. See p. 227 above. The county 'averages', upon which the national
'average' is based, are themselves open to exactly the same criticism.
Moreover, they are formed from the evidence of employers, not that of
labourers.

2. Loc cit., p. 126.

average of unlike quantities; nor may one divide quantities by counties to arrive at an average of value. This is what Clapham has done.

What he was really doing, of course, was to offer a tentative value judgement as to that elusive quality, 'well-being', in the period of maximum enclosure. But to do this, very many more factors – cultural as well as material – should have been brought to bear upon the judgement. Since the judgement springs like an oak out of such a thicket of circumstantial detail – and since it is itself disguised as an 'average' – it is easily mistaken as a statement of fact.

Nor are the facts themselves as clear as Clapham implies. Agricultural earnings, through much of the nineteenth century, stubbornly refuse to be reduced to statistical form.[1] Not only do we face marked seasonal fluctuations in the demand for labour, but we have at least four different kinds of master-servant relationship (1) Farm servants, hired by the year or the quarter. (2) A regular labour-force – on the large farm. – more or less fully employed the year round. (3) Casual labour, paid by day-rate or piece-rate. (4) More or less skilled specialists, who might contract for the job.

In the first category, declining over this period, there is the most security and the least independence: very low wages, long hours, but board and lodging in the farmer's household In the second category will be found some of the best and some of the worst conditions: the ploughman or shepherd kep' in security by a prudent farmer, his wife and children given preference in casual work, with milk and grain sold at cheap rates: at the other extreme. teenage farmhands, housed and fed as poorly as any pauper apprentices in the early mills, liv ing in hay-lofts and subject to dismissal at any time: and in between 'those unhappy men whom necessity has compelled to become the slaves of one man', living in tied cottages. and

1. It is significant that when Clapham did commit himself to estimates of percentage variations in wages and cost-of-living, he relied not upon any collocation of his own data, but upon the work of other scholars, notably Silberling, whose cost-of-living series have recently come under severe criticism: see, e.g. T. S. Ashton, in *Capitalism and the Historians*. For further cautions as to the difficulties of generalization see J. Saville, *Rural Depopulation in England and Wales* (1957), pp. 15–17.

'bound to work for certain low wages all the year'.[1] In the third category there is immense variation: pauper labour: women and children at pauper wages: Irish migratory workers (even textile workers or other urban craftsmen who left their work for the high harvest earnings): and finely graduated piece-rates, such as those for mowing different qualities of hay-field. In the fourth category, we have countless differences of practice, and disguised sub-contracting or family earnings, which play havoc with any statistical table:

Mar. 21	Samson, waterfurrowing in 29 acres	8·9
	Robert, 1 day sawing tops pollards	1·9
May 20	Strangers, hoeing 5 acres of wheat at 3s. 6d.	17·6
July 29	Wright, mowing 7 acres of clover	14·0
	Richardson and Pavely, cleaning farmyard pond	2·12·6

– so runs an Essex farmer's accounts in 1797.[2] 'I was a hurdle-maker and thatcher, and jobbed at hedging,' Joseph Carter told Alexander Somerville, referring to the years 1823–30:

The squire shewed as how I got £64 a-year from him for work of that kind for seven years. But then he did not shew that I had most times a man to help me, and two women besides at times. He did not shew that. I paid as much as £20 some years for helpers.[3]

If the figures 'do not shew that', it is impossible for them to show a score of other influences: payments in kind or at cheap rates: gardens and potato patches: the effect of en-closure: the effect of taxes, tithes, game laws, and poor-rates: fluctuations in rural industrial employment: above all, the operation of the Poor Laws, before and after 1834. The inci-dence of different grievances may be felt quite differently at different times and in different parts. In some areas, and on some farms, payment in kind may be additional to wages and indicate an improvement in standards; but more generally

1. Board of Agriculture, *Agricultural State of the Kingdom* (1816), p. 162. A reply from Lincolnshire, contrasting the state of tied cottagers on one estate with the labourers on another estate where the landlord rents to each of them an acre for potatoes and four acres for a cow.

2. A. F. J. Brown, *English History from Essex Sources* (Chelmsford, 1952), p. 39.

3. A. Somerville, *The Whistler at the Plough* (Manchester, 1852), p. 262.

(an agricultural historian has warned us) we should see these allowances as 'the polite euphemism for truck in agriculture' – a means of holding wages down or in extreme cases dispensing with money-wage altogether.[1]

In all this very difficult tangle of conflicting evidence – between the effect of the Poor Laws here and new potato patches there, this lost common right and that cottage garden – the 'average' labourer proves more than elusive.[2] But if averages evade us, we may still sketch certain of the general processes at work in many parts of the country. And first we should remember that the spirit of agricultural improvements in the eighteenth century was impelled less by altruistic desires to banish ugly wastes or – as the tedious phrase goes – to 'feed a growing population' than by the desire for fatter rent-rolls and larger profits. As such it turned towards the labourer a face of parsimony:

There is a practice which prevails ... of giving them drink both forenoon and afternoon, be the work what it will; which is a ridiculous custom, and ought to be abolished without loss of time. What can be more absurd, than to see a ploughman stopping his horse half an hour, in a cold winter day, to drink ale?[3]

The arguments of the enclosure propagandists were commonly phrased in terms of higher rental values and higher yield per acre. In village after village, enclosure destroyed the scratch-as-scratch-can subsistence economy of the poor. The cottager without legal proof of rights was rarely compensated. The cottager who was able to establish his claim was left with a parcel of land inadequate for subsistence and a disproportionate share of the very high enclosure cost.

Enclosure (when all the sophistications are allowed for) was a plain enough case of class robbery, played according to

1. For this and other related points see O. R. McGregor's valuable introduction to Lord Ernle, *English Farming, Past and Present* (1961 edn), esp. pp. cxviii–cxxi.

2. The best general accounts are still those in J. L. and B. Hammond, *The Village Labourer* and Lord Ernle, *English Farming, Past and Present*, and (for houses, clothing and food) G. E. Fussell, *The English Rural Labourer* (1947).

3. Rennie, Broun and Shirreff, *General View of the Agriculture of the West Riding* (1794), p. 25.

fair rules of property and law laid down by a parliament of property-owners and lawyers. Recent scholarship suggests that the rules of the game were kept to more fairly than was suggested by the Hammonds in their great *Village Labourer*: even very small property-owners received reasonable treatment, many enclosure commissioners acted conscientiously, and so on.[1] But, in making these useful qualifications, it is possible to overlook the larger fact that what was at issue was a redefinition of the nature of agrarian property itself. Thus Chambers and Mingay have noted that, in enclosure,

The *occupiers* of common right cottages ... who enjoyed common right by virtue of their *tenancy* of the cottage, received no compensation because they were not, of course, the owners of the rights. This was a perfectly proper distinction between owner and tenant, and involved no fraud or disregard for cottagers on the part of the commissioners.[2]

But what was 'perfectly proper' in terms of capitalist property-relations involved, none the less, a rupture of the traditional integument of village custom and of right: and the social violence of enclosure consisted precisely in the drastic, total imposition upon the village of capitalist property-definitions. Of course, such definitions had been encroaching within the village for centuries before enclosure: but they had co-existed with those self-governing and customary elements in the structure of the pre-capitalist village community, which

1. A cogent summary of recent work is in J. D. Chambers and G. E. Mingay, *The Agricultural Revolution, 1750–1880* (1966), ch. 4: see also W. E. Tate, *The English Village Community and the Enclosure Movements* (1967), Chapters 8–10, 16. See also my review of the first book in the *Times Literary Supplement* 16 February 1967, upon which I have drawn in the next few paragraphs (inserted into the Penguin edition), in which I raise certain questions about the social consequences of enclosure which may have been examined too cursorily by these authorities. Among the growing number of studies of particular enclosures, I have found most helpful the series of publications by R. C. Russell, including *The Enclosures of Barton-on-Humber and Hibaldstow* (Barton, n.d.); *The Enclosures of Scartho and Grimsby* (Grimsby, 1964); *The Enclosures of Bottesford and Yaddlethorpe, Messingham and Ashby* (Scunthorpe, n.d.). Each of Mr Russell's studies follows through the actual procedure in great detail, from initiation to award.

2. Chambers and Mingay, op. cit. p. 97.

– while they were no doubt crumbling under the pressure of increasing population – persisted with remarkable vigour in many places. Copyhold and even vaguer customary family tenancies (which carried common rights) might prove to be invalid at law although they were endorsed by the collective memory of the community. Those petty rights of the villagers, such as gleaning, access to fuel, and the tethering of stock in the lanes or on the stubble, which are irrelevant to the historian of economic growth, might be of critical importance to the subsistence of the poor.

Enclosure, indeed, was the culmination of a long secular process by which men's customary relations to the agrarian means of production were undermined. It was of profound social consequence because it illuminates, both backwards and forwards, the destruction of the traditional elements in English peasant society. If one looks at English agriculture in the eighteenth century through the pages of Arthur Young's *Annals of Agriculture*, or the various county surveys prepared (at the turn of the century) for the Board of Agriculture, it is possible to suppose that customary sanctions had long lost their force. But if one looks at the scene again from the standpoint of the villager, one finds a dense cluster of claims and usages, which stretch from the common to the market-place and which, taken together, made up the economic and cultural universe of the rural poor.

Professor Chambers has well written:

The appropriation to their own exclusive use of practically the whole of the common waste by the legal owners meant that the curtain which separated the growing army of labourers from utter proletarianization was torn down. It was, no doubt, a thin and squalid curtain ... but it was real, and to deprive them of it without providing a substitute implied the exclusion of the labourers from the benefits which their intensified labour alone made possible.[1]

The loss of the commons entailed, for the poor, a radical sense of displacement. One encounters an exceptional note of vehemence in some of the protests against enclosure which crop

1. J. D. Chambers, 'Enclosure and Labour Supply in the Industrial Revolution', *Econ. Hist. Rev.* 2nd series, V (1952–3), p. 336.

up from time to time in the Home Office papers: as witness
an anonymous letter of 1799 addressed to Oliver Cromwell,
Esquire, of Cheshunt Park:

Whe right these lines to you who are the Combin'd of the Parish
of Cheshunt in the Defence of our Parrish rights which you unlaw-
fully are about to disinherit us of . . .
Resolutions is maid by the aforesaid Combind that if you intend of
inclosing Our Commond Commond fields Lammas Meads Marshes
&c Whe Resolve before . . . that bloudy and unlawful act [it] is
finished to have your hearts bloud if you proceede in the aforesaid
bloudy act Whe like horse leaches will cry give, give until whe have
spilt the bloud of every one that wishes to rob the Inosent unborn.
It shall not be in your power to say I am safe from the hands of
my Enemy for Whe like birds of pray will prively lie in wait to
spil the bloud of the aforesaid Charicters whose names and places
of abode are as prutrified sores in our Nostrils. Whe declair that
thou shall not say I am safe when thou goest to thy bed for beware
that thou liftest not thine eyes up in the most mist of flames . . .[1]

The 'Combin'd' of Cheshunt were unusually articulate and
determined: they succeeded in raising a counter-petition to
parliament, and as a result of their pressure common rights
were taken into account in the enclosure award. But the tone
of such a letter as this reminds one that enclosure must be
seen within the total situation of power and deference in the
countryside. Men in the social and cultural station of the
authors of such letters could only in the most exceptional circumstances – and with the advice of some men of education
and substance – have had recourse to the costly and procrastinating procedures of an alien culture and an alien power.
The fatalism of the cottager in the face of this ever-present
power, and the uneven, piecemeal incidence of enclosure (when
the enclosure of neighbouring villages might be separated by
the passage of several decades), go some way towards explaining the seeming passivity of the victims.

Even so, this passivity may be overstated; there has been
little research into the actual responses of the poor to enclosure, and such research presents peculiar difficulties, being
concerned with the illiterate and the inarticulate enduring distinct experiences in hundreds of different villages over many

1. 27 February 1799, in H.O.42.46.

decades.[1] Enclosure-riots, the breaking of fences, threatening letters, arson, were more common than some agrarian historians suppose. But a reason for the very patchy character of resistance by the poor may be found in the divisions within the poor themselves. We might find a clue in a later passage of the letter of the 'Combin'd' of Cheshunt:

Whe cannot but say that there is plenty of room for Alterations for Whe cannot see why that Ruskins and a few more of them should run our Common over while there is no room for another to put anything on [If] thou hadst made an Alteration in the rights of Commoning thou instead of being contempabel whould thy Name been as Oderriferous Ointment pour'd fourth to us The voice of us and the maguor part of the parrish is for a regulation of commons rights ...

There is evidence at the end of the eighteenth century of increasing pressure on the commons and of an over-stocking, not only by squatters and cottagers but also by large graziers like 'that Ruskins'. In such a context, the dividing lines between the interests of the very small proprietor and the poor cottager became of critical importance. The small proprietor was interested in the strictest stinting and regulation of common rights: it was in the interest of the cottager or squatter that a more lax definition of custom should prevail. The eyes of the small proprietor (like those of any peasant in any age and country) might glitter at the short-term prospect of outright proprietorship – even the four or five acres which enclosure might bring: but the cottager without any proprietary rights by enclosure lost all. In the long run the gains of the small proprietors might prove to be illusory: but the illusion was sustained during the high price years of the French Wars.

Indeed, both of the major objects of the operation (more food and higher rents) were attained throughout the Wars. Rents rose very markedly in areas of recent enclosure,[2] and they were sustained both by higher prices and higher yields

1. One important study of agrarian disturbance now exists: A. J. Peacock, *Bread or Blood. The Agrarian Riots in East Anglia: 1816* (1965).

2. Chambers and Mingay, op. cit., pp. 84-5 estimate that rents on average doubled after enclosure during the peak period of enclosure acts: see also F. M. L. Thompson, *English Landed Society in the Nineteenth Century* (1963), pp. 222-6.

per acre. When prices fell, in 1815–16 and in 1821, rents remained high – or came down as they always do, tardily – thereby spelling the ruin of many smallholders who had clung on to their few acre holdings gained from enclosure.[1] High rents sustained extraordinary luxury and ostentatious expenditure among the landowners, while high prices nourished higher social pretensions – so much lamented by Cobbett – among the farmers and their wives. This was the meridian for those 'country patriots' whom Byron scorched in his *Age of Bronze*.

But greed alone cannot account for the position into which the labourer was driven in these years. How was it possible, when the wealth of the landowners and farmers was rising, for the labourer to be held at brute subsistence level? We must look for an answer in the general counter-revolutionary tone of the whole period. It is probable that the real wages of labourers had been rising in the decades before 1790, especially in areas contiguous to manufacturing or mining districts. 'There wants a war to reduce wages,' was the cry of some northern gentry in the 1790s.[2] And the reflexes, of panic and class antagonism, inflamed in the aristocracy by the French Revolution were such as to remove inhibitions and to aggravate the exploitive relationship between masters and servants. The Wars saw not only the suppression of the urban reformers but also the eclipse of the humane gentry of whom Wyvill is representative. To the argument of greed a new argument was added for general enclosure – that of social discipline. The commons, 'the poor man's heritage for ages past', on which Thomas Bewick could recall independent labourers still dwelling, who had built their cottages with their own hands,[3] were now seen as a dangerous centre of indiscipline. Arthur Young saw them as a breeding-ground for 'barbarians', 'nursing up a mischievous race of people'; of the Lincolnshire Fens, 'so wild a country nurses up a race of people as wild as the fen'.[4]

1. For examples of the decline in peasant landowning, see W. G. Hoskins, *The Midland Peasant* (1957), pp. 265–8.

2. R. Brown, *General View of the Agriculture of the West Riding* (1799), Appendix, p. 13.

3. Bewick, op. cit., pp. 27 ff.

4. A. Young, *General View of the Agriculture of Lincolnshire* (1799), pp. 223, 225, 437.

Ideology was added to self-interest. It became a matter of public-spirited policy for the gentleman to remove cottagers from the commons, reduce his labourers to dependence, pare away at supplementary earnings, drive out the smallholder. At a time when Wordsworth was extolling the virtues of old Michael and his wife, in their struggle to maintain their 'patrimonial fields', the very much more influential *Commercial and Agricultural Magazine* regarded the 'yeoman' in a different light:

A wicked, cross-grained, petty farmer is like the sow in his yard, almost an insulated individual, who has no communication with, and therefore, no reverence for the opinion of the world.

As for the rights of the cottager in enclosure, 'it may seem needless to notice his claims':

But the interest of the other claimants is ultimately concerned in permitting the labouring man to acquire a certain portion of land ... for by this indulgence the poor-rates must be speedily diminished; since a quarter of an acre of garden-ground will go a great way towards rendering the peasant independent of any assistance. However, in this beneficent intention moderation must be observed, or we may chance to transform the labourer into a petty farmer; from the most beneficial to the most useless of all the applications of industry. When a labourer becomes possessed of more land than he and his family can cultivate in the evenings ... the farmer can no longer depend on him for constant work, and the hay-making and harvest ... must suffer to a degree which ... would sometimes prove a national inconvenience.

As for the village poor they are 'designing rogues, who, under various pretences, attempt to cheat the parish', and 'their whole abilities are exerted in the execution of deceit, which may procure from the parish officers an allowance of money for idle and profligate purposes'.[1]

There are, of course, exceptions. But this is the way the grain runs between 1790 and 1810. It was a matter of policy to increase the dependence of cheap reserves of labour – 'applications of industry' for the convenience of the farmer at haymaking and harvest, and for the road-making, fencing and

1. *Commercial and Agricultural Magazine*, July, September, October 1800.

draining incident on enclosure. What Cobbett called 'Scotch feelosofy' and the Hammonds the 'spirit of the age' was endorsed as heartily by landowners as by manufacturers. But whereas it fitted the conditions of the Industrial Revolution like a glove, in agriculture it contested (at best) with older paternalist traditions (the squire's duty to his labourers) and with the tradition of earnings based on need (the older customs of differentials according to age, marital status, children, etc., which were perpetuated under the Speenhamland system of poor relief); while (at worst) it was reinforced by the feudal arrogance of the aristocracy towards the inferior labouring race. The doctrine that labour discovers its own 'natural' price, according to the laws of supply and demand, had long been ousting the notion of the 'just' wage. During the Wars it was propagated by every means. 'The demand for labour must necessarily regulate wages,' wrote a country magistrate in 1800. And he went on to argue that the poor-rates, by maintaining a surplus population and encouraging marriages – thereby ensuring a supply of labour in excess of demand – brought down the total wages bill. Indeed, he showed himself a pioneer in the science of 'averages':

Let us suppose the annual poor-rates, and the amount of wages throughout England added together in one total; I think this total would be less than the *sole* amount of the wages, if the poor-rates had not existed.[1]

The motives which led to the introduction of the various systems of poor-relief which related relief to the price of bread and to the number of children were no doubt various. The Speenhamland decision of 1795 was impelled by both humanity and necessity. But the perpetuation of Speenhamland and 'roundsman' systems, in all their variety, was ensured by the demand of the larger farmers – in an industry which has exceptional requirements for occasional or casual labour – for a permanent cheap labour reserve.

After the Wars there is a new emphasis: farmers are very much more willing to listen to the warnings of Malthus against 'a bounty on population'. Poor-rates had risen from under two

1. Ibid., October 1800.

million pounds per annum in the 1780s, to more than four millions in 1803, and over six millions after 1812. A bounty on population now appeared, as the Poor Law Commission was to describe it in 1834, as 'a bounty on indolence and vice'. Landowners and farmers began to regret the lost commons – the cow, the geese, the turfs – which had enabled the poor to subsist without coming to the parish overseer. Some cows came back: here and there potato patches made some headway: the Board of Agriculture lent its strenuous support to the allotment propaganda. But it was too late to reverse a general process: no common was ever brought back (though many more were enclosed) and few landowners would risk renting land (perhaps four acres for a cow at a minimum of £6 per annum) to a labourer. Farmers who had made a doctrine of parsimony during the years of war prosperity were not inclined to be less parsimonious when wheat prices fell. Moreover, the population of the villages was added to by returned soldiers; the labourers were joined by bankrupt smallholders; the work incidental to enclosure fell off; and the concentration of the textile industries in the north and the Midlands further weakened the position of the labourer in East Anglia, the West Country, and the south. New or expanding rural industries (straw-plaiting or lace) might afford temporary relief in certain counties; but the overall decline (most notably in spinning) is beyond dispute. And as domestic employments failed, so the cheap labour of women as field labourers grew.[1]

High rents or falling prices: war debt and currency crises: taxes on malt, on windows, on horses: Game Laws, with their paraphernalia of gamekeepers, spring-guns, mantraps and (after 1816) sentences of transportation: all served, directly or indirectly, to tighten the screw upon the labourer. 'The Jacobins did not do these things,' exclaimed Cobbett:

And will the Government pretend that 'Providence' did it? ... Poh! These things are the price of efforts to crush freedom in France, *lest the example of France should produce a reform in England.* These things are the price of that undertaking ...[2]

1. I. Pinchbeck, *Women Workers and the Industrial Revolution* (1930), pp. 57 ff.

2. *Rural Rides* (Everyman edn), I, p. 174.

Nor could the labourer expect to find a protector in the 'average' parson – who, to Cobbett, was an absentee pluralist, entertaining his family at Bath while an underpaid curate attended services.

For nearly four decades, there is a sense of the erosion of traditional sanctions and of a countryside governed with counter-revolutionary licence. 'In regard to the *poor-rates*,' one Bedfordshire 'feelosofer' (Dr Macqueen) wrote to the Board of Agriculture in 1816, 'I always view these as coupled with the idleness and depravity of the working class':

The morals as well as the manners of the lower orders of the community have been degenerating since the earliest ages of the French Revolution. The doctrine of equality and the rights of man is not yet forgotten, but fondly cherished and reluctantly abandoned. They consider their respective parishes as their right and inheritance, in which they are entitled to resort . . .[1]

One recalls with difficulty that England belonged to the labourers as well.

In the southern and eastern parishes the long war of attrition centred on the right of poor-relief. After the commons were lost, it was the last – the only – right the labourer had. The young and the single – or the village craftsmen – might venture to the towns, follow the canals (later the railways), or emigrate. But the mature labourer with a family was afraid of losing the security of his 'settlement'; this, as much as his attachment to his own community and rural customs, prevented him from competing wholesale with the Irish poor (who, unluckier even than him, had no settlement to lose) in the industrial labour market. Even in times of labour 'shortage' in the manufacturing districts, his migration was not encouraged. When, after 1834, the Poor Law Commissioners sought to stimulate such migration, principally to the mills of Lancashire and Yorkshire, – perhaps, as a counter-blow at the trade unions – preference was given to 'widows with large families of children, or handicraftsmen . . . with large families. Adult men could not acquire the requisite skill for the superior processes of the factories.' Labour markets were set up in Manchester and Leeds where mill-owners could scan the details of families – age of children

1. *Agricultural State of the Kingdom* (1816), p. 25.

– character as a workman – moral character – remarks ('exceeding healthy', 'fine of their age', 'willing to take on themselves the part of parents to three orphans') – like stock for sale. 'We have numbers of small families,' one hopeful Suffolk guardian appended, 'such as man and wife, willing, if you could engage them together, say man at 8s., woman at 4s.'[1]

The poor-rates, then, were the labourer's last 'inheritance'. From 1815 to 1834 the contest continued. On the side of the gentry and overseers, economies, setttlement litigation, stone-breaking and punitive tasks, cheap labour-gangs, the humiliations of labour-auctions, even of men harnessed in carts. On the side of the poor, threats to the overseers, sporadic sabotage, a 'servile and cunning' or 'sullen and discontented' spirit, an evident demoralization documented in page after page of the Poor Law Commissioners' Reports. 'It would be better for us to be slaves at once than to work under such a system ... when a man has his spirit broken, what is he good for?' In the Speenhamland counties of the south the labourers had their own bitter jest – the farmers 'keep us here [on the poor-rates] like potatoes in a pit, and only take us out for use when they can no longer do without us'.[2]

It is an apt description. Cobbett, in his invectives against wholesale rural depopulation, was right in his description of causes but wrong in his conclusions. It seems probable that the enclosures – especially of arable land in the south and the east during the Wars – did not result in general depopulation. While labourers were migrating – in ripples, from village to town, and from county to county – the general population rise more than compensated for the loss. After the Wars, when prices fell and the farmers could no longer 'get vent for our young men in the army or navy' (a useful disciplinary power, in the hands of a country magistrate), the outcry was about 'surplus population'. But, after the new Poor Law was put into operation in 1834,

1. *First Annual Report of Poor Law Commissioners* (1836), pp. 313–14; W. Dodd, *The Factory System Illustrated* (1842), pp. 246–7. See also A. Redford, *Labour Migration in England, 1800–1850* (1926), ch. 6.

2. *First Annual Report of the Poor Law Commissioners* (1836), p. 212. The same joke was 'well understood' in Wiltshire in 1845 – but the 'pit' had now become the workhouse; A. Somerville, op. cit., p. 385.

this 'surplus' in some villages proved fictitious. In these villages the greater part of the labour bill was being met through the poor-rates; labourers were employed for odd days or half-days and then turned back on the parish. 'If there comes a frost they discharge them,' said one overseer: 'when the season opens they come to me, and take 'em back again. The farmers make my house what we call in our trade a house of call.' Wet weather created a 'surplus': harvest a 'shortage'. Employers, jealous at subsidizing the labour of their neighbours through the poor-rates, would discharge their own men and apply for their labour from the overseer: 'So-and-so has turned off two of his men; if I am to pay to their wages, he shall pay to yours; you must go.' It is a system open to endless permutations of muddle, waste, and extortion – and to a few tricks on the labourer's side as well. But – cunning and sheer mulishness apart – it had a single tendency: to destroy the last vestige of control by the labourer over his own wage or working life.[1]

'A system' – the cant phrase of the political economy of the time runs, when brought to bear on Speenhamland – 'which has broken the bond of mutual dependence between the master and his servant.' In fact, the southern labourer had been reduced to total dependence on the masters as a class. But slave labour is 'uneconomic', especially when it is exacted from men who nourish grievances at lost rights and the inchoate resistances of 'free-born Englishmen'. It is 'uneconomic' to supervise labourers in gangs (although this was done for many years in the eastern counties) – through most of the year labourers must work in twos and threes, with the stock, in the fields, at hedging, by their own initiative. During these years the exploitive relationship was intensified to the point where it simply ceased to 'pay' – this kind of pauper labour turned out to be turnip-pilferers, alehouse scroungers, poachers and layabouts. It was easier to emigrate than to resist; for reinforcing the exploitive relationship was that of political repression. Illiteracy, exhaustion, the emigration from the village of the ambitious,

1. See A. Redford, op. cit., pp. 58–83; and, for fictitious surpluses, *First Annual Report of the Poor Law Commissioners* (1836), pp. 229–38; W. T. Thornton, *Over-Population* (1846), pp. 231–2.

the sharp-witted and the young, the shadow of the squire and parson, the savage punishment of enclosure or bread rioters and of poachers – all combined to induce fatalism and to inhibit the articulation of grievances. Cobbett, the greatest tribune of the labourers, had many supporters among the farmers and in the small market towns. It is doubtful whether before 1830 many labourers knew his name or understood what he was about. As Cobbett rode past the 'Accursed Hill' of Old Sarum, he met a labourer returning from work:

I asked how he *got on*. He said, very badly. I asked him what was the cause of it. He said the *hard times*. 'What *times*,' said I; 'was there ever a finer summer, a finer harvest . . .?' 'Ah!' said he, '*they* make it bad for poor people, for all that.' '*They?*' said I, 'who is *they*?' He was silent. 'Oh, no, no! my friend,' said I, 'it is not *they*; it is that Accursed Hill that has robbed you . . .' [1]

Throughout the Wars the 'grand fabric of society' was supported upon this 'distressful . . . rustic base'. 'It is the wives of these men,' wrote David Davies, 'who rear those hardy broods of children who, besides supplying the country with the hands it wants, fill up the voids which death is continually making in camps and cities.' [2] After the Wars, with soaring prices and the return of soldiers to their villages, there was some stirring of revolt. 'The Burthen that is now laid on us we are Determin'd to bear no longer,' ran a letter from the Yeovil district, signed with a bleeding heart: 'Blood and Blood and Blood, A General Revolution their mus be . . .' [3] But the very violence of such threats points to a sense of impotence. Only in 1816 in East Anglia, where the labourers were frequently employed in large gangs, did serious disturbances break out. The demand for a minimum wage (2*s*. a day) was united with the demand for price maximums; there were food riots, forced levies for money from the gentry, and the destruction of threshing-machines. But disorder was brutally repressed, and

1. *Rural Rides* (Everyman edn), I I, pp. 56–7.
2. W. Belsham, *Remarks on the Bill for the Better Support . . . of the Poor* (1795), p. 5; D. Davies, *The Case of Labourers in Husbandry* (1795), p. 2.
3. Enclosure in Moody to Sidmouth, 13 May 1816, H.O. 42.150.

thrust back into the underground of the poaching war, the anonymous letter, the flaming corn rick.[1]

Revolt, when it came, in 1830, with its curiously indecisive and unbloodthirsty mobs ('the turbulence of demoralized freemen') was met with the same sense of outrage as a rising of the 'blacks'. 'I induced the magistrates to put themselves on horseback,' recorded the victor of Waterloo,

each at the head of his own servants and retainers, grooms, huntsmen, game-keepers, armed with horsewhips, pistols, fowling pieces and what they could get, and to attack in concert . . . these mobs, disperse them, destroy them, and take and put in confinement those who could not escape.[2]

It was not the Duke, however, but the new Whig Ministry (which was to pass the Reform Bill) which sent Special Commissions down to terrorize the insurgents. And it was the organ of middle-class Radicalism, *The Times*, which led the outcry for examples of severity. The advice was followed:

On the 9th of January [1831], judgment of death was recorded against twenty-three prisoners, for the destruction of a paper machine in Buckingham; in Dorset, on the 11th, against three, for extorting money, and two for robbery; at Norwich, fifty-five prisoners were convicted of machine-breaking and rioting; at Ipswich, three, for extorting money; at Petworth, twenty-six for machine-breaking and rioting; at Gloucester, upwards of thirty; at Oxford, twenty-nine; and at Winchester, out of upwards of forty convicted, six were left for execution. . . . At Salisbury, forty-four prisoners were convicted . . .[3]

And it was a Whig Ministry again which sanctioned, three years later, the transportation of the labourers of Tolpuddle in Dorsetshire, who had had the insolence to form a trade union

This revolt of the field labourers extended more widely into East Anglia and the Midlands, as well as the southern counties,

1. H.O. 42.149/51. For the East Anglian labour-gangs, see W. Hasbach, *History of the English Agricultural Labourer* (1908), pp. 192–204.
2. *Wellington Despatches*, second series, viii, p. 388, cit. H. W. C. Davis, op. cit., p. 224.
3. A. Prentice, *Historical Sketches of Manchester*, p. 372. In the end, nine labourers were hanged, 457 transported, and about 400 imprisoned. See J. L. & B. Hammond, *The Village Labourer*, chs. X and XI.

and lasted longer than is apparent from the Hammonds' account. Few first-hand accounts from the labourers' side have survived. In 1845 Somerville took down the story of Joseph Carter, a Hampshire labourer from the village of Sutton Scotney (one of the places where the revolt commenced), who was sentenced to transportation for his part, and who had spent two years in the Portsmouth hulks. 'Everybody was forced like to go,' said Carter: 'There was no denying':

I wor at the meeting across the street there, in that corner house, the night as Joe Mason read the letter to us all, that came from Overton. There was no name to the letter. But Joe said he knowed who it came from. Joe was a good scholard. The letter, I know, came from old D—s; he be dead; and it came out of Newton; never came from Overton. It said we was all to leave off work; and the Sutton men was to go out and stop the ploughs. They was to send home the horses for the farmers to look after them themselves, and was to take the men with them. And they was to go and turn the men out of the barns. And they was all to go and break the sheens as the farmers had got to do the thrashing. . . .

Well; about the letter. Joe Mason read it. We did not then know who it came from. But we knows, all on us now in this here place, that old D—s had a hand in't. He was a great friend of Mr Cobbett. He used to write to Mr Cobbett. He never got into no trouble about it. He was too good a manager to get other people into trouble to get in himself. No; I do not blame this on Mr Cobbett. I mean old D—s, the shoemaker . . .

The labourers then collected or extorted money from gentry and farmers, and Joseph Carter was made treasurer:

They said I wor honest, and they gave it to me to carry. I had £40 at one time – £40 every shilling. Some people ha' told me since that I should ha' gone off with it. I did think of doing that once. The coach came by when we was up on the London Road, and it did come into my head to get on the coach, and get away from the whole business, with the £40. But I thought about leaving my wife behind, and about what a vagabond they would all call me, and the coach was soon past. . . .

I needn't ha' been tried at all. They came to me time and times after I was in Winchester gaol, to get me to speak against the two Masons. They offered to let me clear, if I would only tell what I knowed agin them. Had I told what I knowed, they'd ha' been hung, as sure as Borrowman, and Cooke, and Cooper, was hung.

I was took out with the other prisoners to see they hung. They tried
to frighten us by it to tell all we knowed on one another. But I
wouldn't split. So the Masons was only transported, and they
transported me, too. Ees the mob took me agin my will; but then
that was not enough to make me split, 'cause you see, I stayed with
them. . . . It wor the young fellows did it . . .[1]

The labourers' revolt was a true outburst of machine-breaking, with little indication of ulterior political motive. While
corn ricks and other property were destroyed (as well as some
industrial machinery in country districts) the main assault was
on the threshing-machine, which (despite futurist homilies)
patently was displacing the already starving labourers. Hence
the destruction of the machines did in fact effect some immediate relief.[2] But among the 'young fellows' it is possible that
political ideas of further significance were abroad.[3] A 'scholard'
like Joe Mason may foreshadow George Loveless. Radical
cobblers like D——s were to be found in most small market
towns. In Norfolk it is tempting to suggest that the agitations
of Jacobins and Radicals had left some traces in the villages.
The most strenuous efforts were made in Lincolshire in 1830
and 1831 to intimidate labourers who had been reading Cobbett's *Register*.[4] But if there was a stirring political consciousness, it did not reach the point at which the urban and rural
workers could form common organizations or make common
cause, until several years after the labourers' revolt had been
repressed.[5]

The revolt of 1830 was not wholly without effect. It led to the
temporary raising of wages in the southern counties. And,

1. A. Somerville, op. cit., pp. 262–4.

2. See E. J. Hobsbawm, 'The Machine-Breakers', *Past and Present*, 1,
February 1952, p. 67.

3. A labourer in Kent was widely reported as saying: 'We will destroy
the cornstacks and thrashing machines this year. Next year we will have
a turn with the Parsons, and the third we will make war upon the Statesmen'; see, e.g., handbill in H.O. 40.25.

4. See J. Hughes, 'Tried Beyond Endurance', *The Landworker*, November 1954.

5. In 1833 James Watson appealed to members of the National Union
of Working Classes to make especial efforts to build branches among
the rural workers. *Working Man's Friend*, 3 August 1833. See also *Radical Reformer*, 19 November 1831.

indirectly, it gave a final push to Old Corruption. Many farmers, and a few of the gentry, had been ashamed of the business, had negotiated with the mobs, or given them passive support. The revolt both sapped the confidence of the gentry, and helped to arouse the Reform agitation of 1831-2. 'The important feature in the affair,' wrote Cobbett, 'is, that the *middle class*, who always, heretofore, were arrayed, generally speaking, against the *working class*, are now *with them* in heart and mind, thought not always in act.... Among the tradesmen, even of the metropolis, *ninety-nine out of a hundred are on the side of the labourers*.'[1] The aristocracy lost 'face': the necessity and urgency of Reform was made plainer. And it is from this time forward that articulate political development can be seen among the rural labourers: pockets of trade unionism in the 1830s: Joseph Arch's father ('steady as Old Time, a plodding man') victimized in 1835 for refusing to sign a petition in favour of the Corn Laws: a scatter of Chartist branches in East Anglia and the south.

But the grievances of the labourers had, as it were, a vicarious existence, twisted in with the other strands which made up the consciousness of the urban working class. Although – unlike France or Ireland – it never gave rise to a coherent national agitation, the ground-swell of rural grievance came back always to access to the *land*. 'Times used to be better before Bledlow was enclosed.... We should rejoice to occupy a rood of land, and pay full rent for it' (Buckinghamshire Labourers' Petition, 1834). '... small allotments of land to labourers to be cultivated with a spade ...' (Essex Labourers' Petition, 1837). 'He wished every labouring man to have three or four acres of land at the same rent as the farmers gave. They would pay this, and gladly. (Loud cheers....)' (speech of Wiltshire labourer, 1845). When the labourer or his children moved into the town it was this aspiration which remained. And when the tithes, the Game Laws, and the threshing machines had been forgotten, the sense of lost rights lingered – or, as Clapham has it, was 'exaggerated' in 'popular retrospect'. We shall see how Cobbett and Hunt, farmers both, helped to shape the new urban radicalism; but rural memories were fed into the urban

1. *Political Register*, 4 December 1830.

working-class culture through innumerable personal experiences.[1] Throughout the nineteenth century the urban worker made articulate the hatred for the 'landed aristocrat' which perhaps his grandfather had nourished in secret: he liked to see the squire cast in villainous melodramas, and he preferred even a Board of Guardians to the charity of a Lady Bountiful: he felt that the landowner had no 'right' to his wealth whereas, if only by foul means, the mill-owner had 'earned' his. The response of urban trade unionists to the transportation of the Tolpuddle labourers was immediate and overwhelming; and to the later struggles of Arch's union scarcely less so. And the yearning for land arises again and again, twisted in with the outworker's desire for an 'independence', from the days of Spence to the Chartist Land Plan and beyond. Perhaps its vestiges are still with us today, in allotments and garden-plots. Land always carries associations – of status, security, rights – more profound than the value of its crop.

We see the influence of this as early as the 1790s, in the Jacobin hatred of the landed aristocracy. This was an enduring characteristic of the radicalism of the artisans, nourished by Paine's *Agrarian Justice* and Spence's propaganda for land nationalization. In the severe post-war depression, Dr Watson and other orators won great support from the unemployed, and the discharged sailors and soldiers who attended the meetings at Spa Fields:

... trade and commerce have been annihilated, but still the earth was by nature designed for the support of mankind. The earth is at all times sufficient to place man above distress ... if he had but a spade and a hoe ...[2]

In the next decade, as Owenism changed its form among its plebeian followers, the dream of a cooperative community upon the land acquired extraordinary force.

And so, to the political myth of English freedom before the 'Norman bastard and his armed banditti' there was added the social myth of the golden age of the village community before enclosure and before the Wars:

1. Richard Hoggart has testified as to the survival of rural memories in working-class Leeds in the 1930s. See *Uses of Literacy* (1957), pp. 23–5.
2. W. M. Gurney, *Trial of James Watson* (1817), 1, p. 70.

Here's that we may live to see the restoration of old English times, old English fare, old English holidays, and old English justice, and every man live by the sweat of his brow ... when the weaver worked at his own loom, and stretched his limbs in his own field, when the laws recognized the poor man's right to an abundance of everything ...

– This is Feargus O'Connor, the Chartist leader, who gave to the myth gargantuan dimensions: but Cobbett, Hunt, Oastler and a score of Radical leaders contributed to it. The savage penal code, the privations, the bridewells, of old England were forgotten; but the myth of the lost paternalist community became a force in its own right – perhaps as powerful a force as the utopian projections of Owen and the Socialists. To say it was 'myth' is not to say it was all false; rather, it is a montage of memories, an 'average' in which every loss and every abuse is drawn into one total. In his youth, 'Old Robin' tells the mill-owner (in a pamphlet of O'Connor's) 'all those new streets behind Mr Twist's and Mr Grab's and Mr Screw's ... were all open fields, and children used to be there at eight, nine, ten, eleven, aye, and twelve years of age, idling their time at play, at cricket, at trap, and marbles, and ball ... and leap-frog ...' Then came the time 'when rich folk frightened poor folk out of their sense with "He's a cooming" and "They're a cooming".' 'Who are "they", Robin?'

Why, Boney and the French, to be sure. Well, that time when rich folk frightened poor folk and stole all the land. This was all common, then, Mr Smith ... All reet and left, up away to bastile and barracks was all common. And all folk in Devil's Dust would have a cow, or donkey, or horse on common, and they'd play cricket, and have running matches, and wrestling. ...

... They built barrack at one end and church at 'tother ... and, at last, almost all folk had to sell cow, to pay Lawyer Grind, and Lawyer Squeeze ... and now the son of one of 'em is mayor, and t'other ... is manager of bank. Aye, dearee me, many's the honest man was hung and transported over ould common.[1]

It is an historical irony that it was not the rural labourers but the urban workers who mounted the greatest coherent

1. F. O'Connor, *The Employer and the Employed* (1844), pp. 15, 41-2, 56.

national agitation for the return of the land. Some of them were sons and grandsons of labourers, their wits sharpened by the political life of the towns, freed from the shadows of the squire. Some – the supporters of the Land Plan – were weavers and artisans of rural descent: 'faither, and grandfaither and all folk belonging to I worked on land and it didn't kill them, and why should it kill me?'[1] Faced with hard times and unemployment in the brick wastes of the growing towns, the memories of lost rights rose up with a new bitterness of deprivation.

We have strayed far from averages. And that was our intention. For we cannot make an average of well-being. We have seen something of the other side of the world of Jane Austen's novels; and for those who lived on that side the period *felt* catastrophic enough. 'When farmers became *gentlemen*,' Cobbett wrote, 'their labourers became *slaves*.' If it is possible to argue that there was gain at the end of the process, we must remember that the gain came to other people. In comparing a Suffolk labourer with his grand-daughter in a cotton-mill we are comparing – not two standards – but two ways of life.

There are, however, two relevant points which may be made about these averages. The first is that it is possible, given the same figures, to show both a relative decline and an absolute increase in poverty. Agriculture is an inelastic industry in its demand for labour: if ten labourers were required for a given farm in 1790, there might be ten – or, with improved ploughs and threshing machines – eight in 1830. We might show that the labourer or carter in regular employment increased his real wages over this period; while the increase in population in the village – casual labour and unemployed – led to an absolute increase in the number of the poor. And while this might be most evident in agriculture, the same hypothesis must be borne in mind when discussing the overall national picture. If, for the sake of argument, we take the hypothesis that 40% of the population (10·5 millions) was living below a given poverty-line' in 1790, but only 30% of the population (18·1 millions) in 1841, nevertheless the absolute number of the poor will have increased from about four millions to well over

1. *The Labourer* (1847), p. 46.

five millions. More poverty will be 'felt' and, moreover, there will in fact be more poor people.

This is not juggling with figures. It is possible that something of this sort took place. But at the same time no such assessment of averages can tell us about 'average' human relationships. To judge these, we are forced to pick our way as we can through conflicting subjective evidence. And a judgement on this period must surely take in some impression of the 'average' English gentleman. We need not accept Cobbett's invective – 'the most cruel, the most unfeeling, the most brutally insolent' of all God's creatures. But we surely need not fall back into some of the queerer notions which have recently made a re-appearance: 'The English country gentlemen were indeed perhaps the most remarkable class of men that any society has ever produced anywhere in the world.'[1] In the place of this we may offer a Norfolk labourer's opinion, in an anonymous letter to 'the Gentlemen of Ashill' – 'You have by this time brought us under the heaviest burden & into the hardest Yoke we ever knowed':

It is too hard for us to bear, you have often times blinded us saying that the fault was all in the Place-men of Parliament, but ... they have nothing to do with the regulation of this parish.

You do as you like, you rob the poor of their Commons right, plough the grass up that God send to grow, that a poor man may feed a Cow, Pig, Horse, nor Ass; lay muck and stones on the road to prevent the grass growing. ... There is 5 or 6 of you have gotten all the whole of the Land in this parish in your own hands & you would wish to be rich and starve all the other part of the poor ...

'We have counted up that we have gotten about 60 of us to 1 of you: therefore should you govern, so many to 1?'[2]

But it was for the tithe-consuming clergy that the especial hatred of the rural community was reserved. 'Prepare your wicked Soul for Death,' an Essex vicar was threatened in 1830, in a letter which enclosed two matches: 'You & your whole Crew are biggest Paupers in the parish ...' The Rector of Freshwater (Isle of Wight) received an even more explicit intimation from one of his parishioners, in the form of some

1. R. J. White, *Waterloo to Peterloo* (1957), pp. 40–4.
2. Enclosure in Rev. Edwards to Sidmouth, 22 May 1816, H.O. 42.150.

mild arson, with an accompanying letter. 'For the last 20 years wee have been in a Starving Condition to maintain your Dam Pride':

What we have done now is Soar against our Will but your harts is so hard as the hart of Pharo ... So now as for this fire you must not take it as a front [an affront], for if you hadent been Deserving it wee should not have dont [done it]. As for you my Ould frend you dident hapen to be hear, if that you had been rosted I fear, and if it had been so how the farmers would lagh to see the old Pasen [Parson] rosted at last ...

'As for this litel fire,' the writer concluded, with equable ill-humour, 'Don't be alarmed it will be a damd deal wors when we Burn down your barn ...' [1]

1. Enclosures in Rev. W. M. Hurlock, 14 December 1830, and the Very Rev. Dean Wood, 29 November 1830, in H.O. 52.7.

[8]

Artisans and Others

IF the average is elusive in agriculture, it is no less so when we come to workers in urban industry. Still, in 1830, the characteristic industrial worker worked not in a mill or factory but (as an artisan or 'mechanic') in a small workshop or in his own home, or (as a labourer) in more-or-less casual employment in the streets, on building-sites, on the docks. When Cobbett directed his *Political Register* towards the common people in 1816, he addressed, not the working class, but the 'Journeymen and Labourers'. There were great differences of degree concealed within the term, 'artisan', from the prosperous master-craftsman, employing labour on his own account and independent of any masters, to the sweated garret labourers. For this reason, it is difficult to offer any accurate estimates of the number and status of artisans in different trades. The occupational tables of the Census of 1831 make no effort to differentiate between the master, the self-employed, and the labourer.[1] After the agricultural labourers and domestic servants (670,491 female domestic servants alone being listed for Great Britain in 1831), the building trades made up the next largest group, accounting perhaps for 350,000 to 400,000 men and boys in 1831. Leaving aside the textile industries where outwork still predominated, the largest single artisan trade was that of shoemaking, with 133,000 adult male workers estimated for 1831, followed by tailoring, with 74,000. (Such figures include the employer, the country cobbler or tailor, the outworker, the shopkeeper, and the urban artisan proper.) In London, the greatest artisan centre in the world,

1. Mayhew later described the occupational returns as 'crude, undigested, and essentially unscientific', a document 'whose insufficiency is a national disgrace to us, for there the trading and working classes are all jumbled together in the most perplexing confusion, and the occupations classified in a manner that would shame the merest tyro'.

where Dr Dorothy George appears to lend her authority to a rough estimate of 100,000 journeymen of all types in the early nineteenth century, Sir John Clapham advises us:

... the typical London skilled workman was neither brewery hand, shipwright nor silk weaver, but either a member of the building trades; or a shoemaker, tailor, cabinet-maker, printer, clockmaker, jeweller, baker – to mention the chief trades each of which had over 2,500 adult members in 1831.[1]

The wages of the skilled craftsmen at the beginning of the nineteenth century were often determined less by 'supply and demand' in the labour market than by notions of social prestige, or 'custom'. Customary wage-regulation may cover many things, from the status accorded by tradition to the rural crafts-man to intricate institutional regulation in urban centres. Industry was still widely dispersed throughout the countryside. The tinker, knife-grinder, or pedlar would take his wares or skills from farm to farm and fair to fair. In the large villages there would be stonemasons, thatchers, carpenters, wheel-wrights, shoemakers, the blacksmith's forge: in the small market town there would be saddlers and harness-makers, tan-ners, tailors, shoemakers, weavers, and very possibly some local speciality such as stirrup-making or pillow-lace, as well as all the business of the posting-inns, carriage of farm produce and of coals, milling, baking and the like. Many of these rural craftsmen were better educated and more versatile and felt themselves to be a 'cut above' the urban workers – weavers, stockingers or miners – with whom they came into contact when they came to the towns. They brought their own customs with them; and no doubt these influenced wage-fixing and differentials in those small-town crafts which grew into great urban industries – building, coach-making, even engineering.

Custom, rather than costing (which was rarely understood), governed prices in many village industries, especially where local materials – timber or stone – were used. The blacksmith might work for so much a pound for rough work, a little more for fine. George Sturt, in his classic study of *The Wheelwright's*

1. For these figures, see *Parliamentary Papers*, 1833, *XXXVII*; Clapham, op. cit., esp. pp. 72–4, and ch. 5; R. M. Martin, *Taxation of the British Empire* (1833), pp. 193, 256.

Shop, has described how customary prices still prevailed in Farnham when he took over the family firm in 1884. 'My great difficulty was to find out the customary price,'

I doubt if there was a tradesman in the district – I am sure there was no wheelwright – who really knew what his output cost, or what his profits were, or if he was making money or losing it on a particular job.

Much of the profit came from 'jobbing' and repairs. As for carts and waggons, 'the only chance for me to make a profit would have been by lowering the quality of the output; and this the temper of the men made out of the question'. The men worked at the pace which their craftsmanship demanded: 'they possibly (and properly) exaggerated the respect for good workmanship and material'; and as for the latter, 'it happened not infrequently that a disgusted workman would refuse to use what I had supplied to him'. In the workman was 'stored all the local lore of what good wheelwright's work should be like'.[1]

Customary traditions of craftsmanship normally went to-gether with vestigial notions of a 'fair' price and a 'just' wage. Social and moral criteria – subsistence, self-respect, pride in certain standards of workmanship, customary rewards for different grades of skill – these are as prominent in early trade union disputes as strictly 'economic' arguments. Sturt's wheel-wright's shop perpetuated much older practices, and was coun-try cousin to the city industry of coach-building, in which – in the early nineteenth century – there was a veritable hierarchy whose wage-differentials can scarcely be justified on economic grounds. 'The wages are in proportion to the nicety of the work', we are told in an 1818 *Book of English Trades*: for the body-makers, £2 to £3 a week: the trimmers 'about two guineas': the carriage-makers £1 to £2: the smith about 30s.: while the painters had their own hierarchy – the herald painters, who adorned the carriages of the great and the osten-tatious with emblems, from £3 to £4: the body painters about £2: and journeymen painters 20s. to 30s. The differentials supported, or perhaps reflected, gradations of social prestige:

1. G. Sturt, *The Wheelwright's Shop* (1923), chs. 10, 37.

The body-makers are first on the list; then follow the carriage-makers; then the trimmers; then the smiths; then the spring-makers; then the wheelwrights, painters, platers, bracemakers and so on. The body-makers are the wealthiest of all and compose among themselves a species of aristocracy to which the other workmen look up with feelings half of respect, half of jealousy. They feel their importance and treat the others with various consideration: carriage makers are entitled to a species of condescending familiarity; trimmers are considered too good to be despised; a foreman of painters they may treat with respect, but working painters can at most be favoured with a nod.[1]

These conditions were supported by the activities of a 'Benevolent Society of Coachmakers'; and they survived the conviction under the Combination Acts of the General Secretary and twenty other members of the society in 1819. But it is important, at this stage, to note this early use of the term 'aristocracy', with reference to the skilled artisan.[2] It is sometimes supposed that the phenomenon of a 'labour aristocracy' was coincident with the skilled trade unionism of the 1850s and 1860s – or was even the consequence of imperialism. But in fact there is both an old and a new élite of labour to be found in the years 1800–1850. The old élite was made up of master-artisans who considered themselves as 'good' as masters, shopkeepers, or professional men.[3] (The *Book of English Trades* lists the apothecary, attorney, optician and statutory alongside the carpenter, currier, tailor and potter.) In some industries, the craftsman's privileged position survived into workshop or factory production, through the force of custom, or combination and apprenticeship restriction, or because the craft remained highly skilled and specialized – fine and 'fancy' work in the luxury branches of the glass, wood and metal trades. The new élite arose with new skills in the iron, engineering and manufacturing industries. This is plain enough in en-

1. W. B. Adams, *English Pleasure Carriages* (1837), cited in E. Hobsbawm, 'Custom, Wages and Work-load in Nineteenth Century Industry', in *Essays in Labour History*, ed. A. Briggs and J. Saville, p. 116.

2. Another early use is in the *First Report of the Constabulary Commissioners* (1839), p. 134, in a context which suggests that the term was widespread at the time.

3. For the eighteenth-century 'aristocracy', see M. D. George, op. cit., ch. 4.

gineering; but even in the cotton industry we must remember
the warning, 'we are not cotton-spinners all'. Overlookers,
skilled 'tenters' of various kinds who adjusted and repaired the
machines, pattern-drawers in calico-printing, and scores of
other skilled subsidiary crafts, at which exceptional wages
might be earned, were among the 1,225 sub-divisions of heads
of employment in cotton manufacture enumerated in the 1841
Census.

If a specially favoured aristocracy was to be found in the
London luxury trades and on the border-line between skills
and technical or managerial functions in the great manufacturing industries, there was also a lesser aristocracy of artisans or
privileged workers in almost every skilled industry. We can
see this if we look for a moment through the inquisitive,
humorous eyes of Thomas Large, a Leicester stocking-weaver
who took part in a deputation to London in 1812 to lobby
M.P.s on behalf of a Bill for regulating conditions in the
hosiery industry.[1] Once they had reached London, the
framework knitters – who had at this time no permanent trade
union organization but simply an *ad hoc* committee formed
to promote the passage of their Bill – made contact with trade
unionists in London who, despite the Combination Acts, were
easily located at their houses of call:

We have engaged the same Room, where the carpinter committee
sat [Thomas Large wrote back to his friends in the Midlands]
when they brought on the late Trial on the sistom of colting. We
have had an opportunity of speaking to them on the subject, they
thought we possessed a fund on a permanent principle to answer
any demand, at any time, and if that had been the case would have
lent us two or three thousand pounds, (for there is £20,000 in the
fund belonging to that Trade) but When they understood our Trade
kept no regular fund to support itself, Instead of Lending us money,
Their noses underwent a Mechanical turn upwards, and each
saluted the other with a significant stare, Ejaculating, Lord bless
us ! ! ! what fools ! ! ! they richly deserve all they put! and ten
times more ! ! ! We always thought stockeners a sett of poor creatures! Fellows as wanting of spirit, as their pockets are of money.
What would our Trade be, if we did not combine together? perhaps
as poor as you are, at this day! Look at other Trades! they all

1. See below, pp. 585–90.

Combine, (the Spitalfields weavers excepted, and what a Miserable Condition are they in). See the Tailors, Shoemakers, Bookbinders, Gold beaters, Printers, Bricklayers, Coatmakers, Hatters, Curriers, Masons, Whitesmiths, none of these trades Receive Less than 30/- a week, and from that to five guineas this is all done by Combination, without it their Trades would be as bad as yours . . .[1]

To Thomas Large's list we might add many others. The compositors and pressmen then stood at the edge of the 30s. line of privilege, having had a particularly hard struggle to organize in the face of the combined London masters. Some skilled men were less fortunate. The type-founders' combination had been broken up, and their wages in 1818 were claimed to average only 18s. per week, having seen no advance since 1790. The same was true of the opticians and pipe-makers. The *Gorgon* suggested in 1819 that 25s. might be the wages of the average London 'mechanic', when averaged over the year.[2] But when in 1824 the Combination Acts were repealed, and the craft unions in the London trades openly showed themselves, we can get an idea of the 'lesser aristocracy' by citing some trades which appeared most often in the columns of the *Trades Newspaper* of 1825: to Large's list we can add the coopers, shipwrights, sawyers, ship caulkers, wire-drawers, cock-founders, fell-mongers, leather dressers, ropemakers, brass founders, silk dyers, clock and watch makers, skinners, and others. It is an impressive list; and in London as well as the larger cities such men were the very heart of the artisan culture and political movements of these years. By no means all of these trades were equally privileged. Some of the trades clubs in 1825 had fewer than 100 members, and not many exceeded 500. They varied between exceptionally privileged groups, like the upholsterers (who charged 'enormous premiums' for admission to apprenticeship) to the shoemakers who (as we shall see) were already in the grip of a crisis which was degrading them to the status of outworkers.[3]

1. *Records of the Borough of Nottingham 1800–1835* (1952), VIII, Thomas Large to Framework-knitters Committee, 24 April 1812.
2. See *Gorgon*, 17 October, 21 and 28 November 1818, 6 February and 20 March 1819.
3. *Trades Newspaper*, 1825–6, *passim*.

Similar important groups of privileged artisans or skilled workers will be found in the provinces, not only in the same trades, but in trades scarcely represented in London. This was true, in particular, of the Sheffield cutlery and Birmingham small-ware industries. In the latter, there persisted far into the nineteenth century the numerous petty workshops, which made Birmingham the metropolis of the small master. Boulton's Soho works bulks large in the story of economic growth. But the great majority of the city's population, at the close of the eighteenth century, were employed in very small shops, whether as labourers or as quasi-independent craftsmen. To enumerate some of the Birmingham products is to evoke the intricate constellation of skills: buckles, cutlery, spurs, candlesticks, toys, guns, buttons, whip handles, coffee pots, ink stands, bells, carriage-fittings, steam-engines, snuff-boxes, lead pipes, jewellery, lamps, kitchen implements. 'Every man whom I meet,' Southey wrote in 1807, 'stinks of train-oil and emery.'[1]

Here, in the Black Country, the process of specialization in the first three decades of the nineteenth century tended to take the simpler processes, such as nail and chain-making, to the surrounding villages of outworkers, while the more highly skilled operations remained in the metropolis of Birmingham itself.[2] In such artisan trades the gulf between the small master and the skilled journeyman might, in psychological and sometimes in economic terms, be less than that between the journeyman and the common urban labourer. Entry to a whole trade might be limited to the sons of those already working in it, or might be bought only by a high apprenticeship premium. Restriction upon entry into the trade might be supported by corporate regulations (such as those of the Cutler's Company of Sheffield, not repealed until 1814), encouraged by masters, and maintained by trade unions under the aliases of friendly societies. Among such artisans at the commencement of the nineteenth century (the Webbs suggested) 'we have industrial

1. J. A. Langford, *A Century of Birmingham Life*, I, p. 272; C. Gill, *History of Birmingham*, I, pp. 95–8; Southey, *Letters from England*, Letter XXVI.

2. See S. Timmins (Ed.), *Birmingham and the Midland Hardware District* (1866), pp. 110 *et passim*; H. D. Fong, *Triumph of Factory System in England* (Tientsin, 1930), pp. 165–9.

society still divided vertically trade by trade, instead of horizontally between employers and wage-earners'.[1] Equally, it might be that a privileged section only of the workers in a particular industry succeeded in restricting entry or in elevating their conditions. Thus, a recent study of the London porters has shown the fascinating intricacy of the history of a section of workers – including the Billingsgate porters – who might easily be supposed to be casual labourers but who in fact came under the particular surveillance of the City authorities, and who maintained a privileged position within the ocean of unskilled labour until the middle of the nineteenth century.[2] More commonly, the distinction was between the skilled or apprenticed man and his labourer: the blacksmith and his striker, the bricklayer and his labourer, the calico pattern-drawer and his assistants, and so on.

The distinction between the artisan and the labourer – in terms of status, organization, and economic reward – remained as great, if not greater, in Henry Mayhew's London of the late 1840s and 1850s as it was during the Napoleonic Wars. 'In passing from the skilled operative of the west-end to the unskilled workman of the eastern quarter of London,' Mayhew commented, 'the moral and intellectual change is so great, that it seems as if we were in a new land, and among another race':

The artisans are almost to a man red-hot politicians. They are sufficiently educated and thoughtful to have a sense of their importance in the State. ... The unskilled labourers are a different class of people. As yet they are as unpolitical as footmen, and instead of entertaining violent democratic opinions, they appear to have no political opinions whatever; or, if they do ... they rather lead towards the maintenance of 'things as they are', than towards the ascendancy of the working people.[3]

In the south, it was among the artisans that the membership

1. S. and B. Webb, *The History of Trade Unionism* (1950 edn), pp. 45–6.

2. W. M. Stern, *The Porters of London* (1960).

3. H. Mayhew, *London Labour and the London Poor* (1862), III, p. 243. Against this should be set the statement of one of Mayhew's scavengers: 'I cares nothing about politics neither; but I'm a chartist.'

of friendly societies was largest[1] and trade union organization
was most continuous and stable, that educational and religious
movements flourished, and that Owenism struck deepest root.
It was, again, among the artisans that the custom of 'tramping'
in search of work was so widespread that it has been described
by one historian as 'the artisan's equivalent of the Grand
Tour'.[2] We shall see how their self-esteem and their desire for
independence, coloured the political radicalism of the post-
war years. And, if stripped of his craft and of his trade union
defences, the artisan was one of the most pitiful figures in
Mayhew's London. 'The destitute mechanics,' Mayhew was
told by the Master of the Wandsworth and Clapham Union,
'are entirely a different class from the regular vagrants.' Their
lodging-houses and 'houses of call' were different from those
of the tramps and the fraternity of 'travellers'; they would
turn to the workhouse only in final despair: 'Occasionally
they have sold the shirt and waistcoat off their backs before
they applied for admittance. . .' 'The poor mechanic will sit in
the casual ward like a lost man, scared. . . . When he's beat out
he's like a bird out of a cage; he doesn't know where to go,
or how to get a bit.'[3]

The London artisan was rarely beaten down so low – there
were many half-way stages before the workhouse door was
reached. His history varies greatly from trade to trade. And if
we look out of London to the northern and Midlands centres of
industry, there are other important classes of skilled labourer
or factory operative – miners in certain coalfields, cotton-
spinners, skilled building-workers, skilled workers in the iron
and metal industries – who are among those whom Professor
Ashton describes as being 'able to share in the benefits of
economic progress'. Among such were the Durham miners
whom Cobbett described (in the Sunderland area) in 1832:

You see nothing here that is pretty; but everything seems to be
abundant in value; and one great thing is, the working people live

1. On the social composition of friendly societies, see P. H. J. H. Gosden, *The Friendly Societies in England* (Manchester, 1961), pp. 71 ff.
2. E. J. Hobsbawm, 'The Tramping Artisan', in *Econ. Hist. Review*.
Series 2, III (1950–51), p. 313.
3. Mayhew, op. cit., I, p. 351.

well. .... The pitmen have twenty-four shillings a week; they live
rent-free, their fuel costs them nothing, and their doctor costs them
nothing. Their work is terrible, to be sure; and, perhaps, they do
not have what they ought to have; but, at any rate, they live well,
their houses are good and their furniture good; and ... their lives
seem to be as good as that of the working part of mankind can
reasonably expect.[1]

The miners, who in many districts were almost an 'hereditary
caste', had a reputation as comparatively high wage-earners:

> Collier lads get gowd and silver,
> Factory lads gets nowt but brass ...

Professor Ashton considers it to be probable that their real
wages were higher in the 1840s than in any but the best of the
war years. But their conditions of work were probably worse.[2]

Many such groups increased their real wages between 1790
and 1840. The progress was not as smooth nor as continuous
as is sometimes implied. It was closely related to the success or
failure of trade unionism in each industry, and unemployment
or seasonal short time must be set against 'optimistic' wage-
series. But if we were concerned only with skilled 'society
men' in regular employment, then the controversy as to living
standards would long ago have been settled on the optimistic
side.

But in fact the whole problem presents endless complexities.
The student who comes across a confident statement of this
order in his textbook –

In 1831 the cost of living was 11 per cent higher than in 1790, but
over this span of time urban wages had increased, it appears, by no
less than 43 per cent.[3]

– should at once scent danger. It is not only that the cost of
living indices are themselves the subject of serious dispute –

1. *Rural Rides*, II, p. 294. Against this account should be set the
stormy incidents in the North-eastern coalfield – the rise and destruction
of Hepburn's union between 1830 and 1832, recounted in R. Fynes, *The
Miners of Northumberland and Durham*, chs. 4–6 and *The Skilled
Labourer*, chs. 2 and 3.

2. See T. S. Ashton, 'The Coal-Miners of the Eighteenth Century,'
Econ. Journal (Supplement), I, 1928, pp. 325, 331, 334.

3. T. S. Ashton, *The Industrial Revolution, 1760–1830* (1948), p. 158.

Professor Ashton himself having described the index upon which his own statement is based as being perhaps derived from the diet of a 'diabetic'.[1] We should also realize that the index of urban wages is based, in the main, upon the wages of skilled workers in full work. And it is exactly here that a host of further problems enter. Why should we suppose, in a period of very rapid population-growth, that the proportion of employed and skilled to casual and unemployed workers should move in favour of the former? Why should the social historian repeatedly encounter evidence suggesting that this was an exceptionally painful period for great masses of the people? How was it – if 1820 to 1850 showed an appreciable rise in the standard-of-living – that after thirty more years of unquestioned improvement betwen 1850 and 1880 – the unskilled workers of England still lived in the conditions of extreme deprivation revealed, in the 1890s, by Booth and by Rowntree?

The first half of the nineteenth century must be seen as a period of chronic under-employment, in which the skilled trades are like islands threatened on every side by technological innovation and by the inrush of unskilled or juvenile labour. Skilled wages themselves often conceal a number of enforced outpayments: rent of machinery, payment for the use of motive power, fines for faulty work or indiscipline, or compulsory deductions of other kinds. Sub-contracting was predominant in the mining, iron and pottery industries, and fairly widespread in building, whereby the 'butty' or 'ganger' would himself employ less skilled labourers; while children – pieceners in the mills or hurryers in the pits – were customarily employed by the spinner or the collier. The Manchester cotton-spinners claimed in 1818, that a wage of £2 3s. 4d. was subject to the following outpayments:

1st piecer per week	0	9	2
2nd piecer per week	0	7	2
3rd piecer per week	0	5	3
Candles on the average winter and summer per week	0	1	6
Sick and other incidental expenses	0	1	6
Expense	£1	5	0

1. T. S. Ashton in *Capitalism and the Historians*, p. 146.

– leaving a balance of 18s. 4d.[1] In every industry similar cases can be cited, whereby the wages quoted by workers reveal a different complexion from those quoted by employers. 'Truck', or payment in goods, and 'tommy shops' complicate the picture further; while seamen and waterside workers were subject to peculiar extortions, often at the hands of publicans – for example, the Thames coal-whippers who – until a protective Act in 1843 – could only gain employment through the publicans who, in their turn, would only employ men who consumed up to 50% of their wages in the public house.[2]

Where a skill was involved, the artisan was as much concerned with maintaining his status as against the unskilled man as he was in bringing pressure upon the employers. Trade unions which attempted to cater for both the skilled and the unskilled in the same trade are rare before 1830; and when the builders, in their period of Owenite enthusiasm, adopted proposals embracing the labourers, the distinction was very clearly marked:

These Lodges should, by degrees, consist of architects, masons, bricklayers, carpenters, slaters, plasterers, plumbers, glaziers, painters; and also quarriers, brickmakers, and labourers as soon as they can be prepared with better habits and more knowledge to enable them to act for themselves, assisted by the other branches who will have an overwhelming interest to improve the mind, morals and general conditions of their families in the shortest time.[3]

But we must also bear in mind the general *insecurity* of many skills in a period of rapid technical innovation and of weak trade union defences. Invention simultaneously devalued old skills and elevated new ones. There is little uniformity in the process. As late as 1818 the *Book of English Trades* (a pocketbook based mainly on London skills) does not list the trades of engineer, steam-engine maker, or boiler-maker: the turner was

1. *Black Dwarf*, 9 September 1818. The admission of sick club (and possibly trade union) dues as necessary 'expenses' does however indicate an improvement in living standards.

2. See G. W. Hilton, *The Truck System* (Cambridge, 1960), pp. 81–7 *et passim*.

3. *Pioneer*, September 1833, cited in R. Postgate, *The Builder's History* (1923), p. 93.

still regarded as mainly a woodworker, and the skills of the engineer were united in the 'machinist' – a versatile master of many trades, 'of considerable ingenuity and great mechanical knowledge' who 'requires the talents and experience of the joiner, the brass and iron founder, the smith and the turner, in their most extended variety'. Only ten years later there was published *The Operative Mechanic and British Machinist*, running to no less than 900 pages, showing the extraordinary diversity of what had once been the mill-wright's craft. And the separation off of new skills can be seen in the formation of the early societies or trade unions which were later to make up the engineers: well-organized trades clubs of mill-wrights at the end of the eighteenth century give rise to the Friendly Society of Iron-moulders (1809), the Friendly and Benevolent Society of Vicemen and Turners (London, 1818), the Mechanics' Friendly Union Institution (Bradford, 1822), Steam Engine Makers' Society (Liverpool, 1824), and the Friendly Union of Mechanics (Manchester, 1826).

But the progression of these societies should not lead us to suppose a record of continuing advancement as new skills became established. On the contrary, whereas the mill-wright (at least in London) was an aristocrat, who was protected both by his own organization (which was so strong that it was one of the occasions for the passing of the Combination Act)[1] and by apprenticeship restrictions, and who maintained a wage of two guineas in the first years of the nineteenth century, the repeal of the apprenticeship clauses of the Elizabethan Statute of Artificers in 1814 left him exposed to serious competition. Alexander Galloway, a former assistant Secretary of the L.C.S. and now the leading engineering employer in London, gave evidence in 1824 that after repeal, 'when a man was allowed to work at any employment, whether he had served one, two, or three years, or not at all, that broke the neck of all com-

1. According to a 'Statement of facts respecting the Journeymen Mill-wrights' in P.C. A.158, the mill-wrights had raised their wages from 2s. 6d. to 3s. a day in 1775 to 4s. 6d. a day in 1799. The journeymen worked for small masters who were themselves employed by 'Brewers, Millers and various Manufacturers', whose works were brought to a halt by any strike. Hence striking journeymen were able to contract directly with the latter, cutting out their own masters.

binations'. The old mill-wrights were 'so overwhelmed by new men, that we could do without them', while piece-rates and other incentives completed the trade unionists' discomfiture. Where the mill-wrights 'used to scoff and spurn at the name of an engineer', which was thought to be an inferior, upstart trade, it was now the turn of the mill-wrights to disappear. Unapprenticed engineers could be found at 18s. per week; and the introduction of the self-acting principle to the lathe (the slide-rest or Maudslay's 'Go-Cart') led to an influx of youths and unskilled.

Hence even this industry – surely one of the most remarkable for the introduction of new skills – does not show an easy progression in status and in wages commensurate to the pace of technical innovation. Rather, it shows a peak towards the end of the eighteenth century, a rapid decline in the second decade of the nineteenth accompanied by an influx of unskilled labour, followed by the establishment of a new hierarchy and of new forms of combination. The work was highly differentiated, and for some years (as the diversity of names of the early trade unions suggests) it was doubtful which trade would establish precedence.[1] The rise of the skilled engineer, in the machine-making industry, was facilitated by the scarcity of his experience. The labour turnover in the early engineering workshops was prodigious; Galloway, who employed eighty or ninety men in 1824, claimed to have had between 1,000 and 1,500 men pass through his works in the previous twelve years; that is more than a total turnover of the labour force *per annum*. Agents of foreign employers scoured Britain in the hope of enticing skilled men to France, Russia, Germany, America.[2] London employers naturally suffered especially. A foreign agent (said Galloway) 'has only to watch at my gates as they come out and in, and get the names of the most able men:

1. See Galloway's evidence: 'Our business is composed of six or eight different branches; workers in wood, whom we call pattern-makers; they consist of good cabinet-makers, joiners, millwrights, and others employed in wood; iron and brass founders; smiths, firemen and hammer-men; ... vice-men and filers; and brass, iron and wood turners, in all their variety.'

2. In the effort to protect British industrial supremacy, it was illegal for many classes of skilled worker to leave the country.

and many engagements of this sort have been made in this way'. In consequence, the wages of the best men steadily rose until by the 1830s and 1840s they belonged to a privileged élite. In 1845, at Messrs Hibbert and Platt's (Oldham), the premier textile machinery works in Britain, employing close on 2,000 workers, wages of 30s. and upwards were paid to good men. The engineers (a Methodist workman complained) spent freely, gambled on horses and dogs, trained whippets, and had flesh meat 'twice or thrice a day'. The wheel had now, however, turned full circle. Where Galloway had been forced to bribe his best men to stay in 1824, the engineer's skill had now multiplied so far that Hibbert and Platt's could carefully select only the best-qualified men. 'I saw,' our Methodist recalls, 'many start that were paid off the first day, some at even shorter trial.' Already the engineer could rely no more on the scarcity of his skill to protect his conditions. He was forced to return to trade unionism, and it is significant that Hibbert and Platt's was the storm-centre of the engineers' lock-out of 1851.[1]

We must always bear in mind this overlap between the extinction of old skills and the rise of new. One after another, as the nineteenth century ran its course, old domestic crafts were displaced in the textile industries – the 'shearmen' or 'croppers', the hand calico-printers, the hand woolcombers, the fustian-cutters. And yet there are contrary instances of laborious and ill-paid domestic tasks, sometimes performed by children, which were transformed by technical innovation into jealously defended crafts. Thus, carding in the woollen industry was done with leather-backed 'cards' into which thousands of wire teeth must be set – in the 1820s and 1830s this was done by children at the rate of 1,500 or 1,600 for a $\frac{1}{2}d$., and (we

1. See *The Book of English Trades* (1818), pp. 237–41; J. Nicholson, *The Operative Mechanic and British Machinist* (1829); J. B. Jefferys, *The Story of the Engineers* (1945), pp. 9–18, 35 ff.; *First Report from Select Committee on Artizans and Machinery* (1824), pp. 23–7; Clapham, op. cit., I, pp. 151–7, 550; Thomas Wood, *Autobiography* (Leeds, 1856), p. 12 *et passim*. See also W. H. Chaloner, *The Hungry Forties: A Re-Examination* (Historical Association, 1957), where, however, it is unwisely implied that the good conditions of skilled men at Hibbert and Platt's are more typical of the 'Forties' than the bad conditions of hand-loom weavers.

are told of one West Riding clothing village) 'on almost every cottage hearth little workers who could scarcely walk relieved the monotony of the weary task by putting a tooth into the card for every inhabitant of the village, and calling out each name as the representative wire was inserted'.[1] Less than fifty years later successive inventions in card-setting machinery had enabled the small craft union of Card-Setters and Machine-Tenters to establish itself in a privileged position among the 'aristocracy' of the woollen industry.

But when we follow through the history of particular industries, and see new skills arise as old ones decline, it is possible to forget that the old skill and the new almost always were the perquisite of different people. Manufacturers in the first half of the nineteenth century pressed forward each innovation which enabled them to dispense with adult male craftsmen and to replace them with women or juvenile labour. Even where an old skill was replaced by a new process requiring equal or greater skill, we rarely find the same workers transferred from one to the other, or from domestic to factory production. Insecurity, and hostility in the face of machinery and innovation, was not the consequence of mere prejudice and (as authorities then implied) of insufficient knowledge of 'political economy'. The cropper or woolcomber knew well enough that, while the new machinery might offer skilled employment for his son, or for someone else's son, it would offer none for him. The rewards of the 'march of progress' always seemed to be gathered by someone else.

We shall see this more clearly when we examine Luddism. But even so, we are only at the fringe of the problem; for these particular insecurities were only a facet of the *general* insecurity of all skills during this period. The very notion of regularity of employment – at one place of work over a number of years for regular hours and at a standard wage – is anachronistic. We have seen that the problem in agriculture was that of chronic semi-employment. This was also the problem in most industries, and in urban experience generally. The skilled and apprenticed man, who owned his own tools and worked for a

1. Frank Peel, 'Old Cleckheaton', *Cleckheaton Guardian*, January–April 1884.

lifetime in one trade, was in a minority. It is notorious that in the early stages of industrialization, the growing towns attract uprooted and migrant labour of all types; this is still the experience of Africa and Asia today. Even the settled workers pass rapidly through a succession of employments. Wage-series derived from the rates paid in skilled trades do not give us the awkward, unstatistical reality of the cycle of unemployment and casual labour which comes through in the reminiscences of a Yorkshire Chartist, recalling his boyhood and youth from the late 1820s to the 1840s.

Tom Brown's Schooldays would have had no charm for me, as I had never been to a day school in my life; when very young I had to begin working, and was pulled out of bed between 4 and 5 o'clock ... in summer time to go with a donkey 1½ miles away, and then take part in milking a number of cows; and in the evening had again to go with milk and it would be 8 o'clock before I had done. I went to a card shop afterwards and there had to set 1,500 card teeth for a ½d. From 1842 to 1848 I should not average 9/- per week wages; outdoor and labour was bad to get then and wages were very low. I have been a woollen weaver, a comber, a navvy on the railway, and a barer in the delph that I claim to know some little of the state of the working classes.[1]

There is some evidence to suggest that the problem was becoming worse throughout the 1820s and 1830s and into the 1840s. That is, while wages were moving slowly but favourably in relation to the cost-of-living, the proportion of workers chronically under-employed was moving unfavourably in relation to those in full work. Henry Mayhew, who devoted a section of his great study of the London poor to the problem of casual labour, understood that this was the crux of the problem:

In almost all occupations there is ... a *superfluity of labourers*, and this alone would tend to render the employment of a vast number of the hands of a casual rather than a regular character. In the generality of trades the calculation is that one-third of the hands

1. B. Wilson, *The Struggles of an Old Chartist* (Halifax, 1887), p. 13. A 'barer in the delph' was a quarryman.

are fully employed, one third partially, and one-third unemployed throughout the year.[1]

Mayhew was incomparably the greatest social investigator in the mid-century. Observant, ironic, detached yet compassionate, he had an eye for all the awkward particularities which escape statistical measurement. In a fact-finding age, he looked for the facts which the enumerators forgot: he wrote consciously against the grain of the orthodoxies of his day, discovering his own outrageous 'laws' of political economy – 'under-pay makes over-work' and 'over-work makes under-pay'. He knew that when an easterly wind closed the Thames, 20,000 dock-side workers were at once unemployed. He knew the seasonal fluctuations of the timber trade, or of the bonnet-makers and pastry-cooks. He bothered to find out for how many hours and how many months in the year scavengers or rubbish-carters were actually employed. He held meetings of the workmen in the trades investigated, and took down their life-histories. If (as Professor Ashton has implied) the standard-of-living controversy really depends on a 'guess' as to which group was increasing most – those 'who were able to share in the benefits of economic progress' and 'those who were shut out' – then Mayhew's guess is worth our attention

Mayhew's guess is given in this form:

... estimating the working classes as being between four and five million in number, I think we may safely assert – considering how many depend for their employment on particular times, seasons, fashions, and accidents, and the vast quantity of over-work and scamp-work in nearly all the cheap trades ... the number of women and children who are being continually drafted into the different handicrafts with the view of reducing the earnings of the men, the displacement of human labour in some cases by machinery ... all these things being considered I say I believe that we may safely conclude that ... there is barely sufficient work for the *regular* employment of half of our labourers, so that only 1,500,000 are fully and constantly employed, while 1,500,000 more are em-

1. Mayhew, op. cit., II, p. 338. The parts of Mayhew's work upon which I have drawn most extensively in the next few pages include his account of the tailors and boot-and-shoemakers in the *Morning Chronicle*, 1849, and *London Labour and the London Poor*, II, pp. 335–82, III, pp. 231 ff.

ployed only half their time, and the remaining 1,500,000 wholly unemployed, obtaining a day's work *occasionally* by the displacement of some of the others.[1]

This remains no more than a guess, a grasping at the statistical expression of the complexities of London experience. But it arises from other findings; in particular, that 'as a general rule ... the society-men of every trade comprise about one-tenth of the whole'.[2] The wages of society men were those regulated by custom and trade union enforcement; those of the non-society men were 'determined by competition'. In London by the 1840s there was a clear demarcation between the 'honourable' and 'dishonourable' parts of the same trades; and trades in which this division was notorious included those of cabinet-makers, carpenters and joiners, boot- and shoe-makers, tailors and all clothing workers, and the building industry. The honourable part comprised the luxury and quality branches: the dishonourable comprised the whole range of 'cheap and nasty' – ready-made clothing, gimcrack or plain furniture, veneered workboxes and cheap looking-glasses, sub-contract work (by 'lumpers') in the building of churches, contract work for the Army or Government.

In a number of the trades which Thomas Large noted as being both organized and highly-paid in 1812 there was a serious deterioration in the status and living standards of the artisan over the next thirty years. The debasing of trades took many forms, and was sometimes accomplished only after intense conflict, in some cases as late as the 1830s. When William Lovett, who had been apprenticed as a rope-maker in Penzance came to London in 1821 and – finding no employment at his own trade – sought to get work as a carpenter or cabinet-maker, the distinction between the honourable and dishonourable trades was not so marked. The fact that he had served no apprenticeship weighed heavily against him, but after bad

1. Mayhew, op. cit., II, pp. 364–5. Cf. *Mechanics Magazine*, 6 September 1823: 'It is obvious that the reason why there is no work for one half of our people is, that the other half work twice as much as they ought.'

2. From the evidence Mayhew adduces elsewhere, as to cabinet-makers and tailors, this would appear to be an exaggeration: perhaps one-fifth or one-sixth is a more probable figure.

experiences at a dishonourable shop, and worse experiences attempting to hawk his own products, he finally gained employment at a large cabinet workshop. When it was discovered that he had served no apprenticeship, the men –

talked of 'setting Mother Shorney at me'; this is a cant term in the trade, and meant the putting away of your tools, the injuring of your work, and annoying you in such a way as to drive you out of the shop ... As soon ... as I was made acquainted with their feelings ... I thought it best to call a shop-meeting, and lay my case before them. To call a meeting of this description the first requisite was to send for a quantity of drink (generally a gallon of ale), and then to strike your hammer and holdfast together, which, making a bell-like sound, is a summons causing all the shop to assemble around your bench. A chairman is then appointed, and you are called upon to state your business.

Lovett's explanation of his difficult circumstances satisfied the men: 'but the demands made upon me for drink by individuals among them, for being shown the manner of doing any particular kind of work, together with fines and shop scores, often amounted to seven or eight shillings a week out of my guinea'.[1] Ten or twenty years later he would not have succeeded in gaining employment in a respectable or society shop: the influential Cabinet-Makers Society (of which Lovett himself became President) had consolidated the position of its members in the quality branches of the trade and closed the doors against the mass of unapprenticed or semi-skilled labour clamouring without. At the same time, the dishonourable trade had mushroomed:[2] middlemen had set up 'slaughter-houses' or great furniture warehouses, and poor 'garret-masters' in Bethnal Green and Spitalfields employed their own families and 'apprentices' in making chairs and shoddy furniture for sale to the warehouses at knock-down prices. Even less fortunate workers would buy or scrape together wood to make

1. W. Lovett, *Life and Struggles in Pursuit of Bread, Knowledge, and Freedom* (1920 edn), I, pp. 31–2. For the old customs of 'footing' and 'maiden garnish' (when the new workman or apprentice must buy drinks for the shop), see J. D. Burn, *A Glimpse of the Social Condition of the Working Class* (n.d.), pp. 39–40.

2. Mayhew, III, p. 231, gives 600–700 society men, and 4,000–5,000 non-society men.

workboxes or card-tables which they hawked in the streets or sold to cut-rate East End shops.

The history of each trade is different. But it is possible to suggest the outlines of a general pattern. Whereas it is generally assumed that living standards declined during the price-rises of the war years (and this is certainly true of the labourers, weavers, and wholly unorganized workers), nevertheless the war stimulated many industries and made for fuller employment. In London the arsenal, the shipyards, and the docks were busy, and there were large Government contracts for clothing and equipment for the services. Birmingham prospered similarly until the years of the continental blockade. The later years of the war saw a general erosion of apprenticeship restrictions, both in practice and at law, culminating in the repeal of the apprenticeship clauses of the Elizabethan Statute of Artificers in 1814. According to their position, the artisans reacted vigorously to this threat. We must remember that this was a time when there was little schooling, and neither Mechanics' Institutes nor Technical Colleges, and that almost the entire skill or 'mystery' of the trade was conveyed by precept and example in the workshop, by the journeyman to his apprentice. The artisans regarded this 'mystery' as their *property*, and asserted their unquestionable right to 'the quiet and exclusive use and enjoyment of their ... arts and trades'. Consequently, not only was repeal resisted, a 'nascent trades council' being formed in London, and 60,000 signatures being collected nationally to a petition to *strengthen* the apprenticeship laws;[1] but as a result of the threat there is evidence that the trades clubs were actually strengthened, so that many London artisans emerged from the Wars in a comparatively strong position.

But at this point the histories of different trades begin to diverge. The pressure of the unskilled tide, beating against the doors, broke through in different ways and with different degrees of violence. In some trades the demarcation between an honourable and dishonourable trade was already to be

1. See T. K. Derry, 'Repeal of the Apprenticeship Clauses of the Statute of Apprentices', *Econ. Hist. Review*, III, 1931-2, p. 67. See also below, p. 565.

found in the eighteenth century.[1] That the honourable trade had maintained its position despite this long-standing threat may be accounted for by several reasons. Much of the eighteenth-century trade was in luxury articles, demanding a quality of workmanship not obtainable by sweated labour. Moreover, in times of full employment, the small-scale dishonourable trade might actually offer better conditions than those of the society men. Thus the *Gorgon* noted in 1818 of the opticians and type-founders, that there had grown up –

a smaller class of tradesmen, termed *garret-masters*, who not only sell their manufacture cheaper than those of large capital, and who carry on the trade on a more extensive scale, but they do actually give higher wages to the men they employ. This we believe is the case in all trades . . .[2]

The outline of this demarcation can be seen in the differentiation between the 'Flint' and 'Dung' tailors, and between the militant and well-organized ladies' shoemakers, and the workers in the men's boot and shoe trade. The shoemakers of both groups were, however, among the first to feel the full effect of the influx of 'illegal' men. The position of the Londoners was weakened by the growth of the large outwork boot and shoe industry in Northamptonshire and Staffordshire.[3] Some incidents in the London shoemakers' history were recorded by Allen Davenport, a Spencean socialist:

It was in 1810 that I began to work for Mr Bainbridge, and it was then I first joined a shop meeting, for all the shops that I had worked for before were unconnected with any meetings . . . perhaps they were thought too insignificant . . . I was kindly received by the members of the fifth division of women's men [i.e. makers of women's shoes], then held at the York Arms, Holborn; and in a

1. Dr Dorothy George notes 'garret-masters' and 'chamber-masters' among the watchmakers and shoemakers: see *London Life in the 18th Century*, pp. 172–5, 197–8. See also E. W. Gilboy, *Wages in Eighteenth-Century England* (Cambridge, Mass., 1934).

2. *Gorgon*, 21 November 1818.

3. See Clapham, op. cit., I, pp. 167–70; M. D. George, op. cit., pp. 195–201; A. Fox, *History of the National Union of Boot and Shoe Operatives* (Oxford, 1958), pp. 12, 20–23. For the rules of the Journeymen Boot and Shoe Makers, 1803, see Aspinall, op. cit., pp. 80–82.

short time became a delegate. . . . From the time I became a member to 1813, the women's men acquired great strength as to members and a considerable increase in pecuniary means. We had at one time fourteen divisions in London; besides being in union, kept up by a well regulated correspondence, with the trade in every city and town, of any importance, throughout the kingdom. But about this time the trade commenced a law suit against a master, for employing an illegal man, and refusing to discharge him. The case was conducted by two intelligent shopmates . . . assisted by an attorney in the court of King's Bench. . . . We gained the day, but the prosecution cost the trade a hundred pounds, which was money thrown away, for almost immediately afterwards the law of Elizabeth which made it illegal for a master to employ a man in our trade that had not served an apprenticeship was repealed, and the trade was thrown open to all.

In the spring of 1813 the union held a strike in support of a detailed price-list: 'every demand of the men was conceded, and we all returned comfortably to our work':

But some of the more turbulent of the members, intoxicated with the success of our last strike, madly proposed a few weeks after to commence another strike. . . . This arrogant proceeding brought on a crisis in the trade; the masters who till then had no association, and were strangers to each other, became alarmed, called themselves together, formed an association, and being completely organized, the strike was resisted, the men were defeated, and scattered to the winds and hundreds of men, women and children suffered the greatest privations during the following winter. From this fatal strike, I date the downfall of the power of the men, and the commencement of despotism among the master shoemakers.[1]

The bitterness of the shoemakers' struggle may be gauged by the extreme radicalism of many of their members throughout the post-war years. The ladies' men clung on to their position in the boom years, 1820–5; but the recession of 1826 at once exposed their weakness. The organized men were surrounded by scores of small 'dishonourable' workshops, where shoes were made up by 'snobs' or 'translators' at 8d. or 1s. a pair. In the autumn of 1826 several of their members were tried for

1. Davenport's *Life*, reprinted in *National Co-operative Leader*, 1861. I am indebted to Mr Roydon Harrison for drawing attention to this source.

riot and assault arising from a strike extending over seven or more weeks; a unionist is alleged to have told a 'scab' that he 'ought to have his liver cut out for working under price'.[1] But the boot and shoe workers notwithstanding maintained some national organization, and in the great union wave of 1832–4 the Northamptonshire and Staffordshire outworkers came into the same struggle for 'equalization'.[2] It was only the destruction of general unionism in 1834 which finally deprived them of artisan status.

The tailors maintained their artisan status rather longer. We can take their union as a model of the quasi-legal trades union of the artisan.[3] In 1818 Francis Place published the fullest account which we have of their operation. By effective combination the London tailors had succeeded in pressing up their wages throughout the war, although probably lagging slightly behind the advance in the cost-of-living. The figures run (in Place's average), 1795, 25s.; 1801, 27s.; 1807, 30s.; 1810, 33s.; 1813, 36s. With each advance the resistance of the masters became firmer: 'Not a single shilling was obtained at any one of these periods but by compulsion.' At the many 'houses of call' of the aristocratic 'Flint' tailors books of the members' names were kept, and the masters used the houses virtually as employment agencies.[4] 'No man is allowed to ask for employment' – the masters must apply to the union. The work was allocated by rota, and the union disciplined 'unworkmanlike' men. The tailors had a dual subscription, the larger contribution being reserved for benefits, the smaller for the needs of the union itself. A twelve-hour day was enforced, except in times of full employment. There were levies for unemployed members, and special levies might be made, in preparation for a strike, as to which the members asked no

1. *Trades Newspaper*, 10 September, 10 December 1826.
2. See below, p. 466, for the organization at Nantwich.
3. Place regarded the combination among the tailors as 'by far the most perfect of any'. But he had, of course, exceptional opportunity to discover their secrets.
4. Cf. advertisements such as this in the papers: 'Men competent to superintend any works in the building line may be had by applying at the following houses . . .' (Journeymen Carpenters, advertising in *Trades Newspaper*, 17 July 1825).

questions even if the purpose was not explained. The actual leadership of the union was carefully shielded from prosecution under the Combination Acts. Each house of call had a deputy,

... chosen by a kind of tacit consent, frequently without its being known to a very large majority who is chosen. The deputies form a committee, and they again chuse in a somewhat similar way a very small committee, in whom, on very particular occasions, all power resides ...

'No law could put it down,' Place wrote: 'nothing but want of confidence among the men themselves could prevent it.' And in fact the 'Knights of the Needle' look extremely strong, at least until the recession of 1826. Their organization could be fairly described as 'all but a military system'. But concealed within Place's own account there was a premonition of weakness:

They are divided into two classes, called Flints and Dungs – the Flints have upwards of thirty houses of call, and the Dungs about nine or ten; the Flints work by day, the Dungs by day or piece. Great animosity formerly existed between them, the Dungs generally working for less wages, but of late years there has not been much difference in the wages ... and at some of the latest strikes both parties have usually made common cause.

This may be seen as an impressive attempt to keep the dishonourable trade in some organizational association with the status-conscious 'Flints'. In 1824 Place estimated a proportion of one 'Dung' to three 'Flints'; but the 'Dungs' 'work a great many hours, and their families assist them.' By the early 1830s the tide of the cheap and ready-made trade could be held back no longer. In 1834 the 'Knights' were finally degraded only after a tremendous conflict, when 20,000 were said to be on strike under the slogan of 'equalization'.[1]

John Wade was still able to speak of the London tailors of 1833 as 'enjoying a much higher remuneration than is received

1. *Gorgon*, 26 September, 3 and 10 October 1818; *First Report ... Artizans and Machinery* (1824), pp. 45–6; Cole and Filson, op. cit., pp. 106–7; [T. Carter], *Memoirs of a Working Man* (1845), pp. 122–4. For the 1834 strike see G. D. H. Cole, *Attempts at General Union* (1953). For antagonism between the organized hatters and dishonourable 'corks', see J. D. Burn, op. cit., pp. 41–2, 49–50.

by the generality of workpeople in the metropolis'. Indeed, he cited them as an example of artisans who by the strength of their combination had 'fortified their own interests against the interests of the public and other workpeople'.[1] But when Mayhew commenced his inquiry for the *Morning Chronicle* in 1849 he cited the tailors as one of the worst examples of 'cheap and shoddy' sweated industry. Of 23,517 London tailors in 1849 Mayhew estimated that 2,748 were independent master-tailors. Of the remainder, 3,000 were society men in the honourable trade (as compared to 5,000 or 6,000 in 1821), and 18,000 in the dishonourable trade were wholly dependent upon large middlemen for their earnings in the 'slop' or ready-made businesses.

London conditions should not be seen as exceptional, although London was the Athens of the artisan. And it is important to notice that there is a pattern of exploitation here which runs counter to the evidence of wage-series compiled from the rates of organized men in the honourable trade. This takes the form both of a break-up of customary conditions and restraints, and of trade union defences. It is generally true that the 'artisan' trades go through two critical periods of conflict. The first was in 1812–14, when apprenticeship regulations were repealed. Those trades, such as the shoemakers and tailors, which were already strongly organized in unions or trades clubs, were able in some degree to defend their position after repeal by strikes and other forms of direct action, although the same years saw greater organization among the masters. But consolidation in closed 'society' shops between 1815 and 1830 was at a price. 'Illegal men' were kept out of the better parts of the trade only to swell the numbers in the unorganized 'dishonourable' trade outside. The second critical period is 1833–5, when on the crest of the great trade union wave attempts were made to 'equalize' conditions, shorten working hours in the honourable trade and suppress dishonourable work. These attempts (notably that of the London tailors) not only failed in the face of the combined forces of the employers and the Government; they also led to at least a

1. J. Wade, *History of the Middle and Working Classes* (5th edn, 1835), p. 293.

temporary deterioration in the position of the 'society' men. The economic historian should see the cases of the Tolpuddle Martyrs and the great lock-outs of 1834 as being as consequential for all grades of labour as the radicals and trade unionists of the time held them to be.[1]

But this conflict between the artisans and the large employers was only part of a more general exploitive pattern. The dishonourable part of the trade grew, with the displacement of small masters (employing a few journeymen and apprentices) by large 'manufactories' and middlemen (employing domestic outworkers or sub-contracting): with the collapse of all meaningful apprenticeship safeguards (except in the honourable island) and the influx of unskilled, women and children: with the extension of hours and of Sunday work: and with the beating down of wages, piece-rates and wholesale prices. The form and extent of the deterioration relates directly to the material conditions of the industry – the cost of raw materials – tools – the skill involved – conditions favouring or discouraging trade union organization – the nature of the market. Thus, woodworkers and shoemakers could obtain their own materials cheaply and owned their own tools, so that the unemployed artisan set up as an independent 'garret-master' or 'chamber-master', working his whole family – and perhaps other juveniles – round a seven-day week and hawking the products on his own account. Carpenters requiring a more costly outlay were reduced to 'strapping-shops' where a sickening pace of gimcrack work was kept up under the foreman's patrol and where each man who fell behind was sacked. Tailoring workers, who could rarely purchase their own cloth, became wholly dependent upon the middlemen who farmed out work at sweated prices. Dressmaking – a notoriously 'sweated' trade – was largely done by needlewomen (often country or small-town immigrants) in shops contracted by large establishments. The building worker, who could neither buy his bricks nor hawk a part of a cathedral round the streets, was at the mercy of the sub-contractor; even the skilled 'society' men expected to be laid off in the winter months; and

1. The best – although still incomplete – account of this second period is in G. D. H. Cole, *Attempts at General Union.*

both classes of worker frequently attempted to escape from their predicament by direct speculative building – 'the land,' as Clapham says, 'rented in hope, materials secured on credit, a mortgage raised on the half-built house before it is sold or leased, and a high risk of bankruptcy'.[1] On the other hand, the coach-builder, the shipwright, or engineer, who did not own all his tools nor purchase his own materials, was nevertheless better situated, by reason of the character of his work and the scarcity of his skill, to maintain or extend trade union defences.

A similar collapse in the status of the artisan took place in older provincial centres. There are many complexities and qualifications. On one hand, the boot and shoe industry of Stafford and of Northamptonshire had long lost its artisan character and was conducted on an outwork basis when the London shoemakers were still trying to hold back the dishonourable trade. On the other hand, the extreme specialization of the Sheffield cutlery industry – together with the exceptionally strong political and trade union traditions of the workers who had been the most steadfast Jacobins – had led to the maintenance of the skilled worker's status in a twilight world of semi-independence, where he worked for a merchant (and, sometimes, for more than one), hired his motive-power at a 'public wheel', and adhered to strict price-lists. Despite the Sheffield Cutlers Bill (1814) which repealed the restrictions which had limited the trade to freemen and which left a situation in which 'any person may work at the corporated trades without being a freeman, and may take any number of apprentices for any term', the unions were strong enough – sometimes with the aid of 'rattening' and other forms of intimidation – to hold back the unskilled tide, although there was a continual threat from 'little mesters', sometimes 'illegal' men or self-employed journeymen, who sought to undercut the legal trade.[2] In the Birmingham industries, every kind of variant is to be found, from the large workshop through innumerable mazes

1. Clapham, op. cit., I, p. 174
2. T. A. Ward (ed. A. B. Bell), *Peeps in to the Past* (1909), pp. 216 ff; S. Pollard, *A History of Labour in Sheffield* (Liverpool, 1959), ch. 2; Clapham, op. cit., I, p. 174.

of small shops and self-employed journeymen, honourable and dishonourable, to the half-naked and degraded outworkers in the nail-making villages. An account from Wolverhampton in 1819, shows how the 'garret-master' appeared at a time of depression:

The order of things ... is completely inverted. Now, the last resource of the starving journeyman is to set up master; his employer cannot find him work, on which there is any possible profit, and is therefore obliged to discharge him; the poor wretch then sells his bed, and buys an anvil, procures a little iron, and having manufactured a few articles, hawks them about ... for what he can get. ... He might have previously received 10s a week as a servant; but now he is lucky if he gets 7s as a master manufacturer.[1]

In the Coventry ribbon-weaving industry there was another twilight, half-outworker, half-artisan situation: the 'first-hand weavers' maintained a poor artisan status, owning their own costly looms, and sometimes employing a 'journeyman's journeyman', while other weavers in the city were employed in workshops or factories at comparable wages: but in the weaving villages to the north there was a large reserve pool of semi-unemployed weavers, working at debased rates as casual outworkers.[2]

From one point of view, the true outworker industry can be seen as one which has wholly lost its artisan status and in which no 'honourable' part of the trade remains:

Capitalistic outwork may be said to be fully established only when the material belongs to the trading employer, and is returned to him after the process for which the outworker's skill is required has been completed – the wool given out to be spun, the yarn given out to be woven, the shirt given out for 'seam and gusset and band', the nailrod to be returned as nails, the limbs to be returned as dolls, the leather coming back as boots.[3]

This, Clapham estimates, was the 'predominant form' of industrial organization in the reign of George IV; and if we add

1. New Monthly Magazine, 1 July 1819, cit. S. Maccoby, op. cit., p. 335. See also T. S. Ashton, 'The Domestic System in the Early Lancashire Tool Trade', Econ. Journal (Supplement), 1926–9, I, pp. 131 ff.

2. See the lucid account in J. Prest, The Industrial Revolution in Coventry (Oxford University Press, 1960), chs. 3 and 4.

3. Clapham, op. cit., I, p. 179.

to the true outworkers (hand-loom weavers, nail-makers, most woolcombers, chain-makers, some boot and shoe workers, framework-knitters, fustian-cutters, glove-makers, some potters, pillow-lace-makers, and many others) the workers in the 'dishonourable' parts of the London and urban artisan trades, it probably remained predominant until 1840.

We shall look at the weaver, as an example of the outworker, later. But there are some general points which relate both to the outworkers and to the artisans. First, it will not do to explain away the plight of weavers or of 'slop' workers as 'instances of the decline of old crafts which were displaced by a mechanical process'; nor can we even accept the statement, in its pejorative context, that 'it was not among the factory employees but among the domestic workers, whose traditions and methods were those of the eighteenth century, that earnings were at their lowest'.[1] The suggestion to which these statements lead us is that these conditions can somehow be segregated in our minds from the true improving impulse of the Industrial Revolution – they belong to an 'older', pre-industrial order, whereas the authentic features of the new capitalist order may be seen where there are steam, factory operatives, and meat-eating engineers. But the numbers employed in the outwork industries multiplied enormously between 1780-1830; and very often *steam and the factory were the multipliers*. It was the mills which spun the yarn and the foundries which made the nail-rod upon which the outworkers were employed. Ideology may wish to exalt one and decry the other, but facts must lead us to say that each was a complementary component of a single process. This process first multiplied hand-workers (hand calico-printers, weavers, fustian-cutters, woolcombers) and then extinguished their livelihood with new machinery. Moreover, the degradation of the outworkers was very rarely as simple as the phrase 'displaced by a mechanical process' suggests; it was accomplished by methods of exploitation similar to those in the dishonourable trades and it often preceded machine competition. Nor is it true that 'the traditions and methods' of the domestic workers 'were those of the eighteenth century'.

1. F. A. Hayek and T. S. Ashton in *Capitalism and the Historians*, pp. 27–8, 36.

The only large group of domestic workers in that century whose conditions anticipate those of the semi-employed proletarian outworkers of the nineteenth century are the Spitalfields silk-weavers; and this is because the 'industrial revolution' in silk preceded that in cotton and in wool. Indeed, we may say that large-scale sweated outwork was as intrinsic to this revolution as was factory production and steam. As for the 'traditions and methods' of the 'slop' workers in the dishonourable trade, these, of course, have been endemic for centuries wherever cheap labour has been abundant. They would, nevertheless, appear to constitute a serious reversal of the conditions of late eighteenth-century London artisans.

What we can say with confidence is that the artisan *felt* that his status and standard-of-living were under threat or were deteriorating between 1815 and 1840. Technical innovation and the superabundance of cheap labour weakened his position. He had no political rights and the power of the State was used, if only fitfully, to destroy his trade unions. As Mayhew clearly showed, not only did under-pay (in the dishonourable trades) make for overwork; it also made for *less* work all round. It was this experience which underlay the political radicalization of the artisans and, more drastically, of the outworkers. Ideal and real grievances combined to shape their anger – lost prestige, direct economic degradation, loss of pride as craftsmanship was debased, lost aspirations to rise to being masters (as men in Hardy's and Place's generation could still do). The 'society' men, though more fortunate, were not the least radical – many London and provincial working-class leaders came like William Lovett, from this stratum. They had been able to hold their status only by an accession of trade union militancy; and their livelihood provided them with a running education in the vices of competition and the virtues of collective action. They witnessed less fortunate neighbours or shopmates (an accident, a weakness for drink) fall into the lower depths. Those who were in these depths had most need, but least time, for political reflection.

If the agricultural labourers pined for land, the artisans aspired to an 'independence'. This aspiration colours much of the history of early working-class Radicalism. But in London the dream of becoming a small master (still strong in the 1790s – and still strong in Birmingham in the 1830s) could not stand up, in the 1820s and 1830s, in face of the experiences of 'chamber' or 'garret' masters – an 'independence' which meant week-long slavery to warehouses or slop shops. This helps to explain the sudden surge of support towards Owenism at the end of the 1820s – trade union traditions and the yearning for independence were twisted together in the idea of social control over their own means of livelihood; a *collective* independence.[1] When most of the Owenite ventures failed, the London artisan still fought for his independence to the last: when leather, wood or cloth ran out, he swelled the throng of street-sellers, hawking bootlaces, oranges or nuts. In the main they were rural workers who entered the 'strapping-shops'. The London-born artisan could rarely stand the pace; nor did he wish to become a proletarian.

We have not, perhaps, clarified the wage-indices, but have proposed a way of reading and of criticizing such indices as exist. In particular, we must always find out whether figures are derived from society or non-society men, and how far the division, in any trade, has gone at any given time. There were certain experiences common to most trades and industries. Few did not suffer during the post-war depression, and most were buoyant between 1820 and 1825 – indeed, in such a period of fuller employment the dishonourable trades could actually extend their operation and be little noticed, since they did not threaten the position of society men. The twelve months after the repeal of the Combination Acts was a period of exceptional buoyancy, when general prosperity conjoined to aggressive trade unionism led to considerable advances by many groups of workers. 'n the summer of 1825 a report was published in the *Trades Newspaper* from the Potteries, which admitted their thriving state in language quite unusual in the Radical or working-class journalism of the time. 'It would be difficult to point out a period ... when the working classes, with the exception of the weavers, enjoyed a greater degree of comfort.' The Pot-

1. See the discussion of Owenism below, pp. 857–87.

teries had been swept, in the previous eight months, by a veritable strike wave:

In Staffordshire, the carpenters were the first to strike, and then every other trade turned out in rotation. The colliers knew that the potters could not go on without them, and the moment the latter had obtained an advance, not a pick was lifted, nor a bucket let down. ... The potters held out a second time, and played their cards with such address, that an ordinary hand now earns 6s per day, while superior journeymen who work by the piece, are actually in the receipt of £3 per week. Even the tailors doggedly refused to shape or sew, goose or seam, or wad a collar, unless they knew the reason why and wherefore; while the spirited barbers ... insisted on an advance of 50% ...[1]

Much of this gain was lost in 1826, recovered in the next three years, and lost once again in the early 1830s. And within this wider history there are the particular histories of individual trades. In general, in those industries where much capital, skill and machinery were required, the artisan lost some of his independence but passed by fairly easy stages into becoming a skilled, even privileged, proletarian: the mill-wright became an engineer or metal mechanic, the shipwright's skill was divided among the shipbuilding trades. In those industries where work could be put out, or where juvenile and unskilled labour could be drafted in, the artisan retained some of his independence but only at the cost of an increasing insecurity and a severe loss of status.

It is the outlook of the artisan which will most concern us when we return to the political history of the post-war years. We may therefore be more impressionistic in our treatment of those who inhabited the lower depths beneath him. In fact, less is known about the unskilled workers, in the first decades of the nineteenth century, since they had no unions, they rarely had leaders who articulated their grievances, and few parliamentary committees investigated them except as a sanitary or housing problem.[2] The down-graded artisan rarely had the

1. *Trades Newspaper*, 24 July 1825. See also W. H. Warburton, *History of T.U. Organization in the North Staffordshire Potteries* (1931), pp. 28–32.

physique or aptitude to engage in arduous semi-skilled or un-skilled labouring. Such occupation groups were either self-recruiting, or enlarged by rural and Irish migrants. Some of these earned good wages for irregular work – on the docks, or as navvies or spademen. These shade into the 'casualties', or casual labourers; and the totally unemployed immigrants to the city, who might be reduced, like young William Lovett when he first came to London, to 'a penny loaf a day and a drink from the most convenient pump for several weeks in succession'. He and a Cornish compatriot:

... generally got up at five o'clock and walked about enquiring at different shops and buildings till about nine; we then bought one penny loaf and divided it between us; then walked about again till four or five in the afternoon, when we finished our day's work with another divided loaf; and very early retired to bed footsore and hungry.[1]

But such discipline in eking out the last few pennies were rare. Habitual uncertainty of employment, as all social investigators know, discourages forethought and gives rise to the familiar cycle of hardship alternated with the occasional spending-spree when in work. Distinct from the labourers (stablemen, street-sweepers, waterside-workers, unskilled builders, carters, and so on), were those for whom 'casualty' had become a way of life; street-sellers, beggars and cadgers, paupers, casual and professional criminals, the Army. Some of the street-sellers were prosperous traders; others were irrepressible scroungers; others, like the costermongers, patterers and ballad-vendors, provide a comic, and devastating antithesis to the sententious theses of Edwin Chadwick and Dr Kay. The mind reels at the expedients by which human beings kept themselves alive, col-lecting dog's dung or selling chickweed or writing letters at 1d. or 2d. a time (for love-letters 'there's wanted the best gilt edge, and a fancy 'velop, and a Dictionary'). The greater part of the street-sellers, certainly by the 1840s, were desperately poor. Taking a deep statistical breath, we can hazard the view that the standard-of-living of the average criminal (but not prostitute) rose over the period up to the establishment of an

1. Lovett, op. cit., I, pp. 25-6.

effective police force (in the late 1830s), since opportunities for pilfering from warehouses, markets, canal barges, the docks, and railways, were multiplying. Probably a good many casual workers supplemented their earnings in this way. The genuine professional criminal or 'traveller' would seem, on his own confession, to have had a splendid standard-of-life: he may be accounted an 'optimist'. The standard of the unmarried mother, except in districts such as Lancashire where female employment was abundant, probably fell: she had offended, not only against Wilberforce, but also against Malthus and the laws of political economy.

It was a time when a widow with six children between the ages of five and fifteen might, in a mill-town, be counted fortunate; and when a blind beggar was an 'aristocrat' of the vagrant fraternity, with whom the sighted and able-bodied sought to travel in order to share in his takings. 'A blind man can get a guide at any place, because they know he's sure to get something,' the blind boot-lace seller told Mayhew. Travelling from lodging-house to lodging-house down from his native Northumberland, and becoming 'fly to the dodge' of begging, 'I grew pleaseder, and pleaseder, with the life, and I wondered how anyone could follow any other.' When he finally entered London, 'as I came through the streets ... I didn't know whether I carried the streets or they carried me'.[1]

Other optimists included the highly professional 'cadgers', who had as many disguises as a quick-change repertory actor, and who rang the changes according to the state of trade by assuming the distresses of others – the 'respectable broken-down tradesman or reduced gentleman caper', the 'destitute mechanic's lurk', the 'turnpike sailors':

I ... went out as one of the Shallow Brigade, wearing Guernsey shirt and drawers, or tattered trowsers. There was a school of four. We only got a tidy living – 16s. or £1 a day among us. We used to call every one that came along – coalheavers and all – sea-fighting captains. 'Now, my noble sea-fighting captain,' we used to say, 'fire an odd shot from your larboard locker to us, Nelson's bulldogs;' ... The Shallow got so grannied [known] in London, that the supplies got queer, and I quitted the land navy. Shipwrecks got

1. Mayhew, I, p. 452.

so common in the streets, you see, that people didn't care for them . . .[1]

The impostors, who studied the market and were quick to vary the supplies of suffering to meet the jaded and inelastic demands of human compassion, fared better than the genuine sufferers, who were too proud or too inexperienced to market their misery to its best advantage. By the 1840s many of the tricks of the impostors were known; unless he had the knowledge of humanity of Dickens or Mayhew, the middle-class man saw in every open palm the evidence of idleness and deceit. And, in the centre of London or the big cities, he might well be right, for he walked through a surrealist world: the open palm might be that of a receiver: the half-naked man in the snowstorm might be working the 'shivering dodge' ('a good dodge in tidy inclement season . . . not so good a lurk, by two bob a day as it once was'): the child sobbing in the gutter over a package of spilt tea and a tale of lost change might be schooled in the dodge by her mother. The collier who had lost both arms was a man to be envied, and:

There's the man with the very big leg, who sits on the pavement, and tells a long yarn about the tram carriage having gone over him in the mine. He does very well – remarkable well.[2]

Most of the worst sufferers were not there. They remained, with their families, in the garrets of Spitalfields; the cellars of Ancoats and south Leeds; in the outworkers' villages. We may be fairly confident that the standard-of-living of paupers declined. The thirty years leading up to the new Poor Law of 1834 saw continuous attempts to hold down the poor-rates, to chip away at outdoor relief, or to pioneer the new-type workhouse.[3] It was not of one of Chadwick's 'Bastilles' but of an earlier model that Crabbe wrote in *The Borough* (1810):

1. Ibid., I, p. 461. For some years after the Wars genuine disbanded sailors were the largest group of London mendicants: *Fourth Report of the Society for the Suppression of Mendicity* (1822), p. 6.

2. Ibid., I, p. 465.

3. See J. D. Marshall, 'The Nottinghamshire Reformers and their Contribution to the New Poor Law', *Econ. Hist. Review*, 2nd Series, XIII, 3 April 1961.

feel good

Boots UK Limited
STORE 2774 6 004
(01743) 735 £310

1/12/2011   14:06
Served by: 1011?

Till 03

TOTAL TO PAY   £25.00
CARD SALES   £25.00

ADVANTAGE
Points Redeemed
Points to spend in Store   9920

feel good

AC DEBIT   EXPIRY 10/13

BUDDG 37468122   AUTH 542093
RID:A0000000031010
PIN WAS SUCCESSFULLY VERIFIED
YOU WILL BE DEBITED BY
PLEASE RETAIN THIS FOR YOUR RECORDS

195 6764 0274 110

boots

feel good

MIX
Paper from
responsible sources
FSC® C041232

www.fsc.org

Boots.com 0845 609 0055
Boots Advantage Card: 0845 124 4545
Boots Customer Care: 0845 070 8090
PO Box 5300, Nottingham NG90 1AA

Please keep this receipt…
…and we'll happily give you an exchange, giftcard or
refund if you change your mind. Without a receipt,
we'll give you an exchange. There are some
exceptions and we'll always make these clear. For the
safety of all our customers we can't accept returned
medicines, cosmetics or foods, unless faulty.
This does not affect your statutory rights.

Shopping and information online at www.boots.com

Registered address:
Nottingham NG2 3AA
Registered VAT No. 116300129

Collect 4 points for every

> Your plan I love not; – with a number you
> Have placed your poor, your pitiable few;
> There, in one house, throughout their lives to be,
> The pauper-palace which they hate to see:
> That giant building, that high-bounding wall,
> Those bare-worn walks, that lofty thund'ring hall!
> That large loud clock, which tolls each dreaded hour,
> Those gates and locks, and all those signs of power:
> It is a prison, with a milder name,
> Which few inhabit without dread or shame.

The Act of 1834, and its subsequent administration by men like Chadwick and Kay, was perhaps the most sustained attempt to impose an ideological dogma, in defiance of the evidence of human need, in English history. No discussion of the standard-of-living after 1834 can make sense which does not examine the consequences, as troubled Boards of Guardians tried to apply Chadwick's insane Instructional Circulars as to the abolition or savage restriction of out-relief in depressed industrial centres; and which does not follow the missionary zeal of the Assistant Commissioners as they sought to bring the doctrin-aire light of Malthusian-Benthamism into the empirical north. The doctrine of discipline and restraint was, from the start, more important than that of material 'less eligibility';[1] the most inventive State would have been hard put to it to create insti-tutions which simulated conditions worse than those of garret-masters, Dorset labourers, framework-knitters and nailers. The impractical policy of systematic starvation was displaced by the policy of psychological deterrence: 'labour, discipline and restraint'. 'Our intention,' said one Assistant Commissioner, 'is to make the workhouses as like prisons as possible'; and another, 'our object ... is to establish therein a discipline so severe and repulsive as to make them a terror to the poor and prevent them from entering'. Dr Kay recorded with satis-faction his successes in Norfolk; the reduction in diet proved less effective than 'minute and regular observance of routine', religious exercises, silence during meals, 'prompt obedience', total separation of the sexes, separation of families (even

1. Conditions of paupers in the workhouses after 1834 were intended to be 'less eligible' than those of the worst-situated labourers outside.

where of the same sex), labour and total confinement. 'I had observed,' he recorded, in that bastard ceremonial English which one day may be as quaint as the thumbscrew and the stocks:

that the custom of permitting paupers to retain their possession, while residing within the walls of the workhouse, boxes, china, articles of clothing, &c., had been perpetuated ... I therefore directed these articles to be taken into the possession of the various Governors ... and deposited in the store-room. In effecting this change in the Cosford Union workhouse, Mr Plum found considerable quantities of bread secreted in these boxes (showing how abundant the dietary is), and likewise soap and other articles, purloined from the workhouse stores. ... On the morning after this change twelve able-bodied female paupers left the house, saying they preferred labour out of doors.

Neither widows with families, nor the aged and the infirm, nor the sick, – continued Dr Kay, in full Chadwickian cry – should be spared these workhouse humiliations, for fear of sustaining improvidence and imposture, and of sapping the motives to industry ... frugality ... prudence ... filial duties ... independent exertions of the labourers during their years of ability and activity....

A notable victory for Dr Kay and Mr Plum! Twelve able-bodied females made frugal and prudent (perhaps transmogrified from pessimists to optimists?) at a blow! And yet, despite all their efforts, incomplete returns from 443 Unions in England and Wales in which the new Bastilles were in operation in three months of 1838 (excluding, among other areas, almost all Lancashire and the West Riding) showed 78,536 workhouse inmates. By 1843 the figure had risen to 197,179. The most eloquent testimony to the depths of poverty is in the fact that they were tenanted at all.[1]

1. Dr Kay's evidence is in G. Cornewall Lewis, *Remarks on the Third Report of the Irish Poor Inquiry Commissioners* (1837), pp. 34–5; returns of workhouse inmates, 1838, in the *Fifth Report of the Poor Law Commissioners* (1839), pp. 11, 181; an example of Chadwick's 'insane' instructional letters, when confronted with the need for out-relief in industrial depression, is in his correspondence with the Mansfield Guardians, *Third Annual Report P.L.C.* (1837), pp. 117–19; *Tenth Annual Report* (1844), p. 272. Among the large literature on the Poor Law, the lucid account of resistance to it in the north in C. Driver, *Tory Radical* (1946), chs. 25 and 26 is to be recommended.

[9]

The Weavers

THE history of the weavers in the nineteenth century is haunted
by the legend of better days. The memories are strongest
in Lancashire and Yorkshire. But they obtained in most parts
of Britain and in most branches of textiles. Of the Midlands
stocking-weavers in the 1780s:

When the wake came, the stocking-maker had peas and beans in
his snug garden, and a good barrel of humming ale.

He had 'a week-day suit of clothes and one for Sundays and
plenty of leisure'.[1] Of the Gloucestershire weavers:

Their little cottages seemed happy and contented ... it was seldom
that a weaver appealed to the parish for relief. ... Peace and content sat upon the weaver's brow.[2]

Of the linen-weaving quarter of Belfast:

... a quarter once remarkable for its neatness and order; he remembered their whitewashed houses, and their little flower gardens,
and the decent appearance they made with their families at markets,
or at public worship. These houses were now a mass of filth and
misery ...[3]

Dr Dorothy George, in her lucid and persuasive *England in
Transition*, has argued that the 'golden age' was in general a
myth. And her arguments have carried the day.

They have, perhaps, done so too easily. After all, if we set up
the ninepin of a 'golden age' it is not difficult to knock it

1. W. Gardiner, *Music and Friends* (1838), I, p. 43. See also M. D.
George, *England in Transition* (Penguin edn 1953), p. 63.

2. T. Exell, *Brief History of the Weavers of Gloucestershire*, cited in
E. A. L. Moir, 'The Gentlemen Clothiers', in (ed.) H. P. R. Finberg,
Gloucestershire Studies (Leicester, 1957), p. 247.

3. Emmerson Tennant, M.P. for Belfast, in House of Commons, 28
July 1835. See also (for the Spitalfields silk-weavers) Thelwall's account,
above, p. 157.

down. Certainly, the condition of the Spitalfields silk-weavers in the eighteenth century was not enviable. And it is true that capitalist organization of the woollen and worsted industries of the south-west and of Norwich early gave rise to many forms of antagonism which anticipate later developments in Lancashire and Yorkshire. Certainly, also the conditions of eighteenth-century weaving communities were idealized by Gaskell in his influential *Manufacturing Population of England* (1833); and by Engels when (following Gaskell) he conjured up a picture of the grandparents of the factory operatives of 1844 'leading a righteous and peaceful life in all piety and probity'.

But the fact of eighteenth-century hardship and conflict on the one hand, and of nineteenth-century idealization on the other, does not end the matter. The memories remain. And so does plentiful evidence which does not admit of easy interpretation. The existence of supplementary earnings from small farming or merely slips of garden, spinning, harvest work, etc., is attested from most parts of the country. There is architectural evidence to this day testifying to the solidity of many late eighteenth-century weaving hamlets in the Pennines. The commonest error today is not that of Gaskell and of Engels but that of the optimist who muddles over the difficult and painful nature of the change in status from artisan to depressed outworker in some such comforting phrases as these:

The view that the period before the Industrial Revolution was a sort of golden age is a myth. Many of the evils of the early factory age were no worse than those of an earlier period. Domestic spinners and weavers in the eighteenth century had been 'exploited' by the clothiers as ruthlessly as the factory operatives were 'exploited' by the manufacturers in the 1840s.[1]

We may distinguish between four kinds of weaver-employer relationship to be found in the eighteenth century. (1) The customer-weaver – the Silas Marner, who lived in independent status in a village or small town, much like a master-tailor, making up orders for customers. His numbers were de-

1. Introduction by W. O. Henderson and W. H. Chaloner to F. Engels, *Condition of the Working Class in England in 1844* (1958), p. xiv.

clining, and he need not concern us here. (2) The weaver, with the status of superior artisan, self-employed, and working by the piece for a choice of masters. (3) The journeyman weaver, working either in the shop of the master-clothier, or, more commonly, in his own home and at his own loom for a single master. (4) The farmer or smallholder weaver, working only part-time in the loom.

The last three groups all run into each other, but it is helpful if the distinctions are made. For example in the mid eighteenth century, the Manchester small-ware and check trades were largely conducted by weaver-artisans (group 2), with a high degree of organization. As the cotton industry expanded in the latter half of the century, more and more small farmers (group 4) were attracted by the high wages to becoming part-time weavers. At the same time the West Riding woollen industry remained largely organized on the basis of small working-clothiers employing only a handful of journeymen and apprentices (group 3) in their own domestic unit. We may simplify the experiences of the years 1780–1830 if we say that they saw the merging of all three groups into a group whose status was greatly debased – that of the proletarian outworker, who worked in his own home, sometimes owned and sometimes rented his loom, and who wove up the yarn to the specifications of the factor or agent of a mill or of some middleman. He lost the status and security which groups 2 and 3 might expect, and the side-earnings of group 4: he was exposed to conditions which were, in the sense of the London artisan, wholly 'dishonourable'.

Among the weavers of the north memories of lost status were grounded in authentic experiences and lingered longest. In the West Country by the end of the eighteenth century the weavers were already outworkers, employed by the great gentle-men clothier who 'buys the wool, pays for the spinning, weav-ing, Milling, Dying, Shearing, Dressing, etc.', and who might employ as many as 1,000 workers in these processes. A York-shire witness in 1806 contrasted the two systems. In the West Country,

there is no such thing as what we in Yorkshire call the domestic system; what I mean by the domestic system is the little clothiers living in villages, or in detached places, with all their comforts, carrying on business with their own capital. .... I understand that in the west of England it is quite the reverse of that, the manufacturer there is the same as our common workman in a factory in Yorkshire, except living in a detached house; in the west the wool is delivered out to them to weave, in Yorkshire it is the man's own property.[1]

But in the Yorkshire domestic industry of the eighteenth century, the wool was the property, not of the weaver, but of the little master-clothier. Most weavers were journeymen, working for a single clothier, and (however much this was later idealized) in a dependent status. An 'idyllic' picture of the clothier's life is to be found in a 'Poem Descriptive of the Manners of the Clothiers, written about the year 1730.'[2] The weavers – we do not know whether Tom, Will, Jack, Joe and Mary are journeymen, apprentices, or sons and daughters of the 'Maister' – are shown eating at a common board, after keeping 'time with hand and feet/From five at morn till Eight at *neet*!'

> Quoth Maister – 'Lads, work hard, I pray,
> 'Cloth mun be pearked next Market day.
> 'And Tom mun go to-morn to t'spinners,
> 'And Will mun seek about for t'swingers;
> 'And Jack, to-morn, by time be rising,
> 'And go to t'sizing house for sizing,
> 'And get you web, in warping, done
> 'That ye may get it into t'loom.
> 'Joe – go give my horse some corn
> 'For I design for t'Wolds to-morn;
> 'So mind and clean my boots and shoon,
> 'For I'll be up it 'morn right *soon*!

1. Cited by E. A. L. Moir, op. cit., p. 226. For the West of England industry, see also D. M. Hunter, *The West of England Woollen Industry* (1910) and J. de L. Mann, 'Clothiers and Weavers in Wiltshire during the Eighteenth Century', in (ed.). L. S. Presnell, *Studies in the Industrial Revolution* (1960).

2. The M S. copy in Leeds Reference Library is transcribed by F. B. in *Publications of the Thoresby Society*, XLI, Part 3, No. 95, 1947, pp. 275–9; there are extracts in H. Heaton, *Yorkshire Woollen and Worsted Industries* (1920), pp. 344–7. Professor Heaton's book remains the standard authority on the domestic industry in Yorkshire in the eighteenth century.

'Mary – there's wool – tak thee and dye it
'It's that 'at ligs i th' clouted sheet!'

Mistress: 'So thou's setting me my wark,
'I think I'd more need mend thy sark,
'Prithie, who mun sit at' bobbin wheel?
'And ne'er a cake at top o' the' creel!
'And we to bake, and swing, to blend,
'And milk, and barns to school to send,
'And dumplins for the lads to mak,
'And yeast to seek, and 'syk as that'!
'And washing up, morn, noon and neet,
'And bowls to scald, and milk to fleet,
'And barns to fetch again at neet!'

The picture invites comparison with Cobbett's nostalgic
reconstructions of the patriarchal relations between the small
southern farmer and his labourers, who shared his board and
his fortunes in the eighteenth century. It is a credible picture
of a time when, in the Halifax and Leeds districts, nearly all
the processes of cloth manufacture took place within a single
domestic unit. By the end of the eighteenth century it would
require some qualifications. Master would no longer buy his
wool in the Wolds (he might now buy his yarn direct from a
spinning-mill) and the finishing processes would be undertaken
in specialized shops. Nor was the market for his pieces as 'free',
although the last of the great yeoman Cloth Halls was built at
Halifax as late as 1779, and in the 1790s a new pirate cloth hall
was set up at Leeds, where interlopers, unapprenticed 'shoemakers and tinkers', and self-employed weavers marketed
their cloth. The small clothier was becoming increasingly dependent upon merchants, factors or mills. He might, if successful, be a small capitalist, employing fifteen or twenty
weavers, many of whom worked in their own homes. If unsuccessful, he might find himself being squeezed out of his independence; his profit being lost in a simple payment for the
work undertaken, in working yarn into cloth to the specifications of a middleman. In spells of bad trade he might
become indebted to the merchant. He was on his way to becoming a mere hand-loom weaver; and, as competition

became more intense, so the Mistress's domestic economy was lost in the demands of the trade.

These processes were slow and at first they were not exceptionally painful. Hundreds of yeomen clothiers were among those who rode to York to vote for Wilberforce in 1807. The intricate sub-divisions of the industry enabled some small masters to cling on for fifty more years, while others founded small finishing and cropping shops. Moreover, the great increase in the output of yarn laid a special premium on the weaver's labour; between 1780 and 1820 the clothier's loss of independence and of status was to some degree disguised by the abundance of work. And if Master's status was, in some cases, falling to that of his journeymen, that of Tom, Will, Jack and Joe appeared to be rising. As the mills and the factors were searching for weavers, so the journeyman gained some independence of the master-clothier. He might now pick and choose his masters. This was, in wool as in cotton, the 'golden age' of the journeyman weaver.

In the earlier eighteenth century the relationships described in the poem are idyllic only in a patriarchial sense. On the debit side, the journeyman had little more independence of his master than the yearly hand on the farm. The parish apprentice, if placed with a bad master, was for years in a position of near-servitude. On the credit side, the journeyman considered himself to be a 'clothier' rather than a mere weaver; his work was varied, much of it in the loom, but some of it out and about; he had some hope of obtaining credit to buy wool and of becoming a small master on his own account. If he worked in his own home, rather than in the master's workshop, he was subject to no work-discipline except that of his own making. Relations between small masters and their men were personal and sometimes close: they observed the same customs and owned allegiance to the same community values:

The 'little makers' ... were men who doffed their caps to no one, and recognized no right in either squire or parson to question, or meddle with them. ... Their brusqueness and plain speaking might at times be offensive. ... If the little maker ... rose in the world high enough to employ a few of his neighbours, he did not therefore cease to labour with his own hands, but worked as hard or perhaps harder than anyone he employed. In speech and in dress he claimed no superiority.[1]

The master-clothier was the peasant, or small *kulak*, of the Industrial Revolution; and it is to him that the Yorkshire reputation for bluntness and independence may be traced.

In the cotton industry the story is different. Here the average unit of production was larger, and relationships similar to those in Norwich and the west of England may be found from the late eighteenth century. By the 1750s Manchester small-ware and check-weavers had strongly organized trade societies. Already they were seeking to maintain their status, by resisting the influx of unapprenticed labour. 'Illegal' men began 'to multiply so fast as to be one in the Gate of another'. During the summer (the weavers complained, these men 'betook themselves to Out-work, such as Day labouring', and in the autumn:

would again return to the Loom, and would be content to work upon any Terms, or submit to do any Kind of servile Work, rather than starve in the Winter; and what they thus submitted to, soon became a general Rule . . .[2]

When the Oldham check-weavers sought, in 1759, to secure legal enforcement of apprenticeship restrictions, the Assize Judge delivered a hostile judgement in which the laws of the land were set aside in favour of the as-yet-unstated doctrines of Adam Smith. If apprenticeship were to be enforced, 'that Liberty of setting up Trades (the Foundation of the present flourishing Condition of Manchester) [would be] destroyed':

In the Infancy of Trade, the Acts of Queen Elizabeth might be well calculated for the publick Weal; but now, when it is grown to that Perfection we see it, it might perhaps be of Utility to have those Laws repealed, as tending to cramp and tye down that Knowledge it was at first necessary to obtain by Rule . . .

1. Frank Peel, 'Old Cleckheaton', *Cleckheaton Guardian*, January–April 1884. Peel, a local historian of accuracy, was writing about the 1830s in a region of the West Riding where the master-clothier lingered longest.

2. See A. P. Wadsworth and J. de L. Mann, *The Cotton Trade and Industrial Lancashire* (Manchester, 1931), p. 348.

As for combinations, 'if Inferiors are to prescribe to their Superiors, if the Foot aspire to be the Head ... to what End are Laws enacted?' It was the 'indispensable Duty of every one, as a Friend to the Community, to endeavour to suppress them in their Beginnings'.[1]

This remarkable judgement anticipated the actual repeal of the Statute of Artificers by more than half a century. Although their organizations were by no means extinguished, the weavers were left without any shadow of legal protection when the vast increase in the output of yarn from the early cotton-mills led to the amazing expansion of weaving throughout south-east Lancashire. William Radcliffe's account of these years in the Pennine uplands is well known:

... the old loom-shops being insufficient, every lumber-room, even old barns, cart-houses and outbuildings of any description were re-paired, windows broke through the blank walls, and all were fitted up for loom-shops. This source of making room being at length exhausted, new weavers cottages with loom-shops rose up in every direction ...[2]

It was the loom, and not the cotton-mill, which attracted immigrants in their thousands. From the 1770s onwards the great settlement of the uplands – Middleton, Oldham, Mott-ram, Rochdale – commenced. Bolton leapt from 5,339 in-habitants in 1773 to 11,739 in 1789: at the commencement of the Wars—

notwithstanding the great numbers who have enlisted, houses for the working class are not procured without difficulty; and last summer many houses were built in the skirts of the town, which are now occupied.[3]

Small farmers turned weaver, and agricultural labourers and immigrant artisans entered the trade. It was the fifteen years between 1788 and 1803 which Radcliffe described as 'the golden age of this great trade' for the weaving communities:

1. Ibid., pp. 366–7.
2. W. Radcliffe, *Origin of Power Loom Weaving* (Stockport, 1828), p. 65.
3. J. Aikin, *A Description of the Country ... round Manchester* (1795), p. 262. Note the early use of 'working class'.

Their dwellings and small gardens clean and neat – all the family well clad – the men with each a watch in his pocket, and the women dressed to their own fancy – the church crowded to excess every Sunday – every house well furnished with a clock in elegant mahogany or fancy case – handsome tea services in Staffordshire ware ... Birmingham, Potteries, and Sheffield wares for necessary use and ornament ... many cottage families had their cow ...[1]

Experience and myth are here intermingled, as they are in Gaskell's account of weaving families earning £4 per week at the turn of the century, and in Bamford's description of his own *Early Days* in Middleton. We know from an Oldham diarist that the prosperity did not extend to fustians, the coarsest branch of the trade.[2] In fact, probably only a minority of weavers attained Radcliffe's standard; but many aspired towards it. In these fifteen or twenty years of moderate prosperity a distinct cultural pattern emerges in the weaving communities: a rhythm of work and leisure: a Wesleyanism in some villages softer and more humanized than it was to be in the first decades of the nineteenth century (Bamford's Sunday school taught him to write as well as to read), with class leaders and local preachers among the weavers: a stirring of political radicalism, and a deep attachment to the values of independence.

But the prosperity induced by the soaring output of machine yarn disguised a more essential loss of status. It is in the 'golden age' that the artisan, or journeyman weaver, becomes merged in the generic 'hand-loom weaver'. Except in a few specialized branches, the older artisans (their apprenticeship walls being totally breached) were placed on a par with the new immigrants; while many of the farming-weavers abandoned their smallholdings to concentrate upon the loom. Reduced to

1. Radcliffe, op. cit., p. 167.
2. See S. J. Chapman, *The Lancashire Cotton Industry* (Manchester, 1904), p. 40. There are indications of widespread reductions commencing in about 1797. An Association of Cotton Weavers, based on Bolton, claimed that wages had fallen by a third between 1797 and 1799; Rev. R. Bancroft, 29 April 1799, P.C. A.155; A. Weaver, *Address to the Inhabitants of Bolton* (Bolton, 1799); Radcliffe, op. cit., pp. 72–7. But wages seem to have reached a peak of 45s. to 50s. a week in Blackburn in 1802; *Blackburn Mail*, 26 May 1802.

complete dependence upon the spinning-mill or the 'putters-out' who took yarn into the uplands, the weavers were now exposed to round after round of wage reductions.

Wage cutting had long been sanctioned not only by the employer's greed but by the widely-diffused theory that poverty was an essential goad to industry. The author of the *Memoirs of Wool* had probably the industry of the west of England in mind when he wrote:

It is a fact well known ... that scarcity, to a certain degree, promotes industry, and that the manufacturer who can subsist on three days work will be idle and drunken the remainder of the week. ... The poor in the manufacturing counties will never work any more time in general than is necessary just to live and support their weekly debauches. ... We can fairly aver that a reduction of wages in the woollen manufacture would be a national blessing and advantage, and no real injury to the poor. By this means we might keep our trade, uphold our rents, and reform the people into the bargain.[1]

But the theory is found, almost universally, among employers, as well as among many magistrates and clergy, in the cotton districts as well.[2] The prosperity of the weavers aroused feelings of active alarm in the minds of some masters and magistrates. 'Some years ago,' wrote one magistrate in 1818, the weavers were 'so extravagantly paid that by working three or four days in the week they could maintain themselves in a comparative state of luxury.' They 'spent a great portion of their time and money in alehouses, and at home had their tea-tables twice a day provided with a rum bottle and the finest wheaten bread and butter'.[3]

Reductions, during the Napoleonic Wars, were sometimes forced by the large employers, sometimes by the least scrupulous employers, sometimes by little masters or self-employed weavers working for 'commission houses'. When markets were sluggish, manufacturers took advantage of the situation by putting out work to weavers desperate for employment at any price, thereby compelling them 'to manufacture great quantities of goods at a time, when they are absolutely not

1. J. Smith, *Memoirs of Wool* (1747), II, p. 308.
2. See Wadsworth and Mann, op. cit., pp. 387 ff.
3. Aspinall, op. cit., p. 271.

wanted'.[1] With the return of demand, the goods were then released on the market at cut price; so that each minor recession was succeeded by a period in which the market was glutted with cheap goods thereby holding wages down to their recession level. The practices of some employers were unscrupulous to a degree, both in the exaction of fines for faulty work and in giving false weight in yarn. Yet at the same time as wages were screwed lower and lower, the number of weavers continued to increase over the first three decades of the nineteenth century; for weaving, next to general labouring, was the grand resource of the northern unemployed. Fustian weaving was heavy, monotonous, but easily learned. Agricultural workers, demobilized soldiers, Irish immigrants – all continued to swell the labour force.

The first severe general reductions took place at the turn of the century: there was an improvement in the last year or two of the Wars, followed by further reductions after 1815 and an uninterrupted decline thereafter. The weavers' first demand, from 1790 onwards, was for a legal minimum wage – a demand supported by some employers, as a means of enforcing fair conditions of competition upon their less scrupulous rivals. The rejection of this demand by the House of Commons in May 1808, was followed by a strike, when 10,000 to 15,000 weavers demonstrated on successive days in St George's Fields, Manchester. The demonstration was dispersed by the magistrates with bloodshed, and the full vindictiveness of the authorities was revealed by the State prosecution and imprisonment of a prominent manufacturer, Colonel Joseph Hanson of the Volunteers, who had supported the minimum wage bill, for the crime of riding among the weavers and uttering 'malicious and inflammatory words':

Stick to your cause and you will certainly succeed. Neither Nadin nor any of his faction shall put you off the field to-day. Gentlemen, you cannot live by your labour. ... My father was a weaver; I myself was taught the weaving trade; I am a weaver's real friend.

1. Weavers' petition in favour of a minimum wage bill, 1807, signed – it is claimed – by 130,000 cotton-weavers: see J. L. and B. Hammond, *The Skilled Labourer*, p. 74.

The weavers subsequently presented to Colonel Hanson a tribute, in the form of a silver cup, to which 39,600 persons contributed. 'The effects of this ill-advised prosecution,' commented the Manchester historian, Archibald Prentice, 'were long and injuriously felt. It introduced that bitter feeling of employed against employers which was manifested in 1812, 1817, 1819, and 1826...'[1]

The dates which Prentice singled out are those of the destruction of power-looms (1812, 1826), of the March of the Blanketeers (1817) and Peterloo (1819). With no hope of legal protection the weavers turned more directly towards the channels of political Radicalism.[2] But for some years after 1800 an alliance between Methodism and 'Church and King' rowdyism kept most of the weavers as political 'loyalists'. It was claimed that 20,000 of them joined the Volunteers early in the Wars, and that there was a time when a man would be knocked down if he criticized the monarchy or the Pension List: 'I have two or three individuals in my eye,' declared a Bolton witness before the Select Committee on Hand-loom weavers in 1834, 'who were in serious danger for being reformers of the old school.' It was after the Wars that the real Radical tide set in; and in 1818 a second critical confrontation between the weavers and their employers took place. It was the year of the great Manchester cotton-spinners' strike, and of the first impressive attempt at general unionism (the 'Philanthropic Hercules'). Once again the weavers struck, collecting the shuttles and locking them in chapels or workshops, not only in Manchester but throughout the weaving towns – Bolton, Bury, Burnley. The strike ended in short-lived concessions on the masters' side, and in the prosecution and imprisonment of several of the weavers' leaders.[3] It was the last effective general strike movement of the Lancashire weavers: thereafter wages in most branches continued to be beaten

1. Howell's *State Trials*, Vol. XXXI, pp. 1–98; Prentice, op. cit., p. 33.

2. For the events leading to Luddism (1812), see below, 591.

3. Hammonds, op. cit., pp. 109–21. The Home Office papers on the 1818 strike, drawn upon by the Hammonds, are now available in full in Aspinall, op. cit., pp. 246–310.

down – 9s., 6s., 4s. 6d. and even less per week for irregular work – until the 1830s.

It is an over-simplification to ascribe the cause of the debasement of the weavers' conditions to the power-loom.[1] The status of the weavers had been shattered by 1813, at a time when the total number of power-looms in the U.K. was estimated at 2,400, and when the competition of power with hand was largely psychological. The estimate of power-looms rises to 14,000 in 1820, but even then it was slow and clumsy and had not yet been adapted to the Jacquard principle, so that it was incapable of weaving difficult figured patterns. It can be argued that the very cheapness and superfluity of hand-loom labour *retarded* mechanical invention and the application of capital in weaving. The degradation of the weavers is very similar to that of the workers in the dishonourable artisan trades. Each time their wages were beaten down, their position became more defenceless. The weaver had now to work longer into the night to earn less; in working longer he increased another's chances of unemployment. Even adherents of the new 'political economy' were appalled. 'Did Dr A. Smith ever contemplate such a state of things?' exclaimed one humane employer, whose honourable practices were the cause of his own ruin:

It is vain to read his book to find a remedy for a complaint which he could not conceive existed, vis. 100,000 weavers doing the work of 150,000 when there was no demand (as 'tis said) and that for half meat, and the rest paid by Poor Rates, could he conceive that the profits of a Manufacture should be what one Master could wring from the hard earnings of the poor, more than another?[2]

'100,000 weavers doing the work of 150,000' – this is the essence of the dishonourable trades, as later seen by Mayhew in London: a pool of surplus labour, semi-employed, defenceless, and undercutting each other's wages. The very circumstances of the weaver's work, especially in the upland hamlets,

1. Similar processes can be seen in the Spitalfields silk-weaving industry in the eighteenth century, where no power was involved. See M. D. George, *London Life in the Eighteenth Century*, p. 187.

2. Hammonds, op. cit., p. 123. See also the impressive statement of the Manchester weavers in 1823, in the Hammonds, *Town Labourer*, pp. 298–301.

gave an additional impediment to trade unionism. A Salford weaver explained these conditions to the Select Committee of 1834:

The very peculiar circumstances in which the hand-loom weavers are situated, preclude the possibility of their having the slightest control over the value of their own labour. . . . The fact that the weavers of even one employer may be scattered over an extensive district presents a constant opportunity to that employer, if he be so minded, to make his weavers the means of reducing the wages of one another alternatively; to some he will tell that others are weaving for so much less, and that they must have no more, or go without work, and this in turn he tells to the rest. . . . Now the difficulty, and loss of time it would occasion the weavers to discover the truth or falsehood of this statement, the fear that, in the interval, others would step in and deprive them of the work so offered . . . the jealousy and resentment enkindled in the minds of all, tending to divide them in sentiment and feeling, all conspire to make the reduction certain to be effected . . .

The decline of the Yorkshire woollen and worsted weavers followed a parallel course, although it often lagged fifteen or more years behind the changes in cotton. Evidence before the Committee on the Woollen Trade of 1806 showed the domestic system still commanding the woollen industry. But the 'little makers' were on the decrease: 'many which were masters' houses are now workmen's houses'; while at the same time merchant manufacturers were bringing a number of hand-looms, as well as the finishing processes, under one roof in unpowered 'factories'. ('A factory,' said one witness, 'is where they employ perhaps 200 hands in one and the same building.') The factories – notably those of Benjamin Gott in Leeds – aroused bitter dislike among both small masters and journeymen, because they were creaming the best customers, and in the finishing processes – where the cloth-dressers or croppers were highly organized – they were taking 'illegal' men. Wealth, declared one witness, 'has gone more into lumps'. The journeymen complained that the factories put out more work to out-weavers in brisk times, and dismissed them without compunction in slack, whereas the small master-clothiers still sought to find employment for their own journeymen. Moreover, even before the use of power, the hand-loom 'factories' offended deep-rooted moral prejudices. A trade union – the Clothier's Community or 'the Institution' – existed among the croppers and weavers, its avowed purpose being to join with the small clothiers in petitioning for a restriction upon the factories and for an enforcement of apprenticeship.[1]

Neither the 'little makers' nor the journeymen received any satisfaction from the House of Commons: their petitions served only to draw attention to their combination, and to the old paternalist statutes which were soon afterwards repealed. In the Leeds and Spen Valley clothing districts the small clothiers were tenacious, and their decline was protracted over a further fifty years. It was in the worsted districts of Bradford and Halifax, and in the fancy woollen district to the south of Huddersfield that the putting-out system was most fully developed by the 1820s; and, just as in cotton, the weavers were the victims of wage-cutting, and of 'slaughter-house men' who warehoused stocks of cut-price goods.

Just as the croppers were the artisan élite of the woollen industry, so the woolcombers were the élite workers in worsted. Controlling a bottle-neck in the manufacturing process, they were in a position to uphold their status so long as they could limit entry to their trade. And this they had done with some success, owing to their exceptional trade union organization which reached back at least to the 1740s. In the early nineteenth century, despite the Combination Acts, they had effective national organization, an imposing Constitution, with all the paraphernalia of an underground union, and the reputation for insubordination and lax time-keeping:

They come on a Monday morning, and having lighted the fire in the comb-pot, will frequently go away, and perhaps return no more till Wednesday, or even Thursday. ... A spare bench is always provided in the shop, upon which people on the *tramp* may rest ...[2]

In Bradford, in February 1825, the festival in honour of Bishop Blaize, the woolcomber's saint, was celebrated on a magnificent scale.[3] In June as if to punctuate the transition to

1. See below, pp. 573–6.
2. *Book of English Trades* (1818), p. 441.
3. See below, pp. 465–6.

the new industrialism, there commenced the bitterest strike of
Bradford's history, in which 20,000 woolcombers and weavers
were involved, and which lasted for twenty-three weeks, ending in total defeat for the strikers.[1] The Combination Acts
had been repealed in the previous year. Commencing in demands for wage advances and rationalization, the strike turned
into a struggle for union recognition, the employers going so
far as to dismiss all children from the spinning-mills whose
parents refused to sign a document renouncing the union. The
contest was seen to be crucial throughout the country, and up
to £20,000 was contributed in support of strike funds. After
defeat, the woolcomber was translated almost overnight from
a privileged artisan to a defenceless outworker. Apprenticeship restrictions had already broken down, and in the years
before 1825 thousands had been attracted by high wages into
the trade. While some combers worked in large workshops,
it had been customary for others to club together in threes
and fours sharing an independent shop. Now they were supplemented by hundreds of newcomers whose unhealthy trade
was carried on in their own homes. Although combing machinery was in existence by 1825 it was of doubtful service in
fine combing; and the cheapness of combers' labour enabled
the threat of machinery to be kept above their heads for a
further twenty years. Throughout this time the combers remained noted for their independence and their 'democratic'
politics. The union estimated that 7,000 or 8,000 were employed in the Bradford trade in 1825; twenty years later there
were still 10,000 handcombers in the district. Many came, in
the 1820s, from agricultural districts:

They came from Kendal, North Yorkshire, Leicester, Devonshire,
and even from the Emerald Isle; so that to spend an hour in a
public-house (the comber's calling was a thirsty one) one might have
heard a perfect Babel of different dialects. ... His attachment to
rural life was evidenced by the fact that in hay-time and harvest he

1. For accounts of the strike see J. Burney, *History of Wool and
Woolcombing* (1889), pp. 166 ff.; J. James, *History of the Worsted Manufacture* (1857), pp. 400 ff.; *Trades Newspaper*, June–September 1826;
W. Scruton, 'The Great Strike of 1825', *Bradford Antiquary* (1888), I,
pp. 67–73.

used to lay aside his wool-combs, take up his scythe ... and go to his own country a harvesting. ... He was a bird fancier too, and his comb-shop was often transformed into a perfect aviary. ... Some combers had a talent for elocution, and could recite with wonderful power. ... Others again were so clever at dramatic personation that they even went the length of forming themselves into companies ...

– so runs one Bradford account.[1] An account from Cleckheaton is in more sombre terms:

Perhaps a more wretched class of workmen never existed than the old woolcombers. The work was all done in their own houses, the best part of their cottages being taken up with it. The whole family, of sometimes six or eight, both male and female, worked together round a 'combpot' heated by charcoal, the fumes of which had a very deleterious effect upon their health. When we add that the workshop was also perforce the bedroom, it will not be wondered at that woolcombers were almost invariably haggard looking ... many of them not living half their days ...

Their wives also had 'often to stand at the "pad-posts" and work from six o'clock in the morning till ten at night like their husbands'.

Another peculiarity about these woolcombers was that they were almost without exception rabid politicians. ... The Chartist movement had no more enthusiastic adherents than these men; the 'Northern Star' was their one book of study.[2]

Perhaps no group was thrown so precipitately as the woolcombers from 'honourable' into 'dishonourable' conditions. The worsted- and woollen-weavers had not known so privileged a status as the eighteenth-century combers; and at first they resisted less stubbornly as their wages declined. As late as 1830, the largest employer of hand-loom weavers in Bradford wrote:

1. W. Scruton, *Bradford Fifty Years Ago* (Bradford, 1897), pp. 95–6.
2. Frank Peel, op. cit. The plight of the combers in the 1840s is described in J. Burney, op. cit., pp. 175–85; their sudden extinction by improved combing machinery in Bradford in the late 1840s is described by E. Sigsworth in C. Fay, *Round About Industrial Britain*, 1830–1850 (1952), pp. 123–8; for their extinction in Halifax in 1856, see E. Baines, *Yorkshire Past and Present*, II, p. 145.

The weavers are of all classes we have to do with the most orderly and steady, never at any period, that I know of, constraining an advance of wages, but submitting to every privation and suffering with almost unexampled patience and forbearance.[1]

Two years later, Cobbett rode through the Halifax district, and reported that:

It is truly lamentable to behold so many thousands of men who formerly earned 20 to 30 shillings per week, now compelled to live upon 5s, 4s, or even less. ... It is the more sorrowful to behold these men in their state, as they still retain the frank and bold character formed in the days of their independence.[2]

The depression in the Huddersfield 'fancy' trade had continued without intermission since 1825. In 1826, 3,500 families were on the list of paupers in Delph in the Saddleworth district, and there was some extension of the 'industrial Speenhamland' system (already in operation in some Lancashire cotton districts) whereby weavers were relieved out of the poor-rates while still in work, thereby further reducing their wages. (For two days a week road-work in Saddleworth the weavers received 12 lb. of oatmeal per day.) In Huddersfield a committee of the masters established, in 1829, that there were over 13,000 out of a population of 29,000 who – when the wage was divided between all members of the family – subsisted on 2d. per day per head. But it was a curious 'depression', in which the actual output of woollen cloth exceeded that in any previous period. The conditions of the weavers were bluntly attributed to 'the abominable system of reducing wages'.[3]

Once again the decline preceded serious competition with the power-loom. Power was not introduced into worsted-weaving on any scale until the late 1820s; into 'fancy' woollens until the late 1830s (and then only partially); while the power-loom was not effectively adapted to carpet-weaving until 1851. Even where direct power competition existed, the

1. Cited in W. Cudworth, *Condition of the Industrial Classes of Bradford & District* (Bradford, 1887).

2. *Political Register*, 20 June 1832.

3. W. B. Crump and G. Ghorbal, *History of Huddersfield Woollen Industry* (Huddersfield, 1935), pp. 120–21.

speed of weaving only slowly rose to that by which the hand-loom's output was trebled or quadrupled.[1] But there was un-doubtedly a chain reaction, as weavers forced out of plain cottons and fustians turned to fine work or silk or worsted and thence to 'fancy' woollen or carpets.[2] Power, indeed, con-tinued in many branches of textiles as an auxiliary to hand-loom weaving, for ten, fifteen, or twenty years. 'In Halifax', one witness informed the Select Committee (somewhat illogi-cally):

there are two very extensive manufacturers, two brothers [Messrs Akroyd]; the one weaves by power-looms and the other by hand-looms. ... they have to sell their goods against each other, there-fore they must bring their wages as near in point of comparison as possible ... to obtain a profit.[3]

Here the power-loom might appear as a lever to reduce the hand-loom weavers' wages and *vice versa*. From another aspect, the manufacturer was well satisfied with an arrangement by which he could base his steady trade upon his power-loom sheds and in times of brisk trade give out more work to the hand workers who themselves bore the costs of fixed charges

1. This is a difficult technical argument. Witnesses before the *Select Committee on Hand-Loom Weavers' Petitions* (1834) disagreed as to whether the average ratio of power to hand output in plain cottons should be estimated at $3:1$ or $5:1$. The dandy-loom, a species of hand-loom operated mechanically in so far as the movement of the cloth through the loom was concerned, to which the weaver must keep time by accelerated movements of the hand-thrown shuttle, was alleged to keep pace with the power-loom, but at great cost to the weaver's health. In worsted, J. James, estimated 2,768 power-looms in the West Riding in 1835, as compared with 14,000 hand-looms estimated in the Bradford district in 1838: by 1841 there were 11,458 West Riding power-looms. Estimates in the *Leeds Times* (28 March, 11 April 1835) suggest that the worsted power-loom weaver (generally a girl or woman minding two looms) could produce two and a half to three times as much work as the hand-loom weaver. But in the next fifteen years the speed of shuttle movements of a six-quarter loom more than doubled (H. Forbes, *Rise, Progress, and Present State of the Worsted Manufactures* (1852), p. 318). The Crossley Carpet Power Loom, patented in 1851, could weave twelve to fourteen times the speed of hand ('Reminiscences of Fifty Years by a Workman', *Halifax Courier*, 7 July 1888).

2. See *S.C. on Handloom Weavers' Petitions* (1835), p. 148 (2066).

3. Ibid., 1835, p. 60 (465–6).

for rent, loom, etc. 'In the event of a decreased demand,' reported the Assistant Commissioner enquiring into the West Riding in 1839:

the manufacturer who employs power, as well as hand-looms, will, of course, work his fixed capital as long as possible. Hence the services of the hand-loom weaver are first dispensed with.

The conditions of most weavers, from the 1820s to the 1840s and beyond, are commonly referred to as 'indescribable' or as 'well known'. They deserve, however, to be described and to be better known. There were selected groups of weavers who maintained their artisan-status, owing to some special skill, until the 1830s; the Leeds stuff weavers were better situated than most, while the Norwich worsted weavers, whose Jacobin and trade union traditions were exceptionally strong, succeeded in keeping up wages in the 1830s by a combination of picketing, intimidation of masters and 'illegal' men, municipal politics, and violent opposition to machinery – all of which contributed to the supersession of the Norwich by the West Riding industry.[1] But the great majority of the weavers were living on the edge – and sometimes beyond the edge – of the borders of starvation. The Select Committee on Emigration (1827) was given evidence of conditions in some districts of Lancashire which read like an anticipation of the Irish potato famine:

Mrs Hulton and myself, in visiting the poor, were asked by a person almost starving to go into a house. We there found on one side of the fire a very old man, apparently dying, on the other side a young man about eighteen with a child on his knee, whose mother had just died and been buried. We were going away from that house, when the woman said, 'Sir, you have not seen all.' We went up stairs, and, under some rags, we found another young man, the widower; and on turning down the rags, which he was unable to remove himself, we found another man who was dying, and who did die in the course of the day. I have no doubt that the family were actually starving at the time . . .

1. An account of the strength of the Norwich Weavers' Committee in its resistance to 'that unclean thing called underprice work' is given (from the master's standpoint) in *First Report of the Constabulary Commissioners* (1839), pp. 135–46. See also J. H. Clapham 'The Transference of the Worsted Industry from Norfolk to the West Riding', *Econ. Journal*, XX.

The evidence came from West Houghton, where half of the 5,000 inhabitants were 'totally destitute of bedding, and nearly so of clothes'. Six were described as being in the actual process of starvation.

It is true that the low wages quoted in these years (from 10s. to 4s.) might represent only one of several wages in the same family, since many wives, girls and youths, worked at a second or third loom. But the wages also concealed further outpayments or deductions. The Bradford worsted weavers in 1835 claimed that from an average wage of 10s. there would be an outlay of 4d. for sizing, 3d. for looming, $9\frac{1}{2}d$. for winding the weft, $3\frac{1}{2}d$. for light, while 4d. more should be added for outlay and wear and tear on the loom. If the outlay for rent (1s. 9d.) and fire and washing (1s. 6d.) were added, this totalled deductions amounting to 5s. 3d., although where the wife or son also worked on a second loom some of these overheads could be spread over two wages.[1] In some cases the loom itself was hired by the weaver, in other cases he owned the loom, but had to hire the gearing or slays for pattern-weaving from the employer. Many weavers were in a perpetual state of indebtedness to the 'putter-out', working off their debts by instalments upon their work, and in a condition where they were incapable of refusing any wages however low.

As their conditions worsened, so they had to spend more and more time in unpaid employments – fetching and carrying work, and a dozen other processes. 'I can remember the time,' wrote one observer in 1844,

when manufacturers hired rooms in districts, and the warps and wefts were conveyed to them, by horse and cart, for convenience of the weavers, and the employer inquired after the employed; but the case is now diametrically opposite, the labourer not only undertakes long journeys in quest of work, but is doomed to many disappointments.[2]

An even more graphic description of all his ancillary unpaid work comes from Pudsey:

1. *Leeds Times*, 7 March 1835.
2. R. Howard, Surgeon, *History of the Typhus of Hepstonstall-Slack* (Hebden Bridge, 1844).

It was quite common when trade was not bad to see weavers and spinners going from place to place seeking work. . . . If they succeeded it was mostly on the condition that they helped to break the wool for it; that is, opened the bales, then fleeces, taking off the coarse parts called the *britch*, put it in sheets, then go to the mill and help to scour it, then 'lit' or dye it. . . . All this was for *nothing*, except in some cases a small allowance for a little ale or cheese and bread. . . . When the slubber had doffed the first set of slubbing, it often became a serious question as to whose turn it was to have it, and casting lots would frequently be the mode of deciding it. . . . When the web was warped there was the sizing process to go through, and the weavers, as a rule, had to buy their own size. . . . After sizing the web, one of the most critical of all the processes is to put it out of doors to dry. . . . A place is chosen, the web-sticks or stretchers are put out, and if frosty, a pick-axe is used to make holes in the ground for posts to hold the ends of the web. . . . Sometimes might be seen a man and his wife up to their knees in snow going out with a web to dry . . .

After this, the weaving, late into the evening by candle or oil light, with 'a boy or girl or perhaps a weaver's wife, standing on one side of the loom watching to see when a thread broke down, whilst the weaver watched the other side, because if a thread broke, and another "shoit" was picked, a dozen more might be broken'. And after the weaving, there were half a dozen odd jobs to do again, before the piece was taken off by the carrier to Leeds:

All this odd jobbing, we say, was done for nothing. . . . It was no uncommon thing, too, when the work was done for the weavers to be unable to get paid for some time after. . . . We cannot wonder that a hand-loom weaver came to be called a 'poverty knocker'.[1]

Some of these practices did not obtain in cotton, or had long been devolved to specialist processes in worsted. They indicate the obsolescence of the small-scale woollen trade. But in the worsted and fancy woollen weaving districts there were equally time-wasting forms of jobbing. Among the scattered upland hamlets the 'human packhorse' was known – the man or woman who hired his or her labour to carry the heavy finished pieces five or even ten miles over the moorland roads.

1. J. Lawson, *Letters to the Young on Progress in Pudsey* (Stanningley, 1887), pp. 26–30.

It was in the weaving districts surrounding such centres as Bradford, Keighley, Halifax, Huddersfield, Todmorden, Rochdale, Bolton, Macclesfield, that the largest populations of utterly depressed outworkers were to be found. The Select Committee of 1834 reported that it found 'the sufferings of that large and valuable body of men, not only not exaggerated, but that they have for years continued to an extent and intensity scarcely to be credited or conceived'. John Fielden, giving evidence to the same Committee in 1835, declared that a very great number of the weavers, could not obtain sufficient food of the plainest or cheapest kind; were clothed in rags and ashamed to send their children to Sunday school; had no furniture and in some cases slept on straw; worked 'not unfrequently sixteen hours a day'; were demoralized by cheap spirits, and weakened by undernourishment and ill-health. Possessions gained in the 'golden age' had passed out of the weaving households. A Bolton witness declared:

Since I can recollect, almost every weaver that I knew had a chest of drawers in his house, and a clock and chairs, and bedsteads and candlesticks, and even pictures, articles of luxury; and now I find that those have disappeared; they have either gone into the houses of mechanics, or into houses of persons of higher class.

The same witness, a manufacturer, could not 'recollect an instance but one, where any weaver of mine has bought a new jacket for many years'. A coarse coverlid, of the value of 2s. 6d. when new, often did service for blankets: 'I have seen many houses with only two or three three-legged stools, and some I have seen without a stool or chair, with only a tea chest to put their clothes in, and to sit upon.'

There is unanimity as to the diet of the poor weaver and his family: oatmeal, oatcake, potatoes, onion porridge, blue milk, treacle or home-brewed ale, and as luxuries tea, coffee, bacon. 'They do not know what it is, many of them,' declared Richard Oastler, 'to taste flesh meat from year's end to year's end ... and their children will sometimes run to Huddersfield, and beg, and bring a piece in, and it is quite a luxury....' If confirmation was needed, it was brought by the careful investigations of the Assistant Commissioners who toured the country after the appointment of the Royal Commission in

1838. The very worst conditions, perhaps, were those found in the cellar dwellings of the big towns – Leeds and Manchester – where Irish unemployed attempted to earn a few shillings by the loom.

But it is easy to assume that the country weavers in the solid, stonebuilt cottages, with the long mullioned windows of the loom-shops, in the beautiful Pennine uplands – in the upper Calder Valley or Wharfedale, Saddleworth or Clitheroe – enjoyed amenities which compensated for their poverty. A surgeon who investigated a typhus epidemic in a hamlet near Heptonstall (a thriving little woollen township during the Civil War) has left a terrible picture of the death of one such community. Situated high on the moors, nevertheless the water-supplies were polluted: one open stream, polluted by a slaughter-house, was in summer 'a nursery of loathsome animal life'. The sewer passed directly under the flags of one of the weaver's cottages. The houses were wet and cold, the ground floors beneath the surface of the earth: 'It may be fairly said oatmeal and potatoes are well nigh what they contrive to exist upon', with old milk and treacle. If tea or coffee could not be afforded, an infusion of mint, tansy or hyssop was prepared. Even of this diet 'they have by no means sufficient.... The inhabitants are undergoing a rapid deterioration.' Medical attendance and funeral expenses were generally paid from the poor-rates; only one in ten received any medical aid in childbirth:

What is the situation of the wife of the hand-loom weaver during the parturient efforts? She is upon her feet, with a woman on each side; her arms are placed round their necks; and, in nature's agony, she almost drags her supporters to the floor; and in this state the birth takes place. ... And why is this the case? The answer is, be-cause there is no change of bedclothing ...

'How they contrive to exist at all,' exclaimed this humane surgeon, 'confounds the very faculties of eyes and ears.'[1]

The contemporary reaction against 'the Hammonds' has gone so far that it is almost impossible to quote such sources, with which these years are all too plentiful, without being accused of pejorative intentions. But it is necessary to do so

1. R. Howard, op. cit., *passim*.

because, without such detail, it is possible for the eye to pass over the phrase, 'the decline of the handloom weavers', without any realization of the scale of the tragedy that was enacted. Weaving communities – some in the West Country and the Pennines, with 300 and 400 years of continuous existence, some of much more recent date but with, none the less, their own cultural patterns and traditions – were literally being extinguished. The demographic pattern of Heptonstall-Slack was extraordinary: in a population of 348, over one-half were under twenty (147 under fifteen), while only 30 were over fifty-five; this did not represent a growing community, but a low expectation of life. In the catastrophic years of the 1830s and 1840s, when the power-loom, the Irish influx, and the new Poor Law, finished off what wage-cutting had begun, there were – alongside the insurrectionary hopes of Chartist weavers – the more gruesome stories: the children's burial clubs (where each Sunday-school pupil contributed 1*d.* per week towards his own or a fellow-pupil's funeral); the dissemination and serious discussion of a pamphlet (by 'Marcus') advocating infanticide. But this is not the whole story. Until these final agonies, the older weaving communities offered a way of life which their members greatly preferred to the higher material standards of the factory town. The son of a weaver from the Heptonstall district, who was a child in the 1820s, recalled that the weavers 'had their good times'. 'The atmosphere was not fouled by ... the smoke of the factory.'

There was no bell to ring them up at four or five o'clock ... there was freedom to start and to stay away as they cared. ... In the evenings, while still at work, at anniversary times of the Sunday schools, the young men and women would most heartily join in the hymn singing, while the musical rhythm of the shuttles would keep time ...

Some weavers had fruit, vegetables, and flowers from their gardens. 'My work was at the loom side, and when not winding my father taught me reading, writing and arithmetic.' A Keighley factory child, who left the mill for a hand-loom at the age of eighteen, informed Sadler's Committee (1832) that he preferred the loom to the mill 'a great deal': 'I have more relaxation; I can look about me, and go out and refresh myself a little.' It was the custom in Bradford for the weavers to gather in their dinner break at noon:

... and have a chat with other weavers and combers on the news or gossip of the time. Some of these parties would spend an hour talking about pig-feeding, hen-raising, and bird-catching, and now and then would have very hot disputes about free grace, or whether infant baptism or adult immersion was the correct and scriptural mode of doing the thing. I have many a time seen a number of men ready to fight one another on this ... topic.[1]

A unique blend of social conservatism, local pride, and cultural attainment made up the way of life of the Yorkshire or Lancashire weaving community. In one sense these communities were certainly 'backward' – they clung with equal tenacity to their dialect traditions and regional customs and to gross medical ignorance and superstitions. But the closer we look at their way of life, the more inadequate simple notions of economic progress and 'backwardness' appear. Moreover, there was certainly a leaven amongst the northern weavers of self-educated and articulate men of considerable attainments. Every weaving district had its weaver-poets, biologists, mathematicians, musicians, geologists, botanists: the old weaver in *Mary Barton* is certainly drawn from the life. There are northern museums and natural history societies which still possess records or collections of lepidoptera built up by weavers; while there are accounts of weavers in isolated villages who taught themselves geometry by chalking on their flagstones, and who were eager to discuss the differential calculus.[2] In some kinds of plain work with strong yarn a book could actually be propped on the loom and read at work.

There is also a weaver's poetry, some traditional, some more

1. J. Greenwood, 'Reminiscences', *Todmorden Advertiser*, 10 September 1909; J. Hartley, 'Memorabilia', *Todmorden and District News*, 1903; W. Scruton, op. cit., p. 92.

2. See also J. F. C. Harrison, *Learning and Living* (1961), p. 45; and M. D. George, op. cit., p. 188 for the Spitalfields weavers Such traditions were also strong in the West Country, Norwich, and, most notably, among the Scottish weavers. In Spitalfields the Silk-weavers supported Mathematical, Historical, Floricultural, Entomological, Recitation, and Musical Societies: G. I. Stigler, *Five Lectures on Economic Problems* (1949), p. 26.

sophisticated. The Lancashire 'Jone o' Grinfilt' ballads went through a patriotic cycle at the start of the Wars (with Jacobin counter-ballads) and continued through Chartist times to the Crimean War. The most moving is 'Jone o' Grinfilt Junior', sung at the close of the Wars:

> Aw'm a poor cotton-wayver, as mony a one knaws,
> Aw've nowt t'ate i' th' heawse, un' aw've worn eawt my cloas,
> Yo'd hardly gie sixpence fur o' aw've got on,
> Meh clogs ur' booath baws'n, un' stockins aw've none;
>> You'd think it wur hard, to be sent into th' ward
>> To clem un' do best 'ot yo' con.
>
> Eawr parish-church pa'son's kept tellin' us lung,
> We'st see better toimes, if aw'd but howd my tung;
> Aw've howden my tung, toll aw con hardly draw breoth,
> Aw think i' my heart he meons t'clem me to deoth;
>> Aw knaw he lives weel, wi' backbitin' the de'il,
>> Bur he never pick'd o'er in his loife.
>
> Wey tooart on six weeks, thinkin' aich day wur th' last,
> Wey tarried un' shifted, till neaw wey're quite fast;
> Wey liv't upo' nettles, whoile nettles were good,
> Un' Wayterloo porritch wur' the best o' us food;
>> Aw'm tellin' yo' true, aw con foind foak enoo,
>> Thot're livin' na better nur me . . .

The bailiffs break in, and take their furniture after a fight.

>> Aw said to eawr Marget, as wey lien upo' th' floor,
>> 'Wey ne'er shall be lower i' this wo'ald, aw'm sure . . .'

When he takes his piece back to his master, Jone is told that he is in debt for over-payment on his last piece. He comes out of the warehouse in despair, and returns to his wife.

>> Eawr Marget declares, if hoo'd clooas to put on,
>> Hoo'd go up to Lunnon to see the great mon;
>> Un' if things didno' awter, when theere hoo had been,
>> Hoo says hoo'd begin, un' feight blood up to th' e'en,
>>> Hoo's nout agen th' king, bur hoo loikes a fair thing,
>>> Un' hoo says hoo con tell when hoo's hurt.[1]

The other kind of weaver-poet was the auto-didact. A remarkable example was Samuel Law, a Todmorden weaver,

1. J. Harland, *Ballads and Songs of Lancashire* (1865), pp. 223–7.

who published a poem in 1772 modelled on Thomson's *Seasons*. The poem has few literary merits, but reveals a knowledge of Virgil, Ovid and Homer (in the original), of biology and astronomy:

> Yes, the day long, and in each evening gloom,
> I meditated in the sounding loom . . .
> Meanwhile, I wove the flow'ry waved web,
> With fingers colder than the icy glebe;
> And oftentimes, thro' the whole frame of man,
> Bleak chilling horrors, and a sickness ran.[1]

Later weaver-poets often convey little more than pathos, the self-conscious efforts to emulate alien literary forms (notably 'nature poetry') which catch little of the weaver's authentic experience. A hand-loom weaver from 1820 to 1850, who then obtained work in a power-loom factory, lamented the effect of the change upon his verses:

I then worked in a small chamber, overlooking Luddenden Churchyard. I used to go out in the fields and woods . . . at meal-times, and listen to the songs of the summer birds, or watch the trembling waters of the Luddon. . . . Sometimes I have been roused from those reveries by some forsaken lovesick maiden, who . . . has poured forth her heartwailing to the thankless wind. I have then gone home and have written. . . . But it is all over; I must continue to work amidst the clatter of machinery.

It is sad that years of self-education should result only in a patina of cliché. But it was the attainment itself which brought genuine satisfactions; as a young man in the late 1820s his observation of nature appears far more soundly based than his observation of lovesick maidens:

I collected insects, in company with a number of young men in the village. We formed a library. . . . I believe I and a companion of mine . . . collected twenty-two large boxes of insects; one hundred and twenty different sorts of British birds' eggs; besides a great quantity of shells (land and fresh water), fossils, minerals, ancient and modern coins . . .[2]

1. *A Domestic Winter-piece* . . . by Samuel Law, of Barewise, near Todmorden, Lancashire Weaver (Leeds, 1772).
2. W. Heaton, *The Old Soldier* (1857), pp. xxiii, xix.

Samuel Bamford serves as a bridge between the folk traditions of the eighteenth-century communities (which lingered long into the next century) and the more self-conscious intellectual attainments of the early decades of the nineteenth. Between these two periods there are two deeply transforming experiences – those of Methodism and of political radicalism.[1] But in accounting for the intellectual leaven, we should also remember the number of small clothiers reduced to the status of weavers,[2] sometimes bringing with them educational attainments and small libraries.

The fullest expression of the values of the weaving communities belongs to the history of the Chartist movement. A high proportion of northern and Midlands local Chartist leaders were outworkers, whose formative experiences came in the years between 1810 and 1830. Among such men were Benjamin Rushton of Halifax, born in 1785 and already a 'veteran' reformer by 1832. Or William Ashton, a Barnsley linen-weaver, born in 1806, transported in 1830 for alleged complicity in strike-riots, liberated in 1838 and brought back from Australia by the subscriptions of his fellow-weavers, to play a leading part in the Chartist movement, and to suffer a further term of imprisonment. Or Richard Pilling, a hand-loom weaver who had transferred to power-looms, and who was known as the 'Father' of the Plug Riots in Lancashire. Or John Skevington, local preacher with the Primitive Methodists, stocking-weaver, and Loughborough Chartist leader; William Rider, a Leeds stuff-weaver; and George White, a Bradford woolcomber.[3]

The career of these men would take us beyond the limits of this study. But the Lancashire Radicalism of 1816-20 was in

1. For Methodism and the weavers, see ch. 11 below. For post-war political radicalism, see pp. 704-8.

2. John Fielden declared before the Select Committee of 1835: 'I think three-fourths of the manufacturers at least in the neighbourhood where I reside have been reduced to poverty.'

3. For Rushton, see pp. 439-40 below. For Ashton, various sources in Barnsley Reference Library. For Pilling, see *Chartist Trials* (1843). For Skevington, see J. F. C. Harrison, 'Chartism in Leicester', in A. Briggs, *Chartist Studies* (1959), pp. 130-31. For White and Rider, see Harrison, 'Chartism in Leeds', ibid., pp. 70 ff.

great degree a movement of weavers, and the *making* of these later leaders was in communities of this kind. What they brought to the early working-class movement can scarcely be overestimated. They had, like the city artisan, a sense of lost status, as memories of their 'golden age' lingered; and, with this, they set a high premium on the values of independence. In these respects they provided, in 1816, a natural audience for Cobbett. The vexed question of embezzlement of yarn apart, nearly all witnesses spoke to the honesty and self-reliance of the weavers – 'as faithful, moral, and trust-worthy, as any corporate body amongst his Majesty's subjects....'[1] But they had, more than the city artisan, a deep social egalitarianism. As their way of life, in the better years, had been shared by the community, so their sufferings were those of the whole community; and they were reduced so low that there was no class of unskilled or casual labourers below them against which they had erected economic or social protective walls. This gave a particular moral resonance to their protest, whether voiced in Owenite or biblical language; they appealed to essential rights and elementary notions of human fellow-ship and conduct rather than to sectional interests. It was as a whole community that they demanded betterment, and utopian notions of redesigning society anew at a stroke – Owenite communities, the universal general strike, the Chartist Land Plan – swept through them like fire on the common. But essentially the dream which arose in many different forms was the same – a community of independent small producers, exchanging their products without the distortions of masters and middlemen. As late as 1848 a Barnsley linen-weaver (a fellow transportee with William Ashton) declared at the Chartist National Convention that when the Charter was won 'They would divide the land into small farms, and give every man an opportunity of getting his living by the sweat of his brow'.[2]

At this point we should enquire more strictly into the actual position of the weavers in the 1830s, and possible remedies. It is customary to describe their plight as 'hopeless', in a 'sick'

1. Radcliffe, op. cit., p. 107.   2. *Halifax Guardian*, 8 April 1848.

or 'obsolete' trade, fighting a 'losing battle' and facing 'inevitable decline'. It may be said, on the other hand, that until the late 1820s the power-loom was used as *an excuse* to distract attention from other causes of their decline.[1] Until 1820 it is difficult to establish a case for *direct* competition between power and hand; although power-looms in cotton were multiplying, it is sometimes forgotten that the consumption of cotton was leaping upwards at the same time.[2] Something of the same kind is true for the worsted industry until 1835; and in other branches of wool until the 1840s.[3] Thus there were two phases in the hand-loom weavers' decline. The first, up to 1830 or 1835, in which power was a creeping ancillary cause, although it bulked more largely in psychological terms (and was, in this sense, a lever in reducing wages); the second, in which power actually displaced hand products. It was in the first phase that the major reductions in wages (let us say, from 20s. to 8s.) took place.

Were both phases inevitable? In the judgement of most historians, it would appear that they were, although it is sometimes suggested that the weavers might have received more

1. G. H. Wood, *History of Wages in the Cotton Trade* (1910), p. 112, offers averages for cotton weavers ranging from 18s. 9d. (1797); 21s. (1802); 14s. (1809), 8s. 9d. (1817); 7s. 3d. (1828); 6s. (1832). These probably understate the decline: a weekly average of 4s. 6d. was certainly found in many districts by the 1830s. The decline in most branches of worsted and woollens was much the same, commencing a little later and rarely falling quite so low. The statistically-inclined may consult the voluminous evidence in the Reports of the Select Committee and Assistant Commissioners: useful tables are in *S.C. on Hand-loom Weaver's Petitions*, 1834, pp. 432-3, 446: and in J. Fielden, *National Regeneration* (1834), pp. 27-30.

2. Estimated cotton power-looms in England: 1820, 12,150; 1829, 55,000; 1833, 85,000. Estimated weight of twist consumed: 1820, 87,096 million lb.; 1829, 149,570 million lb. Estimated number of cotton hand-loom weavers in U.K.: 1801, 164,000; 1810, 200,000; 1820, 240,000; 1830, 240,000; 1833, 213,000 1840, 123,000. See N. J. Smelser, *Social Change in the Industrial Revolution* (1959), pp. 137, 148-9, 207.

3. In the parish of Halifax, where worsted was predominant, consumption of wool leapt from 1830, 3,657,000 lb. to 1850, 14,423,000 lb. Over the same period, worsted power-looms multiplied from some hundreds to 4,000. In Bradford worsteds the ratio of power-looms to hand in 1836 was still about 3,000 to 14,000.

assistance or guidance. In the judgement of a great many contemporaries – including the weavers and their representatives – they were not. In the first phase of decline there were a dozen contributory factors, including the general effects of the post-war deflationary decade: but the underlying causes would appear to be, first, the breakdown of both custom and trade union protection; second, the total exposure of the weavers to the worst forms of wage-cutting; third, the over-stocking of the trade by unemployed to whom it had become 'the last refuge of the unsuccessful'. A Bolton manufacturer defined the efficient cause succinctly:

... I find that from the very commencement of the manufacture of muslins at Bolton. the trade of weaving has been subject to arbitrary reductions, commencing at a very high rate. One would suppose that the reward of labour would find its proper level; but from the very commencement of it, it has been in the power of any one manufacturer to set an example of reducing wages; and I know it as a fact, that when they could not obtain a price for the goods, such as they thought they ought to get, they immediately fell to reducing the weavers' wages.

But at the same time, in Bolton in 1834 – a good year – 'there are no weavers out of employment; there is no danger of any being out of employment at this time'.[1]

The breakdown of custom and of trade unionism was directly influenced by State intervention. This was 'inevitable' only if we assume the governing ideology and the counter-revolutionary tone of these years. The weavers and their supporters opposed to this ideology a contrary analysis and contrary policies, which turned on the demand for a regulated minimum wage, enforced by trade boards of manufacturers and weavers. They offered a direct negative to the homilies of 'supply-and-demand'. When asked whether wages ought not to be left to find their own 'level', a Manchester silk-weaver replied that there was no similarity between 'what is called capital and labour':

Capital, I can make out to be nothing else but an accumulation of the products of labour. ... Labour is always carried to market by

1. *S.C. on Hand-Loom Weavers' Petitions*, 1834, p. 381 (4901), p. 408 (5217).

those who have nothing else to keep or to sell, and who, therefore, must part with it immediately. ... The labour which I ... might perform this week, if I, in imitation of the capitalist, refuse to part with it ... because an inadequate price is offered me for it, can I bottle it? can I lay it up in salt? ... These two distinctions between the nature of labour and capital, (viz. that labour is always sold by the poor, and always bought by the rich, and that labour cannot by any possibility be stored, but must be every instant sold or every instant lost,) are sufficient to convince me that labour and capital can never with justice be subjected to the same laws ...[1]

The weavers saw clearly, Richard Oastler testified, that *'capital and property are protected and their labour is left to chance'.* Oastler's evidence before the Select Committee, when he was heckled by one of the partisans of 'political economy', dramatizes the alternative views of social responsibility:

[*Oastler*]. The time of labour ought to be shortened, and ... Government ought to establish a board ... chosen by the masters and the men ... to settle the question of how wages shall be regulated. ...

Q. You would put an end to the freedom of labour?

A. I would put an end to the freedom of murder, and to the freedom of employing labourers beyond their strength; I would put an end to any thing which prevents the poor man getting a good living with fair and reasonable work: and I would put an end to this, because it was destructive of human life.

Q. Would it have the effect you wished for?

A. I am sure the present effect of free labour is poverty, distress and death. ...

Q. Suppose you were to raise the price very considerably, and ... could not export your goods?

A. We can use them at home.

Q. You would not use so much, would you?

A. Three times as much, and a great deal more than that, because the labourers would be better paid, and they would consume them. The capitalists do not use the goods, and there is the great mistake ... If the wages were higher, the labourer would be enabled to clothe himself ... and to feed himself ... and those labourers are the persons who are after all the great consumers of agricultural and manufacturing produce, and not the capitalist, because a great capitalist, however wealthy he is,

1. Ibid., 1835, p. 188 (2686).

wears only one coat at once, at least, he certainly does seldom wear two coats at once; but 1,000 labourers, being enabled to buy a thousand coats, where they cannot now get one, would most certainly increase the trade ...

As to the commission-houses or 'slaughter-houses', Oastler favoured direct legislative interference:

You never make a Law of this House but it interferes with liberty; you make laws to prevent people from stealing, that is an interference with a man's liberty; and you make laws to prevent men from murdering, that is an interference with a man's liberty ... I should say that these slaughter-house men shall not do so ...

The capitalists 'seem as if they were a privileged order of being, but I never knew why they were so'.[1]

'There is the great mistake' – weavers, who wove cloth when they themselves were in rags, were forcibly educated in the vitiating error of the orthodox political economy. It was before the competition of power – and while their numbers were still increasing – that the Lancashire weavers sang their sad 'Lament':

You gentlemen and tradesmen, that ride about at will,
Look down on these poor people; it's enough to make you crill;
Look down on these poor people, as you ride up and down,
I think there is a God above will bring your pride quite down.

Chorus – You tyrants of England, your race may soon be run,
    You may be brought into account for what you've sorely done.

You pull down our wages, shamefully to tell;
You go into the markets, and say you cannot sell;
And when that we do ask you when these bad times will mend,
You quickly give an answer, 'When the wars are at an end'.

The clothing of the weavers' children is in rags, whilst 'yours do dress as manky as monkeys in a show':

You go to church on Sunday, I'm sure it's nought but pride,
There can be no religion where humanity's thrown aside;
If there be a place in heaven, as there is in the Exchange,
Our poor souls must not come near there; like lost sheep they must range.

1. *S.C. on Hand-Loom Weavers' Petitions*, 1834, pp. 283–8.

With the choicest of strong dainties your tables overspread,
With good ale and strong brandy, to make your faces red;
You call'd a set of visitors – it is your whole delight –
And you lay your heads together to make our faces white.

You say that Bonyparty he's been the spoil of all,
And that we have got reason to pray for his downfall;
Now Bonyparty's dead and gone, and it is plainly shown
That we have bigger tyrants in Boneys of our own.[1]

The transparency of their exploitation added to their anger and their suffering: nothing in the process which brought troops to Peterloo or enabled their masters to erect great mansions in the manufacturing districts seemed to them to be 'natural' or 'inevitable'.

Historians who assume that wage-regulation was 'impossible' have not bothered to present a case which can be answered. John Fielden's proposals for a minimum wage periodically reviewed in each district by trade boards was no more 'impossible' than the 10 Hour Bill which was only won after three decades of intensive agitation and in the face of equal opposition. Fielden had on his side not only the weavers but many of the masters who wished to restrict the less scrupulous and the 'slaughter-houses'. The difficulty lay, not (as Professor Smelser has it) in the 'dominant value-system of the day', but in the strong opposition of a minority of masters, and in the mood of Parliament (which Professor Smelser commends for its success in 'handling' and 'channelling' the weavers' 'unjustified disturbance symptoms').[2] In 1834 the House appointed a Select Committee, chaired by a sympathetic Paisley manufacturer, John Maxwell. He and John Fielden (who was a member of the Committee) ensured that it was well supplied with sympathetic witnesses. The Committee, while expressing deep concern at the weavers' plight, came to no firm recommendation in 1834: but in 1835, after taking further evidence, it came out with an unequivocal report in favour of

1. J. Harland, op. cit., pp. 259–61.
2. See N. J. Smelser, op. cit., p. 247. In fairness to Professor Smelser it should be added that his book, while ponderously insensitive in its general arguments, includes some valuable insights into the effect of technological changes upon the cotton workers' family relationships.

Fielden's Minimum Wage Bill: 'the effect of the measure would be to withdraw from the worst-paying masters the power which they now possess of regulating wages'. A trial of the measure was essential, and 'it will at least show that Parliament has sympathised in their distress, and lent a willing ear to their prayers for relief':

To the sentiment that Parliament cannot and ought not to interfere in cases of this nature, Your Committee is decidedly opposed. On the contrary, where the comfort and happiness of any considerable number of British subjects is at stake, Your Committee conceive that Parliament ought not to delay a moment to inquire, and, if possible, to institute redress.

Your Committee, therefore, recommend that a Bill of the nature of the one proposed by Mr Fielden should be immediately introduced . . .[1]

Pursuant to these recommendations, a Bill was actually introduced on 28 July 1835 by John Maxwell. The strength of the opposition was voiced in a speech by Poulett Thomson:

Was it possible for the Government of the country to fix a rate of wages? Was it possible that the labour of man should not be free?

Such a measure would be 'an act of tyranny'. Dr Bowring and Edward Baines (of the *Leeds Mercury*) advised the weavers to 'relieve themselves' by bringing up their children to other employments. John Fielden was written off by *Hansard* as 'inaudible'. The Bill was rejected by 41 to 129. Raised again by Maxwell in 1836, its second reading was repeatedly postponed and finally dropped. Reintroduced in May 1837 by Maxwell on a motion for the adjournment, leave to introduce a Bill was negatived by 39 to 82. In the teeth of a *laissez faire* legislature the manufacturers from Paisley and Todmorden (many of whose constituents were on the edge of starvation) continued to fight. John Fielden moved to introduce a fresh Bill on 21 December 1837: negatived by 11 to 73. But Fielden then stood up in his place and served notice that he would oppose every money bill until the House did something. This

1. *S.C. on Hand-Loom Weavers' Petitions*, 1835, p. xv. I have quoted this section of the Report in order to correct the inaccurate accounts in Smelser, op. cit., pp. 263–4, and Clapham, op. cit., I p. 552

time he was 'audible'. A Royal Commission was appointed, firmly in the hands of that *doyen* of orthodox 'political economy', Nassau Senior, and another stage of 'handling and channelling' commenced. Assistant Commissioners toured the stricken districts in 1838, forewarned by Senior that they would have to 'combat many favourite theories, and may disappoint many vague or extravagant but long-cherished expectations'. Humane and intelligent men in some cases, who enquired minutely into the weavers' circumstances, they were nonetheless ideologues of *laissez faire*. Their reports – and the final report of the Commission – were published in 1839 and 1840. The arid report of the Assistant Commissioner for the West Riding suggests that – unless for the use of future social historians – his labours need never have been undertaken:

The general conclusion which I have endeavoured to establish is, that it is the business of legislation to remove all checks upon the accumulation of capital, and so improve the *demand* for labour; but with the *supply* thereof it has nothing to do.

But this had also been his assumption. 'The power of the Czar of Russia,' it was reported,

could not raise the wages of men so situate ... all that remains, therefore, is to enlighten the handloom weavers as to their real situation, warn them to flee from the trade, and to beware of leading their children into it, as they would beware the commission of the most atrocious of crimes.[1]

All this 'handling and channelling' had at least two effects: it transformed the weavers into confirmed 'physical force' Chartists, and in cotton alone there were 100,000 fewer weavers in 1840 than in 1830. No doubt Fielden's Bill would have been only partially effective, would have afforded only slight relief in the 1830s as power-loom competition increased, and might have pushed the bulge of semi-unemployment into some other industry. But we must be scrupulous about words: 'slight relief' in the 1830s might have been the difference between death and survival. 'I think there has been already too long delay,' Oastler told the Select Committee of 1834: 'I

1. *Journals of House of Commons* and *Hansard, passim*; *Reports of Hand-Loom Weavers' Commissioners*, 1840, Part III, p. 590; A. Briggs, *Chartist Studies*, pp. 8–9.

believe that delay that has been occasioned in this question has sent many hundreds of British operatives to their graves.' Of the 100,000 weavers lost to Lancashire in that decade, it is probable that only a minority found other occupations: a part of the majority died in their natural term while the other part just 'died off' prematurely.[1] (Some would have been supported by their children who had entered the mills.) But it was in 1834 that the Legislature which found itself unable to offer them any measure of relief struck directly and actively at their conditions with the Poor Law Amendment Bill. Out-relief – the stand-by of many communities, sometimes on a 'Speenhamland' scale – was (at least in theory) replaced by the 'Bastilles' from the late 1830s. The effect was truly catastrophic. If Professor Smelser will examine the 'dominant value-system' of the weavers he will find that *all* poor relief was disliked but to the Malthusian workhouse the values of independence and of marriage offered an absolute taboo. The new Poor Law not only denied the weaver and his family relief, and *kept* him in his trade to the final end, but it actually drove others – like some of the poor Irish – into the trade. 'I cannot contemplate this state of things with any degree of patience,' a Bolton muslin-weaver told the Committee of 1834:

I am in a certain situation; I am now at this moment within a twelvemonth of 60 years of age, and I calculate that within the space of eight years I shall myself become a pauper. I am not capable, by my most strenuous exertions, to gain ground to the amount of a shilling; and when I am in health it requires all my exertions to keep soul and body together. . . . I speak feelingly upon the subject as a man in these circumstances; I view the present Poor Law Amendment Bill as a system of coercion upon the poor man, and that very shortly I shall be under its dreadful operation. I have not merited these things. I am a loyal man, strongly attached to the institutions of my country, and a lover of my country. 'England, with all thy faults, I love thee still', is the language of my soul . . .[2]

1. See the diary of W. Varley, a weaver, in W. Bennett, *History of Burnley* (Burnley, 1948), III, pp. 379–89; (February, 1827) 'sickness and disease prevails very much, and well it may, the clamming and starving and hard working which the poor are now undergoing. . . . The pox and measles takes off the children by two or three a house.'

2. Loc. cit., 1834, pp. 456–60.

It was in such weaving districts as Ashton (where the Chartist parson, Joseph Raynor Stephens, made insurrectionary speeches), Todmorden (where Fielden flatly defied the law), Huddersfield and Bradford that resistance to the Poor Law was violent, protracted, and intense.

But when the second phase of the weavers' decline – full competition with the power-loom – was entered, what remedies were there? 'What enactment,' Clapham wrote, 'other than state pensions for weavers, the prohibition of the power-loom, or the prohibition of training in hand-loom weaving, would have been of the least use it is hard to see.'[1] These were not among the weavers' own demands, although they protested against:

... the unrestricted use (or rather abuse) of improved and continually improved machinery ...

... the neglect of providing for the employment and maintenance of the Irish poor, who are compelled to crowd the English labour market for a piece of bread.

... The adaptation of machines, in every improvement, to *children*, and *youth*, and *women*, to the exclusion of those who ought to labour – THE MEN.[2]

The response of the weavers to machinery was, as these resolutions indicate, more discriminating than is often supposed. Direct destruction of power-looms rarely took place except when their introduction coincided with extreme distress and unemployment (West Houghton, 1812: Bradford, 1826). From the late 1820s, the weavers brought forward three consistent proposals.

First, they proposed a tax on power-looms, to equalize conditions of competition, some part of which might be allocated towards the weavers' relief. We should not forget that the hand-loom weaver was not only himself assessed for poor-rates, but paid a heavy burden in indirect taxation:

Their labour has been taken from them by the power-loom; their bread is taxed; their malt is taxed; their sugar, their tax, their soap,

1. Clapham, op. cit., I, p. 552.
2. *Report and Resolutions of a Meeting of Deputies from the Hand-Loom Worsted Weavers residing in and near Bradford, Leeds, Halifax, &c.* (1835).

and almost every other thing they use or consume, is taxed. But the power-loom is not taxed –

so ran a letter from the Leeds stuff weavers in 1835.[1] When we discuss the minutiae of finance we sometimes forget the crazy exploitive basis of taxation after the Wars, as well as its re-distributive function – from the poor to the rich. Among other articles taxed were bricks, hops, vinegar, windows, paper, dogs, tallow, oranges (the poor child's luxury). In 1832, of a revenue of approximately £50 millions, largely raised in indirect taxation on articles of common consumption, more than £28 millions were expended on the National Debt and £13 millions on the armed services as contrasted with £356,000 on the civil service, and £217,000 on the police. A witness before the Select Com-mittee in 1834 offered the following summary of taxation liable to fall annually upon a working man:

No. 1. Tax on malt, £4. 11s. 3d. No. 2. On sugar, 17s. 4d. No. 3. Tea or coffee, £1. 4s. No. 4. On soap, 13s. No. 5. Housing, 12s. No. 6. On food, £3. No. 7. On clothing, 10s. Total taxes on the labourer per annum, £11. 7s. 7d. Taking a labourer's earnings at 1s. 6d. per diem, and computing his working 300 days in the year (which very many do), this income will be £22. 10s.; thus it will be admitted that at the very least, 100 per cent, or half of his income is abstracted from him by taxation ... for do what he will, eating, drinking, or sleeping, he is in some way or other taxed.[2]

The summary includes items which few hand-loom weavers could afford, including, only too often, bread itself:

> Bread-tax'd weaver, all can see
> What that tax hath done for thee,
> And thy children, vilely led,
> Singing hymns for shameful bread,
> Till the stones of every street
> Know their little naked feet.

– so ran one of Ebenezer Elliott's 'Corn Law Rhymes'.[3]
  It is no wonder that Cobbett's attacks on the fund-holders

1. *Leeds Times*, 25 April 1835.
2. *S.C. on Hand-Loom Weavers' Petitions*, 1834, pp. 293 ff. The wit-ness, R. M. Martin, was author of *Taxation of the British Empire* (1833).
3. E. Elliott, *The Splendid Village, &c.* (1834), I, p. 72.

met with a ready reception, and that Feargus O'Connor first
won the applause of the 'fustian jackets and unshorn chins' of
the north by striking the same note:

You think you pay nothing: why, it is you who pay all. It is you
who pay six or eight millions of taxes for keeping up the army; for
what? for keeping up the taxes...[1]

Certainly, a tax on power-looms seems no more 'impossible'
than taxes on windows, oranges, or bricks.

Two other proposals related to the restriction of hours in
power-loom factories, and the employment of adult male
power-loom weavers. The first of these was a powerful influence
leading many hand-loom weavers to give their support to the
10 Hour agitation. Heavy weather has been made of this, from
the 1830s to the present day, with the men coming under the
accusation of 'sheltering behind the skirts of the women' or of
using the plight of the children as a stalking-horse in their own
demand for shorter hours. But, in fact, the aim was openly
declared by factory operatives and weavers. It was intrinsic to
their alternative model of political economy that shorter hours
in the factory should at one and the same time lighten the
labour of children, give a shorter working day to the adult
operatives, and spread the available work more widely among
the hand-workers and unemployed. In the second case, whereas
mule-spinning was generally reserved to male operatives, the
power-loom more often was attended by women or juveniles.
And here we must look further at the reasons for the hand-
loom weaver's opposition to the factory system.

'Reason' is not the appropriate word, since the conflict is
between two cultural modes or ways of life. We have seen that
even before the advent of power the woollen weavers disliked
the hand-loom factories. They resented, first, the discipline;
the factory bell or hooter; the time-keeping which overrode
ill-health, domestic arrangements, or the choice of more varied
occupations. William Child, a journeyman weaver victimized
for his activities with 'the Institution' of 1806, refused to enter
a hand-loom factory because of his objections to 'being con-

1. *Halifax Guardian*, 8 October 1836.

fined to go exactly at such an hour and such a minute, and the bad conduct that was carried on there. . . .'

A tender man when he had his work at home could do it at his leisure; there you must come at the time: the bell rings at half past five, and then again at six, then ten minutes was allowed for the door to be opened; if eleven expired, it was shut against any person either man, woman, or child; there you must stand out of door or return home till eight.[1]

In the 'golden age' it had been a frequent complaint with employers that the weavers kept 'Saint Monday' – and sometimes made a holiday of Tuesday – making up the work on Friday and Saturday nights. According to tradition, the loom went in the first days of the week to the easy pace of 'Plen-ty of time. Plen-ty of time.' But at the week-end the loom clacked, 'A day t' lat. A day t' lat.' Only a minority of weavers in the nineteenth century would have had as varied a life as the smallholder weaver whose diary, in the 1780s, shows him weaving on wet days, jobbing – carting, ditching and draining, mowing, churning – on fine.[2] But variety of some sorts there would have been, until the very worst days – poultry, some gardens, 'wakes' or holidays, even a day out with the harriers:

> So, come all you cotton-weavers, you must rise up very soon,
> For you must work in factories from morning until noon:
> You mustn't walk in your garden for two or three hours a-day,
> For you must stand at their command, and keep your shuttles in play.[3]

To 'stand at their command' – this was the most deeply resented indignity. For he felt himself, at heart, to be the real *maker* of the cloth (and his parents remembered the time when the cotton or wool was spun in the home as well). There had been a time when factories had been thought of as kinds of workhouses for pauper children; and even when this prejudice passed, to enter the mill was to fall in status from a self-motivated man, however poor, to a servant or 'hand'.

1. *Committee on the Woollen Trade* (1806), p. 111 *et passim*.
2. T. W. Hanson, 'Diary of a Grandfather', *Trans. Halifax Antiq. Soc.* 1916.
3. J. Harland, op. cit., p. 253

Next, they resented the effects upon family relationships of the factory system. Weaving had offered an employment to the whole family, even when spinning was withdrawn from the home. The young children winding bobbins, older children watching for faults, picking over the cloth, or helping to throw the shuttle in the broad-loom; adolescents working a second or third loom; the wife taking a turn at weaving in and among her domestic employments. The family was together, and however poor meals were, at least they could sit down at chosen times. A whole pattern of family and community life had grown up around the loom-shops; work did not prevent conversation or singing. The spinning-mills – which offered employment only for their children – and then the power-loom sheds, which generally employed only the wives or adolescents – were resisted until poverty broke down all defences. These places were held to be 'immoral' – places of sexual licence, foul language, cruelty, violent accidents, and alien manners.[1] Witnesses before the Select Committee put now one, now another, objection to the front:

... no man would like to work in a power-loom, they do not like it, there is such a clattering and noise it would almost make some men mad; and next, he would have to be subject to a discipline that a hand-loom weaver can never admit to.

... all persons working on the power-loom are working there by force, because they cannot exist any other way; they are generally people that have been distressed in their families and their affairs broken up ... they are apt to go as little colonies to colonize these mills ...

A Manchester witness whose own son had been killed in a factory accident declared:

I have had seven boys, but if I had 77 I should never send one to a cotton factory. ... One great objection that I have is, that their

1. See statement of the Manchester weavers (1823): 'The evils of a Factory-life are incalculable, – There uninformed, unrestrained youth, of both sexes mingle – absent from parental vigilance. ... Confined in artificial heat to the injury of health, – The mind exposed to corruption, and life and limbs exposed to Machinery – spending youth where the 40th year of the age is the 60th of the constitution ...' (Hammonds, *The Town Labourer* p., 300).

morals are very much corrupted. ... They have to be in the factories from six in the morning till eight at night, consequently they
have no means of instruction ... there is no good example shown
them ...

'I am determined for my part, that if they will invent machines
to supersede manual labour, they must find iron boys to mind
them.'[1]

Finally, we have all these objections, not taken separately,
but taken as indicative of the 'value-system' of the community.
This, indeed, might be valuable material for a study in historical sociology; for we have, in the England of the 1830s, a
'plural society', with factory, weaving, and farming communities impinging on each other, with different traditions,
norms, and expectations. The history of 1815 to 1840 is, in
part, the story of the confluence of the first two in common
political agitation (Radicalism, 1832 Reform, Owenism, 10
Hour agitation, Chartism); while the last stage of Chartism is,
in part, the story of their uneasy coexistence and final dissociation. In the great towns such as Manchester or Leeds where
the hand-loom weavers shared many of the traditions of the
artisans, intermarried with them, and early sent their children
to the mills, these distinctions were least marked. In the upland
weaving villages, the communities were far more clannish;
they despised 'teawn's folk' – all made up of 'offal an' boylin-
pieces'.[2] For years, in such areas as Saddleworth, Clitheroe,
the upper Calder Valley, the weavers in their hillside hamlets
kept apart from the mills in the valley-bottoms, training their
children to take their places at the loom.

Certainly, then, by the 1830s, we may begin to speak of a
'doomed' occupation, which was in part self-condemned by
its own social conservatism. But even where the weavers
accepted their fate, the advice of the Royal Commission 'to
flee from the trade' was often beside the point. The children
might find places in the mills, or the growing daughters turn
to the power-loom:

1. *S.C. on Hand-Loom Weavers' Petitions*, 1834, p. 428 (5473), p. 440
(5618); p. 189 (2643–6).

2. Edwin Waugh, Lancashire Sketches (1869), p. 128.

If you go into a loom-shop, where there's three or four pairs of
looms,
They all are standing empty, encumbrances of the rooms;
And if you ask the reason why, the old mother will tell you
plain,
My daughters have foresaken them, and gone to weave by steam.[1]

But this was not always possible. In many mills, the spinners
or the existing labour force had priority for their own children.
Where it took place, it added to the weaver's shame his dependence upon his wife or children, the enforced and humiliating
reversal of traditional rôles.

We have to remember the lack of balance between adult and
juvenile labour in the early factory system. In the early 1830s
between one-third and one-half of the labour force (all classes
of labour) in cotton-mills was under twenty-one. In worsted the
proportion of juveniles was a good deal higher. Of the adults,
considerably more than half were women. Dr Ure estimated,
from the reports of the Factory Inspectors in 1834, an adult
labour force in all textile mills in the United Kingdom of
191,671, of whom 102,812 were women and only 88,859 were
men.[2] The male employment pattern is clear enough:

In the cotton factories of Lancashire, the wages of the males during the period when there is the greatest number of employed –
from eleven to sixteen – are on the average 4s. 10¼d. a-week; but
in the next period of five years, from sixteen to twenty-one, the
average rises to 10s. 2½d. a-week; and of course the manufacturer
will have as few at that price as he can. .... In the next period of
five years, from twenty-one to twenty-six, the average weekly wages
are 17s. 2½d. Here is a still stronger motive to discontinue employing males as far as it can practically be done. In the subsequent two
periods the average rises still higher, to 20s. 4½d., and to 22s. 8½d.
At such wages, only those men will be employed who are necessary
to do work requiring great bodily strength, or great skill, in some art,
craft, or mystery ... or persons employed in offices of trust and
confidence.[3]

Two obvious, but important, points must be made about

1. J. Harland, op. cit., p. 253.
2. A. Ure, *The Philosophy of Manufactures* (1835), p. 481; J. James,
History of the Worsted Manufacture, pp. 619–20; James, *Continuation
of the History of Bradford* (1866), p. 227. The reports often underestimate the juvenile labour force.   3. Ure, op. cit., p. 474.

this employment pattern. The first – which we have already made in relation to 'dishonourable' trades – is that we cannot artificially segregate in our minds 'good' factory wages from bad wages in 'outmoded' industries. In a system based upon the discontinuance of the employment of adult males 'as far as it can practically be done' the wage of the skilled factory operative and the wage of the unskilled worker displaced from the mill at sixteen or twenty-one must be stamped on different sides of the same coin. Certainly in the wool textiles industries, juvenile workers displaced from the mills were sometimes forced, in their 'teens, back to the hand-loom. The second point is that the adult male hand-loom weaver, even when hardship overcame his prejudices, had little more chance of employment in a mill than an agricultural worker. He was rarely adapted to factory work. He had neither 'great bodily strength' nor skill in any factory craft. One of the best-disposed of masters, John Fielden, recalled of 1835:

I was applied to weekly by scores of hand-loom weavers, who were so pressed down in their conditions as to be obliged to seek such work, and it gave me and my partners no small pain to ... be compelled to refuse work to the many who applied for it.[1]

In the artisan trades of Lancashire in the early 1830s wages were reasonably high – among iron-moulders, engineers, shoemakers, tailors and skilled building workers anything from 15s. to 25s. (and above in engineering). But these rates had been obtained only by the strength of combination, one of whose aims was to keep the discharged factory youth and the hand-loom weaver *out*. If the weaver could have changed jobs – or apprenticed his children – to any *artisan* trade, social conservatism would not have prevented this. Against unskilled labouring there was certainly understandable prejudice: it was seen as a final loss of status:

> But aw'll give o'er this trade, un work wi' a spade.
> Or goo un' break stone upo' th' road ...

– declares 'Jone o' Grinfilt' at the height of his tribulations.

But even here there were difficulties. The Manchester silk-weaver who expounded the elements of a labour theory of

1. J. Fielden, *The Curse of the Factory System* (1836), p. 68.

value to the House of Commons had failed in his attempts to get work as a porter (wages, 14s. to 15s.). The weaver's physique was rarely up to heavy unskilled labouring (the wages of bricklayer's labourer and 'spademen' being 10s. or 12s.), and he competed with Irish labourers who were stronger and willing to work for less.[1] And while weavers in the large towns no doubt found ill-paid odd jobs of many kinds, the middle-aged country weaver could not remove his home and family:

The change had a terrible effect on the minds of some old hand-loom weavers. ... We have seen an old Pudsey weaver with tears in his eyes while ... recounting the good points of his loom. Yes, it was hung on its prods as a loom ought to be, and swung to and fro as a loom should do, the going part easy to put back, yet came freely to its work, and would get any amount of weft in. When that loom first came from one of the best makers in England ... the neighbours all came to see it, and admired and coveted it. But now for some time both this loom and another ... have all been dumb, and are covered with dust and cobwebs ...[2]

The story of the hand-loom weavers impinges at a score of points upon the general question of living standards during the Industrial Revolution. In its first stages it appears to provide evidence on the 'optimistic' side: the spinning-mills are the multipliers which attract thousands of outworkers, and raise their standards. But as their standards are raised, so their status and defences are lowered; and from 1800 to 1840 the record is almost unrelievedly 'pessimistic'. If we are to assess standards in these years, not in 'futuristic' terms, but in terms of the living generations who experienced them, then we must see the weavers as a group who not only did not 'share in the benefits' of economic progress but who suffered a drastic decline. Since textiles were the staple industries of the Industrial Revolution, and since there were far more adults involved in the weaving than in the spinning branches, this would seem as valid a way of describing the experience of these years as any. The customary story, perhaps for reasons of dramatic

1. Wages noted here are those listed as average in 1832 by the Manchester Chamber of Commerce: see *First Annual Report P.L.C.*, 1836, p. 331 and *British Almanac*, 1834, pp. 31–61.

2. J. Lawson, *Progress in Pudsey*, pp. 89–90.

style, fastens attention upon the multiplier (the mule, the mill, and steam): we have looked at the people who were multiplied.

'Optimists', of course, recognize the plight of the weavers; in every account there is some saving clause, excepting 'a few small and specially unhappy sections of the people, such as the hand-loom weavers', 'a small group among a prospering community', or 'pockets of technological underemployment'.[1] But, as Clapham well knew, the weavers could in no sense be described as a 'small' group before the later 1840s. Weavers were, and had probably been for some hundreds of years, the largest single group of industrial workers in England. They were the ploughmen of our staple industries. At any time between 1820 and 1840 they came third in the occupational lists, after agricultural labourers and domestic servants, and greatly exceeding any other industrial group. 'No census of them [i.e. looms in the U.K.] was ever taken: but there cannot have been fewer than 500,000 and there may have been very many more.'[2] Estimates for the United Kingdom, taking in looms in cotton, wool, silk, linen, flax, as well as such specialist branches as ribbon-weaving (but excluding framework-knitting) sometimes rose as high as 740,000. But in many families there would be two, three and four looms. The estimate of the Select Committee of 1834–5 that 800,000 to 840,000 were wholly dependent upon the loom may be as close as we can get.

It is the enduring myth of freedom in an obsolete ideology that for the Legislature to do nothing, and to allow 'natural' economic forces to inflict harm on a part of the community, constitutes a complete defence. The power-loom provided both the State and the employers with a cast iron alibi. But we might equally well see the story of the weavers as the expression of the highly abnormal situation which existed during the Industrial Revolution. In the weavers' history we have a paradigm case of the operation of a repressive and exploitive

1. Clapham, *Economic History* I, p. 565; F. A. Hayek in *Capitalism and the Historians*, p. 28; R. M. Hartwell, 'The Rising Standard of Living in England, 1800–1850', *Econ. Hist. Review*, 2nd Series, XIII, April 1961.

2. Clapham, op. cit., I, p. 179.

system upon a section of workers without trade union defences. Government not only intervened actively against their political organizations and trade unions; it also inflicted upon the weavers the negative dogma of the freedom of capital as intransigently as it was to do upon the victims of the Irish famine.

The ghost of this dogma is still abroad today. Professor Ashton regrets that financial factors retarded investment in power-looms:

It is sometimes suggested that the 'evils' of the industrial revolution were due to the rapidity with which it proceeded: the case of the domestic textile workers suggests the exact opposite. If there had been in weaving a man of the type of Arkwright, if rates of interest had remained low, if there had been no immigration and no Poor Law allowance, the transfer to the factory might have been effected quickly and with less suffering. As it was, large numbers of hand workers continued, for more than a generation, to fight a losing battle against the power of steam.[1]

But, as we have seen, for the power-loom masters it was not a 'battle' but a great convenience to have an auxiliary cheap labour force, as a stand-by in good times and as a means of keeping down the wages of the women and girls (8s. to 12s. Manchester, 1832) who minded the power-looms. Moreover, there *was* scarcely no 'transfer to the factory'. If the introduction of power had been swifter, then – all other things being equal – its consequences would have been even more catastrophic.

Some economic historians appear to be unwilling (perhaps because of a concealed 'progressivism', which equates human progress with economic growth) to face the evident fact that technological innovation during the Industrial Revolution, until the railway age, did displace (except in the metal industries) adult skilled labour. Labour so displaced swelled the limitless supply of cheap labour for the arduous work of sheer human muscle in which the times were so spendthrift. There was little or no mechanization in the mines; in the docks; in brickworks, gasworks, building; in canal and railway building; in carterage and porterage. Coal was still carried on men's

1. T. S. Ashton, *The Industrial Revolution*, p. 117.

backs up the long ladders from ships' holds: in Birmingham men could still, in the 1830s, be hired at 1s. a day to wheel sand in barrows nine miles by road, and nine miles empty back. The disparity between the wages of an engineer (26s. to 30s.) or carpenter (24s.) and the spademan (10s. to 15s.) or weaver (say 8s.) in 1832 is such that we cannot allow social conservatism alone to explain it. It suggests that it is the skilled trades which are exceptional, and that conditions in unskilled manual labour or in outwork industries, so far from being 'specially unhappy', were characteristic of a system designed by employers, legislators and ideologists to cheapen human labour in every way. And the fact that weaving became overstocked at a time when conditions were rapidly declining is eloquent confirmation. It was in the outwork industries, Marx wrote, that exploitation was most 'shameless', 'because in these last resorts of the masses made "redundant" by Modern Industry and Agriculture, competition for work attains its maximum'.[1]

There is, of course, a 'futurist' argument which deserves attention. It is, in fact, an argument which many working men who lived through until better times adopted. However full of suffering the transition, one such working man commented:

... power-loom weavers have not to buy looms and a jenny to spin for them; or bobbins, flaskets, and baskets; or to pay rent and taxes for them standing; nor candles, or gas and coal for lighting and warming the workshop. They have not to pay for repairs, for all wear and tear ... nor have they to buy shuttles, pickers, sideboards, shop-boards, shuttle-boards, picking-sticks, and bands and cords. ... They have not to be propped up on the treadles and seatboards ... or have their wrists bandaged to give strength. ... They have not to fetch slubbing, warp their webs, lay up lists, size, put the webs out to dry, seek gears, leck pieces, tenter, teem, dew, and cuttle them; and least of all would they think of breaking wool, scouring, and dyeing it *all for nothing too*.[2]

If we see the hand-loom weaver's work in this light, it was certainly painful and obsolete, and any transition, however full of suffering, might be justified. But this is an argument which discounts the suffering of one generation against the gains of the future. For those who suffered, this restrospective comfort is cold.

1. *Capital* (1938 edn), p. 465.   2. J. Lawson, op. cit., p. 91.

[10]
Standards and Experiences
I. GOODS

THE controversy as to living standards during the Industrial Revolution has perhaps been of most value when it has passed from the somewhat unreal pursuit of the wage-rates of hypothetical average workers and directed attention to articles of consumption: food, clothing, homes: and, beyond these, health and mortality. Many of the points at issue are complex, and all that can be attempted here is to offer comments upon a continuing discussion. When we consider measurable quantities, it seems clear that over the years 1790–1840 the national product was increasing more rapidly than the population. But it is exceedingly difficult to assess how this product was distributed. Even if we leave other considerations aside (how much of this increase was exported owing to unfavourable terms of trade? how much went in capital investment rather than articles of personal consumption?) it is not easy to discover what share of this increase went to different sections of the population.

The debate as to the people's diet during the Industrial Revolution turns mainly upon cereals, meat, potatoes, beer, sugar and tea. It is probable that *per capita* consumption of wheat declined from late eighteenth-century levels throughout the first four decades of the nineteenth century. Mr Salaman, the historian of the potato, has given a convincing blow by blow account of the 'battle of the loaf', by which landowners, farmers, parsons, manufacturers, and the Government itself sought to drive labourers from a wheaten to a potato diet. The critical year was 1795. Thereafter war-time necessity took second place to the arguments as to the benefits of reducing the poor to a cheap basic diet. The rise in potato acreage during the Wars cannot be attributed to wheat shortage alone: 'some deficiency there was, but unequal division between the different classes of society consequent on inflated prices was a far more potent factor ...' The great majority of the English people, even in the north, had turned over from coarser cereals to wheat by 1790; and the white loaf was regarded jealously as a symbol of their status. The southern rural labourer refused to abandon his diet of bread and cheese, even when near the point of starvation; and for nearly fifty years a regular dietary class-war took place, with potatoes encroaching on bread in the south, and with oatmeal and potatoes encroaching in the north. Indeed, Mr Salaman finds in the potato a social stabilizer even more effective than Halévy found in Methodism:

... the use of the potato ... did, in fact, enable the workers to survive on the lowest possible wage. It may be that in this way the potato prolonged and encouraged, for another hundred years, the impoverishment and degradation of the English masses; but what was the alternative, surely nothing but bloody revolution. That England escaped such a violent upheaval in the early decades of the nineteenth century ... must in large measure be placed to the credit of the potato.[1]

Nutritional experts now advise us that the potato is full of virtue, and certainly whenever standards rose sufficiently for the potato to be an added item, giving variety to the diet, it was a gain. But the substitution of potatoes for bread or oatmeal was felt to be a degradation. The Irish immigrants with their potato diet (Ebenezer Elliott called them, 'Erin's root-fed hordes') were seen as eloquent testimony, and very many Englishmen agreed with Cobbett that the poor were victims of a conspiracy to reduce them to the Irish level. Throughout the Industrial Revolution the price of bread (and of oatmeal) was the first index of living standards, in the estimation of the people. When the Corn Laws were passed in 1815, the Houses of Parliament had to be defended from the populace by troops. 'NO CORN LAWS' was prominent among the banners at Peterloo, and remained so (especially in Lancashire) until the anti-Corn Laws agitation of the 1840s.

1. R. N. Salaman, *The History and Social Influence of the Potato* (Cambridge, 1949), esp. pp. 480, 495, 506, 541–2. J. C. Drummond and A. Wilbraham, the historians of *The Englishman's Food* (1939), also see this as a period of decline.

Meat, like wheat, involved feelings of status over and above its dietary value. The Roast Beef of Old England was the artisan's pride and the aspiration of the labourer. Once again, *per capita* consumption probably fell between 1790 and 1840, but the figures are in dispute. The argument turns mainly upon the number and weight of beasts killed in London slaughter-houses. But even if these figures are established, we still cannot be sure as to which sections of the people ate the meat, and in what proportions. Certainly, meat should be a sensitive indicator of material standards, since it was one of the first items upon which any increase in real wages will have been spent. The seasonal workers did not plan their consumption meticulously over fifty-two Sunday dinners, but, rather, spent their money when in full work and took what chance offered for the rest of the year. 'In the long fine days of summer,' Henry Mayhew was told,

the little daughter of a working brickmaker used to order chops and other choice dainties of a butcher, saying, 'Please, sir, father don't care for the price just a-now; but he must have his chops good; line-chops, sir, and tender, please – 'cause he's a brickmaker.' In the winter, it was, 'O please, sir, here's a fourpenny bit, and you must send father something cheap. He don't care what it is, so long as it's cheap. It's winter, and he hasn't no work, sir – 'cause he's a brick-maker.' [1]

Londoners tended to have higher standards of expectation than labourers in the provinces. In the depth of the 1812 depression, it was the impression of an observer that the London poor fared better than those of the north and the west:

The Poor of the Metropolis, notwithstanding the enormous price of the necessaries of life, are really living comparatively in comfort. The humblest labourer here frequently gets meat (flesh meat) and always bread and cheese, with beer of some sort, for his meals, but a West Country peasant can obtain for his family no such food. [2]

There was, of course, a variety of inferior 'meats' on sale: red herrings and bloaters, cow-heel, sheep's trotters, pig's ear, faggots, tripe and black pudding. The country weavers of

1. Mayhew, op. cit., II, p. 368.   2. *Examiner*, 16 August 1812.

Lancashire despised town food, and preferred 'summat at's deed ov a knife' – a phrase which indicates both the survival of their own direct pig-keeping economy and their suspicion that town meat was diseased – if forced to eat in town 'every mouthful went down among painful speculations as to what the quadruped was when alive, and what particular reason it had for departing this life'.[1] It was not a new thing for town dwellers to be exposed to impure or adulterated food; but as the proportion of urban workers grew, so the exposure became worse.[2]

There is no doubt that *per capita* beer consumption went down between 1800 and 1830, and no doubt that *per capita* consumption of tea and of sugar went up; while between 1820 and 1840 there was a marked increase in the consumption of gin and whiskey. Once again, this is a cultural as well as dietetic matter. Beer was regarded – by agricultural workers, coal-whippers, miners – as essential for any heavy labour (to 'put back the sweat') and in parts of the north beer was synonymous with 'drink'. The home-brewing of small ale was so essential to the household economy that 'if a young woman can bake oatcake and brew well, it is thought she will make a good wife': while 'some Methodist class-leaders say they could not lead their classes without getting a "mugpot" of drink'.[3] The decline was directly attributed to the malt tax – a tax so unpopular that some contemporaries regarded it as being an incitement to revolution. Remove the malt tax, one clerical magistrate in Hampshire argued in 1816, and the labourer –

would go cheerfully to his daily employ, perform it with manly vigour and content, and become attached to his house, his family, and, *above all*, his country, which allows him to share, in common with his superiors, in a plain wholesome beverage, which a poor man looks up to, more, indeed, than to any thing that could possibly be granted them by a British Parliament.[4]

1. E. Waugh, *Lancashire Sketches*, pp. 128–9.
2. See J. Burnett, 'History of Food Adulteration in Great Britain in the Nineteenth Century', *Bulletin of Inst. of Historical Research*, 1959, pp. 104–7.
3. J. Lawson, op. cit., pp. 8, 10.
4. *Agricultural State of the Kingdom* (1816), p. 95.

The additional duty upon strong beer led to widespread evasion: and 'hush-shops' sprang up, like that in which Samuel Bamford was nearly murdered as a suspected exciseman until he was recognized by one of the drinkers as a *bona fide* radical 'on the run'.

The effect of the taxes was undoubtedly to reduce greatly the amount of home-brewing and home-drinking; and, equally, to make drinking less of a part of normal diet and more of an extra-mural activity. (In 1830 the duty on strong beer was repealed and the Beer Act was passed, and within five years 35,000 beer-shops sprang up as if out of the ground.) The increase in tea-drinking was, in part, a replacement of beer and, perhaps also, of milk; and, once again, many contemporaries – with Cobbett well to the fore – saw in this evidence of deterioration. Tea was seen as a poor substitute, and, with the increased consumption of spirits, as an indication of the need for stimulants caused by excessive hours of labour on an inadequate diet. But by 1830 tea was regarded as a necessity: families that were too poor to buy it begged once-used tea-leaves from neighbours, or even simulated its colour by pouring boiling water over a burnt crust.[1]

All in all, it is an unremarkable record. In fifty years of the Industrial Revolution the working-class share of the national product had almost certainly fallen relative to the share of the property-owning and professional classes. The 'average' working man remained very close to subsistence level at a time when he was surrounded by the evidence of the increase of national wealth, much of its transparently the product of his own labour, and passing, by equally transparent means, into the hands of his employers. In psychological terms, this felt very much like a decline in standards. His own share in the 'benefits of economic progress' consisted of more potatoes, a few articles of cotton clothing for his family, soap and candles, some tea and sugar, and a great many articles in the *Economic History Review*.

1. For an indication of some of the points at issue here, see the articles on the standard-of-living by T. S. Ashton, R. M. Hartwell, E. Hobsbawm, and A. J. Taylor cited above.

II. HOMES

The evidence as to the urban environment is little easier to interpret. There were farm labourers at the end of the eighteenth century who lived with their families in one-roomed hovels, damp and below ground-level: such conditions were rarer fifty years later. Despite all that can be said as to the unplanned jerry-building and profiteering that went on in the growing industrial towns, the houses themselves were better than those to which many immigrants from the countryside had been accustomed. But as the new industrial towns grew old, so problems of water supply, sanitation, over-crowding, and of the use of homes for industrial occupations, multiplied, until we arrive at the appalling conditions revealed by the housing and sanitary inquiries of the 1840s. It is true that conditions in rural villages or weaving hamlets may have been quite as bad as conditions in Preston or Leeds. But the size of the problem was certainly worse in the great towns, and the multiplication of bad conditions facilitated the spread of epidemics.

Moreover, conditions in the great towns were – and were felt to be – more actively offensive and inconvenient. Water from the village well, rising next to the graveyard, might be impure: but at least the villagers did not have to rise in the night and queue for a turn at the only stand-pipe serving several streets, nor did they have to pay for it. The industrial town-dweller often could not escape the stench of industrial refuse and of open sewers, and his children played among the garbage and privy middens. Some of the evidence, after all, remains with us in the industrial landscape of the north and of the Midlands today.

This deterioration of the urban environment strikes us today, as it struck many contemporaries, as one of the most disastrous of the consequences of the Industrial Revolution, whether viewed in aesthetic terms, in terms of community amenities, or in terms of sanitation and density of population. Moreover, it took place most markedly in some of the high-wage areas where 'optimistic' evidence as to improving standards is most well based. Common sense would suggest that we must take both kinds of evidence together; but in fact various arguments in mitigation have been offered. Examples have been found of improving mill-owners who attended to the housing conditions of their employees. These may well lead us to think better of human nature; but they do no more than touch the fringe of the general problem, just as the admirable charity hospitals probably affected mortality rates by only a decimal point. Moreover, most of the serious experiments in model communities (New Lanark apart) date from after 1840 – or from after public opinion was aroused by the inquiries into the Sanitary Conditions of the Working Classes (1842) and the Health of Towns (1844), and alerted by the cholera epidemics of 1831 and 1848. Such experiments as antedate 1840, like that of the Ashworths at Turton, were in self-sufficient mill villages.

It is also suggested that worsening conditions may be somehow discounted because they were no one's fault – and least of all the fault of the 'capitalist'. No villain can be found who answers to the name of 'Jerry'. Some of the worst building was undertaken by small jobbers or speculative small tradesmen or even self-employed building workers. A Sheffield investigator allocated blame between the landowner, the petty capitalist (who offered loans at a high rate of interest), and petty building speculators 'who could command only a few hundred pounds', and some of whom 'actually cannot write their names'.[1] Prices were kept high by duties on Baltic timber, bricks, tiles, slates; and Professor Ashton is able to give an absolute discharge to all the accused: 'it was emphatically not the machine, not the Industrial Revolution, not even the speculative bricklayer or carpenter that was at fault'.[2] All this may be true: it is notorious that working-class housing provides illustrations of the proverb as to every flea having 'lesser fleas to bite 'em'. In the 1820s, when many Lancashire weavers went on rent-strike, it was said that some owners of cottage property were thrown on the poor-rate. In the slums of the great towns publicans and small shopkeepers were among those often quoted as owners of the worst 'folds' or human warrens of crumbling mortar. But

1. G. C. Holland, *The Vital Statistics of Sheffield* (1843), pp. 56–8.
2. *Capitalism and the Historians*, pp. 43–51.

none of this mitigates the actual conditions by one jot; nor can debate as to the proper allocation of responsibility exonerate a process by which some men were enabled to prey upon other's necessities.

A more valuable qualification is that which stresses the degree to which, in some of the older towns, improvements in paving, lighting, sewering and slum clearance may be dated to the eighteenth century. But, in the often-cited example of London, it is by no means clear whether improvements in the centre of the City extended to the East End and dockside districts, or how far they were maintained during the Wars. Thus the sanitary reformer, Dr Southwood Smith, reported of London in 1839:

While systematic efforts, on a large scale, have been made to widen the streets ... to extend and perfect the drainage and sewerage ... in the places in which the wealthier classes reside, nothing whatever has been done to improve the condition of the districts inhabited by the poor.[1]

Conditions in the East End were so noisome that doctors and parish officers risked their lives in the course of their duties. Moreover, as the Hammonds pointed out, it was in the boom towns of the Industrial Revolution that the worst conditions were to be found: 'what London suffered [in the Commercial Revolution] Lancashire suffered at the end of the eighteenth and at the beginning of the nineteenth century'.[2] Sheffield, an old and comparatively prosperous town with a high proportion of skilled artisans, almost certainly – despite the jerry-builders – saw an improvement in housing conditions in the first half of the nineteenth century, with an average, in 1840, of five persons per house, most artisans renting a family cottage on their own, with one day room and two sleeping rooms. It was in the textile districts, and in the towns most exposed to Irish immigrations – Liverpool, Manchester, Leeds, Preston, Bolton,

1. *Fifth Annual Report of the Poor Law Commissioners* (1938), p. 170. See also *Fourth Report* (1838), Appendix A, No. 1.

2. See M. D. George, *London Life in the Eighteenth Century*, ch. 2; *England in Transition* (Penguin edn), p. 72; Hammond, *The Town Labourer*, ch. 3 and Preface to 2nd edition; Dr R. Willan, 'Observations on Disease in London', *Medical and Physical Journal*, 1800, p. 299.

Bradford – that the most atrocious evidence of deterioration – dense overcrowding, cellar-dwellings, unspeakable filth – is to be found.[1]

Finally, it is suggested, with tedious repetition, that the slums, the stinking rivers, the spoliation of nature, and the architectural horrors may all be forgiven because all happened so fast, so haphazardly, under intense population pressure, without premeditation and without prior experience. 'It was ignorance rather than avarice that was often the cause of misery.'[2] As a matter of fact, it was demonstrably both; and it is by no means evident that the one is a more amiable charac teristic than the other. The argument is valid only up to a point – to the point in most great towns, in the 1830s or 1840s, when doctors and sanitary reformers, Benthamites and Chartists, fought repeated battles for improvement against the inertia of property-owners and the demagoguery of 'cheap government' rate-payers. By this time the working people were virtually segregated in their stinking enclaves, and the middle classes demonstrated their real opinions of the industrial town by getting as far out of them as equestrian transport made convenient. Even in comparatively well-built Sheffield,

All classes, save the artisan and the needy shopkeeper, are attracted by country comfort and retirement. The attorney – the manufacturer – the grocer – the draper – the shoemaker and the tailor, fix their commanding residences on some beautiful site ...

Of sixty-six Sheffield attorneys in 1841, forty-one lived in the country, and ten of the remaining twenty-five were newcomers to the town. In Manchester the poor in their courts and cellars lived,

... hidden from the view of the higher ranks by piles of stores, mills, warehouses, and manufacturing establishments, less known to their wealthy neighbours – who reside chiefly in the open spaces of Cheetham, Broughton, and Chorlton – than the inhabitants of New Zealand or Kamtschatka.

1. G. C. Holland, op cit., p. 46 *et passim*. An excellent account of the working man's urban environment in mid-century Leeds is in J. F. C. Harrison, *Learning and Living* (1961), pp 7–20.

2. R. M. Hartwell, op. cit., p. 413.

'The rich lose sight of the poor, or only recognize them when attention is forced to their existence by their appearance as vagrants, mendicants, or delinquents.' 'We have improved on the proverb, "One half of the world does not know how the other half lives", changing it into "One half of the world *does not care* how the other half lives." Ardwick knows less about Ancoats than it does about China...'[1]

Certainly, the unprecedented rate of population growth, and of concentration in industrial areas, would have created major problems in any known society, and most of all in a society whose rationale was to be found in profit-seeking and hostility to planning. We should see these as the problems of industrialism, aggravated by the predatory drives of *laissez faire* capitalism. But, however the problems are defined, the definitions are no more than different ways of describing, or interpreting, the same events. And no survey of the industrial heartlands, between 1800 and 1840, can overlook the evidence of visual devastation and deprivation of amenities. The century which rebuilt Bath was not, after all, devoid of aesthetic sensibility nor ignorant of civic responsibility. The first stages of the Industrial Revolution witnessed a decline in both; or, at the very least, a drastic lesson that these values were not to be extended to working people. However appalling the conditions of the poor may have been in large towns before 1750, nevertheless the town in earlier centuries usually embodied some civic values and architectural graces, some balance between occupations, marketing and manufacture, some sense of variety. The 'Coketowns' were perhaps the first towns of above 10,000 inhabitants ever to be dedicated so single-mindedly to work and to 'fact'.

III. LIFE

The questions of health and longevity present even greater difficulties in interpretation. Until recently it was widely accepted that the main factor in Britain's population 'explosion' between 1780 and 1820 was in the declining death-rate, and in particular the decline in the rate of infant mortality. It was

1. G. C. Holland, op cit., p. 51; W. Cooke Taylor, *Notes of a Tour in the Manufacturing Districts of Lancashire* (1842), pp. 12–13, 160.

therefore reasonable to assume that this was effected by improvements in medical knowledge, nutrition (the potato), hygiene (soap and the cotton shirt), water supplies or housing. But this whole line of argument has now been called in question. The population 'explosion' can be seen as an European phenomenon, taking place simultaneously in Britain and in France, and in Spain and Ireland where many of these factors did not operate to the same degree. Second, demographers are now disputing the accepted evidence: and able arguments have been put forward which place renewed emphasis on the rise in the birth-rate, rather than a decline in the death-rate, as the causative factor.[1]

If we accept Dr Krause's view that the birth-rate rose after 1781 and declined after 1831 and that 'no important change in the death-rate is indicated', this by no means provides evidence as to the improving health and longevity of the working class. It is interesting to note that the fertility ratio (that is, the number of children aged 0–4 per 1,000 women in the child-bearing age-groups) was highest in 1821; first, in the heartland of the Industrial Revolution (Lancashire, the West Riding, Cheshire, Staffordshire): second, in the worst hit 'Poor Law counties' of the south. On the face of it, this would appear to provide confirmation for the Malthusian arguments – so widely held at the time, and so much disliked by Cobbett – that Speenhamland relief and the opportunities for employment in the mills (including child labour) boosted the birth-rate. We do not have to suppose that parents consciously decided to have more children in order to provide additional wage-earners or claims on the poor-rate. A rise in the birth-rate might be explicable in terms of the break-up of traditional patterns of community and family life (both Speenhamland and the mills could weaken taboos against early and 'improvident' marriage), the decline in 'living-in' among farm servants and apprentices, the impact of the Wars, concentration in new towns, or even genetic selection of the most fertile. Moreover,

1. See especially J. T. Krause, 'Changes in English Fertility and Mortality, 1781–1850', *Econ. Hist. Review*, 2nd Series, XI, No. 1, August 1958, and 'Some Neglected Factors in the English Industrial Revolution', *Journal of Economic History*, XIX, 4 December 1959.

a rise in the birth-rate is certainly not to be taken as evidence of rising living standards.[1] It was a continual theme of observers in the early nineteenth century that the poorest and most 'improvident' among the workers had the largest families; while in Ireland it took the searing experience of the Great Famine to alter the entire marriage-pattern of Irish peasant life.[2]

The arguments are complex, and are best left, for the time being, with the demographers. But we have reached a point where the evidence – which has customarily been interpreted upon the assumption that the death-rate was declining – needs looking at afresh. It would seem that medical advances can only have had a minimal influence upon the life expectation of working people before 1800. It is possible that some real decline took place in the mid-eighteenth century in London and other older 'artisan' towns, to which the decline in gin-drinking, and early efforts at sanitary improvement and enlightenment contributed. It is also possible that the beginnings of the population 'explosion' date from the mid-century, and arise from the decline in epidemics resulting upon 'changes in virulence and resistance upon which human effort had no influence'.[3] The initial population increase was supported by a long run of good harvests, and by an improvement in living standards which belongs, not to the later, but to the earliest years of the Industrial Revolution, As the Revolution gathered pace, and as we encounter the classic conditions of overcrowding and demoralization in the rapidly growing great towns – swollen by a host of uprooted immigrants – so there

1. See J. T. Krause, 'Some Implications of Recent Work in Historical Demography', *Comparative Studies in Society and History*, I, 2, January 1959.

2. K. H. Connell, 'The Land Legislation and Irish Social Life', *Econ. Hist. Review*, XI, 1 August 1958.

3. T. McKeown and R. G. Brown, 'Medical Evidence Related to English Population Changes in the Eighteenth Century', *Population Studies*, November 1955. See also J. H. Habakkuk, 'English Population in the Eighteenth Century', *Econ. Hist. Review*, VI, 2, 1953; G. Kitson Clark, *The Making of Victorian England* (1962), ch. 3; and, for a thorough examination of economic and demographic data in one region, J. D. Chambers, *The Vale of Trent, 1670–1800* (Economic History Society, Supplement, 1957).

is a serious deterioration in the health of the urban populations. The infant mortality rate in the first three or four decades of the nineteenth century was very much higher – and at times twice as high – in the new industrial towns as it was in the rural areas. 'Not 10% of the inhabitants of large towns enjoy full health,' declared Dr Turner Thackrah of Leeds;[1] and there is abundant literary evidence, much of it from medical men, as to the incidence of disease, malnutrition, infant mortality and occupational malformations in the working population. The evidence is sometimes contradictory, especially as to the effects of child labour in the mills, since when the 10 Hour agitation was at its height in the 1830s doctors sometimes argued from opposing briefs. But it is time that an end was put to the tendency of 'optimistic' historians to dismiss as 'biased' the evidence of doctors favourable to the demands of reformers, while accepting as 'objective' and authoritative the evidence of medical witnesses called in to support the employers' case.[2]

The First Report of the Registrar-General (1839) showed that about 20% of the total death-rate was attributed to consumption: a disease normally associated with poverty and over-crowding, as prevalent in the countryside as in the urban areas. Of ninety-two deaths of adult and juvenile workers in a Leeds woollen mill between the years 1818–27, no fewer than fifty-two were attributed to consumption or 'decline', the next two categories being 'worn out' or 'too old' (9) and asthma (7). It is interesting to examine the more detailed figures presented by Dr Holland, physician to the Sheffield General Infirmary, covering causes of death in the Sheffield registration district in the five years between 1837 and 1842. Out of 11,944 deaths in this period (including infants) the following complaints were each cited as causing the deaths of more than 100 persons in the five-year period:

1. *The Effects of Arts, Trade and Professions ... on Health and Longevity* (1832), ed. A. Meiklejohn (1957), p. 24.
2. The only support for this way of reading the evidence would appear to be the highly unsatisfactory and impressionistic discussion of the medical evidence on child labour in W. H. Hutt, 'The Factory System in the Early Nineteenth Century', *Economica*, March 1926; reprinted in *Capitalism and the Historians*, pp. 166 ff. See below, p. 371.

1.	Consumption	1,604
2.	Convulsions	919
3.	Inflammation of Lungs	874
4.	Decay of Nature	800
5.	Accidents (returned by Coroner)	618
6.	Fever, Scarlet	550
7.	Debility	519
8.	Dentition	426
9.	Inflammation of Bowels	397
10.	Inflammation of Brain	351
11.	Decline	346
12.	Measles	330
13.	Small Pox	315
14.	Hooping Cough	287
15.	Inflammations not distinguished	280
16.	Fever, Common	255
17.	Asthma	206
18.	Croup	166
19.	Paralysis	107
20.	Disease of the liver	106

We do not need to point to the evident inadequacy in diagnosis (neither gastro-enteritis nor diphtheria are listed). Dr Holland commented that the returns were 'not much to be depended upon': 'decline', as well as many cases of 'asthma', should be attributed to consumption. As for the registration of only *one* death from 'want of food':

The observation of any medical practitioner must indeed be very limited, that has not led him to the conclusion, that the deaths of hundreds in this town are to be traced to a deficiency of the necessaries of life. They may die of disease, but this is induced by poor living, conjoined with laborious exertion.

The Sheffield figures, however, show only sixty-four deaths in the five years in childbirth (where errors in diagnosis are scarcely likely). This represents a dramatic improvement over the previous 100 years, to which the diminution of puerperal fever, improved hygiene and midwifery could have substantially contributed. But if maternal mortality was falling in all classes, working-class mothers were surviving only to give birth to more children whose chances of life, in the industrial centres, were diminishing. And if infant mortality was high, we must remember that the critical period in a child's life was not 0–1 but 0–5. Thus, of the 11,944 deaths in Sheffield in this period, the age-distribution is as follows:

Under 1	2,983
1	1,511
2 to 4	1,544

This gives us 6,038 deaths under the age of five, and the remaining 5,906 deaths distributed over the other age-groups. The infant mortality (0–1) rate in Sheffield at this time was about 250 in 1,000, while the 0–5 mortality rate was 506 in 1,000. Much the same is true of Manchester where (Dr Kay noted) 'more than one-half of the off-spring of the poor ... die before they have completed their fifth year', and where the Registrar-General's Report (1839) showed deaths in the 0–5 age-groups of 517 in 1,000. But these figures underestimate – and perhaps seriously underestimate – the actual child mortality rate, because the industrial centres were constantly swelled with adult immigrants. Thus the 1851 Census (which recorded birth-places) showed that 'in almost all the great towns the migrants from elsewhere outnumbered the people born in the town'; and the deaths of immigrants would have the effect of continually diluting the true facts of child mortality. The growth of the great towns cannot be attributed, before 1840, to a greater rate of natural increase than in the countryside. If the tradi-tional view is true, and the bulk of the population, in the older centres, market towns and villages, benefited in some degree in their health from the products (and sanitary enlightenment) of the Industrial Revolution, those who produced those goods did not. The thought occurs to one that in the high-wage industrial centres generation after generation of children were bred, more than half of whom died before they could scarcely speak; while in the low-wage countryside children were kept alive by the poor-rates to supplement, by migration, the heavy adult labour force of the towns.[1]

There is no reason to suppose that the health of adult factory

1. G. C. Holland, op. cit., ch. 8; J. P. Kay, *The Moral and Physical Condition of the Working Classes employed in the Cotton Manufacture of Manchester* (1832); *First Annual Report of the Registrar-General* (1839), *passim*; A. Redford, op. cit., p. 16.

operatives was below average, and some evidence to indicate
that the health of adult cotton-spinners improved between 1810
and 1830 and more rapidly thereafter, as hours were limited,
machinery boxed in, and space, ventilation and whitewashing
improved. But their children appear to have suffered with the
rest of the labour force. In a survey undertaken on behalf of
the employers in Manchester in 1833, it was found that the
married spinners investigated had had 3,166 children (an
average of four and a half to each marriage): 'of these children,
1,922, or 60½ per cent. of the whole, were alive, and 1,244, or
39½ per cent., were dead'.[1] One may reasonably assume that
the 39½% might rise towards 50% by the time that children
who were infants at the time of the survey reached the age of
five, or failed to reach it. This heavy child mortality among
the children of workers who are often cited as beneficiaries of
the Industrial Revolution may be attributed in part to the
general environmental health conditions. It may also have been
due to the characteristic deformation and narrowing of the
pelvic bones in girls who had worked since childhood in the
mills, which made for difficult births:[2] the weakness of infants
born to mothers who worked until the last week of pregnancy:
but above all to the lack of proper child care. Mothers, for fear
of losing their employment, returned to the mill three weeks or
less after the birth: still, in some Lancashire and West Riding
towns, infants were carried in the 1840s to the mills to be
suckled in the meal-break. Girl-mothers, who had perhaps
worked in the mill from the age of eight or nine, had no domestic training: medical ignorance was appalling: the parents were
a prey to fatalistic superstitions (which the churches sometimes
encouraged): opiates, notably laudanum, were used to make
the crying baby quiet. Infants and toddlers were left in the
care of relatives, old baby-farming crones, or children too small
to find work at the mill. Some were given dirty rag-dummies

1. W. Cooke Taylor, op. cit., p. 261.
2. See the evidence of Dr S. Smith, of Leeds, in *Poor Man's Advocate*,
5 May 1832. The low incidence in Sheffield of maternal deaths in childbirth may perhaps be related to the fact that fewer girls were employed
there in occupations which required standing for twelve or fourteen
hours a day.

to suck, 'in which is tied a piece of bread soaked in milk and water', and toddlers of two and three could be seen 'running about with these rags in their mouths, in the neighbourhood of factories'.[1]

'A factory labourer,' one who was himself a cripple wrote:

can be very easily known as he is going along the streets; some of his joints are almost sure to be wrong. Either the knees are in, the ankles swelled, one shoulder lower than the other, or he is round-shouldered, pigeon-breasted, or in some other way deformed.[2]

But the same was true of many industrial occupations, whether conducted within or without a factory. If cotton-spinners were rarely employed after forty (and those who were had been through the long selective process which weeded out the weak), there were also few old miners or old cutlers. Dr Thackrah found a higher incidence of occupational disease among shoddy-workers and rag pickers, while Dr Holland wrote a detailed treatise on the disease and accidents among Sheffield grinders. We have seen the evil working conditions of domestic woolcombers, while weavers were also subject to deformities. The same is true of glass-workers in the Mendips, of bakery workers, and of many of the London sweated trades. Tailors had a characteristic deformity of the shoulders and chest which came from sitting for many hours each day 'cross-legged on a board'.

Dr Turner Thackrah saw little to choose between the worst domestic employments and the cotton-mills. The children leaving the Manchester cotton-mills appeared to him:

... almost universally ill-looking, small, sickly, barefoot and ill-clad. Many *appeared* to be no older than seven. The men, generally from sixteen to twenty-four, and none aged, were almost as pallid and thin as the children. The women were the most respectable in appearance ...

He contrasted them with the workers in the smaller-scale mills and finishing-shops of the West Riding: 'the stout fullers, the hale slubbers, the dirty but merry rosy-faced pieceners'. In the cotton-operatives,

1. W. Dodd, *The Factory System Illustrated* (1842), p. 149.
2. Ibid., pp. 112–13.

I saw, or thought I saw, a degenerate race – human beings stunted, enfeebled, and depraved – men and women that were not to be aged – children that were never to be healthy adults.

He questioned the evidence on health collected by the cotton employers, since most male operatives were laid off in early manhood, and the cotton-spinner whose strength failed would die in some other trade. In both the new mills and many of the older domestic trades, old workers appeared 'vastly inferior in strength and appearance to old peasants'.[1]

We have to see the multiplier and the multiplied at the same time. Against the undoubtedly large number of children who were factory cripples we have to set the toll of rickets among the children of weavers and of the outworkers in general. By 1830 it was taken for granted that the 'average' urban-industrial worker was stunted in growth and unfitted by reason of his weak physique for the heavy manual labour reserved to the Irish poor; when out of work the cotton-spinner was helpless, or at the best might hope to be employed 'in going errands, waiting upon the market-people, selling pins and needles, ballads, tapes and laces, oranges, gingerbread...'[2]

So long as the essential demographic statistics are in dispute, any conclusion must be tentative. Nothing should lead us to underestimate the appalling mortality rates of London during the gin 'epidemic' of the early eighteenth century. But it would seem that the living and working conditions of artisans and of some rural labourers were rather healthier in the second half of the eighteenth century than that of factory operatives or outworkers in the first half of the nineteenth. If London and Birmingham show a declining death-rate in these years, this was perhaps because they remained to a high degree 'artisan' cities with higher standards of child care and slightly less unhealthy working conditions. In the industrial north, in the Potteries and in most coalfields, infant mortality increased, and life became shorter and more painful. Perhaps in consequence the consumption of alcohol, and the use of opiates, increased, adding to the hazards of occupational disease. And sheer misery may have contributed to raising the rate of reproduc-

1. Thackrah, op. cit., esp. pp. 27–31, 146, 203–5.
2. W. Dodd, op. cit., p. 113.

tion. Dr Holland found 'the most dissipated, reckless and improvident' among the worst paid and least organized Sheffield workers: 'we speak from extensive enquiries when we assert, that the more wretched the condition of the artisans and the earlier do they marry'.[1]

If we accept that the national death-rate – and more particularly infant mortality rate – showed a slight decline over the first four decades of the nineteenth century, we must still ask of the statistics exactly the same questions as we have asked of wages and articles of consumption. There is no reason to suppose that dying children or disease were distributed more equitably than clothes or meat. In fact, we know that they were not. The moneyed man might – as Oastler noted – rarely wear two coats at once, but his family had tenfold the chances of diagnosis, medicine, nursing, diet, space, quiet. Attempts were made to assess the average age at death according to different social groups in various centres in 1842:

	Gentry	Tradesmen	Labourers
Rutlandshire	52	41	38
Truro	40	33	28
Derby	49	38	21
Manchester	38	20	17
Bethnal Green	45	26	16
Liverpool	35	22	15

At Leeds, where the figures were estimated at 44, 27, 19 the *aggregate* average of the three groups was 21. In Halifax, a large dispersed parish which compared favourably in its death-rate with more concentrated centres, a local doctor calculated the average age at death of 'gentry, manufacturers and their families' at 55: shopkeepers, 24: operatives, 22.[2]

Demographers would be right to consider this as 'literary rather than statistical evidence. But it indicates that a substantial decline in infant mortality and increase in life expectation among several millions in the middle classes and aristo-

1. G. C. Holland, op. cit., pp. 114–15.
2. *Report on the Sanitary Condition of the Labouring Classes* (1842), p. 153; G. C. Holland, op. cit., p. 128; for Halifax, Dr Alexander, cited in W. Ranger, *Report on ... Halifax* (1851), pp. 100 ff.; for later figures, see James Hole, *The Homes of the Working Classes* (1866), pp. 18 ff.

cracy of labour would mask, in national averages, a worsening position in the working class generally. And in this view, Dr Holland of Sheffield has anticipated us:

We have no hesitation in asserting, that the sufferings of the working classes, and consequently the rate of mortality, are greater now than in former times. Indeed, in most manufacturing districts the rate of mortality in these classes is appalling to contemplate, when it can be studied in reference to them alone, *and not in connexion with the entire population*. The supposed gain on the side of longevity, arises chiefly from ... a relatively much more numerous middle class than formerly existed ...

'We may be deceived,' he continued, by the 'gross returns':

... into the belief, that society is gradually improving in its physical and social condition, when indeed the most numerous class may be stationary, or in the process of deterioration.[1]

IV. CHILDHOOD

We have touched already on child labour: but it deserves further examination. In one sense it is curious that the question can be admitted as controversial: there was a drastic increase in the intensity of exploitation of child labour between 1780 and 1840, and every historian acquainted with the sources knows that this is so. This was true in the mines, both in inefficient small-scale pits where the roadways were sometimes so narrow that children could most easily pass through them; and in several larger coalfields, where – as the coal face drew further away from the shaft – children were in demand as 'hurryers' and to operate the ventilation ports. In the mills, the child and juvenile labour force grew yearly; and in several of the outworker or 'dishonourable' trades the hours of labour became longer and the work more intense. What, then, is left in dispute?

But 'optimists' have, since the time of the Hammonds, surrounded the question with so many qualifications that one might almost suspect a conspiracy to explain child labour away. There was 'nothing new' about it; conditions were as bad in the 'old' industries as in the new: much of the evidence is

1. G. C. Holland, op. cit., p. 124.

partisan and exaggerated: things were already improving before the outcry of the 1830s was made: the operatives themselves were the worst offenders in the treatment of children: the outcry came from 'interested' parties – landowners hostile to the manufacturers, or adult trade unionists wanting limitation of hours for themselves – or from middle-class intellectuals who knew nothing about it: or (paradoxically) the whole question reveals, not the hardship and insensitivity, but the growing humanity of the employing classes. Few questions have been so lost to history by a liberal admixture of special pleading and ideology.

Child labour was not new. The child was an intrinsic part of the agricultural and industrial economy before 1780, and remained so until rescued by the school. Certain occupations – climbing boys or ship's boys – were probably worse than all but the worst conditions in the early mills: an orphan 'apprenticed' by the parish to a Peter Grimes or to a drunken collier at a small 'day-hole' might be subject to cruelty in an isolation even more terrifying.[1] But it is wrong to generalize from such extreme examples as to prevalent attitudes before the Industrial Revolution; and, anyway, one of the points of the story of Peter Grimes is his ostracism by the women of the fishing community, and the guilt which drives him towards his grave.

The most prevalent form of child labour was in the home or within the family economy. Children who were scarcely toddlers might be set to work, fetching and carrying. One of Crompton's sons recollected being put to work 'soon after I was able to walk':

My mother used to bat the cotton on a wire riddle. It was then put into a deep brown mug with a strong ley of soap suds. My mother then tucked up my petticoats about my waist, and put me into the tub to tread upon the cotton at the bottom. ... This process was continued until the mug became so full that I could no longer safely stand in it, when a chair was placed besides it, and I held on to the back ...

Another son recollected 'being placed, when seven years of age, upon a stool to spread cotton upon a breaker preparatory to spinning, an elder brother turning the wheel to put the

1. See M. D. George, *London Life in the Eighteenth Century*, ch. 5.

machine in motion'.[1] Next came the winding of bobbins: and, when ten or eleven, spinning or – if the legs were long enough to reach the treadles – a turn in the loom. So deeply rooted was child labour in the textile industries that these were often held up to the envy of labourers in other occupations where children could not find employment and add to the family earnings; while the early hand-loom 'factories' in the woollen industry met with opposition on the grounds that they would lead to child unemployment. If the factory system were to prevail, declared one witness in 1806,

it will call all the poor labouring men away from their habitations and their homes into Factories, and there ... they will not have the help and the advantage from their families which they have had at home. Supposing I was a parent and had four or five or six children, and one of them was 14, another 12, another 10; if I was working with my family at home, I could give them employment, one to wind bobbins, another to work at the loom and another at the jenny; but if I go to the Factory they will not allow me to take those boys, but I must leave them to the wide world to perish ...[2]

By contemporary standards this was arduous, even brutal. In all homes girls were occupied about the baking, brewing, cleaning and chores. In agriculture, children – often ill-clothed – would work in all weathers in the fields or about the farm. But, when compared with the factory system, there are important qualifications. There was some variety of employment (and monotony is peculiarly cruel to the child). In normal circumstances, work would be intermittent: it would follow a cycle of tasks, and even regular jobs like winding bobbins would not be required all day unless in special circumstances (such as one or two children serving two weavers). No infant had to tread cotton in a tub for eight hours a day and for a six-day week. In short, we may suppose a graduated introduction to work, with some relation to the child's capacities and age, interspersed with running messages, blackberrying, fuel-gathering or play. Above all, the work was within the family economy and under parental care. It is true that parental

1. G. F. French, *Life of Samuel Crompton* (1859), pp. 58–9, 72; see also B. Brierley, *Home Memories* (Manchester, 1886), p. 19.

2. *Committee on the Woollen Trade* (1806), p. 49.

attitudes to children were exceptionally severe in the eighteenth century. But no case has been made out for a general sadism or lack of love.

This interpretation is validated by two other circumstances: the persistence, in the eighteenth century, of games, dances and sports which would have been scarcely possible if children had been confined for factory hours: and the resistance of the hand workers to sending their children into the early mills, which was one cause for the employment in them of pauper apprentices. But it was not the factory only – nor, perhaps, mainly – which led to the intensification of child labour between 1780 and 1830. It was, first, the fact of specialization itself, the increasing differentiation of economic rôles, and the break-up of the family economy. And, second, the breakdown of late eighteenth-century humanitarianism; and the counter-revolutionary climate of the Wars, which nourished the arid dogmatisms of the employing class.

We shall return to the second point. As to the first, nearly all the vices known to the eighteenth century were perpetuated in the early decades of the nineteenth, but in an intensified form. As Dickens knew, Peter Grimes was as likely to be found in early Victorian London as in Georgian Aldeburgh. The reports of the Children's Employment Commissions of 1842 showed new-model Boards of Guardians, in Staffordshire, Lancashire and Yorkshire, still getting rid of pauper boys of six, seven and eight, by apprenticing them to colliers, with a guinea thrown in 'for clothes'. The boys were 'wholly in the power of the butties' and received not a penny of pay; one boy in Halifax who was beaten by his master and had coals thrown at him ran away, slept in disused workings, and ate 'for a long time the candles that I found in the pits that the colliers left overnight'.[1] The mixture of terror and of fatalism of the children comes through in the laconic reports. An eight-year-old girl, employed for thirteen hours a 'day', to open and close traps: 'I have to trap without a light, and I'm scared.... Sometimes I sing when I've light, but not in the dark; I dare not sing then.' Or seventeen-year-old Patience Kershaw, who discussed the merits of different employments:

1. *Children's Employment Commission. Mines* (1842), p. 43.

... the bald place upon my head is made by thrusting the corves; my legs have never swelled, but sisters' did when they went to mill; I hurry the corves a mile and more under ground and back; they weigh 3 cwt. ... the getters that I work for are naked except their caps ... sometimes they beat me, if I am not quick enough. ... I would rather work in mill than in coalpit.[1]

This is no more than the worst eighteenth-century conditions multiplied. But specialization and economic differentiation led to children outside the factories being given special tasks, at piece-rates which demanded monotonous application for ten, twelve or more hours. We have already noted the card-setting village of Cleckheaton, where 'little toddling things of four years old ... were kept hour after hour at the monotonous task of thrusting the wires into cards with their tiny fingers until their little heads were dazed, their eyes red and sore, and the feebler ones grew bent and crooked'. This might still be done at home, and the evidence suggests that sweated child labour of this sort was if anything increasing throughout the early decades of the century in most outwork industries, in rural industries (straw-plaiting, lace), and in the dishonourable trades.[2] The crime of the factory system was to inherit the worst features of the domestic system in a context which had none of the domestic compensations: 'it systematized child labour, pauper and free, and exploited it with persistent brutality ...'[3] In the home, the child's conditions will have varied according to the temper of parents or of master; and to some degree his work will have been scaled according to his ability. In the mill, the machinery dictated environment, discipline, speed and regularity of work and working hours, for the delicate and the strong alike.

We do not have to rehearse the long and miserable chronicle of the child in the mill, from the early pauper apprentice mills to the factory agitation of the 1830s and 1840s. But, since comforting notions are now abroad as to the 'exaggerated' stories of contemporaries and of historians, we should discuss some of the qualifications. Most of them are to be found in a

1. Ibid., pp. 71, 80.
2. It is to be noted that some of the worst examples in Marx's *Capital* are taken from the Children's Employment Commission of the 1860s.
3. H. L. Beales, *The Industrial Revolution* (1928), p. 60.

provocative, almost light-hearted, article published by Professor Hutt in 1926. A spoonful of lemon-juice is sometimes good for the system, but we cannot live on lemon-juice for ever. This slight, scarcely documented, and often directly misleading article, has appeared in footnotes until this day, and has been republished in *Capitalism and the Historians*.[1] Nearly every point which it makes was anticipated and met in the arguments of the 10 Hour advocates; and notably in John Fielden's restrained and well-documented *The Curse of the Factory System* (1836).

It would be tedious to go over all the points. It is true – and a point which is frequently cited – that the evidence brought before Sadler's Committee of 1832 was partisan; and that historians such as the Hammonds, and Hutchins and Harrison (but not Fielden or Engels), may be criticized for drawing upon it too uncritically. With Oastler's help, Short-Time Committees of the workers organized the collection of evidence – notably from the West Riding – for presentation to this Committee; its Chairman, Michael Sadler, was the leading parliamentary champion of the 10 Hour Bill; and its evidence was published before any evidence had been taken from the employers. But it does not follow that the evidence before Sadler's Committee can therefore be assumed to be untrue. In fact, anyone who reads the bulk of the evidence will find that it has an authenticity which compels belief, although care must be taken to discriminate between witnesses, and to note the differences between some of the worst conditions in small mills in smaller centres (for example, Keighley and Dewsbury) as compared with conditions in the larger mills in the great cotton towns. There is no basis for Professor Hutt's assertions that the Factory Commission appointed – on the master's insistence – in the following year provided 'effective answers to nearly all the charges made before [Sadler's] committee'. Much of the evidence before the Commission tends towards different conclusions. Moreover, where the evidence conflicts, one is at a loss to follow the logic by which we are asked to give unhesitating preference to that adduced by the

1. W. H. Hutt, 'The Factory System of the Early Nineteenth Century', *Economica*, March 1926.

masters (and their over-lookers) as against that of their employees.[1]

Those who, like Professors Hutt and Smelser, exalt the evidence of the Factory Commission (1833) as opposed to that of Sadler's Committee, are guilty of the same error as that of which the Hammonds are accused. Rightly or wrongly, Oastler and the Short-Time Committee regarded the appointment of this Commission as a deliberate measure of procrastination, and the Commissioners as instruments of the employers. As a matter of policy they refused to give evidence before them. The movements of the Assistant Commissioners in the factory districts were closely watched. They were criticized for dining and wining with the mill-owners and for spending only a derisory portion of their time in inspection. It was noted that mills were specially whitewashed and cleansed, and under-age children removed from sight, before their visits. The workers contented themselves with mounting hostile demonstrations.[2] The reports of the Commissioners were subjected to as much criticism from the workers' side as that of Sadler's Committee received from the employers.

'I was requested by one of my neighbours,' declared one of Sadler's witnesses,

to recommend the Committee to come to Leeds Bridge at half past five o'clock in the morning, while the poor factory children are passing, and they would then get more evidence in one hour there than they will in seven years examination. I have seen some children running down to the mill crying, with a bit of bread in their hand, and that is all they may have till twelve o'clock at noon: crying for fear of being too late.

Even if we leave the stories of sadistic overlookers aside, there was then commenced a day, for multitudes of children, which

1. *Capitalism and the Historians*, pp. 165–6. Professor Hutt even repeats the gossip of the masters and of Dr Ure, such as the baseless charge that John Doherty had been convicted of a 'gross assault' on a woman.

2. See *The Voice of the West Riding*, 1 June 1833: 'The men of Leeds – the working classes – have nobly done their duty. They have indignantly refused to co-operate with a set of men who, if they had the least spark of honesty amongst them, would have let the Tyrannical Factory Lords do their own dirty work . . .' Also ibid., 15 and 22 June 1833 and Driver, op. cit., ch. 19.

did not end until seven or eight o'clock; and in the last hours of which children were crying or falling asleep on their feet, their hands bleeding from the friction of the yarn in 'piecing', even their parents cuffing them to keep them awake, while the overlookers patrolled with the strap. In the country mills dependent upon water-power, night work or days of fourteen and sixteen hours were common when they were 'thronged'. If Professor Hutt does not regard this as 'systematic cruelty', humane mill-owners like Fielden and Wood were in no doubt.

Nor are there any mysteries as to the attitude of the adult workers, many of whom were the parents or relatives of the children. As Professor Smelser has shown,[1] there is a sense in which the family economy of the domestic system was perpetuated in the factory. The child's earnings were an essential component of the family wage. In many case, although probably not in the majority, the adult spinner or worker might be kin to the child working for him. The demand for the limitation of adult, as well as child, hours was necessitated by the fact that they worked at a common process; if children's hours only were limited, nothing could prevent evasion, or the working of children in double relays (thus lengthening the adult working-day). Only the actual stoppage of the mill machinery could guarantee limitation. If the adults also stood to benefit by shorter hours, this does not mean that they were indifferent to humane considerations nor does it justify the offensive suggestion that the great pilgrimages and demonstrations on behalf of the factory child in the 1830s were hypocritical.

It is perfectly true that the parents not only needed their children's earnings, but expected them to work. But while a few of the operatives were brutal even to their own children, the evidence suggests that the factory community expected certain standards of humanity to be observed. A spinner in the Dewsbury area, noted for his evil-temper and for striking children with the billy-roller, 'could not get any one to work for him in the whole town, and he went to another place . . .' Stories of parents who visited vengeance upon operatives who maltreated their children are not uncommon. Thus a witness before Sadler's Committee described how, when he was a child,

1. N. J. Smelser, op. cit., esp. chs. 9 and 10.

he was beaten by the slubber. 'One of the young men who served the carder went out and found my mother':

> She came in ... and asked of me what instrument it was I was beaten with, but I durst not do it; some of the by-standers pointed out the instrument ... and she seized it ... and beat it about the fellow's head, and gave him one or two black eyes.[1]

This assorts ill with loose statements sometimes made as to the general indifference of the parents. The evidence of both Reports suggests that it was the discipline of the machinery itself, lavishly supplemented by the driving of overlookers or (in small mills) of the master, which was the source of cruelty. To say that practices common to whole industries were continued 'against the will and against the knowledge of the masters' does not require refutation. Many parents certainly connived at the employment of their own children under the legal age enacted in 1819 and 1833. It is to the credit of men like Doherty and of the Short-Time Committees that they campaigned imperiously amongst the operatives against such evils, encouraging dignity among the degraded and explaining the value of education to the uneducated. The Factory Movement also involved many thousands who were not factory operatives: the weavers who wished to 'muzzle the monster steam': parents displaced from the mills by juveniles, and supported by their children's earnings. Gaskell saw (in 1833) that the workers' discontent arose less from simple wage issues than from —

> the separation of families, breaking up of households, the disruption of all those ties which link man's heart to the better portion of his nature – viz. his instincts and social affections ...[2]

The Factory Movement, in its early stages, represented less a growth of middle-class humanitarianism than an affirmation of human rights by the workers themselves.

In fact, few arguments are so specious as that which proposes that because unlimited child labour was tolerated in the

1. Against such stories we have to set the appalling accounts of sadism, employed by adult operatives themselves upon pauper apprentices, during the period of the Wars. See J. Brown, *Memoir of Robert Blincoe* (Manchester, 1832), pp. 40–41.

2. P. Gaskell, *The Manufacturing Population of England*, p. 7.

eighteenth century but, in its new and more intense forms, became less tolerable by the 1830s, this is another sign of the growing humanitarianism of 'the age'. Professor Hayek has referred to 'this awakening of social conscience', to this—

increasing awareness of facts which before had passed unnoticed. ... Economic suffering both became more conspicuous and seemed less justified, because general wealth was increasing faster than ever before.

Professor Ashton has offered a variant of this argument. The Royal Commissions and parliamentary committees of inquiry of the early nineteenth century –

are one of the glories of the early Victorian age. They signalized a quickening of social conscience, a sensitiveness to distress, that had not been evident in any other period or any other country.

And he has shown unaccustomed strength of feeling in his defence of the parliamentary investigators:

... a generation that had the enterprise and industry to assemble the facts, the honesty to reveal them, and the energy to set about the task of reform has been held up to obloquy as the author, not of the Blue Books, but of the evils themselves.[1]

Blue Books in the early nineteenth century served many purposes, but reform comes low on the list. Parliamentary investigations took place as a routine response to petitions: as a means of 'handling and channelling' discontent, procrastinating, or fobbing off ill-behaved M.P.s; or purely from an excess of utilitarian officiousness. Ireland's decline through misery after misery to the seemingly inevitable climax of the Great Famine was accompanied by the absence of any important measure of alleviation – and by an average of five parliamentary enquiries per year.[2] The hand-loom weavers and framework-knitters were duly enquired into as they starved. Eight enquiries in ten years preceded the establishment of the police. (The fact that action resulted in the latter, but not in the

1. *Capitalism and the Historians*, pp. 18–19, 35–6.
2. See E. Strauss, *Irish Nationalism and British Democracy* (1951), p. 80: and Mr Strauss's comment – 'Ignorance of the facts was not one of the causes of Irish misery during the nineteenth century.'

former, cases is instructive.) Mr Gradgrind was most certainly out and about after 1815, but as Dickens knew perfectly well he stood not for an 'awakening of social conscience' or 'sensitiveness to distress' but for efficiency, cheap centralized government, *laissez faire*, and sound 'political economy'.

The Blue Books (at least until we came to the great sanitary enquiries) were not the product of 'an age' or the fruit of 'a generation', but a battle-ground in which reformers and obstructionists fought; and in which humanitarian causes, as often as not, were buried. As for the upper classes, what we see in the 1830s is not a new 'awakening of conscience' but the almost volcanic eruption, in different places and people, of a social conscience quiescent throughout the Napoleonic Wars. This conscience is certainly evident in the second half of the eighteenth century. The campaign to protect the climbing-boys, in which Hanway took a part, reached the statute book, against little opposition, in 1788. Every abuse returned during the Wars, and attempts to secure new legislative protection in their aftermath met direct opposition, and were thrown out in the Lords – for, if boys had been dispensed with, their Lordships might have had to make alterations to their chimneys.[1] All Howard's honourable work on behalf of prisoners left little lasting impression, as conditions reverted after his death. We have noted already how the infection of class hatred and fear corrupted the humanitarian conscience. It is true that Peel's Act of 1802 stands out against this darkness; but its operation was confined to pauper apprentices, and it was less a precedent for new legislation than an attempt to extend customary apprenticeship safeguards in a new context. What is more important – and was more disastrous for the factory child – was the atrophy of the conscience of the country gentry, the only men who had the authority or the traditional duty to protect the poor.

Nothing more confirms this atrophy, and the profound moral alienation of classes, than the manner of the real 'awakening' when it came. Scores of gentlemen and professional men, who gave some support to humanitarian causes in the 1830s and 1840s, appear to have been living in the 1820s in the midst of

1. See J. L. and B. Hammond, *The Town Labourer*, pp. 176–93.

populous manufacturing districts, oblivious to abuses a few hundred yards from their gates. Richard Oastler himself lived on the edge of Huddersfield, but it was not until the Bradford manufacturer, John Wood, *told* him about child labour that he noticed it. When girls were brought half-naked out of pits, the local luminaries seem to have been genuinely astonished:

Mr Holroyd, solicitor, and Mr Brook, surgeon, practising in Stainland, were present, who confessed that, although living within a few miles, they could not have believed that such a system of unchristian cruelty could have existed.[1]

We forget how long abuses can continue 'unknown' until they are articulated: how people can look at misery and not notice it, until misery itself rebels. In the eyes of the rich between 1790 and 1830 factory children were 'busy', 'industrious', 'useful'; they were kept out of their parks and orchards, and they were cheap. If qualms arose, they could generally be silenced by religious scruples: as one honourable Member remarked, of the climbing-boys in 1819, 'the boys generally employed in this profession were not the children of poor persons, but the children of rich men, begotten in an improper manner'.[2] This showed a fine sense of moral propriety, as well as a complete absence of class bias.

But the conscience of 'the rich' in this period is full of complexity. The argument that the impassioned 'Tory' attacks, in the 1830s, upon the abuses of industrialism, voiced by such men as Sadler, Shaftesbury, Oastler, Disraeli, were little more than the revenge of the landowning interest upon the manufacturers and their Anti-Corn Law League makes some sense in 'party political' terms. It is true that they revealed deep sources of resentment and insecurity among traditionalists before the innovations and the growing power of the moneyed middle class. But even a hasty reading of *Sybil*, of the Hammond's Life of Shaftesbury or of Cecil Driver's impressive life of Oastler will reveal the shallowness of any judgement limited to these terms. We seem to be witnesses to a cultural mutation: or, as in the case of eighteenth-century constitu-

1. *Children's Employment Commission. Mines* (1842), p. 80.
2. Cited in *The Town Labourer*, p. 190.

tionalism, to a seemingly hollow and conventional rhetoric
which took fire, in individual minds, as a deliberate and
passionate belief.

Moreover, alongside the older arguments of Tory paternalism we have the newer influence of disappointed Romanticism.
In their recoil from the Enlightenment, Wordsworth, Coleridge,
Southey had reaffirmed traditional sanctities, 'the instincts of
natural and social man'. In returning to order, authority, duty,
they had not forgotten Rousseau's teaching on the child. It
was in Book VIII of *The Excursion* that Wordsworth condemned the factory system in contrast to the older rural family
economy:

> The habitations empty! or perchance
> The Mother left alone – no helping hand
> To rock the cradle of her peevish babe;
> No daughters round her, busy at the wheel,
> Or in dispatch of each day's little growth
> Of household occupation; no nice arts
> Of needle-work; no bustle at the fire,
> Where once the dinner was prepared with pride;
> Nothing to speed the day, or cheer the mind;
> Nothing to praise, to teach, or to command!
>   The Father, if perchance he still retain
> His old employments, goes to field or wood
> No longer led or followed by the sons;
> Idlers perchance they were – but in *his* sight;
> Breathing fresh air and treading the green earth:
> Till their short holiday of childhood ceased,
> Ne'er to return! That birthright now is lost.

The mistake, today, is to assume that paternalist feeling
must be detached and condescending. It can be passionate
and engaged. This current of traditionalist social radicalism,
which moves from Wordsworth and Southey through to
Carlyle and beyond, seems, in its origin and in its growth, to
contain a dialectic by which it is continually prompting revolutionary conclusions. The starting-point of traditionalist and
Jacobin was the same. 'What is a huge manufactory,' exclaimed
Thelwall, 'but a common prison-house, in which a hapless
multitude are sentenced to profligacy and hard labour, that an

individual may rise to unwieldy opulence.'[1] 'I detest the manufacturing system' declared his fellow-Jacobin, Thomas Cooper,
who had experienced the early stages of the Lancashire
Industrial Revolution:

You must on this system have a large portion of the people converted into mere machines, ignorant, debauched, and brutal, that the
surplus value of their labour of 12 or 14 hours a day, may go into
the pockets and supply the luxuries of rich, commercial, and manufacturing capitalists.[2]

Southey enraged the 'philosopher' of manufactures, Dr
Andrew Ure, by his even more sweeping condemnation of the
manufacturing system as 'a wen, a fungous excrescence from
the body politic'.[3] Although Jacobin and Tory are at opposed
political poles, sparks of feeling and of argument are continually exchanged between them. The prophets of the 'march of
intellect' – Brougham, Chadwick, Ure – seem to belong to a
different world. Whenever the traditionalist Tory passed beyond reflective argument about the factory system, and
attempted to give vent to his feelings in action, he found himself forced into an embarrassing alliance with trade unionists
or working-class Radicals. The middle-class Liberal saw in
this only evidence of Tory hypocrisy. When Sadler fought (and
lost) his seat at Leeds in the Reform Bill election of 1832, a
shopkeeper-diarist noted:

... nothing supporting him but a few that are under the yoake of
Tyrany and a few Radicals of the lowest order, it is a Bony job that
the Old Torey Party is Obliged to turn Radical on any thing and
every thing to keepe their sistam ...[4]

Two years later, and the new Poor Law, which outraged with
its Malthusian and Chadwickian provisions every 'instinct of
natural and social man', appeared to present to a few Tory

1. *Monthly Magazine*, 1 November 1799. I am indebted to Dr D. V.
Erdman for this reference.
2. T. Cooper, *Some Information Respecting America* (1794), pp. 77–8.
3. R. Southey, *Sir Thomas More: or, Colloquies* ... (1829), I, p. 711;
A. Ure, *The Philosophy of Manufactures* (1835), pp. 277–8. See also
Raymond Williams, *Culture and Society* (Penguin edn, 1961), pp. 39 ff.
4. MS. Diary of Robert Ayrey, Leeds Reference Library.

Radicals an ultimate choice between the values of order and those of humanity. The majority drew back, and contented themselves with schemes for humanitarian amelioration of different kinds: but a few were prepared to associate, not only with Cobbettites, but with Owenites, free-thinkers, and Chartists. Joseph Raynor Stephens actually called for arson against the 'Bastilles' and Oastler stirred up civil – and, some-times, very uncivil – disobedience and, in his rôle as protector of the factory children, even urged the use of industrial sabotage against mill-owners who violated the law:

I will in that event print a little card about *Needles* and *Sand* and *Rusty Nails*, with proper and with very explicit directions, which will make these law-breakers look about them and repent that they were ever so mad as to laugh at the Law and the King. These cards of mine shall then be the catechism of the factory children.[1]

For ten years Oastler trod the edges of revolution; but the title which he gave to one of his periodicals was *The Home, the Altar, the Throne, and the Cottage.*

We can scarcely attribute this eruption of compassion to an 'age' which also jailed Stephens and vilified Oastler. Many of those who really exerted themselves on behalf of the factory children in the earlier years met with abuse, ostracism by their class, and sometimes personal loss. And as Mr Driver has shown, the crucial moment in Oastler's career was not his awakening to the fact of child labour, but the 'Fixby Hall Compact' between himself and Radical trade unionists. The awakening was not, in any case, characteristic of Toryism as a whole: if we wished to anatomize the Tory conscience of 1800 or 1830, we should commence with the squire's attitude to his own labourers. The humanitarianism of the 1830s can cer-tainly be found to have had a cultural ancestry, both in Tory paternalism and in the more subdued traditions, of service and 'good works', of liberal Dissent. But, as an effective force, it crops up only here and there, in individual men and women; Oastler and Bull are no more representative of the Tory than Fielden and Mrs Gaskell are representative of the liberal-nonconformist conscience.

1. C. Driver, op. cit., pp. 327–8.

If Tawney was right, and the treatment of childhood and of poverty are the two 'touchstones' which reveal 'the true character of a social philosophy',[1] then it is the liberal and nonconformist tradition which suffers most severely, in 1830, from this test. It is true that there is a humble twilight world, half-sceptic, half-dissenting, from which much that is best in early Victorian intellectual and spiritual life was to come. But it is equally true that the years between 1790 and 1830 see an appalling declension in the social conscience of Dissent. And above all, there are the proverbial nonconformist mill-owners, with their Methodist overlookers, and their invidious reputation as week-day child-drivers, working their mills till five minutes before midnight on the Saturday and enforcing the attendance of their children at Sunday school on the Sabbath.

The picture is derived, in part, from Frances Trollope's *Michael Armstrong, The Factory Boy* (1840), where 'Messrs Robert and Joseph Tomlins, the serious gentlemen as owns the factory ... attends their ownselves in person every Sunday morning to see that both master and children puts the time to profit.' It is a fictional and coloured picture, belonging, perhaps, more to 1820 than to 1840, more applicable to secluded country mills where the parish-apprentice system survived than to any great cotton town. But still, in the 1830s, the conditions portrayed in Mrs Trollope's 'Deep Dale' in Derbyshire might be found in many secluded valleys on both the Lancashire and Yorkshire side of the Pennines. A fact-finding tour undertaken by a 10 Hour propagandist in the Upper Calder Valley, and in which especial attention was given to the reactions of the local clergy, shows the complexity of any generalization. At Ripponden the vicar refused his support, but the Methodist chapel was loaned for a 10 Hour meeting. At Hebden Bridge an old Methodist lay preacher declared that he was always preaching against the factory system ' "for", says he, "we may preach while our tongues cleave to the roof of our mouths, but we shall never do any good while the system is allowed to go on as it is at present!" ' But he had made himself so obnoxious that the local Methodist mill-owner at Myth-

1. R. H. Tawney, *Religion and the Rise of Capitalism* (Penguin edn), p. 239.

olmroyd always locked the chapel when it was his turn to preach. At Sowerby Bridge, the Rev. Bull, brother to Parson Bull of Bierley (Oastler's famous colleague in the 10 Hour agitation), refused his support and was confident that the benevolence of the masters 'cannot be surpassed'. A group of operatives, passing the Methodist chapel built by one of the mill-owners, Mr Sutcliffe, 'looked towards the chapel and wished it might sink into hell, and Mr Sutcliffe go with it'.

I said it was too bad, as Mr Sutcliffe had built the chapel for their good. 'Damn him,' said another, 'I know him, I have had a swatch of him, and a corner of that chapel is mine, and it all belongs to his workpeople.'[1]

Cragg Dale, an isolated off-shoot of the Calder, was a veritable 'Deep Dale'. A Minister of unidentified affiliations declared:

If there was one place in England that needed legislative interference, it was this place, for they work 15 and 16 hours a day frequently, and sometimes all night: – Oh! it is a murderous system, and the mill-owners are the pest and disgrace of society. Laws human and divine are insufficient to restrain them; they take no notice of Hobhouse's Bill, and they say 'Let Government make what laws they think fit, they can drive a coach and six through them in that valley.'

He related the story of a boy whom he had recently interred who had been found standing asleep with his arms full of wool and had been beaten awake. This day he had worked seventeen hours; he was carried home by his father, was unable to eat his supper, awoke at 4 a.m. the next morning and asked his brothers if they could see the lights of the mill as he was afraid of being late, and then died. (His younger brother, aged nine, had died previously: the father was 'sober and industrious', a Sunday school teacher.) The Anglican curate here gave his unreserved support to the limitation of child labour:

I have seen the poor in this valley oppressed, I have thought it my duty to expose it ... I am bound, from the responsible nature of my

1. It was believed of many mill-owners that they kept a special fund from the fines raised from their workers, and used it for charitable or chapel-building purposes. A large chapel in Dewsbury is still known among the older generation as 'brokken shoit chapel' after the fines taken for broken threads.

office, to bring it into contrast with the liberal and kindly truth of the Gospel. ... And where oppression is exercised it generally falls most heavily upon those who are least able to bear it ... because the widow has no husband, and her children no earthly father ... we often find them most hardly used ...

As a consequence of his sermons – and of personal protests to the masters – the mill-owners had cursed and insulted him and his daughters in the streets. These exposures were followed by a protest meeting in the valley, which was placarded in Oastler's characteristic style:

... you are more Tyrannical, more Hypocritical than the slave drivers of the West Indies. ... Your vaunted *Liberality* ... I shall prove to be *Tyranny* your boasted *Piety* ... neither more nor less than *Blasphemy*. ... Your system of '*Flogging*' – of '*Fines*', of '*Innings up Time*', of '*Truck*', of '*cleaning machinery during mealtimes*' – of '*Sunday Workings*', of '*Low Wages*' ... shall all undergo the Ordeal of '*Public Examination*' ...

'The very Saturday night when I was returning from the meeting,' Oastler declared:

I saw two mills blazing like fury in the valley. Their inmates, poor little sufferers, had to remain there until 11.30 o'clock, and the owner of one of them I found to be a noted sighing, praying, canting religionist ...[1]

We shall return to the Methodists, and see why it was their peculiar mission to act as the apologists of child labour.[2] There can be no doubt that it was the nonconformist mill-owners whom Parson Bull had chiefly in mind when he attacked the 'race' of masters:

... a race whose whole wisdom consists in that cunning which enables them to devise the cheapest possible means for getting out of the youngest possible workers the greatest possible amount of labour, in the shortest possible amount of time, for the least possible amount of wages ... a race of men of whom Agur would have said:

1. G. Crabtree, operative, *Brief Description of a Tour through Calder Dale* (1833); *Voice of the West Riding*, 20, 27 July 1833; *Account of a Public Meeting Held at Hebden Bridge*, 24 August 1833.

2. It is interesting, however, to note that Cecil Driver, op. cit., p. 110, says that the Primitive Methodists often loaned their chapels to Richard Oastler.

there is a generation, oh how lofty are their eyes! and their eyelids are lifted up. There is a generation whose teeth are as swords, and their jaw teeth are as knives to devour the poor from off the earth, and the needy from among men.[1]

On the other hand, while the virtual unanimity of complicity on the part of official Nonconformity exposed it to the biblical attacks of Bull and Oastler, as well as of Short-time Committee operatives (some of whom had first learned their texts in the mill-owners' own Sunday schools), it should by no means be supposed that the Established Church was working unitedly and without remission on the children's behalf. Indeed, we have it from Shaftesbury himself – who would surely have given credit to the Church if it were due – that with the notable exception of Bull the Anglican clergy as 'a body ... will do nothing'.[2]

The claim, then, as to a general 'awakening of conscience' is misleading. What it does is to belittle the veritable fury of compassion which moved the few score northern professional men who took up the cause of the children; the violence of the opposition to them, which drove them on occasions into near-revolutionary courses; and – as humanitarian historians have tended to do – it underestimates the part played in the agitation over twenty and more strenuous years, by such men as John Doherty and the workers' own Short-Time Committee. More recently, one writer has surveyed the issue with that air of boredom appropriate to the capacious conscience of the Nuclear Age. The modern reader, he says, 'well disciplined by familiarity with concentration camps' is left 'comparatively unmoved' by the spectacle of child labour.[3] We may be allowed to reaffirm a more traditional view: that the exploitation of little children, on this scale and with this intensity, was one of the most shameful events in our history.

1. *Manchester and Salford Advertiser*, 29 November 1835.
2. E. Hodder, *Life of Shaftesbury* (1887 edn), pp. 175, 378.
3. R. M. Hartwell, 'Interpretations of the Industrial Revolution in England', *Journal of Econ. Hist.*, XIX, 2 June 1959.

[11]

The Transforming Power of the Cross

I. MORAL MACHINERY

PURITANISM – Dissent – Nonconformity: the decline collapses into a surrender. *Dissent* still carries the sound of resistance to Apollyon and the Whore of Babylon, *Nonconformity* is self-effacing and apologetic: it asks to be left alone. Mark Rutherford, one of the few men who understand the full desolation of the inner history of nineteenth-century Nonconformity – and who is yet, in himself, evidence of values that somehow survived – noted in his *Autobiography* the form of service customary in his youth:

It generally began with a confession that we were all sinners, but no individual sins were ever confessed, and then ensued a kind of dialogue with God, very much resembling the speeches which in later years I have heard in the House of Commons from the movers and seconders of addresses to the Crown at the opening of Parliament.

The example is taken from the Calvinistic Independents: but it will also serve excellently to describe the stance of Methodism before temporal authority. This surrender was implicit in Methodism's origin – in the Toryism of its founder and in his ambivalent attitude to the Established Church. From the outset the Wesleyans fell ambiguously between Dissent and the Establishment, and did their utmost to make the worst of both worlds, serving as apologists for an authority in whose eyes they were an object of ridicule or condescension, but never of trust. After the French Revolution, successive Annual Conferences were forever professing their submission and their zeal in combating the enemies of established order; drawing attention to their activity 'in raising the standard of public morals, and in promoting loyalty in the middle ranks as well

as subordination and industry in the lower orders of society'.[1]
But Methodists were seldom admitted by the Establishment to
audience – and then only by the back door: never decorated
with any of the honours of status: and if they had been mentioned in despatches it would probably have hindered the kind
of moral espionage which they were most fitted to undertake.

The Wars saw a remarkable increase in the Methodist following.[2] They witnessed also (Halévy tells us) 'an uninterrupted
decline of the revolutionary spirit' among all the Nonconformist sects. Methodism is most remarkable during the War
years for two things: first, its gains were greatest among the
new industrial working class: second, the years after Wesley's
death see the consolidation of a new bureaucracy of ministers
who regarded it as their duty to manipulate the submissiveness
of their followers and to discipline all deviant growths within
the Church which could give offence to authority.

In this they were very effective. For centuries the Established Church had preached to the poor the duties of obedience.
But it was so distanced from them – and its distance was rarely
greater than in this time of absenteeism and plural livings –
that its homilies had ceased to have much effect. The deference
of the countryside was rooted in bitter experience of the power
of the squire rather than in any inward conviction. And there
is little evidence that the evangelical movement within the
Church met with much greater success: many of Hannah
More's halfpenny tracts were left to litter the servants' quarters of the great houses. But the Methodists – or many of them
– *were* the poor. Many of their tracts were confessions of redeemed sinners from among the poor; many of their local
preachers were humble men who found their figures of speech
(as one said) 'behind my spinning-jenny'. And the great expansion after 1790 was in mining and manufacturing districts.
Alongside older Salems and Bethels, new-brick Brunswick and

1. Cited in Halévy, op. cit., III, p. 53. For accounts of Methodism's
political stance during these years, see E. R. Taylor, *Methodism and
Politics, 1791–1850*; and R. F. Wearmouth, *Methodism and the Working Class Movements of England, 1800–1850* (1937), especially the chapters on 'The Methodist Loyalty' and 'The Methodist Neutrality'. See
also *The Town Labourer*, ch. 13, 'The Defences of the Poor'.

2. See below, p. 427.

Hanover chapels proclaimed the Methodist loyalty. 'I hear great things of your amphitheatre in Liverpool,' one minister wrote to the Reverend Jabez Bunting in 1811 :

A man will need strong lungs to blow his words from one end of it to the other. In Bradford and in Keighley they are building chapels nearly as large as Carver Street Chapel in Sheffield. To what will Methodism come in a few years? [1]

Jabez Bunting, whose active ministry covers the full half-century, was the dominant figure of orthodox Wesleyanism from the time of Luddism to the last years of the Chartist movement. His father, a Manchester tailor, had been a 'thorough Radical' who 'warmly espoused the cause of the first French revolutionists', but who was not the less a Methodist for that.[2] But in the late 1790s, and after the secession of the Kilhamite New Connexion, a group of younger ministers emerged, of whom Bunting was one, who were above all concerned to remove from Methodism the Jacobin taint. In 1812 Bunting earned distinction by disowning Methodist Luddites; the next year, in Leeds, he counted 'several Tory magistrates of the old school, Church and King people, who, probably, never crossed the threshold of a conventicle before, among his constant hearers'.[3] He and his fellow-ministers – one of the more obnoxious of whom was called the Reverend Edmund Grindrod – were above all organizers and administrators, busied with endless Connexional intrigues and a surfeit of disciplinary zeal. Wesley's dislike of the self-governing anarchy of Old Dissent was continued by his successors, with authority vested in the Annual Conference (weighted down with ministers designated by Wesley himself) and its Committee of Privileges (1803). The Primitive Methodists were driven out because it was feared that their camp meetings might result in 'tumults' and serve as political precedents (as they did); the 'Tent Methodists' and Bible Christians, or Bryanites, were

1. T. P. Bunting, *Life of Jabez Bunting*, D.D. (1887), p. 338.
2. Ibid., p. 11. It is interesting to note that Oastler's father, a Leeds clothier, was also a Methodist and a 'Tom Painite'. In his maturity, Oastler's opinion of Methodism was scarcely more complimentary than that of Cobbett.
3. J. Wray, 'Methodism in Leeds', Leeds Reference Library.

similarly disciplined; female preaching was prohibited; the powers of Conference and of circuit superintendents were strengthened. Espionage into each other's moral failings was encouraged; discipline tightened up within the classes; and, after 1815, as many local preachers were expelled or struck off the 'plan' for political as for religious 'back-slidings'. Here we find an entry in the Halifax Local Preacher's Minute Book: 'Bro. M. charged with attending a political meeting when he should have been at his class' (16 December 1816): there we find a correspondent writing in alarm from Newcastle to Bunting:

... a subject of painful and distressing concern that two of our local preachers (from North Shields) have attended the tremendous Radical Reform Meeting ... I hope no considerable portion of our brethren is found among the Radicals; but a small number of our leaders are among the most determined friends to their spirit and design ... and some of the really pious, misguided sisterhood have helped to make their colours. On expostulation, I am glad to say, several members have quitted their classes (for they have adopted almost the whole Methodist economy, the terms 'Class Leaders', 'District Meetings', etc., etc., being perfectly current among them). If men are to be drilled at Missionary and Bible meetings to face a multitude with recollection, and acquire facilities of address, and then begin to employ the mighty moral weapon thus gained to the endangering the very existence of the Government of the country, *we* may certainly begin to tremble ...

This was in 1819, the year of Peterloo. The response of the Methodist Committee of Privileges to the events of this year was to issue a circular which 'bears clear traces' of Bunting's composition; expressing –

strong and decided disapprobation of certain tumultuous assemblies which have lately been witnessed in several parts of the country; in which large masses of people have been irregularly collected (often under banners bearing the most shocking and impious inscriptions) ... calculated, both from the infidel principles, the wild and delusive political theories, and the violent and inflammatory declamations ... to bring all government into contempt, and to introduce universal discontent, insubordination, and anarchy.[1]

1. T. P. Bunting, op. cit., pp. 527–8.

Wesley at least had been a great-hearted warhorse; he had never spared himself; he was an enthusiast who had stood up at the market-cross to be pelted. Bunting, with his 'solid, mathematical way of speaking', is a less admirable character. It was his own advice to 'adapt your principles to your exigencies'. 'In our family intercourse,' a friend of his youthful ministry informed his son:

his conversation was uniformly serious and instructive. Like his ministry in the pulpit, every word had its proper place, and every sentence might have been digested previously. . . . Sometimes your dear mother's uncontrollable wit suddenly disturbed our gravity; but he was never seen otherwise than in his own proper character as a minister of the gospel of Christ.

Bunting's uncompromising Sabbatarianism stopped just short at the point of his own convenience: 'he did not hesitate, in the necessary prosecution of his ministerial work, to employ beasts; though always with a self-imposed reserve . . .' With children it was another matter. We are often tempted to forgive Methodism some of its sins when we recollect that at least it gave to children and adults rudimentary education in its Sunday schools; and Bamford's happy picture is sometimes recalled, of the Middleton school in the late 1790s, attended by 'big collier lads and their sisters', and the children of weavers and labourers from Whittle, Bowlee, Jumbo and the White Moss. But it is exactly *this* picture, of the laxness of the early Methodists, which Bunting was unable to forgive. When, in his ministry at Sheffield in 1808, his eye fell upon children in Sunday school being taught to *write*, his indignation knew no bounds. Here was 'an awful abuse of the Sabbath'. There could be no question as to its theological impropriety – for children to learn to read the Scriptures was a 'spiritual good', whereas writing was a 'secular art' from which 'temporal advantage' might accrue. Battle commenced in Sheffield (with the former 'Jacobin', James Montgomery, defending the children's cause in the *Sheffield Iris*), from which Bunting emerged victorious; it was renewed at Liverpool in the next year (1809) with the same result; and Bunting was in the forefront of a movement which succeeded, very largely, in extirpating this insidious 'violation' of the Lord's Day until the 1840s. This was, indeed, one of the ways in which Bunting won his national spurs.[1]

The spurs were needed, perhaps, to stick into the children's sides during the six days of the week. In Bunting and his fellows we seem to touch upon a deformity of the sensibility complementary to the deformities of the factory children whose labour they condoned. In all the copious correspondence of his early ministries in the industrial heartlands (Manchester, Liverpool, Sheffield, Halifax and Leeds, 1804–15), among endless petty Connexional disputes, moralistic humbug, and prurient inquiries into the private conduct of young women, neither he nor his colleagues appear to have suffered a single qualm as to the consequences of industrialism.[2] But the younger leaders of Methodism were not only guilty of complicity in the fact of child labour by default. They weakened the poor from within, by adding to them the active ingredient of submission; and they fostered within the Methodist Church those elements most suited to make up the psychic component of the work-discipline of which the manufacturers stood most in need.

As early as 1787, the first Robert Peel wrote: 'I have left most of my works in Lancashire under the management of Methodists, and they serve me excellently well.'[3] Weber and Tawney have so thoroughly anatomized the interpenetration of the capitalist mode of production and the Puritan ethic that it would seem that there can be little to add. Methodism may be seen as a simple extension of this ethic in a changing social milieu; and an 'economist' argument lies to hand, in the fact that Methodism, in Bunting's day, proved to be exceptionally well adapted, by virtue of its elevation of the values of discipline and of order as well as its moral opacity, both to self-

1. Ibid., pp. 295–7, 312–14, 322–3; Bamford, *Early Days*, pp. 100–101. It is fair to note that the Established Church and other Nonconformist sects also forbade the teaching of writing on Sundays.

2. The only humanitarian cause to which Methodists like Bunting gave consistent support was Anti-Slavery agitation; but as the years go by, and the issue is trotted out again and again, one comes to suspect that it was less a vestigial social conscience than a desire to disarm criticism which propped this banner up.

3. L. Tyerman, *John Wesley* (1870), III, p. 499. See also J. Sutcliffe, *A Review of Methodism* (York, 1805), p. 37.

made mill-owners and manufacturers and to foremen, overlookers, and sub-managerial groups. And this argument – that Methodism served as ideological self-justification for the master-manufacturers and for their satellites – contains an important part of the truth. So much John Wesley – in an often-quoted passage – both foresaw and deplored:

... religion must necessarily produce both industry and frugality, and these cannot but produce riches. But as riches increase, so will pride, anger, and love of the world. ... How then is it possible that Methodism, that is, a religion of the heart, though it flourishes now as a green bay tree, should continue in this state? For the Methodists in every place grow diligent and frugal; consequently they increase in goods. Hence they proportionately increase in pride, in anger, in the desire of the flesh, the desire of the eyes, and the pride of life. So, although the form of religion remains, the spirit is swiftly vanishing away.

Many a Methodist mill-owner – and, indeed, Bunting himself – might serve as confirmation of this in the early nineteenth century.[1] And yet the argument falters at a critical point. For it is exactly at this time that Methodism obtained its greatest success in serving *simultaneously* as the religion of the industrial bourgeoisie (although here it shared the field with other Nonconformist sects) and of wide sections of the proletariat. Nor can there be any doubt as to the deep-rooted allegiance of many working-class communities (equally among miners, weavers, factory workers, seamen, potters and rural labourers) to the Methodist Church. How was it possible for Methodism to perform, with such remarkable vigour, this double service?

This is a problem to which neither Weber nor Tawney addressed themselves. Both were mainly preoccupied with Puritanism in the sixteenth and seventeenth centuries, and with the genesis of commercial capitalism; both addressed themselves, in the main, to the psychic and social development of the middle class, the former stressing the Puritan concept of a 'calling', the latter the values of freedom, self-discipline, individualism and acquisitiveness. But it is intrinsic to both arguments that puritanism contributed to the psychic energy

1. See W. J. Warner, op. cit., pp. 168–80.

and social coherence of middle-class groups which felt themselves to be 'called' or 'elected' and which were engaged (with some success) in acquisitive pursuits. How then should such a religion appeal to the forming proletariat in a period of exceptional hardship, whose multitudes did not dispose them to any sense of group calling, whose experiences at work and in their communities favoured collectivist rather than individualist values, and whose frugality, discipline or acquisitive virtues brought profit to their masters rather than success to themselves?

Both Weber and Tawney, it is true, adduce powerful reasons as to the *utility*, from the point of view of the employers, of the extension of Puritan or pseudo-Puritan values to the working class. Tawney anatomized the 'New Medicine for Poverty', with its denunciation of sloth and improvidence in the labourer, and its convenient belief that – if success was a sign of election – poverty was itself evidence of spiritual turpitude.[1] Weber placed more emphasis on the question which, for the working class, is crucial: work-discipline. 'Wherever modern capitalism has begun its work of increasing the productivity of human labour by increasing its intensity,' wrote Weber, 'it has encountered the immensely stubborn resistance of ... pre-capitalistic labour.'

The capitalistic economy of the present day is an immense cosmos into which the individual is born, and which presents itself to him ... as an unalterable order of things in which he must live. It forces the individual, in so far as he is involved in the system of market relationships, to conform to capitalistic rules of action.

But, as industrial capitalism emerged, these rules of action appeared as unnatural and hateful restraints: the peasant, the rural labourer in the unenclosed village, even the urban artisan or apprentice, did not measure the return of labour exclusively in money-earnings, and they rebelled against the notion of week after week of disciplined labour. In the way of life which Weber describes (unsatisfactorily) as 'traditionalism', 'a man does not "by nature" wish to earn more and more money, but simply to live as he is accustomed to live and to earn as much as is necessary for that purpose'. Even piece-rates and other

1. R. H. Tawney, op. cit., pp. 227 ff.

incentives lose effectiveness at a certain point if there is no inner compulsion; when enough is earned the peasant leaves industry and returns to his village, the artisan goes on a drunken spree. But at the same time, the opposite discipline of low wages is ineffective in work where skill, attentiveness or responsibility is required. What is required – here Fromm amplifies Weber's argument – is an 'inner compulsion' which would prove 'more effective in harnessing all energies to work than any outer compulsion can ever be':

> Against external compulsion there is always a certain amount of rebelliousness which hampers the effectiveness of work or makes people unfit for any differentiated task requiring intelligence, initiative and responsibility. . . . Undoubtedly capitalism could not have been developed had not the greatest part of man's energy been channelled in the direction of work.

The labourer must be turned 'into his own slave driver'.[1]

The ingredients of this compulsion were not new.[2] Weber has noted the difficulties experienced by employers in the 'putting-out' industries – notably weaving – in the seventeenth century, as a result of the irregular working habits (drunkenness, embezzlement of yarn and so on) of the workers. It was in the West of England woollen industry – at Kidderminster – that the Presbyterian divine, Richard Baxter, effected by his ministry a notable change in labour relations; and many elements of the Methodist work-discipline may be found fully-formed in his *Christian Directory* of 1673.[3] Similar difficulties were encountered by mine-owners and northern woollen and cotton manufacturers throughout the eighteenth century. Colliers generally received a monthly pay; it was complained that 'they are naturally turbulent, passionate, and rude in manners and character':

1. Weber, op. cit., esp. pp. 54, 60–67, 160–61, 178; E. Fromm, *The Fear of Freedom* (1960 edn), p. 80.

2. Nor is this work-discipline in any sense limited to Methodism. We are discussing Methodism here as the leading example of developments which belong also to the history of Evangelicism and of most Nonconformist sects during the Industrial Revolution.

3. Weber, op. cit., pp. 66–7, 282; Tawney, op. cit., pp. 198 ff. Baxter's writings were favoured reading among the early Methodists, and were much reprinted in the early decades of the nineteenth century.

Their gains are large and *uncertain*, and their employment is a species of task work, the profit of which can very rarely be previously ascertained. This circumstance gives them the wasteful habits of a gamester. . . .

Another trait in the character of a collier, is his predilection to change of situation. . . . Annual changes are almost as common with the pitman as the return of the seasons. . . . Whatever favours he may have received, he is disposed to consider them all cancelled by the refusal of a single request.[1]

The weaver-smallholder was notorious for dropping his work in the event of any farming emergency; most eighteenth-century workers gladly exchanged their employments for a month of harvesting; many of the adult operatives in the early cotton mills were 'of loose and wandering habits, and seldom remained long in the establishment'.[2] A few of the managerial problems in early enterprises are suggested by the list of fines at Wedgwood's Etruria works:

. . . Any workman striking or likewise abusing an overlooker to lose his place.
Any workman conveying ale or liquor into the manufactory in working hours, forfeit 2/–.
Any person playing at fives against any of the walls where there are windows, forfeit 2/– . . .[3]

Whether his workers were employed in a factory or in their own homes, the master-manufacturer of the Industrial Revolution was obsessed with these problems of discipline. The outworkers required (from the employers' point of view) education

1. *Report of the Society for Bettering the Condition of the Poor*, I (1798), pp. 238 ff.; account of the Duke of Bridgewater's colliers (near Manchester). The Duke's colliers were regarded as 'more moral' than most, and 'some of the duke's agents are men of a religious cast, and have established Sunday schools . . .'

2. A. Redford, op. cit., pp. 19–20. As late as the 1830s, Samuel Greg was complaining of 'that restless and migratory spirit which is one of the peculiar characteristics of the manufacturing population'.

3. V. W. Bladen, 'The Potteries in the Industrial Revolution', *Econ. Journal* (Supplement), 1926–9, I, p. 130. See also M. McKendrick, 'Josiah Wedgwood and Factory Disciple', *Hist. Journal*, IV, I, 1961, p. 30. It was Wedgwood's aim to 'make such *Machines* of the *Men* as cannot err'.

in 'methodical' habits, punctilious attention to instructions, fulfilment of contracts to time, and in the sinfulness of embezzling materials. By the 1820s (we are told by a contemporary) 'the great mass of Weavers' were 'deeply imbued with the doctrines of Methodism'. Some of the self-made men, who were now their employers, were Methodists or Dissenters whose frugality – as Wesley had foreseen – had produced riches. They would tend to favour fellow-religionists, finding in them a 'guarantee for good conduct' and 'a consciousness of the value of character'.[1] The 'artisan' traditions of the weavers, with their emphasis on the values of independence, had already prepared them for some variant of Puritan faith.[2] What of the factory operatives?

It is in Dr Andrew Ure's *Philosophy of Manufactures* (1835) – a book which, with its Satanic advocacy, much influenced Engels and Marx – that we find a complete anticipation of the 'economist' case for the function of religion as a work-discipline. The term *Factory*, for Ure:

involves the idea of a vast automaton, composed of various mechanical and intellectual organs, acting in uninterrupted concert for the production of a common object, all of them being subordinated to a self-regulated moving force.

'The main difficulty' of the factory system was not so much technological but in the 'distribution of the different members of the apparatus into one cooperative body', and, above all, 'in training human beings to renounce their desultory habits of work, and to identify themselves with the unvarying regularity of the complex automaton':

To devise and administer a successful code of factory discipline, suited to the necessities of factory diligence, was the Herculean enterprise, the noble achievement of Arkwright. Even at the present day, when the system is perfectly organized, and its labour lightened to the utmost, it is found nearly impossible to convert persons

1. R. Guest, *A Compendious History of the Cotton Manufacture* (1823), pp. 38, 43.
2. In the seventeenth century the Puritan sects had a large weaver following, but – except in the West of England – this tradition had little life in the early eighteenth century.

past the age of puberty, whether drawn from rural or from handi-craft occupations, into useful factory hands. After struggling for a while to conquer their listless or restive habits, they either renounce the employment spontaneously, or are dismissed by the overlookers on account of inattention.

'It required, in fact, a man of a Napoleonic nerve and am-bition, to subdue the refractory tempers of work-people accus-tomed to irregular paroxysms of diligence. ... Such was Arkwright.' Moreover, the more skilled a workman, the more intractable to discipline he became, 'the more self-willed and ... the less fit a component of a mechanical system, in which, by occasional irregularities, he may do great damage to the whole'. Thus the manufacturers aimed at withdrawing any process which required 'peculiar dexterity and steadiness of hand ... from the *cunning* workman' and placing it in charge of a 'mechanism, so self-regulating, that a child may super-intend it'. 'The grand object therefore of the modern manu-facturer is, through the union of capital and science, to reduce the task of his work-people to the exercise of vigilance and dexterity, – faculties ... speedily brought to perfection in the young.'[1]

For the children, the discipline of the overlooker and of the machinery might suffice; but for those 'past the age of puberty' inner compulsions were required. Hence it followed that Ure devoted a section of his book to the 'Moral Economy of the Factory System', and a special chapter to religion. The un-redeemed operative was a terrible creature in Ure's sight; a prey to 'artful demagogues'; chronically given to secret cabals and combinations; capable of any atrocity against his masters. The high wages of cotton-spinners enabled them 'to pamper themselves into nervous ailments by a diet too rich and excit-ing for their indoor occupations':

1. Ure, op. cit., pp. 13–21. Cf. also p. 23: 'It is in fact the constant aim and tendency of every improvement in machinery to supersede human labour altogether, or to diminish its cost, by substituting the in-dustry of women and children for that of men; or that of ordinary labourers, for trained artisans.' As an expression of the mill-owners' intentions this is interesting, and relevant to the textile industries; but as an expression of a 'law' of capitalist development, Marx and Engels perhaps gave Ure's claims too much credence.

Manufactures naturally condense a vast population within a narrow circuit; they afford every facility for secret cabal ...; they communicate intelligence and energy to the vulgar mind; they supply in their liberal wages the pecuniary sinews of contention ...

In such circumstances, Sunday schools presented a 'sublime spectacle'. The committee of a Stockport Sunday school, erected in 1805, congratulated itself upon the 'decorum' preserved in the town, in 1832, at a time of 'political excitement' elsewhere: 'it is hardly possible to approach the town ... without encountering one or more of these quiet fortresses, which a wise benevolence has erected against the encroachments of vice and ignorance'. And Ure drew from this a moral, not only as to general political subordination, but as to behaviour in the factory itself:

The neglect of moral discipline may be readily detected in any establishment by a practised eye, in the disorder of the general system, the irregularities of the individual machines, the waste of time and material ...

Mere wage-payment could never secure 'zealous services'. The employer who neglected moral considerations and was himself 'a stranger to the self-denying graces of the Gospel' –

knows himself to be entitled to nothing but eye-service, and will therefore exercise the most irksome vigilance, but in vain, to prevent his being overreached by his operatives – the whole of whom, by natural instinct as it were, conspire against such a master. Whatever pains he may take, he can never command superior workmanship. ...

It is, therefore, excessively the interest of every mill-owner *to organize his moral machinery on equally sound principles with his mechanical,* for otherwise he will never command the steady hands, watchful eyes, and prompt cooperation, essential to excellence of product. ... There is, in fact, no case to which the Gospel truth, 'Godliness is great gain,' is more applicable than to the administration of an extensive factory.[1]

The argument is thus complete. The factory system demands a transformation of human nature, the 'working paroxysms' of the artisan or outworker must be methodized until the man is

1. Ibid., III, chs. 1 and 3. My italics.

adapted to the discipline of the machine.[1] But how are these disciplinary virtues to be inculcated in those whose Godliness (unless they become overlookers) is unlikely to bring any temporal gain? It can only be by inculcating 'the first and great lesson ... that man must expect his chief happiness, not in the present, but in a future state'. Work must be undertaken as a '*pure act of virtue* ... inspired by the love of a transcendent Being, operating ... on our will and affections':

Where then shall mankind find this transforming power? – in the cross of Christ. It is the sacrifice which removes the guilt of sin: it is the motive which removes love of sin: it mortifies sin by showing its turpitude to be indelible except by such an awful expiation; it atones for disobedience; it excites to obedience; it purchases strength for obedience; it makes obedience practicable; it makes it acceptable; it makes it in a manner unavoidable, for it constrains to it; it is, finally, not only the motive to obedience, but the pattern of it.[2]

Ure, then, is the Richard Baxter of Cottonopolis. But we may descend, at this point, from his transcendental heights to consider, more briefly, mundane matters of theology. It is evident that there was, in 1800, casuistry enough in the theology of all the available English churches to reinforce the manufacturer's own sense of moral self-esteem. Whether he held an hierarchic faith, or felt himself to be elected, or saw in his success the evidence of grace or godliness, he felt few promptings to exchange his residence beside the mill at Bradford for a monastic cell on Bardsey Island. But Methodist theology, by virtue of its promiscuous opportunism, was better suited than any other to serve as the religion of a proletariat whose members had not the least reason, in social experience, to feel themselves to be 'elected'. In his theology, Wesley appears to have dispensed with the best and selected unhesitatingly the worse elements of Puritanism: if in class terms Methodism was hermaphroditic, in doctrinal terms it was a mule. We have already noted Methodism's rupture with the intellectual and democratic traditions of Old Dissent. But

1. Cf. D. H. Lawrence in *The Rainbow*: 'They believe that they must alter themselves to fit the pits and the place, rather than alter the pits and the place to fit themselves. It is easier.'
2. Ure, op. cit., pp. 423–5.

Luther's doctrines of submission to authority might have served as the text for any Wesleyan Conference in the years after 1789:

Even if those in authority are evil or without faith, nevertheless the authority and its power is good and from God. . . .

God would prefer to suffer the government to exist, no matter how evil, rather than allow the rabble to riot, no matter how justified they are in doing so . . .

(Jabez Bunting, however, unlike Luther, could never have admitted the notion that the rabble could ever be 'justified'.) The general Lutheran bias of Wesleyanism has often been noted.[1] Wesley's espousal of the doctrine of the universality of grace was incompatible with the Calvinist notion of 'election'. If grace was universal, sin was universal too. Any man who came to a conviction of sin might be visited by grace and know himself to be ransomed by Christ's blood. Thus far it is a doctrine of spiritual egalitarianism: there is at least equality of opportunity in sin and grace for rich and poor. And as a religion of 'the heart' rather than of the intellect, the simplest and least educated might hope to attain towards grace. In this sense, Methodism dropped all doctrinal and social barriers and opened its doors wide to the working class. And this reminds us that Lutheranism was also a religion of the poor; and that, as Munzer proclaimed and as Luther learned to his cost, spiritual egalitarianism had a tendency to break its banks and flow into temporal channels, bringing thereby a perpetual tension into Lutheran creeds which Methodism also reproduced.

But Christ's ransom was only provisional. Wesley's doctrine here was not settled. He toyed with the notion of grace being perpetual, once it had visited the penitent; and thus a dejected form of Calvinism (the 'elected' being now the 'saved')

1. Weber, in his brief discussion of Methodism in *The Protestant Ethic and the Spirit of Capitalism*, exaggerates the Calvinist elements in its theology, and thereby fails to see its special adaptability as a religion of the proletariat. He thus presses too far the sense of a 'calling' among the Wesleyans, especially when he seeks to apply it to the 'calling' of the working man, a doctrine which has less significance in England than those of submission and obedience.

re-entered by the back door. But as the eighteenth century wore on the doctrine of justification by faith hardened – perhaps because it was so evident that multitudes of those 'saved' in the revivalist campaigns slid back to their old ways after years or only months. Thus it became doctrine that forgiveness of sin lasted only so long as the penitent went and sinned no more. The brotherhood and sisterhood who were 'saved' were in a state of conditional, provisory election. It was always possible to 'backslide'; and in view of human frailty this was, in the eyes of God and of Jabez Bunting, more than likely. Moreover, Bunting was at pains to point out God's view that –

Sin ... is not changed in its nature, so as to be made less 'exceedingly sinful' ... by the pardon of the sinner. The penalty is remitted; and the obligation to suffer that penalty is dissolved; but it is still naturally due, though graciously remitted. Hence appears the propriety and the duty of continuing to confess and lament even pardoned sin. Though released from its penal consequences by an act of divine clemency, we should still remember, that the dust of self-abasement is our proper place before God ...[1]

But there are further complexities to the doctrine. It would be presumptuous to suppose that a man might save *himself* by an act of his own will. The saving was the prerogative of God, and all that a man could do was to prepare himself, by utter abasement, for redemption. Once convinced of grace, however, and once thoroughly introduced to the Methodist brotherhood, 'backsliding' was no light matter to a working man or woman. It might mean expulsion from the only community-group which they knew in the industrial wilderness; and it meant the ever-present fear as to an eternity of lurid punishment to come:

> There is a dreadful hell
> And everlasting pains,
> Where sinners must with devils dwell
> In darkness, fire and chains.

1. Jabez Bunting, *Sermon on Justification by Faith* (Leeds, 1813), p. 11. Bunting's imagery reminds one that in January of this same year (1813) some Luddites had suffered the full 'penal consequences' on the gallows, while others had had their penalty 'graciously remitted' to fourteen years transportation.

How, then, to keep grace? Not by good works, since Wesley had elevated faith above works: 'You have nothing to do but save souls.' Works were the snares of pride and the best works were mingled with the dross of sin; although – by another opportunist feint – works might be a *sign* of grace. (A vestigial Calvinism here for the mill-owners and shopkeepers.) Since this world is the ante-room to eternity, such temporal things as wealth and poverty matter very little: the rich might show the evidence of grace by serving the Church (notably, by building chapels for their own work-people). The poor were fortunate in being less tempted by 'the desire of the flesh, the desire of the eyes, and the pride of life'. They were more likely to remain graced, not because of their 'calling', but because they faced fewer temptations to backslide.

Three obvious means of maintaining grace presented themselves. First, through service to the Church itself, as a class leader, local preacher, or in more humble capacities. Second, through the cultivation of one's own soul, in religious exercises, tract-reading, but – above all – in attempts to reproduce the emotional convulsions of conversion, conviction of sin, penitence, and visitation by grace. Third, through a methodical discipline in every aspect of life. Above all, in labour itself (which, being humble and unpleasant, should not be confused with good works), undertaken for no ulterior motives but (as Dr Ure has it) as 'a pure act of virtue' there is an evident sign of grace. Moreover, God's curse over Adam, when expelled from the Garden of Eden, provided irrefutable doctrinal support as to the blessedness of hard labour, poverty, and sorrow 'all the days of thy life'.

We can now see the extraordinary correspondence between the virtues which Methodism inculcated in the working class and the desiderata of middle-class Utilitarianism.[1] Dr Ure indicates the point of junction, in his advice to the mill-owner 'to

1. Weber and Tawney, of course, direct attention to the parallel development of Puritan and Utilitarian dogmas: cf. Tawney, op. cit., p. 219: 'Some of the links in the Utilitarian coat of mail were forged ... by the Puritan divines of the seventeenth century.' It was Methodism, however, which forged the last links of the Utilitarian chains riveted upon the proletariat.

organize his moral machinery on equally sound principles with his mechanical'. From this aspect, Methodism was the desolate inner landscape of Utilitarianism in an era of transition to the work-discipline of industrial capitalism. As the 'working paroxysms' of the hand-worker are methodized and his unworkful impulses are brought under control, so his emotional and spiritual paroxysms increase. The abject confessional tracts are the other side of the dehumanized prose style of Edwin Chadwick and Dr Kay. The 'march of intellect' and the repression of the heart go together.

But it was Wesley's claim that Methodism was, above all things, a 'religion of the heart'. It was in its 'enthusiasm' and emotional transports that it differed most evidently from the older Puritan sects.[1] We might note some of the approved stages in religious experience, taken from a characteristic tract which describes the conversion of a sailor, Joshua Marsden, in the 1790s. These tracts normally follow a conventional pattern. First, there are descriptions of a sinful youth: swearing, gaming, drunkenness, idleness, sexual looseness or merely 'desire of the flesh'.[2] There follows either some dramatic experience which makes the sinner mindful of death (miraculous cure in mortal illness, shipwreck or death of wife or children); or some chance-hap encounter with God's word, where the sinner comes to jeer but remains to learn the way to salvation. Our sailor had all these experiences. A shipwreck left him 'trembling with horror upon the verge both of the watery and the fiery gulph ... the ghosts of his past sins stalked before him in ghastly forms'. A severe illness 'sent him often weeping and broken-hearted to a throne of grace', 'consumed and burned up sensual desires', and 'showed the awfulness of dying without an interest in Christ'. Invited by a friend to a Methodist class meeting, 'his heart was melted into a child-like weeping frame. ... Tears trickled down his cheeks like rivulets.' There follows the long ordeal of intercession for forgiveness and of wrestling with temptations to relapse into the former life of sin. Only grace can unloose 'the seven seals with which ignorance, pride, unbelief, enmity, self-will, lust and covetousness

1. Excepting, of course, the Baptists – notably in Wales.
2. For an example, taken from this tract, see p. 62 above.

bind the sinner's heart'. Again and again the penitent in his 'novitiate' succumbs to obscurely-indicated 'temptations':[1]

In spite of all, he was sometimes borne away by the violence and impetuosity of temptation, which brought upon him all the anguish of a broken spirit. After being overtaken with sin he would redouble his prayers. ... Sometimes the fear of dying in an unpardoned state greatly agitated his mind, and prevented his falling asleep for fear of awakening in the eternal world.

When the 'desire of the flesh' is to some degree humbled, the 'Enemy' places more subtle spiritual temptations in the penitent's path. Chief among these are *any* disposition which leads to 'hardness of the heart' – levity, pride, but above all the temptation to 'buy salvation' by good works rather than waiting with patience to 'receive it as the free gift of God, through the infinite merits of the bleeding Reconciler'. The doctrine of good works is 'this Hebrew, this Popish doctrine of human merit'. Thus 'hardness of the heart' consists in any character-trait which resists utter submission:

God ... before he can justify us freely ... must wither our gourd, blast the flower of proud hope, take away the prop of self-dependence, strip us of the gaudy covering of christless righteousness, stop the boasting of pharasaical self-sufficiency, and bring the guilty, abased, ashamed, blushing, self-despairing sinner, to the foot of the Cross.

At this point of abasement, 'all his prospects appeared like a waste howling wilderness'. But 'the time of deliverance was now at hand'. At a love-feast in the Methodist chapel, the penitent knelt in the pew 'and, in an agony of soul, began to wrestle with God'. Although 'the enemy raged and rolled upon him like a flood',

1. The language often suggests that the objective component of the 'sin' was masturbation. And this might well be deduced from three facts: (1) The introversial nature of penitent self-absorption. (2) The obsessional Methodist teaching as to the sinfulness of the sexual organs. (3) The fact that the children of Methodists were expected to come to a sense of sin at about the age of puberty. See G. R. Taylor, *The Angel-Makers* (1958), p. 326 for the increase in literature on the subject in these years.

Some of the leaders, with some pious females, came into the gallery, and united in interceding for him at a throne of grace: the more they prayed, the more his distress and burthen increased, till finally he was nearly spent; and sweat ran off him ... and he lay on the floor of the pew with little power to move. This, however, was the moment of deliverance. ... He felt what no tongue can ever describe; a something seemed to rest upon him like the presence of God that went through his whole frame; he sprang on his feet, and felt he could lay upon Christ by faith.

From this time forward the 'burthen of sin fell off'. 'The new creation was manifested by new moral beauties – love, joy, hope, peace, filial fear, delight in Jesus, tender confidence, desire after closer communion, and fuller conformity. ... A new kingdom of righteousness was planted in the heart.' God's glory became 'the end of each action'. But salvation was conditional; the conviction of grace coexisted with the knowledge that man 'is a poor, blind, fallen, wretched, miserable and (without divine grace) helpless sinner'.[1]

Our sinner has now been 'translated from the power of Satan to the kingdom and image of God's dear Son'. And we may see here in its lurid figurative expression the psychic ordeal in which the character-structure of the rebellious pre-industrial labourer or artisan was violently recast into that of the submissive industrial worker. Here, indeed, is Ure's 'transforming power'. It is a phenomenon, almost diabolic in its penetration into the very sources of human personality, directed towards the repression of emotional and spiritual energies. But 'repression' is a misleading word; these energies were not so much inhibited as displaced from expression in personal and in social life, and confiscated for the service of the Church. The box-like, blackening chapels stood in the industrial districts like great traps for the human psyche. Within the Church itself there was a constant emotional drama of backsliders, confessions, forays against Satan, lost sheep; one suspects that the pious sisterhood, in particular, found in this one of the great 'consolations' of religion. For the more intellectual there was the spiritual drama of:

1. Joshua Marsden, *Sketches of the Early Life of a Sailor* (an autobiography in the third person) (Hull, n.d.), *passim*.

trials, temptations, heart sinkings, doubts, struggles, heaviness, manifestations, victories, coldnesses, wanderings, besetments, deliverances, helps, hopes, answers to prayer, interpositions, reliefs, complaints ... workings of the heart, actings of faith, leadings through the mazes of dark dispensations ... fiery trials, and succour in the sinking moment.[1]

But what must be stressed is the *intermittent character* of Wesleyan emotionalism. Nothing was more often remarked by contemporaries of the workaday Methodist character, or of Methodist home-life, than its methodical, disciplined and repressed disposition. It is the paradox of a 'religion of the heart' that it should be notorious for the inhibition of all spontaneity. Methodism sanctioned 'workings of the heart' only upon the occasions of the Church; Methodists wrote hymns but no secular poetry of note; the idea of a passionate Methodist lover in these years is ludicrous. ('Avoid all manner of passions', advised Wesley.) The word is unpleasant; but it is difficult not to see in Methodism in these years a ritualized form of psychic masturbation. Energies and emotions which were dangerous to social order, or which were merely unproductive (in Dr Ure's sense) were released in the harmless form of sporadic love-feasts, watch-nights, band-meetings or revivalist campaigns. At these love-feasts, after hymns and the ceremonial breaking of cake or water-biscuit, the preacher then spoke, in a raw emotional manner, of his spiritual experiences, temptations and contests with sin:

While the preacher is thus engaged, sighs, groans, devout aspirations, and ... ejaculations of prayer or praise, are issuing from the audience in every direction.

In the tension which succeeded, individual members of the congregation then rose to their feet and made their intimate confessions of sin or temptation, often of a sexual implication. An observer noted the 'bashfulness, and evident signs of inward agitation, which some of the younger part of the females have betrayed, just before they have risen to speak'.[2]

The Methodists made of religion (wrote Southey) 'a thing of

1. *Sketches of the Early Life of a Sailor*, pp. 104, 111.
2. Joseph Nightingale, *Portraiture of Methodism* (1807), pp. 203 ff.

sensation and passion, craving perpetually for sympathy and stimulants'.[1] These Sabbath orgasms of feeling made more possible the single-minded weekday direction of these energies to the consummation of productive labour. Moreover, since salvation was never assured, and temptations lurked on every side, there was a constant inner goading to 'sober and industrious' behaviour – the visible sign of grace – every hour of the day and every day of the year. Not only 'the sack' but also the flames of hell might be the consequence of indiscipline at work. God was the most vigilant overlooker of all. Even above the chimney breast 'Thou God Seest Me' was hung. The Methodist was taught not only to 'bear his Cross' of poverty and humiliation; the crucifixion was (as Ure saw) the very pattern of his obedience: 'True followers of our bleeding Lamb, Now on Thy daily cross we die ...'[2] Work was the Cross from which the 'transformed' industrial worker hung.

But so drastic a redirection of impulses could not be effected without a central disorganization of the human personality. We can see why Hazlitt described the Methodists as 'a collection of religious invalids'.[3] If Wesley took from Luther his authoritarianism, from Calvinism and from the English Puritan divines of the seventeenth century Methodism took over the joylessness: a methodical discipline of life 'combined with the strict avoidance of all spontaneous enjoyments'.[4] From both it took over the almost-Manichaean sense of guilt at man's depravity. And, as gratuitous additions, the Wesleys absorbed and passed on through their hymns and writings the strange phenomenon of early eighteenth-century necrophily and the perverse imagery which is the least pleasant side of the Mora-

1. R. Southey, *Life of Wesley and Rise and Progress of Methodism* (1890 edn), 381 ff.

2. J. E. Rattenbury, *The Eucharistic Hymns of John and Charles Wesley* (1948), p. 240:

> We cast our sins into that fire
> Which did thy sacrifice consume,
> And every base and vain desire
> To daily crucifixion doom.

3. W. Hazlitt, 'On the Causes of Methodism', *The Round Table* (1817), *Works*, IV, pp. 57 ff.

4. Weber, *op. cit.*, p. 53.

vian tradition. Weber has noted the connexion between sexual repression and work-discipline in the teachings of such divines as Baxter:

The sexual asceticism of Puritanism differs only in degree, not in fundamental principle, from that of monasticism; and on account of the Puritan conception of marriage, its practical influence is more far-reaching than that of the latter. For sexual intercourse is permitted, even within marriage, only as the means willed by God for the increase of His glory according to the commandment, 'Be fruitful and multiply.' Along with a moderate vegetable diet and cold baths, the same prescription is given for all sexual temptations as is used against religious doubts and a sense of moral unworthiness: 'Work hard in your calling.' [1]

Methodism is permeated with teaching as to the sinfulness of sexuality, and as to the extreme sinfulness of the sexual organs. These – and especially the male sexual organs (since it became increasingly the convention that women could not feel the 'lust of the flesh') – were the visible fleshly citadels of Satan, the source of perpetual temptation and of countless highly unmethodical and (unless for deliberate and Godly procreation) unproductive impulses.[2] But the obsessional Methodist concern with sexuality reveals itself in the perverted eroticism of Methodist imagery. We have already noted, in John Nelson's conversion, the identification of Satan with the phallus. God is usually a simple father image, vengeful, authoritarian and prohibitive, to whom Christ must intercede, the sacrificial Lamb 'still bleeding and imploring Grace / For every Soul of Man'. But the association of feminine – or, more frequently, ambivalent – sexual imagery with Christ is more perplexing and unpleasant.

Here we are faced with layer upon layer of conflicting symbolism. Christ, the personification of 'Love' to whom the great bulk of Wesleyan hymns are addressed, is by turns maternal, Oedipal, sexual and sado-masochistic. The extraordinary assimilation of wounds and sexual imagery in the

1. Ibid., pp. 158–9.
2. Only an appreciation of the degree to which this obsession came to permeate English culture – and in particular working-class culture – can lead to an understanding of why Lawrence was impelled to write *Lady Chatterley's Lover*.

Moravian tradition has often been noted. Man as a sinful 'worm' must find 'Lodging, Bed and Board in the Lamb's Wounds'. But the sexual imagery is easily transferred to imagery of the womb. The 'dearest little opening of the sacred, precious and thousand times beautiful little side' is also the refuge from sin in which 'the Regenerate rests and breathes':

> O precious Side-hole's cavity
> I want to spend my life in thee. . . .
> There in one Side-hole's joy divine,
> I'll spend all future Days of mine.
> Yes, yes, I will for ever sit
> There, where thy Side was split.[1]

Sexual and 'womb-regressive' imagery appears here to be assimilated. But, after the Wesleys broke with the Moravian brethren, the language of their hymns and the persistent accusation of Antinomian heresy among Moravian communities had become a public scandal. In the hymns of John and Charles Wesley overt sexual imagery was consciously repressed, and gave way to imagery of the womb and the bowels:

> Come, O my guilty brethren, come,
> Groaning beneath your load of sin!
> His bleeding heart shall make you room,
> His open side shall take you in . . .

This imagery, however, is subordinated to the overpowering sacrificial imagery of blood, as if the underground traditions of Mithraic blood-sacrifice which troubled the early Christian Church suddenly gushed up in the language of eighteenth-century Methodist hymnody. Here is Christ's 'bleeding love', the blood of the sacrificial Lamb in which sinners must bathe, the association of sacrifice with the penitent's guilt. Here is the 'fountain' that 'gushes from His side,/Open'd that all may enter in':

> Still the fountain of Thy blood
> Stands for sinners open'd wide;
> Now, even now, my Lord and God,
> I wash me in Thy side.

1. See R. A. Knox, *Enthusiasm* (Oxford, 1950), pp. 408-17; G. R. Taylor, op. cit., pp. 166-7.

And sacrificial, masochistic, and erotic language all find a common nexus in the same blood-symbolism:

> We thirst to drink Thy precious blood,
> We languish in Thy wounds to rest,
> And hunger for immortal food,
> And long on all Thy love to feast.

The union with Christ's love, especially in the eucharistic 'marriage-feast' (which the Church collectively 'offers herself to God' by 'offering to God the Body of Christ'),[1] unites the feelings of self-mortification, the yearning for the oblivion of the womb, and tormented sexual desire, 'harbour'd in the Saviour's breast':

> 'Tis there I would always abide,
> And never a moment depart,
> Conceal'd in the cleft of Thy side,
> Eternally held in Thy heart.[2]

It is difficult to conceive of a more essential disorganization of human life, a pollution of the sources of spontaneity bound to reflect itself in every aspect of personality. Since joy was associated with sin and guilt, and pain (Christ's wounds) with goodness and love, so every impulse became twisted into the reverse, and it became natural to suppose that man or child only found grace in God's eyes when performing painful, laborious or self-denying tasks. To labour and to sorrow was to find pleasure, and masochism was 'Love'.

This strange imagery was perpetuated during the years of the Industrial Revolution, not only in Methodist hymnody but also in the rhetoric of sermons and confessions. Nor did it pass unnoticed. 'The Deity is personified and embodied in the grossest of images,' Leigh Hunt commented in an essay 'On the Indecencies and Profane Rapture of Methodism'. 'If God must be addressed in the language of earthly affection, why

1. J. E. Rattenbury, op. cit., p. 132.
2. Ibid., pp. 109–11, 202–4, 224–34; and J. E. Rattenbury, *The Evangelical Doctrines of Charles Wesley's Hymns* (1941), p. 184. This subject is due for renewed and more expert attention. Mr G. R. Taylor's study of *The Angel-Makers* is suggestive, but his attempt to find a 'sexual' explanation of historical change in patrist and matrist child-orientations is pressed to the point of absurdity.

not address him as a parent rather than a lover?'[1] But by the end of the eighteenth century, the Methodist tradition was undergoing a desolate change. The negation or sublimation of love was tending towards the cult of its opposite: death. Charles Wesley himself had written more than one hymn which presages this change:

> Ah, lovely Appearance of Death!
> No Sight upon Earth is so fair.
> Not all the gay Pageants that *breathe*
> Can with a dead Body compare.

The Methodist tradition here is ambivalent. On the one hand, Methodist preachers perfected techniques to arouse paroxysms of fear of death and of the unlimited pains of Hell. Children, from the age that they could speak, were terrified with images of everlasting punishment for the slightest misbehaviour. Their nights were made lurid by Foxe's *Book of Martyrs* and similar reading.[2] But at the same time, those who could read were deluged throughout the early nineteenth century, with the tracts which celebrated 'Holy Dying'. No Methodist or evangelical magazine, for the mature or for children, was complete without its death-bed scene in which (as Leigh Hunt also noted) death was often anticipated in the language of bride or bridegroom impatient for the wedding-night. Death was the only goal which might be desired without guilt, the reward of peace after a lifetime of suffering and labour.

So much of the history of Methodism has, in recent years, been written by apologists or by fair-minded secularists trying to make allowances for a movement which they cannot under-

1. The Editor of the Examiner [Leigh Hunt], *An Attempt to Shew the Folly and Danger of Methodism* (1809), esp. pp. 54–64, 89–97. The language also laid the Methodists open to charges that love-feasts, watch-nights, and revivalist fervour became occasions for promiscuous sexual intercourse. Among sober critics, Nightingale discounted these accusations, Leigh Hunt supported them, Southey reserved judgement. See such *canaille* as A Professor, *Confessions of a Methodist* (1810).

2. Cf. W. E. H. Lecky, *History of England in the Eighteenth Century* (1891 edn), II, p. 585: 'The ghastly images [the Methodist preachers] continually evoked poisoned their imaginations, haunted them in every hour of weakness or depression, discoloured all their judgements of the world, and added a tenfold horror to the darkness of the grave.'

stand, that one notes with a sense of shock Lecky's judgement at the end of the nineteenth century:

A more appalling system of religious terrorism, one more fitted to unhinge a tottering intellect and to darken and embitter a sensitive nature, has seldom existed.[1]

Over the Industrial Revolution there brooded the figure of the Reverend Jabez Branderham (almost certainly modelled upon Jabez Bunting) who appears in Lockwood's grim nightmare at the opening of *Wuthering Heights*: 'good God! what a sermon; divided into *four hundred and ninety parts* ... and each discussing a separate sin!' It is against this all-enveloping 'Thou Shalt Not!', which permeated *all* religious persuasions in varying degree in these years, that we can appreciate at its full height the stature of William Blake. It was in 1818 that he emerged from his densely allegorical prophetic books into a last phase of gnomic clarity in *The Everlasting Gospel*. Here he reasserted the values, the almost-Antinomian affirmation of the joy of sexuality, and the affirmation of innocence, which were present in his earlier songs. Almost every line may be seen as a declaration of 'mental war' against Methodism and Evangelicalism.[2] Their 'Vision of Christ' was his vision's 'greatest Enemy'. Above all, Blake drew his bow at the teaching of humility and submission. It was this nay-saying humility which 'does the Sun & Moon blot out', 'Distorts the Heavens from Pole to Pole',

> Rooting over with thorns & stems
> The buried Soul & all its Gems.

II. THE CHILIASM OF DESPAIR

The utility of Methodism as a work-discipline is evident. What is less easy to understand is why so many working people were willing to submit to this form of psychic exploitation. How was it that Methodism could perform with such

1. Lecky, op. cit. III, pp. 77–8.
2. Cf. Wilberforce, *A Practical View of Christianity*, p. 437: 'Remember that we are all fallen creatures, born in sin, and naturally depraved, Christianity recognizes no *innocence* or *goodness of heart*.'

success this dual rôle as the religion of both the exploiters and the exploited?

During the years 1790–1830[1] three reasons may be adduced: direct indoctrination, the Methodist community-sense, and the psychic consequences of the counter-revolution.

The first reason – indoctrination – cannot be overstated. The evangelical Sunday schools were ever-active, although it is difficult to know how far their activities may be rightly designated as 'educational'. The Wesleyans had inherited from their founder a peculiarly strong conviction as to the aboriginal sinfulness of the child; and this expressed – in Wesley's case – with a force which might have made some Jesuits blench:

Break their wills betimes. Begin this work before they can run alone, before they can speak plain, perhaps before they can speak at all. Whatever pains it costs, break the will if you would not damn the child. Let a child from a year old be taught to fear the rod and to cry softly; from that age make him do as he is bid, if you whip him ten times running to effect it. . . . Break his will now, and his soul shall live, and he will probably bless you to all eternity.[2]

At Wesley's Kingswood School only severely workful 'recreations' were allowed – chopping wood, digging and the like – since games and play were 'unworthy of a Christian child'. ('I will kill or cure,' said Wesley, who rarely said things he did

1. These years cover the period of the rise and dominance of Jabez Bunting and his circle. After 1830 liberalizing tendencies can be seen at work within the Methodist Connexion; and although Bunting fought a determined rearguard action, by the 1840s Methodism entered a new and somewhat softened stage. On the one hand, some second or third generation mill-owners and employers left the Methodists for the respectability of the Established Church. On the other hand, Methodism appears as the authentic outlook of some in the small shopkeeper and clerical and sub-managerial groups, in which a muted radicalism is joined to the ideology of 'self-help'. See E. R. Taylor, op. cit., chs. 5, 6, and W. J. Warner, op. cit. pp. 122–35.

2. Southey, op. cit., p. 561. We can see, for example from Bamford's memoirs of the 1790s, and from Thomas Cooper's *Life* (when as a Methodist schoolmaster in the 1820s he regarded it as a sign of grace that he should *not* strike his pupils) that Wesley's teachings were humanized by many of his late eighteenth-century and early nineteenth-century followers. But see the orthodox utilitarian advocacy of Jabez Bunting, in *Sermon on a great work described* (1805).

not mean: 'I *will* have one or the other – a Christian school, or none at all.') A brief glance at the 'educational' materials in common use in Sunday schools in the first decades of the nineteenth century exposes their true purpose. The Wesley's lurid hymns, employed in the adult services, were replaced by Isaac Watts' *Divine Songs of Children*, or moralistic variants by later writers. Toddlers were taught to sing that they were 'By nature and by practice too, A wretched slave to sin.' The All-seeing God's 'piercing eye' looked upon their most 'secret actions':

> There's not a sin that we commit,
> Nor wicked word we say,
> But in thy dreadful book 'tis writ,
> Against the judgement-day.

A characteristic moral story of the time exemplifies the general tendency of this 'teaching'.[1] John Wise is the son of 'a very poor man, who had many children, and could scarce get bread for them all by hard labour. He had to work with all his might each day in the week, and lived on oatcake, and oatmeal boiled up with water.' His father, notwithstanding, was a good 'prayerful' man, repeatedly giving thanks for his blessings: for example, 'Some of us might have died, but we are all in the land of the living.' John's mother taught him Watts' hymn of the work-disciplined sun:

> When from the chambers of the east
> His morning race begins,
> He never tires, nor stops to rest,
> But round the world he shines,
>
> So, like the sun, would I fulfil
> The duties of this day,
> Begin my work betimes, and still
> March on my heavenly way.

John's parents teach him the sanctity of the Sabbath, and deliver various homilies on duty, obedience and industry. Then comes the awful story of Betty, John's wicked sister, who goes for a walk on Sunday, and comes back wet and muddy, having

1. *The History of John Wise, a Poor Boy: intended for the Instruction of Children* (Halifax, 1810).

lost a shoe. Her father rebukes her, and reads to the family Moses' decree that the man who gathered sticks on the Sabbath should be stoned to death. Betty's sin is much worse than this man's, but this time she is pardoned. But worse sins follow: some children play truant from Sunday school and play *football* instead! The next Sunday the children are admonished, and told the story of the forty-two children who mocked the aged Elisha and who were torn in pieces, at the behest of a merciful God. The infants then carol another of Watts' hymns:

> When children in their wanton play,
>   Serv'd old Elisha so;
> And bid the prophet go his way,
>   'Go up, thou bald-head, go:'
>
> GOD quickly stopt their wicked breath,
>   And sent two raging bears,
> That tore them limb from limb to death,
>   With blood, and groans, and tears.

In the end, the piety of John and of his father are rewarded by an inheritance from a stranger, deeply moved by their patience and submission to poverty.

One might laugh; but the psychological atrocities committed upon children were terribly real to them. One may doubt the emphasis placed by a recent writer upon the repressive effect of Puritan infant-binding (in tight swaddling clothes) and anal training, although the point cannot be dismissed.[1] But despite all the platitudes repeated in most textbooks as to the 'educational initiatives' of the Churches at this time, the Sunday schools were a dreadful exchange even for village dame's schools. Eighteenth-century provision for the education of the poor – inadequate and patchy as it was – was nevertheless provision *for education*, in some sort, even if (as with Shenstone's schoolmistress) it was little more than naming the flowers and herbs. In the counter-revolutionary years this was poisoned by the dominant attitude of the Evangelicals, that the function of education began and ended with the 'moral rescue' of the children of the poor.[2] Not only was the teaching

1. G. R. Taylor, op. cit.
2. Cf. Raymond Williams, *The Long Revolution* (1961), pp. 135–6.

of writing discouraged, but very many Sunday school scholars left the schools unable to read, and in view of the parts of the Old Testament thought most edifying this at least was a blessing. Others gained little more than the little girl who told one of the Commissioners on Child Labour in the Mines: 'if I died a good girl I should go to heaven – if I were bad I should have to be burned in brimstone and fire: they told me that at school yesterday, I did not know it before'.[1] Long before the age of puberty the child was subject at Sunday school and at home (if his parents were pious) to the worst kind of emotional bullying to confess his sins and come to a sense of salvation; and many, like young Thomas Cooper, went 'into secret places twenty times in a day, to pray for pardon . . .'[2]

Lecky's epithet, 'religious terrorism', is in fact by no means an excessive term to apply to a society which provided no alternative educational arrangements for the children of the poor – at least until the Lancastrian charity school movement, in which the notion of 'moral rescue' was modified by genuine educational intentions and by the utilitarian concern for equipping children for industrial occupations.[3] But – and here we come to our second reason – we should beware of giving too bleak and too unqualified a picture of the evangelical churches from the evidence of Sunday school primers, or from the dogmas of such men as Bunting. What the orthodox Methodist minister intended is one thing; what actually happened in many communities may be another. The old 'Arminian' Methodists had a more humane attitude to Sunday school teaching; the Methodists of the New Connexion were always more intellectual in their approach than those of the Wesleyan orthodoxy; we have noted that James Montgomery (of the *Sheffield Iris*) led the fight among the Sheffield Nonconformists to retain the teaching of writing in the Sunday school syllabus. The lay teachers, who volunteered their ser-

1. Cited in J. L. and B. Hammond, *Lord Shaftesbury* (Penguin edn), p. 74.

2. T. Cooper, *Life*, p. 37.

3. Those writers today who rightly expose the human depreciation resulting from the commercial abuse of the media of communication, seem to me to have matters out of proportion when they overlook the extent and character of mass indoctrination in earlier periods.

vices, were less likely to be doctrinaire; and there was a continuous tension which could at times produce unlikely results. 'Even our Sunday Schools', a Bolton minister wrote to the Duke of Portland in 1798:

> may become in some Instances the Seminaries of Faction. We have discovered one if not two who have taken the Oaths of United Englishmen, who are acting in the capacity of S. Schoolmasters gratis . . .[1]

The 'quiet fortresses' of the Stockport Sunday schools, which Dr Ure so commended in the 1830s, nevertheless had been besieged with a vengeance (and to some degree actually displaced) between 1817 and 1820, when the Reverend Joseph Harrison and the Stockport Political Union sponsored a Radical Sunday School movement which must have been staffed, in part, by former teachers and scholars of the orthodox schools.[2]

And this should be seen, not only in the schools, but also in relation to the general influence of the Methodist churches. As a dogma Methodism appears as a pitiless ideology of work. In practice, this dogma was in varying degrees softened, humanized, or modified by the needs, values, and patterns of social relationship of the community within which it was placed. The Church, after all, was more than a building, and more than the sermons and instructions of its minister. It was embodied also in the class meetings: the sewing groups: the money-raising activities: the local preachers who tramped several miles after work to attend small functions at outlying hamlets which the minister might rarely visit. The picture of the fellowship of the Methodists which is commonly presented is too euphoric; it has been emphasized to the point where all other characteristics of the Church have been forgotten.[3] But it remains both true and important that Methodism, with its open chapel doors, did offer to the uprooted and abandoned

1. Rev. Thomas Bancroft, 12 February 1798, P.C. A. 152.
2. See D. Read, *Peterloo* (Manchester, 1957), pp. 51 ff., and below, p. 788.
3. The sense of fellowship in the early years of the Church is expressed sympathetically in L. F. Church, *The Early Methodist People* (1948). See also, of course, Dr Wearmouth's books, among many others.

people of the Industrial Revolution some kind of community to replace the older community-patterns which were being displaced. As an unestablished (although undemocratic) Church, there was a sense in which working people could make it their own; and the more closely knit the community in which Methodism took root (the mining, fishing or weaving village) the more this was so.

Indeed, for many people in these years the Methodist 'ticket' of church-membership acquired a fetishistic importance; for the migrant worker it could be the ticket of entry into a new community when he moved from town to town. Within this religious community there was (as we have seen) its own drama, its own degrees of status and importance, its own gossip, and a good deal of mutual aid. There was even a slight degree of social mobility, although few of the clergy came from proletarian homes. Men and women felt themselves to have some place in an otherwise hostile world when within the Church. They obtained recognition, perhaps for their sobriety, or chastity, or piety. And there were other positives, such as the contribution to the stability of the family and the home, to which we shall return. The Puritan character-structure, moreover, was not something which could be confiscated solely for the service of the Church and the employer. Once the transference was made, the same dedication which enabled men to serve in these rôles, will be seen in the men who officered trade unions and Hampden Clubs, educated themselves far into the night, and had the responsibility to conduct working-class organizations. In analysing the ideology of Methodism, we have presented an intellectualized picture. In the fluency of social life, plain common sense, compassion, the obstinate vitality of older community traditions, all mingle to soften its forbidding outlines.

There is a third reason, however, why working people were exceptionally exposed to the penetration of Methodism during the years of the Napoleonic Wars. It is, perhaps, the most interesting reason of all, but it has been scarcely noticed. It may best be approached by recalling the hysterical aspect of Methodist and Baptist revivalism, and of the smaller sects. During the worst years of the Industrial Revolution, real opiates were used quite widely in the manufacturing districts. And Charles Kingsley's epithet, 'the opium of the masses', reminds us that many working people turned to religion as a 'consolation', even though the dreams inspired by Methodist doctrine were scarcely happy. The methods of the revivalist preachers were noted for their emotional violence; the tense opening, the vivid descriptions of sudden death and catastrophe, the unspecific rhetoric on the enormity of sin, the dramatic offer of redemption. And the open-air crowds and early congregations of Methodism were also noted for the violence of their 'enthusiasm' – swooning, groaning, crying out, weeping and falling into paroxysms. Southey, indeed, suggested that revivalism was akin to Mesmerism: Wesley 'had produced a new disease, and he accounted for it by a theological theory instead of a physical one'.[1] Sometimes these symptoms took the form of violent mass hysteria, as in the incident at Bristol recorded in Wesley's *Journal* in March 1788 when a 'vehement noise ... shot like lightning through the whole congregation':

The terror and confusion was inexpressible. You might have imagined it was a city taken by storm. The people rushed upon each other with the utmost violence, the benches were broken in pieces, and nine tenths of the congregation appeared to be struck with the same panic.

At Chapel-en-le-Frith, he recorded in 1786, this hysteria had already become habit-forming:

Some of them, perhaps many, scream all together as loud as they possibly can. Some of them use improper, yea, indecent expressions in prayer. Several drop down as dead, and are as still as a corpse; but in a while they start up and cry, Glory, glory ...

Such excesses of hysteria Wesley condemned, as 'bringing the real work into contempt'.[2] But throughout the Industrial Revolution more muted forms of hysteria were intrinsic to Methodist revivalism. Tight communities, miners, hill-farmers or weavers, might at first resist the campaign of field-preaching and prayer-meetings among them; then there might be 'a

1. Southey, op. cit., pp. 382 ff.
2. See the discussion of the 'enthusiasm' in R. A. Knox, op. cit., pp. 520–35.

little moving among the dry bones'; and then 'the fire broke out; and it was just as when the whins on a common are set on fire, – it blazed gloriously'.[1]

The example is taken from propaganda in West Riding weaving villages in 1799–1801, when whole communities declared themselves – at least temporarily – 'saved'. And it is rarely noted that not only did the war years see the greatest expansion of Methodism, notably in the northern working class, but that this was also accompanied by renewed evidence of hysteria. For example, in the years 1805–6, when numbers flocked to the Methodists in Bradford, 'no sooner, in many cases, was the text announced, than the cries of persons in distress so interrupted the preacher, that the service ... was at once exchanged for one of general and earnest intercession'.[2] 'Three fell while I was speaking,' a preacher of the Bible Christians in Devon noted complacently in his diary in 1816: 'we prayed, and soon some more fell; I think six found peace.' The ministrations of this sect among the moorland farmers and labourers were often accompanied by agonies, prostrations, 'shouts of praise', and 'loud and piteous cries of penitents'.[3]

Methodism may have inhibited revolution; but we can affirm with certainty that its rapid growth during the Wars was a component of the psychic processes of counter-revolution. There is a sense in which any religion which places great emphasis on the after-life is the chiliasm of the defeated and the hopeless. 'The utopian vision aroused a contrary vision. The chiliastic optimism of the revolutionaries ultimately gave birth to the formation of the conservative attitude of resignation ...' – the words of Karl Mannheim's describing another movement. And he also gives us a clue to the nature of the psychic process:

Chiliasm has always accompanied revolutionary outbursts and given them their spirit. When this spirit ebbs and deserts these movements, there remains behind in the world a naked mass-frenzy and a despiritualized fury.[4]

1. F. A. West, *Memoirs of Jonathan Saville* (Halifax, 1844).
2. W. M. Stamp, *Historical Notices of Wesleyan Methodism in Bradford* (1841), p. 85.
3. F. W. Bourne, *The Bible Christians* (1905), pp. 36–42.
4. K. Mannheim, *Ideology and Utopia* (1960 edn), pp. 192–6.

Since, in England of the 1790s, the revolutionary impulse was
stifled before it reached the point of 'outburst', so also when
the spirit ebbed, the reaction does not fall to the point of
frenzy. And yet there are many phenomena in these decades
which can scarcely be explained in any other way. Authentic
millennarialism ends in the late-1790s, with the defeat of English
Jacobinism, the onset of the Wars, and the confining of
Richard Brothers in a mad-house. But a number of sects of
'New Jerusalemites' prospered in the next fifteen years.[1] Prophet after prophet arose, like Ebenezer Aldred, a Unitarian
minister in an isolated village in the Derbyshire Peak (Huck-
low):

> There he lived in a kind of solitude, became dreamy and wild; laid
> hold on the prophecies; saw Napoleon in the Book of Revelation:
> at last fancied himself the Prophet who, standing neither on land
> nor water, was to proclaim the destruction of a great city ...

and, clothed in a white garment, his grey hair flowing down
his shoulders, sailed in a boat on the Thames, distributing
booklets and prophesying doom.[2] Radical, mystic and mili-
tarist contested for the robes of Revelation: the lost tribes
of Israel were discovered in Birmingham and Wapping: and
'evidence' was found that 'the British Empire is the peculiar
possession of Messiah, and his promised naval dominion'.[3]

But the most startling evidence of a 'despiritualized fury'
is to be found in the movements surrounding – and outliving
– the greatest Prophetess of all, Joanna Southcott. It was in
1801 that her first cranky prophetic booklet was published,
The Strange Effects of Faith. And the general climate of expectant frenzy is shown by the rapidity with which the reputation of the Devon farmer's daughter and domestic servant
swept the country. Her appeal was curiously compounded of
many elements. There was the vivid superstitious imagination
of the older England, especially tenacious in her own West

---

1. In March 1801, Earl Fitzwilliam was enquiring into the activities of
the followers of Brothers in Bradford, led by Zacchaus Robinson, a
weaver, who 'was for many years a strong Methodist. & what is here
called a Class Leader'. Fitzwilliam Papers, F. 45 (a).
2. T. A. Ward, op. cit., pp. 188–9; Eben-Eser, *The Little Book* (1811).
3. R. Wedgwood, *The Book of Remembrance* (1814).

Country. 'The belief in supernatural agency', wrote the *Taunton Courier* in 1811,

is universally prevalent throughout the Western Counties, and very few villages there are who cannot reckon upon at least one who is versed in 'Hell's Black Grammar'. The Samford Ghost, for a while, gained its thousands of votaries . . .[1]

There was the lurid imagery and fervour of the Methodist communion, to which (according to Southey) Joanna had been 'zealously attached'.[2] There was the strange amalgam of Joanna's own style, in which mystic doggerel was thrown down side by side with shrewd or literal-minded autobiographical prose – accounts of childhood memories, unhappy love affairs, and encounters between the stubborn peasant's daughter and disbelieving parsons and gentry. There was, above all, the misery and war-weariness of these years, and the millennarial expectancy, of a time when the followers of Brothers still lived daily in the hope of fresh revelation – a time when:

One madman printed his dreams, another his day-visions; one had seen an angel come out of the sun with a drawn sword in his hand, another had seen fiery dragons in the air, and hosts of angels in battle array. ... The lower classes ... began to believe that the Seven Seals were about to be opened . . .[3]

Joanna was no Joan of Arc, but she shared one of Joan's appeals to the poor: the sense that revelation might fall upon a peasant's daughter as easily as upon a king. She was acclaimed as the true successor to Brothers, and she gathered around her an entourage which included several educated men and women. (If Blake's prophetic books may be seen, in part, as an idiosyncratic essay in the margin of the prevailing prophetic mood, his acquaintance William Sharp, also an engraver and former 'Jacobin', gave to Joanna his complete allegiance.) But Joanna's appeal was felt most strongly among working people

1. Cited in *Alfred*, 24 August 1811. See also F. W. Bourne, op. cit., pp. 55, 64–5, for accounts of women possessed by the devil, and of a woman 'who declared herself to be Christ'.

2. Southey, *Letters from England* (1808, 2nd edn), III, p. 238.

3. Ibid., III, p. 232.

of the west and north – Bristol, south Lancashire, the West Riding, Stockton-on-Tees.

O England! O England! England! the axe is laid to the tree, and it must and will be cut down; ye know not the days of your visitation ... The midnight-hour is coming for you all, and will burst upon you. I warn you of dangers that now stand before you, for the time is at hand for the fulfilment of all things. 'Who is he that cometh from Edom, with dyed garments from Bozrah; that speaketh in righteousness, mighty to save all that trust in him; but of my enemies I will tread them in mine anger, and trample them in my fury; for the day of vengeance is in my heart, and the year of my redeemed is come.'

Most of Joanna's prophecies convey little more than an apocalyptic mood, and auguries of catastrophe so vague that they were easily applied to the crises and upheavals of Napoleonic Europe, with Bonaparte himself figuring as THE BEAST. Her manner lacked the revolutionary specificity of Brothers; but her apocalypse was most certainly one in which the sheep were to be separated irrevocably from the goats. 'The Earth shall be filled with My Goodness,' the Lord spoke through Joanna, 'and hell shall be filled with My Terrors. ... My fury shall go forth – and My Loving-kindness shall save to the utmost all them that now come unto ME.'

Awake, awake, O Zion, put on thy beautiful garments, O Jerusalem: for the day of the LORD is at hand ... I will break down the pride of the Lofty, and I will exalt the Spirit of the Meek ...

For the saved there was offered a shadowy Utopia:

> When I my people do redeem
> From every power of hell and sin,
> Your houses I shall build anew,
> And palaces bring to your view;
> For golden mines I have in store:
> The foaming seas shall send on shore
> Millions of treasure hid therein,
> And mines of diamonds shall be seen ...
> I've gold of Ophir, that shall come
> To build Jerusalem up again,
> And those that are the first redeem'd
> May say, these promises we claim ...

There was even an echo of Paine's 'Bastard and his armed banditti', and a suggestion that the land would be returned to the labouring people:

> But now the heirs I mean to free,
> And all these bondmen I'll cast out,
> And the true heirs have nought to doubt;
> For I'll cut off the bastard race,
> And in their stead the true heirs place
> For to possess that very land . . .

It is probable that Joanna Southcott was by no means an impostor, but a simple and at times self-doubting woman, the victim of her own imbalance and credulity. (One's judgement as to some members of the circus which 'promoted' her may be more harsh.) There is a pathos in her literal-minded transcriptions of her 'Voices'. The long messages which the Lord instructed her to communicate were full of the highest testimonials to the ability of Joanna herself:

> For on the earth there's something new appears.
> Since earth's foundation plac'd I tell you here,
> Such wondrous woman never was below . . .

So flattered by the best of all Referees, she was able to exert upon the credulous a form of psychic blackmail no less terrifying than that of the hell-fire preachers. One day, while sweeping out a house after a sale, 'she was permitted by the Lord to find, *as if by accident*', a commonplace seal. Thereafter her followers – the 'Johannas' or Southcottians – were able to obtain from her a special seal, a sort of promissory note that the bearer should 'inherit the Tree of Life to be made Heirs of God & joint-heirs with Jesus Christ'. The promise of the millennium was available only to 'THE SEALED PEOPLE', while the scoffers received more dreadful threats:

> And now if foes increase, I tell you here,
> That every sorrow they shall fast increase,
> The Wars, her tumults they shall never cease
> Until the hearts of men will turn to me
> And leave the rage of persecuting thee.

Thousands upon thousands (in one estimate, 100,000) were 'sealed' in this way. There was, indeed, a market in seals at one time comparable to the late medieval market in relics of the Cross. The emotional disequilibrium of the times is revealed not only in the enthusiasm of the 'Johannas' but also in the corresponding violence of feeling of the mobs which sometimes assaulted her under-prophets. Southcottianism was scarcely a form of revolutionary chiliasm; it did not inspire men to effective social action, and scarcely engaged with the real world; its apocalyptic fervour was closely akin to the fervours of Methodism – it brought to a point of hysterical intensity the desire for *personal* salvation. But it was certainly a cult of the poor. Joanna's God cursed the false 'shepherds' of England (landowners and governors) who conspired to raise the price of bread:

My charges will come heavy against them, and my judgements must be great in the land, if they starve the poor in the midst of plenty. ... What I said of Nineveh, Sodom and Gomorrah, what I said of Tyre and Sidon, what I said concerning the Galileans, are now charges against the shepherds of England.

The old imagery of the 'Whore of Babylon' was revived with luxuriating confusion, and all 'the Clergy throughout the land' were pointed out as the 'Lovers and Adulterers' with Jezebel, who 'adulterate my Bible as an adulterous man would commit fornication with an adulterous woman'. As in all the cults of the poor, there was a direct identification between their plight and the tribulations of the Children of Israel: 'as close as Pharaoh pursued the Children of Israel, so close will Satan pursue the Sealed People, by temptations within the persecutions without ...' At times all tissue of sense disappears beneath the riot of such imagery; in which the proper nouns of the Old Testament struggle with the rhythms of Ancient Pistol:

Come out! come out! let Sodom feel its doom. Where now is Lot? At Zoar safe! Where is his wife? Is she not salt all? The writing is on the wall – Thou lewdly revellest with the bowls of God. ... Let Bel asunder burst! ... The saints now judge the earth. The omnipotent is here, in power, and spirit in the word – The sword, white horse, and King of kings has drawn the flaming sword! Rejoice, ye saints, rejoice! ... Great Og and Agag where are ye! The walls of Jericho are thou, fall flat! Joshua's rams horns, the seven and twelve, pass Jordan's stream.   The Lord's anointed reigns – The rods or laws of Ephraim, ten unite in one, and hold by Judah's skirt – The Son of Man o'er Israel reigns – The dry bones now arise. ... The bride is come – The Bridegroom now receives the marriage seal. The law and gospel now unite – The moon and sun appear – Caleb and Joshua pass the stream in triumph to restore – Where now thou Canaanite art thou? Where all thy maddened crew? –

> Hittites be gone! no more appear to hurt or to annoy;
> Now Israel's sons in peace succeed and Canaan's land enjoy.
> Behold, from Edom I appear, with garments dipt in blood:
> My sons are freed, and sav'd and wash'd amidst the purple
>   flood ...[1]

The first frenzy of the cult was in 1801–4; but it achieved a second climax in 1814 when the ageing Joanna had an hysterical pregnancy and promised to give birth to 'Shiloh', the Son of God. In the West Riding 'the whole district was infested with bearded prophets', while Ashton, in Lancashire, later became a sort of 'metropolis' for the 'Johannas' of the north.[2] When the Prophetess died in the last week of 1814, tragically disillusioned in her own 'Voice', the cult proved to be extraordinarily deep-rooted. Successive claimants appeared to inherit her prophetic mantle, the most notable of whom was a Bradford woolcomber, John Wroe. Southcottian derivatives passed through one aberration after another, showing them-

1. This last passage is not Joanna's, but a 'small part of the thoughts' of 'a gentleman of vast respectability' who was among her followers. All the other passages are from Joanna's writings. See *Strange Effects of Faith*, 5th Book, p. 235; 6th Book, p. 275; *A Continuation of Prophecies* (1802), pp. 15, 48–9; *A Word in Season* (1803), p. 17; *A Word to the Wise* (1803), p. 32; *Sound an Alarm in My Holy Mountain* (1804), pp. 31, 45; *A Warning to the World* (1804), p. 8; *Copies and Parts of Copies*, &c. (1804), p. 49; *Letters and Communications* (1804), pp. 44–5; *Answer to Five Charges in the Leeds Mercury* (1805), pp. 20–21; *Divine and Spiritual Communications* (1809), pp. 20, 39. See also G. R. Balleine, *Past Finding Out* (1956), chs. 1 to 7; William Sharp, *An Answer to the World* (1806).

2. Followers of the cult were obliged to wear beards. For Southcottian penetration into the north, see J. Crossley, *Remarks and Inquiries on a Sermon Preached by the Rev. J. Cockin* (Leeds, 1806); G. Turner, *A Vindication for the Honour of God* (Leeds, 1807); W. Cooke Taylor, op. cit., p. 230; F. Peel, *Nonconformity in the Spen Valley*, pp. 187–8.

selves capable of sudden flare-ups of messianic vitality until the last years of the nineteenth century.[1]

There is no doubt that the Southcott cult wreaked great havoc in the Methodist camp, notably in Bristol, Lancashire and Yorkshire. Indeed, Joanna's few essays in theological polemic were directed at the Methodists whom she accused of holding 'Calvinistic' tenets, thereby—

making the great Creator and Father of all a being of such cruelty, that no words can express, or pen describe – instead of a BEING whose LOVE is every where and whose MERCY is *over all* HIS WORKS.[2]

The Methodists, of course, had many advantages over the Southcottians: organizational stability, money, the benign attitude of the authorities. What members they lost to the cult were probably soon regained. But this does not mean that we can dismiss the cult as a mere 'freak', irrelevant to the stolid lines of social growth. On the contrary, we should see the 'Johannas' and the Methodist revival of these years as intimate relations. The Wars were the heyday of the itinerant lay preachers, with their 'pious ejaculations, celestial groans, angelic swoonings'[3] – the 'downright balderdash' which so much enraged Cobbett:

Their heavenly gifts, their calls, their inspirations, their feelings of grace at work within them, and the rest of their canting gibberish, are a gross and outrageous insult to common sense, and a great scandal to the country. It is in vain that we boast of our *enlightened state*, while a sect like this is increasing daily.[4]

As orthodox Wesleyanism throve, so also did breakaway groups of 'Ranters' – the Welsh 'Jumpers' (cousins to the American 'Shakers'), the Primitive Methodists, the 'Tent Methodists', the 'Magic Methodists' of Delemere Forest, who fell into trances or 'visions', the Bryanites or Bible Christians, the

1. See G. R. Balleine, op. cit., chs. 8 to 14; W. H. G. Armytage, *Heavens Below*, pp. 274–6; and below, pp. 879–82.
2. *Divine and Spiritual Communications* (1809), p. 33.
3. Halifax Theatre Royal playbill, 1793.
4. *Political Register*, 12 June 1813.

'Quaker Methodists' of Warrington and the 'Independent Methodists' of Macclesfield. Through the streets of war-time and post-war England went the revivalist missionaries, crying out: 'Turn to the Lord and seek salvation!'

One is struck not only by the sense of disequilibrium, but also by the *impermanence* of the phenomenon of Methodist conversion. Rising graphs of Church membership are misleading; what we have, rather, is a revivalist pulsation or an oscillation between periods of hope and periods of despair and spiritual anguish. After 1795 the poor had once again entered into the Valley of Humiliation. But they entered it unwillingly, with many backward looks; and whenever hope revived. religious revivalism was set aside, only to reappear with renewed fervour upon the ruins of the political messianism which had been overthrown. In this sense, the great Methodist recruitment between 1790 and 1830 may be seen as the chiliasm of despair.

This is not the customary reading of the period; and it is offered as an hypothesis, demanding closer investigation. On the eve of the French Revolution the Methodists claimed about 60,000 adherents in Great Britain. This indicated little more than footholds in all but a few of the industrial districts. Thereafter the figures claimed advance like this: 1800, 90,619; 1810, 137,997; 1820, 191,217; 1830, 248,592.[1] Years especially notable for revivalist recruitment were 1797–1800, 1805–7, 1813–18, 1823–4, 1831–4. These years are so close to those of maximum political awareness and activity that Dr Hobsbawm is justified in directing attention to the 'marked parallelism between the movements of religious, social and political consciousness'.[2] But while the relationship between political and

1. Census of Religious Worship, England and Wales, 1851 (1853), p. lxxviii. Orthodox Wesleyan circuits with over 1,000 members in 1815 were claimed to be: London, Bristol, Redruth, St Ives, Birmingham, Burslem, Macclesfield, Manchester, Bolton, Liverpool, Colne, Nottingham, Sheffield, Leeds, Birstal, Bradford, Halifax, Isle of Man, Sunderland, Wakefield, Dewsbury, Epworth, York, Hull, Darlington, Barnard Castle, Newcastle, Shields. See M. E. Edwards, 'The Social and Political Influence of Methodism in the Napoleonic Period' (London Ph.D. Thesis, 1934), p. 244.

2. *Primitive Rebels*, pp. 129–30.

religious excitement is obviously intimate, the nature of the relationship remains obscure: the conclusion that 'Methodism advanced when Radicalism advanced and not when it grew weaker' does not necessarily follow.[1] On the contrary, it is possible that religious revivalism took over just at the point where 'political' or temporal aspirations met with defeat. Thus we might almost offer a spiritual graph, commencing with the far-reaching emotional disturbances associated with the French Revolution and *Rights of Man*. In the early 1790s we find secular Jacobinism and the millennarial hopes of Richard Brothers: in the late 1790s and the 1800s, Methodist revivalism and the frenzy of the 'Johannas', which more than one contemporary witness saw as being part of the same stock, and appealing to the same audience;[2] in the aftermath of Luddism (1811–12) a renewed wave of revivalism, giving way to the political revival of the winter of 1816–17. In the latter two years the Primitive Methodists broke through into the framework-knitters' villages of Nottinghamshire, Derbyshire and Leicestershire, and the relationship between revivalism and political radicalism appears to have been especially close. On Whit Sunday 1816, 12,000 were claimed at a camp-meeting in Nottingham Forest. From the autumn of 1816 until the summer of 1817 popular energies appear to have been absorbed in radical agitation, culminating in the Pentridge 'rising' of June 1817 in which at least one local preacher took a leading part. But the great Primitive Methodist revival which took place in these counties in 1817 and 1818 ('one of the most remarkable ... ever experienced') would seem to have taken fire *after* the Pentridge disaster.[3] The year of maximum political activity in the post-war decade, 1819, is a year unremarkable for revivalism; while the revivalist fervour of 1831–4 may in part be attributed to the campaigns in the rural counties of

1. See E. J. Hobsbawm, 'Methodism and the Threat of Revolution', *History Today* (1957), VII, p. 124.

2. See e.g. Leigh Hunt, op. cit., p. xiv.

3. H. B. Kendall, *History of the Primitive Methodist Church* (1919), pp. 7–8, 31. The rôle of the revival may be fixed by the legendary incident, recorded by Kendall, of a 'Luddite' of 1817 who was meditating assassination, and was waylaid on his mission and brought to the chapel instead.

the south and east, in the aftermath of the 'Last Labourers' Revolt'.[1]

The suggestion is tentative. To take it further, we should know more about, not the years of revivalism, but the months; not the counties, but the towns and villages. Moreover, the relationship of Primitive Methodists or Bible Christians to political agitation was very different from that of the orthodox Wesleyans. A close examination of all the churches which experienced revivals shows, however, that their progress was not marked by a steady upward movement, interspersed with occasional steep inclines when mass conversions were made. It was more in the nature of a pulsation, a forward surge followed by a withdrawal. Thomas Cooper's account of his own conversion in the 1820s may be taken as characteristic: 'the example was wondrously infectious. Hundreds in the town [Gainsborough] and circuit began to pray for holiness of heart ...' For weeks he felt transfigured, in a 'heaven on earth of holiness'. Then at length he returned to earth, lost his temper with the children at school where he taught, and his sense of transfiguration was lost:

Similar to my experience was that of scores of our members in the town, and in the villages of the circuit. And such is the experience in all circuits of the connexion. Often, what is called a 'Revival' begins with some one or more striving for holiness. The theme kindles desire in others ... and sometimes fills a circuit with glowing excitement for many months. But the decline invariably sets in ...[2]

Cooper gives us the experience. But in terms of the social process we may suppose something like an oscillation, with religious revivalism at the negative, and radical politics (tinged with revolutionary millennarialism) at the positive pole. The connecting notion is always that of the 'Children of Israel'. At one pole, the chiliasm of despair could reduce the Methodist working man to one of the most abject of human beings. He was constantly warned by his ministers against reformers, as 'these sons of Belial': 'We ... ought to wait in silence the

1. Similarly, Professor Armytage finds that the years of maximum emigration from the industrial districts in the 1840s to the Mormon City of Zion were years of Chartist inactivity. See below, p. 882.
2. T. Cooper, *Life*, pp. 85–6.

salvation of the Lord. In due time he will deliver his *own dear peculiar people.*'[1] As such a 'peculiar person' his tools were occasionally destroyed, or he was refused entry to trade unions, upon suspicion of being an employer's 'nark'. Cobbett pressed the attack upon the Methodists further: 'Amongst the people of the north they have served as spies and blood-money men.'[2]

On the other hand, as if to baffle expectation, Methodist working men, and, indeed, local preachers, repeatedly emerged in the nineteenth century – in handfuls here and there – as active workers in different fields of working-class politics. There were a few Methodist Jacobins, more Methodist Luddites, many Methodist weavers demonstrating at Peterloo, Methodist trade unionists and Chartists. They were rarely (with the exception of trade unionism in the pits and, later, in agriculture) initiators; this rôle was more often filled by Owenites and free-thinkers who emerged from a different moral pattern. But they were often to be found as devoted speakers and organizers, who carried with them – even after their expulsion from the Methodist Church – the confidence of their communities.

One reason for this lies in the many tensions at the heart of Wesleyanism. Just as the repressive inhibitions upon sexuality carried the continual danger of provoking the opposite – either in the form of the characteristic Puritan rebel (the forerunner of Lawrence) or in the form of Antinomianism; so the authoritarian doctrines of Methodism at times bred a libertarian antithesis. Methodism (and its evangelical counterparts) were highly politically conscious religions. For 100 years before 1789, Dissent, in its popular rhetoric, had two main enemies: Sin and the Pope. But in the 1790s there is a drastic redirection of hatred; the Pope was displaced from the seat of commination and in his place was elevated Tom Paine. 'Methodism,' Bunting declared, 'hates democracy as much as it hates sin.' But constant sermonizing against Jacobinism served also to keep the matter in the front of the public consciousness. In

1. These words are put into the mouth of a Methodist preacher in a radical tract, *A Dialogue between a Methodist Preacher and a Reformer* (Newcastle, 1819), but they faithfully represent Methodist sermons of the time.   2. *Political Register*, 3 January 1824.

times of hardship or of mounting political excitement all the 'pent-up hostility' [1] in the mind of the Methodist working man might break out; and, with the rapidity of a revivalist campaign, Jacobin or Radical ideas might spread 'like fire in the whins'.

Moreover, we should remember the tension between spiritual and temporal egalitarianism characteristic of Lutheranism. In the Old Testament working people found more than a vengeful authoritarian God; they also found an allegory of their own tribulations. It is this body of symbolism (together with *Pilgrim's Progress*) which was held in common by chiliasts, 'Johannas', 'Jumpers' and orthodox Wesleyans. No ideology is wholly absorbed by its adherents: it breaks down in practice in a thousand ways under the criticism of impulse and of experience: the working-class community injected into the chapels its own values of mutual aid, neighbourliness and solidarity. Moreover, we must realize what incredible mumbo-jumbo those Hebrew genealogies, anathemas, and chronicles must have seemed when set beside the daily experience of weavers or miners. Here and there texts would spring to the eye, applicable to almost any context, and it was as likely that they should appear as figures of the class struggle as of the spiritual pilgrimage. This was the case of the 'underground' of 1801, when it was credibly reported that Lancashire conspirators took an oath based upon Ezekiel:

And thou, profane wicked prince of Israel, whose day is come, when iniquity shall have an end,

Thus saith the Lord God; Remove the diadem, and take off the crown: this shall not be the same: exalt him that is low, and abase him that is high.

I will overturn, overturn, overturn it: and it shall be no more, until he come whose right it is; and I will give it to him ...

The sword, the sword is drawn: for the slaughter it is furbished, to consume because of the glittering.[2]

1. Cf. E. Fromm, *Fear of Freedom* (1960 edn), pp. 81–3.

2. R. F. Wearmouth, *Methodism and Working-Class Movements, 1800–1850*, p. 61: Ezekiel, XXI, 25–28. It is interesting to note that this text was also used by English Levellers: cf. Gerrard Winstanley, *Fire in the Bush* (1650): 'You oppressing powers of the world ... do you remember this? Your overturning, overturning, overturning, is come on to you ...' For another example, see below, p. 560.

We see it also in the language of one of the unpaid Ministers of the Independent Methodists of the Newcastle district – a group which broke away after the expulsions of Radical lay preachers in 1819:

Unequal laws, and a partial administration, plant a thorn in every breast, and spread a gloom in every countenance. . . . It may be justly said of such rulers, Their vine is the vine of Sodom, and the fields of Gomorrah; their grapes are grapes of gall, their clusters are bitter; their wine is the poison of dragons, and the cruel venom of asps. But in the kingdom of the Messiah, peace flows as a river. . . . The rod of God's strength, which comes out of Zion, is not a rod of oppression.[1]

In this way even the 'fortresses' of the Sunday schools might breed rebellion. A collecting sheet [2] of the early nineteenth century from Todmorden, in which all subscribers to the strike fund are listed by their chosen pseudonyms, gives us the feel of this period, when the chapel and the pub made common cause in a moment of industrial crisis:

	£	s.	d.
One who is sorry to see a Man who is crowned with the Silver mantle of time, corroborate the truths of Solomon, Prov. 27th., verse 22nd.	0	2	6
A Salt chap with an Ass	0	0	2
Stand True	0	0	6
Hare and Hounds Inn	0	0	6
Love mercy, do justice	0	0	4
Hang th' old chap	0	0	2
Jam a Tum's wife	0	0	2
Amicus	0	1	0
Royal George Inn	0	1	0
Tell Old Robertshaw to read the 13th. verse in the 22nd chap. of Jeremiah	0	0	6
Eastwood Weavers	0	5	4

1. Hugh Kelly, *The Stone Cut Out of the Mountain* (Newcastle,1821), p. 13: H. Kelly, *An Impartial History of Independent Methodism* (Newcastle, 1824).

2. Placard in author's possession. The recommended reading from Jeremiah is: 'Woe unto him that buildeth his house by unrighteousness, and his chambers by wrong; that useth his neighbour's service without wages, and giveth him not for his work.'

	£	s.	d.
If Dick o' Jos's wife duzzant give ower burning the Reports, Old Thunderbout Clogs will tell about her wareing half a crown of a Sunday Bustle	0	4	3½
A chap bout jacket	0	0	2
Cut his tail off and sew it on again for punishment	0	0	4

But in the years between 1790 and 1830 it would be as ridiculous to describe the participation of rebellious Methodist lay preachers and others in extreme Radical agitations as a 'Methodist contribution' to the working-class movement, as it would be to describe the practice of free love among extreme Antinomians as a 'Puritan contribution' towards sexual liberation. Both are *reactive* cultural patterns; but just as the Puritan sexual rebel (like Lawrence) remains a 'Puritan' in his deep concern for 'a right relation' between men and women, so the Methodist political rebel carried through into his radical or revolutionary activity a profound moral earnestness, a sense of righteousness and of 'calling', a 'Methodist' capacity for sustained organizational dedication and (at its best) a high degree of personal responsibility. We see this in those Methodists who took part in the Pentridge rising – one of whom, executed at Derby for high treason, 'had been the ablest local preacher in the Circuit'.[1] We see it in the better qualities of Samuel Bamford, and in the self-discipline which he brought to the demonstrators of 1819. We see it in Loveless, the Dorchester labourer and 'Tolpuddle Martyr'. Whenever popular agitation grew in intensity, this form of 'heresy' became evident. Indeed, by the 1830s – despite all the attempts of Bunting's old guard to hold the position by anathemas and expulsions – whole communities, in particular of weavers and stockingers, had come to combine their Methodism and their Chartism.

There were other factors which influenced this process. By the early nineteenth century there was a marked tension between the professionalized Wesleyanism of the stipendiary ministry and the voluntarism of the lay preachers. The secession of the Kilhamite New Connexion had by no means ended the feelings of resentment felt by many laymen at the vesting of the supreme government of orthodox Methodism in the

1. Benjamin Gregory, *Autobiographical Recollections* (1903), pp. 126–9.

hands of an arbitrarily nominated circle of ministers. Again
and again Cobbett lampooned the Methodist Conference as
the 'CONCLAVE'. He presented it as a new bureaucracy,
composed of 'the most busy and persevering set of men on
earth', intent upon preserving their worldly interests, and in
perpetuating a new hereditary priesthood, living in comfort
off the tributary pennies of the poor. He saw in Wesley's school,
Kingswood, the machinery for perpetuating a new élite.[1] It
was the professional ministry, and not the local preachers,
whom Cobbett accused of being 'the bitterest foes of freedom
in England':

... hostile to freedom as the established clergy have been, their
hostility has been nothing in point of virulence compared with that
of these ruffian sectarians. ... Books upon books they write. Tracts
upon tracts. Villainous sermons upon villainous sermons they
preach. Rail they do ... against the West Indian slave-holders; but
not a word do you ever hear from them against the slave-holders
in Lancashire and in Ireland. On the contrary, they are continually
telling the people here that they ought to thank the Lord ... not
for a bellyful and a warm back, but for that abundant grace of
which they are the bearers, and for which they charge them only
one penny per week each.[2]

Cobbett's attacks were not wholly disinterested. He had
attacked the Methodists, in the same unmeasured way, but for
the opposite reasons, in his Tory days, when he discovered that
several of Colonel Despard's associates were Methodists.[3] This
was one of his consistent prejudices. And he was enraged, in
the early 1820s, not only by the high Toryism of Bunting and

1. 'The members of this Conference have a School at *King's Wood*,
at which *their* sons (and not the sons of their congregations,) are *educated* ! . . This, too, is maintained at the expense of the congregations.
... The sons, thus educated, sally out, in due time, to be *gentlemen*;
that is to say ... to be Excisemen, Tax-gatherers, Clerks and Officers of
various sorts.' *Political Register*, 27 January 1820.

2. Ibid., 3 January 1824.

3. Ibid., 23 July 1803: 'Of the six traitors ... executed with Despard
... *three* were *Methodists*, and had a methodist teacher to attend them
in their last moments. ... The sect consists chiefly of grovelling wretches
in and about great towns and manufacturing places ...' Cf. T. E. Owen,
Methodism Unmasked (1802).

the 'CONCLAVE' but also by the facility with which the Methodist Church tapped the pennies of the very same men who attended Radical demonstrations. But without doubt many of the lay preachers and class leaders shared his dislike of the full-time ministry, as well as of such practices as pew-rents and privileges for the wealthy. And this dislike Cobbett was at pains to foster. 'A man who had been making shoes all the week,' he wrote, 'will not preach the worse for that on the Sunday.'

There are thousands upon thousands of labourers and artizans and manufacturers, who never yet attempted to preach, and who are better able to do it than the members of the Conference, who for the far greater part have been labourers and artizans, and who have become *preachers*, because it was pleasanter to *preach* than to *work*.

The 'pious and disinterested' unpaid local preachers (in Cobbett's picture) were being '*kept down*' by the 'haughty oligarchy of the Conference:

The Dons of the Conference scowl upon them; treat them as interlopers; send them off into little villages to preach to half dozens, or half scores; while they themselves preach to thousands. Now, it ought to be a point with the Methodists all over the kingdom to go to hear none but these disinterested men; and, if the Conference shut them out of the chapels, they ought to hear them at their own houses, to follow them into barns or under trees.

The other 'remedy' which Cobbett proposed to the Methodists was to '*withold their pennies*'; or, at least, to withhold them from all ministers except reformers.[1]

It is not clear whether many Methodists followed Cobbett's advice; or whether he gave the advice because it was already being taken. But he certainly helps us to understand the character of the many breakaway sects – notably the Primitive Methodists and Bible Christians – in the first decades of the nineteenth century. Whereas the Kilhamite secession had displayed a vertical split within the Church, in which the more intellectual members had broken away, the secessions of this period were, above all, horizontal splits, in which lay preachers and their

1. Ibid., 27 January 1820, 13 January 1821.

congregations severed themselves from the professional ministry. The Bible Christians arose because a zealous layman, William O'Bryan, found that the Methodist Establishment refused to recognize his calling. He took to free-lance preaching in north Devon, ignoring the disciplinary restraints of the society, and was excluded as a 'walking beggar'. He took his groups of converted with him. To read the biography of Bunting beside that of Hugh Bourne, the earnest mill-wright and joiner (called in to improvise machinery, repair timbering, or do iron work at collieries or 'mountain farms' in Staffordshire) who founded the Primitive Methodists, is to pass between two different worlds. 'Our chapels,' Bourne recalled, 'were the coal-pit banks, or any other place; and in our conversation way, we preached the Gospel to all, good or bad, rough or smooth.'[1] The local Wesleyan Establishment was little interested in the converts whom Bourne and Clowes were making in the pits and pottery towns. The evangelistic zeal which led to the first camp-meetings at Mow Cop (1807 and 1808) was promptly disowned.

Bunting looked down upon the workers from the heights of connexional intrigue; Bourne and Clowes were *of* the working people. Bunting was intent upon ushering Methodism to a seat on the right hand of the Establishment; the Primitives still lived in the world of hardship and persecution of Wesleyanism's origin. We can scarcely discuss the two Churches in the same terms. The preaching of the Primitives was as hard as the lives of their congregations; it required (Dr Hobsbawm has said) the sharpest contrast 'between the gold of the redeemed and the flame-shot black of the damned'. But this was not preached *at*, but *by*, the poor. In this and other sects, the local preachers made the Church their own; and for this reason these sects contributed far more directly to the later history of trade unionism and political Radicalism than the orthodox Connexion.[2]

1. J. T. Wilkinson, *Hugh Bourne, 1772–1852* (1952), pp. 21–32. See also the same author's life of William Clowes.

2. See E. J. Hobsbawm, *Primitive Rebels*, ch. 8. The Primitive Methodists numbered 200 in 1811, 7,842 in 1820. See H. B. Kendall, op. cit., p. 31.

There was one other context in which Methodism of *any* variety necessarily assumed a more class-conscious form: in the rural areas. The chapel in the agricultural village was inevitably an affront to the vicar and the squire, and a centre in which the labourer gained independence and self-respect. Once again, it was the influence of the Primitive Methodists – notably in East Anglia – which was to prove most remarkable. But we can see the logic in a pamphlet by an irate country parson of 1805 – several years before the Primitive Methodists were founded.[1] The field labourers converted to Methodism were accused of all kinds of seditious intentions. They say, 'That Corn and all other fruits of the earth, are grown and intended by Providence, as much for the poor as the rich.' They were less content with their wages, less ready 'to work extraordinary hours as the exigencies of their masters might require'. Worse, instead of recouping themselves for the next week's labour, they exhausted themselves on Sundays walking several miles to hear a preacher. On week-nights instead of going straight to bed, they wasted fire and candles, singing hymns – a sight the parson had been horrified to see 'in some of our poorest cottages at so late an hour as nine ... of a winter's evening'. Many years later George Howell emphasized the perpetuation of these attitudes among the gentry, when commenting on the case of the Dorchester labourers. Methodism was 'a shocking offence in those days in many villages, especially in Dorset and other West counties. Indeed, next to poaching, it was the gravest of all offences.'

In all these ways, tensions were continually generated within the heart of a religion whose theological tenets were those of submissiveness and the sanctification of labour. The fullest development of this reactive dialectic belongs to the later history of trade unionism among the miners and rural workers, and to the history of Chartism. But it finds its origin in the decades 1810–30, when such Chartist leaders as Ben Rushton of Halifax and John Skevington of Loughborough went through their formative years. Rushton, a hand-loom weaver born in 1785, and local preacher with the Methodist New

1. *A Letter to a County Gentleman on the Subject of Methodism* (Ipswich, 1805).

Connexion, was active in Radical politics at the time of Peterloo, was probably imprisoned, and either expelled or withdrew
from the Connexion at the time of Cobbett's appeal to Methodists to refuse to pay their dues. He was active again in the Poor
Law agitation and on behalf of the hand-loom weavers in the
early 1830s. In 1839, at one of the first of the great Chartist
camp-meetings (themselves modelled upon the Primitive
Methodists) several local preachers spoke along with Rushton.
One of them, William Thornton, opened the proceedings with
prayer – that 'the wickedness of the wicked may come to an
end' – and Feargus O'Connor clapped him on the shoulder,
saying: 'Well done, Thornton, when we get the People's
Charter I will see that you are made Archbishop of York.'
Another moved a resolution binding the meeting 'not to attend
any place of worship where the administration of services is
inimical to civil liberty ... but to meet in such a way and
manner in our separate localities in future as the circumstances of the case require'. Ben Rushton seconded the resolution, declaring: 'For himself he had given nothing to the
parsons since 1821, and the next penny they had from him
would do them good.' Another local preacher, Hanson, added
his denunciations of the clergy:

> They preached Christ and a crust, passive obedience and non-
> resistance. Let the people keep from those churches and chapels
> ('We will!'). Let them go to those men who preached Christ and a
> full belly, Christ and a well-clothed back – Christ and a good house
> to live in – Christ and Universal Suffrage.[1]

Men like Rushton, Thornton and Hanson made a contribution to the Chartist movement it is impossible to overestimate.
We see it in the character of the camp-meetings, and the fervour
of the Chartist hymns, such as 'Sons of Poverty Assemble':

> See the brave, ye spirit-broken,
> Who uphold your righteous cause:
> Who against them hath not spoken?
> They are, just as Jesus was,
> Persecuted
> By bad men and wicked laws.

1. B. Wilson, op. cit., p. 3; *Halifax Guardian*, 25 May 1839. Hanson
was expelled by the Methodists for this speech.

Rouse them from their silken slumbers,
  Trouble them amidst their pride;
Swell your ranks, augment your numbers,
  Spread the Charter far and wide:
    Truth is with us,
    God himself is on our side.[1]

We see it in the Plug Rioters who marched into Halifax singing the 'Old Hundredth'. We see it in the slogans, such as the great banner carried at one Chartist demonstration by the weavers of Rushton's village of Ovenden: 'Be not ye afraid of them, remember the Lord, who is great and terrible, and fight for your brethren, your sons and your daughters, your wives and your houses.'[2] We see it in the Chartist chapels; in the Spen Valley, where Deacon Priestley had given wheat to 'Christ's poor', where John Nelson had seen Satan on Gomersal Hill-Top, where Southcottians, Antinomians and Methodist Luddites were to be found at the opening of the century, we now have such a chapel, in the 1840s, at which we have an account of Rushton preaching, from the text, 'The poor ye have always with you.' The poor he divided into three classes: the halt and the blind, who were 'God's poor': the idle and reckless, who deserved to be left to look after themselves:

Then, thirdly, there were the poor who had striven and worked hard all their lives, but who had been made poor, or kept poor by the wrong-doing and oppressions of others. . . . With fiery eloquence he went on to denounce the men who refused political justice to their neighbours, and who held them down till their life was made one long desperate struggle for mere existence.

As his eloquence and indignation gathered force, 'the feelings of the audience were manifested by fervid ejaculations . . . until at last one, carried away by Mr Rushton's strong denunciation of oppressors, cried out, "Ay, damn 'em, damn 'em."[3]

While such men as Rushton brought exceptional moral

1. *National Chartist Hymn Book.*
2. *Halifax Guardian*, 21 April 1848. See also the slogans of 1819, below, p. 760.
3. F. Peel, *Spen Valley, Past and Present* (Heckmondwike, 1893), pp. 317–19.

fervour to the movement in many districts nothing would be more mistaken than to suppose that they were predisposed to favour the 'moral force' (as opposed to 'physical force') party within Chartism. On the contrary, they served a God of Battles whom the men of the New Model Army would have understood; and more than a few former lay preachers were willing to speak to the text, 'He that hath no sword let him sell his garment and buy one.' Rushton – described by a friend as 'as steady, fearless, and honest a politician as ever stood upon an English platform' – was willing to lead the Plug Rioters (and to incur another term of imprisonment); and, when in his sixties, he was still campaigning and speaking on behalf of Ernest Jones. The weaver-preacher was in demand until his death; now we find him preaching in worn clothing and clogs at an anniversary service in a weaving hamlet to a congregation in 'their best clothes, namely, clogs and working clothes, including long brats or bishops'; now we find him tramping many miles every night, in an effort to keep the spirit alive in struggling Chartist branches. (Once a young colleague noted that Rushton's clogs were worn through to the sock. 'Ay,' said the old man, pausing only a moment in his political discourse, 'but think of the reward hereafter.') His death, in 1853, was the occasion for a great Chartist funeral; since Rushton had stipulated that no paid priest should officiate, the orations were delivered by Gammage and Ernest Jones.[1]

But Jabez Bunting and Ben Rushton did not belong to the same worlds. It is only by doing violence to the imagination that we can conceive of the Chartist weaver and the authoritarian clergyman as ever having been connected in a common 'movement'. For who was Rushton but the Adam whom Bunting's God had cursed?

1. *Commonwealth*, 16 November 1866; *People's Paper*, 2 July 1853; *History of Luddenden Dean Chapel* (1928), p. 5. For a man of similar force and integrity, from the Primitive Methodists, John Skevington of Loughborough, see Harrison, 'Chartism in Leicester' in A. Briggs, *Chartist Studies* (1959), pp. 70 ff.

[12]

Community

I. LEISURE AND PERSONAL RELATIONS

THE Methodist Revival of the war years mediated the work-discipline of industrialism. It was also, in some part, a reflex of despair among the working population. Methodism and Utilitarianism, taken together, make up the dominant ideology of the Industrial Revolution. But in Methodism we see only the clearest expression of processes at work within a whole society. Many of its features were reproduced in the evangelical movement in all the churches, and in the social teaching of some Utilitarians and Deists. Hannah More held quite as strongly as Wesley to the view that it was a 'fundamental error to consider children as innocent beings', rather than as beings of 'a corrupt nature and evil dispositions'.[1] And in the Sunday schools which were promoted by the Church of England in many villages in the 1790s and 1800s we find exactly the same emphasis (although sometimes with a more paternalist tone) upon discipline and repression as we have noted in the schools of Stockport or Halifax. Their function is uniformly described as being to cherish in the children of the poor 'a spirit of industry, economy, and piety'; Sunday school teachers at Caistor (Lincs) were instructed to—

... tame the ferocity of their unsubdued passions – to repress the excessive rudeness of their manners – to chasten the disgusting and demoralizing obscenity of their language – to subdue the stubborn rebellion of their wills – to render them honest, obedient, courteous, industrious, submissive, and orderly ...[2]

1. H. More, *Strictures on the Modern System of Female Education* (1799), p. 44.
2. R. C. Russell, *History of Elementary Schools & Adult Education in Nettleton and Caistor* (Caistor, 1960), pp. 5, 7.

The pressures towards discipline and order extended from the factory, on one hand, the Sunday school, on the other, into every aspect of life: leisure, personal relationships, speech, manners. Alongside the disciplinary agencies of the mills, churches, schools, and magistrates and military, quasi-official agencies were set up for the enforcement of orderly moral conduct. It was Pitt's moral lieutenant, Wilberforce, who combined the ethos of Methodism with the unction of the Establishment, and who was most active between 1790 and 1810 in this cause. In 1797 he expounded at length 'the grand law of subordination', and laid down articles for the management of the poor:

... that their more lowly path has been allotted to them by the hand of God; that it is their part faithfully to discharge its duties and contentedly to bear its inconveniences; that the present state of things is very short; that the objects, about which wordly men conflict so eagerly, are not worth the contest ...[1]

By 1809 he was satisfied that overt Jacobinism was no longer a danger; but in every manifestation of moral indiscipline he saw the danger of Jacobin revival. 'We are alive to the political offence,' he wrote, 'but to the moral crime we seem utterly insensible.'

In this he was too modest, since his own Society for the Suppression of Vice had clocked up 623 successful prosecutions for breaking the Sabbath laws in 1801 and 1802 alone.[2] But his conviction as to the intimate correlation between moral levity and political sedition among the lower classes is characteristic of his class. Prosecutions for drunken and lewd behaviour increased; Blake's old enemy, Bishop Watson of Llandaff, preached a sermon in 1804 in which he found the rôle of the common informer to be 'a noble Design ... both in a religious and in a political Point of View'. The amusements of the poor were preached and legislated against until even

1. W. Wilberforce, *A Practical View of the Prevailing Religious System of Professed Christians* (1797), pp. 405–6.

2. See L. Radzinowicz, op. cit., III, pp. 504–6, and Parts 3 and 4 *passim*. See also G. R. Taylor, op. cit., p. 36: '... the period of decisive moral change was not at the time of Victoria's accession, or even in the nineteenth century at all, but ... during the decade 1790–1800'.

the most innocuous were regarded in a lurid light. The Society for the Suppression of Vice extended its sphere of interference to 'two-penny hops, gingerbread fairs, and obscene pictures'.[1] Nude sea bathers were persecuted as if they were forerunners of tumbrils and guillotine. 'With regard to adultery,' wrote John Bowdler darkly, 'as it was punished capitally by the Jewish law, some think it ought to be so ... among us.' The Evangelical exhorted the upper classes to reform their own manners as an example to the poor. In 'Society' itself the post-revolutionary years saw 'an increased reserve of manner ... fatal to conviviality and humour'.[2]

The process of social discipline was not uncontested. The attempt of Dr Bowdler's supporters to carry new legislation for the imprisonment of adulterers foundered in the House of Commons; unlike penalties imposed upon common Sabbathbreakers, vagrants, tinkers, stage-dancers and tumblers, ballad-singers, free-thinkers and naked bathers, legislation against adultery was open to objection in that it might discriminate against the amusement of the rich as well as of the poor. And other attempts to interfere with the leisure of the people were thrown out by the House of Commons, on slender majorities made up of one part *laissez faire* inertia, one part Foxite defence of the liberty of the subject, and one part traditional Tory tolerance for 'bread and circuses' and dislike for Methodistical 'fanaticism'. (An irony of the time was the defence by the War Minister, Windham, of bull-baiting against both Evangelicals and reformers – a defence which led to the cry going up, from Satan's strongholds, of 'Windham and Liberty!')

But if the disciplinarians lost a few legislative skirmishes, they won the battle of the Industrial Revolution; and in the process the 'Irish' temperament often attributed to the eighteenth-century English poor in town and countryside was translated into the methodical way of life of industrial capitalism. In the countryside this can be seen most clearly in the triumph of the money-economy over the casual, 'uneconomic' rhythms of peasant semi-subsistence. In the industrial areas it

1. *Gorgon*, 24 April 1819.
2. T. Moore, *Life of Sheridan* (1825), p. 217.

can be seen in the extension of the discipline of the factory bell or clock from working to leisure hours, from the working-day to the Sabbath, and in the assault upon 'Cobbler's Monday' and traditional holidays and fairs.

Although the economic functions of the eighteenth-century fair were still of great importance – annual 'hirings', horse and cattle fairs, sale of miscellaneous commodities – we should not forget their equal importance in the cultural life of the poor. Still, in the early days of the Industrial Revolution, the working man's year was made up of cycles of hardship and short commons, punctuated with 'feast' days when drink and meat were more plentiful, luxuries like oranges and ribbons were bought for the children, dancing, courtship, convivial visiting and sports took place. Until late in the nineteenth century there was still a network of fairs held throughout the country (many of which authority tried in vain to limit or proscribe), at which a fraternity of pedlars, card-sharpers, real or pretended gipsies, ballad-mongers and hawkers were in attendance.[1] A Northumberland diarist of 1750 describes Whit Monday:

... went to Carton Sports – a Saddle, bridle, whip, etc. all to be Gallopt for. ... Abundance of young men and women diverted themselves with the game or pastime here that they call Losing their Suppers. ... And after all they ended their recreation with Carrouzing at the Ale-houses and ye men Kissing and toying away most of the night with their Mistresses ...

Three weeks later there was the Lebberston Sport – 'a Copper Pan was play'd for at Quoites ... there was also a Dove neatly deckt and adorned with Ribbons of divers colours and other fine Trappings which was danced for by the Country Girls ...'[2] In 1783 a Bolton magistrate complained that – at a time when oatmeal was selling at two guineas a load—

there was so little appearance of want in this township that one evening I met a very large procession of young men and women with fiddles, garlands, and other ostentation of rural finery, dancing

1. The reader will recall Hardy's Wessex novels. For an account of some of the fairs in the 1830s, see *First Report of the Constabulary Commission*, pp. 30–42.

2. Beswick MS. Diary, cited in G. R. Taylor, op. cit., p. 16.

Morris dances in the highway merely to celebrate an idle anniversary, or, what they had been pleased to call for a year or two, a fair at a paltry thatched alehouse upon the neighbouring common.[1]

It is tempting to explain the decline of old sports and festivals simply in terms of the displacement of 'rural' by 'urban' values. But this is misleading. The more robust entertainments, whether in their ugly form of animal baiting and pugilism, or in more convivial festivities, were as often, or more often, to be found in the eighteenth century in London or the great towns as in the countryside. They continued into the nineteenth century with a vigour which recalls both the unruly traditions of the London apprentices of Tudor times, and also the very large proportion of nineteenth-century Londoners who were immigrants from the village. The greatest festival of all was Bartholomew Fair, with its menageries, pickpockets, pantomimes of Harlequin and Faustus, card sharpers, plays, exhibitions of wild men and of horsemanship. In 1825 the *Trades Newspaper* complained:

For weeks previous it is denounced from the pulpit and the press, and stories are raked up of apprentices led away from the paths of honesty, of ruined maids of all-work, of broken heads and brawlings ...[2]

In the previous decade the authorities had feared that the Fair would become 'the general rendezvous for sedition and the signal for insurrection'.[3]

On the other hand, the Industrial Revolution, which drained the countryside of some of its industries and destroyed the balance between rural and urban life, created also in our own minds an image of rural isolation and 'idiocy'. The urban culture of eighteenth-century England was more 'rural' (in its customary connotations), while the rural culture was more rich, than we often suppose. 'It is a great error to suppose,' Cobbett insisted, 'that people are rendered stupid by remaining always in the same place.' And most of the new industrial towns did not so much displace the countryside as grow *over*

1. B. T. Barton, *Historical Gleanings of Bolton* (Bolton, 1881), I, p. 263.

2. 11 September 1825.

3. *Sherwin's Weekly Political Register*, 15 September 1817.

it. The most common industrial configuration of the early nineteenth century was a commercial or manufacturing centre which served as the hub for a circle of straggling industrial villages. As the villages became suburbs, and the farmlands were covered over with brick, so the great conurbations of the late nineteenth century were formed.

But there was nothing in this process so violent as to enforce a disruption of older traditions. In south Lancashire, the Potteries, the West Riding and the Black Country local customs, superstitions, and dialect were neither severed nor transplanted: the village or small town craftsman grew into the industrial worker. Bamford has testified in his *Early Days* to the vigour of tradition in Lancashire weaving villages at the turn of the century. There were the tales of witches, boggarts, 'fyerin'; the furious pugilism and the cock-fighting; the customs, such as 'pace-egging' (at Easter) or 'Riding the Black Lad'; the holidays with their traditional celebrations – Christmas, Shrove-Tide, 'Cymbalin Sunday', and 'Rushbearing' in August when morris dancers were to be found in Middleton, Oldham or Rochdale:

> My new shoon they are so good,
> I cou'd doance morrice if I wou'd;
> An' if hat an' sark be drest,
> I will doance morrice wi' the best.

Or there was 'Mischief-neet', on 1 May, when lads would leave signs on the doorsteps of the village women:

A gorse bush indicated a woman notoriously immodest; and a holly bush, one loved in secret; a tup's horn intimated that man or woman was faithless to marriage; a branch of sapling, truth in love; and a sprig of birch, a pretty girl.[1]

We may set beside Bamford's picture of the 1790s Joseph Lawson's reminiscences of a 'backward' clothing village in the West Riding – Pudsey – in the 1820s, with the old and new ways of life at a moment of transition. The houses were scattered 'as if they had sprung up from seeds dropped unawares', the roads unlighted and unflagged, the groups of houses ap-

1. *Early Days*, chs. 13 to 16.

proached by crooked folds and passages. Rooms are low, windows small without sashes:

There is dense ignorance of sanitary science. A doctor comes into a house where there is fever, and he knocks a pane of glass out with his stick, his first dose of medicine being fresh air.

Most of the houses are without ovens but have a 'bakstone' for baking. The stone floors are sanded, furniture is plain and sparse: 'in some houses there is an oaken chest or kist – a family heirloom, or a small cupboard fastened up in a corner, and a delfcase for pots and plates'. Water is scarce, and on wash-days queues of twenty or thirty may form at the wells. Coal and candles are dear, and in the winter neighbours gather to share each other's fires. Baking and brewing are done at home; white bread and meat are regarded as luxuries: 'oatcake, brown bread, porridge pudding, skimmed milk, potatoes, and home-brewed beer, which they always call 'drink', are the principal articles of food'.

The sparse routine is broken by occasional 'tides' or feasts, when 'a bit of beef' is bought, and all go to the fair, where gingerbread, fruit, and toys are sold, there are peep-shows of the Battle of Waterloo, Punch and Judy shows, gambling stalls, swings; and a customary 'love market', where the young men court the girls with 'tidings' of brandy-snaps and nuts. Very few of the working people can read well enough to read a newspaper; although papers are taken (and read aloud) at the blacksmith's, the barber's and several public houses. Much of the news still comes by way of broadsheet vendors and street singers. Old superstitions are a living source of terror to old and young. There are ghosts at Jumble's Well, Bailey Gallows, Boggard Lane; parents commonly discipline their children by shutting them 'in cellars and other dark places for the black boggards to take them'. 'Another most serious and mischievous superstition, everywhere prevalent, was the belief that when any child died, it was the will of the Lord that it should be so.' Sanitary reformers were regarded as 'Infidels'. Dogfighting and cock-fighting were common; and it was also common at feast-times 'to see several rings formed, in which men stripped to their bare skin would fight sometimes by the

hour together, till the combatants were not recognizable ...'
Drunkenness was rife, especially at holidays and on 'Cobbler's
Monday', which was kept by weavers and burlers as well as
cobblers. But there were plenty of less violent pastimes: knur
and spell, 'duck knop', and football through the streets. The
village was clannish within, and a closed community to outsiders from only two or three miles distant. Some very old
traditions survived, such as 'Riding the Stang', whereby if a
man was known to ill-use his wife, or a woman was thought
to be lewd, a straw effigy would be carried through the streets
by a hooting crowd, and then burnt by the offender's door.[1]

So far from extinguishing local traditions, it is possible that
the early years of the Industrial Revolution saw a growth in
provincial pride and self-consciousness. South Lancashire and
the West Riding were not rural wildernesses before 1780; they
had been centres of domestic industry for two centuries. As
the new factory discipline encroached upon the hand-worker's
way of life, and as the Corporation and Coronation Streets
were built over Yep-fowd and Frogg Hole and T'Hollins, so
self-consciousness was sharpened by loss, and a quasi-
nationalist sentiment mingles with class feeling in the culture
of the industrial workers (new machines versus old customs,
London tyranny or 'foreign' capital against the local clothier,
Irish labour undercutting the native weaver). George Condy, a
leading publicist of the 10 Hour Movement, wrote a foreword
to Roby's *Traditions of Lancashire* (1830); Bamford was only
one among a score of plebeian authors who followed in the
steps of the eighteenth-century 'Tim Bobbin', in celebrating
and idealizing local customs and dialect.

But this was a conscious resistance to the passing of an old
way of life, and it was frequently associated with political
Radicalism.[2] As important in this passing as the simple physical
loss of commons and 'playgrounds',[3] was the loss of leisure
in which to play and the repression of playful impulses. The

1. J. Lawson, *Progress n udsey, passim.*
2. Cobbett springs to mind. But William Hone perhaps did more to
record old customs, publishing his *Date Book, Every-Day Book,* and
Table Book, as well as Strutt's *Sports and Pastimes,* all in the 1820s.
3. See the Hammonds, *The Black Age,* ch. 6.

Puritan teaching of Bunyan or Baxter were transmitted in their entirety by Wesley: 'Avoid all lightness, as you would avoid hell-fire; and trifling, as you would cursing and swearing. Touch no woman ...' Card-playing, coloured dresses, personal ornaments, the theatre – all came under Methodist prohibition. Tracts were written against 'profane' songs and dancing;[1] literature and arts which had no devotional bearing were profoundly suspect; the dreadful 'Victorian' Sabbath began to extend its oppression even before Victoria's birth.

A characteristic tract shows the extent of Methodist determination to uproot pre-industrial traditions from the manufacturing districts.[2] It had been noted at a Sheffield Quarterly Meeting in 1799 that some members were not 'altogether free from conforming to the custom of *visiting* or *receiving visits*, at the *annual Feast*'. Such feasts, known variously as 'Wakes' (Derbyshire and Staffordshire), 'Rushbearing' (Lancashire) and 'Revels' (west of England) might in origin have been permissible but had become 'dreadfully prostituted to the most diabolical purposes'. Time was spent in 'eating and drinking intemperately; talking prophanely, or at least unprofitably; in laughing and jesting, fornication and adultery ...' The least participation was 'fellowship with the unfruitful works of darkness'. Money was wasted by the poor which might have been saved; many contracted debts. Methodists who mixed in such festivities were exposed to the worldly ways of the unconverted – backsliding was a common result. They should refuse to entertain even friends and relatives (from among the unconverted) who might call; and if such visitors could not be turned from the door they should be entertained only by Bible-reading, holy discourse and hymn-singing:

1. Apologists had some difficulty with the reference in *Ecclesiastes* to 'a time to dance'. But since 'no instances of dancing are found upon record in the Bible, in which the two sexes united in the exercise', it was argued that the permission could only extend to members of *one* sex (segregated from the other) dancing upon a sacred occasion in full daylight on a weekday. (No such occasions are recorded.) See A. Young, *A Time to Dance* (Glasgow, n.d.); also Southey, op. cit. pp. 546–9.

2. Rev. James Wood, *An Address to the Members of the Methodist Societies* (1799), *passim*.

Oh, Brethren, what are we doing! There is death in the pot. The plague is begun. Wrath is gone forth against fruitless professors. The slumbers of sin are upon us ...

Other customary survivals, such as meat and drink at the funeral 'wake', came in for equal condemnation. Even the visiting of relatives on a normal Sabbath day could not be condoned, unless in cases of sudden sickness.[1]

The warmth of the argument suggests that in many places, like Bamford's Middleton, the struggle between the old way of life and the new discipline was sharp and protracted. And Lawson's account of Pudsey shows the 'chapel folk' as a group set *apart* from the community by their sombre manners. There were many who were brought up in devout families who reacted strongly against their upbringing, as did William Lovett:

... being obliged to frequent a place of worship three times of a Sunday, strictly prohibited all books but the Bible and Prayer Book, and not being allowed to enjoy a walk, unless to chapel ... are sufficient to account for those boyish feelings. My poor mother ... thought that the great power that has formed the numerous gay, sportive, singing things of earth and air, must above all things be gratified with the solemn faces, prim clothes, and half-sleepy demeanour of human beings; and that true religion consists in listening to the reiterated story of man's fall ...[2]

To many men in the post-war generation, such as Lovett, it seemed that it was the Methodists who were uncouth and backward. And this reminds us of the extreme difficulty in generalizing as to the moral tone and manners of working-class communities during the Industrial Revolution. It is clear that

1. The Wakes were important kinship occasions, when the townsfolk visited their kin in the country, and 'the married daughter came to her former home with her children'. Howitt, who described them as 'a short pause in the otherwise ever-going machinery of servitude', recounted how old people in the villages, when asked about their sons and daughters in the towns, would say: 'Well, well, we shall see them at the wake.' Even the disciplinary Wedgwood was defeated by the Wakes, which nust be observ'd though the Worla was to end with them': R. E. Leader, *Reminiscences of Old Sheffield* (Sheffield, 1876), pp. 200–202; W. Howitt, *Rural Life of England* (1838), I, p. 59, pp. 245–54; N. McKendrick, op. cit., p. 46.

2. Lovett, op. cit., I, p. 8.

between 1780 and 1830 important changes took place. The 'average' English working man became more disciplined, more subject to the productive tempo of 'the clock', more reserved and methodical, less violent and less spontaneous. Traditional sports were displaced by more sedentary hobbies:

The Athletic exercises of Quoits, Wrestling, Foot-ball, Prison-bars and Shooting with the Long-bow are become obsolete ... they are now Pigeon-fanciers, Canary-breeders and Tulip-growers —

or so a Lancashire writer complained in 1823.[1] Francis Place often commented upon a change, which he saw in terms of a growth in self-respect and an elevation in 'the character of the working-man'. 'Look even to Lancashire,' he wrote a month after Peterloo:

Within a few years a stranger walking through their towns was 'touted', i.e. hooted, and an 'outcomling' was sometimes pelted with stones. 'Lancashire brute' was the common and appropriate appellation. Until very lately it would have been dangerous to have assembled 500 of them on any occasion. Bakers and butchers would at the least have been plundered. Now 100,000 people may be collected together and no riot ensue ...[2]

It is here that evaluation becomes most difficult. While many contemporary writers, from Cobbett to Engels, lamented the passing of old English customs, it is foolish to see the matter only in idyllic terms. These customs were not all harmless or quaint. The unmarried mother, punished in a Bridewell, and perhaps repudiated by the parish in which she was entitled to relief, had little reason to admire 'merrie England'. The passing of Gin Lane, Tyburn Fair, orgiastic drunkenness, animal sexuality, and mortal combat for prize-money in iron-studded clogs, calls for no lament.

But, between old superstition and new bigotry, it is proper to be cautious when meeting the claims of the Evangelicals to have been an agency of intellectual enlightenment. We have already noted the tendency of the Methodists to harden into a sect, to keep their members apart from the contagion of the unconverted, and to regard themselves as being in a state of civil war with the ale-house and the denizens of Satan's strong-

. Guest, op. cit., pp. 38–9.   2. Wallas, op. cit., pp. 145–6.

holds. Where the Methodists were a minority group within a community, attitudes hardened on both sides; professions of virtue and declamations against sin reveal less about actual manners than they do about the rancour of hostilities. Moreover, the air of the early nineteenth century is thick with assertions and counter-assertions, especially where the values of handworkers and factory workers were in conflict, or those of the opponents and defenders of child labour. Critics of the factory system saw it as destructive of family life and constantly indicted the mills as centres of the grossest sexual immorality; the coarse language and independent manners of Lancashire mill-girls shocked many witnesses. Gaskell contrasted the idyllic innocence of the domestic workers, whose youth was spent in a pagan freedom which entailed the obligation of marriage only if conception took place, with the febrile promiscuity of the factory where some of the employers enacted scenes with the mill-girls which –

put to blush the lascivious Saturnalia of the Romans, the rites of the Pagoda girls of India, and the Harem life of the most voluptuous Ottoman.[1]

Such colourful accounts were, not unnaturally, resented not only by the employers but by the factory workers themselves. They pointed out that the illegitimacy rate in many rural districts compared unfavourably with that in mill-towns. In many mills the greatest propriety was enforced. If there were 'Ottomans' among the mill-owners, there were also paternalists who dismissed any girl detected in a moral lapse.

It is not easy to draw a balance. On the one hand, the claim that the Industrial Revolution raised the status of women would seem to have little meaning when set beside the record of excessive hours of labour, cramped housing, excessive child-bearing and terrifying rates of child mortality. On the other hand, the abundant opportunities for female employment in the textile districts gave to women the status of independent wage-earners. The spinster or the widow was freed from dependence upon relatives or upon parish relief. Even the unmarried mother might be able, through the laxness of 'moral

1. *The Manufacturing Population of England*, p. 64.

discipline' in many mills, to achieve an independence unknown before. In the largest silk-mills at Macclesfield, righteous employers prided themselves upon dismissing girls who made a single 'false step'. A witness who contrasted this with the easier-going manners of Manchester came up with observations disturbing to the moralist:

I find it very generally ... the case, that where the mills and factories are nearly free from mothers of illegitimate children, there the streets are infested with prostitutes; and on the contrary, where the girls are permitted to return to their work, afer giving birth to a child, there the streets are kept comparatively clear of those unhappy beings.[1]

The period reveals many such paradoxes. The war years saw a surfeit of sermonizing and admonitory tracts limiting or refuting claims to women's rights which were associated with 'Jacobinism'. Women's subordination in marriage was dictated in the bleakest terms. 'The Christian scriptures,' declared Paley, enjoin upon the wife an obedience in marriage 'in terms so peremptory and absolute, that it seems to extend to everything not criminal, or not entirely inconsistent with the women's happiness'.[2] But the same years see also a stubborn minority tradition, in the main among professional people and radical artisans in the great cities, which set forward claims more far-reaching than any known before the French Revolution. The claims made in the 1790s by Mary Wollstonecraft, William Blake and Thomas Spence were never wholly abandoned; they recur, not only in Shelley's circle, but also in the Radical publications of the post-war years. They were voiced, self-deprecatingly, in the *Black Dwarf*; more stridently in Richard Carlile's publications; most powerfully by Anna Wheeler and William Thompson and in the Owenite movement.[3] But it was in the textile districts that the changing economic status of

1 .W. Dodd, *The Factory System Illustrated*, p. 194. Margaret Hewitt discusses some of the evidence, in the main from post-1840 sources, in *Wives and Mothers in Victorian Industry* (1958), esp. ch. 5.

2. W. Paley, *Concise Admonitions for Youth* (1809), p. 68. See also T. Gisborne, *Enquiry into the Duties of the Female Sex* (1797), esp. pp. 226–9.

3. *Black Dwarf*, 9 and 30 September 1818; for Carlile and the Owenites, see below, ch. 16.

women gave rise to the earliest widespread participation by
working women in political and social agitation. In the last
years of the eighteenth century female benefit societies and
female Methodist classes may have given experience and self-
confidence – the claim of women to act as local preachers was
a persistent Wesleyan 'heresy'. But the war years, with their
increased demand for labour not only in the spinning-mills
but also at the hand-loom, accelerated the process.[1] In 1818
and 1819 the first Female Reform Societies were founded, in
Blackburn, Preston, Bolton, Manchester, Ashton-under-Lyne.
Samuel Bamford's account – if we may credit it – suggests a
sudden leap forward in consciousness. At a meeting in the
Saddleworth district, on the Lancashire-Yorkshire border,

I, in the course of an address, insisted on the right, and the propriety also, of females who were present at such assemblages voting
by a show of hand for or against the resolutions. This was a new
idea; and the women, who attended numerously on the bleak
ridge, were mightily pleased with it. The men being nothing dissentient, when the resolution was put the women held up their
hands amid much laughter; and ever from that time females voted
with the men at the Radical meetings. ... It became the practice,
female political unions were formed, with their chairwomen, committees, and other officials; and from us the practice was soon borrowed ... [by] religious and charitable institutions.[2]

(In Newcastle, at the same time, one of Jabez Bunting's correspondents was lamenting the default of the 'pious sisterhood'
who were embroidering reform banners.) The twenty years
between 1815 and 1835 see also the first indications of independent trade union action among women workers. John Wade,
commenting upon a strike of 1,500 female card-setters in the
West Riding in 1835, pointed the moral: 'Alarmists may view
these indications of female independence as more menacing
to established institutions than the "education of the lower
orders".'[3]

1. For the increase in the number of women weavers during the Wars,
see Ivy Pinchbeck, *Women Workers and the Industrial Revolution*
(1930), pp. 164–6.

2. *Passages in the Life of a Radical* (1893 edn), pp. 141–2.

3. J. Wade, *History of the Middle and Working Classes* (1835), pp.
570–71.

But there is a paradox of feeling even in this advance. The Radicalism of northern working women was compounded of nostalgia for lost status and the assertion of new-found rights. According to conventions which were deeply felt, the woman's status turned upon her success as a housewife in the family economy, in domestic management and forethought, baking and brewing, cleanliness and child-care. The new independence, in the mill or full-time at the loom, which made new claims possible, was felt simultaneously as a loss in status and in personal independence. Women became more dependent upon the employer or labour market, and they looked back to a 'golden' past in which home earnings from spinning, poultry, and the like, could be gained around their own door. In good times the domestic economy, like the peasant economy, supported a way of life centred upon the home, in which inner whims and compulsions were more obvious than external discipline. Each stage in industrial differentiation and specialization struck also at the family economy, disturbing customary relations between man and wife, parents and children, and differentiating more sharply between 'work' and 'life'. It was to be a full hundred years before this differentiation was to bring returns, in the form of labour-saving devices, back into the working woman's home. Meanwhile, the family was roughly torn apart each morning by the factory bell, and the mother who was also a wage-earner often felt herself to have the worst of both the domestic and the industrial worlds.

'Once we could have welcomed you, by spreading before you a board of English hospitality, furnished by our industry,' the Female Reformers of Bolton addressed William Cobbett in 1819: 'Once, we could have greeted you, with the roseate countenances of English females. ... We could have presented to your view our Cottages, vieing for cleanliness and arrangement with the Palace of our King.' The Female Reformers of Blackburn took up the same theme – their houses 'robbed of all their ornaments', their beds 'torn away ... by the relentless hand of the unfeeling tax-gatherer' so that 'borough-mongering tyrants' might repose on 'beds of down' while their families lay on the straw. Above all, they appealed on behalf of their children: 'we are daily cut to the heart to see them greedily devour the coarse food that some would scarcely give to their swine'. It was natural that they should respond to Cobbett, who was soon to consolidate their support with his *Cottage Economy*, and also to Oastler, with his emphasis upon 'the home'. Neither Cobbett nor Oastler gave the least support to the notion of women's suffrage, nor did the Female Reform Societies raise the demand on their own account. Their rôle was confined to giving moral support to the men, making banners and caps of liberty which were presented with ceremony at reform demonstrations, passing resolutions and addresses, and swelling the numbers at meeings.[1] But even these forms of participation called forth the abuse of their opponents. The 'petticoat reformers' of Manchester were described in the *Courier* as 'degraded females', guilty of 'the worst prostitution of the sex, the prostitution of the heart', 'deserting their station' and putting off the 'sacred characters' of wife and mother 'for turbulent vices of sedition and impiety'. Whatever his view on women's suffrage, Cobbett had no second thoughts about coming to the Female Reformers' aid:

Just as if women were made for nothing but to cook oat-meal and to sweep a room! Just as if women had no minds! Just as if Hannah Moore and the Tract Gentry had reduced the women of England to a level with the Negresses of Africa! Just as if England had never had a queen . . .![2]

II. THE RITUALS OF MUTUALITY

Again and again the 'passing of old England' evades analysis. We may see the lines of change more clearly if we recall that the Industrial Revolution was not a settled social context but a phase of transition between two ways of life. And we must see, not one 'typical' community (Middleton or Pudsey), but many different communities coexisting with each other. In south-east Lancashire alone there were to be found, within

1. The initiation of another tradition may be noted in an informer's report on the Manchester Political Union, 17 November 1819: 'The Union is *miserably poor*, having to solicit aid from the Female Union, not being able to pay their way' (H.O. 42.198).

2. *Political Register*, 23 October, 29 December 1819; Courier, 15 July 1819.

a few miles of each other, the cosmopolitan city of Manchester upon which migrants converged from every point in the kingdom; pit-villages (like the Duke of Bridgewater's collieries) emerging from semi-feudalism; paternal model villages (like Turton); new mill-towns (like Bolton); and older weaving hamlets. In all of these communities there were a number of converging influences at work, all making towards discipline and the growth in working-class consciousness.

The working-class community of the early nineteenth century was the product, neither of paternalism nor of Methodism, but in a high degree of conscious working-class endeavour. In Manchester or Newcastle the traditions of the trade union and the friendly society, with their emphasis upon self-discipline and community purpose, reach far back into the eighteenth century. Rules which survive of the Manchester small-ware weavers in the 1750s show already meticulous attention to procedure and to institutional etiquette. The committee members must sit in a certain order. The doors must be kept locked. There are careful regulations for the safe-keeping of the 'box' Members are reminded that 'Intemperance, Animosity and Profaneness are the Pest and Vermin that gnaw out the very Vitals of all Society.'

If we consider this Society, not as a Company of Men met to regale themselves with Ale and Tobacco, and talk indifferently on all Subjects: but rather as a Society sitting to Protect the Rights and Privileges of a Trade by which some hundreds of People ... subsist ... how awkward does it look to see its Members jumbled promiscuously one amongst another, talking indifferently on all Subjects ...

'Decency and Regularity' are the watchwords; it is even hoped that when 'Gentlemen and Magistrates' observe such order 'they will rather revere than punish such a Society'.[1]

This represents the code of the self-respecting artisan, although the hope that such sobriety would win the favour of the authorities was to be largely disappointed. It was in a similar school that such men as Hardy and Place received their education in London. But as the Industrial Revolution ad-

1. Wadsworth and Mann, op. cit., pp. 345-7.

vanced, it was this code (sometimes in the form of model rules) which was extended to ever-wider sections of working people. Small tradesmen, artisans, labourers – all sought to insure themselves against sickness, unemployment, or funeral expenses[1] through membership of 'box clubs' or friendly societies. But the discipline essential for the safe-keeping of funds, the orderly conduct of meetings and the determination of disputed cases, involved an effort of self-rule as great as the new disciplines of work. An examination of rules and orders of friendly societies in existence in Newcastle and district during the Napoleonic Wars gives us a list of fines and penalties more exacting than those of a Bolton cotton-master. A General Society imposed fines for any member 'reflecting upon' another member in receipt of sick money, being drunk on the Sabbath, striking another, 'calling one another bye-names', coming into the clubroom in liquor, taking God's name in vain. The Brotherhood of Maltsters added fines for drunkenness at *any* time, for failure to attend the funerals of brothers or of their wives. The Glass-Makers (founded as early as 1755) added fines for failure in attending meetings, or for those who refused to take their turn in the rota of officers; for failing to keep silence when ordered, speaking together, answering back the steward, betting in the club, or (a common rule) disclosing secrets outside the society. Further,

Persons that are infamous, of ill character, quarrelsome, or disorderly, shall not be admitted into this society. ... No Pitman, Collier, Sinker, or Waterman to be admitted ...

The Watermen, not to be outdone, added a rule excluding from benefits any brother sick through 'any illness got by lying with an unclean woman, or is clap't or pox'd'. Brothers were to be fined for ridiculing or provoking each other to passion. The Unanimous Society was to cut off benefits if any member in

1. Working people attached an exceptional valuation to the ceremony of funeral. A pauper funeral was the ultimate social disgrace. And ceremony bulked large in folk-lore, and preoccupied dying men. 'I could wish,' wrote a condemned Luddite 'for John Rawson, John Roberts, and John Roper to be my bearers; dear wife, choose the other three thyself': *The Surprising ... History of 'General Ludd'* (Nottingham, n.d.), p. 239.

receipt of sick money was found 'in ale-houses, gaming, or drunk'. To maintain its unanimity there were fines for members proposing 'discourse or dispute upon political or ecclesiastical matters, or government and governors'. The Friendly Society of All Trades had a rule similar to 'huffing' in draughts; there was a fine 'if any member has an opportunity of fining his brother, and does not'. The Cordwainers added fines for calling for drink or tobacco without leave of the stewards. The House-Carpenters and Joiners added a prohibition of 'disloyal sentiments' or 'political songs'.[1]

It is possible that some of these rules, such as the prohibition of political discourse and songs, should be taken with a pinch of salt. While some of these societies were select sick-clubs of as few as twenty or thirty artisans, meeting at an inn, others were probably covers for trade union activity; while at Newcastle, as at Sheffield, it is possible that after the Two Acts the formation of friendly societies was used as a cover for Jacobin organization. (A 'company' friendly society, in 1816, bore testimony to 'the loyal, patriotic, and peaceable regulations' of many Newcastle societies, but complained that these regulations were often insufficient to prevent 'warm debate and violent language'.)[2] The authorities were deeply suspicious of the societies during the war years, and one of the purposes of the rules was to secure registration with the local magistrates. But anyone familiar with procedure and etiquette in some trade unions and working-men's clubs today will recognize the origin of still-extant practices in several of the rules. Taken

1. *Laws and Orders of the Friendly Society who meet at the House of Mr Wm Forster* ... (N. Shields, 1795), p. 11; *Rules and Orders of the Brotherhood of Maltsters* (Newcastle, 1796), p. 6; *Articles, Laws and Rules of the Glass-makers Friendly Society* (Newcastle, 1800), pp. 5, 11, 15; *Articles* ... *of the Friendly Society of Watermen* (Newcastle, 1804), p. 11; *Articles of the Unanimous Society* (Newcastle, 1804), p. 11; *Articles* ... *of the Friendly Society of All Trades* (Newcastle, 1804), p. 9; *Articles* ... *of the Society of Cordwainers* (Hexham, 1806), p. 8; *Rules of the Philanthropic Society of House-Carpenters and Joiners* (Newcastle, 1812), p. 7; *Articles* ... *of the Miners Society* (Newcastle, 1817).

2. *A Short Account of the Benevolent Society* ... *at Messrs Angus Manufactory* (Newcastle, 1816).

together, they indicate an attainment of self-discipline and a diffusion of experience of a truly impressive order.[1]

Estimates of friendly society membership suggest 648,000 in 1793, 704,350 in 1803, 925,429 in 1815. Although registration with the magistrates, under the first Friendly Society Act of 1793, made possible the protection of funds at law in the event of defaulting officers, a large but unknown number of clubs failed to register, either through hostility to the authorities, parochial inertia, or through a deep secretiveness which, Dr Holland found, was still strong enough to baffle his enquiries in Sheffield in the early 1840s. Nearly all societies before 1815 bore a strictly local and self-governing character, and they combined the functions of sick insurance with convivial club nights and annual 'outings' or feasts. An observer in 1805 witnessed near Matlock –

... about fifty women preceded by a solitary fiddler playing a merry tune. This was a female benefit society, who had been to hear a sermon at Eyam, and were going to dine together, a luxury which our female benefit society at Sheffield does not indulge in, having tea only, and generally singing, dancing, smoking, and negus.[2]

Few of the members of friendly societies had a higher social status than that of clerks or small tradesmen; most were artisans. The fact that each brother had funds deposited in the society made for stability in membership and watchful participation in self-government. They had almost no middle-class membership and, while some employers looked upon them favourably, their actual conduct left little room for paternalist control. Failures owing to actuarial inexperience were common; defaulting officers not infrequent. Diffused through every part of the country, they were (often heart-breaking) schools of experience.

In the very secretiveness of the friendly society, and in its opaqueness under upper-class scrutiny, we have authentic evidence of the growth of independent working-class culture and

1. For the legal status of friendly societies at this time, see P. H. J. Gosden, *The Friendly Societies in England* (Manchester, 1961), p. 5. For the social composition of societies in Sheffield, see G. C. Holland, op. cit., ch. 17.

2. T. A. Ward, op. cit., p. 78. See also J. H. Priestley, 'Ripponden Female Society *Trans. Halifax Antiq. Soc.*, 1943.

institutions. This was the sub-culture out of which the less stable trade unions grew, and in which trade union officers were trained.[1] Union rules, in many cases, were more elaborate versions of the same code of conduct as the sick club. Sometimes, as in the case of the Woolcombers, this was supplemented by the procedures of secret masonic orders:

> Strangers, the design of all our Lodges is love and unity,
> With self-protection founded on the laws of equity,
> And when you have our mystic rights gone through,
> Our secrets all will be disclosed to you.[2]

After the 1790s, under the impact of the Jacobin agitation, the preambles to friendly society rules assume a new resonance; one of the strangest consequences of the language of 'social man' of the philosophical Enlightenment is its reproduction in the rules of obscure clubs meeting in the taverns or 'hush-shops' of industrial England. On Tyneside 'Social' and 'Philanthropic' societies expressed their aspirations in terms which ranged from throw-away phrases – 'a sure, lasting, and loving society', 'to promote friendship and true Christian charity', 'man was not born for himself alone' – to more thundering philosophical affirmations:

Man, by the construction of his body, and the disposition of his mind, is a creature formed for society. . . .

We, the members of this society, taking it into our serious consideration, that man is formed a social being ... in continual need of mutual assistance and support; and having interwoven in our constitutions those humane and sympathetic affections which we always feel at the distress of any of our fellow creatures ...[3]

1. It was a continual complaint of the authorities that friendly societies allowed members to withdraw funds when on strike. Macclesfield was described in 1812 as 'a nest of illicit association', 'full of sick and burial societies which are the germ of revolution': C. S. Davies, *History of Macclesfield* (Manchester, 1961), p. 180.

2. [E. C. Tuffnell], *The Character, Objects and Effects of Trades' Unions* (1834, reprinted 1934), pp. 42 ff.

3. *Rules ... of the Sociable Society* (Newcastle, 1812); *Articles of the Friendly Society at West Boldon* (Sunderland, 1811); *Rules of the Good Intent Society* (Newcastle, 1815); *Articles of the Unanimous Society* (Newcastle, 1804); see also H. J. Maltby, 'Early Bradford Friendly Societies', *Bradford Antiquary*, VII, 1933, for examples of Methodist influenced rules.

The friendly societies, found in so many diverse communities, were a unifying cultural influence. Although for financial and legal reasons they were slow to federate themselves, they facilitated regional and national trade union federation. Their language of 'social man' also made towards the growth in working-class consciousness. It joined the language of Christian charity and the slumbering imagery of 'brotherhood' in the Methodist (and Moravian) tradition with the social affirmations of Owenite socialism. Many early Owenite societies and stores prefaced their rules with the line from Isaiah (XLI, 6): 'They helped every one his neighbour; and every one said to his brother, be of good courage.' But the 1830s there were in circulation a score of friendly society or trade union hymns and songs which elaborated this theme.

Mr Raymond Williams has suggested that 'the crucial distinguishing element in English life since the Industrial Revolution is ... between alternative ideas of the nature of social relationship'. As contrasted with middle-class ideas of individualism or (at their best) of service, 'what is properly meant by "working-class culture" ... is the basic collective idea, and the institutions, manners, habits of thought, and intentions which proceed from this'.[1] Friendly societies did not 'proceed from' an idea; both the ideas and the institutions arose in response to certain common experiences. But the distinction is important. In the simple cellular structure of the friendly society, with its workaday ethos of mutual aid, we can see many features which were reproduced in more sophisticated and complex forms in trade unions, cooperatives, Hampden Clubs, Political Unions, and Chartist lodges. At the same time the societies can be seen as crystallizing an ethos of mutuality very much more widely diffused in the 'dense' and 'concrete' particulars of the personal relations of working people, at home and at work. Every kind of witness in the first half of the nineteenth century – clergymen, factory inspectors, Radical publicists – remarked upon the extent of mutual aid in the poorest districts. In times of emergency, unemployment, strikes, sickness, childbirth, then it was the poor who 'helped every one his neighbour'. Twenty years after Place's comment on the

1. *Culture and Society* (Penguin edn), pp. 312–14.

change in Lancashire manners, Cooke Taylor was astounded at the way in which Lancashire working men bore 'the extreme of wretchedness',

with a high tone of moral dignity, a marked sense of propriety, a decency, cleanliness, and order ... which do not merit the intense suffering I have witnessed. I was beholding the gradual immolation of the noblest and most valuable population that ever existed in this country or in any other under heaven.

'Nearly all the distressed operatives whom I met north of Manchester ... had a thorough horror of being forced to receive parish relief.'[1]

It is an error to see this as the *only* effective 'working-class' ethic. The 'aristocratic' aspirations of artisans and mechanics, the values of 'self-help', or criminality and demoralization, were equally widely dispersed. The conflict between alternative ways of life was fought out, not just between the middle and working classes, but within working-class communities themselves. But by the early years of the nineteenth century it is possible to say that collectivist values are dominant in many industrial communities; there is a definite moral code, with sanctions against the blackleg, the 'tools' of the employer or the unneighbourly, and with an intolerance towards the eccentric or individualist. Collectivist values are consciously held and are propagated in political theory, trade union ceremonial, moral rhetoric. It is, indeed, this collective self-consciousness, with its corresponding theory, institutions, discipline, and community values which distinguishes the nineteenth-century working class from the eighteenth-century mob.

Political Radicalism and Owenism both drew upon and enriched this 'basic collectivist idea'. Francis Place may well have been right when he attributed the changed behaviour of Lancashire crowds in 1819, to the advance of political consciousness 'spreading over the face of the country ever since the Constitutional and Corresponding Societies became active in 1792':

Now 100,000 people may be collected together and no riot ensue, and why? ... The people have an object, the pursuit of which gives

1. Cooke Taylor, op. cit., pp. 37–9. Taylor was writing at the time of the cotton depression of 1842.

them importance in their own eyes, elevates them in their own opinion, and thus it is that the very individuals who would have been the leaders of the riot are the keepers of the peace.[1]

Another observer attributed the changes in Lancashire to the influence both of Cobbett and of the Sunday schools and noted a 'general and radical change' in the character of the labouring classes:

The poor, when suffering and dissatisfied, no longer make a riot, but hold a meeting – instead of attacking their neighbours, they arraign the Ministry.[2]

This growth in self-respect and political consciousness was one real gain of the Industrial Revolution. It dispelled some forms of superstition and of deference, and made certain kinds of oppression no longer tolerable. We can find abundant testimony as to the steady growth of the ethos of mutuality in the strength and ceremonial pride of the unions and trades clubs which emerged from quasi-legality when the Combination Acts were repealed.[3] During the Bradford woolcomber's strike of 1825 we find that in Newcastle, where the friendly society was so well rooted, the unions contributing to the Bradford funds included smiths, mill-wrights, joiners, shoemakers, morocco leather dressers, cabinet-makers, shipwrights, sawyers, tailors, woolcombers, hatters tanners, weavers, potters and miners.[4] Moreover, there is a sense in which the friendly society helped to pick up and carry into the trade union movement the love of ceremony and the high sense of status of the craftsman's guild. These traditions, indeed, still had a remarkable vigour in the early nineteenth century, in some of the old Chartered Companies or Guilds of the masters and of master-craftsmen, whose periodical ceremonies expressed the pride of both the masters and of their journeymen in 'the Trade'. In 1802, for example, there was a great jubilee celebration of the Preston

1. Wallas, op. cit., p. 146.

2. A Member of the Manchester Committee for relieving the Sufferings of the 16th of August, 1819 [J. E. Taylor], *Notes and Observations Critical and Explanatory on the Papers relative to the Internal State of the Country* ... (1820).

3. See above, p. 264.

4. *Trades Newspaper*, 11 September 1825.

'Guilds'. In a week of processions and exhibitions, in which the nobility, gentry, merchants, shopkeepers, and manufacturers all took part,[1] the journeymen were given a prominent place:

The Wool-Combers and Cotton Workers ... were preceded by twenty-four young blooming handsome women, each bearing a branch of the cotton tree, then followed a spinning machine borne on men's shoulders, and afterwards a loom drawn on a sledge, each with work-people busily employed at them ...

At Bradford, on the eve of the great strike of 1825, the wool-combers' feast of Bishop Blaize was celebrated with extra-ordinary splendour:

Herald, bearing a flag.

Twenty-four Woolstaplers on horseback, each horse caparisoned with a fleece.

Thirty-eight Worsted-Spinners and Manufacturers on horseback, in white stuff waistcoats, with each a sliver of wool over his shoulder and a white stuff sash: the horses' necks covered with nets made of thick yarn.

And so on until we reach:

BISHOP BLAIZE

Shepherd and Shepherdess.

Shepherd-Swains.

One hundred and sixty Woolsorters on horseback, with ornamented caps and various coloured slivers.

Thirty Comb-makers.

Charcoal Burners.

Combers' Colours.

Band.

Four hundred and seventy Wool-combers, with wool wigs, &c.

Band.

Forty Dyers, with red cockades, blue aprons, and crossed slivers of red and blue.[2]

After the great strike such a ceremony could not be repeated.

1. Companies represented included the tanners, skinners, glovers, cord-wainers, carpenters, butchers, vintners, tailors, smiths, mercers and drapers. See *Leeds Mercury*, 4 September 1802.

2. J. James, *History of Bradford* (1866), pp. 164–7; J. Burnley, *Yorkshire Stories Retold*, (Leeds, n.d.), p. 165–75.

This passage from the old outlook of 'the Trade' to the duality of the masters' organizations, on the one hand, and the trade unions on the other, takes us into the central experience of the Industrial Revolution.[1] But the friendly society and trade union, not less than the organizations of the masters, sought to maintain the ceremonial and the pride of the older tradition; indeed, since the artisans (or, as they still are called, tradesmen) felt themselves to be the *producers* upon whose skill the masters were parasitic, they emphasized the tradition the more. With the repeal of the Combination Acts their banners moved openly through the streets. In London, in 1825, the Thames Ship Caulkers Union (founded in 1794) displayed its mottos: 'Main et Coeur', 'Vigueur, Vérité, Concorde, Dépêche', which reveal the pride of the medieval craft. The Ropemakers Union proceeded with a white banner on which was portrayed a swarm of bees around a hive: 'Sons of Industry! Union gives Strength'. (At the houses of masters who had granted them an increase, they stopped and gave a salute.) John Gast's Thames Shipwrights Provident Union, the pacemaker of the London 'trades', outdid all with a blue silk banner: 'Hearts of Oak Protect the Aged', a handsome ship drawn by six bay horses, three postilions in blue jackets, a band, the Committee, the members with more banners and flags, and delegations representing the trade from Shields, Sunderland, and Newcastle. The members wore blue rosettes and sprigs of oak, and in the ship were old shipwrights who lived in the union's almshouses at Stepney.[2] At Nantwich in 1832 the shoemakers maintained all the sense of status of the artisan's craft union, with their banner, 'full set of secret order regalia, surplices, trimmed aprons ... and a crown and robes for King Crispin'. In 1833 the King rode on horseback through the town attended by train-bearers, officers with the 'Dispensation, the Bible, a large pair of gloves, and also beautiful specimens of ladies' and gents' boots and shoes':

1. For the formation of 'Middle-Class Consciousness' between 1780 and 1846, see Professor Briggs's article with this title, *Past and Present*, April 1956. For the importance of the notion of 'the Trade' in the Luddite movement, see blow, pp. 595–8.

2. *Trades Newspaper*, 14, 21, 28 August 1825. The caulkers had about 300 members, the ropemakers 200, the shipwrights about 1,500.

Nearly 500 joined in the procession, each one wearing a white apron neatly trimmed. The rear was brought up by a shopmate in full tramping order, his kit packed on his back, and walking-stick in hand.[1]

No single explanation will suffice to account for the evident alteration in manner of the working people.[2] Nor should we exaggerate the degree of change. Drunkenness and uproar still often surged through the streets. But it is true that working men often appear most sober and disciplined, in the twenty years after the Wars, when most in earnest to assert their rights. Thus we cannot accept the thesis that sobriety was the consequence only, or even mainly, of the Evangelical propaganda. And we may see this, also, if we turn the coin over and look at the reverse. By 1830 not only the Established Church but also the Methodist revival was meeting sharp opposition in most working-class centres from free-thinkers, Owenites, and non-denominational Christians. In London, Birmingham, south-east Lancashire, Newcastle, Leeds and other cities the Deist adherents of Carlile or Owen had an enormous following. The Methodists had consolidated their position, but they tended increasingly to represent tradesmen and privileged groups of workers, and to be morally isolated from working-class community life. Some old centres of revivalism had relapsed into 'heathenism'. In Newcastle's Sandgate, once 'as noted for praying as for tippling, for psalm-singing as for swearing', the Methodists had lost any following among the poor by the 1840s. In parts of Lancashire weaving communities as well as factory operatives became largely detached from the chapels and were swept up in the current of Owenism and free-thought:

If it had not been for Sunday schools, society would have been in a horrible state before this time. ... Infidelity is growing amazingly. ... The writings of Carlile and Taylor and other infidels are more read than the Bable or any other book. ... I have seen weeks after weeks the weavers assembled in a room, that would contain 400

1. 'Reminiscences of Thomas Dunning', ed. W. H. Chaloner, *Trans. Lancs. & Cheshire Antiq. Soc.*, LIX, 1947. This flamboyant display of strength was followed by the arrest of the Nantwich officers in the general assault on the unions in 1834.

2. For a further discussion of the artisan culture, see below, pp. 781–819.

people, to applaud the people who asserted and argued that there was no God. ... I have gone into the cottages around the chapel where I worship, I have found 20 men assembled reading infidel publications ...[1]

Owenite and secular movements often took fire 'like whins on the common', as revivalism had done before.

Engels, writing from his Lancashire experience in 1844, claimed that 'the workers are not religious, and do not attend church', with the exception of the Irish, 'a few elderly people, and the half-bourgeois, the overlookers, foremen, and the like'. 'Among the masses there prevails almost universally a total in-difference to religion, or at the utmost, some trace of Deism...' Engels weakened his case by overstating it; but Dodd quoted a Stockport factory where nine out of ten did not attend any church, while Cooke Taylor, in 1842, was astonished at the vigour and knowledge of the Scripture shown by Lancashire working men who contested Christian orthodoxies. 'If I thought that the Lord was the cause of all the misery I see around me,' one such man told a Methodist preacher, 'I would quit his service, and say he was not the Lord I took him for.' Similarly, in Newcastle in the Chartist years thousands of artisans and engineers were convinced free-thinkers. In one works employing 200 'there are not more than six or seven who attend a place of worship'. 'The working classes,' said one working-man,

are gathering knowledge, and the more they gather, the wider becomes the breach between them and the different sects. It is not because they are ignorant of the Bible. I revere the Bible myself ... and when I look into it ... I find that the prophets stood between the oppressor and the oppressed, and denounced the wrong doer, however rich and powerful. ... When the preachers go back to the old book, I for one will go back to hear them, but not till then ...

The Sunday schools were bringing an unexpected harvest.[2]

The weakening hold of the churches by no means indicated

1. Evidence of a Bolton employer, *S.C. on Hand-loom Weavers' Petitions* (1834), p. 419.

2. Engels, op. cit., pp. 125–6; Cooke Taylor, op. cit., pp. 153–5; *Newcastle Chronicle, Inquiry into the Condition of the Poor* (Newcastle, 1850), pp. 32, 56. See also Dodd, op. cit., pp. 181, 186.

any erosion of the self-respect and discipline of class. On the contrary, Manchester and Newcastle, with their long tradition of industrial and political organization, were notable in the Chartist years for the discipline of their massive demonstrations. Where the citizens and shopkeepers had once been thrown into alarm when the 'terrible and savage pitmen' entered Newcastle in any force, it now became necessary for the coal-owners to scour the slums of the city for 'candy-men' or rag-collectors to evict the striking miners. In 1838 and 1839 tens of thousands of artisans, miners and labourers marched week after week in good order through the streets, often passing within a few feet of the military, and avoiding all provocation. 'Our people had been well taught,' one of their leaders recalled, 'that it was not riot we wanted, but revolution.'[1]

III. THE IRISH

One ingredient in the new working-class community has necessarily evaded this analysis: the Irish immigration. In 1841 it was estimated that over 400,000 inhabitants of Great Britain had been born in Ireland; many more tens of thousands were born in Britain of Irish parentage. The great majority of these were Catholics, and among the poorest-paid labourers; most of them lived in London and in the industrial towns. In Liverpool and in Manchester anything between one-fifth and one-third of the working population was Irish.

This is not the place to rehearse the appalling story of the immiseration of the Irish people in the first half of the nineteenth century. But the disasters which afflicted Ireland came less from the potato-blight than from the after-effects of a counter-revolution following upon the merciless repression of the United Irishmen's rebellion (1798) far more savage than anything enacted in England; and from the political, economic and social consequences of the Act of Union (1800). In 1794 a clergyman of the Church of Ireland named William Jackson, who was acting as a go-between between William Hamilton Rowan,

1. Fynes, op. cit., p. 19; Thomas Burt, *Autobiography* (1924), p. 34; T. A. Devyr, *The Odd Book of the Nineteenth Century* (New York, 1882), pp. 184–5.

of the United Irishmen, and the French, was seized in Dublin with a paper outlining the position in Ireland and the prospects of support in the event of a French invasion. The population of Ireland was estimated (erroneously) at 4,500,000,[1] of whom 450,000 were supposed to be Anglicans, 900,000 Dissenters, and 3,150,000 Catholics. Of the Dissenters ('the most enlightened body of the Nation') it said:

They are steady Republicans, devoted to Liberty and through all the Stages of the French Revolution have been enthusiastically attached to it. The Catholics, the Great body of the People, are in The Lowest degree of Ignorance and Want, ready for any Change because no Change can make them worse, the Whole Peasantry of Ireland, the Most Oppressed and Wretched in Europe, may be said to be Catholic.

Whereas the anti-Gallican prejudices of the English would 'unite all ranks in opposition to the Invaders', in Ireland 'a Conquered, oppressed and Insulted Country the Name of England and her Power is Universally Odious ...'

The Dissenters are enemies to the English Power from reason and Reflection, the Catholics from a Hatred of the English Name. ...
    In a word, from Reflection, Interest, Prejudice, the spirit of Change, the misery of the great bulk of the nation and above all the Hatred of the English name resulting from the Tyranny of near seven centurys, there seems little doubt but an Invasion would be supported by the People.[2]

It is arguable that the French lost Europe, not before Moscow, but in 1797, when only a Navy in mutiny stood between them and an Ireland on the eve of rebellion.[3] But the invasion, when it came, was of a different order; it was the invasion of England and Scotland by the Irish poor. And Jackson's brief reminds us that the Irish emigration was more differentiated than is often supposed. In the years before and after '98, the Dissenters of Ulster, the most industrialized province, were not the most loyal but the most 'Jacobinical' of the Irish; while

1. The first Census, in 1821, gave a figure of 6,803,000.
2. T. S., 11.3510 A (2); *Trial of the Rev. Wm. Jackson* (1795), pp. 80–81.
3. See E. H. S. Jones, *The Invasion that Failed* (Oxford, 1950).

it was only after the repression of the rebellion that the antagonism between the 'Orangemen' and 'Papists' was deliberately fostered by the Castle, as a means of maintaining power. The emigrants included seasonal harvest-workers from Connaught, fugitive Wexford smallholders, and Ulster artisans, who differed as greatly from each other as Cornish labourers and Manchester cotton-spinners. (The notorious Saturday night brawls were more often between Irish and Irish than between Irish and English; nor were they always religious wars – the rivalries of Leinster, Munster and Connaught were also re-enacted in the folds and courts of Preston and Batley.) Wave followed upon wave of immigration.[1] Between 1790 and 1810 there was still a considerable admixture of Protestants and Ulstermen, many of them tradesmen, artisans, weavers and cotton-operatives, some of them adherents of *Rights of Man*. As the effects of unequal economic competition under the Union became felt, silk- and linen-weavers and cotton workers evacuated their declining industries for Manchester and Glasgow, Barnsley, Bolton and Macclesfield. In this wave came young John Doherty, who had worked in his teens in a cotton-mill in Meath, and who arrived in Manchester towards the end of the Wars, to become within a few years the greatest of the leaders of the Lancashire cotton workers.

From this time forward it was more than ever a Catholic and peasant migration. The yeomanry of Lincolnshire, a local paper noted in 1811, 'have for many years made a point of inviting them by public advertisement'. This referred to the seasonal migrants, the harvest workers whose 'spirit of laborious industry' was commended, as against the 'greedy' Lincolnshire labourer,

who desires to make excessive wages through the necessity of the farmer, and whom half a guinea a day, at the height of the season, will not satisfy,

and who was further reproved for looking upon 'the Irish auxiliary' with jealousy.[2] As the migration-routes became familiar, so more of the immigrants came to stay. Successive

1. For the considerable Irish colony in eighteenth-century London, see M. D. George, *London Life in the Eighteenth Century*, pp. 113 ff.
2. *Boston Gazette*, in *Alfred*, 21 September 1811.

failures of the potato crop, notably the famine of 1821-2, drove forward the migration.

The mass eviction of peasant 'freeholders' between 1828 and 1830 swelled the numbers travelling on the crowded boats to Liverpool and Bristol. But England was 'far from being their Mecca, and is indeed the last place they would willingly approach'. The more fortunate, who could save the passage money, were emigrating to America or Canada, and they were the most destitute who came to this country. Once here, as soon as employment was found, heroic efforts were made to send remittances back to Ireland, and often to raise the small sum needed to bring relatives across and to reunite the family in England.[1]

The conditions which the greater part of the post-war immigrants left behind them were, in the language of the Blue Books, insufficient to support 'the commonest necessaries of life':

Their habitations are wretched hovels, several of a family sleep together upon straw or upon the bare ground ... their food commonly consists of dry potatoes, and with these they are ... obliged to stint themselves to one spare meal on the day. .... They sometimes get a herring, or a little milk, but they never get meat except at Christmas, Easter, and Shrovetide.[2]

As the cheapest labour in Western Europe, this part of their story is familiar. Page after page of the Blue Books concerned with sanitary conditions, crime, housing, hand-loom weavers, are filled with accounts of the squalor which the Irish brought with them to England: of their cellar-dwellings: the paucity of furnishings and bedding: the garbage thrust out at the doors: the overcrowding: the under-cutting of English labour. Their utility to the employers in the last respect needs no stressing. A Manchester silk manufacturer declared, 'the moment I have a turn-out and am fast for hands I send to Ireland for ten, fifteen, or twenty families ...'[3]

1. For the migration generally, see Redford, op. cit., pp. 114 ff.; for an excellent summary of its economic and social causes, see E. Strauss, *Irish Nationalism and British Democracy* (1951), esp. chs. 9 and 10.

2. *Third Report of the Commissioners for Inquiring into the Condition of the Poorer Classes in Ireland* (1836), p. 3.

3. *Report on the State of the Irish Poor in Great Britain* (1836), p. vii.

But the influence of the Irish immigration was more ambivalent and more interesting than this. Paradoxically, it was the very success of the pressures effecting changes in the character-structure of the English working man which called forth the need for a supplementary labour force unmoulded by the industrial work-discipline. This discipline, as we have seen, required steady methodical application, inner motivations of sobriety, forethought, and punctilious observation of contracts; in short, the controlled paying-out of energies in skilled or semi-skilled employments. By contrast, the heavy manual occupations at the base of industrial society required a spendthrift expense of sheer physical energy – an alternation of intensive labour and boisterous relaxation which belongs to pre-industrial labour-rhythms, and for which the English artisan or weaver was unsuited both by reason of his weakened physique and his Puritan temperament.

Thus Irish labour was essential for the Industrial Revolution, not only – and perhaps not primarily – because it was 'cheap' (the labour of English weavers and farm workers was cheap enough in all conscience), but because the Irish peasantry had escaped the imprint of Baxter and Wesley. Demoralized in Ireland by a sub-subsistence economy or by the conacre system (by which they were reduced to semi-slavery to the farmers in return for the use of a potato patch) they had acquired a reputation for lethargy and fecklessness. Energy was no asset in a land where the good tenant was penalized by the doubling of his rent. In England they were capable of astonishing feats, showing a –

... willingness, alacrity and perseverance in the severest, the most irksome and most disagreeable kinds of coarse labour, such for instance as attending on masons, bricklayers and plasterers, excavating earth for harbours, docks, canals and roads, carrying heavy goods, loading and unloading vessels.

Dr Kay, who made inquiries as to the value of Irish labour among Lancashire employers in 1835, found that English labourers were preferred in all skilled occupations, having 'that steady perseverance which factory employment peculiarly requires'. 'The English are more steady, cleanly, skilful labourers, and are more faithful in the fulfilment of contracts made between master and servant.' Although many thousands of Irish were employed in the cotton industry, 'few, if any ... are ever employed in the superior processes ...; they are almost all to be found in the blowing-rooms ...' Scarcely any were placed in 'offices of trust', while few 'attained the rank of spinners'. On the other hand, in unskilled occupations the position was reversed. A Birmingham employer gave evidence in 1836:

The Irish labourers will work any time. ... I consider them very valuable labourers, and we could not do without them. By treating them kindly, they will do anything for you. ... An Englishman could not do the work they do. When you push them they have a willingness to oblige which the English have not; they would die under anything before they would be beat; they would go at hard work till they drop before a man should excel them ...

'They require more looking after; they talk more at work' – personal rather than economic incentives are often noted as being of most effect; good-humoured themselves, they worked best for good-humoured employers who encouraged them to mutual emulation. 'The Irish are more violent and irritable, but they are less stubborn, sullen, and self-willed than the English.' Their generosity and impulsiveness was easily imposed upon; it is literally true that they 'would die ... before they would be beat'. 'In his own country he is notoriously lazy and negligent in the extreme; after crossing the channel he became a model of laboriousness and enterprise.' Paid by piece-rate or gang-rate on the docks or at navvying, 'they are tempted to overwork themselves, and to ruin their health and constitution in a few years. This is the case of porters, coal-heavers, and many common labourers in London,' a high proportion of whom were Irishmen. An observer at the Liverpool docks noted the manner in which oats were loaded on to a vessel:

These men (chiefly Irishmen) received the full sacks as they were lowered by the crane off the hitch on their shoulders and carried them across the road. They pursued their heavy task during the working hours of a summer's day at a uniform, unremitting pace, a trot of at least five miles an hour, the distance from the vessel to the storehouse being fully fifty yards ... At this work a good labourer earned, at 16*d.* per 100 sacks, ten shillings a day; so that consequently he made seven hundred and fifty trips ... carrying for half the distance a full sack of oats on his shoulder, thus performing a distance of ... forty-three miles ...

By the 1830s whole classes of work had passed almost entirely into the hands of Irishmen since the English either refused the menial, unpleasant tasks or could not keep up with the pace.[1]

Thus to an extraordinary degree the employers had the best of a labour supply from the pre-industrial and the industrialized worlds. The disciplined worker at heart disliked his work; the same character-structure which made for application and skill erected also barriers of self-respect which were not amenable to dirty or degrading tasks. A building employer, explaining why the Irish were confined to labouring rôles, gave evidence:

They scarcely ever make good mechanics; they don't look deep into subjects; their knowledge is quick, but superficial; they don't make good millwrights or engineers, or anything which requires thought. ... If a plan is put in an Irishman's hand, he requires looking after continuously, otherwise he will go wrong, or more probably not go on at all.

This was the consequence of 'want of application' rather than any 'natural incapacity'; it was a 'moral' and not an 'intellectual' defect:

A man who has no care for the morrow, and who lives only for the passing moment, cannot bring his mind to undergo the severe discipline, and to make those patient and toilsome exertions which are required to form a good mechanic.[2]

The *Report on the State of the Irish Poor in Great Britain*, which is one of the most impressive essays in sociology among the Blue Books of the Thirties, came to this conclusion:

1. *Report on the State of the Irish Poor in Great Britain* (1836), pp. v, vii–ix, xxx–xxxi; Strauss, op. cit., ch. 14, 'The Irish in Great Britain'; *First Annual Report Poor Law Commissioners* (1836), pp. 305–6; G. C. Lewis, *Remarks on the Third Report of the Irish Poor Inquiry Commissioners* (1837), p. 24; John Wade, *History of the Middle and Working Classes*, pp. 242–3; Sir G. Head, *A Home Tour of Great Britain* (1835), pp. 190–91.

2. *Report on the State of the Irish Poor in Great Britain*, pp. ix, xxx–xxxi.

The Irish emigration into Britain is an example of a less civilized population spreading themselves, as a kind of substratum, beneath a more civilized community; and, without excelling in any branch of industry, obtaining possession of all the lowest departments of manual labour.

The employers found this 'advantageous', one master in the Potteries noted, 'as the native population is fully employed in the more ingenious and skill-requiring works'. Nevertheless, in the view of many employers the immigration 'has not been an unmingled benefit'. For the Irish displayed the same exuberance and indiscipline in their relaxation as in their work. 'A large number of the labouring Irish in the manufacturing towns ... spend their earnings in the following manner':

On the Saturday night, when they receive their wages, they first pay the score at the shop ... and their rent ... and when their debts are thus paid, they go drinking spirits as long as the remnant of their wages holds out. On the Monday morning, they are penniless ...

Maintaining a 'fixed standard of existence, little superior to that which they observed in their own country', they lacked the Puritan virtues of thrift and sobriety as much as those of application and forethought. Every Saturday night the streets of Manchester, Liverpool and other manufacturing towns were taken over by hundreds of drunken and brawling Irishmen.

Moreover, in a score of ways the Irishman's virtues and vices were the opposite of those of the disciplined English artisan. The Irish had a sometimes violent, sometimes good-humoured contempt of English authority. Not only were the rulers' laws and religion alien, but there were no community sanctions which found prosecution in the English law courts a cause of shame. Well-treated, an employer said, they were trustworthy: 'If one among them is detected in a petty theft, the others will avoid him'. But the Irishman detected in pilfering from unpopular employers or farmers or refusing to pay rent was supported not only by the licence of his compatriots but by their collective force. A Manchester cotton master declared, there is 'no recklessness of conduct which they do not at times display'. Constantly fighting among themselves, they turned as one man if any individual was attacked from

outside. Attempts to seize illicit stills led to wars of cutlasses
and brickbats, in which the Irish women were not the most
backward. In Manchester's Little Ireland attempts to serve
legal executions for rent, debt, or taxes, had to be conducted
like a minor military action against an embattled population.
'It is extremely dangerous,' said the Deputy Constable of
Manchester in 1836, 'to execute a warrant in a factory where
many Irish are employed; they will throw bricks and stones on
the officers' heads as they are coming up stairs ...' And the
Superintendent of the Manchester Watch gave evidence that –

... in order to apprehend one Irishman in the Irish parts of the
town, we are forced to take from ten or twenty, or even more,
watchmen. The whole neighbourhood turn out with weapons;
even women, half-naked, carrying brickbats and stones for the men
to throw. A man will resist, fighting and struggling, in order to gain
time till his friends collect for a rescue ...[1]

These Irish were neither stupid nor barbarians. Mayhew
often remarked upon their generosity, their 'powers of speech
and quickness of apprehension'. They adhered to a different
value-system than that of the English artisan; and in shocking
English proprieties one feels that they often enjoyed themselves
and acted up the part. Often, a Bolton attorney recalled, they
played the fool in the dock, bringing forward a tribe of countrymen as 'character witnesses', showing an acute knowledge of
legal procedure in their prevarications, and making magistrates
dizzy with their blarney. The same disregard for veracity made
many of them consummate beggars. Generous to each other,
if they saved money it was for some definite project – emigration to Canada or marriage. To bring wives and children,
brothers and sisters, to England they would 'treasure up
halfpenny after halfpenny' for years, but 'they will *not* save
to preserve either themselves or their children from the degradation of a workhouse ...' As street-sellers they remained in
the poorest grades, as hawkers or rag-dealers; their temperament, Mayhew dryly commented, was not adapted to 'buying
in the cheapest market and selling in the dearest'. To the English Poor Laws they maintained a cheerful predatory attitude.

1. *State of the Irish Poor in Great Britain*, pp. x, xvi–xvii, x; *First
Report of the Constabulary Commissioners* (1839), pp. 167–9.

They turned the obsolete Settlement Laws to their advantage, joy-riding up and down the country at parochial expense (and who would know whether Manchester was or was not the parish of origin of Paddy M'Guire?) and slipping out of the overseer's cart when the stopping-place seemed congenial. They would accept parochial relief 'without the least sense of shame'.[1]

This was an unsettling element in the formative working-class community – a seemingly inexhaustible flow of reinforcements to man the battlements of Satan's strongholds. In some towns the Irish were partially segregated in their own streets and quarters. In London in 1850 Mayhew found them in the labyrinth of alleys off Rosemary-lane, in whose folds could be seen 'rough-headed urchins running with their feet bare through the puddles, and bonnetless girls, huddled in shawls, lolling against the door-posts'. In the cellars of Manchester and Leeds there was a similar segregation. And there was also the segregation of religion. In 1800 the native working-class population which adhered to the Catholic faith was minuscule. In the Irish immigration the Catholic Church saw evidence of a divine plan to recover England to the Faith; and wherever the Irish went, the priests followed closely after. Moreover, this Irish priesthood was poorer and closer to the peasantry than any in Europe. With an average income which has been estimated at £65 a year, in a literal sense they lived off their flocks, taking their meals in the homes of their parishioners and dependent on their goodwill. 'The priest,' said the Protestant Bishop of Waterford,

must follow the impulse of the popular wave, or be left behind on the beach to perish. ... 'Live with me and live as I do; oppress me not with superior learning or refinement, take thankfully what I choose to give you, and earn it by compliance with my political creed or conduct.' Such ... is the language of the Irish cottager to his priest.

The Catholic Bishop of Waterford confirmed this in a striking charge to his clergy in 1797:

1. H. M. Richardson, *Reminiscences of Forty Years in Bolton* (Bolton, 1885), pp. 129–31; Mayhew, op. cit., I, pp. 109, 121.

Do not permit yourselves to be made instruments of the rich of this world, who will try ... to make instruments of you, over the poor, for their own temporal purposes. ... The poor were always your friends – they inflexibly adhered to you, and to their religion, even in the worst of times. They shared their scanty meal with you, and with your predecessors. ... If they had ... imitated the conduct of the rich, who not only shut their doors against you, but not unfrequently hunted you like wild beasts, I should not be able to address the present respectable body of clergy under my spiritual authority ...

A Church which had found a priest to ride at the head of the insurrectionists at Wexford, and another (O'Coigly) to suffer on the scaffold in England, was deeply involved in the national aspirations of the peasantry; for thirty years after 1810, Daniel O'Connell sought (mainly through the Catholic Association) to employ the priesthood as auxiliary political agitators. When the Irish poor came to England, the priesthood used every means – devoted ministration (with a knowledge of the mind of their parishioners which no English clergy could equal), psychological terror, financial aid and financial extortion, pressure on relatives, comfort in distress – to maintain their hold on their flock; and they trusted to the only form of evangelism likely to succeed in Protestant England: the birth-rate. English coal-whippers, navvies, or costermongers were, many of them, 'heathens'; their Irish analogues attended Mass. The priest was the only authority to whom the Irish labourers showed any deference. A Catholic Canon could quell a Saturday night riot in Bolton where the magistrates failed. When Mayhew accompanied one priest on the round of his flock:

Everywhere the people ran out to meet him. ... Women crowded to their door-steps, and came creeping up from the cellars through the trap-doors, merely to curtsey to him. ... Even as the priest walked along the street, boys running at full speed would pull up to touch their hair ...[1]

Indeed, for many of the migrants the power of the priest increased. Torn up by their roots, the priest was the last point

1. Ibid., I, p. 12; E. Wakefield, *An Account of Ireland* (1812), II, p. 557; Halévy, op. cit., III, pp. 93–5; Dr Hussey, *Pastoral Letter to the Catholic Clergy* (Waterford, 1797).

of orientation with their old way of life. Literate but not far removed in social class, free from identification with English employers and authorities, sometimes knowing the Gaelic, the priest passed more frequently between England and Ireland, brought news of home and sometimes of relatives, could be entrusted with remittances, savings or messages. Hence it followed that the most enduring cultural tradition which the Irish peasantry brought – to the third and fourth generation – into England was that of a semi-feudal nationalist Church. In the most squalid cellars there might still be found some of the hocus-pocus of Romanism, the candlesticks, the crucifix, and the 'showy-coloured prints of saints and martyrs' alongside the print of O'Connell, the 'Liberator'. The enormously rich inheritance of Irish song and folklore perished, by contrast, often with the first generation. The immigrants might continue for a time the customs of their villages, visiting each others' dwellings 'where they jig and reel furiously'. But with their children the fiddle, the pipe, and the Gaelic were laid aside.

If they were segregated in some towns, the Irish were never pressed back into ghettoes. It would have been difficult to have made a people who spoke the same language and were British citizens under the Act of Union into a subject minority. There was a great deal of inter-marriage. And it is not the friction but the relative ease with which the Irish were absorbed into working-class communities which is remarkable. There were, of course, many riots, especially where Irish and English unskilled labour was in direct competition – in the building industry or on the docks. In the 1830s and 1840s pitched battles, with mortal casualties, took place among railway navvies. In London in particular anti-Catholic and anti-Irish feeling remained strong; each stage in the long parliamentary contest for Catholic Emancipation (1800–1829) took place against a background of scurrilous anti-Papal broadsheets and ballads, while as late as 1850 the appointment of Catholic bishops led to effigy-burnings and the outcry of 'Papal Aggression'. Mayhew found 'patterers' and 'chaunters' who regarded a good anti-Papal patter as being as lucrative as a good murder:

> Monks and Nuns and fools afloat,
> We'll have no bulls shoved down our throat,
> Cheer up and shout down with the Pope,
> And his bishop cardinal Wiseman.

But none of the chaunts or litanies recorded by Mayhew included any reference to the Irish. Most harked back to the folklore of Smithfield burnings and national sentiment, on the lines of 'Old English John Bull's Reply to the Papal Bull of Rome'. The cellar-dwellers off Rosemary-lane could hardly be assimilated to the folklore of alien aggression.[1]

On the contrary, there were many reasons why English Radicalism or Chartism, and Irish nationalism, should make common cause, although the alliance was never free from tensions. Antagonism could scarcely take racialist forms in the Army, Navy, or in the northern mill-towns, in all of which the Irish fought or worked side-by-side with English fellow victims. From the days of the United Irishmen – and the time when the Irish with their shillelaghs had helped in the defence of Thomas Hardy's house – a conscious political alliance had been maintained. English reformers generally supported the cause of Catholic Emancipation; for years Sir Francis Burdett was its foremost parliamentary champion, while Cobbett furthered the cause not only in the *Political Register* but also in his myth-making *History of the Protestant Reformation in England* (1823) in which the origin of Old Corruption and 'the Thing' was traced back to the Tudor despoliation of monasteries and charitable foundations. Radical publicists also kept alive memories of the savage repression of 1798, and Hone, Cruikshank and Wooler pursued Castlereagh ('Derry-Down-Triangle') without mercy for his complicity in the tortures and floggings. Roger O'Connor, the father of Feargus, was a close friend of Burdett and was at one time mooted as Burdett's fellow member for Westminster. In 1828 the Radical and anti-O'Connellite London Irish formed an Association for Civil and Political Liberty, which had Hunt's and Cobbett's support, which cooperated closely with advanced English Radicals, and which was one of the precursors of the National Union of the

1. Mayhew, op. cit., I, pp. 243, 252–3.

Working Classes (1830) – itself the forerunner of the Chartist London Working Men's Association (1836).[1]

There is thus a clear consecutive alliance between Irish nationalism and English Radicalism between 1790 and 1850, at times enlivened and confused by the fortunes of the O'Connor family. But in the Midlands and the north the influence of the Irish immigration was less explicit. For more than twenty years after 1798 one Irish county after another was swept by agrarian disturbances, in which secret societies – Threshers, Caravats, Shanavests, Tommy Downshires, Carders, Ribbonmen, and the later Molly Maguires – employed different forms of terrorism to defend tenant rights, hold down rents and prices, resist tithes, or drive out English landlords. In 1806 the Threshers virtually controlled Connaught, in 1810 the feuding Caravats and Shanavests were active in Tipperary, Kerry, Waterford; in 1813 disturbances spread to Meath, King's County and Limerick; while during the potato famine of 1821–2 disturbances spread throughout Munster, Leinster and parts of Connaught. Gun-law, the holding of hostages for execution by both sides, local feuds, robbery of arms, forced collections of money – the pent-up waters of agrarian hatred burst out in one place as soon as they had been dammed, by means of executions and transportations, in another. The countryside exhibited, the Irish Solicitor-General lamented in 1811, the 'formidable consequences of an armed peasantry, and a disarmed gentry'. The Lord Chief Baron, sentencing to death a boy scarcely in his teens for stealing arms, declared:

Can it be endured, that those persons who are labouring by day, should be legislating by night? – that those who are tilling the ground by day, should be enacting laws by night to govern the country?

1. See, e.g. Sherwin's *Political Register*, 19 and 26 July 1817; Hone's *Reformists' Register*, 19 July 1817; Cobbett's *Political Register*, 17 January 1818; *Cap of Liberty*, 8 September 1819; Cole, *Life of William Cobbett* (1924), pp. 308–9; D. Read and E. Glasgow, *Feargus O'Connor* (1961), pp. 12–14, 19. Roger O'Connor's connexion with the English movement was complicated by his claim to be the lawful King of Ireland (a claim which Feargus inherited). Roger's proposal to stand for Westminster was quashed by Cobbett on these grounds: 'No: we want not a multitude of Royal Families: the one Royal Family that we have is quite enough to satisfy any nation not destitute of all conscience.'

Many Irish immigrants, like Thomas Devyr of Donegal – who became Secretary to the Chartist Northern Political Union – had been accustomed in their youth to hear the 'heavy tramp' of men 'in semi-military array' through the village street at night.[1]

We can cite no actual biographies (what Irishman, in an English court, would have confessed to former membership of the Carders or 'Levellers'?) but there can be no doubt that some of the immigrants brought with them the traditions of these secret organizations. Their influence will be noted in 1800–1802 and during the Luddite years.[2] The rapid movement of men with blackened faces at night, the robbery of arms, the houghing of horses and cattle – these were methods in which many Irishmen had served an apprenticeship. Moreover, the existence of Irish colonies in all the manufacturing towns made for rapidity of communication. It contributed to the natural freemasonry of the disinherited; if the Irish were quick to quarrel, they were also quick to come to each others' aid.

If many of the peasantry brought their revolutionary inheritance with them, the priesthood did not. It was no part of the Church's desire to attract attention to the growing Catholic minority in Britain or to bring further disabilities down upon it. In the 1830s the politics of the priesthood went no further than allegiance to O'Connell; and O'Connell, who had abandoned the forty-shilling freeholders in Ireland in exchange for Emancipation, who voted against the 10 Hour Bill, and who confused and confounded his more critical countrymen in England by his egotism, his rhetorical royalism, and his in-and-out running with the Whigs, illustrates the alliance between Irish nationalism and English Radicalism at its weakest point. Hence, alone among the churches in England, the Catholic Church produced no 'maverick' clergy who became prominent in national radical movements. And although the Irish labourers were quick to join combinations, most of them worked in

1. See Halévy, op. cit., II, pp. 28–30; Wakefield, op. cit., II, pp. 763 ff.; Strauss, op. cit., pp. 88–9; Trials of the Caravats and Shanavests in Howell, *State Trials* (1823), XXXI, pp. 419, 423, 464; Devyr, op. cit pp. 93, 101.

2. See below, esp. pp. 652–4.

unskilled trades where unionism was weakest. Hence they produced few articulate leaders in the English movement. (John Doherty, with his tenacious attention to trade union organization, and his conscious adaptation of some of O'Connell's organizational methods to the National Association for the Protection of Labour (1829), was an exception.) The Irish influence is most felt in a rebellious disposition in the communities and places of work; in a disposition to challenge authority, to resort to the threat of 'physical force', and to refuse to be intimidated by the inhibitions of constitutionalism. The Irish were, a Catholic priest admitted in 1836, 'more prone to take part in trades unions, combinations and secret societies than the English'. 'They are the talkers and ringleaders on all occasions,' claimed another witness. Engels saw the 'passionate, mercurial Irish temperament' as the precipitate which brought the more disciplined and reserved English workers to the point of political action:

... the mixing of the more facile, exitable, fiery Irish temperament with the stable, reasoning, persevering English must, in the long run, be productive only of good for both. The rough egotism of the English bourgeoisie would have kept its hold on the working-class much more firmly if the Irish nature, generous to a fault, and ruled primarily by sentiment, had not intervened, and softened the cold, rational English character in part by a mixture of the races, and in part by the ordinary contact of life.[1]

We may dispute Engels' language of 'nature' and 'race'. But we need only replace these terms to find that his judgement is valid. It was an advantage to the employers, at a time when precision engineering coexisted with tunnelling by means of shovel and pick, to be able to call upon both types of labour. But the price which had to be paid was the confluence of sophisticated political Radicalism with a more primitive and excitable revolutionism. This confluence came in the Chartist movement; and when Feargus O'Connor broke with O'Connell, and Bronterre O'Brien adapted the socialism of land national-

1. *Report on the State of the Irish Poor*, p. xxiii; Strauss, op. cit., pp. 125–30; Engels, op. cit., p. 124. See also Rachel O'Higgins, 'The Irish Influence in the Chartist Movement', *Past and Present*, XX, November 1961, pp. 84–5.

ization to English conditions, it threatened to bring with it an even greater danger. Once before, in the 1790s, when Feargus's uncle, Arthur O'Connor, had been arrested with O'Coigly and Binns at Maidstone, it seemed possible that English Jacobinism and Irish nationalism would engage in a common revolutionary strategy. If O'Connor had been able to carry Ireland with him as he carried the north of England, then the Chartist and 'Young Ireland' movements might have come to a common insurrectionary flash-point. The reservations of the 'moral force' Chartists on the one hand, and the influence of O'Connell and the priesthood on the other, together with the terrible demoralization of the 'Great Hunger', prevented this from happening. But this lies beyond the limits of this study.

IV. MYRIADS OF ETERNITY

If we can now see more clearly many of the elements which made up the working-class communities of the early nineteenth century, a definitive answer to the 'standard-of-living' controversy must still evade us. For beneath the word 'standard' we must always find judgements of value as well as questions of fact. Values, we hope to have shown, are not 'imponderables' which the historian may safely dismiss with the reflection that, since they are not amenable to measurement, anyone's opinion is as good as anyone else's. They are, on the contrary, those questions of human satisfaction, and of the direction of social change, which the historian ought to ponder if history is to claim a position among the significant humanities.

The historian, or the historical sociologist, must in fact be concerned with judgements of value in two forms. In the first instance, he is concerned with the values actually held by those who lived through the Industrial Revolution. The old and newer modes of production each supported distinct kinds of community with characteristic ways of life. Alternative conventions and notions of human satisfaction were in conflict with each other, and there is no shortage of evidence if we wish to study the ensuing tensions.

In the second instance, he is concerned with making some judgement of value upon the whole process entailed in the

Industrial Revolution of which we ourselves are an end-product. It is our own involvement which makes judgement difficult. And yet we are helped towards a certain detachment, both by the 'romantic' critique of industrialism which stems from one part of the experience, and by the record of tenacious resistance by which hand-loom weaver, artisan or village craftsman confronted this experience and held fast to an alternative culture. As we see them change, so we see how we became what we are. We understand more clearly what was lost, what was driven 'underground', what is still unresolved.

Any evaluation of the quality of life must entail an assessment of the total life-experience, the manifold satisfactions or deprivations, cultural as well as material, of the people concerned. From such a standpoint, the older 'cataclysmic' view of the Industrial Revolution must still be accepted. During the years between 1780 and 1840 the people of Britain suffered an experience of immiseration, even if it is possible to show a small statistical improvement in material conditions. When Sir Charles Snow tells us that 'with singular unanimity ... the poor have walked off the land into the factories as fast as the factories could take them', we must reply, with Dr Leavis, that the 'actual history' of the 'full human problem [was] incomparably and poignantly more complex than that'.[1] Some were lured from the countryside by the glitter and promise of wages of the industrial town; but the old village economy was crumbling at their backs. They moved less by their own will than at the dictate of external compulsions which they could not question: the enclosures, the Wars, the Poor Laws, the decline of rural industries, the counter-revolutionary stance of their rulers.

The process of industrialization is necessarily painful. It must involve the erosion of traditional patterns of life. But it was carried through with exceptional violence in Britain. It was unrelieved by any sense of national participation in communal effort, such as is found in countries undergoing a national revolution. Its ideology was that of the masters alone. Its messianic prophet was Dr Andrew Ure, who saw the factory system as

1. C. P. Snow, *The Two Cultures* (1959); F. R. Leavis, 'The Significance of C. P. Snow', *Spectator*, 9 March 1962.

'the great minister of civilization to the terraqueous globe', diffusing 'the life-blood of science and religion to myriads ... still lying "in the region and shadow of death".'[1] But those who served it did not *feel* this to be so, any more than those 'myriads' who were served. The experience of immiseration came upon them in a hundred different forms; for the field labourer, the loss of his common rights and the vestiges of village democracy; for the artisan, the loss of his craftsman's status; for the weaver, the loss of livelihood and of independence; for the child, the loss of work and play in the home; for many groups of workers whose real earnings improved, the loss of security, leisure and the deterioration of the urban environment. R. M. Martin, who gave evidence before the Hand-Loom Weavers' Committee of 1834, and who had returned to England after an absence from Europe of ten years, was struck by the evidence of physical and spiritual deterioration:

I have observed it not only in the manufacturing but also in agricultural communities in the country; they seem to have lost their animation, their vivacity, their field games and their village sports; they have become a sordid, discontented, miserable, anxious, struggling people, without health, or gaiety, or happiness.

It is misleading to search for explanations in what Professor Ashton has rightly described as 'tedious' phrases, – man's 'divorce' from 'nature' or 'the soil'. After the 'Last Labourers' Revolt', the Wiltshire field labourers – who were close enough to 'nature' – were far worse degraded than the Lancashire mill girls. This violence was done to *human* nature. From one standpoint, it may be seen as the outcome of the pursuit of profit, when the cupidity of the owners of the means of production was freed from old sanctions and had not yet been subjected to new means of social control. In this sense we may still read it, as Marx did, as the violence of the capitalist class. From another standpoint, it may be seen as a violent technological differentiation between work and life.

It is neither poverty nor disease but work itself which casts the blackest shadow over the years of the Industrial Revolu-

1. *Philosophy of Manufactures*, pp. 18–19.

tion. It is Blake, himself a craftsman by training, who gives us the experience:

Then left the sons of Urizen the plow & harrow, the loom,
The hammer & the chisel & and the rule & compasses . . .
And all the arts of life they chang'd into the arts of death.
The hour glass contemn'd because its simple workmanship
Was as the workmanship of the plowman & the water wheel
That raises water into Cisterns, broken & burn'd in fire
Because its workmanship was like the workmanship of the shepherds
And in their stead intricate wheels invented, Wheel without wheel,
To perplex youth in their outgoings & to bind to labours
Of day & night the myriads of Eternity, that they might file
And polish brass & iron hour after hour, laborious workmanship,
Kept ignorant of the use that they might spend the days of wisdom
In sorrowful drudgery to obtain a scanty pittance of bread,
In ignorance to view a small portion & think that All,
And call it demonstration, blind to all the simple rules of life.

These 'myriads of eternity' seem at times to have been sealed in their work like a tomb. Their best efforts, over a lifetime, and supported by their own friendly societies, could scarcely ensure them that to which so high a popular value was attached – a 'Decent Funeral'. New skills were arising, old satisfactions persisted, but over all we feel the general pressure of long hours of unsatisfying labour under severe discipline for alien purposes. This was at the source of that 'ugliness' which, D. H. Lawrence wrote, 'betrayed the spirit of man in the nineteenth century'.[1] After all other impressions fade, this one remains; together with that of the loss of any felt cohesion in the community, save that which the working people, in antagonism to their labour and to their masters, built for themselves.

1. 'Nottingham and the Mining Country', *Selected Essays* (Penguin edn), pp. 119, 122.

Part Three

THE WORKING-CLASS PRESENCE

'The Levelution is begun,
So I'll go home and get my gun,
And shoot the Duke of Wellington.'
Belper street-song

'The people are not apt ... to volunteer a rebellion for
the theatrical éclat of the thing.'
WILLIAM HAZLITT

[13]

Radical Westminster

POPULAR radicalism was not extinguished when the corresponding societies were broken up, Habeas Corpus suspended, and all 'Jacobin' manifestations outlawed. It simply lost coherence. For years it was made inarticulate by censorship and intimidation. It lost its press, it lost its organized expression, it lost its own sense of direction. But it is there, as a palpable presence, throughout the Wars. It is scarcely possible to give a coherent historical account of an incoherent presence, but some attempt must be made.

In 1797, as Pitt's repression settled upon the country, Grey and Fox moved for a last time a motion in the House for household suffrage. Thereafter, Fox and his patrician rump of Whig 'commonwealthsmen' seceded from the House, in protest against the suspension of Habeas Corpus and in opposition to the war. They retired to their country mansions, their amusements and their scholarship, their discussions at Holland House and Brooks' Club. Wealthy and influential, they could not be altogether excluded from political life, since they were secure in the possession of rotten boroughs which their own principles denounced.[1] After 1800 they drifted back and resumed their seats in the House. While the democratic persuasions of most of the group were largely speculative, individual members – Sir Samuel Romilly, Samuel Whitbread, H. G. Bennet – stood up again and again in the House to defend political liberties or social rights. Between 1797 and 1802, Fox appeared to provide the only shelter for reform. Here and there groups met to toast Fox and Grey, to demand the restoration of political liberties, or to petition for peace. In

1. One of the oddest ironies of the time was the return of Horne Tooke in 1800 as Member for the rottenest borough of all – Old Sarum. Tooke was unseated on a technicality – that he was a former Minister of the Church.

Norwich former Jacobins met in this way, and commenced in 1799 'an open Monthly Meeting of the Friends of Liberty'.[1]

But the least evidence of such groups drew the immediate attention of magistrates, and the fire of anti-Jacobin publicists – not the least vitriolic of whom was a new journalist, William Cobbett, who had recently returned from the United States where he had done service as an anti-Jacobin polemicist, and who had been rewarded for his patriotism by being given assistance by the Secretary at War, Windham, in founding his *Political Register* (1802). But if the open reformers were dispersed or driven underground, general disaffection grew throughout the years 1799–1802. Napoleon's continental blockade brought to Britain stagnant industries, unemployment and soaring food prices. Manufacturers petitioned for peace, and were supported by a swell of resentment against the Assessed Taxes. There were food riots throughout the country. And there is evidence to suggest an organized, insurrectionary underground.[2]

The brief Peace of Amiens (April 1802 to May 1803) introduced a new period. Pitt gave way for a time to Addington (later Lord Sidmouth), who was a weaker Prime Minister, although he was firmly in the same anti-Jacobin, repressive tradition. The war had dragged on for nearly ten years, and the peace was received with illuminations and public rejoicing. Napoleon's emissary was drawn in triumph through the London streets. Cobbett's office was wrecked because the *Register* supported the continuance of war. Curious Whigs and reformers, including Fox himself, flocked to Paris to look at the new republic. (Colonel Thornton, who had flung his regimentals to the York 'rabble' in 1795, brought to Paris a pack of fox hounds, horses, and a case of pistols as a gift for the First Consul.)

Peace brought a General Election, in which in half a dozen constituencies advanced candidates, with Jacobin support, achieved surprising success. In Kent, where the corresponding societies had once had such strength in the Medway towns, a

---

1. One of the People, *The Thirty-Sixth of a Letter to the Society which met at The Angel . . . to Celebrate the Birth-Day of C. J. Fox* (Norwich, 1799).   2. See below, pp. 515–28.

Foxite candidate defeated the sitting Member. In Coventry after serious riots a Radical failed to secure election by a mere eight votes. In Norwich Windham, the Secretary at War, was unseated, and two Foxite candidates were elected with very active Jacobin support. At Nottingham there were extraordinary scenes of excitement, when a reformer was elected with the support of the Foxite corporation and the exultant crowd. In a triumphant procession, the band played *Ça Ira* and the 'Marseillaise', the tricolour was hoisted, and (according to an anti-Jacobin pamphleteer) 'a female, representing the Goddess of Reason, in a state of ENTIRE NUDITY was a conspicuous figure! ! !' The Nottingham crowd (commented Cobbett) was 'to all appearances ... a republican, revolutionary mob'. The victor was unseated, in 1803, by the House of Commons, on the plea that rioters had intimidated the electors; and the event was made the occasion for introducing legislation strengthening the power of country magistrates in the manufacturing town.[1]

But the most sensational election was in Middlesex, Wilkes' old constituency. In the previous three years scandals had come to light as to the treatment of the 'Habeas Corpus prisoners' of the L.C.S. and United Englishmen, held without trial in Coldbath Fields prison, under the régime of Governor Aris. Sir Francis Burdett, an M.P. and friend of Horne Tooke, received an appeal from the victims, written – according to a later account by Cobbett – upon the fly-leaf of a book with a splinter of wood dipped in blood. He found several of the prisoners emaciated, 'mere frames of men', and took up their cases – in particular the case of Colonel Despard – inside and outside the House of Commons. Overnight he became the hero of the London crowd, and the cry went up: NO BASTILLE! In 1802 he fought Middlesex against the sitting Member, a ministerial supporter named Mainwaring who was also a

1. J. Bowles, *Thoughts on the late General Election, as demonstrative of the Progress of Jacobinism* (1802), pp. 3–4; and *Salutary Effects of Vigour* (1804), p. 141. Reformers angrily gave the lie to Bowles with respect to the allegation of a naked lady: see *Ten Letters on the Late Contested Election at Nottingham* (Nottingham, 1803), pp. 24–5; Sutton, *Date-Book of Nottingham*, p. 244. The secret perhaps lies in a reference to a woman in the procession 'dressed in salmon or flesh-coloured apparel': *Letter to John Bowles* (Nottingham, 1803), p. 9.

magistrate associated with Governor Aris. The campaign focused the attention of the country, John Frost, who had been pilloried in 1794, was one of Burdett's agents; and other former Jacobins and detainees helped with his campaign. The still-Tory Cobbett lamented that:

The road from Piccadilly to the hustings at Brentford is a scene of confusion and sedition, such as never was beheld, except in the environs of Paris, during the most dreadful times of the revolution. ... The road ... is lined with ragged wretches from St Giles's bawling out 'Sir Francis Burdett and No Bastille' and at the hustings there are daily some half a dozen convicts who have served out their time in the house of correction, employed in amusing the rabble with execrations on the head of Mr Mainwaring.

Burdett's victory was the signal for illuminations almost on the scale of the celebration of the peace. 'It will have this most dreadful effect', mourned Cobbett. 'It will embolden and increase the disorderly and dishonest part of this monstrously overgrown and profligate metropolis.'[1]

Even Lancaster saw a contest in which a 'Jacobinical mob' was addressed by a lady, who told them that 'the contest was between shoes and wooden clogs, between fine shirts and coarse ones, between the opulent and the poor, and that the people were everything if they chose to assert their rights'.[2] It seemed that a movement of greater force than that of 1792–5 was maturing. The course of English history might have been changed if there had been five years of peace. But events occurred which threw all into confusion. In November 1802, Colonel Despard was seized on a charge of high treason; in January executed.[3] In the winter of 1802–3 relations between Britain and France became acrimonious. In May 1803, the two countries were once again at war.

But this appeared to many reformers as a different kind of war. In 1802 Napoleon had become First Consul for life; in

1. Elected, Byng (Whig), 3,843, Burdett (Radical), 3,207. Not elected, Mainwaring (Tory), 2,936. See Cobbett's *Political Register*, 10, 17, 24 July 1802; J. G. Alger, *Napoleon's British Visitors and Captives* (1904); J. Dechamps, *Les Iles Britanniques et La Revolution Française* (Brussels, 1949), ch. 5; M. W. Patterson, *Sir Francis Burdett* (1931), chs. 4 and 7.

2. J. Bowles, *Thoughts on the late General Election*, p. 63.

3. See below, pp. 521–8.

1804 he accepted the crown as hereditary Emperor. No true
follower of Paine could stomach this. The hardened Jacobin
was cut as deeply by this as more moderate reformers had
been dismayed by Robespierre. However much they had sought
to maintain a critical detachment, the morale of English reformers was closely involved with the fortunes of France.
The First Empire struck a blow at English republicanism from
which it never fully recovered. The *Rights of Man* had been
most passionate in its indictment of thrones, Gothic institutions, hereditary distinctions; as the war proceeded, Napoleon's
accommodation with the Vatican, his king-making and his
elevation of a new hereditary nobility, stripped France of its
last revolutionary magnetism. *Ça Ira* faded in the memories
even of the Nottingham crowd. If the Tree of Liberty was to
grow, it must be grafted to English stock.

France appeared to many now simply in the guise of a
commercial and imperial rival, the oppressor of Spanish and
Italian peoples. Between 1803 and 1806 the Grand Army was
poised across the Channel, waiting only for mastery of the
seas. 'Jacobinism is killed and gone,' declared Sheridan, who
had himself joined Addington's Ministry, in December 1802:
'And by whom? By him who can no longer be called the child
and champion of Jacobinism; by Buonaparté.' And Windham,
fresh from his Norwich defeat, made an extraordinary appeal in
the House for national unity in the face of the return of war:

To the Jacobins I would appeal, not as lovers of social order, of
good government, of monarchy, but as men of spirit, as lovers of
what they call liberty, as men of hot and proud blood – I would ask
them if they are content to be put under the yoke, and crushed by
France? [1]

With the renewal of war, the Volunteers drilled Sunday
after Sunday. They were not, perhaps, as popular as contemporary publicists and patriotic legend suggest. 'Volunteers'
is, in any case, a misnomer. Officers came forward a great
deal more readily than the miscellaneous, ill-disciplined, incurably anti-militaristic rank-and-file, who were losing their
only day of rest. Pains were taken, also, to keep arms out of the
hands of the disaffected. 'In large towns,' Sheridan said on

1. Cobbett's *Parliamentary Debates*, II, Supplement, 1667, 1752.

behalf of the Government, 'such as Birmingham, Sheffield, and Nottingham, he should prefer associations of the higher classes, and in the country and villages those of the lower.' In Norwich, *The Times* reported in 1804,

the common people in the city ... and its vicinity have taken an aversion to the system of volunteering. On Monday an attempt was made by them, particularly the females, to obstruct the volunteers of the Norwich regiment from mustering. They abused and insulted the officers, and accused the volunteers of being the cause of small loaves and the advance in corn.

The sons of the squire, the attorney, and the manufacturer, enjoyed dressing up on horseback and attending Volunteer balls. A common understanding grew up between aristocracy and middle class, forming that *esprit de corps* which was later to carry the day on the field at Peterloo; while at the balls their sisters selected husbands who facilitated that cross-fertilization of landed and commercial wealth which distinguished the English Industrial Revolution. The rank-and-file had few such rewards: in one Northumberland village, with a high percentage of 'volunteers', '13 offered to serve in the infantry, 25 in the cavalry, 130 as guides, 260 as waggoners, and 300 as drivers of cattle'.[1]

But despite this undercurrent, Sheridan was right, Jacobinism, as a movement deriving inspiration from France, was almost dead. Between 1802 and 1806 there was certainly a revival of popular patriotic feeling. 'Boney', if he was admired, was admired as a 'warrior', not as an embodiment of popular rights. Britain was inundated with patriotic chap-books, broadsheets, and prints. If the women of Norwich resisted and if Northumberland villagers played dumb, thousands of Lancashire weavers joined the Volunteers. Nelson was as popular a war hero as England had known since Drake; he was thought to be a man with sympathy for popular rights, and his intercession for the life of Colonel Despard was remem-

1. *Cobbett's Parliamentary Debates*, IV, 1191, 1362; *The Times*, 5 November 1804. For a contemporary record of the reconciliation between land and commerce in the Volunteers, see T. A. Ward's Sheffield diary, *Peeps into the Past, passim*. And Jane Austen.

bered; the bitter-sweet victory of Trafalgar (1805) was the
theme of a hundred ballads and the talk of every tavern and
hamlet. In 1806 Fox (in the last year of his life) himself
joined the national coalition – the 'Ministry of All-the-Talents'
– and became resigned to the continuance of war.[1]

Once again, Radicalism was not extinguished. But the terms
of argument shifted beyond recognition. Former Jacobins became patriots, as eager to denounce Napoleon for his apostasy
to the republican cause as legitimists were to denounce him
for his usurpation from the House of Bourbon. (In 1808 a
former Secretary of the L.C.S., John Bone, made a significant
attempt to reawaken the old cause by publishing the *Reasoner*,
a journal which supported both the war and many old
'Jacobin' demands.[2]) Others, like Redhead Yorke of Sheffield,
suffered the classic compulsions of guilt and the desire for
self-exculpation, so familiar in the disenchanted romantics of
more recent times; Yorke had become by 1804 an 'anti-
Jacobin' publicist so virulent that Cobbett was driven by him
towards the reformers out of sheer disgust.

It was in this highly unexpected quarter that the new note of
Radicalism was first sounded. For the same influences which
had dispersed the old kind of Jacobinism had also caused the
old kind of *anti*-Jacobinism to lose some of its force. If
Napoleon was an enemy because he was a despot who had concentrated all power in his hands, what was to be said of Pitt,
who (back in power from 1804 until his death early in 1806)
had eroded British liberties, jailed men without trial, bribed the
press, and used every form of Ministerial influence to shore up
his power? Cobbett, the pugnacious Tory journalist who could
by no stretch of the imagination be accused of Jacobinism, swung
round in 1804 and began to rake the Ministry with polemic:

The tide has turned: from popular enthusiasm it has run back to
despotism: Buonaparté's exaltation to the post of Consul for life
began the great change in men's minds, which has been completed

1. For the literature of popular patriotism, see F. Klingberg and S.
Hustvedt, *The Warning Drum ... Broadsides of 1803* (Univ. of Cali-
fornia, 1944). Even John Thelwall contributed a *Poem and Oration on
the Death of Lord Nelson* (1805).

2. This honourably named periodical failed through lack of support.
See *Reasoner*, 16 April 1808.

by his more recent assumption [i.e. as Emperor], and which not only removes the danger before to be apprehended from the prevalence of notions in favour of liberty, but tends to excite apprehensions of a different kind, to make us fear that, by means of the immense and yet growing influence now deposited in the hands of the minister by the funding and bank-note system, we may, in fact, though not in name, become little better than slaves, and slaves, too, not of the king but of the minister of the day ...

The logic which connected the despotism of Napoleon and of Pitt is by no means clear: Cobbett, so cogent in detailed argument, often blustered through the larger outlines. But the drift of what he said, with increasing force and frequency, was clear. Despotism ought to be fought at home as well as abroad. The press was bought. The Ministry was inefficient and corrupt, supporting a mob of 'court-sycophants, parasites, pensioners, bribed-senators, directors, contractors, jobbers, hireling lords, and ministers of state'. The Civil List was a form of factional bribery, supported by money raised from excessive taxation. The upstart *nouveau riche*, fattened by the war, threatened the rights of the King and the liberties of the people. Only a free Britain could resist foreign invasion. In a queer jumble of Toryism and Radicalism he accused, not the reformers, but the Ministry of:

... endeavouring to sow the seeds of discord amongst [the people]; to divide them again into Jacobins and Anti-Jacobins; to hatch a pretext for measures of extraordinary coercion; to create discontent and disloyalty, to unnerve the arm of war, and to lay us prostrate at the foot of the enemy.[1]

Cobbett's words were no less remarkable than their occasion. Mainwaring had upset the 1802 result on a petition to the House. In 1804 there was a Middlesex by-election, in which every Ministerial resource was employed to push Sir Francis Burdett out, and replace him by Mainwaring's son. Burdett was scarcely a reformer of the calibre to provide national leadership. He was a patrician Radical who consciously modelled his tactics upon Wilkes,[2] and who had acquired great

1. *Political Register*, 1 September 1804.
2. 'I shall ... use my utmost endeavour,' he said on the hustings in 1804, 'that 45 and Liberty shall go down connected together to the latest posterity.'

wealth through his marriage to Miss Sophia Coutts. Histrionic on the hustings, he proved himself to be a weak reform leader in the House in the next ten or fifteen years. But he was one of the only national spokesmen of reform capable of being heard at all. He did not try to repudiate the taint of Jacobinism brought upon him by his friendship with Horne Tooke and Arthur O'Connor. In 1804 he stood his ground, and while the populace huzza'd NO BASTILLE he poured scorn on Whigs and Tories alike. For fifteen days the poll wavered between Mainwaring and Burdett. Every day, at the close of the poll, Burdett addressed enormous, excited crowds, appealing to the Middlesex freeholders under the slogan of 'INDEPENDENCE', urging them again and again to 'be active and canvass'. Could the electors of Middlesex have 'a free and independent voice,' or was the seat to be traded in perpetuity into the control of 'a combination of interested distillers, publicans and brewers, of magistrates and contractors'? Every day at the close of the poll, Mainwaring stepped forward to address the crowd on the hustings, and was howled down with groans. The supporters of Mainwaring placarded London with libels upon Burdett and his 'Jacobin' connexions, challenged his voters, and polled every elector subject to influence – 'the clerks, psalm-singers and bell-ringers of Westminster', 'police-officers, jobbers, and thief-takers'. On the fifteenth and final day it appeared that Burdett had a majority of one: Burdett, 2,833, Mainwaring, 2,832. An exultant crowd dragged him in triumph through London 'amidst a cavalcade, that appeared like a moving wood – the carriages and horsemen being covered with green boughs', while the bands played 'Rule Britannia' and a flag flew above Burdett's carriage painted with Hercules treading on the Hydra. On the next morning the Sheriff reversed the decision on a technicality which turned on the closing time of the poll. But the moral triumph was complete.[1]

Cobbett was right to speak of a turning tide. His own support for Burdett – inconceivable two years before – was a sign of the turn. That so many freeholders should have declared for Burdett indicated an unusual restiveness among the tradesmen, professional men and small gentry, and master-artisans. They

1. *Cobbett's Political Register*, 25 August 1804.

had a dozen grievances, some disinterested – the appeal of the old cries of 'liberty' and 'independence' – some more interested; for example, Government contracts for coach-building, harness, and military clothing were commonly placed with a few big firms or middle-men, passing over the host of smaller masters and master-artisans. Cobbett, in 1804–6, was not initiating but flowing *with* a new reforming tide. In the next few years his *Register* voiced a pugnacious piecemeal Radicalism, which was the more formidable in that each particular abuse was aired and argued with individual detail. Cobbett exposed civil and military mismanagement, peculation, the sale of commissions by the Duke of York's mistress, brutal flogging in the Army, with a force which compelled attention from men of different persuasions, for many of whom the old alignments of the 1790s had lost their meaning. *Because* Cobbett was still something of a Tory, who harked back to a sentimental ideal of a sturdy, independent, plain-speaking people who despised wealth and rank but were loyal to their Constitution, he evaded the anti-Jacobin prejudices and enabled reformers to re-group.

But Burdett's triumph was made possible by the presence of the far more radical London crowd. In 1806 popular feeling found another outlet, and surged through into the electoral process at Westminster. While Middlesex had a freeholder franchise, Westminster was one of the few 'open' constituencies in the south of England, with a householder franchise which admitted many master-artisans and some journeymen to the vote. From 1780 one of its two seats had been held by Fox. Horne Tooke had contested the other seat, and had polled respectably, in 1790 and 1796, but the seat had gone to a Ministerial nominee by tacit agreement. 'Pitt's party put in one Member, and Fox's party put in the other; and, both parties hated all thought of any thing resembling a real election. The affair was settled at a joint meeting of the two factions, as thieves made a division of booty . . .'[1]

On Fox's death, the seat was left open to the Whig faction and the Duke of Northumberland arrogated to himself the

1. See Cobbett's partisan account of the 1806 contest, written twelve years later, *Political Register*, 17 January 1818.

right to nominate his son, Lord Percy, who was 'elected' without a contest. Francis Place watched with disgust, as the Duke's liveried servants threw lumps of bread and cheese, and distributed beer, to the servile, struggling mob.[1] With a General Election approaching, Cobbett addressed four open letters to the electors of Westminster. The themes were simple:

To hear some persons talk of an election for Westminster, a stranger to the state of things would believe, that the electors were the bondsmen, or, at best, the mere menial servants of a few great families. The question ... seems to be, not what man the electors may wish to choose, but what man is preferred by a few of the noblemen ...

Electors should assert their independence, and rid themselves of deference and the fear of influence:

You are nearly *twenty thousand* in number. Your trades and occupations are ... full as necessary to your employers as their employment is necessary to you. If you are turned out of one house, there is always another ready to receive you; if you lose one customer you gain another ...

In particular, 'the *journeymen* who compose no small part of the electors of Westminster, appear to me to be entirely out of the reach of seduction ...' Employers who sought to enforce the votes of their employees should be exposed to 'public scorn': 'the artisans of a workshop, led to the hustings under the command of the master, are degraded to a level with cattle'. Unless some independent candidate offered himself at the General Election, 'Westminster would ... place itself upon a level with Old Sarum or Gatton'.[2]

The Tories brought forward Admiral Hood. The Whigs brought forward Fox's old colleague, Sheridan, who was now Naval Secretary in the Coalition Government, in receipt of £6,000 a year. Cobbett and the reformers would have nothing to do with him. At the eleventh hour, a candidate offered himself who personified the state of confusion in the Radical camp. James Paull, the son of a Perth tailor, was a self-made

1. See above, p. 84.
2. Ibid., 9 August, 20 and 27 September 1806.

wealthy India merchant, who had returned to England in 1804 with the aim of assisting in the impeachment of Governor-General Wellesley. He was taken up by Fox's circle, which then had the support of the Prince of Wales; and as a man likely to embarrass Pitt's administration, he was found (in 1805) a seat in the rotten borough of Newtown, Isle of Wight. The attack on Wellesley was duly launched. But when the Foxites entered the Coalition, Paull was privately told to drop the matter, or at the least 'lay upon my oars'. When Paull indignantly refused he found himself at the dissolution ejected from his seat at Newtown, and repudiated by the men whom he had naïvely supposed to have his cause at heart. His answer was to hurl himself on to the hustings at Westminster.

Paull passed briefly through Radical history, and no one has bothered to find out much about him. It is customary to dismiss him as a quarrelsome little man with a personal grievance. His grievance, however, was more than personal. Wellesley's arrogance, brutality, and bad faith in his dealings with Oudh are incontestable. There is no reason to suppose that Paull was not passionately outraged by these 'acts of wanton aggression and tyranny' in India, which he compared with those for which 'we are daily reproaching' France. If the issues were remote for the Westminster electors, Paull compelled respect as a man whom both the Whigs and the Tories wished to silence. 'What our man wanted in point of talent and knowledge,' Cobbett wrote later,

he amply made up for in *industry* and *pluck*. He was a man of diminutive size; but what there was of him was good. He was game, every inch of him: a real game cock.

He knew little of English politics, had no great eloquence as a speaker or cogency as a writer, but he also had no political inhibitions or ambitions. In three weeks of tumultuous campaigning, a new alliance of reformers was founded: Sir Francis Burdett, the patrician Radical, who nominated Paull on the hustings; Cobbett, the empirical reformer who directed his campaign; and Major Cartwright, the veteran advocate of manhood suffrage, who secured from Paull a pledge that he was a parliamentary reformer.

'We had to contend against the whole force of the Borough-faction, who had united against us in open, active, and desperate hostility,' Cobbett recalled. The first four days of the poll showed Paull in the lead, whereupon Hood and Sheridan, who had ridiculed his chances, formed a coalition against him. Broadsheets, squibs, and songs flew around London:

> Lo! Corruption stalks forward in Liberty's guise,
> Freemen! rally your legions, and guard your rich prize,
> Wave your banners on high, at fair Liberty's call —
> Shout the watch-word aloud — *Independence and Paull*!
>
> Let the place-hunting crew 'gainst our politics rant,
> Call us Jacobins, Traitors, and such idle cant;
> With our King we're determined to stand or to fall —
> So success to our cause — *Independence and Paull*!
>
> He's the friend of the poor, and the freedom of man,
> And will lighten our taxes as fast as he can . . .

Paull's opponents ridiculed his humble origins, and his appearance:

> . . . who is that odd little fellow beyond,
> Who looks like a pickpocket dragg'd to a pond?

On one side, declared Cobbett, were the 'relations of placemen and pensioners', the 'tax-gatherers, magistrates, police-men, and dependent clergy', and Sheridan's personal following of 'play-actors, scene-shifters, candle-snuffers, and persons following . . . immoral callings'. On the other side, there is evidence of the first serious attempts at democratic electoral organization among the artisans and journeymen; parish committees for canvassing; and organized support among the trades clubs of journeymen-shoemakers, printers, and tailors. Night after night the crowd drew Paull in triumph through the streets.

James Paull failed to gain the seat, but he came in only 300 votes behind Sheridan[1] and the campaign broke the grip of both the factions upon Westminster. 'That was the *real struggle*,' declared Cobbett: 'that was the *real triumph* of freedom in Westminster.' When actual victory came in the following year, Paull had no part in it. Burdett had failed to

1. Hood, 5,478, Sheridan, 4,758; Paull, 4,481.

win Middlesex in 1806; some of the freeholders were frightened
by his extremism, although he still commanded the huzzas of
the hustings and on his defeat 'most of the houses in Kensing-
ton and Knightsbridge were illuminated, and the whole had
more the appearance of a triumph ...' But he failed also for
another, and typically quixotic, reason. In previous contests
he had used his great wealth freely in the traditional manner
of electioneering, with the wholesale treating of voters, and
probably as much general oiling with drink and money as was
employed by his opponents. He was now nettled by accusations
of bribery; while Cobbett, who was now his ally, had been
sounding throughout 1806 the demands of electoral austerity.
In a celebrated by-election at Honiton in 1806 Cobbett had
demanded the absolute prohibition of bribery and treating, and
that the candidates should enter into a solemn pledge that if
returned they would accept neither office nor public money.
Burdett, therefore, adopted the austere manner; but, not content with this, he refused to do more than appear each day on
the hustings and call upon the 'independent electors' to come
forward of their own accord. There was to be no canvassing, no
treating, no carriages for elderly voters, no organization whatsoever. When his supporters formed a committee, he repudiated
it upon the hustings and urged them to rely on the 'unassisted
public principle'. The reliance halved his vote.

In 1807 another General Election gave reformers their opportunity. Week after week in the *Political Register* Cobbett
addressed letters to the electors of Westminster, sounding an
alert. Paull's supporters got ready, and a committee was formed
which called on Burdett to fight for the other seat. But Burdett
had given up:

With the omnipotent means of corruption in the power of our
spoilers, all struggle is vain. We must wait for our redress and
regeneration till corruption shall have exhausted the means of corruption. ... Till that time shall arrive, I beg leave to retire from all
parliamentary service ...

A deputation waited upon him, and asked whether if he was
elected without his own permission or intervention, he would be
willing to accept the seat? To this Burdett gave a weary assent:
'If I should be returned for Westminster ... I must obey the

call ... but I will not spend a guinea, nor do anything whatever, to contribute to such election.' There was worse to follow. With this passive assent, the Westminster Committee prepared to bring forward Burdett and Paull as colleagues for the two seats. But Burdett seems to have wished to shake off his plebeian fellow candidate, whereupon the 'game cock' flew into a rage and challenged Burdett to a duel in which both were wounded – Paull so seriously that his supporters dropped his candidature. On the eve of the fifteen-day poll the reformers' cause appeared to have brawled and ridiculed itself out of the field.[1] The last-minute candidature of a little-known Radical sailor, Lord Cochrane, brought a slight revival of hopes. But on the morning when the poll commenced, the members of Burdett's committee 'were very much depressed':

We had no money, no means of making a display, nobody had joined us, the Tories despised us and the Whigs derided us. It was the being laughed at that produced the worst effect of all ... those who could well have borne to have been abused could not bear to be laughed at.

But only a fortnight later the artisans and shopkeepers of Westminster were chairing Burdett and Cochrane in a tumultuous triumph. Burdett had left the others far behind, while Cochrane had won the second seat with a majority of 1,000 over Sheridan. (Cochrane was so sorry for Sheridan on the last day of the poll that he took off his inspectors, and allowed him to poll the same voters many times over in order to achieve a more respectable defeat.) Thereafter Westminster (except for a curious episode in 1819) was never lost to Radicalism. The only popular constituency in London, in which the Houses of Parliament were situated, had been captured by men whom almost the entire press designated as 'Jacobins'.[2]

1. For this incident, see *Annual Register*, 1807, pp. 425–8, 632–9; M. D. George, *Catalogue of Political and Personal Satires* (1947), VIII, pp. 528–9.

2. Cochrane held his seat until 1818, when he resigned it in order to go to the aid of the South American republics. Burdett remained Member for Westminster until 1837, when, with a final quixotic flourish, he crossed the floor of the House, resigned the seat and fought it again as a Conservative, just scraping home. Paull was less fortunate: he survived the duel by little more than a year, taking his own life in 1808.

This was not as wild an accusation at it seems. An interesting incident had taken place in 1806. Paull was informed that a leading member of his committee was a notorious Jacobin of French origin, Mr Lemaitre. In horror he demanded that Lemaitre leave his committee-rooms, and asked Cobbett to deliver the message. Cobbett tried to serve the sentence of dismissal as gently as he could, but he encountered a man of greater strength of will than he expected. Lemaitre was indeed a former Jacobin; an active member of the L.C.S. and a watch-case maker, he had been seized during the 'Pop-Gun Plot' scare of 1794-5, imprisoned again without trial in 1796, and was detained once more between 1798 and 1801, being 'confined a great part of the period between eighteen and twenty-five years of age'. On his release, he had helped Burdett in his Middlesex elections, and had gained considerable experience. Entering Paull's committee-rooms on the third day of the poll, he found the Committee 'had neither plan nor system to regulate the business of the canvass'. For several days he had worked from early morning until midnight to organ-ize an effective plan of canvass. This plan he now brought to Cobbett's attention. 'Upon my honour, Mr Lemaitre, this is the only really useful thing I have yet seen in this commit-tee,' exclaimed Cobbett. Apologies were made, and Lemaitre remained.

The victory of 1807 was entirely the work of the Westminster Committee. Several of its key members were former commit-teemen of the L.C.S. Lemaitre had his plan of street-by-street and court-by-court canvass prepared well in advance. On the third floor of 'a Gin Shop called the Britannia Coffee House', Francis Place worked for three weeks without payment, from dawn until midnight, keeping careful accounts, collating can-vass returns, and preparing reports for the General Committee. Richter, another former detainee, was his lieutenant. 'We were all of us obscure persons,' wrote Place:

... not one man of note among us, not one man in any way known to the electors generally, as insignificant a set of persons as could well have been collected together to undertake so important a matter as a Westminster election against wealth and rank and name and influence ...

They were derided by their opponents as 'nobody, common tailors, and Barbers. ... We were laughed at for our folly, and condemned for our impudence.' Both principle and the shortage of funds demanded electoral austerity:

... there should be no paid counsellors, attorneys, inspectors nor canvassers, no bribing, no paying of rates, no treating, no cockades, no paid constables, excepting two to keep the committee-room doors.

No money was spent, except by a vote of the committee. By far the greatest item of expense (until the flags, bands, and ribbons of the triumph) was in printing handbills and placards. In Place, who only left the committee-rooms once to canvass, the Committee had an organizer of genius.[1]

We must now attempt some survey of the position of the English Radicalism in 1807. In the first place, the term 'radicalism' suggests both a breadth and an imprecision in the movement. The Jacobins of the 1790s were clearly identified by their allegiance to the *Rights of Man* and to certain forms of open organization. 'Radicalism' came to include very diverse tendencies as the nineteenth century advanced. In 1807 it suggests as much about the courage and tone of the movement as it does about any doctrine. It indicated intransigent opposition to the Government; contempt for the weakness of the Whigs; opposition to restrictions upon political liberties; open exposure of corruption and the 'Pitt system'; and general support for parliamentary reform. There was little agreement on social and

1. This account of the 1806 and 1807 elections is based largely upon Cobbett's *Political Register*, 1806 and 1807, *passim*; Ibid., 17 January 1818; Flower's *Political Review*, May 1807; Place's reminiscences, in Wallas, op. cit., pp. 41–7, and in Cole and Filson, *British Working Class Movements*, pp. 79–81; Anon., *History of the Westminster and Middlesex Elections* (1807), pp. 15, 36–7, 145, 157, 345, 379, 437; Westminster Committee, *An Exposition of the Circumstances which gave rise to the Election of Sir F. Burdett, Bart* ... (1807). See also M. W. Patterson, *Sir F. Burdett* (1931), 1, ch. 10; G. D. H. Cole, *Life of Cobbett*, chs. 9 and 10; C. Lloyd, *Lord Cochrane* (1947), Part II, ch. 1; S. Maccoby, *English Radicalism, 1786–1832*, pp. 207–8. Cobbett's account, while not wholly reliable, is a corrective to the accounts supplied by Place (and accepted too uncritically) which neglect the importance of the Middlesex elections of 1802 and 1804, ridicule Paull, and attribute success in 1807 solely to Place's own organizing genius.

economic questions, and while the most consistent radicalism was that of the London populace, it was broad enough to take in at times the unrest of manufacturers or small gentry.

Notwithstanding their confusion, the contests of 1806 and 1807 were of real importance. The cause of reform became articulate once more. There were two extreme Radicals, returned by a plebeian electorate, in the House. There was a weekly journal, edited with genius, which the administration could scarcely ban, and which had proclaimed itself beyond reach of Tory or Whig influence. Even the 'father of reform', Major Cartwright, had secured renewed publicity and popularity.[1] A new name is first heard – a gentleman-farmer, Henry Hunt, who issued an appeal to the freeholders of Wiltshire to follow the example of Westminster. In the city itself a new kind of electoral organization had been built up; and the Westminster Committee did not disband itself, but remained for many years as a prototype of post-war reform organizations. These names – Burdett, Cartwright, Cobbett, Hunt, Place – are prominent in the history of articulate Radicalism for the next fifteen years. Burdett continued for some years to be the darling of the London crowd. Cartwright, whose fixity outlasted every twist of events, was to promote the first Hampden Clubs. Cobbett was to advance step by step from 'independence' to root-and-branch denunciation of 'Old Corruption' – and, indeed, of milk-and-water Radicals like Burdett and Place. Hunt was to act, now as Cobbett's ally, now as his rival, pitting his mastery of mass oratory against Cobbett's mastery of polemic. Place was to develop the policy of reformist permeation, and of the artisan and middle class alliance, and was to act as the link between Benthamite reformers and trade unions and plebeian debating groups.

The victory of 1807 was a half-way house between the patrician techniques of Wilkes and more advanced forms of democratic organization. The gains were important. A new meaning had been given to the notion of 'independence'. Hitherto, the word had been a synonym for opulence and

1. In addition to the support which he gave to Paull and Burdett, Cartwright himself stood in 1806 for his own town of Boston, polling 59 votes against 237 for the successful candidate.

landed interest: Whig and Tory candidates were often recommended on the hustings on account of their wealth, which, it was supposed, would render them 'independent' of the need to curry favour or place from the Ministers or King. Cobbett's notion of independence insisted upon the duty of the *electors*, whether freeholders, tradesmen or artisans, to free themselves by their own exertions from patronage, bribery and deference. The Westminster Committee had gone yet further; in so far as they had organized victory independently of their own candidates, the *menu peuple* of Westminster had emerged as a force in their own right. Moreover, they had provided a striking example of the effectiveness of a new kind of electoral organization, dependent not upon the wealth or influence of the candidate but upon the voluntary exertions of the electors. In this sense the people of Westminster felt the victory to be their own.

It would be wrong, however, to suggest that the Westminster Committee led an independent 'populist', still less working-class, movement. The electorate (comprising about 18,000 householders in 1818)[1] included many independent craftsmen and some artisans. But its tone was increasingly set by the small masters and tradesmen. The degree of Radicalism of these groups was an important factor in post-war political life, and it had an influence on one sector of English liberties which proved to be a continuing embarrassment to the authorities. Most of the important political and press trials took place in London, and it was from this social milieu that the juries were drawn. Shopkeepers and tradesmen had made intractable juries in the 1790s. Lists of possible jurymen are preserved in the Treasury Solicitor's papers, in the cases of Despard and O'Coigly, showing with what care the law officers of the Crown sought to eliminate Jacobin sympathizers from the juries.[2] Despite their precautions, the authorities received new humilia-

---

1. *Gorgon*, 4 July 1818.

2. On one such list, the names from which the jury was to be drawn were marked G. (good), B. (bad), and D. (doubtful). The many B.s included such tradesmen as a scale-maker, a glass-seller, grocers, a sail-maker, and brewers (one Southwark brewer being marked 'very B.') T.S. 11.333.

tions at the hands of London juries between 1817 and 1819.[1]
Thereafter the juries became more compliant, partly because
the authorities developed new refinements of the special jury
system and other means of 'packing', partly because the radicalism of the City (and its representatives, such as Aldermen
Waithman and Wood) was becoming more and more distanced
from the plebeian movement.

Thus the victory at Westminster scarcely belonged to the
artisans, however much they contributed to it. And the victory,
also, was partially illusory. Apart from the fact that the necessary property-qualification confined the choice of candidates
to men of means, no one on Place's General Committee (least
of all Place) would have conceived of putting forward one of
their own number as candidate. The seat was Burdett's, and
the function of the Committee was to bring him support. Moreover, the Committee showed itself in later years to have serious limitations as a democratic organization. In 1807 it was
formed in the heart of a new democratic impulse. In later years
it became essentially a self-appointed body – or, as Cobbett
complained, a 'caucus' – partly under the control of Burdett,
partly representative of tradesmen and masters like Place. By
the end of the Wars, Place had become the confidant of Bentham and James Mill. He grew more and more hostile to Hunt
and to Cobbett, and to methods of agitation among 'members
unlimited'. The Westminster Committee was a useful place
from which discreet wire-pulling could be exercised in the
interests of the sober and studious artisan. When Cochrane's
seat became vacant, in 1818, Cobbett's nominee, Major Cartwright, was passed over in favour of the Benthamite Radical,
Hobhouse. The Committee became increasingly detached from
the working people of London in the same proportion as
Place's sense of 'self-approbation' and his dislike of the demonstration and the hustings grew.[2]

1. The jury which acquitted Dr Watson for his part in the Spa Fields
riots (1817) had as foreman a Lottery Office Keeper, and as members a
Button-maker, Anchor Smith, Woollen-draper, Capellaire-maker, Iron-
monger, Silversmith, Mercer, Shoe-maker, Carrier and Druggist: *People*,
21 June 1817.

2. For an insight into the working of the committee, see A. Aspinall,
'The Westminster Election of 1814', *Eng. Hist. Rev.* XL (1925).

This was, in part, an inevitable outcome of the situation in which the Radicals of 1807 were placed. Anti-Jacobinism was by no means dead. Cobbett broke through the censorship almost by accident, and there was scarcely any other regular Radical press. (In 1810 Cobbett himself was imprisoned for two years for his attack upon the abuses of flogging in the Army). The Westminster Committee survived as an electoral organization, but the authorities had no intention of permitting a new growth of popular clubs. When John Gale Jones, the former L.C.S. leader, overstepped the bounds of prudence in debates which he organized in 'The British Forum', off Covent Garden, the House of Commons committed him to Newgate (1810). And when Burdett denounced its action as illegal, the House committed Burdett to the Tower. It is true that almost the whole population of London seemed to be on Burdett's side. Burdett at first refused to surrender to the House, adopting Wilkes's policy of defiance, and barricading himself in his Piccadilly home. Lord Cochrane drove up in a hackney-coach, rolled a barrel of gunpowder through the door, and prepared to mine all entrances and defend Burdett with arms. The people milled in the streets, and it seemed that riots on the scale of 1780 were inevitable. Place himself thought that the Army was so disaffected that some spasmodic insurrection was possible. But the very nature of the incident, with its histrionic echoes of Wilkes and its confusion among the Radical leaders, underlines the weakness of the reformers. Even when they rode an insurrectionary tide, they had neither organization nor coherent policy. The laws outlawing corresponding societies had open political meetings had atomized the movement, so that the individualistic and quarrelsome behaviour of its leaders was a function of their situation as 'voices' rather than as organizers.

Radicalism remained a defensive movement, an articulate movement of protest, supported by widespread popular disaffection. It was not yet an offensive force. If we are to understand the extremism of Burdett and Cochrane in 1810, we need only read Byron. Such men despised the scramble for power and riches, the hypocrisy of their own class and the pretensions of the new rich. In their frustration they dreamed perhaps at times of some revolutionary spasm which would overthrow the whole fabric of 'Old Corruption'. If we are to understand the anger of Cobbett, we need only think of the things which made him angry: the fat contracts, the squalid scandals of the Royal Dukes, the soaring rents and taxes, and the impoverishment of the rural labourers, the Ministerial subsidies to the press, the destruction of popular amusements by the informers of the Vice Society. Disaffection swelled for a hundred reasons. Hostility to the press-gang, the grievances of disabled soldiers, the grievances of artisans elbowed out by the mushrooming war-contracting firms, and, after Trafalgar, the growing undertow of opposition to a seemingly endless and purposeless war.

'It is very probable,' a Sheffield Dissenting minister wrote, in 1808,

that whenever mankind shall form themselves into societies for the establishment of that kingdom, in which *swords* shall be beat into *ploughshares* ... that great men will be the principal opposers of the glorious work; especially the opposition may be expected from *Generals, Admirals, Contractors, Agents,* and such like; and many of the advocates for *Christ's peaceful reign* may look for severe treatment from their wicked hands.

'Christ's kingdom' could be ushered into the world only after 'much opposition and blood', for the 'Devil and his agents' would not suffer it to come any other way:

How often have I known poor wives and mothers pawn their necessary clothing to redeem their husbands or their sons from the gripe of a *rascally unrelenting crimp*! Oh heavens! what hardships are poor men doomed to ...

'O poverty! thou art the unpardonable offence! ... Thou hast neither rights, charters, immunities nor liberties!'

Come hither, *old* SATAN, old *Murtherer*, and I will do by thee as thou didst by a better than me: I will take thee, in turn, into 'an exceedingly great and high mountain, and I will show thee all the kingdoms of this *christian* world and the glory of them'. ... Now, SATAN, look down upon *christendom*, and behold the motley group; Bibles, Swords – Churches, Barracks – Chapels, Fortresses – Ministers of peace in black, and men of war in red and blue – a *few* men who act as *Saviours*; millions of men whose sole business is to systematize and practice the destruction of men. ... The true *Sons of Peace* lightly esteemed, obscure, neglected and scorned. – The *Heroes of Murder* and Plunder, exalted, extolled, honoured, pensioned, and *immortalized* ...[1]

It is a voice out of the old England of Winstanley and Bunyan, but of an old England which had begun to read Cobbett. And it reminds us of how remote, in Sheffield, Newcastle or Loughborough, the Westminster elections had been. In the taverns and coffee-houses of the city, Radicals could meet to discuss, and could feel the strength of their numbers. Of the provincial centres where the Jacobin propaganda had penetrated most deeply, only Norwich and Nottingham had a franchise wide enough to allow Radicals to make use of the electoral process. Birmingham, Manchester, Leeds, and most of the growing industrial centres were without any representation in the unreformed House. Here, and in the smaller towns and industrial villages, the Church and magistrates watched for any signs of 'sedition'; even a subscriber to Cobbett's *Register* might find himself to be marked. The reformer felt himself to be isolated – 'obscure, neglected and scorned'. The Westminster triumph threw into greater darkness the repression of the provinces.

Hence it was that the Radical movement took markedly different form in the Midlands and industrial north – a difference which was to influence events for half a century. In London the channels between middle-class and working-class reformers remained open; the characteristic form of organization was the committee, in which a few professional men worked alongside self-educated artisans who tended to despise the political backwardness of the labourers and the demoralized and criminal poor. As repression relaxed, the forum, debating society, and discussion group revived. Periodical Westminster elections provided at least a safety-valve, and a sanction for

1. G. Beaumont, Minister of the Gospel of Peace, *The Warrior's Looking-Glass* (Sheffield, 1808). The author was probably a Baptist minister. For a similar note of radical Christian protest against the war, see the *Cambridge Intelligencer*, and letters in the *Tyne Mercury*, e.g. 5 January 1808.

tumults. In the Midlands and the north, Radicalism was driven underground, into the world of the illegal trade union; it became associated with industrial grievances, the secret meeting, and the oath. Until 1815 neither Burdett nor Corbett meant much in the heartlands of the Industrial Revolution. The Westminster Committee had no message for the Luddites. North of the Trent we find the illegal tradition.

[14]

An Army of Redressers

I. THE BLACK LAMP

'BEHOLD the head of a traitor!' In February 1803 the executioner held up before the London crowd the head of Edward Marcus Despard. He and his six fellow victims had been found guilty of high treason (encompassing the death of the King) and all died with fortitude. Despard declared that he was innocent of the charge, but died because he was 'a friend to the poor and the oppressed'. The crowd was angry and compassionate. The London press feared that if the victims had been drawn through the streets and executed at Tyburn or Kennington Common, instead of at Southwark, riots and an attempt at rescue might have ensued. Among those who witnessed the execution was a young apprentice named Jeremiah Brandreth. Fourteen years later his own head was held aloft before the crowd in front of Derby Castle: 'Behold the head of a traitor!'

Between Despard and Brandreth there stretches the illegal tradition. It is a tradition which will never be rescued from its obscurity. But we may approach it from three directions: first, from considering some surviving evidence as to the 'underground' between 1800 and 1802; second, from some criticism of the historical sources; and, third, from some examination of the quasi-legal trade union tradition. Unless we make this preparation, we shall be unable to understand the Luddite movement, and the post-war years of the Pentridge Rising, Oliver the Spy, and the Cato Street Conspiracy.

We have seen the origin of the illegal tradition in the shadowy societies of 'United Englishmen' at the end of the 1790s.[1] In 1800 and 1801 a rash of rioting broke out throughout England. Most of these were food riots, provoked by scarcity and soar-

1. See above, pp. 185–92.

ing prices during Napoleon's continental blockade. But there are suggestions, also, of some sketchy organization. Several riots and consumer's 'strikes' were advertised in advance by handbills, on a scale which argues organization by committees with access to the printing-press. From London, in September 1800:

FELLOW COUNTRYMEN

How long will ye quietly and cowardly suffer yourselves to be imposed upon, and half-starved by a set of mercenary slaves and Government hirelings? Can you still suffer them to proceed in their extensive monopolies, while your children are crying for bread? No! let them exist not a day longer. We are the sovereignty, rise then from your lethargy. Be at the Corn Market on Monday.

For six days there were tumults at the Corn Market. In November handbills called upon 'Tradesmen, Artizans, Journeymen, Labourers, &c., to meet on Kennington Common' – a meeting prevented only by a show of military strength. In Portsmouth the dockyard 'artificers' resolved to 'abstain from making any use of any butter, cream, milk, and potatoes' until prices should come down. In Nottingham army officers were stoned out of a theatre when they tried to make the audience sing 'God Save the King'. In Nottingham, also, where the Liberty Tree was still planted with annual ceremony at the turn of the century, the authorities intercepted a letter which described a successful food riot, with enthusiasm for 'the conduct of the people on tuesday who Stood the fire from the Yeomanry with such an Undaunted Courage that astonished the Gentlemen ...'. But the writer added a significant comment. The crowd was no longer divided between 'Jacobin' and 'Church and King' factions: 'What scarred the Gentlemen the most was to see the Union of parties their being no ... painites nor no such song as God save the King to be heard.' Here was an important shift in popular attitudes, in the sub-political responses of 'the mob'.[1]

Meanwhile, alarming reports were coming into the Home Office. The worst trouble-centres appeared to be Nottingham,

1. H.O. 65.1; J. Ashton, *Dawn of the Nineteenth Century in England* (1906), p. 19; D. V. Erdman, *Blake, Prophet against Empire*, pp. 317–19; Hammonds, *The Town Labourer*, p. 291.

industrial Lancashire (where the United Irishmen and Englishmen were reputed to remain active), and the West Riding. We may piece together what is known of the latter region. The organization spread outward from Jacobin Sheffield. In September 1800, an inflammatory handbill was found nailed openly in a workshop: 'K — G — and the Farmer are busy crambing the empty stomachs of the poor with Bayonets.' In December the Sheffield magistrates found it necessary to issue a proclamation against the 'numerously attended' meetings which were being held in the fields at night. Various reports were sent to Earl Fitzwilliam, the Lord-Lieutenant of the county. At one such meeting, advertised to consider the best means of reducing the price of provisions, a spy heard talk of pikes and arms; when the spy was recognized, he was driven off. People were being enrolled in secret societies, and taking solemn oaths of confederacy: 'there is a system of organization going on – secret committees – and a preparation of hostile weapons'. Frequent meetings were taking place near Sheffield –

at 10 o'clock in the Evening – an orator in a Mask harangues the people – reads letters from distant societies by the light of a candle & immediately burns them.

No one was admitted to the field without giving a watchword to a ring of sentries.[1]

By March 1801, the alarm had spread to Leeds and Huddersfield, where the magistrates feared 'an Insurrection was in contemplation among the lower orders'. There were 'persons going about endeavouring to persuade the People to take an oath, to support each other in regulating and lowering the Price of all necessaries of Life'. A letter from two Lancashire magistrates alleged that some sort of delegate meeting of 'agents' from Yorkshire, Birmingham, Bristol and London had met in January in the neighbourhood of Ashton-under-Lyne. At the same time, Pitt's Two Acts (passed at the end of 1795) banning seditious meetings, as well as the suspension of Habeas Corpus, expired. Although any form of organized correspondence between individual groups remained illegal, it became technically lawful to call public meetings once more.

1. Fitzwilliam Papers, F.44 (d), (e).

Within a matter of weeks protest meetings were being called, often by handwritten handbills, in a score of widely separated places. In Yorkshire meetings were called in Sheffield, Wakefield, Dewsbury, Bingley. In Bingley handbills were distributed secretly under doors and in market stalls early in April, calling on people to attend a demonstration of the 'association of the Friends of Liberty'. The purpose of the meeting was to demonstrate against the exorbitant price of provisions, 'to expose fraud and every species of Hereditary Government, to lessen the oppression of Taxes, to propose plans for the education of helpless infancy and the comfortable support of the aged and destressed ... to exterpate the horrid practice of war':

Will you suffer yourselves to be thus imposed upon by a Majority of mercenary hirelings, Government pimps – corndealers – placemen – pentioners – paracites etc. and yourselves Starving for Bread? No let them exist not one day longer, we are the Sovereignty ... Drag the Constitution from its hidden place – and lay it open to publick inspection – Shake the Earth to its centre ...[1]

'It appears to be in agitation,' reported a Committee of Secrecy of the House of Commons, 'suddenly to call numerous meetings in different parts of the country, at the same day and hour, to an extent which, if not prevented, must materially endanger the public peace.' By the end of April the Seditious Meetings Act was re-enacted, and Habeas Corpus suspended for a further year.

The agitation promptly went underground once more. We may once again try to follow its history in the West Riding. Throughout the summer of 1801 meetings continued, mainly at night; Batley, Ossett, and Saddleworth are added to the list of centres. At Halifax, in July 1801, some kind of delegate committee appears to have met, with representatives from the textile towns and a speaker from Sheffield. There was talk of oath-taking or 'twisting-in' to the United Britons or Englishmen, whose main centre of activities may have been across the Pennines in Bolton. All who joined were required to answer in the affirmative three questions: (1) Did they desire a total

1. Ibid., F. 45 (a).

change of system? (2) Were they willing to risk themselves in a contest to leave their posterity free? (3) 'Are you willing to do all in your power to create the Spirit of Love, Brotherhood & Affection among the friends of freedom & omit no opportunity of getting all the political information you can ...' A further delegate meeting was reported from Leeds in August; it was adjourned, according to a magistrate, upon a resolution that there was 'no occasion for any further Meetings till the French landed'. A Wakefield magistrate concurred: '... a Revolution is their object and the rising of the disaffected depends entirely on the enemy invading the country'.[1]

Meetings had now become so widespread that they were noticed in the *Leeds Mercury*, whose Editor, Edward Baines had once been secretary of a 'Jacobin' club at Preston, but who was now anxious to disassociate himself entirely from 'all secret associations for political purposes'. The practice of midnight political meetings, it was editorially noted, had become 'very frequent'. There were strong reasons to suppose them to be motivated by 'bad designs' and some suspicion of a secret correspondence with France. He accused the reformers of shrinking into 'lurking holes like a lawless banditti'. Baines' note called forth an uncompromising reply from Benjamin Flower, whose *Cambridge Intelligencer* was (with Montgomery's *Sheffield Iris*) the last of the provincial reformers' papers to struggle through to the nineteenth century. In November 1800 Flower had issued a general call for public demonstrations for peace: people (he said) 'perceive and feel that the effect of war and taxes [is] to raise the price of all consumable commodities'. Now Flower accused Baines of being a 'time-server', of aiding the 'Church-and-King' propagandists, of deliberately smearing the reformers (who had no alternative but to meet in secret) with the libel of 'French correspondence', and of bringing comfort to:

that corrupt and profligate system which has desolated a great part of Europe, murdered millions of our fellow creatures, robbed the people of this country of their most valuable rights, and brought the kingdom to the verge of ruin.

1. Ibid., F.45 (a), (d).

This breach, between the old Painite Radicalism of such men
as Flower (who were not afraid to risk prosecution or agitation among the discontented masses), and the cautious 'constitutional' Whiggish Radicalism of Baines, was to grow in
significance as the nineteenth century advanced.[1]

There appears to have been a lull, punctuated with public
rejoicing when Peace Preliminaries were ratified in October.
Then in the winter of 1801–2 there were renewed reports of
'nightly' meetings in the West Riding, and of protests against
the Malt Tax, the Window Tax, and restrictions upon liberty.
Although peace came in March 1802, nocturnal meetings continued, and, despite every effort, the magistrates could not
identify any of the leaders. The fullest account of a meeting is
in a letter from the Mayor of Leeds to Earl Fitzwilliam in
August 1802:

With respect to the nocturnal meetings, they continue, though the
place is never known to others till they take place. On Friday
evening at or near midnight a meeting was held in a hollow way,
or narrow valley about six miles from Leeds and two from Birstall,
at some distance from any public road. A man of perfect veracity
assures me that he attempted to form one of the party, but found
that scouts were stationed on all sides at some distance, the outer-
most of whom accosted him and aimed at drawing him off in a
different direction. On his persevering he found another irregular
and moving line of scouts, who asked his business, and upon his
continuing to proceed towards the 'Black Lamp' of men, a whistling
was made, and he heard expressions and tones of voice that quite
deterred him from his purpose. That some particular persons whom
they called gentlemen were expected and were not then arrived, he
could easily recollect from what he overheard on the way. . . .

From another quarter on which I can depend, I learn that the
committee forming the 'Black Lamp,' and which on Friday night
might be composed of about 200 men, consists of those who have
discoursed on the subject with nine others, and have sworn them in,
each of which again, *ad infinitum*, becomes a Committee man on the
same grounds. 'Abolition of all taxes, and the full enjoyment of
their rights' are the subjects on which the leaders hold forth, and the
cement which holds them together. 'By Christmas they should be

1. *Leeds Mercury*, 1 August 1801; E. Baines, *Life of Edward Baines*,
(1851), p. 51; *Cambridge Intelligencer*, 15 November 1800, 8 August
1801.

able to carry their points, and on one night the rise was to take place in every quarter.'[1]

Whatever organization there was had access to the printing-press. In June 1802 a small eight-page 'Address to United Britons' was sent to the Home Office by a West Riding magistrate. This claimed to unite 'in a chain of affection' all those seeking to overthrow the nation's oppressors:

The independent LIBERTY of a wise people, they deem TREASON, because they dread that justice may fall on their own guilty heads . . .[2]

In the autumn two Sheffield men, William Lee and William Ronkesley, were brought to trial for administering secret oaths. It was alleged that between October 1801 and August 1802 they had been members of a secret association, comprising 1,000 members in Sheffield, which had manufactured pikes and had secret depots of buried arms. The organization was officered by 'Directors & Conductors', who drilled the members at night. Its aims were vague, but (the Mayor of Leeds wrote to Fitzwilliam) 'an Idea has place amongst the poor – that they *should* pay no Taxes. ... Thousands carry about with them a Secret Conviction & Indulge a Hope that Matters are growing Ripe.'[3] Lee and Ronkesley were sentenced to seven years transportation.[4]

In November Despard and his associates were seized in London. There were more reports in December, of the preparation of arms in Sheffield. As late as August 1803 Fitzwilliam was told by an informant that oath-taking and pike-manufacture continued. Secret organization 'has pervaded the great body of the People in the manufacturing district of this Country', he wrote to the Secretary of State, despite his habitual scepticism. 'Vast numbers of the Army & Militia were sworn', with the same oath as taken in the Despard business. There were special envoys between districts: 'Little is committed to

1. H.O. 42.66, printed in full in Aspinall, *Early English Trade Unions*, pp. 52–3. Original in Fitzwilliam Papers, F.45 (d).

2. R. Walker, to H.O. 28 June 1802 (enclosure), H.O. 42.64.

3. J. Dixon, 17 July 1802; W. Cookson, 27 July 1802; J. Lowe, 3 December 1802: all in Fitzwilliam Papers, F.45 (d).

4. L. T. Rede, *York Castle in the Nineteenth Century*, pp. 198–201.

paper, but whatever is, is destroy'd as soon as communicated.'
'The Managers never meet in their own towns: when they have
occasion to deliberate they go to a distance from their homes.'[1]
Thereafter the 'Black Lamp' appears to go out.

Similar reports came in, during the same period, from south
Lancashire and parts of the Midlands. Clearly there was some
underground organization in existence, which sought to turn
discontent at the soaring prices and food shortages into a
revolutionary channel. There is too much evidence, and from
too many independent sources, for it to be possible to uphold
the accepted historical fiction that 'sedition' had no existence
except in the imaginations of Ministers, magistrates and spies.
But at this point the sources lead only into obscurity. Did the
'United Britons' have any real *national* existence? Was Colonel
Despard connected with it, and with the underground in Lancashire and the West Riding? Were there links with France
and with Robert Emmet in Dublin? Did the underground
continue after 1802?

The Despard trial revealed little, although a great deal was
suggested. Colonel Despard (1751–1803) came of an Irish
landowning family, and had a distinguished military record.
'We went on the Spanish Main together,' declared Nelson,
who was called by the Defence at the trial: 'We slept many
nights together in our clothes upon the ground; we have measured the height of the enemies' wall together. In all that period
... no man could have shown more zealous attachment to his
Sovereign and his Country than Colonel Despard.'[2] Nelson
had thought so highly of his comrade-in-arms that he had expected him to rise to one of the most distinguished positions in
the Army. But this was many years before: the two men
had not met since 1780. From 1772, Despard served continuously in the West Indies and British Honduras, until his recall
on half-pay in 1790. He appears to have been the very type of

1. Fitzwilliam Papers, F.45 (e). The informant, Fitzwilliam adds, is 'a
steady, industrious man, not young, I see but little reason to suppose this
the idle tale of a flippant prater...'

2. Cf. *London Gazette*, 18 July 1780; 'There was scarcely a gun fired
but was pointed by Captain Nelson, of the *Hinchinbroke*, or Lieutenant
Despard, chief engineer...'

numbers of officers in this period, who, possessing neither wealth nor influence enough to secure recognition, found themselves defrauded of promotion, overtaken by nincompoops with interest at court, subjected to accusations of misconduct by their rivals, and left to kick their heels for years in the corridors of power.[1] We can see in Despard some of the same mixture of the private grievances of a serving officer and of general disgust at the corruption and insincerities of political life which made Lord Cochrane into a Radical.

But Despard was also an Irishman, and by 1796 or 1797 he had become so deeply committed to the cause of Irish independence that he was serving both on the committee of the London Corresponding Society and in the more shadowy circles of the United Irishmen and United Englishmen in London. He was one of the group with whom O'Coigly had made contact in Furnival's Inn Cellar.[2] Early in 1798 the Privy Council received various reports as to his activities, which suggested that he was building an underground *military* organization, in which the style of the Elizabethan soldier of fortune and that of the nineteenth century revolutionary were curiously compounded. While the aims of the organization were Jacobinical, those enlisting in Despard's service were promised high rank and reward in the event of success. Imprisoned under the suspension of Habeas Corpus between 1798 and 1800, Despard's case was prominent among those which featured in the 'No Bastille' agitation of Sir Francis Burdett and of the London crowd. On his release in 1800, it would seem that Despard set to work once more to construct his revolutionary army.

He was arrested in the last week of November 1802, at 'The Oakley Arms', Lambeth, in the company of about forty working men and soldiers. Certain facts were proved at his trial beyond question. Despard and certain of his associates had been passing in the previous months from one meeting-place to another in the taverns of working-class London: 'The Flying Horse' at Newington, 'The Two Bells' and 'The Coach

---

1. For Despard's early career, see Sir Charles Oman, *The Unfortunate Colonel Despard* (1922); J. Bannantine, *Memoirs of E. M. Despard* (1799).

2. See above, p. 186.

and Horses' in Whitechapel, 'The Ham and Windmill' in the Haymarket, 'The Brown Bear' and 'The Black Horse' in St Giles's, 'The Bleeding Heart' in Hatton Garden. The company in all these places included labourers and soldiers, with a high proportion of Irish, and certainly some kind of Jacobin conspiracy was mooted.

Other facts were adduced, at his trial or in the contemporary press, which must be viewed with a more critical eye. Thus it was alleged that Jacobin guardsmen at both the Chatham and London barracks had enrolled a considerable number of followers, bound to the conspiracy by secret oaths. Papers found on the prisoners gave the 'constitution' of their society:

The independence of Great Britain and Ireland – An equalization of civil, political, and religious rights – An ample provision for the families of the heroes who shall fall in the contest.
A liberal reward for distinguished merit – These are the objects for which we contend, and to obtain these objects we swear to be united.[1]

Soldiers had been invited to join this 'Constitution Society' in order 'to fight, to burst the chain of bondage and slavery'. The organization (it was alleged) had no fewer than seven divisions and eight sub-divisions in Southwark alone, with further divisions in the Borough, Marylebone, Spitalfields and Blackwall, principally among 'day-labourers, journeymen, and common soldiers,' discharged sailors, and Irish dockers. It was a paramilitary organization, with 'ten men in each company, and when they amounted to eleven, the eleventh took the command' of a new company. Each company was commanded by a 'captain', each group of five companies amounted to a 'deputy division', commanded by a 'colonel'. On the other hand, if this was the approved model, it does not appear to have been carried widely into effect. According to one witness Despard said that:

a regular organization in London is dangerous to us, it is under the eye of Government; but a regular organization in the country is necessary, and, I believe, general . . .

1. Identical papers were found in Yorkshire in 1802; Fitzwilliam Papers, F.45 (d).

Such an organization in London would be 'a moral impossibility'. But he mentioned Leeds, Sheffield, Birmingham, Manchester, and Chatham as 'country' centres where such organization existed, with which he claimed to be in touch.

The trial brought further allegations. Colonel Despard and his revolutionary army were accused of preparing an imminent *coup d'état*. The Tower and the Bank were to be stormed, the barracks seized from within, the prisons thrown open, and the King was to be assassinated or taken prisoner. 'I have weighed everything well within myself,' Despard was alleged to have said, 'and God may know, my heart is callous.' The Cabinet were known to the conspirators as 'the Man Eaters'. The seizure of the Tower or of the King's person was to be the signal to the London crowd to rise; and the mail coaches (which all left London from a central point, at Piccadilly) were 'to be stopped, as a signal to the people in the country that they had revolted in town'.

There is no real evidence to suggest that the case against Despard was a 'frame-up', although his innocence was widely believed at the time[1] and the suggestion has been handed down in the Whig tradition of history. It is true that the Crown witnesses were disreputable – notably John Emblin, a former Jacobin watchmaker, and one of the guardsmen, both of whom turned King's evidence, and the second of whom swore away the life of his own brother. It is true also that a good deal of the evidence as to the conspiracy in the Army implicated Despard himself only indirectly, and may have taken place independently of him or even against his advice; while the more colourful details as to the intended assassination of the King and seizure of the Tower may have been trumped up for the occasion. On the other hand, neither Despard nor his counsel offered the least explanation as to the purpose of these frequent meetings in obscure London taverns, in which a gentleman of Despard's rank was an unlikely customer.

1. See, for example, C. F. Mortimer, *A Christian Effort to Exalt the Goodness of the Divine Majesty, even in a Memento, on Edward Marcus Despard, Esq. And Six Other Citizens, undoubtedly now with God in Glory* (1803), which quotes Matthew chap. 28, v. 12: 'They gave large Sums of Money to the Soldiers, &c.'

Derspard broke the silence which he maintained throughout the trials of himself and his fellow conspirators only after sentence of death had been passed. And then it was to expostulate:

Your Lordship has imputed to me the character of being the seducer of these men; I do not conceive that anything appeared in the trial or the evidence adduced against me, to prove that I am the seducer of these men.

In the circumstances this can only be taken as an admission that a conspiracy existed, but that Despard, so far from initiating it, was drawn into it by others, as to whose identity he maintained a loyal silence.

'Colonel Despard,' Francis Place (who had served with him on the Committee of the L.C.S) annotated a manuscript over thirty years later: 'he ... was a singularly mild gentlemanly person – a singularly good-hearted man.' 'Orator' Hunt, whose first contact with Jacobin notions was when (imprisoned in the King's Bench) he met Despard, wrote in similar vein: 'a mild gentleman-like man'. Must we accept the usual accounts – that his following was 'microscopic' or that 'it is hardly possible to explain the folly of his plot except on the supposition that his mind was disordered'?[1] The state of Ireland in 1798 was enough to disorder the mind of any Irish patriot. And if we suppose (as we reasonably may) that Despard and his circle had access to former contacts of the L.C.S. as well as to the 'United Irishmen' in Britain,[2] and that there was some loose link between them and such organizations as the 'Black Lamp' in Yorkshire,[3] then the conspiracy was a serious busi-

1. See Cole and Postgate, *The Common People*, p. 163; H. W. C. Davis, *The Age of Grey and Peel*, p. 95.

2. At least one other of the conspirators, Charles Pendrill, was formerly a leading member of the L.C.S. Confined in 1798–1800 in Gloucester gaol with Binns, he was a journeyman shoemaker (a former master), of Tooley Street. Although cited in the trials as a leading conspirator, he was released under a general pardon after Despard and his associates had been executed; only to reappear in a similar conspiratorial rôle in 1817. See below, p. 715.

3. In 1801 several 'United Englishmen' were arrested at Bolton, and one, Callant, was later executed on a charge of seducing soldiers from their allegiance; W. Brimelaw, *Political History of Bolton* (1882), I, p. 14; G. C. Miller, op. cit., p. 404.

ness. Moreover, the mutinies of the fleet remind us that a revolutionary organization in the Army was by no means inconceivable. No less than the Navy, the Army seethed with grievances – as to pay, food and accommodation, the care of dependants, discipline and floggings. The soldiers, who included many Irish, were allowed to don mufti in the evenings and to mingle with labourers and artisans in the London taverns. There were few security precautions, and Jacobin emissaries might easily gain access to the soldiers' quarters in the barracks – as Bamford and Mitchell were to do in 1817. It may seem unlikely today that a Grenadier Guardsman should christen his son 'Bonaparte'; but such is the case with one of Despard's associates. The Crown's allegation that no fewer than 300 soldiers in the 3rd Battalion of the Guards, and thirty or forty in the 1st Battalion were involved in the conspiracy may appear far-fetched; but the six victims who were selected for trial and execution with Despard were all guardsmen, and such an example suggests that the Government was seriously perturbed by the extent of the conspiracy.

When a full view is taken of the evidence, the Despard affair must be seen as an incident of real significance in British political history. It linked the struggles of the Irish nationalists (Despard had some contact with Robert Emmet) with the grievances of London labourers, and of croppers and weavers in the north of England. It was a last flaring-up of the old Jacobinism of the 1790s, which suffered, with Despard, a most serious defeat. The affair appeared to justify the Government's policy of 'alarm' and of the suspension of popular liberties. It initiated also, among a small circle of ultra-Jacobins, the strategy (or, perhaps, fantasy) of the *coup d'état*. This was to remain the objective of small groups in London until the time of the Cato Street Conspiracy (1820), while the notion of spreading the signal for a general rising by stopping the mail coaches was to recur in Chartist times.

Despard took most of his secrets with him. If he was, as he claimed, innocent of the charge of plotting the assassination of the King and Cabinet, he offered no further explanation as to the objectives of his society. By one account, he said on the scaffold:

I know that, from having been inimical to the bloody, cruel, coercive, and unconstitutional measures of Ministers, they have determined to sacrifice me under what they are pleased to term a legal pretext. ... I wish you, my fellow-citizens, health, happiness, and prosperity; although I shall not live to experience the blessings of the godlike change, be assured, Citizens, that the period will come, and that *speedily*, when the glorious cause of Liberty shall effectually triumph ...

If Despard was innocent of complicity in the plot which existed among the Guards, it is possible that a defence was, in honour, impossible, because it would have implicated others. But the prosecution also underplayed its hand, confining its case to the proof of certain overt acts, and claiming to be in the possession of further information from informers who were not disclosed at the trials, since they 'will remain unsuspected ... for the future security of the State'. When the trial took place Britain was still at peace with France, and it was rumoured that evidence as to French complicity was withheld. Despard 'was impressed with the opinion,' declared the *Morning Post*,

that a revolution was not to be effected by extensive associations ... but by a small party of desperate men, who, having struck one great blow, such as the assassination of the King, and filled the city with consternation, would find thousands to support them.

'The poor ... believe him a martyr.' 'Shall Despard's headless corpse walk into every tap-room, to make proselytes an hundred fold ...?' [1]

1. This account of the Despard conspiracy is based upon: J. H. Gurney, *The Trial of Edward Marcus Despard* (1803), esp. pp. 33, 36, 44–5, 72–3, 79, 115, 127, 137, 174, 269; T.S. 11.332; T.S. 11.333; 'Narrative of John Oxlade' (annotated by Place) in Add. MSS. 27809; *Leeds Mercury*, 27 November 1802; *Morning Post*, 22 February 1803; State Trials at Large, *The Whole Proceedings at the Trials of Colonel Despard* (1803), p. 78. Fifteen years later Oliver the Spy reported upon a conversation with one of the chief conspirators, Charles Pendrill: 'He admitted the Soldiers were very deeply implicated, and very staunch.' On one occasion about 200 soldiers mustered in arms in houses close to the Tower, ready to attempt the *coup*, and Pendrill 'seem'd confident that the Tower might have been very easily taken at that time, and given up by the soldiers, had they mustered any thing like the Intention; but the numbers that appeared were too contemptible'. Narrative of Oliver, in H.O. 40.9.

II. THE OPAQUE SOCIETY

For some years the alarm expressed by the *Morning Post* would seem to have been excessive. It was not until 1811 that the underground revealed itself again, and then it was in the form of violent industrial conflict – the Luddite movement. The Luddite attacks were confined to particular industrial objectives: the destruction of power-looms (Lancashire), shearing-frames (Yorkshire), and resistance to the break-down of custom in the Midlands framework-knitting industry. To explain their actions, need we look any further than into the immediate economic and industrial grievances?

We shall propose a different answer. But in attempting any answer the historian faces difficulties in the interpretation of the sources which must be explained. From the 1790s until 1820 these sources are unusually clouded by partisanship.

First, there is the conscious partisanship of the authorities, From Pitt to Sidmouth, Government pursued a single policy. Disaffection must be ringed round and isolated; and this might be done by attaching to it the suspicion of pro-Bonapartist conspiracy or (after 1815) wild, insurrectionary intention. Successive Committees of Secrecy of the House (1801, 1812, 1817) presented lurid and unsubstantiated allegations of insurrectionary networks. In a sense, the Government needed conspirators, to justify the continuation of repressive legislation which prevented nation-wide popular organization.

But the myth that all reformers were French agents or conspirators set in motion a curious logic. Not only did it mean that reformers were driven perforce into obscure, secretive form of activity. It also meant that, in order to penetrate these forms, the authorities were prompted to employ spies and informers on a scale unknown in any other period. The line between the spy and the *agent provocateur* was indistinct. The informer was paid by piece-rate; the more alarmist his information, the more lucrative his trade. Fabricated information might be eagerly accepted by the authorities who propagated the myth. At a certain stage, it is impossible to know how far they were themselves deluded by conspiracies which their own informers engendered. To isolate and terrorize potential revolutionaries, it was possible to adopt a policy of deliberate provocation. In this sense, it was the policies of Pitt, in repressing the corresponding societies, which set in motion the logic which led to both Oliver the Spy and the Pentridge Rising of 1817. These years reveal such a foul pattern of faked evidence, intimidation and double agents, that it is possible to regret that the logic did not work itself out to its proper conclusion. If the Cato Street conspirators had achieved their object in the assassination of the Cabinet, the Cabinet would have been slain by conspirators whom their own repressive policies had engendered, and their own spies had armed.

Thus, evidence presented by the authorities as to a conspiratorial underground between 1798 and 1820 is dubious and sometimes worthless. This was, indeed, the main line of counter-attack of contemporary reformers, including Burdett and Samuel Whitbread. In a dramatic moment in 1817, H. G. Bennet, the Member for Shrewsbury, hurled the Report of the Committee of Secrecy on to the floor of the House, declaring it to be a libel upon 'the whole people ... trash which I only think fit for trampling under my feet'. Successive historians have taken much the same view, whether prompted by a scrupulous concern for the laws of evidence, by sympathy with the reformers, or, more recently, by the phlegmatic assumption that any determined revolutionary activity may be ruled out without examination as un-English. In reaction against the myths of Jacobin or Spencean conspiracy, they have propagated a counter-myth of English 'constitutionalism', and placed great reliance upon the major alternative source of information: the archives (manuscripts, reminiscences, pamphlets, cuttings, etc.) collected by Francis Place.

These archives are invaluable. But Place was far from being that mythical creature, the 'objective observer'. He also was highly partisan, deeply involved in the Radical quarrels which disfigure the entire period, 1806–32, and impatient of opponents – Cobbett he saw only as 'an unprincipled cowardly bully', Orator Hunt as 'impudent, active, vulgar'. The official fact-finder on working-class problems for the Utilitarians, when he came to write his reminiscences he was anxious to emphasize the contribution of the moderates, and to belittle the importance of the 'mob agitators'. Moreover, he was profoundly suspect among advanced reformers. In 1810 he was foreman of a coroner's jury which had exculpated the unpopular Duke of Cumberland from the well-founded suspicion of having murdered his valet; he was known to associate with people whom Radicals regarded as undesirable; he was publicly accused by both Burdett and Hunt of being a 'spy'. The accusation is ridiculous: spies were an altogether more scruffy order of beings. On the other hand, Place was – after 1810 – so convinced as to the necessity for constitutionalist reform that if he had come into the possession of evidence as to insurrectionary conspiracy he might well have passed it on to the authorities. Hence, when we refer to Place's archives we must remember that while he was well placed to collect information on metropolitan reform movements and on the more 'respectable' trade unions and trades clubs, there were areas in which his information was as sketchy as that of the authorities; he knew little of the Midlands and the north, little about illegal trade union organization, and if there had been any serious political underground its organizers would certainly not have admitted Place into its secrets.[1]

And here we are close to the heart of the problem. For the third great reason why the sources are clouded is that working people *intended* them to be so. And 'intention' is too rational a term. There were, indeed, two cultures in England. In the heartlands of the Industrial Revolution, new institutions, new attitudes, new community-patterns, were emerging which were, consciously and unconsciously, designed to resist the intrusion of the magistrate, the employer, the parson or the spy. The new solidarity was not only a solidarity *with*; it was also a solidarity *against*. From the point of view of the authorities, two-thirds of their problem was to obtain any reliable information at all. Magistrates rode through thronged neighbourhoods a few hundred yards from their seats, and found themselves received like hostile aliens. They were more powerless to uncover trade union lodges than Pizarro's free-

1. Add MSS. 27809, ff. 16, 17. See also W. E. S. Thomas, 'Francis Place and Working Class History', *Hist. Journal* (1962), p. 61.

booters were to uncover golden chalices in the villages of Peru.

Hence the Home Office records (our main first-hand sources) often make perplexing reading. Like uncomprehending travellers, the magistrates and commanding officers were at the mercy of their informants. A friendly society might appear as an engine of sedition to a man who had never thought of the cost of burial to the poor. A ranting field preacher might sound like an agent of Despard. Employers might *wish* to freeze the magistrate's blood with tales of Jacobins in order to ensure harsh treatment for trade unionists. The J.P.s hawked for scraps of news from informers (paid or anonymous), and miscellaneous go-betweens such as publicans, travelling salesmen, and soldiers. Here we find one solemnly passing on to the Lord-Lieutenant of the West Riding the gossip which his barber had brought that morning. There we find another, writing from Barnsley in 1802, to say that 'the women all talk misteriously. There is a general expectation of they know not what.' And there we find a Methodist minister writing to the Duke of Portland about a Grand Association of revolutionaries, based on Bolton in 1801 – the story having come from a 'confidential friend' who got it from the 'leader of the Methodist Singers' at a Sheffield chapel, who in turn got it from someone else.[1]

This kind of tittle-tattle is of course worthless. But here we must look rather more closely at the rôle of informers. It was the fond belief of the English people that the employment of spies in domestic affairs was un-British, and belonged to 'the continental spy system'. In fact it was an ancient part of British Statecraft as well as of police practice. It goes back long before the time at which Christopher Marlowe was caught up in its toils; and espionage and counter-espionage against the Catholics, the Commonwealth, and the Jacobites take us well into

1. Fitzwilliam Papers, F.44 (a), 45 (d); R. F. Wearmouth, *Methodism and the Working-Class Movements of England, 1800–1850*, p. 60. Compare T. A. Abdy to Duke of Portland, 20 December 1795, passing on information from 'my own Gamekeeper, who from his situation has opportunities of learning more than I, as a Magistrate can . . .': H.O. 42.37.

the eighteenth century. It was sustained in criminal practice (and became most widespread in the fifty years between 1780 and 1830) for a quite different reason. The very inadequacy of the regular police forces had led to the system of 'payment by results', or graduated rewards (or Tyburn tickets) for securing different degrees of conviction. And this, in turn, had bred a nauseous kind of middleman, who profited from the disclosure of crimes which it was in his interest to magnify, or even to manufacture. The early nineteenth century saw several appalling disclosures of such provocations in purely criminal cases, and no doubt many others went undetected. The Luddites were pursued, like any group of criminal offenders, by large offers of rewards for information leading to convictions. Joseph Nadin, the notorious Manchester Deputy Constable, had come under suspicion of profiting from the sale of Tyburn tickets obtained by malpractices. In 1817 the Bank of England prosecuted 124 people for forging or uttering forged notes, and the Radical press exposed cases in which blood-money informers 'planted' forged bank notes on innocent victims, and then secured the reward for their conviction.[1]

Thus both a political and a criminal tradition endorsed the employment of spies; and, especially after 1798, this was much strengthened by the experience gained in the 'pacification' of Ireland. But the spies so employed were of very different qualities. In a few cases, when dealing with radical political movements, it was possible for the authorities to select and send in to the movement men of some education and ability: 'Citizen Groves', who succeeded in penetrating into the inner councils of the L.C.S., in 1794, was a man of this sort. The great majority of informers, however, belong much more to the tradition of 'blood-money' mercenaries. Recent attempts to lift some of the odium traditionally placed upon such men as Oliver, by representing them as 'detectives' performing a

1. For the whole system of criminal information and its abuses, see L. Radzinowitcz, op. cit., I. pp. 333 ff.; Southey, *Letters from England* (1808, 2nd edn), I, p. 173; Hazlitt, 'On the Spy System', *Works*, VII, pp. 208 ff. For Nadin, see D. Read, *Peterloo* (Manchester, 1957), p. 65. For the bank note forgeries, see the *Black Dwarf*, 1816–18, *passim*; *Duckett's Dispatch*, 9 February 1818; H. Hunt, *Memoirs* (1822), III, p. 483

dangerous but honourable part, according to their lights, are misplaced.[1] It may be possible to take such a view of a spy in war-time, even in a civil war; but not in such a war as Pitt or Sidmouth waged against the reformers, with forces so unequally disposed. Moreover, these informers fall into two groups. There were, first, those who had fallen foul of authority in some way, and who purchased their immunity from prosecution (or secured their release from gaol) by taking up the trade. The most favoured recruiting grounds for such spies were the debtor's gaols. At the turn of the century a particularly nasty example of such a recruit, named Barlow, was entertaining himself at inns in Manchester and Sheffield (and attempting to implicate middle-class reformers) and was frequently writing plaintively to the Home Office for the money, not only to meet his current expenses but also to pay off previous debts, which (he alleged) had been promised to him upon his entering upon the employment. He exceeded the bounds of discretion, and one of his begging letters is testily endorsed (perhaps by the Duke of Portland): 'If any additional argument had been necessary to get rid of Barlow it is certainly furnished by this Letter. I incline to give him £20 & dismiss him without delay.'[2] The connection between the Government and Castle, Oliver and Edwards (wrote a Scot who had become an informer himself, for less dishonourable reasons, and who had become ashamed of his own trade) 'all originated in the Fleet Prison'.[3]

The second group of informers comprises turncoats who, having been active reformers, became spies to save their own skins or for money; or, more simply, of casual mercenary volunteers attempting to sell information by the 'piece'. Notions

1. See, for example, A. F. Fremantle, 'The Truth about Oliver the Spy', *Eng. Hist. Rev.*, XLVII (1932), p. 601; p. 601; R. J. White, *From Waterloo to Peterloo*, ch. 13.

2. Barlow, 16 November 1799, P.C. A.164. Barlow was not in fact dismissed at this point since (perhaps because he sensed how the wind was blowing) he commenced to send in long circumstantial accounts of illegal combinations.

3. A. B. Richmond, *Narrative of the Condition of the Manufacturing Population* (1825), p. 159. See also (for Oliver) the deposition of Charles Pendrill in Cobbett's *Political Register*, 16 May 1818.

of honour or of professional duty are scarcely relevant to men in either group.[1] On the other hand, it is mistaken to suppose that the reports of these men are therefore all worthless. Bad men can work usefully in a bad cause.[2] If generalizations may be attempted from the extraordinary diverse collection of documents (written reports and letters, transcriptions of verbal depositions, confessions of condemned men, etc.) to be found in the Home Office, Treasury Solicitor's, and Privy Council papers, they might take this form:

1. The informer certainly had (as the Hammonds and others have noted) an occupational bias towards sensationalizing his reports. The more mercenary his motives, the more he was at pains to provide the kind of information his employers wished to buy.

2. The employers, however, were not all fools – a fact which is too often overlooked. They were aware of this bias. It was in the interests of magistrates to obtain accurate information. They disliked being sent on fool's errands after non-existent depots of arms, or wasting their time in pursuit of tavern demagogues. They frequently took the precaution of employing more than one informer (unknown to each other) as a means of checking information. It was the general practice of J.P.s who forwarded information to the Home Office to add some kind of assessment as to the credibility of the information.

3. These informations are, nevertheless, a kind of distorting mirror in which to view history, not only because most spies tended to put a criminal construction upon even 'innocent' activities, but because of the information which they did *not* send. This covers, of course, the concerns and interests of

1. On the political spy system generally, see F. O. Darvall, *Popular Disturbances and Public Order in Regency England* (1934), chs. 12 and 14 Hammonds, *The Skilled Labourer*, ch. 12; F. W. Chandler, *Political Spie and Provocative Agents* (Sheffield, 1933); W. J. Fitzpatrick, *The Secre Service under Pitt* (1892).

2. Fitzwilliam wrote to Pelham of one spy: '. a most consummate Rascal, a fellow of as bad a character as can be found ... Worthless as he may be, he may not be the worse Agent, for the purpose of getting into the secrets of the Disaffected'; 25 September 1802, Fitzwilliam Papers, F.45 (d).

the less political, more apathetic majority. But it also covers whole regions of Britain. We have to think, not only of the motives of the spies, but of the motives of the J.P.s who employed them. From the Public Record Office, Bolton appears to have been the most insurrectionary centre in England, from the late 1790s until 1820. But it is by no means clear whether this was because Boltonians *were* exceptionally revolutionary in disposition; or because Bolton suffered from two unusually zealous magistrates – the Rev. Thomas Bancroft and Colonel Fletcher – both of whom employed spies (or 'missionaries') on an exceptional scale.

The point is important. For the greater part of this period England was governed by the Tories. A magistrate who wrote industriously to the Home Office was likely either to be a fervent anti-Jacobin Tory or to be interested in gaining the notice of Government for some more private reason. In the same period, many reports from Yorkshire were more laconic than those from Lancashire, although there is no reason to believe that Sheffield or Barnsley were less revolutionary in temper than Manchester or Bolton. Yorkshire had a Whiggish magistracy under a Whig Lord-Lieutenant (Fitzwilliam), who had no liking for Tory intervention in his own affairs. And the same argument applies to many J.P.s of the 'old school', whether Whig or Tory in their allegiance. The maintenance of order was a parochial affair, the responsibility of the local aristocracy, and to write long letters to the Home Office was unnecessary, a nuisance, and somewhat humiliating.

This jealousy of central authority in fact led to a number of extraordinary tangles. Successive Home Secretaries came to rely upon certain magistrates, of proven zeal, whose authority was stretched beyond their own borders. Senior military officers and magistrates reported on each others' activity or apathy. In the Luddite crisis, Mr Lloyd, an active Stockport attorney, was encouraged to stretch his authority into Yorkshire, even to the point of spiriting Crown witnesses across the Pennines. In the post-war years Colonel Fletcher of Bolton often had fuller sources of information on the Manchester reformers than the local Bench. When Oliver was sent directly by Sidmouth into the Midlands and north in 1817 he was more than once in danger of being arrested by local J.P.s who thought him to be a *bona fide* revolutionary.

Thus we must see that the Home Office papers give a distorted view, not only in this or that particular, but as a whole. We have to read, not only between the lines of the letters sent in, but also the letters which were never sent.

4. In general it can be said that the authorities succeeded, both nationally and locally, much better in penetrating illegal political organizations than industrial ones, and regional bodies rather than local ones. The reasons for this are self-evident. It was simpler for an informer to pass himself off as a Jacobin or a Radical than as a cropper or a framework-knitter. The political societies were gathered from a wide region and from different social groups; illegal unions or Luddite bodies grew out of workshops and communities in which each man was known. It was always at the point where one town or region linked up with another that the spy found infiltration most easy.

5. When all these points are borne in mind, we are left with only two reflections. The first is the truism that each separate report must be scrutinized with care, according to the normal rules of evidence. It is necessary to say this, since it has become somewhat fashionable to dismiss *all* such reports as unreliable, or at any rate all that do not suit a chosen interpretation. But few reports do not offer some purchase for criticism: corroboration or contradiction by other sources, internal evidence, inherent probability, and the like. We may take two examples, both in 1817. The first is an informer's report of a Manchester reformer's speech:

He then stated the situation of the poor man and his children. The Child says to his Father, give me some bread, the father replies, I have none; the Child says, Is there none? the Father says, yes, plenty but Tyrants or Robbers take it from us. It is for you (meaning the people) to stretch forth your hands and fetch it again.[1]

The second is a letter to a Crown lawyer

Mr Litchfield sir thear is one thing that I am not serten weather I menshened but I have thought it most properest to cumenecate to

1. Report of speech of Bagguley, in H.O. 40.4.

you thear wos to have been small Detachements plased at Diferant
Entereneses in and out of London to prevent Government for
sending despatches to haney part of the Cuntrey as thear was oneley
one hors soulger sent with them . . . proposed by young watson and
thisilwood and a greed to by all.[1]

Need the contrast be pointed further? The first appears to be
as credible as any account by an untrained reporter. Clearly,
the informer was impressed, despite himself, by this passage
in the speech; and he has recorded, more vividly than the
'literary' versions usually published in the Radical press, the
manner of the democratic orator. The author of the second is
the notorious *provocateur*, John Castle – the 'protector' of a
brothel madam whose evidence was torn into shreds at the trial
of Watson in 1817. But even if we did not know this, his style
betrays him in the first line. He is falling over his illiterate pen
in an effort to ingratiate himself further with the authorities.
This does not mean that every word of his deposition is a lie.
It does mean that each word must be critically fumigated
before it may be admitted to historical intercourse.

The other reflection is this. So far from being led a dance by
a series of impostors, one is impressed by the extraordinary
skill with which Government, between 1792 and 1820, succeeded in forestalling serious revolutionary developments, and
in maintaining a steady flow of reliable information as to insurrectionary conspiracies. Spies were placed successfully in the
L.C.S. (although only intermittently at the centre). They
discovered a certain amount about the United Irishmen and
Englishmen. They entered and dispersed Despard's conspiracy.
They were eventually (but only partially and after great difficulty) infiltrated into certain Luddite districts. In the post-war
years, as we shall see, Government knew before it took place
of every detail of the conspiracy which culminated in the
Pentridge Rising; while Arthur Thistlewood was shadowed
from 1816 until his death on the scaffold in 1820. In Manchester 'the Person whom we designate by the letter B' was
appointed Treasurer to collect subscriptions for Colonel
Despard's defence; and the same, or another 'B', was
appointed Treasurer to a quasi-Luddite 'secret committee' in

1. John Castle, 6 March 1817, T.S. 11.351.

1812, while he and other informers were fully conversant with each Lancashire development between 1816 and 1820.[1] Notions as to the traditional stupidity of the British ruling class are dispelled by an acquaintance with the Home Office papers.

Indeed, a convincing history of English Jacobinism and popular Radicalism could be written solely in terms of the impact of espionage upon the movement. In its earliest years the L.C.S. became aware of the over-zealous and provocative attitudes struck by the typical spy. In 1794 one Jones, of Tottenham, was accused (mistakenly) of being a spy, because of his violent resolutions which were alleged to be for the 'purpose of *entrapping* the Society'. Jones (the genuine informer, Groves, reported with wry relish) complained:

If a Citizen made a Motion which seemed anyways spirited he was set down as a Spy sent among them by Government. If a Citizen sat in a Corner & said nothing he was watching their proceedings that he might the better report it. . . . Citizens hardly knew how to act.[2]

In an attempt to tighten security, the L.C.S. in 1795 introduced a new Constitution which included the following Rule of Order:

Persons attempting to trespass on order, under pretence of showing zeal, courage, or any other motive, are to be suspected. A noisy disposition is seldom a sign of courage, and extreme zeal is often a cloak of treachery.[3]

But such rules, once made, could be circumvented by an actor who modified his style. And political Radicalism after the war had scarcely begun to revive before it encountered the shocks of Castle and Oliver. If we seek for one explanation for the fragmentation of post-war Radicalism, and the allegiance given to journalists rather than to organizations, we shall find it here.[4]

For this reason the secret *political* tradition appears either as a series of catastrophes (Despard, Pentridge, Cato Street), or else as a trickle of propaganda so secretive and small-scale,

1. T.S. 11.333 and below, p. 649.   3. Add. MSS. 27813.
2. Groves, 21 July 1794, T.S. 11.3510 A (3).   4. See below, esp. pp. 686–7.

and so hemmed in by suspicion, that it scarcely had any effect, except in those places where it effected a junction with the secret *industrial* tradition. Such a junction took place in the Luddite movement, and in Nottingham and Yorkshire the Luddites resisted permeation by spies with extraordinary success. Here the authorities were faced with a working-class culture so opaque that (unless a Luddite prisoner broke down under questioning and in fear of the scaffold) it resisted all penetration. When two experienced London police magistrates were sent down to Nottingham, they reported to the Home Office: 'almost every creature of the lower order both in town & country are on their side'.[1]

And here we may make several obvious points, as to the study of Luddism in particular. If there had been an underground in these years, by its very nature it would not have left written evidence. It would have had no periodicals, no minute Books, and, since the authorities watched the post, very little correspondence. One might, perhaps, have expected some members to have left personal reminiscences; and yet, to this day, no authenticated first-hand accounts by Luddites have come to light. But many active Luddites, while literate, were not readers and writers. Moreover, we have to look ahead from 1813. Luddism ended on the scaffold; and at any time in the next forty years to have proclaimed oneself as having been a Luddite instigator might have brought unwelcome attention from the authorities, perhaps even recriminations in the community where the relatives of those who had been executed still lived. Those Luddites who had left their past behind them had no more wish than a man with a criminal record to be reminded of their youth. For those who had not, we must remember that the revolutionary and conspiratorial stream runs onwards through 1816–20, 1830–32, and up to the last Chartist years. The working-class culture of the Midlands and north which nurtured physical-force Chartism in 1848 was scarcely less opaque to the genteel investigator than that of the years of war. Of those Luddites 'whose lives were spared, and who remained in the country,' wrote Frank Peel,

1. Reports of Conant and Baker, 26 January 1812, in H.O. 42.119. (Copy also in Nottingham Reference Library.)

it is singular to note that many of them seem to have been all the rest of their lives mixed up with all the political and social movements which followed, and which were to some extent under the ban of the law.

Most became followers of Cobbett, Hunt, and of Feargus O'Connor. One old Luddite (Peel recounts) who would never reveal anything of Luddism's secrets, nevertheless in his dotage sang Luddite songs to his grandchildren; another flitted from Yorkshire to Lancashire, and was imprisoned more than twenty-five years later for his part in the Chartist movement; another remained 'morose and silent' about Luddism until his death.[1] In the Midlands framework-knitting villages, as in the West Riding, midnight meetings, drillings and insurrectionary rhetoric went on for forty years. There are legends of Luddite arms, buried in 1812, and dug up at subsequent crises. Such reminiscences as survived were handed down as a secret tradition.

It is, indeed, not until the 1860s and 1870s that the stories of survivors begin to break the surface of print; and a man who was twenty-one in 1811 would have been eighty in 1870. There were several such survivors in the West Riding, and their stories were gathered by local historians with sympathy and (so far as one may judge) some accuracy. Because these works are the last form of a secret verbal tradition, they must be taken as serious sources.[2]

In Nottingham we are faced with a perplexing and intriguing circumstance. At least one of the framework-knitters' leaders was a man of unusual political and literary ability. Gravener Henson (1785–1852) was a man who challenges comparison with Francis Place, in one sense, with John Doherty, in another. There was (a contemporary wrote) 'no trade combination in the three Midland counties during the first forty years of this century with which ... Henson was not

1. Frank Peel, *The Risings of the Luddites* (Heckmondwike, 1895 edn), pp. 269–70.

2. There is a little in Charlotte Brontë's *Shirley* – nearly all from the 'other' side – and in A. L., *Sad Times* (Huddersfield, 1870) and in D. F. E. Sykes and G. Walker, *Ben o' Bill's, The Luddite* (Huddersfield, n.d.), and Frank Peel, *The Risings of the Luddites* (1st edn, 1880). See my introduction to the 1968 reprint of Peel.

acquainted'. In 1812 he was the moving spirit behind the Framework-Knitter's Committee, which was certainly a cousin to the Luddite movement. In subsequent years he was imprisoned (1817) during the suspension of Habeas Corpus, and later took a leading part in the campaign to repeal the Combination Acts. He was a self-taught man, thick-set, 'with a short neck, keen small eyes, and a head very broad at the base, rising up angularly to an unusual height'. He was enormously well-informed in the laws relating to industry and trade unionism, published the first part of a *History of the Framework-Knitting and Lace Trades* (1831), and contributed to the Radical and local press. In the Nottingham district the reputation clung to him of having been a Luddite, even 'General Ludd' himself. This is almost certainly untrue; but, without any doubt, Henson *knew* the greater part of the Luddite story. And yet so fluent a writer showed, to the end of his life, a 'decided repugnance' to enter into details of the subject. Indeed, it is said that he left valuable manuscripts disclosing the secrets of Luddism in the hands of an 'influential member' of the Nottingham Corporation, 'on the understanding that they will be given to the public when the demise of certain parties shall have removed the only difficulty'. These manuscripts have never turned up – perhaps the 'influential member' preferred to take them with him to his grave.[1]

So far from discounting the story of some effective Luddite underground, Henson's 'repugnance' to disclose the facts lends weight to it. And here we must pass from criticism of the sources to constructive speculation. From Despard to Thistlewood and beyond there is a tract of secret history, buried like the Great Plain of Gwaelod beneath the sea. We must reconstruct what we can.

1. W. Felkin, *History of the Machine-Wrought Hosiery and Lace Manufactures* (1867), pp. xvii, 240–41; *Nottingham Review*, 19 November 1852; W. H. Wylie, *Old and New Nottingham* (1853), p. 234. The influential member, in one account, was Alderman John Bradley. The discovery of these manuscripts would be of the greatest interest.

III. THE LAWS AGAINST COMBINATION

One of the 'hidden hands' behind the disorder, whom the authorities most suspected, was Thomas Spence. Spenceans were believed to have instigated bread riots in 1800 and 1801, although when Spence was tried and imprisoned in the latter year it was on account of his seditious publications. In 1817 once again a Select Committee of the House detected a conspiracy by the 'Society of Spencean Philanthropists'. Place on the other hand, said the Spenceans were 'next to nobody and nothing', 'harmless and simple'.

We shall return to the events of 1816–17. But it is probable that, until Spence's death in 1814, Place's account is nearest to the truth. Spence did not have the discretion, nor the practical application, for a serious conspirator. On the other hand, his group kept some sort of underground discontent alive in London, with chalking and rough handbills. More important, in the context of repression, Spence did not believe in a centralized, disciplined underground. His policy was that of the *diffusion* of agitation. In March 1801, the Spenceans agreed to organize themselves as loosely as possible, with 'field preachers'. Supporters should form societies, meeting in tap-rooms 'after a free and easy manner, without encumbering themselves with rules' – their function was to talk and to circulate Citizen Spence's pamphlets. (A society called the 'Free and Easy' met every Tuesday at 'The Fleece' in Little Windmill Street in 1807.) Their intention seems to have been to make disaffection so amorphous that the authorities could find no centre and no organizing sinews.[1]

This was not the method of the 'Black Lamp' and of Luddism. But it provides a clue, in the very policy of diffusion. For the illegal tradition, from 1800 to 1820, never had a centre. There was no Babouvist Conspiracy of Equals, no Buonarroti who sent emissaries up and down the land; and if we search for one, we make the same mistake as the authorities. Jacobinism had become indigenous in working-class com-

1. O. D. Rudkin, *Thomas Spence and his Connections*, pp. 122–3, 146–7; Add MSS. 27808.

munities at exactly the same time as it had lost any national centre as well as most middle-class support. It was in old centres of Jacobin propaganda – Sheffield, Nottingham, south Lancashire, Leeds – that Thelwall's 'Socratic spirit' was now endemic in the workshops and mills. In part this was a conscious tradition. Groups of Painites, who knew and trusted each other, met together in secret; the *Rights of Man* passed from hand to hand; in Merthyr, according to one colourful account,

a few who thought highly of his *Rights of Man* and *Age of Reason* would assemble in secret places on the mountains, and taking the works from concealed places under a large boulder or so, read them with great unction.[1]

Mayhew took down the account of an old London bookseller who used to sell 'Tom Paine on the sly':

If anybody bought a book and would pay ... three times as much as was marked, he'd *give* the 'Age of Reason' in. ... His stall was quite a godly stall, and he wasn't often without a copy or two of the 'Anti-Jacobin Review' ... though he had 'Tom Paine' in a drawer.[2]

In Sheffield 'old Jacks' still met to toast Paine's health and sing: 'God Save Great Thomas Paine':

7   Facts are seditious things
                    When they touch courts and Kings.
                        Armies are rais'd.
                    Barracks and bastilles built,
                    Innocence charged with guilt,
                    Blood most unjustly spilt,
                        Gods stand amaz'd ...[3]

After Despard's execution, such groups of Painites in manufacturing communities will have lost any national links. They drew back into their own communities, and their influence

1. C. Wilkins, *History of Merthyr Tydfil* (1867). By the same account, 'religious men had the nails in their boots arranged to form T.P., that they might figuratively tread Tom Paine underfoot'.

2. Mayhew, op. cit., I, p. 318.

3. John Wilson, *The Songs of Joseph Mather* (Sheffield, 1862), pp. 56–7. Cf. B. Brierley, *Failsworth, My Native Village*, pp. 14–16.

will have been shaped by local problems and experiences. Only at times of great unrest will they have reached out, with extreme caution, first for regional, later for national, contacts. But, as they drew back, so their ideas were shaped, in their turn, but the peculiarities of each community. The foci of dissatisfaction will have become economic and industrial; it was easier, in Bolton or Leeds, to organize a strike or a demonstration at the price of bread, than a political discussion, a petition, or an insurrection. The Jacobins or Painites disappeared; but the demand for human rights became diffused more widely than ever before. Repression did not destroy the dream of the egalitarian English republic; it dissolved the remaining ties of loyalty between working people and their masters, so that disaffection spread in a world which the authorities could not penetrate. An indignant clerical magistrate, the Rev. J. T. Becher, gave his own version of the origin of Luddism:

I attribute the ... outrages to those Jacobinical principles with which the inferior orders have been sedulously inoculated by our Nottingham Reformers, who have, in many instances, become the objects of that secret organization and malevolent confederacy which they fostered by their pernicious examples, their licentious harangues, and their seditious Press for the attainment of their factious projects. Thus have the evils ... been introduced and cherished until they have become *intimately incorporated with the state of society* in this and other manufacturing districts.[1]

Behind this outburst lie complex animosities. Becher as a Tory (Regent in his own person of both Church and King) felt that Nottingham hosiers had been hoist with their own petard. Some had been reformers in the 1790s; were Dissenters; had petitioned for peace in 1801: had helped to displace a Tory Member in 1802 to the accompaniment of riots and *Ça Ira*. (Ironically, this same Member, Daniel Parker Coke, reinstated to his place in 1803, proved himself more attentive to the framework-knitters' case than their Whig employers.) Now the dragon's teeth which they had sown in the Nottingham marketplace ten years before were springing up in arms all around them. But Becher was right to see that what had once been a

1. Aspinall, op. cit., pp. 170, 174. My italics.

propaganda of a minority had now become 'intimately incorporated with the state of society'. And the stock upon which Jacobinism had been grafted was the illegal trade union.

There is little evidence as to any deliberate decision on the part of Painites to 'permeate' trade unions and friendly societies.[1] But at any time before the 1840s it is a mistake to segregate in our minds political disaffection and industral organization. In friendly societies which, while legal, were debarred from forming regional or national links, the 'no politics' rule was often observed. Some of the old-established trades clubs had a similar tradition. But in most manufacturing communities the initiation of *any* organized movement is likely to have fallen upon a minority of active spirits; and the men who had the courage to organize an illegal union, the ability to conduct its correspondence and finances, and the knowledge to petition Parliament or consult with attorneys, were likely also to have been no strangers to the *Rights of Man*. As younger trade union leaders came forward, they will have quickly been driven toward an extreme Radicalism by the very conditions of their conflict with employers, magistrates, and an indifferent or punitive House of Commons.

It was Pitt who, by passing the Combination Acts, unwittingly brought the Jacobin tradition into association with the illegal unions. This was especially the case in Lancashire and Yorkshire, where the Act of 1799 jolted the Jacobins and trade unionists into a widespread secret combination, half political, half industrial, in emphasis. 'It originated at Sheffield,' an informer (Barlow) reported:

... in the republican society there – is connected with the principal manufacturing towns in Yorkshire – & communicated to this Town [Manchester], Stockport, & particularly Bury.

In Sheffield the same informer found a 'general spirit of disaffection created in every class of artisan & mechanics by the late Bill ... which I am afraid has already caused more to *combine* than would have thought of such a measure but for the Bills'. The trade unionists (he reported) were making returns

1. W. H. Reid, *The Rise and Dissolution of the Infidel Societies*, p. 20, declares that 'the Clubbists' thought 'their business was to worm themselves into convivial societies of every kind', in particular benefit societies.

of the number of workers likely to be adversely affected by the Combination Act, and calculated 60,000 in Lancashire, 50,000 in Yorkshire, and 30,000 in Derbyshire. The secret committees of the new organization were 'under the Management of Republicans'. Thereafter, it is interesting to note, the surviving political clubs in the north and Midlands dropped such titles as 'Patriotic' or 'Constitutional' Societies, and called themselves 'Union Societies' – a term whose ambivalence enabled them to encompass both political and industrial aims. The term (if not the clubs) survived into the Union Societies and Political Unions of the post-war years.[1]

In Lancashire the resistance to the Combination Acts was organized by a committee of skilled unionists, comprising the fustian-cutters, cotton-spinners, shoemakers, machine-makers, and calico-printers.[2] In Yorkshire, persistent reports attributed to the cloth-dressers or croppers the rôle of initiators in secret organizations for both industrial and ulterior purposes. A Memorandum laid before the Privy Council at the time when the Combination Act of 1799 was passed singled out the croppers for particular condemnation: 'the Despotic power they really possess and Exercise almost exceeds belief'.[3] In 1802 Earl Fitzwilliam, the temperate Lord-Lieutenant of the West Riding, sent successive reports to the Home Office, in which the organization of the croppers and more general illegal combination appear to be inextricably intermingled. Fitzwilliam inclined at first to take reports of serious insurrectionary conspiracy with a tablespoonful of salt. 'The true Jacobinical sort of conspiracy,' he wrote in July, 'I fear does exist, in a greater or lesser degree. ... I trust, the real secret is in *very few* hands, that the rest are dupes ...' Most nocturnal meetings, he considered, were only 'for the purpose of raising their wages, and from which nothing is to be apprehended'. As to the propriety of acceding to the request of some large

1. P.C. A.161, 164. At about this time Major Cartwright was 'much consulted in the formation of several infant societies', called Union Societies. F. D. Cartwright, op. cit., I, p. 243.

2. T. Bayley to H.O., 6 November 1799, in P.C. A.164.

3. 'Observations on Combinations among Workmen', in P.C. A.152. See below, p. 573.

manufacturers that such meetings be forcibly put down, he was guarded. The need to suppress seditious meetings ought not to be made into a pretext for 'obtaining more restrictive laws against combinations of journeymen for increase of wages'. Such men were entitled to their share of 'the season of harvest' when trade was good. To penalize their combinations would be unjust:

I am not sure that we should not afford them ground of complaint against the Constitution, that we should not drive them into the service of the true Jacobin, and by our own acts, furnish a justification for theirs ...[1]

Within two months his opinion had changed. There were three reasons. First, he received reports both of the 'Black Lamp' and of secret trade union organization, which were more circumstantial, and in which trade union purposes were inseparably intermingled with rumours of ulterior revolutionary objectives. He was informed that:

... there were three houses at Leeds and three at Wakefield where the committees met – that one of them was expected to be searched some time since, and that their papers were hid under a trapdoor in the floor of the house and amongst the coals; that each member paid 1d. per week to the fund; that there were many committee men made, and that each committee man got ten more ... that they carry their weekly pennies to Leeds; that there would be a rising all over the country on the same night, and everything overturned the next morning.

Second, he received from the Home Office convincing evidence as to the close connexion between the organization of the croppers or shearmen in Yorkshire and the west of England, where gig-mills had recently been destroyed. Third, he became increasingly alarmed at reports of a rising tide of successful trade unionism, involving a score of trades. In early September the Mayor of Leeds wrote to him in dismay at 'the momentous shape which the spirit of combination amongst workmen of almost every class (but particularly amongst shearmen) has now assumed':

Perquisites, privileges, time, mode of labour, rate, who shall be employed, &c., &c. – all are now dependent upon the fiats of our

1. Aspinall, op. cit., pp. 41, 45–6.

workmen, beyond all appeal; and all branches are struggling for their share of these new powers. It is now a confirmed thing that a bricklayer, mason, carpenter, wheelwright, &c., shall have 3s. per week higher wages in Leeds or in Manchester than at Wakefield, York, Hull, Rochdale ...

At the end of September 1802, all of the croppers employed by Gott, the largest woollen manufacturer in Leeds, struck in opposition to the employment of two boys over the recognized age for apprenticeship (fourteen). (The issue was a pretext for a general show-down between Gott and the croppers, and thereby for the whole West Riding trade, on the apprenticeship question.) Earl Fitzwilliam now wrote to Lord Pelham, calling for 'further restriction against the combination of journeymen':

I cannot help feeling a strong opinion that all the meetings, and suspicion of meetings, takes its rise in the combination of the very men I am now speaking about, the croppers. They are the tyrants of the country; their power and influence has grown out of their high wages, which enable them to make deposits that puts them beyond all fear of inconvenience from misconduct. They are, however, an order of men not necessary to the manufacture, and if the merchants had firmness to do without them, their consequence would be lost, their banks would waste, their combinations would fall to the ground, and we should hear no more of meetings of any sort ...[1]

We do not know whether any of the moving spirits in the cropper's union were former members of the society of 'Working Mecanicks' who had written to the L.C.S. five years before.[2] We do know, however, that small producers had established at the turn of the century in Leeds a new hall for free trade in cloth, by-passing the wealthy clothiers, and that it was known universally as the 'Tom Paine Hall'. We know also that the main intermediary for postal communication between the croppers of Yorkshire and the shearmen of the West Country was a Leeds shoemaker, George Palmer, in whom we can surely detect the proverbial radical cobbler? It is reasonable

1. Ibid., pp. 53–64. See also the Hammonds, *The Skilled Labourer*, pp. 174–8.
2. See above, p. 194.

to suppose that some of these literate, skilled, and very able men were Painites.

Moreover, the Combination Acts of 1799 and 1800 had forced the trade unions into an illegal world in which secrecy and hostility to the authorities were intrinsic to their very existence. The position of unions between 1799 and the repeal of the Combination Acts (1824–5) was complex. We have first to face the paradox that it was in the very years when the Acts were in force that trade unionism registered great advances. Not only did unions which reach far back into the eighteenth century – woolcombers, hatters, cordwainers and shoemakers, shipwrights, tailors – continue more or less unperturbed through many of the years in which the Combination Acts were in force; there is also evidence of organization spreading to many new trades, and of the first attempts at general union- ism. The Webbs judged that a number of the London craft trades 'have never been more completely organized ... than between 1800 and 1820'.[1] Many artisan trades, like the tailors, had their network of trades clubs or lodges, houses of call, tickets, support of members on tramp, control over apprentice- ship (which entailed a substantial payment into union funds), benefits, bank deposits, and even on occasion official price-lists drawn up in agreement with the masters. Such evidence has led to suggestions that the Combination Acts were almost 'a dead letter', and that the notion that there was any 'campaign against liberty' during these years is much exaggerated.[2]

This is as untrue as the notion, sometimes found in popular accounts, that the Combination Acts made illegal trade unions which were legal before. There was, in fact, sufficient legisla- tion before the 1790s to make almost any conceivable trade union activity liable to prosecution – as conspiracies in com- mon law, for breach of contract, for leaving work unfinished, or under Statute law covering separate industries. The Com- bination Acts were passed by a Parliament of anti-Jacobins

1. S. and B. Webb, *History of Trade Unionism*, p. 83. See also above, pp. 278–84.

2. See M D. George, 'The Combination Acts', *Economic History Review*, 1936, VI, pp. 172 ff. A useful summary of the legal position before and during the Acts is in Aspinall, op. cit., pp. x–xxx.

and landowners, whose first concern was to add to the existing
legislation intimidating political reformers. They were also
intended to codify existing anti-trade union law, simplifying
the procedure, and enabling two magistrates to proceed by
summary jurisdiction. Their novelty consisted in this; in the
inclusive nature of their prohibition of *all* combination; and
in the fact that, unlike legislation in the earlier paternalist
tradition, they included no compensatory protective clauses.
While technically prohibiting combinations of masters as well,
they were, as Professor Aspinall has shown, 'an odious piece of
class legislation'.[1]

As such, they hung over the heads of all trade unionists for
twenty-five years, and were often employed. 'Two or more
Justices meet daily at one or other of the Manufacturing
Towns,' a Home Office emissary wrote from the west of
England in 1802, 'and as the Combination Act affords a
very convenient pretext for summoning and examining
upon Oath any suspected Persons I have continually some
before them.'[2] It was this blanket nature of the Acts which
proved so 'convenient'. No count has been made of the number of cases brought under them (for this would involve
lengthy research in the provincial press), but no one familiar
with these years can doubt that their general prohibitive influence was ever-present. On the other hand, there were a
number of interesting reasons why they were not as widely
employed as might have been expected. First, despite the
weight of legislation, there was a hazy area in which some
kind of trade union activity was still, in practice, accepted as
permissible. On the one hand, trades clubs – such as those in
the London crafts – which emphasized their function as
benefit societies, and which kept quiet as to their national
correspondence and negotiating functions, might go for years
unmolested, until some conflict or strike offended employers
or the authorities. On the other hand, occasions arose in which
it was lawful for the journeymen in a trade – at least in different towns and districts – to represent their interest in petitions to Parliament, or in attendance at Committees of the
House. Moreover, the Acts did not altogether displace the

1. Loc. cit., p. xvii.   2. Hammonds, *The Skilled Labourer*, p. 176.

older, obsolescent legislation empowering magistrates to arbitrate in wage disputes. For journeymen to apply, whether to a magistrate or to Parliament, for protection (and the authorities were reluctant to block altogether the constitutional outlets for grievances), then they must be permitted some organization in order to select their spokesmen and to raise the necessary expenses.

Here, then, was a disputed area on the border of legality, which proved important in the history which leads to Luddism. But, next, there were several reasons why employers were often reluctant to use the Acts as more than a threat. In the artisan industries, such as tailoring or shoemaking, there were many small masters with little organization amongst themselves. In London or Birmingham a good many of them were themselves Radicals, who despised the repressive legislation of which the Combination Acts were a part, and who had scruples against their use. Relations with their journeymen were often informal and personal; trades clubs had long been accepted as part of the scene; the very small employer still found apprenticeship convenient. He thought of his business as providing him with a reasonable living rather than in terms of expansionism, and consequently he was as jealous as his men of the few large employers who, disregarding custom and apprenticeship, were taking the cream off the market and employing cheap labour. Hence in such trades, the artisan unions existed within an undefined area of toleration. If they overstepped these limits, by strike action or 'unreasonable' demands, they might bring either prosecution or the counter-organization of the masters upon their heads. They were not free from the effects of the Combination Acts, but they had learned to live alongside them.

Outside the artisan trades – indeed, over the greater part of the manufacturing districts of the north, Midlands, and west, other conditions obtained. Wherever we find outwork, factory, or large workshop industry, the repression of trade unionism was very much more severe. The larger the industrial unit or the greater the specialization of skills involved, the sharper were the animosities between capital and labour, and the greater the likelihood of a common understanding among the employers. We find some of the sharpest conflicts involving men with special skills who attempted to attain to, or to hold, a privileged position – cotton-spinners, calico-printers, pattern-makers, mill-wrights, shipwrights, croppers, woolcombers, some grades of building worker. We find others involving large numbers of outworkers – notably weavers and framework-knitters – attempting to resist wage-cutting and the deterioration of status.

But even here the Combination Acts were not always brought into use. In the first place, these put the onus for prosecution upon the employers. But despite a number of early combinations among the masters in different industries, every employer was surrounded by the jealousy of his competitors. The larger his enterprise, the greater the jealousy, and the more likely his rivals were to profit from his embarrassment. (Thus Gott's attempt to beat the croppers in 1802 was defeated by the capitulation of other Leeds manufacturers to the union's demands.) Next wherever the union was strong, prosecution involved many difficulties. It was notoriously difficult to obtain two witnesses among the men to swear to the union's existence. The employer knew that he was likely to lose many of his best craftsmen. If they were not imprisoned or on strike, they would simply peel off in ones and twos and 'black' his workshop or mill. Moreover, the results of a prosecution did not always justify the losses which might be entailed. For a first conviction, the punishment was only three months imprisonment; and while conviction was usually secured, it was not automatic. Employers were further deterred 'by the power of appeal to the Quarter Sessions ... which might hang them up for three months before a determination could be had, during all which time the informer could have carried on no business because his cropping shops would have been under an interdict'.[1]

Thus it was that prosecutions often took place, not under the Acts of 1799–1800, but under previous legislation – the common law of conspiracy, or under the Elizabethan Statute of Artificers (5 Eliz. c.4) penalizing workers for leaving work unfinished. The advantage of the first lay in the fact that it

1. Beckett to Fitzwilliam, 28 January 1803, Fitzwilliam Papers, F.45 (e).

could be used against the 'ring-leaders' or officers of a union (accompanied by the seizure of papers and funds); that more severe penalties could be imposed; and, not least, that the onus for prosecution fell upon the authorities rather than upon individual employers. The advantage of the second was that it was possible, in the event of a strike, for the employer to proceed by summary jurisdiction on the evidence of the strike itself, without securing witnesses who would swear to formal trade union organization. 'Very few prosecutions have been made to effect under the Combination Acts,' wrote Gravener Henson, the framework-knitters' leader:

but hundreds have been made under this law, and the labourer can never be free unless this law is modified; the combination is nothing; it is the law with regards the finishing of work, which masters employ to harrass and keep down the wages of their workpeople.[1]

These qualifications are important; but they should not lead us to conclusions as to any temperate disposition on the part of authority towards trade unionism. From the point of view of the trade unionists, it made little difference whether they were prosecuted under the Acts, or under common law or 5 Eliz. c.4, except that the latter were more severe or more expeditious. To the general public, in any case, *all* this legislation was grouped under the generic term, 'the laws against combination'. The effectiveness of the legislation is not to be judged by the number of prosecutions but by its general deterrent influence. Under one law or another, blows were struck at the unionists at critical moments, or at critical points of development: for example, the west of England woollen workers (1802), the Yorkshire Clothier's 'Institute' (1806), Lancashire cotton-weavers (1808 and 1818), *The Times* compositors (1810), Glasgow weavers (1813), Sheffield cutlers (1814), framework-knitters (1814), calico-printers (1818), and Barnsley linen-weavers (1822). Such cases generally arose at times of widespread and successful organization, or at times when the Government itself had become alarmed at the disorder and 'seditious' agitation surrounding it. The Home Office corre-

1. Cited by M. D. George, op. cit., p. 175.

spondence reveals that such general considerations often took priority over the particular industrial issues; and, further, that a continuous tussle took place between the authorities (Home Office or magistrates) who wished the employers to prosecute, and the masters who wished to throw the onus on Government.[1] Even the larger employers often acted with considerable misgiving. 'The law is harsh,' admitted a Sheffield employer to his protesting fiancée in 1814, 'for wages are difficult to be advanced except by combination, and at a less insubordinate period I would not have attempted to put such a law in force.'[2] Once again we can detect that indefinite area of toleration, which was upset only at the point where unionists became uncomfortably successful or 'insubordinate'.

Thus in the artisan trades, especially in London, there was a twilight world of semi-legality, in which a very high degree of organization was achieved, and considerable funds built up. (We have seen Thomas Large's suggestion that the Carpenters had £20,000 in 1812, and Davenport's account of the shoemakers in the same years.[3]) It was from the London trades that the first periodical concerned with union affairs – the *Gorgon*, edited by John Wade, a wool-sorter, emerged in 1818. But in the northern and Midlands manufacturing districts, in conditions where combination must either be widespread and militant or else ineffectual, one or other of the laws against combination was frequently in use, as an auxiliary to wage-cutting or victimization, breaking up incipient unions and driving others into underground forms. In the textile trades Gravener Henson saw the Acts as –

a tremendous millstone round the neck of the local artisan, which has depressed and debased him to the earth: every act which he has attempted, every measure that he has devised to keep up or raise his wages, he has been told was illegal: the whole force of the civil

1. For an excellent example, see the opinion of Spencer Perceval, then Attorney General, 5 October 1804: 'If Government attends to this application on the part of the boot and shoemakers, similar applications must be expected from every other trade, and it will lead to an opinion that it is not the business of the masters of the trade who feel the injury to prosecute, but that it is the business of Government.' Aspinall, op. cit., pp. 90–92.

2. T. A. Ward, op cit., pp. 216–19.   3. See above, p. 263 and p. 281.

power and influence of the district has been exerted against him
because he was acting illegally: the magistrates, acting, as they
believed, in unison with the views of the legislature, to check and
keep down wages and combination, regarded ... every attempt on
the part of the artisan to ameliorate his situation ... as a species
of sedition and resistance of the Government: every committee
or active man among them was regarded as a turbulent, dangerous
instigator, whom it was necessary to watch and crush if possible.[1]

It was Henson's association of framework-knitters in 1813
whose tickets carried a coat-of-arms with a loom, an arm holding a hammer, and the motto: 'Taisez vous' (Keep Quiet). The
men of Notts county (he said in 1824) consider the combination laws 'so oppressive, their motto has been, "If you will find
gaols, we will find bodies." '[2] The Webbs, whose materials for
The History of Trade Unionism were collected at the end of
the nineteenth century, noted that every old union had its
'romantic legend of its early years': 'the midnight meeting of
patriots in the corner of a field, the buried box of records, the
secret oath, the terms of imprisonment ...'[3] Thus, the Society
of Ironfounders, formed in 1810, is supposed to have met 'on
dark nights on the peaks, moors, and wastes on the highlands
of the Midland Counties'.[4] Where such nocturnal meetings
took place (as undoubtedly they did) the whole atmosphere was
one which will have encouraged revolutionary talk, even when
the immediate objective was industrial. More commonly the
unions met in a private room of a sympathetic inn-keeper. The
form of organization was one which made penetration by spies
difficult. In some cases it was based on 'classes' (a form borrowed from the Methodists),[5] or upon refinements which perhaps owed something to Jacobin and Irish experience. Thus,
by an elaborate system of delegation from the workshop to
the town committee, and from thence to the regional committee, it was possible to shield the names of the officers and
committeemen even from the union membership. (In certain

1. [G. White and Gravener Henson], *A Few Remarks on the State of
the Laws at present in Existence for regulating Masters and Workpeople*
(1823), p. 86.
2. *Fourth Report ... Artizans and Machinery* (1824), p. 281.
3. Loc. cit., p. 64.   4. R. W. Postgate, *The Builders History*, p. 17.
5. See R. F. Wearmouth, op. cit., Part III, ch. 2.

cases, the officers were appointed by a secret ballot within the committee, and their names were known only to the Secretary or Treasurer.)[1] Hence, if one part of the organization became known to the authorities, other parts might remain intact.

Awe-inspiring oaths and initiation ceremonies were probably fairly widespread. There is no reason to doubt the authenticity of the well-known ceremony of the woolcombers (or builders?), with its inside and outside tilers, its bandaging of the eyes, its solemn oath of secrecy sworn before the figure of death:

I call upon God to witness this my most solemn declaration, that neither hopes, fears, rewards, punishments, nor even death itself, shall ever induce me directly or indirectly, to give any information respecting any thing contained in this Lodge, or any similar Lodge connected with the Society; and I will neither write, nor cause to be written, upon paper, wood, sand, stone, or any thing else, whereby it may be known . . .[2]

Such oaths had a long ancestry, owing something to free-masonry, something to old guild traditions, and something to commonplace civil ceremonies, such as the burgess oath. Thus an oath of the 'Freemen of the Company of Basket-Makers', in use in the mid eighteenth century, bound members to 'well and faithfully keep' the secrets of the craft, which might not be taught 'to any Man but to such as be Free of the same Science', and to pay 'all manner of Duties, as becometh a Brother and a Freeman to do'.[3] One of Colonel Fletcher's Bolton 'missionaries' dug up a more horrific oath, supposedly imported by Irish 'ribbon-men':

I do swear in the presence of you my brethren and of our blessed lady Mary that I will maintain and support our holy Religion by destroying Heretics as far as my person and property will go, not one excepted.[4]

From these disparate sources, the oaths of the early nineteenth century were compounded, the Luddites drawing most

1. See A. B. Richmond, op. cit., p. 77.
2. [E. C. Tuffnell], *Character, Objects and Effects of Trades' Unions* (1834; 1933 edn), p. 67.
3. Rules in Brit. Mus. press-mark L.R. 404.a.4. (52). See also the great variety of forms in *The Book of Oaths* (1649).
4. H.O. 42.119.

upon the Irish tradition, the unionists upon the craft and masonic traditions.[1] The union oaths probably fell into disuse earliest among the London crafts and the artisans of the large towns. But initiation ceremonies and oath-taking persisted in the Midlands and north (and elsewhere) for many years after the repeal of the Combination Acts, not only as a measure of security against the employers, but also because they had become part of the moral culture – solidarity, dedication, and intimidation – essential to the union's existence. The Huddersfield branch of the Old Mechanics bought, on its formation in 1831, a pistol, a Bible, and ten yards of curtain material; clearly, the properties of the initiation ceremony were a first charge on the members' funds.[2] During the great wave of general unionism between 1832 and 1834, there appears to have been a revival in oath-taking, especially in the shadowy Yorkshire 'Trades' Union'. Paradoxically, the tradition of *taisez vous* seems to have flared up into a last phase of bombastic ceremony which was far from silent. The gentry were alarmed by rumours of 'solemn and dreadful oaths' binding men to kill traitors or bad masters. Colliers and building workers were seen entering inns where 'they make a noise as if they were at a military drill, and ... forty or fifty pistol shots are commonly fired off in one night. A pistol is fired over every man's head immediately on his taking the oath ...'[3] Simeon Pollard, the Union's leader, denied that any such oaths were taken; but John Tester, a leader of the wool-comber's strike in 1825 (and now a bitter opponent of unionism) wrote caustically about the expense of union paraphernalia – 'swords, death-scenes, gowns, banners, battle-axes, and large empty boxes like military chests'. At an inquest upon a young Irish blackleg who died as a result of being beaten by unidentified assailants at Farsley, near Leeds (December 1832), details came out which seem credible. A branch of the union

1. For the masonic tradition, and for the rôle of ritual and initiation ceremonies generally, see E. J. Hobsbawm, *Primitive Rebels*, ch. 9.

2. See facsimile in J. B. Jefferys, *The Story of the Engineers*, facing p. 20.

3. MS. Diary of Anne Lister (Bankfield Museum, Halifax), 31 August, 9 September 1832.

had met weekly at the 'Bay Mare', paying 3*d.* each week for the use of a private room on the second floor:

Extraordinary precautions were used to prevent what passed in the room from being overheard, the underside of the joists were planked with inch boards, and the interstices filled with wood shavings, and during meetings a guard was stationed on the outside of the door, and all the ale and other liquor was fetched into the room by one of the Unionmen.

The father of the dead man gave evidence as to having joined the Union in order to discover its plans, at his master's request. But his account appears authentic:

When a member is admitted there are two rooms, in one of which the Lodge is assembled. The first operation was to blindfold him; he was then conducted into the Lodge by two members; he was then required to give the pass word, which on that occasion was Alpha and Omega; he was then walked round the room, during which time a great rumbling noise was made by a sheet of iron – a hymn was then sung – and he still continued to walk about the room two or three times, and was asked if his motive was pure – they then took the bandage from his eyes, and the first thing he saw was a picture of death as large as a man, over which was the inscription 'Remember Thy End'. Over this picture there was a drawn sword – his eyes were then bandaged again, and he was walked about the room, when, upon a signal being given, all the members made a great stamping noise with their feet – he was then ordered to kneel down beside a table, and the bandage was again taken from his eyes, when he saw a large bible before him, his hand having been placed upon it. ... The 94th Psalm was then read, when the oath was administered which was to this effect: that he was to obey all the commands of the Union Committee, and to keep all secrets in every particular – the conclusion of the oath contained an imprecation, on which each person sworn is made to wish that if he violates the oath that his soul may be burnt in the lowest pit of hell to all eternity ...[1]

1. *Leeds Mercury*, 15 December 1832. See also ibid., 4 August, 8 December, 22 December 1832, and (for Tester) *Leeds Times*, 7 and 14 June 1832. I have quoted these passages at length since they qualify the otherwise admirable account in Cole, *Attempts at General Union*, chs. 7 and 16.

In an age which has forgotten the God of Battles, we may quote some verses from the psalm which these trade unionists selected to read to the initiates:

O Lord God, to whom vengeance belongeth; O God, to whom vengeance belongeth, shew thyself. . . .

Lord, how long shall the wicked, how long shall the wicked triumph?

How long shall they utter and speak hard things? and all the workers of iniquity boast themselves?

They break in pieces thy people, O Lord, and afflict thine heritage.

They slay the widow and the stranger, and murder the fatherless. . . .

For the Lord will not cast off his people, neither will he forsake his inheritance.

But judgement shall return unto righteousness: and all the upright in heart shall follow it.

Who will rise up for me against the evildoers? or who will stand up for me against the workers of iniquity . . .?

Shall the throne of iniquity have fellowship with thee, which frameth mischief by a law?

They gather themselves together against the soul of the righteous, and condemn the innocent blood.

But the Lord is my defence; and my God is the rock of my refuge.

And he shall bring upon them their own iniquity, and shall cut them off in their own wickedness; yea, the Lord our God shall cut them off.[1]

This oath and this psalm, before the picture of death in the back room of an inn, were serious things for people in whom deep superstitions still stirred – some of whom had, perhaps, believed in Joanna Southcott or been swept into the Wesleyan revival. Moreover, a man need only raise his eyes at work, or perhaps in tap-room or chapel, to meet the eyes of others who shared in the same vows of secrecy. It was for some such oath as this that the Dorchester labourers (or 'Tolpuddle Martyrs') were transported in 1834, after which oath-taking fell rapidly into disuse. And it was at a mass meeting on Hunslet Moor, Leeds, to protest against the Dorchester sentences that a well-known reformer declared publicly:

1. Other oaths were based on *Ezekiel* XXI (see above, p. 431) and *Numbers* XXX, v.2 and *Deuteronomy* XXIII, v.21–3. See E. J. Jones, 'Scotch Cattle and Early Trade Unionism in Wales', *Econ. Journal* (Supplement), 1926–9, I, pp. 389–91.

I have known men of the strictest moral character, in the humbler walks of life, who have taken the same oath. So many ... that to select them and transport them would almost dispopulate the West Riding.[1]

But we must not paint too colourful a picture of the heroic days of illegality. Much of the work done in the back rooms of inns was humdrum. Much of it was the solid and quiet work of the benefit and burial society. Many of the worst problems, in quiet years, came not from the masters but from the in-experience or ignorance of the officers. Funds slowly acquired would be lost with an absconding officer, with no possible re-course to the law, like those of the Tewkesbury branch of the Framework-Knitters which were unwisely entrusted to a Secre-tary who was 'seemingly a Man of Abillities and a religious turn'.[2] If the officers usually served without payment, com-mittee meetings were well lubricated with ale paid for out of union funds. The social functions of the unions were im-portant, but enough evidence has been left in early account books to suggest that another of John Tester's complaints was not without basis:

I have seen scores of committee-men, who seemed to possess no ... qualification, except for an extraordinary swallow. Their powers of deglutition were most prodigious.[3]

There is no reason why the secret tradition should not be-long to the tap-room as well as to the midnight meeting on the moors. Gentlemen would not be found at either place, and a stranger would be noted as soon as he entered the bar. Secrecy must be seen as more than a matter of oaths and cere-monies; it involved, during the years of war and its aftermath, a whole code of conduct, almost a mode of consciousness. At work no leader or deputation need approach the employer with the men's demands; a hint would be dropped, an over-looker would be prompted, or an unsigned note be left for the master to see. If the demands were not met, there was no

1. *Leeds Times*, 19 April 1834. The Chairman, Thomas Barlow, added: 'I am glad to hear that for some time back you have discontinued taking oaths.'

2. Nottingham City Archives, 3984 I, 22 June 1812.

3. *Leeds Times*, 7 June 1834. For examples, see Postgate, op. cit., pp. 21–2.

need – in the small workshop – for a formal strike; men would simply drop away or singly give notice. While the leaders might be known, it might also be impossible to procure evidence as to their activities. 'So cautious are they now become,' wrote a Wakefield magistrate in 1804, 'no general striking or communication with masters is necessary; it is done in a way perfectly intelligible to the masters, but so as impossible to be given in evidence to prove a combination.'[1] There are some few individuals,' wrote Place twenty years later,

who possess the confidence of their fellows, and when any matter relating to the trade has been talked over, either at the club or in a separate room, or in a workshop or a yard, and the matter has become notorious, these men are expected to direct what shall be done, and they do direct – simply by a hint. On this the men act; and one and all support those who may be thrown out of work. . . . Those who direct are not known to the body, and not one man in twenty, perhaps, knows the person of any one who directs. It is a rule among them to ask no questions, and another rule among them who know most, either to give no answer if questioned, or an answer to mislead.[2]

Moreover, conditions of illegality were those in which trade unionists most frequently took recourse to direct action in order to enforce demands which could neither be raised in law nor in open negotiation. This took place in a score of ways. In its milder forms, it was little more than extreme moral pressure. The craftsman working under the union rate would be boycotted; the 'illegal' man would find that his tools were 'lost', or would be 'fined' by his shopmates. In Spitalfields silk would be cut in the loom; in the woollen districts pieces would be slashed; in the framework-knitting industry the 'jacks', vital parts of the stocking-loom, would disappear. Blacklegs or bad masters would know themselves to be watched; a brick might come through the window, or they might be attacked in a lane at night. In Gloucestershire blackleg weavers were carried astride the beam from their own looms and thrown into a pond. At times even more violent forms of intimidation were employed; there was a scatter of cases reported from Glasgow, Dublin, Manchester and Sheffield, of actual or attempted

1. Aspinall, op. cit., p. 93.   2. Webbs, op. cit., pp. 86–7.

assassinations, vitriol-throwing, or charges of gunpowder thrown into workshops. The most sensational cases were widely publicized, and created in the minds of even sympathetic people of the middle class a deep fear of the violent character of the secret unions.[1]

More commonly, such direct action was carefully controlled within limits imposed by the moral culture of the working community. A blackleg was seen as an interloper who threatened to take bread from the mouths of the hard working and the innocent; but, while no tears were wasted on him if he was assaulted and 'taught a lesson', there was no moral sanction for murder or mutilation. Luddism was an extension of this kind of direct action, but it also was carefully controlled within the same unspoken code. Even in the rougher code of pit-villages and of seaports like Sunderland and North Shields, where the rowdy demonstration and the riot preceded more settled forms of organization, violence was still held within limits which were felt rather than defined.

Paradoxically, the persistence of secrecy and of occasional violence encouraged the arguments for the repeal of the Combination Acts. Francis Place's argument is familiar:

The laws against combinations ... induced [working people] to break and disregard the laws. They made them suspect the intentions of every man who tendered his services. They made them hate their employers with a rancour which nothing else could have produced. And they made them hate those of their own class who refused to join them, to such an extent as cordially to seek to do them mischief.[2]

And Place's own account of the successful agitation for their repeal has been repeated so often (and so uncritically) that it is now legendary. According to this, shortly after the Wars ended he commenced, almost single-handedly, to agitate opinion inside and outside the House. In this he received little help and some resistance from trade unionists themselves:

Working-men had been too often deceived to be willing to trust to any one who was not well known to them. Habitually cunning,

---

1. An excellent example of this deep-seated fear is to be found in Mrs Gaskell's treatment of trade unions in her compassionate *Mary Barton* (1848)   2. Wallas, op. cit., p. 239.

and suspicious of all above their own rank in life, and having no expectation of any mitigation, much less of a chance of the laws being repealed, they could not persuade themselves that my communications were of any value to them, and they would not therefore give themselves any trouble about them, much less to give such information as might, they thought, be some day used against them. I understood them thoroughly, and was neither put from my purpose nor offended with them. I was resolved to serve them as much as I could.[1]

Eventually he found in Joseph Hume a Member sufficiently capable, persistent, and within the confidence of the Ministers, to pilot repeal through the House. A Select Committee was packed with supporters. Outside the House, Place set up a permanent H.Q. for the trade union movement, preparing the best witnesses and sending supplies of evidence to Hume; and (in 1824) a Bill was put through under the strategy of *Taisez Vous*, so quietly that even its staunchest supporters were warned not to speak. This Bill not only repealed the obnoxious Acts, but also explicitly excluded trade unionists from prosecution for conspiracy at common law. A wave of open trade union organization and strikes ensued, and in 1825 both the employers and the Government counter-attacked, appointing a new Committee which was expected to recommend the reinstatement of punitive legislation. But, once again, Place and Hume worked ceaselessly to resist or modify such legislation; petitions poured in from the country; the lobbies of the House were filled with delegations demanding to give evidence. In the event, the amending Bill of 1825 tightened up legislation to the point where almost any form of persuasion or intimidation of non-unionists was an offence, but left the main points gained: trade unionism and strikes were no longer offences as such.[2]

This account is not untrue. Place's achievement was a remarkable feat of intelligent wire-pulling and of enormously industrious and well-informed lobbying. Not a point of vantage or of danger was overlooked. He exploited to the full the fact that he was dealing with a House full of gentlemen who found

1. Ibid., p. 204.
2. Place's full account is in Wallas, op. cit., ch. 8; Webbs, op. cit., ch. 2; Postgate, op. cit., ch. 2.

trade union matters boring, some of whom disliked the manufacturing interest, others of whom had made of *laissez faire*
an unquestioned dogma, and most of whom were confused or
indifferent as to the issues. But the story has long been due for
re-examination. And these are among the points which must be
taken into account.

First, trade unionists had reason to suspect Place. Their
bitterness had been roused, not only by the Combination Acts,
but (perhaps even more) by the simultaneous repeal or supersession of all legislation which protected their own interests.[1]
But both Place and Hume were devotees of orthodox 'political
economy', and had given active assistance in the dismantling
of *all* legislation restraining the 'freedom' of capital or of
labour. Thus, in July 1812, Gravener Henson, then lobbying
in the face of strong opposition for the safe passage of a protective Bill for the framework-knitters, wrote sadly back to the
Nottingham committee: 'Mr Hume opposed our Bill on Dr
A. Smith's grounds of letting Trade alone ...' The repeal of
the apprenticeship clauses of 5 Eliz. c.4 was actively engineered
by Place. The committee of the master-manufacturers which
organized the campaign for repeal (1813–14) was under the
chairmanship of Alexander Galloway, the former Assistant
Secretary of the L.C.S., whose Smithfield works was now the
leading engineering shop in London. Its secretary, John
Richter, was for years one of Place's closest associates. The
issue had been bitterly contested by the trade unions, and
hundreds of petitions had been forwarded for the retention or
extension of apprenticeship regulation, carrying a total of
300,000 signatures. The opposition of the workers (and of
many small masters in the London crafts) Place dismissed as
'bigotry' – 'a proof of the ignorance of the journeymen of
their real interests'. It is therefore not surprising that trade
unionists still 'suspected the intentions' of Place and Hume in
1824.[2]

1. See above, p. 279 and (for the croppers and stockingers) below, pp.
595–6.
2. *Records of the Borough of Nottingham*, VIII, p. 156; Webbs,
History of Trade Unionism, pp. 61–2; T. K. Derry, 'Repeal of the Apprenticeship Clauses of the Statute of Apprentices', *Econ. Hist. Rev.*,
III (1931–2), pp. 77, 85.

In the second place, it is by no means true that Place was conducting a 'single-handed' campaign. In fact, Gravener Henson (who carried far more authority among trade unionists, especially north of the Trent), had got so far ahead of Place that he had drawn up a Bill, and enlisted the support of Peter Moore, the Radical M.P. for Coventry, who introduced the Bill in 1823. Place and Hume moved swiftly, as much to sabotage Henson's Bill, as to promote their own. Henson's ideas are usually dismissed in Place's words, as 'complicated and absurd', a 'mass of absurdities'. The Webbs, more cautiously, noted that the Bill was 'elaborate', repealing the Combination Acts but 'substituting a complicated machinery for regulating piecework and settling industrial disputes'. 'Some of these proposals were meritorious anticipations of subsequent factory legislation,' they continued, 'but the time was not ripe for such measures.' And they went on to compliment Place upon his 'great political sagacity' in using particularly devious Fabian techniques to ensure that Henson and Moore were pushed out of the way.[1]

In fact, Place's 'political sagacity' was such that he was convinced that the Combination Acts were the cause, not only of secrecy and outrages, but of strikes and of trade unionism itself. Influenced by his own experience in small tailoring shops, he supposed that if masters and men were in a condition of complete freedom, each master would settle matters more or less amicably with his own workmen, the laws of supply and demand would regulate the price of labour, and in a few cases arbitration by magistrates would settle difficulties.

1. Wallas, op. cit., pp. 207–10; op. cit., p.100, n. 1. Moore's (and Henson's) Bill was certainly cumbersome and tactically ill-judged. It proposed to repeal close on 400 Acts and sections of Acts (including the obnoxious Master and Servants legislation which was employed for many years after the Combination Acts were repealed); and to enact measures 1) obliging employers to give employees a formal ticket stating wages and conditions of labour, 2) limiting overtime, 3) abolishing truck, 4) facilitating actions by employees against their employers for recovery of wages, 5) setting up machinery for arbitration. There were a number of minor clauses covering annual hirings, embezzlement of materials, tools, &c. See *Parliamentary Papers* (1823), II, pp. 253 *et seq.*; *Hansard*, new series, VIII, 366.

'The business is really very simple,' he advised Hume, when suggesting to him how to circumvent Moore:

Repeal every troublesome and vexatious enactment, and enact very little in their place. Leave workmen and their employers as much as possible at liberty to make their own bargains in their own way. This is the way to prevent disputes ...

And in 1825 he wrote to Burdett:

Combinations will soon cease to exist. Men have been kept together for long periods only by the oppression of the laws; these being repealed, combinations will lose the matter which cements them into masses, and they will fall to pieces. All will be as orderly as even a Quaker could desire. He knows nothing of the working people who can suppose that, when left at liberty to act for themselves, without being driven into permanent associations by the oppression of the laws, they will continue to contribute money for distant and doubtful experiments, for uncertain and precarious benefits.[1]

'This is the way to prevent disputes ...' This was the keynote of all Place's lobbying; and it was an article by M'Culloch, the *doyen* of 'political economy', in the *Edinburgh Review*, putting forward similar arguments, which swung many M.P.s in support of repeal. Henson, of course, had no such illusions. But, as an outworker himself, he knew from experience that for the weavers, framework-knitters, and others, trade unionism was not enough; and hence his Bill sought to provide the positive protective machinery for which the House of Commons may not have been 'ripe' but of which the outworkers stood in crying need.

The response of trade unionists to the events of 1824 and 1825 now seems more explicable. They saw Henson's Bill manoeuvred out of the way by men who were known to have opposed trade union demands before and who appeared to have some understanding with the Government. Hence, a decided reluctance to come forward with support in the early stages; and when they did come forward, to give evidence before Hume's Committee, Place found them full of reservations:

1. Wallas, op. cit., pp. 210, 217.

The workmen were not easily managed. It required great care and pains and patience not to shock their prejudices. ... They were filled with false notions, all attributing their distresses to wrong causes. ... All expected a great and sudden rise of wages, when the Combination Laws should be repealed; not one of them had any idea whatever of the connexion between wages and population ...

When they saw what Place was about, they gave him support, not with enthusiasm, but on the principle that half a loaf was better than none. When the Acts were repealed, they made use of their new freedom with vigour. When it seemed likely that they would be reinstated, in 1825, even the Government was shaken by the storm of protests, petitions, meetings, and deputations from every trade. 'Vigilant and intelligent men' came down to watch the parliamentary proceedings, from Lancashire, Glasgow, Yorkshire, Tyneside. Any attempt to re-enact the Combination Acts, John Doherty, the leader of the Lancashire cotton-spinners, wrote to Place, would result in a widespread revolutionary movement.[1]

Place was the main architect of repeal, and thus immortalized himself in trade union history. This he deserved. But we should not for this reason chide the unions for 'apathy' (as did the Webbs)[2] nor understate the almost hilarious confusion of the time. Place was a doctrinaire, who wished the Acts repealed because they offended against good political economy (and also because he was indignant at any repression of working men). He had no notion of 'serving' the trade union movement through consultation and common agreement. He wished to manage their delegates as he manipulated M.P.s: 'I knew well enough that if they could be served ... it must be done with-

1. Wallas, op. cit., pp. 213–14, 228; Webbs, op. cit., pp. 106–7; *Reports of Select Committee on Artizans and Machinery* (1824), *passim*.

2. As early as January 1824 the *Black Dwarf* issued a general appeal for petitions in support of repeal; many scores of such petitions from trades clubs throughout the country flooded in in the first months of 1824. It is of interest to speculate how far members of Government (such as Huskisson) tolerated Hume's Bill as a means of ditching the Bill of Peter Moore. See *Black Dwarf*, 17 January 1824; *Mechanics' Magazine*, 24 January, 7 February 1824; *Journals of the House of Commons*, LXXIX, 1824; Huskisson in the debate of 27 May 1823, *Hansard*, new series, VIII (1823).

out their concurrence, in spite of them.'[1] The trade unionists, for their part, summed him up; saw that he was in earnest and influential; and gave him qualified support, although it was not the Bill that they wanted. Place was almost certainly right that Henson's Bill could never have got through the House, any more than Maxwell and Fielden's Bill for regulating weavers' wages succeeded ten years later. On the other hand, Place was grossly self-deluded as to the probable consequences of repeal; and it was in part the very force of this delusion (that repeal would prevent disputes) which enabled Hume to gather support in a bored or hostile House.

Once repeal was gained, not the 'laws' of M'Culloch but the organizations of such men as John Gast and Doherty, moved into the area of new freedom. The London unionists turned, not to Place, but to Thomas Hodgskin, for their theory. For a brief period, several unions looked with favour upon Place's gospel of the common interests of workers and employers.[2] But the theory of class collaboration had scarcely made its appearance before it came under fire, first from the *Trades Newspaper*, and, second, from the Owenite Socialists.[3] Except in certain craft unions, it was pushed back so far that it scarcely influenced trade union development for fifteen or twenty years. One wonders whether Francis Place, the great wire-puller, was not himself at the end of a trade union wire?

IV. CROPPERS AND STOCKINGERS

This is to anticipate our narrative. For the most cogent arguments for repeal of the Combination Acts were, first, their continuing ineffectiveness in preventing the growth of trade unionism; and, second, the prevalence of violent trade union action, which had been dramatized by Luddism. We have attempted to draw closer to the Luddite movement from three

1. Wallas, op. cit., p. 204.
2. The Sheffield cutlers sent Place a handsome gift, while the Lancashire operative cotton-spinners held a dinner at which Hobhouse, Hume and Place were toasted, and a toast was also drunk to 'The Cotton Manufacturers of Manchester; and may peace and harmony long prevail between them and their workpeople.' See *Trades Newspaper*, 24 July 1825.   3. See below, ch. 16.

directions: the shadowy tradition of some political 'under-ground'; the opacity of the historical sources: and the vigorous traditions of illicit trade unionism. We must now analyse more closely the industrial context within which Luddism took place.

This analysis already exists,[1] but it may be corrected and supplemented by evidence which has more recently come to light. Luddism proper, in the years 1811–17, was confined to three areas and occupations: the West Riding (and the crop-pers), south Lancashire (and the cotton weavers), and the framework-knitting district centred on Nottingham and taking in parts of Leicestershire and Derbyshire.

Of these three groups, the croppers or shearmen[2] were skilled and privileged workers, among the aristocracy of the woollen workers; while the weavers and framework-knitters were outworkers, with long artisan traditions, undergoing a deterioration in status. The croppers come closest to the Lud-dites of popular imagination. They were in direct conflict with machinery which both they and their employers knew per-fectly well would displace them. The cropper's work was des-cribed before the Committee on the Woollen Trade in 1806:

The business of a cloth worker is to take a piece of cloth in its rough state as it comes from the market, or as it comes from the fulling mill; he first raises that cloth; after that, if it is a good piece, it is cropped wet; it is then taken and mossed and rowed; mossing is filling up the bottom of the wool after it has been cut with the shears wet, it is done with a handle set with teazles in each hand; after that it is rowed and tentered ... and dried; if a fine piece it will receive three cuts dry after the tenter ...

After this, the back was cut, and the cloth was examined for faults and repaired, brushed up, cleaned, pressed, and perhaps

1. The Hammonds'. *The Skilled Labourer* remains the best account of the background to Luddism, ch. 4, 'The Cotton Workers', ch. 6, section 4, 'The Shearmen or Croppers', ch. 8, 'The Framework Knitters', and chs. 9 and 10 on Nottingham and Yorkshire Luddism. Frank Peel's *The Rising of the Luddites* (for Yorkshire) is the most lively regional study. F. O. Darvall's *Popular Disturbances and Public Order in Regency Eng-land* draws extensively but unimaginatively upon the Home Office papers.

2. The two terms were interchangeable, although 'croppers' was more commonly in use in Yorkshire and 'shearmen' in the West Country. Sometimes also the generic 'cloth-dressers' or 'cloth-workers' was used.

cut a final time.[1] The cloth-worker or cropper undertook all these processes. Apart from the cleaning, the tentering (or stretching), and the pressing, the cropper's skill resided in the central process, by which the surface or 'nap' of the cloth was raised by means of teazles; the shearing done with very heavy hand shears (four feet in length, from handle to blade, and 40 pounds in weight). Both operations required experience and skill. Moreover, while the croppers' wages were regulated by custom at about 5% of the value of the finished cloth, 'they can make a piece 20 pr. Cent better or worse by due care and labour or the reverse'. They were thus in an unusually strong bargaining position.[2]

By the end of the eighteenth century, the finishing of the cloth had become a highly specialized process. Some large manufacturers undertook the whole process in a single 'factory'; and Gott employed as many as eighty croppers under his own roof. But most merchants bought their pieces in an unfinished state from the small clothiers, and put them out for finishing in workshops employing 'forty, fifty, or sixty' skilled men and apprentices in Leeds, but only five or six in the smaller finishing-shops in the West Riding villages. Estimates in 1806 vary between 3,000 and over 5,000 croppers in the West Riding (the second estimate taking in apprentices), with 500 master dressers. In the west of England there were perhaps one-third of that number.[3]

The croppers thus controlled the finishing processes; and, like the woolcombers, were in a strong position to organize and to keep out unskilled labour. They made up the aristocracy of the West Riding clothing-workers, and, when fully employed, could earn in the first years of the nineteenth century up to 30s. a week. They had a reputation for 'independent' or 'insubordinate' manners, political awareness, and rollicking relaxation. 'The Cropper strictly speaking is not a servant,' wrote a correspondent in the *Leeds Mercury*:

He does not feel, or call himself as such, but a cloth-worker, and

1. Loc. cit., p. 296. A clear elucidation of these processes is in W. B. Crump, *The Leeds Woollen Industry, 1780–1820* (Leeds, 1931), pp. 38–51.
2. 'Observations on Combinations', 1799, P.C. A.152.
3. *Committee on the Woollen Trade* (1806), pp. 239, 289, 297.

partakes much more of the nature of a shoe-maker, joiner, taylor, &c. ... Like them, he comes and goes, stops a longer, or a shorter time ... according as he may chance to have work.[1]

According to another account, they had 'twice or three times as much money at the ale house than the weaver, the dresser or the dyer', and were 'notoriously the least manageable of any persons employed in this important manufacture'.[2]

But at the same time they were well aware that their status had been made insecure by machinery which could change them almost overnight from an élite into 'an order of men not not necessary to the manufacture'. The gig-mill was an old invention; indeed, much of the conflict leading up to Luddism turned on a Statute of Edward VI under which its use was prohibited. Essentially it was a simple device, by which, instead of the nap being raised by hand, the cloth was passed between cylinders set with teazles. The croppers (and some master dressers) maintained that the gig-mill was unsuitable for all but the coarsest cloth, tearing and overstraining cloth of finer quality; but these arguments were themselves overstrained in the attempt to prove the indispensability of hand skill. The gig-mill, however, threatened to dispossess the cropper of only one part of the finishing process. More recent, and in its implications equally serious, was the invention of the shearing-frame – a device by which two or more shears, set in one frame, could be passed over the surface of the cloth, with a simplicity which dispensed with the need for skilled craftsmen.

The struggle against the gig-mill reaches back into the eighteenth century. Long employed in a few parts of the west of England, the clothing-workers had not become reconciled to its use; and, while a few gig-mills were operating in parts of the West Riding at the end of the eighteenth century, the croppers had organized to prevent its introduction into Leeds. For many years croppers had passed between Yorkshire and the West Country, since their skill was interchangeable; and by the 1790s the resistance to the gig-mill was reaching crisis point. In 1791 the cloth merchants of Leeds issued a public manifesto, signify-

1. *Leeds Mercury*, 15 January 1803.
2. *Manchester Exchange Herald*, 21 April 1812, cited in Darvall, op. cit., pp. 60–61, 106.

ing their intention to introduce the new machinery; and more than one Leeds mill was destroyed by the croppers in the next ten years. In 1799 the Privy Council was informed that the croppers had a 'general purse' amounting to above £1,000. They were strong enough to enforce a closed shop, and –

a Workman daring from Gratitude to stand by the Master in the hour of his need, becomes a proscribed *Isolé*. He can never be allowed to work where a Ticket Man is till he has adjured his neutrality and paid the penalty they please to impose.

If any master attempted to short-circuit any of the finishing processes, the croppers insisted upon a fine being paid into their funds. If masters returned work as ill-done, the case was adjudicated by a committee of the workers. A Leeds gig-mill had been destroyed in the presence of 'hundreds' of witnesses, but, despite the offer of liberal rewards, not one could be found to give evidence against the men:

The system exists more in general consent to the few simple rules of their union, than in any written Form, and by way of evading all chance of Conviction they have now formed themselves into a General Sick Club.[1]

This sick club was probably the first form of 'the Institution' or 'Clothier's Community' (1802). Its headquarters were in Leeds, but it was Wiltshire, in 1802, which was the centre where the burning of mills and rioting took place. This was, perhaps, less a sign of strength than of despair. In Leeds the croppers were so strongly organized that it had become out of the question to introduce the gig-mill.[2] In August 1802 the Mayor of Leeds had written to Earl Fitzwilliam:

From a perfect conviction that their threats would be carried into execution here, if any merchant infringed the clothworkers' prescriptions, I have, within these last nine months, by my own personal influence, privately prevailed upon one or two houses who

1. 'Observations on Combinations', P.C. A.152. See also *Committee on the Woollen Trade* (1806), esp. pp. 235, 264–5, 369; W. B. Crump, op. cit., pp. 46, 317–18, 327; Hammonds, *The Skilled Labourer*, pp. 171–80; Aspinall, op. cit., pp. 40 ff.

2. There had, however, been gig-mills in the vicinity of Huddersfield for twenty years, which were 'totally stopt from working' by 'an arrête of the workmen' in 1802: Cookson to Fitzwilliam, 30 August 1803, Fitzwilliam Papers, F.45(d).

meditated the adding a gigmill or a shearing machine to their works, to desist for the present, or I am firmly convinced we should have had such horrid outrages to deplore here, as have been practised in the West.[1]

These 'horrid outrages' had reached their climax in the West Country in the last years of the eighteenth century. Bodies of rioters 1,000 or 2,000 strong, attacked the hated mills, and in Somersetshire in December 1797:

Two or three hundred men with their faces black'd & armed with Bludgeons enter'd the Houses of a Sheergrinder . . . about three miles from Froome, and demolish'd about thirty pounds worth of Shears.[2]

In Wiltshire, however, there is some indication that the croppers were already weakened by the waning position of their own industry in relation to the West Riding. With the discharge of shearmen from the forces during the brief peace, the problem of unemployment was more acute. 'A Souldier Returned to his Wife and weeping Orphans' wrote to a Member of Parliament from Bradford (Wilts) in 1802:

We know that it have been mentioned to our great men and Ministers in Parliament by them that have Factorys how many poor they employ, forgetting at the same time how many more they would employ were they to have it done by hand as they used to do. The Poor house we find full of great lurking Boys. . . . I am informed by many that there will be a Revolution and that there is in Yorkshire about 30 thousand in a Correspondent Society. . . . The burning of Factorys or setting fire to the property of People we know is not right, but Starvation forces Nature to do that which he would not . . .[3]

A Gloucestershire clothier was the recipient of a more alarming letter:

Wee Hear in Formed that you got Shear in mee sheens [i.e. Shearing Machines] and if you Dont Pull them Down in a Forght Nights Time Wee will pull them Down for you Wee will you Damd infernold Dog. And Bee four Almighty God we will pull down all the Mills that heave Heany Shearing me Shens in We will cut out Hall your Damd Hearts as Do Keep them and We will meock the rest Heat them or else We will Searve them the Seam.[4]

1. Aspinall, op. cit., p. 52; Fitzwilliam Papers, F.45(d).
2. Bowen to Duke of Portland, 20 December 1797, H.O. 42.41.
3. Hammonds, op. cit., pp. 172–3.   4. D. M. Hunter, op. cit., p. 21.

However obsolete the statute of Edward VI prohibiting gig-mills may have been, it is important that the croppers were aware of it and held that protection against displacement by machinery was not only their 'right' but also their *constitutional* right. They also knew of the clause in the Elizabethan Statute of Artificers enforcing a seven years' apprenticeship, and of a Statute of Philip and Mary limiting the number of looms which might be employed by one master. Not only did they know of these laws: they attempted to put them in force. In 1802 they canvassed public opinion in the West Riding, and won great sympathy in their contest with Gott. Their opposition to new machinery does not appear to have been unthinking or absolute; proposals were in the air for the gradual introduction of the machinery, with alternative employment found for displaced men, or by a tax of 6*d*. per yard upon cloth dressed by machinery, to be used as a fund for the unemployed seeking work. The croppers seem to have cherished some hope of a general negotiation within the trade, and were chiefly indignant at the attitude of a few masters, motivated by 'Revenge and Avarice', and who sought to press home their advantage in the 'consciousness of ... the facility with which the law favours the conviction of illegal combinations'.[1]

It is here that the flagrant class oppression of the Combination Acts bore down upon them at every point. At a time when the common law of conspiracy or 5 Elizabeth c.4 was being employed to defeat trade union action, every attempt to enforce statute law favourable to the workers' interests ended in failure or financial loss. The west of England woollen workers raised subscriptions to empower attorneys to commence actions against gig-mills and against unapprenticed men, but none were successful.[2] The masters, however, were disturbed enough to petition for the repeal of all protective legislation covering the woollen industry. The Yorkshire woollen workers were drawn

1. See the interesting letters of 'A Looker On' and 'A Merchant' in *Leeds Mercury*, 15, 22, 29 January 1803.

2. See E. A. L. Moir, op. cit., pp. 254 and 258–9; W. E. Minchinton, 'The Beginnings of Trade Unionism in the Gloucestershire Woollen Industry', *Trans. Bristol and Glos. Archaeol. Soc.*, LXX, 1951, pp. 126 et seq.; *Rules & Articles of the Woollen-Cloth Weavers Society* (Gloucester, 1802).

into the same legislative struggle. Heavy expenses were incurred to employ counsel on their behalf to attend the House during 1802–3, and to send witnesses to give evidence on the journeymen's behalf. The master's Bill was checked in 1803, and became lost in a Parliament preoccupied with the resumption of war with France. In successive years, an annual suspending Bill was pushed through the House with almost no discussion, waiving all protective legislation on the workers' behalf, while the quasi-legal Institution incurred endless expenses trying to resist the masters' progress. One of the croppers' witnesses, in 1806, declared that the Yorkshire croppers and weavers alone had raised between £10,000 and £12,000 for legal expenses and attendance on Parliament in the previous three years.

Meanwhile, tempers were rising, and support for the croppers was growing. In Yorkshire the Institution had become a formidable organization. Not only did the croppers claim almost 100% organization ('I do not suppose,' declared one witness, 'that there are twenty Cloth-workers in the county of York but what are in the institution'), but a great many small masters and weavers were subscribing to their funds. When their books were seized in 1806, it appeared that many other groups of workers either belonged to the Institution or had received grants from their funds: colliers, bricklayers, woolsorters, clothiers, joiners, sawyers, flax-dressers, shoemakers, turnpike-men, cabinet-makers, pattern-ring-makers, and paper-makers; while payments had been made to and received from the Manchester cotton-spinners. By 1806, indeed, the case of the croppers had almost melted into the general grievances and demands of the working community. For the croppers the grievance was specific: 'now gigs and shearing frames are like to become general, if they are allowed to go on many hundreds of us will be out of bread'. For the weavers the issue was wider: could the obsolescent apprenticeship clauses of 5 Elizabeth c.4 be re-inforced, thereby stemming the influx of unskilled labour? All artisans saw this as a test case, indicative of the restoration or the total abrogation of the old protective or arbitrative labour code which alone afforded any hope of legal defence against the full impact of wage-cutting and labour dilution. For many of the small masters – thousands of whom were among the 39,000 who petitioned in 1805 in favour of a Bill to limit looms, put down gig-mills, and enforce apprenticeship – it appeared that the domestic system itself was at stake. In 1806 when a new Committee was appointed to enquire into the Woollen Trade, impressive delegations appeared to give evidence from most sections of woollen workers and small masters of both Yorkshire and the west. The witnesses all converged in a general detestation of the factory system; 'they frankly allow,' the Committee reported, 'that they wish to retain this Law [i.e. apprenticeship] on account of its tending to embarrass the carrying on the Factory system, and thereby to counteract its growth'. The threat of the gig-mill was one element only in a general revulsion against the great employers who were breaking down working customs and disrupting a settled way of life.[1]

It would be a sad understatement to say that the men's witnesses before the 1806 Committee met with a frosty reception. They and their counsel were browbeaten and threatened by the advocates of *laissez faire* and the anti-Jacobin tribunes of order. Petitions were seen as evidence of conspiracy. Witnesses whom the croppers had sent to London and maintained at such expense were interrogated like criminals ('I mean to tell the truth as far as comes to my knowledge,' expostulated one cropper: 'my character is my bread.'). It was held to be an outrageous offence that they had collected money from outside their own ranks and had been in contact with the woollen workers of the west. They were forced to reveal the names of their fellow officers. Their books were seized. Their accounts were scrutinized. The Committee dropped all pretence of judicial impartiality, and constituted itself into an investigating tribunal. 'Your Committee need scarcely remark,' it reported to the House of Commons,

that such Institutions are, in their ultimate tendencies, still more alarming in a political, than in a commercial view . . .

1. *Committee on the Woollen Trade*, 1806, pp. 232, 239, 277, 347, 355, Appendix 13; Hammonds, op. cit., pp. 180–86; Aspinall, op. cit., pp. 66–7.

It saw in the croppers' organization 'the existence of a systematic, and organized Plan, at once so efficient and so dangerous, both from the amount of its force, and from the facility and secrecy with which ... that force can be called into action ...' It was this which called for 'the most deliberate and serious consideration of Parliament'.[1]

The Institution, of course, went underground. For two more years suspending Bills were passed. In 1808 the croppers petitioned once more, declaring that 'the great question respecting the use of that Machine ... having been brought in so many Sessions of Parliament, the Expenses have greatly distressed them'. Finally, in 1809 all the protective legislation in the woollen industry – covering apprenticeship, the gig-mill, and the number of looms – was repealed. The road was now open for the factory, the gig-mill, the shearing-frame, the employment of unskilled and juvenile labour. The road to *any* constitutional redress was finally blocked. If there had been a 'constitutional' and a 'Luddite' faction within the croppers' ranks, the latter now carried the day. Already, in 1805, an anonymous letter had been received at the Royal Exchange Insurance Office:

Gent. Directors,

At a general but private meeting of the Chairmen of all the Committees of cloth workers in this county (viz. York) it was ordered to desire you (for your own profit) not to insure any factory where any machinery was in belonging the cloth workers. For it was ordered again to petition parliament for our rights; and, if they will not grant us them, by stopping the machinery belong us, we are determined to grant them ourselves, but does not wish you to be any loser thereby.

By order of the
Cloth Workers.[2]

After 1806 and 1809 every vestige of legislation which suggested that the journeyman in wool might look to Parliament to defend their status had been abrogated. When, in the stagnant and distressed years of the Orders in Council, some large

1. *Committee on the Woollen Trade*, 1806, p. 244, Appendix, pp. 17–18.
2. Ibid., p. 312. This letter is undoubtedly authentic, but there is no evidence that it was authorized by the Institution.

employers hurried to install the new machinery in the hope of cornering, with cheap labour, the little trade that was left, Luddism appeared with an almost inevitable logic. To the croppers Ned Ludd was the defender of ancient right, the upholder of a lost constitution:

We will never lay down Arms [till] The House of Commons passes an Act to put down all Machinery hurtful to Commonality, and repeal that to hang Frame Breakers. But We. We petition no more – that won't do – fighting must.

Signed by the General of the Army of Redressers
Ned Ludd Clerk

Redressers for ever Amen.[1]

However, the signal for Luddism came first, not from the croppers, but from the framework-knitters. Their story is complicated by the fact that there was no single obnoxious machine, like the gig-mill, against which they were in revolt; and because with them, the constitutional and the Luddite strategies do not appear as alternatives so much as tactics simultaneously employed. It is the constitutional thread which we must unravel first.

The general process by which the framework-knitters were beaten down to poverty during the Wars follows very similar lines to that by which the weavers were degraded. The stocking-loom, however, was a more expensive machine than most hand-looms. The industry was controlled by the merchant-hosiers; the manufacture was undertaken by stockingers, working in their own homes, or in small workshops of master-stockingers. While some stockingers[2] owned their own looms or frames, after 1800 these came more and more under the ownership of the hosiers, or of independent speculators who invested small or large sums in looms, upon which they drew the rent in much the same way as owners of cottage-property. Thus, to the general grievances concerning wage-cutting and working customs there was added the running grievance of frame rents. The hosiers, in fact, had two alternative means of lowering wages: to reduce the price paid for the work, or to raise

1. W. B. Crump, op. cit., p. 230.
2. Stockinger and framework-knitter are interchangeable terms.

the frame-rents. And, as in hand-loom weaving, the least scrupulous masters undermined conditions throughout the trade.

In 1811 there were perhaps 29,000 stocking-looms in the country, and 50,000 workers employed in and about the hosiery trade.[1] Although a tiny pocket of the industry remained in London, its seventeenth-century home, the industry was now largely concentrated in the Nottingham-Leicester-Derby triangle. As in the Yorkshire woollen industry, a few large workshops or 'factories' were growing up, but by far the greatest number of stockingers worked in small industrial villages in workshops containing three or four frames. Unlike the skilled croppers, the framework-knitters were outworkers in a position exceptionally exposed to exploitation; like the weavers they looked back to better times. Accounts of the second half of the eighteenth century differ; but from 1785 until 1805 it seems that there was a fairly high level of employment, with wages of 14s. or 15s. a week for a twelve-hour day. But by the turn of the century the industry was facing difficult readjustments. The sombre tone of anti-Jacobin society led to a falling demand for the gorgeous hose of pre-revolutionary years, although this was compensated for to some extent by the increased demand for plain hosiery and the gradual introduction of machine-wrought lace. The stockingers experienced a growing deterioration in their conditions, and reacted with vigour. As in the case of the weavers, magistrates and masters were to be found who attributed the insubordination of the men to the 'luxury and licentiousness' induced by their former affluence: 'Among the men the discussion of politics, the destruction of game, or the dissipation of the ale houses was substituted for the duties of their occupation during the former part of the week, and in the remaining three or four days a sufficiency was earned for defraying the current expenses' — 'the lower orders were almost universally corrupted by profusion and depravity scarcely to be credited . . .'[2]

1. Detailed accounts in Nottingham Archives 3984 II, f. 29 suggest 29,355 hands in the trade. W. Felkin, op. cit., pp. 239, 437, suggests 29,580 frames in 1812, and 50,000 framework-knitters.

2. See Hammonds, op. cit., pp. 222–6; Darvall, op. cit., pp. 28–34.

The grievances of the stockingers were complex, and a full understanding of them demands a minute attention to the details of the trade.[1] Not only plain and fancy hose, but also gloves, braces, mitts, spider-net blouses, pantaloons, cravats, and miscellaneous articles were manufactured in the Midlands; and Leicester, where much fine work was done, was not as badly hit in the Luddite years as Nottingham. But all grievances turned upon the various means by which the least scrupulous hosiers were seeking to economize labour and cheapen production. In some villages 'truck' was so widespread that it had almost displaced payment in wages. Payment for work depended upon complicated piece-rates which turned, in lace, upon the fineness of count in the lace; the men complained that they were consistently underpaid, as for work of coarser quality, and that the masters refused to employ an instrument called the 'rack' which measured the count. The stockingers had to deduct from their inadequate wages out-payments for seaming, needles, oil, the fetching and carrying of work, etc. Unscrupulous middlemen, or interlopers, called 'bag hosiers' visited the villages persuading stockingers who were underemployed, or who wished to save themselves the waste of time involved in taking their work to the large hosiers' warehouses in Nottingham, to do work below the accepted rates. But most serious of all were the grievances as to 'cut-ups' and 'colting'.

'*There is no new machinery in Nottingham, or its neighbourhood, against which the workmen direct their vengeance,*' so wrote the middle-class Radical paper, the *Nottingham Review*:

The machines, or *frames* . . . are not broken for being upon any new construction . . . but in consequence of goods being wrought upon them which are of little worth, are deceptive to the eye, are disreputable to the trade, and therefore pregnant with the seeds of its destruction.[2]

1. The clearest summaries are in Darvall, op. cit., ch. 2, and A. Temple Patterson, *Radical Leicester*, ch. 3. See also F. A. Wells, *History of the Midland Hosiery Trade* (1935).
2. *Nottingham Review*, 6 December 1811.

Cut-up stockings (and other articles) were manufactured from large pieces of knitted material, woven on a wide loom, which was then cut up into the required shape, the articles then being sewn at the seam.[1] The articles were cheap, and – in comparison with the traditional stocking-frame – they could be mass-produced. But they were bitterly disliked in the trade for a number of reasons. The men, and many of the masters also, argued that the product was much inferior and that the seams came apart. To the inexpert eye they resembled the real article, and therefore could undercut hose made 'in a tradesmanlike manner' – and this at a time when the collapse of the South American market and the general stagnation induced by the Orders in Council had led to a falling demand. Further, the poor quality of the 'cut-ups' offended the craftsman's pride in his work, and led to the products of the trade generally falling into disrepute. Moreover, this grievance led directly into the grievance as to 'colting', or the employment of unskilled labour or of too many apprentices. Cheap techniques of production encouraged the influx of cheap and unskilled labour. Framework-knitting was being debased into a 'dishonourable' trade.

The stockingers, like the croppers, had a long history of both constitutional and violent defence of their conditions. A Framework-Knitters' Company had obtained a Charter from Charles II, although in the eighteenth century the Midlands industry had in fact evaded its regulations and it had fallen into obscurity. Between 1778 and 1779 there had been a determined attempt to secure a legal minimum wage. When the Bill was defeated, rioting and frame-breaking ensued. In 1787 a price-list was negotiated between the hosiers and the men, which remained in force to some degree for twenty years. From 1807 onwards wages declined, and the stockingers once again had recourse to constitutional agitation. The old Framework-Knitters' Company was revived, the journeymen paying the heavy subscription of £1 13s. 6d. for admission, and several actions were commenced. A test case against 'colting' succeeded; but the 1s. damages awarded by the jury was insufficient to deter other offenders. Wages declined by one-third

---

1. For opposition to the broad loom as such, see letters in *Leicester Journal*, 13 December 1811, *Derby Mercury*, 19 December 1811.

from their 1807 level. In 1811, Gravener Henson, who now emerged as the outstanding leader of the men, attempted one of the only recorded actions against the masters under the Combination Acts. He produced evidence that some of the hosiers had combined to reduce wages, and had published their resolutions in the Nottingham press. The magistrates refused to attend to his complaint, and the Town Clerk refused to serve a warrant.[1]

Just as in the case of the croppers, the framework-knitters felt that every statute which might have afforded them protection was abrogated or ignored, while every attempt to enforce their rights by trade union action was illegal. Although some of the hosiers, before 1811, also wished to see the suppression of 'cut-ups' and 'colting', class alignments hardened month by month, and the goodwill which had formerly existed between those employers who were political reformers and their journeymen was dissipated. However, there is good reason to suppose that in 1811–12 some of the hosiers who paid customary rates and did not manufacture 'cut-ups' actively sympathized with the Luddites' aims, if not with their methods. For Luddism in Nottingham, as in Yorkshire, was highly selective. Those frames only were broken which manufactured under-price or 'cut-up' work; when goods were slashed, in the loom or when seized from the carrier's cart, the 'cut-ups' were destroyed while those with proper selvedges were left undamaged. The distinction was clearly made in the song, *General Ludd's Triumph*:

> The guilty may fear but no vengeance he aims
> At the honest man's life or Estate,
> His wrath is entirely confined to wide frames
> And to those that old prices abate.
> These Engines of mischief were sentenced to die
> By unanimous vote of the Trade
> And Ludd who can all opposition defy
> Was the Grand executioner made.

1. Hammonds, *Town Labourer*, p. 66; *Skilled Labourer*, p. 227; Darvall, op. cit., p. 43; *Committee on Framework-Knitters' Petitions* (1812); J. D. Chambers, 'The Framework-Knitters' Company', *Economica*, November 1929.

He may censure great Ludd's disrespect for the Laws
Who ne'er for a moment reflects
That *foul Imposition* alone was the cause
Which produced these unhappy effects.
Let the haughty no longer the humble oppress
Then shall Ludd sheath his conquering sword,
His grievances instantly meet with redress
Then peace will be quickly restored.

Let the wise and the great lend their aid and advice
Nor e'er their assistance withdraw
Till full-fashioned work at the old fashioned price
Is established by Custom and Law.
Then the Trade when this arduous contest is o'er
Shall raise in full splendour its head,
And colting and cutting and squaring no more
Shall deprive honest workmen of bread.[1]

Indeed, the framework-knitters claimed a constitutional sanction even for frame-breaking. Under the Charter granted by Charles II there was a clause empowering the Framework-Knitters' Company to appoint deputies to examine goods, and to cut to pieces those badly or deceitfully manufactured. These powers the Luddites now assumed as rights. In reply to magisterial proclamations against their activities, they issued a counter DECLARATION, be-spattered with 'Whereases' and 'Whenevers', declaring both their intention and their right to 'break and destroy all manner of frames whatsoever that make the following spurious articles and all frames whatsoever that do not pay the regular price heretofore agreed to by the Masters and Workmen'. A list of the offensive frames and practices was subjoined.[2]

The major phase of Nottinghamshire Luddism was between March 1811 and February 1812; and within that period there were two peaks, March and April, and November to January, when frame-breaking spread to Leicestershire and Derbyshire. In this phase perhaps 1,000 frames were destroyed, at a cost of between £6,000 and £10,000, and numerous articles damaged. We shall return to these events. But in Nottingham there is

1. Copy in H.Q. 42.119 (to the tune, 'Poor Jack').
2. Conant and Baker to H.O. 42.119 partly reproduced in Darvall, op. cit., p. 170.

an interesting oscillation between Luddite and constitutional protest, and it is possible that both were directed – at least up to 1814 – by the same trade union organization, in which perhaps Luddites and constitutionalists (probably led by Gravener Henson) differed in their counsels. The major phase of Luddism ended with the passage of the Bill to make frame-breaking a capital felony, which was characterized in 'Ned Ludd's' DECLARATION as 'void', since it had been obtained in the 'most fraudulent, interested, and electioneering manner'. Nevertheless, the passage of the Bill in February 1812, so much alarmed the framework-knitters that they set urgently to form themselves into a quasi-legal association, the 'United Committee of Framework-Knitters', many of whose papers (seized in 1814) still survive.

The first step of the Nottingham Committee was to open correspondence with London, Leicester, Derby and even Dublin, Tewkesbury and Glasgow, and to try (unsuccessfully) to secure a postponement in the passage of the offensive Bill in order that their representations could be heard by the House. Responses from their correspondents reveal the extreme difficulties in the way of forming any legal association. From Leicester (20 February 1812):

It was thought necessary to put ourselves under the broad Sheild of the Law and solicite the Concurance of the Magistrates of the Borough ... to hold an aggregate meeting of the Trade ...

From Derby (3 March 1812): 'the Magistrates of this Rotten Borough will not suffer us to have a Meeting of the Trade'. In London, where only 100 or so stockingers still worked, the Hatton Garden magistrates were more helpful, but (4 March 1812) 'two police officers attended our meeting to give satisfaction to the magistrate that our proceedings were legal'. From Tewkesbury a correspondent replied (2 March) that the magistrate had prevented a meeting, and letters were opened. Thomas Latham (who, with Henson, conducted most of the correspondence) wrote a stinging letter to the Mayor of 'Tukesbury':

Know you not, Sir, that the Act, commonly called 'The Gagging Act' is long since dead of its own natural death?

He should beware that people 'may be driven to the commission of crime, for the purpose of exercising their *veangence*, when they cannot exercise their *rights*'. Despite these difficulties committees were formed in all these centres, and correspondence was also maintained with stockingers in Sheffield, Sutton-in-Ashfield, Belper, Heanor, Castle Donnington and Godalming.[1]

The aim of the Nottingham Committee was to promote a Bill giving parliamentary relief to the stockingers. From certain committees there came the suggestion of a petition for a minimum wage Bill. These proposals the Nottingham Committee resisted:

It is well known, that governments will not interfere with the regulation of the *quantum* of wages which shall be paid for a certain *quantum* of labour; because the thing in itself would amount to the odious practice of fixing a *maximum* and *minimum* upon an article, which fluctuates as does our national prosperity, and adversity. . . . It is true that Government has interfered in the regulation of wages in times long since gone by; but the writings of Dr Adam Smith have altered the opinion, of the polished part of society, on this subject. Therefore, to attempt to advance wages by parliamentary influence, would be as absurd as an attempt to regulate the winds.

Clearly, Henson and his colleagues had taken measure of the opposition. If they were to secure the advance of wages which they wanted (the Nottingham Committee argued) it must be more detailed legislation preventing *indirect* abatements:

And the Committee are of opinion . . . that the late outrages in this town and neighbourhood, have had their origin, *with the multifarious impositions practised upon the workmen by the hosiers, for want of parliamentary regulations.*

Hence it was intended to draw up a Bill which included a number of detailed clauses: (1) to regulate the size of hose by the number of jacks (i.e. wires in the stocking-frame), (2) to make the marking of all hose compulsory, so that good quality could be distinguished from poor, (3) to make the use of the 'rack' compulsory in assessing payment for machine-lace,

1. Nottingham Archives and *Records*, VIII, p. 139.

(4) to prohibit inferior copies of good quality goods, (5) to make it compulsory for price-lists to be displayed in every workshop, (6) to give to J.P.s the power to regulate frame-rents.

Accordingly a Bill was drawn up, 'For Preventing Frauds and Abuses in the Frame-Work Knitting Manufacture', containing several of these clauses, as well as the prohibition of payment in 'truck'. Subscription-lists and a petition in favour of the Bill were circulated actively in March 1812. By the end of April over 10,000 signatures had been collected from the framework-knitters ('N.B. All the Males in the Trade may sign but no Women.'):

Nottingham		2,629
– –	County	2,078
Leicester		1,100
– –	County	2,057
Derby		239
– –	County	1,809
Tewkesbury		281
Godalming		114
London		92

The subscription-lists show a breadth of support outside the stockingers' own ranks – donations from publicans, grocers, bakers, butchers, millers, farmers, printers, some master-hosiers, and many artisans. An appeal was issued for donations from Sick Clubs. In June, when the Bill was coming before Parliament, a soldier wrote offering to take a collection in the militia regiment at Great Yarmouth, while the Committee acknowledged 'My Lord Biron's handsome subscription'.

From late April until the end of July Henson, Large, Latham and other delegates were frequently in London, attending to the Bill. Their reports on the City were hardly complimentary. Not only did they find the skilled trade unionists supercilious, they also found their expense allowance from the union stretched to the full. On 22 April they reported that they had slept their first night at 'The Swan with Two Necks', Lad Lane:

When with Cold Supper of Beef, Lodgings, Waiter and Chamber-maid they contrived to ease us of twenty-five shillings; which made

Tommy Small [i.e. Large] exclaim, scratching his Head, Lunnun is the Devil ! ! ! ! ! !'

(Henson, back in Nottingham in May, wrote to inquire of his colleagues whether 'London is improved in Smell'). The expenses of the affair were heavy. Legal and parliamentary costs swallowed most of the funds, but there were also the fares and expenses of the delegates (Henson, in mid-June, paid a flying visit to Dublin), an allowance (14s. per week) to their wives, a further allowance (3s. a day) for Committee members engaged full-time in collecting subscriptions. The response of the stockingers themselves was uneven. Leicester, whose worsted hose manufacture was not yet as badly affected as Nottingham cottons, was lacking in enthusiasm: 'There is not half a dozen good fellows in the Town,' Large had written in April, and 'those principally are composed of Sherwood Lads'.[1] In May a Committee member wrote despairingly of the lack of support in Nottinghamshire villages engaged in the plain (two-needle) trade, whose stockingers suspected that the Bill would benefit mainly those in the lace and silk manufacture: 'I have been out too days and could not get one Peney they look Pleasant as a Cows husband at me.' As the months drew on, questions were asked about the cost of maintaining delegates in London and wives at home. (These jealousies inevitably arose in every early trade union context.) Moreover, while the Committee sought strenuously to suppress machine-breaking which would prejudice their case in Parliament, feelings ran high in Nottingham, where seven Luddites were sentenced to transportation for seven or fourteen years in March. The Committee undoubtedly knew who the leading Luddites of the previous year were, if it did not actually include some of them among its number. In April the only attempted assassination during the Midlands disturbances took place – a hosier named William Trentham being wounded outside his house. The attack was preceded by an anonymous letter from 'the Captain' denouncing Trentham's under-payment of women:

You must be sensible Sir that these unfortunate Girls are under very strong temptations to turn prostitutes, from their extreme

1. i.e. Luddites.

poverty. The Captain authorizes me to say that these People being defenceless he conceives them to be more immediately under his protection as his believes their Wages are the lowest in England.

From Leicester the secretary of the local committee wrote in dismay to the London delegates:

I have been informed that Mr Trantham Hosier of Nottn was shot on Monday night at his own door, report says that on Saturday last he *docked* his hands twopence per pair and told them to tell *Ned Ludd*. How true this may be I know not, certain it is that this is not a proper time to irritate the public mind by gross Insult.

There is an element of pathos in the progress of events in London. The stockingers' representatives – and in particular Henson – gave a most impressive account of their case before the Parliamentary Committee examining the Bill.[1] The delegates also lobbied industriously, showing M.P.s examples of bad workmanship and 'cut-ups', and distributing gifts of their finest work (paid out of Committee funds) to influential persons. Stockings, a silk veil, a silk press, and handkerchiefs were given to the Prince Regent. Sidmouth received the deputation graciously, ordering stockings and a shawl for his daughters, and the delegates seemed at the point of success. On the eve of the Third Reading of the Bill, Henson wrote back to Nottingham with a note of triumph (30 June 1812):

We have Some Reason to [think] the Prince Regent is also favorable, We have only Dr A. Smiths Disciples to contend with whose principles are execrated all over the Kingdom.

Two days later he wrote despondently. Hume had opposed the Bill, and then the House had adjourned, 'there not being Forty Members present, they ran out of the House when our business came on like wild fire'. So much for the months of petitioning and collecting, of victimization and attempts at legal organization. In Committee the House received last-minute representations and petitions from large hosiery houses in Leicester and Nottingham. The House thereupon decided to erase *all* the

1. See *Committee on Framework-Knitters' Petitions* (1812), esp. pp. 38–46. One of the men's witnesses was John Blackner, the historian of Nottingham, who had been a framework-knitter since 1780.

clauses of the Bill relating to hosiery, leaving in only emaciated clauses relating to lace and to truck. This news Henson sent back to Nottingham in a letter with a savage addendum:

P.S. They may Dock, Cut up, Square, Make Single Cotton, and Cheat, Rob, Pilfer and Oppress now to their hearts content.

In the hope of getting some clauses re-instated, the delegates waited on the Radical leader:

Sir Francis Burdett told us that Parliament never interfered with Disputes between Masters and Workmen. ... Sir Francis did not attend to support us but left the House ... it is the *ministerial* Side of the House that is the advocates of our Bill.

The emasculated Bill did indeed pass its Third Reading, despite another long speech in opposition from Hume, on 21 July: 'The Ministers were for the Bill, only 12 in the House when it Passed, all the Patriots went away as usual.' But it is difficult to understand what part the 'ministerial side' were playing, for three days later the Bill was rejected out of hand by the Lords. The strongest speech against it (there were none in its favour) came from Lord Sidmouth: he 'trusted in God that no such principle would be again attempted to be introduced in any Bill brought up to that House'.[1]

This is by no means the end of the story of the framework-knitters' organization. Briefly, on the defeat of the Bill the Committee took measures to strengthen the union. Inquiries were made into 'how the Carpenters, Tailors, Shoemakers, and Cutlers conduct their Union'; a new constitution was drawn up (perhaps with the advice of Sir Samuel Romilly); and the union was given the title of 'The Society for Obtaining Parliamentary Relief, and for the Encouragement of Mechanics in the Improvement of Mechanism'.[2] As such it had an effective existence for nearly two years; benefits, unemployment and strike pay were granted; the union successfully employed some of its own members directly in the manufacture; and its acti-

1. Nottingham Archives, 3984 I and II, *passim*; *Records* VIII, pp. 139–62; Hammonds, op. cit., pp.229, 270.
2. Copy of *Articles and General Regulations* (Nottingham, 1813) in Nottingham Archives, 3984 II, f. 126.

vities were sufficiently powerful to discourage a recrudescence of Luddism. However, in 1814 outbreaks of frame-breaking resumed, according to one account against the wishes of Henson and the 'constitutional' section, according to another account as a supplementary form of trade union enforcement, by which small Luddite bands were actually subsidized out of union funds. A strike at one of the large Nottingham hosier's shops led to action by a 'Secret Committee' of the hosiers and the Corporation, which had long been employing spies to ferret out the union's proceedings. Two of the union's officers were seized and imprisoned and the union's papers were impounded. Frame-breaking continued sporadically until 1817; but it is clear that during the same years the union continued with a vigorous underground existence. Secrecy was giving way year by year to massive and disciplined open demonstrations, as well as to open negotiation.[1]

Much of this history belongs to the aftermath of Luddism. But the history of the abortive Bill to regulate framework-knitting throws into relief the predicament of trade unionists in the Luddite years. Although we do not possess documents which enable us to read the thoughts of the leaders of the weavers and croppers so clearly, they must have encountered very similar experiences in their fruitless and expensive recourse to Parliament between 1800 and 1812. We have already followed in some detail the history of the Lancashire cotton-weavers. But it must be noted that Luddism in Lancashire arose out of a crisis between paternalism and *laissez faire* exactly parallel to those in the hosiery and woollen industries. As late as 1800 and 1803 the weavers, after intensive agitation, had been able to secure at least a formal measure of protection in the Cotton Arbitration Acts. The weavers were already in

1. See the Hammonds, op. cit., pp. 229–54; W. Felkin, op. cit., p. 238; A. Temple Patterson, op. cit., chs. 6, 7; Darvall, op. cit., pp. 139–50, 155–9; Aspinall, op. cit., pp. 169–83, 230, 234–42, 320–28. For a short time Henson was employed full-time by the union. In 1816 he brought two successful actions against hosiers for infringement of the Truck Acts. In 1817 he was arrested while in London where he was petitioning for the lives of condemned Luddites; and he was held without charge for eighteen months during the suspension of Habeas Corpus.

correspondence with the cotton-weavers of Glasgow, and (in the view of Colonel Fletcher of Bolton) their agitation 'originates in the *Jacobin Societies* and is intended as a means to keep the minds of the Weavers in a continual Ferment . . .'[1] The victory of the Arbitration Acts proved illusory. While magistrates were given fresh powers to mediate and to enforce a minimum wage,

> the Magistrates, being more nearly allied to the Masters by rank and fortune, and also more familiar with them by convivial interviews, dealt in the business with but a slack hand.[3]

The agitation for a minimum wage bill reached its first crisis-point in 1807–8, with the petitions, demonstrations, and strikes which resulted in the imprisonment of Colonel Hanson.[3] According to a Scottish witness, who claimed to have taken a leading part in the organization, an impressive nation-wide weavers' union existed from 1809 until the end of 1812, with its centre in Glasgow and with strongholds in Scotland, Lancashire, Carlisle and Northern Ireland.[4] In 1811 the weavers made a renewed effort to obtain a minimum wage bill, petitions appealing for protection against unscrupulous employers being signed by 40,000 Manchester weavers, 30,000 from Scotland, and 7,000 from Bolton. In 1812 there appears to have been some divergence in the weavers' councils, the Lancashire men abandoning all hope of protection and turning towards Luddism, the Glasgow and Carlisle men fighting protracted and expensive test cases in the law courts on the issues of wage-regulation and apprenticeship. The Glasgow men, in fact, won their case, after fighting it at great cost into the higher courts.But the manufacturers promptly refused to pay the minimum which the magistrates had agreed upon at Quarter Sessions, with the result that (November and December 1812) there was a remarkably disciplined and well-supported weavers' strike, from Aberdeen to Carlisle. The men

---

1. Hammonds, op. cit., p. 67, and (for the Arbitration Acts) pp. 62–9, 72 ff.

2. One Who Pities the Oppressed, *The Beggar's Complaint against Rack-Rent Landlords, Corn Factors, Great Farmers, Monopolizers, Paper Money Makers, and War* . . . (Sheffield, 1812), pp. 100 ff.

3. See above, p. 307.   4. A. B. Richmond, op. cit., pp. 14–28.

(said Richmond) were determined to enforce by 'one simultaneous moral effort' the wages awarded by law, and determined also 'to make the last stand for their rank in society'. The Glasgow leaders ('persons of wonderful coolness and ability'), who had been at pains at every point to consult counsel and to act within the law, were thereupon arrested, and awarded sentences ranging from four to eighteen months. When, two years later, the apprenticeship clauses of 5 Eliz. c.4 were repealed, a further petition (this time from Lancashire weavers) declared that 'the present Bill to repeal the aforesaid Law has sunk the spirits of the Petitioners beyond description, having no hope left . . .' [1]

The treatment of the Glasgow weavers' leaders was the most outrageous example of the general predicament of trade unionists at this time. And this is the point at which we may pull together our analysis of the causes which precipitated Luddism. It is of course easy to fall back on an otiose 'economist' explanation, which attributes Luddism to the simple cause and effect of the Orders in Council. It is true that Napoleon's Contintental System and the retaliatory Orders had so disrupted the markets for British textiles that the industries of Lancashire, Yorkshire and the Midlands were stagnant. Both war and successive bad harvests had contributed to raising the price of provisions to 'famine' heights. But this will not do as an explanation of Luddism; it may help to explain its occasion, but not its character. These years of distress, 1811 and 1812, added the supreme grievance of continuous hunger to existing grievances. It made each device by which the least scrupulous masters sought to economize on labour, and cheapen its value (power-looms, shearing-frames, or 'cut-ups'), seem more offensive. But the character of Luddism was not that of a blind protest, or of a food riot (as took place in many other districts). Nor will it do to describe Luddism as a form of 'primitive' trade unionism. As we have seen, the men who organized, sheltered, or condoned Luddism were far from primitive. They were shrewd and humorous; next to the London artisans, some

1. See ibid., pp. 29–40 and Richmond's evidence, *Second Report . . . Artizans and Machinery* (1824), pp. 59 ff.; Hammonds, op. cit., pp. 85–8; Aspinall, op. cit., pp. 137–50, esp. J. J. Dillon to Sidmouth, pp. 143 ff.

of them were amongst the most articulate of the 'industrious classes'. A few had read Adam Smith, more had made some study of trade union law. Croppers, stockingers, and weavers were capable of managing a complex organization; undertaking its finances and correspondence; sending delegates as far as Ireland or maintaining regular communication with the West Country. All of them had had dealings, through their representatives, with Parliament; while duly-apprenticed stockingers in Nottingham were burgesses and electors.

Luddism must be seen as arising at the crisis-point in the abrogation of paternalist legislation, and in the imposition of the political economy of *laissez faire* upon, and against the will and conscience of, the working people. It is the last chapter of a story which begins in the fourteenth and fifteenth centuries, and whose greater part has been told in Tawney's *Religion and the Rise of Capitalism*. True enough, much of this paternalist legislation had been in origin not only restrictive, but, for the working man, punitive. Nevertheless, there was within it the shadowy image of a benevolent corporate state, in which there were legislative as well as moral sanctions against the unscrupulous manufacturer or the unjust employer, and in which the journeymen were a recognized 'estate', however low, in the realm. The J.P. at least in theory could be turned to in the last extremity for arbitration or protection, and even if practice taught working men to expect a dusty answer, it was still by this theory that the magistrate was judged. The function of industry was to provide a livelihood for those employed in it; and practices or inventions evidently destructive of the good of 'the Trade' were reprehensible. The journeyman took pride in his craft, not merely because it increased his value in the labour market, but because he was a craftsman.

These ideals may never have been much more than ideals; by the end of the eighteenth century they may have been threadbare. But they had a powerful reality, none the less, in the notion of what *ought* to be, to which artisans, journeymen, and many small masters appealed. More than this, the ideals lived in the sanctions and customs of the more traditional manufacturing communities. The journeymen celebrated them when they observed, with pomp and gusto, the shoemaker's feast of St Crispin, the jubilee of the Preston 'Guilds', or the wool-comber's feast of Bishop Blaise. The early quasi-legal unions emblemized this tradition in their ornate tickets or membership cards: the shearmen with the coat-of-arms, topped with the crossed shears, between the figure of justice and the figure of liberty; the shoemakers with their motto, 'May the Manufactures of the Sons of Crispin be trod upon by All the World'; all the unions with their proclamations and manifestos, signed 'BY ORDER OF THE TRADE'. As often happens, as the tradition came to its last years, so its was suffused with nostalgic light.

Moreover, it is sometimes forgotten how rapid the abrogation of paternalist legislation was. As late as 1773 the important Spitalfields Act was introduced, which remained in force with modifications for fifty years, under which the silk-weavers secured – what other weavers and stockingers strove in vain to secure – a legal minimum wage.[1] The ineffective cotton Arbitration Acts (1800–1803) at least served to keep alive the notion of protection. Thereafter, in the space of ten years, almost the entire paternalist code was swept away. Between 1803 and 1808 the regulations covering the woollen trade were suspended. In 1809 they were repealed. In 1813 the apprenticeship clauses of 5 Eliz. c.4, were repealed. In 1814 those clauses empowering magistrates to enforce a minimum wage followed. (The clause under which it was an offence to leave work unfinished, however, remained.) In 1814 the apprenticeship restrictions in the cutlery industry were set aside by the Sheffield Cutlers' Bill. During the same ten years workers, penalized under the Combination Acts for any direct trade union action, increasingly had recourse to the courts in attempts to enforce obsolescent legislation. Thus, there were actions by the woollen workers on gig-mills and apprenticeship, by stockingers on 'colting' and 'truck', by cotton-weavers on apprenticeship and minimum wage enforcement, and more than a dozen cases fought by the London trades (coach-makers, lock-

1. For the operation of the Spitalfields Acts, see M. D. George, *London Life in the Eighteenth Century*, ch. 4; Hammonds, op. cit., pp. 209 ff.; J. H. Clapham, 'The Spitalfields Acts', *Economic Journal*, December 1916.

makers, machine-makers, and others) between 1809 and 1813 on similar issues.[1] The great majority of these cases were unsuccessful. The few which succeeded exhausted the funds of the unions and brought derisory damages. Finally, these years also see the dispersal of the last customary or legal controls over price-fixing in the open market, and the failure to reactivate the common law with respect to forestalling and regrating.

We have to imagine the bitter experiences of Henson and Large, in their expensive attendance on Parliament, multiplied one hundredfold. The workers understood quite well what was happening. They were caught squarely between two fires. On the one hand, they faced the fire of established order. By no means all the country magistrates, nor even the Lords-Lieutenant of counties, were doctrinaire supporters of *laissez faire*. On occasions, these men felt real misgivings as to intervening against the journeymen, and even strong dislike of the methods of the large masters. But at the moment when the men's grievances were loudly and effectively voiced, at that moment also they threatened the values of order. The old-fashioned squire might sympathize with a famished stockinger who appeared as a passive plaintiff at his door. He had no sympathy at all with secret committees, demonstrations in the streets, strikes, or the destruction of property.

On the other hand, the men faced the fire of their employers, who gained every day fresh reinforcements from the disciples of *laissez faire*. The Corn Laws of 1815 were to reveal how far the aristocracy and gentry were from real assent to these doctrines. But the war-time Ministry found it convenient to accept the arguments of 'free competition', in so far as they militated against working-class, rather than landed, interests, out of sheer counter-revolutionary opportunism. Indeed, Sidmouth, when moving the repeal of wage-arbitration in 1813, scarcely thought the matter worthy of argument:

It did not require minds so enlightened as those of their Lordships to be aware how pernicious such a state of things must be both to the employer and the servant, but especially to the latter. They

1. See T. K. Derry, 'Repeal of the Apprenticeship Clauses', loc. cit., pp. 71–2.

must all be convinced therefore that it was expedient to pernicious statutes.[1]

If such men as the croppers' and framework-knitter met with rebuffs from the Ministers, they received from Radicals like Hume, or even Burdett. They were opposed at one side by the values of order, at the other side by the values of economic freedom. In between a mass of confused M.P.s, some of whom felt, perhaps, an obscure sense of guilt at the injustice being done, took the easiest way out: 'they ran out of the House when our business came on like wild fire'.

Byron, in his famous speech in the Lords opposing the Bill to make frame-breaking a capital felony, was not indulging in hyperbole: 'When a proposal is made to emancipate or relieve, you hesitate, you deliberate for years, you temporize and tamper with the minds of men; but a death-bill must be passed off hand, without a thought of the consequences.' The workers felt that the bonds, however ideal, which bound them to the rest of the community in reciprocal obligations and duties, were being snapped one after another. They were being thrust beyond the pale of the constitution. The grievance was felt most bitterly by those who, like the weavers and stockingers felt that their status as artisans was being undermined. In 1811 the Plain Silk Hands of Derby appealed to the master-hosiers:

As a body of ingenious artizans employed on materials of great value ... we conceive ourselves entitled to a higher station in society: and that, in point of emolument we ought to rank with mechanics of the first eminence. ... Hedged in by a combination act, we cannot say to you as a public body, that we demand an advance of wages, but we can say that JUSTICE DEMANDS that we should receive a remuneration for extra labour.[2]

'When we consider,' declared a committee of the Lancashire weavers in 1811, 'that the Legislature has already interfered in matters of less moment – has enacted laws for regulating the price of *corn*, for fixing the assize of *bread*, ... for augmenting the salaries of *Judges and Clergymen* ... this Committee are utterly at a loss to conceive on what fair ground Legis-

1. See Hammonds, op. cit., p. 87.
2. *Nottingham Review*, 20 December 1811.

lative interference can be improper under circumstances so necessitous':

Had you possessed 70,000 votes for the election of Members to sit in that House, would your application have been treated with such indifference, not to say inattention? We believe not.[1]

In the first place, then, we must see Luddism in this context. The journeymen and artisans felt themselves to be robbed of constitutional rights, and this was a deeply felt conviction. Ned Ludd was the 'Redresser' or 'Grand Executioner', defending ('by unanimous vote of the Trade') rights too deeply established 'by Custom and Law' for them to be set aside by a few masters or even by Parliament:

> Chant no more your old rhymes about Robin Hood,
> His feats I but little admire.
> I will sing the Atchievements of General Ludd,
> Now the Hero of Nottinghamshire . . .[2]

But, in the second place, we should not over-state the isolation into which the stockingers or croppers had been forced. Throughout the Luddite 'outrages', the machine-breakers had the backing of public opinion in the Midlands and the West Riding. The large employers, and the factory system generally, stirred up profound hostility among thousands of small masters. In 1795 the small master-clothiers of the West Riding were actively canvassing support for a Bill 'for restoring and preserving entire the late system of carrying on the Cloth manufacturing . . .'

Until lately, that System has been by cloth being manufactured by Persons residing in different villages in the County, and sold in the public Halls in Leeds to merchants who did not follow the manufacturing of Cloth.

Of late, several merchants have become manufacturers of Cloth, and, for the better carrying on such manufactory, have erected very large Buildings which are called Factories, wherein they intend to employ Clothiers as their Servants, so that persons, who, with their Families, have been dispersed as before mentioned, will be associated together within, or near those Buildings in a dependant State.

1. H.O. 42.117. See the Hammonds, op. cit., pp. 84–5, for fuller extracts from this remarkable document.
2. *General Ludd's Triumph*, in H.O. 42.119.

The Bill (which sought to prevent merchant-manufacturers from supplementing their orders by buying cloth in the public halls) was 'intended to preserve a System of Trade, which has been productive of more Independence, Prosperity and Morality, and consequently of greater Happiness than any other Branch of Manufacture in the Kingdom'.[1]

The gap in status between a 'servant', a hired wage-labourer subject to the orders and discipline of the master, and an artisan, who might 'come and go' as he pleased, was wide enough for men to shed blood rather than allow themselves to be pushed from one side to the other. And, in the value-system of the community, those who resisted degradation were in the right. In 1797 the first steam-mill was built in Bradford to the accompaniment of menacing and hooting crowds. The 'little makers' of the West Riding saw in the many-chimneyed progeny of Arkwright, across the Pennines, the death-warrant of their own domestic industry. The small masters who supported the 'Institution' or 'Clothier's Community', between 1802 and 1806, had at their backs a general theory of moral economy.

It is easy to forget how evil a reputation the new cotton-mills had acquired. They were centres of exploitation, monstrous prisons in which children were confined, centres of immorality and of industrial conflict;[2] above all, they reduced the industrious artisan to 'a dependant State.' A way of life was at stake for the community, and, hence, we must see the croppers' opposition to particular machines as being very much more than a particular group of skilled workers defending their own livelihood. These machines symbolized the encroachment of the factory *system*. So strongly were the moral presuppositions of some clothiers engaged, that we know of cases where they deliberately suppressed labour-saving inventions, while Richard Oastler's father, in 1800, sold up a prospering

1. MS. 'Heads of Proposed Bill ...', Halifax Reference Library.
2. Compare the Tory Cobbett in the *Political Register*, 23 July 1803; 'On Sunday the children, being let loose from ... those pestiferous prisons ycleped manufactories, may stretch their little cramped up limbs ...'; and the Liberal *Leeds Mercury* (6 March 1802): 'the large manufactories in this and other towns form seminaries for all kinds of profaneness and obscenity. ... The truth of this observation cannot be questioned.'

business rather than employ machinery which he regarded as 'a means of oppression on the part of the rich and of corresponding degradation and misery to the poor'.[1] It was this feeling, among clothiers, master cloth-dressers, artisans and labourers of all descriptions, and even some professional men, which gave a sanction to the Luddites and afforded them protection. General Grey, commanding the troops in the West Riding in 1812, commented with dismay upon:

how much the opinion and wishes of even the more respectable portion of the Inhabitants are in unison with the deluded and ill-disposed populace with respect to the present object of their resentment Gig Mills and Shearing Frames and this extends also to persons having mills of a different description employed in the Manufacturing branch ...[2]

These feelings existed also in the Midlands, where no important improvements in machinery were at issue. The master-stockingers, tradesmen, artisans, and even some of the hosiers were wholly on the framework-knitters' side, most certainly during their appeal to Parliament in 1812. The Bill making frame-breaking a capital offence was deprecated even by those hosiers whose interests it was supposed to defend. And, in this light, the conventional picture of the Luddism of these years as a blind opposition to machinery as such becomes less and less tenable. What was at issue was the 'freedom' of the capitalist to destroy the customs of the trade, whether by new machinery, by the factory-system, or by unrestricted competition, beating-down wages, undercutting his rivals, and undermining standards of craftsmanship. We are so accustomed to the notion that it was both inevitable and 'progressive' that trade should have been freed in the early nineteenth century from 'restrictive practices', that it requires an effort of imagination to understand that the 'free' factory-owner or large hosier or cotton-manufacturer, who built his fortune by these means, was regarded not only with jealousy but as a man engaging in *immoral* and *illegal* practices. The tradition of the just price and the fair wage lived longer among 'the lower orders' than is sometimes supposed. They saw *laissez faire*, not as freedom,

1. Driver, op. cit., pp. 17–18.   2. Darvall, op. cit., p. 62.

but as 'foul Imposition'. They could see no natural law by which one man, or a few men, could engage in practices which brought manifest injury to their fellows.

A 'Declaration Extraordinary', addressed to 'our well-beloved Brother, and Captain in Chief, Edward Ludd', embodies all these notions of the moral economy of the 'Trade'.

Whereas it hath been represented to us, the General Agitators for the Northern Counties, assembled to redress the Grievances of the Operative Mechanics, That Charles Lacy, of the Town of Nottingham, British Lace Manufacturer, has been guilty of diverse fraudulent, and oppressive, Acts – whereby he has reduced to poverty and Misery Seven Hundred of our beloved Brethren ... by making fraudulent Cotton Point Nett, of One Thread Stuff, has obtain'd the Sum of Fifteen Thousand Pounds, whereby he has ruin'd the Cotton-Lace Trade, and consequently our worthy and well-belov'd Brethren; whose support and comfort depended on the continuance of that manufacture.

It appeareth to us that the said Charles Lacy was actuated by the most diabolical motives, we therefore ... do adjudge the said Fifteen Thousand Pounds to be forfeited, and we do hereby ... command Charles Lacy to disburse the said sum, in equal shares among the Workmen, who made Cotton Nett in the year 1807 ...[1]

From this aspect, then, Luddism can be seen as a violent eruption of feeling against unrestrained industrial capitalism, harking back to an obsolescent paternalist code, and sanctioned by traditions of the working community. But at this point the term 'reactionary' comes too easily to some lips. For despite all the homilies addressed to the Luddites (then and subsequently) as to the beneficial consequences of new machinery or of 'free' enterprise, – arguments which, in any case, the Luddites were intelligent enough to weigh in their minds for themselves – the machine-breakers, and not the tract-writers, made the most realistic assessment of the short-term effects. The croppers provide the clearest example of a skill that was simply extinguished:

1. The 'Declaration', in fine copper-plate, is dated November 1811, and empowers Edward Ludd to 'inflict the Punishment of Death' in case of default, and to distribute £50 among the executioners: J. Russell, 'The Luddites', *Trans. Thoroton Society*, X, 1906, pp. 53–62.

Between 1806 and 1817 the number of gig mills in Yorkshire was said to have increased from 5 to 72; the number of shears worked by machinery from 100 to 1,462; and out of 3,378 shearmen no less than 170 were out of work while 1,445 were only partly employed.[1]

Their labour was replaced by that of unskilled men and juveniles. According to an account in 1841:

In 1814, there were 1,733 croppers in Leeds, all in full employment; and now, since the introduction of machinery, the whole of the cloth ... is dressed by a comparatively small number, chiefly boys, at from 5s. to 8s. ... and a few men at from 10s. to 14s. per week. The old croppers have turned themselves to any thing they can get to do; some acting as bailiffs, water-carriers, scavengers, or selling oranges, cakes, tapes and laces, gingerbread, blacking, &c. &c.[2]

This was a sad end to an honourable craft. The later history of the stockingers and cotton-weavers provides scarcely more evidence for the 'progressive' view of the advantages of the breakdown of custom and of 'restrictive practices'. We have already examined in sufficient detail the destruction of the weaver's livelihood. If there is any episode of the Industrial Revolution more harrowing than that of the hand-loom weaver, it is that of the stockinger. By 1819, according to Felkin, very many of them had been reduced to 4s. to 7s. a week for sixteen to eighteen hours daily labour; only emigration to the Cape of Good Hope afforded a means of escape. There was some recovery in the early 1820s, with the introduction of machine-lace (the twist-net or bobbin-net 'fever'), which brought a new influx into the trade, followed by continuing deterioration. 'We've a bit of a spurt now and then,' one of them told Thomas Cooper in 1840: 'But we soon go back again to starvation.' (4s. 6d. was then quoted as an 'average' wage when in employment.) Between the frame-rent, on one side, and a multiplicity of forms of petty exploitation – wage-cutting, 'docking' or fining, truck – on the other, 'the poor framework-knitter was worn down, till you might have known him by his peculiar air of misery and dejection, if you had met him a hundred miles

1. E. Lipson, *The History of the Woollen and Worsted Industries* (1921), p. 181.   2. W. Dodd, *The Factory System Illustrated*, p. 15.

from Leicester'. And this had been effected by 'free competition' alone, without the introduction of any machinery involving steam or water-power.[1]

Even if we make allowances for the cheapening of the product, it is impossible to designate as 'progressive', in any meaningful sense, processes which brought about the degradation, for twenty or thirty years ahead, of the workers employed in the industry. And, viewed from this aspect, we may see Luddism as a moment of *transitional* conflict. On the one hand, it looked backward to old customs and paternalist legislation which could never be revived; on the other hand, it tried to revive ancient rights in order to establish new precedents. At different times their demands included a legal minimum wage; the control of the 'sweating' of women or juveniles; arbitration; the engagement by the masters to find work for skilled men made redundant by machinery; the prohibition of shoddy work; the right to open trade union combination. All these demands looked forwards, as much as backwards; and they contained within them a shadowy image, not so much of a paternalist, but of a democratic community, in which industrial growth should be regulated according to ethical priorities and the pursuit of profit be subordinated to human needs.

Thus we must see the years 1811–13 as a watershed, whose streams run in one direction back to Tudor times, in another forward to the factory legislation of the next hundred years. The Luddites were some of the last guildsmen, and at the same time some of the first to launch the agitations which lead on to the 10 Hour Movement. In both directions lay an alternative political economy and morality to that of *laissez faire*. During the critical decades of the Industrial Revolution, working people suffered total exposure to one of the most humanly degrading dogmas in history – that of irresponsible and unlicensed competition – and generations of outworkers died under this exposure. It was Marx who saw, in the passage of the 10 Hour Bill (1847), evidence that for 'the first time ... in broad daylight the political economy of the middle class

1. Felkin, op. cit., pp. 441 ff.; T. Cooper, *Life*, pp. 137–42. See also J. F. C. Harrison, 'Chartism in Leicester', in A. Briggs, *Chartist Studies*, pp. 121–9.

succumbed to the political economy of the working class'.[1] The men who attacked Cartwright's mill at Rawfolds were announcing this alternative political economy, albeit in a confused midnight encounter.

V. THE SHERWOOD LADS

Luddism lingers in the popular mind as an uncouth, spontaneous affair of illiterate handworkers, blindly resisting machinery. But machine-breaking has a far longer history. The destruction of materials, looms, threshing-machines, the flooding of pits or damage to pit-head gear, or the robbing or firing of houses or property of unpopular employers – these, and other forms of violent direct action, were employed in the eighteenth century and the first half of the nineteenth, while 'rattening' was still endemic in parts of the Sheffield cutlery industry in the 1860s. Such methods were sometimes aimed at machinery held to be obnoxious as such. More often they were a means of enforcing customary conditions, intimidating blacklegs, 'illegal' men, or masters, or were (often effective) ancillary means to strike or other 'trade union' action.[2]

Although related to this tradition, the *Luddite movement* must be distinguished from it, first, by its high degree of organization, second, by the political context within which it flourished. These differences may be summed up in a single characteristic: while finding its origin in particular industrial grievances, Luddism was a *quasi-insurrectionary movement*, which continually trembled on the edge of ulterior revolutionary objectives. This is not to say that it was a wholly conscious revolutionary movement; on the other hand, it had a tendency towards becoming such a movement, and it is this tendency which is most often understated.

The Luddism of Lancashire revealed the highest political content, as well as the greatest spontaneity and confusion. The Luddism of Nottinghamshire was the most highly organized and disciplined, and the most strictly confined to industrial

1. K. Marx, *Selected Works* (1942), II, p. 439.
2. See E. J. Hobsbawm, 'The Machine Breakers', *Past & Present*, I, February 1952, pp. 57 ff.

objectives. The Luddism of Yorkshire moved from industrial to ulterior objectives. Before analysing these differences, we must present a brief narrative.

The main disturbances commenced in Nottingham, in March 1811. A large demonstration of stockingers, 'clamouring for work and a more liberal price' was dispersed by the military. That night sixty stocking-frames were broken at the large village of Arnold by rioters who took no precautions to disguise themselves and who were cheered on by the crowd. For several weeks disturbances continued, mainly at night, throughout the hosiery villages of north-west Nottinghamshire. Although special constables and troops patrolled the villages, no arrests could be made.

Although frame-breaking had extended more widely than at any time for perhaps thirty years, this first outbreak of March and April created no sensation. Riots of one kind or another were endemic in the manufacturing districts, and aroused little comment. But early in November 1811, Luddism appeared in a much more disciplined form. Frame-breaking was no longer the work of 'rioters' but of smaller, disciplined bands, who moved rapidly from village to village at night. From Nottinghamshire it spread to parts of Leicestershire and Derbyshire, and continued without intermission until February 1812. On 10 November there was a serious conflict at Bulwell, where a hosier named Hollingsworth defended his premises. Shots were exchanged, and one of the Luddites (a stockinger from Arnold named John Westley) was killed; but after retreating with his body the Luddites returned, beat down the doors and broke up the frames. Three days later a very large force of Luddites, armed with muskets, pistols, axes and hammers, destroyed seventy frames at a large hosier's workshop in Sutton-in-Ashfield. Night after night, for more than three months, the attacks continued, sometimes in two or three widely separated villages on the same night.

By the end of December the Nottingham correspondent of the *Leeds Mercury* declared: 'the Insurrectional state to which this country has been reduced for the last month has no parallel in history, since the troubled days of Charles the First'. No degree of activity by the magistrates or by large reinforcements of military deterred the Luddites. Every attack revealed planning and method:

They broke only the frames of such as have reduced the price of the men's wages; those who have not lowered the price, have their frames untouched; in one house, last night, they broke four frames out of six; the other two which belonged to masters who had not lowered their wages, they did not meddle with.

The Luddites were masked or disguised; had sentinels and couriers; 'they communicated with each other by means of a watchword, and the firing of a pistol, or gun, is generally the signal of danger, or of a retreat':

The rioters appear suddenly, in armed parties, under regular commanders; the chief of whom, be he whomsoever he may, is styled *General Ludd*, and his orders are as implicitly obeyed as if he had received his authority from the hands of a Monarch.

It was generally believed that the Luddites acted under a solemn oath, and that disobedience to the General's orders was punished with death.[1]

At the same time, raids for arms and the general collection of money for Luddite funds became more general. A letter from Ashover described the authority with which the Luddites acted:

Two men came to this place who called themselves inspectors from the committee; they went to every stockinger's house and discharged them from working under such prices as they gave them a list of. . . . They summoned all the stockingers, about 12 or 14 in number of master men to a public house with as much consequence as if they had had a mandate from the Prince Regent. When they got them hither, all I can learn at present, was for the purpose of collecting money from them for the support of those families who were deprived of getting their bread by having their frames broken. Where they found a frame worked by a person who had not served a regular apprenticeship, or by a woman, they discharged them from working, and if they promised to do so, they stuck a paper upon the frame with these words written upon it – 'Let this frame stand, the colts removed'.[2]

1. Darvall, op. cit., pp. 67–70; Hammonds, op. cit., pp. 261–5; *Leeds Mercury*, 7, 14, 21 December 1811.
2. Aspinall, op. cit., p. 118.

At the village of Pentridge (to become notorious in another context five years later) 'after passing through the village, and examining the frames, and their holders, as to the work they made and the prices they received, they retired without doing any mischief ...' From motives of sympathy or in self-defence, those hosiers who were conforming to the conditions demanded by the stockingers affixed printed bills to their frames: 'THIS FRAME IS MAKING FULL FASHIONED WORK, AT THE FULL PRICE.'[1]

The extraordinary success of the Luddites gave to them a high morale:

> Now by force unsubdued, and by threats undismay'd
> Death itself can't his ardour repress
> The presence of Armies can't make him afraid
> Nor impede his career of success
> Whilst the news of his conquests is spread far and near
> How his Enemies take the alarm
> His courage, his fortitude, strikes them with fear
> For they dread his Omnipotent Arm. . . .
>
> And when in the work of destruction employed
> He himself to no method confines,
> By fire and by water he gets them destroyed
> For the Elements aid his designs.
> Whether guarded by Soldiers along the Highway
> Or closely secured in the room,
> He shivers them up both by night and by day,
> And nothing can soften their doom.[2]

Not only did they openly offer a 'reward' to anyone giving information as to persons who disclosed their secrets, they also issued threats against pseudo-Luddites who collected funds or robbed isolated farms under pretences. The 'General's' discipline is well illustrated by a letter to an 'Unknown Stranger', which accompanied some articles which had been stolen during an attack at Clifton (Notts.), with the request that the articles should be 'Restored to their respective owners':

... it is with extream Regrat that I inform you hau thay Came into my hans when I came out with my men their weir sum joind us that

1. *Alfred*, 9 December 1811.
2. *General Ludd's Triumph*, H.O. 42.119.

I Never had ad with me before and it wear these Villinds that plun-
dred but ass we wear going out of Clifton one of my Men came and
told me that he Believd that those Men ad got some thinck that
they had no Buisiness with I theirfore gave horders that thay should
be searchd ...

The letter ended more grimly:

... we were gust agoen to have hang'd one of the Villends when we
weir informed that Solders weir at hand we thot it Right to Retreat.
N.B. The Men that had the things weir entire strangers to my
horders or they Never dworst not have tuch'd one thinck, but they
have been punished for their vileny for one of them have been
hang'd for 3 Menet and then Let down agane I ham a friend to the
pore and Distrest and a enemy to the oppressors thron.

GENERAL LUDD[1]

In the first week of February 1812, this – the major phase of
Midlands Luddism – died away. There were three reasons.
First, the Luddites were partially successful – the majority of
hosiers had agreed to pay better prices, and wages had generally risen by as much as 2s. a week. Second, there were now
several thousand troops in the area, supplemented by special
constables and local watch parties. Third, the Bill to make
frame-breaking a capital offence was now before Parliament,
and (as we have seen) Luddism gave way suddenly to constitutional agitation – so suddenly that it is impossible not to
believe that the new Committee was not at least partly under
former Luddite direction.[2] But just at the moment that Nottingham Luddism became inactive, Luddism in Lancashire and
Yorkshire was triggered off by its example.

In Yorkshire the reports from Nottingham had been eagerly
followed by the croppers, and according to tradition the
accounts in the *Leeds Mercury* had been read aloud in the workshops. The first intimation of active Luddism came in mid-
January, when a party of men with blackened faces was
surprised on Leeds Bridge. Thereafter Luddism appeared,

1. *Leeds Mercury*, 15 February 1812; *Nottingham Review*, 7 February
1812.

2. Henson claimed that he advised the formation of trades clubs as an
alternative to Ludding: *Fourth Report ... Artizans and Machinery*
(1824), p. 282.

already full-grown, modelled upon the Nottingham discipline and tactics, but accompanied by a greater number of emphatic threatening letters which may, or may not, have stemmed from a central source. In January one of the only Leeds gig-mills was set on fire; by February, nightly attacks were being made in the Huddersfield and Spen Valley districts, where the greatest number of gig-mills and shearing-frames were to be found. After one successful attack,

As soon as the work of destruction was completed, the Leader drew up his men, called over the roll, each man answering to a particular number instead of his name; they then fired off their pistols . . . gave a shout, and marched off in regular military order.

Nothing was destroyed apart from the obnoxious machinery:

. . . one of the party having asked the Leader what they should do with one of the Proprietors, he replied not hurt a hair of his head; but that should they be under the necessity of visiting him again, they could not show him any mercy.[1]

There seem to have been different Luddite 'commands' in the West Riding, centred on Leeds, Halifax, Huddersfield and the small clothing villages of the Spen Valley, whose delegates (from Cleckheaton, Heckmondwike, Gomersal, Birstall, Mirfield, Brighouse, Elland and 'more distant places') are supposed to have met together in February, and to have sent delegates to a further meeting a week or two later at Halifax.[2] A leaflet was distributed in Leeds, in very much more insurrectionary terms than anything attributed to the Nottingham Luddites:

To all Croppers, Weavers &c. & Public at large.
Generous Countrymen,
You are requested to come forward with Arms and help the Redressers to redress their Wrongs and shake off the hateful Yoke of a Silly Old Man, and his Son more silly and their Rogueish Ministers, all Nobles and Tyrants must be brought down. Come let us follow the Noble Example of the brave Citizens of Paris who in Sight of 30,000 Tyrant Redcoats brought A Tyrant to the

1. *Leeds Mercury*, 18 January, 29 February 1812; Frank Peel, op. cit. (1880 edn), p. 17.

2. Peel, op. cit. (1895 edn), pp. 44 ff. It should be noted that wherever Peel's account can be checked it is generally accurate, even in detail.

Ground. by so doing you will be best aiming at your own Interest. Above 40,000 Heroes are ready to break out, to crush the old Government & establish a new one.

Apply to General Ludd Commander of the Army of Redressers.[1]

A Mr Smith, a Huddersfield manufacturer, received a letter even more chilling:

Information has just been given in that you are a holder of those detestable Shearing Frames, and I was desired by my Men to write to you and give you fair Warning to pull them down. . . . You will take Notice that if they are not taken down by the end of next week, I will detach one of my Lieutenants with at least 300 Men to destroy them and furthermore take Notice that if you give us the Trouble of coming so far we will increase your misfortune by burning your Buildings down to Ashes and if you have Impudence to fire upon any of my Men, they have orders to murder you, & burn all your Housing, you will have the Goodness to your Neighbours to inform them that the same fate awaits them if their Frames are not speedily taken down . . .

Mr Smith and his 'Brethren in Sin' were then informed that 'there were 2,782 Sworn Heroes bound in a Bond of Necessity' in the Army of Huddersfield alone, nearly double sworn Men in Leeds':

By the latest letters from our Correspondents we learn that the Manufacturers in the following Places are going to rise and join us in redressing their Wrongs Viz. Manchester, Wakefield, Halifax, Bradford, Sheffield, Oldham, Rochdale and all the Cotton Country where the brave Mr Hanson will lead them on to Victory, the Weavers in Glasgow and many parts of Scotland will join us the Papists in Ireland are rising to a Man, so that they are likely to find the Soldiers something else to do than Idle in Huddersfield and then Woe be to the places now guarded by them . . .[2]

Ten days later (20 March 1812) the most active magistrate in the Huddersfield district was himself the recipient of a threatening letter, purporting to come from the 'Solicitor to General Ludd' at Sherwood Forest, Nottingham, and to carry

1. W. B. Crump, op. cit., p. 229.
2. Ibid., pp. 229–30. Mr Hanson is presumably the Colonel Hanson, imprisoned for supporting the weavers in 1808.

the judgement of the 'Ludds Court at Nottingham'.[1] The successes in Yorkshire, following upon those in the Midlands, the impotence of the military, and the hostility of public opinion, were too much for the smaller manufacturers – especially when they were recipients of such hair-raising mail. Many of them simply capitulated, destroying or storing their own shearing-frames. According to tradition, the Luddites drilled frequently at night: 'musket men, ten abreast, stood first, then those armed with pistols ... pikes and hatchets the third, and an unarmed gang were drawn up in the rear'.[2] But the pride of place, in popular legend, went to the hammermen, who wielded enormous iron sledges called 'Enochs', to break open doors and smash the frames. These frames (as well as hammers) were made by Enoch Taylor, of Marsden, a blacksmith turned machine-maker, and the Luddite cry was: 'Enoch made them, Enoch shall break them.' The assaults were celebrated in the cropper's song, to be rendered in 'true ballad patterer's style':

> And night by night when all is still,
> And the moon is hid behind the hill,
> We forward march to do our will
>   With hatchet, pike and gun!
> Oh, the cropper lads for me,
> Who with lusty stroke
> The shear frames broke,
> The cropper lads for me!
>
> Great Enoch still shall lead the van
> Stop him who dare! stop him who can!
> Press forward every gallant man
>   With hatchet, pike, and gun!
> Oh, the cropper lads for me ...[3]

The major phase of Yorkshire Luddism came to a crisis in mid-April, after only six or seven weeks effective existence. As the number of small manufacturers still using the offensive machines diminished, so it became evident that the Luddites must either rest on these successes or attempt the destruction of the few substantial mills still holding out. They chose the

1. Asa Briggs, *Private and Social Themes in Shirley* (Brontë Society, 1958), p. 9.

2. A. L., *Sad Times*, p. 112.

3. Frank Peel, *Spen Valley: Past and Present*, p. 242.

second course. In the last week of March two mills near Leeds were successfully attacked; on 9 April Joseph Foster's 'extensive' cloth manufactory at Horbury, near Wakefield, was sacked and fired, after an attack by a contingent of up to 300 Luddites, probably assembled from several commands.[1] It was now generally expected that an attack would be made on one of two substantial establishments, whose owners had made themselves notorious for their determination to defy the Luddites. William Horsfall, of Ottiwells near Huddersfield, was choleric and impatient to meet an attack; his men were armed, and he had a cannon mounted in his mill, with embrasures to cover the line of attack; he had boasted that he wished to 'ride up to his saddle-girths' in Luddite blood, and his hatred was so obsessional that even the children taunted him in the streets with shouts of 'I'm General Ludd!' William Cartwright, of Rawfolds in the Spen Valley, was quieter but no less determined; he had soldiers and armed workmen in his premises (where he himself slept) every night, sentinels, and (should his outer defences be broken) barricades of spiked rollers on his stairs and a tub of oil of vitriol at the top. According to tradition, the Luddites drew lots to decide which mill should be their first objective. The choice fell on Rawfolds.

The attack upon Rawfolds has become legendary. Perhaps 150 Luddites took part (it was said that more had been expected, and that the Leeds or Halifax contingents failed to arrive in time). Led by George Mellor, a young cropper from a small finishing shop at Longroyd Bridge near Huddersfield, the Luddites exchanged a brisk fire with the embattled defenders for twenty minutes. Under cover of this fire, a small party of hammermen and men with hatchets made repeated attempts to break down the heavy doors of the mill. This party suffered serious casualties, at least five being wounded, two of whom – mortally wounded – were left behind when the Luddites suddenly retreated. It is said that their commander, Mellor, was the last to be left on the field, and that he could not help the wounded men since he was helping to carry another (his own cousin) to safety. The ground around the mill was littered with muskets, axes, pikes and metal implements.

1. *Leeds Mercury*, 11 April 1812; Darvall, op. cit., p. 114.

A thousand details of this attack and of its aftermath entered into the folklore both of the masters and of the populace. And at this point we should pause to enquire why, as well as looking further at the resources of the authorities, the political context of April and May 1812, and at contemporaneous events in Lancashire.

One part of the background is faithfully given to us in Charlotte Brontë's *Shirley*. The mill-owner, Gérard Moore (modelled on Cartwright), is rightly shown as belonging to the half-Whig, half-Radical, middle class, whose organ was the *Leeds Mercury* – indifferent or hostile to the war, eager to have all restrictions upon trade removed, bitterly critical of Minsterial policies and especially of the Orders in Council. The military parson, Helstone (closely modelled on the Reverend Hammond Roberson), is a rabid 'Church-and-King' Tory, regarding the *Leeds Mercury* as mischievous and the mill-owners as disaffected and as the authors of their own discomforts. All this is authentic. Charlotte Brontë's Jacobin-Whig squire, Mr Yorke, divided between his class allegiance and his sympathy for popular grievances, may also have an original in more than one J.P. who remained strangely inactive during the Luddite outbreaks.

Shirley's limitations, of course, are in the treatment of the Luddites and their sympathisers. But the novel remains a true expression of the middle-class myth. During 1812 traditional class antagonisms were thrown into the crucible of Luddism; mill-owner and squire entered the year in bitter hostility to each other; as the Luddites succeeded in intimidating one manufacturer after another, the contempt of the Robersons grew. Then Cartwright, by his defiant action at Rawfolds, earned the admiration and gratitude of the military officers and the Tory squirearchy. In the north, for a few weeks, he was a hero to be named alongside Wellington. The gunfire at Rawfolds signalled a profound emotional reconciliation between the large mill-owners and the authorities. Economic interest had triumphed, and the ultimate loyalty of the manufacturers when faced with working-class Jacobinism was displayed in one dramatic incident.

But what brought emotional reconciliation to the propertied

classes brought profounder antagonism between them and the working classes. The folk-traditions of the Rawfolds attack emphasized the heroism of the Luddites and the callousness of the defenders. Folklore thrives on incident, on the particular hazards and interplay of character. After the retreat, Cartwright was alleged to have refused water or aid to the two mortally wounded men, unless they divulged Luddite secrets. Hammond Roberson is supposed to have behaved to them more like an inquisitor than a clergyman. Hundreds thronged the street outside the inn where the men lay dying. Stains of *aqua fortis* (perhaps used for cauterization) were found on their bedding, and it was believed that they had been tortured to give information. Roberson is supposed to have hung over the bedside of one of them, John Booth, the nineteen-year-old son of an Anglican clergyman, waiting for a dying confession. At the moment of death, young Booth signalled to Roberson – 'Can you keep a secret?' 'Yes, yes,' replied the eager Roberson, 'I can.' 'So can I,' replied Booth, and shortly after he died.

A letter intercepted by the authorities, from a Nottingham working man, living in Yorkshire (and perhaps a Luddite refugee) to his family at home, gives us the immediate reaction:

There as an engagment been betwixt the Luds & the Army which the Luds was defeated which was oing to Halifax Luds not coming up as they was apointed there was 16 men stormed the Plaice which they had two killed there wounded men was carried of and none of them as been taken since which the two men was buried on Thursday last at Othersfield [Huddersfield] which the Corps was put in a Dark room with six mold Candles which the friends of the Luds followed them every man in Morning with a silk apron edged with Black which the Ministers refused to Burie them but the Luds insisted on them being Buried in the Church which are too have a grand Stone he lived fore and twenty hours after he was taken he was the con of a Church parson which many visited him but He refused to in vulge anything.[1]

1. Radcliffe MSS., 126/32. The writer of the letter in fact confused the details of the funeral of John Booth, who was buried hurriedly in Huddersfield in anticipation of great crowds assembling to pay a tribute, with the funeral of Hartley in Halifax, for which see p. 641 below.

In the days following the attack there was no lack of incident to excite popular imagination: there were many stories of narrow escapes from the military, of wounded men hidden in barns. More than one of the small party of soldiers at Cartwright's mill had shown a marked lack of enthusiasm for duty, and one of them refused to fire his musket during the entire twenty minutes of the affair, 'because I might hit some of my brothers'. The unfortunate soldier (from the Cumberland Militia) was court martialled and sentenced to receive 300 lashes – a probable death sentence. The punishment was administered at Rawfolds, and Cartwright was able to regain a portion of public favour by securing the remission of the greater part of the sentence.

He regained little. In the middle-class myth, Cartwright and Roberson were not only the heroes of the day, but the relentless pursuers of 'evil designing men', mysterious emissaries and agitators from remote parts, who were the instigators of disorders. 'The leaders he did not know,' Charlotte Brontë wrote of Gérard Moore:

> They were strangers: emissaries from the large towns. Most of these were not members of the operative class: they were chiefly 'down-draughts,' bankrupts, men always in debt and often in drink – men who had nothing to lose, and much – in the way of character, cash, and cleanliness – to gain. These persons Moore hunted like any sleuthhound; and well he liked the occupation ... he liked it better than making cloth.

In popular folklore, however, Cartwright and Roberson were simply the 'bloodhounds'. The community closed against them in an extraordinary way. Until the attack on Rawfolds, the Yorkshire Luddites (like those in the Midlands) had confined themselves strictly to frame-breaking. Not they, but Cartwright, had let the first blood. For months, despite the presence of 4,000 troops in the West Riding and the widespread employment of spies, not one of the Rawfolds attackers was clearly identified. Thousands must have known one or another of the participants. Traditions speak of Dissenting Ministers and surgeons who refused to pass on information, small clothiers who sheltered their own Luddite workmen, soldiers who ignored evidence. In whole parishes the 'Watch and Ward' Act was inoperative. Luddite ballads went the rounds:

> You Heroes of England who wish to have a trade
> Be true to each other and be not afraid
> Tho' Bayonet is fixed they can do no good
> As long as we keep up the Rules of General Ludd.[1]

Even the assassination (27 April) of William Horsfall of Otti-well occasioned less revulsion of feeling than might have been expected. The same crisis which had brought the 'Church-and-King' men and the *Leeds Mercury*, Roberson and Cartwright, together, had also cemented popular feeling against the magis-trates and the large employers alike.[2]

Moreover, in April and May 1812, Luddism was the focus for a more diffused (and confused) insurrectionary tension. A part of this arose from the general economic crisis of 1811–12, the growing unpopularity of the war, and the agitation against the Orders in Council. The mutual blockades of Britain and France, and the severance of American trade, had given rise to extreme difficulties in many sections of manufacturing industry – in Birmingham, Sheffield, Liverpool, the textile districts – between 1807 and 1812. Poor harvests added their toll of food shortage and soaring prices. Manufacturers attributed all grievances to the continuation of the war, and specifically to the Orders in Council which placed much of Europe in a state of blockade. It is significant that Luddism broke out in those industries where the large employers had alienated public sup-port by taking advantage of this period of economic extremity to introduce new practices or machines; whereas in those centres – Sheffield, Birmingham and to some extent Man-chester – where the whole industry was partially paralysed, and the employers themselves had initiated demonstrations and

1. Brief, *Rex* v. Milnes and Blakeborough, T.S. 11.2673.
2. The 'folklore' of Luddism is found in A.L., *Sad Times*; F. Peel, *Risings of the Luddites*, and *Spen Valley: Past and Present*; Sykes and Walker, *Ben o' Bill's*. Where possible these accounts have been checked with those in the *Leeds Mercury* and in the ensuing trials. Cartwright's letters, describing the attack and the 'treachery' of his soldiers, are in the Hammonds, op. cit., pp. 305–6; and in H. A. Cadman, *Gomersal: Past and Present* (Leeds, 1930), pp. 114–16.

petitions against the Orders in Council (under the leadership of Brougham and, in Birmingham, young Thomas Attwood) working-class discontent remained largely within 'constitutional' forms.[1]

In fact, by 1812, the old squirearchy was scarcely able to control the manufacturing districts, unless it had the support of the large employers. But, paradoxically, where the employers were hostile to the administration, the problems of order were less. Luddism illustrates this whole problem of order. In the summer of 1812 there were no fewer than 12,000 troops in the disturbed counties, a greater force than Wellington had under his command in the Peninsula. For months at a time these considerable forces were singularly ineffective. This may partly have been due to the fact that many of the common soldiers sympathized with the population, so that the authorities were under the necessity of continually moving them from one district to another for fear of 'disaffection' spreading in their ranks. It was also due to the superb security and communications of the Luddites, who moved silently through well-known terrain while the cavalry trotted noisily from village to village. In the West Riding, whose hills were crossed and re-crossed with bridle-paths and old pack-horse tracks, the Luddites moved with immunity. The movements of the cavalry were 'well-known, and the clash of their swords, the tramp of their horses' feet were to be heard at a long distance at night, it was easy for the Luddites to steal away behind hedges, crouch in plantations, or take by-roads ...'[2] The objectives of the Luddites were in a multitude of dispersed villages and scattered mills. These villages were virtually unpoliced, and the military were reluctant to billet soldiers in fives and sixes in dangerous isolation. The mounted magistrate, who understood little of the industry and of the people, was almost helpless. Only the mill-owner or manufacturer, whose premises and wage-book commanded the village, was able to exert control. Hence, where the

1. See A. Briggs, *The Age of Improvement*, pp. 164–6; A. Prentice. *Historical Sketches of Manchester*, pp. 41–7; Chester New, *Life of Henry Brougham* (Oxford, 1961), chs. 4 and 6.
2. D. F. E. Sykes, *History of the Colne Valley* (Slaithwaite, 1906), p. 309.

employers had lost the allegiance of their workers, the entire structure of order was endangered, and could only be repaired by supplementing their authority as at Rawfolds, where not Roberson but Cartwright was in command. But in those districts, like Sheffield and Birmingham, where the manufacturers and workers were still bound to each other by a common sense of grievance against authority, the danger of actual disorder was kept under the masters' control.

Thus Luddism not only brought magistrate and mill-owner together, it also made inevitable concessions by the administration to the manufacturing interest. And these concessions were received with triumph, with the repeal of the Orders in Council in June 1812.[1] Luddism perhaps hastened this event as much as the constitutional agitation of Attwood and Brougham. But repeal took place against an even more threatening background, for by this time serious disorders in Lancashire had been added to the Luddism of Yorkshire and the Midlands.

It is difficult to know how far the unrest in Lancashire may be described as authentic Luddism. It was made up in part of spontaneous rioting, in part of illegal but 'constitutional' agitation for political reform, in part of incidents fabricated by *provocateurs*, and in part of genuine insurrectionary preparations. Between February and April 1812 'secret committees' of at least two kinds were in being in a number of Lancashire towns. First, there were the committees of the weavers, whose undercover organization had been for several years agitating and petitioning for a minimum wage. Such committees were reported to be in being early in April in Manchester, Stockport, Bolton, Failsworth, Saddleworth, Ashton-under-Lyne, Oldham, Stalybridge, Droylesden, Preston, Lancaster, Hendle, Newton, Drilsdale, Hollinwood, Willington and Eccles.[2] Second, in the Manchester-Stockport district and perhaps else-

1. And also the repeal of 5 Eliz. c.4 in 1813 and 1814.
2. These towns and villages are mentioned as sending delegates to various secret meetings in the statement of Yarwood and reports of 'B' (Bent) for April 1812, in H.O. 40.1. See also Thomas Whittaker's deposition in H.O. 42.121 that at a meeting on 25 March at 'The Good Samaritan', Salford, delegates were present from almost every town within fifteen or twenty miles. For the authenticity of these reports see below, pp. 648f.

where, there was an incipient secret trades council (or 'Committee of Trades') comprising 'the Spinners, Taylors, Shoemakers, Bricklayers, Fustian-Cutters, Joiners and many other Trades'. Such a committee was already in existence in 1799, when the Combination Act was first passed, and no doubt in Manchester the trade unionists consulted formally or informally whenever occasion arose.

On 20 March the warehouse of William Ratcliffe, one of the first manufacturers to use the power-loom, was attacked at Stockport. In April events followed fast upon each other. On 8 April there was a somewhat exuberant riot at the Manchester Exchange. The occasion was, at least indirectly, political. For years it had been supposed that the Prince Regent was a supporter of the Whigs and even of political reform; and he had, for his own factional purposes, encouraged the Foxite opposition in the early years of the war. The expectation had grown that when the restrictions upon his powers came to an end, early in 1812, a 'Peace and Reform' Ministry might be formed, in which Lords Grey and Grenville would take a leading part. However, the Prince Regent had done no more than offer 'some of those persons with whom the early habits of my public life were formed' places in a Coalition, upon terms which he knew beforehand were unacceptable. In the ensuing reshuffle, an even more unpopular administration took office under Perceval, with Castlereagh as Foreign Secretary and Sidmouth (for the first time) as Home Secretary. Popular hopes were dashed more widely than is supposed. There is even a suggestion that this disappointment was the direct occasion for the commencement of Yorkshire Luddism.[1] In Manchester the Church-and-King party seriously misjudged public feeling, and called a public meeting at the Exchange to send a congratulatory address to the Regent for keeping his father's Ministers in office. Reformers placarded Manchester with an appeal to the public to attend the meeting and defeat the address. The Tories backed down, and attempted to cancel the meeting. But great crowds thronged around the Exchange and many of them, mainly weavers, then went to St Anne's Square, where they held their own meeting. Meanwhile, some

1. See below, p. 644.

youngsters broke into the news-room; windows were broken and furniture overturned, and finally a general riot ensued. It was not an important event, but 'indicated a turn in the current of popular opinion. Previously to that time "Church-and-King" was the favourite cry, and hunting "Jacobins" safe sport ...' One old reformer later recalled: 'But we had no Church-and-King mobs after that!'[1]

In the next fortnight there were much more serious riots, in Manchester, Oldham, Ashton, Rochdale, Stockport and Macclesfield. In the main these were food riots, of exceptional violence and extent, with the aim of forcing down the prices of potatoes and bread. At the same time, there were confused reports as to the active instigation and organization of the rioters by 'Luddites' or 'Jacobin' agitators. At Stockport two men in women's clothes, calling themselves 'General Ludd's wives', headed the insurgents. Threatening letters were received, not only by the owners of steam looms, but also by the owners of improved cloth-dressing machinery:

In justice to humanity We think it our Bounin Duty to give you this Notice that is if you do Not Cause those Dressing Machines to be Remov'd Within the Bounds of Seven Days ... your factory and all that it Contains Will and Shall Surely Be Set on fire ... it is Not our Desire to Do you the Least Injury But We are fully Determin'd to Destroy Both Dressing Machines and Steam Looms Let *Who Will* be the Owners ...[2]

(This letter, however, was signed not by Ludd but by 'General Justice'.) On 20 April a major affray took place at Middleton, where Daniel Burton's power-loom mill was attacked by several thousands. The mill was assailed with volley upon volley of stones, and its defenders replied with musket-fire, killing three and wounding some more. On the next morning the threatening crowds assembled in ever greater strength, and were joined at mid-day by –

a body of men, consisting of from one to two hundred, some of them armed with muskets with fixed bayonets, and others with colliers' picks, [who] marched into the village in procession, and joined the

1. Prentice, op. cit., pp. 48–52; Darvall, op. cit., pp. 93–5.
2. Anonymous letter, 19 April 1812, in H.O. 40.1.

rioters. At the head of this armed banditti a *Man of Straw* was carried, representing the *renowned* General Ludd whose standard-bearer waved a sort of red flag . . .[1]

The mill proving impregnable, the rioters burned the mill-owner's house. They were then met by the military, at whose hands at least seven were killed and many more wounded.

This was the climax of Lancashire Luddism, so far as direct attacks on machinery are concerned. It was evidently very much more than a movement of weavers – among the dead were a baker, two weavers, a glazier, and a joiner, while colliers from Holmfield were prominent in the second day's attack. It was also, in terms of casualties, the most serious Luddite affray in the entire country. On 24 April, however, there was a somewhat mysterious sequel – the burning of Wray and Duncroff's mill at Westhoughton. The mystery in this case is not that the mill was attacked – it was an obvious target for destruction. Not only was it the subject of repeated threats, but more than one attempt had been made to attack it, at the instigation of a 'secret committee' in Bolton which was largely directed by *agents provocateurs* employed directly by Colonel Fletcher. The puzzling feature is that, after these provocations had come to very little, a successful attack was then made, independently (as it seems) of the agency of spies.[2]

This episode of Luddism is so full of duplicity that the mind can scarcely follow its tortuous involutions. But the assumption (derived from the Bolton events) that Lancashire Luddism was little more than a provocation superimposed by Colonel Fletcher and Joseph Nadin upon the hunger of the weavers, cannot be sustained. It is true that the overt acts of the Lancashire men show little of that organization and discipline which marked events in Nottingham and the West Riding. On the other hand, the destruction of power-looms raised problems of a different order from that of stocking- or shearing-frames. The power-loom was a costly machine, only recently introduced, employed only in a very few steam-powered mills, and not to

1. *Leeds Mercury*, report from Middleton, 25 April 1812.
2. The tortuous story of 'Old S.' and 'Young S.' is told in the Hammonds, op. cit., ch. 10; Darvall, op. cit., chs. 5, 14; Prentice, op. cit., pp. 52–8; and Anon. *The Blackfaces of 1812* (Bolton, 1839).

be found scattered in small workshops over the countryside. Thus midnight guerrilla tactics were of little avail in Lancashire: each attack must be on the scale of the Rawfolds or Burton's affair, with the probability of a direct encounter with the Army. This scarcely made sense, even in limited tactical terms. At the same time, the people of Lancashire had lived, for several decades, alongside the steam mill in spinning. There must have been very many (and probably a majority) of weavers who doubted the efficacy of resistance to the new machines as such; and this is confirmed by reports as to serious divergences within the weavers' own 'secret committees'. Hence Lancashire Luddism passed through its machine-breaking phase in a matter of three or four weeks. But it is exactly at the moment when attacks on mills came to an end that reports of oath-taking, arming, and drilling became most widespread. Attacks upon power-looms gave way, in May and June, to more serious insurrectionary preparations. Despite savage sentences upon the rioters of April at the Lancashire and Cheshire Assizes at the end of May 1812,[1] disturbances continued until the autumn. In mid-June one of the best-informed Lancashire informants wrote that 'bodies of 100 and upwards of the Luddites have entered houses night after night and made seizures of arms'. The raids were accompanied by signals by gun, rocket, and 'blue-lights' which revealed (in the view of one officer) 'a most extraordinary degree of concert and organization'. For weeks whole districts on the Lancashire-Yorkshire border were virtually under martial law. And one military command, in particular, established a reign of terror, with arbitrary arrests, searches, brutal questionings, and threats, for which we must turn to Irish history in search of a comparison.[2]

It was in the early summer that Luddism reached its crisis-point. In the week of the Middleton and Westhoughton affairs,

1. At Lancaster, of 58 prisoners, 28 were convicted – 8 sentenced to death, and 13 to transportation. At Chester, of 47 prisoners, 29 were convicted – 15 sentenced to death (although only two were hanged), 8 to transportation.

2. Lloyd to H.O., 17 June 1812, H.O. 40.1; F. Raynes, *An Appeal to the Public* (1817), pp. 20–21 *et passim*.

there were also alarming signals from many parts of the country. Serious food riots took place in Bristol, Carlisle, Leeds, Sheffield, Barnsley; in Cornwall the miners struck and marched to the market towns demanding reductions in the price of food; there were disturbances at Plymouth and Falmouth. In several of these places, the food riots displayed more than usual premeditation as a political or civic action to enforce a popular maximum, and at Sheffield, where a militia arms magazine was broken into, the two principal ring-leaders were alleged to be – not starving unemployed, who formed the bulk of the demonstrators – but 'the two most ingenious mechanics in the town', in receipt of wages of four and a half guineas per week.[1] On 27 April, in the West Riding, William Horsfall was assassinated. On 11 May the Prime Minister, Perceval, was assassinated in the House of Commons. For a day the country was in turmoil. Popular elation was undisguised. At Bolton (Colonel Fletcher complained) 'the *Mob* expressed *Joy*' at the news. In the Potteries a witness heard the news when –

A man came running down the street, leaping into the air, waving his hat round his head, and shouting with frantic joy, 'Perceval is shot, hurrah! Perceval is shot, hurrah!'

The crowd in Nottingham celebrated, and 'paraded the town with drums beating and flags flying in triumph'. In London itself crowds gathered outside the House of Commons as the news seeped out, and as the assassin, John Bellingham, was taken away there were repeated shouts of applause from the ignorant or depraved part of the crowd'. The news that Bellingham was probably deranged, and had acted from motives of private grievance, was received almost with disappointment; it had been hoped that another, and more successful, Despard had arisen. When Bellingham went to the scaffold, people cried out 'God bless him', and Coleridge heard them add: 'This is but the beginning.' It was thought inopportune to give Perceval a public funeral.[2]

1. *Leeds Mercury*, 2 May 1812; T.S. 11. 5480.

2. H.O. 40.1; Prentice, op. cit., p. 46; *Leeds Mercury*, 16 May 1812; Peel, *Risings of the Luddites*, pp. 156–7; A. Briggs, *Age of Improvement*, p. 157.

Sheer insurrectionary fury has rarely been more widespread in English history. For some weeks notices had been chalked on West Riding doors and walls, offering 100 guineas for the Prince Regent's head.[1] In mid-May the Regent and his private secretary received scores of threatening letters, one of which signed 'Vox Populi', commenced: 'Provisions Cheaper – Bread or Blood – Tell your Master he is a Damn'd Unfeeling Scoundrel ...'[2] But so far as Yorkshiremen were concerned, the Prince Regent was far away, whereas the mill-owners and magistrates were close at hand. After the defeat at Rawfolds, West Riding Luddism entered a more desperate phase. It had always been more military in its discipline than Nottinghamshire Luddism, and very much more surrounded with secrecy and oaths, since it had come into being at the very moment that frame-breaking had been made a capital offence. The decision to assassinate Horsfall was probably taken by George Mellor himself, the commander of the local district, rather than by any Yorkshire delegate meeting. According to tradition, young Booth, the clergyman's son, was his particular friend and protégé, and he was distracted by his death. Benjamin Walker, the accomplice who turned King's evidence, declared that Mellor and his fellow croppers in John Wood's shop at Longroyd Bridge 'conversed about ... the men killed at Cartwright's':

They said it was a hard matter. Mellor said the method of breaking up the shears must be given up, and instead of it the masters must be shot. That was the most I heard said; they said they had lost two men, and must kill the masters.

To rejoice at the death of a distant Prime Minister was one thing. The assassination, in cold blood from behind a wall, of a man who rode regularly past, and who – for all his unpopularity – 'belonged' in the community was another. It is much too strong a term to suggest that there was a violent revulsion of feeling. Hundreds must have suspected who the assassins were, and yet for months no disclosures were made. It is more true that there was a revulsion of feeling among those who had been passive sympathizers or on-lookers before, while at

1. Radcliffe MSS., 17 March 1812, 126/26.
2. London Gazette, 19 May 1812; H.O. 42.123.

the same time there was a hardening of feeling at both extremes. 'There is not an inhabitant in this Neighbourhood that I know of,' the Rev. Hammond Roberson wrote to Cartwright three days after Horsfall's death,

that is at all alive to the situation of the country, or rather perhaps *that is able* and that *dares* to take any decisive part in directing the operations of the Military besides myself. Were it possible for me to devote my *whole* time to the military I would do my best.[1]

On their side, the Luddites began to lose members, and resorted to threats to restore their flagging discipline. The attacks on shearing-frames ended (although there were now few firms still defiant), and gave way to widespread raids for arms and money. These raids, like those in Lancashire, continued through May, June, July, August and September, although one or two groups of house-breakers masquerading as Luddites confused the picture. Accounts of these raids are comparable with a partisan operation in enemy-occupied territory. A magistrate described, in July 1812, one raid in the village of Clifton (Yorks), and commented upon:

... the precision, intrepidity, & dispatch with which an armed banditti regularly searched a populous village – a mile in length, for arms, and took away six or seven without attempting to touch any other property, firing repeatedly into houses & at individuals who attempted the least resistance, with a promptitude & apparent discipline that no regular troops could exceed . . .[2]

Yorkshire Luddism petered out amidst arrests, betrayals, threats, and disillusion. Once again, the story was handed down in folklore, as well as disclosed in the trials at York in January 1813. Spies, drafted in from other districts, made several discoveries. A group of Painites, including a hatter, John Baines, were arrested at Halifax on the charge of administering Luddite oaths. Then Benjamin Walker, a workmate and accomplice of Mellor's, betrayed the secrets of Horsfall's assassination. Other Luddites turned informer to save their own lives. Some of the men who took part in the Rawfolds affair were tracked down; there were other arrests at Barnsley and Holmfirth. In October Joseph Radcliffe, the

1. See A. Briggs, *Private and Social Themes in Shirley*, p. 12.
2. Fitzwilliam Papers, F.46 (g).

magistrate most active in tracking the Luddites down, received a final threat: 'I most assuredly will make myself another Bellingham and I have the pellit made that shall be sent in your Hart's Blood if I should do it in the house of God.'[1] By November the net was closed. At the York Special Commission in January 1813, Mellor and two colleagues were found guilty of the assassination of Horsfall, and they were at once executed, while the other trials were still in progress. Fifteen others were capitally convicted, one only being commuted to transportation for life, for their part in the Rawfolds attack or in arms raids. Six others, including the old Halifax democrat, Baines, were sentenced to transportation for seven years for administering illegal oaths. Had their offence been committed at the end of July 1812, instead of at the beginning, it would have carried the death-penalty.

Meanwhile, Nottingham and the hosiery districts had been quiet throughout the spring and summer of 1812, in which the Framework-Knitters' Committee had been attempting to secure the passage of their Bill in Parliament. Not one of the leaders of the movement of 1811–12 was ever, with any certainty, convicted. Despite the apparent peace of 1812–13, pressure upon the masters to comply with the stockingers' terms was maintained by anonymous letters and threats of renewed action:

George Rowbottom this is to inform you [ran one such letter, of April 1812] that their is not a man in the town of Arnold Bullwell Hucknall nor Basford that takes work out unless it is full price full fashion and proper price and size and this is to give you Notice that if you bring or give any more work out without its is full fashion full price and proper size you shall work this frame[2] with a rope round your neck ...

There was then a minor recrudescence of Luddism in November and December 1812, but for two years the hosiery

1. Radcliffe MSS., 126–91. Radcliffe was pursued with threats for several more years. 'Ludding is going to start here again,' he was warned, in March 1815, by an anonymous correspondent. The croppers 'swear they will shoot thee first, old Bellsybub they call thee': 126/136.

2. Here there is a rough drawing of a gallows, with the grim note; 'this frame works all full price and fashion'. H.O. 42.122.

workers appear to have placed their faith in the action of their union. Then a few scattered attacks resumed (in 1814), and it seems that some of the hosiery houses actually attempted to provoke frame-breaking in order to gain a pretext for acting against the union.[1] When the union had been broken up, and two of its officers arrested, attacks became more widespread. In September 1814 a Basford stockinger, James Towle, was arrested for his part in one of the attacks, but at the Spring Assizes (1815) he was acquitted. From the summer of 1816 until the first months of 1817 there was a last phase of Midlands Luddism, which reached an intensity not known since 1811. The most sensational attack was at the considerable factory of Heathcote and Boden, Loughborough, whose guards were overpowered by masked men with blunderbusses, and whose costly lace machines were destroyed to shouts of: 'Ludds, do your duty well. It's a Waterloo job, by God.' More than £6,000 worth of damage was done in this one attack. James Towle was once again arrested; this time he was convicted, and, in mid-November, executed. For a month or two attacks continued. According to one account, Towle's brother led a gang which was eager to show 'Jem that they could do something without him'. According to other accounts, this final phase of Luddism was the work of one or two almost 'professional' gangs, who were called in and paid by lodges of the now-underground union. In a confession on the morning of his execution, Jem Towle declared that he had never taken any oath of secrecy, nor heard of any being made use of:

They have no particular fund of money, but when any job is intended, or money wanted for any purpose, it is collected among the stockingers or lace-hands who happen to be in work at the time. ... They have no depot of arms. Many of the gang have a pistol or two concealed in their houses. ... When any job is intended, three or four of the principal people go about to collect hands for it among those whom they know to be well inclined to Ludding.

But Towle's confession may have been designed to throw his questioners off the scent. Early in 1817 other members of his gang were detected, and in April 1817 six were executed at

1. See C. Gray, *Nottingham Through 500 Years* (Nottingham, 1960), p. 165.

Leicester and two more sentenced to transportation. One of the condemned men, Thomas Savage, in depositions in the fortnight before execution, declared that in these last phases 'Ludding and Politicks were closely connected.' He alleged that there was a colony of refugee Luddites in Calais.[1] He sought to implicate Gravener Henson (whom he accused of being 'equal to the perpetration of anything that ever Robespierre committed'), as the 'Headman of the whole'. But his colourful and suspect account did not in fact connect Henson himself at any point with machine-breaking; the accusations were that Henson was the initiator of ultra-Radical agitation among the stockingers which culminated in the Hampden Club movement of the winter of 1816–17, and that he had looked forward to a republican revolution and 'spoke of attacking the barracks at Nottingham'. Whether true or false, Henson was not at liberty to reveal his sympathies when the Pentridge 'rising' of June took place. For, in the same week that Savage had made his accusations, Sidmouth had been informed by a Nottingham correspondent that Henson ('a sensible fellow and very fond of talking') had taken the London mail with the intention of presenting a petition to save the lives of the condemned men. In London he was arrested, and, under the suspension of Habeas Corpus, held for some months. But long before this time the Luddite movement, as we have defined it here, had come to an end.[2]

VI. BY ORDER OF THE TRADE

'Such marchings and counter-marchings!', Byron exclaimed in the House of Lords:

From Nottingham to Bullwell, from Bullwell to Banford, from Banford to Mansfield! and when at length the detachments arrived at their destination, in all 'the pride, pomp, and circumstance of

1. This is not impossible. There was a colony of English framework-knitters at Calais. See Henson's evidence in *Fourth Report ... Artizans and Machinery* (1824), p. 274; and H.O. 79.3 f. 31.

2. Confessions of W. Burton in H.O. 40.4; depositions of Thomas Savage, H.O. 42.163; H. W. C. Davis, *Age of Grey and Peel*, p. 172; Darvall, op. cit., pp. 144–9, 155–9; Hammonds, op. cit., pp. 238–42.

glorious war', they came just in time to witness the mischief which had been done ... and return to their quarters amidst the derision of old women, and the hootings of children.

No doubt some of the local leaders of Luddism were among those who were brought to the scaffold; certainly, both evidence and folk-tradition show that George Mellor and Jem Towle were Luddite 'captains'. But to this day Luddism refuses to give up all its secrets. Who were the 'real' instigators? *Were* there any, or was the movement sparked off spontaneously in one district after another by example? What kind of committees existed in the different districts? Was there any regular communication between them? How far were secret oaths actually administered? What ulterior political or revolutionary aims were held among the Luddites?

To all these questions, only the most tentative answer can be given. It should be said, however, that the answers which are generally accepted are not consonant with some of the evidence. The two most important studies of Luddism are those of the Hammonds and of Darvall. *The Skilled Labourer* is a fine book; but the chapters on Luddism read at times like a brief prepared on behalf of the Whig opposition, and intended to discredit the exaggerated claims made by the authorities as to the conspiratorial and revolutionary aspects of the movement. The rôle of spies and of *agents provocateurs* is emphasized to the point where it is suggested that there was *no* authentic insurrectionary underground and no evidence of delegates passing between the counties. Of oath-taking, the Hammonds declare that 'on the most liberal interpretation, there is no evidence to show that the oath was widespread, *or that it was ever administered* except in districts where spies were busy at work'.[1] Authentic Luddism (it is implied) was without ulterior aims, and was either a matter of spontaneous riot (Lancashire) or an action with strictly limited industrial objectives (Nottingham and Yorkshire).

F. O. Darvall, in his *Popular Disturbances and Public Order in Regency England*, follows most of the Hammonds' judgements. 'There is no evidence whatever,' he declares flatly,

----

1. Loc. cit., p. 339. My italics.

of any political motives on the part of the Luddites. There is not one single instance in which it can be proved that a Luddite attack was directed towards anything deeper than disputes between masters and men, between workmen and their employers. There was not a single Luddite ... against whom a charge of treason was advanced, or could lie. There is no sign, despite the great efforts of the spies to prove such motives, that the Luddites, or indeed any but a few unimportant, unrepresentative, irresponsible agitators, had any large or political designs.

'Despite the most careful search no large dumps of arms, such as the spies talked about, were found. No connexion could be traced between the disaffected in one district and those in others ...' The secret committees in the Lancashire towns were a 'fungoid growth', controlled by spies or by men who made 'petty sedition their source of income'. And of the larger Luddite attacks, 'it does not appear than there was any more organization in these large mobs than there is in the crowd which carries through a spontaneous college "rag"'. There is 'nothing whatever other than the uncorroborated testimony of spies to prove the Luddites ever took any secret or illegal oath at all'.[1]

Caught up in the minutiae of day-to-day reports – phlegmatic officers here, panic-stricken magistrates there, incredibly tortuous stories of espionage in another place – it is possible to doubt the reality of Luddism altogether. But if we stand back from the minutiae for a moment, we shall see that the conclusions of these authorities are as unlikely as the most sensational conspiracy-theory of Luddism. Anyone who has conducted a raffle or organized a darts tournament knows that scores of men cannot be assembled at night, from several districts, at a given point, disguised and armed with muskets, hammers, and hatchets; formed into line; mustered by number; marched several miles to a successful attack, to the accompaniment of signal lights and rockets – and all with the organization of a spontaneous college 'rag'. Anyone who knows the geography of the Midlands and north will find it difficult to believe that the Luddites of three adjoining counties had *no* contact with each other. It requires an exercise of mental

1. Loc. cit., pp. 174-96.

agility to segregate Luddism in our minds, as a purely 'industrial' movement, totally unconnected with 'politics', at a time when disaffected Irish were coming in hundreds into Lancashire, and when people celebrated the assassination of the Prime Minister with triumph in the streets. In short, such views of Luddism can be sustained only by a special pleading which exaggerates the stupidity, rancour, and provocative rôle of the authorities to the point of absurdity; or by an academic failure of imagination, which compartmentalizes and disregards the whole weight of popular tradition.

The fact is, there are *no* sources of evidence as to Luddism's organization which are not in some degree 'tainted' As the Hammonds and Darvall point out, we know only of delegates or of oaths from rumour; or from the stories of 'spies'; or from the magistracy and military; or from confessions of men, condemned to death or in fear of condemnation, and anxious to save their lives. The same is true of Luddism's ulterior aims. But what other kind of evidence could there be? *Every* prisoner automatically becomes subject to duress, *every* informer at once becomes a 'spy'.

We may take oaths as an example. If there is little evidence of oaths being taken by Midland Luddites, there may be a reason for this. The main phase of Midland frame-breaking ended in February 1812. It was only in that month that framebreaking became a capital felony. Yorkshire and Lancashire Luddism commenced in the knowledge that detection meant death : it is therefore likely that some oath of secrecy will have been taken (as both spies and popular tradition insisted). In July 1812 oath-taking, for felonious purposes, was also made a capital offence. Rumour has it that in Yorkshire oaths continued to be administered until the end of the year. But when Luddism recommenced in the Midlands in 1814 to 1816 it is again likely that the small groups engaged will not have wanted to add the extra capital risk involved in the additional offence.

Two of the batches of prisoners tried at the York Assizes in January 1813 were convicted for administering oaths. One case – that of Baines and the Halifax democrats – is highly suspicious. They were convicted on the evidence of two professional spies, of notoriously bad character, drafted in especially from Manchester for the purpose, and there is good reason to believe that the case was a 'frame-up'. Both the Hammonds and Darvall imply that the other case – that of a weaver at Barnsley – was equally suspect, and the work of a professional 'spy'.[1] But this is not quite the case. The informer, Thomas Broughton, was a Barnsley weaver and a freemason, who volunteered information for reasons which are unclear, and who swore a deposition before two Sheffield magistrates in August 1812. According to this, he had joined a 'secret committee' of five Barnsley weavers earlier in the year. They had 'twisted-in' 200 in Barnsley, mainly weavers, but including two publicans, a hatter and a gardener. (No Irishmen were admitted.) His duties were to attend meetings, collect money, and correspond with other committees. Barnsley (where no Luddism took place) was regarded as a new and weak centre, the main strength being in Sheffield and Leeds. Great boasts were made in Luddite circles, of 8,000 'twisted-in' in Sheffield, 7,000 in Leeds, 450 in Holmfirth. Delegates were sent to meetings in Manchester, Stockport and Ashton. In Halifax the Luddites met 'as dissenters under the cloak of Religion'. Many of the Luddites were also members of the militia. 'The Luddites have in view ultimately to overturn the System of Government, by Revolutionizing the Country.' Broughton himself had attended a delegate meeting at Ashton, where another delegate told him the first signal would be an attack on the Houses of Parliament. If the revolution succeeded, Major Cartwright and Burdett were expected to join it. He had received 10s. 10d., as expenses for acting as delegate.[2]

Like many other such depositions, it is next to impossible to sort out truth and falsehood from this. But two points can be made. The first is that Broughton appears to have been a *bona fide* informer; that is, a man who had been an authentic Luddite and had turned traitor. The second is that in the case brought forward at York on Broughton's evidence – against John Eadon, one of the Barnsley Committee – not one word of this deposition was cited. The prosecution sought only to bring evidence to prove the administering of an illegal oath:

1. See Hammonds, op. cit., pp. 314, 325.
2. Deposition in Fitzwilliam Papers, F.46 (g).

I of my own free will and A Coard declare and solemnly sware that I will never reveal to aney. ... Person or Persons aney thing that may lead to discovery of the same Either in or by word sign or action as may lead to aney Discovery under the Penalty of being sent out of this World by the first Brother that May Meet me further more I do sware that I will Punish by death aney trater or trators should there aney arise up amongst us I will persue with unseaceing vengeance, should he fly to the verge of Statude. I will be gust true sober and faithful in all my dealings with all my Brothers So help GOD to keep this my Oath Invoilated Amen.[1]

On the face of it, the oath has an authentic ring.[2] But the point here is to examine a little further the motives of authority. Britain's rulers were callous and indifferent to the working people; but Britain was not a 'police-state'. There were magistrates and officers – the Rev. Hammond Roberson or Colonel Fletcher of Bolton – whose hatred of Luddism was obsessional, and who, like Nadin, the notorious Deputy Constable of Manchester, would stop short at no violence or trick to secure a conviction. And yet there was still another kind of public opinion to contend with. Earl Fitzwilliam, the Whig Lord-Lieutenant of the West Riding, was a man of temperate disposition who was later to lose his Lieutenancy as a result of his public protest about Peterloo and who is unlikely to have licensed actual provocations. The judge, in several Luddite cases in the Midlands, Mr Justice Bayley, was strongly assailed for his leniency. In a more important case in Manchester, in the summer of 1812, the jury refused to convict thirty-eight Radical reformers whom Nadin had tried to 'frame' for Luddite oath-administration. Law officers were well aware that conviction was not automatic.[3]

In these years, moreover, the Government was hated by the working people and actively disliked by many of the middle class. Even if, on the basis of such depositions as that of Broughton, the law officers had advised that a prosecution for

1. *Rex* v. *Eadon*, Howell's *State Trials*, XXXI, 1070.

2. Oaths fabricated by *agents provocateurs* were usually far more grisly – one including a pledge to cut off the head and hands of any traitor and of all his family.

3. This was the reason why the major Luddite trials were by Special Commission.

treason might be instituted, it was not in the interests of the authorities to proceed in this manner. Suspicion that they were acting mainly out of political motives would have inflamed public opinion. It was their business to limit prosecution to *overt criminal acts*: frame-breaking and night attacks, the robbery of arms, oath-taking. Such depositions as those of Broughton were, anyway, poor material for the law courts, especially when the Defence might engage the services of counsel such as Brougham. They rested upon unconfirmed reports of revolutionary rhetoric; meetings with delegates from other districts who generally were unnamed or acted under a pseudonym; obvious exaggerations and highly improbable suggestions – such as the claims that Cartwright, Whitbread, or Burdett would lead the revolution.

In fact, a most curious tussle took place between the local authorities and the Home Office, notably in Yorkshire in the summer and autumn of 1812. 'Mr Lloyd, a very active attorney at Stockport, employed by Government to get information by sending spies around the country' (as one Yorkshire J.P. noted in a letter to Fitzwilliam),[1] was acting under the direct protection of the Home Secretary, seeking to piece together watertight cases, by methods which some country J.P.s might have deplored, and by actually kidnapping and carrying across the Pennines into secret protective custody his key witnesses.[2]

One may suggest a certain divergence in approach. On the one hand, the Home Office (now under Sidmouth) was already following policies which led on to the post-war provocations of Oliver, Edwards and Castle. Sidmouth, Lloyd, Nadin, wanted many arrests, sensational trials and executions, to strike terror into the hearts of Luddites and reformers, and they had very little scruple as to whether their victims were 'genuine' Luddites or not, nor as to the means employed in manufacturing evidence. On the other hand, men like Fitzwilliam and Radcliffe were no less eager to destroy Luddism, but they were more scrupulous as to means and determined to apprehend the real offenders – for example, the assassins of Horsfall and the

1. Fitzwilliam Papers, 9 July 1812. F.46 (g).
2. For this curious tangle, see Hammonds, op. cit., pp. 315 ff. and Darvall, op. cit., pp. 125–33.

men who attacked Cartwright's mill. In the event, the main cases brought to trial (with the exception of the Manchester thirty-eight) were ones which offered secure 'examples of detection, conviction and punishment' for *particular* offences, and in which larger charges of political sedition were kept well in the background. Even in the case of the Halifax democrats, while it is certain that political motives lay behind it,[1] the prosecution was at pains to accuse the prisoners on account of their opinions only indirectly, and to rest its case on the proof of the overt act of the administering of an oath to a certain person on a certain occasion. Thus, if it is asked why no charge of treason was advanced, the answer is that such a charge would have been unpopular, doubtful in law, and might (as in the Manchester case) have resulted in an acquittal.

Nor did the authorities *wish* to institute wholesale trials for oath-taking. They desired simply to bring it to an end.[2] And to do this, they wished to make an example, through trial and transportation, of the most favourable cases. For different reasons, examples were made of the Halifax and Barnsley men. To suppose that authority was motivated by a lust to pursue every possible case to the end is to mistake the nature of power. At York, the 'injured laws' and the values of order were appeased once it was certain that Horsfall's murderers were condemned, that several men were to be transported for

---

1. The brief, *Rex* v. *Baines*, in the Treasury Solicitor's papers, commences: 'the elder Baines is a Hatter, a man notoriously disaffected to the Government': T.S. 11.2673.

2. The evidence of F. Raynes, *An Appeal to the Public* (1817) on all this is overwhelming. Captain Raynes commanded a unit with special responsibility to infiltrate and detect the Luddite instigators, in Lancashire (June–September 1812) and the West Riding (September–December 1812). From motives of private grievance he later published an account of his service, together with his correspondence with superior officers. In several Lancashire districts such as Newton, the oath was 'almost universal amongst the manufacturing and lower classes'. On more than one occasion his agents succeeded in penetrating the conspiracy, but the Luddites (realizing that they were detected) immediately hastened to the nearest magistrate and 'untwisted' themselves by taking the oath of allegiance – to Captain Raynes' intense irritation. Scepticism as to the prevalence of oath-taking cannot survive a careful reading of this pamphlet (Copy in Manchester City Reference Library.)

oath-taking, and that fourteen others should go to the scaffold for robbery of arms and night attacks. To go further would have been to torment public opinion beyond endurance, until every J.P. and mill-owner of the north spent his life amidst execrations. At this point, the book was closed and a proclamation of amnesty issued. Surely there had been revenge enough?

Thus we cannot argue as to Luddism's organization from the cases brought to trial nor from the evidence adduced by the prosecution. Indeed, the authorities generally acted upon evidence or strong suspicions which never appeared at the trials.[1] They were, in fact, in possession of a great deal of evidence as to secret meetings, drilling, oaths and the passage of delegates, some of its shadowy, some of it disreputable, most of it of little value in a court of law. This included scores of anonymous letters, as well as letters and depositions from informers, some of them highly circumstantial, such as one describing the Luddite system of pass-words:

You must raise your right Hand over your right Eye – if there be another Luddite in Company he will raise his left Hand over his left Eye – then you must raise the forefinger of your right Hand to the right Side of your Mouth – the other will raise the little finger of his left Hand to the left Side of his Mouth & will say, What are you? The answer, Determined. He will say, What for? Your answer, Free Liberty.[2]

It is right to say that such statements are worthless as proof in a court of law. But, if we follow the Hammonds and Darvall, in discounting *all* this evidence,[3] we end in a ridiculous posi-

1. This point has been laboured because it also helps to explain some of the confusion surrounding the cases of Despard and of Brandreth. Surviving briefs in the Treasury Solicitor's papers reveal the great care with which the law officers of the Crown sifted their evidence for the overt acts most easily brought to proof. Even in the case of O'Coigly (above, p. 187) the Crown brief is annotated: 'Should the invasion of Ireland be mentioned?' (T.S. 11.333). For the case of Thomas Bacon, see below, p. 729.

2. Fitzwilliam Papers, F.46 (g).

3. There is a considerable amount of this kind of testimony, as to drilling, delegates, revolutionary ambitions, in the Home Office papers. Darvall makes his argument easier by quoting none of it, and dismissing every example, in contemptuous footnotes, as the work of imaginative or interested informers.

tion. We must suppose that the authorities through their agents
actually created conspiratorial organizations and then instituted new capital offences (such as that for oath-taking) which
existed only in the imagination or as a result of the provocations of their own spies. Moreover, this whole line of argument
betrays a failure to imagine Luddism in the context of the local
community. In Nottingham and the West Riding in particular,
the strength of the Luddites was in small industrial villages
where every man was known to his neighbours and bound in
the same close kinship-network. The sanction of an oath would
have been terrible enough to a superstitious-minded people;
but the sanction of the community was even stronger.
Luddite leaders were popular in their own villages, like George
Howarth a weaver who was probably a member of a Yorksire
secret committee – of 'fresh complexion, and stout made; a
great singer in company; conversation vulgar, like a country
man . . .'[1] The authorities had extreme difficulty in persuading
any witness to come forward and name a neighbour. In part,
this was the result of the fear of Luddite reprisals. But, even
more, to act the part of informer was a breach of the moral
economy, entailing a sentence of outlawry from the community. Even the local magistrates could not view Benjamin
Walker, the accomplice who turned King's evidence against
Mellor, in any other light than as a Judas. On the eve of his
execution, Mellor declared: 'That he would rather be in the
situation he was then placed, dreadful as it was, than have to
answer for the crime of their accuser, and that he would not
change situations with him, even for his liberty and two
thousand pounds.' The situation of those Luddites who saved
their lives by giving evidence to the authorities was almost
more pitiful than that of the condemned men. Walker, who was
visited by a Quaker after the executions at York, was found
with a 'countenance . . . pale and ghastly, and his joints, as it
were, so unloosened as if they were scarcely able to support his
body'. In fact he never received the £2,000 blood-money which
was his due; he continued with a miserable vagabond existence, and in the end was reduced to beggary. Two Nottingham
Luddites who turned informer went in fear of their lives, and

1. F. Raynes, op. cit., pp. 114–15.

begged from the Crown their passages to Canada. Others suspected of informing were simply ostracized; one Yorkshireman refused to continue to live with his wife, who had by stupid indiscretions given evidence which led to the execution of one of the Rawfolds assault-party. On a similar occasion, several years later, two Yorkshire informers were ostracized by the community until the end of their lives; if they entered a room or public house, the assembled company would immediately cease talking, or would rise to leave.[1]

We have to imagine the solidarity of the community, the extreme isolation of the authorities. It is this which elevated Cartwright and Roberson to the stature of heroes, in the eyes of Charlotte Brontë, who had herself experienced the same isolation in Haworth parsonage during the Chartist agitations. When Rawfolds was attacked, despite the gunfire no one in the local village stirred to its relief. Only after the Luddites had retired did the three or four local men appear who were willing to declare themselves on the side of the besieged: the Rev. Hammond Roberson, Mr Cockhill (a large master-dyer), Mr Dixon (the manager of a chemical works), a local *bon vivant* named Clough. They were quickly surrounded by a muttering crowd, whose sympathies were very clearly on the side of the wounded Luddites.[2] Moreover, both trials and funerals were made the occasion for demonstrations of public sympathy, which sometimes took the form of intimidation, sometimes of religious fervour. The trials of accused Luddites at Nottingham took place amidst threats, demonstrations, and on one occasion in a packed court-room which was supposed to contain armed men.[3] The foreman of a jury which convicted several men for

1. *An Historical Account of the Luddites* (Huddersfield, 1862), p. 79; Peel, *Risings of the Luddites* (1895 edn), p. 278; Peel, *Spen Valley: Past and Present*, pp. 261, 264; Hammonds, op. cit., pp. 241–2; Sykes and Walker, *Ben o' Bill's*, p. 335. In post-war years it became the practice of the authorities to promise working-class informers their passage to one of the colonies. See also Hammonds, *The Town Labourer*, pp. 259–61.

2. Peel, *Spen Valley*, pp. 255–6. Cf. *Leeds Mercury* (9 May 1812): '... We believe there is a very general disposition amongst the lower classes to view the actions of the persons engaged in this association with complacency, not to say with approbation. This is the strength and life's blood of the Association.'

3. T. Bailey, *Annals of Nottinghamshire* (1855), IV, p. 280.

complicity in Luddite attacks, in Nottingham in March 1812, was pursued to Worksop:

Sir,

by genaral Ludds Express *Express* Commands I am come to Worksop to enquire of your Character towards our cause and I am sorry to say I find it correspond with your conduct you latly shewed towards us. Remember, the time is fast approaching When men of your stamp Will be brought to Repentance, you may be called upon soon. Remember – your a marked man,

Yours for General Ludd,

a true Man.[1]

Despite the fact that the Yorkshire trials took place at York, more than thirty miles from the trouble-centres, the authorities drafted in additional military forces and feared an attempted rescue. Even their opponents admired the fortitude of the condemned men. Mellor and his two companions refused to make any confession. So also did the fourteen who died a few days later. 'If any of these unfortunate men possessed any secret,' wrote the *Leeds Mercury*, 'they suffered it to die with them. Their discoveries were meager in the extreme.'[2] (According to tradition, the presiding judge had allowed himself a little levity on this occasion. Asked whether the fourteen condemned should hang on a single beam, he replied, after a little thought, 'Well, no sir. I consider they would hang more comfortably on two.') The seven who were first brought to execution, in the presence of great crowds, came to the scaffold singing the Methodist hymn:

> Behold the Saviour of Mankind,
> Nail'd to the shameful tree;
> How vast the love that him inclin'd,
> To bleed and die for me.

1. H.O. 42.122.
2. An officer who witnessed the execution wrote to Radcliffe: 'I consider there were eight real *Luds* ... and nine Depredators who took advantage of the Times' [i.e. house-breakers]. He was informed by the Chaplain that the 'real Luds' refused to make any confession: 'I really believe they did not consider it as *any great* if *any* offence.' He adds: 'I believe they were all Methodists.' Colonel Norton to Radcliffe, January 1813, Radcliffe MSS, 126/114.

Hark: how he groans! while nature shakes,
    And earth's strong pillars bend;
The temple's veil in sunder breaks,
    The solid marbles rend.

'Tis done! the precious ransom's paid,
    'Receive my soul', he cries;
See where he bows his sacred head,
    He bows his head and dies.[1]

In all three counties we have an impression of active moral sanction given by the community to all Luddite activities short of actual assassination. The authorities themselves lamented that:

Encouragement was given by the doubts cast on the moral turpitude of these crimes; and evil was raised to its height by the religious fanaticism which unhappily exists in an excessive degree in those populous districts.[2]

Just as the popular myth portrayed all informers as Judases, so Charlotte Brontë followed the middle-class myth when she caricatured in Moses Barraclough, a 'Ranting' preacher and 'a joined Methody', a hypocritical Luddite instigator; and when she gave to the attempted assassin of Gérard Moore an Old Testament tongue: 'When the wicked perisheth, there is shouting; as the whirl-wind passeth, so is the wicked no more ...'[3] The evidence on this is as untidy as usual. Two or three of those executed at York were certainly Methodists. But while many had been nurtured in a Methodist culture (or in its Ranting and Southcottian fringes), even in the condemned cell their ministers – who were exceedingly anxious to exculpate Methodism from complicity – had no power over them. The fervour of the Old Testament had become assimilated to a class solidarity which not even Jabez Bunting could penetrate.

The Luddite funerals illustrate this well. The funeral of John Westley, the Luddite killed in an affray in November 1811,

1. *Proceedings under the Special Commission at York* (Leeds, 1813), pp. 67–9; Hammonds, op. cit., p. 332; H. Clarkson, *Memories of Merry Wakefield* (Wakefield, 1887), p. 40.

2. Authorized introduction to York trials, in Howell, *State Trials* XXXI, 964.

3. *Shirley*, chs. 8, 30.

was made the occasion for a demonstration of popular sympathy in Nottingham. 'The corpse was preceded by a number of the deceased's former club mates, bearing black wands, decked with knots of crape.'

The scene was truly awful. The High Sheriff, the Under-Sheriff, and about half a dozen Magistrates were on the spot, attended by a posse of Constables and about thirty mounted dragoons ... before the body was removed the Riot Act was read in several parts of the town.[1]

The two men who died from their wounds at Rawfolds were attended with the same sympathy. A massive public funeral was prevented at Huddersfield only because the authorities buried Booth quietly in advance of the expected time. Hartley was buried at Halifax, followed by hundreds of mourners, their arms bandaged with white crape. His friends claimed for him a Methodist burial, and when Bunting refused to read the service there were angry scenes. On the following Sunday great crowds assembled for a memorial service. Jonathan Saville, a crippled local preacher, recalled that it was 'the largest congregation that ever assembled in Halifax Chapel':

... the people came from far and wide to show their sorrow for the deceased. They filled the Chapel to overflowing; hundreds stood on the outside, unable to get in, and constables walked before the doors to keep the peace. The preacher who was planned for that afternoon had gone to Huddersfield, probably to get out of the way ...

Bunting again refused to preach, and ordered Saville to deputize. The cripple preached on the contrast in the death of a believer and an infidel:

At that time, perhaps more than ever, infidelity was busy amongst the lower classes ... I exclaimed, 'Infidel, die hard! never strike the black flag when Death confronts you!' It seemed to have great effect ...

The effect, however, was scarcely as Saville intended, and he was stoned on his way from the chapel. 'Vengeance for the Blood of the Innocent' was chalked on walls and doors. For

1. *Leeds Mercury*, 23 November 1811; Bailey, op. cit., IV, p. 247.

weeks after this occasion, Bunting (who also received threatening letters) was afforded an armed guard when he went to country appointments. Similar trouble developed at Holmfirth, and at Greetland (near Halifax) when the Methodist minister refused burial to men executed at York.[1] And the same public demonstrations attended the funeral of James Towle in Nottingham in November 1816, when a clerical magistrate, Dr Wylde, forbade the reading of the Burial Service. Despite this, 3,000 attended the ceremony, and, according to a spy's report:

A School master, I was told, gave out the Hymns that were sung from his House to and at the Grave by Six young women. . . . There was a Starr or Cross upon the Coffin lid, which excited much conjecture, what it could be for. Some said it was because he had died game, others because he had been hung, and some damned Dr Wylde for not allowing the Funeral Service to be read. Badder said . . . it did not signify to Jem, for he wanted no Parsons about him.[2]

No account of Luddism is satisfactory which is confined to a limited industrial interpretation, or which dismisses its insurrectionary undertones with talk of a few 'hotheads'. Even in Nottingham, where Luddism showed greatest discipline in pursuing industrial objectives, the connexion between framebreaking and political sedition was assumed on every side, since not only the framework-knitters but the 'lower orders' generally shared complicity with the Luddites in their contest with hosiers, military, and magistrates. In Lancashire – while the backbone of the organization was made up of weavers – colliers, cotton-spinners, and tradesmen of all kinds shared in the disturbances. In the West Riding, although the objectives of attack were gig-mills and shearing-frames, not only croppers but 'numbers of weavers, tailors, shoemakers, and representatives of almost every handicraft' were associated with the Luddites. John Booth, the parson's son killed in the Rawfolds attack, was apprenticed to a harness-maker.[3] The prisoners brought up for trial before the Special Commission at York

1. J. U. Walker, *History of Wesleyan Methodism in Halifax* (Halifax, 1836), p. 255; E. V. Chapman, *John Wesley & Co (Halifax)* (Halifax, 1952), p. 35; F. A. West, *Memoirs of Jonathan Saville* (1844), pp. 24-5.
2. Hammonds, op. cit., p. 239.   3. Peel, op. cit., pp. 6, 18.

included 28 croppers, 8 labourers, 4 weavers, 3 shoemakers, 3 coal-miners, 3 cotton-spinners, 2 tailors, 2 clothiers, and a butcher, cardmaker, carpenter, carpet-weaver, hatter, hawker, shop-keeper, stonemason, waterman and a woollen-spinner.[1]

We may now hazard an explanation for the course of Luddism. It commenced (1811) in Nottingham as a form of direct 'trade union' enforcement, endorsed by the working community. As such it at once incurred outlawry, and its very situation drove it in a more insurrectionary direction. By the winter of 1811–12 it is likely that 'delegates', whether official or unofficial, did travel to other parts of the north.[2] Yorkshire Luddism (February 1812) commenced in a more insurrectionary temper. On the one hand, the long-rankling grievances of the croppers were blow into flame by the Nottingham example. On the other hand, small groups of democrats or Painites saw in Luddism a more general revolutionary opportunity. The two impulses can be seen in passages from two Luddite letters, both sent in March 1812. The first, probably emanating from Huddersfield, voices the particular grievances of the croppers:

N.B. .... the General ... orders me to inform you how the Cloth Dressers in the Huddersfield District as spent Seven Thousand Pounds in petition Government to put the Laws in force to stop the Shearing Frames and Gig Mills to no purpose so they are trying this method now, and he is informed how you are affraid it will be carried on to another purpose but you need not be apprehensive of that, for as soon as ye Obnoxious machienery is Stop'd or Distroy'd the General and his Brave Army will be disbanded, and Return to their Employment, like other Liege Subjects.[3]

1. *Report of Proceedings under Commissions of Oyer & Terminer ... for the County of York* (Hansard, 1813), pp. xiv–xix. It should be said, however, that a few of these were pseudo-Luddites, accused of house-breaking, while the hatter, shoemakers and cardmaker were the Halifax democrats. Nearly all those indicted for their part in the Rawfolds affair were croppers. See also T.S. 11.2669.

2. See, for example, an intercepted letter from Yorkshire correspondents to a brother in Nottingham, relating to a Nottingham man who was staying with them: 'We ... received him as a friend from you which we believed He is, & we have enjoy'd ourselves over a pot or two of Beer, & he read Mr Luds Song'; 19 April 1812, Radcliffe MSS, 126/32.　　　3. Radcliffe MSS., 126–27.

The other letter, posted a week or so earlier, is the most unlikely of letters from a 'Liege Subject'. It suggests that disappointment in the failure of the Prince Regent to form a
peace and reform ministry (the occasion for the later riot at
the Manchester Exchange) was the trigger for Yorkshire
Luddism:

The immediate Cause of us beginning when we did was that
Rascally letter of the Prince Regents to Lords Grey & Grenville,
which left us no hopes of any Change for the better, & by his falling
in with that Damn'd set of Rogues, Percival & Co to whom we
attribute all the Miseries of our Country. But we hope for assistance
from the French Emperor in shaking off the Yoke of the Rottenest,
Wickedest and most Tyranious Government that ever existed, then
down come the Hanover Tyrants, and all our Tyrants from the
greatest to the smallest, and we will be governed by a just Republic,
and may the Almighty hasten those happy Times is the wish and
Prayer of Millions in this Land . . .[1]

If we accept both letters as authentic, then it would suggest
that Yorkshire Luddism commenced with divided counsels. If
so, the insurrectionary temper became dominant as one event
followed another. Some weight must be placed upon the verbal
tradition, collected by Frank Peel, according to which Baines,
the old Halifax hatter, was indeed at the centre of a group of
'Tom Painers' who formed 'a democratic or republican club'
meeting at the St Crispin's Inn, Halifax. Here an important
meeting of Luddite delegates took place in March, and Baines
welcomed their movement from the Chair:

For thirty years I have struggled to rouse the people against this
evil, and . . . have suffered much for my opinions in body and estate.
I am now nearing the end of my pilgrimage, but I will die as I
have lived; my last few days shall be devoted to the people's cause.
I hail your rising against your oppressors, and hope it may go on
until there is not a tyrant to conquer. I have waited long for the
dawn of the coming day, and it may be, old as I am, I shall yet see
the glorious triumph of democracy.

According to the same tradition, a Nottingham delegate named
Weightman also spoke: 'Our council is in daily communica-

1. W. B. Crump, op. cit., p. 230.

tion with the societies in all the centres of disaffection, and urge a general rising in May.'[1]

There are reasons to suppose that, not the words, but the general tendency of this account, is true. The authorities were clearly determined to secure a conviction against Baines, despite the very shaky evidence of their spies. One witness alleged that Baines had said that he 'was not in the habit of having anything to do with any people, but what were acquainted with the two words Aristocracy and Democracy'; while the Judge regarded it as an aggravation of his offence that he had boasted that 'his eyes had been opened for three and twenty years'.[2] Whether this was just a case of 'framing' the local Radicals, or whether they did indeed have connexions with Luddism is another matter. But light is thrown upon this in the reports of the key Lancashire informer, 'B', in March and April 1812. 'B' claimed to have been visited by a delegate named Walsh from Leeds, and (in April) to have received a letter describing Luddite successes from one Mann, of the same city.[3] Walsh told him that in the Leeds secret committee, 'none of the old Jacks [i.e. Jacobins] are allowed to act, as they have been suspected of late years':

Some of the old Jacks wished to act, but the old Committee had acted so wildly that neither prudence nor success was obtained, so not one is allowed to be on the Committee, but lye in the background.

The Yorkshire organization (Walsh told 'B') was conducted by a 'Committee of Trades', whose meetings were held with extreme secrecy in Leeds:

Committees never hold their meetings in a public house, but in private houses, or when the weather would admit even in the Fields

1. Peel, op. cit. (1880 edn), pp. 23–6. In the preface to the second edition, 1888, Peel recounts how this tradition was preserved.

2. *Report of the Proceedings ... under Oyer and Terminer*, pp. 124, 207.

3. James Mann, a Leeds cropper, was held under the suspension of Habeas Corpus in 1817 (below, p. 733) and later became Leeds' foremost radical bookseller. It would be of interest if these two 'Manns' were the same.

at night, and not as the old business was done to let all the Town know of it.[1]

It may be that while the 'old Jacks' were kept in the background in Leeds, in Halifax the Luddites were less circumspect. And it is consonant with such evidence as exists to suggest that Luddism in Yorkshire took a more generalized insurrectionary form after the failure of the Rawfolds attack. Without doubt by April there was some secret West Riding delegate system in operation. After Rawfolds, the Luddite organization shifted its emphasis to general revolutionary preparations. The months of April to September are months of frequent arms-raids, collections of money, and rumours of oath-taking. Lead (for bullets) disappeared like snow on a warm day; 'pumps and water-spouts are constantly disappearing';[2] even dyeing vats and guttering disappeared. The conspiracy extended to areas like Sheffield and Barnsley where there were neither croppers, gig-mills, nor shearing-frames. The Luddites were inspired by 'crude notions about upsetting the Government itself, when their organization had spread itself throughout the land, and they had collected sufficient arms'.[3]

If Yorkshire Luddism moved outwards from the grievances of the croppers to more general revolutionary aims, there was no single theme binding together the Lancashire discontents. Food riots, inflammatory chalking, *sub rosa* agitation for political reform, secret trade union committees, arms raids, attacks on power-looms, and provocations by spies took place simultaneously, sometimes spontaneously, and often with no direct organizational connexion with each other. The chapter on 'Lancashire Luddism' is the least satisfactory chapter in *The Skilled Labourer*. Some of its statements are plainly false, such as the statement that all disturbances in Lancashire and Cheshire had come to an end by the beginning of May 1812. Others – such as the prodigious influence attributed to a few spies from Bolton and 'B' of Manchester – are based on speculation and special pleading, disguised as narrative. The con-

1. Reports of 'B', 25 March, 18 April 1812, H.O. 40.1. The 'old Committee' and the 'old business' presumably refer to the conspiracy of 1801 and 1802, above pp. 517–21.

2. *Leeds Mercury*, 6 June 1812.   3. Peel, op. cit. (1880 edn), p. 9.

clusions are little short of ridiculous. We are asked to believe that seventy-one companies of infantry, twenty-seven troops of Horse Guards and Dragoons, as well as thousands of special constables (1,500 in the Salford Hundred alone) were on active duty in Lancashire in May 1812 because 'Old S', 'Young S' and 'B' had made their employers' blood run cold with stories of insurrection, and because some spontaneous food riots had taken place.

What is most noticeable in the Hammonds' handling of the sources is a marked disposition to *commence* their research with the assumption that any *bona fide* insurrectionary schemes on the part of working men were either highly improbable or, alternatively, wrong, and undeserving of sympathy, and therefore to be attributed to a lunatic, irresponsible fringe. But it is difficult to see why, in 1812, this should be assumed. With a year's intermission, war had continued for almost twenty years. The people had few civil and no trade union liberties. They were not gifted with historical clairvoyance, so that they might be comforted by the knowledge that in twenty years (when many of them would be dead) the middle class would secure the vote. In 1812 the weavers had experienced a disastrous decline in their status and living standards. People were so hungry that they were willing to risk their lives upsetting a barrow of potatoes. In these conditions, it might appear more surprising if men had not plotted revolutionary uprisings than if they had; and it would seem highly unlikely that such conditions would nourish a crop of gradualist constitutional reformers, acting within a Constitution which did not admit their political existence.

At the least, one might suppose that a democratic culture would approach the predicament of such men with caution and humility. In fact, this has scarcely been the case. Several of the historians who pioneered the study of this period (the Hammonds, the Webbs and Graham Wallas) were men and women of Fabian persuasion, who looked back upon the 'early history of the Labour Movement' in the light of the subsequent Reform Acts, and the growth of T.U.C. and Labour Party. Since Luddites or food rioters do not appear as satisfactory 'fore-runners' of 'the Labour Movement' they merited neither sympathy nor close attention. And this bias was supplemented, from another direction, by the more conservative bias of the orthodox academic tradition. Hence 'history' has dealt fairly with the Tolpuddle Martyrs, and fulsomely with Francis Place; but the hundreds of men and women executed or transported for oath-taking, Jacobin conspiracy, Luddism, the Pentridge and Grange Moor risings, food and enclosure and turnpike riots, the Ely riots and the Labourers' Revolt of 1830, and a score of minor affrays, have been forgotten by all but a few specialists, or, if they are remembered, they are thought to be simpletons or men tainted with criminal folly.

But for those who live through it, history is neither 'early' nor 'late'. 'Forerunners' are also the inheritors of another past. Men must be judged in their own context; and in this context we may see such men as George Mellor, Jem Towle, and Jeremiah Brandreth as men of heroic stature.

Moreover, bias has its way of working into the very minutiae of historical research. This is particularly relevant in the matter of Lancashire Luddism. There is only one reason for believing that the various depositions in the Home Office papers as to its revolutionary features are false, and this is the assumption that any such evidence is bound to be false. Once this is assumed, the Hammonds embark upon the seas of historical fiction. Thus, the most regular Lancashire informant, in Luddite and post-war years, was an individual designated as 'B'. This 'B' had possibly been employed as an informer since 1801 or 1802,[1] and he was in the confidence of Manchester ultra-Radicals. His name was Bent, and he was a small trader, described in 1812 as 'a buyer and seller of cotton waste'.[2] As a man of comparative affluence, he was frequently nominated as Treasurer to different secret committees – an admirable listening-post for a spy. On the face of it, he was well-placed to provide inside information.

1. See *The Skilled Labourer*, pp. 67, 73 and above, p. 538. It is not absolutely certain, however, that this was the same 'B', since other 'B's were employed – for example, Barlow, see above, p. 534.

2. Deposition of H. Yarwood, 22 June 1812, in H.O. 40.1 He was also described as 'a respectable cotton-merchant': see *The Trial at Full length of the 38 Men from Manchester* (Manchester, 1812), p. 137.

In *The Skilled Labour* 'B' appears frequently, in the rôle of a sensationalist and a *provocateur*:

The Home Office Papers contain numbers of illiterate communications from him, full of lurid hints of the approaching outbursts of the lower orders, encouraged by mysterious beings in high stations. The general rising, with the number of thousands who have taken the oath in different parts of the country, is his constant theme.

The Lancashire Luddite oath (declare the Hammonds), 'it is not unreasonable to suppose ... originated in "B."'s fertile brain'. When confronted with evidence that a delegate from Manchester visited a secret committee of the Stockport weavers, and sought to involve them in revolutionary preparations, the Hammonds find the convenient explanation:

Now nobody who has read through the Home Office Papers for this period can fail to recognize in the report of what the Manchester delegate said, the voice of 'B.' ...

Upon this hypothesis (supported by the assumption of superior knowledge which few readers will care to question) the fiction of provocation is elaborated. But a few pages later, when it suits these same authors to give credence to another part of 'B's reports, they blandly inform the reader: 'That Bent ever seriously tried to induce any of his colleagues to work for violent measures is unlikely, as otherwise men of the stamp of John Knight would not have continued to trust him ...' In short 'B's reports are bent in any way which happens to suit the legend of the moment.[1]

One may suggest that the Home Office papers may be read differently. Bent was not a provocateur, he was a plain informer, and he limited his own activities to what was necessary to secure the continued confidence of his fellow Radicals. He appears to have been a somewhat stupid but observant man, a not unusual combination. Hence his evidence can only be trusted when he describes events in which he participated himself, whereas in his reports of ulterior aims or of organization in the rest of the country he passed on the boasts of some

1. Ibid., pp. 274–5, 297, 336–7.

of the more sanguine agitators. The suggestion that Bent was the Manchester delegate who involved the Stockport committee in conspiratorial plans will not stand up to examination.[1]

In fact, if we cease following the false scent of provocation, it is possible to piece together a more coherent account of the inner history of Lancashire Luddism, using very much the same sources as employed by the Hammonds. First, we must recall that Jacobinism had struck deeper roots in Lancashire than in any other manufacturing district, and it had been given a particularly revolutionary tone by the Irish immigration. In Lancashire, almost alone, there is an unbroken thread of *open* anti-war and reform agitation, from the 1790s, through the 'United Englishmen', to the time of Luddism. In 1808 this agitation was reported, not only from Manchester, but from Royton, Bolton and Blackburn. 'Is it not time,' questioned some Bolton weavers, when announcing their intention to demonstrate every Sunday for two months on Charters Moss above the town,

to drag the British Constitution from its lurking hole, and to expose it in its original and naked purity, to show each individual *the laws of his forefathers*.[2]

Year by year, the weavers' fruitless agitation for a minimum wage had driven them in the direction of political agitation, whether of a revolutionary or constitutionalist character.

In the second place, when Luddism commenced in 1811–12, illegal trade unionism was already strongly rooted in Lancashire. We have already noted the degree of organization and consultation of the artisan trades and of the cotton-spinners in Manchester. The weavers' organization, also, was probably extensive and firmly based. In towns and even in some villages

1. Throughout the early Spring of 1812 'B' reported regularly and garrulously. The Hammonds rest their account of the Stockport meeting, in February, upon the confession of Thomas Whittaker in H.O. 42.121. But 'B' reported on 25 March that he still had not succeeded in gaining entry to any of the secret meetings although he hoped to be admitted shortly (H.O. 40.1). He did succeed in attending several of the weavers' meetings in April, but was excluded from an important meeting in May because of a dispute about money (deposition of Yarwood, H.O. 40.1).

2. See Aspinall, op. cit., pp. xxiii n. 2, 98–9 n. 1, 100–101 n. 2.

in Lancashire there were more or less representative 'secret committees' of weavers, accustomed to consulting with each other on applications to Parliament, petitions, the raising of funds, etc.[1]

Thus when Luddism came to Lancashire it did not move into any vacuum. There were already, in Manchester and the larger centres, artisan unions, secret committees of the weavers, and some old and new groups of Painite Radicals, with an ebullient Irish fringe. Lancashire was a rich field for spies and *provocateurs*, not because there was so little, but because there was so much afoot. And the reports are contradictory, not because all the informers were lying, but because there were contradictions in the movement. In a district which was, relatively, as politically sophisticated as Lancashire, there were bound to be divided counsels as to the value of machine-breaking. This conflict in the workers' councils caused much friction between February and the end of April 1812. Thus it would seem that at some time in February the policy of Luddism proper was endorsed by delegate meetings of the weavers, representing secret committees in several towns. According to the deposition of one Yarwood, who was himself a sub-delegate of the Stockport secret committee, the weavers were enrolled (and 'twisted in' with oaths) into an organization whose aims were the destruction of steam looms, the collection of money for arms, and the repulsion of force by force. Subscriptions of 1*d*. a week were collected, and a full-time organizer was actually employed for a month or two, in John Buckley Booth, a former 'dissenting minister'.[2] But at this point Yarwood's statement becomes vague. It seems that other trades, notably the spinners, tailors and shoemakers, had representatives on the secret committees of Manchester and

1. See the evidence of A. B. Richmond, cited above p. 592. There is also a full deposition in the Fitzwilliam Papers, F.46 (g) as to a shadowy 'weavers' union', said to stretch 'from London to Nottingham, and from thence to Manchester and Carlisle', bound by the strictest secrecy, with different degrees of oaths at different levels of the organization, extreme precautions in the transmission of papers – the night assignation on the moor, the message left in a hollow stick in the corner of a designated field, and so on.

2. Perhaps local preacher?

of Stockport, and that many others than weavers were 'twisted in'. But the actual plans of the committees were not known to Yarwood, who was secretary only to a district of the Stockport organization, and who delivered his money and received his instructions from John Buckley Booth.

It is clear, however, from Yarwood's account, as well as others, that the committees were divided. As early as 5 April the Manchester committee refused to 'Lud':

Nothing but Discord reigned amongst them that night. Not money sufficient was produced by the Districts to pay what trifle of liquor had been had by the Secret Committee.

It was necessary to raise the money required to send delegates to Bolton and Stockport 'to inform them that Manchester would not act in concert' by borrowing it (at Yarwood's suggestion) from 'Mr Bent ... whom I had seen with the Secret Committee at the Prince Regent's Arms.' The riots of mid-April would appear, in most cases, to have been spontaneous affairs, not prompted (or even supported) by the secret committees. By the end of April the Manchester trades (notably the spinners and tailors) refused to pay further money, as a result of which the Manchester delegates (including Bent) were excluded from an important delegate meeting at Failsworth on 4 May.

From this time forward, there appear to have been two simultaneous (and perhaps overlapping) forms of organization in Lancashire. On the one hand, one part of the movement concentrated upon renewing the agitation for peace and parliamentary reform. Bent reported a delegate meeting held to prepare a petition for this purpose on 18 May, attended by representatives from several towns in both Lancashire and Yorkshire: as usual, he managed to get himself nominated as Treasurer. This was the agitation with which John Knight and the 'thirty-eight' were associated, who were arrested by Nadin in Manchester in June (as a result of Bent's information) and charged with administering oaths. On the other hand, another part of the movement was certainly engaged in insurrectionary preparations. As early as 28 March Bent claimed to have had a meeting with Irish conspirators, 'dangerously daring fellows, and no less than four of them had been in the Rebellion in Ireland'. In April he claimed that an Irish delegate had actually visited him, having passed through Dublin, Belfast and Glasgow, and intending to continue his journey to Derby, Birmingham and London. He claimed to have been an officer in the rebellion, called himself Patrick Cannovan, and was 'about forty, a genteel appearance, well-drest in black with Hessian boots'. Bent's next visitor was a Birmingham delegate, who passed through Manchester on his way to Glasgow via Preston and Carlisle. A further delegate visited one of the committee in mid-May, from Newcastle in the Potteries, bringing the news that several thousands were sworn in and armed in his district, but that London was 'very backward ... it is not carried on with that spirit as could be expected'. Those in the conspiracy in London were 'chiefly Spitalfields Weavers and Taylors', or 'Knights of the Needle'.

There is no inherent improbability in these stories of an underground, whose main channel of communication was by way of Irish refugees of '98. It is mistaken, however, to attempt to divide the picture too sharply into constitutional reformers here and insurrectionary Irish there. It is equally possible that the more sophisticated political reformers regarded themselves as being more serious revolutionaries than the machine-breakers.[1] 'The Executive,' Bent wrote early in May,

recommends the people to be peaceable, and not to disturb the peace on any account – those people who do are not of those who are twisted in ...

'The fact is,' wrote an anonymous Jacobin from Lancashire on 6 May, signing himself 'Tom Paine',

that there is a regular, general, progressive organization of the people going forward. They may be called Hamdenites, Sidneyites, or Paineites. It has fallen to my lot to unite thousands. WE – for I speak in the name of multitudes – I say we deny and disavow all, or any connexion with machine-breakers, burners of factories, ex-

1. Cf. Peel's comment on the reaction of the Halifax democrats to the assassination of Horsfall : 'Assassination found no advocate or defender in the old democrat Baines.' Peel, op. cit., p. 164.

torters of money, plunderers of private property or assassins. We know that every machine for the abridgement of human labour is a blessing to the great family of which we are a part. We mean to begin at the Source of our grievances as it is of no use to petition, we mean to *demand* and *command* a redress of our grievances ...

One may suggest that by May 1812 Luddism in both Lancashire and Yorkshire had largely given way to revolutionary organization, which was effecting contact, through the medium of Irish emigrés and old Jacobins, with many centres (Sheffield, Barnsley, Birmingham, the Potteries, Glasgow) where no Luddite outbreaks took place. Of Luddism proper, only the name of the General survived. Rough hand-blocked cards, as well as tallies and secret signs and pass-words, were used to secure admission to meetings.[1] An even more tantalizing piece of evidence consists of papers claimed to have been picked up on the road shortly after the Luddite attack on Foster's mill at Horbury, near Wakefield. These consist of two long addresses, in flowery libertarian rhetoric, together with a 'Constitution' and 'Oath' which are *identical with those discovered upon an associate of Despard*, and cited in evidence at his trial.[2] Unless we suppose some deliberate 'plant' (and there is no reason to suppose this), this points unmistakably towards some link between the underground of 1802 and that of 1812.[3]

The evidence as to some kind of underground of this sort comes, in fact, from so many different sources that if it is all to be discounted we must fall back upon some hypothesis which would strain credibility a great deal further – such as the existence of a veritable factory of falsehoods, turning out complementary fantasies, for the sole purpose of deluding the authorities. Thus a quite different informer, a weaver designated 'R.W.', told his local J.P. early in June that a Lancashire delegate meeting had been held in Stockport, attended by men

1. See example on p. 205 above.
2. Enclosures in Rev. W. R. Hay, 16 May 1812, in H.O. 41.
3. Oliver reported of a West Riding delegate meeting (28 April 1817): 'I found there were many among them who did not hesitate to say they were well prepared with Despard &c. in 1802, and that Job was lost entirely by the loss of a few who had neglected to keep up a close Communication between them'. Oliver's 'Narrative', H.O. 40.9.

from Nottingham, Derby and Huddersfield. These delegates blamed –

the hastiness of the People here in beginning the Riots before the time appointed, and before they were sufficiently numerous and furnished with arms.

Pike manufacture was reportedly going ahead in Sheffield, a relatively simple matter in a town with so many small workshops and forges. The rising was now spoken of as planned for the end of September or early October. A midnight meeting was addressed by a 'man of genteel appearance' in a field near Didsbury. There was 'not a word on mills or machinery', but an appeal for a *general*, instead of a 'partial', rising. He was a speaker 'as fit to stand up either in the pulpit or at the bar as any man in the kingdom'.[1]

But it is at the point where we encounter rumours of *national* organization and 'genteel' leaders that we must be most cautious. Obviously, the genuine agitators sought to bolster the morale of their followers with large promises as to national support or even personalities (Cartwright, Burdett, Cochrane, Whitbread, Colonel Wardle and others) who were expected to aid the revolution. But whatever shadowy links the weavers' union, the 'Knights of the Needle', or travelling Irish delegates provided, it is certain that Luddism was a movement without national leadership or centre, and with scarcely any national objectives beyond common distress and the desire to overturn the Government. Above all, the talk (which such men as Bent passed on) of a 'Grand Committee' in London was wholly illusory, and showed a misunderstanding among the provincial revolutionaries as to their true predicament.

General Maitland was probably right when he declared that there was 'no real bottom' to Luddism, and that:

at present the whole of these Revolutionary Movements are limited to the lowest orders of the people generally; to the places where

1. This discussion of Lancashire Luddism is largely based on statements of Bent, Yarwood, Whittaker, 'R.W.', magistrates' reports and anonymous letters in H.O. 40.1 and 42.121 and 42.123.

2. Darvall, op. cit., p. 175. Cf. Beckett to Maitland, 29 August 1812: 'there must be more simultaneous cooperation and more system in what they do before any serious mischief need be feared from them', H.O. 79.2.

they show themselves; and that no concert exists, nor no plan is laid, further than is manifested in the open acts of violence that are daily committed.[2]

We may accept this judgement, provided that we attend closely to what is being said. Less well informed observers than Maitland frightened themselves because they could not conceive of a 'Revolutionary Movement' which did not have some inner knot of 'evil, designing men', some aristocratic or middle-class leaders, who were secretly inspiring the whole. When no such conspirators could be found, opinion swung to the opposite extreme: if there were no directors, then there could have been no revolutionary movement at all. It was inconceivable that croppers, stockingers and weavers should attempt to overthrow authority on their own.[1] 'There was, it seems, no evidence to prove a *setting on*; no evidence to prove a *plot*.' So Cobbett commented on the Report of the Secret Committee of the House of Commons in 1812. 'And this is the circumstance that will most puzzle the ministry. They can find no *agitators*. It is a movement of the *people's own*.'[2]

It was a movement, however, which could engage for a few months 12,000 troops, and which led the Vice-Lieutenant of the West Riding, in June 1812, to declare that the country was taking the 'direct Road to an open Insurrection':

... except for the very spots which were occupied by Soldiers, the Country was virtually in the possession of the lawless ... the disaffected outnumbering by many Degrees the peaceable Inhabitants.[3]

From one aspect, Luddism may be seen as the nearest thing to a 'peasant's revolt' of industrial workers; instead of sacking the *châteaux*, the most immediate object which symbolized their oppression – the gig-mill or power-loom mill – was at-

---

1. See *The Historical Account of the Luddites*, p. 11: 'An opinion prevailed that the views of some of the persons engaged in these excesses extended to revolutionary measures, and contemplated the overthrow of the government; but this opinion seems to have been supported by no satisfactory evidence; and it is admitted on all hands, that the leaders of the riots, although possessed of considerable influence, were all of the labouring classes.'

2. Cole, *Life of Cobbett*, p. 180.   3. Darvall, op. cit., p. 310.

tacked. Coming at the close of twenty years in which the printing-press and the public meeting had been virtually silent, the Luddites knew of no national leadership which they could trust, no national policy with which they could identify their own agitation. Hence it was always strongest in the local community and most coherent when engaged in limited industrial actions.

Even while attacking these symbols of exploitation and of the factory system they became aware of larger objectives. and pockets of 'Tom Painers' existed who could direct them towards ulterior aims. But here the tight organization which served to destroy a mill or stocking-frames was no longer of such service; there was no Old Sarum in their community which they could pull down, and the Houses of Parliament were beyond their reach. Undoubtedly the Luddites of different districts reached out to each other; and undoubtedly, in Yorkshire and Nottingham, some kind of district leadership, known only to a few of the 'Captains' like Towle and Mellor, was established. But if, as is likely, the accounts of delegate meetings at Ashton, Stockport and Halifax are true, it was here that Luddism was at its weakest – most open to penetration by spies, and most given to frothy talk about insurrections with the aid of the French, Irish or Scots. Only in mid-summer 1812 does it appear that a serious conspiratorial organization was coming into existence, which had detached itself from limited industrial grievances and was extending into new districts. By August (in Captain Raynes' view) the Luddites must either 'make a desperate effort to rise in a body', or else the movement must collapse.[1] Two causes brought it to an end. First, the repeal of the Orders in Council, and a rapid improvement in trade. Second, the increasing pressure of the authorities: more troops, more spies, more arrests, and the executions at Chester and Lancaster.

From another aspect we may see the Luddite movement as transitional. We must see through the machine-breaking to the motives of the men who wielded the great hammers. As 'a movement of the *people's own*', one is struck not so much by its backwardness as by its growing maturity. Far from being

1. F. Raynes, op. cit., p. 58.

'primitive' it exhibited, in Nottingham and Yorkshire, discipline, and self-restraint of a high order. One can see Luddism as a manifestation of a working-class culture of greater independence and complexity than any known to the eighteenth century. The twenty years of the illegal tradition before 1811 are years of a richness at which we can only guess; in particular in the trade union movement, new experiments, growing experience and literacy, greater political awareness, are evident on every side. Luddism grew out of this culture – the world of the benefit society, the secret ceremony and oath, the quasi-legal petition to Parliament, the craftsmen's meeting at the house of call – with seeming inevitability. It was a transitional phase when the waters of self-confident trade unionism, dammed up by the Combination Acts, strove to break through and become a manifest and open presence. It was also a transitional moment between Despard and the 'Black Lamp' on one hand, and Peterloo on the other. 'I am otherized to say,' wrote a (probably unauthorized [1]) 'Secretary to General Ludd' from Nottingham to Huddersfield on 1 May 1812,

that it is the opinion of our general and men that as long as that blackgard drunken whoreing fellow called Prince Regent and his servants have anything to do with government that nothing but distress will befall us there [their] foot-stooles. I am further desired to say that it is expected that you will remember that you are mad [made] of the same stuf as Gorg Guelps Juner and corn and wine are sent for you as well as him.

In the three counties, the agitation for parliamentary reform commenced at exactly the point where Luddism was defeated. In Halifax, even before the trial of Baines, one of the first Unions for Parliamentary Reform was founded. 'I have heard you are a Pettitioning for a Parliamentary Reform,' George Mellor wrote to a friend, while awaiting trial in York Castle:

1. In addition to letters probably emanating from *bona fide* Luddite groups, the period was productive of a good deal of free enterprise in letter-writing. Among authors whom I have noted are: 'Mr Pistol', 'Lady Ludd', 'Peter Plush', 'General Justice', 'Thomas Paine', 'A True Man', 'Eliza Ludd', 'No King', 'King Ludd', and 'Joe Firebrand', with such addresses as 'Robin Hoods Cave' and 'Sherwood Forest'.

'I wish these names to be given as follows ...' The names of thirty-nine fellow prisoners were enclosed. ('Remember,' he added, 'a Soul is of more value than Work or Gold.') And, if we follow the logic through to its conclusion, we may credit the exacerbated comment of a Derbyshire magistrate in 1817:

The Luddites are now principally engaged in politics and poaching. They are the principal leaders in the Hampden Clubs which are now formed in almost every village in the angle between Leicester, Derby and Newark.[1]

1. Radcliffe MSS., 126/46 and 126/127A; *An Appeal to the Nation* (Halifax, 1812); Lockett to Beckett, 12 January 1817, H.O. 40.3.

[15]

Demagogues and Martyrs

I. DISAFFECTION

THE Wars ended amidst riots. They had lasted, with one
interval, for twenty-three years. During the passing of the
Corn Laws (1815) the Houses of Parliament were defended
with troops from menacing crowds. Thousands of disbanded
soldiers and sailors returned to find unemployment in their
villages. The next four years are the heroic age of popular
Radicalism.

This Radicalism was not (as in the 1790s) a minority propaganda, identified with a few organizations and writers. After
1815 the claims of *Rights of Man* had little novelty; they were
now assumed. The greatest part of Radical rhetoric and journalism was concerned with the piecemeal exposure of the abuses
of the 'borough-mongering' or 'fund-holding' system – taxes,
fiscal abuses, corruption, sinecures, clerical pluralism; and
these abuses, which were seen as stemming from a venal, self-
interested clique of landowners, courtiers, and placemen,
pointed towards their own remedy – a sweeping parliamentary
reform. This was the groundswell of Radical propaganda,
whose most insistent journalistic voice was that of William
Cobbett and whose most compelling voice on the hustings was
that of Henry Hunt. 'As to the *cause* of our present miseries,'
Cobbett wrote, in his famous Address to the Journeymen and
Labourers (2 November 1816). 'it is the *enormous amount of
the taxes*, which the government compels us to pay for the
support of its army, its placemen, its pensioners, &c. and for
the payment of the interest of its debt.'

'Orator' Hunt handled the same themes. At one of the great
demonstrations in London's Spa Fields at the end of 1816 he
declared:

What was the cause of the want of employment? Taxation. What was the cause of taxation? Corruption. It was corruption that had enabled the borough-mongers to wage that bloody war which had for its object the destruction of the liberties of all countries but principally of our own. ... Everything that concerned their subsistence or comforts was taxed. Was not their loaf taxed? was not their beer taxed? was not everything they ate, drank, wore, and even said, taxed? ... They [taxes] were imposed by the authority of a boroughmongering faction who thought of nothing but oppressing the people, and subsisting on the plunder wrung from their miseries ...[1]

Radicalism was a generalized libertarian rhetoric, a running battle between the people and the unreformed House of Commons within which one issue after another was thrown to the fore. Around this battle there grew up (or, perhaps one should say, Cobbett created) a Radical martyrology and, more especially, a demonology, in which the Prince Regent, Castlereagh, Sidmouth, the spies – Oliver, Castle, and Edwards – the Manchester Yeomanry, Peel and paper-money, and half-hearted or equivocal reformers like Brougham all had ritual parts. Other voices were sometimes more influential than those of Cobbett or Hunt: T. J. Wooler and the *Black Dwarf*; William Hone's satires; Carlile and the *Republican*. But this generalized Radical rhetoric embraced them all, and stretched in the immediate post-war years from its most sophisticated representatives – Byron and Hazlitt, Henry White's *Independent Whig* and John and Leigh Hunt's *Examiner* to the ultra-Radical periodicals like the *Medusa* and *The Cap of Liberty*.

This rhetoric reflected and was supported by the radical disposition of the crowd in London, the cities, and the manufacturing districts. There is a scarcely broken tradition of anti-authoritarian manifestations by the London crowd, from the days of Wilkes, through the great demonstrations called by the L.C.S. in 1795, to the agitations in support of 'Burdett and No Bastille' and thence to the great meetings of post-war Radicalism. Even in 1802–3 this disposition can be seen, not only in the sympathy shown to Despard, but also in the execrations attending Governor Wall to his execution, for the

1. *Examiner*, 17 November 1816.

crime of ordering the flogging to death of an innocent soldier.[1] Ten years later, when Eaton, the old Deist publisher was pilloried for publishing a tract of Paine's under the title of the 'third part' of the *Age of Reason*, there were even more emphatic manifestations. 'I saw Mr Eaton stand in the pillory,' Cobbett recalled some years later;

> The day before, in the same place, a man had been in the pillory for perjury, and had been pelted with rotten eggs, and almost strangled by blood and guts brought from the slaughter-houses, and flung in his face. Very different was the reception that Mr Eaton met with! An immense crowd of people cheered him during the whole hour: some held out biscuits, as if to present him with: others held him out glasses of wine, and others little flags of triumph and bunches of flowers. While the executioner and officers of Justice were hooted! *This it was that was the real cause of putting an end to the punishment of the pillory!*

The crowd said Cobbett) was 'a specimen of London' – 'Gentlemen, Merchants, Tradesmen of all sorts, artizans and labourers, and a pretty fair proportion of females':

> They were not ignorant of the cause of his being in the pillory ... and yet, they could not give their assent to a punishment inflicted for a *matter of opinion*.[2]

Thus the radicalism of the London crowd was no new phenomenon, but in the post-war years it assumed more conscious, organized, and sophisticated forms. What was more new was the shift in the sub-political attitudes of the masses in the provinces, and especially in the Midlands and the north during the war years. In the 1790s only Norwich and Sheffield were regarded as incurably Jacobin centres by the authorities; by the early years of the nineteenth century, Nottingham, Coventry, Bolton were added to the list; by the time of the Luddite movement, most of the Lancashire and West Riding townships, as well as many others in the Midlands, were 'dis-

1. Cobbett's *Political Register*, 6 February 1802. Next to the press-gang, flogging was perhaps the most hated of the institutions of Old England. Cobbett laid the basis for his great popularity among the common people when he was imprisoned in 1810 for denouncing its abuse. For Wall, see also Southey, *Letters from England*, Letter 9.

2. Ibid., 27 January 1820.

affected'; by the end of the Wars, from Carlisle to Colchester and from Newcastle to Bristol, the 'mob' was radical in disposition. Conversely, we may find evidence for this in the extensive programme of war-time barracks-building – between 1792 and 1815, 155 barracks were constructed, many of which were deliberately sited in the 'disaffected' districts of the Midlands and north.[1] England, in 1792, had been governed by consent and deference, supplemented by the gallows and the 'Church-and-King' mob. In 1816 the English people were held down by force.

Hence post-war Radicalism was at times less a movement of an organized minority than the response of the whole community. We might note two examples, both in 1817. The first is the execution of a sailor, Cashman, for his part in an attack upon a gunsmith's shop after the meeting at Spa Fields on 2 December 1816.[2] Cashman was an Irish fisherman, with 'many years' service in the Naval Wars, in which he had been wounded nine times. By his own account, he was owed by the Admiralty more than five years back pay, as well as a considerable sum in prize money. A sum of £1 a month which he had signed over to his poverty-stricken mother in Ireland had never been paid. At the close of the Wars he had been discharged penniless, and in pursuit of restitution he had been referred from one circumlocution office to the next. On the morning of the riot he had been once again to the Admiralty; on his return he had met 'a brother sailor, a warrant officer' who had persuaded him to attend the Spa Fields meeting, treating him to spirits and beer on the way. He had little understanding of the purpose of the meeting and, perhaps, not much recollection of its events.

The authorities could scarcely have chosen a more popular victim than Cashman, and one more likely to bring out all the sympathies and latent radicalism of the London crowd. British 'tars' (of whom many had been present at the Spa Field meeting) were noted for their riotous dispositions: 'they are always the first to *turn out* ... whether to fight, to drink, to dance, or to *kick up a row*'. They were the popular heroes of countless

1. See Halévy, *England in 1815* (Penguin edn), I, p. 104; Hammonds, *The Town Labourer*, p. 85.   2. See below, pp. 694–6.

ballads of the Wars. The shabby treatment of the Cashmans contrasted invidiously with the liberal allowances for sinecure-holders and for the relatives of Ministers and commanding officers, with the £400,000 granted to Wellington for the purchase of a mansion and estate (in addition to other emoluments), with the grants to absentee surveyors of ports or clerkships in the Admiralty. Cashman himself was chiefly indignant at the injustice of his case, at being drawn in a cart through the streets and 'exposed like a common robber'. 'This is not for cowardice,' he exclaimed,

> I am not brought to this for any robbery. ... If I was at my quarters, I would not be killed in the smoke: I'd be in the fire. I have done nothing against my King and country; but fought for them.

The execution assumed the character of a great popular demon-stration, and the scaffold had to be defended by barricades and an 'immense force' of constables:

> As the Sheriffs advanced, the mob expressed the strongest feelings of indignation: groans and hisses burst from all quarters, and attempts were made to rush forward. ..., Cashman ... seemed to enter into the spirit of the spectators, and joined in their exclama-tions with a terrific shout. ... 'Hurra, my hearties in the cause! success! cheer up!'

On the scaffold Cashman rejected the ghastly solicitations to confession and repentance of two Anglican clergymen: 'Don't bother me – it's no use – I want no mercy but from God.' Then, addressing the crowd, 'Now, you buggers, give me three cheers when I trip'; and, after telling the executioner to 'let go the jib-boom', Cashman 'was cheering at the instant the fatal board fell from beneath his feet'. After a few minutes dead silence, the crowd 'renewed the expressions of disgust and in-dignation towards every person who had taken a part in the dreadful exhibition', with cries of 'Murder!' and 'Shame!' It was several hours before the people dispersed.[1]

The other example is taken from Lancashire in the same month. Samuel Bamford, the Middleton weaver and Secretary

1. *Courier*, 12 March 1817; Cobbett's *Weekly Political Pamphlet*, 15 March 1817; *Black Dwarf*, 19 March 1817.

of his local Hampden Club, was arrested by Joseph Nadin and a party of soldiers in his home village. Immediately a crowd gathered around Nadin and his party, and threatened to effect a rescue. Bamford's captors placed him in a coach, escorted by dragoons, and rode on through Chadderton to attempt to make further arrests:

On the road towards Chadderton Hall I advised my conductor to draw up and return to Manchester, assuring him he would not capture any more of my batch that day, and in confirmation I pointed to Chadderton Heights and the neighbouring country, over which scores of people were running like hunters, as if to meet the coach near Royton. All the country was up, I said, and every one whom he might want would be apprised of his coming. He growled a deep oath, saying he had never seen anything like that before; the officer commanding the dragoons, who rode by the coach door, observed that he had seen something like it in Ireland, but never anywhere else.[1]

II. PROBLEMS OF LEADERSHIP

The Hampden Club was founded in London in 1812. In itself it was an unimportant body: a select group of Whig reformers, each in possession of an annual income of over £300 p.a. from landed property. It offered Major Cartwright, however, a platform from which to issue addresses, and a base from which to make crusading tours of the Midlands and the north in the cause of parliamentary reform. 'English gentlemen are perpetually travelling,' he replied to critics of his propaganda: 'Some go to see lakes and mountains. Were it not as allowable to travel for seeing the actual condition of a starving people?'[2]

It is difficult to over-state the importance of Cartwright's evangelizing tours of 1812, 1813, and 1815. For fifteen years the pockets of parliamentary reformers throughout the country had been without a national leadership or strategy, except such as was provided by Burdett and the Westminster Committee, or by Cobbett's *Register*. Both Cartwright and Cobbett saw the

1. S. Bamford, *Passages in the Life of a Radical* (1893 edn), p. 77.
2. F. D. Cartwright, *Life and Correspondence of Major Cartwright* (1826), II, p. 45; E. Halévy, *The Liberal Awakening* (1949 edn), pp. 11 ff.

insurrectionary phase of Luddism as abhorrent and futile. But both of them also looked with renewed interest at the north and Midlands, where unrest was growing. Cobbett's dramatic turn to the 'Journeymen and Labourers' did not take place until 1816. It was the inflexible Major, now over seventy, who decided to enter the Luddite counties.

It was not Cartwright's intention to form a 'working-class' Radical movement. Indeed, he thought it to be his duty to oppose –

any attempt to excite the poor to invade the property of the rich. It is not by an invasion of such property that the conditions of the poor is to be amended, but by ... EQUAL LAWS ...

Pressure for reform might best be obtained 'for the most part by means of the middle classes'. He wished to divert insurrectionary discontent into constitutional forms,[1] and to lay the basis for a nation-wide movement continually petitioning Parliament. In the London Hampden Club he had been forced to put his own belief in manhood suffrage and annual Parliaments into the background, and to compromise with the demand for a ratepayer suffrage. Even so, the patrician reformers complained at his extravagant opinions and failed even to attend the Club's annual dinners. And the Major was contemptuous of timid, Whiggish reformers. He believed still in the agitation among 'members unlimited'. He was more interested in the principles of the men with whom he worked than in their income or occupation.

In this he showed courage. 'I have recently had communication with persons connected with the disturbed districts,' he wrote in May 1812. 'For turning the discontents into a legal channel favourable to Parliamentary Reform, they are anxious to have the advice and countenance of *our Society*.' As early as January 1812 he had visited Derby and Leicester, and had attempted to hold a public reform meeting in Nottingham at the height of the Luddite outbreaks. He had expostulated, in

1. Cartwright to Thomas Hardy, 5 January 1801: 'I do not agree with many, who think it is even now too late so to compose the public mind as to be able to stop at *Reform*, instead of driving on to a *Revolution*. ... The example of France would certainly operate, to prevent our thinking of settling things on a totally new bottom.' F. D. Cartwright, op. cit., I, pp. 292–3.

open letters in the *Nottingham Review*, at the timidity of those gentlemen reformers who had failed to give him support: 'when trade fails, and the workmen *cannot get bread* ... is not this, Sir, a *proper time* to meet?' When John Knight and the 'Thirty-Eight' were imprisoned in Manchester in the summer of 1812, Cartwright wrote immediately to offer encouragement and to give assistance in the defence. In the autumn he decided to enter the 'disturbed districts' again.

In his tour of 1812 he held meetings at Leicester, Loughborough (where 600 attended), Manchester, Sheffield, Halifax, Liverpool and Nottingham. In January and February 1813 he undertook a second tour, holding meetings at thirty-five places in the Midlands, north and west in less than thirty days.[1] (This tour – and Oliver's tours in 1817 – remind us that we are too ready to emphasize the difficulties of communication before the coming of the railways.) At each of these centres there was a nucleus of reformers who had undertaken arrangements for the meeting. Cartwright placed himself at their service, no matter whether they were gentlemen, small tradesmen, artisans or weavers; and he presented a correct cold shoulder to the tepid gentry and large Whig employers who were scandalized at the rabble with which he associated. Even his old colleague Wyvill denounced him, in a pseudonymous pamphlet, for countenancing Luddites and incendiaries. When a dinner was held in his honour at Sheffield by the 'Friends of Parliamentary Reform', a manufacturer who considered himself to be a reformer was outraged because 'the dinner tickets were priced so low that the company, with few exceptions, were of the lowest rank'. The 'Annual Parliament and Universal Suffrage men' predominated, and the Chair was taken by 'one of our violent men'.[2]

1. Lutterworth, Hinckley, Leicester, Loughborough, Chesterfield, Sheffield, Huddersfield, Bradford, Wakefield, Leeds, Preston, Wigan, Liverpool, Bolton, Manchester, Lees, Stockport, Newcastle, Birmingham, Worcester, Tewkesbury, Gloucester, Stroud, Bath, Shepton Mallet, Bridgwater, Taunton, Wellington, Bristol, Calne, Marlborough, Newbury, Hungerford, Abingdon, Reading.

2. F. D. Cartwright, op. cit., I, p. 243, II, pp. 17, 21, 31–55, 110; H.O. 42.119; *Nottingham Review*, 27 December 1811, 3 and 17 January 1812; T. A. Ward, *Peeps into the Past*, p. 191.

Cartwright claimed that he returned from these tours with 200,000 signatures to Reform petitions. (A further tour, in 1815, took him to Scotland.) The meetings did not pass unmolested. At Huddersfield on 22 January 1813 (only a week after the execution of fourteen Luddites) his meeting was invaded by the military, papers and petitions were seized, Cartwright and local reformers (mainly 'working mechanics') were arrested, and only the Major's evident knowledge of constitutional law prevented further persecution. In Bolton, Rochdale, Salford, reformers collecting signatures to his petitions were imprisoned or victimized. We may suppose that as Cartwright passed rapidly from town to town, the incipient clubs which he left behind him had the greatest difficulty in maintaining themselves. It was not until 1816 that they struck root in the manufacturing districts.[1]

The strongholds of Jacobinism had been in artisan centres. It is not possible after 1815 to make a clear definition. At different times between 1815 and 1832 agitation against particular abuses – income tax, tithes, the Corn Laws, sinecures – swept in very many sections of the population. Manufacturers, farmers, small gentry, professional men, as well as artisans and labourers, shared the demand for some measure of parliamentary reform. But the consistent thrust behind the reform movement came from 'the industrious classes' – stockingers, hand-loom weavers, cotton-spinners, artisans, and, in association with these, a widespread scattering of small masters, tradesmen, publicans, booksellers and professional men, from among which groups the officers of local political societies were sometimes drawn.

The complexion of the reform movement differed from one region to another, and this had its bearing upon strategy and emphasis. In Bristol, where Henry Hunt was the spokesman for an impressive agitation before the Wars had ended, the artisans were most prominent, notably the cordwainers and glass-makers.[2] In south Lancashire, where the gulf between the great manufacturers and the workers was deepest, the working-

1. F. D. Cartwright, op. cit., pp. 47–55; Fitzwilliam Papers, F.46 (g); Radcliffe MSS., 126–117.
2. Henry Hunt, *Memoirs* (1822), III, pp. 7–12.

class reform movement was most 'independent', keeping its distance from even the active middle-class reformers of Manchester. In the West Riding economic cleavages were not so sharp, the hand-loom weavers did not enter their worst phase of crisis until the late 1820s, and in Leeds there was some cooperation between artisans and middle-class reformers. In Birmingham, where social gradations shelved less steeply and where the artisan still aspired to becoming a small master, there was a vigorous indigenous Radicalism supported by many employers and to some degree under middle-class leadership.

The Radicalism of Manchester, Birmingham or Leeds, bore a direct relationship to the structure of each community. It is less easy to indicate an authentic London Radicalism deriving from its industrial structure or community patterns. Everyone who aspired to Radical leadership or influence had a London following — Cobbett, Burdett, Carlile, Thistlewood, the Benthamites, Henry Hunt and many more. From the London presses there came a constant outpouring of Radical papers and books. But London itself rarely appeared as a national focus for popular reform organization until the eve of 1832.

The problem lay, in part, in London's size and in the diversity of its occupations. In the manufacturing centres it was possible for local leadership to arise, of men well known in the community and assured of its support. In London there were a number of strong Radical districts — among them, Bethnal Green, Lambeth, Southwark, Finsbury, Islington — from which leaders sometimes emerged. The 'Spenceans' and Cato Street conspirators confidently expected support from the populace in general, and specifically from building-workers, dockers, and the 'navigators' digging the Paddington Canal. At most times the Spitalfields silk-weavers could be relied upon to join Radical demonstrations, while the constitutionally minded Westminster reformers had consistent support among the artisans' trades clubs. But the actual London leadership tended to be superimposed upon this support rather than being drawn directly from it. There was greater opportunity for social mobility, for the intelligent artisan, in London than in

Barnsley or Loughborough. In the industrial villages and smaller towns, the same Radical leaders might remain at their posts, with little change in occupation or status, for twenty or even forty years.

There is a sense of impermanence about the London leadership. Prominent national personalities, orators, wire-pullers, journalists or tavern demagogues, succeeded each other in favour, and often engaged in bitter internecine polemics in full public view. Moreover, London Radicalism emerged from the Wars already much-divided. The obvious contestant for leadership was the old Westminster Committee. But this Committee had now moved decisively in the direction of the alliance between artisan and middle-class reformers. Burdett, whose Radical enthusiasms were cooling, commenced in April 1816 a campaign for admitting to the suffrage all who paid direct taxes. He was supported by the Westminster Committee, which had inaugurated its post-war agitation with a petition against the income-tax (a direct appeal for the support of the propertied classes, and especially of the City reformers whose spokesman was Alderman Waithman). Lord Cochrane still held the other Westminster seat, with the Byronic gusto of the patrician revolutionary, but his reputation was tarnished by scandals on the Stock Exchange, he was little gifted as a political leader, and when he resigned his seat (in order to enlist as a democratic free-booter in the South American wars), he was eventually replaced by the Benthamite, John Cam Hobhouse, whom Burdett and Place preferred to the manhood suffrage nominees, Cartwright or Hunt.[1]

This move at Westminster was not fortuitous. Francis Place and his fellow artisans and small masters (some of them, like Alexander Galloway, now large employers) had abandoned their Jacobin faith: belief in manhood suffrage and in unlimited popular agitation. They were contemptuous of the London rabble, and alarmed by its riotous or insurrectionary elements. They had little contact with the tavern world where a new generation of agitators was now at work. Place was later to declare that Cobbett was 'too ignorant ... to see that the

1. Almost every advanced Radical was opposed to this selection. See Wallas, op. cit., p. 138.

common people must ever be imbecile in this respect [i.e. political organization] when not encouraged and supported by others who have money and influence'. Place himself was directly under the influence of Bentham and of James Mill. While he was no less of a Radical in his contempt for the inefficiency and irrationalism of aristocratic government, and in his indignation at the Corn Laws or at any repressive legislation, he was deeply hostile to any open strategy of popular agitation and organization. On 30 January 1817, when the deputies of the Hampden Clubs were conferring in London, Place drafted an advertising address for Hone's *Reformist's Register* which was a clear attempt to rescue the reform movement from the influence of the manhood suffrage policy. 'It is to the *middle* class *now*, as at *other* times,' the address declared, 'that the salvation of all that ought to be dear to Englishmen must be confided. . . . It is from *this* class ... that whatever of good may be obtained must proceed.'[1]

By 1817 Cobbett had already dubbed the Westminster Committee 'the Rump'. By 1820 he was condemning it as 'a little group of men, who have been intermeddling in the great political affairs of Westminster', a 'nice little snug corporation, which has been kind enough to take upon itself the office of ... the choosing of members to represent that City in Parliament', and as a 'miserable junto ... who have, to all practical purposes, rendered Westminster as much a rotten borough, as Gatton or Old Sarum'.[2] There is little purpose in raking over all the mud which Burdett and Place, on one hand, and Cobbett and Hunt, on the other, threw at each other during these years. It is more important to note that in 1816 the strategy of the best-organized group among the London Radicals was to detach the movement in the country from the influence of Hunt and Cobbett; and to attach a working-class following to a new parliamentary leadership whose rising stars were Hume, Hobhouse and Brougham.

Such a strategy had little appeal for the most ardent reformers in the Jacobin tradition, nor to the most Radical elements

1. Add MSS. 27809 ff. 16, 17, 51. It should be said that Hone did not follow Place's editorial directions.
2. *Political Register*, 9, 16 December 1820.

in the London crowd. The only alternative leadership, however, to the Westminster Committee which offered itself, in 1816, was that of the small 'Society of Spencean Philanthropists'. Thomas Spence himself had died in September 1814 and had been 'buried with some pomp' by 'about forty disciples' from among whom the Society had been organized. Its leading members were supposed to have included the two Watsons, father and son,[1] Arthur Thistlewood, Thomas Preston, Allen Davenport, and the two Evanses, father and son. As a result of Place's reminiscences, they feature in most histories as cranks and nonentities: Watson, the elder, as 'a man of loose habits ... wretchedly poor', his son as 'a wild profligate fellow', Evans, the Librarian to the society, as an eccentric who 'used to march from his house to the public houses where ... the meetings of the *society* were held, with an old bible under his arm'.[2]

The Spenceans were 'next to nobody and nothing', continued Place: they were 'harmless and simple'. But in so far as they were the main contenders with Place and the Westminister Committee, in 1816–17, for the leadership of London Radicalism, Place is not a disinterested witness. To a Benthamite, Thomas Evans's *Christian Polity the Salvation of the Empire* (1816) must have seemed folly. But it may be suggested that Evans's agrarian Socialism was more rational and seminal than Bentham's Felicific Calculus. The Spencean advocates had won much support among the trades clubs, especially among the shoemakers. Their policy – that 'all feudality or lordship in the soil be abolished, and the territory declared to be the people's common farm' – was preparing the minds of artisans for the acceptance of Owen's *New View of Society*.[3]

If the Spenceans were more than 'simple', they were also – in 1816 – of some influence. In Place's vocabulary, to be 'next to nobody and nothing' meant that they had no wires to pull in Parliament nor in influential middle-class circles. But Preston and Thistlewood certainly knew the tavern world of Lon-

1. Neither to be confused with James Watson, the Radical bookseller and associate of Carlile and Hetherington.
2. Add MSS. 27809 ff. 72, 99.
3. For Evans's *Christian Polity*, see above, p. 178.

don better than Place. The Spenceans, throughout the Wars, had advocated the policy of the 'free and easy', the informal meeting in Lambeth or Bethnal Green. The Committee of Secrecy which reported in February 1817 that immediately after the war Spencean societies had multiplied among mechanics and manufacturers, and discharged soldiers and sailors, may not have been as alarmist as is usually supposed. There is some evidence that by the end of 1816 the Spenceans had reorganized their work, in sections and divisions, on the old plan of the London Corresponding Society.[1]

Moreover, there is perhaps some confusion in the very designation, 'Spencean'. Evans was without doubt a disciple of Spence, and he and his son were pursued with exceptional vindictiveness by the authorities because he had the courage to advocate in print the expropriation of the landowners – than which a Parliament of landowners could imagine no greater crime. He and his circle conducted a small, philosophical propaganda for agrarian Socialism in 1816–17.[2] But the more influential political leaders in London – Dr James Watson, Arthur Thistlewood and Thomas Preston – are probably better designated as republicans, or Jacobins in the old Painite tradition, who – during the widespread unemployment of the post-war years – also endorsed the remedy of a return to small farms and 'spade-husbandry' as one solution to the problem of hunger.[3] It is difficult to discover much about Dr Watson. He was perhaps fifty years old in 1816, was described at his trial as a 'medical man and chymist', was poor, and had perhaps been involved in underground political

1. See O. D. Rudkin, *Thomas Spence and his Contemporaries*, pp. 146–9; A. W. Waters, *Spence and his Political Works*; A Davenport, *The Life, Writings and Principles of Thomas Spence*; W. M. Gurney, *Trial of James Watson* (1817), I, p. 45; *Address of the Spencean Philanthropists* (1816), p. 4.

2. See the small periodicals edited by Robert Wedderburn, a coloured man (the son of a Scottish gentleman and a Jamaican slave) and a 'flint' tailor, *The 'Forlorn Hope'* and *The Axe Laid to the Root*, both 1817. The Evanses were imprisoned under the suspension of Habeas Corpus in 1817–18 (for the second time), and their case attracted a great deal of sympathy.

3. See the extract from Dr Watson's speech at Spa Fields, above p. 254.

work for a number of years.[1] He was a friend of that other Jacobin surgeon, John Gale Jones, who addressed several meetings under his chairmanship. Arthur Thistlewood, a former Army officer and former gentleman-farmer, had been in France in the late 1790s and (by one account) had served with the revolutionary armies. Preston, although sometimes referred to as a shoemaker, appears to have been a small employer in the leather trade. 'I have seen so much distress in Spitalfields,' he told the Lord Mayor in December 1816,

that I have prayed to God to swallow me up – I have seen a fine young woman who has not been in a Bed for nine months – I have ruined myself, I have not £1, I have kept forty men at work ...

These men made up the nucleus of London ultra-Radicalism, whether they were Spenceans or 'old Jacks' in the conspiratorial tradition of Despard. Their field of agitation was the trades club and the tavern.[2] Samuel Bamford and his fellow delegates from northern Hampden Clubs attended several such meetings when they were in London in the first months of 1817.[3] It is probable that most of this group inherited Despard's notion that London must perform the rôle of Paris in an English Revolution, either by means of riots culminating in general insurrection directed at the Tower, the prisons and the House of Parliament, or by means of the *coup d'état*. Nor should it be assumed that an insurrectionary movement, in 1817 or 1819, might not – if it had gained sufficient impetus – have achieved some temporary success. But, if several of the group had sad occasion to show that they were brave, nothing can exonerate them from the accusation of culpable amateurishness. They fell victims to their own inflated rhetoric; they plotted with home-made grenades and pikes but were unable to erect, in the London streets, a single defended barricade; on more than one occasion they were caught in romantic deri-

1. See examination of Thomas Preston before the Lord Mayor, 4 December 1816: 'I always considered the Watsons – both of them – the bravest men in England ... they are both surgeons I believe.' T.S. 11.203. See also entry in *D.N.B.*

2. 'Preston talked about a Free and Easy Club as the best way of getting the men together [in Spitalfields].' Deposition of J. Williamson, 24 September 1817, T.S. 11.197.

3. Bamford, op. cit., pp. 25–6.

vative postures. Their underworld of tavern bravado was penetrated with ease by Sidmouth's spies. It was here that Oliver gained the credentials which gave him access to the counsels of reformers in the Midlands and the north. And over the two authentic conspiratorial attempts in London (the Spa Fields riots and Cato Street) there will always hang the suspicion that they were more than one-half the work of Castle and Edwards, the Government's own *provocateurs*.

Thus the London reform movement commenced divided, between cautious contitutionalists on the one hand, and conspirators on the other. The middle ground between these extremes was occupied by Cartwright, Hunt and Cobbett. But we cannot appreciate the full complexity of the problem of Radical organization and leadership unless we look outside London, and also at the situation in which reformers were still placed by the Seditious Societies Act under which the Corresponding Societies were suppressed in 1799.

Under this Act, no national political organization was legal. It was, moreover, illegal to form local societies which were branches of a national society, or which communicated with a national centre by means of correspondence or the exchange of delegates. (This legislation still proved to be an embarrassment to the National Charter Association in 1841.) The only undisputed rights of reformers were, first, to form local, autonomous, clubs or discussion groups;[1] second, the right to petition Parliament or the King, and to meet for that purpose.[2]

The informal club and the tavern meeting was one part of the democratic process which had survived the repression of 1796–1806, in the provinces as well as in London. A correspondent in the *Leeds Mercury* in 1802 referred to the 'societies and clubs' in which tradesmen—

meet nightly in taverns and public houses. Almost every street in a large town has a little senate of this description; and the privileges

1. This was scarcely accepted as a 'right' by some provincial magistrates, who took it upon themselves to intervene and break up meetings. The Leeds Hampden Club was dissolved by magisterial intervention.

2. Even in the worst years of repression, the Government itself paid lip-service to this 'inviolable' right. See also P. Fraser, 'Public Petitioning and Parliament before 1832', *History*, XLVI, 158, October 1961.

of sitting in council over the affairs of the nation, and a pot of porter, has long been claimed by free Britons, and acknowledged by *all* administrations.[1]

In such 'societies' as these Bewick and his fellow Radical tradesmen met in Newcastle during the Wars. From Liverpool during the election of 1812 Brougham wrote to Lord Grey:

You can have no idea of the nature of a Liverpool election. ... You have every night to go to the different clubs, benefit societies, etc., which meet and speechify. ... I had nine nights of the clubs, besides a regular speech each day at close of the poll. I delivered in that time one hundred and sixty speeches odd ...[2]

In 1817 Cobbett could write:

We have *Pitt* Clubs, Whig Clubs, Clubs to suppress Vice, Clubs to detect and punish thieves, Bible Clubs, School Clubs, Benefit Clubs, Methodist Clubs, Hampden Clubs, Spencean Clubs, Military Clubs, Naval Clubs, Gaming Clubs, Eating Clubs, Drinking Clubs, Masters' Clubs, Journeymen's Clubs, and a thousand other sorts of clubs and associations.[3]

But the step from informal tavern group to the avowed Radical club – Hampden Club or Political Union – was a long one. We have interesting records of the discussions which accompanied the formation of the first Hampden Clubs in Lancashire. For example, there is the report of an informer who attended a 'committee meeting of reform' at the Sign of the Dog, Little Bolton, in November 1816:

John Kay began the business by asking us if we had deliberately weighed the consequences in our own minds. He said, are you prepared to suffer persicution, separately and in your own persons for the sake of that great and good cause of reform. ... Our task is an arduous and a dangerous one. Are you who are here willing to engage in it such as it is?

Robeson Bradley said, I know we shall be sufferers, as it is, *I am afraid before the Winter is over*. He said we are brought in to such a situation by our oppressors that both life and liberty is scarce worth preserving. ... Kay said it is legal to seek redress in the way of

1. *Leeds Mercury*, 6 March 1802.
2. Brougham, *Life and Times* (1871), II, p. 62.
3. Cobbett's *Weekly Political Pamphlet*, 1 March 1817.

reform. But when Parliament meets *they can make it illegal* to meet and it is not likely that they will tamely give up their sinecures, pentions &c which they have enjoyed for years. He said the wicked men will rather sacrifice half the people of the nation than give it up peaceably, if they give it up it must be by force, and in their fall they will crush thousands of us . . .

İt was agreed to write to Mr Knight (the Oldham veteran of the trial of the 'Thirty-Eight' in 1812), and also to 'Mr W. Cobbett where he resides', 'desiring them to inform us if it should be legal to take money at the door to defray the expense attending Rent & communication, political tracts &c. . . .' John Knight's reply to this enquiry is also preserved:

Sir, I only received your letter and reply have to state that you may take a room for the purpose of discussing political or other questions (without licencing the room) provided you do not demand money for admission nor fasten the outer door during your stay but people go in & out at pleasure. In a letter I received from London yesterday it is recommended that such meetings are publicly announced, that a Magistrate is informed therof, & in addition thereto that secret meetings had better be avoided & that meetings shd be as numerously attended as possible – the Language used shd be mild & constitutional, but firm & clear. We have engaged a room here [i.e. Manchester] capable of holding a thousand persons. We had thought to *have opened it on Monday next*, but hoping to gain considerable numbers of the upper Classes (as they are called) by delaying it a week we have agreed to do so . . .[1]

Knight was very probably receiving advice from Major Cartwright, or from Thomas Cleary, his lieutenant. In both Lancashire and Leicestershire, in the winter of 1816–17, the various clubs corresponded freely with each other within the county, and even went so far as to convene well-attended delegate meetings or county committees. On 6 January 1817 an informer in the Leicester club was able to report:

A deputation had been sent to Manchester. Graham and Warburton went. Graham stated what great distress they were in, in Lancashire. That the greater part of the poor people could only get a little water and salt and oatmeal – some had one meal a day, and some

1. H.O 40.3, cited in H. W. C. Davis, *Lancashire Reformers, 1816–17*, (Manchester, 1926), pp. 21–2.

had one meal in three days. Then he read a letter from Derby, saying that a person from Manchester would call upon the Leicester club on his way to Birmingham and Bristol. Then reads a letter from Major Cartwright, saying he had received information of fourteen different societies that intend to send Delegates to a Committee in London on 22 January . . .[1]

A few weeks before the Lancashire reformers had gone even further. At a delegate meeting in Middleton, attended by 'deputies from Cheshire & the West Riding' as well as Lancashire, four 'missionaries' were appointed – two to travel through the Potteries to Birmingham, two to hold meetings in Yorkshire. It was even resolved that 'all the petitioning Bodies in all the United Kingdom should send . . . one or more deputies to Manchester . . . to assist in bringing forth all the strength of the Unions into one point of view'.[2]

Thus there was a very remarkable growth of provincial Hampden Clubs or Union societies in the last months of 1816;[3] and within weeks of their formation these clubs were pressing outwards for regional and national contacts which were illegal under the Seditious Societies Act. At one time it seemed that Manchester might assume the national leadership. In the event, however, it was Cartwright and the London Hampden Club which called a Convention of deputies from clubs which met at the end of January 1817 at the 'Crown and Anchor' tavern. This meeting, attended by seventy delegates attempted to steer a way around the Act by meeting in public session and by claiming to represent 'persons who may be deputed from petitioning cities, towns, and other communities to confer together . . . on the best means of effecting a constitutional reform'. Its proceedings were not interrupted by the authorities; and when this is contrasted with the treatment of the 'British Convention' at Edinburgh in 1793, this indicated a slight advance. But the meeting also emphasized the incoherence of the national movement.

1. H. W. C. Davis, *The Age of Grey and Peel*, p. 181.

2. H. W. C. Davis, *Lancashire Reformers*, pp. 27–8.

3. Apart from Lancashire and Leicestershire, the main centres of Hampden Clubs were Nottinghamshire, Derbyshire, Birmingham, Norwich, and parts of the West Riding.

The immediate background to the meeting was the growing popular influence of Cobbett, and the great Spa Fields meetings of November and December 1816, addressed by Henry Hunt. Bamford's account is well known:

At this time the writings of William Cobbett suddenly became of great authority; they were read on nearly every cottage hearth in the manufacturing districts of South Lancashire, in those of Leicester, Derby, and Nottingham; also in many of the Scottish manufacturing towns. ... He directed his readers to the true cause of their sufferings – misgovernment; and to its proper corrective – parliamentary reform. Riots soon became scarce. ... Hampden clubs were now established. ... The Labourers ... became deliberate and systematic in their proceedings ...[1]

'The existence of any political knowledge, or fixed political principles, amongst the poor in this neighbourhood, is of very recent date,' wrote a Manchester reformer in 1820, who also attributed the change to 'Mr Cobbett's masterly essays, upon the financial situation of the country, and the effects of taxation, in reducing the comforts of the labourer':

The cheapness of these publications ensured them a most extensive circulation; and the strong, clear, condensed, and argumentative style of the writer, was happily adapted to suit the capacity of the most numerous class of his readers ..[2]

For several years Cobbett's *Political Register*, priced at 1s. 0½d. owing to the heavy stamp duties, had been gaining circulation in the north.[3] The decisive change came as late as November 1816, when Cobbett, finding a loophole in the stamp regulations, commenced publishing his leading article separately at 2d. as a *Weekly Political Pamphlet* ('Twopenny Trash'). The first pamphlet was his famous 'Address to the Journeymen and Labourers':

Friends and Fellow Countrymen,
    Whatever the Pride of rank, or riches or of scholarship may have induced some men to believe ... the real strength and all the

1. Bamford, op. cit., pp. 11–12.
2. [J. E. Taylor], *Notes and Observations .. on the Papers relative to the Internal State of the Country* (1820).
3. See T. A. Ward, op. cit., p. 163 for references as early as 1810 to 'the club which takes in Cobbett's Register', 'Cobbett's Club', in Sheffield.

resources of a country, ever have sprung and ever must spring, from the *labour* of its people. ... Elegant dresses, superb furniture, stately buildings, fine roads and canals, fleet horses and carriages, numerous and stout ships, warehouses teeming with goods; all these ... are so many marks of national wealth and resources. But all these spring from *labour*. Without the Journeymen and the labourers none of them could exist ...

'The insolent hirelings call you the *mob*, the *rabble*, the *scum*, the *swinish multitude*, and say, that your voice is nothing; that you have no business at public meetings ...' Cobbett demonstrated, in simple terms, the burden upon the people of indirect taxation; the heavy expenditure upon '*Sinecure Placemen* and *Pensioners*'; the constitutional connexion between taxation and representation. He attacked the Malthusian argument that the sufferings of the poor were caused by their early marriages and excessive fertility ('So then, a young man, arm-in-arm with a rosy-cheeked girl, must be a spectacle of evil omen!'), and the argument that the only remedy for unemployment was emigration: 'you who help to maintain them by the taxes which you pay, have as good a right to remain in the country as they have! You have fathers and mothers and sisters and brothers and children and friends as well as they...' The only true remedy was a reformed parliament: 'We must have *that first*, or we shall have nothing good.'

I exhort you to proceed in a peaceable and lawful manner, but at the same time, to proceed with zeal and resolution in the attainment of this object. If the *Skulkers* will not join you, if the 'decent fireside' gentry still keep aloof, proceed by yourselves. Any man can draw up a petition, and any man can carry it up to London ...[1]

Forty-four thousand of the Address were sold by the end of November 1816 – 'Let Corruption *rub that out* if she can.' A sale of 200,000 was claimed for it by the end of 1817.[2] No writing had obtained such popular influence since the *Rights of Man*; and it was followed by weekly pamphlets, in the form of

1. The greater part of this Address is reproduced in G. D. H. and M. Cole, *The Opinions of William Cobbett* (1944), pp. 207–17.

2. See W. H. Wickwar, *The Struggle for the Freedom of the Press, 1819–1832* (1928), pp. 52–4.

open letters – to 'The Good and True Men of Hampshire', to 'All True-Hearted Englishmen', or to individual statesmen – each with an extensive circulation. But Cobbett held back from any step which would give the reform movement organized expression; and, while the Hampden Clubs were fostered by his writing, this was not his intention. The great London reform demonstrations, of 15 November, 2 December and 10 December 1816, at Spa Fields, were convened on the initiative of a committee in which the 'Spenceans' (Dr Watson, Thistlewood, Preston, Hooper) were most influential. Cobbett, indeed, refused an invitation to speak at the first, and the main orator at all three meetings was Henry Hunt.

Hunt was a wealthy gentleman-farmer, who had been a reformer of Cobbett's disposition for ten years and had first won national prominence when he fought an impressive campaign as a Radical in a Bristol election in 1812. Bamford's description of him – as he remembered him in 1817 – is of a handsome man, 'gentlemanly in his manner and attire, six feet and better in height':

His lips were delicately thin and receding. ... His eyes were blue or light grey – not very clear nor quick, but rather heavy; except as I afterwards had opportunities for observing, when he was excited in speaking; at which times they seemed to distend and protrude; and if he worked himself furious ... they became blood-streaked, and almost started from their sockets. Then it was that the expression of his lip was to be observed – the kind smile was exchanged for the curl of scorn, or the curse of indignation. His voice was bellowing; his face swollen and flushed; his griped hand beat as if it were to pulverise; and his whole manner gave token of a painful energy, struggling for utterance.

Hunt's vanity assorted ill with the equally large self-esteem of the Middleton weaver, and Bamford's final judgement upon Hunt was harsh. But Bamford also made an important qualification: Hunt 'was constantly ... placing himself in most arduous situations. ... He was always beating against a tempest of his own or of others' creating. He had thus more to sustain than any other man of his day and station, and should be judged accordingly.'[1] This is true. From the close of the war

1. Bamford, op. cit., pp. 19–20.

until the passage of the Reform Bill, with the exception of several years in the mid-1820s, Hunt was the foremost public orator of the reform movement. He spoke at Spa Fields in 1816. He continued his activity during the suspension of Habeas Corpus in 1817, when Cobbett thought it more politic to retire to America. He was the main speaker at Peterloo, and was imprisoned for his part in the meeting. He was elected to Parliament for the 'scot and lot' constituency of Preston in 1830 and was the solitary champion of the working-class reform movement in the unreformed House of Commons. From 1830 to 1832 he remained loyal to the demand for manhood suffrage, and attacked the 1832 Bill as a betrayal of the plebeian reformers. His very consistency and pugnacity made him a centre of controversy and a target for abuse.

The abuse, however, was not groundless, for Hunt possessed both the qualities and the defects of the demagogue. These characteristics are to be found in a score of leaders of this period so that we must consider them as characteristic of the movement of the time. There was, first, the old Wilkesite tradition, only gradually breaking down, by which even the democratic movement looked to the aristocratic or gentlemanly leader. Only the gentleman – Burdett, Cochrane, Hunt, Feargus O'Connor – knew the forms and language of high politics, could cut a brave figure on the hustings, or belabour the Ministers in their own tongue. The reform movement might use the rhetoric of equality, but many of the old responses of deference were still there even among the huzzaing crowds. Whenever a working man appeared to be rising 'above himself' even in the reform movement he quickly drew the jealousy of many of his own class. Next, there was that demagogic element, inevitable in a popular movement excluded from power or hope of power, which encouraged the wholly unconstructive rhetoric of denunciation. Alongside its martyrs and its intrepid voluntary organizers, the Radical movement had its share of drunkards, runaway Treasurers and ephemeral quarrelsome journalists – and these were not the least bombastic and flamboyant in their language. The very frustrations of a popular movement, in which thousands of powerless men were pitted against an armed Establishment, were released in hyperbole; and Hunt, as the orator at the great reform assemblies, knew how to touch these responses. His style of oratory was given to him by the frustrations of those whom he addressed.

But many other factors contributed to the elevation of the demagogue. At the national level, Radicalism never knew the self-discipline of political organization. Since any party or corresponding centre was illegal, and since no elected executive determined policy and strategy, leadership inevitably fell to individual orators and journalists. Genuine disagreements upon matters of policy spilled over into personal jealousies; and, equally, the leader whose policy was endorsed by popular acclaim found in this food for his personal vanity. The conditions of agitation fostered the personalization of issues. The great mass meeting demanded its colourful figurehead. Hunt, in his white top hat, liked to be known as the 'Champion of Liberty' or (during his imprisonment after Peterloo) as 'Saint Henry of Ilchester', just as Oastler subsequently described himself as 'King of the Factory Children' and O'Connor as 'The Lion of Freedom'.

Moreover, popular Radicalism and Chartism lived, for half a century, with the dilemma which beset Thelwall, Gale Jones, and the Jacobin 'tribunes' of the 1790s. The conflict between 'moral' and 'physical' force reformers is sometimes expressed too dogmatically, as if a clear line can be drawn between determined conspirators like Dr Watson and Thistlewood, on the one hand, and immaculate constitutionalists like Place or Bamford,[1] on the other. In fact, both Radicalism and Chartism inhabited a region somewhere between these two extremes. Few reformers before 1839 engaged in serious preparations for insurrection; but fewer still were willing to disavow altogether the ultimate right of the people to resort to rebellion in the face of tyranny. The Chartist slogan, 'Peaceably if we may, forcibly if we must', expresses also the common notion held

---

1. While Bamford presents himself as a sober constitutional reformer in his *Passages in the Life of a Radical*, written in 1839, there are many indications that the author (who had moved so far from his own agitational past that he was willing to serve as a special constable against the Chartists) took pains to cover over his own connexions with the conspiratorial side of the movement.

by the Radicals of 1816–20 and 1830–32. Major Cartwright insisted on the citizen's right to carry arms. Henry White the editor of the moderate *Independent Whig*, was only one among many Radical journalists who reminded readers of the precedent of the Glorious Revolution of 1688:

It is to a *Revolution* they owe every portion of civil and religious Liberty they are yet permitted to enjoy, and ... it is to a *Revolution* they will be ultimately compelled to resort, if all other legal means be denied of obtaining a Redress of Grievances ...[1]

The name of the Hampden Clubs recalled an even more drastic precedent, and Cobbett was at pains to stress that Revolution was good Whig doctrine. The right to resist oppression by force (he wrote) 'is distinctly claimed and established by the laws and usages of England':

I do not say, that the right ought to be now exercised at all. ... I say, therefore, upon this point, what JUDGE BLACKSTONE says: and that is, that the right to resist oppression always exists, but *that those who compose the nation at any given time must be left to judge for themselves when oppression has arrived at a pitch to justify the exercise of such right.*

More than this, Cobbett was willing to come forward with a defence of the Pentridge Rising: 'What did Brandreth do more than was done by the Whigs at the Revolution?'[2]

Cobbett deliberately pitched upon this ambiguity: the people had the right to rebel, but only if oppression passed a certain undefined point. Wooler adopted the same stance in the *Black Dwarf*: 'the *right* of the people to resist *oppression always exists*, and ... the *requisite power* to do this always resides in the *general will* of the people'.[3] Carlile, in the *Republican*, went further after Peterloo, and advocated tyrannicide.[4] Every popular Radical journal and orator made some reference, oblique or direct, to the right of rebellion. It was part of the essential rhetoric of a movement, which had almost no access to legal redress through the franchise, to hint, warn,

1. *Independent Whig*, 27 July 1817.
2. *Political Register*, 4 April, 6 and 20 June, 26 December 1818.
3. *Black Dwarf*, 30 December, 1818.
4. See below, p. 840. Also Sherwin's *Political Register*, 23 May 1818.

or bluster about the ultimate recourse of the people to physical force. When Henry Hunt addressed the first great Spa Fields meeting (15 November 1816) he went no further than a score of other orators:

He knew the superiority of mental over physical force; nor would he counsel any resort to the latter till the former had been found ineffectual. Before physical force was applied to, it was their duty to petition, to remonstrate, to call aloud for timely reformation. Those who resisted the just demands of the people were the real friends of confusion and bloodshed ... but if the fatal day should be destined to arrive, he assured them that if he knew anything of himself, he would not be found concealed behind a counter, or sheltering himself in the rear.[1]

Such references as these, to the 'fatal day', or 'the day of reckoning', drew the loudest huzzas of the crowds. Nor should we gloss over the vices attendant upon such a style. It fostered also the tap-room demagogue whose Radicalism had more froth than body; and even the paid itinerant orators (whom Bamford so much deprecated) 'who made a trade of speechifying' and who vied with each other for the acclamation of the crowd by indulging in 'the wildest and most extravagant rhodomontade'.[2] The national leaders Cobbett and Wooler with their pens, Hunt with his voice – were adept at pitching their rhetoric just on the right side of treason; but they laid themselves open (as did Oastler and O'Connor after them) to the charge of encouraging other men to take illegal or treasonable actions, from the consequences of which they themselves escaped.

This was one source of quarrels among the Radical leadership. Another perpetual source of strife was money-matters. It was an expensive business being a Radical leader, as both Cobbett and Hunt had reason to know. In addition to speech-making, publications, travelling and correspondence, there were heavy expenses incurred for legal defence or during electoral contests. Cobbett and, more especially, Hunt were extravagant in their tastes – Cobbett in his farming ventures, Hunt in his general style of living. Both were careless in their financial dealings. The incoherent Radical movement, with no elected

1. *Examiner*, 16 November 1816.
2. Bamford, op. cit., p. 36.

executive, and no accredited Treasurer, was perpetually subjected to appeals from *ad hoc* committees to assist with funds
for this or that emergency. Cobbett recouped his losses by his
publishing profits, while Hunt sought to turn propaganda to
his advantage by selling 'radical breakfast powder' (a con-
coction based on roasted corn which was sold as a substitute
for tea or coffee, and which was recommended to Radical, as
a means of boycotting taxed articles). No clear line was drawn
between their private business concerns and the finances of the
movement. Questions as to the use or trusteeship of Radical
funds, or the confusion of public and private interests became
– as they were to become for O'Connor and Ernest Jones –
subjects of humiliating public recrimination.[1]

But the greatest cause of Radical disagreement was sheer
vanity. And vanity was so common a disorder among the
Radical leaders that it appears less as a cause of disagreement
than as a symptom of the general lack of coherent organization.
Nearly all the reform leaders were quick to impugn the motives
of their fellows at the first sign of disagreement. Suspicions
were fed by the disclosure of the parts played by the *provocateurs*, Castle, Oliver and Edwards. From 1817 the air became thick with the rancour of men accusing each other of
being 'spies'.

In default of democratic political organization, Radical
politics were personalized. The movement after 1816 had many
of the virtues of the movement of the 1790s; but not those of
égalité. Cobbett had set a fashion, for which it is scarcely
just to criticize him. The emergence of an independent Radical
press after the Wars was in great degree his personal triumph.
His own account of this achievement (written in 1817 and 1819)
is close to the truth:

Many years ago ... I set out as a sort of *self-dependent politician.*
My opinions were my own. I dashed at all prejudices. I scorned to

1. For example, after Peterloo Hunt was engaged in a long public
wrangle with his fellow reformer, Joseph Johnson of Manchester, in
which the cost of mutual exchanges of hospitality, laundry bills, the
amount of oats fed to Hunt's horse, and the tip given (or not given) to
a chamber-maid at an inn were all exposed to view. See J. Johnson, *A
Letter to Henry Hunt* (Manchester, 1822).

follow any body in matters of opinion. Before my time, every writer of talent enlisted himself under the banners of one party, or one minister, or other. I stood free from all such connexions. ... So that, for many years, I have been an object of hatred with men in power, with men aiming at power ...

By the end of the Wars he had become (in Hazlitt's description) 'a kind of *fourth estate* in the politics of the country', and 'unquestionably the most powerful political writer of the present day'. 'The Reformers read him when he was a Tory, and the Tories read him now that is a Reformer.' Successive acts to raise the tax on newspapers and periodicals, and to tighten the law of seditious libel, were aimed in large part at Cobbett himself. 'There is nothing savouring of *egotism* in my saying this,' Cobbett avowed; and his conclusions are characteristically personal:

That man cannot be guilty of egotism, to check the progress of whose writings a total revolution has been made in the laws of a great kingdom. Such a man necessarily becomes a great subject of discussion and of record; all his actions, his manners, the habits of his life, and almost the size of his body and the colour of his hair, become, with the people of that kingdom, objects of some interest.

Cobbett's favourite subject, indeed, was William Cobbett of Botley. Page after page of his *Register* is filled with his affairs, self-justifications, arguments, feelings chance impressions and encounters. The cause of reform was personalized into the encounter between William Cobbett and Old Corruption. Castlereagh, 'Bolton Fletcher', Wilberforce, Malthus, Brougham, Burdett, were – or became – his *personal* enemies. Fellow reformers moved uneasily within the fickle warmth of his personal approbation; 'he quarrels with his own creatures', Hazlitt noted with some justice, 'as soon as he has written them into a little vogue – and a prison'.

We have to accept Cobbett's vices as the dark side of his genius, a genius which enabled him to exert more influence, week after week for thirty years, than any journalist in English history. It is when these vices are found without his genius that they appear less amiable. For Cobbett set a style which, inevitably, his colleagues and competitors sought to imitate: Hunt, in his *Memoirs*, published in instalments from Ilchester gaol,

Carlile in the *Republican*, and a dozen lesser men. The years between the close of the Wars and the Reform Bill were the age of the 'self-dependent politician'. Every Radical was a political protestant; every leader avowed himself to be an individualist, owing deference to no authority but that of his own judgement and conscience. 'A Reformer,' wrote Hazlitt in 1819, 'is governed habitually by a spirit of contradiction.'

He is a bad tool to work with; a part of a machine that never fits its place; he cannot be trained to discipline, for ... the first principle of his mind is the supremacy of conscience, and the independent right of private judgement. ... His understanding must be satisfied in the first place, or he will not budge an inch; he cannot for the world give up a principle to a party. He would rather have slavery than liberty, unless it is a liberty precisely after his own fashion ...

One reform leader (Hazlitt continued) 'quarrels with all those who are labouring at the same oar ... and thinks he has done a good piece service to the cause, because he has glutted his own ill-humour and self-will, which he mistakes for the love of liberty and the zeal for truth!'

Others ... get into committees ... set up for the heads of a party, in opposition to another party; abuse, vilify, expose, betray, counteract and undermine each other in every way, and throw the game into the hands of the common enemy ...[1]

The virtues of this intractable individualism can be seen in Carlile's long contest with authority.[2] But, whether in Hunt or in Carlile, the vices were offensive, and were thoroughly damaging to the reform movement. From the surging unrest of the people, the vanity of great or petty leaders rose like vapour. Place saw everyone except himself and a few Benthamites as fools who must be manipulated. Bamford exemplifies the complacent self-esteem of the autodidact; his principles were proof against persecution, but were not proof against a kind word from Lord Sidmouth or a compliment from a gentleman upon his verses. Carlile was the ultimate individualist, so confident of his own judgement that he repudiated the very notion

1. W. Hazlitt, Preface to *Political Essays* (1819), *Works*, VII, pp. 13–17.
2. See below, pp. 838–44.

of political consultation or organization. Hunt (if we are to believe only a part of the charges brought against him by colleagues like Bamford and Johnson) was at times contemptible in his vanity. On one occasion, Hunt and his co-defendants after Peterloo made a public progress, while awaiting trial, through the Lancashire cotton towns. 'I was amused,' recalled Bamford, 'as well as a little humiliated, by what was continually occurring near me':

Hunt sat on the box-seat. . . . Moorhouse stood on the roof of the coach, holding by a rope which was fastened to the irons at each side. He had kept that position all the way from Bolton. . . . Hunt continually doffed his hat, waved it lowly, bowed gracefully, and now and then spoke a few words to the people; but if some five or ten minutes elapsed without a huzza or two, or the still more pleasing sound, 'Hunt for Ever.' . . . he would rise from his seat, turn round, and, cursing poor Moorhouse in limbs, soul, or eyes, he would say, 'Why don't you shout man? Why don't you shout? Give them the hip, — you, don't you see they're fagging?' [1]

We have to remember, when we consider Hunt or Burdett or Oastler or O'Connor, that their progresses resembled those of the most popular Royalty, and their appearances those of a *prima donna*. Hunt was received in one Lancashire village in 1819 with the road carpeted with flowers. To the slogans – 'Burdett and No Bastille!', 'Hunt and Liberty!' – there were added the songs:

> With Henry Hunt we'll go, we'll go,
> With Henry Hunt we'll go;
> We'll raise the cap of liberty,
> In spite of Nadin Joe. [2]

At the Manchester Radical Sunday school, the monitors wore locket-portraits of Hunt around their necks in place of crucifixes. [3] No meeting was complete unless the horses had been unharnessed from the carriage of the main speaker, and he had been drawn in triumph by the people through the streets. The great demonstrations had a ritualistic character, in which the speaker moved through declamations and rhetorical questions,

1. Loc. cit., p. 200.
2. J. Harland, *Ballads and Songs of Lancashire*, p. 262.
3. D. Read, *Peterloo* (Manchester, 1957), p. 54.

playing for the expected tumultuous responses.[1] The charismatic orators were those with a taste for self-dramatization. The roar of approbation from the throats of 20,000 people would have inflated the self-esteem of most men. As vanity grew, so the orators became addicted to the sight and sound of the throng cheering below the hustings. 'His appetite,' Prentice noted of Hunt, 'grew with what it fed on.' He became jealous of rivalry, constantly on the look-out for opportunities to strike a dramatic pose, and careless and off-hand with his less important colleagues, who in their turn found their vanity bruised by popular neglect – why not 'Johnson and Liberty!' or 'Bamford and Liberty!'?

The demagogue is a bad or ineffectual leader. Hunt voiced, not principle nor even well-formulated Radical strategy, but the emotions of the movement. Striving always to say whatever would provoke the loudest cheer, he was not the leader but the captive of the least stable portion of the crowd. According to Place,

Hunt says his mode of acting is to dash at good points, and to care for no one; that he will mix with no committee, or any party ; he will act by himself; that he does not intend to affront anyone, but cares not who is offended.

But Place also wrote (in a letter to Hobhouse) in more generous terms of Hunt, after his triumphal reception in London at the summit of his popularity after Peterloo:

Aye, and he deserved it [i.e. London's welcome] too, and more than he got. If the people – I mean the working people – are to have but one man, they will, as they ought, support that man at least with their shouts. And there are very many cases too in which they would fight with him, or for him. Whose fault is it that no better man goes among the people? Not theirs; they will cling to the best man that makes common cause with them. I remember how I felt when I was a working man. ... If none shows himself but Hunt, Hunt must be their man.[2]

1. For example, Saxton at Rochdale: 'the whole country has only to be *united ... and demand* their rights as MEN determined to be free, or die nobly in the struggle. – (*Great applause*)' Sherwin's *Weekly Political Register*, 7 August 1819.

2. Wallas, op. cit., pp. 120, 146.

III. THE HAMPDEN CLUBS

We cannot understand the extraordinary untidiness of post-war Radicalism unless these problems of personality and leadership are borne in mind. It was the heroic age of popular Radicalism, but, on the national scene, its leaders rarely looked heroic and sometimes looked ridiculous. From 1815 until the Chartist years, the movement always appeared most vigorous, consistent, and healthy at the base, and especially in such provincial centres as Barnsley and Halifax, Loughborough and Rochdale. Its true heroes were the local booksellers and news-vendors, trade union organizers, secretaries and local speakers for the Hampden Clubs and Political Unions – men who did not expect to become honoured life-pensioners of the move-ment as a reward for imprisonment, and who, in many cases, were too obscure to do more than leave a few records of their activity in the local press or the Home Office papers. These men provided the platform without which their disputatious, protestant leaders would have been impotent; and they often watched the quarrels among the leadership with dismay.

The confusion of the events of the winter and spring, 1816–17, illustrates these problems of a growing national move-ment which had failed to find a national centre. The meeting of delegates from the local Hampden Clubs at the 'Crown and Anchor' (January 1817) was convened on the initiative of Major Cartwright; and it was the culmination of a national campaign of petitioning, in which petitions for Reform (the majority in favour of Annual Parliaments, Universal Manhood Suffrage, and Vote by Ballot) were presented with a total variously estimated at between half a million and one and a half million signatures.

But between the time when Cartwright had sent out his circular letter calling the meeting (September 1816) and the meeting itself, there had been the riots connected with the second great Spa Fields meeting of 2 December. The origin and significance of these riots remains obscure. As early as March 1816 there appears to have been some kind of ultra-Jacobin agitation in London, directed at the debtors' jails. The

authorities intercepted a letter addressed to 'Our Fellow Countrymen suffering Incarceration', purporting to come from 'The
Tri-Coloured Committee', and announcing the intention of
raising the 'tri-coloured standard' on 2 March. On that day
'the prison doors will be opened, ... [and] your lofty *Bastiles*
be reduced to Ashes':

It is requested you will make known our Plans to every Prison in
London – *Bench, Fleet, Marshalsea, Horsemonger Lane* &c that you
may *all act* at the same time.[1]

Nor is such an agitation altogether unlikely. The little
masters of London and Birmingham, who had been working
on war contracts, were some of the worst sufferers in the post-
war depression. There had been many failures. During the war
many of these small masters had been doing sub-contract work
for large agents, who took the larger share of the profit. They
now saw the middlemen comfortably established, as a result of
their labours, while they were left supporting the burden of
taxation and of poor relief in the worst-hit districts.[2] Such
experiences impelled them towards an extreme Radicalism for
which they had been long prepared by the propaganda of the
L.C.S. and of successive Westminster elections. If the debtor's
jails were places where spies might, on occasion, be recruited,
they were also to a more important extent, finishing-schools for
Radicals, where the victims who languished under the punitive
rigours of the laws of debt were able to read, to argue, and to
enlarge their acquaintance.[3]

1. T.S. 11.203; H.O. 40.7/8.
2. This was a standing grievance of the small masters and artisans
assessed for poor rate in the East End. Thus (in the 1790s) in bad years
the poor rate was from 5s. to 10s. in the £ in Spitalfields and Mile End,
but only 2s. to 2s. 6d. in the West End. See A Magistrate, *An Account
of a Meat and Soup Charity in the Metropolis* (1797); W. Hale, *Letter
to S. Whitbread on the Distresses of the Poor in Spitalfields* (1806); T. F.
Buxton, *The Distress in Spitalfields* (1816); *Trades Newspaper*, 15 October 1826.
3. Although Acts of Insolvency were passed in 1797 and 1801, these
did not relieve small debtors, who were forced to remain imprisoned
while the charges for their own detention added to their debts. See J.
Neild, *Account of the Society for the Relief of Small Debtors* (1802), pp.
301, 335–7. The Home Office papers for 1816 and 1817 contain many
piteous petitions from debtors.

Nothing came of the threats of March 1816. But the theme of an attack on the prison recurs in the Spa Fields affair of December. We have to pick our way through at least three contradictory accounts of this event: that presented by the Prosecution at the subsequent trial of Dr James Watson: that offered by Henry Hunt in his 'Memoirs' in 1822: and that presented by the Defence or by Watson himself. None of these accounts is reliable. The Crown's case rested largely on the evidence of an accomplice who had turned *provocateur*, John Castle: he proved to be a thoroughly disreputable witness, a perjurer and the protector of a brothel 'madam'.[1] Hunt, writing from Ilchester Gaol in the aftermath of the Cato Street Conspiracy – and after he had himself quarrelled decisively with Watson – was interested in offering a version which minimized his own participation; while Watson, in a polemic with Hunt in the press in the autumn of 1819, refused to disclose his side of the story, on the grounds that the time was not yet opportune.

The true story may perhaps be this. The autumn of 1816 was a period of extreme misery and post-war unemployment, affecting equally Lancashire, Yorkshire, the Birmingham trades and London. In the metropolis there was a simultaneous depression of two staple industries – the watch and clock trade, and the silk industry. In Spitalfields alone, it was alleged, there were 45,000 in want of food, and clamouring to enter the workhouses, in November.[2] At the same time London was thronged with discharged soldiers and sailors. But it became abundantly clear that the Westminster Committee was dragging its feet, and refusing to attempt any agitation among the London masses. Apart from the Westminster hustings at election-time (and City elections, when great throngs gathered before the Guildhall), no wholly 'unlimited' demonstration of a Radical character had been called in London since 1795. A small ultra-Jacobin (or 'Spencean') committee was therefore formed, whose most active members were Watson and his son, Preston, Thistlewood, Hooper and Castle, the spy. This

1. See above, pp. 534, 538.
2. See especially the *People*, 19 April 1817; T. F. Buxton, *The Distress in Spitalfields* (1816).

committee issued a call for a demonstration in Spa Fields on 15 November 1816, and approached a number of leading Radicals with invitations to attend. Cobbett kept his distance, and only Hunt agreed to speak. Hunt met the organizers only on the eve of the meeting, when he substituted more moderate resolutions for those which the committee had proposed. At the meeting itself, inadequate arrangements had been made even for a proper hustings; but an enormous gathering presented itself, quite beyond the expectations of the organizers, which Hunt addressed from a window overlooking the fields.

The meeting was 'adjourned' until 2 December. In Hunt's account, the organizers were cock-a-hoop at their success, accompanying him back to his inn, engaging in a good deal of revolutionary bluster over dinner, at which none other than Castle proposed the toast: 'May the last of Kings be strangled with the guts of the last priest.' (Watson and Thistlewood waited upon Hunt the next day, and apologized for Castle's behaviour!) At about the same time, some 'committee of trades' was formed in the metropolis, with which Preston was actively associated, and of which yet another spy (T. Thomas) succeeded in being elected as Chairman. According to Thomas, Preston was meeting with success in organizing the Spitalfields weavers; in private conversation he was speaking of doing away with all landowners and fund holders, and was mooting a rising in which the Bank, the Tower and prisons were to be attacked. Castle eagerly seconded these proposals, and actually placed a few arms in a cart which was taken to Spa Fields on 2 December. The crowd at this meeting was even greater than that at the former one, and it included many soldiers and sailors. The rumour had got abroad that 'something' was going to 'happen' at the meeting, and the rumour had even travelled as far as the north of England.[1] In Preston's view the Army was on the edge of mutiny, not only because of the grievances of the soldiers but also because of general

---

1. In Manchester on 3 December expectant groups of delegates from the surrounding Hampden Clubs awaited the coming of the London mail. There were similar expectations in Sheffield.

sympathy with the people.[1] One of the banners displayed at Spa Fields declared: 'The brave soldiers are our friends, treat them kindly.'

'... the wants of the Belly creates a fever of the Brain ...' So ran a fragment of a handbill, drafted for use among the troops, allegedly found in Dr Watson's home after the Spa Fields affair. But the most notable fever of the brain, on 2 December, would appear to have been, not that of the soldiers, but that of Dr Watson's son. Both Watsons (Preston said) had been drinking before the meeting, and young Watson had drunk immoderately. Arriving early at the hustings, he harangued a part of the crowd, many of whose members (like Cashman) would appear to have been as drunk as himself. Then, leaping off the cart, he plunged into the crowd and led a contingent in the direction of the Tower. Other fragments surged off in different directions. Several gunsmith's shops were looted. Some of the rioters reached the Tower, and a man (perhaps Preston or Thistlewood) climbed on the wall and called upon the troops to join the people. In the Minories there was rioting for several hours, on a scale reminiscent of the Gordon Riots, complete with a man (whose identity was unknown both to the authorities and to the conspirators) who led the mob on horseback. The Government, forewarned of some attempted outbreak, had taken precautions, and Hunt was surprised to see 'great numbers of constables and police officers' stationed in front of Cold Bath Fields prison. But the riots never involved more than a portion of the great crowd. The greater part remained to hear Hunt's address,[2] and then dispersed peacefully, after agreeing once again to 'adjourn' the meeting until 9 December.

This third Spa Fields meeting was, in fact, held, with an

1. Preston declared: 'their situation is more comfortable than the mechanic – but the miserable state of their friends and relatives weigh on their minds'. (T.S. 11.203.) The troops had, in fact, shown a marked lack of ardour when called out against the Corn Law riots of 1815: Hammonds, *The Town Labourer*, p. 86.

2. Dr Watson also claimed that he had remained behind and had attempted to pacify the crowd. See *Independent Whig*, 3 August 1817.

attendance even greater than before.[1] It is not easy to select any explanation which accords with all these confused events. The riots were not a simple drunken outbreak, nor a carefully planned provocation, nor yet a definite attempt to simulate the fall of the Bastille, but they partook in some degree of all three. Dr Watson may perhaps have looked no further than to the effect of the demonstration itself. But it is equally possible that Thistlewood and young Watson (abetted by Castle) had some sketchy notion of sparking off a 'spontaneous' riot which would open the way to a popular *coup d'état*. Young Watson went into hiding, and some months later was smuggled on to a ship bound for America from the Thames, disguised as a Quaker, and with his face disfigured with caustic.[2] Hunt certainly had no part in any insurrectionary conspiracy; but, equally, he was willing to come forward as a witness for the Defence at Dr Watson's trial, and to testify as to his moderating influence,[3] and he continued to work closely with the Doctor for a further two years.

Place called the Spa Fields rioters 'a contemptible set of fools and miscreants'. But there is no reason to suppose that the majority of Londoners saw them in that light. If they suffered from an amateurish and attitudinizing leadership, this was in part the consequence of the failure of the Westminster Committee to stand true to its former Jacobin principles. But the Spa Fields affair had at least three serious consequences. First, it afforded the authorities the pretext they required for acting against the reformers. Second, at the very outset of the post-war agitation it frightened moderate middle-class reformers away from the popular Radical movement.[4] Third, it

1. Further attempts to hold demonstrations in Spa Fields in February and March 1817 (after the Two Acts and the suspension of Habeas Corpus) were unsuccessful. The account above is derived, in the main, from W. M. Gurney, *Trial of James Watson* (1817), esp. I, pp. 45–51, 56–61, 73, 531, II, p. 190; *Memoirs of H. Hunt* (1822), III, pp. 329, 344, 369–72, 447; examination of Preston by the Lord Mayor, 4 and 5 December 1816, in T.S. 11.203; T. Thomas to Sir N. Conant, 9 and 27 November 1816, in H.O. 40.4; papers in H.O. 40.3 and 7; *D.N.B.*

2. *Independent Whig*, 27 July, 12 October 1817.

3. Hunt also took the Chair at a dinner held in celebration of Dr Watson's acquittal on the charge of high treason, ibid., 3 August 1817.

4. See Halévy, op. cit., pp. 18–22.

threw the reformers' leaders into confusion on the eve of the meeting of delegates of the Hampden Clubs. Burdett, who had signed Cartwright's original circular convening the delegate meeting on behalf of the London Hampden Club, absented himself on his Leicester estates, and did not attend at the 'Crown and Anchor'. Cobbett, by his own account, havered until the eve of the meeting; he believed that 'such a Meeting, at such a crisis, would present a most desirable mark for the shafts of Corruption', and that the delegates would be exposed, if not to arrest, at least to the attention of Government spies.[1] He also had a shrewder insight than most reformers into the Government's system of provocation, and into its strategy of splitting the movement by goading extreme Radicals into abortive acts of insurrection. 'They sigh for a PLOT,' he wrote in December 1816: 'Oh, how they sigh! They are working and slaving and fretting and stewing; they are sweating all over; they are absolutely pining and dying for a plot!'[2]

At the last minute Cobbett agreed to attend (as a 'deputy' from Westminster), with Hunt (the deputy from Bristol and Bath). Major Cartwright took the Chair in his imperturbable manner, 'in his long brown surtout and plain brown wig, walking up the room, and seating himself placidly in the head seat'.[3] But the delegates from the vigorous clubs in Lancashire and Leicestershire were dismayed to find the meeting at once plunged into controversy. An attempt was made (with Cobbett's support) to follow the absent Burdett's wishes, and to limit the demands of the reformers to household suffrage. Hunt declared for manhood suffrage, and was supported by provincial delegates. Cobbett then announced himself converted, for typically pragmatic reasons. He had supported household suffrage (he explained) only because he could not see how 'men who had no settled and visible dwelling in the safety of which they were interested ... could be polled with accuracy':

1. *Political Register*, 11 April 1818. See also ibid., 18 April 1818: 'I always told [Burdett] that the effect would be to expose a parcel of defenceless men to the fangs of Corruption.'

2. *Political Register*, 14 December 1816. See also Cole, *Life of Cobbett*, p. 216   3. Bamford, op. cit., p. 20.

I did not see how large crowds of men could be prevented from marching from one parish to another, and thereby voting twice or thrice in the same day, and for five or six different members.

At last 'a very sensible and modest man, whose name I am sorry I have forgotten, and who came from *Middleton* in Lancashire' answered his objections, by pointing out that under the militia laws muster-rolls existed of all male inhabitants in every parish; and that the same means might be used to draw up electoral lists. 'This was enough for me. The thing had never struck me before...'[1]

The 'sensible and modest man from Middleton' was Samuel Bamford, the weaver and – when every criticism has been made – the greatest chronicler of early nineteenth-century Radicalism. Indeed, it is probable that the favourable impression made upon Cobbett by such men as Bamford did more to convert him to the cause of manhood suffrage than the point about the militia lists. The line between householder and manhood suffrage was, in practical terms, the line of demarcation for many years between middle-class and working-class reform movements; and Cobbett's adhesion to the latter was of great importance. But his adhesion by no means solved the problems of organization and of leadership which the Hampden Clubs were facing. Cobbett disliked equally the compromising policies of Burdett and the Westminster 'Rump', and the conspiratorial underground of the London tavern clubs. The alternative course of agitation, to which Cobbett gave formal support, was that proposed by old Major Cartwright. But Cartwright's notions still belonged, in many ways, to the days of Wyvill and the County Associations of small gentlemen reformers. If the gentry failed to come forward, then the Major was happy to associate with artisans or little masters. But he placed his faith still in the old style of activity, the petition and the county meeting. Secret Committees might come and go, suspension might follow upon suspension of Habeas Corpus: Major Cartwright remained at his post, daring the authorities to imprison him, issuing Addresses, looking up antique constitutional precedents (for he still lived in the era of Anglo-Saxon example) and expedients half a shade on the

1. Cobbett's *Weekly Political Pamphlet*, 22 February 1817.

right side of the law. Canning paid hostile tribute to him when he described him as 'the old heart in London from which the veins of sedition in the country are supplied'.[1] But Bamford's tribute is, from the standpoint of a country Radical, more accurate: during the suspension of Habeas Corpus in 1817 (he wrote) 'the worthy old Major remained at his post, brave as a lion, serene as an unconscious child; and also, in the rush and tumult of that time, as little noticed'.[2]

Little more could be asked of him. But in 1817 Cobbett took over Cartwright's outdated notions of organization, adding little except an unlimited confidence in the power of his own writings. To the end of his life he had a lingering fear of Jacobin societies; he was unhappy in any movement which was not subdued to his influence. He exaggerated the power of the written word acting upon 'the public', and belittled the importance of those organizations through which public opinion must be mediated to become effective. Moreover, at the commencement of 1817 he had private as well as public reasons for exercising extreme caution. He had had enough of persecution during his war-time imprisonment. He was in one of his periodic phases of acute financial embarrassment, and he was privately determined to avoid the further attentions of the authorities.

All these factors, both of personality and of ideology, help us to understand why – scarcely a week after the Hampden Club Convention in London at the end of January 1817 – the Radical movement fragmented in confusion. The Convention, in any case, had taken no serious organizational decisions. After a week-end of debate it had broken up, having secured a pledge from Lord Cochrane to present the petitions. On returning from the opening of Parliament on 28 January, the Prince Regent was mobbed and his carriage window broken. The Government at once set in motion the machinery of 'alarm' which it had inherited from Pitt and the events of 1795, and Committees of Secrecy were appointed. While these were sifting the 'Green Bags' with their supposed evidence of treason, a large demonstration of reformers chaired Lord

1. See R. J. White, *Waterloo to Peterloo* (1957), p. 134.
2. Bamford, op. cit., p. 44.

Cochrane to the House of Commons, with a petition (from Bristol) in his arms 'about the size of a tolerable barrel'. The Committee of the House of Lords reported in mid-February, delineating the activities of the Spenceans, the Spa Fields rioters, and the Hampden Clubs in the most lurid terms. It found evidence to prove that:

... a traitorous conspiracy has been formed in the metropolis for the purpose of overthrowing, by means of a general insurrection, the established Government, laws, and Constitution of this kingdom, and of effecting a general plunder and division of property ... and that such designs ... extended widely in some of the most populous and manufacturing districts.[1]

In the last days of February and in March a succession of measures were passed against the reformers, re-enacting in their full severity the repressive legislation of the 1790s. Habeas Corpus was suspended until 1 July 1817.[2] The Seditious Meetings Act (to continue in force until 24 July 1818) was designed to ensure that all reforming 'Societies and Clubs ... should be utterly suppressed and prohibited as unlawful combinations and confederacies'. No meeting might be held of more than fifty persons without prior notice to the magistrates, who were given powers to disperse any such meetings as were (in their own judgement) of a seditious tendency. At the same time, Sidmouth sent out from the Home Office a circular drawing the attention of magistrates to their power to arrest persons suspected of disseminating seditious libel.

At this moment Cobbett defected. His defection was two-fold. First, he chose the moment when the authorities were

1. Report of House of Lords Committee, Hansard, 1817, XXXV, p. 411. Sidmouth could see in the Hampden Clubs only 'Combinations, which, under the Mask of Parliamentary Reform, are aiming at Public Confusion and Revolution'. – Sidmouth to Fitzwilliam, 10 December 1816, Fitzwilliam Papers, F.45 (g).

2. The Habeas Corpus Suspension Act, passed on 4 March 1817, was re-enacted in July, and did not expire until January 1818. Place estimated that by the autumn of 1817 ninety-six people were confined on charges of treason in England, and thirty-seven in Scotland – most of whom were subsequently discharged without trial. Returns for England in H.O. 42.172, however, show only forty-three detainees. For a summary of this phase of repression, see H. Jephson, The Platform, I, pp. 399–434.

moving against the Hampden Clubs to issue his own blanket rejection of *all* reformers' societies:

I advise my countrymen to have nothing to do with any *Political Clubs*, any secret *Cabals*, any *Correspondencies*; but to trust to *individual exertions* and *open meetings*. . . . There are very worthy and zealous men, belonging to such Clubs; but, I shall be very difficult to be made believe, that they are thus employing themselves in the best and most effectual way.

This warning, in mid-February, was followed by an even stronger disclaimer two weeks later: 'I have *always* most earnestly endeavoured to persuade the public that Clubs OF ALL SORTS were of *mischievous tendency* in general, and, *in no possible case*, could be productive of *good*':

I have said . . . that if the object were not to be obtained by the general, free, unpacked, unbiassed, impression and expression of the public mind, it never could be, and never ought to be obtained at all.[1]

This absolute renunciation of popular organization, published in the very week of the suspension of Habeas Corpus, provoked Wooler, in the *Black Dwarf*, to expostulate: 'For heaven's sake, sir, do not thus betray us into the hands of our enemies, by advice that can only produce mischief':

Our enemies are *clubbed* in every direction round us. Do military clubs, and naval clubs, and clubs of borough mongers do no good to the cause of corruption? . . . I have always thought that clubs of every description were the most important means of collecting and condensing that general, free, unpacked, and unbiassed opinion of the public voice, which you say is essential. . . . Sir, you are playing very mischievously with the cause of reform, by thus giving its opponents your sanction to the worst arguments against it. . . . The man who would *divide* the public, in effect *destroys* the public mind.[2]

The end of March saw Cobbett's second defection. Arguing that the Government's repressive legislation was aimed especi-

1. *Weekly Political Pamphlet*, 15 February, 1 March 1817.
2. *Black Dwarf*, 5 March 1817.

ally at himself, he went into voluntary exile in America.[1] A score of other journals sought to fill the gap – notably the *Black Dwarf*, Hone's *Reformists' Register*, and Sherwin's *Political Register* – and, by successfully resisting persecution, threw Cobbett's defection into darker shadow. But his flight brought immediate dismay and demoralization; and in the ensuing confusion no national centre for the reform movement can be seen.

This coincidence of persecution and confusion is the background to the tangled story of the March of the Blanketeers, the Ardwick Conspiracy, and the Pentridge Rising. In many parts of the Midlands and the north the local reform movement was strong. Impressive public meetings had been held in the previous autumn and winter.[2] The political crisis of the early spring coincided with extreme economic distress, unemployment in the textile and iron districts, and soaring prices – all of which continued until the late summer of 1817. In the winter of 1816–17 the habit of political meeting, and of reading and discussion, had spread throughout most of the manufacturing districts. From such centres as Leicester, Manchester, Nottingham, Derby, Sheffield and Birmingham there radiated a network of contacts to reforming groups in the industrial villages. In the larger centres, which provided the focal organization, the reformers usually included a number of artisans and small tradesmen, a few labourers, and several extreme 'Huntites' of the middle class. These gained support, not only in their own urban centre, but also amongst the artisans or hand-workers in the surrounding area. Once the cause of re-

1. Cobbett did not return until the end of 1819. But, after an interval, he resumed publication of the *Register*, commenting at long distance on English events, often five or six months after they had taken place. Thus his comments on the Derby executions (7 November 1817) appeared in the *Register*, 11 April 1818. His comments, however, were generally well-informed, as a result of his correspondence and also of the reports of refugee reformers who came to the United States.

2. For example, reform meetings were held at Nottingham, Bolton, and Sheffield (8,000 in attendance) in September and October 1816, and at Birmingham in January 1817: *Nottingham Review*, 27 September, 4 and 11 October 1816; Langford, *A Century of Birmingham Life*, II, pp. 414–16.

form had struck root in the framework-knitting, pottery, nail-making, or hand-loom weaving village, then local township or village clubs were formed, almost wholly proletarian in character and having the same kind of command over the sympathy of the local community as the Luddite activists.

We have most information as to the movement in Leicestershire and Lancashire. The Leicester club was founded in October 1816. Its President was a dyer and timber merchant, its Vice-President a cobbler, its most active members included a printer, a framesmith, and leaders of the local framework-knitters. In a month's time, its membership (with a penny a week subscription) had grown to over 500. A spy reported on the events of a general meeting at the end of November 1816. More than 200 attended; for more than an hour of the time was spent in drinking, talking, and collecting subscriptions. Then the Chairman of the evening was appointed – William Scott, the framesmith, a veteran Painite of the 1790s. He addressed the meeting, introducing a copy of the Court Calendar and reading out a list of pensioners, to the accompaniment of hisses and commentary from the audience:

Some one said, We are met to get shut of some of these fellows. . . . Another answered, 'Let them die in their garters.' Another said, 'Send them to the Tower.' Another said, 'Wait only *two* years' . . . Standing armies loudly condemned. . . . A man named Riley made a motion that 100 copies of Cobbett's *Register* be purchased every week. . . . It was carried by a show of hands.

On a vote of thanks to the Chairman, Scott responded with a song:

He said it was the same that he was singing when the ruffians broke in at the Three Crowns about eighteen years ago; *Millions be free!* Loud applause. He sung a revolutionary song.

By the end of 1816 more than thirty Hampden Clubs were claimed in Leicestershire towns and villages. There is some suggestion that the spread of the clubs was coincident with the framework-knitters' trade union organization, and more than one alarmed magistrate saw the clubs as an 'attempt to graft Parliamentary Reform upon Luddism'. The authorities viewed

the penetration of political Radicalism into the villages with
the greatest anxiety, alleging that the stockingers 'were solely
impressed with the belief that Revolution was the object, and
were no further interested than to hold themselves in readiness
to fight when necessary'. The immediate cessation of overt
activity by the Leicester Hampden Clubs, on the suspension of
Habeas Corpus, was interpreted by the same authorities (with
good reason) as evidence that the reformers had retreated into
secret forms of organization for which the experiences of
Luddism had prepared them.[1]

In Lancashire the picture is somewhat similar. Manchester
was the great reform metropolis, although other centres –
Oldham, Stockport, Bolton, Rochdale – were large enough to
provide alternative models, and to steady the movement when
the Manchester reformers buried themselves in quarrels. Bamford's reminiscences commence with a roll-call of 'the leading
reformers of Lancashire' at the end of 1816:

These were John Knight, of Manchester, cotton manufacturer;
William Ogden, of Manchester, letter-press printer ... William
Benbow, of Manchester, shoemaker; — Bradbury, of Manchester,
stone cutter; Charles Walker, of Ashton, weaver; Joseph Watson,
of Mossley, clogger; Joseph Ramsden, of Mossley, woollen weaver;
William Nicholson, of Lees, letter-press printer; John Haigh, of
Oldham, silk weaver; Joseph Taylor, of Oldham, hatter; John
Kay, of Royton, cotton manufacturer, William Fitton, of Royton,
student in surgery; Robert Pilkington, of Bury, cotton weaver;
Amos Ogden, of Middleton, silk weaver; Caleb Johnson, of Middleton, cotton weaver; – and Samuel Bamford, of Middleton, silk
weaver. Soon afterwards we were joined by John Johnston, of
Manchester, tailor; and Joseph Mitchell, of Liverpool, draper.[2]

To these we might add other names, of men prominent between 1816 and 1819: John Browe, of Oldham, a journeyman

1. H.O. 40.3; A. T. Patterson, *Radical Leicester*, pp. 107 et. seq.;
H. W. C. Davis, *The Age of Grey and Peel*, pp. 180–83.

2. Bamford, op. cit. (3rd edition, Heywood, n.d.), p. 9. A magistrate's
note in 1816 (H. W. C. Davis, *Lancashire Reformers*, p. 24) describes
Knight as 'a man of no property or character', Kay and Fitton as weavers. Mitchell was a journeyman printer, whose wife had a draper's business.

machine-maker and lay preacher in the Methodist Unitarian Chapel; Bamford's comic friend, Joseph Healey, the barber and 'quack' doctor; John Bagguley, a servant, and Samuel Drummond, of Stockport, the chief organizers of the 'Blanketeers' march; Joseph Johnson, of Manchester, a small brush manufacturer; and the group around the Radical *Manchester Observer*, founded early in 1819, notably Wardle, James Wroe and J. T. Saxton. In addition, the men held on suspicion for complicity in the Ardwick conspiracy included a knife-grinder, a cooper, and a bleacher.

One account of the early months of the Lancashire movement comes from the somewhat unreliable pen of the printer, Joseph Mitchell. Early in 1816 he had been a member of the Liverpool Concentric Society, a largely middle-class society which disgusted him by its refusal to engage in public propaganda:

They would drink, and sing, and smoke, and toast, and pun, and speechify, after a good dinner, and over a bottle, and puff such men as Brougham and the like ... but they would not do one single act towards favouring the people's cause.[1]

Mitchell travelled to south Lancashire in search of work, meeting many 'professing' but inactive reformers, and deciding 'to mix among the people, to spread moral and political information'. He became the first self-appointed political missionary, visiting town after town, and maintaining himself by the sale of Cartwright's pamphlets and his own *Address to the People: or A.B.C. of politics*. Early in November 1816 he visited Cartwright in London, and met Cobbett, who gave him the Lancashire agency of the *Political Register* (a post which he seems to have shared with Benbow). From this point his story merges with that of the Hampden Clubs.[2]

Although there was a handful of small manufacturers and professional men active in the Lancashire movement, these should be clearly distinguished from the small group of active

1. For the Concentric Society, see B. Whittingham-Jones, 'Liverpool's Political Clubs', *Trans. Lancs. & Cheshire Hist. Soc.*, 1959, p. 129.

2. *Blanketteer*, 27 November 1819; *Address to the People* (1816) in H.O. 40.9.

middle-class reformers in Manchester. These had their own press, their distinct Benthamite ideology, and were at pains to distance themselves from the Huntite reformers even on those occasions when they took part in common agitations or (as after Peterloo) rendered important assistance to them.[1] It is curious to note that no cotton-spinner or mill-hand features among the local Radical leadership. There can be little doubt as to the Radical sympathies of the spinners. The Manchester authorities noted in February 1817 that reformers' meetings 'are swelled much in numbers from the moment the Spinning Factories in the neighbourhood leave off working – a proof that the discontent is not confined to those who are distressed, the circumstances of the Spinners being comparatively good. This body have of late contributed out of their funds assistance to the Reformers.'[2] The spinners, who were undergoing reductions in these years, were approaching the first peak of their trade union strength. 1818 was to see the great spinners' strike, and the first impressive attempts to organize a 'General Union of Trades'. During the strike the letters of magistrates to the Home Office contained many complaints as to the influence of Radical agitators like Bagguley and Drummond over the spinners as well as the weavers.[3]

The Lancashire spinners were, thus, at the core of northern trade unionism and, indeed, were pioneering new forms of organization in the national scene. Why did they produce no notable reform leaders? The reasons may be partly of circumstance, and partly political and ideological. The spinners' union was (under the Combination Act) a quasi-legal body. Over the years, the workers had become adept at keeping their effective leaders in the background. They were much more vulnerable than weavers or artisans to victimization by their employers; and the Lancashire mill-owners had a tradition of

1. For the middle-class reformers, see A. Prentice, op. cit., pp. 73–4; D. Read, *Peterloo*, ch. 5.

2. H. W. C. Davis, *Lancashire Reformers*, p. 30.

3. See the Hammonds, *The Skilled Labourer*, ch. 5; Aspinall, *Early English Trade Unions*, ch. 7; Cole, *Attempts at General Union*, ch. 2. For the impressive letter by a cotton-spinner in the *Black Dwarf* in 1818, see pp. 218–21 above.

black-listing political agitators.[1] In this sense, the factory worker was less 'independent' than the weaver, even though the latter might be living on the edge of famine. Moreover, we must remember the long hours worked in the cotton-mills. The way of life described by Bamford, whereby at the peak periods of agitation, the semi-employed weavers and artisans might take time off to tramp many miles to delegate meetings, or to harangue gatherings of reformers, was not open to the adult cotton-spinner.

But it is not difficult to suggest further reasons why the spinners held back from a leading position among the reformers. The Radicalism of Cobbett and of Hunt, with its emphasis upon the values of economic independence, its emotional hostility to the factory system, and its criticism of the present in the light of an ideal past of mutual ties and economic reciprocity, did not speak for the factory workers' predicament. Until the 1820s, when a confluence began to take place between Owenism and trade unionism, it is difficult to point to a Radicalism in key with the experience of those within the cotton-mills; although there is some evidence that groups of spinners here and there preferred the tauter and more utilitarian appeal of Wooler and Carlile to the moralizing of Cobbett's *Register*. Huntite Radicalism had little to say about factory reform, or social questions in general. The main channel for the energy of the factory workers of 1816–20 was within their own trade union organization. Here results were immediate, the issue tangible. Most of the cotton-spinners were Radicals; but the authorities feared no spinners' rising, nor march on London.

To this we may add that Manchester had already some of the weaknesses, as well as strengths, of a metropolis. Its great size, diversity of occupations, spreading slum districts, and the constant passage through it of immigrants, gave to it less of a sense of cohesion than existed in the upland townships. The very large Irish population, while sympathizing with the agitation of 1816–

1. In the early 1800s Lancashire mill-owners were encouraged to dismiss suspected Jacobins (Aspinall, op. cit., p. xxiii). In October 1816 the 'tyrannic Proprietors' sacked workers attending Radical meetings (H.O. 40.9). In the 1830s there was a purge of Owenite factory hands: G. Simmons, *The Working Classes* (1849), p. 70.

20, did not become integrated with the movement. Moreover, if some of the cotton towns (notably Bolton) had zealous loyalist magistrates, many of the smaller ones were almost wholly proletarian in character and were scarcely policed.[1] In Manchester the permanent Deputy Constable, Joseph Nadin, had gained experience in Radical-hunting during the Luddite years. The known Radical leaders were marked and watched, and spies continually infiltrated into the Manchester Constitutional Society or Political Union. In Manchester, in 1817 and 1819, Nadin's men and the reformers' leaders brushed against each other in the streets, and sometimes stayed to exchange banter or threats. William Ogden, arrested in March 1817, testified that 'the notorious J. Nadin ... had for six weeks before declared to me, from time to time, that if I did not discontinue my attendance at the public meetings, he would apprehend me'.[2] 'Theaw'rt a moderate length to begin wi',' Nadin remarked on one occasion, to encourage the morale of one of his prisoners, 'but theaw'll be lunger afore theaw comes back to Reighton: ween ha' thee hang'd.'[3] But the 'country folk' only suffered on rare occasions from his uncouth attentions.

The 'rural patriots', then, were the backbone of the reform movements of these years. They felt this to be so themselves. After an open-air meeting in Manchester at the end of October 1816, an informant returned 'with a herd of the Failsworth reformists':

They vented the bitterest curses & reproaches against the people of Manchester but chiefly against the higher classes. They consoled themselves by ascribing the absence of the Manchester people to the coercion of the Masters. ... Of the number present Informant thinks one half were people from the country.[4]

1. A. T. Patterson makes the same point about Leicestershire, where, at this time, Loughborough had only one resident J.P.; and draws a distinction between the 'physical force' tradition of the villages of north Leicestershire, and (by comparison) the law-abiding reputation of Leicester itself. See 'Luddism, Hampden Clubs, and Trades Unions in Leicestershire', *English Historical Review*, LXIII (1948), p. 172.

2. Cobbett's *Political Register*, 16 May 1818.

3. Bamford (3rd edn, Heywood), p. 174.

4. H. W. C. Davis, *Lancashire Reformers*, p. 24. It should be noted that at this meeting repeated applications to middle-class reformers in Manchester to take the Chair had met with refusals.

A majority of those who set off from Manchester with their petitions and blankets to march to London (March 1817) were country weavers.[1]

Although in 1818 Stockport provided an important model of a rather different type of urban reform movement, under the leadership of the Reverend Joseph Harrison, a Methodist minister turned Radical orator and schoolmaster,[2] the 'country' people were again dominant in 1819: These were the men whose nightly drillings, of which Bamford has left idyllic and over-innocent descriptions, were the prelude to Peterloo. (The mill-hands of Manchester had neither the time for such preparations, nor the secluded moors upon which to undertake them.) These were the people, too, whose great orderly contingents – from Lees and Saddleworth, Middleton and Rochdale, Oldham and Bury – filled so large a part of St Peter's Fields on 16 August 1819. And, just as the more extreme 'physical force' party in the provinces waited upon London for a signal, so many of the upland weavers waited impatiently for Manchester to commence the insurrection. Fury, not only against the authorities, but also (one suspects) against this apathetic Babylon of the factory-system, nourished the talk in 1817, and again in 1819, of starting the insurrection by making a 'Moscow of Manchester'. And, at the end of 1819, when the Manchester movement was beginning to break up in a welter of personal disputes and warring factions, an entertaining report by a spy upon an appallingly rancorous and disorderly meeting of the Manchester Union concludes:

... at this moment presented themselves two Country-Men, one of which got up and wished to know if this was the Union. – it was some time before any one spoke. – at last some person said it should be – the Stranger then said he came from Flixton, to see

1. Lists of the arrested men (in H.O. 42.172) show a great preponderance of weavers. In one batch of 48 prisoners, 29 were weavers, 2 were spinners, 2 labourers, and 1 each of the following: cabinet-maker, sawyer, book-binder, joiner, machine-maker, tallow chandler, dyer, shoemaker, rope-maker, 'calendar man'. In another batch of 173 prisoners there were rather more spinners, carders, bleachers, piecers, etc., but the great majority were weavers.

2. For the Stockport Union Society, see D. Read, op. cit., pp. 47 ff., and below p. 788.

how Reform was going on – some one cried out, 'did Justice Wright send you?' the Old Man took no Notice but continued that in their Country hundreds were daily joining their Sections, and if he was to tell them what he had seen this Night they would never put any confidence in the Manchester Union. – Several of the Leaders got round the Strangers and persuaded them not to mention what they had seen that Night.[1]

These people were, of course, in the main hand-loom weavers, whose problems and way of life we have examined in an earlier chapter. By 1819 whole communities of Lancashire weavers had adhered to the cause of reform; and from this time until the last Chartist years, weavers and stockingers were always among its staunchest and most extreme adherents. Successive failures in their agitations for parliamentary protection led directly to the question of the reform – or overthrow – of the seat of government itself. They could not hope to improve their position by trade union action alone; and the failure of the great weavers' strike of 1818 to bring any enduring gains underlined the lesson. If the ideology of economic 'independence' and sturdy political individualism, voiced by Cobbett and Hunt, was out of key with the factory-hands' experience, it fitted that of the weavers like a glove. The weavers shared Cobbett's dislike of the noise and oppression of the mills; his emphasis upon every man's right to obtain, by the sweat of his own brow, a square meal, a decent coat, and physical well-being; his suspicion of London, paper-money, 'the Thing'; his preference for moral, rather than utilitarian, argument; his nostalgia for passing rural values. Indeed, they responded eagerly to most of the views of Cobbett in 1817 – except for his disavowal of political societies and clubs.

The strength of the extreme reformers, then, lay in the hand-workers' villages of the Midlands and the north. We hope to have disposed of the misconception that these industrial villagers were 'bumpkins' or 'yokels', among the most 'backward' sections of the people. While the artisan strongholds in the cities – London, Birmingham, Norwich, Sheffield, Newcastle – provided the earliest following for Carlile's Deism and Owen's Socialism, the hand-workers perhaps ranked next to

1. H.O. 42.198, quoted in full in D. Read, op. cit., Appendix B, p. 221.

them in the scale of intelligence and literacy, in which they compared favourably with other industrial groups – iron-workers and miners, the city poor, manual labourers, and many mill-workers.[1] The comparative prosperity of the early years of the Industrial Revolution, in consequence of the machine-yarn boom, had led to a rise not only in material but also in cultural values. It was the undermining of this way of life which gave extreme force to the hand-workers' protest. If the centres of Radical 'conspiracy' were to be for thirty years in such places as Pentridge, Loughborough and Barnsley – if plots were discussed in a chapel at Middleton, a pub at Thornhill Lees, and a gravel-pit in Heckmondwike – this was not because these places were on the edge of nowhere, but because the people of these townships and villages were at the heart of the conflict between unplanned economic individualism and an older way of life. Weavers and stockingers were the worst victims of *laissez faire*, and therefore they merited also the closest attentions of Lord Sidmouth and Oliver. They were – not the backward – but the characteristic workers of this phase of the Industrial Revolution.

IV. BRANDRETH AND OLIVER

But all the great centres of the hand-workers were from 100 to 200 miles away from London. Had the textile centres been in Essex, the nail-making villages in Sussex – had the weavers brought their banners to Spa Fields instead of St Peter's Fields – the course of English history would have been changed. As it was, whenever insurrectionary sentiment smouldered in the Pennines or in Warwickshire, it had no obvious objective close at hand. Luddism, by 1817, was largely discredited. How was the weight of feeling in the provinces to be brought to bear on Government itself? The March of the Blanketeers (which, per-haps, in its early planning stages, Cartwright and Cobbett may have known about and encouraged) was an attempt to bring

1. See R. K. Webb, 'Working-Class Readers in Early Victorian England', *English Historical Review*, LXV (1950), pp. 333 ff., for evidence that (despite persistent complaints as to a recent decline) the standard of literacy of hand-loom weavers in 1840 compared favourably with other groups.

this pressure to bear. The Lancashire men were to march peacefully with their petitions upon London, holding meetings and gathering support on the way. There was some expectation of support from other groups of marchers from Yorkshire and the Midlands, and one of the Manchester leaders is reported to have said, 'If we could get you as far as Birmingham, the whole wd. be done, for I have no doubt you will be 100,000 strong.'[1] As to what was intended in London, various rumours were afoot. The organizers declared that no more was intended than the presentation of their petitions to the Prince Regent. But a tumultuous welcome was expected from the London populace, and there may have been some expectation that the marchers could perform a similar rôle to that of the men of Marseilles in Paris in 1792.

Again we must ask a question. It is not only what was intended, but who intended it? The geographical situation of the hand-workers not only made for their isolation from the centre of power; it also made for a crucial weakness in communication and organization. We have noted the cohesion of the smaller industrial communities, and their opacity to the scrutiny of the authorities. The weak points in their organization were always the *links* between them and the regional centres, and above all, between these centres and London. It was relatively easy for the authorities to infiltrate spies into the organization at Manchester, and even at Sheffield and Nottingham; and these spies, by their forwardness and ability to take time off work, very often succeeded in becoming delegated to the regional committees. It was most easy of all to place spies among the London tavern extremists.

A widely accepted account of the events of the spring and summer of 1817 is as follows:

In March and again in June the magistrates pounced upon meetings of working-class delegates and arrested them all. These men were supposed to be engaged on making plans for a general insurrection; but apart from the evidence supplied by paid spies and informers,

1. H. W. C. Davis, *Lancashire Reformers*, p. 31. The Staffordshire miners had set a precedent in 1816 with the first attempted 'hunger march'. The 'Blanketeers' were in fact prevented from marching by the military, more than 200 were arrested, and few got further than Leek.

there is nothing to show that any such movement existed. Wild talk there doubtless was; but of any organized conspiracy there is no untainted evidence at all.[1]

This is the classic Whig interpretation of 1817, and it is also the defence used by the reformers of the time themselves. It is an interpretation which received scholarly backing in the Hammonds' *Skilled Labourer* (chapter 12), which remains the most authoritative reconstruction of the career of the notorious Oliver.[2]

The Whig case, however, is a serious over-simplification. We need not go over once again our discussion of what constitutes 'untainted' evidence. But there are overwhelming reasons for supposing that some kind of 'physical force' conspiracy was under preparation in 1817, which was inextricably intertwined with the counter-conspiracy of Government *provocateurs*. As early as December 1816 there was loose contact between the 'Jacobin' party in London and extreme reformers in the provinces. At least two of the missionaries appointed by the Lancashire delegate meeting in the same month, with instructions to visit Yorkshire and the Midlands, were of the 'physical force' party – William Benbow and Joseph Mitchell. From this time forward Mitchell (whom a well-informed Lancashire magistrate described as 'a sort of chief for the whole of this part of the country'[3]) moved frequently between London, the Midlands, and the north. When Bamford attended the Hampden Club 'convention' in January 1817, both Mitchell and Benbow had made many London contacts. Benbow acted 'almost as master of ceremonies', and Mitchell accompanied Bamford on a visit to the barracks where (by accident, in Bamford's disingenuous account) they distributed Radical pamphlets. Since Cartwright, Cobbett and Hunt offered no serious organized leadership, some of the provincial delegates had further meetings at 'The Cock' in Grafton-Street with Dr

1. Cole and Postgate, *The Common People*, p. 217.

2. A. F. Fremantle's article, 'The Truth about Oliver the Spy', *Eng. Hist. Review* XLVII (1932), pp. 601 ff. is drawn upon largely by R. J. White in his recent account of the Pentridge rising in *From Waterloo to Peterloo*, ch. 13. Both these accounts are, however, inferior to that of the Hammonds.

3. See H. W. C. Davis, *Lancashire Reformers*, p. 28.

Watson and his group, where plans of national communication and (perhaps) of secret organization were discussed.[1]

Thus when Habeas Corpus was suspended in the first week of March some sketchy system of national organization already existed. The authorities claimed that there were four centres of organization controlled by 'secret committees': 1. Nottingham, Derby and Leicester. 2. Birmingham and district. 3. Lancashire. 4. Yorkshire. There was undoubtedly a considerable passage of delegates and also of Radical correspondence. Mitchell has left some account of these months, when he, Benbow, and Knight eluded the authorities, 'scarce ever resting two nights at a place'.[2] Bamford has also described his days 'on the run' with Healey, at a time when some Lancashire reformers did not dare to come out 'save like owls at nightfall', while others 'assembled under various pretexts':

Sometimes they were termed 'benefit societies', sometimes 'botanical meetings', 'meetings for the relief of the families of imprisoned reformers', or 'of those who had fled the country'; but their real purpose, divulged only to the initiated, was to carry into effect the night attack on Manchester . . .

An informer at one such meeting, at Chadderton in March, reports in terms which are familiar from Luddite until Chartist times :

The Chadderton man said that most of the people had arms already. He said he thought they would muster about 70 Firelocks. . . .

It was agreed to come to M'chester on Friday afternoon at 3 o'clock & to meet at the Royal Oak at Ardwick Bridge, to hear what news had come from B'ham, Sheffield & any other places from wh. information was expected. The Chadderton man said he had seen the Deputy from Bury & he [had] been at Huddersfield & Leeds & he was confident the people were all ready to begin at any hour as they had been getting up a deal of arms that had been hid since the time of the Luddites.[3]

'They were to advance when they saw a Rocket . . .' Almost identical passages can be found in the Home Office papers for

1. Bamford (1893 edn), pp. 21, 32–3; H. Hunt, *The Green Bag Plot* (1819), p. 9.

2. *Blanketteer*, 23 October 1819.

3. Bamford, op. cit., p. 44; H. W. C. Davis, op. cit., p. 35.

1839 and 1848. The physical force party was always waiting
'to hear what news had come' from Birmingham ... or London
... or Newport. From one standpoint the story is pathetic. It
was out of half a dozen meetings of this sort that the 'Ardwick
Conspiracy' was built, at the end of March, on the pretext of
which several of the most active Lancashire leaders were
seized. From another aspect it is more serious. On dozens of
occasions and at a dozen places men assembled with a few guns
and home-made arms in villages of the Midlands and north,
and made irresolute movements, less through timidity than
through their fear of betrayal and their sense of geographic
isolation. If at any of these crises the 'news' *had* come, if a
major centre had been 'captured' by revolutionaries, then
insurrection might have spread rapidly to other districts.

By May revolutionary feeling was rising in several districts,
and there was sporadic communication between them. But
there was no responsible organizing centre. The country waited
upon London; but the Londoners with whom they were in
sketchy contact were less able to initiate an insurrectionary
attempt than the countrymen. William Stevens, a Nottingham
needlemaker who took an active part in the conspiracy and
later escaped to America, later deposed that after the suspension
of Habeas Corpus 'many hundreds ... and, as he believes,
many Thousands, said that ... it was time to *resist*':

... this was the way of thinking of a great part of the people in his
Town in the months of March, April, and May 1817 ...

But 'though the means of resistance were anxiously wished for
... no plan of resistance was formed until some time in the
month of May'. It was first mooted when, in April, 'Mr
Mitchell went through Nottingham ... on his way to London'.[1]

Mitchell (said Bamford) 'moved in a sphere of his own, the
extent of which no man knew save himself'. In April he visited
in London Charles Pendrill, the Jacobin shoemaker and former
associate of Despard, who was then making preparations to
escape to America. Pendrill had recently helped a friend,
known to him as William Oliver, out of debtor's gaol: soon
after this Oliver 'began to make very vehement professions of
patriotism, and expressed uncommon anxiety to know whether

1. Deposition in Cobbett's *Political Register*, 16 May 1818.

there were any Political Associations into which he might obtain admittance'.[1] Oliver's professions were believed and by March he had been admitted to the inner circle of London reformers. On 28 March he requested an interview with Lord Sidmouth. In April he was introduced by Pendrill and other reformers to Mitchell, who waited upon him in his rooms and was impressed by his 'full length bronze figure of Napoleon' on the chimney-piece, and the portraits of Burdett, Cobbett, Horne Tooke and Fox:

He told me that it was the desire of the London friends to form a connexion with the country friends. I said ... it was also much wished by the country.

But when Mitchell requested a meeting with the London committee, Oliver assured him that it was too dangerous a time to call them together.[2]

Oliver prevailed upon Mitchell to be permitted to accompany him on his next tour in the provinces. The two men set off on 23 April on a tour which was to last (for Oliver) for twenty-three days and which was to secure for him introductions to leading reformers in the main centres of the Midlands and the north.[3] It was a splendid coup of espionage, and Sidmouth was well served by Oliver's reports. On 5 May he reported attending a central delegate meeting at Wakefield, attended by men from Birmingham, Sheffield, Huddersfield, Barnsley, Leeds, and by Thomas Bacon for the North Midlands district – large promises were made as to the number of men

1. Pendrill's deposition in Cobbett's *Political Register*, 16 May 1818. Pendrill had known Oliver since 1811, at which time he had been foreman to a carpenter. Oliver has variously been described as a builder, carpenter and accountant; he was in fact, a superior clerk or book-keeper and surveyor.

2. *Blanketteer*, 23 October 1819.

3. Oliver left London 24 April: 25, Birmingham: 26, Sheffield via Derby: 27, 28, Wakefield, Dewsbury: 29, Leeds: 30, Manchester: 1 and 2 May, Liverpool: 3, Manchester: 5, Wakefield: 6, Huddersfield: 7, Wakefield: 8, Huddersfield: 9, Barnsley: 10, Ossett: 11, Spen Valley: 12, Bradford: 13, Leeds: 15, London. On the journey between Birmingham and Leeds, Mitchell introduced Oliver to a leading Derby reformer 'whilst the coach horses were changing'. H. Hunt, *The Green Bag Plot*. See also paper headed 'O's Tour' in T.S. 11.351, and Oliver's 'Narrative' (H.O. 40.9) and letters (H.O. 40.10).

who would rise in each district. The date of the rising was planned for 26 May, and Oliver promised that London 'would be ready'. Privately, he reported that it was 'a weak and impractical scheme, and that if it could be delayed it would blow up of itself'.[1]

But – perhaps by a miscalculation – Mitchell had been arrested on 4 May, and Oliver proceeded, as 'the London delegate', on his own.[2] Thereafter an extraordinary situation existed, in which insurrectionary preparations were going forward in several districts, but in which the only London contact-man who can be identified was a Government agent. In London Watson, Thistlewod, Preston and Hooper were still awaiting trial for high treason for their part in the Spa Fields affair, and a conviction was generally expected. Some leading reformers were in hiding; others had followed Cobbett to America; still others were already in prison. Up to this point matters seem clear enough. But from this point the sources became heavily partisan. The reformers and Whig critics of Government (such as Bennet in the House of Commons and Baines in the *Leeds Mercury*) were at pains to present every piece of evidence to show that Oliver was the main instigator and organizer of the events of 9 June. The authorities, on the other hand, alleged that Oliver's rôle was solely that of an informer, that if he intervened in revolutionary plans it was only to postpone or disorganize them, and that it was only thanks to their vigilance that a dangerous insurrection was averted.

The truth is probably more complex than either account. Oliver was not the only spy in the secret organization. The magistrates in Lancashire and Nottingham were kept well briefed by their own local informers. But, at the same time, it is not true that the only instigators of revolution were spies. Bamford was visited at Middleton in May, not by Oliver, but by delegates from Derby – Thomas Bacon and Turner – both of whom were to be involved in the Pentridge Rising. William

1. Hunt, op. cit.; and deposition of Stevens.
2. By one account, Mitchell was travelling under an assumed name, dressed like a weaver in fustian clothes & had an apron round him'. T. W. Tattie to Fitzwilliam, 22 January 1820, Fitzwilliam Papers, F.52 (c).

Stevens deposed that when Thomas Bacon brought his report back to the North Midlands committee, from the Wakefield meeting of 5 May,

Brandreth, Turner, and Ludlam were present, as well as a great many more persons. ... About five or six days before the 26th of May, a letter from our friends at Sheffield came to Nottingham, informing us that the rising has been put off to the 9th of June in consequence of the advice of Oliver . . . because the nights would then be dark, and because the whole country would by that time be in a more perfect state for rising. ... In consequence of this, preparations continued to be made in Nottingham and the neighbourhood until the day of rising.

Oliver had, meanwhile, returned to report to his masters in London, not neglecting to look up his old colleague Mitchell in Cold Bath Fields prison (thereby attaching to him the long-lasting suspicion that he also was a spy).[1] On 23 May (according to the authorities) Sidmouth was advised by the magistrates of the Midlands and north that the insurrection would take place on 9 June, with or without the support of London. 'He sent Oliver by the mail into the country.'[2]

But on this second tour Oliver acted like a man with a quite different brief. His talk was now full of large promises. Formerly he had on occasion represented himself as 'delegated' by Burdett, Cochrane, Hunt or Major Cartwright.[3] Now he added

1. Baines, who exposed Oliver in the *Leeds Mercury*, also led the attack on Mitchell. Mitchell was an amateurish and foolish conspirator, but he was not a spy. His name was cleared by a formal Radical investigation, headed by Jones Burdett. Bamford devoted a chapter to his vindication, concluding, in capital letters – 'Had he been a spy, he would have betrayed those who never were betrayed', an admission that there was more to the plot than even Oliver knew. On his release from prison Mitchell disregarded Major Cartwright's advice that, if he was an honest man, he should retire from public life; re-entered Radical politics; defended his reputation against Baines's accusations in his *Blanketteer*; was stoned and thrown into the canal at Leeds; and was imprisoned in 1820 for seditious libel. See Bamford, op. cit., chs. 12, 26; *Life of Edward Baines*, p. 109; *Blanketteer*, 23 October to 20 November 1819; Fitzwilliam Papers, F.52 (c); L. T. Rede, *York Castle in the Nineteenth Century*, p. 630.

2. See H. Hunt, op. cit.

3. See, for example, the deposition of Scholes in *Leeds Mercury*, 21 June 1817; W. Cliff (of Derby) in *Duckett's Dispatch*, 9 December 1818.

talk of the plans of the Wolverhampton reformers to take Weedon Barracks: Wooler, the editor of the *Black Dwarf*, 'was then at work in London printing the Proclamations to be issued by the Provisional Government': preparations (he said) were always further advanced in every place than the one in which he happened to be. His attentions were concentrated upon the West Riding and Nottingham in particular.[1]

It is significant that Oliver settled upon the two districts in which the secret Luddite organization had been strongest. Moreover, both were the centres of an even older revolutionary tradition. 'The People of Nottingham,' Sherwin wrote, 'have ... an habitual feeling of hatred against oppression that perhaps is not to be surpassed by any town in the world.'[2] Benbow held a meeting at Pentridge as early as December 1816. The leading reformer in this district, Thomas Bacon, was an 'old Jack', probably in his forties, who had worked for some years as a fettler or dresser of cast iron at the Butterey Iron Works. (Victimized for his political activities, in 1817 he fell back upon the trade of framework-knitting.) According to the brief prepared by the Crown against him (but, in the sequel, never used), he had been from 1791 'an active Supporter of the Doctrines of Liberty and Equality and a zealous disciple of Thomas Paine'. He held that property should be 'equalized', the landed estates broken up, and 8 acres be distributed to each man. For Bacon, Cobbett's *Register* and the Hampden Clubs 'did not go far enough'.[3]

In the other revolutionary centre, the West Riding, the

1. Paper headed 'O's Tour (T.S. 11.351) gives the following itinerary: 23 May, left London; 24, Birmingham; 25, Derby; 26, Derby; 27, Nottingham; 28, villages near Nottingham; 29, Sheffield to Wakefield; 30, Bradford and Halifax; 31, Manchester; 1 June, Liverpool; 2, Manchester to Wakefield; 3, Wakefield; 4, at Camps Mount (General Byng's H.Q. near Wakefield); 5, Leeds; 6, Thornhill Lees, near Dewsbury: left with mail for Nottingham; 7, Nottingham: left on London mail. In Lancashire, according to Bamford and Prentice, both middle-class and working-class reformers already suspected him and issued warnings against his schemes. See also Sherwin's *Political Register*, 15 November 1817, 14 February 1818; Oliver's 'Narrative' and letters, in H.O. 40.9/10; evidence of Bradley and Dickenson, H.O. 42.165 and 167.

2. Sherwin's *Political Register*, 21 June 1817.

3. *Rex v. Thomas Bacon*; brief in T.S. 11.351.

situation was somewhat more confused, since Fitzwilliam's Whig magistracy and Lord Sidmouth were often at cross-purposes. (It seems probable that the Lord-Lieutenant himself was not apprised of Oliver's identity and objectives.) In the last week of May active Sheffield magistrates, acting on their own information, surprised a midnight meeting of the 'Leaders of Tens' at 'the Grinding Wheel of Mr Chandler'. 'When the meeting took the alarm men rushed from the doors & Windows & hastened to the Wood.' Wolstenholme, one of the local leaders, and three others were seized, and thereafter the Sheffield movement was in confusion.[1]

From Nottingham, in these days, we are able to compare two independent sources, in which the bias might be expected to have opposing tendencies. In the first, a local informer (who did not know of Oliver's true identity) reported to a local magistrate:

I ... went to Jerry Brandreth's between 6 and 7 this evening. ... We left his House ... and met [Stevens] against the gaol. We walked up Sandy Lane ... Stevens said I should have been here on Monday night. ... He stated that there was a London Delegate, who reported that there was about 70,000 in London ready to act with us; and that they were very ripe in Birmingham. ... It was not stated where he lived, but that he was a staunch friend, and that ... he was to be here again on Wednesday or Thursday, and to bring the determination of the time to be fixed upon for the Insurrection.[2]

In the second, Stevens gives his own account nearly a year later:

... on the 1st or 2d day of June, Oliver came to Nottingham ... to the house of this deponent. He said, that all would be ready in London for the 9th of June ... Oliver had a meeting with us now, at which meeting Brandreth and Turner, and many others were present. At this meeting he laid before us a paper which he called a Plan of the Campaign. ...

When Oliver had thus settled every thing with us, he prepared to set off to organize things in Yorkshire, that all might be ready to move in the Country at the moment that the rising took place in

1. Parker to Fitzwilliam, 29 May 1817, Fitzwilliam Papers, F.45 (i).
2. Informer (H. Sampson of Bullwell?) enclosed in Enfield to Sidmouth, 1 June 1817, H.O. 40.6.

London, where he told us there were Fifty Thousand Men with arms prepared, and that they would take the Tower . . .

A 'convention' of northern delegates was to meet at Sheffield on 7 June to make the final arrangements:

When it had met, the members were to separate and go to the several great Towns; and the members were to go, not to their own places of abode, but to other places, in order that mutual confidence might be established, and in order that true information might be interchanged . . .

Stevens, indeed, set off for Sheffield on 7 June, but 'was overtaken by a Boy on horse-back', as a result of which he returned to Nottingham:

At his own house he found Oliver, who now said, that some treachery had taken place in Yorkshire; but that, as all was ready in London, all would go on well, if they did but remain firm to their promises at Nottingham and Derby. A meeting now took place, at which Oliver was present . . .

After this meeting Oliver immediately took post to London, explaining that he must 'give the risers in London an assurance of the hearty cooperation of the Country'.[1]

A good deal came to light as to the movements of Oliver in Yorkshire between 2 and 6 June. He moved rapidly from town to town, in preparation for a delegate meeting at Thornhill Lees, near Dewsbury, on 6 June. Two days before this, he had a private interview with Major-General John Byng, commanding the troops in the north. The Thornhill Lees meeting was surrounded, and the delegates seized, by troops under General Byng's personal command.[2] Oliver was allowed to 'escape', but was seen a few hours later by a reformer in a Wakefield hotel (shortly before his departure on the Sheffield coach) in conversation with a servant of General Byng's, and the truth leaked out. By the time Oliver reached Nottingham,

1. Deposition of William Stevens in Cobbett's *Political Register* 16 May 1818. These references contradict the suggestions by A. F. Fremantle and R. J. White that Oliver had never had any contact with Brandreth. See also *Nottingham Review*, 7 November 1817.

2. These arrests were not intended by Sidmouth or Byng, but were forced by a zealous magistrate. See Hammonds, op. cit., p. 358.

on the evening of the seventh, some rumours of treachery had already reached the town; and the final meeting described by Stevens included a gruelling cross-examination of the spy, which he was lucky to survive. A tall man said (Oliver reported) 'they were not so fond of being hung for nothing at Nottingham as they were in Lancashire, and if I did not stop he did not know what to think of me.'[1]

But 'Jerry' Brandreth was not at this final meeting. As early as 5 June the Nottingham Town Clerk had been notified by his own informer:

> I saw Jerry at his own house ... I asked him if they had any Communication with any other person than the London Delegate – he said they had not but some of the chaps had. ... He told me he was going to Pentridge for good, to command the men who were to rise there, and that he was to bring them here ... and to collect from all the Towns they came through ...

Later that day the informer was told by Brandreth's wife that he had already gone. 'She thought he would not return till the job Began.'[2] Of all these events Lord Sidmouth was apprised. From 7 June the Government, the Army, and the magistrates were standing by, awaiting the Pentridge revolt. On the seventh the Town Clerk of Nottingham was in conference all day with the magistrates on 'the means for preventing and suppressing an expected insurrection of the populace in this town and neighbourhood'. On the ninth the Town Clerk wrote: 'My confidential clerk is on the look-out near Pentridge, watching the result of old Bacon's threatened movements. ... We sat in council waiting for it through the first part of the night.'[3]

'Oliver drew towards London, leaving his victims successively in the traps that he had prepared for them. ... The employers of Oliver might, in an hour, have put a total stop to those preparations, and have blown them to air. ... [They] wished, not to prevent, but to produce those acts ...'[4] This was

1. For these days see H.O. 40.9 and *Leeds Mercury*, esp. 21 June 1817.
2. H.O. 40.6.
3. D. Gray, *Nottingham Through 500 Years* (Nottingham, 1960), p. 169; S. Maccoby, op. cit., p. 352.
4. Cobbett's *Political Register*, 16 May 1818.

Cobbett's interpretation and it is difficult to see how any other construction can be put upon the evidence. Recent suggestions that Oliver was not a *provocateur*, or, alternatively, that if he was, he exceeded Sidmouth's instructions,[1] cannot be sustained. Nor is there any reason to suppose that members of the Liverpool administration were squeamish – or, indeed, felt any sense of guilt – at the notion of shedding blood. 'One can never feel that the King is secure upon his throne till he has dared to spill traitors' blood,' Lord Liverpool himself had written, when refusing to intercede for the life of Marshal Ney.[2] Castlereagh had served his apprenticeship in the suppression of Irish rebellion. Lord Chancellor Eldon was fighting a rearguard action against Romilly and the penal reformers, in defence of capital penalties.[3] The Government was at that time preparing to try for high treason not only Dr Watson and his colleagues, but also groups of Sheffield and Glasgow reformers.[4] *The Masque of Anarchy* does not reveal the 'ignorant injustice' of Shelley's judgement,[5] but judgements which the greater part of Shelley's countrymen came to share. The Government wanted blood – not a holocaust, but enough to make an example.

The story of Pentridge is soon told. Brandreth, the 'Nottingham Captain', performed the part which he had undertaken. For two or three days before 9 June he was making open preparations, recruiting and holding council in one of the Pentridge inns. On the night of the ninth two or, at the most, three hundred men were gathered from villages at the foot of the Derby Peak – Pentridge, South Wingfield, Ripley. They were stockingers, quarrymen, iron workers (from the Butterley

1. See A. F. Fremantle and R. J. White, *ubi supra*.

2. See R. J. White, op. cit., p. 95; E. P. Thompson, 'God and King and Law', *New Reasoner*, 3, 1957–8.

3. For example, in 1813 he sought to maintain the medieval penalties for high treason. See L. Radzinowicz, op. cit., I, pp. 519–20.

4. The six Sheffield workers seized at the end of May were charged with high treason, but were never brought to trial – partly because Yorkshire opinion, including that of many of the gentry, was outraged by the Oliver disclosures. In February a number of Glasgow reformers had been arrested, but owing to the courage of the main prosecution witness they were acquitted in July.

5. R. J. White, op. cit., p. 70.

Iron Works) and labourers, with a few guns and more pikes, scythes, and bludgeons. Many of them – the Ludlams, Weight-mans, and Turners – were related to each other. They set off in the rain to march the fourteen miles to Nottingham, calling at farms and houses and demanding arms and support on the way. At one of these farms the only blood of the rising was shed; Brandreth, demanding imperiously entrance to a house where it was believed there was a gun, fired through the window and killed a farm servant. Brandreth led the increasingly despondent (and dwindling) party with grim determination. He had repeated some verses, which catch the mood of that night:

> Every man his skill must try,
> He must turn out and not deny;
> No bloody soldier must he dread,
> He must turn out and fight for bread.
> The time is come you plainly see
> The government opposed must be.

One of his lieutenants assured a follower that:

He believed the day and hour were fixed when the whole nation was expected to rise; and before the middle of the week, he believed there would be hundreds of thousands in arms ... there were men appointed all over the nation ...

Brandreth added more promises, suited to the morale of the moment, or to his audience: 'Nottingham would be given up before they got there', 'they should proceed from Nottingham to London, and wipe off the National Debt', forces 'would come in the morning out of Yorkshire like a cloud', and:

... by a letter which he had seen from London yesterday, the keys of the Tower would be given up to the Hampden club party, if they were not already.

To some reluctant recruits there was promised 'roast beef and ale', rum, and even a pleasure trip on the Trent. 'A provisional government' would be formed, and it would send relief into the country to the wives and children of those who had taken up arms. Always he promised that the 'Northern clouds' would come, 'men from the North would ... sweep all before them, and every man that refused should be shot upon the place'.

Throughout the night the surrounding villages were disturbed by 'guns fired, horns blowing, shouts, and different noises'. As the column approached Nottingham the next day and found no support awaiting it, the men became more and more downcast, and began to slip away, while Brandreth became more imperious, and threatened to shoot deserters. At length they saw approaching them a small force of Hussars. The insurrection ended in panic, as the men dropped their weapons and ran for cover, while the troops rode after them, or rounded them up in the next few days.[1]

Pentridge was not the only village which rose on the night of 8 and 9 June. Despite the arrest of the Yorkshire delegates at Thornhill Lees,[2] several hundred clothing workers, mainly from the Holmfirth valley, advanced upon Huddersfield under a leader who told them: 'Now, my lads, all England is in arms – our liberties are secure – the rich will be poor, and the poor will be rich.' An explanation as to why this attempt took place, despite the fact that Oliver's treachery was already known in Yorkshire, is offered in depositions of two of the insurgents. One of the local leaders (in one account) read the *Leeds Mercury* and 'said all was up, for the Plan was completely broke into, and he said that it must either be done now or we shall all be hanged ...' In another account, a leader said: 'We must go, Lads, for it will do nothing dodging on it, the business must be done tonight,' – 'he reckoned we were like to fight for Liberty ...' The incident reproduces in many details the Pentridge Rising; but in the 'Folley Hall' rising, the insurgents were very much more fortunate than their Derbyshire fellows. A few shots were exchanged with a small party of military, but no life was lost. When the military returned with reinforcements,

1. W. B. Gurney, *Trials of Jeremiah Brandreth &c.* (1817), I, 87, 152, II, 398, 420, 443, 450. One of the villages the rebels went through was Eastwood – D. H. Lawrence's 'old wild England'.

2. These delegates, from Leeds, Wakefield, Dewsbury, Holmfirth, Huddersfield, Bradford, and the Spen Valley, *may* only have been working-class reformers whom Oliver had lured to the meeting. But at least one of them, James Mann, the Leeds cropper, was a local reform leader, later to become the leading Radical bookseller in Leeds. It is more likely that they were in fact 'delegates' of some sort. See *Leeds Mercury*, 14 and 21 June 1817.

the insurgents (perhaps disheartened to find no revolutionists in command of Huddersfield) had disappeared into the night. Two of the leaders went into hiding. Those who were apprehended benefited from the revulsion of feeling occasioned by the *Leeds Mercury* disclosures as to the rôle of Oliver; when they were brought to trial in July, the jury refused to convict.[1]

We have told the story of Oliver at length because it is one of the great stories of English history which came to partake almost of the quality of myth. Oliver was the archetype of the Radical Judas, and his legendary rôle was to carry influence throughout nineteenth-century history. We may distinguish between the immediate and the longer-term influence. The employment of informers had become virtually a routine practice on the part of magistrates in the larger industrial centres during the Luddite years; and ever since the 1790s a part of the Government's own resources had been appropriated for such secret service purposes. But the practice was regarded by a very wide section of public opinion as being wholly alien to the spirit of English law. The notion of 'preventive' police action even in criminal cases was shocking, and when this was extended to matters of 'domestic' political belief it was an affront to every prejudice of the free-born Englishman. The exposure in the *Leeds Mercury* of Oliver's rôle as an *agent provocateur* literally astounded public opinion. While the historian may read Oliver's reports in the Home Office papers with little surprise – seeing in him only one of the most industrious and daring of a corps of informers – there were thousands of shopkeepers, country squires, Dissenting Ministers, and professional men who, in 1817 had no idea that such things could take place in England.

Hence the *Leeds Mercury* disclosures, published less than a week after the risings, had a disastrous effect upon the reputation of the Government. In the very week that the Pentridge affair took place, Dr Watson was standing his trial for high treason. The Defence tore the leading prosecution witness, Castle, into shreds, and the jury had time to hear of the first

---

1. *Leeds Mercury*, 19 and 26 July 1817; D. F. E. Sykes, *History of Huddersfield* (1908), pp. 292–4; depositions of John Buckley and John Langley, in Fitzwilliam Papers, F.45 (k); T.S. 11.3336 and 4134 (2).

revelations about Oliver before reaching their verdict. It was 'Not Guilty'. This was only one of a series of defeats in the courts: the acquittals of the Glasgow and Folley Hall 'conspirators', and of Wooler and (in December) of Hone on charges of seditious libel. Although throughout 1817 many reformers remained imprisoned under the suspension of Habeas Corpus, the clamour grew throughout the country against the 'continental spy system'. Instead of isolating the 'physical force' reformers, the revulsion against the actions of Oliver brought extreme and moderate groups together. 'The most abominable practices recorded in history,' wrote John Wade in the *Gorgon*. Ten years later Francis Place wrote: 'I despair of being able adequately to express correct ideas of the singular baseness, the detestable infamy, of their equally mean and murderous conduct':

They who passed the Gagging Acts, in 1817 and the Six Acts in 1819 were such miscreants, that could they have acted thus in a well-ordered community they would all have been hanged . . .[1]

Cobbett's reaction (in America) was inevitably delayed; but from his first comments in 1818 he never allowed the names of Brandreth or of Oliver to be forgotten. The Government had outraged not only the reformers but also all those who valued the old rhetoric of libertarian constitutionalism by which the very purpose of government was to safeguard individual rights.

This profound alienation of feeling was made only the more profound by the subsequent trial and execution of the Derby rioters. While Brandreth's case was a foregone conclusion (since he had killed a man), his followers might well have been accused only of riot. But the administration was determined to exact its full measure of blood. Thirty-five men were arraigned for high treason. Extraordinary care was taken in hand-picking the most compliant jury.[2] Ten lawyers acted for the Prosecution, against the two assigned to the Defence. The trial, postponed until October, took place in an atmosphere of terror. The prisoners had been held for weeks on bread and water, and denied visitors. ('Hang All Jacobins' was chalked on the

1. *Gorgon*, 27 June 1818; Wallas, op. cit., p. 123.
2. See Hammonds, op. cit., p. 366–8.

walls of Derby's All Saint's Church.) Moreover, the trial itself took a curious course. The whole country was talking of Oliver, and it was confidently expected that the Defence would attempt to prove his instigation. But the spy's name was never mentioned. The Prosecution (who held Oliver in reserve at Derby *incognito*) rested their case upon proof of the overt acts committed by the accused. The Defence in Brandreth's case, in the person of 'Lawyer Cross', claimed that the prisoner had been instigated and deluded – not by Oliver – but by *Cobbett* and by the 'artful and insidious publications' of the Radical press:

I cannot help alluding ... to one of the most malignant and diabolical publications ever issued from the English press. ... It is entitled – 'An Address to the Journeymen and Labourers ...'

These were 'the most mischievous publications that were ever put into the hand of man'.[1] With Brandreth convicted, the Defence switched its emphasis, and pleaded that his associates had been under the spell of their charismatic leader – Denman likening the Nottingham Captain to Byron's *Corsair*:

> There breathe but few whose aspect might defy
> The full encounter of his searching eye;
> There was a laughing devil in his sneer,
> That raised emotions both of rage and fear ...

This did not appear as a sufficient plea in mitigation to the farmers on the Derby jury, however much it may have enhanced Denman's reputation at the Bar. Turner, Ludlam and Weightman were all found guilty and condemned to death; whereupon the remaining prisoners, including the veteran reformer Thomas Bacon, tendered a plea of guilty on the understanding that their lives would be spared. Over Oliver's part a 'veil was drawn'.[2]

It is an extraordinary business, not the less so since there were reformers in the country who had volunteered to go to Derby and testify as to Oliver's activities, even at the danger of incriminating themselves.[3] We cannot accept the explanation

1. W. B. Gurney, *Trials*, I, pp. 198–200.

2. Weightman was respited, and joined thirteen others who were transported.

3. See Sherwin's *Political Register*, 15 November 1817.

that the Defence did not cite Oliver because Oliver in fact had
no connexion with Brandreth. In the first place, we know that
he had. In the second place, Denman knew this. Before the
trial he wrote to a friend that he had reason to believe that
Oliver was at the bottom of the 'whole business'. Defending
his conduct in 1820 in the House of Commons he said that he
had 'not the smallest doubt' that the rising was instigated by
Oliver, 'from the information which he had obtained at the
time, as counsel for the prisoners, and which he had subsequently followed up ...' He thought it unwise, however, to call
spies as Defence witnesses because under the rules of legal procedure he could not cross-examine his own witnesses: 'they
would, when cross-examination was impracticable, have
thrown all the weight of their testimony against the prisoners'.
And there was a further (and perhaps more important) consideration: to have adduced Oliver 'to speak of his conversations with Brandreth would only have proved that the plan of
insurrection was more deeply laid than it was the prisoners'
business to contend it was'. Indeed, we now know that the brief
for the prisoners' Defence is endorsed with a note to the effect
that proof of instigation by Oliver 'is inadmissable, and if
admissable, it does not lessen the Malignity of the Offence ...'[1]

This is a plausible explanation. But it is difficult to believe
that some procedural means might not have been found to
expose so flagrant a case of provocation. While proof of instigation by Oliver might not constitute a legal basis for a defence, juries in London and in Yorkshire had revealed how
powerful an effect, in fact, such suspicions produced. There are
other possible explanations. The authorities were desperate for
a conviction. (Lord Sidmouth was ill in October but 'derived
more benefit from the termination of the Derby trials than
from all that the medical men could give him.') They were also
willing to take extraordinary measures to prevent Oliver's
name from being introduced. It is clear from the briefs in the
Treasury Solicitor's papers that the Crown had at first intended to put Thomas Bacon (who had not been involved in the

1. J. Arnold, *Memoir of ... Lord Denman* (1873), I, p. 116; *Hansard*
(new series) I, 267; R. J. White, op. cit., p. 173. See also *Nottingham
Review*, 8 August 1817.

actual rising) on trial first, for treason and insurrection. But while (as the brief shows) the Crown could have mounted a case against Bacon without calling upon Oliver's evidence, the veteran reformer would certainly have forced the issue in some way, and might even have defended himself. At the eleventh hour, the Crown changed its tactics: 'we have resolved not to bring forward any prosecution in which [Oliver's] name can be brought in question'. With Brandreth as the leading defendant, it was possible to limit the charges to the overt acts of rebellion.

Moreover, the prisoners themselves were isolated until the time of their trial, and may not have known the full story of Oliver's rôle. Although their relatives sold everything, down to their beds, to provide funds for the defence, it was only in the autumn, when a Radical wire-worker in London named West formed a defence committee (and, at the last moment, persuaded Hunt to attend at Derby), that any national aid was forthcoming. Indeed, it is not impossible that Government brought some pressure to bear on the Defence. Even on the scaffold, pains were taken to prevent the victims from exercising their customary right to their 'last words', the chaplain interposing himself between the condemned men and the crowd. The Radical press argued with some colour that an understanding had been reached with the Prosecution, attributing the worst motives to 'Lawyer Cross'. Brandreth's case was hopeless. Might the Crown have hinted that the lives of some, or all, of his fellows might be spared, if the Defence made no mention of Oliver's part? Or might the Prosecution have threatened to implicate many more reformers if Oliver's testimony had been called upon?[1]

But in this speculation it is easy to forget the prisoners. Who *was* Jeremiah Brandreth? The Hammonds, characteristically, describe him as 'a half-starved, illiterate, and unemployed framework-knitter', 'ready to ... forward any proposal however wild'. This is pejorative writing. We know that Brandreth

1. T. S. 11.351; H. Hunt, *Memoirs*, III, pp. 499–502; *Black Dwarf*, 12 November 1817; Cobbett's *Political Register*, 25 April 1818; Hammonds, op. cit., p. 368; R. J. White, op. cit., p. 172; E. P. Thompson, op. cit, pp. 73–4.

was not illiterate. If he was half-starved and unemployed, so were many hundreds of his fellow stockingers, notably in the 'Derbyshire Ribs' trade in which he was employed. We know that he had a house in Nottingham, and that when he was arrested his wife was sent as a pauper to her settlement in Sutton-in-Ashfield. From there she wrote to her husband, on learning from him of his sentence:

... if you have (which is the general opinion) been drawn in by that wretch Oliver, forgive him, and leave him to God and his own conscience. That God will give to every man his reward, though, when I call him a human being I scarce think him so (though in the shape of one). O that I could atone for all and save your life.

(Even this letter was suppressed from Brandreth by the jailor.) Ann Brandreth, being penniless, walked from Sutton to Derby to say farewell to her husband. His own last letter to her was written in a 'clear, plain and steady' hand:

I feel no fear in passing through the shadow of death to eternal life; so I hope you will make the promise of God as I have, to your own soul, as we may meet in Heaven. .... My beloved ... this is the account of what I send to you — one work bag, two balls of worsted and one of cotton, and a handkerchief, an old pair of stockings and a shirt, and the letter I received from my beloved sister ...[1]

It is from such detail, as well as from the trial, that we must reconstruct a picture of Brandreth, and for an interesting reason. Until the end he refused 'to say where he was born, the different stations in life he has been engaged in, or any particular concerning his parentage'. He was rumoured to have had different trades, and to come from Exeter. In prison he declared himself to be 'of the Baptist persuasion'. 'Much is said,' related Denman to a friend, 'of the stern and inflexible patriotism of his character.' To a magistrate who sought a confession from him in jail, he poured out 'a volley of abuse and mockery', but at other times he was singularly silent and determined.[2]

In fact, these conspirators were not all the unlettered yokels

1. Hammonds, op. cit., p. 358; Arnould, op. cit., p. 116; Cobbett's *Political Register*, 25 April 1818.

2. *Leeds Mercury*, 8 and 15 November 1817; Arnould, op. cit., p. 115.

which some historians would have them to be.[1] Because one of their followers thought that a 'provisional government' had something to do with 'provisions', we need not suppose that they all had straw in their hair. A number were former soldiers, who travelled widely in their service. Of Brandreth's fellows, William Turner was a stone-mason, aged forty-seven, who had served in Egypt and elsewhere in the Militia.[2] Weightman was a sawyer – 'a very civil and decent character', 'a sober peaceable man'. Isaac Ludlam 'was a man of some small property, being part owner of a stone quarry' near Derby, and 'well known for some miles around as a Methodist preacher'.[3] In prison he consoled himself by reading Baxter's *Call to the Unconverted*. The arrested Yorkshire delegates were, in the main, superior artisans,[4] while nine of the twenty-four men charged with offences after the Folley Hall rising were croppers.

This suggests another way of viewing the insurgents. Persistent rumour suggested that Brandreth himself had been a Luddite – perhaps even a Luddite 'captain'.[5] The Holmfirth valley, from which the 'Folley Hall' insurgents came, was an area persistently connected with the Luddite oath-takings of 1812. At least one of the insurgents had 'an old Halbert which he said had been used in Ludding time'. An officer noted that the attempt was accompanied by signal lights on the hills and the

1. Of 35 arraigned at the Derby trials, 13 were framework-knitters, 7 were labourers, 5 colliers, 2 stonecutters, 2 farmers, and one each of the following: stone-mason, moulder, blacksmith, engineer, sawyer, tailor, T.S. 11.351.

2. *Independent Whig*, 23 October 1817.

3. *Leeds Mercury*, 30 October 1817. This was denied the next week, by 'request', but Ludlam may have belonged to one of the seceding Methodist bodies – New Connexion or Primitives. See also B. Gregory's evidence, above, p. 433.

4. Two croppers, three clothiers, a shoemaker, carpenter, weaver, cardmaker, and publican. Ibid, 14 June 1817.

5. See e.g. *Legislator*, 1 March 1818, and Lord G. Cavendish to Fitzwilliam, 25 August 1817, Fitzwilliam Papers, F.45 (k). More remarkably, Brandreth was present at Despard's execution – when offered an explanation of the forms of the penalty for high treason, he said that this could be spared, as he had witnessed it in the case of Colonel Despard (*Independent Whig*, 9 November 1817). Two other conspirators of this time were involved in the Despard affair – Pendrill, and Scholes of Wakefield. See also Oliver's testimony, above, p. 654 n. 3.

firing of signal-guns: 'the system seems to be exactly similar to that practised at the time of the Luddites'. The Leeds cropper, James Mann, may have been a leader of Leeds Luddism, while another of the arrested delegates at Thornhill Lees (Smaller) was said to be 'a notorious stealer of arms in 1812'. 'A Rising on the 8th or 9th,' a Leeds magistrate reported, 'has been the common Conversation in the Croppers' Shops for 2 or 3 weeks past.'[1]

There is reason, then, to suppose that some of those involved were not dupes but experienced revolutionaries. Brandreth's long silence had in it a heroism which has been little understood. It is probable that he kept silent about Oliver in the hope that his own death would atone for the offences of his fellows, and in order to prevent the involvement of fellow reformers. 'Brandreth,' according to one account, 'is said to have declared, that his blood ought to be shed, as he had shed blood; but he hoped he should be the only victim.' But, at the same time, he 'felt no contrition' for the murder which he had committed. Although 'ready to join in any act of religion', he was 'insensible of any remorse, and proof against all fear'. 'God gave me great fortitude.' he wrote to his wife, 'to bear up my spirits on trial.'[2]

We may see the Pentridge rising as one of the first attempts in history to mount a wholly proletarian insurrection, without any middle-class support. The objectives of this revolutionary movement cannot perhaps be better characterized than in the words of the Belper street song – 'The Levelution is begun ...'[3] The attempt throws light upon the extreme isolation into which the northern and Midlands workers had been forced during the Wars, and it is a transitional moment between Luddism and the 'populist' Radicalism of 1818–20 and 1830–32. Even without Oliver's patent provocations, some kind of insurrection would probably have been attempted, and perhaps with a

1. Wood to Fitzwilliam, 6–7 and 9 June 1817; deposition of John Buckley; Capt. J. Armytage to Fitzwilliam; all in Fitzwilliam Papers, F.45 (i) and (k). For Mann see above, p. 645.

2. *Independent Whig*, 9 November 1817; *Nottingham Review*, 24 October 1817.

3. B. Gregory, *Autobiographical Recollections*, p. 129. The Pentridge men styled themselves 'the Regenerators'.

greater measure of success.[1] Indeed, in the Crown's view, not Oliver nor Mitchell, but Thomas Bacon, who himself had travelled between Nottingham, Derby, Yorkshire, Lancashire and Birmingham, was the main instigator of rebellion.[2]

This offers, in terms of *realpolitik*, a shred of justification for the actions of Sidmouth and the Government. Believing that some outbreak was inevitable, they determined to handle it in such a way as to exact an example of terror and punishment which would silence, once for all, the monstrous sedition of the 'lower orders'. But this is not to suggest that in any circumstances in 1817 a working-class insurrection had any hope of success. Every detail of the story illustrates the weakness of the revolutionary organization, and the lack of an experienced leadership. The testimony of the Nottingham informer, who was also evidently employed (with the knowledge of the Town Clerk and of Sidmouth) in a provocative rôle, illustrates the position of reformers in a hundred industrial villages. On 6 June he visited Charles Smith at Arnold (formerly a notable Luddite centre) 'and began to talk with him about the Job and asked him if he had got anybody ready':

He said all the Town were ready, if there was a probability of succeeding, but he did not think there was a chance – He said, there could be nothing done unless they were properly organized and had a good leader, and he advised me to keep clear from the hands of Justice, as the intended attempt would only get many hanged . . .[3]

V. PETERLOO

In the following months such men as Charles Smith mourned Brandreth in their thousands. Cashman apart, this was the first blood shed in the encounter. The psychic consequences were

1. See the deposition of one of those deeply involved, James Birkin, that he had no doubt that insurrection would have broken out 'in various places in Nottingham, Yorkshire, Lancashire and Staffordshire' without Oliver's intervention (H.O. 42.172).

2. *The King* v. *Thomas Bacon*, brief in T.S. 11.351; Lord G. Cavendish to Fitzwilliam, 25 August 1817, Fitzwilliam Papers, F.45 (k).

3. H.O. 40.6. A week previously Smith had told the informer: 'He has read of many Revolutions but none that succeeded without the co-operation of some great men & he thinks there are not any to aid the present proceedings . . .'

profound, and thereafter both Government and reformers saw the issue as a sheer contest of power. And yet the longer-term influence of the Oliver affair was to strengthen the constitutionalist, as opposed to the revolutionary, wing of the reform movement. A rising *without* Oliver would have panicked the middle class to the side of the administration. A rising *with* Oliver threw Whigs and middle-class reformers on to the alert. For three years the crucial political contests centred upon the defence of civil liberties, and the rights of the Press, where the middle class itself was most sensitive. The Oliver affair gave to the working-class reform movement after 1817 a determined but constitutionalist outlook. 'Peaceably if we may' took precedence over 'forcibly if we must'. The acquittals of Wooler, Hone, the Folley Hall insurgents, and the protests at the 'spy system' of such men as Earl Fitzwilliam and Coke of Norfolk (and of much of the Press), emphasized the importance of vestigial rights and of the constitutionalist tradition. The failure at Pentridge emphasized the extreme danger of conspiracy. Only the shock of Peterloo (August 1819) threw a part of the movement back into revolutionary courses; and the Cato Street Conspiracy (February 1820) served to reinforce the lesson of Oliver and of Pentridge. From 1817 until Chartist times, the central working-class tradition was that which exploited every means of agitation and protest short of active insurrectionary preparation.

Moreover, moderate reformers and Whigs were not slow to turn the lesson of Oliver to their own advantage. Indeed, the *Leeds Mercury* drew a lesson from the exposures which was, in effect, that the working class must place itself under the guidance and protection of the Whigs and middle-class reformers. In its editorial on the Derby trials it advised reformers to:

... shun as an enemy every political missionary who should seek to instil the deadly seeds of rebellion into their minds. ... Every one should be suspected henceforth as a spy, or an informer, or an incendiary, who talks of any force but that of reason ...[1]

In London the Burdettite *Independent Whig* drew much the

1. *Leeds Mercury*, 30 October 1817.

same lesson: one of the victims at Derby had, earlier in 1817, cancelled his subscription to the *Whig* and announced his intention of subscribing to the *Political Register*, and the rising was seen as a consequence of the propagation of Cobbett's 'poisonous doctrines'.[1] Cobbett, for his part saw his warnings against all 'clubs and correspondencies' confirmed, while Hunt, on more than one occasion in the future, raised the cry of 'Oliver' to silence critics such as Watson, Cleary and Thistlewood. For forty more years, the name of Oliver tolled in the memory of physical force reformers and Chartists, and gave a fatal irresolution to all their preparations.

There is a sense in which Peterloo followed directly, and inevitably, upon Pentridge. It was the outcome of an extraordinarily powerful and determined 'constitutionalist' agitation, largely working class in character, within a potentially revolutionary context. What was displayed, in 1819, was not the strength but the growing weakness of the English *ancien régime*. Fragmented and terrorized, with many local leaders under arrest, the reform movement had little organized expression through much of 1818. But, in a curious way, the authorities were powerless also. The Government met in a hostile London, where juries had refused to convict Wooler and Hone, where grotesque prints and lampoons were displayed in the windows, and where publications which were, in the eyes of the authorities, seditious atrocities, were disseminated with impunity. One by one they were forced to release the reformers – Thomas Evans, Gravener Hensen, Knight, Bamford, Johnson, Bagguley, Mitchell and many others – held on suspicion in 1817. The released men refused to lie down: they addressed meetings, attended dinners in their honour, and attempted to sue the Government for illegal arrest. In Lancashire and the Midlands there were great strikes in which supposedly illegal trade unions paraded the streets. The repression of the 1790s had been endorsed not only by the landowners and many employers, but by enough public opinion in both the middle and working classes, to silence the Jacobins. The repression of 1817 provoked, on the contrary, an accession of strength to the radical reformers, while a large section of middle-class opinion held

1. *Independent Whig*, 23 October 1817.

aloof from the Government. In 1795 Pitt could present himself as defending the Constitution against French innovation. In 1819 Liverpool, Sidmouth, Eldon and Castlereagh were seen as men intent upon displacing constitutional rights by despotic 'continental' rule.

1819 was a rehearsal for 1832. In both years a revolution was possible (and in the second year it was very close) because the Government was isolated and there were sharp differences within the ruling class. And in 1819 the reformers appeared more powerful than they had ever been before, *because* they came forward in the rôle of constitutionalists. They laid claim to rights, some of which it was difficult to deny at law, which had never been intended for extension to the 'lower orders'. But if these rights were gained, it meant, sooner or later, the end of the old régime: as scores of magistrates wrote in to the Home Office, in very similar terms, if meetings or unions or seditious pamphlets were allowed, *at what point would this stop*? For no one supposed that the structure of power rested upon Pitt's barracks alone. The integument of power, in the countryside or in the corporate town, was composed of deference and fear. If riots or strikes were, from time to time, inevitable, there must still be enough of these two requisites for insubordination to be cowed as soon as an example was made of the ring-leaders.

In 1817 this world was passing. By 1819, in whole regions of England, it had passed. The defences of deference had been weakened by Dissent and (despite itself) by Methodism. They had been challenged by Luddism and Hampden Clubs. In May 1817 Sherwin carried further Thelwall's insight into the influence of manufactures on the working man. 'The nature of his calling forces him into the society of his fellow men.' In a manufacturing district political discussion is inevitable, while the workers have the means of organization in clubbing their pennies together. Numbers bring an absence of deference:

If an Aristocrat happen to meet a Weaver in the street, and the latter does not choose to *off with his hat*, the man of consequence cannot harm him. Hence arises that contempt for assuming greatness and petty despotism, which we may observe in all manufacturing towns. And from this contempt proceeds ... that downright rooted hatred, that we may observe when we hear an Aristocratical minded man speak of those parts of the country wherein manufactures and political information have flourished . . .[1]

The rights to which reformers laid claim in 1819 were those of political organization, the freedom of the press, and the freedom of public meeting; beyond these three, there was the right to vote. We may take these in order. For the first, the British working class had already become – as it was to remain for a hundred years – perhaps the most 'clubbable' working class in Europe. The facility with which English working men formed societies in the early nineteenth century is formidable. The influence of Methodism and of Dissenting chapels; the lengthening experience of the friendly societies and trade unions; the forms of parliamentary constitutionalism, as observed on the hustings or as mediated by middle-class and self-educated reformers to the working-class movement – all these influences had diffused a general addiction to the forms and proprieties of organizational constitutionalism. It seems at times that half a dozen working men could scarcely sit in a room together without appointing a Chairman, raising a point-of-order, or moving the Previous Question:

. . . a Motion was made, 'That no person but Leaders of Sections should vote' – one Gentn. got up and spoke as follows – Mr Chair! Mr Chair!! Mr Chair!!! I *desire* you will do Your Duty in keeping Order – after he had repeated this so often I was afraid of his Lungs, the Chairman called out Order! Order!! and with such a voice that made me tremble. . . . He then proceeded, – Mr Chair I look upon *us* here, as being Members sent to *this here* place, to transact the business of Reform, in same manner as our business should be done in Parliament, to which I compare us here. . . . He then took his Seat when up started two or three others . . . one of them saying he had only a few words to say in Opposition to that Gentn. who had compared this place to the House of Commons – that House of Corruption – that Den of Thieves, as Cobbett properly called it, if he thought they resembled that Company in any way he would never come into this place again . . .[2]

The account is from Manchester. But, if another informer's report is to be believed, the Cato Street Conspirators, while

1. Sherwin's *Political Register*, 24 May 1817.
2. H.O. 42.198, reprinted in full in D. Read, op. cit., pp. 219–20.

plotting in a garret the assassination of the Cabinet, found it necessary to appoint one of their number as Chairman (with a pike as symbol of office), and to take the questions of beheading Castlereagh and firing the Tower of London in proper form, with a vote upon the substantive motion.

This playing at Parliament was only the ridiculous side of the creative tradition of organization. To unite in the face of exploitation or oppression was almost the instinctual response of such men as weavers and colliers. They themselves had come to understand that it was only through organization that they could transform themselves from a mob into a political movement. Moreover, while Pitt's legislation against *national* delegate or corresponding societies remained on the statute book, when the 'Gagging Acts' expired in 1818 the right of local organization could only with difficulty be challenged at law. The last months of 1818 and the first of 1819 saw a number of new models of local reform societies: the Stockport Political Union: the Hull Political Protestants: the British Forum in London. When compared with the Corresponding Societies or Hampden Clubs, they are distinguished by their *open* character. They were, above all, centres for debate and political discussion (in Newcastle they were called 'Political Reading Societies'), and for the sale of Radical publications. As such, they were less open to provocations by spies. The spies could enter, but what else could they do? [1]

In the absence of national organization, the local societies took their lead from the Radical press. It was because this press provided the very tissues without which the movement would have fallen apart, that the claim for the fullest liberty of the press was one of the foremost Radical demands. 1816–20 were, above all, years in which popular Radicalism took its style from the hand-press and the weekly periodical. This means of propaganda was in its fullest egalitarian phase. Steam-printing had scarcely made headway (commencing with *The Times* in 1814), and the plebeian Radical group had as easy access to the hand-press as Church or King. Transport was too

1. For an account of the impressive Stockport model, see below, p. 788, for the Political Protestants, Wearmouth, op. cit., pp. 88 ff. and Halévy, op. cit., pp. 59–60.

slow for the national (or London) newspaper to weaken the position of the provincial press; but rapid enough to enable the weekly *Political Register* or *Black Dwarf* to maintain a running commentary on the news. The means of production of the printed page were sufficiently cheap to mean that neither capital nor advertising revenue gave much advantage; while the successful Radical periodical provided a living not only for the editor, but also for regional agents, booksellers, and itinerant hawkers, thereby making of Radicalism, for the first time, a profession which could maintain its own full-time agitators. In favourable conditions the circulation of the publications of Cobbett, Carlile, Wooler and Wade competed with, or greatly exceeded, all but a handful of the established journals.[1]

From the time of Cobbett's defection, it was the *Black Dwarf* which commanded the largest Radical audience. Its editor, T. J. Wooler (1786–1853) was a Yorkshire-born printer, who had served his apprenticeship in Shoreditch, and his apprenticeship to politics in the small debating societies (such as the Socratic Union, which met at the 'Mermaid Tavern', Hackney) and periodicals of the war years.[2] In 1815 he had founded *The Stage*, whose mixture of heavy-handed satire and libertarian rhetoric set the tone also for the *Black Dwarf*. He had the moral support (and perhaps the subsidies) of Major Cartwright, and was himself exceptionally fluent both as an orator and as a writer – composing, on occasions, his articles directly on the stone. He was a consistent advocate of Radical organization, upon the open and constitutionalist pattern:

Those who condemn clubs either do not understand what they can accomplish, or they wish nothing to be done. ... Let us look at, and emulate the patient resolution of the Quakers. They have conquered *without arms* – without *violence* – without threats. They conquered by union.

The 'Political Protestants' (whose first club was founded at Hull in July 1818) exemplified, for him, the expedient organizational form, with classes (of not more than twenty), a weekly penny subscription, and the main function of selling and discussing Radical publications. 'Larger meetings are not so well

1. On all these points, see below, pp. 789 ff.
2. See entry in *D.N.B.*

calculated for discussions.' By a rule all 'secret transactions' were disavowed, and members proposing such could be censured or expelled. 'Our books and accounts ... shall at all times be laid open for the inspection of the magistrates.' Against such measures (he proclaimed) 'spies will be useless', and – in his characteristically overblown style – 'the agents of a Sidmouth and a Castlereagh will be as harmless as the scowling fiend that was startled at the ear of the Eve by the touch of Ithuriel'.[1]

Wooler had many competitors. In London, Henry White's *Independent Whig* was a substantial weekly newspaper, admirable in its coverage, but (from its Whiggish or Burdettite politics) little interested in Radical organization. John Hunt's *Examiner* served with brilliance as the weekly of the Radical intelligentsia, with Hazlitt as a regular contributor. John Thelwall had re-emerged to undertake the editorship of the *Champion*. These journals all held aloof from the plebeian movement – John and Leigh Hunt were irritated at being confused with their namesake, whose 'vulgarity' they disliked. (The *Examiner* dissociated itself editorially from the Orator after the first Spa Fields meeting – 'he never utters a sentence worth hearing' – with a discrimination that was both precious and obtuse.) [2] Among the score of pamphlet-sized periodicals, the most influential were Sherwin's *Political Register* and the *Gorgon*. Sherwin had been dismissed from the keepership of Southwell Bridewell for avowing himself a disciple of Paine. Although he was scarcely eighteen, his *Register* was (next to the *Gorgon*) perhaps the most cogent and well written of the periodicals. Moreover, it holds its place in the history of Radical theory because of Sherwin's association with Richard Carlile, who took over first the publishing and then the editorial control of the *Register*, finally transforming it into the renowned *Republican*.[3] The penny *Gorgon* had a smaller circulation, confined to London and Manchester. Edited by John Wade, a former journey-

1. *Black Dwarf*, 9 September 1818.
2. *Examiner*, 24 November 1816.
3. For its first few weeks, Sherwin's *Register* had carried this title. For Sherwin, see Wickwar, op. cit., pp. 69 ff., and for Carlile, see below, pp. 791–9.

man woolsorter, it was the most austere and reputable in intellectual terms. Wade was also the author of the extremely impressive *Black Book*, whose well-researched evidence as to parliamentary corruption, sinecures, pluralism and absenteeism in the Church, and nepotism and extravagance in the Bank and the East India Company, was published in fortnightly sixpenny parts, with a sale of 10,000 for each. The *Gorgon*'s main influence was upon the shaping theory of the working-class movement, where it served as a junction between the Utilitarians and the Radical trade unionists: 'we wish' (declared Wade) 'the Ultra Reformers, the Universal Suffrage men, to whom we belong, to make some advances to the moderate Reformers'.[1] On the other flank of Wooler and Cobbett, there were a dozen more or less ephemeral periodicals of the physical-force party, the most long-lived of which was the *Medusa: or Penny Politician*, edited by Thomas Davison, a Smithfield bookseller, which carried editorials on such themes as 'The Blowing Up of the Present System', and which warned its critics that –

... there are trees, lamp-posts, and halters everywhere, if summary justice is required, to make examples of any hardened and incorrigible villain, or any *great* or little plunderer of property.[2]

These were the periodicals which radiated Radicalism out from London to the provinces, whose editors, publishers, booksellers, hawkers, and even bill-stickers were in the front of the contest for the liberty of the press between 1817 and 1822. A main business of the Radicals was to increase their sales. But, as the movement grew, the provincial centres began to develop their own press. By far the most impressive was the *Manchester Observer*, a newspaper rather than a periodical, whose circulation at the end of 1819 approached that of the *Black Dwarf*, and which had a greater sense of the *news* of the movement than any competitor. The *Observer* was, of course, closely involved in Manchester politics; and local politics gave rise to the need for journals in other centres. George Edmonds in Birmingham fought a sharp Radical campaign which secured his elec-

1. *Gorgon*, 25 July 1818. See also below, p. 848, and Wickwar, op. cit., pp. 60–61, 67.
2. *Medusa*, 1 and 29 May 1819. See also Wickwar, op. cit., pp. 63–4.

tion, in April 1819, to the Birmingham Board of Guardians. He conducted his fight in a series of *Letters*[1] which later gave rise to *Edmond's Weekly Register*. In Norwich where the old Jacobin-Whig alliance which had returned William Smith to Parliament in 1802 still had some reality, the General Election of 1818 gave rise to a *Blue and White Dwarf*. Small sheets appeared in Coventry, Dudley and no doubt elsewhere.

'Dustmen and porters read and discuss politics; and labourers, journeymen, and masters speak *one language of disaffection and defiance.*'[2] It would be tedious to rehearse the alarm voiced by magistrates or Ministers at this phenomenon. The effect of the press, in the eyes of one observer, was that –

a line of demarcation was drawn between the different ranks of society, and a rooted antipathy and ferocious spirit of retaliation was engendered in the minds of the labouring classes.[3]

At the end of 1819, during the high tide of Hone and Cruikshank's brilliant lampoons (*The Political House that Jack Built* was supposed to have sold 100,000 copies) Eldon declared with indignation:

When he was in office [as Attorney-General in 1794] he never heard of waggons filled with seditious papers in order to be distributed through every village, to be scattered over the highways, to be introduced into cottages. ... There was ... scarcely a village in the Kingdom that had not its little shop in which nothing was sold but blasphemy and sedition.[4]

'There is scarcely a street or a post in the Land but that is placarded with something seditious,' wrote 'Bolton Fletcher'. Prosecutions apart, there were many attempts to 'write Cobbett down', with subsidized loyalist journals: Merle's *White Dwarf*, *Shadgett's Weekly Review of Cobbett, Wooler, Sherwin, and Other Democratical and Infidel Writers*, the Manchester *Patriot*, and scurrilous pamphleteers of the 'Job Nott'

1. G. Edmonds, *Letters to the Parishioners of Birmingham* (1819). See also a collection of anti-Edmonds tracts (British Museum, 8135 cc. 6); and *Birmingham Inspector* (1817).
2. See R. K. Webb, *The British Working Class Reader*, p. 47 et seq.
3. A. B. Richmond, *Narrative*, p. 54.
4. See Wickwar, op. cit. pp. 135 et seq.

tribe in Birmingham. (The perpetual quarrels in the reformers' own ranks provided these journals with a good deal of their copy.)

We may take one example of such publications, as an indication of the tone of panic which is to be found at the end of 1819. It is a bogus *Reformer's Guide* (designed to impersonate the genuine article), published in Leeds, a copy of which was sent by its proud authors to Lord Sidmouth, in the hope of gaining the eye of the Minister:

A radical reform means a complete revolution. It is a change of government, founded on republican principles, and its object is a new modification of the rights of mankind. This is its true character, and its features are pillage, murder, and massacre.

Reformers held to a 'levelling principle', and 'if we have an equal right to the property of others ... the same argument ... would palliate and excuse the violation of their wives and daughters'.

Who are these that fatten on your folly? Turn to the political booksellers. ... At first like certain venemous reptiles, they were found in dark alleys and holes, and hiding places, not daring to creep forth ...

But now they were reaping profits from the people's gullibility:

Bless God for his mercies to you. You cannot do that honestly, and be a factious discontented character. Be thankful that you are an Englishman. ... Read your Bible. ... Keep your wives and daughters at home ... [1]

The third right to which the constitutionalist reformers laid claim in 1819 was to the public meeting and open-air demonstration. Twenty years lay between the last demonstrations of the L.C.S. and the Spa Fields meetings. For all this time, popular political meetings had been largely in abeyance, except at times of elections or on those occasions when local Whig authorities had convened county meetings presided over by the gentry. In the provinces the very notion of working men attend-

1. *Reformer's Guide or The Rights of Man Considered* (Leeds, 1819).

ing meetings under the auspices of men of their own rank was, in the minds of loyalist gentry, synonymous with riot and insubordination. When a clerical magistrate prevented the holding of an orderly reform meeting in Birmingham early in 1817, the words which rose to his lips were 'riotous and disgraceful proceedings – clamour and violence of a misguided populace – tumultuous proceedings ... machinations of a few designing individuals ... wicked artifices'.[1] When the first open-air reform meeting was held in the Potteries (at Burslem, January 1817), Earl Talbot, the Lord-Lieutenant of Staffordshire, and a group of magistrates thought it necessary to attend in person, while troops were held at a short distance out of sight.[2]

It was, above all, in Lancashire that the new pattern of the constitutionalist reform demonstration first matured. As early as October 1816 there is a record of an orderly open-air demonstration in Blackburn. In January 1817 an Oldham meeting was preceded by a procession, complete with band, which was headed symbolically by a Quaker apothecary.[3] The Spa Fields affair – and then the experience of Pentridge – redoubled the determination of the constitutionalists to refute the accusations that they were a disorderly and ragged rabble. Bamford's account of the preparations for Peteloo is well known:

It was deemed expedient that this meeting should be as morally effective as possible, and that it should exhibit a spectacle such as had never before been witnessed in England. We had frequently been taunted in the press with our ragged, dirty appearance ... with the confusion of our proceedings, and the mob-like crowds in which our members were mustered ...

' "Cleanliness", "sobriety", "order", were the first injunctions issued by the committee, to which, on the suggestion of Mr Hunt, was subsequently added that of "peace".' This was a main purpose of the nightly or early morning drillings which preceded 16 August 1819. This was also a function of the

1. G. Edmonds, *Letter to the Inhabitants of Birmingham* (1817), p. 15.
2. H.O. 40.4. Earl Talbot, however, was favourably impressed by the orderliness of the crowd of 3,000, and recommended to Lord Sidmouth that the Hampden Club (rather than the right of meeting) should be suppressed.
3. H.O. 40.4.

discipline and pageantry with which the contingents moved towards Manchester – a leader to every hundred men (distinguished by a sprig of laurel in his hat), the bands and the great embroidered banners (presented with ceremony by the Female Unions), the contingent of 'our handsomest girls' at the front.[1]

But Bamford overstates the novelty of this discipline and display. For the forms taken over by the Radicals came from several sources. The camp-meetings of the Primitive Methodists contributed something, but their influence can be seen more clearly in the camp-meetings of the northern Chartists. Something was also contributed by the Army veterans who became Radical drill-sergeants. The reformers owed much more to the Radical political tradition, to the trade unions and friendly societies. From the time of Wilkes the people of London had revelled in the ceremonial of the great political occasion. Even Place's sober Westminster Committee expended more on the post-victory celebrations in 1807 than on the entire election campaign.[2] Each great occasion was planned by a special committee, which arranged for the order of the procession, its route, the appropriate favours and slogans to be displayed, the disposition of the bands and banners. When Henry Hunt made his triumphal entry into London on 15 September 1819 (in the interval between Peterloo and his trial), the orders for the day occupy a whole column of small print: 'Some hundreds of footmen bearing large branches of oak, poplar, &c.' 'A footman, bearing the emblem of union – a bundle of sticks stuck on a pitchfork ...', 'The Committees, bearing white wands, and all wearing knots of red ribband and laurel leaves in their hats', 'A green silk flag, with gold letters and Irish harp', bands, horsemen, 'A white flag surmounted and bordered with crape', and inscribed in black to the victims of Peterloo, 'The old red flag, with the inscription "Universal Suffrage"', a carriage containing Messrs Watson, Thistlewood and Preston and other friends of Mr Hunt, more bands, more flags, more horsemen, Mr H U N T .. and so on, down the page. Even a dog wore a favour, with 'No Dog Tax' on his collar. 'It would take me a whole day and a quire of paper to give you

1. Bamford, 1893 edn, chs. 24, 25.   2. See above, p. 507.

anything like detail,' Keats wrote to his brother George, 'The whole distance from the Angel at Islington to the Crown and Anchor was lined with multitudes.' [1]

This tradition was obviously less strong in the north, which had no Burdett and no Westminster elections. More influential here were the friendly society and trade unions. We have noted the medieval ceremonial of the Preston Guilds and of the wool-combers, from which the legal benefit societies had largely borrowed.[2] In the post-war years there is a growing evidence that the 'illegal' trade unions were openly displaying their strength. The miners at Dewsbury proceeded through the town, in 1819, with bands and banners flying; the framework-knitters formed orderly demonstrations in Nottingham in 1819; in Manchester, during the great strike of 1818, the spinners 'marched By piccadilly on Tuesday and was $23\frac{1}{2}$ minets in going Bye', reported the informer, Bent: 'One man from Eich shop is chose by the People and he commands them he forms them in Ranks and ... they obey him as Strickley as the armey do their Colonel and as Little Talking as in a Regiment.' [3]

'The peaceable demeanour of so many thousand unemployed Men is not natural,' General Byng commented on this occasion. It is a phrase worth pausing over. The gentry, who had decried the reformers as a rabble, were appalled and some were even panic-stricken when they found that they were *not*.

> ... that very ORDER they cried up before
> Did afterwards gall them ten thousand times more,
> When they found that these men, in their 'Radical Rags',
> March'd peacably on, with their Banners and Flags.[4]

The comment, from Newcastle, serves with redoubled force for Manchester. Norris, the Chairman of the Bench, when committing Hunt for trial after Peterloo, spoke (perhaps in self-extenuation) of a meeting,

1. *Cap of Liberty*, 15 September 1819; *Independent Whig*, 19 September 1819; John Keats, *Works* (Glasgow, 1911), V, p. 108.

2. See above, pp. 465-7.

3. Dewsbury, see Aspinall, op. cit., p. 341; Nottingham, see ibid., p. 320; Manchester, see *The Skilled Labourer*, p. 100.

4. 'Bob in Gotham', *Radical Monday* (Newcastle, 1821), p. 4.

assembled, with such insignia and in such a manner, with the *black flag*, the *bloody dagger*, with 'Equal Representation or Death'. ... They came in a threatening manner – they came under the banners of death, thereby showing they meant to overturn the Government.[1]

Bamford admitted that the pitch-black flag of the Lees and Saddleworth Union, lettered in white paint with 'Love', two hands joined and a heart, was 'one of the most sepulchral looking objects that could be contrived'. But it was not the flags so much as the *discipline* of the sixty or a hundred thousand who assembled on St Peter's Fields which aroused such alarm. The drilling, in the weeks preceding the meeting, sometimes undertaken by old Waterloo men – and, on occasion, with staves at the shoulder like muskets, or hand-claps to simulate firing – gave colour to the prosecution witnesses who spoke of a 'military array'. (Hunt himself had deprecated this 'playing at soldiers'.) Beneath this contingent response, however, we must understand the profounder fear evoked by the evidence of the translation of the rabble into a disciplined *class*.

Even the middle-class reformers witnessed this development with alarm: the 'bustle and loss of time' of the 'constant succession of meetings', the 'violent resolutions' and 'intemperate harangues', all do 'infinite mischief – which utterly preclude moderate men from wishing them success'.[2] For the loyalist authorities, the challenge appeared as one between order and the loss of all moral, and even physical, authority. 'Armed or unarmed, Sir,' wrote a Yorkshire loyalist,

I consider such meetings, as that held at Manchester, to be nothing more or less than risings of the people; and I believe, that these risings of the people, if suffered to continue, would end in open rebellion ...[3]

The effect upon the reformers' morale of each successive demonstration was instantaneous. With each breach in the walls of deference, the waters of insubordination swept through. The morale of each individual weaver or shoemaker

1. An Observer, *Peterloo Massacre* (Manchester, 1819), p. 46.
2. *Manchester Gazette*, cited in D. Read, op. cit., p. 71.
3. A Yorkshire Freeholder, *A Letter to S. W. Nicholl, Esq.* (1819), p. 8.

was higher from the reassurance of the numbers, the pageantry, the rhetoric. If the open organization of the people had continued on this scale it would have become impossible to govern. The weeks before Peterloo saw scores of small meetings and (week by week) ever more impressive demonstrations in the regional centres: at Manchester and Stockport in June, at Birmingham, Leeds and London in July.[1] The policy of open constitutionalism was proving more revolutionary in its implication than the policy of conspiracy and insurrection. Wooler and Hunt had achieved, without any secret 'correspondencies' or system of delegates, a position in which they could call out a national movement. The election (at Birmingham in July) of Sir Charles Wolseley as 'legislatory attorney' to represent the unrepresented, pointed the way to an even more dangerous development: a National Convention, appointed by Radical suffrage, challenging Parliament. Confronted by this swelling power, Old Corruption faced the alternatives of meeting the reformers with repression or concession. But concession, in 1819, would have meant concession to a largely working-class reform movement; the middle-class reformers were not yet strong enough (as they were in 1832) to offer a more moderate line of advance. This is why Peterloo took place.

This has to be said again, since it has been suggested recently that Peterloo was an affair, in part unpremeditated, in part arising from the exacerbated relations in Manchester itself, but in no sense any part of a considered policy of Government repression. Mr Donald Read, in a study of Peterloo which does much to place the event in its local context, holds the view:

Peterloo, as the evidence of the Home Office shows, was never desired or precipitated by the Liverpool Ministry as a bloody repressive gesture for keeping down the lower orders. If the Manchester magistrates had followed the spirit of Home Office policy there would never have been a 'massacre'.

We shall probably never be able to determine with certainty whether or not Liverpool and Sidmouth were parties to the

1. See Halévy, op. cit., pp. 62–3.

decision to disperse the meeting with force.[1] But we can no more understand the significance of Peterloo in terms of the local politics of Manchester than we can understand the strategic importance of Waterloo in terms of the field and the orders of the day. If the Government was unprepared for the news of Peterloo, no authorities have ever acted so vigorously to make themselves accomplices after the fact. Within a fortnight the congratulations of Sidmouth and the thanks of the Prince Regent were communicated to the magistrates and military 'for their prompt, decisive, and efficient measures for the preservation of the public peace'. Demands for a parliamentary enquiry were resolutely rejected. Attorney and Solicitor-Generals were 'fully satisfied' as to the legality of the magistrates' actions. The Lord Chancellor (Eldon) was of the 'clear opinion' that the meeting 'was an overt act of treason'; he saw ahead 'a shocking choice between military government and anarchy'. State prosecutions were commenced, not against the perpetrators, but against the victims of the day – Hunt, Saxton, Bamford and others – and the first intention of charging them with high treason was only abandoned with reluctance. If the Manchester magistrates initiated the policy of repression, the Government endorsed it with every resource at its disposal.

1. Loc. cit., p. 207. Mr Read places great weight (p. 120) on a letter of Sidmouth's twelve days before Peterloo, advising the Manchester magistrates to 'abstain from any endeavour to disperse the mob'. But if any 'Peterloo decision' was reached by Sidmouth and the magistrates it is likely to have been reached privately in the week before the meeting. And it is highly unlikely that any record would have been left in the official Home Office papers for subsequent inspection. The 'Private and Secret' correspondence between Hobhouse and Byng and Norris (in H.O. 79.3) is curiously ambiguous. Several letters (which have the air of being 'for the record') deprecate 'hasty' or forcible action against the crowd (folios 479, 480, 483); but there is an air of anticipation without precedent, a private address is given to Norris (Chairman of the Manchester Bench) for correspondence (folio 489), and two days after Peterloo Hobhouse records Sidmouth's satisfaction in the judgement of Colonel L'Estrange in 'his employing the Yeomanry in the Van, agreeably to the Plan on which I know you intended to act' (folio 510). My opinion is (a) that the Manchester authorities certainly intended to employ force, (b) that Sidmouth knew – and assented to – their intention to arrest Hunt in the midst of the assembly and to disperse the crowd, but that he was unprepared for the violence with which this was effected.

Hunt, Cartwright, Burdett, Carlile, Sir Charles Wolseley, Wroe
(of the *Manchester Observer*), Edmonds (of Birmingham) –
these are only a few of those imprisoned or awaiting prosecution by the end of 1819. Hay, the clerical magistrate prominent
on the Peterloo bench, was rewarded with the £2,000 living of
Rochdale. Earl Fitzwilliam, for protesting at the massacre, was
removed from his Lord-Lieutenancy. The Six Acts sealed what
16 August initiated. If the Peterloo decision was unpremeditated, it would appear to have been the signal for which the
Government was waiting.[1]

Lord Liverpool declared that the action of the Manchester
magistrates was 'substantially right', although it was not altogether 'prudent'. 'There remained no alternative but to support
them.' At some point, the encounter was inevitable. But what
made it less than 'prudent' was its peculiar savagery, and for
this we must look to the Manchester context for the explanation. An exceptional antagonism obtained between the Manchester loyalists and the working-class reformers. In part this
was the result of the maturity of the working-class movement;
in part of a dozen factors – the loyalist sentiments of many of
the great commercial and manufacturing houses; their antagonism to the trade unions; the legacy of Luddism and of 1817;
the influence of Nadin; the influence of Tory churchmen. 'These
Manchester yeomen and magistrates are a greater set of brutes
than you form a conception of,' Place wrote to Hobhouse:

I know one of these fellows who swears 'Damn his eyes, seven
shillings a week is plenty for them'; and when he goes round to
see how much work his weavers have in their looms, he takes a
well-fed dog with him. . . . He said some time ago that 'The sons of
bitches had eaten up all the stinging nettles for ten miles around
Manchester, and now they had no greens to their broth.' Upon my
expressing indignation, he said, 'Damn their eyes, what need you
care about them? How could I sell you goods so cheap if I cared
anything about them.'

'They cut down and trampled down the people; and then it
was to end just as cutting and trampling the furze bushes on a

1. See *inter alia* C. D. Yonge, *Life of Lord Liverpool* (1868), II, pp.
378, 409, 419–22, 432; H. Twiss, *Life of Lord Eldon*, II, pp. 337–40;
Wickwar, op. cit., pp. 129–31 *et passim*; Pellew, *Life of Lord Sidmouth*,
pp. 283 ff.

common would end.'[1] A writer in the *Manchester Observer* in the week before Peterloo addressed the 'official gentlemen of Manchester': 'I defy the blood-thirsty partisans of Danton, Marat, Robespierre, to furnish a more despotic, tyrannical crew.'[2] A month after Peterloo a clerical magistrate afforded himself the privilege of the Bench to address the accused:

I believe you are a downright blackguard reformer. Some of you reformers ought to be hanged, and some of you are sure to be hanged – the rope is already round your necks . . .[3]

There are two points about Peterloo which have, somehow, become lost in recent accounts. The first is the actual bloody violence of the day. It really was a massacre. We need not give the hour by hour account once again.[4] But, whatever some of the drilling weavers had in mind, Hunt had exerted himself effectually in the week before the event to ensure obedience to his request for 'quietness and order', and a *'steady, firm* and *temperate* deportment'. The leaders of the contingents had warned their followers to ignore all provocations. Many staves – or 'walking-sticks' – had been left behind. The presence of so many women and children was overwhelming testimony to the pacific character of a meeting which (the reformers knew) all England was watching. The attack was made on this multitude with the venom of panic.

But the panic was not (as has been suggested) the panic of bad horsemen hemmed in by a crowd. It was the panic of class hatred. It was the *Yeomanry* – the Manchester manufacturers, merchants, publicans, and shopkeepers on horseback – which did more damage than the regulars (Hussars). In the Yeomanry (a middle-class reformer testified) 'there are ... individuals

1. Wallas, op. cit., p. 141.   2. *Manchester Observer*, 7 August 1819.

3. *The Times*, 27 September 1819.

4. See the accounts in Bamford, Prentice, J. E. Taylor; the contemporary reports by Tyas in *The Times*, by Baines in the *Leeds Mercury*, and by Carlile in Sherwin's *Political Register*; the evidence of witnesses and participants in the *Trial* of Henry Hunt, the *Inquest on John Lees* of Oldham and the action against Colonel Birley; F. A. Bruton, *The Story of Peterloo* (1919) and *Three Accounts of Peterloo* (1921), and (in defence) [Francis Philips], *An Exposure of the Calumnies &c.* (1819).

whose political rancour approaches to absolute insanity'.[1] These were the men who pursued the banners, knew the speakers by name and sought to pay off old scores, and who mustered and cheered at the end of their triumph. 'There was whiz this way and whiz that way,' declared one cotton-spinner: 'whenever any cried out "mercy", they said, "Damn you, what brought you here?".' We may get the feel of the confused field from such a passage as this:

I picked up a Cap of Liberty; one of the Cavalry rode after me and demanded it; I refused to give it up. Two others then came up and asked what was the matter, when the first said, this fellow won't give up this Cap of Liberty. One of the others then said, damn him, cut him down. Upon this, I ran. ... One of the Cavalry cut at Saxton, but his horse seemed restive, and he missed his blow. He then called out to another, 'There's Saxton, damn him, run him through.' The other said, 'I had rather not, I'll leave that for you to do.' When I got to the end of Watson-street, I saw ten or twelve of the Yeomanry Cavalry, and two of the Hussars cutting at the people, who were wedged close together, when an officer of Hussars rode up to his own men, and knocking up their swords said, 'Damn you what do you mean by this work?' He then called out to the Yeomanry, 'For shame, gentlemen; what are you about? the people cannot get away.' They desisted for a time, but no sooner had the officer rode to another part of the field, than they fell to work again.[2]

There is no term for this but class war. But it was a pitifully one-sided war. The people, closely packed and trampling upon each other in the effort to escape, made no effort at retaliation until the very edges of the field, where a few trapped remnants – finding themselves pursued into the streets and yards – threw

1. J. E. Taylor, op. cit., pp. 175–6. Hunt published a list of the occupations of the Yeomanry who actually served on 16 August: these included several sons of publicans and manufacturers, a wine-merchant, commission-agent, dancing-master, cheese-monger, butcher, &c.; *Address to the Radical Reformers*, 29 October 1822, pp. 13–16. See also D. Read, op. cit., p. 81.

2. *Inquest on John Lees* (1820), pp. 70, 180. Compare Tyas's account in *The Times*: 'Two Yeomanry privates rode up to Saxton. "There ... is that villain, Saxton; do you run him through the body." – "No," replied the other, "I had rather not – I leave it to you." The man immediately made a lunge at Saxton.'

brick-bats at their pursuers. Eleven were killed or died from their wounds. That evening, on every road out of Manchester the injured were to be seen. The Peterloo Relief Committee had, by the end of 1819, authenticated 421 claims for relief for injuries received on the field (a further 150 cases still awaited investigation). Of these, 161 cases were of sabre wounds, the remainder were injuries sustained while lying beneath the crowd or beneath the horses' hooves. More than 100 of the injured were women or girls. While there will have been some impostors, there will also have been scores of injured who did not claim relief, because their wounds were slight or because they feared victimization.[1] We may leave the field with Bamford's unforgettable picture:

In ten minutes . . . the field was an open and almost deserted space. . . . The hustings remained, with a few broken and hewed flag-staves erect, and a torn and gashed banner or two drooping; whilst over the whole field were strewed caps, bonnets, hats, shawls, and shoes, and other parts of male and female dress, trampled, torn, and bloody. The yeomanry had dismounted – some were easing their horses' girths, others adjusting their accoutrements, and some were wiping their sabres . . .[2]

The second point about Peterloo which has somehow evaded definition is the sheer *size* of the event, in terms of its psychological impact and manifold repercussions.[3] It was without question a formative experience in British political and social history. Once again, as with Pentridge, we may distinguish between the short-term and long-term repercussons. Within two days of Peterloo, all England knew of the event. Within a week every detail of the massacre was being canvassed in alehouses, chapels, workshops, private houses. At first it is difficult to distinguish any clear pattern of response. The key-note, among the reformers and their supporters, was certainly indignation, anger, or compassion, rather than alarm. Already, on the field, Henry Hunt (who showed at his best during the moment of crisis) seemed to sense that for the Radicals Peter-

1. J. E. Taylor, op. cit., p. 170.   2. Bamford, op. cit., p. 157.
3. See, however, the useful discussion of the aftermath of Peterloo in Read, op. cit., chs. 9–14.

loo was a moral victory. He had been himself the victim of the Yeomanry's violence. After his arrest he had been forced to run the gauntlet between the special constables, who had struck him with their staves: General Clay 'with a large stick struck him over the head with both hands as he was ascending the steps to the Magistrate's house', a blow which knocked down his famous white hat and 'packed it over his face'. Notwithstanding this treatment, when he emerged from the house (a fair-minded opponent recalled):

I thought I could perceive a smile of triumph on his countenance. A person (Nadin, I believe) offered to take his arm, but he drew himself back, and in a sort of whisper said: 'No, no, that's rather too good a thing . . .'[1]

For several days, in Lancashire, the immediate talk was of vengeance. Manchester appeared as if under martial law; there were riots, and rumours of the 'country' people advancing in military order; Bamford has described the grinding of scythes, and the preparation of 'old hatchets . . . screw-drivers, rusty swords, pikels, and mop-nails'.[2] But by the end of August the impulse to insurrection was checked and steadied by the evidence of overwhelming moral support in the country. The epithet itself – 'Peter-Loo' – with its savagely sardonic confidence, indicates better than any other evidence, the tone of feeling. In the succeeding weeks, the storm of the Radical press was to be swelled by the inspired lampoons of Cruikshank and Hone; the 'butchers' of Manchester met not only with the full-blown libertarian rhetoric of Hunt and Wooler but with bitter jeering which it was more hard to bear. 'These are THE PEOPLE all tatter'd and torn,' ran *The Political House that Jack Built*,

> Who curse the day wherein they were born,
> On account of Taxation too great to be borne,
> And pray for relief, from night to morn,
> Who, in vain, Petition in every form,
> Who, peaceably Meeting to ask for Reform,
> Were sabred by Yeomanry Cavalry, who

1. F. A. Bruton, *Three Accounts of Peterloo*, pp. 20–21, 68.
2. Bamford, op. cit., p. 163; see also *Independent Whig*, 22 August 1819.

Were thank'd by THE MAN, all shaven and shorn,
All cover'd with Orders – and all forlorn;
THE DANDY OF SIXTY, who bows with a grace,
And has *taste* in wigs, collars, curiasses, and lace;
Who, to tricksters, and fools, leaves the State and its treasure,
And when Britain's in tears, sails about at his pleasure ...

Even the Prince Regent's speech at the opening of Parliament
was matter for another parody:

but lo!
CONSPIRACY and TREASON are abroad!
Those imps of darkness, gender'd in the wombs
Of spinning-jennies, winding-wheels, and looms,
In Lunashire –
O Lord!
My L—ds and G—tl—n, we've much to fear!
Reform, Reform, the swinish rabble cry –
Meaning of course rebellion, blood, and riot –
Audacious rascals! you, my Lords, and I,
Know 'tis their duty to be starved in quiet ... [1]

Peterloo outraged every belief and prejudice of the 'free-born
Englishman' – the right of free speech, the desire for 'fair play',
the taboo against attacking the defenceless. For a time, ultra-
Radicals and moderates buried their differences in a protest
movement with which many Whigs were willing to associate.
Protest meetings were held: on 29 August in Smithfield, with
Dr Watson in the chair, and Arthur Thistlewood as a speaker:
on 5 September a much larger meeting in Westminster, with
Burdett, Cartwright, Hobhouse and John Thelwall among the
speakers.[2] When Hunt made his triumphal entry into London
ten days later, *The Times* estimated that 300,000 were in the
streets.

No one can suppose that the tradition of the 'free-born Englishman' was merely notional who studies the response to the
news of Peterloo. In the months which followed, political
antagonism hardened. No one could remain neutral; in Manchester itself the 'loyalists' were placed in an extreme isolation,
and the Methodists were the only body with a popular follow-

1. W. Hone. (with Cruikshank), *The Man in the Moon* (1819).
2. *Independent Whig*, 29 August, 5 September 1819.

ing to come (with fulsome declarations) to their side.[1] But if there were many gentry and professional men who were shocked by Peterloo, at the same time they had no desire to conjure up *further* monster demonstrations of the people.[2] Thus the effective movement after Peterloo, which swung from the cry of 'vengeance' back into constitutionalist forms of protest, was largely working class in initiation and character.

If Peterloo was intended to curb the right of public meeting it had exactly the opposite consequences. Indignation provoked Radical organization where it had never before existed, and open-air demonstrations were held in regions hitherto under the spell of the 'loyalists'. At Coseley, near Wolverhampton, a Political Union was formed – the first in that part of the Black Country. 'Disaffection,' a local J.P. complained,

in this neighbourhood certainly cannot arise from distress, for in point of employment and Wages the Workmen in Mines and Iron Works are perhaps in a better situation than the Working Classes in any other branches in the kingdom.[3]

The most remarkable accession to the movement came from Newcastle, and from the pitmen of Northumberland and Durham. Here – despite a continuous tradition of Radicalism since the 1790s (Bewick and his fellow tradesmen and artisans, and the strong friendly societies and trade unions) – the Church and King party controlled the Corporation and had intimidated the reformers from open organization. It had 'long been the boast of the Pitt faction,' wrote the *Independent Whig*, 'that the population of this part of England was perfectly passive and destitute of spirit.' In July and August 1819 the Radical 'Reading Societies' gave rise to Political Protestants (on the model commended by the *Black Dwarf*). After Peterloo the whole district seemed to turn over to the reformers. An

1. H.O. 42.198. The Committee of the Manchester Sunday Schools resolved (24 September 1819) to exclude all children who attended in white hats or wearing radical badges. See, however, D. Read, op. cit., p. 203 for dissensions in the Methodist body.

2. There were exceptions: for example, in Yorkshire and in Norfolk protest meetings were held under Whig auspices.

3. H.O. 42.98. The committee consisted of two bakers, and a blacksmith, colliery agent, forge hammer-man, collier, small farmer, and shoemaker.

open-air protest demonstration was called (with the permission of the Mayor) on 11 October. It was expected that the 'comparative steadiness' of the coal trade, together with the threat of certain colliery viewers to dismiss men who attended, would limit support. In the event,

From the North, from the South, from the East, from the West,
The RADICALS march'd into Town, six-a-breast,

to the accompaniment of a band playing 'Johnnie Cope, are ye waukin' yet?'

From fifty to one hundred thousand people 'started up, as if by magic', and observers were astonished to see the instructions for 'Order, Spirit, Unanimity' observed, not only by the dreaded pitmen, but by sailors from Sunderland and Shields. After marching eight miles, the Shields contingent refused even 'to partake of a barrel of ale provided for them', being 'determined not ... to do anything which might endanger the harmony of the day'. The speakers included a weaver, a schoolmaster, a tailor, a master printer, a bookseller and a cobbler. After 'Radical Monday' (claimed as Newcastle's 'first public political meeting ever held in the open air') the city never lost its position among the three or four leading Radical and Chartist centres. Radical 'classes' were formed in the next few weeks, with the rapidity of a revivalist campaign, in all the surrounding industrial villages and ports: in Jarrow, Sheriff Hill, Penshaw, Rainton, Houghton, Newbattle, Hetton, Hebbern, South Shields, Winlaton, Sunderland – the *Black Dwarf* could be seen 'in the hat-crown of almost every pitman you meet'. Sedition spread as far as the pitmen of Bishop Wearmouth, who (an exasperated magistrate wrote to Sidmouth) 'have had the Assurance to propose that Tradesmen known to be Radicals should be employed in supplying the collieries with Articles of consumption'.[1]

Against this threat the Newcastle loyalists formed an Armed Association. Against the Armed Association the pitmen and

1. *A Full Account of the General Meeting of the Inhabitants of Newcastle* (Newcastle, 1819); 'Bob in Gotham', *Radical Monday*; *Black Dwarf* and *Newcastle Chronicle*, passim; *Durham Advertiser*, quoted in *Political Observer*, 19 December 1819; H.O. 42.198; *Independent Whig*, 17 October 1819; R. G. Wearmouth, op. cit., pp. 102–3, above pp. 388, 432.

forgemen began to arm in their turn. These are the preliminaries to civil war. We have been overmuch influenced by Bamford's picture of the sober and restrained response of all but a few hotheads to Peterloo. For in the months of October and November Radical constitutionalism itself took a revolutionary turn. If their opponents were armed and acted unconstitutionally then they also would exercise the right (which Major Cartwright had long proclaimed) of every citizen to bear arms. If meetings were to be ridden down, then they would attend them with the means of defence. The staple means were pikes, stout wooden staves with a groove at one end into which a sharp blade (carried in a pocket) could be inserted. The blades could be easily made (at different sizes, from 1*s.* to 3*s.*, according to the reformer's means) in one of the small smithies in which Newcastle, Sheffield, Birmingham and Manchester abounded. We have some knowledge of one such Manchester *entrepreneur* (with one eye on his *Black Dwarf* and the other on a thriving market) called Naaman Carter. He was so incautious as to employ as his main agent (whose business it was to tout samples of the pikes around the inns and 'hush shops' in the weaving villages, and collect the instalments from those who bought their pike blades on the 'never-never') a man who was employed in another capacity – as informer 'Y'. 'Y's' circumstantial and often irrelevant accounts can scarcely be dismissed as fabrications. On one occasion, when he called upon the Radical smith,

I found him and his wife fighting – I told him it was foolish to fight on the Sabbath-day, they had better adjourn it till Monday, when they might fight it out. The Wife said, I shall not be beaten by you, I will have you put into the New Bayley for making Pikes – She said this, just as he was pushing and kicking her out of the door ...

But Naaman Carter's problems of marital adjustment did not affect the pike trade, which was thriving in the first week of November. 'Y' found plenty of customers who admired the samples which (one said) 'would do the business for the Prince and every Bugger of them'. One of his customers was none other than Bamford, who in the reports of 'Y', scarcely resembles the self-portrait which he drew twenty years later.

At a hush-shop where the transaction was settled, Bamford gave the toast: 'May the Tree of Liberty be planted in Hell, and may the bloody Butchers of Manchester be the Fruit of it!' As the fumes of the illicit brew rose, one of his companions said, they would give the Manchester butchers 'a damn good piking, and he would go home and work, till God damn him, his hands would fly off, and sing Brittania, and the Devil would fetch them all'.[1]

There is no doubt that these sentiments were general in the manufacturing districts. It was rumoured that pistols were being smuggled from Birmingham to the north in the 'pot-carts'. From town after town, in October and November, there came reports of arming, drilling, and demonstrations in arms: Newcastle, Wolverhampton, Wigan, Bolton, Blackburn. The Halifax reformers returned from a meeting at Huddersfield in November 'marching in ranks about eight or ten abreast, with music, and six or seven flags, and lighted candles; many of them had sticks ...' At a certain point they 'shouted and fired many pistols in the air'. At Burnley ten or fifteen thousand attended a demonstration, despite placards from the magistrates cautioning them not to do so. At their head was a man with a board on which was 'Order, Order' but here also they 'fired scores of pistols'. At Halifax, at an earlier meeting, one of the forty-one banners had been inscribed: 'We groan, being burdened, waiting to be delivered. ... But we rejoice in hopes of a Jubilee.' (It was not the jubilee of George the Third that was anticipated.) Another declared: 'He that sheddeth man's blood by man shall his blood be shed.' The contingent from Ripponden carried a picture of a half-starved weaver in his loom: 'The poor man's labour is as dear to him as the rich man's property.' At Sheffield a monster procession marched to the Brocco behind bands playing the 'Dead March in Saul' and 'Scots wha hae wi' Wallace bled.'[2]

1. 'Y's' verbal deposition to Manchester Boroughreeve, 6 and 8 November 1819, in H.O. 42.198.

2. 'Papers relative to the Internal State of the Country', *Parliamentary Debates*, XLI (1820), *passim* (a somewhat sensational selection of magistrates' reports, &c); H.O. 42.198; J. E. Taylor, op. cit., pp. 102–34; *Briton*, 11 November 1819; *Independent Whig*, 10, 17, 31 October 1819; Halévy, op. cit., p. 66.

But by the end of December 1819 the movement was in a virtual state of collapse. For this there were two reasons: the divisions among the Radical leaders, and the repression of the Six Acts. The first makes up a tangled story which has not yet been successfully unravelled. We have noted that the London Radical organization was always weak and amorphous. There was, in London, in 1818 and in the early part of 1819, no coherent central body similar to the Political Unions and Protestants of the Midlands and north. Activities were often called on an *ad hoc* basis – meetings of 'the friends of Mr Wooler' or special dinners at the 'Crown and Anchor'. The two Westminster elections of 1818 had aroused much dissension between the supporters of Burdett (who insisted upon giving first a banker friend, Kinnaird, and then John Cam Hobhouse, his support as second candidate as against the claims of Cartwright, Cobbett, or Hunt), and other Radical groupings.

Despite the fiasco of Spa Fields, Dr Watson and Thistlewood remained at the centre of the most determined attempts at the organization of London's popular Radicalism. If the reports of yet one more well-placed informer (John Williamson) are to be believed, Thistlewood and Preston started once again, in the autumn of 1817, the attempt to create the sinews of conspiracy.[1] They found the going hard, in the aftermath of the Pentridge rising. The distress in Spitalfields was no longer so severe. In September (according to Williamson) Preston said 'he had been in Spitalfields ... to two or three of his old acquaintances and he found they had got work and such men as he they did not like'. Instead of stopping to hear his 'discourse', they kept on working in the loom. Thistlewood moved from one midnight meeting to another. There was obscure talk of getting a subsidy from an Englishman in Paris, a refugee of the 1790s. Oaths were taken, but the organization remained minuscule because 'Preston said that nobody should know

1. According to *Sherwin's Political Register* (13 September 1817) the authorities panicked at the rumour that an insurrection was planned to coincide with Bartholomew Fair. Four regiments of horse were called out, and the Lord Mayor searched for weapons among the 'oyster-tubs, sausage-stalls, and gingerbread baskets'. See H.O. 40.7 and 8 for details of this conspiracy.

what their plans were to be' until three hours before they were to be set in motion. Preston paid a brief visit (December 1817) to Birmingham, and reported the men there in 'good spirits'. Williamson himself was sent by Thistlewood to reconnoitre a barracks, and find out how many cannon were there. But apart from insurrectionary fantasies, the actual achievements of the group were very small. They provided Lord Sidmouth with some alarmist reading, they formed a few tavern groups, and they acted as cheer-leaders on several occasions for demonstrations of the London crowd.[1]

While Dr Watson was still associated with Thistlewood, he was probably no party to this attempt at conspiracy.[2] In February 1818 Sidmouth found a convenient means of putting Thistlewood out of the way, without recourse to a trial. Thistlewood had published an open letter, in which public and private grievances were confused, demanding 'satisfaction' from the Home Secretary – that is, challenging him to a duel. As a result he was confined in the King's Bench prison, as a disturber of the peace, Lord Sidmouth paying for his maintenance there out of his own pocket. In 1819 Radical London re-awoke, and scores of tavern groups and debating societies (some of them called Union Societies) were formed. Once again Watson attempted to build up some central organization, and he was joined in the summer of 1819 by Thistlewood, now released, who – it seems – accepted the policy of constitutional agitation and turned his back, for a time, upon plotting a *coup d'état*. By the summer of 1819 a London 'Committee of Two Hundred' was formed.[3] From June until October Watson, Thistlewood, Preston and Waddington were the most active and influential London leaders, especially among working people. They had the support of the old Jacobin orator, John Gale Jones, as well as of Carlile's *Republican*, the *Cap of Liberty*, and the *Medusa*. It was the 'Committee of Two Hundred' which

1. See, e.g deposition of Williamson, 18 December 1817; Thistlewood said 'Carlile was going to be tried tomorrow and that he hoped they would all come and bring as many as ever they could with them to give him three cheers.' T.S. 11.197.

2. Ibid., 27 September 1817: 'Thistlewood did not say much after Watson came. I think he does not like Watson.' Also 11 February 1818 in H.O. 40.9.   3. *Medusa*, 31 July 1819.

took the initiative in the well-prepared arrangements for Hunt's entry into London after Peterloo,[1] and the 'Doctor' himself performed the ceremonies of welcome, showing considerable self-restraint and tact in the face of the swollen arrogance and political fastidiousness of Hunt.

In 1820, after the Cato Street Conspiracy, a hostile observer gave an account of the 'Radical Committee Room', at the 'White Lion', Wych-street, which was regarded as a centre for London's Radical 'underground'. In the tap-room:

sat a set of suspicious, ill-looking fellows ... whilst at a small deal table to the right sat Mr —, with a book and some papers and printed bills before him; from the obscurity of the place, having no light but what proceeded from a candle placed before Mr —, or from that in the bar, a stranger coming in would not be able to recognize any of the faces on seeing them afterwards elsewhere. On the right hand ... is a small parlour; here of an evening a select committee assembled, and no others were admitted. This was the room in which the most private transactions were carried on; Mr Thistlewood or Dr Watson always came out into the passage to speak to any person who called there on business. In a very large room upstairs ... upwards of a hundred ill-looking persons have assembled of an evening; in it the open committee and loose members of the society met. .... Here their processions, &c., were arranged; their flags ... kept; whilst the more private business was carried on below in the parlour.[2]

Such a centre was, inevitably, the subject for the constant attention of Government spies. But it does not follow that all its proceedings were ridiculous. The London 'ultra' Radicals were, after Peterloo, placed in a very difficult predicament. 'Reform cannot be obtained without bloodshed,' the *Cap of Liberty* declared flatly in October, while the more irresponsible *Medusa* wrote:

There is not a Post from every part of the Kingdom, which does not furnish some new and striking instance of the necessity of constantly wearing arms.[3]

1. There were two preparatory committees: Dr Watson's, and a rival committee which included Thomas Evans, Galloway, and Carlile. But both merged under Watson's chairmanship. See *Independent Whig*, 12 September 1819.

2. G. T. Wilkinson, *The Cato-Street Conspiracy* (1820), pp. 56-7.

3. *Medusa*, 9 October 1819.

Carlile (two years later) summed up the message of all his writings in this period: 'Reform will be obtained when the existing authorities have no longer the power to withold it, and not before ...'[1] Moreover, the two months after Peterloo displayed in its fullest extent the weakness of the national leadership. Hunt's pusillanimity was at its worst. After Peterloo he held the centre of the stage, and both the reformers and the authorities watched anxiously his every move. This was rich meat for his vanity. Peterloo might have been a personal affront, and his processions through Lancashire and London personal triumphs. He disliked Watson having any share in the honours of the London demonstration; quarrelled with the route which the Committee had chosen, and upon which thousands of expectant Londoners were kept waiting for half the day. (He had a grudge against London, anyway, since he had been roughly handled and booed on the Westminster hustings in 1818.) He quarrelled with Watson about the Chairman (Gale Jones) chosen for his dinner of welcome, shouting at him in public: 'You are a damned officious meddling fellow; why not I take the chair, as well as Sir Francis Burdett after *his* procession?' He then commenced to quarrel about money-matters. In Lancashire he succeeded in giving offence to most of the local reform leaders, while he allowed a funeral pro-cession of some thousands to attend the burial of his favourite horse. He was in fact (and not without reason) more pre-occupied with manoeuvring for a position of vantage in the approaching trials than with attending to the movement in the country.[2]

By September the reformers were dividing into revolutionary and constitutionalist wings. The policy sanctioned by Hunt and Wooler was that of passive resistance, remonstrance, legal action against the perpetrators of Peterloo, and abstinence from all taxed articles. In August the policy had a good deal to

1. R. Carlile, *An Effort to set at rest some little disputes and misunder-standings between the reformers of Leeds* (1821), p. 10.
2. *Peterloo Massacre*, p. 72; Bamford, op. cit., pp. 247 ff.; *Cap of Liberty*, 15 September 1819; J. Johnson, *Letter to Henry Hunt, passim*; letters between Hunt, Watson and Thistlewood exchanged in the general press, October and November 1819.

recommend it, and was loyally supported by all sections of the movement. But by October it was wearing thin. It was abunantly evident that hopes of legal redress were empty, most of all in Lancashire; while it was superfluous to recommend abstinence to the northern weavers. Moreover, as week by week the protest movement grew larger, the moderates offered no advice except to await in patience the opening of Parliament. Then, if no enquiry into Peterloo was instituted – or if Habeas Corpus was suspended – some other, undefined, advice might be given. But Parliament did not meet until 23 November – more than *three months* after Peterloo. The 'ultra' Radicals argued, with some colour, that Hunt's advice meant damping down the movement in the country, abandoning popular initiative, and, in effect, handing over the leadership to the parliamentary Whigs. Like other demagogues, Hunt appears to have been alarmed at the spirits which he himself had helped to conjure up.

After waiting nearly two months, the 'ultra' Radicals put forward an alternative policy, which was supported by Watson and Carlile. This was for 'meetings ... throughout the Kingdom on one and the same day'. The day first proposed was 1 November, although it was later twice postponed. On the face of it, this was only to take the constitutionalist movement a stage further, although the genuine conspirators (of whom Arthur Thistlewood was one) may have hoped the simultaneous meetings would lead directly to insurrection. Throughout October the policy gathered support, and meetings were planned at Newcastle, Carlisle, Leeds, Halifax, Huddersfield, Barnsley, Manchester, Bolton, Wigan, Blackburn, Burnley, Newcastle-under-Lyne, Nottingham, Leicester and Coventry. By the end of the month the usually well-informed General Byng considered that Thistlewood 'has superceded Hunt in [the] idolatry' of the London people. Thistlewood visited Manchester (where there was now an ultra-Radical Union as well as the Huntite Patriotic Society) where the proposal won wide support. Some meetings in fact took place, and further plans were made for 15 November. But in the middle of October, Hunt, observing that the movement was slipping out of his hands, exerted himself to reassert control. In a 'Letter to the Reformers of the North', published in Wroe's *Manchester Observer* (19 October) he denounced the plan of simultaneous meetings. He followed this up with a further letter, recalling the name of Oliver, and specifically attaching to Thistlewood the imputation of being a spy.

Thereafter for weeks the press was open to angry letters passing between Thistlewood and Watson, on one hand, and Hunt and his supporters, on the other, which the loyalist press reprinted with delight under the sardonic heading: 'Radical State Papers'. Dr Watson had been imprisoned for debt for the non-payment of a bill at Hunt's reception, and Hunt made shifty attempts to explain what he had done with moneys collected towards the expenses. Much of the controversy was irresponsible on both sides. Beneath it, it would appear that Hunt had well-founded suspicions as to Thistlewood's conspiratorial intentions, and as to Dr Watson's weak and amateurish grasp as a political leader. On the other hand, it would appear that Thistlewood had indeed succeeded in building up an underground chain of communication in the country, which in parts of the Midlands and the north survived Hunt's attacks.[1] The Manchester Political Union was downcast by the refusal of 'Hunt and his Junto' to support the proposed meetings. Revised plans were made for delegates of the 'underground', from London, west Scotland, Lancashire, Yorkshire, Birmingham and the Potteries, to meet in Nottingham on the day that Parliament reassembled, and to remain in permanent secret session as an 'executive' with instructions to call simultaneous meetings in the event of the suspension of Habeas Corpus. Hunt's bitter opposition prevented these plans from maturing.[2]

1. Only two or three thousand attended a Smithfield meeting called by the Committee of Two Hundred in the first week of November, and addressed by Thistlewood and Preston. But it is not clear whether this was the consequence of Hunt's attacks in the previous two weeks, or of the very bad weather. See *Independent Whig*, 7 November 1819.

2. This account is based on various sources in H.O. 42.198 and 199; A. B. Richmond, op. cit., pp. 181–4; J. E. Taylor, op cit, p. 134; *Cap of Liberty*, 13 October and 15 December 1819; *Republican*, 12 November 1819; General Byng to Wellington, 28 October 1819, in *Wellington Despatches*, I, p 84. See also D. Read, op. cit., pp. 147–50, 155–8. The Secre-

If Thistlewood can be accused of folly (for which he was to suffer with his own life) he acted under great provocation. The response of the national Radical leaders to the Six Acts, which were rushed through the House in December, was feeble in the extreme. At the beginning of November, Cobbett had returned from his exile, landing at Liverpool and meeting with a triumphant reception from the Lancashire people. Disorientated after his absence, and having not the least desire to head a working-class insurrection, he seemed like a man who had lost his head. At Liverpool he announced that he had brought back with him the bones of one of England's greatest sons – Tom Paine. Then (it turned out) it was not Paine's republicanism but his notions of currency reform which Cobbett wished to honour. The *Register* carried alternate bluster ('the great mass have a right to arm in their own *defence*') and cold water: 'My earnest hope is that the people will place their grand reliance on the Debt.' This *'Hole-Digger'* would bring down Old Corruption by its own operation, without the people's exertion:

It is the *most effectual* as well as the safest way, to let the trout exhaust himself, while we hold the rod and line and the hook.

After the passing of the Six Acts he brought forward one great new proposal for 'carrying on the struggle for the rights and liberties of our country'. The proposal was for a Fund for Reform, of about £5,000, to be raised in tuppeny subscriptions by reformers and trades unionists 'and lodged in my hands':

----

tary of the ultra-Radical Manchester Political Union, W. C. Walker, whose notorious character and 'two wives' caused such uproar at one meeting, was considered by the Manchester stipendiary, Norris, to be the 'Thistlewood of this part'. But Colonel Fletcher, of Bolton, and Lord Sidmouth knew better. From internal evidence it would seem that Walker (who was to be one of the delegates to the 'executive' at Nottingham) was none other than 'Alpha', who was in Colonel Fletcher's employment. Walker ('Alpha' informed Fletcher, with some self-satisfaction) 'has formed the most usefull connections possible and has given proof against the crafty wiles of the Police'. See 'Alpha' to Fletcher, 15 and 17 November 1819, in H.O. 42.198 and compare with D. Read, op. cit., pp. 157, 218–23.

to be used solely by me, of course, and without the check or countroul of any-body; and without any one ever having a right to ask me what I am going to do with it ... I will tell nobody how I intend to employ the money: I will answer no questions ...[1]

The Six Acts appear as a codification and extension of the legislation of 1795 and 1817. The first Act prohibited drilling and 'military' training: the second authorized justices to enter and search houses, without warrants, on suspicion of there being arms: the third prohibited meetings exceeding fifty in number, with certain exceptions (county and parish meetings) and additions (designed to suppress Radical lecture-meetings): the fourth Act (of great importance in the next twelve years) increased the stamp duty on periodical publications, raising their cost to 6d. and above: the fifth and sixth Acts were designed to extend for seditious the powers of the authorities, especially in actions and expedite libel.[2] The only measure of the earlier repressions which was not repeated was the suspension of Habeas Corpus. Thereafter the Government launched upon the most sustained campaign of prosecutions in the courts in British history. By the summer of 1820 Hunt, and four Manchester reformers (indicted for their part at Peterloo), Wooler, Burdett, Sir Charles Wolseley, the Rev. J. Harrison, Knight, Carlile, Edmonds, Wroe, Johnston, Bagguley, Drummond and Mitchell were all imprisoned. A major assault had commenced against the 'seditious' and 'blasphemous' press. Scores of prosecutions, against publishers or newsvendors, had been instituted by the private prosecuting societies or dealt with by summary jurisdiction. And Arthur Thistlewood had at length made his public exit from the scaffold.

1. Cobbett's *Political Register*, 6 November, 5 December 1819, 6 January 1820. The Fund only amounted to a few hundreds, and was largely expended by Cobbett in his own candidature at Coventry in 1820. This politically discreditable incident is somewhat glossed over in Cole, *Life of Cobbett*, p. 242.

2. For useful summaries, see Halévy, op. cit., pp. 67 ff.; Jephson, op. cit., II, pp. 502 ff.; Maccoby, op. cit., chap. 20. For the press prosecutions, see below, pp. 791-7.

VI. THE CATO STREET CONSPIRACY

The Two Acts of 1795 were at least passed in the face of
monster demonstrations, which Fox himself condescended to
address. In December 1819 Hunt, Cobbett, Wooler or Burdett
could have filled the streets of London, the Midlands, the
north and Scotland with demonstrations.[1] It is difficult not to
conclude that the Radical leaders themselves were alarmed at
the character of their following in the industrial centres. Hunt
was busily dissociating himself from extremists and abstaining
from any action which might arouse prejudice at his forthcoming trial. Cobbett instructed his readers in the use of
roasted wheat as a substitute for coffee and the superiority of
water over wine. On 22 January 1820 he issued, at last, 'A
P L A N'. It was addressed 'To the Ladies', and was for 'Promoting Sobriety and Frugality, and an Abhorrence of Gaming'.[2]
It was in these circumstances that the final episode of the post-
war agitation took place.

We do not know much about Arthur Thistlewood and the
Cato Street conspirators.[3] Thistlewood was a gentleman,
who had suffered various misfortunes, mostly (it would seem)
of his own making. Not many men who had been arraigned
once for high treason were willing to put their heads in the
noose a second and a third time, as Thistlewood did in 1817–
18 and again in 1820. His courage was more than three parts
foolhardiness; but so was that of Emmett, or of the men of
'Easter '16'. The scurrilous biographies appearing in the press

1. See the comment in *Union: Prospective of a New Publication* (1831),
(John Rylands Lib. R.106147): 'The Government in 1819 owed its safety
to Mr Hunt's forbearance.'

2. *Political Register*, 4 December 1819, 22 January 1820.

3. Much remains to be found out. John Stanhope's *Cato Street Conspiracy* (1962), is entertaining in the familiar 'whodunit' tradition. It
establishes beyond any doubt the provocative role of Edwards, drawing
upon the evidence of H.O. 44.4/6. It does not, however, place the conspiracy in context, and biographical details are largely drawn from the
hostile reports in the press and in G. T. Wilkinson's version of the trials.
A number of documents, endorsed on the back 'Thistlewood Papers',
remain to be investigated in H.O. 42 and H.O. 40.7/10.

at the time of his death have perpetuated a tradition which lingers in writing today.[1] But the case is, to say the least, not proven; and it assorts ill with his conduct on the scaffold. To George Borrow, who may have romanticized the lore of the underworld, Thistlewood was one of the 'Old Radicals' – 'a brave soldier' who 'had served with distinction as an officer in the French service', and 'one of the excellent swordsmen of Europe'. He had 'never unsheathed his sword ... but in defence of the feeble and insulted – he was kind and open-hearted, but of too great simplicity ...' 'Oh, there was something in those fellows!'[2]

We can scarcely accept unreservedly the accounts of his opponents or of Borrow. He was, it is certain, an 'old Jack' and thorough Republican. And, when too many of his associates gave expression to their republicanism in the rhetoric of the print-shop and the harangue, he may be given credit for a comparative taciturnity and attention to practical organization. Bu it is more important to appreciate the predicament in which such a man was placed. At a meeting at the 'White Lion' in early November (a spy informed Lord Sidmouth) Dr Watson informed the committee 'that the communication between himself and the Country Places had dropped for that they had sided with Hunt'. At this time 'Thistlewood was with the weavers in Spitalfields'.[3] By other accounts, Thistlewood himself was deeply and bitterly affected by Hunt's charge that he was a spy, and determined to remove the aspersion by some bold action. As the Six Acts were passing through Parliament, he rebuilt some underground connexions, especially with York-

1. See, for example, R. J. White, op. cit., p. 199, where he is compared to an 'atom-bomb traitor', assisted by 'ruffianly guttersnipes'; and Mr Stanhope's references (pp. 28, 57) to 'psychopathic personalities', with 'personal neuroses'. As a matter of fact, one of the only men of 1819–20 to whom we are entitled to apply these epithets with clinical accuracy is Lord Castlereagh. See H. M. Hyde, *The Strange Death of Lord Castlereagh* (1959).

2. G. Borrow, *Romany Rye*, Appendix, ch. 10. Borrow also says that Thistlewood lost his fortune, not (as in the scurrilous accounts) by gaming, but by an injudicious loan to a friend.

3. H.O. 42.198. Report of 'I.S.', 10 November 1819.

shire and Glasgow.[1] By December the Cato Street Conspiracy
was afoot.

It was a repetition, even in some particulars, of the Despard
and Spa Fields affairs. But it was rather more violent, more
pathetic. Thistlewood felt that there rested upon himself the
duty to rescue the country from repression. If only the *initial*
blow could be struck – at the Tower, at the Bank, at Parliament or at the King – then the signal would be given (he was
assured) when Spitalfields, the Minories, Smithfield would rise;
and the 'Country Places' would sweep all before them. More
than this, it would seem that Thistlewood had pledged his
honour to provincial emissaries that London *would* act in this
way. If he behaved with a rashness that was scarcely sane in
January and February 1820, it was the rashness of desperation.
He moved anxiously (himself in extreme poverty) among the
London ultra-Radicals; the Deist artisans, labourers, and tradesmen who read and approved of Thomas Davison's *Medusa* or
Shorter's *Theological Comet*, in which the sanguinary overthrow of priests as well as of kings was eagerly awaited.[2]

There were many men who applauded the idea of a rising –
the shoemakers, in particular, were ready, and their union was
virtually a Jacobin organization,[3] while Irishmen of '98 were
said to be in London in November, meeting at Davison's shop,
and '*again* endeavouring to stir up the Lower order of the
Irish to *Rebellion*'.[4] Moreover, there were men who had ideas

1. See especially A. B. Richmond, op. cit, pp. 183–4. On 23 December
1819, nine delegates of the Lancashire secret organization were arrested,
presumably on the information of 'Alpha'. See *Independent Whig*, 1
January 1820.

2. See, for example, *The Theological Comet: or Free-Thinking Englishman*, 28 August 1819: 'To the Manchester Blood Hounds' – 'Are you so
religiously inclined as to delight in the barbarities and massacres of that
monstrous butcher Moses . . .?'

3. The Jacobin tradition among the shoemakers runs from Thomas
Hardy and John Ashley (both Secretaries of the L.C.S.) through Charles
Pendrill (and other associates of Despard) and Davenport, the Spencean,
to the ultra-Radicals, Preston and Waddington. The majority of the Cato
Street conspirators were boot and shoemakers, and the Central and
West London branches each voted £50 towards their defence (*Indepen-
dent Whig*, 12 March 1820).

4. Reports of 'I.S.', 15 November 1819, H.O. 42. 198.

as to how the first blow might be struck. George Edwards, an artist of sorts, who had executed a bust of Paine for Carlile and who was brother to a former Secretary of the Spenceans, was particularly fertile in suggestions. 'He proposed,' declared Thistlewood in his defiant speech before receiving sentence of death,

> a plan for blowing up the House of Commons. This was not my view: I wished to punish the guilty only, and therefore I declined it. He next proposed that we should attack the Ministers at the *fête* given by the Spanish Ambassador. This I resolutely opposed ... there were ladies invited to the entertainment – and I, who am shortly to ascend to the scaffold, shuddered with horror at the idea of that, a sample of which had previously been given by the Agents of Government at Manchester ...

'Edwards was ever at invention; and at length he proposed attacking them at a cabinet-dinner.' Meetings were held in several rooms and in the loft at Cato Street. James Ings, a butcher prone to vivid fantasies, was carried away in anticipation by his rôle when (in accordance with the plan) the house would be entered and the door thrown open upon the diners: 'I shall say, "My Lords, I have got as good men here as the Manchester yeomanry – Enter citizens, and do your duty."' The heads of Castlereagh and Sidmouth were to be placed on pikes – proclamations of a 'Provisional Government' posted in the city – minor diversions started at the Tower and the Mansion House. As the time of the proposed attack approached, Thistlewood appears to have held to it only with a desperate kind of honour. *Something* must be attempted. 'I hope you will not give up what you are going to do,' he said. 'If you do, this will be another Despard's business.'

The plan had, of course, long been known to those heads which it was proposed to carry on pikes through the streets. Even the advertisement, in the *New Times*, announcing the cabinet dinner was a hoax. The conspirators were duly apprehended, though not without a skirmish in which Thistlewood ran through one of the Bow Street Runners. The arrests created the sensation which the Government required to justify the Six Acts, and also to help them through a General Election.[1]

1. See Maccoby, op. cit., p. 366.

The effects of the sensation wore off when the trials took place (in mid-April) and when Edwards's part as a *provocateur* was exposed.

At their trials and on the scaffold, Thistlewood and his companions bore themselves with courage, and even bravado. (Thistlewood's only sense of disillusion seems to have come, in the weeks before the trial, when the prisoners passed through London and there was no attempt at rescue by the London crowd.) All except for Davidson (a 'man of colour' from Jamaica who had some Methodist associations) appear to have been Deists, and refused the consolations of the prison chaplain. More than one of the prisoners composed defiant verses while awaiting sentence:

> Tyrants. Ye fill the poor with dread
> And take way his right
> And raise the price of meat and bread
> And thus his labour blight.
>
> You never labour, never toil,
> But you can eat and drink;
> You never cultivate the soil,
> Nor of the poor man think ...

'My dear Celia,' James Ings wrote to his wife:

I must die according to law, and leave you in a land full of corruption, where justice and liberty has taken their flight from, to other distant shores. ... Now, my dear, I hope you will bear in mind that the cause of my being consigned to the scaffold was a pure motive. I thought I should have rendered my starving fellow-men, women, and children, a service ...

John Brunt, a shoemaker, declared in court before sentence was passed, 'in a particularly bold and unembarrassed manner',

he had, by his industry, been able to earn about £3 or £4 a-week, and while this was the case, he never meddled with politics; but when he found his income reduced to 10s. a-week, he began to look about him. ... And what did he find? Why, men in power, who met to deliberate how they might starve and plunder the country. He looked on the Manchester transactions as most dreadful. ... He had joined the conspiracy for the public good. He was not the man who would have stopt. O no: he would have gone through with it to the very bottom. . . . He would die as the descendant of an ancient Briton . . .

On the scaffold, Thistlewood declared, in his strong Lincolnshire accent: 'I desire all here to remember, that I die in the cause of liberty . . .' Cobbett, in a moving and plain-spoken account, recalled the name of Sir Thomas More. Hobhouse, who witnessed the executions, noted in his diary:

The men died like heroes. Ings, perhaps, was too obstreperous in singing 'Death or Liberty', and Thistlewood said, 'Be quiet, Ings; we can die without all this noise.'

The crowd was barricaded at a distance from the scaffold so that no rescue could be attempted and no dying speeches be heard. When the heads of the victims were displayed, the crowd was wild with anger – 'the yells and execrations from the assembled crowds exceeded all conception'.[1]

So ended the 'old Radicalism', which, in its way, was an extension into the nineteenth century of the Jacobinism of the 1790s. (The shoemakers of Cato Street were some of the last to use the term 'Citizen' and other Jacobin forms.) We have sought to redress, a little, the customary picture of a gang of criminal desperadoes. Thistlewood was certainly guilty of folly, in exposing the lives of his followers to such patent provocation. ('I am like a bullock drove into Smithfield market to be sold,' Ings burst out at his trial: 'Lord Sidmouth knew all about this for two months.') His plans – to seize cannon and arsenals, fire the barracks, and set up a Provisional Government in the Mansion House – were little more than fantasies. He derived a justification for his plot from the Roman apologists of tyrannicide. At his trial he declared that 'high treason was committed against the people at Manchester':

Brutus and Cassius were lauded to the very skies for slaying Caesar; indeed, when any man, or set of men, place themselves above the

1. Thistlewood, Ings, Brunt, Tidd and Davidson were executed on 1 May. Five others were transported. This account is based on G. T. Wilkinson, op. cit., *passim*; H. Stanhope, *The Cato Street Conspiracy*, esp. ch. 6 (for the rôle of Edwards); Cobbett's *Political Register*, 6 May 1820; R. F. Wearmouth, op. cit., p. 71; *Independent Whig*, 7 May 1820; Lord Broughton, *Recollections of a Long Life*, (1909), II, p. 126; E. Aylmer, *Memoirs of George Edwards* (1820).

laws of their country, there is no other means of bringing them to justice than through the arm of a private individual.

But even if some variant of the Cato Street Conspiracy had succeeded in its immediate objective, it is difficult to see what would have followed. Perhaps, for a few days, the 'Gordon Riots' on a larger and much bloodier scale; followed, in all probability, by a 'White Terror', with Peterloo re-enacted in a dozen English and Scottish towns. Thistlewood had overlooked Shakespeare's ironic comment, set in the mouth of Brutus:

> Stoop, Romans, stoop,
> And let us bathe our hands in Caesar's blood
> Up to the elbows, and besmear our swords:
> Then walk we forth, even to the market-place,
> And, waving our red weapons o'er our heads,
> Let's all cry, 'Peace, freedom and liberty.'

But those who suffered with Thistlewood, and who were most entitled to condemn him for his folly, appear to have felt for him the greatest loyalty. Susan Thistlewood, also, appears not as a cypher but as a spirited Jacobin in her own right, with a cold and intellectual manner and a readiness to take an active part in the defence.[1] How far the Cato Street Conspiracy was linked to any genuine national plan is unclear. There were three attempted risings shortly after the arrest of the conspirators – one in Glasgow, and two in Yorkshire. In the neighbourhood of Glasgow small parties of weavers rose on 5 and 6 April (with their famous banner, 'Scotland Free or a Desart'), there was a sharp encounter with the military at the 'Battle of Bonnymuir', and in the outcome three men were executed. One – James Wilson – was an 'old Jack'; another was a forebear of Keir Hardie; both were self-educated men of unusual attainments.[2] It seems that the insurgents believed that they were acting their part in a plan for simultaneous risings in

1. G. T. Wilkinson, op. cit., pp. 73–4; Cobbett's *Political Register*, 6 May 1820; Bamford, op. cit., p. 299.
2. [Peter Mackenzie], *An Exposure of the Spy System Pursued in Glasgow* (Glasgow, 1832), pp. 71–232, and *The Trial of James Wilson* (Glasgow, 1832); A. B. Richmond, op. cit., p. 184.

Scotland, Yorkshire, Lancashire, and Carlisle – in all the weavers' strongholds.

Six days before (31 March 1820) there had been an irresolute movement in the textile villages around Huddersfield. The croppers, as usual, were deeply involved. After Peterloo, scores of clubs had been formed, where the *Black Dwarf*, *Cap of Liberty*, and *Manchester Observer* had been taken in. A cropper who had attended demonstrations holding a banner inscribed 'Rouse Britons and assert your Rights: The Lion awake to a Sense of Danger', deposed that a rising had been planned in November, 'in consequence of an investigation as to the proceedings at Manchester not having been carried on according to their wishes'. Cards, torn in half, and inscribed 'Demo' were distributed, the signal for the rising being the delivery of the other half ('cracy'). The aim was to 'establish a free Government'. To the accompaniment of beacon-signals 200 insurgents assembled, with pikes, pitchforks, and guns, only to disperse when other parties failed to materialize. On the night of 11 April, the last attempt took place, at Grange Moor, near Barnsley. Forty or fifty Radical 'classes' existed among the linen-weavers and colliers of the town, linked by a general delegate committee, and thence to a secret committee of seven. The subjects discussed at their meetings were:

Oppression of the Poor, the Taxation and the National Debt, and what was laid upon the necessaries of life ... and Corruption of Ministers and how many thousands a year were expended on them and on pensions and places out of our earnings.

The Barnsley Radicals expected all the north and the Midlands to rise on the same night. They were to proceed to Grange Moor, where they would *rendezvous* with other contingents, and then proceed:

through Barnsley to Sheffield and on to London. It was said the Scotsmen would be at Leeds as soon as us or not above a day's march behind us.

Perhaps 300 assembled, with drums, weapons, haversacks (with three days provisions) and a green flag with black fringe: 'He that smiteth a man so that he die, shall surely be put to death.' They were marshalled by two former soldiers, Comstive (a

'Waterloo man' and a 'good penman') and Addy (who wore the symbolic white hat). They trudged the twelve miles to Grange Moor, picking up small parties on the way, arriving in the small hours to find the *rendezvous* deserted. After waiting for some time, the rumour of a Government plot spread through the ranks, and they scattered in dismay. For these two attempts, Comstive, Addy, and several others were transported.

Rumours swept through the manufacturing districts. 'It is reported that the Scots will shortly invade England and join the English Radicals,' a Burnley weaver noted in his diary (7 April); but ten days later he noted that three ultra-Radicals 'leaves the country, but where they are gone remains a secret, though it is said they are gone to the sea'. On 14 April a weaver, Joseph Tyas, was apprehended near Huddersfield, and in his wife's cap a letter was found, addressed by him to 'our brethren in Lankaster Shire':

Dearly beloved—

We hope you are comeng on pretty well though your Captifeity is painful. . . . Our Musick in Yorkshire as played twise where yours in Lankashire has never struck at all, is your Musicians sick? . . .

Melancholy, Melancholy, Melancholy Yorkshire, your Reformers stand true. . . . About 300 at Grange Moor, they marched all night, each man had is Blanket Spare [Spear] or Gon & well filed with ammunition poor Men to be so deceived by short sighted men it would have tuck an afect on your feelings to have seen the brave men stand under their arms all that weet night after a march of 12 miles and Not one Man to meet them according to Apointment all their pike shafts were left on the more the blades taken out except 3 or 4 which was to feast in [too fast in], the poor Men stud with charefull [cheerful] hearts till daylight beating the drums and their breast but no other partity joyned them. All at a loss to know what to do. Return to Barnsley they could no think of but when there was no other prospect they all begain to shed tears Most bitterly with Crys of the most distracted . . .

'I hope,' the letter concludes, 'that we may all meet in one Body and one Voice yet . . .'[1]

'Again and again,' counselled the *Manchester Observer*, 'do

1. T.S. 11.4131 and 3573; Peel, Spen Valley, pp. 262–4 and *Risings of the Luddites* (1888 edn), pp. 313–19; Bennett, *History of Burnley*, III, p. 380; H.O. 40.11/12.

we caution our ... countrymen against listening to any *strangers* ... under *any pretended authority as delegates from distant places.*[1] Cato Street brought back to the minds of reformers, with redoubled force, the message of Oliver. With meetings banned and the press under fire, political unions began to fall apart. As this happened, two other events occurred which altered the character and direction of the movement. The first was the onset of the years of general prosperity, from 1820 to 1825. Falling prices and fuller employment took the edge off Radical anger. And, at the same time, the surviving Radical journalists settled (almost with relief) upon a new cause – the agitation on behalf of the honour and regal rights of Queen Caroline, whom George IV wished to set aside for misconduct, and who was the latest victim of a 'Green Bag'. Into the humbug of the Queen's case we need not inquire. It displayed every vice of the Radical movement (as well as of the loyalists) on the largest scale. The glory of it (from the Radical standpoint) was that it placed Old, Corruption in the most ludicrous and defensive postures. It allowed Radical addresses, remonstrances, protests, petitions, to be drawn up in defence of honour, chastity, justice and 'sincere attachment to the Throne'. It enabled, also, Hone and Cruikshank to produce some of their most glorious lampoons. Week after week during 1820 Cobbett devoted his *Register* entirely to the defence of the Queen. Brougham, Cobbett and Alderman' Wood handled the Queen's affairs, and even wrote her replies to Addresses (which they might also have written), until the ultra-loyalist *John Bull* could say with justification: 'She is as much the leader of the Radicals as Hunt was before her':

These spouting, mouthing, blind devotees to disorder and riot, care as little for the Queen as they did for Hunt. She serves as the pole to hoist the revolutionary Cap of Liberty on. Burdett was the pole at one time ... Hunt was the last pole before the Queen: and now her Majesty is established the *veritable* Mother Red-Cap of the faction.[2]

But it was no longer the 'revolutionary Cap of Liberty' that was hung on the Queen. This had been lost, somewhere on the

1. *Manchester Observer*, 15 April 1820.
2. *John Bull*, 24 December (cited in Maccoby, op. cit., p. 354).

way between Peterloo and Cato Street. Indeed, the prominence in the agitation of Brougham, Wood and Hobhouse was a portent of the shape of the new movement of the 1820s, under the guidance of the middle-class Utilitarians and younger Whigs.[1]

It was, perhaps, not Cato Street nor the Six Acts which had the most lasting influence upon the British political tradition, but Peterloo. For after the short-term reactions, a longer-term response can be felt. First, it served notice upon the middle-class reformers and Whigs as to the consequences that would flow from their loss of influence over the unrepresented masses. Even Wilberforce felt that some moderate reformers ought, perhaps, to come forward 'to rescue the multitude out of. the hands of the Hunts and Thistlewoods'.[2] After the clamour of 1819 had died down, the middle-class reform movement assumed a more determined aspect. Second, the experience of the post-war agitation shook the confidence of the *ancien régime* in itself; and some of the loyalists of 1819 became, in the 1820s, willing to admit the need for limited concessions. Thus even Colonel Birley of the Manchester Yeomanry was to be found in the 1820s campaigning for the transfer of seats from rotten boroughs to Manchester.[3] In the minds of such men as Peel the conviction was growing that some alliance must be made, between the manufacturing and landed interest, and against the working-class.

But the enduring influence of Peterloo lay in the sheer horror of the day's events. In 1819 the action of the loyalists found many defenders in their own class. Ten years later it was an event to be remembered, even among the gentry, with guilt. As a *massacre* and as 'Peter-Loo' it went down to the next generation. And because of the odium attaching to the event, we may say that in the annals of the 'free-born Englishman' the massacre was yet in its way a victory. Even Old Corruption knew, in its heart, that it dare not do this again. Since the

1. For the Queen Caroline affair, see Chester New, *Life of Henry Brougham*, ch. 13; Halévy, *The Liberal Awakening*, pp. 80–106; Maccoby, op. cit., ch. 20; Cole, *Life of Cobbett*, ch. 16.

2. Wilberforce, *Life*, V, p. 37.

3. See D. Read, op. cit., ch. 11.

moral consensus of the nation outlawed the riding down and
sabreing of an unarmed crowd, the corollary followed – that
the right of public meeting had been gained. Henceforward
strikers or agricultural workers might be ridden down or dispersed with violence. But never since Peterloo has authority
dared to use equal force against a peaceful British crowd. Even
the handling of the 'Plug Riots' (1842) and Bloody Sunday
(1887) saw a violence that was carefully controlled. The most
portentous incident of 16 August took place not on St Peter's
Fields but some time later on the road leading out of Manchester. Samuel Bamford, after searching anxiously for his
wife, turned homewards up the road along which hundreds
were streaming in disarray to the upland districts. In Harpurhay
he caught up with a great number of the Middleton and Rochdale contingents:

I rejoined my comrades, and forming about a thousand of them into
file, we set off to the sound of fife and drum, with our only banner
waving, and in that form we re-entered the town of Middleton.

[16]

Class Consciousness

I. THE RADICAL CULTURE

WHEN contrasted with the Radical years which preceded and the Chartist years which succeeded it, the decade of the 1820s seems strangely quiet – a mildly prosperous plateau of social peace. But many years later a London costermonger warned Mayhew:

People fancy that when all's quiet that all's stagnating. Propagandism is going on for all that. It's when all's quiet that the seed's a-growing. Republicans and Socialists are pressing their doctrines.[1]

These quiet years were the years of Richard Carlile's contest for the liberty of the press; of growing trade union strength and the repeal of the Combination Acts; of the growth of free thought, cooperative experiment, and Owenite theory. They are years in which individuals and groups sought to render into theory the twin experiences which we have described – the experience of the Industrial Revolution, and the experience of popular Radicalism insurgent and in defeat. And at the end of the decade, when there came the climactic contest between Old Corruption and Reform, it is possible to speak in a new way of the working people's consciousness of their interests and of their predicament as a class.

There is a sense in which we may describe popular Radicalism in these years as an intellectual culture. The articulate consciousness of the self-taught was above all a political consciousness. For the first half of the nineteenth century, when the formal education of a great part of the people entailed little more than instruction in the Three R's, was by no means a period of intellectual atrophy. The towns, and even the villages, hummed with the energy of the autodidact. Given the elementary techniques of literacy, labourers, artisans, shopkeepers

1. Mayhew, op. cit., I, p. 22.

and clerks and schoolmasters, proceeded to instruct themselves, severally or in groups. And the books or instructors were very often those sanctioned by reforming opinion. A shoemaker, who had been taught his letters in the Old Testament, would labour through the *Age of Reason*; a schoolmaster, whose education had taken him little further than worthy religious homilies, would attempt Voltaire, Gibbon, Ricardo; here and there local Radical leaders, weavers, booksellers, tailors, would amass shelves of Radical periodicals and learn how to use parliamentary Blue Books; illiterate labourers would, nevertheless, go each week to a pub where Cobbett's editorial letter was read aloud and discussed.

Thus working men formed a picture of the organization of society, out of their own experience and with the help of their hard-won and erratic education, which was above all a political picture. They learned to see their own lives as part of a general history of conflict between the loosely defined 'industrious classes' on the one hand, and the unreformed House of Commons on the other. From 1830 onwards a more clearly defined class consciousness, in the customary Marxist sense, was maturing, in which working people were aware of continuing both old and new battles on their own.

It is difficult to generalize as to the diffusion of literacy in the early years of the century. The 'industrious classes' touched, at one pole, the million or more who were illiterate, or whose literacy amounted to little more than the ability to spell out a few words or write their names. At the other pole there were men of considerable intellectual attainment. Illiteracy (we should remember) by no means excluded men from political discourse. In Mayhew's England the ballad-singers and 'patterers' still had a thriving occupation, with their pavement farces and street-corner parodies, following the popular mood and giving a Radical or anti-Papal twist to their satirical monologues or chaunts, according to the state of the market.'[1] The illiterate worker might tramp miles to hear a Radical orator, just as the same man (or another) might tramp to taste a sermon. In times of political ferment the illiterate would get their workmates to read aloud from the periodicals; while at

1. See esp. Mayhew, op. cit., I, p. 252 ff.

Houses of Call the news was read, and at political meetings a prodigious time was spent in reading addresses and passing long strings of resolutions. The earnest Radical might even attach a talismanic virtue to the possession of favoured works which he was unable, by his own efforts, to read. A Cheltenham shoemaker who called punctually each Sunday on W. E. Adams to have 'Feargus's letter' read to him, nevertheless was the proud owner of several of Cobbett's books, carefully preserved in wash leather cases.[1]

Recent studies have thrown much light on the predicament of the working-class reader in these years.[2] To simplify a difficult discussion, we may say that something like two out of every three working men were able to read after some fashion in the early part of the century, although rather fewer could write. As the effect of the Sunday schools and day schools increasingly became felt, as well as the drive for self-improvement among working people themselves, so the number of the illiterate fell, although in the worst child labour areas the fall was delayed. But the ability to read was only the elementary technique. The ability to handle abstract and consecutive argument was by no means inborn; it had to be discovered against almost overwhelming difficulties – the lack of leisure, the cost of candles (or of spectacles), as well as educational deprivation. Ideas and terms were sometimes employed in the early Radical movement which, it is evident, had for some ardent followers a fetishistic rather than rational value. Some of the Pentridge rebels thought that a 'Provisional Government' would ensure a more plentiful supply of 'provisions'; while, in one account of the pitmen of the north-east in 1819, 'Universal Suffrage is understood by many of them to mean universal suffering ... "if one member suffers, all must suffer".'[3]

Such evidence as survives as to the literary accomplishment

1. W. E. Adams, *Memoirs of a Social Atom* (1903), I, p. 164.
2. See especially R. K. Webb, *The British Working Class Reader, 1790–1848* (1955), the same author's article, 'Working-Class Readers in Early Victorian England', *English Hist. Rev.*, LXV (1950); R. D. Altick, *The English Common Reader* (Chicago, 1957), esp. chs. 4, 7, 11; and J. F. C. Harrison, *Learning and Living* (1961), Part One.
3. *Political Observer*, 19 December 1819.

of working men in the first two decades of the century serves only to illustrate the folly of generalization. In the Luddite times (when few but working men would have supported their actions) anonymous messages vary from self-conscious apostrophes to 'Liberty with her Smiling Attributes' to scarcely decipherable chalking on walls. We may take examples of both kinds. In 1812 the Salford Coroner, who had returned a verdict of 'Justifiable Homicide' upon the body of a man shot while attacking Burton's mill was warned:

... know thou cursed insinuater, if Burton's infamous action was 'justifiable', the Laws of Tyrants are Reasons Dictates. – Beware, Beware! A month's bathing in the Stygian Lake would not wash this sanguinary deed from our minds, it but augments the heritable cause, that stirs us up in indignation.[1]

The letter concludes, 'Ludd finis est' – a reminder that Manchester boasted a grammar school (which Bamford himself for a short time attended) as well as private schools where the sons of artisans might obtain Latin enough for this. The other paper was found in Chesterfield Market. It is much to the same purpose but (despite the educational disadvantages of the writer) it somehow carries a greater conviction:

I Ham going to inform you that there is Six Thousand men coming to you in Apral and then We Will go and Blow Parlement house up and Blow up all afour hus/labring Peple Cant Stand it No Longer/dam all Such Roges as England governes but Never mind Ned lud when general nody and his harmey Comes We Will soon bring about the greate Revelution then all these greate mens heads gose of.

Others of the promised benefits of 'general nody' were: 'We Will Nock doon the Prisions and the Judge we Will murde whan he is aslepe.'[2]

The difference (the critics will tell us) is not only a matter of style: it is also one of sensibility. The first we might suppose to be written by a bespectacled, greying, artisan – a cobbler

1. Another letter ('Eliza Ludd' to Rev. W. R. Hay, 1 May 1812) commences: 'Sir, Doubtless you are well acquainted with the Political History of America'; both in H.O. 40.1.   2. H.O. 42.121.

(or hatter or instrument-maker) with Voltaire, Volney and Paine on his shelf, and a taste for the great tragedians. Among the State prisoners of 1817 there were other men of this order from Lancashire: the seventy-year-old William Ogden, a letter-press printer, who wrote to his wife from prison: 'though I am in Irons, I will face my enemies like the Great Caractacus when in the same situation'; Joseph Mitchell, another printing worker, whose daughters were called Mirtilla, Carolina and Cordelia, and who – when another daughter was born while he was in prison – wrote in haste to his wife proposing that the baby be called Portia: or Samuel Bamford himself, whose instructions to his wife were more specific: 'a Reformers Wife ought to be an heroine'.[1] The second letter (we can be almost sure) is the work of a collier or a village stockinger. It is of much the same order as the more playful letter left by a pitman in the north-east coalfield in the house of a colliery viewer in 1831, into which he and some mates had broken during a strike riot:

I was at yor hoose last neet, and meyd mysel very comfortable. Ye hey nee family, and yor just won man on the colliery, I see ye hev a greet lot of rooms, and big cellars, and plenty wine and beer in them, which I got ma share on. Noo I naw some at wor colliery that has three or fower lads and lesses, and they live in won room not half as gude as yor cellar. I don't pretend to naw very much, but I naw there shudn't be that much difference. The only place we can gan to o the week ends is the yel hoose and hev a pint. I dinna pretend to be a profit, but I naw this, and lots o ma marrows na's te, that wer not tret as we owt to be, and a great filosopher says, to get noledge is to naw wer ignerent. But weve just begun to find that oot, and ye maisters and owners may luk oot, for yor not gan to get se much o yor own way, wer gan to hev some o wors now . . .[2]

'If the Bible Societies, and the Sunday School societies have been attended by no other good,' Sherwin noted, 'they have at least produced one beneficial effect; – they have been the means of teaching many thousands of children to read.'[3] The letters of Brandreth and his wife, of Cato Street conspirators,

1. H.O. 42.163; *Blanketteer*, 20 November 1819.
2. R. Fynes, *The Miners of Northumberland and Durham* (1923 edn), p. 21
3. Sherwin's *Political Register*, 17 May 1817.

and of other State prisoners, give us some insight into that great area between the attainments of the skilled artisan and those of the barely literate. Somewhere in the middle we may place Mrs Johnston, addressing her husband ('My Dear Johnston'), who was a journeyman tailor, in prison:

... believe me my Dear if thare is not a day nor a hour in the day but what my mind is less or more engage about you. I can appeal to the almighty that it is true and when I retire to rest I pray God to forgive all my enimies and change thare heart ...

Beside this we may set the letter of the Sheffield joiner, Wolstenholme, to his wife:

Our Minaster hath lent me four vollams of the Missionary Register witch give me grat satisfaction to se ou the Lord is carin on is work of grais in distant contres.

The writing of this letter was attended with difficulties, since 'Have broke my spettacles'.[1] Such letters were written in unaccustomed leisure. We can almost see Wolstenholme laboriously spelling out his words, and stopping to consult a more 'well-lettered' prisoner when he came to the hurdle of 'satisfaction'. Mrs Johnston may have consulted (but probably did not) one of the 'professional' letter-writers to be found in most towns and villages, who wrote the appropriate form of letter at 1d. a time. For, even among the literate, letter-writing was an unusual pursuit. The cost of postage alone prohibited it except at infrequent intervals. For a letter to pass between the north and London might cost 1s. 10d., and we know that both Mrs Johnston and Mrs Wolstenholme were suffering privations in the absence of their husbands – Mrs Johnston's shoes were full of water and she had been able to buy no more since her husband was taken up.

All the Cato Street prisoners, it seems, could write after some fashion. Brunt, the shoemaker, salted some sardonic verses with French, while James Wilson wrote:

1. H.O. 42.172. These correspondents, who were impatiently awaiting release from detention, knew that their mail was read by the prison governor, and were therefore especially prone to insert references to for-giveness, grace, and improving reading.

> the Cause wich nerved a Brutus arm
> to strike a Tirant with alarm
> the cause for wich brave Hamden died
> for wich the Galant Tell defied
> a Tirants insolence and pride.

Richard Tidd, another shoemaker, on the other hand, could only muster: 'Sir I Ham a very Bad Hand at Righting'.[1] We cannot, of course, take such men as a 'sample', since their involvement in political activity indicates that they belonged to the more conscious minority who followed the Radical press. But they may serve to warn us against *under*stating the diffusion of effective literacy.[2] The artisans are a special case – the intellectual *élite* of the class. But there were, scattered throughout all parts of England, an abundance of educational institutions for working people, even if 'institution' is too formal a word for the dame school, the penny-a-week evening school run by a factory cripple or injured pitman, or the Sunday school itself. In the Pennine valleys, where the weavers' children were too poor to pay for slates or paper, they were taught their letters by drawing them with their fingers in a sand-table. If thousands lost these elementary attainments when they reached adult life, on the other hand the work of the Nonconformist Churches, of friendly societies and trade unions, and the needs of industry itself, all demanded that such learning be consolidated and advanced. 'I have found,' Alexander Galloway, the master-engineer, reported in 1824,

from the mode of managing my business, by drawings and written descriptions, a man is not of much use to me unless he can read and write; if a man applies for work, and says he cannot read and write, he is asked no more questions . . .[3]

In most artisan trades the journeymen and petty masters found some reading and work with figures an occupational necessity. Not only the ballad-singer but also the 'number man' or

1. See J. Stanhope, op. cit., pp. 161–7.

2. Some of the earliest trade union correspondence which survives – that of the framework-knitters in the Nottingham City Archives – shows a widespread diffusion of literary attainment. See above, pp. 585–90.

3. *First Report . . . on Artizans and Machinery* (1824), p. 25.

'calendar man' went round the working-class districts, hawking chap-books,[1] almanacs, dying speeches and (between 1816 and 1820, and at intervals thereafter) Radical periodicals. (One such 'calendar man', who travelled for Cowdrey and Black, the 'seditious [i.e. Whig] printers in Manchester', was taken up by the magistrates in 1812 because it was found that on his catalogues was written: 'No blind king – Ned Ludd for ever.'[2]) One of the most impressive features of post-war Radicalism was its sustained effort to extend these attainments and to raise the level of political awareness. At Barnsley as early as January 1816 a penny-a-month club of weavers was formed, for the purpose of buying Radical newspapers and periodicals. The Hampden Clubs and Political Unions took great pains to build up 'Reading Societies' and in the larger centres they opened permanent newsrooms or reading-rooms, such as that at Hanley in the Potteries. This room was open from 8 a.m. till 10 p.m. There were penalties for swearing, for the use of indecent language and for drunkenness. Each evening the London papers were to be 'publicly read'. At the rooms of the Stockport Union in 1818, according to Joseph Mitchell, there was a meeting of class leaders on Monday nights; on Tuesday, 'moral and political readings'; on Wednesdays, 'a conversation or debate'; on Thursdays, 'Grammar, Arithmetic, &c' was taught; Saturday was a social evening; while Sunday was school day for adults and children alike. In Blackburn the members of the Female Reform Society pledged themselves 'to use our utmost endeavour to instil into the minds of our children a deep and rooted hatred of our corrupt and tyrannical rulers.' One means was the use of 'The Bad Alphabet for the use of the Children of Female Reformers': B was for Bible, Bishop, and Bigotry; K for King, King's evil, Knave and Kidnapper; W for Whig, Weakness, Wavering, and Wicked.

Despite the repression after 1819, the tradition of providing such newsrooms (sometimes attached to the shop of a Radical bookseller) continued through the 1820s. In London after the

1. Catnach's 'Trial of Thurtell', 500,000 (1823): 'Confession and Execution of Corder', 1,166,000 (1828).
2. H.O. 40.1.

war there was a boom in coffee-houses, many of which served this double function. By 1833, at John Doherty's famous 'Coffee and Newsroom' attached to his Manchester bookshop, no fewer than ninety-six newspapers were taken every week, including the illegal 'unstamped'. In the smaller towns and villages the reading-groups were less formal but no less important. Sometimes they met at inns, 'hush-shops', or private houses; sometimes the periodical was read and discussed in the workshop. The high cost of periodicals during the time of the heaviest 'taxes on knowledge' led to thousands of *ad hoc* arrangements by which small groups clubbed together to buy their chosen paper. During the Reform Bill agitation Thomas Dunning, a Nantwich shoemaker, joined with his shopmates and 'our Unitarian minister . . . in subscribing to the *Weekly Dispatch*, price 8½*d*., the stamp duty being 4*d*. It was too expensive for *one* ill-paid crispin . . .'[1]

The circulation of the Radical press fluctuated violently. Cobbett's 2*d*. *Register* at its meridian, between October 1816 and February 1817, was running at something between 40,000 and 60,000 each week, a figure many times in excess of any competitor of any sort.[2] The *Black Dwarf* ran at about 12,000 in 1819, although this figure was probably exceeded after Peterloo. Thereafter the stamp tax (and the recession of the movement) severely curtailed circulation, although Carlile's periodicals ran in the thousands through much of the Twenties. With the Reform Bill agitation, the Radical press broke through to a larger circulation once more: Doherty's *Voice of the People*, and *The Pioneer* all had circulations above ten thousand, Carlile's *Gauntlet*, Hetherington's *Poor Man's Guardian*, while a dozen smaller periodicals, like the *Destructive*, ran to some thousands. The slump in the sale of costly weekly periodicals

1. For Radical reading-rooms, see A. Aspinall, *Politics and the Press* (1949), pp. 25-8, 395-6; Wearmouth, op. cit., pp. 24-5, 88-9, 97-8, 111-12. For Dunning, 'Reminiscences' (ed., W. H. Chaloner), *Trans. Lancs. & Cheshire Antiq. Soc.*, LIX, 1947, p. 97. For Stockport, see *Blanketteer*, 27 November 1819, and D. Read, op. cit., p. 48 f. For Blackburn, W. W. Kinsey, 'Some Aspects of Lancashire Radicalism', (M. A. Thesis, Manchester 1927), pp. 667.

2. In 1822 the circulation of the leading daily, *The Times*, was 5,730; the *Observer* (weekly), 6,860.

(at anything from 7*d.* to 1*s.*) during the stamp tax decade was
to great degree made up by the growth in the sales of cheap
books and individual pamphlets, ranging from *The Political
House that Jack Built* (100,000) to Cobbett's *Cottage Economy*
(50,000, 1822–8), *History of the Protestant 'Reformation'*, and
Sermons (211,000, 1821–8). In the same period, in most of the
great centres there were one or more (and in London a dozen)
dailies or weeklies which, while not being avowedly 'Radical',
nevertheless catered for this large Radical public. And the
growth in this very large *petit-bourgeois* and working-class
reading public was recognized by those influential agencies –
notably the Society for the Promotion of Christian Knowledge
and the Society for the Diffusion of Useful Knowledge –
which made prodigious and lavishly subsidized efforts to
divert the readers to more wholesome and improving
matter.[1]

This was the culture – with its eager disputations around
the booksellers' stalls, in the taverns, workshops, and coffee-
houses – which Shelley saluted in his 'Song to the Men of
England' and within which the genius of Dickens matured.
But it is a mistake to see it as a single, undifferentiated 'reading
public'. We may say that there were several different 'publics'
impinging upon and overlapping each other, but nevertheless
organized according to different principles. Among the more
important were the commercial public, pure and simple, which
might be exploited at times of Radical excitement (the trials
of Brandreth or of Thistlewood were as marketable as other
'dying confessions'), but which was followed according to
the simple criteria of profitability; the various more or less
organized publics, around the Churches or the Mechanics'
Institutes; the passive public which the improving societies
sought to get at and redeem; and the active, Radical public,
which organized itself in the face of the Six Acts and the taxes
on knowledge.

The struggle to build and hold this last public has been
admirably told in W. D. Wickwar's *The Struggle for the Free-*

1. For the attempts to replace the radical press with safe and improving matter, see R. K. Webb, op. cit., chs. 2, 3, 4 and J. F. C. Harrison,
op. cit., chs. 1 and 2.

dom of the Press.[1] There is perhaps no country in the world in which the contest for the rights of the press was so sharp, so emphatically victorious, and so peculiarly identified with the cause of the artisans and labourers. If Peterloo established (by a parodox of feeling) the right of public demonstration, the rights of a 'free press' were won in a campaign extending over fifteen or more years which has no comparison for its pig-headed, bloody-minded, and indomitable audacity. Carlile (a tinsmith who had nevertheless received a year or two of grammar school education at Ashburton in Devon) rightly saw that the repression of 1819 made the rights of the press the fulcrum of the Radical movement. But, unlike Cobbett and Wooler, who modified their tone to meet the Six Acts in the hope of living to fight another day (and who lost circulation accordingly), Carlile hoisted the black ensign of unqualified defiance and, like a pirate cock-boat, sailed straight into the middle of the combined fleets of the State and Church. As, in the aftermath of Peterloo, he came up for trial (for publishing the Works of Paine), the entire Radical press saluted his courage, but gave him up for lost. When he finally emerged, after years of imprisonment, the combined fleets were scattered beyond the horizon in disarray. He had exhausted the ammunition of the Government, and turned its *ex officio* informations and special juries into laughing-stocks. He had plainly sunk the private prosecuting societies, the Constitutional Association (or 'Bridge-Street Gang') and the Vice Society, which were supported by the patronage and the subscriptions of the nobility, bishops and Wilberforce.

Carlile did not, of course, achieve this triumph on his own. The first round of the battle was fought in 1817, when there were twenty-six prosecutions for seditious and blasphemous libel and sixteen *ex officio* informations filed by the law officers

---

1. His account, covering the period 1817–32 is mainly concerned with the first phase of the battle – the right of publication – particularly associated with Richard Carlile. The second phase, the struggle of the 'Great Unstamped' (1830–35), associated particularly with the names of Carpenter, Hetherington, Watson, Cleave and Hobson, has not yet found its historian, although see C. D. Collett, *History of the Taxes on Knowledge* (1933 edn), ch. 2, and A. G. Barker, *Henry Hetherington* (n.d.).

of the Crown.[1] The laurels of victory, in this year, went to Wooler and Hone, and to the London juries which refused to convict. Wooler conducted his own defence; he was a capable speaker, with some experience of the courts, and defended himself with ability in the grandiloquent libertarian manner. The result of his two trials (5 June 1817) was one verdict of 'Not Guilty' and one muddled verdict of 'Guilty' (from which three jurymen demurred) which was later upset in the Court of King's Bench.[2] The three trials of William Hone in December 1817 are some of the most hilarious legal proceedings on record. Hone, a poor bookseller and former member of the L.C.S., was indicted for publishing blasphemous libels, in the form of parodies upon the Catechism, Litany, and Creed. Hone, in fact, was only a particularly witty exponent of a form of political squib long established among the newsvendors and patterers, and practised in more sophisticated form by men of all parties, from Wilkes to the writers in the *Anti-Jacobin*. Hone, indeed, had not thought his parodies worth risking liberty for. When the repression of February 1817 commenced, he had sought to withdraw them; and it was Carlile, by republishing them, who had forced the Government's hand. Here is a sample:

Our Lord who art in the Treasury, whatsoever be thy name, thy power be prolonged, thy will be done throughout the empire, as it is in each session. Give us our usual sops, and forgive us our occasional absences on divisions; as we promise not to forgive those that divide against thee. Turn us not out of our places; but keep us in the House of Commons, the land of Pensions and Plenty; and deliver us from the People. Amen.

Hone was held in prison, in poor health, from May until December, because he was unable to find £1,000 bail. Not much was expected when it was learned that he intended to conduct his own defence. But Hone had been improving the time in prison by collecting examples, from the past and present, of other parodists; and in his first trial before Justice

1. Wickwar, op. cit., p. 315. See also ibid, pp. 38–9 for the peculiarly unfair form of persecution, the *ex officio* information, which virtually permitted imprisonment without trial.
2. *The Two Trials of T. J. Wooler* (1817).

Abbott he secured an acquittal. In the next two days the old, ill and testy Lord Chief Justice Ellenborough himself presided over the trials. Page after page of the record is filled with Ellenborough's interruptions, Hone's unruffled reproofs to the Chief Justice on his conduct, the reading of ludicrous parodies culled from various sources, and threats by the Sheriff to arrest 'the first man I see laugh'. Despite Ellenborough's unqualified charge ('... in obedience to his conscience and his God, he pronounced this to be a most impious and profane libel') the jury returned two further verdicts of 'Not Guilty', with the consequence (it is said) that Ellenborough retired to his sick-room never to return. From that time forward – even in 1819 and 1820 – all parodies and squibs were immune from prosecution.[1]

Persecution cannot easily stand up in the face of ridicule. Indeed, there are two things that strike one about the press battles of these years. The first is, not the solemnity but the delight with which Hone, Cruikshank, Carlile, Davison, Benbow and others baited authority. (This tradition was continued by Hetherington, who for weeks passed under the noses of the constables, in his business as editor of the unstamped *Poor Man's Guardian*, in the highly unlikely disguise of a Quaker.) Imprisonment as a Radical publisher brought, not odium, but honour. Once the publishers had decided that they were ready to go to prison, they outdid each other with new expedients to exhibit their opponents in the most ludicrous light. Radical England was delighted (and no one more than Hazlitt) at the resurrection by Sherwin of *Wat Tyler* – the republican indiscretion of Southey's youth. Southey, now Poet Laureate, was foremost in the clamour to curb the seditious licence of the press, and sought an injunction against Sherwin for infringement of copyright. Lord Eldon refused the

1. *Second Trial of William Hone* (1818), pp. 17, 45; *Proceedings at the Public Meeting* to form a subscription for Hone (1818); F. W. Hackwood, *William Hone* (1912), chs. 9–11; Wickwar, op. cit., pp. 58–9. An old patterer told Mayhew (I, p. 252) that despite the acquittals, it remained difficult to 'work' Hone's parodies in the streets: 'there was plenty of officers and constables ready to pull the fellows up, and ... a beak that wanted to please the high dons, would find some way of stopping them. . .'

injunction: the Court could not take notice of property in the 'unhallowed profits of libellous publications'. 'Is it not a little strange,' Hazlitt inquired, 'that while this gentleman is getting an injunction against himself as the author of *Wat Tyler*, he is recommending gagging bills against us, and thus making up by force for his deficiency in argument?'[1] On the other hand, Carlile (who had taken over Sherwin's business) was more than pleased that the injunction was refused – for the sales of the poem were a staple source of profit in his difficult period at the start of business. 'Glory be to thee, O Southey!', he wrote six years later: '*Wat Tyler* continued to be a source of profit when every other political publication failed. The world does not know what it may yet owe to Southey.'[2]

The incidents of the pirating of *Queen Mab* and the *Vision of Judgement* were part of the same ebullient strategy. No British monarch has ever been portrayed in more ridiculous postures nor in more odious terms than George IV during the Queen Caroline agitation, and notably in Hone and Cruik- shank's *Right Divine of Kings to Govern Wrong*, *The Queen's Matrimonial Ladder*, *Non Mi Ricordo*, and *The Man in the Moon*. The same author's *Slap at Slop and the Bridge-Street Gang* (1822) appeared in the format of the Government- subsidized *New Times*, complete with a mock newspaper-stamp with the design of a cat's paw and the motto: 'On Every Thing He Claps His Claw', and with mock advertisements and mock lists of births and deaths:

MARRIAGE

His Imperial Majesty Prince Despotism, in a consumption, to Her Supreme Antiquity, The IGNORANCE of Eighteen Centuries, in a decline. The bridal dresses were most superb.

While Carlile fought on from prison, the satirists raked his prosecutors with fire.

1. Hazlitt, *Works*, VII, pp. 176 ff. 'Instead of applying for an injunc- tion against *Wat Tyler*,' Hazlitt opined, 'Mr Southey would do well to apply for an injunction against Mr Coleridge, who has undertaken his defence in *The Courier*.'

2. Sherwin's *Republican*, 29 March 1817; Carlile's *Republican*, 30 May 1823.

The second point is the real toughness of the libertarian and constitutional tradition, notwithstanding the Government's assault. It is not only a question of support in unexpected places – Hone's subscription list was headed by donations from a Whig duke, a marquis, and two earls – which indicates an uneasiness in the ruling class itself. What is apparent from the reports of the law officers of the Crown, in all political trials, is the caution with which they proceeded. In particular they were aware of the unreliability (for their purposes) of the jury system. By Fox's Libel Act of 1792 the jury were judges of the libel as well as of the fact of publishing; and however judges might seek to set this aside, this meant in effect that twelve Englishmen had to decide whether they thought the 'libel' dangerous enough to merit imprisonment or not. One State prosecution which failed was a blow at the morale of authority which could only be repaired by three which succeeded. Even in 1819–21 when the Government and the prosecuting societies carried almost every case[1] (in part as a result of their better deployment of legal resources and their influence upon juries, in part because Carlile was at his most provocative and had shifted the battlefield from sedition to blasphemy), it still is not possible to speak of 'totalitarian' or 'Asiatic' despotism. Reports of the trials were widely circulated, containing the very passages – sometimes, indeed, whole books read by the defendants in court – for which the accused were sentenced. Carlile continued imperturbably to edit the *Republican* from gaol; some of his shopmen, indeed, undertook in prison the editing of another journal, as a means of self-improvement. If Wooler's *Black Dwarf* failed in 1824, Cobbett remained in the field. He was, it is true, much subdued in the early Twenties. He did not like Carlile's Republicanism and Deism, nor their hold on the artisans of the great centres; and he turned increasingly back to the countryside and distanced himself from the working-class movement. (In 1821 he undertook the first of his *Rural Rides*, in which his genius seems at last to have found its inevitable form and matter.) But, even at this distance, the *Political Register* was always there, with its columns – like

1. In these three years there were 115 prosecutions and 45 *ex officio* informations.

those of the *Republican* – open to expose any case of persecution, from Bodmin to Berwick.

The honours of this contest did not belong to a single class. John Hunt and Thelwall (now firmly among the middle-class moderates) were among those pestered by the 'Bridge-Street Gang'; Sir Charles Wolseley, Burdett, the Reverend Joseph Harrison, were among those imprisoned for sedition. But Carlile and his shopmen were those who pressed defiance to its furthest point. The main battle was over by 1823, although there were renewed prosecutions in the late Twenties and early Thirties, and blasphemy cases trickled on into Victorian times. Carlile's greatest offence was to proceed with the unabashed publication of the *Political Works*, and then the *Theological Works*, of Tom Paine – works which, while circulating surreptitiously in the enclaves of 'old Jacks' in the cities, had been banned ever since Paine's trial *in absentia* in 1792, and Daniel Isaac Eaton's successive trials during the Wars. To this he added many further offences as the struggle wore on, and as he himself moved from Deism to Atheism, and as he threw in provocations – such as the advocacy of assassination – which in any view of the case were incitements to prosecution. He was an indomitable man, but he was scarcely loveable, and his years of imprisonment did not improve him. His strength lay in two things. First, he would not even admit of the possibility of defeat. And second, he had at his back the culture of the artisans.

The first point is not as evident as it appears. Determined men have often (as in the 1790s) been silenced or defeated. It is true that Carlile's brand of determination ('THE SHOP IN FLEET STREET WILL NOT BE CLOSED AS A MATTER OF COURSE') was peculiarly difficult for the authorities to meet. No matter how much law they had on their side, they must always incur odium by prosecutions. But they had provided themselves, under the Six Acts, with the power to *banish* the authors of sedition for offences far less than those which Carlile both committed and proudly admitted. It is testimony to the delicate equilibrium of the time, and to the limits imposed upon power by the consensus of constitutional opinion, that even in 1820 this provision of the Act was not employed.

Banishment apart, Carlile could not be silenced, unless he were
to be beheaded, or, more possibly, placed in solitary confinement. But there are two reasons why the Government did not
proceed to extreme measures: first, already by 1821 it seemed
to them less necessary, for the increased stamp duties were
taking effect. Second, it was apparent after the first encounters
that if Carlile were to be silenced, half a dozen new Carliles
would step into his place. The first two who did so *were*, in
fact, Carliles: his wife and his sister. Thereafter the 'shopmen'
came forward. By one count, before the battle had ended
Carlile had received the help of 150 volunteers, who – shopmen, printers, newsvendors – had between them served 200
years of imprisonment. The volunteers were advertised for in
the *Republican* – men 'who were free, able, and willing to serve
in General Carlile's Corps':

it is most distinctly to be understood that a love of propagating the
principles, and a sacrifice of liberty to that end ... AND NOT GAIN,
must be the motive to call forth such volunteers; for – though R.
Carlile pledges himself to ... give such men the best support in his
power – should any great number be imprisoned, he is not so
situated as to property or prospects as to be able to promise any
particular sum weekly ...[1]

From that time forward the 'Temple of Reason' off Fleet Street
was scarcely left untenanted for more than a day. The men
and women who came forward were, in nearly every case,
entirely unknown to Carlile. They simply came out of London;
or arrived on the coach from Lincolnshire, Dorset, Liverpool
and Leeds. They came out of a culture.

It was not the 'working-class' culture of the weavers or
Tyneside pitmen. The people most prominent in the fight included clerks, shop assistants, a farmer's son; Benbow, the
shoemaker turned bookseller; James Watson, the Leeds warehouseman who 'had the charge of a saddlehorse' at a dry-
salter's; James Mann, the cropper turned bookseller (also of
Leeds). The intellectual tradition was in part derived from the
Jacobin years, the circle which had once moved around Godwin
and Mary Wollstonecraft, or the members of the L.C.S., the

1. Wickwar, op. cit., p. 231.

last authentic spokesman of which – John Gale Jones – was one of Carlile's most constant supporters. In part it was a new tradition, owing something to Bentham's growing influence and something to the 'free-thinking Christians' and Unitarians, such as Benjamin Flower and W. J. Fox. It touched that vigorous sub-culture of the 'editors of Sunday newspapers and lecturers at the Surrey Institute' which *Blackwood*'s and the literary Establishment so scorned – schoolmasters, poor medical students, or civil servants who read Byron and Shelley and the *Examiner*, and among whom, not Whig or Tory, but 'right and wrong considered by each man abstractedly, is the fashion'.[1]

It is scarcely helpful to label this culture *bourgeois* or *petit-bourgeois*, although Carlile had more than his share of the individualism which (it is generally supposed) characterizes the latter. It would seem to be closer to the truth that the impulse of rational enlightenment which (in the years of the wars) had been largely confined to the Radical intelligentsia was now seized upon by the artisans and some of the skilled workers (such as many cotton-spinners) with an evangelistic zeal to carry it to 'numbers unlimited' – a propagandist zeal scarcely to be found in Bentham, James Mill or Keats. The subscription lists for Carlile's campaign drew heavily upon London; and, next, upon Manchester and Leeds. The artisan culture was, above all, that of the self-taught. 'During this twelve-month,' Watson recalled of his imprisonment, 'I read with deep interest and much profit Gibbon's *Decline and Fall of the Roman Empire*, Hume's *History of England*, and ... Mosheim's *Ecclesiastical History*.'[2] The artisans, who formed the nuclei of Carlile's supporting 'Zetetic Societies' (as well as of the later Rotunda) were profoundly suspicious of an estab-

1. Keats to his brother George, 17 September 1819, *Works* (1901), V, p. 108. The letter continues: 'This makes the business of Carlile the bookseller of great moment in my mind. He has been selling deistical pamphlets, republished Tom Paine, and many other works held in superstitious horror. ... After all, they are afraid to prosecute. They are afraid of his defence; it would be published in all the papers all over the empire. They shudder at this. The trials would light a flame they could not extinguish. Do you not think this of great import?'

2. W. J. Linton, *James Watson*, (Manchester 1880), p. 19.

lished culture which had excluded them from power and knowledge and which had answered their protests with homilies
and tracts. The works of the Enlightenment came to them with
the force of revelation.

In this way a reading public which was increasingly working
class in character was forced to *organize itself*. The war and
immediate post-war years had seen a 'kept' press, on the one
hand, and a Radical press on the other. In the Twenties much
of the middle-class press freed itself from direct Government
influence, and made some use of the advantages which Cobbett
and Carlile had gained. *The Times* and Lord Brougham, who
disliked the 'pauper press' perhaps as much as Lord Eldon
(although for different reasons), gave to the term 'Radicalism'
a quite different meaning – free trade, cheap government, and
utilitarian reform. To some degree (although by no means
entirely) they carried the Radical middle-class with them – the
schoolmasters, surgeons, and shopkeepers, some of whom had
once supported Cobbett and Wooler – so that by 1832 there
were two Radical publics: the middle-class, which looked forward to the Anti-Corn Law League, and the working-class,
whose journalists (Hetherington, Watson, Cleave, Lovett,
Benbow, O'Brien) were already maturing the Chartist movement. Throughout the Twenties the working-class press
struggled under the crushing weight of the stamp duties,[1] while
Cobbett remained loosely and temperamentally affiliated to
the plebeian rather than to the middle-class movement. The
dividing-line came to be, increasingly, not alternative 'reform'
strategies (for middle-class reformers could on occasion be as
revolutionary in their tone as their working-class counterparts)
but alternative notions of political economy. The touchstone
can be seen during the field labourer's 'revolt' in 1830, when
The Times (Cobbett's 'BLOODY OLD TIMES') led the demand
for salutary examples to be made of the rioters, while both
Cobbett and Carlile were prosecuted once again on charges
of inflammatory writing.

In 1830 and 1831 the black ensign of defiance was hoisted

1. In 1830 these taxes amounted to a 4*d.* stamp on each newspaper or
weekly periodical, a duty of 3*s.* 6*d.* on each advertisement, a small paper
duty, and a large surety against action for libel.

once again. Cobbett found a loophole in the law, and recommenced his *Twopenny Trash*. But this time it was Hetherington, a printing worker, who led the frontal attack. His *Poor Man's Guardian* carried the emblem of a hand-press, the motto 'Knowledge is Power', and the heading: 'Published contrary to "Law" to try the power of "Might" against "Right".' His opening address, quoted clause by clause the laws he intended to defy:

> ... the *Poor Man's Guardian* ... will contain *'news, intelligence and occurrences,'* and *'remarks and observations thereon,'* and *'upon matters of Church and State tending,'* decidedly, *'to excite hatred and contempt of the Government and Constitution of ... this country, as* BY LAW *established,'* and also, *'to vilify the* ABUSES *of Religion'* ...

It would also defy every clause of the stamp tax legislation,

> or any other acts whatsoever and despite the 'laws' or the will and pleasure of *any tyrant* or *body of tyrants* whatsoever, any thing herein-before, or any-where-else ... to the contrary notwithstanding.

His fourth number carried the advertisement, 'WANTED': 'Some hundreds of POOR MEN out of employ who have NOTHING TO RISK ... to sell to the poor and ignorant' this paper. Not only were the volunteers found, but a score of other unstamped papers sprang up, notably Carlile's *Gauntlet*, and Joshua Hobson's *Voice of the West Riding*. By 1836 the struggle was substantially over, and the way had been opened for the Chartist press.

But the 'great unstamped' was emphatically a working-class press. The *Poor Man's Guardian* and the *Working Man's Friend* were in effect, organs of the National Union of the Working Classes; Doherty's *Poor Man's Advocate* was an organ of the Factory Movement; Joshua Hobson was a former hand-loom weaver, who had built a wooden hand-press by his own labour; Bronterre O'Brien's *Destructive* consciously sought to develop working-class Radical theory. These small, closely printed, weeklies carried news of the great struggle for General Unionism in these years, the lock-outs of 1834 and the protests at the Tolpuddle case, or searching debate and exposition of Socialist and trade union theory. An examination of this period would take us beyond the limits of this study, to a time when the working class was no longer in the making but (in its Chartist form) already made. The point we must note is the degree to which the fight for press liberties was a central formative influence upon the shaping movement. Perhaps 500 people were prosecuted for the production and sale of the 'unstamped'.[1] From 1816 (indeed, from 1792) until 1836 the contest involved, not only the editors, booksellers, and printers, but also many hundreds of newsvendors, hawkers, and voluntary agents.[2]

Year after year the annals of persecution continue. In 1817 two men selling Cobbett's pamphlets in Shropshire, whom a clerical magistrate 'caused ... to be apprehended under the Vagrant Act ... and had *well flogged at the whipping-post*'; in the same year hawkers in Plymouth, Exeter, the Black Country, Oxford, the north; in 1819 even a peep-show huckster, who showed a print of Peterloo in a Devon village. The imprisonments were rarely for more than a year (often newsvendors were committed to prison for a few weeks and then released without trial) but they could be more serious in their effects upon the victims than the more widely publicized imprisonments of editors. Men were thrown into verminous 'Houses of Correction'; often chained and fettered; often without knowledge of the law or means of defence. Unless their cases were noted by Cobbett, Carlile or some section of the Radicals, their families were left without any income and might be forced into the workhouse.[3] It was, indeed, in the smaller centres that the contest for freedom was most hard-fought. Manchester or Nottingham or Leeds had Radical enclaves and meeting-

1. Abel Heywood, the Manchester bookseller, claimed the figure to be 750.

2. Societies for the Diffusion of 'Really Useful Knowledge' were formed to assist the 'unstamped'. See *Working Man's Friend*, 18 May 1833.

3. See Wickwar, op. cit., pp. 40, 103–14; *Second Trial of William Hone* (1818), p. 19; for the case of Robert Swindells, confined in Chester castle, while his wife and baby died from neglect, and his remaining child was placed in the poorhouse; Sherwin's *Political Register*, 14 March 1818, for the cases of Mellor and Pilling of Warrington, held for nineteen weeks chained to felons in Preston Gaol, sent for trial at the Court of King's Bench in London – the 200 miles to which they had to walk – the trial removed to Lancaster (200 miles back) – and then discharged.

places, and were ready to support the victimized. In the market town or industrial village the cobbler or teacher who took in Cobbett or Carlile in the Twenties might expect to be watched and to suffer persecution in indirect forms. (Often Cobbett's parcels of *Registers* to country subscribers simply failed to arrive – they were 'lost' in the mail.) A whole pattern of distribution, with its own folklore, grew up around the militant press. Hawkers (Mayhew was told), in order to avoid 'selling' the *Republican*, sold straws instead, and then *gave* the paper to their customers. In the Spen Valley, in the days of the 'unstamped', a penny was dropped through a grating and the paper would 'appear'. In other parts, men would slip down alleys or across fields at night to the known rendezvous. More than once the 'unstamped' were transported under the noses of the authorities in a coffin and with a godly cortège of free-thinkers.

We may take two examples of the shopmen and vendors. The first, a shop*woman*, serves to remind us that, in these rationalist and Owenite circles, the claim for women's rights (almost silent since the 1790s) was once again being made, and was slowly extending from the intelligentsia to the artisans. Carlile's womenfolk, who underwent trial and imprisonment, did so more out of loyalty than out of conviction. Very different was Mrs Wright, a Nottingham lace-mender, who was one of Carlile's volunteers and who was prosecuted for selling one of his *Addresses* containing opinions in his characteristic manner:

A Representative System of Government would soon see the propriety of turning our Churches and Chapels into Temples of Science and ... cherishing the Philosopher instead of the Priest. Kingcraft and Priestcraft I hold to be the bane of Society. ... Those two evils operate jointly against the welfare both of the body and mind, and to palliate our miseries in this life, the latter endeavour to bamboozle us with a hope of eternal happiness.

She conducted her long defence herself [1] and was rarely interrupted. Towards the end of her defence,

Mrs Wright requested permission to retire and suckle her infant child that was crying. This was granted, and she was absent from the Court twenty minutes. In passing to and fro, to the Castle Coffee

1. Most of Carlile's shopmen were provided with long written defences by Carlile, and this was probably so in her case.

House, she was applauded and loudly cheered by assembled thousands, all encouraging her to be of good cheer and to persevere.

Some time later she was thrown into Newgate, on a November night, with her six-months' baby and nothing to lie on but a mat. Such women as Mrs Wright (and Mrs Mann of Leeds) had to meet not only the customary prosecutions, but also the abuse and insinuations of an outraged loyalist press. 'This wretched and shameless woman,' wrote the *New Times*, was attended by '*several females*. Are not these circumstances enough to shock every reflecting mind?' She was an 'abandoned creature' (the conventional epithet for prostitutes) 'who has cast off all the distinctive shame and fear and decency of her sex'. By her 'horrid example' she had depraved the minds of other mothers: 'these monsters in female form stand forward, with hardened visages, in the face of day, to give their public countenance and support – *for the first time in the history of the Christian world* – to gross, vulgar, horrid blasphemy'. She was a woman, wrote Carlile, 'of very delicate health, and truly all spirit and no matter'.[1]

The longest sentences endured by a newsvendor were probably those served by Joseph Swann, a hat-maker of Macclesfield. He was arrested in 1819 for selling pamphlets and a seditious poem:

> Off with your fetters; spurn the slavish yoke;
> Now, now, or never, can your chain be broke;
> Swift then rise and give the fatal stroke.

Shunted from gaol to gaol, and chained with felons, he was eventually sentenced to two years imprisonment for seditious conspiracy, two years for blasphemous libel, and a further six months for seditious libel to run consecutively. When these monstrous sentences had been passed, Swann held up his white hat and enquired of the magistrate: 'Han ye done? Is that all? Why I thowt ye'd got a bit of hemp for me, and hung me.' His wife also was briefly arrested (for continuing the sale of pamphlets); she and her four children survived on a parish allowance of 9s. a week, with some help from Carlile and

1. See Wickwar, op. cit., pp. 222–3; *Trial of Mrs Susannah Wright* (1822), pp. 8, 44, 56; *New Times*, 16 November 1822.

Cobbett. Cobbett, indeed, interested himself particularly in the case of Swann, and when Castlereagh committed suicide it was to Swann that Cobbett addressed his triumphant obituary obloquies: 'CASTLEREAGH HAS CUT HIS OWN THROAT AND IS DEAD! Let that sound reach you in the depth of your dungeon ... and carry consolation to your suffering soul.' After serving his four and a half years, Swann 'passed the gate of Chester Castle ... in mind as stubborn as ever', and resumed his trade as a hatter. But he had not yet been discharged from service. In November 1831 the *Poor Man's Guardian* reported proceedings at the Stockport magistrate's court, where Joseph Swann was charged with selling the 'unstamped'. The Chairman of the Bench, Captain Clarke, asked him what he had to say in his defence:

Defendant. – Well, Sir, I have been out of employment for some time; neither can I obtain work; my family are all starving. ... And for another reason, the weightiest of all; I sell them for the good of my fellow countrymen; to let them see how they are misrepresented in Parliament ... I wish to let the people know how they are humbugged ...

Bench. – Hold your tongue a moment.

Defendant. – I shall not! for I wish every man to read these publications ...

Bench. – You are very insolent, therefore you are committed to three months' imprisonment in Knutsford House of Correction, to hard labour.

Defendant. – I've nothing to thank you for; and whenever I come out, I'll hawk them again. And *mind you* [looking at Captain Clark] the first that I hawk shall be to your house ...

Joseph Swann was then forcibly removed from the dock.[1]

In the twentieth-century rhetoric of democracy most of these men and women have been forgotten, because they were impudent, vulgar, over-earnest, or 'fanatical'. In their wake the subsidized vehicles of 'improvement', the *Penny Magazine* and the *Saturday Magazine* (whose vendors no one prosecuted) moved in; and afterwards the commercial press, with its much larger resources, although it did not really begin to capture the

1. Wickwar, op. cit., pp. 105–7; *Independent Whig*, 16 January 1820; Cobbett's *Political Register*, 17 August 1822; *Poor Man's Guardian*, 12 November 1831; A. G. Barker, *Henry Hetherington*, pp. 12–13.

Radical reading public until the Forties and the Fifties. (Even then the popular press – the publications of Cleave, Howitt, Chambers, Reynolds, and Lloyd – came from this Radical background.) Two consequences of the contest may be particularly noticed. The first (and most obvious) is that the working-class ideology which matured in the Thirties (and which has endured, through various translations, ever since) put an exceptionally high value upon the rights of the press, of speech, of meeting and of personal liberty. The tradition of the 'free-born Englishman' is of course far older. But the notion to be found in some late 'Marxist' interpretations, by which these claims appear as a heritage of 'bourgeois individualism' will scarcely do. In the contest between 1792 and 1836 the artisans and workers made this tradition peculiarly their own, adding to the claim for free speech and thought their own claim for the untrammelled propagation, in the cheapest possible form, of the products of this thought.

In this, it is true, they shared a characteristic illusion of the epoch, applying it with force to the context of working-class struggle. All the enlighteners and improvers of the time thought that the only limit imposed to the diffusion of reason and knowledge was that imposed by the inadequacy of the means. The analogies which were drawn were frequently mechanical. The educational method of Lancaster and Bell, with its attempt at the cheap multiplication of learning by child monitors, was called (by Bell) the 'STEAM ENGINE of the MORAL WORLD'. Peacock aimed with deadly accuracy when he called Brougham's Society for the Diffusion of Useful Knowledge the 'Steam Intellect Society'. Carlile was supremely confident that 'pamphlet-reading is destined to work the great necessary moral and political changes among mankind':

The Printing-press may be strictly denominated a Multiplication Table as applicable to the mind of man. The art of Printing is a multiplication of mind. . . . Pamphlet-vendors are the most important springs in the machinery of Reform.[1]

Owen contemplated the institution, by means of propaganda, of the NEW MORAL WORLD with messianic, but mechanical, optimism.

1. See Wickwar, op. cit., p. 214.

But if this was, in part, the rationalist illusion, we must remember the second – and more immediate – consequence: between 1816 and 1836 this 'multiplication' seemed to *work*. For the Radical and unstamped journalists were seizing the multiplying-machine on behalf of the working class; and in every part of the country the experiences of the previous quarter-century had prepared men's minds for what they now could read. The importance of the propaganda can be seen in the steady extension of Radical organization from the great towns and manufacturing areas into the small boroughs and market towns. One of the Six Acts of 1819 (that authorizing the search for weapons) was specificially confined only to designated 'disturbed districts' of the Midlands and the north.[1] By 1832 – and on into Chartist times – there is a Radical nucleus to be found in every county, in the smallest market towns and even in the larger rural villages, and in nearly every case it is based on the local artisans. In such centres as Croydon, Colchester and Ipswich, Tiverton and Taunton, Nantwich or Cheltenham, there were hardy and militant Radical or Chartist bodies. In Ipswich we find weavers, saddlers, harness-makers, tailors, shoemakers; in Cheltenham shoemakers, tailors, stonemasons, cabinet-makers, gardeners, a plasterer and a blacksmith – 'earnest and reputable people – much above the average in intelligence'.[2] These are the people whom Cobbett, Carlile, Hetherington and their newsvendors had 'multiplied'.

'Ernest and reputable people . . .' – this autodidact culture has never been adequately analysed.[3] The majority of these people had received some elementary education, although its inadequacy is testified from many sources:

1. The counties of Lancaster, Chester, the West Riding, Warwick, Stafford, Derby, Leicester, Nottingham, Cumberland, Westmorland, Northumberland, Durham, the city of Coventry, and the country boroughs of Newcastle-upon-Tyne and Nottingham.

2. W. E. Adams, op. cit., p. 169. I am indebted to Mr A. J. Brown for information about Ipswich. See also *Chartist Studies*, ed. A. Briggs, for Chartism in Somerset and East Anglia

3. J. F. C. Harrison's admirable account in *Learning and Living* tends to underestimate the vigour of radical culture before 1832. The best firsthand accounts are in William Lovett's autobiography and (for Chartist times) Thomas Frost, *Forty Years Recollections* (1880).

I well remember the first half-time school in Bingley. It was a cottage at the entrance to the mill-yard. The teacher, a poor old man who had done odd jobs of a simple kind for about 12s. a week, was set to teach the half-timers. Lest, however, he should teach too much or the process be too costly, he had to stamp washers out of cloth with a heavy wooden mallet on a large block of wood during school hours.[1]

This is, perhaps, the 'schooling' of the early 1830s at its worst. Better village schools, or cheap fee-paying schools patronized by artisans, could be found in the Twenties. By this time, also, the Sunday schools were liberating themselves (although slowly) from the taboo upon the teaching of writing, while the first British and National schools (for all their inadequacies) were beginning to have some effect. But, for any secondary education, the artisans, weavers, or spinners had to teach themselves. The extent to which they were doing this is attested by the sales of Cobbett's educational writings, and notably of his *Grammar of the English Language*, published in 1818, selling 13,000 within six months, and a further 100,000 in the next fifteen years.[2] And we must remember that in translating sales (or the circulation of periodicals) into estimates of readership, the same book or paper was loaned, read aloud and passed through many hands.

But the 'secondary education' of the workers took many forms, of which private study in solitude was only one. The artisans, in particular, were not as rooted in benighted communities as it is easy to assume. They tramped freely about the country in search of work; apart from the enforced travels of the Wars, many mechanics travelled abroad, and the relative facility with which thousands upon thousands emigrated to America and the colonies (driven not only by poverty but also by the desire for opportunity or political freedom) suggests a general fluency of social life. In the cities a vigorous and bawdy plebeian culture coexisted with more polite traditions among the artisans. Many collections of early nineteenth-

1. Thomas Wood, *Autobiography (1822–80)* (Leeds, 1956). See also An Old Potter, *When I Was a Child* 1903), ch. 1.
2. M. L. Pearl, *William Cobbett* (1953), pp. 105–7. There were also many pirated editions.

century ballads testify to the fervour with which the battle between Loyalists and Radicals was carried into song. Perhaps it was the melodramatic popular theatre which accorded best with the gusto of the Jacobins and of the 'old Radicals' of 1816–20. From the early 1790s the theatre, especially in provincial centres, was a forum in which the opposed factions confronted each other, and provoked each other by 'calling the tunes' in the intervals. A 'Jacobin Revolutionist and Leveller' described a visit to the theatre, in 1795, in a northern port:

... and as the theatre is generally the field in which the Volunteer Officers fight their Campaigns, these military heroes ... called for the tune of *God Save the King*, and ordered the audience to stand uncovered ... I sat covered in defiance of the military.[1]

It was in the years of repression that this song (with its denunciation of the 'knavish tricks' of the Jacobins) replaced 'The Roast Beef of Old England' as a 'national anthem'. But as the Wars dragged on, the audience often proved itself to be less easily cowed by 'Church and King' bullies than later generations. A riot in Sheffield in 1812 commenced when 'the South Devon officers insist on having "God Save the King" sung, and the mobility in the gallery insist on its not being sung. . . . A disturber has been sent to prison.'[2]

Most early nineteenth-century theatre-riots had some Radical tinge to them, even if they only expressed the simple antagonism between the stalls and the gods. The jealousy of the monopolistic Patent Theatres to their little rivals, with their 'burlettas' and their shows 'disgraced ... by the introduction of Horses, Elephants, Monkeys, Dogs, Fencers, Tumblers, and Rope Dancers',[3] was reinforced by the dislike felt by employers for the dangerous ebullience of the audience. In 1798 the 'opulent Merchants, Shipbuilders, Ropemakers' and other

1. *Philanthropist*, 22 June 1795.
2. T. A. Ward, op. cit., p. 196. See also the Nottingham example, above p. 516.
3. See H.O. 119.3/4 for the accusations and counter-accusations passing between Covent Garden and Drury Lane, on the one hand, and the 'illegitimate' little theatres on the other, 1812–18.

employers around London Docks memorialized the Government, complaining that the performances at the Royalty Theatre, near the Tower, encouraged 'habits of dissipation and profligacy' among 'their numerous Manufacturers, Workmen, Servants, &c.'[1] (The complaint had been going on for more than two hundred years.) In 1819 disorder raged through central London, night after night, and week after week, in the notorious 'O.P.' riots, when the prices were raised at Drury Lane. It was Authority's particular dislike of the theatre's blend of disorder and sedition which enabled the Patent Theatres to preserve at least the forms of their monopoly until as late as 1843.

The vitality of the plebeian theatre was not matched by its artistic merit. The most positive influence upon the sensibility of the Radicals came less from the little theatres than from the Shakespearian revival – not only Hazlitt, but also Wooler, Bamford, Cooper, and a score of self-taught Radical and Chartist journalists were wont to cap their arguments with Shakespearian quotations. Wooler's apprenticeship had been in dramatic criticism; while the strictly trades unionist *Trades Newspaper* commenced, in 1825, with a theatre critic as well as a sporting column (covering prize-fighting and the contest between 'the Lion Nero and Six Dogs').[2] But there was one popular art which, in the years between 1780 and 1830, attained to a peak of complexity and excellence – the political print.

This was the age, first, of Gillray and of Rowlandson, and then of George Cruikshank, as well as of scores of other caricaturists, some competent, some atrociously crude. Theirs was, above all, a metropolitan art. The models for the cartoonists drove in their coaches past the print-shops where their political (or personal) sins were mercilessly lampooned. No holds whatsoever were barred, on either side. Thelwall or Burdett or Hunt would be portrayed by the loyalists as savage incendiaries, a flaming torch in one hand, a pistol in the other,

1. H.O. 65.1.

2. *Trades Newspaper*, 31 July, 21 August 1825 et seq. The Editor felt called upon to apologize for carrying news of prize-fighting and animal-baiting; but the paper was governed by a committee of London trades unions, and the members' wishes had to be met.

and with belts crammed with butchers' knives; while Cruikshank portrayed the King (in 1820) lolling blind drunk in his
throne, surrounded by broken bottles and in front of a screen
decorated with satyrs and large-breasted trollops. (The Bishops
fared no better.) The popular print was by no means an art for
the illiterate, as the balloons full of minute print, issuing from
the mouths of the figures, testify. But the illiterate also could
participate in this culture, standing by the hour in front of the
print-shop window and deciphering the intricate visual
minutiae in the latest Gillray or Cruikshank: at Knight's in
Sweeting's Alley, Fairburn's off Ludgate Hill, or Hone's in
Fleet Street (Thackeray recalled), 'there used to be a crowd ...
of grinning, good-natured mechanics, who spelt the songs, and
spoke them out for the benefit of the company, and who received the points of humour with a general sympathizing roar'.
On occasions, the impact was sensational; Fleet Street would
be blocked by the crowds; Cruikshank believed that his 'Bank
Restriction Note' (1818) resulted in the abolition of the death-
penalty for passing forged money. In the 1790s the ·Govern-
ment actually suborned Gillray into anti-Jacobin service.
During the Wars the mainstream of prints was patriotic and
anti-Gallican (John Bull took on his classic shape in these
years), but on domestic issues the prints were savagely polemical and frequently Burdettite in sympathy. After the Wars
a flood of Radical prints was unloosed, which remained immune
from prosecution, even during the Queen Caroline agitation,
because prosecution would have incurred greater ridicule.
Through all its transformations (and despite the crudities of
many practitioners) it remained a highly sophisticated city art:
it could be acutely witty, or cruelly blunt and obscene, but in
either case it depended upon a frame of reference of shared
gossip and of intimate knowledge of the manners and foibles
of even minor participants in public affairs – a patina of intricate allusiveness.[1]

The culture of the theatre and the print-shop was popular in

1. Some notion of the complexity of this output can be gained from Dr
Dorothy George's very learned *Catalogues of Political and Personal
Satire in the British Museum*, volumes 7, 8, and 9 and 10. See also
Blanchard Jerrold, *George Cruikshank* (1894), ch. 4.

a wider sense than the literary culture of the Radical artisans. For the keynote of the autodidact culture of the Twenties and early Thirties was moral sobriety. It is customary to attribute this to the influence of Methodism, and undoubtedly, both directly and indirectly, this influence can be felt. The Puritan character-structure underlies the moral earnestness and self-discipline which enabled men to work on by candle-light after a day of labour. But we have to make two important reservations. The first is that Methodism was a strongly *anti-intellectual* influence, from which British popular culture has never wholly recovered. The circle to which Wesley would have confined the reading of Methodists (Southey noted) 'was narrow enough; his own works, and his own series of abridgements, would have constituted the main part of a Methodist's library'.[1] In the early nineteenth century local preachers and class leaders were encouraged to read more: reprints of Baxter, the hagiography of the movement, or 'vollams of the Missionary Register'. But poetry was suspect, and philosophy, biblical criticism, or political theory taboo. The whole weight of Methodist teaching fell upon the blessedness of the 'pure in heart', no matter what their rank or accomplishments. This gave to the Church its egalitarian spiritual appeal. But it also fed (sometimes to gargantuan proportions) the philistine defences of the scarcely-literate. 'It is *carte blanche* for ignorance and folly,' Hazlitt exploded:

Those ... who are either unable or unwilling to think connectedly or rationally on any subject, are at once released from every obligation of the kind, by being told that faith and reason are opposed to one another.[2]

From the successive shocks of Paine, Cobbett, Carlile, the Methodist ministers defended their flocks: the evidence was abundant that unmonitored literacy was the 'snare of the devil'.

Some of the off-shoots from the main Methodist stem – the Methodist Unitarians (an odd conjunction) and notably the New Connexion – were more intellectual in inclination, and their congregations resemble the older Dissenting Churches.

1. Southey, *Life of Wesley*, p. 558.
2. *Works*, IV, pp. 57 ff., from *The Round Table* (1817).

But the main Methodist tradition responded to the thirst for enlightenment in a different way. We have already noted [1] the submerged affinities between Methodism and middle-class Utilitarianism. Strange as it may seem, when we think of Bentham and his hatred of 'juggical' superstition, the spirit of the times was working for a conjunction of the two traditions. If intellectual enquiry was discouraged by the Methodists, the acquistion of *useful* knowledge could be seen as godly and full of merit. The emphasis, of course, was upon the *use*. Work-discipline alone was not enough, it was necessary for the labour force to advance towards more sophisticated levels of attaintment. The old opportunist Baconian argument – that there could be no evil in the study of nature, which is the visible evidence of God's laws – had now been assimilated within Christian apologetics. Hence arose that peculiar phenomenon of early Victorian culture, the Nonconformist minister with his hand on the Old Testament and his eye on a microscope.

The effects of this conjunction can already be felt within the working-class culture of the Twenties. Science – botany, biology, geology, chemistry, mathematics, and, in particular, the applied sciences – the Methodists looked upon with favour, provided that these pursuits were not intermixed with politics or speculative philosophy. The solid, statistical, intellectual world which the Utilitarians were building was congenial also to the Methodist Conference. They also compiled their statistical tables of Sunday school attendances, and Bunting (one feels) would have been happy if he could have calculated degrees of spiritual grace with the accuracy that Chadwick calculated the minimum diet that might keep a pauper in strength to work. Hence came that alliance between Nonconformists and Utilitarians in educational endeavour, and in the dissemination of 'improving' knowledge alongside godly exhortation. Already in the Twenties this kind of literature is well established, in which moral admonishments (and accounts of the drunken orgies of Tom Paine on his unvisited deathbed) appear side by side with little notes on the flora of Venezuela, statistics of the death-roll in the Lisbon earthquake, recipes for boiled vegetables, and notes on hydraulics:

1. See above, p. 401.

Every species ... requires a different kind of food. ... Linnaeus has remarked, that the cow eats 276 species of plants and rejects 218; the goat eats 449 and rejects 126; the sheep eats 387 and rejects 141; the horse eats 262 and rejects 212; and the hog, more nice in its taste than any of those, eats but 72 plants and rejects all the rest. Yet such is the unbounded munificence of the Creator, that all these countless myriads of sentient beings are amply provided for and nourished by his bounty! 'The eyes of all these look unto Him, and he openeth his hand and satisfieth the desire of every living being.' [1]

And already in the Twenties, Political Economy can be seen as a third partner alongside Morality and Useful Knowledge, in the shape of homilies upon the God-given and immutable laws of supply and demand. Capital, even nicer in its taste than the hog, would select only the industrious and obedient worker and reject all others.

Thus Methodism and Evangelicism contributed few active intellectual ingredients to the articulate culture of the working people, although they can be said to have added an earnestness to the pursuit of *information*. (Arnold was later to see the Nonconformist tradition as deeply philistine, and indifferent to 'sweetness and light'.) And there is a second reservation to be made, when the sobriety of the artisan's world is attributed to this source. Moral sobriety was in fact demonstrably a product of the Radical and rationalist agitation itself; and owed much to the old Dissenting and Jacobin traditions. This is not to say that there were no drunken Radicals nor disorderly demonstrations. Wooler was only one of the Radical leaders who, it was said, was too fond of the bottle; while we have seen that the London taverns and Lancashire hush-shops were important meeting-places. But the Radicals sought to rescue the people from the imputation of being a 'mob'; and their leaders sought continually to present an image of sobriety.

Moreover, there were other motives for this emphasis. One of

1. Thomas Dick, *On the Improvement of Society by the Diffusion of Knowledge* (Glasgow, 1833), p. 175. See also p. 213, where it is argued that 'arithmetic, algebra, geometry, conic sections, and other departments of mathematics' are particularly godly studies since they 'contain truths that are eternal and unchangeable'.

the Rules of the Bath Union Society for Parliamentary Reform (established in January 1817) is characteristic:

It is earnestly recommended to every Member not to spend his Money at public houses, because half of the said Money goes in Taxes, to feed the Maggots of Corruption.[1]

In the post-war years Hunt and Cobbett made much of the call for abstinence from all taxed articles, and in particular of the virtues of water over spirits or beer. The sobriety of the Methodists was the one (and only) attribute of their 'sect' which Cobbett found it possible to praise: 'I look upon drunkenness as the root of much more than half the mischief, misery and crimes with which society is afflicted.'[2] This was not always Cobbett's tone; on other occasions he could lament the price, for the labourer, of beer. But a general moral primness is to be found in most quarters. It was, particularly, the ideology of the artisan or of the skilled worker who had held his position in the face of the boisterous unskilled tide. It is to be found in Carlile's account of his early manhood:

I was a regular, active, and industrious man, working early and late ... and when out of the workshop never so happy anywhere as at home with my wife and two children. The alehouse I always detested ... I had a notion that a man ... was a fool not to make a right application of every shilling.[3]

Many a day he had missed out a meal, and 'carried home some sixpenny publication to read at night'. It is to be found, in its most admirable and moving form, in William Lovett's *Life and Struggles ... in Pursuit of Bread, Knowledge and Freedom,* a title which, in itself, condenses all that we are seeking to describe.

It was a disposition strengthened, among the republicans and free-thinkers, by the character of the attacks upon them. Denounced in loyalist lampoons and from Church pulpits as disreputable exemplars of every vice, they sought to exhibit themselves as bearing, alongside their unorthodox opinions, an

1. H.O. 40.4.
2. *Political Register,* 13 January 1821. The Temperance Movement can be traced to this post-war campaign of abstinence.
3. See Wickwar, op. cit., p. 68.

irreproachable character. They struggled against the loyalist legends of revolutionary France, which was presented as a sanguinary thieves' kitchen, whose Temples of Reason were brothels. They were particularly sensitive to any accusation of sexual impropriety, of financial misconduct, or of lack of attachment to the familial virtues.[1] Carlile published in 1830 a little book of homilies, *The Moralist*, while Cobbett's *Advice to Young Men* was only a more hearty and readable essay upon the same themes of industry, perseverance, independence. The rationalists, of course, were especially anxious to counter the accusation that the rejection of the Christian faith must inevitably entail the dissolution of all moral restraints. Alongside Volney's influential *Ruins of Empire* there was translated, and circulated as a tract, his *Law of Nature*, which served to argue – in the form of a dialogue – that the respectable virtues must all be adhered to according to the laws of social utility:

Q. Why do you say that conjugal love is a virtue?
A. Because the concord and union which are the consequence of the affection subsisting between married persons, establish in the bosom of their family a multitude of habits which contribute to its prosperity and conservation ...

So on for the greater part of a page. And so, through chapters on Knowledge, Continence, Temperance, Cleanliness, the Domestic Virtues, which read like a prospectus for the Victorian age. Where heterodoxy appeared on matters of sexual relations, as it did among the Owenite communitarians, it generally did so with a zeal characteristic of the Puritan temperament.[2] The very small group of neo-Malthusians who

1. Cf. T. Frost, *Forty Years' Recollections*, p. 20 (of the anti-Owenite propaganda of the Thirties): 'It was a very common device for complainants and witnesses to say of a person charged with larceny, wife desertion, or almost any other offence, 'He is a Socialist'; and reports of all such cases had the side-head, 'Effect of Owenism' ...'

2. See, for example, William Hodson in the *Social Pioneer*, 20 April 1839 (*et passim*): 'Allow me, Sir, to state ... my views upon the [Marriage] Question . . . neither *man nor woman* can be happy, until they have *equal rights*; to marry each other for a home, as is often the case now, is the buying of human flesh; it is slave dealing of the worst description. . . . I contend that all unions ought to be solely from affection – to continue the unions when that affection ceases to exist is perfect ... *prostitution.*'

with considerable courage propagated among the working people, in the early Twenties, knowledge of the means of contraception did so out of the conviction that the only way in which the 'industrious classes' could raise their physical and cultural standards was by limiting their own numbers. Place and his companions would have been utterly shocked if it had been suggested that these means contributed to sexual or personal freedom.[1]

Levity or hedonism was as alien to the Radical or rationalist disposition as it was to the Methodist, and we are reminded of how much the Jacobins and Deists owed to the traditions of old Dissent. But it is possible to judge too much from the written record, and the public image of the orator. In the actual movement, cheerfulness keeps breaking in, not only with Hone, but, increasingly, with Hetherington, Lovett and their circle, who were softer, more humorous, more responsive to the people, less didactic, but not less determined, than their master, Carlile. It is tempting to offer the paradox that the rationalist artisans on Carlile's or Volney's model exhibited the same behaviour-patterns as their Methodist analogues; whereas in one case sobriety and cleanliness were recommended in obedience to God and to Authority, in the other case they were requisite virtues in those who made up the army which would overthrow Priestcraft and Kingcraft. To an observer who did not know the language the moral attributes of both might have appeared indistinguishable. But this is only partly so. For Volney's chapter-headings continue, 'Of the Social Virtues, and of Justice'. There was a profound difference between disciplines recommended for the salvation of one's own soul, and the same disciplines recommended as means to the salvation of a class. The Radical and free-thinking artisan was at his most earnest in his belief in the *active* duties of citizenship.

Moreover, together with this sobriety, the artisan culture nurtured the values of intellectual enquiry and of mutuality.

1. See Wallas, op. cit., pp. 166–72; N. Himes, 'J. S. Mill's Attitude toward Neo-Malthusianism', *Econ. Journal* (Supplement), 1926–9, I, pp. 459–62; M. Stopes, *Contraception* (1923); N. Himes, 'The Birth Control Handbills of 1823', *The Lancet*, 6 August 1927; M. St. J. Packe, *Life of John Stuart Mill* (1954), pp. 56–9. See also below, p. 855.

We have seen much of the first quality, displayed in the fight for press freedom. The autodidact had often an uneven, laboured, understanding, but it was his own. Since he had been forced to find his intellectual way, he took little on trust: his mind did not move within the established ruts of a formal education. Many of his ideas challenged authority, and authority had tried to suppress them. He was willing, therefore, to give a hearing to any new anti-authoritarian ideas. This was one cause for the instability of the working-class movement, especially in the years between 1825 and 1835; it also helps us to understand the rapidity with which Owenism spread, and the readiness of men to swing from one to another of the utopian and communitarian schemes which were put forward. (This artisan culture can be seen, also, as a leaven still at work in Victorian times, as the self-made men or the children of artisans of the Twenties contributed to the vigour and diversity of its intellectual life.) By mutuality we mean the tradition of mutual study, disputation, and improvement. We have seen something of this in the days of the L.C.S. The custom of reading aloud the Radical periodicals, for the benefit of the illiterate, also entailed – as a necessary consequence – that each reading devolved into an *ad hoc* group discussion: Cobbett had set out his arguments, as plainly as he could, and now the weavers, stockingers, or shoemakers, debated them.

A cousin of this kind of group was the mutual improvement society, whether formal or informal, which met week by week with the intention of acquiring knowledge, generally under the leadership of one of its own members.[1] Here, and in the Mechanics' Institutes, there was some coming-together of the traditions of the chapel and of the Radicals. But the coexistence was uneasy, and not always peaceful. The early history of the Mechanics' Institutes, from the formation of the London Institute in 1823 until the 1830s, is a story of ideological conflict. From the standpoint of the Radical artisan or trade unionist, the enthusiasm of Dr Birkbeck and of some Dissenting clergy and Benthamite professional men to assist them to establish centres for the promotion of knowledge was very much to be welcomed. But they certainly were not prepared to have this

1. See J. F. C. Harrison, op. cit., pp. 43 et. seq.

help *on any terms*. If Brougham appears in some recent writing as a great, but opportunist, Radical, this was not at all how he was viewed by the 'old Radicals' of 1823. They had seen him provide apologies for the spy system in 1817 (in a speech which Cobbett raked up again and again); and they were to see him stand up in the House at the climax of Carlile's campaign and declare that he 'rejoiced at the result of some recent trials' and regarded the prisoners as having published 'a mass of the grossest and most criminal matter'.[1] Brougham's zeal for the Institutes was enough to make them suspect at the outset; and Place's attempts to act as go-between between Brougham (whom he secretly despised) and the London trades unionists (who less secretly suspected him) were not likely to dispel this. The crucial conflicts took place on the questions of control, of financial independence, and on whether or not the Institutes should debate political economy (and, if so, *whose* political economy). Thomas Hodgskin was defeated in the latter conflict by Place and Brougham. In the former conflicts Birkbeck, in his zeal to raise money to expand the facilities of the Institute, overruled the advice of Robertson, Hodgskin and John Gast that – if the matter was undertaken less ambitiously – the artisans themselves could raise the necessary funds, and own and control the whole.

These two defeats, and the inauguration of Brougham's lectures on political economy (1825), meant that control passed to the middle-class supporters, whose ideology also dominated the political economy of the syllabus. By 1825 the *Trades Newspaper* regarded the London Institute as a lost cause, which was dependent upon 'the great and wealthy':

When it was founded, there was such a strong and general feeling excited on its behalf among the Mechanics of the Metropolis, that we felt perfectly convinced, had not that feeling been damped ... the Mechanics themselves might and would have furnished all the means requisite for ensuring it the most splendid success ...

In the provinces the history of the Mechanics' Institutes is more chequered. In Leeds (as Dr Harrison has shown) the Institute was from the outset controlled by sponsors from the

1. See Wickwar, op. cit., p. 147; and Place's comment, *'Well done, hypocrite; you who are not a Christian yourself.'*

middle class, and notably by Nonconformist manufacturers; in Bradford and in Huddersfield it was, for a period, controlled by Radical artisans. After the mid-Twenties the tendency was general for the custom of artisans to give way to that of the lower middle class, and for orthodox political economy to come into the syllabus. But still in 1830 the movement looked unorthodox enough (by reason of its galaxy of Utilitarian and Unitarian sponsors) for many Anglican and Wesleyan clergy to hold aloof. A Yorkshire vicar, in 1826, saw the Institutes as agencies of universal suffrage and 'universal free-thinking', which would 'in time degenerate into Jacobin clubs, and become nurseries of disaffection'. In the early 1830s a curate attacked the management of the Leicester Mechanics' Institute for perverting it into a school 'for the diffusion of infidel, republican, and levelling principles'. Among the papers taken by its library was Carlile's *Gauntlet*.[1]

We have spoken of the *artisan* culture of the Twenties. It is the most accurate term to hand, and yet it is not more than approximate. We have seen that '*petit-bourgeois*' (with its usual pejorative associations) will not do; while to speak of a 'working-class' culture would be premature. But by artisan we should understand a milieu which touched the London shipwrights and Manchester factory operatives at one side, and the degraded artisans, the outworkers, at the other. To Cobbett these comprised the 'journeymen and labourers', or, more briefly, 'the people'. 'I am of opinion,' he wrote to the Bishop of Llandaff in 1820, 'that your Lordship is very much deceived in supposing the People, or the vulgar, as you were pleased to call them, to be *incapable of comprehending argument*':

The people do not, I assure your Lordship, at all relish little simple tales. Neither do they delight in declamatory language, or in loose

1. See especially J. F. C. Harrison, op. cit., pp. 57–88, 173–8; *Mechanic's Magazine*, 11 and 18 October 1823; T. Kelly, *George Birkbeck* (Liverpool, 1957), chs. 5 and 6; E. Halévy, *Thomas Hodgskin* (1956), pp. 87–91; Chester New, op. cit., ch 17; *Trades Newspaper*, 17 July 1825; F. B. Lott, *Story of the Leicester Mechanic's Institute* (1935); M. Tylecote, *The Mechanic's Institutes of Lancashire and Yorkshire before 1851* (Manchester, 1957).

assertion, their minds have, within the last ten years, undergone a very great revolution. . . .

Give me leave . . . to say that . . . these classes are, to my certain knowledge, at this time, more enlightened than the other classes of the community. . . . They see further into the future than the Parliament and the Ministers. – There is this advantage attending their pursuit of knowledge. – They have no particular interest to answer; and, therefore, their judgement is unclouded by prejudice and selfishness. Besides which, their communication with each other is perfectly free. The thoughts of one man produce other thoughts in another man. Notions are canvassed without the restraint imposed upon suspicion, by false pride, or false delicacy. And hence the truth is speedily arrived at.[1]

Which argument, which truths?

II. WILLIAM COBBETT

Cobbett throws his influence across the years from the end of the Wars until the passing of the Reform Bill. To say that he was in no sense a systematic thinker is not to say that his was not a serious intellectual influence. It was Cobbett who *created* this Radical intellectual culture, not because he offered its most original ideas, but in the sense that he found the tone, the style, and the arguments which could bring the weaver, the schoolmaster, and the shipwright, into a common discourse. Out of the diversity of grievances and interests he brought a Radical consensus. His *Political Registers* were like a circulating medium which provided a common means of exchange between the experiences of men of widely differing attainments.

We can see this if we look, less at his ideas, than at his tone. And one way to do this is to contrast his manner with that of Hazlitt, the most 'Jacobin' of the middle-class Radicals and the one who – over a long period of years – came closest to the same movement as that of the artisans. Hazlitt is using his knife on the fund-holders and sinecurists:

Legitimate Governments (flatter them as we will) are not another Heathen mythology. They are neither so cheap nor so splendid as the Delphin edition of Ovid's Metamorphoses. They are indeed 'Gods to punish,' but in other respects 'men of our infirmity.' They

1. *Political Register*, 27 January 1820.

do not feed on ambrosia or drink nectar; but live on the common fruits of the earth, of which they get the largest share, and the best. The wine they drink is made of grapes: the blood they shed is that of their subjects: the laws they make are not against themselves: the taxes they vote, they afterwards devour. They have the same wants that we have: and, having the option, very naturally help themselves first, out of the common stock, without thinking that others are to come after them. ... Our State-paupers have their hands in every man's dish, and fare sumptuously every day. They live in palaces, and loll in coaches. In spite of Mr Málthus, their studs of horses consume the produce of our fields, their dog-kennels are glutted with the food that would maintain the children of the poor. They cost us so much a year in dress and furniture, so much in stars and garters, blue ribbons, and grand crosses, – so much in dinners, breakfasts, and suppers, and so much in suppers, breakfasts, and dinners. These heroes of the Income-tax, Worthies of the Civil List, Saints of the Court calendar (*compagnons du lys*), have their naturals and non-naturals, like the rest of the world, but at a dearer rate. ... You will find it easier to keep them a week than a month; and at the end of that time, waking from the sweet dream of Legitimacy, you may say with Caliban. 'Why, what a fool was I to take this drunken monster for a God.' [1]

Hazlitt's was a complex and admirable sensibility. He was one of the few intellectuals who received the full shock of the experience of the French Revolution, and, while rejecting the naïveties of the Enlightenment, reaffirmed the traditions of *liberté* and *égalité*. His style reveals, at every point, not only that he was measuring himself against Burke, Coleridge, and Wordsworth (and, more immediately, against *Blackwood*'s and the *Quarterly Review*), but that he was aware of the strength of some of their positions, and shared some of their responses. Even in his most engaged Radical journalism (of which this is an example) he aimed his polemic, not towards the popular, but towards the polite culture of his time. His *Political Essays* might be published by Hone,[2] but, when writing them, he will have thought less of Hone's audience than of the hope that he

1. 'What is the People?', from *Political Essays* (1819), in Works, VII, p. 263.

2. Hone said in his advertisement: 'The Publisher conscientiously affirms, that there is more Original and just Thinking, luminously expressed in this Volume, than in any other Work of a living Author.'

might make Southey squirm, make the *Quarterly* apoplectic, or even stop Coleridge short in mid-sentence.

This is in no sense a criticism. Hazlitt had a width of reference and a sense of commitment to a *European* conflict of historical significance which makes the plebeian Radicals appear provincial both in space and time. It is a question of rôles. Cobbett could never have written a sentence of this passage. He could not admit (even as a figure of speech) that we might *will* to flatter Legitimacy; he could not have accepted the norms of 'the world', which Hazlitt assumes, if only to punish; he could not have written '*our* State-paupers', since his every sinew was strained to make his audience see the stock-jobbers and placemen as *them*; and, as a corollary, he could not have written, with this sense of distance, of 'the children of the poor,' – he would either have said (to his audience) '*your* children' or he would have given a particular example. He is not likely to have said 'they cost us so much a year'; he would have put down a definite figure, even if it was at hazard. 'These heroes of the Income-tax' is closer to Cobbett's trick of naming;[1] but with Hazlitt there is still the drawl of the patrician Friend of the People (like Wilkes or Burdett, a pinch of snuff just at the moment when poised in the House for the most deadly thrust); with Cobbett there is no ironic pretence of ceremony – out come the names, *Parson* Malthus, *Bolton* Fletcher, the *Thing*, with a bluntness which made even Shelley blench ('Cobbett's snuff, revenge').

It is a matter of tone; and yet, in tone, will be found at least one half of Cobbett's political meaning. Hazlitt's style, with its sustained and controlled rhythms, and its antithetical movement, belongs to the polite culture of the essayist. Despite *Rural Rides*, one cannot easily think of Cobbett as an essayist. Indeed, Hazlitt's fertile allusiveness and studied manner, since it belonged to a culture which was not available to the artisans, might well arouse their hostility. When Cobbett wrote about sinecures it was in some such terms as this:

There are of these places and pensions all sizes, from *twenty pounds* to *thirty thousands* and nearly *forty thousand pounds a year*! ...

1. Cf. Cobbett's 'Seigneurs of the Twist, Sovereigns of the Spinning Jenny, great Yeomen of the Yarn.'

There are several individual placemen, the profits of *each* of which would maintain *a thousand families.* .... Mr PRESTON ... who is a *Member of Parliament* and has a large estate, says, upon this subject, 'Every family, even of the poorest labourers, consisting of five persons, may be considered as paying in *indirect taxes*, at least *ten pounds a year*, or more than half his wages at seven shillings a week!' And yet the insolent hirelings call you the *mob*, the *rabble*, the *swinish multitude*, and say, that your voice is nothing ...[1]

Everything here is solid, and related, not to a literary culture, but to commonly available experience. Even Mr Preston is placed. Cobbett brought the rhythms of speech back into prose; but of strenuously argumentative, emphatic speech.

Observe him writing on the familiar theme that the clergy should be judged, not by their professions, but their actions:

There is something unfortunate, to say the least of it, in this perfect union of action between the Church and the Methodist Convocation. Religion is not an abstract idea. It is not something metaphysical. It is to produce effect upon men's conduct, or it is good for nothing. It is to have an effect upon the actions of men. It is to have a good influence in the affairs and on the condition of men. Now, if the Church religion ...[2]

Cobbett's relationship to his audience in such passages as this (and the example falls from the first *Register* which comes to hand – almost any *Register* would provide the same) is so palpable that one might reach out one's hand and touch it. It is an argument. There is a proposition. Cobbett writes 'metaphysical', looks up at his audience, and wonders whether the word communicates. He explains the relevance of the term. He repeats his explanation in the plainest language. He repeats it again, but this time he enlarges the definition to carry wider social and political implications. Then, these short sentences finished with, he commences exposition once more. In the word 'Now' we feel is implied: 'if all of you have taken my point, let us proceed together ...'

It is not difficult to show that Cobbett had some very stupid

1. 'Address to the Journeymen and Labourers', *Political Register*, 2 November 1816.

2. Ibid., 27 January 1820.

and contradictory ideas, and sometimes bludgeoned his readers with specious arguments.[1] But such demonstrations are beside the point unless the profound, the truly profound, democratic influence of Cobbett's attitude to his audience is understood. Paine anticipates the tone; but Cobbett, for thirty years, talked to his audience like this, until men were talking and arguing like Cobbett all over the land. He assumed, as a matter scarcely in need of demonstration, that every citizen whatsoever had the power of reason, and that it was by argument addressed to the common understanding that matters should be settled. During the past ten years (he wrote in 1820) –

I have addressed nothing to [the people] which did not rely, for success, upon *fact*, and upon the best arguments which I was able to produce. My subjects have been generally of the most intricate nature. . . . I have made use of no means to attract curiosity or to humour the fancy. All has been an appeal to the understanding, the discernment and the justice of the reader.

It is not, of course, true that Cobbett employed no devices to 'attract curiosity'. If he treated his readers as equals he treated Ministers, Bishops, and Lords as something less. ('Wilberforce,' one of his open letters began: 'I have you before me in a canting pamphlet.') To this we should add two other devices. The first is the homely, practical analogy, most commonly taken from rural life. In this he had an unerring sense of the experience available to the whole body of his readers. Such figures, with him, were not decorative in function, or passing allusions. They were taken up, held in the hand, turned over, deliberately deployed to advance the argument, and then set down. We may take the example of Cobbett's famous description of Brougham and the moderate reformers as scarecrows or S H O Y-H O Y S – 'and now I will tell you why':

A shoy-hoy is a sham man or woman, made of straw or other stuff, twisted round a stake, stuck into the ground . . . with a stick or gun put into his hand. These shoy-hoys are set up for the purpose of driving birds from injuring the corn or the seeds, and sometimes

1. The loyalist press delighted in publishing lists of Cobbett's self-contradictions. So also, from an opposite standpoint, did his ultra-Radical opponents: see Gale Jones' damaging *Vindication of the Press, against the Aspersions of William Cobbett, including a Retrospect of his Political Life and Opinions* (1823).

to frighten them from cherries, or other fruit. The people want a reform of the parliament, and there has for a long time . . . been a little band, who have professed the desire to get parliamentary reform. They have made motions and speeches and divisions, with a view of keeping the hopes of the people alive, and have thereby been able to keep them quiet from time to time. They have never desired to *succeed*, because success would put an end to their hopes of emolument; but they have amused the people. The great body of the factions, knowing the reality of their views, have been highly diverted by their sham efforts, which have never interrupted them in the smallest degree in their enjoyment of the general plunder. Just as it happens with the birds and the shoy-hoys in the fields or gardens. At first, the birds take the shoy-hoys for a *real* man or woman; and, so long as they do this, they abstain from their work of plunder; but after having for some little while watched the shoy-hoy with their quick and piercing eyes, and perceived that it never moves hand or foot, they totally disregard it, and are no more obstructed by it than if it were a post. Just so it is with these political shoy-hoys; but . . . they *do mischief*. . . . I remember an instance . . . which very aptly illustrates the functions of these political deceivers. The birds were committing great ravages upon some turnip-seed that I had at Botley. 'Stick up a shoy-hoy,' said I to my bailiff. 'That will do *no good*, sir,' . . . he replied . . . telling me, that he had, that morning, in the garden of his neighbour MORELL . . . actually seen a sparrow settled, with a *pod*, upon the *shoy-hoy's* hat, and there, as upon a dining-table, actually pecking out the peas and eating them, which he could do with greater security there where he could look about him and see the approach of an enemy, than he could have done upon the ground, where he might have been taken by *surprise*. Just exactly such are the functions of our political shoy-hoys. The agricultural . . . shoy-hoys deceive the depredating birds but a very short time; but they continue to deceive those who stick them up and rely upon them, who, instead of rousing in the morning, and sallying upon the depredators with powder and shot, trust to the miserable shoy-hoys, and thus lose their corn and their seeds. Just thus it is with the people, who are the dupes of all political shoy-hoys. In Suffolk, and other eastern counties, they call them *mawkses* . . .[1]

What is one to make of such writing? From one aspect it is imaginative writing of genius. The analogy commences a

1. *Political Register*, 1 September 1830. See G. D. H. and M. Cole, *The Opinions of William Cobbett*, pp. 253–4.

little stiffly; politics and agriculture run on converging lines, but we feel the image to be far-fetched. Then – at 'quick and piercing eyes' – the two arguments are fused, with an uprush of polemical delight. Cobbett is half in jest, the image grows to surrealist proportions – Brougham with a sparrow on his hat, the reformers with powder and shot, turnip-seed and neighbour MORELL (who will probably never make his appearance again). From another aspect, what an extraordinary thing it is, this part of the English political tradition! This is more than polemic: it is also political theory. Cobbett has defined, in terms that a labourer or artisan could well understand, the function of a very English form of reformist accommodation. More than this, he illuminates, across more than a century, the *mawkses* of other parties and other times.

The other device, which we have already noted,[1] is the personalization of political issues – a personalization centred upon Cobbett of Botley himself. But if Cobbett was his own subject, he handled this subject with unusual objectivity. His egotism transcended itself to the point where the reader is aware, not of Cobbett's ego, but of a plain-spoken, matter-of-fact, observant sensibility, with which he is encouraged to identify himself. He is asked to look, not *at* Cobbett, but *with* him. The triumph of this manner can be seen in his *Rural Rides*, where not only his contemporaries but successive generations have felt his palpable presence as he talked with labourers in the fields, rode through the villages, and stopped to bait his horses. The force of his indignation is all the more compelling because of his delight at anything which pleased him. At Tenterden—

the afternoon was very fine, and, just as I rose the hill and entered the street, the people had come out of church and were moving along towards their houses. It was a very fine sight. *Shabbily-dressed people do not go to church.* I saw, in short, drawn out before me, the dress and beauty of the town; and a great many very, very pretty girls I saw; and saw them, too, in their best attire. I remember the girls in the *Pays de Caux*, and, really, I think those of Tenterden resemble them. I do not know why they should not; for there is the *Pays de Caux* only just over the water, just opposite this very place.

1. See above, p. 687.

Or, in a village in Surrey, the absence of poverty is made into a telling point against its general incidence:

As I came along between Upwaltham and Eastdean, I called to me a young man, who, along with other turnip-hoers, was sitting under the shelter of a hedge at breakfast. He came running to me with his victuals in his hand; and I was glad to see that his food consisted of a good lump of household bread and not a very small piece of *bacon*. ... In parting with him, I said, 'You do get some *bacon* then?' 'Oh, yes! Sir,' said he, and with an emphasis and a swag of the head which seemed to say, 'We *must* and *will* have *that*.' I saw, and with great delight, a pig at almost every labourer's house. The houses are good and warm; and the gardens some of the very best that I have seen in England. What a difference, good God! what a difference between this country and the neighbourhood of those corrupt places *Great Bedwin* and *Cricklade*. What sort of *breakfast* would this man have had in a mess of *cold potatoes*? Could he have *worked*, and worked in the wet, too, with such food? Monstrous! No society ought to exist where the labourers live in a hog-like sort of way.

'There is the *Pays de Caux* ... just opposite this very place', 'this country', 'this man' – wherever he was, Cobbett always compelled his readers, by the immediacy of his vision, the confusion of reflection and description, the solidity of detail, and the physical sense of place, to identify themselves with his own standpoint. And 'standpoint' is the proper word, for Cobbet placed himself firmly in some physical setting – on his farm at Botley or on the road into Tenterden – and then led outwards from the evidence of his senses to his general conclusions. Even during his American exile (1817–19) it was important for him to convey this sense of place:

From one side of my room I look out into a farm yard, full of fodder and of cattle, sheep, hogs, and multitudes of poultry, while, at a few paces, beyond the yard, runs the river Susquehannah, which is wider than the Thames and has innumerable islands lying in it, from a quarter of an acre to five or six acres in extent. From the other side of my room I look into an Orchard of Apples and Peaches of forty acres, lying in a narrow valley, which runs up between two mountains, about a quarter of a mile high, formed precisely like the ridge of a house, the gable ends being towards the river. Last night it rained: it froze before morning, and the frost caught the drops hanging upon the trees; so that the sun, which is now shining as bright as in England in the month of May, exhibits these icicles in countless millions of sparkling diamonds.

But this setting was turned to effect to dramatize the more strongly his feelings (expressed in a letter to Hunt) inspired by the news of the execution of Brandreth and his fellows:

I have, my dear Hunt, the little thatched cottages of Waltham Chase and of Botley Common now full in my mind's eye, and I feel at this day, with more force than ever, that passion, which would make me prefer the occupation of the meanest of those most humble abodes, accompanied with the character of Englishman, to the mastership over, and the actual possession of, all that I have above described, unaccompanied, with that character. As I said, when I left England, so I still say, that I never can like any people so well as I like the people of England.

If Cobbett made, from the struggle of the reform movement, something of a martyrology and demonology, he was himself the central figure of the myth. But we should hesitate before we accuse him too far of personal vanity. For the myth demanded also that William Cobbett be seen as a plain Englishman, unusually belligerent and persevering, but not especially talented – such a man as the reader might think himself to be, or the labourer in the turnip-field, or (given this or that turn of circumstance) as the landlady's son in a small inn in a Sussex village might become:

The landlady sent her son to get me some cream, and he was just such a chap as I was at his age, and dressed just in the same sort of way, his main garment being a blue smock-frock, faded from wear, and mended with pieces of *new* stuff. ... The sight of this smock-frock brought to my recollection many things very dear to me. This boy will, I dare say, perform his part at Billingshurst, or at some place not far from it. If accident had not taken me from a similar scene, how many villains and fools, who have been well teazed and tormented, would have slept in peace at night, and have fearlessly swaggered about by day!

His compassion for the poor always had this quality: 'there, but for the grace of God, goes Will Cobbett'. His affectation was to appear to be more 'normal' than he was. He never allowed his readers to forget that he had once followed the plough, and that he served as a common soldier. As he prospered, so he affected the dress, not of a journalist (which he pretended not to be), but of an old-fashioned gentleman-farmer. In Hazlitt's description, he wore 'a scarlet broadcloth waistcoat with the flaps of the pockets hanging down, as was the custom for gentleman-farmers in the last century'; in Bamford's, 'dressed in a blue coat, yellow swansdown waistcoat, drab jersey small-clothes, and top boots ... he was the perfect representation of what he always wished to be – an English gentleman-farmer'. It is Hazlitt who gives the justest character to Cobbett on the score of vanity:

His egotism is delightful, for there is no affectation in it. He does not talk of himself for lack of something to write about, but because some circumstance that has happened to himself is the best possible illustration of the subject, and he is not the man to shrink from giving the best possible illustration of the subject from a squeamish delicacy. He likes both himself and his subject too well. He does not put himself before it, and say, 'Admire me first', but places us in the same situation with himself, and makes us see all that he does. There is no ... abstract, senseless self-complacency, no smuggled admiration of his own person by proxy: it is all plain and above-board. He writes himself plain William Cobbett, strips himself quite as naked as anybody could wish – in a word, his egotism is full of individuality and has room for very little vanity in it.[1]

This is a generous literary judgement. But a political judgement must be more qualified. The great change in the tone and style of popular Radicalism, exemplified in the contrast between Paine and Cobbett, was (once again) first defined by Hazlitt:

Paine affected to reduce things to first principles, to announce self-evident truths. Cobbett troubles himself about little but the details and local circumstances. ... Paine's writings are a sort of introduction to political arithmetic on a new plan: Cobbett keeps a day-book, and makes an entry at full of all the occurrences and troublesome questions that start up throughout the year.

The personalization of politics – this labourer in his cottage-garden, this speech in the House of Commons, that example

1. *Political Register*, June 1817, 11 April 1818, 2 October 1819; *Rural Rides*, passim; Bamford, op. cit., p. 21; Hazlitt, *Table Talk* (1821).

of persecution – was well adapted to the pragmatic approach of an audience only awakening to political consciousness. It also had an opportunist value, in that, by fixing attention upon circumstantial ephemera and particular grievances, and by eschewing theoretical absolutes, it enabled royalists and republicans, Deists and Churchmen, to engage in a common movement. But the argument can be taken too far. Paine's *Rights of Man* had found an equal response in an audience no more literate, and had encouraged a more principled theory of popular rights; while the contemporaneous success of more theoretical journals proves the existence of a large working-class public which could take its politics neat. Cobbett, in fact, helped to create and nourish the anti-intellectualism, and the theoretical opportunism (masked as 'practical' empiricism) which remained an important characteristic of the British labour movement.

'I remembered my mother being in the habit of reading Cobbett's *Register*, and saying she wondered people spoke so much against it; she saw nothing bad in it, but she saw a great many good things in it.'[1] James Watson's mother was a domestic servant in a clergyman's house, and a Sunday School teacher. 'Mr Cobbett's *Weekly Political Pamphlets*,' wrote Hone, in 1817,

should be bound up, and be on the same shelf with the History of England, the Pilgrim's Progress, Robinson Crusoe, and the Young Man's Book of Knowledge. Every cottage and kitchen library in the kingdom is incomplete without it . . .

It should be 'as common and familiar' as the Housekeeper's Instructor and Buchan's Domestic Medicine.[2] This was, in fact, to be much what happened. Wooler or Carlile might, with their more sophisticated and intellectual manner, have

---

1. W. J. Linton, *James Watson*, p. 17. Cf. T. Frost, op. cit., p. 6: 'the only books I ever saw in my father's house, besides the bible and a few old school books . . . were some odd numbers of Cobbett's *Register*.'

2. Hone's *Reformist's Register*, 5 April 1817, on Cobbett's departure to America. See, however, Wooler's angry rejoinder: 'We are almost inclined to wish that Mr Cobbett had confined himself to writing . . . upon such subjects, that he might have . . . deceived none but kitchen maids and scullions.' *Black Dwarf*, 9 April 1817.

given expression to the Radicalism of the city artisans; but only Cobbett could have succeeded, in 1816, in bringing stockingers and weavers into the same dialogue.

The curious way in which he had graduated from Toryism to Radicalism entailed a certain opportunism in his position. He had been able to side-step the anti-Gallican and anti-Jacobin prejudices of the war years. He was able to disown the French Revolution and Tom Paine as things in whose defence he had had no part. Eventually (as he himself acknowledged in generous terms) he came to accept many of Paine's arguments. But he always ducked away from the intransigent Jacobin rejection of the hereditary principle in any form, and thus was able to present himself both as a radical reformer and as a constitutionalist. In the 'Address to Journeymen and Labourers' he warned against men who 'would persuade you, that, because things have been perverted from their true ends, there is *nothing good* in our *constitution and laws*. For what, then, did Hampden die in the field, and Sydney on the scaffold?' The Americans, in seceding from Britain, had taken care to preserve 'Magna Carta, the Bill of Rights, the Habeas Corpus' and the body of the Common Law:

We want *great alteration*, but we want *nothing new*. Alteration, modification to suit the times and circumstances; but the great principles ought to be and must be, the same, or else confusion will follow.

Even when (in the last year of his life) he urged the people to resist the New Poor Law with force, he did so in the name of constitutional rights and the sanctities of custom. His attitude to the rationalists showed the same blend of Radicalism and traditionalism. He defended with force their right to publish arguments against the Christian religion. But when Carlile went further and committed what was (in Cobbett's eyes) offensive blasphemy by dating the *Republican* 'in the year 1822 of the Carpenter's wife's son' he appealed to mob law. If this had been done in America (he roared) –

You would ... be instantly dressed in a coat of tar and feathers, and ... be ridden *bare-rumped upon a rail*, till you dropped off by the side of some wood or swamp, where you would be left to ruminate on the wisdom (to say nothing of the modesty) of setting up for a maker of span-new governments and religions.[1]

There can scarcely have been another writer in our history who has written so many and such telling attacks upon the Anglican clergy (and, in particular, the rural clergy) as Cobbett. And yet, for no reason which was ever seriously advanced, he frequently announced his attachment, not only to the Throne (which he nearly brought down in the Queen Caroline agitation) and the Constitution (which his followers all but slew in 1819 and 1832) but also to the Established Church. He was even capable of writing, on occasion, of 'our duty to hold in abhorrence Turks and Jews', because Christianity was 'part and parcel of the law'.

Such opportunism made impossible the development of any systematic political theory out of Cobbettism. And his economic prejudices were of a piece with this kind of evasion. Just as he developed, not a critique of a political *system*, nor even of 'Legitimacy', but an invective against 'Old Corruption', so he reduced economic analysis to a polemic against the *parasitism* of certain vested interests. He could not allow a critique which centred on ownership; therefore he expounded (with much repetition) a demonology, in which the people's evils were caused by taxation, the National Debt, and the paper-money system, and by the hordes of parasites – fund-holders, placemen, brokers and tax-collectors – who had battened upon these three. This is not to say that this critique was baseless – there was fuel enough for Cobbett's fire, in the grossly exploitive pattern of taxation, and in the parasitic activities of the East India Company and the Banks. But, characteristically, Cobbett's prejudices keyed in with the grievances of the small producers, shopkeepers, artisans, small farmers, and consumers. Attention was diverted from the landowner or industrial capitalist and focussed upon the middleman – the factor or broker who cornered markets, profited from the people's shortages, or lived, in any way not closely attached to land or industry, upon unearned income. The arguments were moral as much as economic. Men were entitled to wealth, but only if they could

1. *Political Register*, 2 February 1822.

be *seen* to be hard at work. Next to sinecurists Cobbett hated Quaker speculators.

Deficient in theory he was also sometimes plainly mischievous in his immediate influence upon political strategy, while he was by no means always as straightforward in personal and public dealings as he asked other men to be. For his failings as a political leader he was not fully responsible. He was a journalist, and not a political leader or organizer, and it was only the accident of the context (the outlawing of effective political organization) which forced him into the other rôle. But, if he did not choose to be a political leader, he was (like other men in this predicament) reluctant to see the movement go in any way but the way which he prescribed. When all these – and other – failings are accounted, it is easy to underestimate him, as a nostalgic romantic or a bully.

But the commonplace judgement so often met with, that Cobbett was 'really a Tory', is unhelpful. One reason we have sufficiently examined: the democratic character of his tone. His relationship with his audience was peculiarly intimate: we must remember that he was continually talking with his readers. He addressed them at reform meetings. He made lecture-tours'. Even when he was in America, his post-bag was heavy, and deputations of Scottish mechanics and émigré reformers waited upon him on the banks of the Susquehannah. He rode into the countryside to find out how men were thinking and talking. Hence Cobbett's ideas can be seen less as a one-way propagandist flow than as the incandescence of an alternating current, between his readers and himself. 'I always say that I have derived from the people ... ten times the light that I have communicated to them':

A writer engaged in the instruction of such a people, is constantly upheld, not only by the applause that he receives from them, and by perceiving that his labours are attended with effect; but also by the aid which he is continually deriving from those new thoughts which his thoughts produce in their minds. It is the flint and the steel meeting that brings forth the fire.[1]

How moving is this insight into the dialectical nature of the very process by which his own ideas were formed! Few writers

1. *Political Register*, 27 January 1820.

can be found who were so much the 'voice' of their own audience. It is possible to follow Cobbett's genius as an indicator
of the movement for which he spoke. At times of crisis there
is this bright incandescence. At times when the movement
flagged, he becomes most cranky and idiosyncratic: ·his style
glows only dully. And this is true until his very last years; as
his audience changed, so he changed with it.

This is what Raymond Williams has well described as Cobbett's 'extraordinary sureness of instinct'. And yet, instinct for
what? In the first place it was an instinct which disclosed the
real nature of changing relationships of production, which he
judged, in part, against an idealized patriarchal past, and in
part against an assertion of the worth of every individual
labourer which is, in no sense, backward-looking. In the second
place, Cobbett was the 'free-born Englishman' incarnate. He
gathered up all the vigour of the eighteenth-century tradition
and took it forward, with new emphasis, into the nineteenth.
His outlook approximated most closely to the ideology of the
small producers. The values which he endorsed with his whole
being (and he wrote at his best when he gave his prejudices full
rein) were those of sturdy individualism and independence. He
lamented the passing of small farmers; of small tradesmen; the
drawing of the resources of the country into 'great heaps'; the
loss by the weavers of 'the frank and bold character formed in
the days of their independence'.[1] The small farmer who resented the great estate of the brewer or absentee Lord; the
small clothier who petitioned against the growth of the factory
system; the small tailor or bootmaker who found that middlemen were receiving Government contracts or creaming the
market – these were among his natural audience. They also
felt the same diffuse hostility to 'speculation' and the 'commercial system'; but (like Cobbett) they stopped short before any
radical critique of property-rights.

If this had been all, Cobbett might have remained as the
political spokesman of the little bourgeoisie. But his audience
– the Radical movement itself – took him further. 'We are daily
advancing to the state in which there are but two classes of

1. *Political Register*, 30 January 1832. See also R. Williams, *Culture
and Society* (Pelican edn), pp. 32–4.

men, *masters*, and *abject dependants*.' When Cobbett considered the position of the artisan or the cotton-spinner, he extrapolated from the experience of the small masters who were being forced down into the working class. He saw the factory proletariat of Manchester less as new-fangled men than as little producers who had lost their independence and rights. As such, the work-discipline of the mills was an outrage upon their dignity. They were right to rebel, as he would rebel in the same position. As for child labour, it was simply 'unnatural'.

His attitude to the field labourers was somewhat different. Although he struggled to understand a commercial and manufacturing society, the essential model of political economy in his mind was drawn from agriculture. And here he accepted a social structure in which the landowner, the good tenant, the petty land-holder, and the labourer all had their part, provided that productive and social relationships were governed by certain mutual obligations and sanctions. Defending his own conduct as a landlord, he cited the case of an old cottager, living in retirement on the farm at Botley when he took it up:

The old man paid me no rent; when he died I had a headstone put to his grave to record, that he had been an honest, skilful, and industrious labouring man; and I gave his widow a shilling a week as long as I was at Botley.[1]

Here he is indistinguishable from the better kind of squire whose passing he so often lamented. But this is not all. There is also that uncomfortable sentence: 'No society ought to exist where the labourers live in a hog-like sort of way.' *No society ought to exist* – the very touchstone of his social criticism is the condition of the labouring man. When, as at the time of the labourers' revolt or the New Poor Law, he judged this condition to be unendurable, then he was willing to challenge the received social order:

God gave them life upon this land; they have as much right to be upon it as you have; they have a clear right to a maintenance out of the land, in exchange for their labour; and, if you cannot so

1. *Twopenny Trash*, 1 October 1830.

manage your lands yourselves as to take labour from them, in exchange for a living, give the land up to them . . .[1]

This was written less than six months before he died.

This is why Cobbett (and John Fielden, his friend and fellow Member for Oldham after 1832) came so close to being spokesmen of the working class. Once the real condition of the working people – for Cobbett, the labourer, for Fielden, the factory child – is made, not *one*, but *the* test of all other political expedients, then we are close to revolutionary conclusions. Concealed within the seemingly 'nostalgic' notion of the 'historic rights of the poor', which, in different ways, was voiced by Cobbett, Oastler and Carlile, there were also *new* claims maturing, for the community to succour the needy and the helpless, not out of charity, but as of right.[2] Cobbett loathed the 'comforting system' of charity and moral rescue, and, in his *History of the Protestant 'Reformation'*, he was chiefly intent upon giving historical backing to his notion of social rights. The lands of the medieval Church had been held in trust for the poor. Wrongfully misappropriated or dispersed, nevertheless the poor still had a claim upon them, which (in Cobbett's eyes) was recognized through the mediation of the old Poor Laws. The repeal of those laws constituted the last act in a shameful series of robberies by which the poor had been cheated of their rights:

Among these rights was, the right to live in the country of our birth; the right to have a living out of the land of our birth in exchange for our labour duly and honestly performed; the right, in case we fell into distress, to have our wants sufficiently relieved out of the produce of the land, whether that distress arose from sickness, from decrepitude, from old age, or from inability to find employment. ... For a thousand years, necessity was relieved out of the produce of the Tithes. When the Tithes were taken away by the aristocracy, and by them kept to themselves, or given wholly to the parsons, provision was made out of the land, as compensation for what had been taken away. That compensation was given in the rates as settled by the poor-law. The taking away those rates was to violate the agreement, which gave as much right to receive in

1. *Political Register*, 28 February 1835.
2. See Asa Briggs, 'The Welfare State in Historical Perspective', *Archiv. Europ. Sociol.*, II (1961), p. 235.

case of need, relief out of the land, as it left the landowner a right to his rent.[1]

This historical myth, which assumes some medieval social compact between the Church and the gentry, on one hand, and the labourers, on the other, was employed to justify claims to new social rights in much the same way as the theory of Alfred's free constitution and of the Norman yoke had been used to justify the claim to new political rights. According to this view, the landowners' tenure of their land was not of absolute right, but was dependent upon their fulfilling their social obligations. Neither Cobbett nor Fielden started from the assumption that the working people had any right to expropriate landed property or capital; but both accepted that if the existing property-relations violated, for the labourer or his child, essential claims to human realization, then any remedy, however drastic, was open to discussion. (For Fielden it meant that he – the third greatest 'Seigneur of the Twist' in Lancashire – was willing to work with John Doherty in pursuit of a General Strike for the eight-hour day.)

Cobbett's touchstone was at the same time an insurmountable barrier between his kind of political theory and the ideology of the middle-class Utilitarians. If Malthus's conclusions led to the preaching of emigration or of restraints upon the marriage of the poor, then they were faulted by this touchstone. If the 'Scotch feelosofers' and Brougham could do no more than destroy the poor man's rights under the old Poor Law, leave the weavers to starve, and sanction the labour of little children in the mills, then this touchstone proclaimed them to be designing rogues. It is sometimes less an argument than an affirmation, an imprecation, a leap of feeling. But it was enough. Cobbett did more than any other writer to preserve the Radicals and Chartists from becoming the camp-followers of Utilitarians or of Anti-Corn Law League. He nourished the culture of a class, whose wrongs he felt, but whose remedies he could not understand.

1. *Tour of Scotland* (1833), cited in W. Reitzel (ed.), *The Autobiography of William Cobbett*, pp. 224–5.

III. CARLILE, WADE AND GAST

Yet we must not forget the inconsistencies, the bullying, the anti-intellectualism, the professions of loyalty to Throne and Church, the theoretical opportunism, the turns and twists of Cobbett's ephemeral political writing. These weaknesses were more than evident to the more articulate Radicals. Already in 1817 he was under sharp fire from other periodicals. By 1820 many Radical artisans had ceased to take Cobbett seriously as a thinker, although they had not ceased to enjoy his gargantuan polemics. They continued to read him, but they began to read some other journal as well. Among these lesser journals, between 1817 and 1832, there was much original and demanding thought, which was to give shape to the political consciousness of the class after 1832. We may select from this four tendencies: the Paine-Carlile tradition: the working-class Utilitarians and the *Gorgon*; the trade unionists around the *Trades Newspaper* of John Gast: and the variety of tendencies associated with Owenism.

We have already examined the main stock of ideas of the first, in *Rights of Man*, and its most important contribution in Carlile's fight for the free press. The derivation from Paine is explicit. It is not only the acknowledgement of a debt, but the assertion of a doctrinal orthodoxy:

The writings of Thomas Paine, alone, form a standard for anything worthy of being called Radical Reform. They are not Radical Reformers who do not come up to the whole of the political principles of Thomas Paine. . . . There can be no Radical Reform short of . . . a Republican form of Government.[1]

We get a sense of the force and loyalty with which this doctrine was held from an account of a meeting of the Cheltenham Chartist branch, whose Chairman was an old blacksmith:

One night . . . somebody spoke of Tom Paine. Up jumped the chairman. 'I will not sit in the chair,' he cried in great wrath, 'and hear that great man reviled. Bear in mind he was not a prize-

1. R. Carlile, *An Effort to set at rest . . . the Reformers of Leeds* (1821), p. 7.

fighter. There is no such person as Tom Paine. Mister Thomas Paine, if you please.'[1]

Uncompromising hostility to the hereditary principle and to 'Gothic' superstition and survivals, defiant affirmation of the rights of the private citizen – these are among its virtues. But in England, at least by the later Twenties, the Paine-Carlile tradition had acquired a certain stridency and air of unreality. The cry, *à bas les aristos*, has less force when we consider the real structure of power in England as the Industrial Revolution advanced, the complex interpenetration of aristocratic privilege and commercial and industrial wealth. The rationalist lampoons upon the 'priesthood', as the hired apologists of privilege and the emissaries of an ignorance designed to hold the people in thrall, are somehow just wide of the mark; they might touch the fox-hunting rural rector or the clerical magistrate, but they flew past the ear of the Evangelicals and the Nonconformist ministers who were already active with British and National schools. The polemic tends to disperse itself in abstractions; it does not grip and engage, as Cobbett's nearly always does. Carlile's 'priest' was depicted as busy with 'Kneeling, tenths, pilgrimages, exorcisms, sprinkling, crosses, sacraments, ablutions, circumcision, and gibberish' in the intervals of 'lasciviousness ... and drunkenness.'[2] Although Carlile knew more of English gaols than any other Radical he continued to confuse them with the Bastille. If George IV *had* been strangled in the entrails of the Bishop of Llandaff it would have been a triumph, but not the triumph which he supposed. He would still have had to deal with the last city alderman and the last local preacher.

As is characteristic of the doctrinaire, at times he tried to manipulate reality so that it might confirm his doctrines. He fed his persecutors with fresh provocations:

As I consider that the majority of the present Ministers are tyrants and enemies to the interests and welfare of the people of this country, so also am I bold to confess that, if any man that has suffered unjustly under their administration, should be so indifferent

1. W. E. Adams, op. cit., I, p. 169.
2. Philanthropus, *The Character of a Priest* (1822), pp. 4, 6.

about his own life as to slay any one or more of them, I would tune my lyre to sing his praises.

But such a tyrannicide would show 'a want of virtue' if he sought companions to perform the act; he should have the resolution to do it single-handed: 'I condemn an association for such purposes.'[1] And the passage leads us to others of his weaknesses. There is, first, the irresponsibility of his individualism. This is an incitement which he could publish (as he published others) simply *as* an incitement, without thought of the consequences. Like other men who have codified ideas into an orthodoxy, it is not true that he simply passed on the notions of his master. He ossified them *by* turning them into doctrine; he took one part of Paine's ideas (the doctrine of individual rights), and neglected others. And the part which he adopted he pushed to its extremity, the *ne plus ultra* of individualism.

Every citizen owed no deference to authority and should act as if it did not exist. This he did himself, and was ready to take the consequences. But he held that the citizen owed only a duty to his own reason; he was not bound to consult others, even of his own party, nor to submit to their judgement. Indeed, the notion of party was offensive. The power of reason was the only organizer which he admitted, and the press the only multiplier:

When the political principles laid down by Thomas Paine are well understood by the great body of the people, everything that is necessary to put them in practice will suggest itself, and then plots and delegate meetings will be wholly unnecessary. . . . In the present state of this country the people have no other real duty than to make themselves individually well acquainted with what constitutes their political rights. . . . In the interim, each individual ought to prepare and hold himself ready, as an armed individual, without relation to or consulting with his neighbours, in case circumstances should ever require him to take up arms, to preserve what liberty and property he may already possess against any tyrannical attempts to lessen them. . . . Let each do his duty, and that openly, without reference to what his neighbour does . . .

1. *Republican*, 19 January 1821. Carlile also republished Sexby's 'Killing No Murder'.

The power of popular knowledge he called the 'zetetic principle':

> Let us then endeavour to progress in knowledge, since knowledge is demonstrably proved to be power. It is the power of knowledge that checks the crimes of cabinets and courts; it is the power of knowledge that must put a stop to bloody wars and the direful effects of devastating armies.[1]

The first passage was written in the dark year, 1820, and Carlile was in part anxious to protect Radicals from the kind of organization so easily penetrated by *provocateurs*. But here is this absence of the concrete – 'liberty', 'knowledge', 'bloody wars', and 'cabinets and courts'. And here also is this serious misunderstanding of his audience: 'Let each do his duty ... without reference to what his neighbour does ...' Did he not know that the essence of the working-class Radical movement consisted in each man 'consulting with his neighbours'? Without this consultation, his shopmen would not have come forward, his country agents would not have held to their posts. The key to his blindness lies perhaps in the phrase: 'to preserve what liberty and property he may already possess against any tyrannical attempts ...' For this is not only Paine, it is also Locke.

Once again the term arises in the mind: 'petit-bourgeois individualism'. And, if we make the difficult effort to discard some of the pejorative associations of the term, we can see that, in the case of Carlile, it is helpful. The model in the back of his mind is perhaps that of the little master, the hatter, the brushmaker, the bookseller; we can see, in Carlile, not only the limitations of the little bourgeoisie, but also, in this insurgent time, their strengths. Bewick, if he had been a somewhat younger man, might have read the *Republican*. What Carlile was doing was taking the bourgeois jealousy of the power of the Crown, in defence of their political and property rights, and extending it to the Shoreditch hatter or the Birmingham toymaker and his artisans.

In terms of rights of press and speech, the results were as dramatic as was Cobbett's democratic tone. But in terms of

1. *Republican*, 4 October 1820, 26 April 1822; see Wickwar, op. cit., pp. 213–15.

political and economic theory, the position was either barren or delusive. The strength of the Lockeian ideology lay in the fact that the bourgeois *were* men of large property; the demand for an end to State control or interference was (for them) a liberating demand. But the hatter had little property and his artisans still less. To demand an absence of State regulation meant simply giving their larger competitors (or 'market forces') fuller rein. And this was so evident that Carlile, no less than Cobbett, was forced to make a demonology of sinecurists, placemen, and tax-eaters. The great evil afflicting the little masters must be seen to be taxation. There must be as little Government as possible, and that little must be cheap.

This was close to anarchism, but only at its most negative and defensive sense. Every man must be free to think, to write, to trade, or to carry a gun. The first two were his main pre-occupation, to the point where the freedom of the press was no longer a means but, in itself, an end. The vista of social proposals opened up in the second part of *Rights of Man* was that part of the master's work which touched him least. He had the self-made man's contempt of the feckless, and the autodidact's impatience with those who did not take up the opportunities of self-improvement which were offered. He served imprisonment to open the gates of Reason: and if the workers did not flock through that was their own fault: 'The Alehouse, I know, has charms insuperable to the great body of mechanics.'[1] He was a minority-minded man.

His rationalism, like his political theory, was made up of negations. He took pleasure in exposing biblical absurdities, and in publishing passages of obscenity to be found in the Bible. When he offered a primer of positive virtues, in the *Moralist*, it was (as we have seen) a tepid rationalist apologia for the virtues of a bourgeois family man. In his attitude to poetry (or towards any imaginative attributes) he showed a 'single-vision' as narrow as that of Bentham. Although he pirated *Cain* and *The Vision of Judgement* he was at pains to point out that he did this 'not from any admiration of the works, but because I saw them menaced by my enemies'. The half-dozen Cantos of *Don Juan* which he had read were 'in

1. *Republican*, 23 August 1822.

my opinion *mere slip-slop*, good for nothing useful to mankind'. (He does not appear to have noticed that any of them were witty):

I am not a poet, nor an admirer of poetry beyond those qualities which it might have in common with prose – the power of instructing mankind in useful knowledge.[1]

'In my opinion ...' – this reminds us that the culture of the autodidact can also be philistine. The democracy of intellect was in danger of becoming a sort of Bartholomew Fair. Here everyone might set out his stall, anyone's opinions were as good as anyone else's, the strangest sideshows – headless women and poor old dancing bears – might all be on offer. The artisans strayed in and paid their pennies; they were encouraged at once to set up stall for themselves, to argue and debate before they had served any apprenticeship to the trade. The more strenuous minds who offered their work in the same market – Hodgskin or Thompson, O'Brien or Bray – must have many a time cursed the opinionated hucksters bawling all around them.

Nevertheless, when all these criticisms have been made – and they are many, and they go far to explain the stridency of the militant rationalist tradition in the nineteenth century – when all this has been said, it was Carlile who set up the market. Nor is this a figure of speech. His publications were one market – it was he who published Paine, Volney, Palmer, Holbach and many others. But he also set up the market for spoken debate. In 1830 he founded the Rotunda in which the formative debates of the London working-class movement took place. Its proceedings were published regularly in his *Prompter*. The journal might have been better entitled the *Promoter*, for this is what, in effect, Carlile had become. He was the Showman of Free Thought, and no one had more right to the situation. He cast around for star performers who would draw in the crowds. John Gale Jones, the veteran Jacobin surgeon, still commanded a following. But his greatest success was the promotion of the Reverend Robert Taylor, an apostate Anglican and former chaplain to the King, who preached – in full canonicals –

1. See Wickwar, op. cit., p. 272.

atheistic sermons attacking the 'selfish and wicked priesthood'. Taylor was an earnest and scholarly man, who also served his turn in prison, and who did something to bring 'her Divine Majesty, the IGNORANCE of Eighteen Centuries' into a further decline. But his sermons, copiously illustrated with linguistic criticism of the hebraic text, were, for the audience, something rich and strange: a headless woman. So also was another of the Rotunda showpieces, Zion Ward, an inheritor of the Southcottian mantle, who spellbound audiences with stupefying harangues upon Revelation and Reform. Despite such attractions, Carlile reported a sad falling-off in the attendances at the weekly religious debates (August 1831). The Rotunda was now being used on Wednesday evenings by a new tenant, the National Union of the Working Classes. Carlile (once again in prison) was a little irritated that this Union was proposing to *organize* the next round in the fight for press liberties, the 'unstamped'. 'I have nothing to do with any association,' he wrote, 'and do not seek ... assistance from anything of the kind.' Like other individualists, his egotism had engrossed the cause, and he resented the idea that others might make it theirs. 'Beware of Political Clubs,' he wrote a month later. He had the strongest feeling against clubs, societies and even trade unions or benefit clubs. 'Almost every horror of the first French Revolution sprung out of political clubs. ... I pronounce them all to be dastardly associations, contemptible, frivolous, paltry nothings.' As the contest for the Reform Bill became week by week more critical, he published information about barricades, hand-grenades, and burning acids: 'LET EVERY MAN ORGANIZE HIMSELF.' But the National Union continued to meet in the Rotunda, and many of its most impressive leaders Watson, Hetherington, Lovett, Cleave, Hibbert – were men nurtured in the tradition of Carlile, who had long left him behind while still holding fast to his first principle: 'Free Discussion is the only necessary Constitution – the only necessary Law to the Constitution.'[1]

Twenty years of homilies from Hannah More and the Bishop

1. *Republican*, 11 July 1823; *Devil's Pulpit*, 4 and 18 March 1831; *Prompter*, 30 August, 31 September, 15 October 1831; *Radical*, 24 September 1831; H.O. 40.25.

of Llandaff, Wilberforce and the Methodist Conference, had built up a head of anti-clerical pressure among the Radicals. The *Gorgon* could write as a matter of course of 'the meek and gentle Moses, who led the scabby and mangy Israelites out of Egypt':

We will not say that Moses was as subtle and as great an impostor as Mahomet. We will not say that Aaron, the high priest, was as necessary to Moses, as Perigord Talleyrand once was to Buona-parte. We will not say that Joshua was as great a military ruffian as old Blucher or Suvaroff: and that the cruelties and butcheries committed in Canaan were ten times more atrocious than any committed during the twenty-five years of revolutionary warfare . . .[1]

Nevertheless, this *is* what the *Gorgon* managed to say. This is one point where it touches the Carlile tradition; and the two are related, also, by their affinities to Utilitarianism. In Carlile this is implicit; even poetry must be *useful* and impart *knowledge*. The *Gorgon*'s intellectual history is more exciting. It was an explicit attempt to effect a junction between Benthamism and working-class experience. It was not (as Place might have made it if he had captured it) an attempt simply to relay the ideas of the middle-class Utilitarians to a working-class audience. John Wade, the former journeyman wool-sorter who edited it (in 1818–19), was a man of originality and great application, who did not take his ideas on trust. In the result, the *Gorgon* seems not so much to accept these ideas as to wrestle with them: the enquiry is being made – can Utilitarianism in the context of working-class experience be put to *use*?

The influence of Place was important, and we must come nearer to understanding the man. We have kept a watchful eye upon him throughout this study because, as an archivist and historian (of the L.C.S., of Westminster Radicalism, of the repeal of the Combination Acts) his bias has been gravely misleading. He has risen from being a journeyman breeches-maker into a prosperous shopkeeper and employer, the close confidant of Bentham and the Mills, and the adviser of M.P.s. From the early 1800s his emphasis has been upon the building

1. *Gorgon*, 24 April 1819. Shelley, writing *Prometheus Unbound* in 1818–19 gave to the obscure revolutionary god the name 'Demogorgon': one wonders if there was any association of ideas?

of bridges between the artisans and the middle class; he has lent his support to the Lancastrian schools movement and the Mechanics' Institute; his concern has been with the sober, respectable artisan and his efforts at self-improvement. But because he was so obviously a founding father of the Fabian tradition (and was taken uncritically as such by Graham Wallas) we should not see him just as a 'captive' of the middle class, nor should we suppose that he was incapable of taking up the most intransigent positions. On matters of free thought and expression he was still half a Jacobin; he had helped to publish the first edition in England of the *Age of Reason*, and even though he came to regard Carlile as a 'fanatic' he gave him a great deal of assistance in his earlier struggles. We have seen his fury at the repression of 1817 and 1819, and the enormous application with which he was to work for trade union rights, even though his zeal for the cause of the unionists was curiously compounded with the political economy of M'Culloch. In intellectual terms, by 1818 he really was a captive of Bentham: he *learned* the doctrines of Bentham and the elder Mill rather than inquiring into them, and in his own writing he added almost nothing to them except the illustrative facts which he collected with such industry. But in political terms he was a force in his own right; he gave to the Utilitarians, not just a seat at Westminster which was within his manipulation, but a point of contact with the world of the Radical tradesmen and artisans. The very fact that such a man could perform this rôle, both ideologically and politically, is a new phenomenon.

Place's main contribution to the *Gorgon* was the collection of factual material on the London trades (notably the tailors).[1] John Wade set the tone and emphases of the periodical. Wade was (beside Place) the most impressive fact-finder among the Radicals. His *Black Book* is greatly superior to any other Radical investigation of the kind. One can see that he was at-

1. See above, p. 283. It is not clear whether Wade accepted Place's notes as they came in, or took editorial liberties with them. Although Place assisted the *Gorgon*, he never met Wade, and the paper 'was not altogether such a publication as I should have preferred'. See Wallas, op. cit., pp. 204–5.

tracted to the Benthamites by their solidity of research, and their concern for the practical particulars of reform – in the law, the prisons, education. From the outset the *Gorgon* expressed irritation at the prevailing rhetoric of popular Radicalism. On the one hand, it struck hard at the specious arguments of constitutional antiquity – most frequently to be found in the *Black Dwarf*, where Major Cartwright was still writing of witenagemots and perpetuating the theory of the Norman yoke:

We really think we cannot better advance the cause of Reform than by excluding from the consideration of the subject, all allusions to a former state of society . . .

Arguments derived from the 'good old times', Wade pointed out, came strangely from the mouths of working-class reformers. Much of the '*ancient lore* that has been raked together' was part and parcel of severely repressive legislation *against* the labourers. Can the reformers' leaders (he asked),

bring nothing to bear against the old rotten borough-mongering system but musty parchment, black letter and latin quotations? Is there nothing in the situation of our finances, in our belated paper system, in the number of paupers –

for comment and indictment? But if he rejected the specious appeal to precedent, he also rejected Paine's confidence in the claims of 'natural rights'. If it was argued that all men had a *natural* right to the vote, then how could one gainsay the same right in women? For Wade (as for Cobbett) this was the *reductio ad absurdum*. Lunatics and workhouse inmates were (just like women) denied the vote for evident reasons of social utility; and this seemed the soundest basis upon which working-class Radicals (or at least the male half of them) might rest their claims:

GENERAL UTILITY is the sole and ultimate object of society; and we shall never consider either sacred or valuable any natural or prescriptive claims that may be opposed to it.[1]

It was not difficult to justify a claim to the vote upon such

1. *Gorgon*, 20 June, 18 July, 22 August 1818.

a basis. But here came the rub. Wade was refreshingly pre-occupied with social reform and trade union organization. If Utilitarianism was to be extended as an ideology of the working class, it was necessary to have some theory of social structure and of political economy. How was the good of the greatest number to be determined, and might it be that what was useful to employers might be oppressive to working people? Wade's theory of social structure was impressionistic and derivative, but at least he offered more than Cobbett's 'Old Corruption' or the rhetoric of the 'borough-mongering system'. He divided society into the parasitic and the productive classes. In the first group were (a) the upper classes, including the dignitaries of the Church and the Law, and the nobility, and (b) the 'mid-dling classes' – loyal parsons, Commissioners of Taxes, officials in the departments of Revenue. These he identified with Cor-ruption. In the second group were the 'productive classes': the term was wide enough to include professional men and em-ployers, but the emphasis was upon 'those who, by their labours, increase the funds of the community, as husbandmen, mechanics, labourers, &c.' Below this group he placed the nondescripts, such as paupers and State creditors:

The industrious orders may be compared to the soil, out of which everything is evolved and produced; the other classes to the trees, tares, weeds and vegetables, drawing their nutriment ... on its surface ...

When mankind attained to a state of 'greater perfectibility', then the industrious classes alone ought to exist. 'The other classes have mostly originated in our vices and ignorance ... having no employment, their name and office will cease in the social state.'[1]

At this point Wade enlisted the help of Place, and the *Gorgon* began to feature material every week on the state of the work-ing classes. It is not clear whose hand is most influential. On the one hand, there is a strong emphasis upon labour as the source of value, an emphasis perhaps strengthened by Ricardo's

1. *Gorgon*, 8 August 1818, and *The Extraordinary Black Book* (1831 edn), pp. 217–18. See also A. Briggs, 'The Language of Class in early nineteenth-century Britain', *Essays in Labour History*, p. 50.

Principles of Economics, published in the previous year.[1] 'Labour is the superabundant product of this country,' wrote the *Gorgon*, 'and is the chief commodity we export':

Of the four staple manufactures, namely, cotton, linen, cloth, and iron, perhaps, on an average, the raw material does not constitute one-tenth of their value, the remaining nine-tenths being created by the labours of the weaver, spinner, dyer, smith, cutler, and fifty others. ... The labours of these men form the chief article of traffic in this country. It is by trading in the blood and bones of the journeymen and labourers of England that our merchants have derived their riches, and the country its glory ...

The statement is emotive rather than exact. It reminds us that the notion of labour as the source of all value was found, not only in Thelwall's *Rights of Nature*, but also in an emphatic tone in Cobbett's 'Address to the Journeymen and Labourers' of 1816. Cobbett, one feels, had in his mind's eye, while writing, his own farm, and the labourers busy with the stock, at the plough, repairing buildings. Wade (or Place) had in his eye the craftsman and outworker, the wool-sorter or tailor, who was given raw material in some form and, by his labour or skill, processed the material. To the raw material, one-tenth; to the labour and skill the rest.[2]

But the same article in the *Gorgon* at once commenced to instruct trade unionists in the platitudes of political economy. The reward for labour was regulated by demand and supply. 'An increase in the wages of journeymen is attended with a proportionate decrease in the profits of masters' – the wages fund. When the price of labour advances it has 'a tendency to force capital out of that branch of industry'. And (very much in the language of the Place who assisted in the repeal of the Statute of Artificers) –

Both masters and journeymen, ought in all cases to act *individually*, not *collectively*. When either party has recourse to *unnatural* or *artificial* expedients, they produce unnatural effects.

1. Ricardo is cited in *Gorgon*, 26 September 1818.
2. Ibid., 12 September 1818. For the origins of the labour theory of value, touched upon briefly and inexpertly in this chapter, see G. D. H. Cole, *History of Socialist Thought, The Forerunners* (1953), A. Menger, *The Right to the Whole Produce of Labour* (1898); R. N. Meek, *Studies in the Labour Theory of Value* (1956).

The theory of natural laws or rights, shut out by Wade at the front door, has been invited in at the back. For, by this time, it is scarcely possible to think of middle-class Utilitarianism without thinking also of Malthus and of orthodox political economy: the doctrine of utility could only be interpreted in the light of the 'laws' of population and those of supply and demand. If Utilitarianism was to enter working-class ideology it would make it captive to the employing class.

And yet the matter was not to be settled so easily. Through September, October and November 1818 the *Gorgon* carried detailed examinations of the position of some of the London trades: tailors, type-founders, opticians, compositors.[1] At the same time it conducted a defence of the Manchester cotton-spinners, whose strike was attracting the bitterest attacks in both the loyalist and the new-style middle-class Radical press (notably *The Times*). The comparison of wage-rates over the previous twenty years in organized and unorganized trades led to an inescapable conclusion. Whether 'natural' or 'artificial', combination *worked*:

... we had always thought that the prosperity of masters and work-men were simultaneous and inseparable. But the fact is not so, and we have no hesitation in saying that the cause of the *deterioration* in the circumstances of workmen generally, and the different degrees of deterioration among different classes of journeymen, de-pends entirely on the degree of perfection that prevails among them, which the law has pronounced a crime – namely, COMBINA-TION. The circumstances of the workmen do not in the least de-pend on the prosperity or profits of the masters, but on the power of the workmen to *command* – nay to *extort* a high price for their labour ...[2]

This can scarcely be Place, in view of the arguments which he is known to have adopted in 1814 and 1824.[3] But if the author was Wade, he did not long hold to this position. Sub-sequently he adopted the ideology of the middle-class Utili-

1. For some of its findings, see above, p. 280.
2. Ibid., 21 November 1818.
3. Place informed the Select Committee on Artizans and Machinery (*First Report* (1824), p. 46): 'no principle of political economy [is] better established than this of wages: increase of wages must come from profits'.

tarians, and his popular *History of the Middle and Working Classes* (1835) has this characteristic blend of the Radical politics and orthodox economics, together with industrious compilation of fact. It is, however, a disappointing work to have come from the author of the *Black Book* and the editor of the *Gorgon*.

Gast's history is different. He was, with Gravener Henson and John Doherty, one of the three truly impressive trade union leaders who emerged in these early years. Each came from industries undergoing greatly different experiences, and the characteristic contribution of each was for this reason different. Henson exemplifies the struggle of the outworkers, touching the fringes of Luddism, organizing their illegal union, sharing their advanced political Radicalism, and attempting until 1824 to enforce or enact protective legislation in their favour. Doherty of the cotton-spinners was able to place more emphasis upon the workers' own power to improve their conditions, or to change the entire system, by the force of combination; he was, by 1830, at the heart of the great movements of the northern workers for general unionism, factory reform, cooperative organization, and 'national regeneration'. Gast, coming from a smaller but highly organized skilled trade, was constantly concerned with problems of the organization and mutual support of the London and national *trades*.

Gast was a shipwright, who served his apprenticeship in Bristol (where he had been born in 1772), and came to London around 1790. Of his 'thirty or forty' years on the Thames (he said in 1825) twenty-eight had been spent in one Deptford yard, in which he was the 'leading hand', with sixteen or so men under his charge: 'I there assisted in building not less than from twenty to thirty sail of men-of-war ... exclusive of merchant ships.' In 1793 the shipwrights had been organized in the St Helena Benefit Society – there were 'not ten men in the river who were not members'. The society failed, but in 1812 there was a shipwright's strike and the Hearts of Oak Benefit Society was formed in which Gast took a leading part. The society was so successful that it not only provided the usual benefits, for sickness, death, and accident, but also erected from its funds thirteen alms-houses for retired shipwrights.

When the Thames Shipwrights Provident Union was founded
in August 1824, Gast was its first Secretary. He must by this
time have been in his mid-fifties.[1]

After the repeal of the Combination Acts the shipwrights
were involved in a particularly bitter struggle with their employers, who led the lobby pressing for new anti-trade union
legislation in 1825.[2] Thus Gast and his union were thrown into
prominence. But long before this he had won respect in London trade union circles. We have seen that he was associated
with the *Gorgon*, while he was prominent at the same time in
the attempts (in Manchester and London) to form the 'Philanthropic Hercules', the first General Union of all trades.[3] It is
clear that by 1818 Gast was the leading figure in more than
one committee of London 'trades'. Moreover, an interesting
translation took place in London working-class Radicalism
between 1819 and 1822. In the former year, Hunt's triumphal
entry into London after Peterloo had been prepared by a committee in which such men as Dr Watson, Gale Jones, Evans
and Thistlewood, were prominent – in the main old Jacobins,
professional men, small masters, and a few artisans. When
Hunt was released from Ilchester Gaol at the end of 1822 he
was welcomed to London by John Gast, on behalf of 'The
Committee of the Useful Classes'.[4] From this time forwards
London working-class Radicalism acquires a new cogency: it
is more easy to see from which industries its strength is drawn.
In Gast's committee it is possible to see an incipent 'trades
council'. In 1825, with the repeal of the Combination Acts, and
with the threat of their reimposition, the trades felt strong
enough to found their own weekly *Trades Newspaper*.[5]

1. *Trades Newspaper*, 31 July 1825.
2. See the Hammonds, *The Town Labourer*, pp. 138–40.
3. Ibid., p. 311; Webbs, *History of Trade Unionism*, pp. 85–5; Wallas
op. cit., p. 189; G. D. H. Cole, *Attempts at General Union*, pp. 81–2.
4. Hunt's *Address to the Radical Reformers*, 9 December 1822.
5. The paper was planned by 'those Town and Country Representatives
of Trades who had assembled in London to watch the progress of the
late Inquiry respecting the Combination Laws'. £1,000 was subscribed by
the trades themselves to found the paper, and apart from the shipwrights,
the sawyers, coopers, carpenters, ladies' shoemakers, caulkers, and silk
weavers appear to have been directly involved. The paper was governed
by a committee of the trades.

The *Trades Newspaper*, with its motto, 'They helped every one his neighbour', is important not only because it throws a flood of light upon the strength of trade unionism which, until this time, one must follow through the shadows of the Courts and the Home Office papers.[1] It also indicates a point of complete rupture between middle-class Utilitarianism, on one hand, and emergent 'trade union theory' on the other. The conflict was quite explicit. It is as if the orthodox parts of the *Gorgon* had gone on with Place and Wade, while the unorthodox claims for the value of combination became the basis for Gast's new venture. Some of the polemics were aimed specifically at Place, and in a manner both unfortunate and unfair; and this may help to explain why Gast and the London trades feature so little in Place's own account of these years. The controversy had in fact been opened in the previous year, in the pages of Wooler's *Black Dwarf*, now in the last year of its life.[2] It was provoked by the wedding which had been solemnized, in the pages of James Mill, between Malthusianism and political economy. Baldly stated, this proposed that the problem of unemployment[3] was a natural, rather than artificial, one, arising from the 'surplus' of population; as such it was insoluble; being insoluble, it was the underlying determinant of wage-rates, since – however much skilled groups might attain to a privileged position by means of restricting entry into their craft – the mass of the workers would find that the natural laws of supply-and-demand would cheapen the value of a service which was in excess supply.

1. See above, p. 264.

2. See the controversy on population, commencing on 12 November 1823, and continuing through successive issues. Mr P. M. Jackson informs me that he has found evidence (in the Place collection) which identify the Malthusian correspondent 'A.M.' as John Stuart Mill.

3. There is a legend abroad that 'unemployment' was outside the semantic frame of the 1820s. Perhaps it stems from an unwise statement in G. M. Young, *Victorian England* (Oxford, 1936), p. 27, that 'unemployment was beyond the scope of any idea which Early Victorian reformers had at their command, largely because they had no word for it': to which is added the authority of a footnote: 'I have not observed it earlier than the sixties.' In fact (as is often the case with these semantic 'datings') the statement is wrong. (Cuckoos generally arrive in these islands some weeks before they are announced in *The Times*.) 'Unem-

To this Cobbett had long given a passionate and explosive negative ('PARSON Malthus! Scotch feelosofers!'). The 'Black Dwarf' offered more strenuous arguments. 'The quantity of employment is unlimited,' he wrote:

I have seen men and women without stockings in this great manufacturing country, which furnishes stockings to all quarters of the world. ... If every one in these islands alone were as well clothed as they could wish to be, the home consumption would be ten times as extensive as it is.

'It is not by diminishing their numbers,' he concluded (in replying to objections from Place), 'but by sharpening their intellects, that the condition of the human race is to be bettered.'[1]

The argument was resumed in the first number of the *Trades Newspaper*, whose first editor was the advanced Radical, J. C. Robertson, the pioneer of the London Mechanics' Institute and colleague of Thomas Hodgskin.[2] The editorial took issue with M'Culloch for adopting Malthusian theory and advising the workers: 'Restrict your numbers so as not to overstock the demand for labourers.' 'This,' the editorial commented, 'is to conspire against nature, against morality, and against happiness.' The available means for such restriction were either abstinence from marriage, or from the enjoyment of marriage, or else the use of contraceptives. Now Place had firmly endorsed the Malthusian position, and had taken it upon himself to propagate it amongst the working class; but, having no confidence in their capacity for sexual abstinence, he had further assisted in the covert dissemination of handbills providing in-

---

ployed', 'the unemployed', and (less frequently) 'unemployment' are all to be found in trade union and Radical or Owenite writing of the 1820s and 1830s: the inhibitions of 'Early Victorian reformers' must be explained in some other way.

1. *Black Dwarf*, 3 and 31 December 1823.

2. Dr Iorwerth Prothero has drawn my attention to evidence which suggests that J. C. Robertson wrote the early editorial articles in the paper (which he edited until March 1826) rather than Gast (to whom I attributed them in the first edition of this book). But Gast, as chairman of the committee of controlling trades, undoubtedly had great influence upon the paper's policy and conduct.

formation as to the means of birth control.[1] Place now attempted to defend M'Culloch in the columns of the *Trades Newspaper.*

If Place had taken part in a courageous action for the most wrong-headed of Utilitarian reasons, the *Trades Newspaper* attacked him bitterly on both counts. On the one hand, it was insinuated that Place was associated with a 'nameless' and immoral advocacy, too disgusting to be described. (We should remember that this response to contraception was shared on every side, and there is no reason to suppose that Gast was not genuinely shocked.) On the other hand, he opened a critique which was of far greater significance:

If Messrs Malthus, M'Culloch, Place & Co are to be believed, the working classes have only to consider how they can most effectually restrict their numbers, in order to arrive at a complete solution of all their difficulties ... Malthus & Co ... would reduce the whole matter to a question between Mechanics and their sweethearts and wives [rather than] a question between the employed and their employers – between the Mechanic and the corn-grower and monopolist – between the tax-payer and the tax-inflictor.[2]

The note is quite clear. Gast and Robertson had rejected the model of a 'natural' and self-adjusting political economy, which, left unrestrained, would operate to the benefit of employers and employed alike. An essential antagonism of interests is assumed, and its resolution or adjustment must be a matter of force. What might be of utility to capital might well be oppressive to labour. And for this shaping working-class theory there came important intellectual reinforcements. There was published in 1825 *Labour Defended Against the Claims of Capital* (over the pseudonym 'A Labourer') by Thomas Hodgskin, a retired naval lieutenant on half-pay. Gast, Robertson, and Hodgskin had already been associated in the Mechanics' Institute, for which the latter lectured in political economy. In the second half of 1825 the greater part of *Labour Defended* was published in extracts in the *Trades Newspaper*, and a series

1. See F. Place, *Illustrations and Proofs of the Principle of Population* (1822). Also see above, p. 816 n. 1.

2. *Trades Newspaper*, 17, 24, 31 July, 11 September 1825. Place appears to have given assistance to an unsuccessful rival to the *Trades Newspaper*, the *Artizan's London and Provincial Chronicle* (1825).

of editorial articles gave to it a warm, but not uncritical, welcome, selecting from Hodgskin's work, with particular approval, the elements of the labour theory of value: 'the *only* thing which can be said to be stored up is the skill of *the labourer*':

All the capitalists of Europe, with all their circulating capital, cannot of themselves supply a single week's food and clothing . . .[1]

Hodgskin's primitive socialist theory was particularly well adapted to the experience of the London trades – and from this experience his theory was in great part derived. In the face of renewed threats of legislation, he defended trade unionism with strong and common-sense arguments: 'Combination is of itself no crime; on the contrary, it is the principle on which societies are held together.' His particular fire was directed against the capitalist in his rôle as entrepreneur or middleman:

Betwixt him who produces food and him who produces clothing, betwixt him who makes instruments and him who uses them, in steps the capitalist, who neither makes nor uses them and appropriates to himself the produce of both. . . . Gradually and successively has he insinuated himself betwixt them, expanding in bulk as he has been nourished by their increasingly productive labours, and separating them so widely from each other that neither can see whence that supply is drawn which each receives through the capitalist. While he despoils both, so completely does he exclude one from the view of the other that both believe they are indebted to him for subsistence.

In his active technical or managerial rôle, the capitalist was seen as productive; in this rôle he also was a labourer, and should be rewarded as such. But as a middleman or speculator he was merely parasitic:

The most successful and widest-spread possible combination to obtain an augmentation of wages would have no other injurious effect than to reduce the incomes of those who live on profit and interest, and who have no just claim but custom to any share of the national produce.

Hodgskin did not offer an alternative *system* (unless it was the supersession of all systems in a Godwinian sense) and there is

1. *Trades Newspaper*, 21 and 28 August 1825 et. seq.

a sense in which he side-stepped the question of property-rights. What he sanctioned was a mounting organized pressure, by all the strength and intellectual and moral resources of the working class, to confiscate the gross wealth of the capitalist interloper. This war of capital and labour, between 'honest industry' and 'idle profligacy', would not end until the workers received the full product of their own labour, and 'till *man* shall be held more in honour than the clod he treads on or the machine he guides.'

IV. OWENISM

The publication of *Labour Defended*, and its reception in the *Trades Newspaper*, represents the first clear point of junction between the 'labour economists' or the Owenites and a part of the working-class *movement*.[1] But of course Owen had preceded him; and even if Owen, Gray, Pare and Thompson had not been writing, Hodgskin's work was bound to lead on to the further question: if capital was largely parasitic upon labour, might not labour simply dispense with it or replace it by a new system. Moreover, by a curious twist it was possible for Utilitarianism to lead on to the same question: if the only criterion by which a social system might be judged was *use*, and if the greatest number in that society were toilers, clearly no veneration for custom or Gothic notions should prevent one from contriving the most useful possible *plan* by which the masses might exchange and enjoy their own products. Hence Owenite Socialism always contained two elements which never wholly fused: the philanthropy of the Enlightenment, devising 'span-new systems' according to principles of utility and bene-

1. In the following pages I cannot hope to re-examine the thought of Owen or of the 'labour economists'. My purpose is to illustrate at one or two points the way theory impinged upon working-class experience and the way the new ideas were selected or changed in the process; that is, my concern is more with the sociology of these ideas than with their identity. For Hodgskin see G. D. H. Cole's edition of *Labour Defended* (1922) and E. Halévy, *Thomas Hodgskin* (1956, trans. A. J. Taylor). For a lucid and brief discussion of Owen and the labour economists, see H. L. Beales, *The Early English Socialists* (1933), chs. 4 and 5; and for a fuller summary, G. D. H. Cole, *History of Socialist Thought*, I, *The Forerunners*, and M. Beer, *A History of British Socialism*, Part III.

volence: and the experience of those sections of workers who selected notions from the Owenite stock, and adapted or developed them to meet their particular context.

The story of Robert Owen of New Lanark is well known, even legendary. The model paternalist mill-owner and self-made man who canvassed the royalty, courtiers and governments of Europe with his philanthropic proposals; the growing exasperation of Owen's tone as he met with polite applause and practical discouragement; his propaganda to all classes and his proclamation of the Millennium the growing interest in his ideas and promises among some working people; the rise and fall of the early experimental communities, notably Orbiston; Owen's departure to America for more experiments in community-building (1824–29); the growing support for Owenism during his absence, the enriching of his theory by Thompson, Gray and others, and the adoption of a form of Owenism by some of the trade unionists; the initiative of Dr King at Brighton with his *Cooperator* (1828–30) and the widely scattered experiments in cooperative trading; the initiative of some London artisans, among whom Lovett was prominent, in promoting national propaganda in cooperative principles (the British Association for Promoting Cooperative Knowledge), in 1829–30; the swelling tide after Owen's return, when he found himself almost despite himself at the head of a movement which led on to the Grand National Consolidated Trades Union.

It is an extraordinary story; and yet there is a sense in which parts of it *had* to be so. We may start at the point of entry, with the paternalist tradition. And we must see that the great experiments at New Lanark were instituted to meet the same difficulties of labour discipline, and the adaptation of the unruly Scottish labourers to new industrial work-patterns that we have already encountered in our discussion of Methodism and of Dr Ure. 'At that time the lower classes in Scotland ... had strong prejudices against strangers ...', 'the persons employed at these works were therefore strongly prejudiced against the new director ...':

... they possessed almost all the vices and very few of the virtues of a social community. Theft and the receipt of stolen goods was their trade, idleness and drunkenness their habit, falsehood and deception their garb, dissensions, civil and religious, their daily practice; they united only in a zealous systematic opposition to their employers.

These passages, from *A New View of Society* (1813), are much the common run of the new mill-owner or iron-master's experience. The problem was to indoctrinate the youth in 'habits of attention, celerity, and order'. It is wholly to Owen's credit that he chose neither the psychic terrors of Methodism nor the discipline of the overlooker and of fines to attain his ends. But we must see, all the time, that Owen's later Socialism retained the marks of its origin. He was cast as the kindly Papa of Socialism: Mr Owen, the Philanthropist, who secured entrée to the Court and the Cabinet-room in the post-war years (until he committed his *faux pas* of dismissing, with kindly tolerance, all received religions whatsoever as mischievous irrationalism), merges without any sense of crisis into 'the benevolent Mr Owen' who was addressed by and issued addresses to the working classes. He was in one sense the *ne plus ultra* of Utilitarianism, planning society as a gigantic industrial panopticon; in another, and most admirable and kindly sense, he was an industrial Hanway, who thought a good deal about children, liked to see them happy, and really was outraged at their callous exploitation. But the notion of working-class advance, by its own self-activity towards its own goals, was alien to Owen, even though he was drawn, between 1829 and 1834, into exactly this kind of movement. This can be seen in the tone of all his writings. He wished (he said in 1817) to 'remoralize the Lower Orders'. Next to 'benevolent' the words most commonly encountered in early Owenite writings are 'provided for them'. Education should 'impress on the young ideas and habits which shall contribute to the future happiness of the individual and the State; and this can be accomplished only by instructing them to become rational beings':

Fourth, – What are the best arrangements under which these men and their families can be well and economically *lodged, fed, clothed, trained, educated, employed, and governed*?[1]

1. R. Owen. *A New View of Society and other writings* (Everyman edn), pp. 74, 260.

This tone presented an almost insuperable barrier between Owen and the popular Radical as well as trade union movement. 'The operatives and working classes were at this time strangers to me and to all my views and intentions,' Owen noted (in his *Autobiography*) of the immediate post-war years. 'Their democratic and much-mistaken leaders taught them that I was their enemy and that I desired to make slaves of them in these villages of unity and mutual cooperation.' But in the circumstances this was scarcely surprising. The Philanthropist, Mr Owen, swam into their view during the desperate post-war depression years. Many of the gentry were themselves appalled at the extent of unemployment and distress, while they were also anxious as to the insurrectionary temper of the unemployed. More than this, the poor-rates had risen to over £6 millions at a time when agriculture had fallen from its wartime prosperity. The poor were unsightly, a source of guilt, a heavy charge on the country, and a danger. The columns of the reviews were full of discussions on the emendation of the Poor Laws, all of which had greater economy as their goal. Mr Owen (whose extensive properties at New Lanark became a fashionable addition to genteel tours) now came forward with a Plan, which really could not have been nicer. He proposed to put the poor into 'Villages of Cooperation', where – after an initial capital grant out of taxes – they would *pay their own way*, and become 'useful', 'industrious', 'rational', self-disciplined, and temperate as well. The Archbishop of Canterbury liked the idea, and Lord Sidmouth went over it quite closely with Mr Owen. 'My Lord Sidmouth will forgive me,' Owen wrote in one of his public letters on poor relief which appeared in the London press in the summer of 1817, 'for he knows I intend no personal offence. His dispositions are known to be mild and amiable...' This was published a fortnight after the Pentridge rising and the exposure of Oliver.

The Plan smelled of Malthus and of those rigorous experiments of magistrates (like the strangely named 'Nottingham Reformers') who were already working out the Chadwickian plan of economical workhouse relief. Even if Owen was himself (as some of the Radicals were willing to allow) deeply in earnest and dismayed by the distress of the people, his plan, if taken up by Government, would certainly be orientated in this way. Cobbett has been too easily accused of 'prejudice' in denouncing Owen's 'Villages of Cooperation' as 'parallelograms of paupers'. Not only did they savour to him of the 'comforting system' of patronage and charity which he loathed, but his instinct was probably right – that Owen's ideas, if they *had* been taken up by the authorities in 1817, would probably have given rise to an extension of 'productive employment' within the workhouse system. But Cobbett was only voicing the general Radical response. His proposed institutions (wrote Sherwin) would be 'prisons', 'a community of vassals':

Mr Owen's object appears to me to be to cover the face of the country with workhouses, to rear up a community of slaves, and consequently to render the labouring part of the People absolutely dependant upon the men of property.[1]

When Owen attempted to interest the Radicals in his proposals, at a crowded meeting in the City of London Tavern, the Radical leaders, one after another – Cartwright, Wooler Alderman Waithman – opposed him in similar terms. When Gale Jones proposed that the plan at least deserved examination he was shouted down and accused of apostasy.[2]

The debate served only to display the weakness of both sides. On the one hand, Owen simply had a vacant place in his mind where most men have political responses. One part of the *New View* was dedicated to the Prince Regent, another to Wilberforce. Fifteen years later his paper, the *Crisis* sailed blandly through the waters of 1831 and 1832, carrying cargoes of reports on cooperative congresses and on trading stores at Slaithwaite, without noticing that the country was *in fact* in a state of revolutionary crisis. This vacancy had its endearing aspects: when it occurred to Mr Owen that the royalty was an irrational institution and that Bishops were a costly and unnecessary tribute to Gothic ignorance, he had no hesitation in pointing this out to the present incumbents, being sure that they would

1. Sherwin's *Political Register*, 26 April, 9 August, 20 September 1817.
2. See *Independent Whig*, 24 August 1817. The only radical papers which appear to have given Owen a favourable hearing in 1817–19 were the short-lived *People* and the *Independent Whig* which sent a correspondent to New Lanark.

see that he intended 'no personal offence' and that they would duly liquidate themselves in submission to rational suasion. But this was scarcely endearing to the 'old Radicals' of 1817. Their weaknesses, on the other hand, consisted in a lack of any constructive social theory, whose place was taken by a rhetoric in which all ills were attributed to taxation and sinecures, which all could be remedied by Reform.

Hazlitt's response to the *New View* was the most complex, and shows the bruised Jacobin in him struggling against the weight of Burke: 'Why does Mr Owen put the word 'New', in black-letter at the head of the advertisement of his plan of reform?' 'The doctrine of Universal Benevolence, the belief in the Omnipotence of Truth, and in the Perfectibility of Human Nature, are not new, but "Old, old," Master Robert Owen':

Does not Mr Owen know that the same scheme, the same principles, the same philosophy of motives and actions ... of virtue and happiness, were rife in the year 1793, were noised abroad then, were spoken on the house-tops, were whispered in secret, were published in quarto and duodecimo, in political treatises, in plays, poems, songs and romances – made their way to the bar, crept into the church, ascended the rostrum, thinned the classes of the universities ... that these 'New Views of Society' got into the hearts of poets and the brains of metaphysicians, took possession of the fancies of boys and women, and turned the heads of almost the whole kingdom: but that there was one head which they never got possession of, that turned the heads of the whole kingdom round again ...?

Thus repelled (Hazlitt mocked) it seems that *philosophy* was driven from the country,

and forced to take refuge and to lie snug for twenty years in the New Lanark mills, with the connivance of the worthy proprietor, among the tow and spindles; from whence he lets us understand that it is coming up again to Whitehall-stairs, like a spring-tide with the full of the moon, and floating on the blood that has flowed for the restoration of the Bourbons, under the patronage of the nobility, the gentry, Mr Wilberforce, and the Prince Regent, and all those who are governed, like those great personages, by no other principle than truth, and no other wish than the good of mankind! This puff will not take with us: we are old birds, not to be caught with chaff ...

Hazlitt's insight is extraordinarily acute. For Owen indeed was not the first of the modern Socialist theorists (Hodgskin was much closer to being that) but one of the last of the eighteenth-century rationalists – he was Godwin, now setting out from New Lanark to claim the Chairmanship of the Board of Directors of the Industrial Revolution. In his new disguise, as a practical and eminently successful man, he had entrée where the old philosophers were reviled and spurned. 'A man that comes all the way from the banks of the Clyde acquires a projectile force that makes him irresistible':

He has access, we understand, to the men in office, to the members of parliament, to lords and gentlemen. He comes . . . to batter down all their establishments, new or old, in church or state . . . and he quietly walks into their houses with his credentials in his pocket, and reconciles them to innumerable Houses of Industry he is about to erect on the site of their present sinecures . . .

'We do not,' continued Hazlitt, 'wish him to alter his tone.' But he prophesied, with uncanny accuracy, some of the consequences, if he did not:

His schemes thus far are tolerated, because they are remote, visionary, inapplicable. Neither the great world nor the world in general care any thing about New Lanark, nor trouble themselves whether the workmen there go to bed drunk or sober, or whether the wenches are got with child before or after the marriage ceremony. Lanark is distant, Lanark is insignificant. Our statesmen are not afraid of the perfect system of reform he talks of, and, in the meantime, his cant against reform in parliament . . . serves as a practical diversion in their favour. But let the good which Mr Owen says he has done in one poor village be in danger of becoming general . . . and his dreams of elevated patronage will vanish. . . . Let his 'New View of Society' but make as many disciples as the 'Enquiry concerning Political Justice', and we shall see how the tide will turn about. . . . He will be marked as a Jacobin, a leveller, an incendiary, in all parts of the three kingdoms; he will be avoided by his friends, and become a bye-word to his enemies . . . and he will find out that it is not so easy or safe a task as to be imagined to . . . make mankind understand their own interests, or those who govern them care for any interest but their own.[1]

1. *Examiner*, 4 August 1816; see *Works*, VII, p. 97 et. seq.

The quality in Owen which his patrons discovered with consternation (and into which Hazlitt had some insight) was that of sheer propagandist zeal. He believed, equally with Carlile, in the multiplication of 'reason' by means of its diffusion. He spent a small fortune in posting his Addresses to men of influence throughout the country; and a larger fortune upon the experimental communities. By 1819 his patrons had grown weary of him, and he in turn was addressing himself more particularly to the working class. He had long held the view that working people were the creatures of circumstances; he deplored their 'gross ferocity of character' and one feels that (like Shaw) his chief reason for being a Socialist was the desire that they should be abolished. But here there comes a twist in his thought, productive of large consequences. If the workers were creatures of circumstances, so also − the thought may have occurred to him while walking in the park after an unsatisfactory interview − were Lord Sidmouth and the Archbishop. The thought was communicated in an Address to the Working Classes (1819):

From infancy, you ... have been made to despise and hate those who differ from you in manners, language, and sentiments. ... Those feelings of anger must be withdrawn before any being who has your real interest at heart can place power in your hands. ... You will then distinctly perceive that no rational ground for anger exists. ... An endless multiplicity of circumstances, over which you had not the smallest control, placed you where you are. ... In the same manner, others of your fellow-men have been formed by circumstances, equally uncontrollable by them, to become your enemies and grievous oppressors. .. Splendid as their exterior may be, this state of matters often causes them to suffer even more poignantly than you. ... While you show by your conduct any desire violently to dispossess them of this power, these emoluments and privileges − is it not evident that they must continue to regard you with jealous and hostile feelings .. ?

'The rich and the poor, the governors and the governed, have really but one interest' − to form a new cooperative society. But the rich no less than the poor, being creatures of circumstance, were unable to see their true interests. (The 'sudden admission of strong light' from Owen's writings was in danger of destroying their 'infant powers of vision'). The workers (or those of them who had seen the light of reason) should disengage from class conflict. 'This irrational and useless contest must cease', and the *avant garde* (by establishing model communities and by propaganda) might blaze a path by means of which the working people could simply *by-pass* the property-rights and power of the rich.[1]

However admirable Owen was as a man, he was a preposterous thinker, and, while he had the courage of the eccentric, he was a mischievous political leader. Of the theorists of Owenism, Thompson is more sane and challenging, while Gray, Pare, Dr King and others had a firmer sense of reality. There comes through his writings not the least sense of the dialectical processes of social change, of 'revolutionizing practice':

The materialist doctrine that men are products of circumstances and upbringing and that, therefore, changed men are products of other circumstances and changed upbringing, forgets that circumstances are changed precisely by men and that the educator must himself be educated. Hence this doctrine necessarily arrives at dividing society into two parts, of which one towers above society (in Robert Owen, for example) –

So ran Marx's third thesis on Ludwig Feuerbach. If social character was (as Owen held) the involuntary product of 'an endless multiplicity of circumstances,' how was it to be changed? One answer lay in education, where one of the most creative influences of the Owenite tradition can be seen. But Owen knew that until 'circumstances' changed he could not gain access to the schooling of a generation. The answer must therefore lie in the sudden change of heart, the millenarial leap. The very rigour of his environmental and mechanical materialism meant that he must either despair or proclaim a secular chiliasm.

Mr Owen, the Philanthropist, threw the mantle of Joanna Southcott across his shoulders. The tone of the ranter was noted, not only by Hazlitt, but by others of his contemporaries. A writer in Sherwin's *Register* compared him to Joanna, who—

deluded thousands for the moment, by telling them that a Shiloh was about to come into the world; a Prince of Peace, under whose

1. See Owen, op. cit., pp. 148–55.

standard all the nations of the earth were to unite; by telling them
that ... swords were to be converted into plough-shares.[1]

It was also to be examined by Engels and by Marx, and the
more recent promulgation of the discovery in academic circles
is not original.[2] Owen was promising, in 1820, to '*let prosperity
loose on the country*', and in his communities he offered no
less than 'Paradise'. By 1820 an Owenite society was forming in
the metropolis, and the hand-bill advertising its periodical, the
Economist, declared:

Plenty will overspread the land! – Knowledge will increase! —
Virtue will flourish! – Happiness will be recognized, secured, and
enjoyed.

Owen frequently used analogies drawn from the great advance
in productive techniques during the Industrial Revolution:
some individuals 'forget that it is a modern invention to enable
one man, with the aid of a little steam, to perform the labour
of 1,000 men'. Might not knowledge and moral improvement
advance at the same pace? His followers took up the same
imagery:

... the construction of a great social and moral machine, calculated
to produce wealth, knowledge, and happiness, with unprecedented
precision and rapidity ...

A correspondent to the *Economist* noted that 'the tone of joy
and exultation which pervades your writings is really most infectious'.

The members of the London society were aware –

that their proceedings must be comparatively imperfect, whilst
they remain in their present dwellings, remote ... from one
another.

With an enthusiasm reminiscent of the early Moravians, they
acquired some new houses on Spa Fields (no longer to be a
meeting-place), with a schoolroom and common eating-room.
The pages of the *Economist* and other early journals were full

1. Sherwin's *Political Register*, 20 September 1817.
2. See, however, Engels' generous tribute to Owen in *Anti-Dühring*
(1878; Lawrence & Wishart, 1936), pp. 287-92: 'a man of almost
sublimely child-like simplicity of character, and at the same time a born
leader of men'.

of speculations as to how capital might be raised – if it were supposed (an odd supposition) that there were 50,000 families of the working classes in the metropolis, these would, if brought into association, have an average income of £50 p.a. or £2½ millions collectively. And so on. The communitarians at Orbiston were enrolled in a 'Society of Divine Revelation'. By 1830 when Owen, returning from America, found himself at the head of a movement of the masses, this messianic tone had the force of a secular religion. On 1 May 1833, Owen delivered an Address at the National Equitable Labour Exchange 'denouncing the Old System of the World and announcing the Commencement of the New'. Not only would the profit motive be displaced by cooperation, the vices of individualism by the virtues of mutuality, but *all* existing social arrangements would give way to the federations of mixed agricultural and industrial villages:

We ... abandon all the arrangements to which [sectional] interests have given birth; such as large cities, towns, villages, and universities. ...

Courts of law and all the paraphernalia and folly of law ... cannot be found in a rational state of society ...

Hitherto the world had been 'in gross darkness'. All ceremonial worship of an unknown Power was 'much worse than useless'. Marriages will be recognized as a 'union of affection only'. 'Celibacy, in either sex, beyond the period designed by nature, will be no longer considered a virtue', but 'a crime against nature'. The new society would offer a balance between intellectual and physical labour, entertainment and the cultivation of the physical powers as in Greece and Rome. All citizens would abandon all ambition, envy, jealousy, and other named vices:

I therefore now proclaim to the world the commencement, on this day, of the promised millennium, founded on rational principles and consistent practice.[1]

1. *Economist*, 4 August, 20 and 27 October 1821 *et passim*. For the proclamation of the Millennium, I have used the account appended to Bronterre O'Brien's edition of *Buonarrotti's History of Babeuf's Conspiracy of Equals* (1836), pp. 438–45.

This proclamation might startle some Women's Cooperative Guilds today. It also appears, at first sight, an unlikely ideology to be accepted by the working people, whose formative experiences have been the subject of this study. And yet, if we look more closely, we will find that it was not some psychic frenzy or 'collective paranoia' which gave rise to the rapid spread of Owenism. In the first place, *Owenism* from the late Twenties onwards, was a very different thing from the writings and proclamations of Robert Owen. It was the very imprecision of his theories, which offered, none the less, an image of an alternative system of society, and which made them adaptable to different groups of working people. From the writings of the Owenites, artisans, weavers and skilled workers selected those parts which most closely related to their own predicament and modified them through discussion and practice. If Cobbett's writings can be seen as a relationship with his readers, Owen's can be seen as ideological raw material diffused among working people, and worked up by them into different products.

The artisans are the clearest case. The editor of the *Economist* admitted, in 1821, that few of his readers were among the working classes. But we gain an idea of the first members of the London 'Cooperative and Economical Society' who set up the community on Spa Fields from a circular sent to the Nobility and Gentry, soliciting their patronage for their wares. They offered to execute carving and gilding, boot and shoe-making, hardware (including grates and stoves), cutlery, clothing, sewing and dress-making, cabinet-making, book-selling and book-binding, drawings in water colours and on velvet, and Transparent Landscape Window Blinds. This suggests artisans and self-employed craftsmen, who abounded in two of the greatest cooperative centres – London and Birmingham. The spirit of these endeavours (of which there were a number, some antedating Owen) is expressed in a letter sent to the *Economist*:

... the working classes, if they will but exert themselves *manfully*, have no need to solicit the smallest assistance from any *other* class, but have within themselves ... superabundant resources.[1]

1. *Economist*, 13 October 1821, 9 March 1822. See Armytage, op. cit., pp. 92–4 for a brief account of the Spa Fields experiment.

This is not Owen's tone. But it is certainly the tone which we have met repeatedly when following the *political* Radicalism of the artisans. Individualism was only one part of their outlook; they were also inheritors of long traditions of mutuality – the benefit society, the trades club, and chapel, the reading or social club, the Corresponding Society or Political Union. Owen taught that the profit-motive was wrong and unnecessary: this keyed in with the craftsman's sense of custom and the fair price. Owen endorsed the view, held also by Cobbett, Carlile and Hodgskin, that the capitalist was largely parasitic in his function: 'that manual labour, properly directed, is the source of all wealth': this keyed in with grievances of artisans or little craftsmen-masters against the contractors and middlemen. Owen taught that '*the natural standard of human labour*' should be taken as 'the *practical* standard of value',[1] and that products ought to be exchanged according to the labour embodied in them: this keyed in with the outlook of the shoemaker, cabinet-maker, and brushmaker, who lived in the same court and who did in any case on occasion exchange services.

Indeed, the germ of most of Owen's ideas can be seen in practices which anticipate or occur independently of his writings.[2] Not only did the benefit societies on occasion extend their activities to the building of social clubs or alms-houses; there are also a number of instances of pre-Owenite trade unions when on strike, employing their own members and marketing the product.[3] The artisan was only slowly losing his

1. See 'Report to the County of Lanark' (1820), in Owen, op. cit., esp. pp. 261–2.

2. An attempt was made, as early as 1796, to form a British Fraternal Society, which was to unite the resources of the benefit societies with forms of organization derived from the Corresponding Society. It originated among the Spitalfields weavers, and it was proposed that old age and unemployed benefits should be paid, the Society should employ its own out-of-work members and the products of silk weavers, tailors, shoemakers, &c., should be exchanged with each other. See Andrew Larcher, *A Remedy for Establishing Universal Peace and Happiness* (Spitalfields, 1795) and *Address to the British Fraternal Society* (1796).

3. E.g., the Journeymen Tobacco Pipe Manufacturers who, after an eleven-week strike in the winter of 1818–19, commenced direct manufacture in the Maze, Borough – 'a friend' having 'procured us a factory'. See *Gorgon*, 6 and 13 February 1819.

status as a self-employed man, or as a man who did work for several masters; and in doing this or that contract he might enlist the aid of other craftsmen with different skills. The covered market, or bazaar, with its hundreds of little stalls, was an old institution; but at the close of the Wars new bazaars were opened, which attracted attention in philanthropic and Owenite circles, where a section of counter was let (by the foot) for the week, the day, or even part of the day. Wares of every type were invited – even artists might exhibit – and one may suppose that the craftsmen and 'garret-masters' who were struggling for 'an independence' were the tenants.[1] By 1827 a new bazaar was in being, which acted as a centre for the exchange of products made by unemployed members of London trades – carpenters, tailors, shoemakers, and others who were put to work on materials bought out of trade union funds.[2]

Thus the Equitable Labour Exchanges, founded at London and Birmingham in 1832-3, with their labour notes and exchange of small products, were not conjured out of the air by paranoiac prophets. If we list the products which were brought for exchange to the Cooperative Congress in Liverpool in October 1832 we can also see the people. From Sheffield, cutlery and coffee-pots: from Leicester, stockings and lace: from Huddersfield, waistcoat pieces and shawls: from Rochdale, flannels. There were diapers from Barnsley, stuffs from Halifax, shoes and clogs from Kendal, and prints from Birkacre. A spokesman of the Birmingham Equitable Labour Exchange said that the people of his district 'knew not what to do with their masses of iron, brass, steel and japan wares': why should they not be exchanged for Lancashire cottons and Leicester stockings? The long list of trades who proposed to bring their wares to the Birmingham Exchange includes (in the 'Bs') blacking-makers, bell-ringers, birch broom makers, button and trimming makers, brace-makers, braziers, brush-makers,

1. J. Nightingale, *The Bazaar* (1816). Particularly commended was the New Bazaar, 5 Soho Square, opened that year; a Beehive Bazaar in Holborn was also mentioned.

2. *Cooperative Magazine* (1827), pp. 230-31, cited in S. Pollard, 'Nineteenth-Century Cooperation: from Community Building to Shopkeeping', *Essays in Labour History*, p. 87.

bakers, bellows-makers, bedstead-makers, basket-makers. In the 'Ss' we find straw hat and bonnet-makers, scale makers, stove grate makers, silkweavers, blacksmiths and whitesmiths, and stationers. There are not (and could scarcely be) boiler-makers, blast furnace-men, or builders; shipwrights or cotton-spinners; miners or engineers.[1]

The list includes not only the little masters and artisans but also outworkers. As their position (weavers and stockingers) was the most desperate, so Owenism was only one of the solutions at which they clutched in the Thirties. The appeal of the Labour Exchange was not so immediate in the vicinity of Huddersfield or Burnley, for the obvious reason that in districts where the staple product was weaving, and where hundreds were semi-employed or employed on starvation wages on the same products, there was no obvious mart. Hence the northerners were impelled, at the outset, to look towards a national plan of cooperation. 'If our Birmingham friends will engage to appear in our fabrics,' wrote a Halifax cooperator:

We will engage to cut our beef and pudding (when we can get any) with their knives and forks, and sup our broth and oatmeal porridge with their spoons; and if our London brethren will do so too, we will appear, as soon as possible, with their silk handkerchiefs round our necks.[2]

It was in Lancashire and Yorkshire that we find the most rapid development of a *general theory* of a new 'system', whereby on a national scale equitable exchange might take place, as well as some of the hardiest and most practical support for 'utopian' experiments in community building. The Manchester and Salford Association for the Promotion of Cooperative Knowledge, founded in 1830, gained immediate support. The weavers hoped to find in cooperation the strength to compete with the power-loom. A great cause of social evils, wrote the *United Trades' Cooperative Journal*, was—

in the erroneous arrangement of our domestic, social and commercial affairs, by means of which machinery is made to compete with and against human labour instead of cooperating with him.

1. *Crisis*, 30 June, 27 October, 8 and 15 December 1832.
2. *Lancashire and Yorkshire Cooperator*, No. 2. (date unidentified).

'We can fairly trace that all the miseries which society suffers are mostly owing to the unfair distribution of wealth,' wrote the *Lancashire and Yorkshire Cooperator*.[1] In these districts with their long traditions of trade unionism and mutual aid, cooperation offered a movement in which rationalists and Christians, Radicals and the politically neutral, could work together. The movement gathered up also the traditions of self-improvement and educational effort, providing reading-rooms, schools, and itinerant lecturers. By 1832 perhaps 500 cooperative societies were in existence in the whole country, with at least 20,000 members.[2]

While Owen (bruised somewhat, despite his optimism, by the failures at Orbiston and New Harmony) was awaiting large capital gifts before further experiments could be risked, the cooperators in scores of centres, from Brighton to Bacup, were impatient to raise themselves immediately by their own efforts. At the Liverpool Congress of 1832 the proceedings offer the contrast between long evangelistic harangues and such interventions as this:

Mr WILSON, a delegate from Halifax, stated that in May 1829, he and 8 other persons laid down a shilling each, and ... commenced business in a small room in a back entry. Their numbers had increased; they ... were now worth £240 and had begun to find labour for some of their members (*Hear, hear.*)[3]

This juxtaposition of the little store and the millenarial plan is of the essence of the cooperative mood between 1829 and 1834. (It is found also in the diversity of particular grievances and organizations which held up for a brief while the edifice of the Grand National Consolidated Trades Union.)

In the neighbourhood of Huddersfield and Halifax, where cooperation spread among the weavers with such speed, one hope was that the store might purchase the warp and weft for the weaver and then sell the product, short-circuiting the employers. Cooperators might also, by a penny-a-week subscription, accumulate the capital to employ unemployed members.

1. 6 March 1830; 26 November 1831. See A. E. Musson, 'The Ideology of Early Cooperation in Lancashire and Cheshire', *Transactions Lancs. & Cheshire Antiq. Soc.*, LXVII, 1957.

2. S. Pollard, op. cit., p. 86.   3. *Crisis*, 27 October 1832.

But most of these motives may be better expressed by quoting the rules of a society formed in 1832 in Ripponden, a weaving village in the Pennines:

From the astonishing changes which the course of a series of years have produced to the labouring classes ... from competition and the increase of machinery which supersedes hand labour, combined with various other causes, over which, as yet, the labouring classes have no control – the minds of thinking men are lost in a labyrinth of suggestions what plan to adopt in order to better, if possible, their conditions. ...

By the increase of capital the working classes may better their condition, if they only *unite* and set their shoulder to the work; by uniting we do not mean strikes and turning out for wages, but like men of one family, strive to begin to work for ourselves. ...

The plan of cooperation which we are recommending to the public is not a visionary one but is acted upon in various parts of the Kingdom; we all live by the produce of the land, and exchange labour for labour, which is the object aimed at by all Cooperative Societies. We labourers do all the work and produce all the comforts of life; – why then should we not labour for ourselves and strive to improve our conditions?

Fundamental Principles

First. – That labour is the source of all wealth; consequently the working classes have created all wealth.

Secondly. – That the working classes, although the producers of wealth, instead of being the richest, are the poorest of the community; hence, they cannot be receiving a just recompense for their labour.

The objects of the society included the mutual protection of all members against poverty and 'the attainment of independence by means of a common capital'. The means of obtaining these objects included a weekly subscription into a common fund, the employment of the capital in trade, the employment of its members 'as circumstances will permit', and—

Lastly. – By living in community with each other, on the principles of mutual cooperation, united possessions, equality of exertions, and of the means of enjoyments.[1]

1. J. H. Priestley, *History of Ripponden Cooperative Society* (Halifax, 1932), ch. 4. It is not clear whether these rules date from 1833 or 1839.

This is not just a translation of Owen's doctrines to the context of a weaving village. The ideas have been shaped laboriously, in terms of the weavers' experience; the emphases have shifted; in place of the messianic stridency, there is the simple question: Why not? One of the small cooperative journals was aptly entitled *Common Sense*: its emphasis was on the 'Trading Associations':

The object of a Trading Association is briefly this: to furnish most of the articles of food in ordinary consumption to its members, and to accumulate a fund for the purpose of renting land for cultivation, and the formation thereon of a cooperative community.

A weekly sum from wages could be used for the wholesale purchase of tea, sugar, bread or oatmeal.[1] From Brighton Dr King's *Cooperator* was advocating this in greater detail.[2] The idea keyed in with other needs; the need to escape from the 'tommy shop' or the profiteer; the need to buy staple foods cheap, and free from the criminal adulteration which was only too common – the flour mixed with 'plaster of Paris, burnt bones, and an earthy substance ... called Derbyshire White'.[3]

But this idea had also an appeal to the skilled and organized workers in the larger industries, whose approach to Owenism was more circumspect. The *Trades Newspaper* carried some notes on Orbiston in 1825, but Owen's plans for communities were held to be 'impracticable from the dislike that free-born, independent men, must have to be told what they must eat ... and what they must do'.[4] Moreover, the very notion of acquiring an economic independence, which appealed to some small craftsmen and outworkers, offered an objection to the shipwright or the worker in large-scale industry – what use a Village of Cooperation to him?

1. *Common Sense*, 11 December 1830.

2. See S. Pollard, *Dr William King* (Loughborough Cooperative College Papers, 6, 1959).

3. *Trades Newspaper*, 31 July 1825. For the quasi-cooperative corn mills founded as a result of the near-famine of 1795, see G. J. Holyoake, *Self Help A Hundred Years Ago* (1891), ch. 11, and J. A. Langford, *A Century of Birmingham Life*, II, pp. 157–60. In some MS 'Notes and Observations on Cooperative Societies' Lovett records that there were many societies, especially consumer groups, during the wars, and mentions the Spitalfields Weavers: Add. MSS., 27, 791 ff. 245, 258.

4. Ibid., 14 August 1825.

By the close of the Twenties, however, Gast had declared for Owenism. A more important adhesion was that of the Manchester Cotton Spinners after their six-month strike in 1829. Doherty pioneered, in 1830, the National Association for the Protection of Labour, whose organ, the *United Trades Cooperative Journal* soon became the *Voice of the People*. Soon after this another skilled body, the Builders' Union, whose products could not possibly be taken to the Equitable Labour Exchange, set its course towards the greatest of all the experiments in cooperative direct action. What made the difference?

One answer may simply be that by the end of the Twenties one variant or another of cooperative and 'labour' economic theory had taken hold of the cadre of the working-class movement. Cobbett offered no coherent theory. Carlile's individualism was repellent. Hodgskin, by implication, pointed towards mature socialist theory, but his analysis pulled up before that point, and was in any case compatible with co-operative theory as William Thompson showed. The rationalist propaganda of the previous decade had been effective; but it had also been narrow and negative, and had given rise to a thirst for a more positive moral doctrine which was met by Owen's messianism. Owen's imprecision of thought made it possible for different intellectual tendencies to coexist within the movement. And we must insist again that Owenism was both saner, and more strenuous in intellectual terms, than the thought of its master. For the skilled workers the movement which began to take shape in 1830 at last seemed to give body to their long-held aspiration – general national unionism. From the Philanthropic Hercules of 1818 to the Combination Acts lobby of 1825 there had been much reaching out for united action. Throughout the summer and autumn of 1825 the *Trades Newspaper* reported each stage of the Bradford wool-combers' strike, and the support flowing in from all parts of the country. It declared emphatically: 'It is all the workers of England against a few masters at Bradford.'[1] Doherty saw in the failure of the great spinners' strike of 1829 another lesson: 'It was

1. *Trades Newspaper*, 11 September 1825.

then shown that no individual trade could stand against the combined efforts of the masters of that particular trade: it was therefore sought to combine all the trades.'[1] One result was the formation of the Operative Spinners of England, Ireland, and Scotland, whose first conference, on the Isle of Man in December 1829, showed an impressive attempt to surmount the organizational complexities of united organization in three disparate regions.[2] From this basis, the National Association for the Protection of Labour brought together, for a short time, wool textile workers, mechanics, potters, miners, builders, and many other trades; 'but after it had extended about one hundred miles round this town (Manchester) a fatality came upon it that almost threatened its existence'.[3] The 'fatality' came from divisions and jealousies within the Operative Spinners itself; excessive or premature demands upon the strike funds of the Association; and Doherty's unwise attempt to move the office of the *Voice of the People* to London. But despite its failure, the National Association gave new notations to the idea of cooperation; and while the Manchester movement entered a phase of recriminations, the movement continued to flourish in the Potteries and in Yorkshire.[4] Doherty may have attempted to take the movement forward too precipitately; but he rightly saw, in the growing popularity of Owenite ideas, a means of bringing the organized workers of the country into a common movement. Thenceforward, the history of Owenism and of general unionism must be taken together.[5]

1. Hammonds, *The Town Labourer*, p. 312.

2. *Report of the Proceedings of a Delegate Meeting of Cotton Spinners, &c.* (Manchester, 1830).

3. *Union Pilot and Cooperative Intelligence*, 24 March 1832.

4. See Doherty's *Poor Man's Advocate*, 21 January 1832: 'The management [of the Association] has passed into the hands of the spirited and intelligent operatives of Yorkshire, where we hope the same spirit of jealousy and faction which, in a great measure, neutralized the best influence of the Association here, will be avoided.'

5. See especially G. D. H. Cole, *Attempts at General Union*; Postgate *The Builders' Union*, chs. 3 to 5; W. H. Warburton, *History of T.U. Organization in the Potteries* (1931), chs. 2 to 4. Some details of the 'fatality' which beset the N.A.P.L. are to be found in D. Caradog Morris, 'The History of the Labour Movement in England, 1825–51' (Ph.D. thesis, London, 1952).

The experimental communities failed, although one or two – like that at Ralahine – were partially successful. While the most ambitious ventures, like that of the builders, collapsed, some of the smaller cooperative ventures did in fact struggle on. Most of the societies and shops of the early Thirties collapsed, only to be re-born on the Rochdale model in a few years time. The Labour Exchange or Bazaar, in Gray's Inn Road, was a spectacular muddle. And yet there is nothing wholly inexplicable in the Owenite ferment. We have seen the way in which artisans, outworkers, and trade unionists all have a place within it. Its most unstable millenarial elements came largely from two sources: the benevolent well-wishers and the very poor. For the first Owenism (since it professed not to be a doctrine of class conflict or expropriation) attracted to it in some numbers philanthropic gentlemen and clergy – Godwinians, Quakers, intellectual rebels, and cranks. Some of these, like Dr King and, most notably, William Thompson, the Irish landowner and author of the *Inquiry into the Distribution of Wealth* (1824), *Labour Rewarded* (1827), and (with Anna Wheeler) *An Appeal of One-Half of the Human Race Women, against the Pretensions of the Other Half, Men, to retain them in Political and thence in Civil and Domestic Slavery* (1825), greatly enriched the movement. Others gave money without which its experiments could not have been undertaken. Nevertheless in most of the communities there is the figure of one or more cranky gentlemen, whose inexperience in the practice of any collective unit, and whose utopian experimentalism, drove the Owenite artisans to fury. To declare that men must make a new social system was one thing; to declare that men could make any kind of new system they liked was another. One artisan Socialist, Allen Davenport the former Spencean, left a somewhat sardonic picture of the London Labour Exchange:

The public mind was completely electrified by this new and extraordinary movement. ... The great assembly room, originally fitted up in the most elegant style ... the ceiling was magnificently embossed, and the ornamental parts richly gilded with gold; and capacious enough to hold two thousand individuals. But this ... was not sufficient to satisfy Mr Owen's ideas of beauty. A splendid platform was raised, on which was placed a superb and majestic organ. ... On festival nights ... the avenues were brilliantly illuminated with ... costly Grecian lamps. Ten or a dozen musical instruments were employed; and ladies and gentlemen sung to the sweetest airs. ...

The festivals were opened with a short lecture, on the subjects of social love, universal charity, and the advantages of cooperation. ... The lecture was followed by a concert, and the concert by a ball. ...

Meantime every avenue to the Exchange, during the whole week, was literally blocked up by the crowds of people that constantly assembled – some attracted by the novelty of the institution; some to watch its progress ...; some to make deposits and exchanges. ... But alas! it was soon discovered that the beautiful labour notes ... could not by any means be forced into general circulation, on which account the supply of provisions failed and a complete failure was the result of one of the most extraordinary movements that was ever attempted in this or in any other country. Still, the principles on which the system was founded remain unimpeachable, and ought to be cherished in the public mind ...

The Owen of this account is the Owen whom Peacock ridiculed in *Crotchet Castle*. Too many of the Owenite ventures overshot themselves, and ended in this sort of muddle of waste, benevolence and bad planning. If Owen was the greatest propagandist of Owenism, he was also one of its worst enemies. If the Labour Exchange had been left in the hands of such men as Lovett, the outcome might have been different.[1]

The other aspect of this millenarial instability came, more directly, out of the chiliasm of the poor. Just as at the time of the French Revolution, there is a revival of messianic movements during the excitement of the Reform Bill agitation and its aftermath. There remained many offshoots from the Southcottian movement, whose sects were now taking

1. For Thompson, see R. Pankhurst, *William Thompson* (1954). For accounts of the Labour Exchange, see R. Podmore, *Robert Owen* (1906), II; G. D. H. Cole, *Life of Robert Owen* (1930), pp. 260–66, and Lovett, op. cit., I, pp. 43 ff. Davenport's account is in *National Cooperative Leader*, 15 March 1861.

peculiar and perverted forms[1] which perhaps require more attention from the psychiatrist than the historian. But three examples of this continuing millenarial instability may be noted.

The first is the enormous following gained, between 1829 and 1836, by a crippled shoemaker, 'Zion' Ward, one of the inheritors of Joanna's mantle. Ward, formerly a zealous Methodist, had convinced himself by allegorical acrobatics, that he was the 'Shiloh' whose birth the ageing Joanna had announced. Soon afterwards, he came to believe that he was Christ (and had formerly been Satan), and that the entire Bible was an allegorical prophecy of his annunciation. (The story in the New Testament of Christ's life was a false report – if the Redeemer had come, 'why is not man redeemed?') What was unusual in Ward's paranoia (apart from its surrealist solipsism) was, first, that he buttressed it with arguments derived from Carlile and the Deists; and, second, that he directed his messianic appeal towards the dynamic of Radicalism. His following grew up in Southwark, Hackney, Walworth; in Chatham, Nottingham, Birmingham, Derby, Chesterfield, Leeds – many of these old Southcottian strongholds. At Barnsley he called forth stormy applause when he launched an attack on all the clergy 'who from the Archbishop to the least are perjured persons and the False Prophets mentioned in the Bible'. This became, more and more, the keynote of his prophecies: 'Priestcraft detected! Its Overthrow projected!' The King must 'take away the enormous salaries of the bishops, and expend the money for the public good'. He launched a weekly periodical, *The Judgement Seat of Christ* – perhaps the only occasion in which Christ has been credited with the week-by-week editorial conduct of a popular journal. Throughout the summer of 1831 he drew enormous audiences for his lectures, often filling the 2,000 places in Carlile's Rotunda:

1. See T. Fielden, *An Exposition of the Fallacies and Absurdities of that Deluded Church generally known as Christian Israelites or 'Johannas'* ... (1850), for details of the 'mysteries' of initiation and discipline at the hands of the pious sisterhood: 'the woman takes the man by his privates while in his stooping attitude ... she holds him by one hand, and gives him the stripes by the other ...'

N.B. The writings of the Messiah sold at the ... Rotunda, Black-friars Road. Preaching at the Rotunda on Thursday evenings at 7.30 and on Sunday afternoons at 3.

Early in 1832 he was found guilty of blasphemy at Derby ('The Bishops and Clergy are Religious Impostors, and as such by the Laws of England liable to Corporal Punishment' – surely risky ground to argue upon?) and with a fellow prophet imprisoned for two years. Despite illness and partial paralysis, he continued his mission until his death in 1837.[1]

The second example is that of the extraordinary 'Sir William Courtenay' (or J. N. Tom), who arrived in a startled Canterbury in 1832, wearing Eastern dress and accompanied by rumours of great wealth, received 400 freak votes in the General Election, and, after being sentenced for perjury, published his *Lion*, with the views of:

Sir William Courtenay ... King of Jerusalem, Prince of Arabia, King of the Gypsies, Defender of his King and Country ... now in the City Gaol, Canterbury.

Tom, who was a wine-merchant who originally came from Joanna Southcott's West Country, had been for a short time a Spencean. His *Lion* denounced equally all infidels and clergy:

> The Root of all Evil is in the Church.
> Lucre! Lucre!! Lucre!!!
> Heaven protect the Widow, Fatherless and Distressed.

Released from prison and lunatic asylum, he went to live in the homes of the peasantry in villages near Canterbury. In May 1838 he commenced moving around the villages, on horse-back and armed with pistols and a sword, at the head of fifty or a hundred labourers, armed with bludgeons. A loaf of bread was carried on a pole beneath a blue and white flag with a rampant lion, and Tom is supposed to have read to his followers from James, Chapter V:

Go to now, ye rich men, weep and howl for your miseries that shall come upon you. . . .
Behold, the hire of the labourers who have reaped down your fields, which is of you kept back by fraud, crieth: . . .

1. G. R. Balleine, *Past Finding Out*, ch. 11; ed. H. B. Hollingsworth, *Zion's Works* (1899), I, pp. 300 ff.; Zion Ward, *A Serious Call: or The Messiah's Address to the People of England* (1831).

The women, in particular, believed that he had miraculous powers. A labourer said later, 'he loved Sir William' –

He talked in such a manner to them, and was always reading the Scripture, that they did not look upon him as a common man and would have cheerfuly died for his sake.

Like Oastler and Stephens in the north, he denounced the New Poor Law as a breach of divine law. Eventually a constable was sent to arrest him, whom Courtenay (or Tom) killed. But the labourers did not leave him. More than fifty of them retired with him to Blean Wood, where in the dense undergrowth they awaited the military. Tom exhibited the prints of nails in his hands and feet, and announced that if he should be killed he would rise again:

This is the day of judgement – this is the first day of the Millennium – and this day I will put the crown on my head. Behold, a greater than Sampson is with you!

To his followers he promised land – perhaps 50 acres each. As the soldiers approached, he sounded a trumpet and said it was heard at Jerusalem where 10,000 were ready to obey his command. At length the battle was joined – perhaps the most desperate on English soil since 1745. Against firearms and bayonets the Kentish labourers had only bludgeons: 'I never witnessed more determination in my life,' said one witness: 'I never saw men more furious or mad-like in their attack upon us in my life.' One officer was killed, as well as Courtenay and eleven or twelve of his followers. It was a higher death-roll than Pentridge or Peterloo.[1]

The affair of Blean Wood belongs more to the older cultural patterns than the new. It was the last peasants' revolt. It is interesting that the 'ranting' Bryanites, or Bible Christians, had one of their strongholds in Kent; and at a time when men's psychic world was filled with violent images from hell-fire and Revelation, and their real world filled with poverty and oppression, it is surprising that such explosions were not more

1. P. G. Rogers, *Battle in Bossenden Wood* (1961), pp. 4, 96; *An Account of the Desperate Affray in Blean Wood* (Faversham, 1838); *Essay on the Character of Sir William Courtenay* (Canterbury, 1833); *The Lion*, 6 and 27 April 1833; *Globe*, 1 June, 10 August 1838.

frequent. The third example, which takes us closer to Owenism, is that of the extraordinary success of the Mormon propaganda in industrial districts in England in the late 1830s and 1840s. Thousands of converts were baptized in a few years, and thousands of these 'Latter-Day Saints' set sail from Liverpool to the City of Zion. The first converts were 'mainly manufacturers and other mechanics ... extremely poor, most of them not having a change of clothes to be baptized in'. Many of them, who were aided with passage money, walked and pushed hand-carts all the way from Council Bluffs to Salt Lake City.[1]

These examples all serve to emphasize that it is premature, in the 1830s, to think of the English working people as being wholly open to secular ideology. The Radical culture which we have examined was the culture of skilled men, artisans, and of some outworkers. Beneath this culture (or coexisting with it) there were more obscure levels of response, from which the charismatic leaders like Oastler and O'Connor drew some of their support. (In the Chartist movement, men like Lovett were never finally to find a common outlook and strategy with the 'unshorn chins and fustian jackets' of the north.) The instability was particularly to be found where the new rationalist and the older-style Methodist or Baptist patterns impinged upon each other, or were in conflict within the same mind. But, whereas Dissent and rationalism seem to have ordered and tamed the character of the southern artisan, in those parts where the Methodist pattern was dominant during the Wars, emotional energies seem to have been stored or repressed. Strike a spade into the working-class culture of the north at any time in the Thirties, and passion seems to spring from the ground.

Hence Owenism gathered up some of this passion also. With Owen and his lecturers prophesying that 'prosperity would be let loose', it was inevitable that they should gather around them the Children of Israel. The communitarian yearning revived, and the language of rationality was translated into that of brotherhood. As in all such phases of ferment, antinomianism also revived, with its mystical equivalents of the

1. See Armytage, op. cit., part III, ch. 7, 'Liverpool: Gateway to Zion'; P. A. M. Taylor, *Expectations Westward* (1965).

secular notions of sexual liberation held among some Owenite communitarians: 'If you love one another,' Zion Ward told young people in his 'chapels',' go together at any time without any law or ceremony.' (Ward also had a scheme for a Land Colony, 'where those who are willing to leave the world can live together as one family'.) Moreover, for the poor, Owenism touched one of their deepest responses – the dream that, somehow, by some miracle, they might once again have *some stake in the land*.

One feels that, in the 1830s, many English people felt that the structure of industrial capitalism had been only partly built, and the roof not yet set upon the structure. Owenism was only one of the gigantic, but ephemeral, impulses which caught the enthusiasm of the masses, presenting the vision of a quite different structure which might be built in a matter of years or months if only people were united and determined enough. A spirit of combination has grown up, Bronterre O'Brien wrote in 1833, whose object:

is the sublimest that can be conceived, namely – to establish for the productive classes a complete dominion over the fruits of their own industry. ... An entire change in society – a change amounting to a complete subversion of the existing 'order of the world' – is contemplated by the working classes. They aspire to be at the top instead of at the bottom of society – or rather that there should be no bottom or top at all.[1]

It is easy, in retrospect, to see this spirit as naïve or 'utopian'. But there is nothing in it which entitles us to regard it with academic superiority. The poor were desperately poor, and the prospects of a community in which they might not only blend intellectual culture with the athletic pursuits of Greece and Rome, but also *eat*, were attractive. Moreover, there was this important difference between Owenism and earlier creeds which gathered millenarial impetus. With the Owenites the Millennium was not to arrive, it was to be *made*, by their own efforts.

And this is where we may gather all the lines of Owenism together: the artisans, with their dreams of short-circuiting

1. *Poor Man's Guardian*, 19 October 1833. See M. Morris, *From Cobbett to the Chartists* (1948), p. 87.

the market-economy: the skilled workers, with their thrust towards general unionism: the philanthropic gentry, with their desire for a rational, planned society: the poor, with their dream of land or of Zion: the weavers, with their hopes of self-employment: and all of these, with their image of an equitable brotherly community, in which mutual aid would replace aggression and competition. Maurice wrote in 1838:

When the poor men say, 'we, too, will acknowledge circumstances to be all in all, we will cast away any belief in that which is invisible, this world shall be the only home in which we will dwell', the language may well appall all who hear. ... Nevertheless ... it is the 'we will' ... which imparts to the dry chips of Mr Owen's theory the semblance of vitality.[1]

This 'we will' is evidence that working people were approaching maturity, becoming conscious of their own interests and aspirations as a class. There was nothing irrational or messianic in their offering a critique of capitalism as a system, or in projecting 'utopian' ideas of an alternative and more rational system. It was not Owen who was 'mad', but, from the standpoint of the toilers, a social system in which steam and new machinery evidently displaced and degraded labourers, and in which the markets could be 'glutted' while the unshod weaver sat in his loom and the shoemaker sat in his workshop with no coat to his back. These men knew from their experience that Owen was sane when he said that:

... the present arrangement of society is the most anti-social, impolitic, and irrational that can be devised; that under its influence all the superior and valuable qualities of human nature are repressed from infancy, and that the most unnatural means are used to bring out the most injurious propensities ...[2]

So far from being backward-looking in its outlook, Owenism was the first of the great social doctrines to grip the imagination of the masses in this period, which commenced with an acceptance of the enlarged productive powers of steam and the mill. What was at issue was not the machine so much as the

1. F. D. Maurice, *The Kingdom of Christ*, cited in Armytage, op. cit., p. 85.   2. Owen, op. cit., p. 269.

profit-motive; not the size of the industrial enterprise but the control of the social capital behind it. The building craftsmen and small masters, who resented control and the lion's share of the profits passing to master-builders or contractors, did not suppose that the solution lay in a multitude of petty entrepreneurs.[1] Rather, they wished the cooperation of skills involved in building to be reflected in cooperative social control. It is ironic that a movement which is sometimes supposed to have drawn much of its strength from the 'petit-bourgeois' should have made more earnest attempts to pioneer new forms of community life than any in our history. 'All the fervour and earnestness of the early Cooperative Societies,' Holyoake wrote many years later, 'was ... about communistic life. The "Socialists" ... hoped to found voluntary, self-supporting, self-controlled industrial cities, in which the wealth created was to be equitably shared by all those whose labour produced it.'[2] Those who see, in the failure of these experiments, only a proof of their folly may perhaps be too confident that 'history' has shown them to be a dead end.

What was irrational in Owenism (or 'utopian' in its common pejorative meaning) was the impatience of the propaganda, the faith in the multiplication of reason by lectures and tracts, the inadequate attention to the means. Above all, there was Owen's fatal evasion of the realities of political power, and his attempt to by-pass the question of property-rights. Cooperative Socialism was simply to displace capitalism, painlessly and without any encounter, by example, by education, and by growing up within it from its own villages, workshops, and stores. Cooperation has no 'levelling tendency', the *Economist* was anxious to reassure its readers. Its purpose was to 'elevate all'; its wealth would not be taken from existing possessors but would be 'newly produced wealth'.[3] 'We ... do not come here as levellers,' declared a Warrington clergyman: 'We do not come here to deprive any human being of any of his or her property.'[4] In 1834, at the furthest point in the Owenite movement, a 'Charter of the Rights of Humanity' declared:

1. See Postgate, op. cit., pp. 72–3.   2. See S. Pollard, op. cit., p. 90.
3. *Economist*, 11 August 1821.   4. A. E. Musson, op. cit., p. 126.

The present property of all individuals, acquired and possessed by the usages and practices of old society, to be held sacred until ... it can no longer be of any use or exchangeable value ...[1]

This was the vitiating weakness of Owenism. Even the little group of Spencean Philanthropists, at the end of the Wars, could see that Socialism entailed the expropriation of the great landowners. 'It is childish,' Spence had written in his *Restorer of Society to its Natural State* (1800):

... to expect ever to see Small Farms again, or ever to see anything else than the utmost screwing and grinding of the poor, till you quite overturn the present system of Landed Property. For they have got more completely into the spirit and power of oppression now than was ever known before. ... Therefore anything short of total Destruction of the power of these Samsons will not do ... nothing less than the complete Extermination of the present system of holding Land ... will ever bring the World again to a state worth living in.

It was this which aroused the particular fury of Britain's rulers, who held the mild Thomas Evans, author of *Christian Polity*, without trial for a year, at a time when Lord Sidmouth was discussing the proposals of the enlightened Mr Owen. In that year one of the last Spenceans, a coloured tailor called Robert Wedderburn, promoted a little ill-printed journal; *The 'Forlorn Hope'*:

Mr Owen ... will find that the lower classes are pretty well convinced that he is a tool to the land-holders and Ministers ...[2]

The Spenceans and old Radicals of 1817 proved to be wrong in their estimation of Owen; and Spence's and Evans's pre-occupation with agrarian Socialism was inadequate for industrial England. But the Spenceans were at least willing to pose the problems of ownership and class power.

It was because Owen refused to look squarely at either that he was able to remain quite indifferent to political Radicalism, and to lead the movement frequently up illusory paths. For years the cooperative movement continued with this coexistence of philanthropists and working-class Radicals. By 1832, how-

1. O'Brien, op. cit., p. 437.

2. *The 'Forlorn Hope', or a Call to the Supine*, 4 and 11 October 1817.

ever, men like Hetherington, O'Brien, and James Watson had quite different emphases, and were rejecting Owen's dismissal of all political means. Owenism was for them always a great and constructive influence. They had learned from it to see capitalism, not as a collection of discrete events, but as a *system*. They had learned to project an alternative, utopian system of mutuality. They had passed beyond Cobbett's nostalgia for an older world and had acquired the confidence to plan the new. They had gained an understanding of the importance of education, and of the force of environmental conditioning. They had learned, from Thompson and Anna Wheeler, to assert new claims for the rights of women. Henceforward, nothing in capitalist society seemed given and inevitable, the product of 'natural' law. This is all expressed in the Last Will and Testament of Henry Hetherington:

These are my views and feelings in quitting an existence that has been chequered with the plagues and pleasures of a competitive, scrambling, selfish system; a system by which the moral and social aspirations of the noblest human beings are nullified by incessant toil and physical deprivations; by which, indeed, all men are trained to be either slaves, hypocrites, or criminals. Hence my ardent attachment to the principles of that great and good man — ROBERT OWEN.

V. 'A SORT OF MACHINE'

'The present mischief these two men [Owen and Hodgskin] have in some respects done is incalculable,' noted Francis Place.[1] The 'mischief' is written across the years 1831–5. And at this point the limits of this study have been reached; for there is a sense in which the working class is no longer in the making, but has been made. To step over the threshold, from 1832 to 1833, is to step into a world in which the working-class presence can be felt in every county in England, and in most fields of life.

The new class consciousness of working people may be viewed from two aspects. On the one hand, there was a consciousness of the identity of interests between working men of the most diverse occupations and levels of attainment, which

1. Add. MSS. 27,791 f. 270.

was embodied in many institutional forms, and which was expressed on an unprecedented scale in the general unionism of 1830–34. This consciousness and these institutions were only to be found in fragmentary form in the England of 1780.

On the other hand, there was a consciousness of the identity of the interests of the working class, or 'productive classes' as against those of other classes; and within this there was maturing the claim for an alternative *system*. But the final definition of this class consciousness was, in large part, the consequence of the response to working-class strength of the middle class. The line was drawn, with extreme care, in the franchise qualifications of 1832. It had been the peculiar feature of English development that, where we would expect to find a growing middle-class reform movement, with a working-class tail, only later succeeded by an independent agitation of the working class, in fact this process was reversed. The example of the French Revolution had initiated three simultaneous processes: a panic-struck counter-revolutionary response on the part of the landed and commercial aristocracy; a withdrawal on the part of the industrial bourgeoisie and an accommodation (on favourable terms) with the *status quo*; and a rapid radicalization of the popular reform movement until the Jacobin cadres who were tough enough to survive through the Wars were in the main little masters, artisans, stockingers and croppers, and other working men. The twenty-five years after 1795 may be seen as the years of the long counter-revolution, and in consequence the Radical movement remained largely working-class in character, with an advanced democratic populism as its theory. But the triumph of such a movement was scarcely to be welcomed by the mill-owners, iron-masters and manufacturers. Hence the peculiarly repressive and anti-egalitarian ideology of the English middle classes (Godwin giving way to Bentham, Bentham giving way to Malthus, M'Culloch, and Dr Ure, and these giving rise to Baines, Macaulay and Edwin Chadwick). Hence also the fact that the mildest measure of reform, to meet the evident irrationalities of Old Corruption, was actually *delayed*, by the resistance of the old order on the one hand, and the timidity of the manufacturers on the other.

The Reform Bill crisis of 1832 – or, to be more accurate, the successive crises from early in 1831 until the 'days of May' in 1832 – illustrates these theses at almost every point. The agitation arose from 'the people' and rapidly displayed the most astonishing consensus of opinion as to the imperative necessity for 'reform'. Viewed from one aspect, England was without any doubt passing through a crisis in these twelve months in which revolution was possible. The rapidity with which the agitation extended indicates the degree to which experience in every type of constitutional and quasi-legal agitation was present among the people:

The systematic way in which the people proceeded, their steady perseverance, their activity and skill astounded the enemies of reform. Meetings of almost every description of persons were held in cities, towns, and parishes; by journeymen tradesmen in their clubs, and by common workmen who had no trade clubs or associations of any kind . . .

So Place wrote of the autumn of 1830, adding (of February 1831):

. . . yet there was not even the smallest communication between places in the same neighbourhood; each portion of the people appeared to understand what ought to be done . . . [1]

'The great majority' of those who attended the swelling demonstrations, the King's private Secretary complained in March 1831 to Grey, 'are of the very lowest class.' The enormous demonstrations, rising to above 100,000 in Birmingham and London in the autumn of 1831 and May 1832, were overwhelmingly composed of artisans and working men.[2]

'We did not cause the excitement about reform,' Grey wrote a little peevishly to the King, in March 1831: 'We found it in full vigour when we came into office.' And, viewed from another aspect, we can see why throughout these crisis months a revolution was in fact improbable. The reason is to be found in the very strength of the working-class Radical movement; the skill with which the middle-class leaders, Brougham, *The Times*, the *Leeds Mercury* both used this threat of working-

1. Add. MSS 27,789. For an example of this facility in spontaneous organization, see Prentice, op. cit., pp. 408–10.
2. See Jephson, *The Platform*, II, ch. 15.

class force, and negotiated a line of retreat acceptable to all but the most die-hard defenders of the *ancien régime*; and the awareness on the part of the Whigs and the least intransigent Tories that, while Brougham and Baines were only blackmailing them, nevertheless if a compromise was not come to, the middle-class reformers might no longer be able to hold in check the agitation at their backs.

The industrial bourgeoisie desired, with heart and soul, that a revolution should not take place, since they knew that on the very day of its commencement there would be a dramatic process of radicalization, in which Huntite, trade unionist, and Owenite leaders would command growing support in nearly all the manufacturing centres. 'Threats of a "revolution" are employed by the middle classes and petty masters,' wrote the *Poor Man's Guardian*. But –

a violent revolution is not only beyond the means of those who threaten it, but is to them their greatest object of alarm; for they know that such a revolution can only be effected by the poor and despised millions, who, if excited to the step, might use it for their own advantage, as well as for that of themselves, who would thus … have their dear rights of property endangered: be assured that a violent revolution is their greatest dread …[1]

The middle-class reformers fought skilfully on both fronts. On the one hand *The Times* came forward as the actual organizer of mass agitation: 'We trust there is not a county, town, or village in the United Kingdom which will not meet and petition for a reform. …' It even urged upon the people 'the solemn duty of forming themselves into political societies throughout the whole realm'. It supported – as did Edward Baines, before cheering throngs, at Leeds – measures of enforcement which led directly on towards revolution: the run on the Banks, refusal to pay taxes, and the arming of members of Political Unions. On the other hand, the riots at Nottingham, Derby and Bristol in October 1831 underlined the dual function of the Political Unions on the Birmingham model:

These Unions were to be for the promotion of the cause of reform, for the protection of life and property against the detailed but

1. October 1831.

irregular outrages of the mob, as well as for the maintenance of *other* great interests against the systematic violences of an oligarchy ...[1]

These middle-class incendiaries carried in their knapsacks a special constable's baton. There were occasions when the Tories themselves hoped to outwit them, by encouraging the independent working-class reform movement to display itself in a form so alarming that Brougham and Baines would run to Old Corruption for protection. When the National Union of the Working Classes proposed to call a demonstration in London for manhood suffrage, and in resistance to the Whig Reform Bill, the King himself wrote (4 November 1831):

His Majesty is by no means displeased that the measures contemplated by the meeting in question are so violent, and ... objectionable, as he trusts that the manifestation of such intentions and such purposes may afford the opportunity ... of checking the progress of the Political Unions ...[2]

Throughout the country middle-class and working-class reformers manoeuvred for control of the movement. In the earliest stages, until the summer of 1831, the middle-class Radicals held the advantage. Seven years before Wooler had closed the *Black Dwarf* with a sadly disillusioned final Address. There was (in 1824) no 'public devotedly attached to the cause of parliamentary reform'. Where hundreds and thousands had once clamoured for reform, it now seemed to him that they had only 'clamoured for bread'; the orators and journalists of 1816–20 had only been 'bubbles thrown up in the fermentation of society'.[3] Many of the working-class leaders of the late 1820s shared his disillusion, and accepted the anti-political stance of their master, Owen. It was not until the summer of 1830, with the rural labourers' 'revolt' and the July Revolution in France, that the tide of popular interest began to turn

1. *The Times*, 1 December 1830, 27 October 1831; see Jephson, op. cit., II, pp. 69, 107. During the Bristol riots, the authorities were forced to call in the leaders of the Bristol Political Union to restore order. See *Bristol Mercury*, 1 November 1831; Prentice, op. cit., p. 401.

2. Cited in Jephson, op. cit., II, p. 111. The demonstration of the National Union was, in fact, pronounced seditious and prohibited. It was a risk too great to take.

3. Final Address, prefacing *Black Dwarf*, XII (1824).

back to political agitation. And thenceforward the insanely stubborn last-ditch resistance of the die-hards (the Duke of Wellington, the Lords, the Bishops) to *any* measure of reform dictated a strategy (which was exploited to the full by the middle-class Radicals) by which popular agitation was brought to bear behind Grey and Russell, and in support of a Bill from which the majority had nothing to gain.

Thus the configuration of forces of 1816–20 (and, indeed, of 1791–4), in which the popular demand for Reform was identified with Major Cartwright's platform of manhood suffrage, was broken up. 'If any persons suppose that this Reform will lead to ulterior measures,' Grey declared in the House in November 1831:

they are mistaken; for there is no one more decided against annual parliaments, universal suffrage, and the ballot, than I am. My object is not to favour, but to put an end to such hopes and projects.

This was clearly enough seen by the older Radicals, the majority of whose articulate spokesmen poured scorn on the Whig Bill until the final 'days of May'. 'It mattered not to him,' declared a Macclesfield Radical, 'whether he was governed by a boroughmonger, or a whoremonger, or a cheese-monger, if the system of monopoly and corruption was still to be upheld.'[1] Hunt, from his place as Member for Preston (1830–32), maintained the same propositions, in only slightly more decorous language. George Edmonds, the witty and courageous Radical schoolmaster, who had chaired Birmingham's first great post-war demonstration on Newhall Hill (January 1817), declared:

I am not a house-holder. – I can, on a push, be a musket-holder. The nothing-but-the-Bill does not recognize George Edmonds as a citizen! – George Edmonds scorns the nothing-but-the-Bill, except as cut the first at the national robber.[2]

This was the position also of the élite of London's Radical artisans, enrolled in the National Union of Working Classes and Others, whose weekly debates in the Rotunda in 1831 and

1. *Poor Man's Guardian*, 10 December 1831.

2. G. Edmonds, *The English Revolution* (1831), p. 5. Edmonds went on to play an active part in the Chartist movement.

1832 were reported in Hetherington's *Poor Man's Guardian* – undoubtedly the finest working-class weekly which had (until that time) been published in Britain. The debates were attended by Hetherington himself (when not in prison), William Lovett, James Watson, John Gast, the brilliant and ill-fated Julian Hibbert, and old William Benbow (the former colleague of Bamford and of Mitchell), now pressing his proposal for a 'Grand National Holiday', or month's general strike, in the course of which the productive classes would assume control of the nation's government and resources.[1] The debates increasingly turned upon the definition of class. William Carpenter, who shared with Hetherington the honour of initiating the struggle for the 'unstamped' press, offered a dissentient opinion. The Whig Bill ought to be supported, as a 'wedge'. He complained that the *Poor Man's Guardian* used the words 'middle men' and 'middle class' as 'convertible terms', whereas the middle classes 'are not only *not* a class of persons having interests different from your own. They are the *same* class; they are, generally speaking, *working* or *labouring* men.'[2] Throughout the entire crisis the controversy continued. After the Bill had passed, the *Poor Man's Guardian* recorded its conclusion:

The promoters of the Reform Bill projected it, not with a view to subvert, or even remodel our aristocratic institutions, but to consolidate them by a reinforcement of sub-aristocracy from the middle-classes. ... The only difference between the Whigs and the Tories is this – the Whigs would give the shadow to preserve the substance; the Tories would not give the shadow, because stupid as they are, the millions will not stop at shadows but proceed onwards to realities.[3]

It is problematical how far the militant Owenites of the Rotunda represented any massive body of working-class opinion. They commenced by representing only the intelligentsia

1. See A. J. C. Rüter, 'Benbow's Grand National Holiday', *International Review of Social History* (Leiden), I, 1936, pp. 217 et seq.

2. W. Carpenter, *An Address to the Working Classes on the Reform Bill* (October 1831). See also the ensuing controversy in the *Poor Man's Guardian*.

3. *Poor Man's Guardian*, 25 October 1832; see A. Briggs, *The Age of Improvement*, p. 258.

of the artisans. But they gathered influence most rapidly; by October 1831 they were able to organize a massive demonstration, perhaps 70,000 strong, many wearing the white scarves emblematic of manhood suffrage; perhaps 100,000 joined their demonstrations against the National Fast in March 1832. Place regarded the Rotundists (many of whom he wrote off as 'atrocious') as constituting the greatest of threats to the middle-class strategy, and much of his manuscript history of the Reform Bill crisis (upon which historians have placed too much reliance) is devoted to the unscrupulous manoeuvres by which he sought to limit their influence, and displace it by that of his rival National Political Union. The Duke of Wellington himself saw the contest as one between the Establishment and the Rotunda, which he compared to two armies *'en présence'*. It confused his military mind very much to reflect that he could place no river between the armies, with adequate sentinels and posts on the bridges. The enemy was installed at sensitive points within his own camp.[1]

The procession of October 1831, however, was mainly composed (it seems) of 'shopkeepers and superior artisans'. And while the numbers called out were impressive, they compare poorly with the even greater demonstrations at Birmingham, drawn from a smaller population. It would seem that, while the London artisans had at last succeeded in building a cohesive and highly articulate leadership, there remained a wide gulf between them and the mass of London labourers, and workers in the dishonourable trades. (This problem was to recur time and again in the history of London Chartism.) The position was caricatured in the pages of a scurrilous and alarmist pamphlet by Edward Gibbon Wakefield. He saw the Rotundists as 'Desperadoes' and idealists, whose danger lay in the fact that they might unleash the destructive energies of the criminal classes, 'the helots of society', who were crammed in the lanes and alleys off Orchard Street, Westminster, or Whitechapel. Here were the thousands of unpolitical (but dangerous) 'coster-

1. See J. R. M. Butler, *The Passing of the Great Reform Bill* (1914), pp. 292–3, 350; Add. MSS., 27,791 f. 51; Memorandum on 'Measures to be taken to put an End to the Seditious Meetings at the Rotunda', *Wellington Despatches*, second series (1878), VII, p. 353.

mongers, drovers, slaughterers of cattle, knackers, dealers in dead bodies and dogs' meat, cads, brick-makers, chimney-sweepers, nightmen, scavengers, &c.' His attitude to the Owenite Socialists of the Rotunda was ambiguous. On the one hand, they were mostly 'sober men, who maintain themselves by industry' – men plainly marked off by superior talents from the dangerous classes. On the other hand, many were 'loose single men living here and there in lodgings, who might set fire to London without anxiety for helpless beings at home':

In manner they are rather gentle than rough; but touch one of them on his tender point; – only say that you think the stimulus of competition indispensable to the production of wealth; – and he will either turn from you in scorn, or ... tell you, with flashing eyes, that you are paid by the Government to talk nonsense. Any thing like a compromise is what annoys them even more than decided opposition.

Many, he said (with some truth), 'are provided with arms':

If an insurrection of the London populace should take place, they will be found at the most dangerous posts, leading the thieves and rabble, pointing out the most effectual measures, and dying, if the lot fall on them, with cries of defiance.

'These will be the fighting men of our revolution, if we must have one.'[1]

The picture is overdrawn; but it is not wholly without truth.[2] The danger, from the point of view of authority (whether Whig or Tory), lay in a possible conjunction between the artisan Socialists and the 'criminal classes'. But the unskilled masses in London inhabited another world from that of the artisans – a world of extreme hardship, illiteracy, very widespread demoralization, and disease, which was dramatized by the cholera outbreak of the winter of 1831–2. Here we have all the classic problems, the hand-to-mouth insecurity, of a

1. E. G. Wakefield, *Householders in Danger from the Populace* (n.d. October 1831?).
2. While Lovett and his circle believed in the maximum of pressure short of physical force (and maintained some relations with Place), others, including Benbow and Hibbert, were preparing for an armed struggle.

metropolitan city swollen with immigrants in a period of rapid population-growth.[1]

The unskilled had no spokesmen and no organizations (apart from friendly societies). They were as likely to have followed the lead of a gentleman as of an artisan. And yet the severity of the political crisis which commenced in October 1831 was sufficient to crack the crust of fatalism, deference, and need, within which their lives were enclosed. The riots of that month in Derby, the sacking of Nottingham Castle, the extensive riots at Bristol – all were indicative of a deep disturbance at the foundations of society, which observers anxiously expected to be followed by the uprising of London's East End.

The Birmingham Political Union was an acceptable model, which *The Times* itself could commend, because the local industrial context favoured a reform movement of the masses which still remained firmly under middle-class control. The history of Birmingham Radicalism is significantly different from that of the north Midlands and the north. There was no basis in its small-scale industries for Luddism, and the 'father' of the Political Unions, Thomas Attwood, first gained public prominence when he led, in 1812, a united agitation of the masters and artisans against the Orders in Council. There were undoubtedly groups of 'physical force' Radicals in the Black Country in 1817–20, but – whether by good fortune or good judgement – they were never exposed by any abortive movement like the Pentridge and Grange Moor affairs.[2] As Professor Briggs has shown, Thomas Attwood was able in 1830 to 'har-

1. It is interesting to speculate upon how far Place's frequent assertions as to the improvement in the manners and morals of the London populace expressed the truth, or merely the widening gulf between the artisans and unskilled, the narrowing of Place's own circle of experience, and the pushing of poverty out of the City's centre towards the east and the south. On the whole problem of metropolitan growth and demoralization (and its 'biological' foundation), see L. Chevalier, *Classes Laborieuses et Classes Dangereuses à Paris Pendant La Première Moitié Du XIXème Siècle* (Paris, 1958), which suggests many new lines of research into London conditions.

2. It is difficult to discount Oliver's circumstantial account of Birmingham contracts (Narrative in H.O. 40.9). See also evidence in H.O. 40.3 and 6.

monize and unite' the diverse 'materials of discontent' because the Industrial Revolution in Birmingham had 'multiplied the number of producing units rather than added to the scale of existing enterprises'. There had been little displacement of skilled labour by machinery; the numberless small workshops meant that the social gradients shelved more gently, and the artisan might still rise to the status of a small master; in times of economic recession masters and journeymen were afflicted alike.[1] Hence, class antagonism was more muted than in Manchester, Newcastle, and Leeds. Throughout the Reform Bill crisis, Attwood controlled the Birmingham Union with 'such a show of good-nature' (O'Brien later recalled) 'that the Brummagem operatives seemed really to believe that they would be *virtually*, though not actually, represented in the 'reformed' parliament'. And, in a tribute impressive from so stern a critic, O'Brien added:

> To this body, more than to any other, is confessedly due the triumph (such as it was) of the Reform Bill. Its well-ordered proceedings, extended organization, and immense assemblages of people, at critical periods of its progress, rendered the measure irresistible.[2]

In such centres as Leeds, Manchester, and Nottingham the position of the middle-class reformers was very much more uneasy. At Manchester (as in London) rival political Unions coexisted, and from October 1831 onwards the manhood suffrage Union made the running. At Bolton in the same month the rejection of the Bill by the House of Lords resulted in a split in the Political Union, the largest (manhood suffrage) section organizing a demonstration, 6,000 strong, behind the banners: 'Down with the Bishops!', 'No Peers.'[3] In the

---

1. See Cobbett's angry comment: 'Do you imagine that the great manufacturers, and merchants, and bankers are crying for REFORM, because they have been converted to a love of *popular rights*! Bah! . . . [Financial causes] have made them raise their wages; these they cannot pay and *pay tithes and taxes* also. . . . Therefore, are they *reformers*; therefore, they throw their lusty arms around the waist of the Goddess': *Political Register*, 17 October 1831.

2. *Destructive*, 2 February and 9 March 1833; A. Briggs, 'The Background of the Parliamentary Reform Movement in Three English Cities', *Camb. Hist. Journal*, 1952, p. 293, and *The Age of Improvement*, p. 247.

3. W. Brimelow, *Political History of Bolton* (1882), I, p. 111.

Midlands and the north such incidents were repeated dozens of times. 'Walk into any lane or public-house, where a number of operatives are congregated together,' wrote Doherty in January 1832:

and listen, for ten minutes, to the conversation ... In at least seven out of every ten cases, the subjects of debate will be found to bear upon the appalling question of *whether it would be more advantageous to attack the lives or the property of the rich?* [1]

Indeed in the winter of 1831–2 the ridicule poured upon the Bill and upon its attendant proceedings in the *Poor Man's Guardian* takes on a somewhat academic air. No doubt the Rotundists were right to designate the Bill as a trap (and as a betrayal of the Radical movement). But the well-nigh neolithic obstinacy with which Old Corruption resisted *any* reform led on to a situation in which the nation stepped, swiftly and without premeditation, on to the threshold of revolution. Belatedly, the *Poor Man's Guardian* adjusted its tactics, publishing as a special supplement extracts from Colonel Macerone's *Defensive Instructions for the People* (a manual in street-fighting).[2] Throughout the 'eleven days of England's apprehension and turmoil' which preceded the final passage of the Bill through the Lords in May, Francis Place held his breath. On the evening of the day when it passed, he returned home and noted:

We were within a moment of general rebellion, and had it been possible for the Duke of Wellington to have formed an administration the Thing and the people would have been at issue.

There would have been 'Barricadoes of the principal towns – stopping circulation of paper money'; if a revolution had commenced, it 'would have been the act of the whole people to a greater extent than any which had ever before been accomplished'.[3]

In the autumn of 1831 and in the 'days of May' Britain was within an ace of a revolution which, once commenced, might well (if we consider the simultaneous advance in cooperative and trade union theory) have prefigured, in its rapid radical-

1. *Poor Man's Advocate*, 21 January 1832.
2. *Poor Man's Guardian*, 11 April 1832.
3. Add. MSS., 27, 795 ff. 26–7.

ization, the revolutions of 1848 and the Paris Commune. J. R.M. Butler's *The Passing of the Great Reform Bill* gives us some sense of the magnitude of the crisis; but his study is weakened by an insufficient awareness of the potential openness of the whole situation, evinced in such comments as this (upon the National Union of the Working Classes):

... it disgusted sensible people ... by its arrogant silliness, as when the Bethnal Green branch petitioned the King to abolish the House of Lords, or the Finsbury section urged the Commons to confiscate the estates of the 199 peers ...[1]

Some assessment less complacent than this is required. The fact that revolution did not occur was due, in part, to the deep constitutionalism of that part of the Radical tradition[2] of which Cobbett (urging the acceptance of half a loaf) was the spokesman; and in part to the skill of the middle-class Radicals in offering exactly that compromise which might, not weaken, but strengthen both the State and property-rights against the working-class threat.

The Whig leaders saw their rôle as being that of finding the means to 'attach numbers to property and good order'. 'It is of the utmost importance,' Grey said, 'to associate the middle with the higher orders of society in the love and support of the institutions and government of the country.'[3] The extreme care with which this line was drawn is evinced by a survey undertaken by Baines in 1831, to discover 'the numbers and respectability of the £10 householders in Leeds'. The results were communicated to Lord John Russell in a letter which should be taken as one of the classic documents of the Reform Bill crisis. Baines's pioneering psephological canvassers –

1. Butler, op. cit., p. 303.

2. See Gladstone's comment: 'I held forth to a working man ... on the established text, reform was revolution ... I said, "Why, look at the revolutions in foreign countries", meaning of course France and Belgium. The man looked hard at me and said ... "Damn all foreign countries, what has old England to do with foreign countries"; This is not the only time that I have received an important lesson from a humble source.' J. Morley, *Life of Gladstone* (1908), I, p. 54.

3. See A. Briggs, 'The Language of "Class" in Early Nineteenth-Century England', op. cit., p. 56.

stated *unanimously*, that the £10 qualification did not admit to the exercise of the elective franchise a single person who might not safely and wisely be enfranchised: that they were surprised to find how comparatively few would be allowed to vote.

In answer to Russell's enquiry as to the proportion which £10 householders bore to the rest of the population, the canvassers reported:

... in the parts occupied chiefly by the working classes, not one householder in fifty would have a vote. In the streets principally occupied by shops, almost every householder had a vote. ... In the township of Holbeck, containing 11,000 inhabitants, chiefly of the working classes, but containing several mills, dye-houses, public-houses, and respectable dwellings, there are only 150 voters. ... Out of 140 householders, heads of families, working in the mill of Messrs Marshall and Co, there are *only two* who will have votes. ... Out of 160 or 170 householders in the mill of Messrs O. Willan and Sons, Holbeck, there is *not one* vote. Out of about 100 householders in the employment of Messrs Taylor and Words-worth, machine-makers, – the highest class of mechanics, – *only one* has a vote. It appeared that of the working classes not more than one in fifty would be enfranchised by the Bill.

Even this estimate would appear to have been excessive. Returns made to the Government in May 1832 showed that in Leeds (population, 124,000) 355 'workmen' would be admitted to the franchise, of whom 143 'are clerks, warehousemen, over-lookers, &c.' The remaining 212 were in a privileged status, earning between 30s. and 40s. a week.[1]

Such surveys no doubt reassured the Cabinet, which had meditated raising the £10 franchise qualification to £15. 'The great body of the people,' Place wrote, 'were self-assured that either the Reform Bills would be passed by Parliament, or that they should, by their own physical force, obtain much more than they contained, if they were rejected ...'[2] It is the threat of this 'much more' which hung over both Tories and Whigs in 1832, and which enabled that accommodation to be made, between landed and industrial wealth, between privilege and money, which has been an enduring configuration of English

1. Baines, *Life of Edward Baines*, pp. 157–9.
2. Add. MSS., 27790.

Upon the banners of Baines and Cobden were not
nd *liberté* (still less *fraternité*) but 'Free Trade' and
ament'. The rhetoric of Brougham was that of
, security, interest. 'If there is a mob,' Brougham said
eech on the second reading of the Reform Bill,

there is ...e people also. I speak now of the middle classes – of those
hundreds of thousands of respectable persons – the most numerous
and by far the most wealthy order in the community, for if all your
Lordships' castles, manors, rights of warren and rights of chase,
with all your broad acres, were brought to the hammer, and sold
at fifty years' purchase, the price would fly up and kick the beam
when counterpoised by the vast and solid riches of those middle
classes, who are also the genuine depositaries of sober, rational,
intelligent, and honest English feeling. ... Rouse not, I beseech
you, a peace-loving, but a resolute people. ... As your friend, as
the friend of my order, as the friend of my country, as the faithful
servant of my sovereign, I counsel you to assist with your uttermost
efforts in preserving the peace, and upholding and perpetuating
the Constitution ...[1]

Divested of its rhetoric, the demands of the middle-class
Radicals were voiced by Baines, when the Bill had been
passed:

The fruits of Reform are to be gathered. Vast commercial and
agricultural monopolies are to be abolished. The Church is to be
reformed. ... Close corporations are to be thrown open. Retrenchment and economy are to be enforced. The shackles of the Slave
are to be broken.[2]

The demands of working-class Radicalism were less clearly
formulated. A minimum political programme may be cited
from the manifesto of Hetherington's *Republican*:

Extirpation of the Fiend Aristocracy; Establishment of a Republic,
viz. Democracy by Representatives elected by Universal Suffrage;
Extinction of hereditary offices, titles and distinctions; Abolition
of the ... law of primogeniture; ... Cheap and rapid administration
of justice; Abolition of the Game Laws; Repeal of the diabolical
imposts on Newspapers ...; emancipation of our fellow-citizens
the Jews; Introduction of Poor Laws into Ireland; Abolition of the

1. See J. R. M. Butler, op. cit., pp. 284–5.   2. Baines, op. cit., p. 167.

Punishment of Death for offences against property; Appropriation of the Revenues of the 'Fathers in God', the Bishops, towards maintenance of the Poor; Abolition of Tithes; Payment of every Priest or Minister by his Sect; The 'National Debt' not the debt of the Nation; Discharge of the Machinery of Despotism, the Soldiers; Establishment of a National Guard.

This is the old programme of Jacobinism, with little development from the 1790s. (The first principle of a declaration of the National Union, drawn up by Lovett and James Watson, in November 1831, was: 'All property (honestly acquired) to be sacred and inviolable.')[1] But around this 'much more' other demands accrued, according to the grievances foremost in different districts and industries. In Lancashire, Doherty and his supporters argued that 'universal suffrage means nothing more than a power given to every man to protect his own labour from being devoured by others'.[2] The Owenites, the factory reformers, and 'physical force' revolutionaries like the irrepressible William Benbow were pressing still further demands. But, in the event, the terms of the contest were successfully confined within the limits desired by Brougham and Baines. It was (as Shelley had foreseen in 1822) a contest between 'blood and gold'; and in its outcome, blood compromised with gold to keep out the claims of *égalité*. For the years between the French Revolution and the Reform Bill had seen the formation of a middle-class 'class consciousness', more conservative, more wary of the large idealist causes (except, perhaps, those of other nations), more narrowly self-interested than in any other industrialized nation. Henceforward, in Victorian England, the middle-class Radical and the idealist intellectual were forced to take sides between the 'two nations'. It is a matter of honour that there were many individuals who preferred to be known as Chartists or Republicans rather than as special constables. But such men – Wakley, Frost of Newport, Duncombe, Oastler, Ernest Jones, John Fielden, W. P. Roberts, and on to Ruskin and William Morris – were always disaffected individuals or intellectual 'voices'. They represent in no sense the ideology of the middle class.

What Edward Baines had done, in his correspondence with

1. See Lovett, op. cit., I, p. 74.   2. A. Briggs, op. cit., p. 66.

Russell, was to offer a definition of class of almost arithmetical exactitude. In 1832 the line was drawn in social consciousness by the franchise qualifications, with the crudity of an indelible pencil. Moreover, these years found also a theorist of stature to define the working-class predicament. It appears almost inevitable that he should have been an Irish intellectual, uniting in himself a hatred of the English Whigs with the experience of English ultra-Radicalism and Owenite Socialism. James 'Bronterre' O'Brien (1805–64), the son of an Irish wine merchant, and a distinguished graduate of Trinity College, Dublin, arrived in London in 1829 'to study Law and Radical Reform':

My friends sent me to study law; I took to radical reform on my own account ... While I have made no progress at all in law, I have made immense progress in radical reform. So much so, that were a professorship of radical reform to be instituted tomorrow in King's College (no very probable event by the way), I think I would stand candidate ... I feel as though every drop of blood in my veins was radical blood ...[1]

After editing the *Midlands Representative* during the Reform Bill crisis, he moved to London and assumed the editorship of the *Poor Man's Guardian*.

'We foresaw,' he wrote of the Reform Bill, 'that its effect would be to detach from the working classes a large portion of the middle ranks, who were *then* more inclined to act with the people than with the aristocracy that excluded them.'[2] And in his Introduction to Buonarotti's history of the Conspiracy of Equals, he drew a parallel: 'The Girondists would extend the franchise to the small middlemen (just as our English Whigs did by the Reform Bill) in order the more effectively to keep down the working classes.' 'Of all governments, a government of the middle classes is the most grinding and remorseless.'[3]

It was a theme to which he often returned. His anger was refreshed by each new action of the Whig administration – the

1. *Bronterre's National Reformer*, 7 January 1837. O'Brien in fact was qualified in law at the Bar in Dublin.

2. *Destructive*, 9 March 1833.

3. O'Brien, op. cit., pp. xv, xx. For O'Brien, see G. D. H. Cole, *Chartist Portraits* (1941), ch. 9; T. Rothstein, *From Chartism to Labourism* (1929), pp. 93–123; Beer, op. cit., II, pp. 17–22.

Irish Coercion Bill, the rejection of the 10 Hour Bill, the attack on the trades unions, the Poor Law Amendment Act. 'Previously to the passing of the Reform Bill,' he wrote in 1836:

the middle orders were supposed to have some community of feeling with the labourers. That delusion has passed away. It barely survived the Irish Coercion Bill, it vanished completely with the enactment of the Starvation Law. No working man will ever again expect justice, morals or mercy at the hands of a profit-mongering legislature.[1]

A refugee from a middle-class culture himself, he took especial pleasure in writing of his own class in terms which imitated its own drawing-room small-talk about the servant classes: 'The pursuits and habits [of the middle classes] are essentially debasing. Their life is necessarily a life of low cunning and speculation . . .':

These two classes never had, and never will have, any community of interest. It is the workman's interest to do as little work, and to get as much for it as possible. It is the middleman's interest to get as much work as he can out of the man, and to give as little for it. Here then are their respective interests as directly opposed to each other as two fighting bulls.

And he sought, with considerable genius, to twist together the tradition of ultra-Radicalism with that of Owenism, into a revolutionary Socialism, whose goals were political revolution, the expropriation of the propertied classes, and a network of Owenite communities:

We must have what Southey calls 'a revolution of revolutions'; such an one as Robespierre and St Just projected in France in the beginning of 1794; that is to say, a complete subversion of the institutions by which wealth is distributed. . . . Property – property – this is the thing we must be at. Without a change in the institution of property, no improvement can take place.

Such a revolution (he hoped) would come, without violence, in the immediate aftermath of the attainment of manhood suffrage: 'From the *laws of the few* have the existing inequalities sprung; by the laws of the many shall they be destroyed.'[2]

1. *Twopenny Despatch*, 10 September 1836.
2. *Destructive*, 9 March, 24 August 1833; *People's Conservative; and Trade's Union Gazette*, 14 December 1833.

Historians today would certainly not accept O'Brien's over-crude assimilation of the post-Reform Whig administration to the interests of the 'middle class'.[1] (Old Corruption had more vitality than that, as the protracted struggle for the repeal of the Corn Laws was to show.) Nor is it proper to select this one theorist (middle-class in his own origins) as expressive of the new consciousness of the working class. But at the same time, O'Brien was very far from being an eccentric at the edges of the movement. As editor of the *Poor Man's Guardian* and other journals he commanded a large, and growing, working-class audience; he was later to earn the title of the 'School-master' of Chartism. His writings are a central thread through the abundant agitations of the early 1830s, providing a nexus for the old democratic claims, the social agitations (against the New Poor Law and for Factory Reform), the Owenite communitarian experiments, and the syndicalist struggles of the trade unions. O'Brien was, as much as Cobbett and Wooler in the post-war years, an authentic voice of his times.

For most working men, of course, disillusion in the Reform Bill came in less theoretical forms. The proof of the pudding was in the eating. We may see the eating in microcosm in a few of the incidents at one of the contests in the ensuing General Election – at Leeds. Here Baines, who had already used his influence to instate Brougham as the Yorkshire member, brought forward in the Whig interest Marshall, one of the largest employers in Leeds, and Macaulay (or 'Mr Mackholy' as one of the tail of Whig shopkeepers noted in his diary). Macaulay was one of the most complacent of the ideologists of the Reform Bill settlement, translating into new terms the Tory doctrine of 'virtual representation':

The higher and middling orders are the natural representatives of the human race. Their interest may be opposed, in some things, to that of their proper contemporaries, but it is identical with that of the innumerable generations which are to follow.

1. O'Brien himself came to regret the vehemence of his dismissal of the entire 'middle class', when an opportunity for alliance between the Chartists and elements from the middle class occurred in the 1840s: see Beer, op. cit., I I, p. 126.

'The inequality with which wealth is distributed forces itself on everybody's notice,' he lamented, while 'the reasons which irrefragably proved this inequality to be necessary to the well-being of all classes are not equally obvious.' Mr Marshall was not equal to him as a theorist; but, if a Radical election sheet is to be believed, he was of the view that 12s. a week was a good wage for a man with a family, he considered that the working classes might better their conditions by emigration, and:

In Mr Marshall's mill, a boy of 9 years of age was stripped to the skin, bound to an iron pillar, and mercilessly beaten with straps, until he fainted.[1]

The Tory candidate, on the other hand, was Sadler, leading parliamentary spokesman of the 10 Hour Movement. Oastler had launched, with the Short-Time Committees, his passionate campaign against child labour two years before. The amazing 'Pilgrimage to York' had taken place in the previous April; and the 10 Hour agitation (like the Owenite agitation) continued without pause during the Reform Bill crisis months. In such a contest, therefore, Oastler could be counted upon to side with Sadler against Baines, who had conducted a mealy-mouthed defence of the mill-owners in the *Leeds Mercury*. Cobbett could be counted upon to do the same. Indeed, he gave a reference for Baines which reminds us of the latitude of the libel laws of the time:

This great LYING PUFFER of Brougham ... who has always taken care to have one member, at least, to do more mischief to public liberty than any other fifty members in the House of Commons; this swelled-up, greedy, and unprincipled puffer, who has been the deluder of Yorkshire for twenty years past ...[2]

A Tory-Radical alliance was therefore inevitable behind Sadler. It was also inevitable that the greater part of the Noncon-formist 'shopocrat' vote would go to 'Mr Marshall Our Towns-man and Mr Mackholy the Scotchman' (as our diarist put it):

1. J. R. M. Butler, op. cit., pp. 262–5; *Cracker*, 8 December 1832.
2. *Political Register*, 24 November 1832. Cobbett was recalling the former Yorkshire county member, Wilberforce.

... as to Sadler he never has done any good nor he never will do ... for he has always been inventing something that has tended to injure the inhabitants of the Town of Leeds ... he was the first promoter of the Improvement Act and that has cost the Inhabitants a manny thousands and the Burthen has cheefly fallen upon Shop-keepers and what I call the Middling Class of People ... its true he is one of our Magestrate Party but he is not better for that ...[1]

The working-class Radicals in Leeds, maintained their inde-pendent press and organization. The men of Leeds (they de-clared) who 'have assembled in evil report and good report; ... been instant in season and out of season', had now been betrayed by the men who, in the days of May, had addressed their great assemblies and promised Reform or barricades:

Messrs Marshall and Macaulay may ... be very friendly to Reforms of all sorts and sizes, both in church and state; they may also be in favour of the abolition of all monopolies except their own, those of mill-men and placemen; but the operatives of Leeds remember that if they support them, they do what they can to put Legislative power into the hands of their enemies.

Moreover, the Radicals declared that the old forms of electoral bribery and influence employed by the aristocratic interest were now finding insidious new forms in the service of the manu-facturing interest. Although the workers did not have votes, great efforts were made to offset the effects of 10 Hour demon-strations in favour of Sadler by compelling factory-hands to declare for Marshall and Macaulay at the hustings:

We could name more than a dozen mills, all the hands of which have received positive orders to be in the Yard on Monday, and to hold up their hands for the Orange candidates ... on pain of instant privation of employment. ... They have each their stations assigned in the yard, where they are to be penned like flocks of sheep, sur-rounded on all sides by overlookers, clerks and other under-strappers, for the purpose of enforcing the high mandate of the counting-house.

In the event, the scene on the hustings turned into riot, where Oastler and the 10 Hour men 'rang matins on the thick skulls of the flying oranges'. When Sadler was defeated at the poll,

1. MS Letterbook of Ayrey (Leeds Reference Library).

Marshall and Macaulay were burned in effigy in the same city centre where Paine had been burnt by the loyalists in 1792.[1]

This Leeds election of 1832 was of more than local significance. It had focused the attention of factory reformers throughout the country, drawing addresses in Sadler's favour from thousands of signatories in northern towns. There is no mistaking the new tone after 1832. In every manufacturing district a hundred experiences confirmed the new consciousness of class which the Bill had, by its own provisions, so carefully defined. It was the 'reformed' House of Commons which sanctioned the transportation of the Dorchester labourers in 1834 ('a blow directed at the whole body of united operatives'),[2] and who launched, with 'the document' and the lock-out, the struggle to break the trade unions, whose intensity and whose significance (in both political and economic terms) is still too little understood. Against the manifesto of the masters, the Yorkshire Trades Union issued its own:

The war cry of the masters has not only been sounded, but the havoc of war; war against freedom; war against opinion; war against justice; and war without justifying cause ...

'The very men,' declared one Leeds trade unionist, 'who had pampered Political Unions, when they could be made subservient to their own purposes, were now endeavouring to crush the Trades Unions':

It was but the other day that the operatives were led in great numbers to the West Riding meeting at Wakefield, for the purpose of carrying the Reform Bill. At that time, the very individuals who were now attempting to put down trades' unions, were arraying them to carry by the force of numbers, a political reform which he was sure would not otherwise have been obtained from the aristocracy of this country. That reform which had thus been obtained appeared to him to have been the ultimate means of strengthening the hands of corruption and oppression.[3]

1. *Cracker*, 8, 10, 21 December 1832. See also A. Briggs, 'The Background of the Parliamentary Reform Movement in Three English Cities', op. cit., pp. 311–14; E. Baines, *Life*, pp. 164–7; C. Driver, *Tory Radical*, pp. 197–202.

2. Speech of William Rider, Leeds stuff-weaver and later to be a prominent Chartist Leader, *Leeds Times*, 12 April 1834.

3. *Leeds Times*, 12, 17, 24 May 1834.

The line from 1832 to Chartism is not a haphazard pendulum alternation of 'political' and 'economic' agitations but a direct progression, in which simultaneous and related movements converge towards a single point. This point was the vote. There is a sense in which the Chartist movement commenced, not in 1838 with the promulgation of the 'Six Points', but at the moment when the Reform Bill received Royal Assent. Many of the provincial Political Unions never disbanded, but commenced at once to agitate against the 'shopocrat' franchise. In January 1833 the *Working Man's Friend* was able to announce that the fortress of middle-class Radicalism had been stormed: '... in spite of all the opposition and chicanery of a RAG MERCHANT MONARCHY, the Midland Union of the Working Classes was formed by the brave, but, till then, misled people of that country'.[1] The characteristic ideology of Birmingham Radicalism, which united employers and journeymen in opposition to the aristocracy, the Banks, the National Debt, and the 'paper-money system', was beginning to fall apart. For a time Attwood himself was carried with the new current, partly through loyalty to the regiments to which he had made large promises before. Once again, a monster demonstration gathered on Newhall Hill (May 1833), at which an attendance of 180,000 was claimed, and at which there was expressed –

... a sentiment of common hatred to the parties whom, having been mainly instrumental in forcing into power, they now assembled to express their disgust of the ... treachery which they had manifested.

The attendance was swelled by colliers from Walsall, ironworkers from Wolverhampton, outworkers from Dudley. The process of radicalization which was to make Birmingham a Chartist metropolis had begun.[2]

But the content of this renewed agitation was such that the vote itself implied 'much more', and that is why it had to be denied. (The Birmingham of 1833 was not the Birmingham of 1831: it was now the home of an Equitable Labour Exchange, it was the headquarters of the socialist Builders' Union, it

1. *Working Man's Friend and Political Magazine*, 5 January 1833.
2. *Report of the Proceedings of the Great Public Meeting &c.*, 20 May 1833.

housed the editorial office of the *Pioneer*.) The vote, for the
workers of this and the next decade, was a symbol whose importance it is difficult for us to appreciate, our eyes dimmed
by more than a century of the smog of 'two-party parliamentary politics'. It implied, first, *égalité*: equality of citizenship,
personal dignity, worth. 'Instead of bricks, mortar, and dirt,
MAN ought to be represented,' wrote one pamphleteer, lamenting the lot of 'the miserable, so-called "free-born" Englishman,
excluded from the most valuable right that man can enjoy in
political society.'[1] 'Be we, of the working millions,' wrote
George Edmonds –

never more seen at baby-shows, Lord Mayor penny-peeps, and
gingerbread Coronations – be not present as accomplices in such
national fooleries. Let the tawdry actors have all the fun to themselves.

'Like the wild Irish of old, the British millions have been too
long insolently placed without the pale of social governments':

I now speak the thoughts of my unrepresented fellow millions, the
Wild English, the free-born slaves of the nineteenth century.[2]

But in the context of the Owenite and Chartist years, the
claim for the vote implied also further claims: a new way of
reaching out by the working people for *social control* over their
conditions of life and labour. At first, and inevitably, the exclusion of the working class provoked a contrary rejection, by
the working class, of all forms of political action. Owen had
long prepared the ground for this, with his indifference to
political Radicalism. But in the post-1832 swing to general
unionism, this anti-political bias was not quietist but embattled,
militant, and even revolutionary. To examine the richness of
the political thought of these years would take us further into
the history of general unionism – and, indeed, into the early
years of Chartism – than we intend to go. They are years in
which Benbow canvassed his notion of the 'Grand National
Holiday' in the industrial districts; in which the printing-
worker, John Francis Bray, carried forward Hodgskin's
ideas, in lectures to Leeds artisans, later published as *Labour's*

1. 'I.H.B.L.', *Ought Every Man to Vote?* (1832).
2. G. Edmonds, *The English Revolution* (1831), pp. 5, 8.

Wrongs and Labour's Remedies; in which the Builders' Union and the Grand National Consolidated Trades Union rose and fell; and in which Doherty and Fielden founded the 'Society for National Regeneration' with its remedy of the General Strike for the Eight-Hour Day. The Owenite communitarians were fertile with notions and experiments prefiguring advances in the care of children, the relations between the sexes, education, housing, and social policy. Nor were these ideas canvassed among a limited intelligentsia only; building workers, potters, weavers, and artisans were willing, for a while, to risk their livelihood to put experiments to the test. The swarming variety of journals, many of which made exacting demands upon the readers, were addressed to an authentic working-class audience. In the silk mills of the Colden Valley, isolated on the Pennines between Yorkshire and Lancashire, the Owenite journals were read.

Two themes only may be mentioned of those which arose again and again in these years. The first is that of internationalism. This was, to be sure, part of the old Jacobin heritage; and one which the Radicals had never forgotten. When Oliver tramped with the Leeds cropper, James Mann, and another revolutionary, to the rendezvous at Thornhill Lees (in 1817) he found, from their discourse, that 'the recent news from the Brazils seemed to cheer them with greater hopes than ever'.[1] Cobbett could always find time to add a stop-press to his journals:

I have just room to tell you, that the people of BELGIUM, the *common people*, have *beaten the Dutch armies*, who were marched against them to compel them to *pay enormous taxes*. This is excellent news.[2]

The French Revolution of 1830 had a profound impact upon the people, electrifying not only the London Radicals but working-class reformers in distant industrial villages. The struggle for Polish independence was followed anxiously in the working-class press; while Julian Hibbert, in the Rotunda, carried a vote of sympathy with the Lyons weavers, in their

1. Narrative of Oliver, H.O. 40.9.
2. *Two-Penny Trash*, 1 October 1830.

ill-fated insurrection, likening them to the weavers of Spital-fields. In the Owenite movement this political tradition was extended to embrace social and class solidarities. In 1833 a 'Manifesto of the Productive Classes of Great Britain and Ireland' was addressed to 'the Governments and People of the Continents of Europe and of North and South America', commencing: 'Men of the Great Family of Mankind ...' By the end of the same year, the question of some common alliance between the trade unionists of England, France, and Germany had already come under discussion.[1]

The other theme was that of industrial syndicalism. When Marx was still in his teens, the battle for the minds of English trade unionists, between a capitalist and a socialist political economy, had been (at least temporarily) won. The winners were Hodgskin, Thompson, James Morrison and O'Brien; the losers were James Mill and Place. 'What is capital?' asked a writer in the *Pioneer*. 'It is reserved labour!' cries M'Culloch. '... From whom and what was it reserved? From the clothing and food of the wretched.'[2] Hence the workers who had been 'insolently placed without the pale of social government' developed, stage by stage, a theory of syndicalism, or of 'Inverted Masonry'.[3] 'The Trades Unions will not only strike for less work, and more wages,' wrote 'A Member of the Builder's Union',

but they will ultimately ABOLISH WAGES, become their own masters, and work for each other; labour and capital will no longer be separate but they will be indissolubly joined together in the hands of the workmen and work-women.

The unions themselves could solve the problem of political power; a 'Parliament' of the industrious classes could be formed, delegated directly from workshops and mills: 'the Lodges send Delegates from local to district, and from district to National Assemblies. Here are Universal Suffrage, Annual Election, and No Property Qualification, instanter.'[4] The idea was developed (in the *Pioneer*) of such a House of Trades:

1. See, e.g., *Destructive*, 7 December 1833. 2. *Pioneer*, 13 October 1833.
3. *Man*, 13 October 1833.   4. *Man*, 22 December 1833.

which must supply the place of the present House of Commons, and direct the commercial affairs of the country, according to the will of the trades which compose associations of the industry. This is the ascendancy scale by which we arrive to universal suffrage. It will begin in our lodges, extend to our general union, embrace the management of trade, and finally swallow up the whole political power.[1]

This vision was lost, almost as soon as it had been found, in the terrible defeats of 1834 and 1835. And, when they had recovered their wind, the workers returned to the vote, as the more practical key to political power. Something was lost: but Chartism never entirely forgot this preoccupation with social control, to the attainment of which the vote was seen as a means. These years reveal a passing beyond the characteristic outlook of the artisan, with his desire for an independent livelihood 'by the sweat of his brow', to a newer outlook, more reconciled to the new means of production, but seeking to exert the collective power of the class to humanize the environment: – by this community or that cooperative society, by this check on the blind operation of the market-economy, this legal enactment, that measure of relief for the poor. And implicit, if not always explicit, in their outlook was the dangerous tenet: production must be, not for profit, but for use.

This collective self-consciousness was indeed the great spiritual gain of the Industrial Revolution, against which the disruption of an older and in many ways more humanly comprehensible way of life must be set. It was perhaps a unique formation, this British working class of 1832. The slow, piecemeal accretions of capital accumulation had meant that the preliminaries to the Industrial Revolution stretched backwards for hundreds of years. From Tudor times onwards this artisan culture had grown more complex with each phase of technical and social change. Delaney, Dekker and Nashe: Winstanley and Lilburne: Bunyan and Defoe – all had at times addressed themselves to it. Enriched by the experiences of the seventeenth century, carrying through the eighteenth century the intellectual and libertarian traditions which we have described, forming their own traditions of mutuality in the friendly

1. *Pioneer*, 31 May 1834.

society and trades club, these men did not pass, in one generation, from the peasantry to the new industrial town. They suffered the experience of the Industrial Revolution as articulate,
free-born Englishmen. Those who were sent to gaol might
know the Bible better than those on the Bench, and those who
were transported to Van Diemen's Land might ask their relatives to send Cobbett's *Register* after them.

This was, perhaps, the most distinguished popular culture
England has known. It contained the massive diversity of skills,
of the workers in metal, wood, textiles and ceramics, without
whose inherited 'mysteries' and superb ingenuity with primitive
tools the inventions of the Industrial Revolution could scarcely
have got further than the drawing-board. From this culture of
the craftsman and the self-taught there came scores of in-
ventors, organizers, journalists and political theorists of impressive quality. It is easy enough to say that this culture was
backward-looking or conservative. True enough, one direction of the great agitations of the artisans and outworkers,
continued over fifty years, was to *resist* being turned into a
proletariat. When they knew that this cause was lost, yet they
reached out again, in the Thirties and Forties, and sought to
achieve new and only imagined forms of social control. During
all this time they were, as a class, repressed and segregated in
their own communities. But what the counter-revolution sought
to repress grew only more determined in the quasi-legal institutions of the underground. Whenever the pressure of the rulers
relaxed, men came from the petty workshops or the weavers'
hamlets and asserted new claims. They were told that they had
no rights, but they knew that they were born free. The Yeomanry rode down their meeting, and the right of public meeting was gained. The pamphleteers were gaoled, and from the
gaols they edited pamphlets. The trade unionists were imprisoned, and they were attended to prison by processions with
bands and union banners.

Segregated in this way, their institutions acquired a peculiar
toughness and resilience. Class also acquired a peculiar resonance in English life: everything, from their schools to their
shops, their chapels to their amusements, was turned into a
battleground of class. The marks of this remain, but by the

outsider they are not always understood. If we have in our social life little of the tradition of *égalité*, yet the class-consciousness of the working man has little in it of deference. 'Orphans we are, and bastards of society,' wrote James Morrison in 1834.[1] The tone is not one of resignation but of pride.

Again and again in these years working men expressed it thus: 'they wish to make us tools', or 'implements', or 'machines'. A witness before the parliamentary committee enquiring into the hand-loom weavers (1835) was asked to state the view of his fellows on the Reform Bill:

Q. Are the working classes better satisfied with the institutions of the country since the change has taken place?

A. I do not think they are. They viewed the Reform Bill as a measure calculated to join the middle and upper classes to Government, and leave them in the hands of Government as a sort of machine to work according to the pleasure of Government.

Such men met Utilitarianism in their daily lives, and they sought to throw it back, not blindly, but with intelligence and moral passion. They fought, not the machine, but the exploitive and oppressive relationships intrinsic to industrial capitalism. In these same years, the great Romantic criticism of Utilitarianism was running its parallel but altogether separate course. After William Blake, no mind was at home in both cultures, nor had the genius to interpret the two traditions to each other. It was a muddled Mr Owen who offered to disclose the 'new moral world', while Wordsworth and Coleridge had withdrawn behind their own ramparts of disenchantment. Hence these years appear at times to display, not a revolutionary challenge, but a resistance movement, in which both the Romantics and the Radical craftsmen opposed the annunciation of Acquisitive Man. In the failure of the two traditions to come to a point of junction, something was lost. How much we cannot be sure, for we are among the losers.

Yet the working people should not be seen only as the lost myriads of eternity. They had also nourished, for fifty years, and with incomparable fortitude, the Liberty Tree. We may thank them for these years of heroic culture.

1. *Pioneer*, 22 March 1834; see A. Briggs, 'The Language of "Class" in Early Nineteenth Century England', loc. cit., p. 68.

Postscript

THE five years which have elapsed between this book's first publication and the present edition is too short a period to allow for major redefinitions. I have therefore contented myself with the minimum of revisions. I have corrected some errors and infelicities, struck out a few lazy passages, and attempted to clarify the argument in the chapter on 'The Field Labourers' – a chapter which still remains inadequate to its theme.

One other chapter is clearly inadequate: that on 'Standards and Experiences'. This was shaped by a particular historical controversy – the 'standard-of-living argument' – which recent historiography is already assimilating and passing beyond. It now seems to me to be an ungenerous chapter, which adds little in information or analysis. My comments on the exceedingly complex and developing research in demography are trivial: and the reader who wishes to inform himself on this, or on problems of health, housing, and urban growth, must on most occasions turn to the work of those economic historians whose assumptions are, in this chapter, under criticism. Nevertheless. One still hears of examples, from this or that well-established school of economic history, of a commitment to the ideology of economic growth so blatant that it is in danger of reducing a discipline to a propaganda. Since this is so I have decided to let the chapter stand: *as* a polemic.

The rest of the book I defend. I accept, of course, that it has many serious omissions. The artisans and outworkers are in the centre of my picture, but the figures at both edges of it are blurred. One critic fairly takes me to task for understating the experiences of the early factory workers, the miners, iron-workers, engineering and building trades, and transport workers.[1] Another, equally fairly, criticizes me for giving too little account of the 'flag-saluting, foreigner-hating, peer-respecting side of the plebian mind.'[2] I have shown too little of both; and, while there

1. J. D. Chambers, 'The Making of the English Working Class', *History*, 1 June 1966, p. 187.

2. Geoffrey Best, 'The Making of the English Working Class', *Historical Journal*, VIII, 1965, p. 278.

are sound books – including *The Skilled Labourer* – to which we can turn for some of the workers in the first group, we have, as yet, almost everything to find out about the second. I have shown too little, not only of the first factory workers, but also of the ebullience of the British tar, the audience for the anti-Gallican broadside, the criminal sub-cultures of the great cities, the insulated parochialism of the small industrial and mining enclaves, the deep deference of some parts of the countryside. We need to know more about all these things. More knowledge will not, however, explain away the emergence of a class movement in the 1830's; although it may make the emergence of such a common movement, out of so many disparate elements and despite so many sociological resistances, appear all the more remarkable.

When it first appeared, this book met with a generous but critical reception in the academic press. The criticisms have been directed towards three areas: the treatment of Methodism: the treatment of episodes in the years 1811–19: and general questions of method, relating especially to the analysis of social class.

It would be easier to take into account the criticisms of my treatment of Methodism if the critics had been more precise. R. Currie and R. M. Hartwell criticize, usefully, my figures for national Methodist growth. They then relapse into a caricature in which I am supposed to welcome Methodist revivalism as 'a counter-revolutionary tool'. They are (like several aghast reviewers) much taken by the metaphor of 'psychic masturbation', which they manage to quote three times in four paragraphs, without indicating its context or the problem (the contrast between weekday Methodist discipline and the raw emotionalism of Methodist conversion, sermons, love-feasts, confessionals, spiritual journals and tracts, etc.) which the metaphor illustrates.[1] Professor Chambers is also a caricaturist, although in a more boisterous, knockabout, manner. I am represented by him as arguing that –

The Methodists ... were really frustrated revolutionaries; being prevented from dying on the barricades, they trooped into the chapels; vainly thirsting for the blood of the bourgeois, they consoled themselves by bawling about the Blood of the Lamb.[2]

In fact, the direct political influence of Methodism was only of secondary interest to me when I wrote chapters 2 and 11. I was anxious to find out what the experience of Methodism – in

1. R. Currie and R. M. Hartwell, 'The Making of the English Working Class?' *Economic History Review*, 2nd series XVIII, no 3, December 1965.   2. Chambers, op. cit., p. 186.

particular between 1780 and 1820 – was *about* – why working people who had been deserting, or were resistant to, the more rational dissenting churches, should accept this passionate Lutheranism. Too much writing on Methodism commences with the assumption that we all know what Methodism was, and gets on with discussing its growth-rates or its organizational structures. But we cannot deduce the quality of the Methodist experience from this kind of evidence. Moreover, while Christian and non-Christian historians can co-operate equably in establishing quantities or analysing organizations, the dialogue becomes more difficult when one is evaluating experiences – John Wesley's journals or the multitude of confessional tracts. Certainly the dialogue should continue;[1] but, in the end, one must ask: are we studying a genuine spiritual experience, or is it only to be understood as a rendering of, or displacement of, other mental energies?

My answer (since I am not a Christian) directed attention to the cultural shock entailed in the transition to mature industrialism. Methodism's function as a carrier of work-discipline was shared with Evangelicalism more generally, but in no other church is it to be seen so clearly.[2] The Wesleyans first, and the Primitive Methodists after them, repeatedly sought for outright confrontations with the older, half-pagan popular culture, with its fairs, its sports, its drink, and its picaresque hedonism.

One bias no doubt produces another. So much that has been written about Methodism has been apologetic or bland that I may have offered too severe a corrective. We may agree, with one historian of Methodism, that the life of the chapel did (for many people at many places) offer 'to the lonely and insecure a whole network of intimate social relationships'.[3] Yet we should also allow those to speak who found themselves stifled in this network by their fellows' 'ignorance, their hatred of those who differed from them, their intolerance and their scandalous mountebank tricks in the pulpit.'[4]

1. A common ground may be found in literary criticism.
2. I have argued the wider case in 'Time, Work-Discipline, and Industrial Capitalism', *Past and Present*, December 1967.
3. John Walsh, 'Methodism at the End of the Eighteenth Century', in *A History of the Methodist Church in Great Britain*, eds. Rupert Davies and Gordon Rupp (1965), I, p. 311.
4. Mrs A. Mathews, *Memoirs of Charles Mathews, Comedian* (1838), I, p. 39. The evidence on this side of the question is substantial and I will offer more if I am goaded to it. A glimpse into the more light-hearted anti-Methodist literature is in A. M. Lyles, *Methodism Mocked* (1960).

The comments of several of my critics suggest more familiarity with the shopkeeper Wesleyanism of the Victorian years than with the volatile emotionalism of this period. Thus Currie and Hartwell insist: 'the most revivalist Methodists were politically the most radical'. I see little evidence for this before 1815. The Cornish tinners (perhaps the most revivalist of any Wesleyan group) were not radical, nor, so far as I know, were the Welsh Jumpers. Again, they lay it down: 'Methodism is not and never has been "chiliastic"'. This was not of course my point. Nevertheless, a millenarian instability can certainly be found, repeatedly, in Methodist environs, from the time of Brothers to that of Zion Ward.

This instability could also be political. I note, with alarm, that after the 'Halévy Thesis' (Methodism prevented revolution) we are likely to have a 'Thompson Thesis' (Methodist expansion was the consequence of counter-revolution) held up for debate. Miss Himmelfarb even deplores that 'an occasion for significant historical controversy' has been evaded: Dr E. J Hobsbawm has suggested that 'Methodism advanced when Radicalism advanced', whereas I have suggested that 'religious revivalism took over just at the point where "political" or temporal aspirations met with defeat': she sees in the muted terms of our argument a conspiracy of Marxists to present 'a united front against a common enemy'.[1]

There may, however, be a more simple reason than ideological conspiracy for our caution: we are both aware that the evidence is inconclusive. Revivalism is not a phenomenon which admits of a single hold-all explanation. Given the initial propensity to instability, it may be set in motion by any sombre or dramatic event – a Lisbon earthquake, plague, famine, national crisis, war, a local pit-disaster, or (in a village) the sudden death of an individual. It may be induced by missionary evangelism from outside, or, within a church, there may be periodic self-induced revivals, following an internal generational pattern, as successive cohorts of the young are brought to an emotional commitment to the church of their parents.[2] Moreover, different contexts may require different explanatory methods. Methodist history breaks down into several distinct periods, and we must, at the least, distinguish between the years of Wesley's own pastorate, the volatile war

1. G. Himmelfarb, *Victorian Minds* (New York, 1968), pp. 292–9.

2. I find useful for comparative purposes the study of enthusiastic religion in western New York by Whitney R. Cross, *The Burned-Over District* (Cornell University, 1950). A late and melancholy account of induced revivalism is to be found in E. J. Thompson, *Introducing the Arnisons* (1935), ch. XI.

years (some of whose features are long continued in rural and mining districts, especially among the Primitives), and the sober years of ascending respectability and social status, and of connexional disputes, from the early 1820s to 1849.

My concern is, in particular, with the middle period, and it is to these years that I applied the description, 'the chiliasm of despair'. These years see the highest growth-rates of Methodism in the nineteenth century.[1] Revivalism, between 1791 and 1835, sometimes appears in close association with political disturbance, and sometimes it does not. The Cornish Methodists, who stubbornly resisted radicalism until the Chartist years,[2] appear to fall outside my 'thesis'; their greatest revival, of 1814, appears to have had no overt political connexions.[3] On the other hand, the revival (Wesleyan and Primitive) in industrial Shropshire in 1821–2 appears to fit the thesis exactly: it followed directly upon political and industrial excitement climaxed by the Cinderhill Riots, in which two colliers were killed by the yeomanry and another (for his part in the riots) was executed.[4]

More commonly, we are dealing with relationships – and psychic disturbances – so obscure that we may never be able to advance beyond hypotheses. The war years were years also of three major food crises, of rumours of battles and of crowned heads falling. The grand year of evangelism, 1798 – which saw revivalism spreading far beyond the ranks of the Methodists – took place after the food-crisis years of 1795–6, the Mutiny of 1797, and against the background of invasion threat.[5] An observer in Wales in the same

1. See Robert Currie, 'A Micro-Theory of Methodist Growth', *Proceedings of the Wesley Historical Society*, XXXVI, October 1967, p. 66.

2. See Brian Harrison and Patricia Hollis, 'Chartism, Liberalism and the Life of Robert Lowery', Eng. Hist. Rev., LXXII, 1967, p. 508.

3. Official Wesleyan opposition to revivalism developed at the beginning of the century less because of its political consequences (which were not yet apparent) than because 'the revivalistic spirit developed a centrifugal force which threatened to fling off into space innumerable ecclesiastical fragments': see M. S. Edwards, *The Divisions of Cornish Methodism, 1802 to 1857* (Cornish Methodist Historical Association, 1964, pp. 15–16. I am indebted to Mr John G. Rule, of the University of Southampton, for much information and insight into Cornish Methodism.

4. Barrie Trinder, *The Methodist New Connexion in Dawley and Madeley* (Wesley Historical Society, West Midlands, 1967), pp. 3–5.

5. See D. J. Jeremy, 'A Local Crisis between Establishment and Nonconformity', *Wilts. Archaeological and Nat. Hist. Magazine*, LXI, 1966, pp. 63–84. Nonconformity (mainly Independents, but also

year – at a time when the Welsh Jumpers were in hysterical par-oxysms – found that the rumour was abroad that 'the Irish were coming to eat them with a horn of salt.'[1]

The Primitive revival in the East Midlands in 1816–18 may, however, provide evidence for the 'Hobsbawm Thesis'. On 5 June 1817, four days *before* the Pentridge rising, a Nottinghamshire magistrate was writing anxiously to Sidmouth of meetings of thousands of 'Ranters' on the commons, wastes, and lanes. No sedition was being openly promulgated, 'but in the present inflamed state of their minds, and when discontent is so universal among the lower orders, we cannot but think these meetings highly danger-ous.'[2] And yet, in a period of repeated insurgency and repeated failure, at what point is the 'Thompson Thesis' to be brought into operation? The revival of 1817 commenced in the previous year: a year of economic crisis, of the suspension of Habeas Corpus and the frustration of 'legitimate' outlets in petitions and Hampden Clubs, of the repression of the East Anglian labourers' revolt. And after Pentridge, the revival was to take on even greater dimensions.

My thesis was never offered for universal, instant application. I proposed only that, taking this period as a whole, the emotional evangelism, and the 'inflamed state of mind' accompanying it, can be seen as the chiliasm of despair. There are exceptions, and after 1832 we are in a different territory, although Hobsbawm and Rudé have found important evidence of revivalism taking hold in the South and East after the failure of the labourers' revolt of 1830–31.[3] In this case the revivalism may be seen, immediately, as a displace-ment of energies from 'temporal' to other-worldly concerns: but the village chapel, with its self-discipline and its resistance to defer-ence, became the seed-bed from which the next generation of rural

---

Methodists and Baptists) saw an "astonishing explosion" of growth in 1797–9 in Wiltshire, with the registration in three years of 115 new meeting houses in Wiltshire and Berkshire, compared with 80 in the previous six years and 112 in the succeeding eight.

1. William Sampson, *Memoirs* (Leesburg, V, 1817), pp. 57–9. 'Poli-tics' is too limited a term for the expectations and anxieties of these years. Thus during West Riding disturbance after Despard's arrest in 1802 an observer noted of the women: '. . . there is a general expectation of they know not what. Like the second advent, the time is coming, the Day is at hand': Fitzwilliam Papers, J. Beckett, 22 November 1802, F. 45 (d).

2. Thomas Beaumont to Sidmouth, 5 June 1817, H.O. 42.166.

3. E. J. Hobsbawm and G. Rudé, *Captain Swing: the Agricultural Labourers' Rising of 1830* (1968).

radicals and trade unionists would arise. This eventuation should not be read back into its origins.

Currie and Hartwell find unconvincing my theory 'of a popular oscillation between politics and religion – negative and positive poles of the social process':

Thompson leaves the oscillation undefined: does the whole population oscillate first to political action, then, when it fails, to religious? Or does one section of the population oscillate to political action, and a second to religious, when the first is disappointed? . . . In either case the oscillation should leave some mark on Methodism.

The answer, of course, is both. One might cite scores of life-histories of individual oscillators, including such highly articulate men as Joseph Barker and Thomas Cooper. But a simpler answer would be: the oscillators were the 'floating voters', who would now flock to the chapel, now would follow the Jacobin or Radical hard-core. When the latter were themselves oscillators (lay preachers of the Wesleyans or Primitives) then one got that coincidence of inflamed politics and evangelism which did, indeed, leave some mark on Methodism, notably (in this period) in the West Riding. Here, in the aftermath of Peterloo and during the preparations for the Grange Moor rising, one alarmed clergyman wrote to Sidmouth:

I find that the greater part of the people called Methodists are united with the *Radicals*; they assemble in the evenings in certain cottages in the country, under the pretence of religious worship, but . . . at these meetings they are in the constant habit of reading the works of Wooler, Cobbett, &c. At these meetings also they form plans for advancing the wages of operative manufacturers, by means of association.[1]

Such moments were generally ephemeral. Wesleyan orthodoxy had abundant means of disciplining heresy, and pressing congregations back into quietism.[2] The unequivocal conservatism of the

1. Rev. T. Westmorland, Vicar of Sandal, nr. Wakefield, 10 December 1819, H.O. 42. 200. The brief against Richard Lee, one of the 'Folley Hall' insurrectionaries of 1817, suggests that he recruited for his revolution 'when Chapel loosed' – i.e. as the men came out: T.S. 11.4134 (2). It was commonly believed that the "Ranters" in 1819 were preaching the enjoyment of "all worldly things in common": *Champion*, 25 July 1819.

2. It should be noted, however, that the Wesleyan growth-rate started to fall in 1816–17, and there was an absolute decrease in Wesleyan membership in 1819–20, associated with the growth of the Primitive and other breakaway groups: Robert Currie, op. cit., pp. 70–1. From this point onward the Currie-Hartwell view that the revivalist sects were also the most radical is perhaps correct.

Methodist establishment during these years is now, fortunately, no longer a matter of controversy. Dr John Kent, who dislikes the tone of certain critics of Methodism, has neverethless confirmed this finding:

Some critics have . . . said that Wesleyanism ought to have shown more sympathy towards the aspirations of the working classes. Such criticism often seems to imply that no decent Christian could have been a Tory in the 1830s.[1]

The controversy as to what 'decent Christians' should have done in the 1830s, and as to *which* Christians were decent ones, is one which a non-Christian historian would be tactless to enter.

No theme in my book has been received with more scepticism than my suggestion that there is a continuous underground tradition, linking the Jacobins of the 1790s to the movements of 1816–20. Currie and Hartwell find the notion 'unprovable', Chambers sees me as the victim of 'obsession' and 'fantasy'. In fact, I now think that I was too reticent about this underground. The 'United Men' were a good deal more active in Lancashire in 1797–8 than I have suggested; and the Rev. W. R. Hay, who was to preside at Peterloo, was winning his spurs in 1801 chasing large crowds of Jacobinical conspirators around the hills of Saddleworth.[2] The agitations in Lancashire in 1801 were on a greater scale than the 'Black Lamp' of 1802 in Yorkshire; and while the background to the agitation lay, no doubt, in the combinations of the weavers, there was also an ulterior conspiracy afoot. A plan was in circulation 'for conducting the business without incommoding it by flustration'. Reformers in every town were, on a given night, to send a drummer in the small hours through the streets, drumming to arms. As the startled troops came out of their billets they were to be seized and disarmed by the reformers, who were then to 'secure the end of every street, keep the flag of Liberty flying, [and] give strict orders that no man plunder the people.'[3]

There is an element of fantasy here, but it is not of my invention. The Despard conspiracy (I am now convinced) was more firmly based, and had more provincial links, than I have suggested.[4]

1. John Kent, *The Age of Disunity* (1966), p. 133.
2. W. R. Hay, 4 May 1801, H.O. 42. 62.
3. Ibid., folios 214, 298. Other specimens of this 'plan' were found in Yorkshire.
4. Professor Alfred Cobban, shortly before his death, passed on to me, at the suggestion of Professor Rudé, his own file on the Despard case, which does much to confirm its existence: I hope to publish these findings later.

Slender links between the conspiracies of 1801–2, Luddism, and 1817 – have yet to be shown to be 'unprovable'. Charles Pendrill provides one such link: a member of the committee of the L.C.S. which was arrested in 1798,[1] he was held for a short time in Gloucester jail with John Binns,[2] was lucky to escape with his life from the Despard affair,[3] was involved in the Spa Fields affair[4] and was the means of introducing Mitchell to Oliver in 1817.[5] Pendrill, indeed, told Oliver that he 'was deeply committed in Despard's Business – that made him so well acquainted with them in Yorkshire and Lancashire. They told me so themselves.'[6]

I did not labour these links (although I indicated them to the careful reader[7]) because I was not offering a thin minority tradition of disaster-dogged insurrectionists as an explanatory key. The links are more important on the local than the national scale: in town after town a handful of old Jacobins of the 1790s will be found among the leading trade unionists and reformers of 1816. Even so, the interesting historical question should not be posed at a conspiratorial level. Why did men and ideas which were isolated from the mainstream in 1795 receive such widespread support twenty years later?

The most substantial critique of my treatment of this period is in a study by R. A. Church and S. D. Chapman of 'Gravener Henson and the Making of the English Working Class'[8] which calls in question my analysis of Nottinghamshire Luddism. Church and Chapman are serious, if somewhat ideologically mounted, historians, with a good command of Nottingham sources. Their study is based upon an expert understanding of the hosiery and lace trades, and fills in much that was unknown about Henson's bio-

1. P.C. 1. 43. A 150.

2. *Leeds Mercury*, 27 November 1802.

3. He told Oliver that he owed his escape to the solidarity of the soldiers: when he was summoned with them before the Privy Council 'those who actually knew him, declared they had never seen him to their knowledge before': narrative of Oliver in H.O. 40.9.

4. Examination of Robert Moggridge, May 1817, in H.O. 40.10, which suggests that Pendrill was among the Spenceans.

5. See above, p. 716.

6. Examination of Oliver by Ponsonby and Bathurst, 15 June 1817, H.O. 42. 166. An informer, Sangster, wrote to Sidmouth in 1817 describing Pendrill as a man 'equal to Guy Fawkes': H.O. 42. 163.

7. See above pp. 528, 645, 654, 732 ff.

8. In *Land, Labour and Population in the Industrial Revolution*, eds. E. L. Jones and G. E. Mingay (1967).

graphy after 1817. But I remain unconvinced as to their account of Nottingham Luddism.

Church and Chapman take issue with me on these points. I have argued (p. 585) that 'in Nottingham there is an interesting oscillation between Luddite and constitutionalist protest, and it is possible that both were directed – at least up to 1814 – by the same trade union organization, in which perhaps Luddites and constitutionalists (probably led by Gravener Henson) differed in their counsels.' They render this very qualified suggestion down to –

The implication is that Henson's organization worked through constitutional channels by day, and by night engaged in industrial sabotage, a view that clearly warrants careful scrutiny.

Careful scrutiny would show that these are not quite the same propositions. It is possible for men to share a common culture and, within limits, common interests, to be informed of each others' tactics, to meet in the same taverns or serve on the same committees, and for first one counsel, and then the other, to carry the day without destroying a larger loyalty to each other. But Church and Chapman would not accept this hypothesis either. In their view, the Luddite and the constitutionalist strategies were wholly divorced from each other. The first they see as characteristic of the workers in the debased conditions of the out-villages:

The Luddites were based in the country districts, in the industrial villages of Arnold, Basford, Bulwell, Sutton-in-Ashfield, and Ilkeston, where the common and lower-paid branches of the manufacture were carried on.

These villagers they see as rude, riotous, unorganized, and rancorously radical. Henson and the constitutionalists, by contrast,

were based in Nottingham and (to a lesser extent) in Leicester, where the finer and better-paid branches of the hosiery manufacture were carried on.

The framework knitters here were moderately radical burgesses who had no need to 'resort to mask-and-hammer politics':

... within the limits possible when a country is at war, the views of the working classes, like those of other sections of the community, could find outlets for expression, and through the correspondence columns of the newspapers their grievances and aspirations were subjects for public debate.

If there was any relationship between constitutionalism and violence, it was unplanned and fortuitous: 'the country knitters took to smashing frames when the established leadership, which was in the hands of Henson and his associates in the town, either failed or was discredited.'

This is all very reasonable. Church and Chapman, in true black-coated style see history as peopled with reasonable men doing their best each according to his own lights. When Nottingham framework knitters were gaoled under the Combination Acts they were 'temporarily deprived of their freedom'; when Henson spoke for Reform and against the suspension of Habeas Corpus he 'attacked aristocratic manipulation of membership of the House of Commons'; his experience as a small master 'broadened his political outlook' and gave him 'new horizons' (opposition to Chartism being among them). The only unreasonable men were the Luddites.

I am led into my error by two misconceptions. We will examine each in turn. First, I argue that Luddism gave way so suddenly, in February 1812, to the constitutional action of the United Framework Knitters 'that it is impossible not to believe that the new Committee was not at least partly under former Luddite direction' (p. 608 and 585). I attributed this change in strategy to three causes, one of which was the introduction of the Bill to make frame-breaking a capital offence. Church and Chapman prefer to see no connexion between these events, and note that 'the decision to organize was taken on 11 February 1812, i.e. before the Bill had been read for the first time.'[1] This is true but the reader is unlikely to guess from their tone, and their uninformative documentation of the point, that what is at issue is only *three days*.[2] Moreover, death bills, even in these reasonable years, did not drop out of a blue sky. If Church and Chapman refer to *Hansard* they will find that Lord Liverpool announced impending measures (it would be 'necessary to apply to parliament for some additional powers') on 4 February,[3] a week before the Framework Knitters met. It might puzzle a twentieth-century historian, but it was un-

1. Ibid., p. 135, note 6.
2. Leave to bring in a Bill 'for the more exemplary Punishment of persons destroying or injuring any Stocking or Lace Frames' was granted on 14 February; presented and read on the same day; committed on 17 February; reported on the 18th; given a third reading on the 20th; and received the royal assent (after amendments in the Lords) on 20 march: *Commons Journals*, LXVIII.
3. *Hansard*, XXI, cols. 602-3, 671. The first official announcement of the Framework Knitters Committee appeared in the *Nottingham Review*, 14 February, signed by Gravenor Henson.

likely to puzzle a framework-knitter in 1812, to know what was meant by 'additional powers'. Government had been canvassing the intended measure for some days,[1] and it would be surprising if their intention had not become known. The fact that the new Committee hoped to delay the bill is confirmed from their own papers;[2] the fact that the advocates of Luddite activism were also watching events closely would appear to be confirmed from the Home Office papers.[3]

Thus the relationship between the death Bill and the organization of the Committee is confirmed under Church and Chapman's 'scrutiny'. This does not, of course, prove that constitutionalists and Luddites were in direct consultation with each other. This is my second misconception: although many of Henson's contemporaries believed him to have Luddite associations, it can be shown from his subsequent statements and actions that this was not so.[4] In fact, I inclined towards the same view, and said (although Church and Chapman neglect to mention this) that it is 'almost certainly untrue' that he was ever a Luddite, although, without any doubt, he knew the Luddite story (p. 542).

But the matter is a great deal more complex than Church and Chapman suppose. And they make matters more complicated for themselves by taking a view of the evidence which is sometimes

1. Thus the Duke of Newcastle, Lord Lieutenant of Nottingham-shire, was writing on 5 February that he found Government's inten-tion of making the punishment for frame-breaking capital 'highly salutary': Newcastle to Ryder, H.O. 42. 120.

2. One of the first letters received by the Committee was from Daniel Parker Coke, M.P. for Nottingham, replying to a request from the Committee that he should try to secure ten or twelve days' postpone-ment of the parliamentary proceedings, in order that they could pre-sent evidence: *Records of the Borough of Nottingham* (1952), VIII, p. 138.

3. See e.g. letter of General 'E. Ludd', dated Shirewood Camp, 22 February 1812, in H.O. 42. 120, commencing: 'I have waited patiently to see if any measures were likely to be adopted by Parlia-ment to alleviate distress in any Shape whatever; but the hand of con-ciliation is shut & my poor suffering country is left without a ray of hope.'

4. Church and Chapman imply (op. cit. p. 138, note 2) that I have falsified the evidence by omitting to cite Felkin's opinion that Henson took no part in Luddism. I did not cite it because it was not relevant in that context and because a score of *opinions* as to Henson's com-plicity could have been quoted, on both sides of the question. I decided to cite none.

tortuous,[1] sometimes simple-minded,[2] and often nugatory.[3] No one supposes that Henson went out at night, with blackened face and a hammer. The point is: did he ever (in 1811-12 or 1814) assent to the signal which sent other men out, did he raise money for them, or coordinate his tactics with theirs?

I remain, guardedly, of the view that — at least from February 1812 — he used his influence to dissuade his fellow knitters from Luddite tactics. This is what he said himself twelve years later:[4] and to say so was, in itself, to admit that he had been within talking distance. Certainly, during his successive campaigns for parliamentary relief it was of paramount importance to prevent 'outrages' and (despite the circumstances in which the letter was written) I am inclined to accept the general tenor of his account to Lord Sidmouth of his efforts to pacify the minds of the stockingers when their Bill was rejected (in July 1812):

I undertook to soothe and moderate the public mind in Nottingham ... [and] succeeded, but in a manner that gave additional offence to some of the masters, by advising the workmen to seek for redress by combinations. ... The plan indeed was objectionable but in the midst of so wild a commotion it was the only expedient possible.[5]

This account assorts fairly well with a confidential report of Coldham's in June 1812, before the Bill was rejected. The passage of

1. Thus they use the evidence of two London magistrates who visited Nottingham in 1812 to cast discredit upon the evidence of all the town and county magistrates from 1811 to 1817. The evidence of the Town Clerk of Nottingham, Coldham, who was secretary to the hosiers' 'secret committee', they disregard since 'he had no experience of the hosiery industry' (pp. 138-9, 139, note 5). They are not good on magistrates. The 'London magistrate' (p. 134) who described Henson as a 'sensible fellow and very fond of talking' was in fact James Hooley, a Nottingham hosier, who was willing to swear an affidavit that Henson was engaged in treasonable practices: Hooley to Sidmouth, 8 April 1817, H.O. 42. 163.

2. They appear to accept at its face value every denial of Luddite associations, even when Henson is writing from prison to Sidmouth and petitioning for release (p. 140). If one supposes that he *had* these associations, what would he have said?

3. Until Henson's missing history of Luddism turns up, the major source for Nottingham Luddism must remain the voluminous documentation in the Public Record Office: but every reference by Chapman and Church to these papers appears to be through a secondary source: the Hammonds, Darvall, Patterson, or myself.

4. See Church and Chapman, op. cit., p. 140.

5. Henson to Sidmouth, Cold Bath Fields, 10 June 1817, H.O. 42.166.

the death Bill in the previous March had 'dried up our channels of information and darkened such of them as are still open':

I believe that the measures in Parliament [i.e. the discussion of the Framework-Knitters' Bill] have very much interested the Framework-knitters & that those who were lately turbulently disposed & some of whom are now willing if necessary to go to more horrid extremities (if necessary to keep up the system of Terror) are willing to await the success of the Bill intended to be brought into Parliament.

Coldham feared, however, that the workers might soon commence a general agitation for peace:

In the meantime I cannot but applaud the policy of *those supporters of General Ludd* [the italicized words deleted, and overwritten 'Framework-knitters'] who affect to impute all their Distresses to the Conduct of their Masters & to fraudulent Goods . . .[1]

Both Henson and Coldham were negotiating extremely treacherous political waters in 1812 and 1813. If Henson was a constitutionalist, he was a framework-knitter's leader first and a constitutionalist second. If he was to hold back the Luddites he must show that his alternative methods could bring results. This he failed to do with his Bill, and the formation of the 'Union Society' was the next means proposed. But Coldham, equally, knew that the 'constitutionalist' strategy – however illegal it was under the Combination Acts – was a defence against Luddism. Only this can explain why the Union Society got as far as it did.

Even so, there are ambiguities as to Henson's position not fully cleared up. As Church and Chapman mention, Francis Place, who talked with Henson in 1824 when the troubles were long past, seems to have thought he was 'King Ludd'.[2] It remains possible that the Framework knitters (by whom Henson was actually employed as full-time organizer at times between 1812 and 1814[3]) did keep the right arm of Luddite enforcement in reserve for times when the constitutionalist left arm proved too weak. Certainly, there is some evidence that until 1817 Henson and his successive committees were raising funds and securing legal aid for Luddite prisoners.[4] Church and Chapman argue that, if Henson had really

1. Coldham, 2 June 1812, H.O. 42.123.

2. British Museum, Add. MSS. 27, 809, f. 17–18.

3. J. T. Becher, 24 May 1814, H.O. 42.139.

4. A letter of H. Enfield, 21 October 1816, H.O. 42. 154, suggests that prosecutions of masters for truck were not (as Church and Chapman suggest, p. 136) a 'private' campaign of Henson's. Subscriptions were being organized by committees, which applied the money to trade-union purposes, the prosecution of masters, and the defence of Luddite prisoners.

been implicated, the evidence would have been found in his correspondence.[1] But Henson was far too wily to have subscribed his signature as an accomplice to a capital offence. What was, however, intercepted in the post, in April 1817, was an interesting letter from Anderson, a colleague of Henson's, to an English frameworkknitter in Calais, soliciting employment for 'a very youseful young man ... a very good hand either in wharp or pint net', who was patently a Luddite refugee from justice The letter continued:

I have some very unpleasant news to tel you whe sent a peticion up to government to save the lives of those unfortunate men that sufferd this day at Leister. And whe sent it by gravener henson and Wm Robinson. And when they got there they seised gravener and put Im in the towr for I treason and told him that he had saved them troble of fetching Im ...

Clearly both correspondents were well acquainted with the executed Luddites ('little Sam the desarter', etc.), and the letter concluded: 'Mr and Mrs Henson and all give their respects to you.' [2]

A 'close scrutiny' of the evidence, then, will leave us undecided as to Henson's exact connexions with the Luddites. But in all this evidence nothing has come to light to substantiate the ChurchChapman thesis as to the moderation and hostility to Luddism of the Nottingham workers when contrasted with their country cousins. As they note, the 'social and political significance' of this division 'has been overlooked hitherto.' [3] And remarkably so. What is so patently clear to these historians was unaccountably overlooked by scores of magistrates, soldiers, and observers of the time, who continued to send in biased accounts of the solidarity of the Nottingham stockingers, their refusal to give information, their collections in aid of Luddism, and their impassioned radicalism. It is possible that it is Church and Chapman who have overlooked a simple point.

Fewer frames were broken in Nottingham than in the outvillages because the organization of the town workers was *stronger* than in the countryside. Their conditions of work and pay were better, and the conditions which they demanded were more quickly enforced upon the employers.[4] It was exactly in the out-villages and industrial hinterland where the bag hosiers operated and the cheap cut-ups were made that the threat to their position was

1. Op. cit., p. 140.

2. J. Anderson to Wood (of Calais), 16 April 1817 in H.O. 42.163.

3. Op cit., p. 140.

4. See J. L. and B. Hammond, *The Skilled Labourer* (2nd edition, 1920), pp. 262. 264–5.

developing. The villages were the battleground, because they were the frontier between organization and disorganization.

A parallel may be drawn with Luddism in the West Riding. There were no Luddite outbreaks in Leeds, simply because the croppers' organization was so strong, and there were no machines to break. It was, again, in the hinterland, in the Spen Valley and around Huddersfield, that the conflict was fought out. And the conflict can be seen even within workshops. In Wood's workshop, where George Mellor worked, Benjamin Walker (who turned informer) had been prevented from working in Leeds because he was not a member of the Clothier's 'Institute'; but he knew about the Institute, 'long before Ludding began': 'much money has been subscribed and expended in London about acts of parliament'. James Haigh, on the other hand, had been in the union, but not for the previous four years. Moreover, an examination of this workshop quickly dispels that crass economism, which was once to be found in popular Marxist texts but which has now taken refuge in the work of orthodox economic historians, whereby it is assumed that the lowest-paid and most depressed workers must be the most militant. George Mellor, in fact, was the stepson of his employer ('He was above me, and never kept company with me', complained Walker), earned as much as 35s. a week, and, having no family, was rumoured to have saved £100.[1] It was exactly, as I have argued sufficiently, the privileged worker who saw his whole status endangered who provided the Luddite leader.

Thus we have no need of the Church–Chapman thesis to understand the first phase of Nottingham Luddism. After the failure of the parliamentary campaign in the summer of 1812 the thesis is more helpful. The unity between the town workers and the organized workers in the hinterland was already under strain;[2] and after the Bill's defeat the trade union, in its new form, was being forced back upon its base in the town.[3]

1. Examinations of Walker and Haigh before Joseph Radcliffe in K.B. 8.91, folios 11, 153, 192, 198.

2. See pp. 656–7 above and *Records of the Borough of Nottingham*, VIII, p. 148.

3. During the campaign for the Bill, there was substantial support for the petition in the country: signatures – Nottingham town. 2,629; county, 2,078; *Records*, VIII, p. 144. But the First Annual Conference of the 'Union Society' in 1813 saw a serious decline of country support: members – Nottingham, 1,455; Lambley, 59; Basford, 72; Ilkeston, 95; Sutton and Mansfield, 79 (county total, 305): H.O. 42. 139.

The failure of the agitation may have made the country workers more desperate or more defeatist; but it indicates nothing of the moderation of the workers in the town. Church and Chapman dispute my suggestion that Henson 'shared the Luddites' 'advanced political radicalism',[1] since (as we have seen) the views of Nottingham burgesses 'could find outlets . . . through the correspondence columns of the newspaper'. The failure of the historical imagination here is daunting. Members of senior common rooms in the 1960s may be satisfied with an occasional 'outlet' in a letter to *The Times*, but the grievances of the people in England between 1811 and 1820 were not so readily met. It may be true (as our authors remark somewhat portentously) that 'less is known about what is typical [i.e. of working people's political attitudes] than is sometimes supposed.'[2] If the major sources of information, in the Home Office papers, are to be disregarded, then we must long be contented with a little knowledge and a modish agnosticism.

I never proposed, of course, that the populist radicalism of the 'disturbed districts' in these years was confined to some economically circumscribed working class, still less to the most depressed sections of workers. Tradesmen, small masters, professional men and others were vocal in the agitations. Many years later Place was still writing of 'the detestable infamy' and the 'mean and murderous conduct' of the post-war administration.[3] Moreover, I was at pains to indicate that Midlands Luddism, more than the Luddism of Yorkshire and Lancashire, was confined to industrial objectives. But this does not diminish the overwhelming evidence that Nottingham Luddism took place against a general background of radical agitation and expectation. In May 1812, when Church and Chapman suppose the Nottingham workers to have been engrossed by moderate constitutionalism, the news of the assassination of the Prime Minister 'was received with the greatest joy by the Populace here', with 'exultation, such as shouting, making bonfires, and . . . carrying a Flag and a Drum.'[4] The disturbances could only be silenced by military force and the reading of the Riot Act.

1. Op. cit., p. 137. What I have actually said (above p. 851) is that Henson 'exemplifies the struggle of the outworkers, touching the fringes of Luddism, organizing their illegal union, sharing their advanced political Radicalism, and attempting to . . . enact protective legislation in their favour.' 'Their' clearly applies to the outworkers, and not to Luddism.

2. Op. cit., p. 161.   3. British Museum Add. MSS. 27, 809 ff., 69–70.
4. Coldham, 14 May 1812, H.O. 42. 123.

That Henson aligned himself with this radicalism is indubitable, but the evidence as to his direct involvement in 1816 and 1817 is so contradictory as to require an open verdict. There were poison-pen writers around who were anxious to 'shop' him. One such writer, in 1817, fingered Henson and six of his 'mates of the Hembdon Club ... werry darring Wegabonds ... worse than High-waymen Man.'[1] Thomas Savage, a Luddite awaiting execution, attempted to save his life in the same year by incriminating Henson (See p. 628). But his evidence tended only to link Henson with Major Cartwright, Burdett, and Benbow, and was too highly seasoned ('Savage heard Gravener Henson say about a year & a half since that the depot at Derby might be taken') to be palatable.[2]

After Henson's release from prison he moved steadily away from the framework knitters, both in his life experience and in his political values. Church and Chapman's study is valuable on these later years.. But the evolution of an individual can scarcely invalidate (as they seem to believe) generalizations about the Luddites – or about the working class. Such evolutions, in opinions and in social status, are not wholly unknown. There is an element of pathos in Henson's progress. With his energy and his unusual intellectual equipment, he had often given way to impatience with his fellows: 'Damn the Trade', he wrote to a fellow committee man in May 1812, 'they are the most backward dilatory, *unwilling to do good* race of Men on Earth. ... If any Man in the Trade refuses to do his Duty in the making of Articles for the Recovery of his Trade Knock his Teeth down his Throat instantly.'[3] Now that his strategy had failed, he appears increasingly as an isolated, opinionated man, and as something of a 'sea-lawyer'. He was suspected by those whom he had served,[4] and it is clear that by 1825

1. Anon. (Sam Weller?), dated Nottingham, 15 June 1817, H.O. 42. 166.

2. The magistrate who took Savage's deposition thought him 'a sensible well educated man ... well situated for a leading man in a committee of working manufacturers'. Some of those mentioned in his deposition were, in fact, Hampden Club men. But the desperate circumstances of such a confession make it highly suspect: deposition of Savage, 8 April 1817, and C. G. Mundy to Sidmouth, 4 April and 17 April 1817, H.O. 42. 163. See also H.O. 40. 10.

3. *Records*, VIII, p. 147.

4. See the report of a spy, 4 May 1819, of an open-air meeting of framework knitters in Nottingham: 'Gravenor Henson was there – Some of them expressed to others, in confidence, their suspicions of his being a Traitor to them. They said, "Beware he does not turn Oliver".' H.O. 42. 187.

he had lost his influence. Perhaps this rejection accentuated his criticisms of a younger generation of radical and Chartist leaders.

I have followed Church and Chapman into their arguments very closely, and for a reason. The Hammonds, in their lifetime, turned too often towards their critics a genteel cheek of silence; and, after that, they were dead. For more than twenty years the ideological school of history has been able to knock the 'sentimentalists' with impunity, in articles and seminars. Meeting only with silence, they have become careless: a certain professional scowl, a suggestion of anti-sentimental rigour, has served to cover any lacunae in scholarship.

But I am neither genteel, nor, as yet, dead. If I have answered with asperity, it is in the interests of the history itself. By all means let there be arguments. But let them be about the actual historical evidence, rather than in defence of prior ideological presuppositions. The question of Henson illustrates the complexity of the evidence at one point. I by no means suppose that, in handling a score of equally complex points touched on in this book, I have always uncovered the truth. I have done no more than sample the hundreds of thousands of papers in the Public Record Office, and other points will become clear only after the study of local sources which I have not touched.[1] No single historian can hope to cover, in any detail, all this ground. The fuller understanding must await many closer and more patient studies which work through all the available evidence – studies with such titles as 'Gravenor Henson and the Making of the English Working Class'.

Church and Chapman conclude their demolition of me with a number of ideological homilies:

... when some labour historians write of 'the working class', its norms and values, it is the behaviour and attitudes of the non-apathetic section of the working classes which they knowingly or unwittingly attribute to the whole of the working classes: thus 'the working classes' are indentified with 'the working class'. It is legitimate to ask whether one is justified in attributing to the apathetic and silent masses those views which only some of the minority are demonstrated to have held ...[2]

(I particularly enjoy the police-court flavour of 'knowingly or unwittingly', followed by 'it is legitimate ...') Since other critics

1. An admirable example of such local research has been the activities of the Pentrich Revolution 150th anniversary committee, in which librarians, archivists, and historians uncovered and collected important new material on the event.

2. Op. cit., p. 165.

have loitered in this general area, with similar intent, I may, in
conclusion, touch on these points of categories and methods.

The complaint is that I impose the notion of class upon the
evidence instead of observing a 'plural society'. Currie and Hartwell
suggest that I do this partly by exaggerating the size of popular
agitations:

> For example, he cites (p. 909) the 1832 meeting at Newhall Hill, Bir-
> mingham 'at which an attendance of 180,000 was claimed' (and not
> challenged by Mr Thompson). Even allowing that the attendance 'was
> swelled by colliers from Walsall, ironworkers from Wolverhampton,
> outworkers from Dudley', the figure is preposterous. In 1831 the total
> population of Birmingham, Dudley, Walsall and Wolverhampton was
> less than 140,000. Many of Mr Thompson's figures of mass meetings are
> similarly exaggerated . . .

Since they give no other examples of exaggeration, we might look
at this one, although the meeting (in 1833 and not in 1832) was
the subject of only a passing reference and I was not concerned to
dispute or to confirm the claim. I appear to have a different census
from the one kept at Nuffield College, and mine shows a population in Birmingham, in 1831, in excess of 140,000. If we take the
boroughs of Birmingham, Dudley, Walsall and the township of
Wolverhampton together we get a total of 209,827; if we take the
Poor Law Unions of these centres, we get 284,863; if we add the
Unions of West Bromwich (including Wednesbury) and of Stour-
bridge (including Halesowen and Tipton) – and according to press
reports both areas were heavily represented – we get 360,390,
within the general population catchment area. Further outlying
areas could be added (the press reported contingents from Coventry, Warwick, Leamington, Tewksbury, etc.).

Even so, 180,000, or half the population of the area, seems
unlikely. It would seem less 'preposterous' if Currie and Hartwell
attended more closely to much-scorned 'literary' sources. The meeting (one of whose purposes was to call for the dismissal of
Ministers) was a centre of national interest and was watched by
Government with anxiety. It was one of those well-planned and
publicized meetings which the Birmingham Union had experience
in organizing, with stands and scaffolding erected on the hustings,
and with neighbourhood contingents marching in behind horsemen
and attended by marshalls. For the general populace it was part
spectacle, part festival: the *Times* reporter said Newhall Hill had
the appearance of 'a great fair': '. . . we have no doubt that the
good folks of Birmingham and its vicinity looked upon the meeting

as an excellent ... excuse for making holyday'. Around the skirts of the meeting were refreshment booths: ginger-beer, table-ale, oranges, biscuits. Every account (and especially in the hostile press) noted the vast number of women and children. All first-hand reports, from *Aris's Birmingham Gazette* to *The Times*, found the meeting 'immense', but precise estimates are less satisfactory. The reformers claimed up to 230,000; *The Times*, which was both hostile and sceptical, noted that the space covered would without difficulty accommodate 150,000 to 200,000, the hill was filled 'in every part' by a 'dense mass' and an 'immense sea of human beings', and, estimating the attendance at from 70,000 to 80,000, did not make clear whether women and children were included within the estimate or not.

180,000 still seems large, but not 'preposterous'. It is of course true: the organizers of meetings tend to exaggerate their size, and the opponents to diminish them. I am perfectly willing to make a downward allowance from the popular side if my critics will make an upward allowance on theirs. But the point of substance is whether I persistently exaggerate the scope of popular movements, in which only a minority were interested, while the 'apathetic and silent masses' stood outside. And here I suspect that Currie and Hartwell are so habituated to the modes of more institutionalized politics that they do not appreciate the very different modes of this period, and the massive support which, at moments of peak agitation, was aroused. At such times, not scores, but hundreds and sometimes thousands were prepared to walk many miles to hear an orator (or evangelist). In 1801 Hay found thousands at Buckton Castle, 'a situation very high and where the counties of Lancaster, York, Chester, and Derby meet',[1] some of whom had been coming in from 4 a.m. from as far away as Manchester (12 miles) and Stockport (9 miles).[1] Thousands of weavers and spinners were ready, in 1817, to march from Manchester to London; the thousands who marched in Oastler's 'pilgrimage' to York are well attested; the Chartists of Lancashire and Yorkshire held rallies on Blackstone Edge, miles from any large centre. When rallies were held, at times of excitement, in the centre of populous areas – the Newhall Hill meetings or the Chartist rally at Peep Green in 1839 – the attendance was undoubtedly 'immense'. One should look, perhaps, to nationalist rallies in recent years in Africa or Asia to find comparisons for the mode.

This does not mean that reformers were consistently and steadily

1. W. R. Hay, 4 May 1801, folios 11–15, H.O. 42. 62.

supported by masses. A leader could find himself deserted overnight (as was Henson); in the early 1830s even the staunch John
Gast, who had been agitating for forty years, could burst out: 'the
only way to an Englishman's Brains is through his guts. ... Burk
was not much out of the way when he called them the Swinish
Multitude, for feed a Pig well and you may do anything with
him.' [1] Although this is also the view of English popular history
of W. W. Rostow and of some contributors to the *Economic History
Review*, it is not the whole truth. There is, throughout this period
until Chartism, a rising standard of popular political expectation.
Currie and Hartwell, and other critics, think I have shown no
movement of a class, but only the radicalization of a minority
of artisans, who had little common identity with 'the labouring
poor'.[2] 'Mr Thompson's working class ... remains, even after 850
pages, a myth, a construct of determined imagination and theoretical
presuppositions.'

Whether this is so must be judged by my readers. I have tried
to distinguish between the experiences of different groups —
artisans, outworkers, and labourers — and to show how they were
coming to act, think, and feel, not in the old modes of deference
and parochial seclusion, but in class ways. Currie and Hartwell
perhaps require something more definite, some card-of-membership
of a class, before they will be convinced. Since class relations and
class consciousness are cultural formations, they are never as
definite or matter-of-fact as that. Nor does history have terminal
points. The outcome of this period of 'making' lies beyond this
book, in the Chartist years, when these several groups found
common institutions, programmes, forms of action, and modes of
thought. Even so, the differing outlooks of each group were not
extinguished, and they can be felt as a tension within the common
movement even in 1839. With the failure of Chartism (and contributing to that failure) the groups pulled apart from each other
once more, and a new phase of class relationships and institutions
commenced.[3]

What happened in this period of 'making' was twofold. First,
there was a shift in the whole background, as well as in the minority

1. Gast to Place, British Museum Add. MSS. 27, 829 f. 20.

2. Currie and Hartwell, op. cit., pp. 638–9. I am at a loss to understand why they think I 'do not like the artisans'.

3. I have argued this point more fully, and tried to clarify my notion
of 'class', in 'The Peculiarities of the English', *The Socialist Register,
1965*, edited Ralph Miliband and John Saville (1965), especially
pp. 357–8

foreground, of popular dispositions. The active minority (certainly, in the main, artisans and outworkers) no longer found themselves hemmed in by Church-and-King bruisers or engulfed in mass apathy. The shift did not happen once and for all and everywhere. It was noted in London by 1795,[1] in Nottingham in 1796,[2] in Birmingham at about the same time;[3] in Newcastle it was perhaps delayed until 1819,[4] while in Merthyr the change came with climactic force in 1831.[5]

Second, from 1816 onwards, at first in a few places only and in a few minds, but soon with greater frequency and diversity, ideas were worked out, actions were taken, and experiments were made with organizations, which prefigure the developments of the 1830s, which show that working men were putting themselves into a new stance in relation to other social groups and were developing new solidarities.

It is partly a question of *morale*. At its simplest level it meant that it was possible for individual working men to have a sense – not just of sporadic crowd turbulence – but of sustained commitment to a movement for their own class objectives, and a confidence which enabled them to stand up against the physical and moral resources of their opponents. In March 1817 a young Blanketeer was seized at Ashburn, in Derbyshire, on his way to London, and this note was found in his pocket:

Father and Mother

I Arived in this Town to night and I hope to stop in this Town all Night. All is Confusion, some of us the[y] alow to Come in town and

1. A correspondent in *The Brazen Trumpet*, 17 March 1798, notes: '. . . a combination of pampered, lazy, and insolent priests could not, at this day, engage a mob in their cause' as in 1792. 'The dark age rolls away a pace.'

2. J. F. Sutton, *The Date-Book of Nottingham* (Nottingham, 1880), p. 212.

3. See R. B. Rose's careful study of 'The Origins of Working-Class Radicalism in Birmingham', *Labour History* (Canberra), November, 1965, pp. 6–14; Victoria County History, Warwickshire, VII (1964), pp. 284–5.

4. See above p. 758 I do not accept N. McCord's argument in 'Tyneside Discontents and Peterloo', *Northern History* (Leeds), II, 1967, pp. 91–111, that there is little evidence of the pitmen's support for 'Radical Monday'. He takes too limited a view of the evidence, and treats even this too selectively. I have cited above some of the contrary evidence.

5. See G. A. Williams's superb study of 'The Insurrection at Merthyr Tydfil in 1831', *Trans. Hon. Soc. of Cymmrodorion*, 1965, pp. 222–243.

some the[y] keep out – All the way we have come we have been Garded by the Soldiers and a Grate Many have gon back agen ... We se[e] very plane the[y] are Determined to stop us, a great many of us as been put in prison in nearly all the towns we have come throw – thear sordes gliter round our heades but the thing is as it is ...

'Tell all the men', the letter concluded, 'that I ham in good spirets as ever tho I do not know but I may be in prison in ten minetes from now, I ham a trew Reformer yet and i do not Care who knows it.'[1] This is what I mean by the new confidence of class.

As for the theoretical definition of class, I can only repeat what I have written in another place:

Sociologists who have stopped the time-machine and, with a good deal of conceptual huffing and puffing, have gone down to the engine-room to look, tell us that nowhere at all have they been able to locate and classify a class. They can only find a multitude of people with different occupations, incomes, status-hierarchies, and the rest. Of course they are right, since class is not this or that part of the machine, but *the way the machine works* once it is set in motion – not this and that interest, but the *friction* of interests – the movement itself, the heat, the thundering noise. Class is a social and cultural formation (often finding institutional expression) which cannot be defined abstractly, or in isolation, but only in terms of relationship with other classes; and, ultimately, the definition can only be made in the medium of *time* – that is, action and reaction, change and conflict. When we speak of *a* class we are thinking of a very loosely defined body of people who share the same congeries of interests, social experiences, traditions and value-system, who have a *disposition* to *behave* as a class, to define themselves in their actions and in their consciousness in relation to other groups of people in class ways. But class itself is not a thing, it is a happening.

This book is an attempt to describe this happening, this process of self-discovery and of self-definition.[2]

University of Warwick, May 1968.

1. Jonathan Hutton, 11 March 1817, H.O. 40. 5.
2. 'Peculiarities of the English', op. cit., p. 357.

Bibliographical Note

I HAVE drawn upon manuscript sources selectively, and in particular at those points where it seemed to me advisable to reexamine the accepted accounts. In the Public Record Office the most valuable sources have been the *Home Office Papers* (H.O.), especially series 40 and 42: miscellaneous bundles relating to the London Corresponding Society, food riots, &c., in the *Privy Council Papers* (P.C.); and the *Treasury Solicitor's Papers* (T.S.), which sometimes contain the evidence (informers' reports, depositions, intercepted letters, &c.) from which the Crown briefs against State prisoners were prepared. I have also consulted the *Place Collection* in the British Museum (Add. MSS.), and have found most useful Place's 'Autobiography', the Minute Books and Letter Books of the L.C.S., notes on aspects of L.C.S. history by Hardy, Richter, Lemaitre, and Oxlade: Place's materials on the life of Spence and his notes on 1816–20: and Lovett's notes on the history of the National Union of the Working Classes and Others. I have explained in my text some reasons why it is advisable to use Place's historical materials with some caution.

The *Fitzwilliam Papers* are part of the large Wentworth collection now in the care of Sheffield Reference Library. They include some part of the correspondence on public affairs of Earl Fitzwilliam, together with reports from Yorkshire J.P.s and other informants, during the time when he was Lord Lieutenant of the West Riding. I have drawn on series F. 44, 45 and 52, which are of interest for the early 1790s, the years 1801–3, and for Luddism. Two other sources have been of value for Luddism. The *Radcliffe Papers* include some correspondence preserved by Sir Joseph Radcliffe, the exceedingly active Huddersfield magistrate who received his knighthood in recognition of his services in bringing leading Yorkshire Luddites to trial. The manuscripts remain in the custodianship of his descendant, Captain J. B. E. Radcliffe, at Rudding Park, Harrogate, and they are catalogued by the National Register of Archives. The *Papers of the Framework-Knitters' Committee* were seized in 1814 and remain in the Nottingham City Archives. They cover the years 1812–14, and an admirable selection has been published in the *Records of the Borough of Nottingham, 1800–1832* (1952). These have been my main manuscript sources.

Most of the scarcer pamphlets, periodicals, &c., cited in the text are to be found in the British Museum or in the John Rylands Library (Manchester). It has not been possible to follow the press intensively for the fifty years covered by my narrative, and I have therefore, once again, consulted newspapers and periodicals selectively, in the attempt to throw light upon certain problems and periods. I have referred frequently to Cobbett's *Political Register*, *The Times*, the *Leeds Mercury*, and the *Nottingham Review*, and on occasions to other provincial papers. Among Jacobin, Radical, trade unionist, or Owenite periodicals which I have consulted are:

For the 1790s: Eaton's *Politics for the People*; *The Patriot* (Sheffield); Thelwall's *Tribune*; *The Cabinet* (Norwich); Perry's *Argus*; *The Philanthropist*; *The Moral and Political Magazine*; *The Cambridge Intelligencer*, *The Sheffield Iris*. (The most interesting writing in the 1790s, however, is in pamphlet, rather than periodical, form).

For the Wars, and the years 1816–20: Flower's *Political Review*; Bone's *Reasoner*; *The Alfred*; *The Independent Whig*; Hone's *Reformist's Register*; Sherwin's *Republican*; Sherwin's *Political Register*; *The Black Dwarf*; *The 'Forlorn Hope'*; *The Axe Laid to the Root*; *The People*; *The Political Observer*; *The Legislator*; *The Briton*; *Duckett's Despatch*; *The Gorgon*; *The Black Book* (originally published in periodical parts); *The Examiner*; *The Champion*; *The Cap of Liberty*; *The Medusa*; *The Manchester Observer*; *The White Hat*; *The Theological Comet, or Free-Thinking Englishman*; *The Blanketteer*; Carlile's *Republican*; *The Birmingham Inspector*; *Hunt's Addresses to Radical Reformers*.

For the 1820s and early 1830s: *The Economist*; *The Mechanic's Magazine*; *The Trades Newspaper*; *The Artizan's London and Provincial Chronicle*; Carlile's *Prompter*; Cobbett's *Two-Penny Trash*; *The Devil's Pulpit*; *The Voice of the People*; Dr King's *Cooperator*; *Common Sense*; *The Union Pilot*; *The Lancashire and Yorkshire Cooperator*; *The Poor Man's Advocate*; *The Voice of the West Riding*; *The Poor Man's Guardian*; *The Working Man's Friend*; *The Radical Reformer*; *The Cosmopolite*; *The Cracker*; *The Crisis*; *The Destructive*; *The People's Conservative*; *The Man*; *The Pioneer*; *The Herald of the Rights of Industry*. Also (for later periods) *Bronterre's National Reformer*; *The Social Pioneer*; *The Ten Hours' Advocate*; *The Labourer*; *The Northern Star*; *Notes to the People*.

On the title-page to Part One there are reproduced the two sides to one of the token coins issued by the London Corresponding Society. Many such coins were issued – they were struck, for example, in honour of the juries which acquitted Hardy, Tooke and Thelwall, and Daniel Isaac Eaton – and Thomas Spence struck many others. On the title-page to Part Two there is a rough wood-blocked card, supposedly used as a ticket of admission to secret Luddite meetings in Lancashire (1812). On the title-page to Part Three, Cruikshank's mock memorial to the victors of Peterloo is from William Hone and George Cruikshank's *A Slap at Slop* (1822).

Finally, there are a few secondary authorities which demand mention since I have been (like all students of this period) very much indebted to them. A. Aspinall, *The Early English Trade Unions* (1949) provides an excellent selection of documents from the Home Office Papers for the years when the Combination Acts were in force. G. D. H. Cole and A. W. Filson, *British Working Class Movements: Select Documents* (1951) provides a wider selection of source-material, and M. Morris, *From Cobbett to the Chartists* (1948) a more abbreviated selection. Those who cannot gain access to Cobbett's *Political Register* (his *Rural Rides* are available in the Everyman edition) will find ably edited selections in G. D. H. and M. Cole, *The Opinions of William Cobbett* (1944) and in W. Reitzel, *The Progress of a Ploughboy* (1933). Both H. L. Jephson, *The Platform* (1892) and G. Wallas, *Life of Francis Place* (1898) draw extensively and verbatim from Place's manuscripts, very often too uncritically. Of the books by J. L. and B. Hammond, *The Skilled Labourer* (1919) remains of outstanding importance, and *The Village Labourer* (1911) is scarcely less important. (*The Town Labourer* (1917) is a more impressionistic work). M. D. George, *London Life in the Eighteenth Century* (1930); J. H. Clapham, *Economic History of Modern Britain*, (Cambridge, 1927); S. and B. Webb, *History of Trade Unionism* (1894: revised 1920); and I. Pinchbeck, *Women Workers and the Industrial Revolution* (1930) have all earned their place as reference books. There is no volume of comparable weight on early democratic and Radical history; perhaps the best introductions remain, G. S. Veitch, *The Genesis of Parliamentary Reform* (1913) – although Veitch's English Jacobins are too pious and constitutionalist for belief – and, for later years, W. D. Wickwar, *The Struggle for the Freedom of the Press* (1928) and J. R. M. Butler, *The Passing of the Great Reform Bill* (1914). (S. Maccoby's interesting volume on *English Radicalism, 1786–1832* (1955), is in general too much oriented towards parliamentary goings-on to throw light on the kinds of problem examined in this book). Samuel Bamford's *Passages in the Life of a Radical* (Heywood, 1841) and William Lovett's *Life and Struggles in Pursuit of Bread, Knowledge, and Freedom* (1876) – both of which have appeared in subsequent editions – are essential reading for any Englishman. Students who wish to place this history in a wider framework will find in E. Hobsbawm, *The Age of Revolution* (1962) and Asa Briggs, *The Age of Improvement* (1959) the material for an European and a British frame of reference; while E. Halévy, *England in 1815* (1924) remains the outstanding general survey of early nineteenth-century British society.

To attempt a full bibliography in a book which covers such an extensive period and so many topics must either appear pretentious or incomplete. In each section of the book I have been at pains to indicate in my footnotes the most relevant secondary authorities; and I hope that I have given sufficient indication of my main primary sources in the same place. I must therefore ask for the reader's indulgence, and leave him with the envoi of a Spitalfields silk weaver (from Samuel Sholl's *Historical Account of the Silk Manufacture* – 1811) by way of apology:

> My loom's entirely out of square,
> My rolls now worm-eaten are;
> My clamps and treadles they are broke,
> By battons, they won't strike a stroke;
> My porry's covered with the dust,
> My shears and pickers eat with rust;
> My reed and harness are worn out,
> My wheel won't turn a quill about;
> My shuttle's broke, my glass is run,
> My droplee's shot – my cane is done!

Acknowledgements

ACKNOWLEDGEMENT is due to the authorities and libraries which have allowed me to quote from manuscript sources. Unpublished Crown copyright material in the Public Record Office has been reproduced by permission of the Controller of H.M. Stationery Office. Material from the Wentworth Woodhouse Muniments (Fitzwilliam Papers) has been reproduced by permission of Earl Fitzwilliam and Earl Fitzwilliam's Wentworth Estates Company, through the courtesy of the Sheffield City Librarian. I must also make acknowledgement to the Keeper of Manuscripts, British Museum (Place Collection); the Corporation of Nottingham (Framework-knitters Papers); Nottingham Public Libraries; the City Librarian, Leeds; and Captain J. B. E. Radcliffe, M.C. (Radcliffe Papers). I should also like to thank the librarians and staff at all these institutions for their assistance, as well as the librarians and staff at the John Rylands Library, Manchester, the Manchester Central Reference Library, the Norwich Central Reference Library, the Brotherton Library (Leeds University), the public libraries at Bradford, Halifax, and Wakefield, and the Tolson Memorial Museum, Huddersfield. The Luddite 'ticket' reproduced on p. 205 is Crown copyright, and is reproduced by permission of the Controller of H.M. Stationery Office.

I am also indebted to the following houses for permission to cite passages in copyright works: George Allen & Unwin Ltd (*The Protestant Ethic and the Spirit of Capitalism* by M. Weber, 1930); the Cambridge University Press (*Economic History of Modern Britain* by Sir John Clapham, 1929, Volume I, and *The History and Social influence of the Potato* by R. N. Salaman, 1949); the Clarendon Press, Oxford (*Wilkes and Liberty* by G. Rudé, 1962); Longmans, Green & Co. Ltd (*The Town Labourer*, 1917, and *The Skilled Labourer*, 1919, both by J. L. and B. Hammond); the Manchester University Press (*Primitive Rebels* by E. Hobsbawm, 1959); and the Oxford University Press (*The Industrial Revolution* by T. S. Ashton, 1948). The text of the Authorized Version of the Bible is Crown copyright and the extracts used herein are reproduced by permission.

Index